P9-CMW-126

3 9082 06943419 2

REFERENCE

THE NEW INTERPRETER'S® BIBLE
IN TWELVE VOLUMES

VOLUME NINE

THE GOSPEL OF
LUKE

THE GOSPEL OF
JOHN

EDITORIAL BOARD

THE NEW INTERPRETER'S® BIBLE

GENERAL ARTICLES
&
INTRODUCTION, COMMENTARY, & REFLECTIONS
FOR EACH BOOK OF THE BIBLE
INCLUDING
THE APOCRYPHAL / DEUTEROCANONICAL BOOKS
IN
TWELVE VOLUMES

VOLUME
IX

ABINGDON PRESS
Nashville

THE NEW INTERPRETER'S® BIBLE
VOLUME IX

Copyright © 1995 by Abingdon Press

This book is printed on recycled, acid-free paper.

Library of Congress Cataloging-in-Publication Data

The New Interpreter's Bible: general articles & introduction, commentary, & reflections for each book of the Bible, including the Apocryphal/Deuterocanonical books.
    p. cm.
    Full texts and critical notes of the New International Version and the New Revised Standard Version of the Bible in parallel columns.
    Includes bibliographical references.
    ISBN 0-687-27822-8 (v. 9: alk. paper)
    1. Bible----Commentaries. 2. Abingdon Press. I. Bible. English. New International. 1994. II. Bible. English. New Revised Standard. 1994.
BS491.2.N484   1994
220.7'7----dc20
                        94-21092
                        CIP

The Hebraica® and Graeca® fonts used to print this work are available from Linguist's Software, Inc., PO Box 580, Edmonds, WA 98020-0580 tel (206) 775-1130.

PUBLICATION STAFF
President and Publisher: Robert K. Feaster
Editorial Director: Neil M. Alexander
Managing Editor: Michael E. Lawrence
Project Director: Jack A. Keller, Jr.
Assistant Editor: Eli D. Fisher, Jr.
Production Editor: Linda S. Allen
Art Director: Nancy R. Bozeman
Designer: J. S. Laughbaum
Copy Processing Manager: Sylvia S. Marlow
Composition Specialist: Kathy M. Harding
Publishing Systems Analyst: Glenn R. Hinton
Prepress Manager: William E. Gentry
Prepress Systems Technicians: Thomas E. Mullins
                              J. Calvin Buckner
Production Coordinator: James E. Leath
Scheduling: Laurene M. Brazzell
            Helen M. Pouliot
Print Procurement Coordinator: David M. Sanders

98 99 00 01 02 03 04----10 9 8 7 6 5 4 3 2

MANUFACTURED IN THE UNITED STATES OF AMERICA

CONSULTANTS

NEIL M. ALEXANDER
Vice President/Editorial Director
Abingdon Press
Nashville, Tennessee

OWEN F. CAMPION
Associate Publisher
Our Sunday Visitor
Huntington, Indiana

MINERVA G. CARCAÑO
Minister-in-Charge
South Valley Cooperative Ministry
Albuquerque, New Mexico

V. L. DAUGHTERY, JR.
Pastor
Park Avenue United Methodist Church
Valdosta, Georgia

SHARON NEUFER EMSWILER
Pastor
First United Methodist Church
Rock Island, Illinois

JUAN G. FELICIANO VALERA
Pastor
Iglesia Metodista "Juan Wesley"
Arecibo, Puerto Rico

CELIA BREWER MARSHALL
Lecturer
University of North Carolina at Charlotte
Charlotte, North Carolina

NANCY C. MILLER-HERRON
Attorney and clergy member of the
Tennessee Conference
The United Methodist Church
Dresden, Tennessee

ROBERT C. SCHNASE
Pastor
First United Methodist Church
McAllen, Texas

BILL SHERMAN
Pastor
Woodmont Baptist Church
Nashville, Tennessee

RODNEY T. SMOTHERS
Pastor
Central United Methodist Church
Atlanta, Georgia

WILLIAM D. WATLEY
Pastor
St. James African Methodist Episcopal Church
Newark, New Jersey

TALLULAH FISHER WILLIAMS
Pastor
Trinity United Methodist Church
Mt. Prospect, Illinois

SUK-CHONG YU
Pastor
San Francisco Korean United Methodist Church
San Francisco, California

CONTRIBUTORS

ELIZABETH ACHTEMEIER
Adjunct Professor of Bible and Homiletics
Union Theological Seminary in Virginia
Richmond, Virginia
(Presbyterian Church [U.S.A.])
Joel

LESLIE C. ALLEN
Professor of Old Testament
Fuller Theological Seminary
Pasadena, California
(Baptist)
1 & 2 Chronicles

GARY A. ANDERSON
Associate Professor of Religious Studies
University of Virginia
Charlottesville, Virginia
(The Roman Catholic Church)
Introduction to Israelite Religion

DAVID L. BARTLETT
Lantz Professor of Preaching and
Communication
The Divinity School
Yale University
New Haven, Connecticut
(American Baptist Churches in the U.S.A.)
1 Peter

ROBERT A. BENNETT
Professor of Old Testament
Episcopal Divinity School
Cambridge, Massachusetts
(The Episcopal Church)
Zephaniah

ADELE BERLIN
Professor of Hebrew and East Asian
Languages and Literature
University of Maryland
College Park, Maryland
Introduction to Hebrew Poetry

BRUCE C. BIRCH
Professor of Old Testament
Wesley Theological Seminary
Washington, DC
(The United Methodist Church)
1 & 2 Samuel

PHYLLIS A. BIRD
Associate Professor of Old Testament
Interpretation
Garrett-Evangelical Theological Seminary
Evanston, Illinois
(The United Methodist Church)
The Authority of the Bible

C. CLIFTON BLACK
Associate Professor of New Testament
Perkins School of Theology
Southern Methodist University
Dallas, Texas
(The United Methodist Church)
1, 2, & 3 John

JOSEPH BLENKINSOPP
John A. O'Brien Professor of Biblical Studies
Department of Theology
University of Notre Dame
Notre Dame, Indiana
(The Roman Catholic Church)
Introduction to the Pentateuch

M. EUGENE BORING
I. Wylie and Elizabeth M. Briscoe Professor of
New Testament
Brite Divinity School
Texas Christian University
Fort Worth, Texas
(Christian Church [Disciples of Christ])
Matthew

WALTER BRUEGGEMANN
William Marcellus McPheeters Professor of Old
Testament
Columbia Theological Seminary
Decatur, Georgia
(United Church of Christ)
Exodus

DAVID G. BUTTRICK
Professor of Homiletics and Liturgics
The Divinity School
Vanderbilt University
Nashville, Tennessee
(United Church of Christ)
The Use of the Bible in Preaching

RONALD E. CLEMENTS
Samuel Davidson Professor of Old Testament
King's College
University of London
London, England
(Baptist Union of Great Britain and Ireland)
Deuteronomy

RICHARD J. CLIFFORD
Professor of Old Testament
Weston School of Theology
Cambridge, Massachusetts
(The Roman Catholic Church)
Introduction to Wisdom Literature

JOHN J. COLLINS
Professor of Hebrew Bible
The Divinity School
University of Chicago
Chicago, Illinois
(The Roman Catholic Church)
Introduction to Early Jewish Religion

ROBERT B. COOTE
Professor of Old Testament
San Francisco Theological Seminary
San Anselmo, California
(Presbyterian Church [U.S.A.])
Joshua

FRED B. CRADDOCK
Bandy Distinguished Professor of Preaching
and New Testament, Emeritus
Candler School of Theology
Emory University
Atlanta, Georgia
(Christian Church [Disciples of Christ])
Hebrews

TONI CRAVEN
Professor of Hebrew Bible
Brite Divinity School
Texas Christian University
Fort Worth, Texas
(The Roman Catholic Church)
Introduction to Narrative Literature

JAMES L. CRENSHAW
Robert L. Flowers Professor of Old Testament
The Divinity School
Duke University
Durham, North Carolina
(Baptist)
Sirach

KEITH R. CRIM
Pastor
New Concord Presbyterian Church
Concord, Virginia
(Presbyterian Church [U.S.A.])
Modern English Versions of the Bible

R. ALAN CULPEPPER
Dean
The School of Theology
Mercer University
Atlanta, Georgia
(Southern Baptist Convention)
Luke

KATHERYN PFISTERER DARR
Associate Professor of Hebrew Bible
The School of Theology
Boston University
Boston, Massachusetts
(The United Methodist Church)
Ezekiel

ROBERT DORAN
Professor of Religion
Amherst College
Amherst, Massachusetts
1 & 2 Maccabees

THOMAS B. DOZEMAN
Professor of Old Testament
United Theological Seminary
Dayton, Ohio
(Presbyterian Church [U.S.A.])
Numbers

JAMES D. G. DUNN
Lightfoot Professor of Divinity
Department of Theology
University of Durham
Durham, England
(The Methodist Church [Great Britain])
1 & 2 Timothy; Titus

ELDON JAY EPP
Harkness Professor of Biblical Literature
and Chairman of the Department of Religion
Case Western Reserve University
Cleveland, Ohio
(The Episcopal Church)
Ancient Texts and Versions of the New Testament

KATHLEEN ROBERTSON FARMER
Professor of Old Testament
United Theological Seminary
Dayton, Ohio
(The United Methodist Church)
Ruth

CAIN HOPE FELDER
Professor of New Testament Language
and Literature
The School of Divinity
Howard University
Washington, DC
(The United Methodist Church)
Philemon

TERENCE E. FRETHEIM
Professor of Old Testament
Luther Seminary
Saint Paul, Minnesota
(Evangelical Lutheran Church in America)
Genesis

FRANCISCO O. GARCÍA-TRETO
Professor of Religion and Chairman of the
Department of Religion
Trinity University
San Antonio, Texas
(Presbyterian Church [U.S.A.])
Nahum

CATHERINE GUNSALUS GONZÁLEZ
Professor of Church History
Columbia Theological Seminary
Decatur, Georgia
(Presbyterian Church [U.S.A.])
The Use of the Bible in Hymns, Liturgy, and Education

JUSTO L. GONZÁLEZ
Adjunct Professor of Church History
Columbia Theological Seminary
Decatur, Georgia
(The United Methodist Church)
How the Bible Has Been Interpreted in Christian Tradition

DONALD E. GOWAN
Robert Cleveland Holland Professor of Old
Testament
Pittsburgh Theological Seminary
Pittsburgh, Pennsylvania
(Presbyterian Church [U.S.A.])
Amos

JUDITH MARIE GUNDRY-VOLF
Assistant Professor of New Testament
Fuller Theological Seminary
Pasadena, California
(Presbyterian Church [U.S.A.])
Ephesians

DANIEL J. HARRINGTON
Professor of New Testament
Weston School of Theology
Cambridge, Massachusetts
(The Roman Catholic Church)
Introduction to the Canon

RICHARD B. HAYS
Associate Professor of New Testament
The Divinity School
Duke University
Durham, North Carolina
(The United Methodist Church)
Galatians

THEODORE HIEBERT
Professor of Hebrew Bible
McCormick Theological
Seminary
Chicago, Illinois
(Mennonite Church)
Habakkuk

CARL R. HOLLADAY
Professor of New Testament
Candler School of Theology
Emory University
Atlanta, Georgia
Contemporary Methods of Reading the Bible

MORNA D. HOOKER
  Lady Margaret's Professor of Divinity
  The Divinity School
  University of Cambridge
  Cambridge, England
  (The Methodist Church [Great Britain])
    Philippians

DAVID C. HOPKINS
  Professor of Old Testament
  Wesley Theological Seminary
  Washington, DC
  (United Church of Christ)
    Life in Ancient Palestine

DENISE DOMBKOWSKI HOPKINS
  Professor of Old Testament
  Wesley Theological Seminary
  Washington, DC
  (United Church of Christ)
    Judith

LUKE T. JOHNSON
  Robert W. Woodruff Professor of New
    Testament and Christian Origins
  Candler School of Theology
  Emory University
  Atlanta, Georgia
  (The Roman Catholic Church)
    James

WALTER C. KAISER, JR.
  Colman Mockler Distinguished Professor
    of Old Testament
  Gordon-Conwell Theological Seminary
  South Hamilton, Massachusetts
  (The Evangelical Free Church of America)
    Leviticus

LEANDER E. KECK
  Winkley Professor of Biblical Theology
  The Divinity School
  Yale University
  New Haven, Connecticut
  (Christian Church [Disciples of Christ])
    Introduction to The New Interpreter's Bible

CHAN-HIE KIM
  Professor of New Testament and Director of
    Korean Studies
  The School of Theology at Claremont
  Claremont, California
  (The United Methodist Church)
    Reading the Bible as Asian Americans

RALPH W. KLEIN
  Dean and Christ Seminary-Seminex Professor of
    Old Testament
  Lutheran School of Theology at Chicago
  Chicago, Illinois
  (Evangelical Lutheran Church in America)
    Ezra; Nehemiah

MICHAEL KOLARCIK, S.J.
  Assistant Professor
  Regis College
  Toronto, Ontario
  Canada
  (The Roman Catholic Church)
    Book of Wisdom

WILLIAM L. LANE
  Paul T. Walls Professor of Wesleyan
    and Biblical Studies
  Department of Religion
  Seattle Pacific University
  Seattle, Washington
  (Free Methodist Church of North America)
    2 Corinthians

ANDREW T. LINCOLN
  Department of Biblical Studies
  University of Sheffield
  Sheffield, England
  (The Church of England)
    Colossians

J. CLINTON McCANN, JR.
  Assistant Professor of Old Testament
  Eden Theological Seminary
  St. Louis, Missouri
  (Presbyterian Church [U.S.A.])
    Psalms

ABRAHAM J. MALHERBE
  Buckingham Professor of New Testament
    Criticism and Interpretation, Emeritus
  The Divinity School
  Yale University
  New Haven, Connecticut
  (Church of Christ)
    *The Cultural Context of the New Testament:
    The Greco-Roman World*

W. EUGENE MARCH
    Arnold Black Rhodes Professor of Old
      Testament
    Louisville Presbyterian Theological Seminary
    Louisville, Kentucky
    (Presbyterian Church [U.S.A.])
      Haggai

JAMES EARL MASSEY
    Dean Emeritus and
      Distinguished Professor-at-Large
    The School of Theology
    Anderson University
    Preacher-in-Residence, Park Place Church
      Anderson, Indiana
    (Church of God [Anderson, Ind.])
      Reading the Bible from Particular Social
        Locations: An Introduction;
      Reading the Bible as African Americans

J. MAXWELL MILLER
    Professor of Old Testament
    Candler School of Theology
    Emory University
    Atlanta, Georgia
    (The United Methodist Church)
      Introduction to the History of Ancient Israel

PATRICK D. MILLER
    Charles T. Haley Professor of Old Testament
      Theology
    Princeton Theological Seminary
    Princeton, New Jersey
    (Presbyterian Church [U.S.A.])
      Jeremiah

FREDERICK J. MURPHY
    Associate Professor and Chair of the
      Department of Religious Studies
    College of the Holy Cross
    Worcester, Massachusetts
    (The Roman Catholic Church)
      Introduction to Apocalyptic Literature

CAROL A. NEWSOM
    Associate Professor of Old Testament
    Candler School of Theology
    Emory University
    Atlanta, Georgia
    (The Episcopal Church)
      Job

GEORGE W. E. NICKELSBURG
    Professor of Christian Origins and Early Judaism
    School of Religion
    University of Iowa
    Iowa City, Iowa
    (Evangelical Lutheran Church in America)
      The Jewish Context of the New
        Testament

IRENE NOWELL
    Associate Professor of Religious Studies
    Benedictine College
    Atchison, Kansas
    (The Roman Catholic Church)
      Tobit

KATHLEEN M. O'CONNOR
    Associate Professor of Biblical Studies
    Maryknoll School of Theology
    Maryknoll, New York
    (The Roman Catholic Church)
      Lamentations

GAIL R. O'DAY
    Almar H. Shatford Associate Professor of Homiletics
    Candler School of Theology
    Emory University
    Atlanta, Georgia
    (United Church of Christ)
      John

BEN C. OLLENBURGER
    Associate Professor of Old Testament
    Associated Mennonite Biblical Seminaries
    Elkhart, Indiana
    (Mennonite Church)
      Zechariah

DENNIS T. OLSON
    Assistant Professor of Old Testament
    Princeton Theological Seminary
    Princeton, New Jersey
    (Evangelical Lutheran Church in America)
      Judges

CAROLYN OSIEK
    Professor of New Testament
    Department of Biblical Languages
      and Literature
    Catholic Theological Union
    Chicago, Illinois
    (The Roman Catholic Church)
      Reading the Bible as Women

SAMUEL PAGÁN
Evangelical Seminary of Puerto Rico
San Juan, Puerto Rico
(Christian Church [Disciples of Christ])
Obadiah

SIMON B. PARKER
Associate Professor of Hebrew Bible and
Harrell F. Beck Scholar in Hebrew Scripture
The School of Theology
Boston University
Boston, Massachusetts
(The United Methodist Church)
*The Ancient Near Eastern Literary
Background of the Old Testament*

PHEME PERKINS
Professor of New Testament
Boston College
Chestnut Hill, Massachusetts
(The Roman Catholic Church)
Mark

DAVID L. PETERSEN
Professor of Old Testament
The Iliff School of Theology
Denver, Colorado
(Presbyterian Church [U.S.A.])
Introduction to Prophetic Literature

CHRISTOPHER C. ROWLAND
Dean Ireland's Professor of the Exegesis
of Holy Scripture
The Queen's College
Oxford, England
(The Church of England)
Revelation

ANTHONY J. SALDARINI
Professor of Biblical Studies
Boston College
Chestnut Hill, Massachusetts
(The Roman Catholic Church)
Baruch; Letter of Jeremiah

J. PAUL SAMPLEY
Professor of New Testament and
Christian Origins
The School of Theology and The Graduate Division
Boston University
Boston, Massachusetts
(The United Methodist Church)
1 Corinthians

JUDITH E. SANDERSON
Assistant Professor of Hebrew Bible
Department of Theology and Religious Studies
Seattle University
Seattle, Washington
*Ancient Texts and Versions of the Old
Testament*

EILEEN M. SCHULLER
Associate Professor
Department of Religious Studies
McMaster University
Hamilton, Ontario
Canada
(The Roman Catholic Church)
Malachi

FERNANDO F. SEGOVIA
Associate Professor of New Testament
and Early Christianity
The Divinity School
Vanderbilt University
Nashville, Tennessee
(The Roman Catholic Church)
Reading the Bible as Hispanic Americans

CHRISTOPHER R. SEITZ
Associate Professor of Old Testament
The Divinity School
Yale University
New Haven, Connecticut
(The Episcopal Church)
Isaiah 40–66

CHOON-LEONG SEOW
Associate Professor of Old Testament
Princeton Theological Seminary
Princeton, New Jersey
(Presbyterian Church [U.S.A.])
1 & 2 Kings

MICHAEL A. SIGNER
Abrams Professor of Jewish Thought and
Culture
Department of Theology
University of Notre Dame
Notre Dame, Indiana
*How the Bible Has Been Interpreted in
Jewish Tradition*

MOISÉS SILVA
Professor of New Testament
Westminster Theological Seminary
Philadelphia, Pennsylvania
(The Orthodox Presbyterian Church)
*Contemporary Theories of Biblical
Interpretation*

DANIEL J. SIMUNDSON
Professor of Old Testament
Luther Seminary
Saint Paul, Minnesota
(Evangelical Lutheran Church in America)
Micah

ABRAHAM SMITH
Assistant Professor of New Testament
and Christian Origins
The School of Theology
Boston University
Boston, Massachusetts
(The National Baptist Convention, USA, Inc.)
1 & 2 Thessalonians

DANIEL L. SMITH-CHRISTOPHER
Associate Professor of Theological Studies
Department of Theology
Loyola Marymount University
Los Angeles, California
(The Society of Friends [Quaker])
*Daniel; Bel and the Dragon; Prayer of
Azariah; Susannah*

MARION L. SOARDS
Professor of New Testament Studies
Louisville Presbyterian Theological Seminary
Louisville, Kentucky
(Presbyterian Church [U.S.A.])
Acts

ROBERT C. TANNEHILL
Academic Dean and Harold B. Williams
Professor of Biblical Studies
Methodist Theological School in Ohio
Delaware, Ohio
(The United Methodist Church)
The Gospels and Narrative Literature

GEORGE E. TINKER
Associate Professor of Cross-Cultural Ministries
The Iliff School of Theology
Denver, Colorado
(Evangelical Lutheran Church in America)
Reading the Bible as Native Americans

W. SIBLEY TOWNER
The Reverend Archibald McFadyen Professor of
Biblical Interpretation
Union Theological Seminary in Virginia
Richmond, Virginia
(Presbyterian Church [U.S.A.])
Ecclesiastes

PHYLLIS TRIBLE
Baldwin Professor of Sacred Literature
Union Theological Seminary
New York, New York
Jonah

GENE M. TUCKER
Professor of Old Testament, Emeritus
Candler School of Theology
Emory University
Atlanta, Georgia
(The United Methodist Church)
Isaiah 1–39

CHRISTOPHER M. TUCKETT
Rylands Professor of Biblical Criticism
and Exegesis
Faculty of Theology
University of Manchester
Manchester, England
(The Church of England)
Jesus and the Gospels

RAYMOND C. VAN LEEUWEN
Professor of Religion and Theology
Eastern College
Saint Davids, Pennsylvania
(Christian Reformed Church in North America)
Proverbs

ROBERT W. WALL
Professor of Biblical Studies
Department of Religion
Seattle Pacific University
Seattle, Washington
(Free Methodist Church of North America)
Introduction to Epistolary Literature

DUANE F. WATSON
Associate Professor of New Testament Studies
Department of Religion and Philosophy
Malone College
Canton, Ohio
(The United Methodist Church)
2 Peter; Jude

RENITA J. WEEMS
Associate Professor of Hebrew Bible
The Divinity School
Vanderbilt University
Nashville, Tennessee
(African Methodist Episcopal Church)
Song of Songs

SIDNIE A. WHITE
Assistant Professor of Religion
Department of Religion
Albright College
Reading, Pennsylvania
(The Episcopal Church)
Esther; Additions to Esther

VINCENT L. WIMBUSH
Professor of New Testament and
    Christian Origins
Union Theological Seminary
New York, New York
(Progressive National Baptist Convention, Inc.)
*The Ecclesiastical Context of the New
    Testament*

N. THOMAS WRIGHT
Lecturer in New Testament Studies
Fellow, Tutor, and Chaplain
Worcester College
Oxford, England
(The Church of England)
Romans

GALE A. YEE
Associate Professor of Old Testament
Department of Theology
University of Saint Thomas
Saint Paul, Minnesota
(The Roman Catholic Church)
Hosea

FEATURES OF
THE NEW INTERPRETER'S BIBLE

The general aim of *The New Interpreter's Bible* is to bring the best in contemporary biblical scholarship into the service of the church to enhance preaching, teaching, and study of the Scriptures. To accomplish that general aim, the design of *The New Interpreter's Bible* has been shaped by two controlling principles: (1) form serves function, and (2) maximize ease of use.

General articles provide the reader with concise, up-to-date, balanced introductions and assessments of selected topics. In most cases, a brief bibliography points the way to further exploration of a topic. Many of the general articles are placed in volumes 1 and 8, at the beginning of the coverage of the Old and New Testaments, respectively. Others have been inserted in those volumes where the reader will encounter the corresponding type of literature (e.g., "Introduction to Prophetic Literature" appears in Volume 6 alongside several of the prophetic books).

Coverage of each biblical book begins with an "Introduction" that acquaints the reader with the essential historical, sociocultural, literary, and theological issues necessary to understand the biblical book. A short bibliography and an outline of the biblical book are found at the end of each Introduction. The introductory sections are the only material in *The New Interpreter's Bible* printed in a single wide-column format.

The biblical text is divided into coherent and manageable primary units, which are located within larger sections of Scripture. At the opening discussion of any large section of Scripture, readers will often find material identified as "Overview," which includes remarks applicable to the large section of text. The primary unit of text may be as short as a few verses or as long as a chapter or more. This is the point at which the biblical text itself is reprinted in *The New Interpreter's Bible*. Dealing with Scripture in terms of these primary units allows discussion of important issues that are overlooked in a verse-by-verse treatment. Each scriptural unit is identified by text citation and a short title.

The full texts and critical notes of the New International Version and the New Revised Standard Version of the Bible are presented in parallel columns for quick reference. Since every translation is to some extent an interpretation as well, the inclusion of these two widely known and influential modern translations provides an easy comparison that in many cases will lead to a better understanding of a passage. Biblical passages are set in a two-column format and placed in green tint-blocks to make it easy to recognize them at a glance. The NIV and NRSV material is clearly identified on each page on which the text appears.

Immediately following each biblical text is a section marked "Commentary," which provides an exegetical analysis informed by linguistic, text-critical, historical-critical, literary, social-scientific, and theological methods. The Commentary serves as a reliable, judicious guide through the text, pointing out the critical problems as well as key interpretive issues.

The exegetical approach is "text-centered." That is, the commentators focus primarily on the text in its final form rather than on (a) a meticulous rehearsal of problems of scholarship associated with a text, (b) a thorough reconstruction of the pre-history of the text, or (c) an exhaustive rehearsal of the text's interpretive history. Of course, some attention to scholarly problems, to the pre-history of a text, and to historic interpretations that have shaped streams of tradition is important in particular cases precisely in order to illumine the several levels of meaning in the final form of the text. But the *primary* focus is on the canonical text itself. Moreover, the Commentary not only describes pertinent aspects of the text, but also teaches the reader what to look for in the text so as to develop the reader's own capacity to analyze and interpret the text.

Commentary material runs serially for a few paragraphs or a few pages, depending on what is required by the biblical passage under discussion.

Commentary material is set in a two-column format. Occasional subheads appear in a bold green font. The next level of subdivisions appears as bold black fonts and a third level as black italic fonts. Footnotes are placed at the bottom of the column in which the superscripts appear.

Key words in Hebrew, Aramaic, or Greek are printed in the original-language font, accompanied by a transliteration and a translation or explanation.

Immediately following the Commentary, in most cases, is the section called "Reflections." A detailed exposition growing directly out of the discussion and issues dealt with in the Commentary, Reflections are geared specifically toward helping those who interpret Scripture in the life of the church by providing "handles" for grasping the significance of Scripture for faith and life today. Recognizing that the text has the capacity to shape the life of the Christian community, this section presents multiple possibilities for preaching and teaching in light of each biblical text. That is, instead of providing the preacher or teacher full illustrations, poems, outlines, and the like, the Reflections offer *several* trajectories of possible interpretation that connect with the situation of the contemporary listeners. Recognizing the power of Scripture to speak anew to diverse situations, not all of the suggested trajectories could be appropriated on any one occasion. Preachers and teachers want some specificity about the implications of the text, but not so much specificity that the work is done for them. The ideas in the Reflections are meant to stimulate the thought of preachers and teachers, not to replace it.

Three-quarter width columns distinguish Reflections materials from biblical text and Commentary.

Occasional excursuses have been inserted in some volumes to address topics of special importance that are best treated apart from the flow of Commentary and Reflections on specific passages. Set in three-quarter width columns, excursuses are identified graphically by a green color bar that runs down the outside margin of the page.

Occasional maps, charts, and illustrations appear throughout the volumes at points where they are most likely to be immediately useful to the reader.

CONTENTS
VOLUME IX

THE GOSPEL OF LUKE

INTRODUCTION, COMMENTARY, AND REFLECTIONS
BY
R. ALAN CULPEPPER

THE GOSPEL OF
LUKE

INTRODUCTION

The Gospel according to Luke, as readers through the centuries have discovered, is one of the treasures of biblical literature. It merits sustained attention and disciplined reading and calls for a radical openness to its challenges. This commentary gives special attention to the literary and theological treasures of the third book of the New Testament. The Overview sections interpret the larger divisions in structure of the text. The Commentary sections lead the reader to grasp the intricacies of the text by examining its primary themes, its narrative character, the structure of individual sections, its contacts with the Old Testament, its place in the development of various Gospel themes, and its christology. The Reflections sections offer a variety of approaches to the interpretation of specific passages for the church and contemporary believers: extensions of key themes, theological reflections, musings over the continuing challenge of key phrases, hermeneutical suggestions, applications to contemporary situations, examples from church history, and quotations or allusions to poetry and other literary works that resonate with the text. The commentary, however, is only a starting point for the reader's own engagement with the text and reflections on its meaning. Interpretation is a personal odyssey. The commentary can guide readers and offer reference points, but readers make their own journeys, and the text will move, inspire, and challenge different readers in different ways.

Each of the Gospels presents the story of Jesus in a different way, and much of their richness is lost if one tries to harmonize them into one consistent account. Each Gospel contains a different structure, develops different themes, and portrays the person of Jesus in its own unique way. The Markan Jesus is an enigmatic and tragic figure, misunderstood and abandoned. Being a disciple of the Markan Jesus means taking up the cross and following him. The Matthean Jesus is a new Moses who fulfills the Scripture and establishes the authority of his own words. Being a disciple of the Matthean Jesus, therefore, means keeping his teachings and making other disciples. The Johannine Jesus is the Word incarnate, the heavenly revealer who is not of this world but who was sent to reveal the Father. Being a disciple of the Johannine Jesus means responding to the revelation with belief, being born from above, imbibing living water and eating the bread of life, and fulfilling one's place and vocation in the community of the "children of God."

The Lukan Jesus is compassionate, a friend to outcasts. Luke also relates Jesus to the history of Israel, the Scriptures, contemporary world history, and the unfolding of God's redemptive purposes in human history. Jesus is the Savior sent to seek and to save the lost. For Israel, Jesus' ministry has ironic and tragic consequences. The religious leaders reject Jesus, and like those who killed God's prophets in the past, they hand Jesus over to be crucified. The people, however, are far more receptive to Jesus than are their leaders, and they are only temporarily implicated in his death during the trial before Pilate. The Gospel ends with the disciples being commissioned as witnesses for the mission they will undertake in the book of Acts.

In order to enter more deeply into the reading of this Gospel, one needs to consider its place among the Gospels, recognize its distinctive structure, sensitize oneself to its dominant christological emphases, and summarize its leading themes.

LUKE AMONG THE GOSPELS

Like the other Gospels, Luke's author is anonymous; it does not indicate who wrote it or where or when it was written. According to early tradition that can be traced to the second century, Luke, the physician and companion of Paul, wrote both Luke and Acts. The earliest manuscript of the Gospel, $\mathfrak{P}^{75}$, dates from 175–225 CE and contains extensive portions of the Gospel. This manuscript contains the earliest occurrence of the title "Gospel According to Luke." How much earlier the titles of the Gospels may be traced is a matter of debate. The titles were apparently attached to the Gospels, however, when they began to circulate and it became necessary to distinguish one from another.

The NT provides meager information about Luke. Philemon lists Luke among Paul's "fellow workers" (Philemon 24). Colossians, which was probably written about the same time, names Luke among Paul's companions and identifies him as "the beloved physician" (Col 4:14). Second Timothy, which was probably composed later by one of Paul's associates, reports of Paul's final imprisonment, "Only Luke is with me" (2 Tim 4:11).

The "we" passages in Acts (16:10-17; 20:5-15; 21:1-18; 27:1–28:16) have contributed further to the tradition of Luke's association with Paul. In these verses the narrator in Acts shifts from third-person to first-person narrative. These passages have been interpreted in various ways: as evidence that the author was present with Paul on these occasions and wrote from firsthand experience (or, in a variation of this view, that he used his own diaries); that he drew from a diary written by one of Paul's companions and did not change the voice of the narrator to make it consistent with the rest of his account; or that he wrote in the first person at this point in the narrative to heighten interest or to follow a literary convention in the reporting of sea voyages.

Even if one takes the NT references to Luke at face value and agrees that Luke was the author of Luke and Acts and that the "we" sections report Luke's firsthand experiences, the NT does not tell us how much Luke was influenced by Paul's thought. Since Luke is listed among those who "send greetings" (Col 4:14; Philemon 24), one might presume that Luke knew of Paul's letter writing. Nevertheless, we do not know that Luke read Paul's letters; we do not know how long Luke was with Paul or how familiar he was with the patterns of Paul's theology and preaching. As a result, we must read the Gospel according to Luke on its own terms and not against the background of Pauline theology.

The earliest references to Lukan authorship in the writings of the Church Fathers appear in ancient prologues and in the writings of Irenaeus and Tertullian. The latter are easier to date than the former.

Irenaeus (c. 130–200), bishop of Lyon and defender of the fourfold Gospel, wrote *Against Heresies,* a lengthy apologetic work in five books, around 185 CE. At issue in the interpretation of Irenaeus's testimony is how much he knew of Luke and the composition of the Gospel beyond the New Testament references surveyed above. Irenaeus wrote: "Luke also, the companion of Paul, recorded in a book the Gospel preached by him."[1] Irenaeus, therefore, attributes to Luke a role in relation to Paul similar to the role that tradition from Papias accorded to Mark: "Mark, the disciple and interpreter of Peter, did also hand down to us in writing what had been preached by Peter."[2] Citing the "we" passages, Irenaeus claims further that "Luke was inseparable from Paul" and that he "performed the work of an evangelist, and was entrusted to hand down to us a Gospel."[3] In doing so, Luke, who was "not merely a follower, but also a fellow-labourer of the Apostles," learned from the apostles what they had learned from the Lord and delivered to us "what he had learned from them," as he himself testified in Luke 1:1-4.[4] Valuable as his testimony is, therefore, Irenaeus, our earliest witness, tells us nothing more than can be found in the NT references.

In his treatise *Against Marcion,* Tertullian (c. 150–c. 225, writing c. 207–208) attacks both Marcion's rejection of the other three Gospels and his abridgment of the Gospel according to Luke. Regarding the first, Tertullian insists on the succession of the Lord, the apostles (Matthew, John, and later Paul), and those who followed the apostles (Mark and Luke).

1. Irenaeus *Against Heresies* 3.1.1 (ANF, 1:414).
2. Ibid.
3. Ibid., 3.14.1 (ANF, 1:437-38).
4. Ibid., 3.14.1-2 (ANF, 1:438).

Of the apostles, therefore, John and Matthew first instil faith into us; whilst of apostolic men, Luke and Mark renew it afterwards. . . . Luke however, was not an apostle, but only an apostolic man; not a master, but a disciple, and so inferior to a master—at least as far subsequent to him as the apostle whom he followed (and that, no doubt was Paul) was subsequent to the others. . . . Inasmuch, therefore, as the enlightener of St. Luke himself [Paul] desired the authority of his predecessors for both his own faith and preaching, how much more may not I require for Luke's Gospel that which was necessary for the Gospel of his master.[5]

Nevertheless, Tertullian affirms the authority of the Gospel and defends the credibility of its transmission prior to Marcion's proposed emendation of it. Marcion must have found it in its original form, since he argued that it had been "interpolated by defenders of Judaism."[6] Luke's Gospel, Tertullian affirms, "has stood its ground from its very first publication. . . . For even Luke's form of the Gospel men usually ascribe to Paul" and "Luke's Gospel also has come down to us in like integrity [as the other Gospels] until the sacrilegious treatment of Marcion."[7] Tertullian, therefore, attests the authority of Luke and the reliability of its original form, rejecting Marcion's argument for an abridged version of the Gospel.

The date of the Muratorian Canon, which survives in an eighth-century manuscript, is debated. It has been suggested that it comes from Rome around 200 CE, but more recently arguments for a fourth-century date and provenance have gained ground.[8] The introduction to Luke, at least, contains little that could not have been gleaned from the NT.

> The third Gospel book, that according to Luke. This physician Luke after Christ's ascension (resurrection?), since Paul had taken him with him as an expert in the way (of the teaching), composed it in his own name according to (his) thinking. Yet neither did he himself see the Lord in the flesh; and therefore, as he was able to ascertain it, so he begins to tell the story from the birth of John.[9]

The prologue to Luke in the ancient Gospel prologues contains further biographical information. The "Oldest Gospel Prologues" were once thought to have been composed together as anti-Marcionite prologues to the four Gospels, but they are now generally treated as independent documents. R. G. Heard concluded that the prologue to Luke in its present form dates from the third century. Nevertheless, he suggested that the first part of it "incorporates, if not an earlier and purely biographical Prologue, at least earlier and very valuable biographical data."[10] The first part of the prologue reads as follows:

> Luke is a Syrian of Antioch, a doctor by profession, who was a disciple of apostles, and later followed Paul until his martyrdom. He served the Lord, without distraction, unmarried, childless, and fell asleep at the age of 84 in Boetia, full of the Holy Spirit.[11]

5. Tertullian *Against Marcion* 4.2 (ANF, 3:347-48).
6. Ibid., 4:4 (ANF, 3:349).
7. Ibid., 4:5 (ANF, 3:350).
8. See A. C. Sundberg, Jr., "Canon Muratori: A Fourth-Century List," *HTR* 66 (1973) 1-41; and Sundberg, "Muratorian Fragment," in *IDBSup* (Nashville: Abingdon, 1976) 609-10.
9. Wilhelm Schneemelcher, ed., *New Testament Apocrypha,* rev. ed., trans. R. McL. Wilson (Louisville: Westminster/John Knox, 1991) 1:34.
10. R. G. Heard, "The Old Gospel Prologues," *JTS* 6 (1955) 11.
11. Ibid., 7.

The second part adds that he wrote the Gospel "in the regions of Achaea." While these biographical details are credible, they are also unsubstantiated, making it difficult to know how much value to assign to them.

As this brief survey of the testimony of the Church Fathers indicates, from late in the second century the tradition that Luke wrote the Gospel and Acts was widely accepted. Most of what we know about Luke, however, comes from the NT itself. By the third century, added details about Luke and the circumstances of the composition of the Gospel appear in the old Gospel prologues, but this data cannot be corroborated from other sources. In view of this impasse, scholars have turned to the Gospel of Luke itself and its relationship to the other Gospels for further information regarding the evangelist and the composition of the Gospel.

This commentary is primarily concerned with the Gospel of Luke as an independent composition with its own literary and theological integrity. Nevertheless, it is often instructive to note parallels (or a lack of them) in Mark or Matthew. Luke himself indicates that he knows of other written accounts (see 1:1). Luke does not number himself among the eyewitnesses, however, but among those who came later and learned the tradition "handed on to us by those who from the beginning were eyewitnesses and servants of the word" (1:2-3).

For comparative purposes, the commentary adopts the widely held view that Mark was the earliest of the Gospels and that Luke used a second written source, identified by the letter Q. The latter seems to have been a collection of the teachings of Jesus that pre-dated the writing of the narrative Gospels. Luke, like Matthew, also contains material that is not found in any other Gospel. The resulting pattern of relationships can be diagrammed as follows.

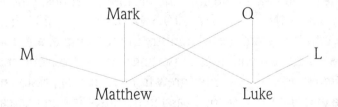

The Gospel of John is the result of a similarly complicated, but probably independent, composition history. Using the Two Source hypothesis (Mark and Q) one can derive the following rough outline of Luke's use of his sources.

Luke 1:1–2:52	L
Luke 3:1–6:19	Mark (and Q for material about John the Baptist and the Temptations)
Luke 6:20–8:3	Q and L
Luke 8:4–9:50	Mark
Luke 9:51–18:14	Q and L
Luke 18:15–24:11	Mark and L
Luke 24:12–24:53	L

The infancy narrative has no parallel in the other Gospels and is quite different from the birth account in Matthew 1–2. Whereas Matthew features Joseph's role in the birth of Jesus, Luke's account highlights Mary's role. The only elements common to the two accounts can be summarized in a confessional statement: Jesus was born of the virgin Mary in Bethlehem. Luke defers the genealogy of Jesus until after the baptism and temptations, and the genealogy is quite different from that found in Matthew 1:1-18, except that both are genealogies of Joseph and both trace the line of Jesus to David and Abraham.

Luke also brings forward Jesus' visit to Nazareth (Mark 6:1-6) and uses the scene in the synagogue at Nazareth (Luke 4:16-30) as the keynote for Jesus' public ministry. For the ministry in Galilee, Luke (4:31–6:19) follows Mark (1:21–3:19) until the Sermon on the Plain, which is not found in Mark but has parallels in Matthew's Sermon on the Mount.

Following the sermon, Luke adds a collection of miracles and teachings (7:1–8:3) that clarify Jesus' role in relation to John the Baptist and his identity as one greater than the prophets. This section, which is compiled from tradition drawn from Q and L, has been called the "little interpolation."

Through the rest of the Galilean ministry (Luke 8:4–9:50) Luke follows Mark (Mark 4:1–9:40). Curiously, Luke's account of the Galilean ministry skips sections of the Markan account: the so-called big omission (Mark 6:45–8:26 at Luke 9:17) and the "little omission" (Mark 9:41–10:12 at Luke 9:50).

The "big interpolation" follows (9:51–18:14). Luke fills nine chapters of the extended journey to Jerusalem with incidents and teachings drawn from Q and L. Luke, therefore, places most of the Q material in the little and big interpolations, whereas Matthew places it in five sermon blocks (Matt 5:1–7:27; 10:5-42; 13:3-52; 18:3-35; 23:2–25:46).

For the entry into Jerusalem, Jesus' ministry in the Temple, and the passion narrative, Luke again follows Mark, expanding and inserting material from one or more other sources. Scholars have often suggested that Luke drew from a separate passion narrative in addition to Mark, but the evidence for a second passion narrative is thin and can be accounted for by appeal to oral tradition and Lukan redaction.

Mark has no resurrection appearances of Jesus in its earliest form (which concludes with Mark 16:8), so Luke again goes his own way at this point, narrating the appearance to the two on the road to Emmaus and the appearance to the eleven back in Jerusalem (neither appearance has a parallel in Matthew). Throughout Luke 24 there are fascinating points at which Luke and John share common traditions.

Since the Gospel according to Mark is usually dated about the year 70, a date for Luke in the mid-eighties appears likely. Moreover, because the book of Acts makes no mention of Paul's letters or letter writing (as does 2 Pet 3:16), it also appears likely that Luke and Acts were written before Paul's letters were collected and circulated as a collection. Unless the prologue to the book of Acts was added later, it indicates that the Gospel was written first: "In the first book, Theophilus, I wrote about all that Jesus did and taught from the beginning until the day when he was taken up to heaven" (Acts 1:1-2 NRSV). A further factor in the date of Luke's composition of the Gospel is his handling of Jesus' predictions of the destruction of Jerusalem (esp. the embankments in 19:43-44 and the camps in 21:20). Without disputing that Jesus may well have forecast the destruction of Jerusalem, the commentary on these passages cites Josephus's report of the events leading to the destruction of the city and suggests that Luke has drawn from the tradition of Jesus' words, reflected on them in light of Old Testament prophecies of destruction, and set forth the predictions in such a way that readers in his own time could easily see that Jesus' words had been fulfilled in the bloody days at the end of the war of 66–70 CE. A date for the composition of the Gospel in the mid-eighties is based, therefore, on Luke's use of Mark, the absence of references to Paul's letters in Acts, and the Lukan form of Jesus' predictions of the destruction of Jerusalem.

Some definition of the character of the evangelist can be gleaned from the Gospel itself. Luke is a skilled writer who is adept with the Greek language, knows the conventions of Hellenistic historiography, demonstrates a remarkable knowledge of the OT, has been influenced by the style of the Septuagint, and has carefully compiled a full record of the ministry of Jesus and the development of the early church. Luke is both a miniaturist and a master designer. Repeatedly, the commentary notes that an individual story or pericope is a Gospel in miniature, artfully depicting Jesus' message, his ministry among the outcasts, or the central elements of the kerygma. Luke is a good storyteller. He knows how to use character and color and paints scenes vividly with his words. Luke is also a master designer in the sense that he gives structure to the whole of his work. Luke situates Jesus in the context of the history of his time and also in the long history of the purposes of God and God's redemption of Israel and of all people. Moreover, Luke expands the genre of Gospel writing by linking the story of Jesus more securely to the leading figures of Jesus' time, by narrating both the annunciations and the births of John and Jesus, by inserting a genealogy that traces Jesus' lineage back to Adam, "the son of God" (3:38), by including in his Gospel more of Jesus' teachings, and by tying the Gospel story to the events that followed in the Acts of the Apostles. Luke chronicles God's call for the repentance of Israel, Israel's rejection of the gospel, and the beginnings of the mission to the Gentiles. Luke's skills and artistry are evident, therefore, both from the examination of particular scenes and stories and from the design and thematic development of the two books.

Luke was probably a Gentile, but apparently one who was knowledgeable in the OT and had a working grasp of Jewish practices and institutions. His description of houses (5:19), cities, and social classes (e.g., 14:15-24) shows that he was familiar with the structure and social organization of a Hellenistic city like Antioch or Ephesus. The evangelist's deference to Theophilus ("most excellent Theophilus," 1:3) indicates that he himself was probably a member of the artisan class rather than the elite—Theophilus's subordinate, not his equal. Even if the tradition based on Col 4:14 is correct and the evangelist was a physician, that would not make him wealthy or a member of the elite.

In the first century, physicians were artisans. Efforts have been made to show that Luke's descriptions of illnesses, afflictions, and healings in the Gospel are more precise than those in other accounts, but the evidence will not support the argument that the Gospel must have been written by a physician. Moreover, the theological differences between Luke and Paul mean that even if Luke was Paul's associate and companion for a period of time, the Gospel of Luke must be read on its own terms and not against the background of Paul's writings. One important step in the reading of the Gospel is the recognition of its design or structure.

STRUCTURE

Banal as it may seem to say so, the Gospel according to Luke is about Jesus. For that reason, it owes a great deal in form to ancient biography. It begins with a literary prologue that confirms the author's qualifications and guarantees the reliability of the biography. The events surrounding the birth of the hero serve as divine omens of his future greatness. An event from his youth foreshadows the work he will do in his maturity. Similarly, the events at the beginning of his public life characterize the significance of the work he is about to do. The heart of the work, then, is a record of his mighty acts and sage teachings. The narrative ends, appropriately, with accounts of the hero's farewell discourse, the manner of his death, the mysterious events that followed his death (appearances to his acquaintances and a translation into heaven), and his parting words to his followers. Distinctive as the Gospel is, each of these elements appears in other Jewish and Greco-Roman biographies.[12]

Some parts of the Gospel's structure are clearly discernible and universally recognized. At other points, the structure is open to various interpretations. The major units of the Gospel are often marked by transitions, introductions and conclusions, lapses in time, changes of geographical location, and the introduction of new characters. From such indications, the following structure emerges.

Luke 1:1-4	The Prologue
Luke 1:5–2:52	The Infancy Narrative
Luke 3:1–4:13	Preparation for the Ministry of Jesus
Luke 4:14–9:50	The Ministry in Galilee
Luke 9:51–19:27	The Journey to Jerusalem
Luke 19:28–21:38	The Ministry in Jerusalem
Luke 22:1–24:53	The Passion and Resurrection Narratives

The Gospel contains seven main sections, most of which contain subsections indicated in the outline below and the commentary. The prologue is distinguished both by its content

---

12. See esp. Charles H. Talbert, *What Is a Gospel? The Genre of the Canonical Gospels* (Philadelphia: Fortress, 1977); and Richard A. Burridge, *What Are the Gospels? A Comparison with Graeco-Roman Biography* (Cambridge: Cambridge University Press, 1992).

and by its style. The first four verses of the Gospel follow the pattern of the prologues of other historical works and are written in some of the most polished and elevated Greek of the entire NT. With v. 5, the style changes dramatically, becoming much more Semitic.

Luke's infancy narrative is distinctive in that it constructs parallels and contrasts between the births and roles of John the Baptist and Jesus. Seven sections are clearly visible; the annunciation of the birth of John the Baptist to Zechariah in the Temple (1:5-25), the annunciation of the birth of Jesus to Mary (1:26-38), Mary's visit to Elizabeth (1:39-56), the birth of John the Baptist (1:57-80), the birth of Jesus and the visit of the shepherds (2:1-20), the presentation of Jesus in the Temple (2:21-40), and Jesus in the Temple at the age of twelve (2:41-52). Luke is also the only Gospel to report any event from Jesus' boyhood. Unlike the legends in the *Infancy Gospel of Thomas,* however, Luke's story of Jesus in the Temple points ahead to his ministry, and especially to his teaching in the Temple in Luke 19:47–21:38.

The elapse of years and the extended introduction to the historical context in 3:1-2 indicate the beginning of a new section of the Gospel, one that is devoted to the preparations for the ministry of Jesus. The individual units of this section are also clearly identifiable. The first three describe John's ministry, the second three Jesus' preparation for ministry: (1) the setting of John's ministry (3:1-6), (2) John's preaching (3:7-18), (3) the imprisonment of John (3:19-20), (4) the baptism of Jesus (3:21-22), (5) the genealogy of Jesus (3:23-38), and (6) the temptation of Jesus (4:1-13).

Luke divides the ministry of Jesus into three periods: the ministry in Galilee (4:14–9:50), the ministry en route to Jerusalem (9:51–19:27), and the ministry in Jerusalem (19:28–21:38). The primary ambiguity in the structure of Luke concerns the end of the journey to Jerusalem and the beginning of the ministry there. Most commentators regard Jesus' parable on kingship in 19:11-27 as the conclusion of the journey section and the transition to his entry into the city. Others, however, mark the end of the Lukan journey section at 18:14 (after which Markan parallels resume) or at 18:34 (after which the sequence of events and the geographical references become significant to the progress of the narrative), and the beginning of Jesus' ministry in Jerusalem at 19:41 (his weeping over the city) or at 19:45 (his entry into the Temple).

The structure of the journey section is also vigorously contested. Fitzmyer divides the journey into three parts using the references to Jerusalem as indications of the beginning of a new section (9:51–13:21; 13:22–17:10; 17:11–18:14, with a return to Markan material in 18:15–19:27), but he recognizes that this scheme is "a mere convenience, since the division at these points is otherwise insignificant and somewhat arbitrary."[13] Evans contends that the journey section is patterned on the arrangement of materials in Deuteronomy 1–26.[14] Others find lectionary cycles or chiastic structures as the basis for

13. Joseph A. Fitzmyer, *The Gospel According to Luke (I–IX),* AB 28 (Garden City, N.Y.: Doubleday, 1981) 825.
14. C. F. Evans, "The Central Section of St. Luke's Gospel," in *Studies in the Gospels: Essays in Memory of R. H. Lightfoot,* ed. D. E. Nineham (Oxford: Blackwell, 1955) 37-53.

the organization of this section of the Gospel. The lack of consensus and the variety of approaches to solving the problem of the structure of the journey section underline the reality that Luke has neither related the material in these ten chapters to the journey motif nor made the basis for its organization clear.

Rather than attempting to fit the material into a consistent pattern on the basis of geographical references, the sequence of the parables, or perceived parallels with Deuteronomy, the following commentary has attempted to mark the internal linkages, organization, and subject matter of these chapters while despairing of achieving a neat, balanced, or consistent structure. For example, Jesus' visit to the home of Mary and Martha is coupled with the lawyer's question and the parable of the good Samaritan in 10:25-42. Luke 11:1-13 offers instruction on prayer. The debates and exchanges of 11:14-36 fit under the subject of responses to charges of deviancy. The extended unit in 12:1–13:9 collects instructions on readiness for the coming judgment. Luke 13:10-35 contains events and parables that concern the unexpected reversals brought by the kingdom of God (the stooped woman, the mustard seed and the yeast, the narrow door, and warnings for Jesus and Jerusalem). Luke 14 returns to the meal scenes that are characteristic of Luke. Luke 15 is a famous collection of parables on the joy of recovery and return (the lost sheep, the lost coin, and the prodigal son). Luke 16 contains two parables on rich men and lovers of money that are joined by a miscellaneous collection of sayings in 16:14-18. Luke 17 does not offer a thematic unity as readily as other sections, since it contains the demands of forgiveness and faith (17:1-10), the healing of the ten lepers (17:11-19), and sayings on the kingdom and its coming (17:20-37). Much of the travel section develops Luke's emphasis on Jesus' gospel to the rich and the poor, and this theme provides a unifying thread for the various paragraphs of Luke 18:1–19:27 (the unjust judge and the persistent widow, the Pharisee and the tax collector, the little children and the rich ruler, the blind beggar, Zacchaeus, and the parable of the greedy and vengeful king).

The structure of the rest of the Gospel falls in place more easily. Jesus' ministry in Jerusalem (19:8–21:38) is set in the Temple. After Jesus enters the city (19:28-40), he weeps over the city and drives the merchants from the Temple (19:41-46), preparing it for his ministry there and pointing ahead to its imminent destruction. Teaching in the Temple each day, Jesus is supported by the people and opposed by their leaders. First he is questioned by one group after another as they seek to trap him in his answers. Then he warns of the coming wars and persecutions, the destruction of Jerusalem, and the coming of the Son of Man.

The passion and resurrection narratives (22:1–24:53) report the preparations for the Passover (22:1-13), the last supper (22:14-20), and the Lukan farewell discourse (22:21-38). The events that lead up to Jesus' trial before Pilate follow in succession: Jesus is arrested (22:47-53); Peter denies Jesus in the courtyard (22:54-62); Jesus is challenged to prophesy (22:63-65) and is then brought before the Sanhedrin (22:66-71). Luke arranges the trial before Pilate neatly in five scenes in 23:1-25: Pilate's first declaration of Jesus' innocence, Jesus' appearance before Herod, Pilate's second declaration of Jesus' innocence, Pilate's third declaration of Jesus' innocence, and Pilate's capitulation to the crowd. Luke's artistry is also visible in his account of the crucifixion, death, and burial of Jesus (23:26-56). On the way to the cross, Jesus is supported by three individuals or groups (Simon of Cyrene, the people, including women from Jerusalem, and the two crucified with him). Following the crucifixion, Luke notes the responses of three other individuals or groups (the centurion, the crowds, and his acquaintances, including the women from Galilee).

The resurrection narratives in Luke 24 cluster in three sections: the discovery of the empty tomb (24:1-12), the appearance on the road to Emmaus (24:13-35), and the appearance to the eleven (24:36-53). The latter is composed of three subsections: proofs of the resurrection (24:36-43), Jesus' interpretation of the Scripture and commissioning of the disciples (24:44-49), and the blessing of the disciples and Jesus' departure (24:50-53), which also serves as the conclusion of the Gospel. Significant as the structure of the Gospel is, however, most of the freight is carried not by its structure but by Luke's christology and the various themes for which Luke is famous.

CHRISTOLOGICAL EMPHASES

Not only is Luke centered around the person of Jesus, but also it focuses the question of his identity so that it becomes part of the plot of the Gospel during the Galilean ministry. The scribes and Pharisees question, "Who is this who is speaking blasphemies?" (5:21). John sends two of his disciples to ask, "Are you the one who is to come, or are we to wait for another?" (7:20). Those at the table in Simon the Pharisee's house ask, "Who is this who even forgives sins?" (7:49). Then, Jesus' own disciples ask one another, "Who then is this?" (8:25). In the next chapter Herod asks the same question, "John I beheaded; but who is this about whom I hear such things?" (9:9). Shortly thereafter, Jesus asks his disciples the question of his identity: "Who do the crowds say that I am?" (9:18). The repeated question sustains the issue, and the characters search for an answer while the identity of Jesus, revealed from the annunciation of his birth, is confirmed and amplified for the reader. The Galilean ministry concludes, then, with Peter's confession, "The Messiah of God" (9:20) and the voice from heaven, which says, "This is my Son, my Chosen" (9:35).

While much of Luke's characterization of Jesus is conveyed by the biographical form of the Gospel and the presentation of the events and teachings that typified his ministry, the titles employed at various points in the Gospel also serve to characterize Jesus in various roles. The titles, however, are not static entities with consistent meanings. On the contrary, they are fluid, and their meaning develops and changes with the unfolding narrative, the interaction between context and title, and the tensions and complementarity among the different titles. The reader may find it helpful, therefore, to survey Luke's use of the leading christological titles in order to sensitize oneself to this aspect of the narrative.

1. Son of God. This title occurs surprisingly seldom in Luke—only six times, once in the annunciation (1:35), twice in the devil's temptations of Jesus (4:3, 9), twice in the outcry of the demons (4:41; 8:28), and once in the accusations of the chief priests, the scribes, and the council (22:70). The disciples never confess or worship Jesus as "Son of God," and where the centurion confesses that Jesus was the Son of God at his death in Mark, Luke has altered the confession so that the centurion says instead, "Certainly this man was innocent" (23:47). The difference between the roles of the title "Son of God" in Mark and Luke is all the more striking when one realizes that it appears in the first line of the Gospel (Mark 1:1) and then at the christological high point of the Gospel, which comes with the centurion's confession in Mark 15:39. Luke has neither of these. From such observations, one might conclude that Luke denies or diminishes the significance of this title for Jesus by using it to characterize the distorted perception of Jesus by the devil, the demons, and Jesus' adversaries.

On the other hand, the title also appears obliquely in very positive contexts. Jesus is first introduced in the annunciation with the words "He will be great, and will be called the Son of the Most High" (1:32). The only occurrence of the actual title in a positive context follows immediately (1:35). At his baptism, the voice from heaven declares, "You are my Son, the Beloved" (3:22), and at the transfiguration the voice from heaven says, "This is my Son, my Chosen" (9:35). Thereafter, Jesus himself appears to adopt the title in his words to the disciples, "No one knows who the Son is except the Father, or who the Father is except the Son and anyone to whom the Son chooses to reveal him" (10:22). The last occurrence is even more oblique; in the parable of the wicked tenants Jesus echoes the language of the voice from heaven when he says that the owner of the vineyard resolves, "I will send my beloved son" (20:13).

In effect, the title is not part of the public discourse in the Gospel but part of the privileged communication to the reader. Only one who has heard the words of Gabriel at the annunciations and the voice from heaven at Jesus' baptism and transfiguration would understand the significance of Jesus' allusions to the title in 10:22 and 20:13. Jesus never uses the title directly with the crowds or his opponents and only indirectly ("the Son") with his disciples. Luke appears to endorse the title "Son of God" and uses it indirectly to define Jesus' relationship to God as Son to the Father, while treating it as a mystery known to the spiritual beings (Gabriel, the devil, and the demons) and a scandal to his adversaries. If the title was originally used metaphorically or suggested kingship (as in 1:32, "and the Lord God will give to him the throne of his ancestor David"), the virgin birth narrative affirms the literal sense rather than the metaphorical meaning of the title.

The heart of the issue is not whether Jesus is the Son of God (that is made clear at the annunciation, the baptism, and the transfiguration) but how Jesus will fulfill his identity. What is the role of the Son of God? The devil challenges him to turn a stone into bread or throw himself down from the Temple (4:3, 9). Ironically, eating with outcasts and feeding his followers, blessing, breaking, and giving bread will indeed characterize his ministry, as will his teaching in the Temple—but not in this way.[15]

2. Prophet—One Greater Than the Prophets. At least one aspect of Jesus' identity revolves around his role as a prophet. Jesus is a prophet who fulfills Moses and the prophets, but he is also one greater than the prophets.

Jesus' prophetic identity is tied to his relationship with John. The annunciation to Zechariah declares that John will possess the spirit and power of Elijah (1:17), and his work is described in terms that echo the OT prophets. By contrast, Jesus will be the Son of the Most High (1:32) and the "mighty savior" from the house of David (1:32-33, 69). Zechariah later affirms the angelic announcement concerning John when he says, "And you, child, will be called the prophet of the Most High" (1:76). John's prophetic role is confirmed in the accounts of his ministry (e.g., 3:1-6) and even by Jesus himself: "A prophet? Yes, I tell you, and more than a prophet" (7:26). Jesus is greater than John, who is the forerunner of Jesus; therefore, it follows that Jesus, too, is greater than the prophets.

Nevertheless, at significant points Luke portrays Jesus as a prophet and as one who fulfills the prophets. As a description of his ministry, Jesus reads from the prophet Isaiah (Luke 4:18-19). In the dispute that follows, Jesus characterizes the crowd's antagonism by saying, "No prophet is accepted in the prophet's hometown" (4:24); and he defends his interpretation of Isaiah by appealing to events in the ministries of Elijah and Elisha (4:25-28).

The issue of Jesus' relation to John and the prophets takes center stage in Luke 7. Luke's account of the raising of the widow's son in 7:11-17 exhibits clear parallels with Elijah's raising of a widow's son in 1 Kings 17 (see the Commentary on Luke 7:11-17). The crowd perceives the significance of the event and responds, "A great prophet has arisen among us" (7:16). Such a confession is especially significant in view of the widespread notion that the spirit of prophecy had been taken from Israel and that there would be no other prophets until the end times (see, e.g., 1 Macc 9:27; cf. Luke 4:46; 14:41).[16]

John's disciples come to Jesus to ask if he is "the coming one," an allusion to Mal 3:1; 4:5-6, but Jesus attributes that messenger role to John himself (7:27), while defining his ministry in terms of fulfillment of the prophets (esp. Isaiah and Elijah/Elisha; see the Commentary on 7:21-22). John fulfilled the role of the one who would prepare the way for the Messiah. Thus he was greater than the prophets (7:26, 28), but even the least in the kingdom is greater than he. This clarification opens the way for Jesus to assume other, more adequate titles while he fulfills the work of the prophets.

Simon the Pharisee mistakenly thinks Jesus is not even a prophet (7:39), while others think he is a prophet, or one of the prophets (9:8, 19; 24:19). At the transfiguration, Moses and Elijah appear with Jesus and talk with him about his "exodus" in Jerusalem (9:30-31). Perhaps elevating Jesus' authority over that of even Moses and Elijah, the voice from

15. See further Martin Hengel, *The Son of God: The Origin of Christology and the History of Jewish-Hellenistic Religion* (Philadelphia: Fortress, 1976).

16. Josephus *Against Apion* 1.41.

heaven then claims Jesus as "my Son" and admonishes the disciples to "listen to *him*" (9:35, italics added). As a prophet, and indeed the one who fulfills the prophets, it is appropriate that he die in Jerusalem (13:33). Finally, the resurrection narratives emphasize that Jesus fulfilled the prophets and that the gospel story must be understood in their light (24:25, 27, 44). While Luke recognizes that Jesus was more than a prophet, it also insists that he must be understood as "a prophet mighty in deed and word before God and all the people" (24:19).

3. Lord. The importance of the title "Lord" in Luke is evident first by its frequency. The term occurs 103 times in Luke, but in some forty of these instances it refers to God as "the Lord." In another 24 instances the term is used of persons besides Jesus (19:33) or characters in Jesus' parables (12:36, 37, 42-47; 16:3, 5; 20:13, 15). Of the remaining instances, when "Lord" refers to Jesus, eighteen are in the vocative, where others address Jesus as "Lord." In these instances, it is difficult to decide when the title means simply "sir" and when it carries the meaning "Lord" (as it seems to at least in 5:8; 6:46; 9:61; and 10:17). Most important, however, the narrator frequently calls Jesus "Lord" in the narration (7:13, 19; 10:1, 39, 41; 11:39; 12:42; 13:15; 17:5-6; 18:6; 19:8; 22:61; 24:3). Since the narrator's speech patterns carry great authority, it is significant that while the narrator refers to Jesus as "the Lord," the narrator does not commonly call Jesus "the Messiah" (see 2:26; 4:41), "the Savior," or "the Son of Man" (see 5:24).

Statistics do not tell the whole story, however, and the categories are neither as clear nor as static as they may appear. The repeated use of "Lord" to refer to God in the infancy narratives colors its use in reference to Jesus later in the Gospel. Fitzmyer suggests, further, that the title was first used of Jesus in reference to his status as risen Lord and then retrojected back into the ministry of Jesus.[17] The title was used of rulers and masters in the Greco-Roman world, and it apparently was used as a term of respect for teachers and great men and in an elevated sense in reference to God in pre-Christian Judaism.

Interesting subtleties become evident when Luke's use of "Lord" to refer to Jesus is examined systematically. After encountering the term in reference to God ten times in Luke 1:6-38, the reader hears Elizabeth ask, "Why has this happened to me, that the mother of my Lord comes to me?" (1:43). Then, at the birth of Jesus, the angels announce, "To you is born this day in the city of David a Savior, who is the Messiah, the Lord" (2:11). The uses of "Lord" in the vocative begin in Luke 5:8, and there the juxtaposition of "Lord" and "sinner" implies that the term means more than "sir": "Go away from me, Lord, for I am a sinful man!" Jesus uses the title in a Son of Man saying in Luke 6:5, "The Son of Man is lord of the sabbath." Shortly thereafter, he asks his disciples, "Why do you call me 'Lord, Lord,' and do not do what I tell you?" (6:46). The narrator's references to Jesus as "the Lord" start in the next chapter (7:13, 19).

At points there are interesting relationships between the metaphorical use of "Lord"

17. Fitzmyer, *The Gospel According to Luke (I–IX)*, 203.

and the use of the title in the vocative or by the narrator. For example, the term occurs nine times in 12:36-47. In Luke 12:36-37, Jesus speaks of a master or lord in a parable, where the master seems to represent the coming Son of Man. In 12:41, Peter asks, "Lord, are you telling this parable for us or for everyone?" and the narrator continues, "And the Lord said" (12:42), after which Jesus uses the term five more times in an explanation of the parable and in related sayings in 12:42-47. Similarly, the vocative occurs in 13:23, "Lord, will only a few be saved?" and Jesus gives a parabolic or metaphorical answer in which many seek entrance, saying, "Lord, open to us" (13:25), but the owner of the house will not let them in. The metaphorical and the absolute uses of the term are again difficult to distinguish in 16:8, where interpreters have debated whether the verse is part of Jesus' parable or a comment by the narrator following the parable (see the Commentary on this verse). The precise connotations of the term are also difficult to determine in Luke 19:31, 34, where the disciples take a colt for Jesus to ride on and tell its owners, "The Lord [or its lord] needs it." By the end of the Gospel, the disciples use the term not only in the vocative but also in the absolute when they echo the Easter confession, "The Lord has risen indeed, and he has appeared to Simon" (24:34).

The title "Lord," therefore, subtly infuses the Gospel with the church's post-Easter confession of the risen Lord. Luke affirms the confession of Jesus as Lord. Even from his birth, Jesus is the Lord who would rise from the dead.

4. Messiah or Christ. Much like the title "Son of God," the title "Messiah" or "Christ" also belongs to the privileged knowledge of who Jesus is that is communicated by the Gospel. Literally, *Messiah* means "the anointed one" or "the Christ." The title first appears at the birth of Jesus, where the angels announce, "To you is born this day in the city of David a Savior, who is the Messiah, the Lord" (2:11). Of all the constructions using these titles in the NT, this verse is the only place where this one (χριστὸς κύριος *christos kyrios*) occurs, but it resembles the combination of the two titles in Luke 2:26, "the Lord's Messiah," and Acts 2:36, "know with certainty that God has made him both Lord and Messiah, this Jesus whom you crucified." Anointing was connected with kingship (cf. 1 Sam 24:6), and "the Lord's anointed" was the one anointed by God to serve as king.

The identity of Jesus as the Messiah is then treated as "inside information" known to the narrator, the reader, and the angels and demons, but not to the other characters. The Holy Spirit revealed to Simeon that he would not die until he saw "the Lord's Messiah" (2:26), and then guided Simeon to recognize Jesus as the Messiah. The people question whether John might be the Messiah (3:15), but the reader knows better. In an interpretive comment, the narrator explains that the demons also knew that Jesus was the Messiah (4:41).

The knowledge of Jesus' full identity as the Messiah breaks upon the disciples in 9:20 when Peter confesses that Jesus is "the Messiah of God." Even so, they do not understand the fate that awaits Jesus in Jerusalem. The superiority of the Messiah to David is explained in 20:41-44. Jesus' messiahship becomes the source of ironic mockery at his trial and crucifixion. The council of the religious leaders demands, "If you are the Messiah, tell us" (22:67). One of the three charges leveled against Jesus when he is brought before Pilate is that he says "that he himself is the Messiah, a king" (23:2). The charge may arise out of Jesus' words about the Messiah and the son of David in 20:41-44, but he does not openly claim these titles in Luke. The mockery of the leaders of the people at the cross connects the title with the words of the voice from heaven in 9:35: "Let him save himself if he is the Messiah of God, his chosen one!" (23:35; cf. Isa 42:1). Similarly, one of those crucified with Jesus challenges him, "Are you not the Messiah? Save yourself and us!" (23:39).

The title "Messiah," therefore, conveys the hidden identity of Jesus, as does the title "Son of God," but it also serves as a bridge to the more functional title "Savior" (see below). Further aspects of Jesus' role are conveyed by the title "Son of Man," and these must be examined before we turn to the title that defines the dying Christ in Luke ("Savior"). The title "Son of Man" appears repeatedly in the passion predictions, but in the resurrection narratives, "Messiah" replaces it in sayings where we might have expected to find "Son of Man": "Was it not necessary that the Messiah should suffer these things and then enter into his glory?" (24:26), and "Thus it is written, that the Messiah is to suffer and to rise from the dead on the third day" (24:46).

5. Son of Man. In Luke, Jesus speaks of himself as "the Son of Man" more frequently than with any other form of self-reference. The title "Son of Man" occurs 25 times in Luke (not counting the variant in 9:56). Moreover, with the possible exception of Luke 5:24, which may be a comment by the narrator, the term occurs only on the lips of Jesus in Luke. All three of the traditional categories of Son of Man sayings occur in the Gospel. The sayings that describe Jesus' earthly ministry (8 sayings) are the most diverse and the most like circumlocutions (where "the Son of Man" simply stands for "I"). The Son of Man has authority to forgive sins on earth (5:24); he is lord of the sabbath (6:5); his followers will be persecuted on his account (6:22); in contrast to John the Baptist, he came eating and drinking (7:34); he has no place to lay his head (9:58); those who speak against him will be forgiven (12:10); he came to seek and to save the lost (19:10); and Judas betrays him with a kiss (22:48). Five times the title "Son of Man" occurs in predictions of Jesus' suffering and death (9:22, 44; 18:31; 22:22; 24:7), and twelve times in sayings that refer to the future coming of the Son of Man in glory (9:26; 11:30; 12:8, 40; 17:22, 24, 26, 30; 18:8; 21:27, 36; 22:69). Moreover, Luke has added the title to sayings where it does not appear in Mark or Matthew (e.g., 6:22; 9:22; 12:8, 40; 19:10).

The background of the use of "Son of Man" in the Gospels is still vigorously debated. It occurs in Dan 7:13: "I saw one like a human being/ coming with the clouds of heaven" (NRSV), where it seems to refer to the exaltation of the holy ones of Israel to God. Use of the term to designate an apocalyptic figure (as in the parables of *1 Enoch*) is attested in later sources, as is the use of "the son of man" as a circumlocution in Aramaic. Jesus may have used the term in its generic sense ("a human being") or as a self-reference. Alternatively, he may have used the term because it was sufficiently ambiguous to force the hearer to discern its intended meaning. The various uses of the title in Luke, however, alternate between emphasizing Jesus' humanity and his future role as risen Lord. The lowly one seen in Jesus' ministry will suffer and die, but God will vindicate him and he will return in the future as the exalted Son of Man. One's response to the Son of Man who died on the cross determines the judgment that one will receive when the Son of Man comes in the future. Thus the title "Son of Man" serves an important role in the Gospel, because it links Jesus' ministry, his death, and the future judgment.

6. Savior. Luke is the only one of the Synoptics to call Jesus "Savior." Yet, as significant as the characterization of Jesus as the Savior is in Luke, the title occurs only twice in the Gospel, both times in the infancy narrative. In the first instance it is applied to God (1:47), and in the second the angel of the Lord announces to the shepherds: "To you is born this day in the city of David a Savior, who is the Messiah, the Lord" (2:11).

In this case, however, one cannot gauge the importance of a term merely by counting the frequency of its occurrence. Although the title "Savior" occurs only twice, Jesus is repeatedly identified as God's salvation or as the one who saves. Zechariah rejoices that God has "raised up a horn of salvation for us/ in the house of his servant David" (1:69; cf. 1:71, 77), clearly a reference to Jesus. When Simeon sees Jesus, after he had been promised that he would see the Messiah, he too gives thanks to God, "for my eyes have seen your salvation" (2:30; cf. 3:6).

During the course of his ministry, Jesus assures various ones that their faith has "saved" them or made them whole (7:50; 8:48; 17:19; 18:42). Then, in Jericho, he tells Zacchaeus, "Today salvation has come to this house. . . . For the Son of Man came to seek out and to save the lost" (19:9-10). Fittingly, the theme reaches its climax at the crucifixion of Jesus, where through the irony of the mockery Jesus is portrayed as the taunted Savior. First the leaders of the people scoff, "He saved others; let him save himself if he is the Messiah of God, his chosen one!" (23:35). Then the soldiers join the sport, introducing another title: "If you are the King of the Jews, save yourself!" (23:37). The third time it is one of the two crucified with Jesus who says, "Are you not the Messiah? Save yourself and us!" (23:39). The functional sense of the title has displaced the title itself while also defining the role of the Messiah, the King of the Jews. By the end of the passion narrative, the reader understands clearly the import of both the angelic announcement at Jesus' birth and Simeon's ominous words that a sword would pierce Mary's heart (2:35).

Other titles also serve to characterize Jesus: "servant," "master," and other titles.[18] Luke's characterization of Jesus is distinctive, however, not for the defining role of its titles but for the variety of themes that flesh out these confessions.

18. See ibid., 197-219.

THEMES

Luke is noted for its richness of themes. No other Gospel develops so many themes as fully as does Luke. For this reason, the reader will find numerous references in the commentary to related verses in the Gospel. Seeing the relationship of a particular verse to others that develop a common theme is vital to gaining appreciation for any given passage in the Gospel. The reader is encouraged, therefore, to take the time to read the related verses in context. As an aid to such thematic study of the Gospel, the development of some of its principal themes is traced here. This part of the Introduction can serve as a handy reference point and as a compendium that enables the reader to study the relationship between the Gospel's most important themes.

1. God's Redemptive Purposes. Luke sets the life of Jesus both in its historical context and in a theological context. All that happens in the Gospel and in Acts is ultimately a part of God's redemptive plan for the salvation of all humanity. The phrase "God's purpose" occurs only once in Luke, but several times in Acts (Luke 7:30; Acts 2:23; 13:36; 20:27). Luke's development of this theme is evident in the Gospel's treatment of three related emphases: the sovereignty of God, the fulfillment of Scripture, and the scope of Jesus' redemptive work.

The sovereignty of God means that God's purposes direct events in human history. Some events "must" happen, and there is a divine purpose at work even in puzzling and tragic events. Jesus must be about his Father's business (or in his Father's house; 2:49). He must proclaim the kingdom of God (4:43) and suffer and die (9:22; 17:25; 24:7, 26). It was necessary in God's purposes that Jesus come to Zacchaeus's house (19:5). Even wars and insurrections must occur before the end (21:9). The Scriptures too must be fulfilled (22:37; 24:44).

Gabriel, God's emissary, inaugurates the new era chronicled in the Gospel by declaring first to Zechariah and then to Mary the births and the future work of John the Baptist and Jesus. From the beginning, they are to be understood as carrying out what God has purposed. All things are possible with God, even things that are not possible for ordinary mortals (1:37; 18:27). God is our Savior (1:47), and we are saved by God's mercy (1:78). If it were necessary, God could even raise up children to Abraham from the stones (3:8). In a manner reminiscent of the records of the prophets of old, Luke says that the Word of God came to John the son of Zechariah (3:2), and the Spirit of the Lord anointed Jesus for his ministry (4:18). It was "necessary" (δεῖ *dei*) that he proclaim the kingdom of God (4:43), so each of the succeeding references to the kingdom is to be understood in this light. Jesus' mighty acts are also transparently God's acts. For example, when he raises the son of the widow of Nain, the people respond: "God has looked favorably on his people!" (7:16). The Pharisees and the lawyers are characterized as those who rejected "God's purpose" (7:30). When Jesus exorcised the unclean spirits from the Gerasene demoniac, he instructed him to go and "declare how much God has done for you" (8:39). Such exorcisms are evidence both that Jesus acts "by the finger of God" and that "the kingdom of God has come to you" (11:20). God's providence extends even to sparrows that are sold at a rate of five for two copper coins worth only a sixteenth of a denarius each (12:6). God feeds even the ravens (12:24) and clothes the grass of the field (12:28). Consequently, God also "knows your hearts" (16:15) and will respond quickly to grant justice to the chosen ones who cry out night and day (18:7-8). In a sense, the whole Gospel declares what God has done and leads the reader to follow the example of the disciples in praising God in response (24:53).

Because God is sovereign, the Scriptures must be fulfilled (22:37; 24:44). In no sense can the Gospel according to Luke be pitted over against the OT in a Marcionite fashion.[19] Luke takes care to relate the events of the Gospel to the Scriptures, so that an attentive reader must constantly consult OT passages that are quoted or alluded to in the Gospel. Luke refers to "all that is written" three times (18:31; 21:22; 24:44) and to that which "is written" thirteen times (in various forms: 2:23; 3:4; 4:4, 8, 10, 17; 7:27; 10:26; 19:46; 20:17, 28; 22:37; 24:46). Jesus declares that "today" the Scriptures are fulfilled (4:21), and three times in the resurrection narratives Luke says that Jesus opened the Scriptures for his disciples (24:27, 32, 45). The Scriptures are an expression of God's purposes, so the roles of John and Jesus are characterized at the annunciation in allusions to Scripture; the disciples do not fully understand the events that have transpired among them until they understand them in the light of Scripture. The fulfillment of the Scriptures, consequently, is a further confirmation for the reader that the plan of God is being accomplished.

The plan of God reaches from the works of God among Moses and the prophets through the ministries of John and Jesus to the mission of the church in Acts. The preaching of the gospel to the Gentiles is a direct consequence and outworking of the purposes of God that guided Jesus, but will not be fulfilled until the coming of the Son of Man in glory. The plan of God in Luke and Acts extends temporally through the history of Israel, the ministry of Jesus, and the mission of the church; geographically, from the Temple to the ends of the earth; and ethnically, from the religious leaders to the outcasts, and from the Jews to all peoples. As a result, many of the themes that are treated below could be subsumed under the rubric of the fulfillment of God's redemptive purposes.

2. Salvation for All Alike. Perhaps Luke's most dramatic insight is his perception that Jesus announced salvation for all people alike. Although Jesus' initiatives toward all persons regardless of their social standing are a common feature of all the Gospels, no other Gospel is so clear and emphatic on this point. If Luke was influenced by Paul's mission and Paul's grasp of the gospel, it may have been at this point. Paul declares that the gospel is for "the Jew first and also to the Greek" (Rom 1:16 NRSV). In the blessing of John the Baptist, traditionally called the *Benedictus,* Zechariah praises God for fulfilling the covenant with Abraham and bringing salvation to Israel (1:68-79). Simeon, in the blessing traditionally called the *Nunc Dimittis,* declares that God has prepared this salvation

---

19. Marcion, c. 140 CE, rejected the OT, deleted OT references from Luke, and held that only his edited version of Luke and ten Pauline letters were Scripture.

"in the presence of all peoples,/ a light for revelation to the Gentiles/ and for glory to your people Israel" (2:31-32). Luke then extends the quotation from Isa 40:3, which is found at the beginning of Mark, reading also the next two verses:

"Every valley shall be filled,
  and every mountain and hill shall be made low,
and the crooked shall be made straight,
  and the rough ways made smooth;
and all flesh shall see the salvation of God." (Isa 40:4-5; Luke 3:5-6)

At the synagogue in Nazareth, where Jesus interprets a later passage in Isaiah, he provokes the anger of his townsmen by reminding them that God sent the prophets Elijah and Elisha to a widow in Sidon and to a leper from Syria (4:24-30). The mighty works of God's deliverance were not for Israel alone. In his parables and teachings, Jesus emphasizes further that the inclusiveness of God's mercy knows no bounds: "Then people will come from east and west, from north and south, and will eat in the kingdom of God" (13:29). It will be like a master sending his servant out again and again, saying, "Go out at once into the streets and lanes of the town and bring in the poor, the crippled, the blind, and the lame" (14:21) and "Go out into the roads and lanes, and compel people to come in, so that my house may be filled" (14:23). At the end of the Gospel, Jesus commissions his disciples for this task, sending them out because the fulfillment of the Scriptures, the fulfillment of God's purposes, requires that "repentance and forgiveness of sins is to be proclaimed . . . to all nations, beginning from Jerusalem" (24:47; cf. Acts 1:8). The universalism of the gospel means that what God has done in Christ, God has done for all people, but it does not mean that all people will repent and accept God's mercy. The very proclamation of such a radical gospel leads some to exclude themselves from it. The people at Nazareth seek to kill Jesus (4:29). The patriarchs and the prophets will feast in the kingdom of God, but "you yourselves [will be] thrown out," Jesus warns those who took offense at his gospel (13:28), and the master of the banquet fills his house with nondescript guests so that "none of those who were invited will taste my dinner" (14:24). Tragically, the gospel of God's universal grace will not be universally accepted.

Luke's concern to present the radical inclusiveness of Jesus' ministry is evident in the numerous scenes in this Gospel in which Jesus reaches out to sinners, Samaritans, tax collectors, women, and outcasts. Both social and religious factors conditioned the prevailing attitude to the privileged toward these groups. A vital part of Jesus' proclamation of the new order of the kingdom of God, therefore, consisted in his challenge to the collusion of the religious authorities in the social prejudices of his day. Although the various groups of the oppressed and outcasts of society all illustrate this aspect of Jesus' ministry, by handling them separately we can see the role each plays in the Gospel.

Luke refers to *sinners* more than does any other Gospel (17 times). Interestingly, the term does not occur in the annunciations or the poetic sections of the infancy narrative, and the only reference in the passion and resurrection narratives is the echo of the passion predictions in Luke 24:7. Peter acknowledges that he is a sinner (5:8). The pattern of the majority of the references to sinners in the Gospel reveals that "sinners" are often associated with tax collectors. The term often emerges in the context of table fellowship and Jesus' practice of eating with those scorned by the religious authorities, and it often represents the viewpoint of the Pharisees and religious leaders. When Jesus' disciples are criticized for eating with "tax collectors and sinners" (5:30), Jesus responds that he has not come to call the righteous but sinners to repentance (5:32). In the Sermon on the Plain (6:17-49), Jesus challenges his disciples to do more than the sinners who love those who love them, do good to those who do good to them, and lend to those from whom they hope to receive (6:32-34). Jesus again refers to sinners when he quotes his critics as saying that "the Son of Man has come eating and drinking, and you say, 'Look, a glutton and a drunkard, a friend of tax collectors and sinners' " (7:34). The narrator identifies the woman who approaches Jesus in the house of Simon the Pharisee as "a woman in the city, who was a sinner" (7:37), and Simon refers to her as a sinner (7:39). When the Pharisees and scribes see the tax collectors and sinners coming to Jesus, they grumble and complain that Jesus "welcomes sinners and eats with them" (15:1-2). Jesus responds by telling the parables of the lost sheep, the lost coin, and the prodigal son. The first two of these parables end with the lesson, "Just so, I tell you, there will be more joy in heaven over one sinner who repents than over ninety-nine righteous persons who need no repentance" (15:7; cf. 15:10). In the parable of the Pharisee and the tax collector (18:9-14), the tax collector beats his breast and says, "God, be merciful to me, a sinner" (18:13), and Jesus assures his audience that "this man went down to his home justified" (18:14). Once more, when Jesus went to the home of Zacchaeus, the people complained, "He has gone to be the guest of one who is a sinner" (19:7). The only other references to sinners in Luke come in 13:2, where Jesus asks whether the Galileans who perished were worse sinners than others, and in 24:7, where the angel at the tomb recalls Jesus' warning that he would be "handed over to sinners." The contexts in which most of the references to sinners occur in Luke serve to define "sinners" primarily as those who were shunned by the Pharisees and scribes. They are the tax collectors, harlots, and others with whom Jesus ate and drank, thereby violating the social codes and prescriptions of the Pharisees.

The *Samaritans* were another stereotypical group of outcasts from the perspective of pious Jews. The Samaritans are shown in a positive light in each of the three instances where they appear in the Gospel. When the disciples want to call down fire on a Samaritan village, Jesus rebukes them (9:51-56). The "good Samaritan" (10:33) has become one of the most famous figures in Jesus' teachings, and when Jesus heals ten lepers only a Samaritan sees what has happened and returns praising God (17:11-19). To this one also Jesus gives the assurance, "Go on your way; your faith has made you well" (17:19).

Women play a significant role also, and Luke often features male and female characters in pairs. The infancy narrative features the role of Zechariah and Elizabeth, Joseph and Mary, and Simeon and Anna. In contrast to the Gospel of Matthew, Mary rather than

Joseph is the principal character in Luke's account of the birth of Jesus. Later in the Gospel, Jesus exorcises an unclean spirit from a man in the synagogue in Capernaum and then heals Peter's mother-in-law (4:31-39). He heals a centurion's servant and then raises a widow's son (7:1-17). Jesus vindicates the sinful woman over Simon the Pharisee (7:36-50). Luke is also the only Gospel to note that Jesus was accompanied by a group of women who supported him and the male disciples (8:1-3). Jesus' mother and brothers are not dismissed but are held up as "those who hear the word of God and do it" (8:21; cf. 11:27-28). Jesus heals a woman with a hemorrhage and then raises Jairus's daughter (8:40-56). The account of Jesus' words to Mary and Martha, defending Mary's sitting at his feet and attending to his teachings like a disciple, is unique to Luke (10:38-42). The account of the healing of the crippled woman who could not stand up straight clearly declares Luke's understanding of Jesus' concern for the dignity and wholeness of the woman (13:10-17; for further development of this theme, see the Commentary on this passage). The story has often been linked with the healing of the man with dropsy (14:1-6). Jesus draws his parables from the experience of women as well as from male experiences: The kingdom is like "yeast that a woman took and mixed in with three measures of flour" (13:21). Elsewhere Jesus' parables feature both male and female characters: a shepherd who loses a sheep and a woman who loses a coin (15:3-10), an unjust judge and a persistent widow (18:1-8). Later, in the Temple, Jesus castigates the scribes who "devour widows' houses" (20:47) and praises the poor widow who gives two copper coins (21:1-4). When Jesus predicts the destruction of Jerusalem, he laments in particular the suffering it will inflict on mothers and infants (21:23). Only in Luke does Jesus call upon the daughters of Jerusalem to weep not for him but for the suffering that they will experience in the coming days (23:27-29). Luke again notes the role of the women from Galilee following Jesus' death (23:49, 55-56). At the tomb, the angel declares the Easter tidings to the women; they are not merely messengers to the male disciples (24:1-12).

The various references to women in Luke's Gospel demonstrate both Jesus' concern to extend God's mercy to women as well as to men and Luke's sensitivity to Jesus' radical departure from the social conventions of his time. Luke portrays Jesus associating freely with women and calling for a new pattern of relationships both by his actions and in his teachings. Recent interpreters have pointed out, however, that Luke distances women from the prophetic ministry and confines women to traditional roles: "prayerful, quiet, grateful women, supportive of male leadership, forgoing the prophetic ministry."[20] Luke remains grounded in the social context of the first century. Nevertheless, if its portrayal of Jesus' relationships with women falls short by contemporary standards, it was radical in a first-century context. Jesus permits a woman to touch his feet in public and to sit at his feet with male disciples, and he defends a woman from the scorn of Simon the Pharisee. While Luke's Jesus does not succeed in freeing women from the shackles of societal

20. Jane Schaberg, "Luke," in *The Women's Bible Commentary,* ed. Carol Newsom and Sharon H. Ringe (Louisville: Westminster/John Knox, 1992) 275.

repression, he specifically includes women among those for whom the coming of the kingdom is good news and points to the inauguration of a new community in which freedom, dignity, and equality may be realized.

3. The Blessings of Poverty and the Dangers of Wealth. The poor are also prominent in Luke. Just as Jesus habitually associates with tax collectors and sinners, so he also declares God's vindication of the poor and divine judgment upon the rich. Popular theology held that the rich were blessed of God, but Jesus turned popular theology on its head, maintaining that God would lift up the poor and cast out the rich. From the time of the exile, poverty had come to be associated with humility and dependence on God. Whereas Matthew spiritualizes the beatitudes, "Blessed are the poor in spirit" (Matt 5:3 NRSV), Luke faces the economic realities of poverty, "Blessed are you who are poor" (6:20) and laments the condition of the rich, "But woe to you who are rich,/ for you have received your consolation" (6:24).

Luke's handling of the beatitudes and woes is part of the pattern of his characterization of Jesus' responses to wealth and poverty throughout the Gospel. Not surprisingly, Luke refers to the poor and the rich more than does any other Gospel. Modern readers must, therefore, guard against efforts to pull the prophetic sting from Luke or spiritualize poverty in spite of Luke's efforts to prevent us from doing so. The canticles of the infancy narrative announce the theme. The Lord has "looked with favor" on his lowly servant (Mary), "brought down the powerful from their thrones and lifted up the lowly," and "sent the rich away empty" (1:48, 52-53). In his opening address at Nazareth, Jesus reveals that he has been sent to "bring good news to the poor" (4:18), and he refuses to allow those in Nazareth to hear the Scriptures as promises of deliverance for themselves only. To John's disciples, Jesus responds that the preaching of good news to the poor is one of the signs that validates his ministry (7:22). Embarrassingly, Jesus exhorts the guests at a banquet to invite the poor, the crippled, the lame, and the blind when they give a banquet (14:13, 21). The rich fool thought he was fixed for life, that his future was secure, but the Lord demanded his life of him that night (12:16-21). "Life does not consist in the abundance of possessions," Jesus warned (12:15). Indeed, some of the seed is choked out by "the cares and riches and pleasures of life" (8:14). The poor man Lazarus, who lay at the rich man's gate, is carried to Abraham's bosom, while the rich man who feasted every day is condemned to perpetual torment. They are two men separated by a table, and in the hereafter the tables are turned (16:19-31). How hard it is, Jesus laments, for those who have wealth to enter the kingdom of God (18:24). His exhortation to the ruler who sought eternal life is to sell what he has and give to the poor (18:22), which is just what Zacchaeus pledges to do: "Half of my possessions, Lord, I will give to the poor" (19:8). When the poor widow gives all she has, however, she is praised above the rich who give great sums of money (21:1-4).

Contemporary interpreters face the temptation either to dismiss or to spiritualize Luke's teachings on the dangers of wealth on the one hand or to literalize and absolutize them on the other hand. The challenge is to deal seriously with this aspect of the Gospel in the context of individual life-styles and caring communities in a materialistic and technological society that has widened the gap between rich and poor.

4. Table Fellowship. One of the most characteristic settings for the ministry of Jesus in the Gospel according to Luke is the meal scene. Jesus eats with tax collectors and sinners, with Pharisees, with the crowd, and with the disciples. According to a perceptive quip, "Jesus is either going to a meal, at a meal, or coming from a meal."[21] The meals in Luke become a "type scene," a scene repeated at intervals with subtle variations. The importance of the meal scenes is suggested both by the significance of table fellowship in the first century and by the repetition and complexity of the meal scenes in this Gospel.[22]

Immediately after Jesus called Levi, the tax collector, to follow him, Levi gave a banquet for Jesus. For the first time, we hear the charge that Jesus eats and drinks "with tax collectors and sinners" (5:29-32). In chap. 7, Simon the Pharisee invites Jesus to a meal at his house, where a sinful woman weeps at Jesus' feet and anoints them (7:36-50). When the crowds follow Jesus to a deserted place, Jesus feeds the multitude with five loaves and two fish (9:12-17). When another Pharisee invites Jesus to a meal, Jesus scandalizes his host first by not washing before the meal and then by castigating the Pharisees for being more concerned about washing the outside of vessels than about inner purity (11:37-52). In chap. 14 Jesus is again invited to the house of a leader of the Pharisees (14:1-24). This time he challenges the guests to take the lower seats rather than the seats of honor and then admonishes the host not to invite friends and relatives to a dinner but to invite "the poor, the crippled, the lame, and the blind" (14:11). The parable of the great banquet follows (14:15-24).

Related to the meal scenes is the parable of the rich man and Lazarus, which features the offending table of the rich man (16:19-31). Against this background, the institution of the Lord's Supper (22:14-20) and the meal at Emmaus (24:13-35) take on a special significance. The meal is connected with Jesus' death. His breach of the social boundaries through his inclusive table fellowship fueled the opposition that led to his death. Whenever the Lord's supper is observed both his table fellowship with outcasts and his death for sinners is commemorated. The Table becomes the place where disputes over greatness are set aside and divisive barriers are overturned by means of voluntary servanthood (22:24-27). Table fellowship also characterizes both the eschatological promise and the experience of the church. The hope of the disciples and the promise Jesus offers is that they will eat and drink at Jesus' table in the kingdom (23:30). The risen Lord, moreover, is present with the believing community and makes himself known to them in "the breaking of bread" (24:35). Here then is *the heart of Luke's hermeneutic:* After investigating everything carefully (1:3), Luke has found that he recognizes "the truth concerning the

21. Robert J. Karris, *Luke: Artist and Theologian, Luke's Passion Account as Literature* (New York: Paulist, 1985) 47.

22. For an insightful analysis of the role of the Lukan meal scenes, see Craig Thomas McMahan, "Meals as Type-Scenes in the Gospel of Luke" (Ph.D. diss., Southern Baptist Theological Seminary, 1987).

things about which you have been instructed" when memory of the actions and teachings of Jesus' ministry is enlightened by the Scriptures and reenacted in the hospitality and table fellowship of the community of believers.

5. The Role of a Disciple. Christology and discipleship are always connected. How one understands the role of Jesus as the Christ shapes one's understanding of discipleship. Luke takes the hard edge off Mark's portrayal of the disciples, omitting the statement that the disciples' hearts were hardened (Mark 6:52), Jesus' rebuke of the disciples for their failure to understand about the loaves (Mark 8:17-21), Jesus' rebuke to Peter, "Get behind me, Satan" (Mark 8:32-33), and the disciples' final abandonment of Jesus (Mark 14:50-52). At other places Luke softens the critique of the disciples. At the transfiguration, when Peter asked if they could build booths and stay there, Luke adds "not knowing what he said" (Luke 9:33). In the Gethsemane scene, Jesus finds the disciples "sleeping because of grief" (22:45). The disciples are called not to die with Jesus but to take up their cross *daily* and follow him (9:23).

Jesus is the model to be imitated. He is empowered by the Spirit, he is compassionate toward the poor and oppressed, he heals and forgives, he prays, and he dies a model martyr's death. The disciples are called with an unconditional, absolute, person-centered call: "Follow me" (5:27; 9:59). Complementing the Gospel's emphasis on the dangers of wealth and possessions, Luke notes that the disciples "left everything and followed him" (5:11, 28). Those who offer to follow him but cannot leave other concerns behind are rejected (9:57-62).

Aspects of Luke's characterization of Jesus need to be explored further, therefore, as reflections of the model that Jesus offers for his disciples. Jesus' obedience to God's direction is a model for his followers. He "must" be in his Father's house, or "about my Father's interests" (see 2:49). Jesus rebuffs the devil's attempts to gain his allegiance or direct the course of his ministry; Jesus follows the direction of Scripture and chooses to worship God "and serve only him" (4:8). What the Lord has anointed Jesus to do (4:18), he faithfully accomplishes in the following chapters. His prayer at the end of his ministry, "not my will but yours be done" (22:42), is consistent with all that he has done to that point.

Related to both Jesus' empowerment by the Spirit and his obedience to God is the role of prayer in Luke's account of Jesus' ministry. The Spirit descends on Jesus "when Jesus also had been baptized *and was praying*" (3:21, italics added). Jesus regularly withdrew from the crowds to deserted places to pray (5:16). He prayed all night in the mountains before he chose the twelve disciples (6:12), then he taught the disciples to pray for those who abused them (6:28). Jesus' conversation with the disciples and Peter's confession that he was the Messiah occur while Jesus was praying (9:18). Similarly, the three disciples witness the transfiguration when they accompany Jesus on another of his retreats to the mountains for prayer (9:28). Jesus teaches the disciples the model prayer on another occasion when they have seen him praying (11:1-4). In addition, several of Jesus' parables are related to prayer: the parable of the neighbor in need at midnight (11:5-8; cf. 11:9-13), the parable of the widow and the unjust judge (18:1-8, esp. v. 1), and the parable of the Pharisee and the tax collector (18:9-14). In contrast to Jesus' practice and teaching regarding prayer, the scribes say long prayers for the sake of appearance (20:47).

Like various other themes, the emphasis on prayer as a facet of Jesus' character that is modeled for the disciples culminates in the passion narrative. Jesus prays on the Mount of Olives before he is arrested. He instructs the disciples to "pray that you may not come into the time of trial" (22:40, 46). Then, he kneels and prays for deliverance from the suffering he knows lies ahead, and in a textually dubious verse is strengthened by an angel (see the Commentary on 22:43-44). Later, when Jesus is dying, he dies praying: "Father, forgive them; for they do not know what they are doing" (23:34, which is absent in some MSS; see the Commentary); and "Father, into your hands I commend my spirit" (23:46). Both of these prayers from the cross, moreover, are unique to Luke, and Jesus' role as a model of martyrdom is confirmed when in the book of Acts Stephen echoes the two prayers of Jesus as he dies (Acts 7:59-60). If following Jesus in Luke means doing as Jesus does, then prayer is a vital part of being a follower of Jesus.

The trial and death of Jesus also confirm his identification with the oppressed, and that he was innocent under the law—a righteous man. Just as it was characteristic of Jesus that he ate with tax collectors and sinners, so also at his death "he was counted among the lawless" (22:37) and died with criminals (23:33). The beginning of Luke's passion narrative makes it clear that the religious leaders were "looking for a way to put Jesus to death" (22:2) and that Satan facilitated their plot against Jesus (22:3-6).

Luke underscores the innocence of Jesus repeatedly throughout the trial and crucifixion scenes. The Gospel takes pains to ensure that the reader understands that the accusations against Jesus are false charges. Jesus did not forbid the payment of taxes (23:2; cf. 20:20-26). His role as the Messiah was diametrically opposed to that of an earthly king (23:2; cf. 19:11-27), and by the end of the trial Luke has shown that it is the leaders themselves who pervert the people (23:2; cf. 23:13-18). The trial before Pilate is structured around Pilate's three declarations that he finds no crime in Jesus (23:4, 14, 22). When Pilate sends Jesus to Herod, Herod returns him and Pilate reports that Herod found him innocent also (23:6-12, 15). Jesus' innocence is confirmed by two authorities, but Pilate nevertheless capitulates to the will of the leaders of the people (23:25). At the cross, the "penitent thief" crucified with Jesus also maintains that Jesus has done nothing wrong (23:41), and the centurion who witnessed Jesus' death "praised God and said, 'Certainly this man was innocent' " (23:47).

The function or functions of Luke's emphasis on Jesus' innocence can again be interpreted variously. If Theophilus is a Roman official, Luke may be concerned to make the point that Jesus (and the disciples and Paul in Acts) was repeatedly declared innocent by the Roman authorities, confirming that from its inception Christianity was not an illegal religion and was not perceived as a threat to Roman authority. On the other hand, if (as seems more likely) the Gospel is intended for the believing community, the repeated declarations of innocence in the Gospel and Acts may serve to reassure believers of the rightness of their convictions and to give them precedents to which they can appeal when they too are "brought before kings and governors" (21:12).

The centurion's praise of God and affirmation that Jesus was δίκαιος (*dikaios*) moves the characterization of Jesus to another level. The term may mean "innocent," but Luke uses it elsewhere with the sense of "just" or "righteous." Among those whom Luke characterizes as "just" are Zechariah and Elizabeth (1:6), Simeon (2:25), and—in the same context as the centurion's confession—Joseph of Arimathea (23:50). In Acts, moreover, Jesus is called "the Righteous One" (Acts 3:14; 7:52; 22:14).

The prominence of *joy* and *the praise of God* in Luke defines the response of those who see God's power at work in John the Baptist and Jesus and hear the good news of the kingdom. The birth of John brought joy and gladness (1:14, 44, 58), and at the birth of Jesus the angels brought the shepherds "good news of great joy for all the people" (2:10). Some who receive the gospel with joy, however, are like seed sown in rocky ground: "They believe only for a while and in a time of testing fall away" (8:13). The seventy Jesus sent out on mission returned filled with joy at what they had seen (10:17), and Jesus reminds the scribes and Pharisees that there is joy in heaven over one sinner who repents (15:7, 10). Joy also characterizes the response of the disciples to the appearances of the risen Lord (24:41-52).

In Luke those who see the power of God at work or hear the good news are not only filled with joy, but their characteristic response is to glorify or praise God as well. This doxological undertone to the Gospel is evident in the response of the shepherds at Jesus' birth, who returned, "glorifying and praising God for all they had heard and seen" (2:20). Thereafter, both terms, "glorify" (δοξάζω *doxazō*) and "praise" (αἰνέω *aineō*), occur in various contexts, but not together. The more common term is "glorify" (*doxazō*). The paralytic and those who witness his healing glorify God (5:25-26). The raising of the son of the widow at Nain (7:16) leads the crowd to glorify God, and the crippled woman (13:13), the Samaritan leper (17:15), and the blind beggar in Jericho (18:43) respond to their healings by glorifying God. Then, when the centurion witnesses Jesus' death, another of God's mighty acts, he too glorifies God (23:47).

The other term Luke uses to describe responses of awe, penitence, gratitude, and worship is *aineō* ("to praise God"). The angelic host that announces Jesus' birth praises God (2:13), and then the shepherds answer the angels with their own praise of God (2:20). Later, the disciples add their antiphonal response, praising God (19:37) with a variation of the angels' words, saying, "Peace in heaven,/ and glory in the highest heaven!" (19:38).

Significantly, the Gospel ends with the disciples' praising God (24:53). Here a third verb occurs: "blessing" God (εὐλογέω *eulogeō*). Codex Bezae (D) has the more common "praise" God (*aineō;* which also occurs in Acts 2:47; 3:8-9), but the idiom "to bless God" also occurs earlier in the Gospel when Zechariah praises God (1:64) and when Simeon takes Jesus in his arms and praises God (2:28). The choice of the verb in 24:53 may be due to the occurrence of the verb twice earlier in the same scene (24:50-51), where Jesus blesses the disciples. Appropriately, the Gospel ends on a note of blessing and doxology.

6. The Importance of an Accurate Witness. This theme is more important to Luke than a tallying of the frequency of its occurrence in the Gospel might indicate. The only occurrence of the verb "to bear witness" (μαρτυρέω *martyreō*) is in 4:22, where the people of Nazareth initially respond to Jesus by bearing witness to him. The two related words for the witness borne occur only four times (μαρτυρία *martyria,* 22:71; and μαρτύριον *martyrion,* 5:14; 9:5; 21:13). The Sanhedrin asks what further need there is for testimony after Jesus responds to their question as to whether he is the Son of God by saying, "You say that I am" (22:70-71). The disciples, however, are to be witnesses for Jesus and the gospel. Thus the term evokes a judicial context. When the disciples are persecuted and brought before kings and governors, "This will give you an opportunity to testify" (21:13). The concept of "witness" develops in the course of the NT writings from the role of an eyewitness, to one who can testify to the gospel, to one who dies for the sake of the gospel ("a martyr" [μάρτυς *martys*]). The special Lukan use of this term links two senses of it: The disciples can bear witness to the fact of Jesus' death and resurrection, and they can testify to its significance. Luke 24:48 links both senses (see the discussion of this verse in the Commentary). By the time we come to Paul (Acts 22:15), the sense has already shifted from the first to the second sense. Paul can bear a confessing witness, but he was not an eyewitness to the events of Jesus' ministry (Acts 1:22).

For their work as witnesses, the disciples will be empowered by the Holy Spirit. The Gospel of Luke plays an important role in shaping the biblical doctrine of the Spirit in that it affirms that the Holy Spirit was active before the birth of Jesus (1:35, 41, 67; 2:25-27), the Spirit rested upon Jesus during his ministry (3:22; 4:1, 14, 18; 10:21), and Jesus charged the disciples to wait in Jerusalem until the Spirit had come upon them (24:49; cf. 11:13). The witness of the disciples, therefore, is guided and empowered by the Spirit. Confirming this promise, the book of Acts notes that the Spirit guides the disciples and the early church in each of its major new ventures. The linkage between witness and Spirit is explicit in Acts 5:32: "And we are witnesses to these things, and so is the Holy Spirit whom God has given to those who obey him" (NRSV). The concern for an accurate and continuing witness also guided Luke in the writing of the Gospel, "So that you may know the truth concerning the things about which you have been instructed" (1:4).

READING THE GOSPEL OF LUKE

The study of the Gospel according to Luke is a richly rewarding experience. Luke is a good storyteller and has the penetrating insight of a prophet. As a result, the Gospel is engaging and offers a perspective on the redemptive events of Jesus' ministry. It continually calls the Christian community to model more fully Jesus' concern for the oppressed, the overlooked, and the outcast. The kingdom community is one in which the social barriers that divide and exclude are torn down and God's grace can begin to flow to and among the wealthy and the poor, the sick and the self-righteous, the powerful and the excluded. The study and teaching of such a Gospel can serve to actualize in individuals and in congregations the redemptive purposes of God that guided Jesus' ministry and resulted in his death and resurrection. If the Spirit empowered the witness of this Gospel, then by opening ourselves to it we may also be guided by God's Spirit to be a part of God's ongoing redemptive work. The study of the Gospel, therefore, calls us to see the sights and hear the words of Jesus' ministry as if we had been among the eyewitnesses, to grasp Luke's distinctive perspective on the person and work of Jesus, and to see the implications of the Gospel for the times and circumstances in which we live.

BIBLIOGRAPHY

Commentaries

Craddock, Fred B. *Luke.* Interpretation. Louisville: Westminster/John Knox, 1990. Treats Luke as preaching and offers fresh insights for preaching the Gospel.

Danker, Frederick W. *Jesus and the New Age: A Commentary on St. Luke's Gospel.* Rev. ed. Philadelphia: Fortress, 1988. Danker's masterful grasp of the literature of the Greco-Roman world leads him to read Luke as a bridge builder between the Jewish and Gentile cultural-religious experiences who portrays Jesus as the Great Benefactor who introduces the New Age.

Ellis, E. Earl. *The Gospel of Luke.* NCB. Greenwood, SC: Attic, 1966. A commentary on the RSV that treats with respect the view that the Gospel was written by Luke, the companion of Paul, shortly after Paul's death.

Evans, Craig A. *Luke.* New International Biblical Commentary. Peabody, Mass.: Hendrickson, 1990. A readable commentary on the NIV that offers an interpretation of each section followed by additional notes that explain technical textual issues for a general readership.

Fitzmyer, Joseph A. *The Gospel According to Luke.* AB 28 and 28A. Garden City, N.Y.: Doubleday, 1981, 1985. The standard reference commentary that provides a thorough and reliable treatment of the introductory, textual, philological, historical, form critical, redaction critical, and theological issues.

Johnson, Luke Timothy. *The Gospel of Luke.* Sacra Pagina 3. Collegeville: Liturgical Press, 1991. This recent commentary offers a fresh reading of the Gospel as a literary whole that focuses on the theme of Jesus as the prophet for the people of God. The introduction is especially good.

Marshall, I. Howard. *The Gospel of Luke: A Commentary on the Greek Text.* NIGTC. Grand Rapids: Eerdmans, 1978. A reference commentary that is particularly valuable for its attention to philological and historical issues.

Nolland, John. *Luke.* 3 vols. WBC 35A-C. Dallas: Word, 1989–93. This encyclopedic work canvasses the various possible interpretations of each section and verse and guides the reader to a judicious handling of the options.

Schweizer, Eduard. *The Good News According to Luke.* Translated by David E. Green. Atlanta: John Knox, 1984. A commentary that is well worth consulting for the theological insights that emerge from Schweizer's reading of the Gospel.

Stein, Robert H. *Luke.* The New American Commentary, 24. Nashville: Broadman, 1992. A useful resource for preachers and teachers, the text of this commentary is structured under three rubrics (Context,

Comment, and the Lukan Message). Stein, an accomplished redaction critic, highlights the christology of the Gospel.

Talbert, Charles H. *Reading Luke: A Literary and Theological Commentary on the Third Gospel.* New York: Crossroad, 1982. Valuable for its reading of Luke in light of parallels from Greco-Roman literature and for its analysis of the Gospel's literary patterns and theological motifs.

Tannehill, Robert C. *The Narrative Unity of Luke–Acts: A Literary Interpretation,* vol. 1: *The Gospel According to Luke.* Philadelphia: Fortress, 1986. A narrative critical reading of Luke and Acts as a theological interpretation of the purpose of God for Israel and all humanity.

Tiede, David L. *Luke.* Augsburg Commentary on the New Testament. Minneapolis: Augsburg, 1988. This commentary highlights the narrative of the Gospel, Luke's interpretation of the Scriptures of Israel, and Luke's witness to God's judgment and salvation.

Specialized Studies

Brown, Raymond E. *The Birth of the Messiah: A Commentary on the Infancy Narratives in the Gospels of Matthew and Luke.* New York: Doubleday, 1977. The definitive work on the birth narratives in Matthew and Luke. Brown shows how the birth accounts are rooted in the OT and how they develop theological perspectives that are integral to the Gospels in which they appear.

————. *The Death of the Messiah: A Commentary on the Passion Narratives.* 2 vols. New York: Doubleday, 1994. This magisterial work minutely examines each element of the passion narratives in the four Gospels, showing how historical traditions serve theological purposes in the Gospel accounts.

Conzelmann, Hans. *The Theology of St. Luke.* Translated by Geoffrey Buswell. New York: Harper & Row, 1961. This standard work was the first monograph to use redaction criticism in an effort to discern the theological perspectives of the Third Evangelist.

Darr, John A. *On Character Building: The Reader and the Rhetoric of Characterization in Luke–Acts.* Louisville: Westminster/John Knox, 1992. In studies of the characterization of John the Baptist, the Pharisees, and Herod, Darr develops a reader-response approach to characterization in the Gospel and casts new light on each of these characters.

Karris, Robert J. *Luke: Artist and Theologian.* New York: Paulist, 1985. Karris provides a valuable perspective on the Lukan passion narrative by showing how it handles some of the Gospel's leading themes, especially justice, food, and innocent suffering.

Kingsbury, Jack Dean. *Conflict in Luke: Jesus, Authorities, Disciples.* Minneapolis: Fortress, 1991. Following a narrative-critical approach, Kingsbury shows how the Gospel develops three separate but intersecting stories. By examining the stories of Jesus, the authorities, and the disciples, Kingsbury brings to light the various levels of conflict in the plot of the Gospel and reflects on their significance for its christology.

Kurz, William S. *Reading Luke–Acts: Dynamics of Biblical Narrative.* Louisville: Westminster/John Knox, 1993. Reading Luke–Acts as a continuous narrative, Kurz highlights the role of the narrator and the importance of narration, gaps, and implicit commentary for the reading of the Gospel and Acts.

Maddox, Robert. *The Purpose of Luke–Acts.* Göttingen: Vandenhoeck & Ruprecht, 1982. In this meticulous and rewarding monograph, Maddox sought further understanding of the purpose(s) of Luke and Acts by considering the potential significance of their treatment of Jews, Gentiles, and Christians; the picture of Paul; Christians in the Roman Empire; Luke's eschatology; the affinities of Luke and John; and Luke's purpose in the church of his time.

Malina, Bruce J., and Richard L. Rohrbaugh. *A Social-Science Commentary on the Synoptic Gospels.* Minneapolis: Fortress, 1992. A handy, nontechnical interpretation of the synoptic Gospels in the light of insights drawn from social-science criticism.

Navone, John. *Themes of St. Luke.* Rome: Gregorian University Press, 1970. Navone shows how twenty different themes are developed in Luke.

Neyrey, Jerome H., ed. *The Social World of Luke–Acts: Models for Interpretation.* Peabody, Mass.: Hendrickson, 1991. This challenging collection of essays harvests the promise of social-science criticism for understanding the social codes and norms that are implicit in Luke–Acts.

Parsons, Mikeal C. *The Departure of Jesus in Luke–Acts: The Ascension Narratives in Context.* JSNTSup 21. Sheffield: Sheffield Academic, 1987. Drawing on recent developments in both textual criticism and narrative criticism, Parsons shows how the departure of Jesus brings closure to the Gospel and a narrative opening for Acts.

Powell, Mark Alan. *What Are They Saying About Luke?* New York: Paulist, 1989. This brief review assesses the state of scholarship on the composition of the Gospel, the concerns of Luke's community, christology and soteriology, political and social issues, and spiritual and pastoral concerns in Luke.

Schaberg, Jane. "Luke." In *The Women's Bible Commentary.* Edited by Carol Newsom and Sharon H. Ringe. Louisville: Westminster/John Knox, 1992. In a brief commentary on selected passages, Schaberg contends that Luke is a dangerous Gospel because it reinforces the subjugation of women by defining subordinate roles for women while denying them positions of leadership.

Sheeley, Steven M. *Narrative Asides in Luke–Acts.* JSNTSup 72. Sheffield: *JSOT,* 1992. Sheeley calls attention to a neglected feature of the Lukan narrative and analyzes the functions of the asides in the light of their role in other ancient narratives.

OUTLINE OF LUKE

I. Luke 1:1-4, The Prologue

II. Luke 1:5–2:52, The Infancy Narrative

A. 1:5-25, The Annunciation of the Birth of John the Baptist
B. 1:26-38, The Annunciation of the Birth of Jesus
C. 1:39-56, Mary's Visit with Elizabeth
D. 1:57-80, The Birth of John the Baptist
E. 2:1-20, The Birth of Jesus
F. 2:21-40, The Presentation of Jesus in the Temple
G. 2:41-52, The Boy Jesus in the Temple

III. Luke 3:1–4:13, Preparation for the Ministry of Jesus

A. 3:1-6, The Setting of John's Ministry
B. 3:7-18, John's Preaching
C. 3:19-20, The Imprisonment of John
D. 3:21-22, The Baptism of Jesus
E. 3:23-38, The Genealogy of Jesus
F. 4:1-13, The Temptation of Jesus

THE PROLOGUE

1 Many have undertaken to draw up an account of the things that have been fulfilled[a] among us, [2]just as they were handed down to us by those who from the first were eyewitnesses and servants of the word. [3]Therefore, since I myself have carefully investigated everything from the beginning, it seemed good also to me to write an orderly account for you, most excellent Theophilus, [4]so that you may know the certainty of the things you have been taught.

a1 Or been surely believed

1 Since many have undertaken to set down an orderly account of the events that have been fulfilled among us, [2]just as they were handed on to us by those who from the beginning were eyewitnesses and servants of the word, [3]I too decided, after investigating everything carefully from the very first,[a] to write an orderly account for you, most excellent Theophilus, [4]so that you may know the truth concerning the things about which you have been instructed.

aOr for a long time

COMMENTARY

Luke opens the Gospel with a perfectly constructed prologue, setting forth the occasion and purpose for his writing. That being the case, it is surprising how little the prologue tells us. It seems to be both carefully worded and deliberately vague, simultaneously clarifying and obscuring.

As a prefatory statement, Luke 1:1-4 is one of the most literary, stylized sentences in the New Testament, rivalled only by John 1:1-18; Eph 1:3-14; and Heb 1:1-4. In contrast to the other opening statements, however, Luke's prologue clearly reflects the conventional form of prologues found in contemporary historical and biographical works. Such prologues contain most or all of the following components: (1) a statement about the author's predecessors, (2) the work's subject matter, (3) the author's qualifications, (4) the plan or arrangement of the work, (5) the purpose of the writing, (6) the author's name, and (7) the official addressee.[23] While all of these elements

(except the author's name) are present in Luke, the prologue leaves a number of questions unanswered. It does not mention Jesus by name or title (cf. Matt 1:1; Mark 1:1; John 1:1), and it gives no indication of the subject matter of the work. Neither does it name any of the author's predecessors or sources, nor does it state the plan or scope of the work. The statement of purpose is cryptic, and Theophilus's role and relationship to Luke are not stated. What then does the prologue tell us?

Verses 1-4 are an extended, periodic sentence in which verses 1-2 comprise the protasis ("if . . . " or "since . . . ") and verses 3-4 the apodosis ("then . . . " or "therefore . . . "). Within each member there are three parts, with some corresponding elements. These relationships, which are more visible in Greek than in English, may be set forth as follows.

The italics identify three corresponding elements. The English translation creates the apparent repetition of "an orderly account," since there is no noun for the writing in verse 3.

23. See Charles H. Talbert, *Reading Luke: A Literary and Theological Commentary on the Third Gospel* (New York: Crossroad, 1982) 7-11. See also, e.g., Josephus *Against Apion* 1.1.1-3; 2.1.1; *Antiquities of the Jews* 1.1-9; Philo *Life of Moses.*

Protasis (vv. 1-2)	Apodosis (vv. 3-4)
Since many have undertaken	*I too* decided, after investigating everything carefully from the very first,
to set forth an orderly account	*to write* an orderly account for you, most excellent Theophilus, so that you may know the truth
of the events that have been fulfilled among us, just as they were handed on to us by those who from the beginning were eyewitnesses and servants of the word,	*concerning the things about which you have been instructed*

In contrast to other prologues, Luke's does not criticize other accounts as inaccurate. At most there is the implication that his work will supply "the truth." This term can mean "security," "safety," "assurance," or "certainty." One debated issue that arises from these verses concerns Luke's aim and purpose in writing a gospel. Is he supplying (a) an orderly account to correct (historical) inaccuracies in other accounts, (b) (doctrinal) truth where false teaching was a threat, or (c) assurance where uncertainty had prevailed? While various interpretations have emphasized Luke's historical, theological, or pastoral concerns, it may not be possible or desirable to settle on one interest and exclude the others.

Although Luke does not name the others who had written—possibly because at this early date their writings were not yet called Gospels and individual names had not been attached to the accounts—he obviously knows of other accounts of the life and teachings of Jesus (probably at least Mark and Q, possibly a passion narrative, and

traditions found also in John). Luke was not an eyewitness, and he may not have included himself among the "servants of the word." Instead, he had followed the events closely, received the traditions handed on by the eyewitnesses and servants of the word, and profited from the writings of his predecessors. Evidently, he had collected his material from both oral traditions and earlier writings. He himself, however, stood at some distance from the events, and possibly even from those who were eyewitnesses to the events of Jesus' ministry.

Luke's concern is not merely historical, though. He signals that his narrative will relate the things "that have been fulfilled," that the events are "the word" (the Christian message or preaching), and that his account will provide Theophilus with "assurance." Beyond the honorific title "most excellent," which probably indicates an elevated social status, we are told nothing further about Theophilus. The references to "us" and "the things about which you have been instructed," as well as the understanding of Scripture assumed throughout the Gospel, suggest that Theophilus was a believer or a God-fearer, but nothing else is known of him. The reference may indicate that he was Luke's patron, but there is no evidence that Theophilus was a Roman official or that the name identifies every reader who is a "friend of God," as Origen suggested. Theophilus is addressed again in Acts 1:1, following a reference to "the first book." While the prologue to Luke may have been intended to introduce both volumes, the references to "the beginning," "the word," and "the things about which you have been instructed" are better understood as allusions to the Gospel traditions than as terms for the story of the church in Jerusalem and Paul's work among the Gentiles.

REFLECTIONS

In literary terms, the prologue serves not only as an introduction but also as a narrative frame. As one begins to read a narrative, the narrator or voice telling the story ushers the reader into a narrative world. The prologue is the air lock to this new atmosphere, the crackle on the screen as the picture appears, the vestibule connecting the sanctuary to the world outside. The prologue is not the beginning of the story; rather, it is an introductory comment about the story, its author, readers, and purposes. Because the prologue leaves so many of these issues uncertain, it invites us to read further while setting a tone for the narrative that follows.

Actually, the reader has no explicit information about the content of the story. Commentators have remarked both on the "secular" character of the prologue and on its elevated, polished style. It has a sophisticated appeal. The style is literate, the terms are lofty, and the appeal is couched in the conventions of historical writing. Every detail creates the impression of an educated, informed writer who is concerned to give the reader a lucid, informed, and reliable report of significant events. The writer has prepared carefully and addresses Theophilus as one held in great esteem. The prologue, therefore, can serve as a provocative pattern for the church's proclamation of the gospel. What can we learn from it regarding how the church should address the secular world in order to gain a hearing for its message?

Three words foreshadow concerns that will recur in the Gospel: *fulfilled, eyewitnesses,* and *assurance.* The reference to the things that have been "fulfilled among us" looks back on God's redemptive acts in the history of Israel. In a word, Luke acknowledges that the story of Jesus is also the story of the fulfillment of God's redemptive purposes, the climactic episode in a sequence of events that stretches back through the promises of the prophets. Repeatedly Luke will emphasize the pattern of the fulfillment of Scripture in the events of the Gospel (cf. Luke 1:20; 4:21; 9:31; 24:44). For both interpretation and proclamation the warning is clear: These events can be understood only in the context of Scripture. Apart from this context, or more technically the relationships between these texts (Hebrew Scriptures and the Gospel), one misses the dynamic tensions, motifs, echoes, and continuity that are vital to a perceptive reading of the Gospel. Theologically, it is vital that the continuity of the Gospel with the redemptive acts of God in the history of Israel be preserved. Without that continuity, the Gospel is truncated and distorted; the twin demons of Marcionism and anti-Jewish sentiment lie close at hand.

The prologue also signals Luke's emphasis on the importance of *eyewitness* testimony (cf. Luke 11:48; 24:48; Acts 1:8, 22; 2:32). While Luke's intent to write accurately and completely does not mean that he worked with the sensitivities or methods of a modern historian, he has taken pains to ensure that his account stands in continuity with the history of Israel and with the preaching of the apostles and the witness of those who had been with Jesus.

The third word, which connotes *truth* and *assurance,* has been interpreted alternatively as the content of the gospel and its fulfillment in the experience of the hearer. Because God's promises to Israel have been fulfilled through the life and teachings of Jesus, we can know the assurance that is grounded in God's redemptive love, praise God with unbounded joy, fervently follow Jesus' example and teachings, open our lives to the leading of God's Spirit, and respond to the call to join the company of witnesses spreading to the ends of the earth the good news of Jesus' coming.

LUKE 1:5–2:52

THE INFANCY NARRATIVE

OVERVIEW

In order to appreciate the significance of Luke's infancy narrative, one must recognize the conventions of its genre, its role as a miniature Gospel, and its principal themes.

Whereas Mark and John begin without any accounts of the birth of Jesus, Matthew opens with a genealogy and an account of Jesus' birth in Bethlehem, the family's subsequent flight to Egypt, and their return to Nazareth. Luke is distinctive; it is the only Gospel to report the births of both John and Jesus. Luke also elevates the roles of Mary and Elizabeth, whereas the story in Matthew is guided by Joseph's dreams. Angelophanies, prophetic predictions, and references to the fulfillment of Scripture all serve to alert the reader that the events surrounding the births of John and Jesus are part of a larger story—the fulfillment of the hopes of Israel and the Scriptures through the coming of the Messiah.

Careful attention to each of these elements opens new insights into the initial chapters of Luke. They are not a dispensable preamble, insignificant for Luke's theology; the infancy narrative is both the Gospel in miniature and the opening statement of themes that will be developed throughout Luke (and in a new key in Acts). Luke 1:5–2:52 sets the literary and theological context apart from which the rest of Luke would be greatly diminished.

First impressions are always important, and the infancy narrative both introduces us to the narrative world of the Gospel and provides us with the scriptural, thematic, and theological norms by which we are to respond to the rest of the story. Reading the infancy narrative closely is an essential part of our education as readers of the Gospel. The "primacy effect" means that we will judge later episodes by the expectations created in these opening chapters.

Greco-Roman biographies often opened with accounts of the wondrous omens that accompanied the births of great leaders.[24] The events surrounding the births of great heroes gave evidence of their future greatness and important clues as to what their roles were to be. Luke employs this convention by defining the roles of John and Jesus through the prophecies given at their births. The annunciations also draw upon the pattern of Old Testament annunciations that foretold the births of Ishmael (Gen 16:7-13), Isaac (Gen 17:1-3, 15-21; 18:1-2, 10-15), and Samson (Judg 13:2-23). Five features form the pattern of these "type scenes" of the announcement of one who will play a significant role in the divine design for the destiny of God's people:

1. The *appearance* of an angel (or of the Lord)
2. The response of *fear*
3. The divine *message*
4. An *objection*
5. The giving of a *sign* to guarantee the divine announcement[25]

Standard features also mark the divine *message:* The visionary is addressed by name; a qualifying phrase describes the one to whom the announcement is made; the subject is encouraged not to be afraid; the woman will give birth to a male child; instructions are given regarding the name of the child, often with an etymology interpreting the name; and the future role of the child is announced. Variations, contrasts, or expansions of this pattern can all signal significant implications. Indeed, Luke uses references to the fulfillment of various scriptures and subtle contrasts in

---

24. See Charles H. Talbert, "Prophecies of Future Greatness: The Contribution of Greco-Roman Biographies to an Understanding of Luke 1:5–4:15," in *The Divine Helmsman,* ed. James L. Crenshaw and Samuel Sandmel (New York: KTAV, 1980) 129-41.

25. Raymond E. Brown, *The Birth of the Messiah: A Commentary on the Infancy Narratives of Matthew and Luke* (New York: Doubleday, 1977) 156.

the announcements to show that while John will prepare the way, Jesus will be the Messiah.

The infancy narrative, therefore, both announces themes that will be developed later and functions as a Gospel in miniature. Among the typically Lukan themes that appear in these scenes are the importance of God's redemptive purposes, the fulfillment of Scripture, the role of the Spirit, the redemption of the poor and oppressed, the special role of women in the Gospel story, the role of the Temple and Israel's religious authorities, the witness of those who receive God's mercy, the atmosphere of joy, and the praise of God.

The infancy narrative announces the end of the period of waiting. God is beginning to do a new and wonderful thing. The Son of God is coming into the world, breaking into and putting an end to the ordinary. Those who are able to see in the births of these children the mighty act of God that will lead to redemption for all God's people respond with joy, celebration, and praise. But not all will respond with openness to what God is doing. The child who will bring deliverance will himself be delivered to a cross. In a vital but still embryonic form, therefore, the narrative announces the gospel and calls for all to receive it. But it is not merely a tale of the birth of a child, for as William Wordsworth said, "the Child is father of the Man," and this man was the Son of God.

LUKE 1:5-25, THE ANNUNCIATION OF THE BIRTH OF JOHN THE BAPTIST

NIV

[5]In the time of Herod king of Judea there was a priest named Zechariah, who belonged to the priestly division of Abijah; his wife Elizabeth was also a descendant of Aaron. [6]Both of them were upright in the sight of God, observing all the Lord's commandments and regulations blamelessly. [7]But they had no children, because Elizabeth was barren; and they were both well along in years.

[8]Once when Zechariah's division was on duty and he was serving as priest before God, [9]he was chosen by lot, according to the custom of the priesthood, to go into the temple of the Lord and burn incense. [10]And when the time for the burning of incense came, all the assembled worshipers were praying outside.

[11]Then an angel of the Lord appeared to him, standing at the right side of the altar of incense. [12]When Zechariah saw him, he was startled and was gripped with fear. [13]But the angel said to him: "Do not be afraid, Zechariah; your prayer has been heard. Your wife Elizabeth will bear you a son, and you are to give him the name John. [14]He will be a joy and delight to you, and many will rejoice because of his birth, [15]for he will be great in the

NRSV

[5]In the days of King Herod of Judea, there was a priest named Zechariah, who belonged to the priestly order of Abijah. His wife was a descendant of Aaron, and her name was Elizabeth. [6]Both of them were righteous before God, living blamelessly according to all the commandments and regulations of the Lord. [7]But they had no children, because Elizabeth was barren, and both were getting on in years.

[8]Once when he was serving as priest before God and his section was on duty, [9]he was chosen by lot, according to the custom of the priesthood, to enter the sanctuary of the Lord and offer incense. [10]Now at the time of the incense offering, the whole assembly of the people was praying outside. [11]Then there appeared to him an angel of the Lord, standing at the right side of the altar of incense. [12]When Zechariah saw him, he was terrified; and fear overwhelmed him. [13]But the angel said to him, "Do not be afraid, Zechariah, for your prayer has been heard. Your wife Elizabeth will bear you a son, and you will name him John. [14]You will have joy and gladness, and many will rejoice at his birth, [15]for he will be great in the sight of the Lord. He must never drink wine

NIV

sight of the Lord. He is never to take wine or other fermented drink, and he will be filled with the Holy Spirit even from birth.[a] ¹⁶Many of the people of Israel will he bring back to the Lord their God. ¹⁷And he will go on before the Lord, in the spirit and power of Elijah, to turn the hearts of the fathers to their children and the disobedient to the wisdom of the righteous—to make ready a people prepared for the Lord."

¹⁸Zechariah asked the angel, "How can I be sure of this? I am an old man and my wife is well along in years."

¹⁹The angel answered, "I am Gabriel. I stand in the presence of God, and I have been sent to speak to you and to tell you this good news. ²⁰And now you will be silent and not able to speak until the day this happens, because you did not believe my words, which will come true at their proper time."

²¹Meanwhile, the people were waiting for Zechariah and wondering why he stayed so long in the temple. ²²When he came out, he could not speak to them. They realized he had seen a vision in the temple, for he kept making signs to them but remained unable to speak.

²³When his time of service was completed, he returned home. ²⁴After this his wife Elizabeth became pregnant and for five months remained in seclusion. ²⁵"The Lord has done this for me," she said. "In these days he has shown his favor and taken away my disgrace among the people."

[a]15 Or *from his mother's womb*

NRSV

or strong drink; even before his birth he will be filled with the Holy Spirit. ¹⁶He will turn many of the people of Israel to the Lord their God. ¹⁷With the spirit and power of Elijah he will go before him, to turn the hearts of parents to their children, and the disobedient to the wisdom of the righteous, to make ready a people prepared for the Lord." ¹⁸Zechariah said to the angel, "How will I know that this is so? For I am an old man, and my wife is getting on in years." ¹⁹The angel replied, "I am Gabriel. I stand in the presence of God, and I have been sent to speak to you and to bring you this good news. ²⁰But now, because you did not believe my words, which will be fulfilled in their time, you will become mute, unable to speak, until the day these things occur."

21Meanwhile the people were waiting for Zechariah, and wondered at his delay in the sanctuary. ²²When he did come out, he could not speak to them, and they realized that he had seen a vision in the sanctuary. He kept motioning to them and remained unable to speak. ²³When his time of service was ended, he went to his home.

24After those days his wife Elizabeth conceived, and for five months she remained in seclusion. She said, ²⁵"This is what the Lord has done for me when he looked favorably on me and took away the disgrace I have endured among my people."

COMMENTARY

The first scene is a carefully structured unit: the introduction of Zechariah and Elizabeth (vv. 5-7); the setting of the annunciation—in the Temple (vv. 8-12); the angelic announcement (vv. 13-17); Zechariah's response (vv. 18-20); Zechariah's departure from the Temple (vv. 21-23); and the conception of the child, fulfilling the angelic announcement (vv. 24-25).

The thematic center of the scene is the announcement of John's birth and future greatness, but the scene also fulfills other significant func-

tions. Through it the narrator draws the reader into the story world of the Gospel. The beginning point for all that follows is Jewish piety, the Temple, and the fulfillment of Scripture. By means of angelic revelations, authoritative predictions, commissionings, and references to the fulfillment of Scripture, the text conveys the sense that everything that is reported happens as the unfolding of God's foreordained redemptive plan. Later events are foreshadowed, and expectations are created that are crucial to the reading of later chapters of the Gospel narrative. The appearance of a heavenly messenger in the opening scene lends an air of mystery and wonder to the Gospel from the very beginning. This is not a story of ordinary people or mundane events.

1:5-7. By means of the reference to the days of a king and the introduction of a righteous old couple, the first words transport the reader from the secular literary context of the prologue into a Semitic context. Luke's words "In the days of King Herod of Judea, there was a priest . . . " echo historical references from the prophets: "The words of Jeremiah son of Hilkiah, of the priests . . . in the days of King Josiah. . . . It came also in the days of King Jehoiakim . . . " (Jer 1:1-3 NRSV); "The words of Amos . . . in the days of King Uzziah of Judah . . . " (Amos 1:1 NRSV). The consistent element is the phrase "in the days of" a king who is named. The name of the prophet is then given. Any reader familiar with the Hebrew Scriptures will recognize from Luke's idiom that the Gospel record is being narrated in the voice and style of the Scriptures.

The first temporal reference is very general: "in the days of King Herod." Nothing happens in vv. 5-7. They provide the stable setting for the reader's introduction to the story world; the reader is told who the characters are and how they live. The events of the story begin in the next verse. In Luke the temporal references become increasingly specific so that the reader has the sense of watching a camera zoom in on a particular character: "In the days of King Herod" (v. 5), "Once when he was serving as priest" (v. 8), "at the time of the incense offering" (v. 10), "then there appeared to him an angel" (v. 11), and finally, "but the angel said to him . . . " (v. 13). From verses 5 to 13 the speed of the narrative slows from years to days to hours to the moment of the first dialogue in the Gospel, and we are brought directly into the scene of the angelic appearance.

Rather than letting the reader gather clues to the characters' identities from what they do and say (indirect characterization), in this opening scene the narrator tells the reader who the characters are (direct characterization). Even their names are appropriate to the pervasive piety of the setting: *Zechariah* means "God has remembered," and *Elizabeth* means something like "My God's oath." Zechariah is a priest from the order

of Abijah (1 Chr 24:10; Neh 12:4, 17). Elizabeth also came from a priestly family and had fulfilled the expectations for a daughter of a priest by marrying a priest. Two words characterize the devout couple: "righteous" (δίκαιοι *dikaioi*) and "blameless" (ἄμεμπτοι *amemptoi*; v. 6). The words evoke a picture of one who has fully participated in the provisions of the covenant (see Gen 26:5 [Abraham]; Job 1:1 [Job]; Phil 3:6 [Paul]). *Blameless* does not appear again in Luke or Acts (cf. Phil 2:15; 3:6; 1 Thess 2:10; 3:13; Heb 8:7), but Luke will later characterize Simeon (2:25) and report that Jesus told the parable of the Pharisee and the tax collector to those who thought they were righteous (18:9; cf. 20:20). At the death of Jesus, the centurion pronounces him righteous (23:47), and Joseph of Arimathea is introduced as "a good and righteous man" (23:50). Later, in Acts 7:52, Jesus is called "the Righteous One."

Verse 7 introduces the complication that sets the course for the events that will follow. The narrator reports that the devout couple was childless, Elizabeth was barren, and they were both getting on in years. This note completes the introduction of the characters. Any reader familiar with the Scriptures will be reminded of the stories of Abraham and Sarah (Gen 16:1; 18:11), Isaac and Rebecca (Gen 25:21), Jacob and Rachel (Gen 30:1), Manoah and his wife (Judg 13:2), and Elkanah and Hannah (1 Sam 1:1-2). The bearing of children was considered a great blessing, and it was essential for carrying on the family name, perpetuating God's covenant with Israel, and providing oneself with care in one's old age. Barrenness was regarded as a tragedy, a disgrace, and even a sign of God's punishment. The wonder of John's birth is heightened by the report of the couple's age. Like Sarah, Elizabeth was beyond the age of child bearing. Like Isaac (Gen 25:21) and Hannah (1 Sam 1:9-18), Zechariah and Elizabeth had prayed for a child.

1:8-12. Echoes of the story of the birth of Samuel increase as we are told that the setting for the announcement was Zechariah's service in the Temple. The priests were divided into 24 groups, and each group served twice a year for a week at a time in the Temple. On this occasion, Zechariah was chosen to enter the sanctuary and offer the incense. A sacrifice was offered twice a day, both on the outer altar and on the inner altar, inside the sanctuary. A list was compiled of those priests who had never been chosen to enter the sanctuary, and then lots were cast to determine the priests who would bring the sacrifice to the altar and clean the ashes off of it. This honor normally came only once in a lifetime. The Mishnah describes the ceremony as follows:

> He to whom fell the lot of [offering] the incense took the ladle. . . . He whose lot it was to bear the firepan took the silver firepan and went to the top of the Altar and cleared away the cinders on this side and on that, scooped up fire with the firepan, came down and emptied it out into the golden [firepan] . . . . Then they began to go up the steps to the Porch. They went first whose lot it was to clear the ashes from the inner Altar and the Candlestick. He whose lot it was to clear the ashes from the inner Altar went in and took the ash-bin, prostrated himself, and came out. . . . He whose lot it was to bear the firepan piled up the cinders on the [inner] Altar, smoothed them with the back of the firepan, prostrated himself, and came out. He whose lot it was to bring the incense took the dish from the midst of the ladle and gave it to his friend or kinsman. . . . He began to smooth it down and came out. He that offered the incense did not offer it until the officer said to him, 'Offer the incense!' . . . When all were gone away he offered the incense and prostrated himself and came away.[26]

Once all of the priests had come out onto the porch, they pronounced the priestly blessing (Num 6:22ff.).

At this high moment—the hour of the sacrifice, the pinnacle of Zechariah's life of priestly service, while all the multitude of the people were praying outside, waiting for Zechariah to emerge from the sanctuary—an angel of the Lord appeared on the right side of the altar. The temporal references and explanations of vv. 8-10 delay the action and heighten its drama as the reader waits to learn what happened inside the sanctuary. The specificity of the location of the appearance lends credibility and creates a mental image in the mind of the reader.

The intrusion of the divine into the mundane interrupts and brings an end even to the sacred ceremonies of worship. We are not told whether Zechariah had burned the incense; all that matters from this point on is his response to the Lord's charge to him. Following the pattern of other angelic appearances, Zechariah's initial response is

one of terror and fear. What mortal can stand to be in the presence of the Divine?

1:13-17. The angel's first words (v. 13), and significantly the first words of dialogue in the Gospel, are an encouragement not to be afraid (cf. Dan 10:12, 19). Zechariah's prayer has been heard. From this report we fill an earlier gap in the narrative; apparently Zechariah had been praying, perhaps even as he entered the sanctuary, that God would give them a child. As we soon learn, not only will God give the aging couple a son, but their child will be the forerunner of the Messiah as well. What greater blessing could come to a faithful priest? Zechariah, therefore, as the father will name the child "John," which means "Yahweh has shown favor" or "Yahweh is gracious."

The second prediction (v. 14) is the first announcement of the joy and gladness that will accompany not only the birth of John (1:44, 58) but also the coming of the Messiah to Israel (2:10; 8:13; 15:7, 10; 24:41, 52). Throughout Luke, joy and praise are the spontaneous responses of God's people to the mighty acts they witnessed.

The angelic announcement also declares the child's future greatness. Zechariah's son would be "great before the Lord" (Luke 7:28), and—as was appropriate for a descendant of Aaron (Lev 10:9), a Nazirite (Num 6:3; Judg 13:4), or a prophet (1 Sam 1:11; Mic 2:11)—John would drink no wine or intoxicating drink (7:33). References to individuals being "filled with the Spirit" (1:15, 41, 67) occur frequently in Luke and Acts. The promise of the Spirit indicates that divine power would be active in John. It was commonly held that there had been no prophets in Israel since the time of Malachi, so the announcement that John would be filled with the Spirit was a signal that the messianic age was dawning.

Priestly and prophetic functions are blended in the announcement that John would turn the people of Israel to the Lord (Mic 2:6). The idiom is used in Acts and elsewhere as a technical term for Christian conversion (Acts 3:19; 9:35; 14:15). No Jewish writings depict Elijah as the forerunner of the Messiah. Rather, in Jewish thought Elijah was expected to make peace, reassemble the tribe, purify Israel, restore manna, and raise the dead.[27]

---

26. See *m. Tamid* 5.4–6.3.

27. See J. Louis Martyn, *The Gospel of John in Christian History* (New York: Paulist, 1978) 18n. 25.

In Christian interpretation, however, Elijah would return before the coming of the kingdom of God. The angelic announcement in Luke echoes Mal 4:5-6:

> Lo, I will send you the prophet Elijah before the great and terrible day of the LORD comes. He will turn the hearts of parents to their children and the hearts of children to their parents. (NRSV; cf. Sir 48:10)

The last line of v. 17 associates the references in Mal 3:1; 4:5-6 with Isa 40:3, which is linked to John the Baptist in the Synoptics. John will prepare the people for the Lord's coming (cf. Matt 3:3; Mark 1:2-3; Luke 3:4-6; John 1:23), and his preparatory role will be forecast again in Zechariah's blessing of the child (1:76).

Although Luke has no parallel to Mark 9:9-13, in which Jesus alludes to John's fulfillment of the role of Elijah (cf. Matt 11:13-14; 17:3), the references to Elijah at the annunciation of John's birth alert the reader that the accounts of John's ministry (3:1-20; 7:18-35) are to be read in the light of this role. Indeed, echoes of the announcement occur in the later passages ("prophet," 7:26; "father . . . children," 3:8; "wisdom is vindicated by all her children," 7:35), where again Isa 40:3-5 and Mal 3:1 are cited (3:4-6; 7:27). The role of John announced at his birth will be confirmed by Luke's later reports of his preaching and his calls for repentance. Significantly, however, John was no healer or miracle worker, like Elijah. That role was fulfilled by Jesus.

1:18-20. Zechariah's response is a direct quotation of Gen 15:8, "How will I know that this is so?" (v. 18). The allusion to Abraham is underscored by a reminder of what the narrator has already told the reader (v. 7): Zechariah and his wife were getting on in years. The reader can hardly miss the implication: A new child of the covenant is about to be born; God is acting in a mighty way, just as in the days of Abraham.

The angel returns Zechariah's emphatic "I am old" with an equally emphatic "I am Gabriel" (Dan 8:15-16; 9:21; *1 Enoch* 9:1; 20:7; 40:2, 9). His function is to stand before the Lord (cf. Tob 12:15), and his mission is to bring good news to Zechariah. Gabriel was sent to speak for God, but because Zechariah did not receive the good news, he would not be able to speak until the annunciation was fulfilled and the child was born. Zechariah was concerned that his "days" had

passed (v. 18); now he will count the days until the angelic announcement is fulfilled (v. 20). All in due time! The next words that Zechariah speaks will begin with the pronouncement "Blessed be the Lord God of Israel" (v. 68) and continue to confirm the role announced for the child by Gabriel (v. 76).

1:21-23. As the scene closes, time once again speeds up. The focus cuts from Gabriel's second *speech* (vv. 19-20), to the awkward *moments* when Zechariah is unable to pronounce the blessing (vv. 21-22), the closing *days* of Zechariah's duties (v. 23), the time of Elizabeth's conception, and the *months* of her seclusion (vv. 24-25). The scene is also framed by travel reports—Zechariah's travel to Jerusalem and his return home.

The people who had been at prayer (v. 10), and whom John would prepare for the coming of the Lord (v. 17), were amazed at how long Zechariah stayed in the sanctuary and waited for him (v. 21). According to custom, the priest was not to linger in the sanctuary.[28] When Zechariah emerged, he was not able to speak. The first sign of the fulfillment of the angelic announcement, ironically, was Zechariah's inability to tell anyone what the angel had said. At this point, the priest was supposed to pronounce the priestly blessing (Num 6:24-26) over the people,[29] but Zechariah could not speak a word. Zechariah's inability to speak, however, was a sign to the people that he had seen a vision in the sanctuary, as others had before him.[30] Daniel also had been unable to speak following the angelic appearance to him (Dan 10:15). The scene concludes with Zechariah's departure from Jerusalem at the end of his priestly service.

1:24-25. Thereafter, Elizabeth conceived. Here too the report echoes related passages in the Old Testament. The Lord remembered Hannah, and she conceived after she had returned home (1 Sam 1:19-20). Similarly, God remembered Rachel, and she too conceived and then gave thanks, saying, "God has taken away my reproach" (Gen 30:23 NRSV). Elizabeth's five-month seclusion sets the stage for the angelic revelation of Elizabeth's condition to Mary (1:36). Because of Elizabeth's seclusion, the reader will understand that

---

28. *m. Yoma* 5.1.
29. *m. Tamid* 7.2.
30. Josephus *Antiquities of the Jews* 13.282-83.

Mary did not learn that Elizabeth was expecting a child until Gabriel revealed it to her.

The annunciation of John's birth, therefore, is communicated in a setting of Jewish piety (a priest burning incense in the sanctuary of the Temple), through the dramatic appearance of the angel Gabriel (who is previously mentioned only in Daniel and *1 Enoch*), and at every point the angel's words and the narrator's report echo annunciations of births in the Old Testament. In every respect, therefore, the scene is filled with numinous wonder, divine purpose, and the promise of joy for God's people.

REFLECTIONS

The opening scene in the Gospel tells of the end of Israel's waiting for the decisive, history-fulfilling acts of God. It presumes the suspense created by the centuries of waiting, promise, and prophetic anticipation in the OT. Israel's plight is paralleled and dramatized by an aging couple's waiting and hoping for the birth of a child. In both cases the waiting was so prolonged that hope was beginning to seem futile. The announcement of the coming birth of John, therefore, is a call for the renewing of hope and a challenge for the despairing to believe that it is never too late for those who wait upon the Lord.

1. Both continuity and surprise characterize the pattern of God's redemptive work. The annunciation is given in the Temple, at the hour of the burning of the incense, to a priest, the husband of one of the daughters of Aaron. In this new thing that God was about to do, God was not abandoning Israel. This theme will be developed throughout Luke and Acts (see Acts 3:26; 13:46). It is the Lukan equivalent of the Pauline formulation "to the Jew first and also to the Greek" (Rom 1:16; 2:9, 10). If, by the time Luke wrote, Christianity had become a predominantly Gentile religion, it was not because God had abandoned or rejected Israel. Both Luke and Acts begin at the heart of Judaism, in the Temple, with announcements of the fulfillment of Israel's hopes. Fulfillment, however, required a response of openness to God's redemptive works. Israel's failure to embrace the Messiah when he came constitutes the tragic element of this history and once again pushes into the future the culmination of God's redemptive work.

If the beginning of Luke stands in continuity with the OT, repeating the familiar pattern of an annunciation, it also offers its own surprises. The angelic announcement says nothing about the restoration of the kingdom to Israel (Acts 1:6) and gives no promise of the expulsion of the Gentiles (*Psalms of Solomon* 17). Instead, John will be a successor to the prophets, calling Israel to repentance, reconciliation, and obedience. Justice is required of a people prepared for what God is about to do.

2. The annunciation subtly asserts the relationship between the indicative (what God has done, is doing, and will do) and the consequent imperative (what the faithful should do in response):

Indicative	*Imperative*
he will be great	he shall drink no wine (v. 15)
he will be filled with the Holy Spirit	he will turn many of the people of Israel to the Lord their God (v. 16)
with the spirit and power of Elijah . . .	to turn the hearts of parents to their children . . . (v. 17)

Implicit in each of the predictions of John's greatness is a call for faithful, obedient response. How does the announcement of gladness (v. 14) fit into this scheme? Does the gladness that arises from God's act lead us to obedience? Or is the gladness the result of obedience? The answers to these questions go beyond what is said in this scene, but they are probably both/and rather than either/or.

3. After the stately and formal prologue, the reader may be prepared to read a history of kings and generals, the wealthy and the mighty. The opening words of v. 5, "in the days of King Herod of Judea," seem to confirm this false expectation. Instead, the story of God's mighty acts does not involve Herod but a devout old couple. The world's standards lead us to attribute power and worth to the royal functionary, who was but a puppet of Rome. God chose instead the poor and humble as the venue for the great work of redemption. History would remember Herod only as the king at the time when John the Baptist and Jesus were born. Yet, Herod was not even aware of the events for which he would be remembered. The church can easily continue to perpetuate the false assumptions that can lead the reader of the opening verses of Luke to false expectations. The old, the poor, the humble, and the insignificant are not to be overlooked; they are God's chosen people.

4. Even the faithful may grow dull in their expectations, however. Here is a story of a priest who was praying fervently but who was not prepared for his prayers to be answered. He was officiating in the sanctuary itself, but he did not really expect to experience God's presence. The scene once again challenges us, this time to trust in God expectantly and to be prepared for God's response to our needs. We go through the motions of prayer and worship, but we hardly expect to meet God in the midst of our daily activities—not even in the holy moments of worship. Even the faithful, like Zechariah, need to recover the vitality of worship. Our cynical response often echoes Zechariah's: "How will I know that this is so?" The response as always is to witness what God has done and what God continues to do in our midst. Can we see in the birth of a child God's continuing affirmation of hope for the world in which we live?

5. Throughout, the opening scene of Luke trumpets the fulfillment of the age. Time is important. The period of waiting is over. God is about to bring redemption to all who look to God with hope and faith. The story tells of years, days, and moments, but ultimately it tells of the *kairos* of God's redemption of Israel and of all people. The time that God gives each of us is important, and its importance is heightened by the awareness that God gives meaning and worth to life. Each day is the day the Lord has made, a day for us to be glad and seek in each moment to join our activities to the fulfillment of God's redeeming glory. When that message breaks through the shells of our cynicism, we too can join Elizabeth in the joyful exclamation, "This is what the Lord has done for me!"

LUKE 1:26-38, THE ANNUNCIATION OF THE BIRTH OF JESUS

NIV

26In the sixth month, God sent the angel Gabriel to Nazareth, a town in Galilee, 27to a virgin pledged to be married to a man named Joseph, a descendant of David. The virgin's name was Mary. 28The angel went to her and said, "Greetings, you who are highly favored! The Lord is with you."

29Mary was greatly troubled at his words and

NRSV

26In the sixth month the angel Gabriel was sent by God to a town in Galilee called Nazareth, 27to a virgin engaged to a man whose name was Joseph, of the house of David. The virgin's name was Mary. 28And he came to her and said, "Greetings, favored one! The Lord is with you."*a* 29But she was much perplexed by his words and pon-

a Other ancient authorities add *Blessed are you among women*

NIV

wondered what kind of greeting this might be. [30]But the angel said to her, "Do not be afraid, Mary, you have found favor with God. [31]You will be with child and give birth to a son, and you are to give him the name Jesus. [32]He will be great and will be called the Son of the Most High. The Lord God will give him the throne of his father David, [33]and he will reign over the house of Jacob forever; his kingdom will never end."

[34]"How will this be," Mary asked the angel, "since I am a virgin?"

[35]The angel answered, "The Holy Spirit will come upon you, and the power of the Most High will overshadow you. So the holy one to be born will be called[a] the Son of God. [36]Even Elizabeth your relative is going to have a child in her old age, and she who was said to be barren is in her sixth month. [37]For nothing is impossible with God."

[38]"I am the Lord's servant," Mary answered. "May it be to me as you have said." Then the angel left her.

[a]35 Or So the child to be born will be called holy,

NRSV

dered what sort of greeting this might be. [30]The angel said to her, "Do not be afraid, Mary, for you have found favor with God. [31]And now, you will conceive in your womb and bear a son, and you will name him Jesus. [32]He will be great, and will be called the Son of the Most High, and the Lord God will give to him the throne of his ancestor David. [33]He will reign over the house of Jacob forever, and of his kingdom there will be no end." [34]Mary said to the angel, "How can this be, since I am a virgin?"[a] [35]The angel said to her, "The Holy Spirit will come upon you, and the power of the Most High will overshadow you; therefore the child to be born[b] will be holy; he will be called Son of God. [36]And now, your relative Elizabeth in her old age has also conceived a son; and this is the sixth month for her who was said to be barren. [37]For nothing will be impossible with God." [38]Then Mary said, "Here am I, the servant of the Lord; let it be with me according to your word." Then the angel departed from her.

[a]Gk I do not know a man   [b]Other ancient authorities add of you

COMMENTARY

The next scene opens as though it will continue to tell of the birth of the child promised to Zechariah and Elizabeth. Instead, it tells of a greater miracle and the birth of one who would be even greater than John. In many respects the scene that follows is similar to the annunciation of the birth of John. The angel Gabriel appears to announce the birth of the child, and the annunciation follows the pattern of birth annunciations in the OT: The angel says, "Do not be afraid," calls the recipient of the vision by name, assures him or her of God's favor, announces the birth of the child, discloses the name of the child to be born, and reveals the future role of the child in language drawn from the Scriptures. After their respective announcements, Zechariah and Mary each ask a question, a sign is given, and the scene closes with a departure. The similarity of structure and content between the two scenes invites the reader to consider the differences between them all the more closely. For example, the first an-

nouncement came as an answer to fervent prayer; the second was completely unanticipated. John would be born to parents past the age of child bearing, but the miracle of Jesus' birth would be even greater. Jesus would be born to a virgin. The announcement of Jesus' future role also shows that at every point Jesus would be even greater than his forerunner. Watch how these nuances are developed in the course of the details of this scene.

1:26-28. The opening phrase locates the scene temporally and connects it to the preceding announcement. The credibility of what is about to take place is already underscored by the subtle reminder that what Gabriel announced to Zechariah has already begun to take place. Since we have already met Gabriel, no further introduction is needed. What is about to take place, however, is a further unfolding of God's design for the salvation of all humanity. Gabriel is just God's agent. The central figure in the annunciation is neither Gabriel nor Mary—it is the gracious God of Israel.

Time flies—from the sweeping reference to the interval of six months to the moment of Gabriel's words to Mary. As readers, we are imaginatively drawn into the scene through the frame of the shifting spatial references. Notice how they move from general to specific: from God to a city, of Galilee, Nazareth, to a virgin, betrothed to a man named Joseph, to Mary. By this careful arrangement, Luke lets us sense the coming of the angel.

The angel greets Mary, "Greetings, favored one! The Lord is with you" (v. 28). The words echo the distant words of Hannah, the mother of the prophet Samuel: "Let your servant find favor in your sight" (1 Sam 1:18 NRSV). The words also parallel assurances of power and favor given to the judges of Israel: "The LORD is with you" (Judg 6:12 NRSV). Matthew conveys the same assurance that the birth of Jesus meant the promise of God's redeeming love by means of the name Emmanuel, "God is with us" (Matt 1:23).

1:29-33. Mary was greatly troubled. Tobit, a popular folk tale included in the apocrypha, tells of a jealous angel who appeared on a bride's wedding night each time she married and killed her bridegroom. Against the background of this popular story, the fear of a betrothed girl at the appearance of an angel is all the more understandable. Could it be that she thought an evil spirit was threatening to prevent her marriage?

Although Mary was not yet married, she was betrothed. According to ancient customs, the marriage would have been arranged by her father. She would live at home for a year after her betrothal. Then the groom would come to take her to his home, and the wedding celebration would last for an entire week. Legally, the marriage was sealed after the engagement. Thus, if Joseph had died before the wedding, Mary would have been considered a widow.

Immediately, the angel reassures Mary with the all-important promise that she had found favor with God. Then came the staggering announcement: She—Mary—was going to have a baby, and he would be the Son of God! His name would be called Jesus. The explanation that followed the announcement told of Jesus' role in God's plan. In contrast to John, who would prepare the people (1:16-17), Jesus would be called

"the Son of the Most High" (v. 32). Jesus would be superior to John, therefore, even though John came first. Jesus would reign over Israel as had his forefather David. This prediction adds significance to Luke's earlier report that Joseph was a descendant of David (v. 27).

Again, we hear echoes of past promises. Second Samuel records the promise, "I will make for you a great name" (7:9 NRSV), and Gabriel confirmed, "He will be great" (v. 32). In 2 Samuel, the prophet Nathan was told that through David's son God would "establish the throne of his kingdom forever" (7:13 NRSV). Similarly, the angel announced that Mary's child would "reign over the house of Jacob forever" (v. 33). The same OT passage records God's promise, "I will be his father, and he will be my son" (7:14 NIV). God's promises to David, therefore, were about to be fulfilled in a way David could not have imagined. Jesus' kingdom, however, would not be an earthly, political reign but a spiritual kingdom that would never end.

1:34-35. In response to this angelic announcement, Mary asks a question reminiscent of Zechariah's query, "How can this be?" She had not had sexual relations with a man. Gabriel's response emphasizes that the baby would be born by the power of God. Like the presence of God in the cloud at the transfiguration (9:34), the Holy Spirit would come upon her and overshadow her. The child, therefore, would be God's child, and he would be called the Son of God. As with all the annunciations in Scripture and in ancient biographical accounts, the purpose of the annunciation is to declare something vital about the identity of the child. The Lukan account repeatedly affirms that Mary's son would be called "Son of the Most High" (v. 32a), son of David (v. 32b), and finally the title by which he would be most widely recognized, "Son of God" (v. 35).

1:36. The announcement to Mary, apparently, was a double announcement. The implication of v. 36 is that Mary did not know that Elizabeth was carrying a child also. The interpretation that Elizabeth and Mary were cousins can be traced to Wycliffe, but Luke leaves the nature of their relationship vague ("relative," v. 36). The earlier reference that Elizabeth remained in seclusion makes this lack of communication plausible. The announcement of Elizabeth's joy to Mary, therefore, serves as a sign to her. If Elizabeth, who had been called barren, could bear a child, then Mary could be sure that what had been told to her would come to pass also.

The repetition of the temporal notice, that it was the sixth month of Elizabeth's pregnancy, closes this scene with a return to its opening words in v. 26. At least since the fourth century, churches have observed the births of John the Baptist and Jesus six months apart. The traditional dates are June 24 and December 25, which co-incide with the pagan celebrations of the summer and winter solstices, though nothing in the New Testament confirms these dates. The church may have chosen these dates for several reasons. December 25 falls nine months after March 25, which was traditionally regarded as the first day of creation. In this view, the conception of Jesus was viewed as the beginning of a new creation. In addition, December 25 comes just after the winter solstice, when the days start growing longer. Christians saw Jesus as the true light of the world that would enlighten all people (John 1:9).

1:37. Gabriel's parting words ring with reassurance: "Nothing will be impossible with God." They echo the wonder of Sarah: "Is anything too wonderful for the LORD?" (Gen 18:14 NRSV) and Jesus' later declaration, "What is impossible for mortals is possible for God" (18:27). A barren woman can bear a child. A virgin can conceive. The Lord can enter into human history as a child. From a tomb can come resurrection, and the Holy Spirit can empower the church for its worldwide mission. It is a promise in the future tense: With God nothing *will be* impossible.

1:38. The conclusion to this scene wraps the mantle of Hannah around Mary as she echoes the words of her OT predecessor: "Here am I, the servant of the Lord; let it be with me according to your word" (v. 38; cf. 1 Sam 1:18), and shortly Mary will sing praise to God, just as Hannah had long before (cf. vv. 46-55 and 1 Sam 2:1-10). Throughout the Gospel of Luke, Mary is portrayed in a positive light as one obedient to the Lord (1:39-56; 2:34, 51), and Jesus will later declare, "My mother and my brothers are those who hear the word of God and do it" (8:21).

Gabriel has completed his mission successfully. The annunciation would not have been complete without Mary's trusting, obedient response. Mary had been chosen, "favored," to have an important part in God's plan to bring salvation to God's people, but it is unthinkable that God would have forced Mary to have the child against her will. Mary is an important example, therefore, of one who is obedient to God even at great risk to self.

Just as the scene of the annunciation to Zechariah concludes with his departure from Jerusalem, so also this scene ends with Gabriel's departure. The departure, moreover, complements the detailed announcement of Gabriel's coming at the beginning of the scene. The repetition of temporal and spatial notices at the end of the scene serve, therefore, as a transition from the dialogue between Mary and Gabriel to the narration that follows.

REFLECTIONS

Luke's distinctive attention to God's work among ordinary people continues to be evident. The angel Gabriel appeared first to Zechariah, an old priest going about his duties in the Temple, and then to a young girl not yet married. God chose the lowly rather than the high and mighty to fulfill the plan of redemption. Instead of sending Gabriel to a queen or princess, God sent the angel to a young girl betrothed to a carpenter. They lived in an insignificant town in an unimportant province of the Roman Empire. Nothing about their circumstances would have led anyone to suspect the role they would play in God's plan.

1. Mary had been chosen, "favored" by God. But what a strange blessing. It brought with it none of the ideals or goals that so consume our daily striving. Today many assume that those whom God favors will enjoy the things we equate with a good life: social standing, wealth, and good health. Yet Mary, God's favored one, was blessed with having a child out of wedlock who would later be executed as a criminal. Acceptability, prosperity, and comfort have never been the essence of God's blessing. The story is so familiar that we let its familiarity mask its scandal.

2. If Mary embodies the scandal, she also exemplifies the obedience that should flow from blessing. Mary was favored and would bear a king, but only if she gave herself obediently in response to God's call. The greatest blessings are bound up in the fellowship God shares with us. They are not rewards separate from that fellowship. Perhaps we would inject more realism into our Advent celebrations if we recognized that the glory of Christmas came about by the willingness of ordinary people to obey God's claim on their lives.

3. The ultimate scandal is that God would enter human life with all its depravity, violence, and corruption. Therefore, the annunciation ultimately is an announcement of hope for humankind. God has not abandoned us to the consequences of our own sinfulness. Rather, God has sent Jesus as our deliverer. There is another way, a commonwealth under Jesus' Lordship that is without end.

LUKE 1:39-56, MARY'S VISIT WITH ELIZABETH

NIV

39At that time Mary got ready and hurried to a town in the hill country of Judea, 40where she entered Zechariah's home and greeted Elizabeth. 41When Elizabeth heard Mary's greeting, the baby leaped in her womb, and Elizabeth was filled with the Holy Spirit. 42In a loud voice she exclaimed: "Blessed are you among women, and blessed is the child you will bear! 43But why am I so favored, that the mother of my Lord should come to me? 44As soon as the sound of your greeting reached my ears, the baby in my womb leaped for joy. 45Blessed is she who has believed that what the Lord has said to her will be accomplished!"

46And Mary said:

"My soul glorifies the Lord
47 and my spirit rejoices in God my Savior,
48for he has been mindful
of the humble state of his servant.
From now on all generations will call me
blessed,
49 for the Mighty One has done great things for
me—
holy is his name.
50His mercy extends to those who fear him,
from generation to generation.
51He has performed mighty deeds with his arm;
he has scattered those who are proud in their
inmost thoughts.

NRSV

39In those days Mary set out and went with haste to a Judean town in the hill country, 40where she entered the house of Zechariah and greeted Elizabeth. 41When Elizabeth heard Mary's greeting, the child leaped in her womb. And Elizabeth was filled with the Holy Spirit 42and exclaimed with a loud cry, "Blessed are you among women, and blessed is the fruit of your womb. 43And why has this happened to me, that the mother of my Lord comes to me? 44For as soon as I heard the sound of your greeting, the child in my womb leaped for joy. 45And blessed is she who believed that there would be*a* a fulfillment of what was spoken to her by the Lord."

46And Mary*b* said,

"My soul magnifies the Lord,
47 and my spirit rejoices in God my Savior,
48 for he has looked with favor on the lowliness
of his servant.
Surely, from now on all generations will call
me blessed;
49 for the Mighty One has done great things for
me,
and holy is his name.
50 His mercy is for those who fear him
from generation to generation.

a Or believed, for there will be   *b Other ancient authorities read Elizabeth*

NIV

⁵²He has brought down rulers from their thrones
  but has lifted up the humble.
⁵³He has filled the hungry with good things
  but has sent the rich away empty.
⁵⁴He has helped his servant Israel,
  remembering to be merciful
⁵⁵to Abraham and his descendants forever,
  even as he said to our fathers."

⁵⁶Mary stayed with Elizabeth for about three months and then returned home.

NRSV

⁵¹ He has shown strength with his arm;
  he has scattered the proud in the thoughts
    of their hearts.
⁵² He has brought down the powerful from their
    thrones,
  and lifted up the lowly;
⁵³ he has filled the hungry with good things,
  and sent the rich away empty.
⁵⁴ He has helped his servant Israel,
  in remembrance of his mercy,
⁵⁵ according to the promise he made to our
    ancestors,
  to Abraham and to his descendants forever."
⁵⁶And Mary remained with her about three months and then returned to her home.

COMMENTARY

A master storyteller, Luke has begun the Gospel with a stately literary prologue and two separate but parallel birth announcements. At the end of the second announcement, Mary was told that Elizabeth was expecting a child. The two separate story lines merge when Mary visits Elizabeth. The significance of this scene arises from the following observations: The sparse narrative in these verses (vv. 39-41, 56) serves primarily to frame the prophetic oracles uttered by Elizabeth (vv. 42-45) and Mary (vv. 46-55). The oracles, in turn, offer praise for the faithfulness of Mary, the blessedness of the Lord's birth, and the wonder of God's work of redemption.

1:39-41. The opening and closing words of the scene again describe a coming and going, this time Mary's. As in the previous scene, Mary's approach to Elizabeth moves the reader into the dialogue between Mary and Elizabeth by shifting from general to increasingly specific spatial references: She went to the hill country, to a village of Judea, to the house of Zechariah, to Elizabeth. Her haste may convey obedience, but since she was not told to go to Elizabeth, it is more likely an indication of joy and wonder. There is no question or doubt. The verbs convey the movement, the urgency, and the joy of her journey:

Mary set out, went with haste, entered the house, and greeted Elizabeth.

The meeting of the women is also accompanied by a sign: The child in Elizabeth's womb leaps. The report of the movement of a child in the womb recalls, for those familiar with the Scriptures of Israel, other prenatal signs. Jacob and Esau struggled so fiercely in Rebekah's womb that she lamented: "If it is to be this way, why do I live?" (Gen 25:22 NRSV). Similarly, the birth struggles of Perez and Zerah are noted in Gen 38:27-30. The movement of her unborn child is interpreted immediately by Elizabeth.

1:42-45. These verses contain four oracles. Indeed, there are two signs at the encounter between Mary and Elizabeth. Not only does the child leap, but also Elizabeth is filled with the Holy Spirit and prophesies. Another of the words of announcement to Zechariah is thereby fulfilled. Zechariah remained speechless (vv. 20, 22), Elizabeth conceived (vv. 13, 24), and now the babe has leaped in the womb at the approach of Mary and Elizabeth has been filled with the Spirit, fulfilling the announcement that "even before his birth he will be filled with the Holy Spirit" (v. 15). The report that Elizabeth was filled with the Holy Spirit also serves to alert us that what she says will come as an inspired prophetic utterance, the word of God. Her loud cry, while it may remind one of a birth pang, is the cry of the Spirit in song.

The first oracle declares the blessedness of Mary and the child that will be born to her. Luke has given no indication that Elizabeth knew of the angelic announcement to Mary. The implication is that her knowledge of Mary's pregnancy was given to her by the Spirit. Her oracle did not confer God's blessing on Mary but recognized that she was already blessed. Luke 11:27 will later resonate with Elizabeth's cry, much in the same way that the cry of the disciples at the entry into Jerusalem (19:38) answers the angelic blessing at the birth of Jesus (2:14). Elizabeth's words also evoke the blessings pronounced on Jael (Judg 5:24) and Judith (Jdt 13:18; see also 2 Bar 54:10). Whereas Jael and Judith were praised for their heroism in wielding the sword, however, Mary will experience the point of the sword in her own heart (2:35).

The second oracle takes the form of a question, but discloses more explicitly the identity of the child in Mary's womb. Her reference to Mary as "the mother of my Lord" is already a Christian confession, signaling that as with the rest of the birth narratives, Luke has told this part of his story in light of the entire story. To the blessing of the answer to her prayer for a child has now been added the blessing of a visit from the one who would be the mother of the Lord.

The third oracle explains the meaning of the movement of the babe in her womb. It was a leap of joy. The angel had promised Zechariah that he would have joy, and now joy has come to Elizabeth at the visitation of Mary (cf. vv. 14, 44). John has already begun to fulfill his calling as one who would declare the Lord's coming and prepare the way for him. Later, Jesus would rejoice that the Lord of heaven and earth who had hidden things from the wise had revealed them to infants (10:21)!

The fourth oracle is a beatitude on Mary for her faith that the promise to her would be fulfilled. The oracle, therefore, recalls both the annunciation to Mary and her humble response. Blessing always comes from trusting that God's Word will be fulfilled.

1:46-55. The oracles from Elizabeth are matched by the song of praise from Mary—the Magnificat. A few manuscripts attribute the Magnificat to Elizabeth, but the structure of parallel scenes describing the annunciations and birth of John and Jesus favors the traditional reading that the Magnificat is Mary's answer to the words of Elizabeth. Whether the words fit the situation of Mary or Elizabeth better is moot if, as has often been suggested, the words of the canticles in Luke were drawn from early Jewish-Christian liturgical compositions. The song of Mary turns, therefore, to the effects of the Lord's coming for all God's people. Just as surely as the annunciations, these words echo the promises to Israel through the generations and declare their fulfillment. Only v. 48 speaks directly to the situation, and it echoes the words of blessing that have already been pronounced upon Mary. Just as the annunciations followed the pattern of angelic annunciations in the OT, so also the Magnificat clearly owes much of its inspiration to the song of Hannah in 1 Sam 2:1-10. Both open with a couplet exalting the Lord. Verse 48 declares the reason for Mary's praise and identifies her with the lowly, foreshadowing both the promise of exaltation of the lowly later in the Magnificat and the fulfillment of this promise in the ministry of Jesus. The words of praise, however, speak of God's redeeming work not as future but as already having been fulfilled. Such is the confidence of faith. The overthrow of the powerful has not come about through the mounting up of the weak in rebellion but through the coming of God in the weakness of a child. The couplets describe the dramatic reversal that is the signature of God's mighty acts. The proud are scattered. The powerful are deposed. By contrast, the lowly are exalted and the hungry are fed while the rich are sent away empty. According to the promises, the Lord has helped Israel to remember God's mercies. More than predictions of what is to come, the Magnificat praises God for the goodness of God's nature and the redemption that Israel and the church have experienced. The Magnificat also makes clear the pattern of God's activity. In every line there are echoes of the Scriptures of Israel.

1:56. The scene ends with Mary's departure about three months later. The temporal reference effectively fills the span of time between the annunciation to Mary and the birth of John in the next scene.

REFLECTIONS

1. What mother has not waited for the first stirrings of a child or felt the goodness of God's blessing in the fullness of her womb? The joy of Mary and Elizabeth is the joy of all who look forward with wonder and thankfulness to the birth of a child. The joining of this wonder with God's saving work invites us to consider how the experience of expectancy teaches us the ways of God's gracious work in human experience. Joy is peaked by waiting. Love is disclosed in tenderness and promise. Every birth, therefore, can be a sign of salvation, of finding favor, of being blessed, of living with promise, and of realizing its fulfillment. The experience of Israel and of Jesus are but extensions of these same realities.

2. The joy of the mother will be the job of the son. Mary rejoiced that God had looked on her with favor, that God had shown the strength of God's arm, and that God would overthrow the powerful and exalt the poor. Echoes of her words come to the fore again in Jesus' address in the synagogue at Nazareth and in his parables of the rich man and Lazarus and the Pharisee and the tax collector. Mary praises God as Savior (v. 46), yet it is Jesus who will bring about that salvation.

3. Joy is a recurring theme throughout Luke. The joy of the annunciations and the births in the first two chapters recurs in the joy of forgiveness, healings, raising the dead, and receiving the outcasts throughout the ministry of Jesus. Appropriately, at the end of the Gospel, the disciples return to Jerusalem with joy and are in the Temple praising God. God's redemptive work brings joy to expression in human experience, and that joy is most fully expressed in the praise of God.

4. Mary's praise of God as Savior should not escape notice. The confession "Savior" expresses the desperate need of the lowly, the poor, the oppressed, and the hungry. Those who have power and means, privilege and position have no need sufficient to lead them to voice such a term that is itself a plea for help. "Savior" gives evidence of one's sense of need greater than one's own strength. The proud are thereby excluded from the beginning from the confession that leads to joy and salvation. "Savior" also confesses that the need for deliverance has been met by another. The whole history of redemption, therefore, is evoked by a single word that runs the gamut from desperate need to joyous fulfillment: Savior.

Verse 47 is theologically clear: God is our Savior. The title should never be limited to our confession of Jesus, as though it did not apply to God. All that Jesus does in the Gospel of Luke to effect salvation—calling for repentance, forgiving sinners, healing the sick, casting out demons, eating with outcasts, and dying a redemptive death—he does according to God's purpose and intent. In Jesus, therefore, the role of God as Savior is transparent.

To confess that God is our Savior means that we will not look to some other power for salvation from the chaos we have created. Neither technology nor social progress, neither education nor legislated reforms will deliver us in and of themselves from meaningless lives, amoral secularism, and the various forms of degradation that are rampant in society. God may use any of these processes, but the basis of our trust, hope, and commitment should be clear: God is our Savior.

LUKE 1:57-80, THE BIRTH OF JOHN THE BAPTIST

NIV

57When it was time for Elizabeth to have her baby, she gave birth to a son. 58Her neighbors and relatives heard that the Lord had shown her great mercy, and they shared her joy.

59On the eighth day they came to circumcise the child, and they were going to name him after his father Zechariah, 60but his mother spoke up and said, "No! He is to be called John."

61They said to her, "There is no one among your relatives who has that name."

62Then they made signs to his father, to find out what he would like to name the child. 63He asked for a writing tablet, and to everyone's astonishment he wrote, "His name is John." 64Immediately his mouth was opened and his tongue was loosed, and he began to speak, praising God. 65The neighbors were all filled with awe, and throughout the hill country of Judea people were talking about all these things. 66Everyone who heard this wondered about it, asking, "What then is this child going to be?" For the Lord's hand was with him.

67His father Zechariah was filled with the Holy Spirit and prophesied:

68"Praise be to the Lord, the God of Israel,
>   because he has come and has redeemed his
>   people.
69He has raised up a horn*a* of salvation for us
>   in the house of his servant David
70(as he said through his holy prophets of long ago),
71salvation from our enemies
>   and from the hand of all who hate us—
72to show mercy to our fathers
>   and to remember his holy covenant,
73   the oath he swore to our father Abraham:
74to rescue us from the hand of our enemies,
>   and to enable us to serve him without fear
75   in holiness and righteousness before him all
>   our days.

76And you, my child, will be called a prophet of
>   the Most High;

a69 Horn here symbolizes strength.

NRSV

57Now the time came for Elizabeth to give birth, and she bore a son. 58Her neighbors and relatives heard that the Lord had shown his great mercy to her, and they rejoiced with her.

59On the eighth day they came to circumcise the child, and they were going to name him Zechariah after his father. 60But his mother said, "No; he is to be called John." 61They said to her, "None of your relatives has this name." 62Then they began motioning to his father to find out what name he wanted to give him. 63He asked for a writing tablet and wrote, "His name is John." And all of them were amazed. 64Immediately his mouth was opened and his tongue freed, and he began to speak, praising God. 65Fear came over all their neighbors, and all these things were talked about throughout the entire hill country of Judea. 66All who heard them pondered them and said, "What then will this child become?" For, indeed, the hand of the Lord was with him.

67Then his father Zechariah was filled with the Holy Spirit and spoke this prophecy:

68 "Blessed be the Lord God of Israel,
>   for he has looked favorably on his people
>   and redeemed them.
69 He has raised up a mighty savior*a* for us
>   in the house of his servant David,
70 as he spoke through the mouth of his holy
>   prophets from of old,
71   that we would be saved from our enemies
>   and from the hand of all who hate us.
72 Thus he has shown the mercy promised to our
>   ancestors,
>   and has remembered his holy covenant,
73 the oath that he swore to our ancestor
>   Abraham,
>   to grant us 74that we, being rescued from
>   the hands of our enemies,
>   might serve him without fear, 75in holiness and
>   righteousness
>   before him all our days.
76 And you, child, will be called the prophet of
>   the Most High;

aGk a horn of salvation

NIV

for you will go on before the Lord to prepare
the way for him,
77to give his people the knowledge of salvation
through the forgiveness of their sins,
78because of the tender mercy of our God,
by which the rising sun will come to us from
heaven
79to shine on those living in darkness
and in the shadow of death,
to guide our feet into the path of peace."

80And the child grew and became strong in spirit; and he lived in the desert until he appeared publicly to Israel.

NRSV

for you will go before the Lord to prepare
his ways,
77 to give knowledge of salvation to his people
by the forgiveness of their sins.
78 By the tender mercy of our God,
the dawn from on high will break upon[a] us,
79 to give light to those who sit in darkness and
in the shadow of death,
to guide our feet into the way of peace."

80The child grew and became strong in spirit, and he was in the wilderness until the day he appeared publicly to Israel.

[a] Other ancient authorities read *has broken upon*

COMMENTARY

Following the meeting of Mary and Elizabeth, the story line returns to the fulfillment of the announcement to Zechariah. This section falls into two parts. The first describes the birth, circumcision, and naming of the child (vv. 57-66). The second contains Zechariah's blessing of the child (the *Benedictus,* vv. 67-79). A concluding verse (80) bridges the time between the birth and the beginning of John's ministry.

1:57-66. The birth of John the Baptist is narrated with striking brevity (vv. 57-58). The emphasis throughout this section continues to fall on the phenomena that accompany the birth, the fulfillment of the angelic announcement, Luke's theological interpretation of the event, and the foreshadowing of John's future role. The fulfillment of the announcement of John's birth in such a dramatic fashion also serves to heighten the reader's anticipation of the fulfillment of the even greater predictions regarding the birth of Jesus.

Each element of Luke's narrative of the birth and accompanying phenomena confirms the fulfillment of the annunciation. Elizabeth bore a son. Even this bare report of the birth echoes the words "Your wife Elizabeth will bear you a son" (v. 13). When her neighbors and relatives heard of the birth, they rejoiced with her, fulfilling the prediction that "many will rejoice at his birth" (v. 14). What the neighbors heard, however, is reported as a theological interpretation of the birth:

"that the Lord had shown his great mercy to her" (cf. vv. 50, 54, 72, 78). The cause for rejoicing, therefore, is subtly shifted from the birth to the demonstration of God's mercy.

The report of John's circumcision on the eighth day in accordance with the Mosaic Law (Gen 17:12; Lev 12:3) adds one more facet to Luke's portrayal of the origins of the Christian story from the heart of the heritage and piety of Israel. The naming of the child serves also to confirm the fulfillment of the annunciation of John's birth. At the circumcision he was being called by his father's name: Zechariah. His mother's protest may be taken as evidence either that Zechariah had communicated the angel's instructions to her or that in some wondrous way she had arrived at the same name independently. Naming a son was normally the father's prerogative, and in the naming he claimed the child as his own. The name "John" is found in priestly families, but not exclusively among priests, and means "God has been gracious" (1 Chr 26:3; Ezra 10:6). When the others present responded that no one in her family was named John, they made signs to Zechariah for him to indicate the name that should be given to the child; evidently, Zechariah was deaf as well as mute. The detailed account of the naming contrasts with the brevity of the report of John's birth. The drama of the naming, however, fulfills the sign of Zechariah's speechlessness. What

Gabriel foretold has now come to pass (v. 20). When Zechariah requests a writing tablet and writes "His name is John," the people are amazed, his tongue is freed, and he begins praising God (cf. Dan 10:15-16).

The naming of John and Zechariah's recovery brought fear and amazement both to the neighbors and throughout the hill country of Judea. Fear is a typical response in Luke to a disclosure of God's power (cf. 5:26; 7:16; 8:37; Acts 2:43). Similarly, like Mary (2:19), all who heard these things "placed them in their hearts." In the OT this idiom means that the person perceives that something significant has happened and is prepared to act on it (see Gen 37:11; 1 Sam 21:12; Dan 7:28). The effect of their amazement is to lead the people to speculate over the identity of this child. Their question, "What then will this child become?" has already been answered for the reader by the annunciation to Zechariah, who answers the question in the blessing that follows. The last phrase of v. 66, "For, indeed, the hand of the Lord was with him," may be taken either as a continuation of the previous question or as a comment by the narrator. The latter is preferable (and is followed by the NRSV) because of the past tense verb. The idiom is peculiar to Luke in the NT (cf. Acts 11:21) but common in the OT (Isa. 31:3; 41:20; 66:14).

Every element of this paragraph, therefore, either heightens the fulfillment of the prophecies regarding John's birth or fuels such Lukan themes as fear, joy, and praise as the appropriate response to God's mercy and God's mighty deeds. Every aspect of these events occurred following God's design and led to the fulfillment of God's redemptive work in Israel and beyond.

1:67-79. Zechariah's blessing, traditionally called the *Benedictus,* locates the work of John in reference to both God's promises to Israel and the saving work of Jesus. Gabriel had said that John would be filled with the Spirit (v. 15), then Elizabeth was filled with the Holy Spirit (v. 41; cf. v. 57), and now Zechariah is likewise "filled with the Holy Spirit." Once again we are prepared to receive the words that follow as a divine oracle.

Interpreters have debated the extent and origin of the hymn of praise that follows, assigning the core of it to Jewish Christians or to a traditional Jewish psalm. The traditional source is found in vv. 68-75, with the possible addition of vv. 78-79. If the earlier verses were drawn from a traditional psalm, then vv. 76-77 were inserted by Luke to make the hymn fit the context as Zechariah's answer to the question "What then will this child become?" These two verses are also thoroughly Lukan in style. If vv. 78-79 are treated as part of the Lukan addition, then one avoids the problem of identifying the antecedent of v. 78. On the other hand, one is still faced with the vexing problem that many interpreters have thought that vv. 78-79 characterize the ministry of Jesus rather than John's ministry. At least this addition links the Christian community to those in Israel who were looking forward to God's deliverance of the people.

The language of vv. 68-75 is thoroughly covenantal and frequently echoes phrases from the OT. Luke understood the births of John and Jesus as a part of God's fulfillment of the promises to David (2 Sam 7:8-16) and to Abraham (Gen 12:1-3; 26:3). Jesus was the promised "horn of salvation" (v. 69; cf. Ezek 29:21; 1 Sam 2:10; Ps 18:2). The people of Israel had long expected that God's deliverance would take the form of deliverance from the domination of foreign powers. The deliverance would be a new exodus (v. 71; cf. Pss 18:17; 106:10; 2 Sam 22:18). The progression of thought in the *Benedictus* shows, however, that the true end of God's redemption is not merely deliverance from political domination—as important as that is—but the creation of conditions in which God's people can worship and serve God without fear. As Schweizer perceptively observes: "The ultimate purpose of God's salvation presupposes deliverance from the enemy but is in fact undisturbed worship."[31] Deliverance makes worship in peace—unhindered worship—possible.

We are a covenant people, saved and rescued by God's hand. God has thereby fulfilled the promises to Abraham and to David. Holiness and righteousness—two important elements of the covenants—are to mark God's people "all the days of our life" (v. 75). The worshiping community is therefore invited to join their voices with Zechariah's and Luke's, to serve God, and to live in holiness and righteousness.

---

31. Eduard Schweizer, *The Good News According to Luke,* trans. David E. Green (Atlanta: John Knox, 1984) 43.

The hymn comes to a climax as it describes the place of John in God's redemptive work. John's birth announced God's new deliverance. John would be a prophet (v. 76; cf. 7:26-27) who would go before the Lord (fulfilling Isa 40:3 and Mal 3:1; 4:5). Four infinitives outline the progress of God's redemptive work. The first two describe the role of John the Baptist (vv. 76-77). The last two (v. 79) allude to the inauguration of the kingdom, "when the day shall dawn upon us from on high" (see v. 78).

John would prepare the way (Isa 40:3; Mal 3:1), turning the hearts of parents to their children, turning the disobedient to the wisdom of the just, and making a people prepared (cf. v. 17). John would also "give knowledge of salvation" to the people, calling them to repentance and pointing them to Jesus. Through the knowledge of salvation, the new covenant, foreseen by Jeremiah (31:34), would be fulfilled and inaugurated. According to Jeremiah, the new covenant would mean that each person would "know the LORD . . . for I will forgive their iniquity, and remember their sin no more" (NRSV).

The reference to the knowledge of God leads quickly to the announcement of "light to those who sit in darkness" (v. 79; see Isa 9:2; 42:6-7). The mark of the redeemed is that they live out of the knowledge of God that has been given to them. Darkness is dispelled by the revelation of God's being and God's grace toward us. Finally, through John's call for justice and righteousness (see Luke 3:7-14), and far more through Jesus' exemplary ministry, God would "guide our feet into the way of peace" (v. 79).

REFLECTIONS

What constitutes evidence that "the hand of the Lord" (v. 66) is with us? The hand of the Lord is seen wherever one arises to call for peace and to bring deliverance and reconciliation to the oppressed and the estranged.

The historical context of the *Benedictus* is as important as its literary context. As Luke was concerned to remind his readers, the births of John the Baptist and Jesus, heralding God's redemption, occurred while Israel suffered under the domination of Rome and the vassal king, Herod. It can hardly be accidental that Luke began his "orderly account" by setting the time of God's wonderful new deed "in the days of King Herod of Judea" (1:5). But God did not act through Herod. Instead, God visited an elderly priest and his barren wife. Luke also sets the birth of Jesus in the context of a decree from Caesar Augustus that the conquered people be enrolled by name and city—presumably for the purpose of taxation (2:1-3). God was visiting the people in the midst of their oppression.

That haunting phrase, "to guide our feet into the way of peace," ends Zechariah's blessing upon John, his newborn son. This is the first of fourteen references to peace in the Gospel of Luke. The *Benedictus* links the promise of salvation and redemption inseparably to the achievement of peace. God's people cannot have redemption without peace, for each is necessary for the realization of the other.

Throughout the Gospel peace is closely associated with God's redemptive work and the salvation that comes to God's people. Angels announced Jesus' birth with the refrain of "peace on earth" (see 2:14), and those who followed Jesus answered antiphonally, "Peace in heaven,/ and glory in the highest heaven!" (19:38). Jesus brought peace to those who received him: Simeon (2:29), the woman who wept on Jesus' feet (7:50), and the woman with a hemorrhage (8:48). Through faith, each found peace.

Luke also explores the ways of peace. Disciples on mission announce peace and are received by sons and daughters of peace (10:5-6; Acts 10:36). There are various kinds of peace. Peace that is achieved by strength is always vulnerable to the attack of one who is stronger (11:21-22). A king whose troops are outnumbered will, therefore, make peace with his enemy (14:32). Paradoxically, in a saying regarding the sifting that revelation inevitably causes, Jesus says that he has not come to bring peace but division (12:51). Affirmation of the "way of peace" provokes hostility, often with terrible consequences. Jesus himself suffered violence from those to whom he offered peace, for Jerusalem did not know "the things that make for peace" (19:42). Bringing peace, he died, but (following the reading now favored by text critics) when Jesus appeared to the disciples his words of common greeting still echoed his ultimate purpose: "Peace be to you" (24:36). The *Benedictus* affirms that God's purposes are being fulfilled in the delivering of God's people from their oppressors. Their feet are being guided in the way of peace so that they may worship without fear. Where then are the sons and daughters of peace who can receive this word of faith?

LUKE 2:1-20, THE BIRTH OF JESUS

NIV

2 In those days Caesar Augustus issued a decree that a census should be taken of the entire Roman world. [2](This was the first census that took place while Quirinius was governor of Syria.) [3]And everyone went to his own town to register.

[4]So Joseph also went up from the town of Nazareth in Galilee to Judea, to Bethlehem the town of David, because he belonged to the house and line of David. [5]He went there to register with Mary, who was pledged to be married to him and was expecting a child. [6]While they were there, the time came for the baby to be born, [7]and she gave birth to her firstborn, a son. She wrapped him in cloths and placed him in a manger, because there was no room for them in the inn.

[8]And there were shepherds living out in the fields nearby, keeping watch over their flocks at night. [9]An angel of the Lord appeared to them, and the glory of the Lord shone around them, and they were terrified. [10]But the angel said to them, "Do not be afraid. I bring you good news of great joy that will be for all the people. [11]Today in the town of David a Savior has been born to you; he is Christ[a] the Lord. [12]This will be a sign to you: You will find a baby wrapped in cloths and lying in a manger."

[13]Suddenly a great company of the heavenly host appeared with the angel, praising God and saying,

[14]"Glory to God in the highest,

[a]11 Or *Messiah*. "The Christ" (Greek) and "the Messiah" (Hebrew) both mean "the Anointed One"; also in verse 26.

NRSV

2 In those days a decree went out from Emperor Augustus that all the world should be registered. [2]This was the first registration and was taken while Quirinius was governor of Syria. [3]All went to their own towns to be registered. [4]Joseph also went from the town of Nazareth in Galilee to Judea, to the city of David called Bethlehem, because he was descended from the house and family of David. [5]He went to be registered with Mary, to whom he was engaged and who was expecting a child. [6]While they were there, the time came for her to deliver her child. [7]And she gave birth to her firstborn son and wrapped him in bands of cloth, and laid him in a manger, because there was no place for them in the inn.

[8]In that region there were shepherds living in the fields, keeping watch over their flock by night. [9]Then an angel of the Lord stood before them, and the glory of the Lord shone around them, and they were terrified. [10]But the angel said to them, "Do not be afraid; for see—I am bringing you good news of great joy for all the people: [11]to you is born this day in the city of David a Savior, who is the Messiah,[a] the Lord. [12]This will be a sign for you: you will find a child wrapped in bands of cloth and lying in a manger." [13]And suddenly there was with the angel a multitude of the heavenly host,[b] praising God and saying,

[14] "Glory to God in the highest heaven,
   and on earth peace among those whom he favors!"[c]

[a]Or *the Christ*   [b]Gk *army*   [c]Other ancient authorities read peace, goodwill among people

NIV

and on earth peace to men on whom his favor rests."

¹⁵When the angels had left them and gone into heaven, the shepherds said to one another, "Let's go to Bethlehem and see this thing that has happened, which the Lord has told us about."

¹⁶So they hurried off and found Mary and Joseph, and the baby, who was lying in the manger. ¹⁷When they had seen him, they spread the word concerning what had been told them about this child, ¹⁸and all who heard it were amazed at what the shepherds said to them. ¹⁹But Mary treasured up all these things and pondered them in her heart. ²⁰The shepherds returned, glorifying and praising God for all the things they had heard and seen, which were just as they had been told.

NRSV

15When the angels had left them and gone into heaven, the shepherds said to one another, "Let us go now to Bethlehem and see this thing that has taken place, which the Lord has made known to us." 16So they went with haste and found Mary and Joseph, and the child lying in the manger. 17When they saw this, they made known what had been told them about this child; 18and all who heard it were amazed at what the shepherds told them. 19But Mary treasured all these words and pondered them in her heart. 20The shepherds returned, glorifying and praising God for all they had heard and seen, as it had been told them.

COMMENTARY

Surprisingly, after a long chapter describing the annunciations of the two births, the meeting of Mary and Elizabeth, and the events surrounding the birth and naming of John, the birth of Jesus is reported with a minimum of detail. The first seven verses describe the setting of Jesus' birth in the context of the census. Only vv. 6 and 7 are devoted to the birth itself. Verses 8-20 then record the angelic annunciation to the shepherds and their visit to the Christ child. The structure of the account suggests, therefore, that Luke interprets the significance of the birth in relation to world history, the content of the angelic announcement, and the visit of the shepherds. The few details in this sparse account, such as the references to the manger and the bands of cloth in which the child was wrapped, are also likely to be significant.

2:1-7. Luke's reference to Caesar Augustus, Quirinius, and the census has caused no end of difficulty for those who have sought to verify the chronology from other ancient sources. The difficulty is evident even in the dates of the principal figures. Augustus reigned in various capacities from 44/42 BCE until his death in 14 CE. Luke 1:5 dates the annunciations "In the days of King Herod of Judea" (40/37 BCE–4 CE). Quirinius, however, became governor or legate of Syria only in 6 CE, at which time he conducted a census of Judea. Other considera-

tions add to the difficulties. There is no record of a registration of "all the world" (or the whole Roman Empire) under Augustus, and Josephus does not record an earlier census of Judea. Such a census for tax purposes would not have occurred during the time that Judea was under the charge of Herod, because the collection of taxes was delegated to him. Moreover, the Roman system of registration did not require one to return to one's place of birth or family origin. Property was registered at its location. Neither would Mary have been required to accompany Joseph.[32]

If the historical evidence for a worldwide census cannot be sustained, we must look for reasons why Luke might have recorded the story of Jesus' birth in this way. One suggestion is that he knew of the census, which is also referred to in Acts 5:37, but was confused about its date. While this suggestion is entirely plausible, it does not explain why the census was linked to Jesus' birth. Another suggestion is that Luke was influenced by Ps 87:6.

"The LORD records, as he registers the peoples,
 'This one was born there.' "

32. For detailed discussions of the difficulties posed by Luke's description of the census, see Raymond E. Brown, *The Birth of the Messiah* (New York: Doubleday, 1977) 547-55; Emil Schürer, *The History of the Jewish People in the Age of Jesus Christ (175 B.C.–A.D. 135)*, 2 vols., rev. and ed. Geza Vermes and Fergus Millar (Edinburgh: T. & T. Clark, 1973) 1:399-427.

This verse links census taking with birth, but it is hardly prominent enough to explain why Luke related Jesus' birth to the census. The linkage, however, serves several important purposes. First, it continues the pattern Luke established in the first chapter of relating the gospel story to significant events and rulers of the time (1:5). Luke returns to this pattern again in 3:1-2. Second, Augustus was widely acclaimed as a bringer of peace. By relating Jesus' birth—and the accompanying angelic announcement of "peace on earth" (2:14)—to Augustus's decree, Luke is able subtly to proclaim that the true bringer of peace was not Caesar Augustus but Jesus the Savior. Third, the census enrollment casts the family as complying with Roman law (cf. 20:20-26; 23:2, 47). Fourth, the census, with the assumed requirement that Joseph had to return to Bethlehem for it, allows Luke to explain how it was that Jesus was born in Bethlehem but grew up in Nazareth. Matthew resolves this difficulty by means of the dream warnings that Joseph should take the family from Bethlehem and flee to Egypt, and later that he should return not to Bethlehem but to Nazareth after the death of Herod the Great. In both Matthew and Luke the birth of Jesus in Bethlehem and the lineage of Joseph establish his claim to the title "son of David." References to David are prominent in the birth account in Luke (1:27, 32, 69; and the title "Son of David" occurs three times in Luke: 18:38, 39; 20:41).

The context of Jesus' birth, therefore, has thematic and theological significance. Jesus, the son of David, the bringer of peace, was born in Bethlehem, the city of David. The Savior of all people was born under the reign of Caesar Augustus, whose peace paled before that announced by the angels. The Messiah born under Roman oppression, which was so evident in the forced registration, would overthrow the powerful and raise up the oppressed. In yet another respect, therefore, the context of Jesus' birth—like the annunciations—serves as commentary on his future role. It is an omen or sign. Understood in this way, undue emphasis should not be given to either Luke's precision as a historian or the significance of the historical problems posed by his reference to the census.

As has been noted, Luke describes the birth itself with surprising brevity. All we are told is that while they were in Bethlehem, Mary "gave birth to her firstborn son and wrapped him in bands of cloth, and laid him in a manger, because there was no place for them in the inn" (2:7). The narrator gives no other details. We are not told where they were or what time of the year it was. The innkeeper is never mentioned, and there is no reference to a cave, the traditional site of Jesus' birth. This absence of detail has led to intense scrutiny of the four particulars that are reported: (1) Jesus was Mary's "firstborn"; (2) she wrapped him in "bands of cloth" and (3) laid him in a manger because (4) there was no place for them in "the inn."

The term *firstborn* has sparked discussion because it has implications for the Roman Catholic teaching regarding the perpetual virginity of Mary. Lucian of Samosata put the matter sharply in another context: "If the first, not the only; if the only, not the first."[33] In this context, however, the term may mean no more than that Mary had no other children at the time Jesus was born, but it may also mean that Luke either knew of other children or was not concerned to emphasize Jesus' uniqueness as Mary's only child.

Wrapping a child in bands of cloth was a common practice. It demonstrated maternal care and may have kept the child's limbs straight (Wisd Sol 7:4). The manger was probably a feeding trough, but sometimes the term refers to a stall. The "inn" may refer to a place where caravaners and pilgrims could spend the night, a guest room in a house (cf. 22:11), or to the sleeping area in a single-room Palestinian peasant home. Since there was no place in the sleeping area, the child was placed in a feed trough. This detail may emphasize the humble origins of Jesus, but interpreters have often read it as foreshadowing the failure of humanity to receive the Lord. In this regard, it has been connected with Isa 1:3:

> The ox knows its owner,
>   and the donkey its master's crib;
> but Israel does not know,
>   my people do not understand.

2:8-20. The next scene describes the angelic announcement to the shepherds and their visit to

33. Lucian of Samosata *Demonax* 29, cited by Raymond E. Brown, *The Birth of the Messiah* (New York: Doubleday, 1977) 398.

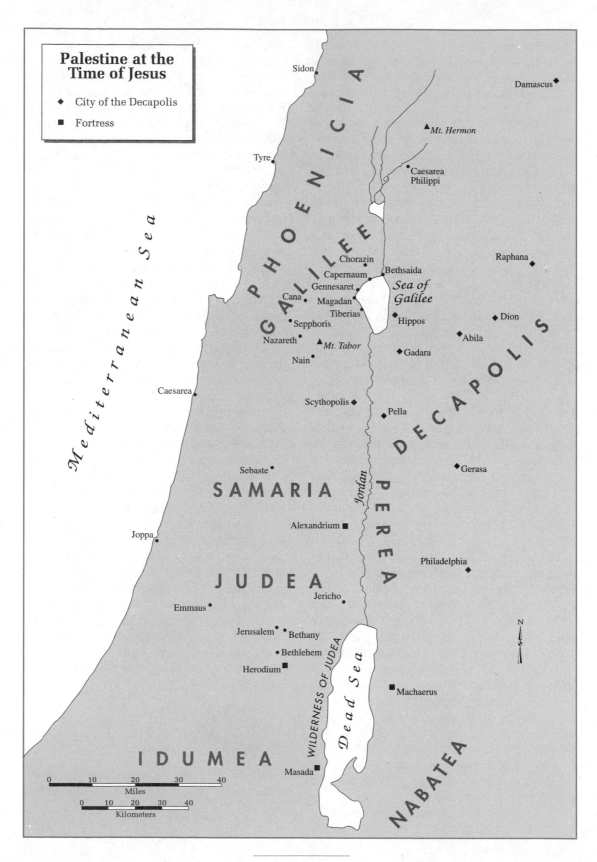

Palestine at the Time of Jesus

♦ City of the Decapolis
■ Fortress

Sidon

Damascus ♦

PHOENICIA

▲ *Mt. Hermon*

Tyre •

• Caesarea Philippi

Mediterranean Sea

GALILEE

Chorazin •

Raphana ♦

Capernaum •

Bethsaida ♦

Gennesaret •

Sea of Galilee

Cana •

Magadan •

Tiberias •

Hippos ♦

Dion ♦

Sepphoris •

Abila ♦

Nazareth •

▲ *Mt. Tabor*

Gadara ♦

Nain •

DECAPOLIS

Caesarea •

Scythopolis ♦

Pella ■

Sebaste •

Gerasa ♦

SAMARIA

Jordan

PEREA

Alexandrium ■

Joppa •

Philadelphia ♦

JUDEA

Jericho •

Emmaus •

Jerusalem • • Bethany

WILDERNESS OF JUDEA

Bethlehem •

Dead Sea

Herodium •

Machaerus ■

IDUMEA

NABATEA

Masada ■

N

| 0 | 10 | 20 | 30 | 40 |

Miles

| 0 | 10 | 20 | 30 | 40 |

Kilometers

the Christ child. Luke and Matthew tell different stories at this point also. Whereas in Matthew the magi follow a star to Bethlehem sometime after the birth of the child, in Luke it is the humble shepherds from the local area to whom a sign of the birth is given. The first two verses set the scene for the announcement; v. 8 describes the shepherds, and v. 9 the appearance of the angel. The announcement and the heavenly chorus follow in vv. 10-14.

Shepherding was a despised occupation at the time. Although the reference to shepherds evokes a positive, pastoral image for the modern reader and underscores Jesus' association with the line of David (1 Sam 16:11; 17:15; Ps 78:70), in the first century, shepherds were scorned as shiftless, dishonest people who grazed their flocks on others' lands. Against this background, it is possible that Luke gets double duty from the shepherds—first, developing further Jesus' connection with David and Bethlehem, and, second, graphically picturing Jesus as one sent to the lowly and outcast. It is to some of their number, shepherds, that the birth is announced. Typically, the story, which begins with a reference to Caesar Augustus, ends with the shepherds' visit to the birth scene in Bethlehem.

Luke describes the appearance of the angel in three statements: The angel stood before them; the glory of the Lord shone around them; and they were greatly afraid. These descriptions carry us again to the angelophanies of the OT and to the angelic annunciations in Luke 1. The words that will be spoken will provide a divine interpretation of the events just described. The darkness is showered with brilliance as the people who wait in darkness see a great light (Isa 9:2). The contrast between the humble setting of the birth and the glory of the angelic announcement could hardly be more dramatic.

The angels announce good news. The verb here is the same one that is used for the proclamation of the gospel. The effect of the good news, as is typical in Luke, will be joy for all the people. The familiarity of these words should not prevent us from overhearing that, first and foremost, the birth of Jesus was a sign of God's abundant grace. Joy and celebration are the only appropriate responses. The birth of Jesus, however, is a sign for all the people—all Israel, all God's people. The

occasion for celebration is described in formal language familiar to everyone who has ever heard the Christmas story. The declaration emphasizes the fulfillment of Israel's messianic expectations "today"; the long-awaited child has been born (cf. Isa 9:6). The titles all define Jesus' role: a savior (a deliverer; Judg 3:9, 15), "Christ the Lord," in the city of David. The title "Christ the Lord," however, occurs nowhere else in the NT. Next, a sign is given, just as signs accompanied each of the previous angelic announcements in Luke. The sign this time is no more than the humble surroundings of the birth that were described in the previous verses: a child wrapped in cloth bands and lying in a manger. Before the shepherds can respond to the announcement, however, a great army of angels (cf. Isaiah 6) appears in the heavens. From the heavenly host a song rises in praise to God (as in Rev 5:9-10; 12:10-12).

The song of the angels is a couplet with three parallel members in each line: (1) glory—peace; (2) in the highest (heaven)—on earth; and (3) to God—among people of goodwill. No verbs or articles clutter this joyful song. Praise for peace is again implicitly directed not to Caesar Augustus but to God. Later in Luke, the disciples entering Jerusalem will provide an antiphonal response:

Peace in heaven,
and glory in the highest heaven! (19:38)

The last word of the song of praise has been interpreted variously. The KJV follows the reading of some ancient MSS in which goodwill, like peace, is given: "peace, goodwill toward men," but the MS evidence no longer favors this reading. The NRSV follows the interpretation that God's goodwill—not that of the people—is intended: "and on earth peace among those whom he favors." This interpretation is now sustained by parallel constructions in the Qumran scrolls.[34]

The response of the shepherds is described in three stages: their conversations with each other (v. 15); finding Mary, Joseph, and the child (v. 16); and their report of the angelic appearance (vv. 17-18). Mary's response (v. 19) and the shepherds' return (v. 20) conclude the scene. Throughout, the emphasis falls on the confirmation of the things that had been spoken to them—

34. 1QH 4.32-33; 11.9.

the angelic announcement. The center of the entire birth scene (2:1-20), therefore, is the christological affirmation of the angel (vv. 10-12) and the response from the heavenly chorus (v. 14). The child is the Messiah. The words of the prophet Isaiah had been fulfilled in an even more wonderful fashion than he could have imagined. The Lord, the savior of God's people, had been born. The whole creation would celebrate, but at first only the shepherds knew what had happened in Bethlehem.

The departure of the angels leaves the spotlight on the shepherds. They immediately resolve to go to Bethlehem. The key point is the way the purpose of their journey is described: to "see this thing that has taken place, which the Lord has made known to us" (v. 15). The angelic announcement was a revelation from the Lord. The reader's interest is implicitly focused on the confirmation of that revelation. The child in the manger was a sign to them that they had found the child of whom that angel had spoken. The manger, therefore, is mentioned in each part of Luke's birth story (vv. 7, 12, 16).

When the shepherds saw the child in the manger, the sign they had been given, they reported to all who were there the things they had been told about the child. Even without a detailed summary, the reader's attention is drawn back to the angelic announcement. A double response follows—from all who heard the shepherds' report (v. 18) and from Mary (v. 19). All were amazed, but Mary kept the words in her heart (cf. 1:66; 2:51; cf. Gen 37:11; Dan 7:28). Another stroke is added to the characterization of Mary with this report from the narrator. Mary is not only the servant of the Lord, but also she quietly considers the meaning of these wonderful events. Luke repeatedly emphasizes the theme of faithful witness to the gospel. The shepherds now join the chorus of witnesses, for they have seen and heard. The result of the whole episode is the response that should arise from all God's people: The shepherds returned to their flocks glorifying and praising God. The focus of the birth scene is underscored one last time, "as it had been told them" (v. 20).

REFLECTIONS

Each year during the Advent and Christmas seasons, we worry about how we are going to get to Bethlehem this year. Bethlehem is the place where God came to us through the birth of a child. It is a place of mystery and wonder, far removed from the ordinary world in which we live. Angels populate the skies and may appear at any time to shepherds in the fields. Although there is a foreign king and an oppressive tax structure, all is well in that tranquil rural setting. Far from the problems of the world, the mother and father hover over their firstborn child lying in a manger. This child will be the Messiah, the Savior for all the earth.

Familiar as it is, the Christmas scene often seems to be little more than a fairy tale, a wonderful story that provides a brief escape from the real world we face each day. A meaningful experience of the good news of the season, however, must inevitably involve entering imaginatively into the story, feeling the wonder of God's grace, and considering the choices that the story puts before us.

1. The first question is, how will we get to Bethlehem? In Matthew, the magi are directed by great learning, by their ability to interpret the movements of stars and planets in the heavens, and by the learning of the sages in Jerusalem. In Luke, however, Mary and Joseph travel to Bethlehem as a family going about the business of life. The shepherds go to Bethlehem by dramatic, heavenly revelation. By all these roads travelers can reach Bethlehem. Not all will follow the road of scholarship or historical investigation. Many will come as families surprised to hear God's Word in the midst of life. Others will come as the result of dramatic, moving experiences of the immediacy of the spiritual and the wondrous in the fabric of ordinary existence. By whatever road we take, the story invites us all to Bethlehem.

2. At Bethlehem, we also witness the scandal of the Christmas story. Neither the familiarity nor the season's festivities should prevent us from realizing the scandal that God came into human history completely helpless, as a newborn, and was laid in a feeding trough. Consider in what splendor God might have come, but instead God slipped unobtrusively into a small province far from the seat of earthly power, born to a young couple, unwed or only recently married. No elaborate preparations were made for the birth. God was born on the road. The crib was a feed trough, and those who came to visit were shepherds, not kings. By entering human history in this way, God identified with the powerless, the oppressed, the poor, and the homeless. Among them, God could do the divine new work. A humility born of need may be the prerequisite for entry into this new kingdom.

3. The Christmas story tells of the birth of a new king. This child would be given the throne of his father, David. The world was moving according to the orders of Caesar Augustus, but although he was hailed as the great bringer of peace, real peace on earth would be realized only through the sovereignty of the child born in Bethlehem. This is the story of the birth of a new kind of king. The birth reveals a new world order, a world not under Caesar but under the direction of God's design for the redemption of all peoples. In this world, God's Word is heard by the humble. There is a place even for shepherds. There is hope for the oppressed, and those who heard what God is doing were filled with joy. God has not forgotten us or abandoned us to the brokenness we have created. The story of Christmas, therefore, is both an announcement of hope and a call to humility.

LUKE 2:21-40, THE PRESENTATION OF JESUS IN THE TEMPLE

NIV

²¹On the eighth day, when it was time to circumcise him, he was named Jesus, the name the angel had given him before he had been conceived.

²²When the time of their purification according to the Law of Moses had been completed, Joseph and Mary took him to Jerusalem to present him to the Lord ²³(as it is written in the Law of the Lord, "Every firstborn male is to be consecrated to the Lord"ᵃ), ²⁴and to offer a sacrifice in keeping with what is said in the Law of the Lord: "a pair of doves or two young pigeons."ᵇ

²⁵Now there was a man in Jerusalem called Simeon, who was righteous and devout. He was waiting for the consolation of Israel, and the Holy Spirit was upon him. ²⁶It had been revealed to him by the Holy Spirit that he would not die before he had seen the Lord's Christ. ²⁷Moved by the Spirit, he went into the temple courts. When the parents brought in the child Jesus to do for

ᵃ23 Exodus 13:2,12   ᵇ24 Lev. 12:8

NRSV

21After eight days had passed, it was time to circumcise the child; and he was called Jesus, the name given by the angel before he was conceived in the womb.

22When the time came for their purification according to the law of Moses, they brought him up to Jerusalem to present him to the Lord ²³(as it is written in the law of the Lord, "Every firstborn male shall be designated as holy to the Lord"), ²⁴and they offered a sacrifice according to what is stated in the law of the Lord, "a pair of turtledoves or two young pigeons."

25Now there was a man in Jerusalem whose name was Simeon;ᵃ this man was righteous and devout, looking forward to the consolation of Israel, and the Holy Spirit rested on him. ²⁶It had been revealed to him by the Holy Spirit that he would not see death before he had seen the Lord's Messiah.ᵇ ²⁷Guided by the Spirit, Simeonᶜ came into the temple; and when the parents brought

ᵃGk Symeon   ᵇOr the Lord's Christ   ᶜGk In the Spirit, he

NIV

him what the custom of the Law required, [28]Simeon took him in his arms and praised God, saying:

[29]"Sovereign Lord, as you have promised,
     you now dismiss[a] your servant in peace.
[30]For my eyes have seen your salvation,
[31]   which you have prepared in the sight of all
          people,
[32]a light for revelation to the Gentiles
     and for glory to your people Israel."

[33]The child's father and mother marveled at what was said about him. [34]Then Simeon blessed them and said to Mary, his mother: "This child is destined to cause the falling and rising of many in Israel, and to be a sign that will be spoken against, [35]so that the thoughts of many hearts will be revealed. And a sword will pierce your own soul too."

[36]There was also a prophetess, Anna, the daughter of Phanuel, of the tribe of Asher. She was very old; she had lived with her husband seven years after her marriage, [37]and then was a widow until she was eighty-four.[b] She never left the temple but worshiped night and day, fasting and praying. [38]Coming up to them at that very moment, she gave thanks to God and spoke about the child to all who were looking forward to the redemption of Jerusalem.

[39]When Joseph and Mary had done everything required by the Law of the Lord, they returned to Galilee to their own town of Nazareth. [40]And the child grew and became strong; he was filled with wisdom, and the grace of God was upon him.

a29 Or promised, / now dismiss   b37 Or widow for eighty-four years

NRSV

in the child Jesus, to do for him what was customary under the law, [28]Simeon[a] took him in his arms and praised God, saying,

[29] "Master, now you are dismissing your servant[b]
          in peace,
       according to your word;
[30] for my eyes have seen your salvation,
[31]   which you have prepared in the presence of
          all peoples,
[32] a light for revelation to the Gentiles
       and for glory to your people Israel."

[33]And the child's father and mother were amazed at what was being said about him. [34]Then Simeon[c] blessed them and said to his mother Mary, "This child is destined for the falling and the rising of many in Israel, and to be a sign that will be opposed [35]so that the inner thoughts of many will be revealed—and a sword will pierce your own soul too."

[36]There was also a prophet, Anna[d] the daughter of Phanuel, of the tribe of Asher. She was of a great age, having lived with her husband seven years after her marriage, [37]then as a widow to the age of eighty-four. She never left the temple but worshiped there with fasting and prayer night and day. [38]At that moment she came, and began to praise God and to speak about the child[e] to all who were looking for the redemption of Jerusalem.

[39]When they had finished everything required by the law of the Lord, they returned to Galilee, to their own town of Nazareth. [40]The child grew and became strong, filled with wisdom; and the favor of God was upon him.

a Gk he   b Gk slave   c Gk Symeon   d Gk Hanna   e Gk him

COMMENTARY

This section brings the birth narrative to a close. Luke's account of the birth of Jesus began with the notice that Joseph and Mary journeyed from Nazareth in Galilee to Bethlehem (2:4). Appropriately, the birth narrative ends with the report that they returned to Galilee, to Nazareth (2:39). Within the sequence of scenes in the birth narratives, it is the counterpart to the naming and dedication of John (1:57-80).

The major motif of this section is that the law of the Lord was fulfilled at Jesus' birth. This section is held together by repeated references to the law (vv. 22-24, 27, and 39), all of the actions taken by Joseph and Mary fulfill what the law prescribes (circumcision and purification), and the transition to their departure from Jerusalem is marked by Luke's report that "they had finished everything required by the law of the Lord"

(v. 39). Other significant motifs include the importance of Jerusalem (vv. 22, 25, 38), the Temple (vv. 27, 37), the guidance of the Holy Spirit (vv. 25-27), and the fulfillment of God's promise of salvation (vv. 25, 30, 38) for both Israel (vv. 25, 32, 34, 38) and the Gentiles (vv. 31-32).

In spite of its unity, the section unfolds in five clearly marked units: the circumcision of Jesus (v. 21), the purification (vv. 22-24), Simeon's blessing (vv. 25-35), Anna's blessing (vv. 36-38), and the conclusion to the birth account (vv. 39-40). The first four units are paired: The circumcision and purification are linked together, as are the roles of Simeon and Anna. Just as a devout couple, Zechariah and Elizabeth, were featured in the birth of John the Baptist, so also another male and female pair of devout persons is introduced in these verses: Simeon and Anna. Neither the acts of obedience in the Temple nor the introduction of Simeon and Anna hold the key to the importance of this section, however. As in Luke's account of the annunciation and birth of Jesus, the real cargo conveyed by these verses is found in what they say about the role of Jesus and his birth in the fulfillment of God's promise of salvation. Simeon and Anna, as devout persons, are important because they recognize and prophetically articulate what Jesus' role will be. Although this section involves arcane details of the law regarding circumcision of the child and purification of the mother after birth, the reader should not miss the point that it conveys the gospel; its primary purpose is to declare who Jesus is and foreshadow what he would do.

2:21, The Circumcision of Jesus. Circumcision of the male child marked his acceptance into the covenant community (Gen 17:9-14). Both rites, circumcision and naming, gave the child an identity. As was often the case, the granting of a biblical or religious name was an act of blessing, a dedication of the child to God, and a declaration of the child's heritage and character.

The law specified that circumcision was to take place on the eighth day (Gen 17:12; Lev 12:3; cf. Luke 1:59; Phil 3:5). The introductory temporal phrase that introduces v. 21 occurs frequently in these early chapters to report completion or fulfillment (1:23, 57; 2:6, 22). The same verb is also used in this context to describe the work of the Spirit (1:15, 41, 67).

The emphasis in v. 21 falls not on the act of circumcision, but on the conferring of the name *Jesus* (cf. the naming of John in 1:59-63; cf. also Matt 1:21). The names of both children, John and Jesus, were given at the annunciation of their births. Luke underscores the significance of the name by reminding the reader that the name *Jesus* had been given not by Joseph but by the angel of the Lord. It declared the child's future role as "Savior" of all people. The conferring of the name, therefore, was itself an act of fulfillment.

2:22-24, The Purification. Two further acts were required of devout parents: the redemption of the firstborn and the purification of the mother. Luke seems to describe both in these verses, though interpreters have debated whether Luke understood the prescriptions of the Jewish Law in these matters. As a reminder of the exodus, the firstborn child was consecrated to the Lord (Exod 13:2, 11-16). The firstborn male was to be redeemed (i.e., bought back) at a price of five shekels of silver (Num 18:15-16). Eventually, the Levites were designated to offer service to God and atonement for the people in place of the firstborn (Num 8:14-19). An entire tractate of the Mishnah is devoted to "the firstlings."[35] The redemption of the firstborn apparently did not require that the child be presented in the Temple (but see Neh 10:35-36). Neither does Luke mention the redemption of Jesus—either because he was not aware of this requirement or because he deliberately omitted it to imply that Jesus continued to be devoted to the Lord. The latter interpretation, however, requires a level of familiarity with Jewish law that could hardly have been assumed among Gentile Christians.

The other ritual prescribed by the Law was the purification of the mother. After the birth of a male child, the mother was ceremonially unclean for seven days and underwent purification for 33 days (the period was twice as long for a female child; Lev 12:1-5). During this time, she was not permitted to enter the Temple or touch any holy object. After the 40 (or 80) days, she was to offer a lamb and a pigeon or turtledove. If she could not afford a lamb, she could offer instead two turtledoves or pigeons (Lev 12:6-8).

35. See *m. Bekhoroth.*

Luke's account of the presentation of Jesus in the Temple underscores the fulfillment of all that the law required at the birth of a child. The descriptions in these verses continue to evoke echoes from the Hebrew Scriptures, especially the dedication of Samuel in the sanctuary at Shiloh. The parallels between the two dedications are unmistakable: The birth of Samuel was promised beforehand; Hannah brought Samuel to the sanctuary and dedicated him to the Lord; Eli blessed Samuel's parents; and the biblical account mentions the women who ministered at the sanctuary (1 Sam 1:24-28; 2:20-22). Each of these elements is repeated in the presentation of Jesus and the blessings by Simeon and Anna.

The scene returns to the Temple, where the Gospel began (1:5-25). The reference to "their" purification may indicate that Luke did not understand that purification was required for the mother only. Alternatively, some interpreters have sought to relieve Luke of the onus of misunderstanding by suggesting that he viewed the act as a family matter. Five of the nine references to the Law in Luke occur in these verses (2:22, 23, 24, 27, 39; cf. 10:26; 16:16, 17; 24:44), and the only two quotations from the OT in Luke 1–2 occur in vv. 23 and 24 (Exod 13:12 [or Exod 13:2, 15] and Lev 12:8 [or Lev 5:11] respectively). Luke does not mention the requirement to offer a lamb, but the reference to the offering of two turtledoves or pigeons may underscore the point that Jesus was born to the poor of Israel. Attention to the details, allusions, and overtones of the passage, therefore, cast fresh light on its significance.

2:25-35, Simeon's Blessing. The account of Simeon's blessing of the child unfolds in the following manner: the narrator's introduction of Simeon (vv. 25-26), Simeon's meeting with the holy family in the Temple (vv. 27-28), Simeon's blessing of the child (vv. 29-32, traditionally known as the *Nunc Dimittis*), the response of Jesus' parents (v. 33), and Simeon's blessing of Mary (vv. 34-35). Throughout, the aura of piety illuminates the scene: It is set in the Temple, the speaker is guided by the Spirit, the parents of the child have come to fulfill the Law, words of Scripture echo in Simeon's oracle, the scene evokes the account of the blessing of Samuel, and the event marks the fulfillment of the promise

that Simeon would see the consolation of Israel and the coming of the Messiah.

The introduction of Simeon follows the common biblical pattern (cf. Job 1:1; John 1:6), conveying his location and his name. Luke characterizes him as "righteous," like Zechariah and Elizabeth (1:6; cf. 23:50; Acts 10:22) and "devout" (cf. Acts 2:4; 8:2; 22:12). The characterization extends two steps further. First, Luke records Simeon's piety and hope in looking forward to the "consolation of Israel." Then the narrator informs the reader that the Holy Spirit was upon Simeon and that the Spirit had revealed to him that he would see the coming of the Messiah before his death. Simeon, therefore, exemplified a devout response to God's promise and God's response to human devotion. The "consolation of Israel" was a term for the restoration of the people and the fulfillment of God's redemptive work. Like much of the language of the *Nunc Dimittis,* the term comes from references in Isaiah:

> Comfort, O comfort my people,
>   says your God
> Speak tenderly to Jerusalem. (Isa 40:1-2 NRSV; cf. 49:13)

> For the LORD will comfort Zion. (Isa 51:3 NRSV)

> Break forth together into singing,
>   you ruins of Jerusalem;
> for the LORD has comforted his people,
>   he has redeemed Jerusalem. (Isa 52:9 NRSV; cf. 66:10-13)

Just as the Spirit had come upon John (1:15, 80), Mary (1:35), Elizabeth (1:41), and Zechariah (1:67), so also now Simeon is identified as one on whom the Spirit rests. "The Lord's anointed" functions in 1 Samuel to designate the king (24:6, 10; 26:9, 11). For Simeon, therefore, the birth of Jesus fulfilled Israel's hope for a royal Messiah. Just as the Spirit had revealed to Simeon (cf. Acts 10:22) that he would not see death before he witnessed the arrival of the Messiah, so also later Jesus would promise his disciples that some of them would not "taste death" before they saw the kingdom of God (Luke 9:27).

Following this extended introduction of Simeon, the narrator reports that the meeting in the Temple was no accident. Simeon was guided there by the Holy Spirit. For the third time the Spirit is mentioned in the introduction to this scene (vv. 25-27). What is about to happen is

God's doing. Devout Simeon was in the Temple because he was prompted to be there by the Spirit; Jesus' parents were there because they were fulfilling the requirements of the Law (see Commentary on vv. 21-24).

The birth of a child, the fulfillment of God's promises, the consolation of Israel, and the coming of the Messiah are all occasions for praising God. The doxological motif in Luke echoes again in this scene (cf. 1:64; 2:34; 24:53). Like the other Lukan canticles (1:46-55, 68-79), the *Nunc Dimittis* is only loosely related to the occasion of the birth of Jesus. It declares the praise of God for faithfulness and the redemption of the people, so it has often been suggested that these verses were not originally composed for this setting. Luke may have drawn them from the canticles used in worship by Jewish Christians and added them at a secondary stage to the birth narratives. On the other hand, the introduction of the *Nunc Dimittis* fits the context and characterization of Simeon so closely that it is difficult to separate it from its narrative context.

The assurance that a patriarch can die in peace because he has seen the fulfillment of God's promises is an OT motif (Abraham, Gen 15:15; Jacob, Gen 46:30). The opening of the *Nunc Dimittis* need not refer to Simeon's death, however. Simeon had been watching for the coming of the Lord's anointed, and now as a faithful watchman he is dismissed from his post by his master. As the NRSV emphasizes, the verb translated "dismiss" (ἀπολύω *apolyō*) is indicative, not imperative. The form may be imperative, but the context of praise favors the indicative. The *Nunc Dimittis* follows a discernible structure: Simeon recognizes that he is being released from his mission to watch for the coming of the Messiah (v. 29) because he has now seen the coming of the one who will bring salvation (v. 30). Compare the emphasis on God's word in Luke 1:38 and 2:29. God has prepared this salvation for all peoples (v. 31), both Gentiles and Israelites (v. 32; cf. 4:25, 27; 7:9). Simeon's blessing, therefore, again relates the birth of Jesus to the fulfillment of the promise of salvation found in the Scriptures of Israel, especially in Isaiah, and looks ahead to the inclusion of Gentiles as well as Jews in the experience of God's blessings.

"Peace" (εἰρήνη *eirēnē*) occurs 14 times in Luke, where it is both the goal and the result of God's redemptive work in Jesus. Simeon saw God's salvation not because he happened to live at the right moment in history but because his devotion and the work of the Spirit in him had led him to understand that God's hand was at work in Jesus' birth. The OT prophets had looked forward to the time when God would establish peace on earth (Ps 72:7; Isa 9:5-6; Zech 8:12; cf. Luke 10:23-24). "Salvation" (σωτήριον *sōtērion*) is actually an adjective used as a noun and denotes here the means of salvation, or the bringer of salvation. Verses 30-31 illustrate "stair-step" parallelism, with v. 31 extending the thought of v. 30. The two lines of v. 32 are an example of synonymous parallelism: light for the Gentiles, glory for Israel.

The themes of these verses—salvation for all peoples, a light for the Gentiles, and the glory of the Lord in Israel—echo various passages in Isaiah (40:5; 42:6; 46:13; 49:6; 52:9-10). The words of Isaiah (42:6; 49:6) concerning light for the Gentiles will be cited later in Acts 13:47 and 26:23, which suggests that Luke understands the whole course of events recorded in these two volumes as the fulfillment of God's promise of salvation for both Jews and Gentiles. The announcement occurs in the Temple, just as had the announcement of the birth of John the Baptist. The Gospel ends with the disciples in the Temple (24:53), and in the early chapters of Acts the disciples are repeatedly in the Temple. But rather than the Gentiles coming to Jerusalem, those who have seen God's salvation will go to the nations. The promises were fulfilled, but not quite as Isaiah had envisioned.

Verse 33 records the reaction of Joseph and Mary, "the child's father and mother." While there is no evidence that the material that follows Luke's account of the birth of Jesus was shaped in light of the virgin birth tradition, by this point Luke has recorded the annunciation and birth in detail and does not need to assert its uniqueness again. Amazement often follows an oracle or dominical saying in Luke (1:63; 2:18; 4:22; 8:25; 20:26; 24:41).

Simeon's second oracle follows in vv. 34-35. Again following the pattern of the dedication of Samuel (1 Sam 2:20), both parents are blessed. As Hannah dominated the 1 Samuel story, so in

Luke's account the second oracle is directed to Mary. This oracle foreshadows the rejection of Jesus. Not all will receive the salvation that has been prepared, see the light of revelation, or recognize the glory of God in the coming of Jesus. The counterpart of this oracle in Matthew is the slaughter of the innocents in Bethlehem and the flight of the holy family to Egypt. While the particular references are often obscure, each of the four lines of this oracle speaks of discrimination and judgment.

(1) "This child is destined for the falling and the rising of many in Israel. . . . " This motif is similar to the combination of the stone passages from Isaiah (8:14; 28:16) and Psalms (118:22) that one finds in Luke 20:17-18; Rom 9:32-33; 1 Pet 2:6-8.[36] The one who would bring salvation would also bring judgment; the cornerstone would be the stone of stumbling for others. "Falling" and "rising," therefore, refer to two different groups, not to a sequence of falling and then rising. The precedence of "falling" signals that this oracle concerns judgment and rejection. Jesus will be rejected by his own people (Luke 4:29; 13:33-35; 19:44, 47-48; 20:14-17). This oracle makes much the same point as Jesus' warning that he had not come to bring peace but division (Luke 12:51-53). Israel would be divided, and as the book of Acts will show, many rejected the gospel.

(2) " . . . and to be a sign that will be opposed. . . . " Later in the Gospel, Jesus warns that just as the sign of Jonah announced judgment on Nineveh, so also the Son of Man would be a sign of judgment on that generation (11:29-30). Acts chronicles the Jewish rejection of Paul using the same verb (ἀντιλέγω *antilegō*; Acts 13:45; 28:19, 22).

(3) " . . . so that the inner thoughts of many will be revealed. . . . " The NRSV (followed here) reverses the sequence of the third and fourth lines of the oracle. The two lines are independent, as the translation suggests. The exposing of inner thoughts continues the theme of discrimination and judgment. Many would "fall and rise" (v. 34), and the thoughts of "many" will be exposed. Undoubtedly, the "thoughts" in question are doubts and refutations; Jesus perceived that the scribes and Pharisees were questioning in their

hearts (5:22; 6:8), and he was also aware of the inner thoughts of the disciples (9:46-47; 24:38).

(4) ". . . and a sword will pierce your own soul too." This line, which so interrupts the flow of the oracle that it is set off by dashes, has at times been interpreted as a secondary insertion, but it is consistent with the context and content of the rest of the oracle. Many interpretations have been advanced that relate this line to the role of Mary in John 19:25-27 and later mariology, but as Raymond E. Brown points out, these interpretations are not supported by Luke.[37] Luke does not record that Mary was present at the cross, nor does he record the piercing of Jesus' side (John 19:34). The reference to a sword passing through echoes Ezek 14:17, where the Lord warns of judgment by saying, "Let a sword pass through the land." The language and theme of the verse are consistent with the oracle in Luke. The statement is obscure and starkly symbolic. The most we can say is that Mary is presented here in a positive light (as in Luke 8:19-21); she will share in the pain of the rejection of Jesus and the division of Israel.

2:36-38, Anna's Blessing. Luke is fond of pairing male and female figures in his narrative. The role of Simeon and Anna in the Temple at the end of the birth narrative balances the role of the aged Zechariah and Elizabeth at the beginning of the narrative. Anna's character and piety are emphasized, but not her words. As a prophet, Anna continues the tradition of female prophets in the OT (Miriam, Exod 15:20; Deborah, Judg 4:4; Huldah, 2 Kgs 22:14; and Isaiah's wife, Isa 8:3) and anticipates the role of female prophets in the early church (Acts 2:17; 21:9; 1 Cor 11:5). She was a descendant of a family from the northern kingdom, and a devout widow, advanced in age. The chronology in v. 37 is not entirely clear. Anna evidently married young and was widowed seven years later. The reference to 84 years probably records her age, but may be read as the number of years she had lived as a widow. In her piety she corresponds closely both to the figure of Judith and to the description of pious widows in 1 Tim 5:3-16. Judith was from the northern kingdom (Jdt 8:1); she fasted regularly (8:6), lived to an advanced age without remarrying (16:22-

---

36. Raymond E. Brown, *The Birth of the Messiah* (New York: Doubleday, 1977) 461.

37. Ibid., 462-63.

23), and praised God for the deliverance of Israel (15:14–16:17). The ideal for widows in the Pauline churches stipulated that a widow supported by the church should not be less than 60 years of age, have married only once, be known for her good works, and pray "night and day" (1 Tim 5:5, 9-10). Anna, therefore, exemplifies the pious widow in both Judaism and the early church, and she prepares the reader for the frequent references to widows in the rest of Luke (where widows are mentioned a total of 9 times) and Acts (6:1; 9:39, 41).

Anna's blessing, though not recorded, is characterized as praising God (cf. v. 28) and speaking about the child. Since this description corresponds to the content of Simeon's oracles, the reader is left to understand that Anna's prophecy matched his. Similarly, the reference to "all who were looking for the redemption of Jerusalem" (v. 38; cf. Isa 52:9) serves as an inclusion, balancing the description of Simeon as one who was "looking forward to the consolation of Israel" at the beginning of this scene. Simeon and Anna, who represent the pious ones, declare that Jesus is the one who will bring salvation for Israel, but not all would receive this salvation. Jesus himself would be rejected, and many in Israel would reject the gospel, but it was also meant for "a light for revelation to the Gentiles" (v. 32).

2:39-40, Conclusion. These verses neatly recapitulate the presentation in the Temple and conclude the birth narrative. The three references to the Law in vv. 22-24 characterized Joseph and Mary's desire to do "everything required by the law of the Lord." This reference in v. 39, therefore, serves as an inclusio that lends cohesion to the scene. The acclamation of Jesus, which gives it its real significance, is not mentioned. Instead, the second part of v. 39 brings the birth narrative to an appropriate conclusion, recording the family's return to Nazareth (cf. 2:4).

Both Matthew and Luke relate that Jesus was born in Bethlehem, yet that he was from Nazareth. At the end of both birth narratives, the family travels to Nazareth, but there the similarity ends. In Matthew there is no evidence that the family had been to Nazareth previously and no record of the census as the pretext for their journey to Bethlehem, so Joseph is directed by a dream to take the family to Galilee to escape Herod Archelaus. In Luke there is no sojourn in Egypt; at the end of the birth narrative, the family returns to their home in Nazareth.

Verse 40 serves as a transition between the birth narrative and what follows. The repetition of a similar description of the growth of the child in v. 52 has led interpreters to suspect that the story of Jesus in the Temple in vv. 41-51 may have been added as an appendage to the birth narrative after it was already substantially finished. The description echoes growth statements from the OT (Isaac, Gen 21:8; Samson, Judg 13:24; and Samuel, 1 Sam 2:21, 26; 3:19). In its Lukan context, however, it also continues the pattern of affirmations that John was great but that Jesus was greater. At the conclusion of the account of John's birth, Luke records: "The child grew and became strong in spirit" (1:80). The first part of v. 40 is the same, but the second part surpasses the earlier growth statement: "The child grew and became strong, filled with wisdom; and the favor of God was upon him." (See Commentary on 2:52 below.)

The two terms used in the latter part of this verse—"wisdom" (σοφία *sophia*) and "grace" (χάρις *charis*, or "favor")—are significant in Luke. Each appears more frequently in Luke than in the other Gospel. In fact, *grace* does not occur at all in Matthew or Mark. Luke uses both terms to characterize Jesus. *Wisdom* is used in both vv. 40 and 52 to describe Jesus' growth. Later, Luke records that Jesus spoke "the Wisdom of God" (11:49; cf. Matt 23:34). Jesus bestowed wisdom on the disciples (21:15), and the seven chosen by the church were men of wisdom (Acts 6:3, 10). At Nazareth, Jesus spoke "gracious words" (4:22). Similarly, the grace of God and the favor of the people would characterize the early church (Acts 2:47; 4:33; 6:8; 7:10, 46). Just as Luke's account of the annunciation, birth, and presentation of Jesus serve to proclaim his identity, so also the conclusion to the birth narrative prepares the reader for Jesus' ministry.

REFLECTIONS

As Joseph and Mary went about the process of fulfilling the requirements of the Jewish law regarding circumcision of the child and purification of the mother, they received God's blessing through Simeon and Anna. This episode merits careful reflection among modern Christians. The observance of religious requirements and rituals has fallen on hard times. Essential to Judaism is the praise of God in all of life. The Jewish law taught that God was to be honored in one's rising up and lying down, in going out and coming in, in how one dressed and what one ate. The danger, however, was always that adherence to external requirements could mask a disregard for purity of heart and sincerity in one's love of God and neighbor. Jesus attacked the hypocrisy of some of the Pharisees of his day, and early Christians soon moved to distinguish themselves from Jewish practices. Ritual observances had a well-established place in Christian devotion in the Middle Ages, but the Reformation again precipitated a separation of the interior aspects of faith from the believer's ritual expressions of that faith.

The pressures of secularism and modern life have again reduced the significance of ritual observances in the lives of most Christians. Busy schedules, dual-career marriages, and after-school activities mean that families eat fewer meals together. Prayer before meals and family Bible study are observed in fewer homes today than just a generation ago. For many, religious rituals are reduced to church attendance at Christmas and Easter and to socially required ceremonies at births, weddings, and funerals. The marking of both daily and special events with rituals that recognize the sacredness of life and the presence of God in the everyday is practically extinct. In the minds of many it is associated either with superstitions and cultic practices of the past or the peculiar excesses of religious fanatics. The result has been that God has receded from the awareness and experience of everyday life. Many assume that God is found only in certain places, in sacred buildings, in holy books, or in observances led by holy persons. Their lives, on the other hand, move in a secular realm devoid of the presence of the holy. Daily experiences are reduced and impoverished. They have no meaning beyond themselves, no opening to transcendence. Little room for mystery remains in the everyday as it becomes increasingly subject to secularism and technology. What have we lost by removing ritual observances from our daily experience?

Reflection on the presentation of Jesus in the Temple can serve to challenge modern believers to recover the mystery of life and the transcendence of everyday experience through ritual celebrations.

Where is God found? The oral law of the rabbis, codified in the Mishnah, recognized that God was present wherever the Torah was studied: "If two sit together and words of the Law [are spoken] between them, the Divine Presence rests between them."[38] For Christians, Jesus took the place of the study of Torah: "For where two or three are gathered in my name, I am there among them" (Matt 18:20). A saying attributed to Jesus in an early Christian papyrus text that dates from early in the third century recognizes the possibility of discovering the divine presence in the ordinary:

"Wheresoever there are (two, they are not without) God: and where there is one alone I say I am with him. Lift the stone and there shalt thou find me: cleave the wood, and I am there."[39]

The last part of this saying may speak either to the cosmic presence of Christ or to the sanctity of work (contrast Eccl 10:9). Either way, the author of this saying recognized that one could meet Christ in the ordinary experiences of life, apart from any temples or priests, even in hard work with stone and wood.

The challenge to modern Christians, therefore, is to find effective rituals for celebrating the

---

38. *M. 'Abot* 3.2.
39. *Oxyrhynchus Papyrus 1.* See M. R. James, *The Apocryphal New Testament* (Oxford: Clarendon, 1924) 27.

presence of God in the ordinary. We need to learn to greet the morning with gratitude; to celebrate the goodness of food, family, and friendship at meals; to recognize mystery in beauty; and to mark rites of passage—like a sixteenth birthday and the freedom and responsibility that come with a driver's license. Rituals are not restrictive; they celebrate the goodness and mystery of life.

Words can be powerful, especially in the context of rituals and celebrations. Commitments are made. Love is given a voice. Promises shape relationships. The words spoken to Joseph and Mary are the center of this scene, but they stand in a powerful context: obedience to the Law, celebration of a birth, worship in the Temple, and recognition that God's promises were being fulfilled. The ceremony was not a foreign intrusion into their lives but an expression of their deepest awarenesses and commitments. Joseph and Mary saw God at work in events they had experienced. They lived within a covenant community, and they sought to fulfill vows they had made as well as to introduce their son into that covenant community. Simeon and Anna, whose lives of devotion had made them sensitive to God's presence in the events of their time, responded to Joseph and Mary's obedience by speaking words of blessing. The blessing gave the ceremony meaning that it would not have had otherwise. Mary and Joseph would remember that blessing the rest of their lives. Each of these elements of ritual and blessing merit reflection as we search for ways to dramatize our gratitude for the goodness and mystery of life.

LUKE 2:41-52, THE BOY JESUS IN THE TEMPLE

NIV

⁴¹Every year his parents went to Jerusalem for the Feast of the Passover. ⁴²When he was twelve years old, they went up to the Feast, according to the custom. ⁴³After the Feast was over, while his parents were returning home, the boy Jesus stayed behind in Jerusalem, but they were unaware of it. ⁴⁴Thinking he was in their company, they traveled on for a day. Then they began looking for him among their relatives and friends. ⁴⁵When they did not find him, they went back to Jerusalem to look for him. ⁴⁶After three days they found him in the temple courts, sitting among the teachers, listening to them and asking them questions. ⁴⁷Everyone who heard him was amazed at his understanding and his answers. ⁴⁸When his parents saw him, they were astonished. His mother said to him, "Son, why have you treated us like this? Your father and I have been anxiously searching for you."

⁴⁹"Why were you searching for me?" he asked. "Didn't you know I had to be in my Father's house?" ⁵⁰But they did not understand what he was saying to them.

⁵¹Then he went down to Nazareth with them

NRSV

41Now every year his parents went to Jerusalem for the festival of the Passover. ⁴²And when he was twelve years old, they went up as usual for the festival. ⁴³When the festival was ended and they started to return, the boy Jesus stayed behind in Jerusalem, but his parents did not know it. ⁴⁴Assuming that he was in the group of travelers, they went a day's journey. Then they started to look for him among their relatives and friends. ⁴⁵When they did not find him, they returned to Jerusalem to search for him. ⁴⁶After three days they found him in the temple, sitting among the teachers, listening to them and asking them questions. ⁴⁷And all who heard him were amazed at his understanding and his answers. ⁴⁸When his parents[a] saw him they were astonished; and his mother said to him, "Child, why have you treated us like this? Look, your father and I have been searching for you in great anxiety." ⁴⁹He said to them, "Why were you searching for me? Did you not know that I must be in my Father's house?"[b] ⁵⁰But they did not understand what he said to

_a_ Gk _they_   _b_ Or _be about my Father's interests?_

NIV	NRSV
and was obedient to them. But his mother treasured all these things in her heart. [52]And Jesus grew in wisdom and stature, and in favor with God and men.	them. [51]Then he went down with them and came to Nazareth, and was obedient to them. His mother treasured all these things in her heart. 52And Jesus increased in wisdom and in years,[a] and in divine and human favor. a Or *in stature*

COMMENTARY

Luke is the only Gospel to include a story from Jesus' childhood. Stories of the precocious wisdom of the hero or philosopher were standard fare in ancient biographical accounts.[40]

The apocryphal infancy gospels contain fanciful stories of the miracles Jesus performed as a child. By comparison, Luke's account of Jesus in the Temple at the age of twelve is restrained. The *Infancy Gospel of Thomas* concludes with a version of this story that contains expansions that report that Jesus "put to silence the elders and teachers of the people, expounding the sections of the law and sayings of the prophets" (19.2). The scribes and the Pharisees responded to Mary with praise for Jesus, exclaiming, "For such glory and such excellence and wisdom we have never seen nor heard" (19.4).

The story of Jesus in the Temple also serves as a transition from the birth narratives to the ministry of Jesus. The former announced Jesus' birth as the birth of the "Son of God" (1:32, 35). Luke's account of Jesus' ministry returns to this title frequently (e.g., 3:22; 4:3, 9, 41; 9:35; 22:70). This transitional story records Jesus' dawning awareness of his identity and foreshadows his relationship to his divine Father, the teachers of Israel, and the Temple (see 19:45, 47-48; 20:1). Luke 2:40 records that as a child Jesus was "filled with wisdom," so it is not out of place for the next pericope to illustrate his wisdom while he was still a child. Wisdom and divine sonship were already linked together in the Jewish wisdom materials: The wise man "professes to have

knowledge of God/ and calls himself a child of the Lord" (Wisd Sol 2:13 NRSV).

Neither Matthew nor Luke integrates the virgin birth accounts with later sections of the Gospel in such a way that the events of the birth of Jesus are recalled or alluded to later. Just as the parents of Jesus are referred to in Luke 2:33 without any explanation or clarification, so also the events of Jesus' birth do not seem to have any effect on Mary's or Joseph's response to Jesus in this account. The story of Jesus in the Temple at the age of twelve makes a christological point about Jesus' wisdom and his divine sonship. It does not furnish psychological data for interpreting the emergence of Jesus' messianic consciousness or Mary's understanding of Jesus' ministry.

The story begins and ends with travel notices, as do other sections of Luke 1–2. Some interpreters find a chiastic structure centering on Jesus and the teachers (vv. 46b-47), but the dramatic center of the story in Luke is not the teachers' praise of Jesus' wisdom—as in the *Infancy Gospel of Thomas*—but Jesus' response to his parents in v. 49. These are the first words Jesus speaks in the Gospel of Luke. In this respect, the unit is similar to the pronouncement stories later in the Gospel, which provide narrative settings for sayings of Jesus. The saying always conveys the main point of the story.

The previous scene emphasized that Joseph and Mary carefully observed the Jewish laws. Thus the family's journey to Jerusalem each year for the Passover celebration fulfilled the requirements that all male Israelites should make a pilgrimage to Jerusalem for Passover, Pentecost, and Tabernacles (see Exod 34:23). Moving at a pace of fifteen miles a day, their journey to Jerusalem would have taken four or five days.

2:41-45. According to later Jewish custom, a

---

40. Each of the following accounts records an event—often set when the hero was twelve—which gives an indication of his future vocation: Moses: Philo *Life of Moses* 1.20-24, and Josephus *Antiquities of the Jews* 2.228-38; Samuel: Josephus *Antiquities of the Jews* 5.348; Solomon: 1 Kings 2:12 (LXX); Epicurus: Diogenes Laertius *Lives of Eminent Philosophers* 10.14; Josephus: Josephus *Life* 8-9.

male child became a man and embraced the traditions of his ancestors at the age of thirteen. At twelve, therefore, Jesus was still a child. Verses 41-42 describe the setting of the story, providing geographical and chronological notices and describing the occasion for the journey to Jerusalem. Verse 43 supplies the complication: Jesus stayed behind in Jerusalem without his parents' knowledge or permission. Verses 44-45 explain how Jesus might have been left behind and describe his parents' search for him. The explanation and the description of the search build suspense by prolonging the interval between the complication and the resolution. In form it is a quest story: When, where, and how will they find Jesus? When Jesus' parents do not find him among the company of travelers, they return to Jerusalem to search for him.

2:46-47. Jesus had been in the Temple, among the teachers. Care should be taken not to overinterpret the details of this story. The reference to three days is not entirely clear, since no indication is given of whether Luke is counting from their departure from Jerusalem, their discovery that Jesus was missing, or their return to Jerusalem. Some interpreters find here an allusion to the resurrection, but the connection is not obvious and the formula "after three days" does not appear elsewhere in Luke. Similarly, although sitting was the normal posture for a teacher, students also sat. Luke may or may not infer that Jesus had joined the ranks of the teachers of Israel or that he was actually teaching the teachers. Nevertheless, they were all amazed at his understanding (cf. Isa 11:2). Although Jesus' first public appearance finds him "in the midst" of teachers in the Temple, he would serve in their midst as a servant (22:27; cf. 24:36).

2:48-50. This is the climax of the story. Narration gives way to dialogue. The parents' amazement is similar to their response to Simeon's blessing (v. 33). It is an expected part of such a story (cf. 4:32) and should not be interpreted as inconsistent with the birth annunciation and birth accounts. Neither should one conjecture that the parents were astonished only at the way Jesus was developing his unique identity and role. Their reaction is true to life. What parent cannot empathize with their distress? A tone of reproach crosses Mary's question as she conveys their anxiety while searching for Jesus.

Jesus' response to his parents contains the logion on which the whole episode hangs. His second question expects a positive answer. It assumes that his parents would know where he was or what he was doing. The phrasing of the question is ambiguous, however, and perhaps deliberately so. In Greek it lacks the noun for "house" or "affairs" or "interests." The translation "in my Father's house" has often been favored because it fits the narrative of Jesus' parents' searching for Jesus and finding him in the Temple. The Temple is called God's house in Luke 19:46 (see also John 2:16 and the reference to the tabernacle as God's house in Luke 6:4). The alternative translation, "about my Father's business" (KJV), also fits the context in terms of both Jesus' involvement with the teachers and the function of this story as a transition to Jesus' public ministry.

Hidden in Jesus' response, but not to be missed, is his pronouncement of the necessity of what he was doing: "I must be. . . . " The statement connotes an awareness of God's purposes that makes the fulfillment of certain activities imperative (see, e.g., 4:43; 9:22; 11:42; 17:25; 22:37). Jesus was responding to the divine imperative that he fulfill God's purposes for his life. His life was not driven by fate—the force that many ancients believed controlled one's destiny. Neither was he driven by political coercion or religious legalism. Instead, his life was bound to God's design for it.

The sharpness of Jesus' response is set up by the reference in Mary's question to "your father and I." The counterpoint of Jesus' insistence that he had to be in his *Father's* house (or about his Father's business) forcefully sets forth Jesus' identity as the Son of God and shows that his life would be guided by his unique relationship to the Father. That is the point of this story, and the main point of the infancy narratives as a whole.

2:51-52. The verses that follow Jesus' pronouncement bring closure to the scene and relate it to its narrative context. Jesus would not begin his public ministry until he was about thirty years old (3:23). Luke makes clear that in the intervening years Jesus fulfilled the commandment to honor one's father and mother. The event in the Temple did not result in open rebellion against his parents. The return to Nazareth closes the episode here, just as the return to Nazareth signaled the conclusion of the birth narrative in 2:39.

Mary and Joseph reacted with wonder at what

Jesus had said. They were not privy to Jesus' understanding of his identity as the Son of God. Although the events of Jesus' birth did not prepare Jesus' parents for the events of his ministry, Mary is depicted in Luke as consistently responsive to the revelatory experiences in her life. Treasuring experiences that are infused with God's presence can bring insight later and provide a firm foundation for a life of obedient discipleship (see 2:19).

For comments on v. 52, see the Commentary on Luke 2:40. The repetition of a similar growth state- ment here adds a further reason for suspecting that the evangelist added Luke 2:41-52 after the birth narrative had already been composed. Verse 52 does not just take us back to the conclusion of the birth narrative, however. It brackets the story of Jesus in the Temple within references to his growth in wisdom and affirms that this one who was already advanced in wisdom grew still further in his understanding. The son who was both divine and human was shaped by the experience of the grace of others and the grace of God.

REFLECTIONS

This episode from Jesus' life evokes a host of reflections that may lead to appropriate preaching themes. Rather than focus on just one aspect of the text, let us walk around it and wonder at its richness.

1. As a story from Jesus' childhood, this account is unique among the canonical Gospels. As much as any other passage of Scripture, it calls for reflection on Jesus' uniquely divine and human personhood. Apparently independent of the virgin birth accounts that precede it, this pericope pushes Jesus' recognition of his identity as God's Son back prior to his baptism. Jesus was fully human, yet fully cognizant that God was his Father.

2. One of the developmental tasks of childhood, teenage, and young adulthood is discovering and affirming one's identity. What defines one's identity—family ties, religious experience, a sense of vocation, a personal creed, or one's dreams and ideals? Jesus found his identity by affirming his relationship to God.

3. Is faith in God a peripheral matter for you, or does it shape your life in some profound way? What role has God in your life? Is religion for you a matter of appealing to a divine being for help in times of need, finding forgiveness, or fulfilling prescribed religious obligations? The story of Jesus in the Temple at the age of twelve provides a ready source of reflection on the significance of God's claim on our lives.

4. God's claims may stand in tension or open conflict with human desires for social acceptance, loyalty to family, economic prosperity, and other worthy ideals. The hard decisions are not those between right and wrong but those that call for us to choose between options when both represent worthy claims. In this event, Jesus was already subordinating other priorities to his sense of God's purpose for his life.

5. Both *searching* and *finding* occur frequently in Luke. Together they mirror the human experience of questing for something better, for truth or knowledge, for love, or for God. What are you searching for, and where or how do you expect to find it? Jesus' parents were searching for Jesus while he sought to be about the tasks that his divine Father had set for him. What we are searching for reveals a great deal about who we are.

6. There are two ways of approaching obedience to God. Some define their religious beliefs and practices with lists of things they may not do: "Thou shalt not. . . . " Such lists set boundaries, but they do not define goals. A commitment to God that is born of the experience of God's love and presence is expressed in grateful participation in God's redemptive work. There are some things we have to do just because of who we are: "I *must* be about my Father's business."

LUKE 3:1–4:13

Preparation for the Ministry of Jesus

Overview

Luke's account of the preparation for Jesus' ministry begins with the work of John the Baptist. Following the parallel accounts of the annunciations and births of John and Jesus, Luke describes John's preaching and baptizing. John prepares the way for Jesus. The record of Jesus' ancestry then reaffirms his identity as the Son of God. Jesus' preparation for his ministry includes baptism, prayer, and a period of withdrawal to the wilderness, during which he is tempted by the devil.

LUKE 3:1-6, THE SETTING OF JOHN'S MINISTRY

NIV

3 In the fifteenth year of the reign of Tiberius Caesar—when Pontius Pilate was governor of Judea, Herod tetrarch of Galilee, his brother Philip tetrarch of Iturea and Traconitis, and Lysanias tetrarch of Abilene— ²during the high priesthood of Annas and Caiaphas, the word of God came to John son of Zechariah in the desert. ³He went into all the country around the Jordan, preaching a baptism of repentance for the forgiveness of sins. ⁴As is written in the book of the words of Isaiah the prophet:

"A voice of one calling in the desert,
'Prepare the way for the Lord,
   make straight paths for him.
⁵Every valley shall be filled in,
   every mountain and hill made low.
The crooked roads shall become straight,
   the rough ways smooth.
⁶And all mankind will see God's salvation.'"ᵃ

ᵃ6 Isaiah 40:3-5

NRSV

3 In the fifteenth year of the reign of Emperor Tiberius, when Pontius Pilate was governor of Judea, and Herod was rulerᵃ of Galilee, and his brother Philip rulerᵃ of the region of Ituraea and Trachonitis, and Lysanias rulerᵃ of Abilene, ²during the high priesthood of Annas and Caiaphas, the word of God came to John son of Zechariah in the wilderness. ³He went into all the region around the Jordan, proclaiming a baptism of repentance for the forgiveness of sins, ⁴as it is written in the book of the words of the prophet Isaiah,

"The voice of one crying out in the wilderness:
'Prepare the way of the Lord,
   make his paths straight.
⁵ Every valley shall be filled,
   and every mountain and hill shall be made low,
and the crooked shall be made straight,
   and the rough ways made smooth;
⁶ and all flesh shall see the salvation of God.'"

ᵃ Gk tetrarch

COMMENTARY

The introduction to John's prophetic ministry blends patterns from Greco-Roman historiography (chronology) and the Hebrew prophets (call). The date of John's call is fixed (vv. 1-2a), and the call is described in a manner reminiscent of the prophets (v. 2b). The location and essence of John's ministry are recorded (v. 3), and its fulfillment of the Scriptures is noted with a quotation from Isaiah (vv. 4-6). The chronological data given here are more detailed than earlier references in 1:5 and 2:1-2, signaling that John's ministry of preaching and baptizing marks the real beginning of the period of Jesus' ministry.

In the days before events were dated according to the years of the Christian era (which was initiated in 533 CE by Dionysius Exiguus), events were dated in relation to the rulers of the period or the number of years since the founding of Rome. Luke follows the former method, fixing the date of John's call by six chronological vectors. Even taken together, however, they do not provide a precise date because of the uncertainties that surround ancient calendars and systems of reckoning. "The fifteenth year of the reign of Emperor Tiberius" is the most promising vector, but it does not furnish us with a reliable date because we do not know which calendar Luke was using or the event from which he counted the years. The Julian, Jewish, Syrian-Macedonian, and Egyptian calendars each reckoned the years differently. Neither is the date of the beginning of Tiberius's reign clearly established. Tiberius's co-regency with Augustus began in 11 or 12 CE; Augustus died in 14 CE; and we do not know whether Luke counted the year of Tiberius's accession as one of the years of his reign. Counting from 14 CE, and counting part of a year as a whole year, brings us to about 28 CE, which accords well with Luke's later note that Jesus was "about thirty years old when he began his work" (3:23; see Commentary on v. 23).

The five other references are less helpful. Procurators governed Judea following the removal of Archelaus from office in 6 CE. Pontius Pilate was procurator from 26 to 36 CE. Herod Antipas remained tetrarch over Galilee, serving the Romans from the death of Herod the Great (4 BCE) until 39 CE, while Herod Philip governed his territories east of the Jordan until 34 CE. Luke's reference to "Lysanias ruler of Abilene [in Syria]" cannot be identified with any known tetrarch and therefore provides no further chronological information.

This detailed correlation of the events of John's ministry with the political events of the period reflects Luke's attention to the form of historical writing, but it also resonates with his emphasis that through Jesus God brought salvation for all persons. The coming of the kingdom of God is set in relation to the events of the reign of human rulers. The reference to "the high priesthood of Annas and Caiaphas" (v. 2) also sets the inauguration of the work of John and Jesus in opposition to the priestly hierarchy. The ambiguous references to both Annas and Caiaphas reflect the continued influence of Annas and his family. Annas was high priest from 6 to 15 CE, and his son-in-law, Caiaphas, was high priest from 18 to 36 CE (see John 11:49; 18:13, 19; Acts 4:6). Pilate, Herod Antipas, and the high priest are also important later in the Gospel. Jesus is brought before the high priest and is tried by Pilate. Herod Antipas, similarly, plays a greater role in Luke than in any of the other Gospels: He imprisoned John (3:19-20), speculated that Jesus was John redivivus (9:7, 9), sought to kill Jesus (13:31), and questioned Jesus before his death (23:7-8, 11-12, 15).

If the chronological data of vv. 1-2 reflect the conventions of Greco-Roman historiography, the call of John echoes the call of a prophet. (The parallels are especially clear in Jer 1:1-5, but see also Isa 6:1; Ezek 1:1-3; and Hos 1:1.) Typically the call of a prophet records that (a) "the word of the Lord came" to or upon (b) the prophet; (c) the son of (the name of his father) is recorded; (d) it occurred in a certain location; and that (e) it came "in the days of" a certain king. The last element is expanded and placed first in Luke 3:1-2a. The remaining elements of the story of the call of a prophet follow in v. 2b. The reference to Zechariah serves also to recall the earlier account of John's annunciation and birth, and the note that John was in the wilderness ties his call to the last previous reference to John in 1:80. It also sets the scene for the events that follow. Here for the first time Luke's account employs traditional material found in the other Gospels. The account of John's ministry and preaching weaves together material from the Gospel of Mark and Q, a collection of the teachings of Jesus used by both Matthew and Luke. At various points Luke's handling of his source material sets his thematic and theological interests in relief.

The wilderness was a desolate area. Some scholars have speculated that John may have lived with the Essenes for a period of time and that his practice of baptizing those who responded to his call for repentance was drawn from the Essene initiation ceremonies and repeated washings. John's baptism predates by fifty years the first reference in Jewish writings to a baptism of proselytes to Judaism, nevertheless a connection with Essene practices cannot be taken for granted. Like the Essenes, John called Israelites to repentance in the wilderness and subjected converts to a ceremony of water cleansing that either expressed their repentance or conveyed God's cleansing to the convert. The water ritual was not effective apart from genuine repentance. In both cases, the washing was probably also understood as a fulfillment of the levitical requirements for purification (see Leviticus 15) and metaphorical references to washing in the OT (see Ps 51:7; Isa 1:16; Jer 4:14).

The Gospel of Mark begins with a quotation from Isaiah 40 and a description of John's baptizing ministry. Luke sets the quotation in the context of the infancy material and the preceding account of John's call. Luke also extends the quotation from Isaiah and deletes the description of John's clothing and diet, while adding an extended account of John's preaching. The effect is to emphasize three Lukan themes: (1) John's role

as a prophet, (2) the call for an ethical renewal in Israel, and (3) the extension of the work of salvation to all peoples.

Luke's omission of the description of John as "clothed with camel's hair, with a leather belt around his waist, and he ate locusts and wild honey" (Mark 1:6 NRSV; cf. Lev 11:21-22; 2 Kgs 1:8) is puzzling because it would have served to further characterize John as a prophet. The association of John with the role of Elijah has been affirmed from even before John's birth, however: "With the spirit and power of Elijah he will go before him, to turn the hearts of parents to their children, and the disobedient to the wisdom of the righteous, to make ready a people prepared for the Lord" (1:17). The quotation of Isaiah 40 repeats not only v. 3 but the next two verses as well. Although Isa 40:3 is quoted in Matt 3:3; Mark 1:3; and John 1:23, only Luke quotes Isa 40:4-5 with its universalizing allusions to "every valley," "every mountain and hill," and "all flesh." The quotation follows the Septuagint text with minor changes. Luke changes "make our God's paths straight" to "make his paths straight" so that it can apply to Jesus more easily, and omits the following clause from v. 6: "and the glory of the Lord will be seen" (cf. Luke 2:9). The last phrase, "the salvation of God," also appears in Acts 28:28 (see also Luke 2:30).

The introduction to this chapter, therefore, fixes the call of John to a prophetic ministry chronologically and describes that ministry as both the fulfillment of the prophets and the preparation for Jesus' ministry. John's preaching was an important part of God's plan for Israel.

REFLECTIONS

1. The first several verses fix the time and political circumstances of John's call. The story begins with a roll call of important persons: governors and kings, even the high priest. In surprising contrast, however, "the word of God" comes not to any of these but to an unknown prophet out in the wilderness. The redemptive work of which Mary sang in the Magnificat is under way: "He has brought down the powerful from their thrones,/ and lifted up the lowly" (1:52). In all ages, God's work proceeds among the poor and the dispossessed. A middle-class church in a nominally Christian society that enjoys religious liberty will have a hard time grasping the fact that Luke does not use these terms in a merely metaphorical or spiritual sense.

2. Moreover, the redemptive events that began with John in a remote corner of Judea were, by God's design, the beginning of the fulfillment of God's concern for the salvation of "all flesh." Repeatedly in Luke we find this theme underscored. Our human tendency is to circumscribe God's activity and limit it to our own kind of people and the causes that are socially and ethically important to us. But God's concern for all continually pushes us to break across the boundaries that we set for it. In many respects, the story of the ministry of Jesus in Luke and the spread of the early church in Acts is the story of God's challenge to social, ethnic, economic, and racial barriers to the spread of the gospel. "All flesh" always includes precisely those groups who are not present in our religious assemblies, either because we have not allowed them to be there or because we have maintained cultural patterns that have excluded them.

3. Because God's redemptive work is still unfinished—the salvation of "all flesh" has not yet been realized—John serves as a role model for the church. The Gospel announces not only what God has done through Jesus but also what God is still in the process of doing. All who hear "the word of God" (v. 2) are called to declare what God is doing in our midst and to point ahead to the fulfillment of God's reign as king. John was a forerunner, announcing the great things of God that are yet to come, a vision of a society redeemed and renewed by the vision of the prophets. As John's preaching (in the next section) shows, he held the vision before others, issued a challenge for them, and called for repentance. He is, therefore, an appropriate model for the church as it seeks to recover its vocation as a prophetic voice in a secular culture.

LUKE 3:7-18, JOHN'S PREACHING

NIV

7John said to the crowds coming out to be baptized by him, "You brood of vipers! Who warned you to flee from the coming wrath? 8Produce fruit in keeping with repentance. And do not begin to say to yourselves, 'We have Abraham as our father.' For I tell you that out of these stones God can raise up children for Abraham. 9The ax is already at the root of the trees, and every tree that does not produce good fruit will be cut down and thrown into the fire."

10"What should we do then?" the crowd asked.

11John answered, "The man with two tunics should share with him who has none, and the one who has food should do the same."

12Tax collectors also came to be baptized. "Teacher," they asked, "what should we do?"

13"Don't collect any more than you are required to," he told them.

14Then some soldiers asked him, "And what should we do?"

He replied, "Don't extort money and don't accuse people falsely—be content with your pay."

15The people were waiting expectantly and

NRSV

7John said to the crowds that came out to be baptized by him, "You brood of vipers! Who warned you to flee from the wrath to come? 8Bear fruits worthy of repentance. Do not begin to say to yourselves, 'We have Abraham as our ancestor'; for I tell you, God is able from these stones to raise up children to Abraham. 9Even now the ax is lying at the root of the trees; every tree therefore that does not bear good fruit is cut down and thrown into the fire."

10And the crowds asked him, "What then should we do?" 11In reply he said to them, "Whoever has two coats must share with anyone who has none; and whoever has food must do likewise." 12Even tax collectors came to be baptized, and they asked him, "Teacher, what should we do?" 13He said to them, "Collect no more than the amount prescribed for you." 14Soldiers also asked him, "And we, what should we do?" He said to them, "Do not extort money from anyone by threats or false accusation, and be satisfied with your wages."

15As the people were filled with expectation, and all were questioning in their hearts concern-

NIV	NRSV

NIV

were all wondering in their hearts if John might possibly be the Christ.[a] [16]John answered them all, "I baptize you with[b] water. But one more powerful than I will come, the thongs of whose sandals I am not worthy to untie. He will baptize you with the Holy Spirit and with fire. [17]His winnowing fork is in his hand to clear his threshing floor and to gather the wheat into his barn, but he will burn up the chaff with unquenchable fire." [18]And with many other words John exhorted the people and preached the good news to them.

[a]15 Or *Messiah*   [b]16 Or *in*

NRSV

ing John, whether he might be the Messiah,[a] [16]John answered all of them by saying, "I baptize you with water; but one who is more powerful than I is coming; I am not worthy to untie the thong of his sandals. He will baptize you with[b] the Holy Spirit and fire. [17]His winnowing fork is in his hand, to clear his threshing floor and to gather the wheat into his granary; but the chaff he will burn with unquenchable fire."

18So, with many other exhortations, he proclaimed the good news to the people.

[a]Or *the Christ*   [b]Or *in*

COMMENTARY

Luke combines Q sayings with sayings drawn from elsewhere to give us the most complete account of John's preaching in the NT. Luke's account of John's preaching is organized into three groups of sayings, each with its own theme: warnings of the coming judgment (vv. 7-9), a call for ethical reforms (vv. 10-14), and an announcement of the coming Messiah (vv. 15-17).[41] Verse 18 is the evangelist's summary of John's preaching ministry.

3:7-9. John's devastating warning of eschatological judgment is addressed to the Pharisees and Sadducees in Matthew (3:7) rather than to the crowds, as it is in Luke. Compare the references to crowds in vv. 7 and 10 with the references to "the people" in vv. 15 and 18. "The people" have already been established in Luke as the people of Israel and the responsive recipients of God's redemptive work (1:10, 17, 68, 77; 2:10, 31-32), but these are the first references to "the crowds" in Luke.

If John's preaching is part of the preparation for Jesus' ministry, Luke could hardly have found a more disturbing introduction than John's address to the crowds: "You brood of vipers!" For readers whose hopes for the blessings of God's salvation of Israel have been stirred by the oracles of the birth narratives (see 1:77; 2:30-32), the announcement of judgment is as alarming as it is unexpected. As a prophetic call, the address "You

brood of vipers" has no clear parallels in the OT, but the image of malicious evildoers as poisonous snakes is readily intelligible. John's question "Who warned you?" introduces the theme of the coming judgment and evokes an image of crowds hurrying to be baptized in order to escape that judgment. John likens the crowds to snakes slithering in flight, as they might to escape the danger of a fire. The warning of the coming eschatological judgment places John in the tradition of the prophets of Israel who issued warnings of the "day of the LORD" or "the day of the LORD's wrath" (Isa 2:11-22; 13:9; Amos 5:18-20; Zeph 1:14-15, 18; 2:2; see also "wrath" in Luke 21:23).

John challenges the crowds that have come for baptism to "bear fruits worthy of repentance." The metaphor of reformed or repentant living as "good works" and, therefore, "fruits" (v. 8) or "good fruit" (v. 9) is common in ancient ethical teachings and in Jewish wisdom materials (cf. 6:43-44; 13:6-9). The calls for repentance in Luke raise interesting questions: Who is called to repentance? Are any not called to repent? The preaching of John the Baptist is characterized as "a baptism of repentance for the forgiveness of sins" (3:3), and the challenge to bear fruit worthy of repentance follows in this context. Here the preaching is addressed to the descendants of Abraham. Later, when Jesus is challenged for eating with tax collectors and sinners, he responds, "I have come to call not the righteous but sinners to repentance" (5:32). Who are the righteous, and

41. See Joseph A. Fitzmyer, *The Gospel According to Luke (I–IX)*, AB28 (Garden City, N.Y.: Doubleday, 1981) 463.

who are the sinners? The righteous persons need no repentance (15:7). It may be that the poor whom Jesus blesses are considered righteous, while the rich are sinners (see 6:20-21, 24-25), but in the context of John's keynote to Jesus' ministry, the challenge is that all whose lives do not exemplify the righteousness of God as described by the prophets are in danger of judgment and need to repent. Eventually, the call for repentance will extend beyond Israel to all peoples (see 24:47).

Neither the ritual of baptism nor the rights of birth will substitute for repentance and ethical reform. The covenant with Abraham (Gen 12:1-3) was often interpreted as a promise of salvation for all of his descendants (Isa 51:2-3; Sir 44:21; *Jub* 12:22-24). In the NT as well, Paul (Romans 4; 9–11; Galatians 3) and John (8:39-58) wrestled with Israel's appeal to the covenant and rejected the interpretation that it ensured salvation for all who claimed Abraham as their father regardless of whether they lived by faith and practiced righteousness. Ethnic heritage apart from righteousness, the Baptist warned, offers no assurance of salvation (cf. 16:19-31).

Indeed, God is not dependent on the physical descent of Israelites in order to accomplish the redemptive work. If necessary, God can cause the stones to produce children to Abraham. This saying is related to Isa 51:1-2:

Look to the rock from which you were hewn,
    and to the quarry from which you were dug.
Look to Abraham your father
    and to Sarah who bore you. (NRSV)[42]

John the Baptist reverses the line of dependence implied here. If, metaphorically, the Israelites are stones hewn from Abraham, then *a fortiori* God can use stones to produce other children to Abraham. And every Israelite knew there was no shortage of stones in the wilderness! God could produce children from lifeless stones. The stone motif will be developed further later in Luke (see 19:40). Jesus himself is identified as a stone (20:18).

The last saying in this section (vv. 7-9) returns to the warning of imminent judgment. The ax has already been placed on the exposed root to measure the blow that is about to come. The burning of rotten or unproductive trees was a prophetic

42. See Joachim Jeremias, λίθος *TDNT*, 4:270-71.

image for judgment (Isa 6:13; 10:33-34; Dan 4:14; Mal 4:1) that appears in Jesus' parables also (Luke 13:6-9; John 15:1-6). In fact, the last part of v. 9 is attributed to Jesus in Matt 7:19. The image of Israel as a vine or a tree was common, and God expected good fruit from it (see esp. the song of the vineyard in Isa 5:1-7).

3:10-14. The crowds understand the prophetic call to an ethical reform and ask what they are to do. The next section of John's preaching (which does not appear in Matthew) unfolds in three parts as three groups (the crowds, v. 10; toll collectors, v. 12; and soldiers, v. 14) each ask John the same question: "What should we do?" John's answers give concrete examples of the ethical reform he called for in the previous verses. All three answers call for an end to a life-style based on greed and the accumulation of material possessions. Such actions of unqualified concern for one's neighbor illustrate the "fruits worthy of repentance" (v. 7).

To the crowds, John answers that if anyone has two tunics (garments worn next to the skin), that person should give one to someone who has none (cf. Jas 2:15-17; 1 John 3:17). Traditionally, repentance was expressed by putting on sackcloth and ashes or offering sacrifices. For John, repentance should take the form of a radicalizing of the commandment to love one's neighbor as oneself (Lev 19:18) and to do deeds of loving kindness (חסד *hesed*; Mic 6:8). John does not call for the crowds to withdraw from society (like the Essenes at Qumran) or to seek a military solution (like the Zealot groups). He addresses individual needs rather than societal problems, and the answer begins with the individual. If one has more than is needed to sustain life, one who does not have such abundance should lay claim to it. He does not say that one who does not have food or clothing should take from one who has more than needed. His interest is in repentance and ethical reform rather than revolution. The first step toward a redeemed community is for those who have to share with those who have not.

To those who collected tolls for the Romans, John said to collect no more than the prescribed amount. Direct taxes (poll tax, land tax) were collected by tax collectors employed by the Romans, while tolls, tariffs, and customs fees were collected at toll houses by toll collectors, the group that appears frequently in the Gospels and is not entirely accurately identified as "tax collectors."[43] Toll collectors paid in advance for the right to collect tolls, so the system was open to abuse and corruption. Zacchaeus, a chief toll collector who would have had others working for him, pledges to pay back any whom he has defrauded (19:1-10).

The soldiers in view here were probably not Romans but local mercenaries serving the Herods or the Roman procurator. Their role, therefore, was similar to that of the toll collectors, whom they may have protected. Both were hated by the local population. The practice of extorting payments by threats was apparently common. Josephus records that both he and John of Gischala warned their troops to avoid theft, extortion, and rape and to be content with their rations.[44] Since a soldier's allowance was minimal, there may even have been the expectation that he would supplement it by extortion. The verb used here for "to accuse falsely" (συκοφαντέω *sykophanteō*) is a colorful one meaning literally "to make figs visible." It refers to those in Athens who informed against anyone exporting figs from Attica. Such informers were "fig showers," from which we get the English word *sycophant*—a swindler or extortionist.

All three of the practical, ethical examples that John gives to illustrate the "fruits worthy of repentance" call for ethical reform. The tax collectors and soldiers are to refrain from exploiting their positions for personal gain at the expense of others, while the crowds are challenged to demonstrate their concern for the well-being of others by sharing whatever they do not need for their own survival.

3:15-17. These verses contain John's announcement of the coming of the Messiah. Following the pattern established in the birth narratives, John points to Jesus as one greater than he. The sayings of vv. 16-17 have parallels in Mark 1:7-8; Matt 3:11-12; and John 1:26-27. Luke's narrative introduction to the sayings, which reports that the people were questioning whether John might be the expected Messiah, summarizes the kind of questioning that John describes in more detail (1:19-28). In Luke, however, the questioning arises from "the people"

rather than from the authorities and expresses expectancy rather than opposition. The change from the references to the crowds in vv. 7 and 10 to "the people" further characterizes the people of Israel as receptive to God's mighty work (see 1:10, 17, 21, 68, 77; 2:10, 31-32).

Nowhere in John's preaching does he announce the kingdom of God, and to this point he has made no reference to the Messiah. In the last two centuries BCE the expectation of a Davidic Messiah had emerged in Palestinian Judaism. Nathan's oracle to David (2 Sam 7:8-16) fueled speculation regarding a future David (Jer 30:9; Ezek 37:23-24). Evidence of the expectation of one or more messiahs remains in the Psalms of Solomon (chaps. 17–18) and the Qumran scrolls (1QS 9:11; 1QSa 2:14, 20).

Twice Luke underscores the significance of the coming of the Messiah by emphasizing that what was happening was for *all* people (vv. 15-16). John was the forerunner of the Messiah, and not the Messiah himself (cf. John 1:20). The "coming One" would be greater than John. The reference echoes Malachi's prophecy of the coming of the Lord (Mal 3:1; 4:5-6). Luke follows the sequence of the sayings in Q rather than Mark 1:7-8, although v. 16 follows the wording of Mark 1:7.

John baptizes in water, a baptism of repentance (cf. Matt 3:11). The coming One would be so much greater than he that John would not be worthy even to untie the thong of his sandals. Untying sandals was such a menial duty that it was expected only of slaves; disciples were not expected to untie their master's sandals (see Acts 13:24-25). Luke will return to the theme of the coming One in 7:19-20, where John asks Jesus if he is the One who is to come.

The nature of the baptism of the coming One has evoked various interpretations. In agreement with Matt 3:11, Luke declares that the One to come "will baptize you with the Holy Spirit and fire" (v. 16). The reference to fire is omitted in Mark 1:8 and the parallels in Acts 1:5; 11:16. What is the relationship between Spirit and fire in this saying? The following interpretations have been advanced: (1) fire describes the inflaming, purifying work of the Spirit; (2) the repentant will receive the Spirit, while the unrepentant will experience the judgment of fire; (3) since the Greek term for "Spirit" can also mean "wind," the meaning is that Jesus' baptism will bring the

43. See John R. Donahue, "Tax Collectors and Sinners: An Attempt at Identification," *CBQ* 33 (1971) 39-61.

44. Josephus *Life* 244; *The Jewish War* 2.581.

judgment of a mighty wind and fire; (4) as might be implicit in the first option, "Spirit" or "wind" and "fire" reflect the Christian interpretation of the Pentecost experience; or (5) John saw in Spirit and fire the means of eschatological purification: the refiner's fire for the repentant and destruction for the unrepentant.[45] The last combines elements of (2) and (3) and fits both the historical context of John's preaching and the literary context in which the saying about winnowing follows. Luke, of course, may have seen the fulfillment of this saying at Pentecost in ways John could not have imagined.

The double proclamation continues in v. 17. At the harvest, grain was gathered to a threshing floor, where the farmer would pitch the grain into the air with a winnowing fork. The wind would blow away the lighter chaff, but the grain itself would fall back to the floor where it could be gathered for use. In the picture painted by this saying, the separation has already taken place and the farmer is at the point of gathering the grain into the granary and burning the chaff. The saying,

therefore, warns of the imminence of the judgment (cf. v. 9). The added detail that the fire is "unquenchable" removes this parabolic saying from ordinary life, unless the term means only that the fire will burn so ferociously that it cannot be extinguished. The detail may be allegorical, however, describing the fire of judgment (Isa 34:8-10; 66:24) or the fires of the garbage heap in the Valley of Hinnom—Gehenna (cf. Matt 18:8; 25:41; Mark 9:43-48; Jude 7; Rev 20:9-15).

While announcing the coming of the Messiah, therefore, John emphasizes in four different ways that the Messiah will be greater than he: (1) John baptizes in water, while the Messiah will baptize with Holy Spirit and fire; (2) the coming One is more powerful than he; (3) John is not worthy to untie the sandal of the coming One; and (4) the coming One will bring salvation for the repentant and judgment for the unrepentant.

3:18. The closing verse of this section (v. 18) concludes the summary of John's preaching and characterizes his work as "exhorting," or in this context calling for repentance, while preaching "good news" to the people of Israel.

45. See Fitzmyer, *The Gospel According to Luke (I–IX)*, 473-74; John Nolland, *Luke 1–9:20*, WBC 35A (Dallas: Word, 1989) 152-53.

REFLECTIONS

1. John rebuked the Israelites who dismissed God's claims on them by appealing to their heritage as the descendants of Abraham. The temptation to self-justification is universal, however. With what rationalizations do we dismiss God's calls to us? The civil-religion rationalization claims that God needs us because we are a Christian nation. The pietist rationalization offers individual piety as a substitute for genuine commitment, while limiting religion to matters of the heart and one's private relationship to God. The universalist rationalization maintains that one's response to God really doesn't make a great deal of difference, since ultimately all will experience God's grace anyway. Whatever our modern equivalent to the appeal to Abraham, John's call comes ringing, "From these very stones. . . . "

2. Another of the haunting phrases from John's preaching is "fruits worthy of repentance." To say that we can never be worthy of God's grace is to miss the point of John's challenge. John calls instead for a change of life-style that reflects the genuineness of our repentance. Just as a false love is not love at all, so also repentance that is not sincere is not repentance. There is an integrity to the repentant. They are whole numbers, integers. Their way of life, their priorities, commitments, personal relationships, passion for peace and justice, and their unplanned acts of compassion all give evidence of their repentance.

3. John's preaching contains three emphases: a prophetic warning against the coming judgment, a call to justice and compassion in our dealings with others, and a confession of the coming Messiah. Think for a moment about the relationship among these three emphases and their expressions in contemporary churches. Each congregation has its own unique blend of heritage, theological distinctives, setting in the community, style of worship, and homogeneity or diversity among its members. Some churches strongly emphasize one or another of the themes of John's preaching—some spend their time interpreting prophecy; others are involved in social action; while others just praise Jesus. Is any one of these emphases by itself a sufficient gospel? More often than not a church will combine christological confession with one of the other two emphases; conservative churches and fundamentalist churches tend to blend praise and prophecy, while liberal mainline Protestant churches often call for social reform as an expression of commitment to Christ. Less frequent is a church that finds a way to maintain both a prophetic/eschatological urgency and an involvement with social issues related to poverty, abuse, hunger, and world peace. Is it desirable for the church today to embody all three strands of John's preaching? If so, how can this be done? By listening to one another, churches that are socially and theologically quite different might learn from each other.

4. Finally, what John points to is a religious experience that is beyond our control. Because it arises from a responsiveness to what God is doing among us, such experience cannot be channeled or domesticated to our tastes. There is the mystery: God acts among us in ways that defy explanation or institutionalization. God calls for a genuine repentance and a commitment to the life-style of a covenant people. Nevertheless, our experience of God is always as Spirit and fire.

LUKE 3:19-20, THE IMPRISONMENT OF JOHN

NIV

¹⁹But when John rebuked Herod the tetrarch because of Herodias, his brother's wife, and all the other evil things he had done, ²⁰Herod added this to them all: He locked John up in prison.

NRSV

¹⁹But Herod the ruler,ᵃ who had been rebuked by him because of Herodias, his brother's wife, and because of all the evil things that Herod had done, ²⁰added to them all by shutting up John in prison.

ᵃ Gk *tetrarch*

COMMENTARY

Luke is distinctive among the Gospels in recording the imprisonment of John prior to the baptism of Jesus. Theologically, the Lukan sequence neatly separates the preparatory work of John from the ministry of Jesus.[46] As narrative artistry, it concludes Luke's account of John's ministry with an account of his departure from the scene that is reminiscent of the references to departures at the end of various scenes in the Lukan birth narratives. Apologetically, it parries possible claims by followers of John the Baptist that John was the greater because he had baptized Jesus (see the discussion of Jesus' baptism below).

46. See Hans Conzelmann, *The Theology of St. Luke,* trans. Geoffrey Buswell (New York: Harper & Row, 1961).

Luke seems to draw from Mark 1:14, which places the beginning of Jesus' ministry after the imprisonment of John (cf. John 3:22-24; 4:1, which envision a period of parallel ministries; Mark 6:17-29, which describes John's death). Nevertheless, Luke changes Mark's sequence of baptism-arrest-beginning of Jesus' ministry and offers no account of John's death. Instead, Luke adds a sequence (7:18-35) that has no parallel in Mark.

The story of Herod Antipas's relationship with Herodias is as colorful as it is scandalous. Herodias was born between 9 and 7 BCE, the daughter of Aristobulus (a son of Herod the Great) and Bernice. Herodias married a son of Herod the Great by another of his ten wives. Herodias's first husband is identified in Mark 6:17 as Philip, while Josephus gives his name as Herod.[47] Scholars have sought to harmonize the two accounts by use of the conflated name "Herod Philip," which does not appear in any ancient account. Luke refrains from naming Herodias's first husband, noting only that he was Herod Antipas's brother (i.e., half-brother). Josephus indicates that Herodias and her first husband had a child, Salome.[48] Herod Antipas, tetrarch of Galilee and Perea, was married to the daughter of King Aretas of Nabatea. Antipas had rebuilt Sepphoris (near Nazareth) and built Tiberius even though the construction of the city defiled a cemetery. Consequently, Antipas had to use forced settlement to populate the new city. On the other hand, Antipas showed sensitivity to Jewish complaints about images on shields and coins in Jerusalem.[49] While visiting Herodias and his half-brother prior to a trip to Rome, Antipas proposed marriage to Herodias, and she consented on the condition that he send away his first wife. The marriage was an offense to pious Jews because it violated the law against such a relationship (Lev 18:16; 20:21).

Luke records that Herod arrested John because of John's condemnation of Herod's marriage. The marriage also resulted in the ruin of Herod Antipas's army. Antipas's first wife fled to her father, who then attacked Antipas. Josephus records that the destruction of Herod Antipas's army was viewed by some Jews as God's judgment on Herod for the death of John the Baptist:

> But to some of the Jews the destruction of Herod's army seemed to be divine vengeance, and certainly a just vengeance, for his treatment of John, surnamed the Baptist. For Herod had put him to death, though he was a good man

and had exhorted the Jews to lead righteous lives, to practice justice towards their fellows and piety towards God, and so doing to join in baptism. In his view this was a necessary preliminary if baptism was to be acceptable to God. They must not employ it to gain pardon for whatever sins they committed, but as a consecration of the body implying that the soul was already thoroughly cleansed by right behaviour. When others too joined the crowds about him, because they were aroused to the highest degree by his sermons, Herod became alarmed. Eloquence that had so great an effect on mankind might lead to some form of sedition, for it looked as if they would be guided by John in everything they did. Herod decided therefore that it would be much better to strike first and be rid of him before his work led to an uprising, than to wait for an upheaval, get involved in a difficult situation and see his mistake. Though John, because of Herod's suspicions, was brought in chains to Machaerus, the stronghold that we have previously mentioned, and there put to death, yet the verdict of the Jews was that the destruction visited upon Herod's army was a vindication of John, since God saw fit to inflict such a blow on Herod.[50]

Josephus gives a political interpretation of Herod's motive for arresting John, but Luke's explanation that it was because of John's condemnation of Herod's marriage is entirely plausible. Herodias ultimately brought a further and final defeat to Herod Antipas. When her brother Agrippa I was given the title of king, she convinced Herod Antipas to appeal to the emperor for the same title. Agrippa, however, sent envoys who persuaded the emperor that Antipas was guilty of treason with the king of Parthia. As a result, the emperor deposed Antipas, and Herodias followed her husband into exile in either Lyons or northern Spain.[51]

---

47. Josephus *Antiquities of the Jews* 18.109.
48. Ibid., 18.136.
49. See H. W. Hoehner, *Herod Antipas*, SNTSMS 17 (Cambridge: Cambridge University Press, 1972; reprint 1980).

50. Josephus, *Antiquities of the Jews*, 18.116-19, in Louis H. Feldman, trans., *Josephus: Jewish Antiquities XVIII–XX*, LCL (Cambridge, Mass.: Harvard University Press, 1965) 81-85.
51. See Josephus *Antiquities of the Jews* 18:240-55; *The Jewish War* 2:183.

REFLECTIONS

The sordid story of Antipas and Herodias is a study in human evil and its consequences. How ironic that the prophet calling for repentance, justice, and compassion is put to death by those seeking only their own pleasure and position. John had done his work, however—the one coming after him would be even mightier than he. On the other hand, Antipas and Herodias would eventually reach for more than they could grasp and bring about their own ruin. The righteous do not always succeed, and the wicked are not always overthrown, but evil is eventually self-destructive. And in the end God will triumph over the worst that we can do.

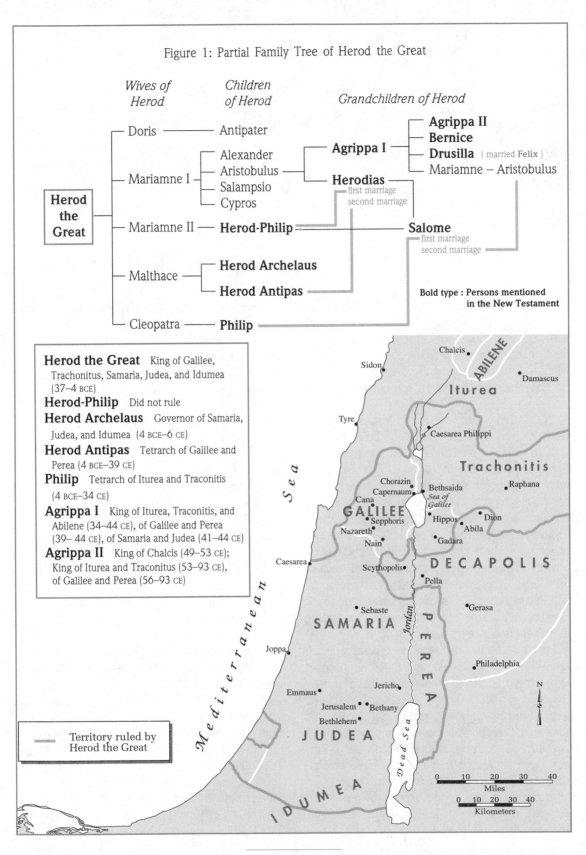

Figure 1: Partial Family Tree of Herod the Great

Wives of Herod — *Children of Herod* — *Grandchildren of Herod*

Doris —— Antipater

Mariamne I —— Alexander
Aristobulus
Salampsio
Cypros

Agrippa I
Herodias
first marriage
second marriage

Mariamne II —— **Herod-Philip** —— **Salome**
first marriage
second marriage

Agrippa II
Bernice
Drusilla (married **Felix**)
Mariamne – Aristobulus

Malthace —— **Herod Archelaus**
Herod Antipas

Cleopatra —— **Philip**

Herod the Great

Bold type : Persons mentioned in the New Testament

Herod the Great King of Galilee, Trachonitus, Samaria, Judea, and Idumea (37–4 BCE)

Herod-Philip Did not rule

Herod Archelaus Governor of Samaria, Judea, and Idumea (4 BCE–6 CE)

Herod Antipas Tetrarch of Galilee and Perea (4 BCE–39 CE)

Philip Tetrarch of Iturea and Traconitis (4 BCE–34 CE)

Agrippa I King of Iturea, Traconitis, and Abilene (34–44 CE), of Galilee and Perea (39– 44 CE), of Samaria and Judea (41–44 CE)

Agrippa II King of Chalcis (49–53 CE); King of Iturea and Traconitis (53–93 CE), of Galilee and Perea (56–93 CE)

Territory ruled by Herod the Great

Chalcis
ABILENE
Sidon
Damascus
Iturea
Tyre
Caesarea Philippi
Trachonitis
Chorazin
Capernaum
Bethsaida
Raphana
Cana
Sea of Galilee
GALILEE
Sepphoris
Hippos
Dion
Nazareth
Abila
Nain
Gadara
Sea
DECAPOLIS
Caesarea
Scythopolis
Pella
Gerasa
Sebaste
SAMARIA
PEREA
Jordan
Philadelphia
Joppa
Jericho
Emmaus
Jerusalem
Bethany
Bethlehem
JUDEA
Dead Sea
Mediterranean
IDUMEA

N

0   10   20   30   40
Miles
0 10 20 30 40
Kilometers

LUKE 3:21-22, THE BAPTISM OF JESUS

NIV

21When all the people were being baptized, Jesus was baptized too. And as he was praying, heaven was opened 22and the Holy Spirit descended on him in bodily form like a dove. And a voice came from heaven: "You are my Son, whom I love; with you I am well pleased."

NRSV

21Now when all the people were baptized, and when Jesus also had been baptized and was praying, the heaven was opened, 22and the Holy Spirit descended upon him in bodily form like a dove. And a voice came from heaven, "You are my Son, the Beloved;[a] with you I am well pleased."[b]

[a]Or my beloved Son   [b]Other ancient authorities read You are my Son, today I have begotten you

COMMENTARY

Each of the Gospels treats the baptism of Jesus differently. In Mark, which lacks a birth narrative and begins with the work of John the Baptist, the baptism of Jesus serves to identify who Jesus is. Mark is distinctive among the Gospels in reflecting no apparent embarrassment at saying that Jesus was baptized by John.

In Matthew, John the Baptist voices the pious reader's objection, saying "I need to be baptized by you, and do you come to me?" (3:14), which allows Jesus to explain that the baptism is necessary "to fulfill all righteousness"—a theme important to Matthew. In John, the baptism of Jesus is not actually narrated. Instead, it is referred to in John's testimony to Jesus. John the Baptist's only role in the Gospel of John is to bear witness to Jesus, so there is no account of his preaching such as we read in Luke 3:7-17. And those who were followers of John the Baptist could not claim to follow his preaching unless they began to follow Jesus as the one whose coming John had announced.

Luke's account is distinctive in several respects: It follows the report that John was imprisoned; John is not mentioned by name; the baptism itself is not reported, only the events that followed Jesus' baptism; prayer is emphasized; and Luke adds that the Spirit descended "in bodily form" as a dove. These peculiarities probably serve various Lukan interests. In particular, Luke emphasizes Jesus' practice of prayer, the apocalyptic fulfillment signaled by the baptism of Jesus, and the twin distinctives of Jesus' identity: the Spirit and sonship.

Luke does not explain why Jesus was baptized or how Luke understands the significance of Jesus' baptism. For answers to these questions, we must interpret the Gospel of Luke on the bases of both the Lukan pattern of the relationship between John and Jesus and the details of Luke's account. The birth narratives establish John as the prophetic forerunner of Jesus, the Son. John will "make ready a people prepared for the Lord" (1:17). Jesus will be called "Son of the Most High" (1:32); he will bring a kingdom (1:33) and salvation (2:30). There could be no question, however, that Jesus required "a baptism of repentance for the forgiveness of sins" (3:3). The baptism of Jesus, therefore, which is reported after the arrest of John the Baptist, marks the succession. John's work has been completed, and Jesus' is just beginning.

Prayer is a recurring emphasis in Luke. The announcement of John's birth occurred at the hour of prayer (1:10). Jesus prays at significant junctures in his ministry: before calling the disciples (6:12), at Caesarea Philippi (9:18), before the transfiguration (9:28), before his death (22:40-46), and on the cross (23:34, 46). It is not surprising, therefore, that Luke should emphasize that Jesus was praying at the time that the Spirit came upon him. Prayer will again be emphasized at the disciples' preparation for the coming of the Spirit at Pentecost (Acts 1:14).

The opening of heaven is an apocalyptic motif found in the OT and in apocalyptic writings (Ezek 1:1; Isa 64:1; John 1:51; Acts 7:56; 10:11; Rev 19:11). The opening of heaven at the baptism of

Jesus signals that he is the Messiah and that the fulfillment of Israel's eschatological expectations is at hand. If the closing of heaven brought drought (Luke 4:25), the opening of heaven would bring God's blessings. God's power and mercy is about to be unleashed.

The blessing that descends from heaven is the Spirit in the form of a dove, descending upon Jesus. The descent of the Spirit is referred to in the OT only in Isa 63:14 LXX. Luke heightens Mark's description of the Spirit "as a dove" by adding the word for "bodily" (σωματικός *sōmatikos*). As in the later description of the coming of the Spirit upon the disciples at Pentecost "like the rush of a violent wind" and with "tongues, as of fire" (Acts 2:2-3), the language here emphasizes both tangibility and inexpressibility. The Spirit was not a dove, but it appeared as something like a dove. The addition of the term *bodily* is also consistent with the "bodily" form of the risen Lord, who in Luke's accounts of the post-resurrection appearances walks, talks, eats, and finally is removed from earth by the ascension.

The antecedent of the choice of a dove as the symbol for the Spirit at Jesus' baptism has been sought in several OT references—e.g., the Spirit of God hovering over the chaos at the creation (Gen 1:2); the dove Noah released after the flood (Gen 8:8); or the eagle that stirs its young to leave the nest in Deut 32:11. In none of these references, however, is the Spirit of God represented by a dove. Even if its origin cannot be traced with confidence, the power of the image of the dove descending on Jesus is attested to by its prominence in Christian art. Jesus' declaration that the Spirit was upon him in his reading of Isa 61:1 in Luke 4:18 should probably be taken as an indication that the reference in Isaiah was fulfilled at Jesus' baptism. The Spirit will also play an important role in Luke and Acts; Luke takes care to point out that the work of John, Jesus, and the apostles was empowered and guided by the Spirit.

The coming of the Spirit upon Jesus commissioned and empowered him for his ministry. The voice from heaven was another common feature of apocalyptic literature (Ezek 1:25, 28; 4 Ezra 6:13-17; John 12:28; Rev 4:1; 10:4). The rabbis taught that the Spirit had departed from the earth with the last of the prophets of Israel, but that on occasion God caused a voice to come forth from heaven. This voice (called the "daughter voice," בת קול *bat qôl*) was not to be regarded as a continuation of the revelation in the Torah or the Prophets or as a substitute for the Holy Spirit.[52]

The voice from heaven is reported in Matthew as a declaration that could be heard by others: "This is my Son" (Matt 3:17). But Luke follows Mark in interpreting the voice as something that only Jesus may have heard: "You are my Son" (Mark 1:11; Luke 3:22). The affirmation of Jesus as God's Son resonates with declarations of sonship throughout Israel's history. Isaac was the promised child of the covenant, the son whom Abraham loved (Gen 22:2). The king of Israel was acclaimed the son of God, as the coronation psalm suggests (Ps 2:7). Later, Israel itself was designated as God's son (Jer 31:20; Hos 11:1), and the servant songs of Isaiah declare that God's election of the servant/child (Isa 42:1). From before Jesus' birth Luke has traced the affirmation of Jesus as God's Son (see 1:32, he will be called "the Son of the Most High"; 1:35, "he will be called Son of God"). At twelve years of age, the precocious child referred to the Temple as "my Father's house" (2:50), and now the voice from heaven confirms both the angelic annunciation and the child's intuition. In the Gospel narrative, Jesus will need to respond to this confirmation of his divine identity, but the reader can have no doubt that Luke confirms the things that have been taught regarding Jesus (1:4).

Two descriptors characterize the Father's relationship to the Son: "the Beloved" and "with whom I am well pleased." The term rendered "beloved" (ἀγαπητός *agapētos*) is used in Luke only on two other occasions, and in each it refers to Jesus: When the voice from heaven speaks again at the transfiguration of Jesus (9:35), and in the parable of the wicked tenants, in which the owner's son interprets Israel's rejection of Jesus, at least in the Lukan form of the parable (20:13). Being "well pleased" (εὐδοκέω *eudokeō*) is also an attribute reserved only for God in the Gospel of Luke. The angelic chorus at Jesus' birth announces God's favor (2:14); it is God's gracious will to hide the revelation from the wise but to give all things to the Son (10:21-22); but it is God's good pleasure to give the kingdom to those

---

52. See Otto Betz, φωνή *TDNT,* 9:288-90.

who are prepared to receive it (12:32). The voice at the baptism of Jesus, therefore, discloses both the identity of the Son and the character of the Father.

REFLECTIONS

1. The text invites reflection at various levels. Theologically, it approaches the mystery of Jesus' relationship to God, the Son's awareness of his relationship to God as Father. It confesses that Jesus could not have done what he did apart from God's empowerment and blessing. Here we find one of the taproots of the confessions the church later shaped regarding the divinity of Jesus and the triune nature of God. With none of the later language of essence and being, the narrative characterizes both Jesus and the divine Father through familial terms and expressions of endearment. Before it is abstracted in creedal language, therefore, our theology expresses our human experience of acceptance, love, and well-being within the family.

2. Pastorally, the description of Jesus' baptism points to the significance of the experience of baptism or confirmation, in which the individual submits to God's grace and finds identity and affirmation. On the part of the one being baptized, baptism expresses repentance, trust, and faith. The people of God, however, participate as those who live out God's words of affirmation to those who submit to God's grace. Here baptism finds new meaning as the pastor and the congregation follow God's example in responding with affirmation and blessing to the one who comes for baptism.

3. For parents, the words of the voice from heaven serve as a reminder that declarations of the parents' love and affirmation of the child are vital to the child's development. Any child who strives to affirm his or her own identity and self-worth without having heard that affirmation from his or her parents faces intense struggles. The voice from heaven, on the other hand, models for us the parental blessing. We who are made in the image of God, and whom God allows to be co-creators in the process of birth, are obligated in return to emulate God in our blessing of the children God gives to us.

LUKE 3:23-38, THE GENEALOGY OF JESUS

NIV

²³Now Jesus himself was about thirty years old when he began his ministry. He was the son, so it was thought, of Joseph,

the son of Heli, ²⁴the son of Matthat,
the son of Levi, the son of Melki,
the son of Jannai, the son of Joseph,
²⁵the son of Mattathias, the son of Amos,
the son of Nahum, the son of Esli,
the son of Naggai, ²⁶the son of Maath,
the son of Mattathias, the son of Semein,
the son of Josech, the son of Joda,
²⁷the son of Joanan, the son of Rhesa,
the son of Zerubbabel, the son of Shealtiel,

NRSV

23Jesus was about thirty years old when he began his work. He was the son (as was thought) of Joseph son of Heli, ²⁴son of Matthat, son of Levi, son of Melchi, son of Jannai, son of Joseph, ²⁵son of Mattathias, son of Amos, son of Nahum, son of Esli, son of Naggai, ²⁶son of Maath, son of Mattathias, son of Semein, son of Josech, son of Joda, ²⁷son of Joanan, son of Rhesa, son of Zerubbabel, son of Shealtiel,^a son of Neri, ²⁸son of Melchi, son of Addi, son of Cosam, son of Elmadam, son of Er, ²⁹son of Joshua, son of Eliezer, son of Jorim, son of Matthat, son of Levi, ³⁰son

^a Gk *Salathiel*

NIV

the son of Neri, [28]the son of Melki,
the son of Addi, the son of Cosam,
the son of Elmadam, the son of Er,
[29]the son of Joshua, the son of Eliezer,
the son of Jorim, the son of Matthat,
the son of Levi, [30]the son of Simeon,
the son of Judah, the son of Joseph,
the son of Jonam, the son of Eliakim,
[31]the son of Melea, the son of Menna,
the son of Mattatha, the son of Nathan,
the son of David, [32]the son of Jesse,
the son of Obed, the son of Boaz,
the son of Salmon,[a] the son of Nahshon,
[33]the son of Amminadab, the son of Ram,[b]
the son of Hezron, the son of Perez,
the son of Judah, [34]the son of Jacob,
the son of Isaac, the son of Abraham,
the son of Terah, the son of Nahor,
[35]the son of Serug, the son of Reu,
the son of Peleg, the son of Eber,
the son of Shelah, [36]the son of Cainan,
the son of Arphaxad, the son of Shem,
the son of Noah, the son of Lamech,
[37]the son of Methuselah, the son of Enoch,
the son of Jared, the son of Mahalalel,
the son of Kenan, [38]the son of Enosh,
the son of Seth, the son of Adam,
the son of God.

[a]32 Some early manuscripts *Sala*   [b]33 Some manuscripts *Amminadab,
the son of Admin, the son of Arni;* other manuscripts vary widely.

NRSV

of Simeon, son of Judah, son of Joseph, son of Jonam,
son of Eliakim, [31]son of Melea, son of Menna, son of
Mattatha, son of Nathan, son of David, [32]son of Jesse,
son of Obed, son of Boaz, son of Sala,[a] son of
Nahshon, [33]son of Amminadab, son of Admin, son
of Arni,[b] son of Hezron, son of Perez, son of Judah,
[34]son of Jacob, son of Isaac, son of Abraham, son of
Terah, son of Nahor, [35]son of Serug, son of Reu,
son of Peleg, son of Eber, son of Shelah, [36]son of
Cainan, son of Arphaxad, son of Shem, son of Noah,
son of Lamech, [37]son of Methuselah, son of Enoch,
son of Jared, son of Mahalaleel, son of Cainan, [38]son
of Enos, son of Seth, son of Adam, son of God.

[a]Other ancient authorities read *Salmon*   [b]Other ancient authorities read *Amminadab, son of Aram;* others vary widely

COMMENTARY

Luke is the only Gospel to record Jesus' age at the time of his baptism: "about thirty." Chronologically, this datum conforms well with other reference points: the birth of Jesus (perhaps two years before the death of Herod the Great in 4 BCE); a ministry of about three years' duration (based on the three Passovers in the Gospel of John); and the death of Jesus at Passover in the year 30. These reference points put the baptism of Jesus in 27 or 28, when Jesus would have been a few months past his thirtieth birthday.

Of what significance is this reference? Some interpreters have sought to relate it to the other chronological references in Luke 3:1, but this effort does not yield a more precise date for Jesus' birth. Alternatively, the reference may be compared to notices that OT figures began their careers at thirty years of age: Joseph (Gen 41:46), the sons of Kohath (Num 4:3), David (2 Sam 5:4), and Ezekiel (Ezek 1:1). Contemporary references indicate that the age of thirty was viewed as the age of maturity.[53]

Modern readers have no sense of how to read a genealogy, so they usually skip them and go on to more interesting parts of the Gospels. The frequency of genealogies in the OT—where there

53. See Josephus *Life* 80; *m. 'Abot* 5.21; 1QSa 1.13.

are about twenty-five genealogies—shows that they fulfilled an important social function and suggests that there were established conventions for written genealogies. Documentation of ancestry was especially common among royal and priestly families. Succession and kinship conferred power and privilege. Genealogies established lines of relationship among families and tribes, but they could also describe the character of an individual. In order to fulfill such purposes, genealogies were often oral and marked by fluidity. First Timothy 1:4 warns against those who are preoccupied with "myths and endless genealogies that promote speculations."

The NT contains two genealogies, both in the Gospels and both genealogies of Jesus. The nearest equivalents are the lists of the twelve disciples, Paul's list of the resurrection appearances (1 Cor 15:5-8), and the heroes of the faith in Hebrews 11. The genealogies of Jesus in Matthew and Luke both reflect attention to their structure, deliberate numerical patterns, and evidence of their author's theological interests. On the other hand, the differences between the two are more pronounced than their similarities. Matthew places the genealogy in the infancy material, prior to the birth of Jesus; Luke places it after the baptism of Jesus. Matthew traces the line of Jesus from Abraham through David to Joseph; Luke works backward from Joseph to Adam. Matthew includes references to four women and occasional significant parenthetical comments; Luke never interrupts the succession of "A son of B, B son of C. . . . " Matthew calls attention to the intended structure of his genealogy: "So all the generations from Abraham to David are fourteen generations; and from David to the deportation to Babylon, fourteen generations; and from the deportation to Babylon to the Messiah, fourteen generations" (1:17). Luke gives no such interpretation of the structure of his genealogy.

Among the agreements and divergences between the two genealogies, the following are notable. First, contrary to some interpretations, both Matthew and Luke trace the line of Jesus through Joseph. The phrase "as was thought" in Luke 3:23 does not indicate that Luke traces the line through Mary; it suggests, rather, that contrary to popular thought Joseph was not the actual father of Jesus—and the genealogy reveals who

his true father was. The first point of divergence occurs with the father of Joseph, whose name is Jacob in Matthew and Heli in Luke. With the exception that the list may occasionally preserve variations in spelling of the same name (e.g., Matthat and Matthan), the next point of agreement occurs with the names Zerubbabel and Shealtiel. Whereas, counting from Jesus, these are the twenty-first and twenty-second names in Luke's list, they are the twelfth and thirteenth names in Matthew's. The two genealogies diverge again at the point of Shealtiel's father and do not converge again until David. In Luke's genealogy, there are twenty-first generations from Shealtiel to David; in Matthew there are only fifteen. Significantly, Luke traces the line from David through Nathan, whereas Matthew traces it through Solomon. The greatest parallels between the two genealogies are to be found in the genealogy of David, where the only differences (except for spelling) are found in the generation(s) between Hezron and Amminadab. From these comparisons, it is clear that any attempt to harmonize the two genealogies is futile. Both evangelists presumably worked with traditional genealogies (which followed biblical accounts of the genealogy of David), and Luke seems to employ the genealogies in Genesis 5 and 11 to complete the line back to Adam. Each evangelist exercised considerable freedom in constructing the genealogy, therefore, and each genealogy, by its selection and arrangement of the names, serves as a comment on the identity of Jesus.

Matthew features Jesus' lineage through Abraham and David (1:1). Parenthetical comments highlight the significance of the twelve tribes of Israel ("Judah and his brothers," 1:2) and the unusual role of women in Jesus' ancestry, perhaps in preparation for the role of Mary in the birth account. David is given the title "King," and the time of the "deportation to Babylon" is marked.

While both the structure and the intent of Luke's genealogy are less explicit, there are sufficient clues to give us some indication of its significance. In Luke, as in Matthew, the genealogy appears to feature sequences of sevens. In all, there are seventy-eight names, counting Jesus and Adam, or seventy-seven generations, and these seem to have been divided into sequences of seven. Counting from Jesus, significant names appear at multiples of 7 generations: 21 generations from Jesus to Shealtiel, 42 generations to David, 56 generations to Abraham, and 70 generations to Enoch. In other words, Luke has so structured Jesus' genealogy that there are 3 sevens of generations from Jesus to Shealtiel, 3 sevens from Shealtiel to David, 2 sevens from David to Abraham, and 3 sevens from Abraham to Adam. Therefore, Jesus begins the twelfth sequence of seven. Like Matthew, Luke records for Jesus a royal lineage through David and an Israelite lineage through Abraham, but ultimately he sets Jesus in the context of all human history, as a descendant of Adam.

The real emphasis, however, is not on Adam but on the last link in the chain: "son of God." Luke seems not to be so concerned with a "second Adam" christology but with the affirmation that Jesus was "son of God." The final position of this title ties the genealogy to its context. The voice from heaven at the baptism of Jesus declared, "You are my son," so the genealogy offers another indication of how Jesus is the Son of God. Its function, therefore, is to serve as further support and clarification for Luke's presentation of Jesus as the Son of God. The angel announced Jesus as the Son of God before his birth, and Jesus was born of a virgin. Jesus' birth was received with joy by the host of angels and by those who recognized its significance. In the Temple, Jesus gave an indication of his divine sonship. When the Word of God came to John in the wilderness, John announced Jesus' coming. At the baptism, the voice from heaven declared, "You are my Son," and the genealogy—which concludes as no other known genealogy, with the designation "son of God"—underscores this same christological theme.

Various interpretations of the Lukan genealogy are possible, therefore: (1) It emphasizes the beginning of the messianic age with Jesus, who inaugurates the twelfth series of seven. (2) It juxtaposes Jesus and Adam, so that Jesus may be seen as the second Adam. (3) It relates Jesus to the history of Israel, through David and Abraham. (4) It places the ministry of Jesus in the context of universal, human history, reaching back to Adam. (5) It affirms Jesus' divine sonship, which is highlighted at the beginning and end of the genealogy. Objections may be raised to each of these interpretations, and it is certainly possible, even probable, that Luke had more than one interest in mind, but the options are listed here in order of ascending significance. The first two are elusive. The first depends on assigning a certain significance to the structure of sevens. The second lacks support elsewhere in Luke. The third is weakened by the consideration that the genealogy continues on to Adam (in contrast to Matthew's). The fourth is more probable, but does not account for the emphatic last link, and exclusive emphasis on the fifth risks treating all the generations between Jesus and God as items within a parenthesis. The best solution, therefore, seems to be to recognize the force of each of these interpretations, especially the last three.

The fifth interpretation, affirming Jesus as the Son of God, has the added strength of explaining the placement of the genealogy between the baptism of Jesus and the temptations. Immediately prior to the genealogy the voice from heaven declares that Jesus is "my Son," and immediately after it the temptation of Jesus begins with the challenge "If you are the Son of God...." The identity of Jesus is now fixed for the reader, so the next section of the Gospel can begin: the fulfillment of Jesus' role as the Son of God during his ministry in Galilee.

REFLECTIONS

Why do so many families find it important to try to reconstruct their family tree? Genealogies seldom confer real power in American society. Nevertheless, establishing one's ancestry and distant relatives seems to meet an important need. Several years ago the nation was galvanized by Alex Haley's retelling of his family history in the television miniseries "Roots." Family stories are passed down from generation to generation, and each name evokes a story and a set of shared experiences, traits, or values.

Theologically, the genealogy of Jesus is important, regardless of the difficulties one faces in establishing its historical accuracy, because it connects Jesus with God, with Israel, and with humanity. These three relationships define his identity and the significance of all that comes later in the Gospel. Jesus is the Son of God who was born to bring salvation to God's people. Jesus stands within the history of God's covenant with Israel; yet, the story of his life has significance for all people. Jesus is the Son of God who entered human history to declare the arrival of God's reign in human history, to call together a new community, and to redeem humanity. Read in this way, the genealogy, like the birth narratives, is a gospel in miniature.

LUKE 4:1-13, THE TEMPTATION OF JESUS

NIV

4 Jesus, full of the Holy Spirit, returned from the Jordan and was led by the Spirit in the desert, [2]where for forty days he was tempted by the devil. He ate nothing during those days, and at the end of them he was hungry.

[3]The devil said to him, "If you are the Son of God, tell this stone to become bread."

[4]Jesus answered, "It is written: 'Man does not live on bread alone.'[a]"

[5]The devil led him up to a high place and showed him in an instant all the kingdoms of the world. [6]And he said to him, "I will give you all their authority and splendor, for it has been given to me, and I can give it to anyone I want to. [7]So if you worship me, it will all be yours."

[8]Jesus answered, "It is written: 'Worship the Lord your God and serve him only.'[b]"

[9]The devil led him to Jerusalem and had him stand on the highest point of the temple. "If you are the Son of God," he said, "throw yourself down from here. [10]For it is written:

"'He will command his angels concerning you
    to guard you carefully;
[11]they will lift you up in their hands,
    so that you will not strike your foot against
        a stone.'[c]"

[12]Jesus answered, "It says: 'Do not put the Lord your God to the test.'[d]"

[13]When the devil had finished all this tempting, he left him until an opportune time.

a4 Deut. 8:3   b8 Deut. 6:13   c11 Psalm 91:11,12   d12 Deut. 6:16

NRSV

4 Jesus, full of the Holy Spirit, returned from the Jordan and was led by the Spirit in the wilderness, [2]where for forty days he was tempted by the devil. He ate nothing at all during those days, and when they were over, he was famished. [3]The devil said to him, "If you are the Son of God, command this stone to become a loaf of bread." [4]Jesus answered him, "It is written, 'One does not live by bread alone.'[a]"

[5]Then the devil[a] led him up and showed him in an instant all the kingdoms of the world. [6]And the devil[a] said to him, "To you I will give their glory and all this authority; for it has been given over to me, and I give it to anyone I please. [7]If you, then, will worship me, it will all be yours." [8]Jesus answered him, "It is written,

'Worship the Lord your God,
    and serve only him.'"

[9]Then the devil[a] took him to Jerusalem, and placed him on the pinnacle of the temple, saying to him, "If you are the Son of God, throw yourself down from here, [10]for it is written,

'He will command his angels concerning you,
    to protect you,'
[11]and

'On their hands they will bear you up,
    so that you will not dash your foot against
        a stone.'"

[12]Jesus answered him, "It is said, 'Do not put the Lord your God to the test.'" [13]When the devil had finished every test, he departed from him until an opportune time.

a Gk he

COMMENTARY

The sonship of Jesus has been confirmed for the reader by this point in the narrative, but the reader has been given few clues as to the nature of the Son of God's work. Expectations varied. Some expected a royal Davidic Messiah, one who would reestablish the kingdom of Israel (see Acts 1:6). This expectation fanned hopes that the Messiah would overthrow the Roman overlords.[54] Others looked for a priestly Messiah who would purify the worship of Israel.[55] Linked with messianic expectations was the promise of a prophet like Moses (Deut 18:15, 18), one who would lead the people as Moses had led the Israelites. Speculation fanned fantastic visions of the messianic age. Even the vineyards would yield fantastic harvests.[56] Having established the sonship of Jesus, Luke turns immediately, before the beginning of Jesus' public ministry, to the story of the temptations. On one level the story describes Jesus' response to calls for misuse of his power and sonship. On another level, the story educates, disabusing the reader of any expectation that Jesus would manifest his sonship by a series of theatrical demonstrations. The work of the Spirit requires faithfulness; neither compromise with Satan nor concessions to popular demands could be allowed.

The form and function of the temptation scene in Luke emerge more clearly when it is compared with the parallel scenes in the other Gospels. Mark's account contains features on which the Lukan account builds: the Spirit, the wilderness, forty days, tempted by Satan. The three separate temptations are described in Matthew, but in a different order: bread, Temple, mountain. The sequence in Matthew, which many commentators consider to be the sequence in the source common to Matthew and Luke, moves from the desert to the pinnacle of the Temple to a high mountain. The sequence may have been attractive to Matthew because it concludes on a high mountain, just as Matthew's Gospel concludes on a mountain in Galilee. The Matthean structure holds in sequence the two temptations that begin "if you are the son of God. . . . " It also cites the quota-

tions from Deuteronomy in reverse order: Deut 8:3; 6:16, 13. At the conclusion, Matthew reports that the devil left Jesus.

The Lukan sequence reverses the last two temptations so that the climactic scene occurs at the Temple, where the Gospel begins and ends. Luke's sequence also allows the temptations to begin and end with references to Jesus' sonship (4:3, 9); and after Jesus has responded twice, citing Scripture, the devil tempts Jesus the third time by citing verses from the Psalms. While the Matthean order may be the more original, therefore, there are good reasons why Luke preferred the sequence in which he presents the three scenes.

The temptation scene is peculiar for several reasons: The devil appears and speaks to Jesus directly; Jesus responds three times, and each time his response is a quotation from the Scriptures; no one is present to witness or report these events; and the settings as well as the temptations themselves project important symbolic overtones. It has been suggested that the temptation scenes are based on Jesus' responses to actual requests for a sign during his ministry (see Luke 11:16, 29). At this point the Gospel of John, which contains no account of the temptations following the baptism of Jesus, may be helpful. More clearly than the other Gospels, John shows how the temptations may have had a basis in the ministry of Jesus as it was understood by the evangelists. Following the feeding of the 5,000, the crowd seeks Jesus out again, hoping that he will make bread for them (John 6:26, 30-31). The coming of the Greeks in John 12:20 brings Jesus as close to temptation as he ever comes in the Fourth Gospel, as he considers whether he should ask to be delivered from his hour (John 12:27). Later, at the death of Jesus, his kingship is declared in Hebrew, the language of religion; in Greek, the language of culture; and in Latin, the language of the state. The brothers of Jesus tempt him to go up to Jerusalem and show the people assembled there the works he could do (John 7:3). John further declares that Jesus' brothers did not believe in him, and Jesus said they belonged to the world (John 7:5-7). John, therefore, shows how Jesus faced the temptations in the course of his ministry, and it may actually be closer to the historical basis for the stylized and symbolic accounts of the temptations in Matthew and Luke.

---

54. See Psalms of Solomon 17.
55. 1QS 9.11; 1QSa 2.19.
56. 2 Bar 29:5-8.

The temptation scene serves several important functions in Luke. (1) *The temptations clarify the nature of Jesus' work as the Son of God.* Following the birth accounts, the episode in the Temple when Jesus was twelve years old, the baptism of Jesus at which he was declared the Son of God by the voice from heaven, and the genealogy, which concludes with the designation "Son of God," the temptations serve to interpret the implications of his identity for his coming ministry. Jesus will fulfill the heritage of Israel, combat the rule of Satan, and fulfill his work as Savior by his faithfulness.

(2) *The temptations identify Jesus with the heritage of Israel.* Like Israel, Jesus was led by the Spirit in the wilderness. The period of forty days also evokes the period of Israel's testing. The temptation to make bread evokes memories of the manna God supplied Israel. Even more clearly, the three quotations from Deuteronomy link the temptation scene with Israel's experience. Consequently, the three temptations themselves may be seen as corresponding to the temptations of Israel, which involved bread (Exod 16:15), testing the Lord (Exod 17:1-7), and idolatry (Exodus 32); for the remembrance of these events, see Psalm 106; 1 Cor 10:6-9.[57]

(3) *The temptations mirror the conflict of God's reign with the reign of Satan.* The interpretation of the parable of the sower explains that some do not receive the Word because, like the birds who peck the seeds, the devil comes and snatches the Word from them (8:12). The success of the mission of the seventy signaled the fall of Satan from heaven (10:18). Later, Jesus explains that he did not cast out demons by the power of Beelzebul, but that the coming of the kingdom is a sign of Satan's defeat (11:14-23). Similarly, the crippled woman is identified as "a daughter of Abraham whom Satan bound for eighteen long years" (13:16). Not surprising is Luke's emphasis that the failures of Jesus' disciples during the events of Jesus' passion are due to Satan's temptations (22:3, 31). Jesus' conflict with Satan at the beginning of his ministry, therefore, serves as an interpretive frame that enables the reader to understand the whole of Jesus' ministry as an attack on the enslaving and destructive effects of Satan's work.

(4) *The temptations emphasize that Jesus' ministry should be understood as the fulfillment of*

the Scriptures. As we have noted, one of the striking features of these verses is that in Jesus' three responses to the devil he quotes scriptures. There is no other dialogue or interpretation; these are the only words Jesus speaks. The effect is to focus attention on both the power and the fulfillment of Scripture. Throughout Luke, the Scriptures form the context for understanding the meaning of the Gospel narrative. The annunciations echo biblical hopes and expectations. John's work is a fulfillment of the prophets (see 3:4-6). Jesus' inaugural address in Nazareth announces the fulfillment of Isaiah 61 (see 4:18-19), and his response to John's queries again points to the fulfillment of the prophets (see 7:18-23). The end of the Gospel makes the same point: Jesus fulfilled what was written in the Law of Moses, the Prophets, and the Psalms (24:44), and those who would understand Jesus must have their minds open to the Scriptures (24:45).

(5) *The temptations offer Jesus' followers a model for resisting temptation.* In various respects, Luke paints a picture of Jesus as a model for his followers. At the risk of caricaturing the nuanced themes of discipleship in each of the Gospels, one might say that for Matthew discipleship means living by Jesus' teachings, "observing" all that Jesus taught (Matt 28:20). The enigmatic Jesus of the Fourth Gospel is hardly one to be imitated; for John discipleship begins with being born from above. Luke stands closer to Mark, but in Mark the imitation or following is focused more narrowly on the call to suffering servanthood: self-denial, taking up the cross, and being a servant to others (Mark 8:34; 9:35; 10:44-45). In Luke Jesus is more frequently portrayed as exemplifying characteristically Christian virtues: Jesus is empowered by the Spirit; he prays regularly; he is compassionate toward the outcast and afflicted; he associates with women, sinners, and tax collectors; and he dies a martyr's death, praying for his persecutors. In the temptation scene, therefore, Jesus faithfully resists temptations to do less than or other than he was called to do. He relies on Scripture and refuses to put God to the test. The temptation scene, therefore, can serve as an example story for all who are tempted.

The temptation scene is neatly arranged in five parts: A. The setting (vv. 1-2); B. The first temptation: turn stones into bread (vv. 3-4); Jesus' response: Deut 8:3; C. The second temptation:

---

57. See Charles H. Talbert, *Reading Luke: A Literary and Theological Commentary on the Third Gospel* (New York: Crossroad, 1982) 47.

the kingdoms of the world (vv. 5-8) Jesus' response: Deut 6:13; 10:20; D. The third temptation: jump from the pinnacle of the Temple (Ps 91:11-12; vv. 9-12) Jesus' response: Deut 6:16; E. Conclusion: The devil's departure (v. 13).

4:1-2. Detailed features of the account are interesting as well as its grand design. The temptation is closely connected with the baptism, giving rise to theories that the genealogy is a later insertion between the two. Jesus, "filled with the Spirit," leaves the Jordan. Although this phrase does not occur elsewhere in Luke, it is common to his vocabulary for describing Christian leaders in Acts (the Seven, 6:3; Stephen, 6:5; 7:55; Barnabas, 11:24). Jesus was led "in the Spirit," "in the wilderness." The first phrase may be understood either instrumentally, "by means of the Spirit," or locatively, "in the Spirit."

The period of forty days evokes Israel's forty years of testing (Num 14:34; Deut 8:2; Ps 95:10; Ezek 4:6). In the early theology of Israel, God tested the people (Gen 22:1; 2 Sam 24:1). Later, testing was attributed to Satan (Gen 3:1-19; 1 Chr 21:1; Job 1:6-12). Luke's account represents a conflation of Mark and Q. For forty days, Jesus was tempted (Mark) and ate nothing (Matthew). Consequently, in Luke, the three temptations actually come after the period of forty days. By implication, then, the temptations catch Jesus in a vulnerable condition, weakened by hunger. Here Luke's skill as a storyteller is evident. The three temptations convey a sense of the nature of the temptations during the forty-day period, they are psychologically plausible, and the first temptation arises out of Jesus' physical need.

4:3-4. The first temptation may be understood on several levels: as a challenge to Jesus' sonship, as a temptation for him to use his sonship to perform a popular sign for the people, as a temptation to exploit his sonship for his own benefit, or as an expression of his independence from God. The construction of the conditional sentence "If . . . then . . . " may imply either a testing of the condition ("If you really are . . . ") or an acceptance of the condition ("Since you are . . . "). The immediate temptation is to make one loaf of bread (cf. Matthew). The references to testing, the wilderness, and the forty days, and the quotations from Deuteronomy all evoke parallels with the provision of manna in the wilderness. Furthermore, manna is mentioned in the verse Jesus quotes

in response (Deut 8:3). Jesus is challenged to repeat the sign of God's provision for the people, but if he makes bread for himself, he abuses his sonship by serving his own needs rather than depending on God's provision for his needs. The fact that the temptation was to give his ministry to meeting the physical needs of the people is less clearly supported. Such an interpretation is plausible when the first temptation is read in conjunction with the other two, which more directly concern the issue of the nature of Jesus' ministry, but the singular loaf, the nature of Jesus' reply, and the fact that he later feeds the multitude weaken this view of the nature of the first temptation.

In Luke, Jesus responds with only the first part of Deut 8:3. Luke does not add the rest of the verse, which offers a positive alternative: "but by every word. . . . " The negative response is sufficient to define human life as more than meeting one's own physical needs. The work of the Son of God would have to involve more than that.

4:5-8. The second temptation is the gain of power by compromise. Luke describes the setting only elliptically: The devil "led him up" and showed him all the kingdoms of the earth in an instant. The devil then claims both authority over the kingdoms and the prerogative to give that authority to whomever he chooses. A Faustian deal is offered: Worship me, and it will all be yours. The Son of God would indeed have authority over the kingdoms of the earth, but his authority would come from God. This is the first reference to authority in the Gospel, but Luke is more concerned with the exercise of authority than any of the other Gospels. Jesus taught with authority (4:32) and commanded the unclean spirits (who were subject to the devil) with such authority that they came out (4:36). He had authority to forgive sins (5:24). A centurion recognized his authority (7:8). Jesus gave the Twelve authority over demons and diseases (9:1). Jesus claimed that he saw Satan fall from heaven and gave his disciples authority to tread on snakes and scorpions (10:19). He instructed them to fear the one who has authority to cast them into hell (12:5). In Luke, therefore, the authority of God, exercised by Jesus, is superior to that of the authority of the devil, exercised through unclean spirits and "the kingdoms of the world."

In response to this temptation, Jesus quotes Deut 6:13 (see also Deut 10:20), but the Lukan form of the text changes the word for "worship" (προσκυνέω *proskyneō*) to the same word used in the devil's proposition in v. 7, and he adds the word for "only" (μόνος *monos*) in the second part of the verse for emphasis.

4:9-12. The climactic scene occurs in Jerusalem, where the devil takes Jesus to the "winglet" of the Temple. There are no contemporary references to this feature of the Temple, but it is often supposed that the site intended is the southeast corner of the Temple wall, its highest point above the valley below. According to later legend, James the brother of Jesus was thrown from the "winglet" of the Temple.[58] In a wonderfully devious manner, the devil frames the third temptation in a quotation from Scripture. Twice Jesus has fended off temptations with words from Scripture, so this time the devil addresses Jesus by citing a text from the Psalms, in effect saying: "Did the psalmist not promise angels to protect you and to bear you up so that you would not even strike your foot against a stone?" (See Ps 91:11-12.) "If you are the Son of God," he challenges Jesus once more, "throw yourself down from here."

This time the temptation is to put God's promises to the test. Specifically, Jesus was tempted to call upon God to deliver him from death in Jerusalem. Ironically, as every Christian reader knows, Jesus would eventually face death in Jerusalem, and when he did he would choose not his own deliverance but faithfulness to his Father's will (see 22:42). Jesus' response to the devil on the

pinnacle of the Temple, therefore, is the counterpart to his prayer in the Garden of Gethsemane. Jesus would fulfill his divine sonship not by escaping death but by accepting death and defeating it. Unlike Israel of old, Jesus refused to put God to the test (Deut 6:16). The words of Deuteronomy are not a prohibition that Jesus challenges the devil to obey, but a command to which Jesus submits himself.

Thus the verses from Deuteronomy with which Jesus wards off temptation are each applicable to all people, not just to Jesus. Taken together, they declare that we are to make life more than just the pursuit of our physical needs; we are to worship and serve God and God alone, and it is not for us to test God. The first and third responses are negative, but both imply the positive that is stated in the second response: The supreme purpose of all life is the worship of God. Any pursuit, priority, or preoccupation that diverts us from that purpose should be seen for what it is: the devil's temptation.

4:13. The notice of the devil's departure is a typical Lukan device for closing a scene. The three temptations are exemplary of all the temptations Jesus faced and would face during his ministry. The reference to the devil's departure "until an opportune time" foreshadows Satan's return later in the Gospel story, in the events leading up to Jesus' death (see 22:3, 31, 53).

---

58. See Eusebius *Ecclesiastical History* 2.23.11.

REFLECTIONS

1. In the temptation scene Jesus fulfills the command that was at the heart of Judaism: "Hear, O Israel: The LORD is our God, the LORD alone. You shall love the LORD your God with all your heart, and with all your soul, and with all your might." These words introduce the Shema, Israel's confession of faith (Deut 6:4-9; 11:13-31; Num 15:37-41). According to tradition, these words were to be recited twice a day, morning and evening. Two of the verses of Scripture quoted by Jesus follow immediately after the opening section of the Shema (Deut 6:13, 16). Jesus responds to the temptation to make bread, thereby dividing his heart between love of God and craving to satisfy his physical needs. He rejects the temptation to compromise his devotion to God for the sake of the world's mammon; he loves God with all his might. And in the third temptation, he refuses to demand that God save his life ("soul") by deliberately placing himself in jeopardy. If Jesus' temptations represent a fulfillment of the Shema, then in yet another way Luke has shown that Jesus was a model Jew. He was the fulfillment of Israel's heritage, the Son of God who loved the Lord with all his heart.

2. Temptation is a universal human experience. Had Jesus not been tempted, he would not really have been human. The temptations, therefore, are a vital part of the narrative christology, which portrays Jesus as fully human. The author of Hebrews, writing in a different genre, asserts that Jesus "in every respect has been tested as we are, yet without sin" (4:15). The wonder is not that Jesus was incapable of sinning but that he was able to avoid sinning although he was tempted. Along with the birth narrative, therefore, the temptations make an important anti-docetic statement: Jesus was fully human and knew what it meant to be tempted.

3. Fascination with the thought of making a deal with the devil has propelled the story of Faust through the past four centuries. The story is based on the life of a German magician (c. 1480–1540) who claimed to be in league with Satan. Marvelous tales developed around his exploits. After Faust died of mysterious causes, "Philipp Melanchthon, Luther's collaborator, reported that Faust was strangled by the Devil in a rural inn in Würtemberg on the day his evil pact came due."[59] From the sixteenth century on, the story of Faust has been told in various forms. In the early accounts, he sells his soul to the devil in return for magical powers—usually for a period of 24 years. At the end of the agreed upon period, the devil takes Faust to hell. The story of Faust was spread as a reaction against Roman Catholicism and as a warning that learning must be kept within limits. Faust's quest for forbidden knowledge finally led him to damnation. Christopher Marlowe, the British dramatist, turned the story into a play, and later Johann Wolfgang von Goethe introduced elements from the book of Job into the story: God permitted the devil to mislead Faust, but God redeemed him in the end. In Goethe's imagination, Faust becomes "a universal hero, a self in quest of fulfillment" who discovers that he is to be judged "not by his finding but by his seeking."[60]

4. For modern readers, the problem with the temptation story is that it seems unreal, far removed from our experience. The devil does not appear to us and transport us from place to place. The temptations we experience are often not so clearly recognizable. The choice is not between good and bad but between bad and worse or good and better. We deal in "gray areas" and do not have the choice of rejecting "Mr. In-between." In the classic westerns, the good guys wear white hats and the bad guys black hats, and ultimately the clash between them is settled on Main Street at high noon. But this type scene has broken down. We seldom experience such clear choices any longer, and even if we have the moral fortitude to handle the clearly recognizable evils, we often lack the wisdom to deal with the moral choices we face more typically. When does what is good for the corporate body outweigh the need of an individual? Which has the higher claim, the needs of the unemployed for a job or anti-pollution standards that protect the ecology but close down certain industries? Should the medical community allow fetal research or the use of fetal tissue to save one life at the expense of another? Where are the guiding words of Scripture for questions like these?

Although the temptation story does not offer ethical instructions that cover every eventuality, it does describe the perennial ethical challenges that Christians face: the temptations to forget one's baptismal identity, to attempt to use one's religion for personal gain, to try to be successful rather than faithful, to be dazzled by the riches of the world, to make compromises where one is called to stand firm, and to avoid the path of sacrifice and suffering. The story is first a christological statement, but secondarily it offers an example for others to follow. Faced with pressing decisions regarding his identity and vocation, Jesus allowed himself to be led by the Spirit. In the experience of wrestling with the temptations, Jesus responded to the Scripture's admonitions regarding God's purpose for life and the call to worship and serve God. In the specific situations that would follow he would have to work out the shape of his obedience to these admonitions. Christian ethics does not come prepackaged. The call is not to adherence to a list of rules and regulations but to faithfulness to the call and purposes of God.

---

59. Daniel J. Boorstin, *The Creators: A History of Heroes of the Imagination* (New York: Random House, 1992) 604.
60. Ibid., 605, 607.

THE MINISTRY IN GALILEE

OVERVIEW

Luke follows the structure of the Gospel of Mark, in which the ministry of Jesus takes place in Galilee, with only brief forays to the north and to the Decapolis (Mark 7:24, 31; 8:27). With the exception of these passages, Jesus is in Galilee throughout Mark 1:15–9:50. He then travels to Jerusalem, where he may have spent no more than a week before his death at Passover. By comparison, Luke abbreviates the period of Jesus' ministry in Galilee and greatly expands the period of Jesus' journey to Jerusalem (Luke 9:51–19:28).

The ministry in Galilee is introduced by Jesus' reading and interpretation of the words of Isaiah in the synagogue at Nazareth. This scene, therefore, functions as a keynote to the entire ministry of Jesus, setting forth the perspective from which it is to be understood. Consequently, there is no subsequent visit to Nazareth corresponding to Mark 6:1-6. Other passages have also been omitted: the so-called longer omission (at Luke 9:17, where Mark 6:45–8:26 is omitted) and the shorter omission (at 9:50, omitting Mark 9:41–10:21). The most notable addition to the Galilean ministry in Luke is the section 6:20–8:3, which includes the Sermon on the Plain. But Luke has inserted other sections of the Galilean ministry into the Markan framework (e.g., Luke 4:16-30; 5:1-11). The rest of the material has parallels in the Gospel of Mark, but often contains minor differences that accentuate Lukan themes.

LUKE 4:14-15, INTRODUCTION TO THE MINISTRY IN GALILEE

[14]Jesus returned to Galilee in the power of the Spirit, and news about him spread through the whole countryside. [15]He taught in their synagogues, and everyone praised him.

14Then Jesus, filled with the power of the Spirit, returned to Galilee, and a report about him spread through all the surrounding country. [15]He began to teach in their synagogues and was praised by everyone.

COMMENTARY

The Gospel of Mark introduces the ministry in Galilee with a reference to the imprisonment of John the Baptist and a declaration of the coming of the kingdom of God. Luke has already reported John's imprisonment (prior to Jesus' baptism; Luke 3:20) and hence does not repeat it. Neither is the announcement of the kingdom given in the introductory summary. Instead, Luke devotes the first major pericope of the Galilean ministry to the announcement of the coming of the kingdom (4:16-30), though the phrase "the kingdom of God" does not occur until 4:43.

The opening phrase notes Jesus' return from the temptations in the wilderness. Luke often uses geographical notices and reports of comings and goings to open and close sections of the narrative. In a manner reminiscent of OT references, Luke describes the disclosure of the power of God's Spirit in Jesus. Just as Jesus' birth had been characterized by Spirit and power (1:35), so also now the Spirit empowers Jesus at the beginning of his ministry. References to the Holy Spirit form a *leitmotif* linking John's preaching (3:16), the baptism of Jesus (3:22), the temptations (4:1), and the beginning of his ministry in Galilee (4:14). Manifestations of the power of the Lord will also be evident in Jesus' works in this section of the Gospel (see 4:36; 5:17; 6:19; 8:46; 9:1).

Luke's reference to the reports of Jesus' works establishes the fact that what Jesus does in Nazareth (4:16-30) and Capernaum (4:31-41) is typical of his work in other locales also. These episodes are paradigmatic and representative of this period of Jesus' ministry. Luke characterizes Jesus' work as teaching rather than preaching (cf. Mark 1:14), though the term "to preach, proclaim" (κηρύσσω *kēryssō*) will be featured in 4:18-19 and in another summary verse at the end of this chapter (4:44). The reference to teaching in the introduction to this section is appropriate, however, because Luke repeatedly describes Jesus as teaching (4:31; 5:3, 17; 6:6). Similarly, synagogues will be the setting for Jesus' work in Nazareth and Capernaum, in Judea (4:44), and in other scenes (6:6; 13:10). The universal acclaim of Jesus, which will play an important role in the next scene, is also a favorite Lukan emphasis. Among the many references to the universal scope of Jesus' work in the ensuing scenes we read that "all" testified to Jesus (4:22), all the crowd sought to touch him (6:19), and all were amazed at what he was doing (9:43).

The praise of God also forms an underlying theme throughout the Gospel of Luke. It is the only appropriate human response to God's disclosure of Jesus as the Savior. Three times in the ministry in Galilee, Luke reports that those who had been touched by Jesus' power departed praising God (5:25, 26; 7:16). Brief as it is, therefore, Luke's introduction to the ministry in Galilee gives the reader an indication of the nature of Jesus' work (teaching), one of its common settings (the synagogues), the source of its power (the Spirit), its result (praise), and its extent (to all).

The rest of Luke 4 is carefully structured. Between the summary of Jesus' return to Galilee in 4:14-15 and the summary of his departure to Judea in 4:44, Luke summarizes Jesus' work in two villages: Nazareth (4:16-30) and Capernaum (4:31-41). In Nazareth, Jesus teaches in the synagogue; in Capernaum, while he is teaching, he casts out an unclean spirit and then heals Peter's mother-in-law and various others. Together, these scenes portray the power of the Spirit in both word and deed, in Jesus' teaching and in his healing. What he proclaimed in Nazareth, he began to do immediately thereafter in Capernaum.

LUKE 4:16-30, PREACHING IN NAZARETH

NIV	NRSV
[16]He went to Nazareth, where he had been brought up, and on the Sabbath day he went into the synagogue, as was his custom. And he stood up to read. [17]The scroll of the prophet Isaiah was handed to him. Unrolling it, he found the place where it is written:	16When he came to Nazareth, where he had been brought up, he went to the synagogue on the sabbath day, as was his custom. He stood up to read, [17]and the scroll of the prophet Isaiah was given to him. He unrolled the scroll and found the place where it was written:

[18]"The Spirit of the Lord is on me,
    because he has anointed me
    to preach good news to the poor.
He has sent me to proclaim freedom for the
        prisoners
	[18] "The Spirit of the Lord is upon me,
	    because he has anointed me
	        to bring good news to the poor.
	He has sent me to proclaim release to the
	        captives
	    and recovery of sight to the blind,

NIV

and recovery of sight for the blind,
to release the oppressed,
[19] to proclaim the year of the Lord's favor."[a]

[20]Then he rolled up the scroll, gave it back to the attendant and sat down. The eyes of everyone in the synagogue were fastened on him, [21]and he began by saying to them, "Today this scripture is fulfilled in your hearing."

[22]All spoke well of him and were amazed at the gracious words that came from his lips. "Isn't this Joseph's son?" they asked.

[23]Jesus said to them, "Surely you will quote this proverb to me: 'Physician, heal yourself! Do here in your hometown what we have heard that you did in Capernaum.'"

[24]"I tell you the truth," he continued, "no prophet is accepted in his hometown. [25]I assure you that there were many widows in Israel in Elijah's time, when the sky was shut for three and a half years and there was a severe famine throughout the land. [26]Yet Elijah was not sent to any of them, but to a widow in Zarephath in the region of Sidon. [27]And there were many in Israel with leprosy[b] in the time of Elisha the prophet, yet not one of them was cleansed—only Naaman the Syrian."

[28]All the people in the synagogue were furious when they heard this. [29]They got up, drove him out of the town, and took him to the brow of the hill on which the town was built, in order to throw him down the cliff. [30]But he walked right through the crowd and went on his way.

a19 Isaiah 61:1, 2   *b27* The Greek word was used for various diseases affecting the skin—not necessarily leprosy.

NRSV

to let the oppressed go free,
[19] to proclaim the year of the Lord's favor."
[20]And he rolled up the scroll, gave it back to the attendant, and sat down. The eyes of all in the synagogue were fixed on him. [21]Then he began to say to them, "Today this scripture has been fulfilled in your hearing." [22]All spoke well of him and were amazed at the gracious words that came from his mouth. They said, "Is not this Joseph's son?" [23]He said to them, "Doubtless you will quote to me this proverb, 'Doctor, cure yourself!' And you will say, 'Do here also in your hometown the things that we have heard you did at Capernaum.'" [24]And he said, "Truly I tell you, no prophet is accepted in the prophet's hometown. [25]But the truth is, there were many widows in Israel in the time of Elijah, when the heaven was shut up three years and six months, and there was a severe famine over all the land; [26]yet Elijah was sent to none of them except to a widow at Zarephath in Sidon. [27]There were also many lepers[a] in Israel in the time of the prophet Elisha, and none of them was cleansed except Naaman the Syrian." [28]When they heard this, all in the synagogue were filled with rage. [29]They got up, drove him out of the town, and led him to the brow of the hill on which their town was built, so that they might hurl him off the cliff. [30]But he passed through the midst of them and went on his way.

a The terms *leper* and *leprosy* can refer to several diseases

COMMENTARY

Scholars generally agree that Luke's account of Jesus' preaching in Nazareth is based on the parallel account in Mark 6 and that it represents the conflation of various sources, so that tensions and rough transitions remain within Luke's account. Turned another way, the arguments for various sources also confirm that Luke did not find other accounts adequate and, therefore, constructed aspects of the following scene to serve as an exemplary introduction to Jesus' ministry.

In these few verses we find the following motifs: the anointing of the Spirit, the fulfillment of Scripture, the pattern of prophetic activities, the announcement of the gospel "to the Jew first," a specific illustration of acceptance being followed by rejection, and a dramatic reminder that the work of God that began in Galilee would extend to "the ends of the earth" (Acts 1:8). We will note the significance of each of these themes in the commentary that follows.

4:16-19, Reading the Prophet Isaiah.

The narrator's summary in vv. 16-17 guides the reader into the scene and prepares for the first spoken words in v. 18. Nazareth has figured prominently in the infancy narratives (1:26; 2:4, 39, 51), but Luke reminds us that this is where Jesus had been brought up. This first synagogue scene follows the reference to Jesus' teaching in the synagogues of Galilee in the previous verse and therefore sets up the teaching that follows as typical of what Jesus was doing throughout Galilee.

Jesus stood to read, as was customary. He would then sit while he taught (4:20; 5:3). Although we do not know exactly what transpired in the worship of a Jewish synagogue of that time, the following elements seem to have been present: the Shema, recitation of the Decalogue, the eighteen benedictions, the reading of Scripture, the Psalms, the exposition, and the blessing. Various people might have been asked to lead in reading and praying. Luke reports only part of the event. The Hazzan, or assistant, would have handed Jesus the scroll. By the first century there was a fixed triennial cycle of readings from the Torah, but arguments that the readings from the Prophets were also fixed by this date are inconclusive. Presumably Jesus was able to read the Scriptures in Hebrew and then interpret them in Aramaic, as would have been customary. (The practice of giving a translation and exposition of the text can be traced to Neh 8:8.) There was usually more than one reader, and each was expected to read at least three verses. The readings from the prophets were probably chosen because they had substantial or linguistic affinities with the reading from the Torah. Luke's description of Jesus' finding the place where the verses quoted from Isaiah occur probably means that Luke understood that Jesus himself chose this passage.

Luke 4:18-19 brings together in modified form verses from the Septuagint (LXX) version of Isa 61:1 and 58:6. Once more, the reader is given indications that Luke has carefully chosen and arranged elements of this account in order to tell the story in a particular way and convey certain understandings to the reader. The Lukan modifications are indicated in italics:

"The Spirit of the Lord is upon me,
because he has anointed me
to bring good news to the poor
[Luke omits: *to bind up the brokenhearted*.]
He has sent me to proclaim
release to the captives
and recovery of sight to the blind,
to let the oppressed go free [Isa 58:6],
to proclaim the year of the Lord's favor."

The phrase translated "he has sent me" (ἀπέσταλκέν με *apestalken me*) can be taken either with the preceding line or with what follows. Luke has also changed the verb in Isa 58:6 to an infinitive so that it fits the context and results in a sequence of four infinitives: to bring good news, to proclaim, to let go free, and to proclaim. The threefold repetition of the pronoun *me* also underscores the role of this passage as a description of Jesus' ministry. Significantly, Jesus does not go on to read the next phrase in Isa 61:2: "and the day of vengeance of our God."

The reference to the anointing of the Spirit connects these verses with the baptism of Jesus (3:22), and the description of the work of God's anointed prophet serves as a positive counterpoint to the temptations. It does not signal a separate anointing. The first part of the quotation explains the significance of the Spirit at the baptism and serves as a confirmation of Jesus' authority when later we read of activities that illustrate Jesus' fulfillment of the four infinitive phrases in this text. In Matthew, this same text underlies the first two of the beatitudes in the Sermon on the Mount.

Significantly, Jesus' work will be good news to the poor. The Magnificat praises the Lord for lifting up the lowly and sending the rich away empty (1:52-53). Later, Jesus announces God's blessing on the poor (6:20) and then refers to the fulfillment of the charge to bring good news to the poor in his response to John (7:22). The poor also figure more prominently in Jesus' teachings in Luke than in any other Gospel (14:13, 21; 16:20, 22; 18:22; 21:3).

The term used here for "captives" (αἰχμαλώτοι *aichmalōtoi*) does not appear elsewhere in the NT, and elsewhere Luke uses the term "release" (ἄφεσις *aphesis*) only for forgiveness of sins, but various events later in Jesus' ministry can be understood as illustrating the fulfillment of this aspect of his commission. The word for "release" recurs in the line from Isa 58:6, inserted here by Luke: release for the oppressed. Jesus released persons from various forms of bondage and oppression: economic (the poor), physical (the lame, the crippled), political (the condemned), and demonic. Forgiveness of sin, therefore, can also be seen as a form of release from bondage to iniquity (Acts 8:22-23).

The restoration of sight to the blind was closely associated with the prophetic vision of the fulfillment of God's promises to Israel (Isa 35:5; 42:6-7). When Jesus restores sight to the blind (as he does in Luke 7:21-22; 18:35), he is figuratively fulfilling God's work of salvation as foreseen by the prophet Isaiah. Jesus is dramatically fulfilling the role of the one who would be a "light for the nations" (see 2:32; Acts 13:47).[61] Like Jesus, his followers are to be light for others (Luke 8:16; 11:33).

The proclamation of the "year of the Lord's favor" in Isaiah 61 is connected with the Jubilee year legislation in Leviticus 25. Following a series of seven sevens, the fiftieth year was to be a time when "you shall proclaim liberty throughout the land to all its inhabitants" (Lev 25:10). It has occasionally been suggested that Jesus was actually proclaiming the observance of the Jubilee year through his reading of Isaiah 61, but this is far from certain. More likely is the interpretation that Jesus related the figure of "the year of the Lord's favor" to the kingdom of God (cf. Luke 4:43). Jesus' ministry signaled that the time for the liberation of the impoverished and oppressed had come, and in that respect at least his work would fulfill the ideal and the social concern of the Jubilee year.

The importance of the reading of Isaiah in this scene can scarcely be exaggerated. For Luke it proclaimed the fulfillment of Scripture and the hopes of Israel through Jesus' ministry as the Son of God. It stated the social concern that guided Jesus' work and allowed the reader to understand all that Jesus did as the fulfillment of his anointing by the Spirit. What Jesus understood by these verses, however, differed sharply from what those gathered in the synagogue assumed they meant.

4:20-27, Declaring the Inclusiveness of God's Mercy. From this point on, the scene in the synagogue becomes difficult to interpret. The

motivation and intent of Jesus' response to the people is not clear. Interpreters have, therefore, attempted various solutions: source critical—"Various traditions have been welded together here";[62] psychological—"Hidden in the hearts of his townsfolk are attitudes of which they, perhaps, are not yet conscious: resistance to God's purpose combined with jealous motives."[63] The challenge is to make sense of the text without reading into it.

The narrator provides a transition between the reading from Isaiah and Jesus' first words. Following the practice of synagogue worship, Jesus rolled up the scroll and handed it back to the attendant. He then sat down to teach. The tension and suspense are heightened by Luke's reporting that all eyes were fixed on Jesus.

Jesus' first words are electric. He announces that the centuries of waiting on God's blessing have ended: "Today this scripture has been fulfilled in your hearing." The words from Isaiah spoke of an anointing by the Spirit, the work of a prophet, and dramatic signs of God's redemption. The townspeople had heard reports of Jesus' teaching elsewhere and might reasonably have expected that if he was a prophet endowed by the Spirit of God he would favor his hometown with his mightiest works. Thus they would share in the fame of the prophet from Nazareth so that no longer would anyone be able to say (however wrongly) that there were no prophets from Galilee (John 7:52). In short, they heard Jesus' declaration of fulfillment as a promise of special favor for his own people and his "hometown" (i.e., his πατρίς *patris*).

As confirmation of the crowd's initial enthusiasm for Jesus' announcement, Luke reports that they bore witness to him and marveled at the "gracious words" he spoke. Luke is depicting a positive response to Jesus based on the content of Jesus' proclamation. If the people find him eloquent it is because they are pleased by what he has said. Their question "Is this not Joseph's son?" may be read with varying degrees of approval or skepticism. (1) Who would have thought that Joseph's boy would someday be God's prophet? (2) Isn't this the son of Joseph (whom we all know)? Does he really expect that we are going

---

61. See Robert C. Tannehill, *The Narrative Unity of Luke–Acts: A Literary Interpretation,* vol. 1: *The Gospel According to Luke,* FFNT (Philadelphia: Fortress, 1986) 67.

62. John Nolland, *Luke 1–9:20,* WBC 35A (Dallas: Word, 1989) 192.
63. Tannehill, *The Narrative Unity of Luke–Acts,* 69.

to believe that he is a prophet? (3) There may further be the irony that the townspeople think of Jesus as the son of Joseph when Luke has repeatedly established that he is the Son of God. Luke often reports reactions in universalizing terms—"all spoke well of him." Because the first part of v. 23 establishes a positive response to Jesus, there is no reason to read a hostile intent into the question. Therefore, the first paraphrase (1) is probably closer than the second, but the developments that come later in the story also render the irony of (3) possible also.

Verse 23, in which Jesus quotes the proverb "Doctor, cure yourself," is the crux of the difficulty. The alternatives facing the interpreter are (1) to take it as a retort or insult directed at Jesus personally. This is the natural sense of the proverb and is consistent with how it is used elsewhere, but it does not explain the sharp shift in tone from the preceding verse. (2) The proverb may be read as an extension of the preceding response to Jesus, if one takes the singular "yourself" as a reference to Jesus' hometown, as in the request that follows. The singular more appropriately refers to Jesus than to Nazareth, but the story flows more smoothly if one follows the latter reading of the proverb. The meaning of the proverb Jesus quotes to the crowd is explained by the rest of v. 23. Jesus has understood the crowd's positive response; they are eager for him to begin to do the works of God's grace among them. They are ready to share in the benefits that might accrue to the prophet's hometown and miffed because he has already done wonderful things in Capernaum.

The second proverb occurs four times in the Gospels, each time in a different form:

Mark 6:4 "Prophets are not without honor [ἄτιμος *atimos*], except in their hometown [πατρίδι *patridi*], and among their own kin, and in their own house."

Matthew 13:57 "Prophets are not without honor [*atimos*] except in their own country (*patridi*) and in their own house."

Luke 4:24 "Truly [ἀμήν *amēn*] I tell you, no prophet is accepted [δεκτός *dektos*] in the prophet's hometown [*patridi*]."

John 4:44 "A prophet has no honor [τιμήν *timēn*] in the prophet's own country [*patridi*]."

The NRSV changes the singular "prophet" in Mark 6:4 and Matt 13:57 into a plural in order to avoid using a masculine pronoun later, and *patridi* is translated variously as "hometown" (Mark and Luke) or "country" (Matthew and John). Only Luke introduces the proverb with the initial *amēn,* which does not occur outside of Jesus' words in the NT and is unprecedented in earlier sources. Three points are notable regarding Luke's use of the proverb: (1) Luke and John give the proverb in a negative form, without an exception clause; (2) Luke uses *dektos* (as in Isaiah; see v. 19) rather than *atimos* or *timē* as in the other forms of the proverb; and (3) the term *patris* can mean either "hometown" or "home country," an ambiguity that will become important in the rest of this scene, since Jesus' interpretation of Isaiah moves from the first (Nazareth) to the second (Israel). Not only will Jesus be rejected by his hometown, but he will also be rejected by his own people; by the end of Acts, Paul will turn to the Gentiles as well.

The people of Nazareth had heard Jesus' declaration of the fulfillment of God's promises as a guarantee of God's blessing on them, but Jesus affirmed a fulfillment that was not limited to Israel only—God would bless all the poor, all the captives. Neither was the fulfillment Jesus announced radically different from the work of the prophets. Israel's Scriptures themselves bear witness to God's blessing on Gentiles as well as Jews. Reminders of the mighty works of Elijah and Elisha follow naturally after the proverb about the prophet and the prophet's home. (The relationship between Jesus and Elijah will be developed further in Luke 7:11-17.)

The comparison between Jesus and Elijah is double edged. On the one hand, many in Israel did not receive God's blessing. On the other hand, some Gentiles did. The time of Elijah was remembered as the period when the heavens were shut and it did not rain for three and a half years (1 Kgs 18:1; cf. Jas 5:17). By the time of Jesus the period of three and a half years had also been connected with the period of similar duration during which the Syrians persecuted Israel during the time of Antiochus IV Epiphanes and the Maccabees (Dan 7:25; 12:7; cf. Rev 11:2; 12:6, 14). Elijah, however, was sent to Zarephath, which belonged to Sidon, and there he met a widow who was responsive to the instructions God had given Elijah. When her son died, Elijah restored him to life (1 Kgs 17:17-24). Similarly, there were many lepers in Israel during the time of Elisha who had a "double portion" of Elijah's spirit (2 Kgs 2:9). The passive verbs imply God's direction: God closed the heavens (4:25), God sent Elijah (4:26), and God cleansed Naaman (4:27; see 2 Kgs 5:1-14).

4:28-30, Jesus Driven Out of Town. The people of Nazareth were filled with rage. This time the passive verb does not imply God's action. At first Jesus had seemed to be promising that God's blessing would be poured out on them. They would share in the unexpected bounty of having a prophet arise from their midst. But now Jesus has told them that God's blessing would not come upon them but upon others. No historical or ethnic boundaries would contain or limit what God was about to do. The poor would hear good news, and the rich would hear woes. Those with faith would be blessed, while others would hear judgment.

The people of Nazareth then began to act on their rage. They drove Jesus out of town (cf. 23:26; Acts 7:58). The end of this scene is so condensed and elliptical that interpreters have often felt the need to fill in conjectural details. The site in question cannot be located with any certainty. Nor is it necessary to speculate about a miraculous deliverance or the force of Jesus' personality or presence. The intent of the crowd was hostile, but Luke emphasizes that Jesus was not stopped by them. The emphasis is on the last word, which in the Greek text is a verb that implies a continuous action: "He was going on" (ἐπορεύετο *eporeueto*). The verb (πορεύομαι *poreuomai*) recurs frequently in Luke as the Gospel narrates the journeys that eventually lead Jesus to Jerusalem and the cross.

REFLECTIONS

This scene is more significant than its brevity might suggest. Its position at the beginning of Jesus' ministry, its emphasis on the Spirit and Scripture, and its depiction of themes that will dominate the rest of the Gospel all point to its paradigmatic character. Readers of the Gospel now understand that all Jesus does in the coming chapters occurs by the power of the Spirit. Jesus teaches, preaches, heals, and casts out demons. He moves among the poor, the outcast, the sick, and the blind. His actions fulfill the Scriptures, especially the Prophets, but even those who awaited the fulfillment of the Scriptures took offense at Jesus and eventually put him to death. This scene suggests that the basis for their hostility toward Jesus was a difference in the way they read the Scriptures. The people of Jesus' hometown read the Scriptures as promises of God's exclusive covenant with them, a covenant that involved promises of deliverance from their oppressors. Jesus came announcing deliverance, but it was not a national deliverance but God's promise of liberation for all the poor and oppressed regardless of nationality, gender, or race. When the radical inclusiveness of Jesus' announcement became clear to those gathered in the synagogue in Nazareth, their commitment to their own community boundaries took precedence over their joy that God had sent a prophet among them. In the end, because they were not open to the prospect of others' sharing in the bounty of God's deliverance, they themselves were unable to receive it.

Not only is this scene paradigmatic of Jesus' life and ministry, but it is also a reminder that God's grace is never subject to the limitations and boundaries of any nation, church, group, or race. Those who would exclude others thereby exclude themselves. Human beings may be instruments of God's grace for others, but we are never free to set limits on who may receive that grace. Throughout history, the gospel has always been more radically inclusive than any group, denomination, or church, so we continually struggle for a breadth of love and acceptance that more nearly approximates the breadth of God's love. The paradox of the gospel, therefore, is that the unlimited grace that it offers so scandalizes us that we are unable to receive it. Jesus could not do more for his hometown because they were not open to him. How much more might God be able to do with us if we were ready to transcend the boundaries of community and limits of love that we ourselves have erected?

LUKE 4:31-44, TEACHING AND HEALING IN CAPERNAUM

NIV

³¹Then he went down to Capernaum, a town in Galilee, and on the Sabbath began to teach the people. ³²They were amazed at his teaching, because his message had authority.

³³In the synagogue there was a man possessed by a demon, an evil[a] spirit. He cried out at the top of his voice, ³⁴"Ha! What do you want with us, Jesus of Nazareth? Have you come to destroy us? I know who you are—the Holy One of God!"

³⁵"Be quiet!" Jesus said sternly. "Come out of him!" Then the demon threw the man down before them all and came out without injuring him.

³⁶All the people were amazed and said to each other, "What is this teaching? With authority and power he gives orders to evil spirits and they come out!" ³⁷And the news about him spread throughout the surrounding area.

³⁸Jesus left the synagogue and went to the home of Simon. Now Simon's mother-in-law was suffering from a high fever, and they asked Jesus to help her. ³⁹So he bent over her and rebuked the fever, and it left her. She got up at once and began to wait on them.

⁴⁰When the sun was setting, the people brought to Jesus all who had various kinds of sickness, and laying his hands on each one, he healed them. ⁴¹Moreover, demons came out of many people, shouting, "You are the Son of God!" But he rebuked them and would not allow them to speak, because they knew he was the Christ.[b]

⁴²At daybreak Jesus went out to a solitary place. The people were looking for him and when they came to where he was, they tried to keep him from leaving them. ⁴³But he said, "I must preach the good news of the kingdom of God to the other towns also, because that is why I was sent." ⁴⁴And he kept on preaching in the synagogues of Judea.[c]

a33 Greek unclean; also in verse 36   b41 Or Messiah   c44 Or the land of the Jews; some manuscripts Galilee

NRSV

31He went down to Capernaum, a city in Galilee, and was teaching them on the sabbath. ³²They were astounded at his teaching, because he spoke with authority. ³³In the synagogue there was a man who had the spirit of an unclean demon, and he cried out with a loud voice, ³⁴"Let us alone! What have you to do with us, Jesus of Nazareth? Have you come to destroy us? I know who you are, the Holy One of God." ³⁵But Jesus rebuked him, saying, "Be silent, and come out of him!" When the demon had thrown him down before them, he came out of him without having done him any harm. ³⁶They were all amazed and kept saying to one another, "What kind of utterance is this? For with authority and power he commands the unclean spirits, and out they come!" ³⁷And a report about him began to reach every place in the region.

38After leaving the synagogue he entered Simon's house. Now Simon's mother-in-law was suffering from a high fever, and they asked him about her. ³⁹Then he stood over her and rebuked the fever, and it left her. Immediately she got up and began to serve them.

40As the sun was setting, all those who had any who were sick with various kinds of diseases brought them to him; and he laid his hands on each of them and cured them. ⁴¹Demons also came out of many, shouting, "You are the Son of God!" But he rebuked them and would not allow them to speak, because they knew that he was the Messiah.[a]

42At daybreak he departed and went into a deserted place. And the crowds were looking for him; and when they reached him, they wanted to prevent him from leaving them. ⁴³But he said to them, "I must proclaim the good news of the kingdom of God to the other cities also; for I was sent for this purpose." ⁴⁴So he continued proclaiming the message in the synagogues of Judea.[b]

aOr the Christ   bOther ancient authorities read Galilee

COMMENTARY

The rest of this chapter amplifies the nature of Jesus' ministry in a parallel setting. Jesus travels to Capernaum, where he is again in the synagogue, again meets conflict, and ultimately moves on. The scene in Capernaum is not simply a repetition of the scene in Nazareth, however. Jesus heals the sick and casts out demons, and then declares that he has been sent to preach the kingdom in other cities also. Luke's account of Jesus' work in Capernaum is divided into four distinct scenes, the last of which also leads Jesus out of Galilee and concludes the initial period of Jesus' ministry there (cf. 4:14).

4:31-37, Teaching and Healing in the Synagogue at Capernaum. The tradition underlying this scene is also found in Mark 1:21-28, but whereas redaction critics have generally read Luke against the text of Mark, attention to Luke's narrative rhetoric demands that we also read it in the context of the foregoing scene in Nazareth.

From the hill country around Nazareth, Jesus went down to Capernaum, a fishing village on the shore of the Sea of Galilee. The reference to Capernaum as "a city in Galilee" may serve to identify it for readers unfamiliar with the geography of Palestine, but it also ties the coming episode to the initial phase of the Galilean ministry that was introduced in Luke 4:14. Verses 15-16 link together teaching on the sabbath and the synagogue, so that Luke is now able to report teaching on the sabbath in 4:31 without explicitly mentioning the synagogue setting until v. 33. The repetition of the setting (teaching on the sabbath in a synagogue) prepares the reader for a repetition of the events of the previous scene. The amazement of the people (v. 32) echoes the initial response of the people of Nazareth (v. 22), and in both contexts Luke comments on the character of Jesus' words. This time it is the authority of his word (cf. vv. 22, 32). This is the first reference to Jesus' authority (there is no direct reference to authority in the infancy material), so its occurrence here stands in direct relation to the devil's lure of the promise of authority (4:6). The devil promised Jesus authority and glory; here the people marvel because he teaches with authority. Jesus possessed the authority of the Spirit, and

that authority was evident in his teaching. In the previous episode he did not cite a succession of rabbis as his authority (as others did) but read a passage of Scripture with three first-person singular pronouns and declared it fulfilled in their hearing. We should imagine that his teaching in Capernaum followed the same pattern.

At this point the story departs from the previous scene. A man with "an unclean spirit" challenges Jesus. This is one of four exorcisms in Luke and the first of the miracle stories. In effect it demonstrates that the power and authority of Jesus' words (now recorded in the Gospel) were also demonstrated in his mighty works. A contest of spirits is also implicit here. What Jesus did, he did because the Spirit of the Lord was upon him (v. 18), and the spirit of an unclean demon was no match for the Spirit of the Lord. Calling the name of the opponent was a means of exposing him or gaining control over him. In this context there is a certain irony to the title "Jesus of Nazareth," since his hometown had rejected Jesus and he would not return there again. The demon rightly perceives Jesus as a threat; what Jesus was doing would eventually break the oppressing, dehumanizing power of all that is demonic in human experience.

"The Holy One of God" is a title drawn from tradition (Mark 1:24) that does not occur elsewhere in Luke (but cf. 1:35). Jesus silenced the unclean spirit and commanded it to come out of the man. Luke heightens the miracle by reporting that although the demon threw the man down it did not harm him. The noun Luke uses to describe the response of the crowd is found only in Luke and Acts (θάμβος *thambos*) in the NT (Luke 5:9; Acts 3:10). Jesus silences the demon with a word, so the people question among themselves, "What kind of word is this?" As readers who have just read the programmatic teaching of Jesus in Nazareth, we understand the character of the word in question. Jesus has not only declared fulfillment of the promise of deliverance of the captives, but by his word he has also released one who has been held captive by a demonic spirit. Jesus had returned to Galilee "in the power of the Spirit" (4:14); now that power was becoming evident to others. The initial response, however, is amazement and questioning, not confession. The question raised in the synagogue in Capernaum will be echoed repeatedly in the coming chapters as various characters in the Gospel strive to understand who Jesus is. The result is that Jesus' fame spread (cf. again 4:14). Although Jesus does not leave Capernaum, this first scene of his work there concludes with a typical Lukan report of a coming or going; news of Jesus *went out* to *every* place in that region.

4:38-39, Healing Simon's Mother-in-Law.
A second demonstration of the power of Jesus' word follows immediately. The scene begins with a transitional report of Jesus' movement from the synagogue to Peter's house. At this stage in Luke's account, Jesus has not yet called any disciples, so there is no reference to Andrew, James, and John as there is in Mark (1:29). In the Lukan sequence, therefore, the healing of Peter's mother-in-law may serve as part of the preparation for Peter's call to discipleship (5:10-11).

Lacking a modern understanding of disease, infection, and fever, Luke describes the mother-in-law's illness in terms that border on possession. Luke uses a term that suggests that she was oppressed, ruled, or "held captive" (συνέχω *synechō*) by the fever. The fever is seen as the cause of her illness, not a symptom of an infection. When "they" (the family?) ask Jesus about her, he assumes a commanding position—"he stood over her"—and commands the fever to leave her. Jesus rebukes the fever, just as he had rebuked the unclean spirit (cf. 4:39; 4:35, 41), and the fever "released" her, just as Jesus had declared that he had come to "proclaim release to the captives." In both instances the verb used is the same.

Luke's account of the healing of Peter's mother-in-law functions differently from Mark's in that it demonstrates the fulfillment of Jesus' prophetic announcement in Nazareth, and it dramatizes the power of Jesus' word, which was also emphasized in the first scene in the Capernaum cycle (see 4:36). The scene closes with the report that Peter's mother-in-law recovered instantly and that she began to serve them. In this respect, she serves as a pattern for all who would subsequently be delivered by Jesus' word and then express their gratitude through serving (see esp. the role of the women in 8:1-3; 10:38-42; 23:49, 55; 24:24).

4:40-41, Healing the Sick. The third healing scene in Capernaum culminates in the confession of Jesus as the Son of God and the Christ. This third scene continues the portrayal of Jesus as healer and exorcist, as in the previous scenes, and the verb translated "rebuke" (ἐπιτιμάω *epitimaō*), which occurs in each of the three scenes, provides another link between them.

The third scene occurs following sundown, significant in this instance because it marks the end of the sabbath. Carrying the sick and healing those with chronic conditions would have been considered a violation of sabbath laws, but it is not clear whether Luke is sensitive to this point or would have expected his readers to grasp it (cf. the more cumbersome temporal references in Mark 1:32-34). Luke streamlines the narrative. The sick are brought to Jesus, and he heals them by laying his hands on them. The laying on of hands was accompanied by prayer in the OT and was used to invoke God's blessing on the person. References to laying on hands for healing do not occur in Jewish literature until the NT period.[64]

As some were being healed, demons came out of them. Thus the line between healings and exorcisms is blurred. In the previous scene Jesus healed by rebuking the fever (as he had previously rebuked the demons); now he exorcises by laying his hands on the sick. This Lukan summary of Jesus' power to heal and exorcise culminates in two christological titles that have no parallel in the Markan account. The demons shouted "You are the Son of God" because they knew that he was the Christ. The combination of these two titles in this summary greatly enhances its significance in the plot of the Gospel. Luke 4 opened with the devil tempting Jesus with the challenge, "If you are the Son of God" (4:3, 9). The townspeople of Nazareth supposed that Jesus was the son of Joseph (4:22), but the chapter ends with the demons broadcasting Jesus' divine sonship. Others will confess Jesus as the Son of God only in Luke 8:28 (the Gerasene demoniac); 9:35 (the voice from heaven); and 22:70 (the unbelieving question of the council of elders, chief priests, and scribes). Adding further weight to the demons' cry is the narrator's comment that they knew that he was the Christ. Jesus was announced as the

---

64. See Joseph A. Fitzmyer, *The Gospel According to Luke (I–IX),* AB 28 (Garden City, N.Y.: Doubleday, 1981) 555.

Christ at his birth (2:11, 26; cf. 3:15), but prior to the trial and death of Jesus the term occurs only here, in 9:20 (Peter's confession) and 20:41 (Jesus' question regarding the Davidic sonship of the Messiah). The two christological titles serve, therefore, to bring the chapter to a climax at the end of the Capernaum cycle. What is implicit in the reading from Isaiah in Nazareth has become explicit in the healings and exorcisms in Capernaum. Only at Peter's confession in Luke 9 and in the trial and death of Jesus will the Gospel again declare Jesus' identity so clearly. The silencing of the demons may explain why such titles do not recur more frequently, but the function of the silencing is not as clear in Luke as it is in Mark.

4:42-44, Departure from Capernaum. The fourth scene concludes both the Capernaum cycle and the beginning of Jesus' ministry in Galilee (4:14-44). The next day Jesus goes to a deserted place, presumably alone, but Luke does not mention prayer as does Mark (1:35) even though Luke normally emphasizes the importance of prayer for Jesus. The crowds seek Jesus to prevent him from leaving them. In Mark those who wanted to prevail on Jesus to stay in Capernaum were "Peter and those with him," but Luke has not yet related the calling of Peter, and the reference to the crowds creates a parallel with the response Jesus received in Nazareth. There too the people wanted to keep Jesus' mighty works for themselves only. In both cases Jesus refused to allow the crowds to impose their restrictions on the work of the kingdom. The same verb is used in both places: Jesus must "travel on"

(πορεύομαι *poreuomai*; 4:30, 42, 43), carrying the good news of the kingdom to other towns.

As with the confession of Jesus as the Son of God, so references to the kingdom of the earth and the kingdom of God bracket the chapter (4:5, 43). The intent of proclaiming the kingdom also serves to make explicit the message of Jesus that began with the reading of Isaiah 61 in Nazareth and that will repeatedly occupy the teachings of Jesus from Luke 6:20 on. Similarly, just as Jesus had declared in Nazareth that the Spirit of the Lord had "sent" (ἀποστέλλω *apostellō*) him to proclaim release to the captives (4:18), so also Jesus left Capernaum referring to the purpose for which he had been "sent." Again, the passive suggests that God is the one who sent him (cf. 9:48; 10:16). God's redemptive purpose, which guides the course of the action in Luke and Acts, propels Jesus to carry the preaching of the kingdom—which included healing the sick and exorcising demons—throughout all the land of the Jews. The reference to Judea in v. 44 is sufficiently puzzling that scribes altered it to Galilee in various manuscripts, but the effect of the reference is not to mark the end of Jesus' ministry in Galilee but to drive home the point of its spread throughout all the region of Palestine. Both in Luke and in other sources "Judea" is occasionally used to designate not the particular region south of Galilee and Samaria, but all of the land of the Jews (see Luke 1:5; 7:17; 23:5; Acts 10:37; 1 Thess 2:14).

REFLECTIONS

The Capernaum cycle is composed of a series of four scenes in which Jesus performs the first healings and exorcisms in the Gospel of Luke. The interpreter must decide at what level to engage these accounts: literary motif, theology, or history. The foregoing commentary has set this cycle in its literary context and illustrated how it coheres and functions as a unit within the Gospel.

1. As we move to the second level, the following questions press themselves upon us: What does it mean theologically to affirm that Jesus healed and exorcised demons? Is there a didactic purpose for these stories? What do they mean for our understanding of christology or providence? The place to start is with the text itself. Luke's account of the healings in Capernaum makes several connections. It connects the healings and exorcisms with Jesus' teaching so that the power of his words is dramatically demonstrated in his mighty works. By implication, where his words are heard, there the power that was manifested in the miracles continues to be active. In the contemporary congregation, the hearing of the gospel leads to acts of ministry in which the hungry are fed (soup kitchens), the blind see (eye clinics, literacy programs), the lame walk (programs for the disabled), and prisoners are set free (prison ministries and rehabilitation programs).

Running through both the Nazareth and the Capernaum episode, however, is the warning that the power of God cannot be possessed, contained, or limited for our own purposes. It moves on, and it is always reaching across the barriers that separate communities and peoples from one another. The mighty works of Jesus' ministry, however, are a manifestation of the power of the Spirit. As the Lord's anointed, Jesus was empowered to extend the work of the prophets and begin the work of the kingdom. What was stated in the reading from Isaiah 61 saw its first small beginnings in the healings in Capernaum. God was moving to free persons from the debilitating and dehumanizing conditions that prevented human beings from living as God willed life to be. In that respect, the text gives up a significant clue when as a result of Jesus' healings, demons flee from those who have been delivered from their illness or impairment. The healings are theologically significant, therefore, because they convey important insights into God's intention for human life and God's unrelenting efforts to free captives and give sight to the blind. Healing and deliverance are manifestations of the work of the kingdom.

What the text does not answer is why some are healed and others are not. Naaman the Syrian and the widow at Zarephath were persons of faith, but the demoniac in the synagogue cried out against Jesus, so that Luke describes his cry as the utterance of the spirit of an unclean demon. Yet this man too was delivered from the demon. Faith or lack thereof may be part of the answer (Luke does not record any miracles performed in Nazareth), but it is not the whole answer. There is still a freedom to God's grace that is not controlled by human response.

2. The most difficult level of reflection is the third, the historical. Did Jesus heal persons? Did Jesus "cast out demons"? What does it mean to say that Jesus exorcised demons? The quest for the historical Jesus began in earnest with the Rationalists who could not accept the miracle accounts of the Gospels at face value. The mighty acts of the Gospels were called "miracles," or acts contrary to the "laws of nature." The Rationalists then proposed non-miraculous, "rational," or reasonable interpretations of the miracle stories. Jesus cured psychosomatic conditions; he appeared to be walking on water while walking beside the lake; he led the multitude to share their food with one another or instructed the disciples to bring food out of a hidden cave; and he "raised" those who had swooned or had been comatose for a brief period. Recently, however, theologians have contended that there is more mystery in human experience than the Rationalists admitted, that God should not be seen as invading natural processes from outside them but as working within natural processes. The line between natural and supernatural has blurred considerably. Historians of Jesus have likewise asserted that Jesus was a healer, as were other charismatic Galilean Jews.[65] While the debate is far from settled, most would agree that the healings and exorcisms of the Gospel narratives cannot be dismissed as first-century superstition. They represent an early Christian interpretation of an aspect of Jesus' historical ministry, and to that extent they are vital to our understanding of Jesus.

By healing the sick, Jesus fulfilled the work and words of the prophets, as we will have occasion to note in coming chapters. Jesus does not perform just any miracles; he does works that are similar to the works of Moses, Elijah and Elisha, and the words of Isaiah. The miracles, therefore, declare the continuance of God's mighty presence among God's people. The miracles declare the fulfillment of Moses and the prophets in Jesus.

The casting out of demons, however, is not a part of the OT tradition. Here we are drawn into the culture and worldview of first-century Palestine. Whereas today we tend to attribute symptoms to internal causes such as chemical disorders or mental illness, first-century Jews

---

65. See, e.g., John Dominic Crossan, *The Historical Jesus: The Life of a Mediterranean Jewish Peasant* (San Francisco: HarperCollins, 1991).

attributed similar phenomena to external powers acting on the person. Perhaps the most honest response for an interpreter is to acknowledge how limited our understanding of spiritual and demonic forces is. While we may not wish to encourage belief in demons that invade human persons, neither are the explanations of the Rationalists very satisfying. The Gospels declare that Jesus approached the mystery of evil in human experience and conquered it. In his presence and by his word or act, human beings were delivered from their bondage, derangement, or illness and restored to wholeness. In such stories we understand God's nature and work among us even if we do not also always understand the mystery of the spiritual or demonic forces that some human beings experience.

LUKE 5:1–6:16, CALLING AND TRAINING DISCIPLES

OVERVIEW

To this point Jesus has acted alone, unaccompanied by disciples. In the next major section (5:1–6:16), however, Jesus begins to call others to leave everything and join him in the work of the kingdom. This section is framed by two scenes that feature the disciples: the call of Simon and the fishermen (5:1-11) and the appointment of the Twelve (6:12-16). Between these two scenes Jesus heals a leper (5:12-16) and a paralytic (5:17-26), calls Levi to follow him and eats with tax collectors (5:27-39), allows his disciples to pluck grain on the sabbath (6:1-5), and heals a man with a withered hand on the sabbath (6:6-11). Throughout this section we see the work of the kingdom spreading and separating those who respond from those who refuse Jesus' call. The latter are often represented by the scribes and Pharisees.

Striking comparisons can be made between Mark and Luke in their handling of these scenes. Throughout this section, Luke reproduces Markan material with varying degrees of revision:

Luke 5:1-3—Mark 1:16-20; 4:1-2
Luke 5:8-11—Mark 1:16-20
Luke 5:12-16—Mark 1:40-45
Luke 5:17-26—Mark 2:1-12
Luke 5:27-32—Mark 2:13-17
Luke 5:33-38—Mark 2:18-22

Luke 6:1-5—Mark 2:23-28
Luke 6:6-11—Mark 3:1-6

The similarities between the two accounts should not mask the significant differences. The call of the first disciples (paralleled in Luke 5:1-11) comes just fifteen verses into Mark's Gospel (1:16-20). Mark races through the ministry of John, the baptism of Jesus, the temptation in the wilderness, and the announcement of the gospel of the kingdom. By contrast, Luke has provided extensive interpretation of Jesus' birth and identity as the Son of God, God's redemptive work has been highlighted, the prophetic context of Jesus' work has been presented, and Jesus' teaching in Capernaum and healing of Peter's mother-in-law have been reported. In terms of the characterization of Peter and the other fishermen, Luke's sequence makes their response to his call to discipleship psychologically plausible. Perhaps more significantly, Luke has delayed the introduction of characters who might serve as role models for the reader's response to the challenge of the gospel until the identity of Jesus and the nature of his ministry have been clearly developed. The reader is now ready to begin to consider a response to the call to follow Jesus, just as the first disciples turned away from their daily pursuits to give themselves to the kingdom work to which Jesus called them.

Luke 5:1-11, Calling the Fishermen

NIV

5 One day as Jesus was standing by the Lake of Gennesaret,[a] with the people crowding around him and listening to the word of God, [2]he saw at the water's edge two boats, left there by the fishermen, who were washing their nets. [3]He got into one of the boats, the one belonging to Simon, and asked him to put out a little from shore. Then he sat down and taught the people from the boat.

[4]When he had finished speaking, he said to Simon, "Put out into deep water, and let down[b] the nets for a catch."

[5]Simon answered, "Master, we've worked hard all night and haven't caught anything. But because you say so, I will let down the nets."

[6]When they had done so, they caught such a large number of fish that their nets began to break. [7]So they signaled their partners in the other boat to come and help them, and they came and filled both boats so full that they began to sink.

[8]When Simon Peter saw this, he fell at Jesus' knees and said, "Go away from me, Lord; I am a sinful man!" [9]For he and all his companions were astonished at the catch of fish they had taken, [10]and so were James and John, the sons of Zebedee, Simon's partners.

Then Jesus said to Simon, "Don't be afraid; from now on you will catch men." [11]So they pulled their boats up on shore, left everything and followed him.

a1 That is, Sea of Galilee   b4 The Greek verb is plural.

NRSV

5 Once while Jesus[a] was standing beside the lake of Gennesaret, and the crowd was pressing in on him to hear the word of God, [2]he saw two boats there at the shore of the lake; the fishermen had gone out of them and were washing their nets. [3]He got into one of the boats, the one belonging to Simon, and asked him to put out a little way from the shore. Then he sat down and taught the crowds from the boat. [4]When he had finished speaking, he said to Simon, "Put out into the deep water and let down your nets for a catch." [5]Simon answered, "Master, we have worked all night long but have caught nothing. Yet if you say so, I will let down the nets." [6]When they had done this, they caught so many fish that their nets were beginning to break. [7]So they signaled their partners in the other boat to come and help them. And they came and filled both boats, so that they began to sink. [8]But when Simon Peter saw it, he fell down at Jesus' knees, saying, "Go away from me, Lord, for I am a sinful man!" [9]For he and all who were with him were amazed at the catch of fish that they had taken; [10]and so also were James and John, sons of Zebedee, who were partners with Simon. Then Jesus said to Simon, "Do not be afraid; from now on you will be catching people." [11]When they had brought their boats to shore, they left everything and followed him.

a Gk he

COMMENTARY

The call of the fishermen takes the form of an extended pronouncement story (a story that features a saying of Jesus) centered around Jesus' challenge to Simon in v. 10b. The larger unit is a composite constructed from three distinct parts: the setting by the lake (5:1-3), for which Luke used Mark 4:1-2; a miracle story—the catch of fish (5:4-7), for which there is a parallel in John 21:3-8; and the call of the fishermen (5:8-11), for which Luke used Mark 1:16-20. The first three verses set the scene and introduce the characters. The catch of fish introduces the first dialogue between Jesus and Simon Peter and prepares for the call to discipleship at the end of the scene. Isolating the dialogue serves to highlight its role in this scene:

Jesus: "Put out into the deep water and let down your nets for a catch."

Simon: "Master, we have worked all night long

but have caught nothing. Yet if you say so, I will let down the nets."

. . . .

Simon: "Go away from me, Lord, for I am a sinful man!"

Jesus: "Do not be afraid; from now on you will be catching people."

Following the narrative technique of framing scenes or episodes by means of entrances and departures that Luke uses repeatedly, the scene is introduced by a reference to the crowd's coming to Jesus and closes with the report that the fishermen left everything to follow Jesus.

5:1-3, Teaching the Crowd Beside the Lake. The temporal relationship between this scene and the preceding one is left vague. Whereas Luke 4:42-44 indicates that Jesus left Capernaum and went to Judea, the beginning of Luke 5 finds Jesus still in Galilee, beside the lake. This is the only place in the NT where the lake is identified by reference to the adjacent territory (Gennesaret, south of Capernaum; cf. Matt 14:34; Mark 6:53), but the designation is found in Josephus, who knew Galilee well.[66] The crowd is presumably the same crowd introduced in 4:42, who were thronging to Jesus because of the mighty works he was doing. Consistent with Jesus' announcement in 4:43 that he had to declare the good news of the kingdom of God, Jesus is not healing but preaching "the word of God" (cf. 8:11, 21; 11:28). In the light of Luke 4, the reader is prepared to associate "the word of God" with the work of the prophets, God's redemptive work declared in the canticles of the birth narratives, the preaching of John the Baptist, and above all the teaching of Jesus in the synagogue in Nazareth.

The primary elements of this scene are all found in Mark in the call of the fishermen and the introduction to the parables in Mark 4: the lake, the boat, the crowd, and the fishermen washing their nets. As in Mark 4:1-2, Jesus gets into the boat to teach the crowd on the shore. The second boat will be summoned following the catch of fish (cf. v. 7).

5:4-7, Enclosing a Catch of Fish. Fish was one of the staples in first-century Palestine, where more fish was eaten than any other meat (see Luke 11:11; 24:42) and a thriving fishing industry flourished on the Sea of Galilee. Fish was eaten fresh, processed, salted, dried, or pickled, for export. The fish of the Sea of Galilee are of three main varieties: the *cichlidae,* a family of large panfish that includes "St. Peter's fish"; the *cyprinidae,* or carp family; and the *siluridae,* or catfish. The Jews did not eat catfish, however, because it did not have "fins and scales" (Lev 11:9-12; Deut 14:9-10).

The various types of nets mentioned in the NT were probably similar to the nets used by Arab fishermen until recent decades. These include (1) the casting net (ἀμφίβληστρον *amphiblēstron,* Matt 4:18), a circular net that was cast by a wading fisherman; (2) the trammel net (though this word is used generically for various nets [δίκτυον *diktyon,* Matt 4:20]), or a line of three nets hanging from floats, the inner net having a small mesh that trapped the fish; and (3) the drag net (σαγήνη *sagēnē,* Matt 13:47), which could be several hundred yards long. Luke's description of putting out into deep water and letting down nets suggests that the fishermen were using the trammel nets.

Luke underscores the wonder of the catch of fish by saying that it filled the boats so much that they began to sink. Recently, a first-century fishing boat was recovered from the mud near the edge of the Sea of Galilee. The shell of the boat is 26.5 feet long, 7.5 feet wide, and 4.5 feet deep and could be rowed or sailed.[67]

By placing the call of Simon Peter and the other fishermen after the miraculous catch of fish, Luke provides a psychologically plausible account of why they left everything to follow Jesus. Luke 5:4-7 seems to depend on a traditional story found also in John 21:1-14, where a strikingly similar catch of fish is reported in a post-resurrection context. Raymond E. Brown lists ten points shared by the two accounts: (1) The disciples had fished all night with no results, (2) Jesus challenged them to let down the nets, (3) the disciples enclosed an enormous catch, (4) the effect on the nets is mentioned, (5) Peter reacts, (6) Jesus is

---

66. Josephus *The Jewish War* 3:463, 506.

67. For a more detailed discussion of the fishing industry and the status of Galilean fishermen, see R. Alan Culpepper, *John, the Son of Zebedee: The Life of a Legend* (Columbia: University of South Carolina Press, 1994) 10-15.

called Lord, (7) other fishermen take part in the catch but say nothing, (8) the theme of following Jesus, (9) the catch of fish "symbolizes a successful Christian missionary endeavor," and (10) the same words appear at various points in the two stories.[68] In spite of all these similarities, the differences between the two accounts should also be noted, the foremost being its setting in Luke as the call of Simon Peter rather than as his post-resurrection reconciliation to Jesus following Peter's treachery in the courtyard during the trial of Jesus. Other differences between the two accounts arise from the fact that in John 21 Jesus is not in the boat but on the shore, there is only one boat, and the nets are untorn despite the large catch.

What are we to make of these parallel accounts? Do the traditions reach back to one event or two? If one event lies behind both accounts, was it originally the call of Peter to discipleship or a post-resurrection appearance? The tradition has apparently gone through an extended process of development, but the similarities are sufficient to point to a common tradition lying behind both Luke 5 and John 21. Three considerations tilt the balance in favor of the hypothesis that Luke has taken a post-Easter appearance tradition and placed it back in the ministry of Jesus. First, other accounts of the call of Peter and the other fishermen to discipleship do not involve a miraculous catch of fish (Mark 1:16-20; Matt 4:18-21; John 1:35-42). In Luke, moreover, the account of the catch of fish is sandwiched between other traditional elements of the call of the disciples (Luke 5:1-3, 10-11), suggesting that Luke has created this setting for the story. Second, following Luke's geographical scheme of the ministry in Galilee—the journey to Jerusalem, and the mission beginning from Jerusalem following Jesus' death and resurrection—there is no place for a Galilean appearance (as in Mark and Matthew). The story of the catch of fish from the Sea of Galilee, if included, had to be placed somewhere during Jesus' ministry in Galilee. Third, Peter's response

("Go away from me, Lord, for I am a sinful man!") would have a special force if it followed his denials of Jesus in the courtyard. Luke seems to have retrojected the tradition of the catch of fish into the ministry as a call story. The alternative is that John 21:1-14 is a story from the ministry of Jesus that has been recast around the themes of resurrection and eucharist. Whether the miracle story was originally an appearance tradition is indeed debatable, since no other appearance takes the form of a miracle story. This story, therefore, may have had a complicated history that we cannot now recover with any confidence.

5:8-11, Calling the First Disciples. The story concerns Simon Peter and his commissioning as a disciple. Peter is the only disciple introduced prior to this scene (see 4:38-39), he is the only one to speak to Jesus, and Jesus' commission is addressed to Peter. The others, James and John, are introduced as Simon's partners, almost as an afterthought.

At the heart of this scene is Jesus' call to the fishermen to leave their nets and give themselves to the work of the kingdom. The metaphor "fishers of men," or "catching people," is striking both because it arises out of the situation and because it is a clever play on words. The fishermen are themselves caught by Jesus and given a new vocation. In the OT and the Dead Sea Scrolls fishing is used metaphorically for gathering people for judgment (Amos 4:2; Hab 1:14-15; Jer 16:16; 1QH 5:7-8). Seen against this background, the call to the disciples was a commission to gather people for judgment, a theme found in the preaching of John the Baptist (3:7-9). The metaphor of fishing was also common in Greek literature as a metaphor for the activity of philosopher-teachers. In the Gospels, however, the call to become fishers of men becomes a call to gather men and women for the kingdom. It retains eschatological overtones from the biblical traditions, it authorizes the disciples as representatives of their teacher and agents of the kingdom, and it looks forward to the church's evangelistic mission.[69]

---

68. Raymond E. Brown, *The Gospel According to John (XIII–XXI)*, AB 29A (Garden City, N.Y.: Doubleday, 1970) 1090.

69. See Culpepper, *John, the Son of Zebedee*, 20-21.

REFLECTIONS

1. Peter's call to leave everything and "catch people" is the counterpart in Luke of the call of Paul in Acts, where the commission is actually communicated through Ananias (Acts 9:15). Both Peter and Paul were called dramatically, through a miraculous event, while they were in the midst of their routine activities, and both were given a commission to devote themselves to bringing others to Jesus. Peter would become the leader of the early church in Jerusalem; Paul would become the great apostle to the Gentiles. These call scenes are important because, although not everyone experiences such a dramatic conversion or call, these scenes contain elements that continue to mark experiences of God's calling in our own context.

2. Christologically, the miraculous catch of fish should probably be understood as a sign that, as the Messiah (4:41) anointed by the Spirit, Jesus did mighty works not unlike the works of Moses, Elijah, and Elisha. This is the first miracle that was not a healing or an exorcism. Jesus does not command the sea or the fish, nor does he instruct the fishermen to do anything out of the ordinary. Like Moses, whom God used to supply manna and water in the wilderness, or Elijah, who supplied an abundance of meal and oil (1 Kgs 17:8-16), and Elisha, who provided an endless supply of oil and fed a hundred people with twenty loaves of barley bread (2 Kgs 4:1-7, 42-44), Jesus provided an abundance of fish. The work of the kingdom, therefore, will be accompanied by signs of God's gracious love. It will inaugurate a time of abundance and blessing.

3. The counterpart to christology is the Gospel's teaching on discipleship. Three observations can be made in this context. First, the fishermen had done nothing to warrant or merit Jesus' call to them. Regardless of what Jesus may have seen in the fishermen, to contend that he called the most capable or most qualified to be his disciples would contradict an important element in the Gospel story. The fishermen were not called because of their qualifications, character, or potential. God's call is as unpredictable as it is unmerited. Second, the call to discipleship did not come in a holy place (the temple or a synagogue) but in the midst of the fishermen's daily work. The point is significant not because God does not call people in a holy place (cf. Zechariah in Luke 1) but because it is a further sign of the work of God's kingdom reaching into the arena of human life. Third, the call to discipleship in Luke's account does not include the familiar words "follow me," as in Mark 1:16-20. Rather, Jesus commissions the fishermen for kingdom service: "catching people." Fourth, the metaphor of fishing suggests various facets of the disciples' role in relation to Jesus and the kingdom. Henceforth they will live by Jesus' teachings and call others to him just as they themselves have been called. Their work will be evangelistic in nature and infused with eschatological urgency. Finally, the call of the kingdom requires a reversal of priorities and a reordering of commitments. The disciples left everything (a more inclusive term than is used in the call accounts in Mark and Matthew), and "they followed him." The language of following Jesus echoes both Elijah's call to Elisha (1 Kgs 19:19-21) and Socrates' call to Strepsiades: "But come and follow me."[70] The last word in Luke's story is Jesus. He will order their lives from now on.

---

70. Aristophanes *The Clouds* 497-517; Diogenes Laertius *Lives* II.48.

Luke 5:12-16, Cleansing a Leper

NIV

¹²While Jesus was in one of the towns, a man came along who was covered with leprosy.ᵃ When he saw Jesus, he fell with his face to the ground and begged him, "Lord, if you are willing, you can make me clean."

¹³Jesus reached out his hand and touched the man. "I am willing," he said. "Be clean!" And immediately the leprosy left him.

¹⁴Then Jesus ordered him, "Don't tell anyone, but go, show yourself to the priest and offer the sacrifices that Moses commanded for your cleansing, as a testimony to them."

¹⁵Yet the news about him spread all the more, so that crowds of people came to hear him and to be healed of their sicknesses. ¹⁶But Jesus often withdrew to lonely places and prayed.

ᵃ12 The Greek word was used for various diseases affecting the skin—not necessarily leprosy.

NRSV

12Once, when he was in one of the cities, there was a man covered with leprosy.ᵃ When he saw Jesus, he bowed with his face to the ground and begged him, "Lord, if you choose, you can make me clean." ¹³Then Jesusᵇ stretched out his hand, touched him, and said, "I do choose. Be made clean." Immediately the leprosyᵃ left him. ¹⁴And he ordered him to tell no one. "Go," he said, "and show yourself to the priest, and, as Moses commanded, make an offering for your cleansing, for a testimony to them." ¹⁵But now more than ever the word about Jesusᶜ spread abroad; many crowds would gather to hear him and to be cured of their diseases. ¹⁶But he would withdraw to deserted places and pray.

ᵃThe terms *leper* and *leprosy* can refer to several diseases
ᵇGk *he*   ᶜGk *him*

COMMENTARY

The characterization of Jesus as the Messiah anointed by the Spirit to fulfill the work of the prophets by his mighty words and deeds continues in this pericope. In the synagogue at Nazareth, Jesus interpreted the words of Isaiah by referring to Elisha's healing of Naaman the Syrian. The reader can hardly miss the connection when Jesus now heals a leper.

In the NT, "leprosy" seems not to be limited to Hansen's disease but denotes various skin diseases that could produce scales, inflammation, or lesions. The priestly legislation regarding the detection and treatment of leprosy is reported in detail in Leviticus 13–14, but the symptoms described there do not conform to what is known of Hansen's disease today. The Levitical law required that the afflicted person be examined by a priest. If the priest determined that the person had leprosy, he or she was to be quarantined for seven days. At the end of the week, the priest might extend the quarantine a second week or pronounce the person clean or leprous. The law required that a leprous person wear torn clothing and disheveled hair and live alone or with other lepers. When approached by another person, the leper was to cover his or her upper lip and call out, "Unclean, unclean" (Lev 13:45-46). Leviticus 14 prescribes a detailed ritual for the cleansing of a leper who has been healed from the disease. The leper must be examined by a priest, a ritual involving two birds was performed, and then the cleansed leper would bathe, shave, and wash his or her clothes before returning to the community.

For the core of the story, Luke follows Mark 1:40-45. The two accounts agree very closely in the dialogue between Jesus and the leper and differ most noticeably in the introduction and conclusion to the story. In the introduction to both this pericope and the next, Luke adopts the Semitic style of the Septuagint: "And it happened that" (καὶ ἐγένετο *kai egeneto*; cf. 1:23, 41, 59, 65; 2:15; 5:17). Luke further situates the healing "in one of the cities," which suggests either that the levitical legislation requiring the leper to remain outside the community was not being followed or that Luke was unfamiliar with the requirement. In comparison with Mark, the leper's condition is heightened: "covered with leprosy." When the leper sees Jesus, he falls on his face and begs Jesus to make him clean. Apparently, from the reports of Jesus' mighty works (4:37), the leper had heard of the healings Jesus had performed and trusted that Jesus could heal him too. Whereas a priest could only pronounce the leper clean or unclean, the man believed that Jesus could actually free him from the disease.

The means by which Jesus heals the leper, which is not usually significant, is important in this pericope. Whereas in other instances Jesus heals at a distance, or simply by his command, in this case he extends his hand, touches the leper, and commands him to be clean. Not only does the healing continue Luke's emphasis on the power of Jesus' word (see 4:36, 39, 41), but also it violates both the Mosiac law and natural human reactions to one afflicted by a disfiguring and contagious skin condition. Jesus touched the leper, thereby rendering himself unclean. Moreover, although the rituals for certifying that a leper was healed were elaborate, Jesus healed the man by a touch and a word. The power to heal, therefore, resides in Jesus even more directly than it had in the prophet Elisha, who sent Naaman to wash seven times in the Jordan River. The cure was instantaneous—the leprosy left him. There was no seven-day quarantine or waiting period.

The charge that the leper should fulfill the law by showing himself to a priest and completing the ritual for cleansing is difficult to interpret. While it repeats verbatim the instruction given in Mark 1:44, in the Lukan context at least the intent seems to be positive. Jesus was concerned that the man keep silent about his cure until he had been certified clean by a priest. The fulfillment of the Mosaic commands is consistent with the offering of the required sacrifices at the presentation of Jesus in the Temple (2:21-24; cf. 17:14, where the same command is repeated). The only way in which the sacrifices could function as a testimony or proof for them (the priests?) would be if the leper also told the priests how Jesus had healed him. The story of the healing of the leper gives us, therefore, a rather perplexing glimpse of Luke's characterization of Jesus' relationship to the religious authorities of Israel. While Jesus heals by the power of the Spirit, touching a leper in the process, he commands observance of the law and provides a witness for the priests. In this instance at least, Jesus, while independent of the religious authorities and structures, was not deliberately antagonistic toward them.

The ending of the story in Luke is markedly different from the Markan account. Luke says nothing further about the leper who was healed. Instead, Luke declares that the reports about Jesus spread even more widely. The effect was that crowds gathered to Jesus all the more. The twin emphases on Jesus' teaching and his healing are extended in this conclusion, but to them is added a reference to prayer, which will become a recurring theme in coming chapters (6:12, 28; 9:18, 28-29). Jesus is thereby characterized as a holy man, a man of Spirit and prayer who is consequently mighty in word and deed, teaching and healing. The crowds pursue him, but Jesus withdraws to desolate places to pray.

REFLECTIONS

This brief account is filled with reversals that carry the deeper meaning of the event. The story opens in the city, where Jesus meets a leper (who by law was barred from the community). By the end of the story, the leper has become clean and has returned to society, but because Jesus touched the leper and healed him, Jesus is himself forced out of the cities and into the wilderness. The turning point is the touch, which renders the man clean and at least by implication makes Jesus unclean. Ironically, Jesus then suffers the estrangement that the law imposed on lepers—he was exiled to desolate places.

1. At one level the conclusion of the story extends the pattern of the previous chapter. Being driven from his hometown and fleeing the crowds that gathered around him in Capernaum, Jesus moved on to other cities (4:44; 5:12), but now he is forced out of all the cities.

At another level, the story reflects Jesus' conflict with sin. Leprosy was a natural symbol for sin. It was repugnant, defiling, and destructive of human community. When the leper fell before Jesus, Jesus "made him clean" (καθαρίζω *katharizō*), a term that could mean forgiveness as well as healing. The healing changed both Jesus and the leper. In a symbolic sense, Jesus took the leper's uncleanness upon himself and suffered the estrangement from society that was normally a leper's lot. By the end of the Gospel, this plot will have been writ large across the narrative. Jesus will die forgiving sinners, and they will be given life. The healing of the leper, therefore, is the gospel in miniature.

2. A contemporary equivalent of leprosy, socially and religiously, is AIDS. It carries with it a social and moral stigma in the eyes of many. It is feared and little understood, and victims often find themselves exiled from the rest of society in the equivalent of leper colonies. Part of the scandal of this story lies in the report that Jesus *touched* the leper, thereby exposing himself to the man's disease and rendering himself ritually unclean. Jesus could hardly have chosen a more dramatic act by which to affirm the importance of the individual, whether leper or person living with AIDS. Jesus' rejection of his culture's judgment on lepers may, therefore, also be seen as judgment on our culture's denial of dignity, humanity, and at times care for persons with AIDS.

3. A further invitation for reflection arises from the leper's confident claim, "Lord, if you choose, you can make me clean." Who told this leper that he did not need to follow the prescribed treatments and sanctions for his condition? What led him to believe that Jesus could (and would) respond to his need? Here is another example of the simple faith that is at times associated with "the poor" in Luke—who depend totally on God's mercy. For such as these, Jesus had come to proclaim the good news of the kingdom. But only those who recognize their need and turn to God for mercy can hear the response: "I do choose. Be made clean."

Luke 5:17-26, Healing the Paralyzed

NIV

[17]One day as he was teaching, Pharisees and teachers of the law, who had come from every village of Galilee and from Judea and Jerusalem, were sitting there. And the power of the Lord was present for him to heal the sick. [18]Some men came carrying a paralytic on a mat and tried to take him into the house to lay him before Jesus. [19]When they could not find a way to do this because of the crowd, they went up on the roof and lowered him on his mat through the tiles into the middle of the crowd, right in front of Jesus.

[20]When Jesus saw their faith, he said, "Friend, your sins are forgiven."

[21]The Pharisees and the teachers of the law began thinking to themselves, "Who is this fellow who speaks blasphemy? Who can forgive sins but God alone?"

[22]Jesus knew what they were thinking and asked, "Why are you thinking these things in your hearts? [23]Which is easier: to say, 'Your sins are

NRSV

17One day, while he was teaching, Pharisees and teachers of the law were sitting near by (they had come from every village of Galilee and Judea and from Jerusalem); and the power of the Lord was with him to heal.[a] 18Just then some men came, carrying a paralyzed man on a bed. They were trying to bring him in and lay him before Jesus;[b] 19but finding no way to bring him in because of the crowd, they went up on the roof and let him down with his bed through the tiles into the middle of the crowd[c] in front of Jesus. 20When he saw their faith, he said, "Friend,[d] your sins are forgiven you." 21Then the scribes and the Pharisees began to question, "Who is this who is speaking blasphemies? Who can forgive sins but God alone?" 22When Jesus perceived their questionings, he answered them, "Why do you raise such questions in your hearts? 23Which is easier,

[a]Other ancient authorities read *was present to heal them* [b]Gk *him* [c]Gk *into the midst* [d]Gk *Man*

NIV	NRSV
forgiven,' or to say, 'Get up and walk'? ²⁴But that you may know that the Son of Man has authority on earth to forgive sins. . . ." He said to the paralyzed man, "I tell you, get up, take your mat and go home." ²⁵Immediately he stood up in front of them, took what he had been lying on and went home praising God. ²⁶Everyone was amazed and gave praise to God. They were filled with awe and said, "We have seen remarkable things today."	to say, 'Your sins are forgiven you,' or to say, 'Stand up and walk'? ²⁴But so that you may know that the Son of Man has authority on earth to forgive sins"—he said to the one who was paralyzed—"I say to you, stand up and take your bed and go to your home." ²⁵Immediately he stood up before them, took what he had been lying on, and went to his home, glorifying God. ²⁶Amazement seized all of them, and they glorified God and were filled with awe, saying, "We have seen strange things today."

COMMENTARY

The healing of the paralytic introduces a series of four controversy stories. The religious authorities, the Pharisees and scribes, are introduced for the first time. The general resistance Jesus met in Nazareth now becomes much more focused, and a specific charge is considered: blasphemy. The story also weaves together even more closely than earlier scenes the twin themes of the power of Jesus' words and his power to heal. For the first time also faith and forgiveness of sins are introduced.

In this story, as in the entire sequence that began with the healing of the leper in Luke 5:12-16, Luke at the same time follows and adapts Mark's account of these events. Since Mark seems to have been Luke's only source for these accounts, the points at which he departs from Mark become all the more important. Originally the story may have reported a healing (Mark 2:1-5*a*, 11-12) without the debate about blasphemy and the authority to forgive sins (Mark 2:5*b*-10). By the time Luke became acquainted with it, however, the story already combined the themes of teaching and healing that Luke has cultivated in the preceding scenes. His redaction of Mark's account, however, sets in relief the literary strategies he is developing in this section of the Gospel.

5:17. As in the preceding scene, Luke's most extensive and telling editing of the story occurs in its introduction and conclusion. The introductory phrase (literally "And it happened one day while he was teaching . . .") echoes the introduction to the story of the leper in v. 12. The characterization of Jesus' activity as teaching extends the emphasis on Jesus' word that we have traced in 4:15, 31, 36, 43-44; 5:3.

This time, rather than noting the press of the crowds around Jesus (as in previous scenes and as in Mark's account), Luke reports that Jesus was surrounded by Pharisees and teachers of the Law who had come from "every village" in Galilee and Judea and from Jerusalem. This is the only reference to "teachers of the law" in the Gospels (but see Acts 5:34, where Gamaliel is identified by this title). There is still a great deal of debate about the role of the Pharisees in first-century Jewish society and in the villages of Galilee in particular. Josephus traces the Pharisees to the Maccabean period.[71] Whatever their political involvements during the period of the Hasmoneans, by the first century they appear to have been a non-priestly group concerned primarily with the teaching, interpretation, and observance of the Law. If there were reports that Jesus was claiming a special, personal authority derived from the Spirit that enabled him to interpret the Scriptures, that he was healing on the sabbath, or that he was violating the rules regarding contact with unclean persons, it is entirely plausible that the Pharisees would have become concerned about Jesus' teachings and activities. There is still a great deal of uncertainty, however, about their role and authority in the villages of Galilee and their relationship to the priestly authorities in Jerusalem. It is also

71. See Josephus *Antiquities of the Jews* 13.171.

unclear whether the religious figures gathered around Jesus in order to investigate him or whether they were genuinely interested in his teaching. In other words, is their presence a sign of their opposition to Jesus or did that opposition arise later as a result of his claim to be able to forgive sins? Once earlier Jesus had been seated among the teachers of Israel (2:46-47), but this time they have come to hear him, and probably to examine his teachings.

Luke's note that they had come from "every village" in the surrounding areas introduces an interesting tension with the earlier reports that news of Jesus' activities had spread through the area (4:37; 5:15). Not only have the reports drawn crowds that have prevented Jesus from moving about in the cities, but also now they have drawn the attention of the Pharisees, setting the stage for the controversy stories that follow.

Equally significant is Luke's comment that "the power of the Lord was with him to heal." The comment, which is not present in Mark, highlights an aspect of Luke's characterization of Jesus and prepares the reader for the healing that follows. The use of "Lord" to refer to God rather than Jesus is consistent with Luke's use of the term throughout the infancy narratives (where the term occurs 27 times). It also resonates with the reading of Isaiah 61 in Luke 4:18 and Luke's characterization of Jesus as being empowered by the Spirit (4:14) and commanding the unclean spirits with power (4:36). As the Messiah who fulfilled the work of the prophets, Jesus had been empowered by the Spirit (cf. the interpretation of Jesus' healing in 4:38-41; 5:12-16; and hereafter in 6:18-19; 7:7; 8:47; 9:2, 11, 42).

5:18-19. The introduction of the third set of characters (the paralyzed man and those who bring him to Jesus) precipitates the exchange between Jesus and the Pharisees. Luke omits Mark's report that the paralytic was being carried by *four* men but adds that he was being carried on a bed or stretcher. Luke also shows greater sensitivity in describing him as "a man who was paralyzed" rather than as "a paralytic." The crowd around Jesus has become a barrier separating him from the man in need. In an act of persistence and determination that will be interpreted as faith (v. 20), the men go up on the housetop and lower the paralyzed man down through the roof. Luke's

departure from Mark at this point suggests that Luke envisions a different style of house, and apparently a different social setting. Mark says that the men dug through the roof—that is, they dug through the reeds and baked mud that were used to cover a Palestinian peasant's house. Yet Luke says they removed the "tiles," which would have covered more affluent Hellenistic homes.

5:20. Here the surprise comes: By underscoring Jesus' power to heal (v. 17) and the bringing of a crippled man to Jesus, the narrator has led the reader to expect that Jesus will heal the man—just as he has healed others. Instead, Jesus pronounces the man's sins forgiven. The first reference to faith in the Gospel of Luke refers to the confidence and determination of those bringing the crippled man to Jesus—confidence that Jesus could heal him and determination to get the man through the crowd. Jesus pronounces the man's sins forgiven, using a formula of forgiveness that recurs again in Luke 5:23; 7:47-48. To this point the forgiveness of sins has been more closely associated with John the Baptist than Jesus (see 1:77; 3:3), but Christian readers would already have understood that John's work was preparatory and that Jesus was the one who brought forgiveness. In this scene, faith, healing, and forgiveness are closely related. Jesus sees the faith of the men who brought the paralytic, and he pronounces the man's sins forgiven. This surprise pronouncement leaves unresolved the man's paralytic condition while also aggravating the tension between Jesus and the Pharisees. A popular theological view interpreted physical afflictions as punishment for sin (Exod 20:5; cf. Luke 13:2-3), but the relation between the two is ambiguous in this scene. Jesus does not treat sin as the cause of the man's affliction. Rather, he uses the healing to confirm his authority to forgive sin.

5:21. The response of the "scribes and Pharisees" (cf. 5:30; 6:7; 11:53; 15:2) is to question Jesus' authority to make such a pronouncement. Luke states their questions in such a way that they focus the issue on Jesus' identity: "Who is this who is speaking blasphemies? Who can forgive sins but God alone?" (see the similar questions in 7:49; 8:25; 9:9). The punishment for blasphemy was death (Lev 24:10-16; *m. Sanh.* 7.5). Blasphemy normally implied that one had spoken the divine name, but it could also be construed more broadly as failure to recognize God's glory, ungodly speech or action, or violation of God's majesty. In the eyes of the religious authorities, by claiming a divine prerogative Jesus had committed blasphemy. By adding the word for "alone" (μόνος *monos*) to the question "Who can forgive sins?" Luke heightens the authority that the scene confers upon Jesus.

5:22-23. Jesus perceived that they harbored these thoughts (cf. 4:23) and responded with a question of his own. The entire exchange assumes that the reader recognizes the importance of vindicating one's honor and avoiding shame. By presenting the paralytic for healing, the men who brought him lodged a positive challenge to Jesus' honor. By healing the man he could vindicate his honor. If he did not do so, he would be shamed. Jesus escalated the issue by claiming an even higher level of honor—a divine prerogative. When the scribes and Pharisees questioned his right to such a claim, Jesus further escalated the conflict by stating their question openly for all the crowd to hear, placing the honor of the scribes and Pharisees in jeopardy if they could not sustain their charge.

The question Jesus poses to the assembled authorities is nuanced with a fine ambiguity. On the one hand, it would be easier *to say* that a person's sins are forgiven than to pronounce him or her healed because the latter is subject to verification, while the former is not. On the other hand, the claim to forgive sins was the higher claim because others had been known to have the power to heal. Added to the nuance of Jesus' question was the lurking suspicion that the man's sin and his paralysis were related. Was Jesus moving directly to the root cause of the man's condition by forgiving his sin, dealing with the weightier rather than the lighter, the cause rather than the result?

5:24. The first part of this verse can be read in three ways. (1) Most translations treat it as part of Jesus' response to the scribes and Pharisees: " 'But so that you may know that the Son of Man has authority on earth to forgive sins'—he said to the one who was paralyzed—'I say to you, stand up and take your bed and go to your home.' "

Alternatively, (2) the first part of the verse may be read as an aside or parenthetical comment to the reader. Accordingly, the "you" refers to the

readers rather than to the scribes and Pharisees: "But to let you know that the Son of Man has authority on earth to forgive sins, he said to the paralyzed man, 'I say to you, "Get up, pick up your pallet, and go home!" ' "[72] Other asides have been found in Luke 1:1-4; 2:22-23; 7:29-30; and 14:35, but these are not really comparable to this verse.[73]

The grammatical construction at the beginning of the verse may also be read as (3) an imperative addressed to the reader: "Know that the Son of Man has authority to forgive sins!—He said to the paralyzed man, 'I say to you, get up and, when you have picked up your bed, go home.' "[74]

At issue here are the syntax of the verse, its probable meaning, and whether this verse is an exception to the consistent pattern that in the Gospels the title "Son of Man" occurs only on the lips of Jesus. The common translation of this verse (1) assumes the syntax is broken and places a dash before "he said to the paralyzed man." The third proposal forces a construction that normally expresses purpose ("but in order that . . .") to be read as an imperative. The second translation creates a disjunction between v. 23 and v. 24, and assumes a change in the speaker (the narrator, not Jesus) and a change in the addressee (the readers rather than the scribes and Pharisees). It also places the title "Son of Man" in a comment by the narrator rather than in Jesus' speech, but it relieves the need to conjecture that the syntax is broken or that the subjunctive verb should be read as an imperative. Thus none of the solutions is completely satisfactory, but the second, which treats the first part of v. 24 as a narrative aside, is the least objectionable since it allows for a smooth reading of v. 24.

The Son of Man saying, whether a dominical saying or a narrative aside, is important both for the plot of the story and for its theology. In the synoptic Gospels, Jesus speaks of himself as "the Son of Man" more frequently than with any other form of self-address. Interpreters have suggested that this title is derived from Dan 7:13, or that it renders an Aramaic circumlocution for "I," or that

72. Joseph A. Fitzmyer, *The Gospel According to Luke (I–IX)*, AB 28 (Garden City, N.Y.: Doubleday, 1981) 577.
73. See, e.g., Steven M. Sheeley, *Narrative Asides in Luke–Acts*, JSNTSup 72 (Sheffield: JSOT Press, 1992) 154.
74. John Nolland, *Luke 1–9:20*, WBC 35A (Dallas: Word, 1989) 230, 237.

it is a title for an apocalyptic figure, as in *1 Enoch.* The date of the relevant portion of *1 Enoch* is debated, however. It is clear, nevertheless, that the title was used in a generic sense for "man" in pre-Christian usage, and that Luke has added it to sayings where the term does not appear in Mark or Matthew (6:22; 9:22; 12:8; 12:40; 19:10). For Luke, therefore, it is a familiar title for Jesus. The question of what the title meant for Luke may be separated from the issue of what Jesus meant in using it. Although the issue is far from settled, it appears that Jesus used the title in its generic sense or as a common self-address. Alternatively, he may have used the title because it was not clearly defined and forced the hearer to search for its meaning. For Luke, "Son of Man" combines or alternates between emphasizing Jesus' humanity and his future role as risen Lord. In this respect, it is tensive and not susceptible to any simple interpretation—a human being has authority to forgive sin, will be exalted, will judge the nations, and will raise the dead. Ultimately, the enigma resides not in the title but in the person of Jesus.

5:25-26. The rest of the pericope follows the form of a typical healing story: the action of the healer, confirmation of the healing, and the response of the crowd. Luke has edited Mark's account of the ending of the story rather freely, improving its syntax and vocabulary; Luke avoids Mark's rough term for "pallet" (κράβαττος *krabattos*) and uses the diminutive of "bed" (κλινίδιον *klinidion*) instead. He changes the term for "immediately" from εὐθύς (*euthys*), which occurs 42 times in Mark but only once in Luke, to παραχρῆμα (*parachrēma*), which occurs 10 times in Luke and 6 times in Acts but never in Mark. He uses participial phrases more skillfully, and doubles the report of glorifying God. First, the man who had been healed glorifies God (v. 25); then, all who were gathered glorify God (v. 26).

This story is rich and complicated both in form and in meaning. It presents Jesus both as healer and as teacher, and more as the Son of Man who forgives sins. The healing is used to confirm an even higher authority—Jesus' authority as the Son of Man—and all of this in the context of examination by the scribes and Pharisees, so that the story serves both to develop Jesus' character and to advance the conflict between Jesus and the religious authorities.

Each of the Gospels points to a different meaning in the conclusion to the story. In Matthew the crowds glorify God for giving "such authority to human beings" (9:8). In Mark the response seems to magnify the healing: "We have never seen anything like this!" (2:12). Luke uses a term that occurs nowhere else in the NT: "We have seen strange things [παράδοξα *paradoxa*] today." The scene, therefore, extends the characterization of Jesus as the prophetic, miracle-working Messiah, adding now the themes of faith and the forgiveness of sin and the designation "Son of Man." These strange and wonderful things properly elicit the response of awe and glorifying God.

REFLECTIONS

The power and fascination of this story lie to a great extent in the way it combines significant themes. The one who heals is also the one who forgives. Faith consists not in affirming a particular tradition's theological creeds but in the conviction that Jesus is able to mediate God's power. Because of the determination of friends, a man who could not come to Jesus on his own is forgiven and healed. Faith is found not in the assembly of scribes and Pharisees from all the surrounding region, but in four unnamed neighbors. The mystery of the relationship between sin and human bondage or affliction is approached. While the mystery is not resolved, the solution is revealed: Jesus came to free us from all that cripples, binds, and enslaves. The priority in this story is clearly placed not on religious orthodoxy but on concern for meeting human need. Because those who brought the paralyzed man to Jesus let no obstacle stand in the way of getting God's help for him, their quest was rewarded. On the other hand, because the scribes and Pharisees were more concerned about defending orthodoxy, their quest was frustrated.

By doubling the reference to glorifying God at the end of the scene, Luke underscores the irony that runs quietly through it from beginning to end. The authorities whispered blasphemy, which technically could include anything that disparaged or denied God's glory. Yet, by what he says Jesus brings all of those present to glorify God. The charge of blasphemy, therefore, is overturned by the response of the authorities themselves. Thus the real blasphemy, by implication, is found in those who resisted Jesus' ministry to the afflicted, bound, and oppressed.

As we have seen, Jesus worked in a context of suspicion that the man's paralysis was a result of his sinfulness. The scandal was that Jesus responded to the man's need and pronounced his sins forgiven. He did not even extract a confession of sin from the man before forgiving him and healing him—a scandalous demonstration of God's unconditional mercy. Today we generally do not attach to illness the implication of sin, but many still view AIDS as God's punishment of practicing homosexuals and sexual promiscuity. AIDS, however, is no longer confined to one segment of the population, and the theological implications of a God who would respond to any sin by unleashing such a disease on humanity are so terrible that no thoughtful person could ever seriously advocate this view. Nevertheless, this distorted theological view persists, offering the interpreter a ready analogy to the link between paralysis and sin that was accepted by many in first-century Palestine.

In this story, by choosing to meet the man's needs for forgiveness and healing rather than attempt to guard God's glory or heap condemnation on the victim, Jesus made the man whole and brought glory to God by doing so. The defense of orthodoxy is not the goal of discipleship, therefore—it is the by-product of ministering to the needs of others.

Luke 5:27-32, Calling Levi, Eating with Outcasts

NIV

27After this, Jesus went out and saw a tax collector by the name of Levi sitting at his tax booth. "Follow me," Jesus said to him, 28and Levi got up, left everything and followed him.

29Then Levi held a great banquet for Jesus at his house, and a large crowd of tax collectors and others were eating with them. 30But the Pharisees and the teachers of the law who belonged to their sect complained to his disciples, "Why do you eat and drink with tax collectors and 'sinners'?"

31Jesus answered them, "It is not the healthy who need a doctor, but the sick. 32I have not come to call the righteous, but sinners to repentance."

NRSV

27After this he went out and saw a tax collector named Levi, sitting at the tax booth; and he said to him, "Follow me." 28And he got up, left everything, and followed him.

29Then Levi gave a great banquet for him in his house; and there was a large crowd of tax collectors and others sitting at the table*a* with them. 30The Pharisees and their scribes were complaining to his disciples, saying, "Why do you eat and drink with tax collectors and sinners?" 31Jesus answered, "Those who are well have no need of a physician, but those who are sick; 32I have come to call not the righteous but sinners to repentance."

a Gk *reclining*

COMMENTARY

The call of Levi and the pronouncements of Jesus at the banquet that follows take us deeper into first-century Palestinian society. More important, they expose the scandal of Jesus' mission and his call to discipleship. In order to grasp the force of this scene, the reader must understand the social values and functions attached to its characters and settings. The scene places Jesus and those who followed him between two sharply different groups: the Pharisees and the toll collectors.

Direct taxes (poll tax, land tax) were collected by tax collectors employed by the Romans, while tolls, tariffs, and customs fees were collected at toll houses by toll collectors, the group that appears frequently in the Gospels and is not entirely accurately identified as "tax collectors."[75] Toll collectors paid in advance for the right to collect tolls, so the system was open to abuse and corruption. The toll collectors were often not natives of the area where they worked, and their wealth and collusion with the Roman oppressors made them targets of scorn.

In contrast, the Pharisees lived out their devotion to God through the study and observance of the Torah and by maintaining purity in all matters. Discipleship to a rabbi meant mastering the oral tradition, "the hedge about the law."[76] Detailed interpretations of the Law guided the Pharisees in matters pertaining to food and meals, so the Pharisees maintained a separation from others and ate only with those who, like them, observed the laws of purity.

Meals are especially prominent in Luke. Indeed, so frequent are meal scenes that someone once commented that in Luke Jesus seems always to be on his way to or from a meal,[77] usually with outcasts and those viewed as sinners (7:29, 31-34; 14:1-24; 15:1-2; 19:1-10). Jesus himself cites the reputation he has earned: "The Son of man has come eating and drinking, and you say, 'Look, a glutton and a drunkard, a friend of tax collectors and sinners!' " (7:34). Meals were important social occasions. A banquet such as the one Levi gave in Jesus' honor expressed joy and celebration. The meals during the ministry of Jesus were then part of the ritual and memory of the early church as it observed fellowship meals. Eating together, and not fasting, became the way in which the church remembered Jesus and declared the coming of the kingdom.

Luke moved directly to the value-laden settings: the toll collector's station and then the banquet at Levi's home. Mark's summary reference to teaching the crowd by the lake is omitted (cf. Mark 2:13). Jesus spotted Levi, or looked intently at him, or looked at him with love foreseeing how God would transform his life. The term "he saw" (ἐθεάσατο etheasato) is one Luke has chosen in place of the more common term found in Mark, but probably one should not read too much into it.

Jesus' call to Levi echoes Jesus' call to the fishermen in Mark's account (Mark 1:16-20). Here Jesus, whom Luke has earlier introduced as the one who would fulfill the prophets (see 4:16-30), now repeats the words with which Elijah had called Elisha: "Follow me" (1 Kgs 19:19-21; cf. 5:11). As a disciple, Jesus chose a toll collector— one who had no apparent qualifications and no virtue or reputation to commend him. The call of God is sheer grace. Levi may even serve as an example of the "foremost of sinners." If Jesus could call a toll collector, he could call anyone. No one else could have more dramatically illustrated Jesus' commitment to the rejected.

It is difficult to make sense of the names of the disciples. Mark 2:14 identifies Levi as "the son of Alphaeus." However, Levi does not appear subsequently in the list of the Twelve, but Matthew, who appears in all the lists, is identified as "the tax collector" in the Gospel of Matthew (10:3). One James, "the son of Alphaeus," also appears in each of the lists. Whether Levi/Matthew had a double name or whether these were two persons is, therefore, uncertain.

Levi's acceptance of the call is expressed in two ways. First, he left everything (cf. 5:11), arose, and began to follow Jesus. Luke adds the reference to forsaking everything—a point that becomes important in the light of Jesus' later teachings on poverty and wealth. The verb "to arise" (ἀνίστημι anistēmi) is also the same one Luke used in v. 25 to describe the action of the man who had been paralyzed. The same call that lifted the paralytic from his mat now lifts Levi from his toll station. Both events illustrate the transforming power of God in the life of a sinner.

Second, Levi gave a great feast for Jesus (cf. 14:13). The call of God requires a complete reorientation of life. Levi's leaving everything behind does not mean that he would not have had the means with which to give a feast. It speaks, rather, of his abandoning of the past to give himself completely to following Jesus. Luke makes it clear (in contrast to Mark 2:15) that Levi gave the feast in his own house. In a Galilean village a "great feast" was a public affair. Even those who

---

75. See John R. Donahue, "Tax Collectors and Sinners: An Attempt at Identification," *CBQ* 33 (1971) 39-61.

76. *M. 'Abot* 1.1.

77. Robert J. Karris, *Luke: Artist and Theologian* (New York: Paulist, 1985) 47.

were not invited gathered around to watch the event, hence the presence of "the Pharisees and their scribes," who were obviously not eating with Levi's friends. Similarly, Luke reports that a "woman of the city" approached Jesus while he was eating in the home of a Pharisee (7:36-37).

Luke refrains from calling Levi's guests "tax collectors and sinners" (Mark 2:15-16), allowing that phrase to be used by the Pharisees. Instead, he reports that a "large crowd of tax collectors and others [was] sitting at table with them." Jesus had commissioned the fishermen to "catch people"; Levi was already drawing others to Jesus.

Scribes were first those who could read and write, and later those trained in the law. Since the law was both civil and religious (a distinction the scribes would not have made), the scribes were both lawyers and religious experts. Here Luke adapts Mark's phrase, envisioning scribes who were allied with the Pharisees. To them, the spectacle of the prophet-healer-teacher eating with a crowd of tax collectors at a tax collector's home was scandalous. They complained (literally "grumbled" [γογγύζω gongyzō]) to Jesus' disciples; the very sound of the Greek verb suggests its meaning. Luke uses the cognate form of this verb elsewhere (15:2; 19:7) to describe the response of those who took offense at Jesus' association with toll collectors or sinners. The report that the critics complained not to Jesus but to his disciples may mean that Luke is aware that the church faced similar criticism—they ate together with sinners and outcasts. Rather than associating with those who would bring honor to them, they were bringing shame upon themselves. Jesus at table with sinners, therefore, is an apt paradigm for the life of the church. The Pharisees put the question to the disciples, but Jesus gives the answer for them. Luke's addition of the phrase "and drinking" to Mark's "eating" brings the activity in line with his characterization of Jesus in Luke 7:33-34 and elsewhere (13:26; 22:30), but references to eating and drinking occur frequently in Luke. The offense was probably twofold. By eating with toll collectors, they were making themselves unclean, but further they were showing their acceptance of the toll collectors. The Pharisees would have

had no problem with Jesus for calling sinners to repentance. Had he called all the toll collectors to repentance, the Pharisees would have made him a national hero. The offense was that Jesus was demonstrating God's grace by not requiring repentance before he would eat with toll collectors and sinners.

Jesus answered with a proverb and a statement that characterized his mission and purpose. These two sayings are the climax of the whole scene. The proverb of the physician is similar to that in Luke 4:23, "Doctor, cure yourself!" (cf. 8:43). Its meaning is largely determined by its context. The proverb states the obvious, but it leaves open the issue of the metaphorical identification of the healthy and the sick. In context, Jesus justifies his association with the tax collectors and those reputed to be sinners. In the previous scene the Pharisees had first questioned and then glorified God because Jesus had forgiven the crippled man and then healed him. If a healer was needed by the sick, not the healthy, then was not the forgiver of sins needed among the sinners? The mission of the righteous was thereby redefined. Discipleship consists not in separation (as was practiced by the Pharisees) but in association. Jesus' worldview, his definition of God's work, and the value he placed on other persons completely overturned his critics.

The scene concludes with the same theme with which it opened: Jesus' call to sinners. The closing statement is tensive, opposing the righteous and the sinners, raising the question of who is actually righteous and who is sinful, and forcing readers to choose paradoxically to place themselves not with the righteous (the Pharisees) but with the sinners (those at table with Jesus). Luke emphasizes repentance, but it is Jesus' purpose, not the condition of his fellowship with sinners. Neither acceptance on the condition of repentance nor acceptance without the call to repentance characterizes Jesus' association with sinners, though inevitably the church has often erred on one side or the other. The preaching of repentance is a consistent theme that ties together John the Baptist's preaching (3:3, 8), Jesus (13:3, 5; 15:7, 10; 17:3-4), and the commission to Jesus' disciples (24:47).

REFLECTIONS

1. This brief scene is important because it describes not just the calling of one disciple but Jesus' call to every person. The stubborn stuff of history demands, however, that we wrestle with the brute fact that Jesus called the outcast, the despised, and the hated. He did not move through Galilean society, handpicking the most religious, most virtuous, or most popular to follow him. He built his movement from the castoffs of society. The key is not to lose sight of the specific scandal—that Jesus called a toll collector to follow him—when we reflect on the general characteristics of the call to discipleship that are mirrored in this scene.

Our tendency to domesticate the tradition and find a place for the righteous at the table can be seen in the history of Jesus' saying: "I have come to call not the righteous but sinners to repentance." First, in Luke 19:10, we find a version of the saying in which the exclusion of the righteous is dropped, removing the tensiveness from the saying: "For the Son of Man came to seek out and to save the lost." A later stage in its interpretation appears in 1 Tim 1:15: "The saying is sure and worthy of full acceptance, that Christ Jesus came into the world to save sinners—of whom I am the foremost." At this point the righteous have been included in the mission to save and have been identified as the "foremost" of sinners. What remains of the rejection of the righteous?

The scandal of this scene in the eyes of the religious people was that Jesus called for and modeled a style of discipleship based on association with sinners rather than separation from them. On a scale running from separation to association with the outcasts of society, where would most churches fall? Again, by whatever interpretive sleight of hand, we have taken the tradition of the Savior who came to seek and to save sinners and have evolved a style of church life based on separation rather than association.

What good is a physician who will treat only the healthy and will not associate with the sick? This scene calls us to a radical and daring reorientation of our understanding of discipleship. The question the Pharisees put to the disciples is not a bad litmus test for faithfulness to Jesus' mission: When the righteous and religious ask why you are associating with the unwashed and the unwanted (by whatever name), there the work that Jesus began is continuing.

2. Jesus' call to discipleship is startlingly brief: "Follow me." In contrast to other forms of discipleship, Jesus called for a personal commitment. He did not challenge others to find a teacher, as did the Pharisees. He did not call for commitment to a philosophy or set of teachings, as did the street-corner philosophers. He did not call for commitment to a political program, as did the revolutionary leaders. He did not promise rewards or allow for a trial period. His call was absolute, unconditional, and person-centered: You follow me. Neither should the context of the call be disregarded. The call to follow Jesus is given in a scene in which Jesus' character and the character of Christian discipleship are further defined by his scandalous association with tax collectors and sinners.

Luke 5:33-39, Debate About Fasting

NIV

33They said to him, "John's disciples often fast and pray, and so do the disciples of the Pharisees, but yours go on eating and drinking." 34Jesus answered, "Can you make the guests of the bridegroom fast while he is with them? 35But

NRSV

33Then they said to him, "John's disciples, like the disciples of the Pharisees, frequently fast and pray, but your disciples eat and drink." 34Jesus said to them, "You cannot make wedding guests fast while the bridegroom is with them, can you?

NIV

the time will come when the bridegroom will be taken from them; in those days they will fast."

³⁶He told them this parable: "No one tears a patch from a new garment and sews it on an old one. If he does, he will have torn the new garment, and the patch from the new will not match the old. ³⁷And no one pours new wine into old wineskins. If he does, the new wine will burst the skins, the wine will run out and the wineskins will be ruined. ³⁸No, new wine must be poured into new wineskins. ³⁹And no one after drinking old wine wants the new, for he says, 'The old is better.'"

NRSV

³⁵The days will come when the bridegroom will be taken away from them, and then they will fast in those days." ³⁶He also told them a parable: "No one tears a piece from a new garment and sews it on an old garment; otherwise the new will be torn, and the piece from the new will not match the old. ³⁷And no one puts new wine into old wineskins; otherwise the new wine will burst the skins and will be spilled, and the skins will be destroyed. ³⁸But new wine must be put into fresh wineskins. ³⁹And no one after drinking old wine desires new wine, but says, 'The old is good.'"ᵃ

ᵃOther ancient authorities read *better*; others lack verse 39

COMMENTARY

Luke has dropped Mark's narrative introduction to the question about fasting, thereby allowing the conversation in the previous scene to continue. The exchange that follows is related to the preceding material by motif (the meal setting), by theme (the relationship between Jesus' piety and that of the Pharisees), and by catchword ("eating and drinking," vv. 30, 33). The linkage Luke has created (cf. Mark 2:18) is not altogether successful, however. The tension between the banquet setting and the discussion of fasting remains, and the reference to "the disciples of the Pharisees" in v. 33 is jarring if one is expected to assume that the question has been raised by the Pharisees who had questioned Jesus' eating with the toll collectors.

The practices of Jesus' disciples are set in contrast to those of both John the Baptist and the Pharisees. Indeed, Jesus here takes a position that is dissimilar from both the Jewish practices of the time and the practices of the early church. Fasting is "the deliberate, temporary abstention from food for religious reasons."[78] In the OT, fasting meant complete abstention from food and water (Exod 34:28; Deut 9:9). Originally, the only national day of fasting was the Day of Atonement, but later other fast days were added (Ezra 8:21-23; Neh 9:1; Zech 8:19). Individual fasts were held for a variety of reasons, including penance (1 Sam 14:24), mourning (2 Sam 1:12; 3:35-36; 12:16), reinforce-

ment of prayer (Tob 12:8; Luke 2:27), and divination or preparation for a divine revelation (Exod 34:28; Dan 9:3). According to Luke (18:12) and the Didache (8:1), Pharisees fasted twice a week. The early church continued the practice of individual fasts (Acts 13:2-3; 14:23) and later required fasting on Good Friday. And Jesus himself fasted during the temptations (Luke 4:2), and taught that fasting should not be practiced for the purpose of public commendation (Matt 6:16-18).

Against this background, the present scene is all the more distinctive. It is the only passage in the NT that questions the value of fasting or signals a change in the place of fasting in Christian devotion. Luke makes the question concern both fasting and prayer, but prayer is not mentioned in the response. Jesus answers the question with a metaphor of a wedding and then adds three metaphorical sayings, each of which contrasts the new with the old. The sayings, therefore, generalize and escalate the issue. More than just the question of whether Jesus' disciples will fast, the issue to which Jesus responds concerns the relation of Christian discipleship to Jewish piety.

Since mourning was one of the reasons for fasting, Jesus points out that mourning would be inappropriate in the context of a wedding (cf. Matt 9:15). In the extended metaphor, which easily lends itself to Christian allegorization (*bridegroom, friends, wedding* mean *Jesus, disciples, the earthly ministry of Jesus*), Jesus may have

78. John Muddiman, "Fast, Fasting," *Anchor Bible Dictionary* (New York: Doubleday, 1992) 2:773.

been claiming his time, the time of the coming of the kingdom, as a time of joy and celebration, not unlike that of a wedding. Fasting might be appropriate at other times (and Luke may have an interest in grounding the Christian practice of fasting in Jesus' own pronouncements), but the time of the announcement of God's good news to the poor and the outcast was a time for celebration, not fasting. The statement "the days will come" is repeated in eschatological warnings later in the Gospel (17:22; 19:43; 21:6; 23:29).

Luke explicitly introduces the three appended sayings, or at least the first of them, as a parable. Such introductions are common in Luke (see, e.g., 6:39; 8:4; 12:16; 13:6). Luke significantly alters the wording of the first saying, underscoring the contrast between new and old and describing the destructive effect of tearing up a new garment to make a patch for an old one. The point is thereby shifted slightly from the Markan form of the saying in which the problem is not the destruction of the new garment in the process of trying to patch an old one but the shrinkage of the new patch so that the patch is ineffective and results in a worse tear. The new is inherently different from the old; it has its own integrity and will not match the old.

Similarly, no one would pour new wine into old wineskins. Here Luke repeats the similitude from Mark almost verbatim but still adds a clarifying and emphatic reference to the "new" wine in v. 37. The point of this saying, which may well have been proverbial, is that as the new wine ferments it will give off gas and stretch the wineskin. If the wineskin is old and brittle, it will break rather than stretch, and the wine will be lost. The result of putting new wine in old wineskins is that both the wine and the wineskins will be lost. Everyone knew that new wine required new wineskins. The challenge of the sayings, therefore, is to see Jesus and his teachings as a new garment that cannot be used to patch up the old, or as new wine that will require new wineskins. By implication, it also defines fasting and other contemporary religious practices as "old wineskins." The contrast, therefore, is a double one, between wine and wineskins and between the old and the new. Those who took offense because Jesus' disciples were not fasting had failed to see that something new had come, and they were unable to distinguish the wine from the wineskins. Their concern was simply with patching the old garment and preserving the old wineskins.

That attitude is wryly exposed by the third saying (v. 39). Those who drink old wine prize it as better than the new. Jesus was not trying to reverse the connoisseur's judgment on the quality of vintage wines (cf. Sir 9:10). Instead, he pointed out with subtlety, wit, and humor that those who drink old wines do not appreciate the new. Since the old wines were more expensive, Jesus' dry humor may have also implied a critique—from the perspective of the poor—of those who could afford expensive tastes.

REFLECTIONS

Each successive controversy story has driven wider the rift between Jesus and his critics. At one level this controversy concerns the place of fasting in Christian devotion. At that level it allows a place for fasting but points to the overriding concern with the celebration of Jesus' coming as the bridegroom who inaugurates the eschatological banquet (a theme to which Luke will return in 14:15-24).

At a deeper level, Jesus' metaphorical sayings declare that there can be no accommodation between the old and the new. The new will supersede and displace the old. The kingdom is greater than anything that went before it. Jesus' ministry stands in the tradition of the prophets, but it cannot be made to fit into the traditional patterns of piety of the past. Fasting was tied to a social system of purity that was antithetical to Jesus' extension of God's grace to the outcasts. The new could not be patched to the old. The entire system by which persons were judged clean or unclean would have to go. As will become clear later (14:15-24), in the social strata of the kingdom there are only those who accept the invitation to the kingdom and those who refuse the king's hospitality. All who eat at table with the Lord are "tax collectors and sinners," but if we are honest, most of us are mirrored in the crowd of the religious people who complained about what Jesus was doing.

The challenge to the church has always been to distinguish the wine from the wineskins and to be ready always to find new skins for the new wine. Repeatedly, however, the church has fought to preserve its old wineskins. Traditional patterns of worship and organization easily become confused with the new wine of Jesus' announcement of good news to the poor and his mission to the outcast.

The closing, wry observation may be one of the Gospel's most piercing judgments. As Christians in a privileged society, have we cultivated such a taste for the old wine that we despise the new? How different the taste of one who would welcome even a cup of cold water! Have we had "the good stuff" (houses, cars, freedoms) for so long that we have lost sight of the power of Jesus' invitation to a toll collector to follow him, his touch of the leper, or his table fellowship with outcasts? That is the celebration of a new vintage. The new wine has arrived bearing the date "the acceptable year of the Lord," and nothing in our relationships with others—especially the wretched, despised, and overlooked among us—can continue as it was.

Luke 6:1-11, Debate About Sabbath

NIV

6 One Sabbath Jesus was going through the grainfields, and his disciples began to pick some heads of grain, rub them in their hands and eat the kernels. [2]Some of the Pharisees asked, "Why are you doing what is unlawful on the Sabbath?"

[3]Jesus answered them, "Have you never read what David did when he and his companions were hungry? [4]He entered the house of God, and taking the consecrated bread, he ate what is lawful only for priests to eat. And he also gave some to his companions." [5]Then Jesus said to them, "The Son of Man is Lord of the Sabbath."

[6]On another Sabbath he went into the synagogue and was teaching, and a man was there whose right hand was shriveled. [7]The Pharisees and the teachers of the law were looking for a reason to accuse Jesus, so they watched him closely to see if he would heal on the Sabbath. [8]But Jesus knew what they were thinking and said to the man with the shriveled hand, "Get up and stand in front of everyone." So he got up and stood there.

[9]Then Jesus said to them, "I ask you, which is lawful on the Sabbath: to do good or to do evil, to save life or to destroy it?"

[10]He looked around at them all, and then said to the man, "Stretch out your hand." He did so, and his hand was completely restored. [11]But they were furious and began to discuss with one another what they might do to Jesus.

NRSV

6 One sabbath[a] while Jesus[b] was going through the grainfields, his disciples plucked some heads of grain, rubbed them in their hands, and ate them. [2]But some of the Pharisees said, "Why are you doing what is not lawful[c] on the sabbath?" [3]Jesus answered, "Have you not read what David did when he and his companions were hungry? [4]He entered the house of God and took and ate the bread of the Presence, which it is not lawful for any but the priests to eat, and gave some to his companions?" [5]Then he said to them, "The Son of Man is lord of the sabbath."

[6]On another sabbath he entered the synagogue and taught, and there was a man there whose right hand was withered. [7]The scribes and the Pharisees watched him to see whether he would cure on the sabbath, so that they might find an accusation against him. [8]Even though he knew what they were thinking, he said to the man who had the withered hand, "Come and stand here." He got up and stood there. [9]Then Jesus said to them, "I ask you, is it lawful to do good or to do harm on the sabbath, to save life or to destroy it?" [10]After looking around at all of them, he said to him, "Stretch out your hand." He did so, and his hand was restored. [11]But they were filled with fury and discussed with one another what they might do to Jesus.

[a]Other ancient authorities read *On the second first sabbath*
[b]Gk *he*   [c]Other ancient authorities add *to do*

COMMENTARY

The succession of discipleship, healing, and controversy stories in Luke 5:1–6:16 continues now with two sabbath controversy scenes. The structure of this part of the Gospel is clarified in part by the introductory phrases, for the first three and the last three units of this section are each introduced with the construction "And it came to pass" (καὶ ἐγένετο *kai egeneto,* or ἐγένετο δέ *egeneto de*) followed by a temporal clause. The parallelism is lost in translation, but the temporal transitions are still clear in 5:1, 12, 17 and in 6:1, 6, 12. In the latter three units, the temporal clause is followed in each instance by an infinitive. The two healing stories in 5:12-16 and 5:17-26 are balanced by the two sabbath controversies in 6:1-5 and 6:6-11, which are introduced with the phrases "One sabbath" (6:1) and "On another sabbath" (6:6). The calling of Levi at the center of this section underscores the theme of discipleship in the opening and closing scenes: the call of the fishermen (5:1-11) and the call of the Twelve (6:12-16). The banquet with toll collectors and sinners celebrated the inauguration of the new era and sharpened its conflict with the old. Jesus' announcement of the new priorities of the kingdom leads him into conflict with the Pharisees over sabbath observance in the next two scenes.

6:1-5, Plucking Grain on the Sabbath. The first sabbath controversy is a pronouncement story that presents the claim that Jesus as the Son of Man is "lord of the sabbath" (v. 5). While the story is drawn from Mark 2:23-28, Luke has simplified and clarified the description of the disciples' actions, dropped the anachronistic reference to Abiathar, and omitted the pronouncement that the sabbath was made for humans and not humans for the sabbath (Mark 2:27).

The actions of Jesus' disciples provide the setting for Jesus' pronouncement. The issue is sabbath violation, not stealing from a neighbor's field. Hebrew law allowed a person to go into another's field and pluck the ears of grain so long as that person did not harvest it with a sickle (Deut 23:24-25). Luke's addition of the phrase "rubbed them in their hands" describes what one would do with an ear of grain in order to separate it from the chaff before eating it. Both reaping and threshing, however, were considered to be forms of work forbidden on the sabbath. The preparation of food was also forbidden on the sabbath.[79]

The reference to "some of the Pharisees" and the continuation of the motif of eating link this scene with the preceding one. Having set aside the system of purity as it pertained to eating with outcasts and fasting, Jesus now authorizes the provision of food for the hungry even if it means violation of the sabbath. The effects of the new era inaugurated by Jesus continue to ripple outward, sweeping away old conventions, requiring the revaluing of ritual observances in relation to persons, and eliciting opposition from the guardians of religious tradition.

The Pharisees' question focuses the issue Luke is concerned with: *why* the disciples were violating Pharisaic tradition regarding the sabbath. Jesus responds, challenging the Pharisees on their own grounds, by arguing from Scripture. In Luke, Jesus' question has an added sting, literally: "Have you not read this—what David did?" The event that Jesus recalls is recorded in 1 Sam 21:1-6. David confronted the priest Ahimelech (not Abiathar, as in Mark 2:26, a difficulty Luke remedies by omitting any reference to the priest) at Nob (not the Temple at Jerusalem, as may be intended by "the house of the Lord"). Jesus' summary of the event in Luke highlights the authority of David to overturn the Levitical rules with reference to the eating not just of ordinary bread but the bread of the Presence. Leviticus 24:5-9 prescribes that the priests should arrange twelve loaves of bread in two rows on the table each sabbath "as a commitment of the people of Israel. . . . They shall be for Aaron and his descendants, who shall eat them in a holy place, for they are most holy portions for him from the offerings by fire to the LORD, a perpetual due." David claimed the authority to offer this bread to his men, vowing that they had kept themselves pure. There is no reference to the sabbath in 1 Sam 21:1-6; the parallel lies in Jesus' authority to set aside prescriptions regarding sacred time, just as David had superseded the law regarding sacred bread. In each instance, hunger—human need—is

---

79. See *Jub.* 2:29; *m. Šabb.* 3.1–4.2; 7.2; 9.5.

given priority over ritual observance of what God has decreed as sacred.

The juxtaposition of Jesus with David in this scene is consistent with Luke's presentation of Jesus as the son of David. In the infancy narrative Jesus was introduced as one born to the house of David (1:27) and who would receive the throne of David (1:32). Later, Jesus will be addressed as "son of David" (18:38-39) and will defend his claim to be one who is greater even than David (20:41-44). The positive evaluation of David is expressed most clearly in Acts 13:22, where David is described as "a man after my heart, who will carry out all my wishes."

In the Markan account on which Luke depends, Jesus affirms that "the sabbath was made for humankind, and not humankind for the sabbath" (Mark 2:27). The effect of this saying is to clarify that sabbath observance was intended as a gift for humanity, not as an onerous duty. The sabbath could, therefore, be violated by work when that work met a real human need. The saying in Mark 2:28 seems to be an early Christian interpretation based on the christological claims implicit in this scene: "So the Son of Man is lord even of the sabbath." Luke has omitted the saying in Mark 2:27, perhaps because it seemed to permit too much latitude in sabbath observance, or perhaps because Luke was more concerned with the christological emphasis of the pronouncement in Mark 2:28. Regardless of Luke's motivation, the effect of his handling of the tradition is to place what probably was originally an early Christian interpretation of Jesus' sabbath saying on the lips of Jesus: "The Son of Man is lord of the sabbath." In this saying "the Son of Man" is clearly used in its titular sense as a reference to Jesus, the risen Lord.

6:6-11, Healing on the Sabbath. The second sabbath controversy story sets in opposition the obligation to save life and the obligation to keep the sabbath. At least according to later rabbinic tradition, one was allowed to heal on the sabbath only when faced with a life-threatening condition: "And whenever there is doubt whether life is in danger this overrides the Sabbath."[80]

The introductory temporal clause is similar to the one Luke has used repeatedly in this section (see 6:1). Luke tells the reader at the outset that the day is the sabbath and adds that Jesus went into the synagogue *to teach* (cf. 4:15, 31; 5:3, 17). Jesus seizes a teachable moment and teaches not just with words but by means of a dramatic life situation. On an earlier occasion there had been a man with an unclean spirit in the synagogue (4:33); this time there is a man with a withered, shriveled, or crippled right hand. Only Luke adds that it was the man's right hand, the hand normally used for work, gesturing, and greeting. Since one performed chores of bodily hygiene with one's left hand, that hand was not to be presented in public.[81] The man had lost the use of his good hand, presumably forcing him to use his left hand in public, thereby adding shame to his physical disability.

Luke also adds that "the scribes and Pharisees" were present (cf. 5:21, 30), watching Jesus closely to see whether he would heal on the sabbath so that they might have something with which to accuse him. The scene is set, therefore, with three parties, which allows the reader to interpret the scene from various perspectives. From the crippled man's point of view, Jesus is a potential healer or source of help, while the scribes and Pharisees pose an obstacle or threat to the possibility that Jesus might heal him. From Jesus' point of view, each of the other parties represents a competing priority, whether to heal the man or to keep the sabbath, thereby complying with the scribes and Pharisees' interpretation that sabbath observance takes precedence, since the man's condition is chronic and not life threatening. From the scribes' and Pharisees' point of view, the man with the withered hand offers the opportunity to put Jesus, who has violated the sabbath in the past, in a no-win situation. If Jesus heals the man, they can accuse him of sabbath violation. If he refuses to heal the man, he has complied with their authority and denied his mission to "release the captives."

Because he knows what they are thinking (cf. 4:23; 5:22), Jesus instructs the man to stand in their midst (cf. 4:35). Contrary to any suspicions the scribes and Pharisees may have that he would try to do something that would escape their notice, Jesus makes a public example of this man. All will see what he is about to do. Instead of

---

healing the man directly, however, Jesus asks a question, just as earlier he had asked the scribes and Pharisees a disarming question before healing the man who was paralyzed (cf. 5:22-23). This device strengthens the parallels between the two earlier healing stories (5:12-16, 17-26) and the two sabbath stories here. The question also serves as a pronouncement, again blending elements of a healing miracle and a pronouncement story.

Verses 6-8, therefore, are preparatory for what follows. They set the scene, introduce the characters, pose the alternatives, and heighten suspense. Jesus' question reinterprets the situation in two respects. First, he sharpens the issue by posing two sets of antitheses: to do good or to do evil, to save life or to destroy it. The second set both interprets and escalates the conflict between the alternatives of the first antithesis. The tensive power of the statement arises from its ambiguity. Does the question apply to Jesus, to the scribes and Pharisees, or to both? For Jesus, if to do good is to save life, he should heal the man. The Pharisees, however, are also faced with a choice. How are they observing the sabbath: By doing good or doing evil? Specifically, while Jesus is seeking to do good, are they not doing evil? Are they seeking to destroy him while he is seeking to heal? The question places the alternatives in a new light. Sabbath observance is defined positively, not in terms of what one will not do, but in terms of what one must do.

The scribes and Pharisees offer no response, though Luke omits Mark's report that they were silent. Luke also omits Mark's description of Jesus' anger and its justification (Mark 3:5). Jesus' look means that his question has scored a direct hit. All present can see that Jesus has silenced his opposition. Having dealt with the scribes and Pharisees, and in the process taught an important lesson, Jesus turns to heal the man. No touch or cleansing process is needed. Just as Jesus had defeated his critics with a word, so also he heals with a word: "Stretch out your hand."

As the scene closes, Luke notes the effects of Jesus' words on each of the other parties. The man's hand is restored, and the scribes and Pharisees are filled with fury—mindless rage. Luke omits Mark's report that the Pharisees began to plot Jesus' death with the Herodians (Mark 3:6). The Pharisees' mindless fury (ἄνοια *anoia*) is not far, however, from the ignorance (ἄγνοια *agnoia*) that will lead to Jesus' death (cf. Acts 3:17; 13:27).[82] Before the authorities move to charge Jesus, however, Luke will report two other healings on the sabbath that will sharpen the issues and the conflict between the old and the new (see 13:1-17; 14:1-6).

---

82. See Robert C. Tannehill, *The Narrative Unity of Luke–Acts: A Literary Interpretation,* vol. 1: *The Gospel According to Luke* (Philadelphia: Fortress, 1986) 176.

REFLECTIONS

The two sabbath stories expose the conflict between competing values and duties. The issue of the relative claims of the duty to meet human need and the duty to observe religious traditions is still with us in various forms. When preaching on these texts, the interpreter needs to avoid the temptation to set up the Pharisees as "straw men" representing a hollow point of view. To do so leaves the conflict in the first century, where it will have little meaning for contemporary Christians, and may even invite them to understand the texts as a Christian polemic against Judaism. While Luke may be chronicling the tragedy of the rejection of Jesus by the religious authorities, the point of identification for modern Christians is not with Jesus over against the Pharisees, but with the Pharisees in their struggle to choose between competing obligations and the difficulty in accepting Jesus' "new" teachings.

Both sabbath controversies set God's command to observe the sabbath in conflict with the command to love one's neighbor. Which takes precedence, the duty of sabbath rest or the duty to feed the hungry and heal the sick? Can the love of God be separated from and juxtaposed with love of neighbor, or is the love of neighbor an expression of our love of God (cf. Luke 10:25-27)?

In the first story, the language of taking holy bread, giving it, and eating it reverberates in Christian ears with the accounts of the feeding of the five thousand and with the observance of the Lord's Supper. Thus when Jesus gives bread to others in the course of the Gospel, it is no less a holy act than the eating of the bread of the Presence. All bread becomes holy when it is given to the hungry in obedience to Jesus.

Jesus' penetrating question in the second story asks not only what is permitted (6:2) on the sabbath, but also what is required. Can one honor God if one neglects human need? On the contrary, then, does not the sabbath require that we take initiative to restore those who are hungry or sick to wholeness and health? Even more sharply, to refuse to do good, to save life, is tantamount to a decision to do evil, to destroy life. From this perspective, rather than defining piety negatively—by what one does not do or what one opposes—Jesus' challenge calls us to demonstrate our faith by the good and beneficial things we do.

The two sabbath controversies present Jesus as the lord of the sabbath, the bringer of the new that sweeps away the old. The process of realizing the implications of that confession, however, forces us constantly to confront the residue of the old in our own efforts to love God and love our neighbor.

Luke 6:12-16, Choosing the Twelve

NIV

¹²One of those days Jesus went out to a mountainside to pray, and spent the night praying to God. ¹³When morning came, he called his disciples to him and chose twelve of them, whom he also designated apostles: ¹⁴Simon (whom he named Peter), his brother Andrew, James, John, Philip, Bartholomew, ¹⁵Matthew, Thomas, James son of Alphaeus, Simon who was called the Zealot, ¹⁶Judas son of James, and Judas Iscariot, who became a traitor.

NRSV

12Now during those days he went out to the mountain to pray; and he spent the night in prayer to God. ¹³And when day came, he called his disciples and chose twelve of them, whom he also named apostles: ¹⁴Simon, whom he named Peter, and his brother Andrew, and James, and John, and Philip, and Bartholomew, ¹⁵and Matthew, and Thomas, and James son of Alphaeus, and Simon, who was called the Zealot, ¹⁶and Judas son of James, and Judas Iscariot, who became a traitor.

COMMENTARY

The naming of the twelve apostles stands at a critical point in Luke's narrative. Structurally, it concludes the section devoted to discipleship and controversy that begins at Luke 5:1 and features the calling of the fishermen in the first scene (5:1-11) and the call of Levi at its center (5:17-26). By placing the appointment of the Twelve immediately after the controversies with the Pharisees—and the dramatic distinction between old and new that these controversies exposed—Luke presents the appointment of the Twelve as the constitution of a new nucleus for the people of God, perhaps in deliberate succession to the twelve tribes of Israel. The conflicts between Jesus and the scribes and Pharisees have already shown that they represent the old and that, therefore, they are no more fit for leadership in the kingdom than old wineskins are fit for new wine. The events at this juncture of the Gospel foreshadow the opposition that will lead to Jesus' death and the witness of the apostles in Acts.

The appointment of the Twelve also prepares for Jesus' preaching to the disciples in the latter part of chap. 6. Here Jesus turns from debates with the Pharisees to instruction for those who have been receptive to his announcement of the kingdom. Luke's highlighting of these developments is set in relief by comparing his arrangement of the material with that of the other evangelists. Luke depends primarily on Mark, but Luke has reversed the sequence of two paragraphs at this point: Mark 3:7-12, a summary statement; and Mark 3:13-19, the appointment of the Twelve. By reversing these two, Luke is able to make the appointment of the Twelve the conclusion of 5:1–6:16, on controversy and discipleship, and to use the summary statement as the introduction to the Sermon on the Plain. Matthew also adapts the Markan summary statement in his introduction to the Sermon on the Mount (Matthew 5–7), but delays the appointment of the Twelve until later in the Gospel (Matt 10:1-4). John has neither a list of the Twelve nor anything like the Sermon on the Plain.

Luke again signals the introduction of a new scene by means of "Now it came to pass" (ἐγένετο δέ *egeneto de*) and a temporal phrase: "Now during those days." The significance of the coming scene is indicated both by its setting on a mountain and the report that Jesus spent the night in prayer. The only other time Jesus goes up on a mountain to pray in Luke is the occasion of the transfiguration (9:28), just prior to the start of his journey to Jerusalem. Prayer is a regular feature of Luke's account of the ministry of Jesus and the growth of the church, and references to prayer often occur in connection with significant turning points in this history (Luke 3:21, the coming of the Spirit upon Jesus; 9:18, Peter's confession that Jesus is the Messiah; 9:28, the transfiguration; 11:1, the Lord's prayer; and 22:40-46, Gethsemane). It is not surprising, therefore, that Luke adds a reference to prayer at this point, even though Mark has none.

In one verse, Luke refers to "the disciples," "the Twelve," and "apostles," but the terms are not synonymous and do not refer to the same groups. In Luke's account, in contrast to Mark and Matthew, the Twelve are distinct from the larger group of disciples: "He called his disciples and chose twelve of them." In the next scene Jesus is still surrounded by "a great crowd of his disciples" (6:17). Luke also departs from Mark by omitting Mark's twofold statement of the purpose for Jesus' appointment of the Twelve (Mark 3:14-15). Instead, Luke declares that Jesus named the Twelve "apostles," thereby characterizing their role as witnesses. The references to apostles in the early church in Acts and in the rest of the NT make it clear that many who were not among the Twelve were still called apostles; Paul contrasts the Twelve with "all the apostles" in his list of the appearances of Jesus (1 Cor 15:3-8); Paul repeatedly claims for himself the title "apostle" (Rom 1:1; 1 Cor 1:1; 9:1-5); Luke calls Barnabas and Paul apostles (Acts 14:14); and Paul refers to Andronicus and Junia as apostles (Rom 16:7). In Luke's account of the Jerusalem conference, the phrase "the apostles and elders" occurs six times (Acts 15:2, 4, 6, 22, 23; 16:4), but the apostles disappear from Luke's account at that point.

Two aspects of Luke's characterization of the Twelve stand out prominently: (1) the relationship between the twelve apostles and the twelve tribes of Israel and (2) the role of the Twelve in the leadership of the early church. The relationship of the Twelve to the tribes of Israel becomes explicit in Luke 22:29-30, "I confer on you, just as my Father has conferred on me, a kingdom, so that you may eat and drink at my table in my kingdom, and you will sit on thrones judging the twelve tribes of Israel." This association probably also explains the importance Luke attaches to the choice of Matthias to take Judas's place as the twelfth apostle. In this process, the following criteria for apostleship are stated: (1) a man, (2) who accompanied Jesus and the other disciples during Jesus' ministry and (3) was a witness to the resurrection (cf. 1 Cor 9:1; 15:8). Implicit in the election process is also the requirement of a commission (cf. Acts 9:15; Gal 1:15-16).[83] In the context of these references, the importance of election also emerges clearly. Jesus "chose" the apostles (Luke 6:13), just as God chose the twelve tribes of Israel (Acts 13:17; cf. Deut 4:37; 10:15). Similarly, Paul was "a chosen instrument" (Acts 9:15), the church prayed to be guided to the person God had "chosen" to replace Judas (Acts 1:24), and Peter was chosen to take the gospel to the Gentile house of Cornelius (Acts 15:7). Luke's use of the term for "chose" (ἐκλέγομαι *eklegomai*) in connection with the appointment of the Twelve, therefore, is hardly incidental; it designates the Twelve as witnesses and leaders chosen by God, just as God had chosen the twelve tribes of Israel.

83. See Joseph A. Fitzmyer, *The Gospel According to Luke (I–IX)*, AB 28 (Garden City, N.Y.: Doubleday, 1981) 615-16.

The second facet of Luke's characterization of the Twelve—their role as apostles—stands out all the more clearly when one recognizes how seldom the Twelve appear in the NT outside of the synoptic Gospels. John mentions the Twelve only four times, and then without listing their names (6:67, 70, 71; 20:24). The expression "the Twelve" designates the apostles only three times outside of the Gospels. Paul mentions the Twelve only once, in the tradition of the appearances (1 Cor 15:5); Revelation links the number twelve with the apostles in 21:14; and the only other reference to the Twelve is in Acts 6:2. If Luke had not linked the Twelve with the role of the apostles in Acts, their place in the leadership of the early church would have been even more puzzling and short-lived than it appears to be when Acts is considered.

Luke's list of the Twelve also bears close inspection. None of the four lists of the Twelve in the NT agrees exactly with any other (see Fig. 2).

Each list tells a story, but one that we can only partially recover. While none of the lists is exactly like any other, they are remarkably similar. All four traditions agree that there were twelve disciples, and all four lists transmit the names in three groups of four. The lead name in each group is the same in each list: Simon Peter, Philip, and James son of Alphaeus. Moreover, the first and second groups of four names are the same in each of the lists, with variations only in the sequence of the names. The differences in the names included in each list appear only in the last group: Matthew and Mark have Thaddaeus, Luke and Acts have Judas son of James. Judas Iscariot, who is always last, is

---

Figure 2: "The Twelve" Identified in Matthew, Mark, Luke, and Acts

Matthew 10	Mark 3	Luke 6	Acts 1
Simon, also known as Peter	Simon (to whom he gave the name Peter)	Simon, whom he named Peter	Peter
Andrew his brother	James son of Zebedee	Andrew his brother	John
James son of Zebedee	John the brother of James (to whom he gave the name Boanerges, that is Sons of Thunder)	James	James
John his brother	Andrew	John	Andrew
Philip	Philip	Philip	Philip
Bartholomew	Bartholomew	Bartholomew	Thomas
Thomas	Matthew	Matthew	Bartholomew
Matthew the tax collector	Thomas	Thomas	Matthew
James son of Alphaeus	James son of Alphaeus	James son of Alphaeus	James son of Alphaeus
Thaddaeus	Thaddaeus	Simon, who was called the Zealot	Simon the Zealot
Simon the Cananaean	Simon the Cananaean	Judas son of James	Judas son of James
Judas Iscariot, the one who betrayed him	Judas Iscariot who betrayed him	Judas Iscariot who became a traitor	

identified in Matthew and Mark as the one who handed Jesus over; Luke is the only one to use the term "betrayer" (προδότης *prodotēs*).

The stories told about the names in the first group are more familiar to us. Matthew and Luke list together the names of the two sets of brothers, recalling the story of the call of the fishermen. This story is recorded in Mark 1:16-20 and Matt 4:18-22. Because Luke's account in 5:1-11 features Peter and the great catch of fish, James and John are mentioned only in passing, and Andrew is not even named. The sequence of the first four names in Luke, therefore, recalls a tradition that Luke has obscured by his redaction of Mark 1:16-20. Mark lists first the "inner three," who are featured more prominently in Mark than in any other Gospel, although we would not have been surprised if Luke had followed this sequence, placing Andrew last, since Andrew's name was omitted from the story of the call of the fishermen. The group of three does not have the same importance for Luke that it does for Mark, since Luke does not separate them from the other disciples at Gethsemane (cf. Mark 14:33; Luke 22:40). The sequence of the first four names in Acts 1 tells a different story; it foreshadows the prominence of Peter and John in the narrative that will follow (Acts 3:1, 3-4, 11; 4:13, 19; 8:14). The naming of Peter and John as the two disciples who were sent to prepare the Passover meal (Luke 22:8) prepares the reader for the appearance of this pair in Acts. Each of the lists, therefore, reflects particular traditions about the disciples. Unfortunately, we know so little about most of the disciples that we cannot reconstruct their stories.

REFLECTIONS

Several themes can be drawn from this brief report of the naming of the apostles that would bear further theological or homiletical reflection:

1. Throughout the biblical record, God calls individuals for particular tasks. Sometimes the person has gifts that are uniquely suited to the task (e.g., Samuel, Jeremiah, Barnabas), but more often than not the person either discovers his or her gifts after setting about the task or succeeds in spite of apparent shortcomings and obstacles (e.g., Moses, Gideon, David, Peter, or Paul). In each case, however, the call begins with an experience of being addressed by God or an inner conviction that God has called the person to serve God and the community in a particular way. Usually, the community of faith recognizes God's call of the individual, but again the recognition may not come immediately, and sometimes not for years thereafter. Both the person and the community of faith need to be alert, therefore, to the leadings of God's Spirit.

2. If the number of the disciples is significant in relation to the twelve tribes of Israel, then Jesus' calling and appointment of the Twelve signals that the new movement that he began and that resulted in the birth of the church stands in continuity with the community of Israel. One may see here varying degrees of fulfillment, reconstitution, or replacement, but at a minimum one may say that what God began in the election of Israel, God has continued to do in the calling of persons to discipleship to Jesus. God is still calling together a people of faith through whom God can bless all the peoples of the earth (Gen 12:1-3). Consequently, blessing and mission are vital aspects of God's purpose for the community of faith, whether it be Israel or the church.

3. Particularly in Luke, the call to follow Jesus is a call to imitate him, and in Acts we see the disciples continuing to do what Jesus began during his ministry. Jesus blessed the poor and the outcast; he ate with the excluded and defended them against the religious authorities. Jesus showed compassion on the weak, the sick, and the small, and in these matters the disciples had a particularly hard time in following Jesus' example. Nevertheless, if discipleship and lordship are directly related, then the Gospel's portrayal of Jesus is vital for the church. We can follow Jesus in the Lukan sense only when we see clearly who he is. Ultimately, of course, the Gospel challenges each reader to respond to the call to discipleship and join the Twelve as followers of Jesus.

LUKE 6:17-49, JESUS' INSTRUCTION TO HIS DISCIPLES

OVERVIEW

The conclusion to the previous section (5:1–6:16) and the insertion of a summary statement (6:17-19) at this point prepare the reader for the opening of a new section: Jesus' instruction of his disciples (6:20-49). The previous chapters have led the reader through a section in which the focus was on christology and the announcement of the Messiah's work (4:14-44) and then a series of controversy and call stories that introduced the disciples and illustrated various responses to Jesus (5:1–6:16). The coming section reports Jesus' teachings on the nature and demands of discipleship (6:20-49).[84]

Luke's account of Jesus' Sermon on the Plain has been so overshadowed by Matthew's Sermon on the Mount that it is difficult to read the former

without comparing it to Matthew and noting what is missing or different in Luke. While the Sermon on the Mount extends over three chapters (109 verses), the Sermon on the Plain is packed into part of one chapter (30 verses). Despite the disparity in content, the sequence of the sermon in Luke agrees with that of Matthew, giving rise to the assumption that there must have been a version of the sermon that predated both Matthew and Luke. It should be noted that at this point in the Gospel Luke departs from Mark and inserts material not found in Mark. Hence Luke 6:20–8:3 has often been called the Little Interpolation. Luke's editorial work, drawing from Q and other sources, however, would not account for the parallels to the Sermon on the Mount illustrated in the synopsis of the two accounts in Fig. 3.

---

84. See John Nolland, *Luke 1–9:20,* WBC 35A (Dallas: Word, 1989) 274.

Figure 3: Synopsis of the Sermon on the Mount/Sermon on the Plain

Matthew 5:7		Luke 6:20-49	
5:3-12	9 beatitudes	6:20-23	4 beatitudes
		6:24-26	4 woes
5:13	The salt of the earth		(cf. 14:34-35)
5:14-16	The light of the world		(cf. 8:16)
5:17-20	The law and the prophets		(cf. 16:16-17)
5:21-26	Murder and anger		(cf. 12:57-59)
5:27-32	Adultery and divorce		(cf. 16:18)
5:33-37	Oaths		
5:38-42	Retaliation	6:29-30	
5:43-48	Love of one's enemies	6:27-28, 32-36	
6:1-6	Almsgiving, prayer		
6:7-15	The Lord's Prayer		(cf. 11:1-4)
6:16-18	Fasting		
6:19-21	Treasures		(cf. 12:33-34)
6:22-23	The sound eye		(cf. 11:34-36)
6:24	Serving two masters		(cf. 16:13)
6:25-34	Anxiety		(cf. 12:22-32)
7:1-5	Judging	6:37-42	
7:6	Profaning the holy		
7:7-11	God's answer to prayer		(cf. 11:9-13)
7:12	The Golden Rule		(6:31)
7:13-14	The two ways		(cf. 13:23-24)
7:15-20	Trees and their fruit	6:43-45	
7:21-23	"Lord, Lord"	6:46	(cf. 13:25-27)
7:24-27	The house built on rock	6:47-49	

This overview quickly reveals five features of Luke's work: (1) Much of what is present in Matthew but absent in Luke concerns the relationship between Jesus' teachings and the Law (e.g., 5:17-20 and the structure of six antitheses in 5:21-48), matters that would have been of more interest to Jewish Christians than to Gentile Christians. It is difficult to tell whether these sections were added to the traditional sermon by Matthew or omitted from it by Luke. (2) Luke has sharpened the edge of Jesus' teachings on wealth and poverty by refusing to spiritualize Jesus' words and by adding the four woes, which are the only significant addition to the tradition found in Matthew. (3) Luke has preserved the instruction dealing with loving one's enemies, judging, bearing fruit, and heeding Jesus' words (6:27-36, 37-42, 43-45, 46, 47-49). (4) The sequence of the sermon in Luke runs parallel to the sequence of the material in Matthew, with omissions, insertions, and a slight change of sequence in 6:27-36. (5) Some of the material omitted from the Sermon on the Mount is found elsewhere in Luke, but even here the material is often abbreviated, as a careful comparison of the numbers of verses in the Lukan material and the Matthean parallels reveals. While respecting the tradition, therefore, Luke has been free to alter the sequence, length, and wording of his materials, thereby shaping the tradition of Jesus' teachings for his own purposes.

Our synopsis defines some of the basic units of Luke's sermon, but it does not resolve the question of its structure. Because the sermon flows from one theme to another in a rather loose fashion, any structure is probably artificial, reflecting the interpreter's reading strategy. Nevertheless, the interpretive options are exposed by surveying the structures that have been proposed. Commentators have proposed dividing the sermon into three parts (6:20-26, 27-38, 39-49), four parts (6:20-26, 27-36, 37-42, 43-49), five parts (6:20-26, 27-36, 37-42, 43-45, 46-49), or six parts (6:20-26, 27-35, 36-38, 39-42, 43-45, 46-49).

All agree that the blessings and woes in 6:20-26 constitute the first section, which defines God's relationship to the disciples. Those who follow the three-part division have the strongest evidence to appeal to because the only formal divisions are indicated by the address in v. 27, "But I say to you that listen," and the aside in v. 39, "He also told them a parable." This division also accords with the character of the material in each section of the sermon: blessings and woes (vv. 20-26), paraenetic exhortations (vv. 27-38), and parables (vv. 39-49). Any other proposed divisions are based on changes in theme (e.g., at v. 36 or 37) or breaks between individual units (e.g., at v. 43 or 46). In the analysis that follows, therefore, the tripartite structure is followed, and the breaks between units are recognized as secondary divisions.

Luke 6:17-19, The Setting for Jesus' Instruction

NIV

17He went down with them and stood on a level place. A large crowd of his disciples was there and a great number of people from all over Judea, from Jerusalem, and from the coast of Tyre and Sidon, 18who had come to hear him and to be healed of their diseases. Those troubled by evil[a] spirits were cured, 19and the people all tried to touch him, because power was coming from him and healing them all.

[a]18 Greek *unclean*

NRSV

17He came down with them and stood on a level place, with a great crowd of his disciples and a great multitude of people from all Judea, Jerusalem, and the coast of Tyre and Sidon. 18They had come to hear him and to be healed of their diseases; and those who were troubled with unclean spirits were cured. 19And all in the crowd were trying to touch him, for power came out from him and healed all of them.

COMMENTARY

Luke has freely adapted Mark 3:7-10 (Mark 3:11-12, the remainder of the Markan summary statement, has already been used in Luke 4:41). Luke picks up the emphasis on healing from Mark and adds the focus on hearing Jesus' teaching so that the summary may serve as a suitable introduction to the sermon in the following verses.

Because Jesus has been up on a mountain with the Twelve, Luke notes that he descended to a level place. Mark's reference to the sea is omitted, and hence also his mention of the boat (which will not reenter the story until 8:22). The crowd is more precisely identified as "a great crowd of his disciples," which picks up the theme of discipleship, further distinguishes the special role of the Twelve, and prepares for Jesus' teaching on discipleship. "The people" (λαός *laos*), who seem to respond to Jesus more positively than the "crowd" (ὄχλος *ochlos*), also reenter the story for the first time since 3:21. This is a gathering of those who have been responsive to Jesus' work and his call to discipleship. They have not come to test Jesus or out of idle curiosity. They have come, rather, to *hear* Jesus and to be healed by

him. The motif of hearing Jesus continues throughout the sermon (see 6:27, 47, 49), so its introduction here sets up an inclusion with vv. 47 and 49 and adds force to the sermon's conclusion.

Luke preserves Mark's list of surrounding territories, omitting only Idumea and the Transjordan. Because Luke does not present the crowd as being hostile, the threat of its crushing Jesus is omitted (cf. Mark 3:9). Exorcisms of unclean spirits will be a recurring feature in the rest of the Galilean ministry (see 7:21; 8:2, 26-39; 9:37-43). In this respect, these summary verses introduce not only the sermon but also the next phase of the Galilean ministry (cf. the summary statement in 4:14-15). Luke's notice that the crowd sought to touch Jesus because power issued from him continues the characterization of Jesus as a Spirit-endowed, charismatic healer. Characteristically, Luke also emphasizes the universal scope of Jesus' power; the people came from *all* Judea and Jerusalem, *all* the crowd sought to touch him, and Jesus healed *all* of them.

Luke 6:20-26, Blessings on the Poor and Woes to the Rich

NIV

20Looking at his disciples, he said:
"Blessed are you who are poor,
for yours is the kingdom of God.
21Blessed are you who hunger now,
for you will be satisfied.
Blessed are you who weep now,
for you will laugh.
22Blessed are you when men hate you,
when they exclude you and insult you
and reject your name as evil,
because of the Son of Man.

23"Rejoice in that day and leap for joy, because great is your reward in heaven. For that is how their fathers treated the prophets.

24"But woe to you who are rich,
for you have already received your comfort.

NRSV

20Then he looked up at his disciples and said:
"Blessed are you who are poor,
for yours is the kingdom of God.
21 "Blessed are you who are hungry now,
for you will be filled.
"Blessed are you who weep now,
for you will laugh.
22"Blessed are you when people hate you, and when they exclude you, revile you, and defame you[a] on account of the Son of Man. 23Rejoice in that day and leap for joy, for surely your reward is great in heaven; for that is what their ancestors did to the prophets.
24 "But woe to you who are rich,
for you have received your consolation.
25 "Woe to you who are full now,

aGk *cast out your name as evil*

NIV

25Woe to you who are well fed now,
  for you will go hungry.
 Woe to you who laugh now,
  for you will mourn and weep.
26Woe to you when all men speak well of you,
  for that is how their fathers treated the false
   prophets.

NRSV

 for you will be hungry.
 "Woe to you who are laughing now,
  for you will mourn and weep.
26"Woe to you when all speak well of you, for
that is what their ancestors did to the false prophets.

COMMENTARY

When Jesus speaks, he speaks specifically to his disciples. What follows is the standard for which every disciple should strive. Nevertheless, the sermon does not begin with admonitions and exhortations, but with the pronouncement of God's blessings on the disciples. The beatitudes are active and performative; they declare God's favor on the poor, the hungry, those who weep, and those who are hated. How fortunate they are because theirs is the kingdom. At the same time, the woes declare that those who prosper now will be judged. Alas, how terrible it will be for them. A note of eschatological expectancy pervades both the beatitudes and the woes; the word *now* (νῦν *nyn*) occurs four times in vv. 21 and 25, suggesting the disparity between the conditions of this age and the rewards of the age to come and underscoring the force of the future tense verbs. Luke's beatitudes differ from Matthew's in that Luke's speak in the second person rather than the third person, they speak to real socioeconomic conditions rather than to spiritual conditions or attitudes, and they declare God's partisan commitment to the poor and the oppressed. Luke includes the beatitudes that stand first, fourth, and ninth in the Matthean sermon, while the blessing on those who weep has no parallel in Matthew. The four woes correspond to the four beatitudes and follow in the same sequence.

6:20-23. The first beatitude sets the tone for all that follows. Whereas the next two beatitudes merely pronounce a reversal—the hungry will be filled and those who weep will laugh—the causal section of the first beatitude declares that the kingdom of God belongs to the poor. This is the second of thirty-two references to "the kingdom of God" in Luke. The first reference, in 4:43—"I

must proclaim the good news of the kingdom of God to the other cities also"—echoes Jesus' announcement of good news to the poor in Nazareth (cf. 4:18). These earlier references to the poor, to the kingdom of God, and to good news prepare the reader to understand that the first beatitude is tied to Jesus' fulfillment of Isaiah 61 and that the teaching for disciples that follows is an extension of what Jesus has already been doing.

The blessing of the poor neither idealizes nor glorifies poverty. It declares God's prejudicial commitment to the poor. The coming of the kingdom will bring a reversal of fortunes (cf. Lazarus, 16:19-31). Indeed, the first two references to the kingdom in Luke (4:43; 6:20) make it clear that one of the principal hallmarks of the kingdom will be the redemption of the poor. They will be released from their degradation. Oppressed now, they will enjoy God's blessings in the kingdom. The hungry will be fed, and those who weep (cf. "mourn" in Isa 61:2; Matt 5:4; Luke 6:25) will laugh.

Jesus' teachings are scandalous because they overturn every conventional expectation. The scandal of his ministry was his association with outcasts, and it was on them that he pronounced God's blessing, just as Jacob had pronounced his blessing on his sons (Genesis 49), thereby passing on God's blessing of Abraham's descendants (Gen 12:1-3). Henceforth, God's presence, advocacy, and redemptive work will be seen among the poor. On the one hand, this declaration makes no mention of Israel, but on the other hand, it is consistent with the prophetic calls for justice for the poor. In the OT God is the protector and defender of the poor.

So scandalous is Jesus' message that revisionist interpretations began as early as Matthew's change of the "poor" to the "poor in spirit" and his change of those who "hunger" to those who "hunger and thirst for righteousness." Spiritualizing the beatitudes grants those who are not poor access to them, but it also domesticates Jesus' scandalous gospel.

Hunger and weeping are treated as aspects of poverty, preventing any romanticized view of the poor. God's promise is that the hungry will be fed. This promise echoes the OT expectations of an eschatological banquet for the elect (Ps 107:9; Isa 25:6; cf. Luke 12:37; 13:29; 14:14-24), but the beatitude will also be fulfilled by Jesus (6:1-5; 9:12-17) and by the early church (Acts 2:46; 6:1-4; 11:28-30). Laughter and joy among the oppressed will characterize the kingdom (Psalm 126). Although the verb used for "to laugh" (γελάω *gelaō*) does not recur in Luke, joy among the people at what God was doing is a common theme in this gospel (1:14; 2:10; 8:13; 10:17; 15:7, 10; 24:41, 52).

The fourth beatitude is different in form and assumes the situation of the early church (see esp. its reference to the "Son of Man"). It envisions four situations in which the disciple may suffer abuse: being hated, excluded, reviled, and defamed. This beatitude has parallels in other early Christian exhortations (1 Pet 3:14; 4:14), so it may well rest on an earlier form: "Blessed are you when you are hated [v. 22*a*], for your reward is great in heaven [v. 23*b*]." The condition of being despised is then related to the church's experience of being persecuted, and reward is promised for those who are faithful to the Lord even when they are cast out and reviled (cf. Isa 66:5; Jas 2:7). The use of "Son of Man" in this context clearly reflects the post-Easter confession of Jesus as the exalted Lord. Persecution of the prophets, however, further demonstrates the opposition of Israel's religious leaders to God's redemptive work, and the stirrings of rejection have already begun (3:19-20; 4:29; 6:11; see later 11:49-51; 13:33-34). The admonition to the reviled persists even in this redacted form of the beatitude: Rejoice in your oppression (cf. Jas 1:2) because God's favor is with those who are reviled.

6:24-26. The four woes drive home the message of the four beatitudes by following them in sequence and stating the inverse. Drawing from its use in the Septuagint, Luke makes more frequent use of the "woe" form than do any of the other Gospels (15 times; cf. 10:13; 11:42-47, 52;

17:1; 21:23; 22:22). Just as the beatitudes announce God's favor, which is an occasion for joy among the poor, so also the woes announce God's judgment, which should be a cause for grief and remorse among the rich. Alas, how terrible it will be for them!

More than any other Gospel, Luke expounds the dangers of wealth. The woe picks up the thread from the Magnificat: God sends the rich away empty (1:53). The rich are shortsighted and are lulled into a false security when they think that their present abundance ensures their future comfort (12:15-21). However, if there is a correlation between treasures on earth and treasures in heaven, it is an inverse one (12:21). The rich are apt to be so preoccupied with their possessions that they fail to respond to God's invitation (14:15-24). The rich who neglect the poor at their gate will find that in the hereafter they will have none of the abundance they enjoyed in this life (16:19-31). Because the kingdom of God means God's vindication of the poor, it is nearly impossible for the rich to enter the kingdom (18:22-25). Nevertheless, those like Zacchaeus, who was rich (19:2), can still repent. Repentance for the rich, however, requires more than just giving generous gifts (21:1-4); it means divesting oneself of wealth that encumbers a genuine dependence on God (18:22) and making restitution for unjust profits (19:8).

Echoing Matthew's warning to those who practice their piety for public approval, Luke declares that the rich have already received their reward in full (6:24; cf. Matt 6:2, 5, 16). They can expect no more. Similarly, those who are full now will hunger. Laughing here is not a joyful response to God's work, as it is in v. 21. It is instead the laughter of the fool who is both unaware and unconcerned about the priorities of the kingdom. That laughter will turn to the mourning of remorse (Jas 5:1).

Like the fourth beatitude, the fourth woe differs in form and follows the pattern of the last beatitude. A good reputation may be desirable (Luke 2:52; Acts 2:47; 5:13), but when *all* speak well of you it is probably a sign either of the flattery accorded the rich or the popularity of the false prophets (Jer 5:31; Mic 2:11). The reference to false prophets in 6:26 corresponds to the reference to the persecuted prophets in 6:23, and the emphatic reference to "their ancestors" (6:23, 26) identifies the flatterers and persecutors with the ancestors who eventually suffered God's judgment in exile. The beatitudes and woes announce that the end is not yet; when God establishes a just reign there will be a radical reversal in the fortunes of the rich and the poor.

REFLECTIONS

1. One of our problems today is that we have forgotten the power and the art of blessing. The election of Israel began with God's promise to bless Abraham and his descendants and make them a blessing to all the peoples of the earth (Gen 12:1-3). It is no wonder, then, that the words preserved on the oldest scrap of Scripture that we possess are the familiar words of the blessing of Aaron in Numbers 6, which begin: "The LORD bless you and keep you. . . . " The blessing of Aaron was recently found on a piece of silver in a tomb at Ketef Hinnom, just south of Jerusalem, that dates from about 600 BCE. The biblical message is not only that God redeems us, but that God blesses us as well.

But what has happened to the art of blessing? The church has abandoned blessing to the charismatics and televangelists. Families have given up the rituals and ceremonies of blessing. Yet, nothing is more important to the development of children than to have their parents' blessing. Without the sure knowledge of that blessing, children may spend their whole lives seeking approval or the substitutes of success.

Beyond their individual words, the beatitudes call us back to the power of blessing and being blessed. They are not first and foremost ethical demands or eschatological promises. They are pronouncements of blessing. The word for "blessed" (μακάριος *makarios*) means something like "Oh, how fortunate." God as Father rejoices in his children and voices his fondest hopes for them. The beatitudes characterize God's people both in their attributes and in the reality that they are blessed by God.

2. The first beatitude describes a way of life, and we, who are not poor—not really—run to Matthew in relief. But our preference for Matthew says much more about us than about the words of Jesus. The poor are those whose desperate need and inability to help themselves have driven them to turn to God for their hope, but we are now being called upon to recognize that Jesus really meant the poor and not just the humble. Gustavo Gutiérrez, the liberation theologian, has commented that

> God has a preferential love for the poor not because they are necessarily better than others, morally or religiously, but simply because they are poor and living in an inhuman situation that is contrary to God's will. The ultimate basis for the privileged position of the poor is not in the poor themselves but in God, in the gratuitousness and universality of God's *agapeic love*.[85]

Because we are not poor, this beatitude either mystifies us or leaves us feeling guilt rather than joy. Like the rich young ruler, we hear the Lord's word and go away sorrowful because our possessions are many. Our pride and our ability to provide for ourselves have blocked the channels of blessing. Our first response, therefore, needs to be repentance and a reordering of the priorities we have set for our lives. But what a hard thing that is!

3. The last beatitude implies that those who live by God's blessing will find themselves so estranged from the world that others will persecute them. The world has little tolerance for saints who set their sights on values and principles the world does not share. But those who are persecuted for participating in God's work will find that God has prepared the kingdom for them. These words of blessing are a two-edged sword. What is blessing and promise to the poor at the same time is a pronouncement of judgment and woe to those who reject God's sovereignty (see Reflections at 6:37-38).

---

85. Gustavo Gutiérrez, "Song and Deliverance," in *Voices from the Margin: Interpreting the Bible in the Third World,* ed. R. S. Sugirtharajah (Maryknoll, N.Y.: Orbis, 1991) 131.

Luke 6:27-36, Love Your Enemies

NIV

27"But I tell you who hear me: Love your enemies, do good to those who hate you, 28bless those who curse you, pray for those who mistreat you. 29If someone strikes you on one cheek, turn to him the other also. If someone takes your cloak, do not stop him from taking your tunic. 30Give to everyone who asks you, and if anyone takes what belongs to you, do not demand it back. 31Do to others as you would have them do to you.

32"If you love those who love you, what credit is that to you? Even 'sinners' love those who love them. 33And if you do good to those who are good to you, what credit is that to you? Even 'sinners' do that. 34And if you lend to those from whom you expect repayment, what credit is that to you? Even 'sinners' lend to 'sinners,' expecting to be repaid in full. 35But love your enemies, do good to them, and lend to them without expecting to get anything back. Then your reward will be great, and you will be sons of the Most High, because he is kind to the ungrateful and wicked. 36Be merciful, just as your Father is merciful."

NRSV

27"But I say to you that listen, Love your enemies, do good to those who hate you, 28bless those who curse you, pray for those who abuse you. 29If anyone strikes you on the cheek, offer the other also; and from anyone who takes away your coat do not withhold even your shirt. 30Give to everyone who begs from you; and if anyone takes away your goods, do not ask for them again. 31Do to others as you would have them do to you.

32"If you love those who love you, what credit is that to you? For even sinners love those who love them. 33If you do good to those who do good to you, what credit is that to you? For even sinners do the same. 34If you lend to those from whom you hope to receive, what credit is that to you? Even sinners lend to sinners, to receive as much again. 35But love your enemies, do good, and lend, expecting nothing in return.[a] Your reward will be great, and you will be children of the Most High; for he is kind to the ungrateful and the wicked. 36Be merciful, just as your Father is merciful."

[a]Other ancient authorities read *despairing of no one*

COMMENTARY

The first part of the sermon dealt with the assurance of God's blessing on the poor, with whom the Christian community is closely identified, and conversely, God's judgment on the rich who persecute the community. The next part of the sermon, however, instructs disciples to love their enemies. There is no place in the Christian ethic for vengeance or retaliation.

6:27-28. The beginning of a new section of the sermon is marked by an appeal "to you that listen" (cf. 6:18, 47, 49). Verses 27-28 contain a fourfold repetition; the principle of love for one's enemies is stated and then repeated in three variations. The principle itself is found in a verbatim parallel in Matt 5:44, and the last variation, to pray for those who abuse you, is similar to the command to pray for those who persecute you in the same verse. The first and second variations of the principle have no parallel in Matthew.

6:29-31. Four applications or illustrations of the principle of love for enemies follow in vv. 29-30: turn the other cheek, do not withhold your shirt, give to the one who asks of you, and if your goods are taken do not ask for them back. In context, the third example, giving to one who asks of you, probably does not concern the duty of a generous response to the destitute, but willing compliance to the requests of one who is more powerful. In this sense, it is closely related to the fourth example. A positive form of the Golden Rule (cf. Matt 7:12) follows at this point, summing up the preceding statements and illustrations of the principle of love for one's enemy. By moving the Golden Rule to this earlier position in the sermon, Luke has placed it more directly in the context of instructions regarding the disciples' response to adversaries.

6:32-36. Verses 32-34 contain a threefold

repetition of questions that expose the deficiency of an ethic that does not extend love beyond the circle of those who are already doing good to one another. Each time, the question has the same form: (1) If you love/do good/lend (2) to those who love/do good/lend to you, (3) what credit is that to you? And each time, the answer is: For even sinners do the same. Verse 35 sums up the preceding section of the sermon with three injunctions: "love your enemies" (cf. vv. 27, 32), "do good" (cf. vv. 27, 33), "and lend, expecting nothing in return" (cf. vv. 30, 34). The result of such love for one's enemies is great, but more—"you will be children of the Most High" (v. 35). Here again, Luke's connection between loving one's enemies and being children of God resembles the peculiarly Matthean beatitude "Blessed are the peacemakers, for they will be called children of God" (Matt 5:9). The disciple's relationship to God is based on the axiom that the child is like the parent, so the character of God dictates that we practice a love that is not limited by others' responses to us, for God "is kind to the ungrateful and the wicked" (v. 35). The injunction to "be merciful, just as your Father is merciful" (v. 36) adapts the OT command to "be holy, for I the LORD your God am holy" (Lev 19:2), which in the Sermon on the Mount has become "Be perfect, therefore, as your heavenly Father is perfect" (Matt 5:48). Whereas this injunction stands at the conclusion of the six antitheses in Matthew 5, here it caps the section on love for one's enemy by placing the ethical imperative in a theological context.

The imperative to love one's enemies can have a range of meanings, depending on its context: Win over your opponent by kindness; take the moral high road; shame your enemy by your superior goodness; deflect hostility or prevent further abuse by offering no resistance; rise above pettiness; or demonstrate a Christ-like character as a Christian witness. These interpretations are neither exhaustive nor mutually exclusive, but they do suggest the range of meanings the command can have. Especially when taken individually, the exhortations in this section can be applied widely and virtually indiscriminately. The problems for interpretation concern the source of these teachings, their settings in the ministry of Jesus and in Luke, and the determination of contemporary contexts in which their application would be appropriate.

Both Jesus and Luke employed ethical teachings that circulated rather widely in parallel forms in Greco-Roman, Jewish, and early Christian traditions. In many instances, however, Jesus responded to and went far beyond the ethical standards of his day, and Luke provided his own interpretation of Jesus' teachings in the composition of this sermon.

One of the key issues is whether Jesus' teachings address the problem of oppression by the Romans and their collaborators—who were often also rich—or whether Jesus' teachings more narrowly concern the relationship of Christians to those who reject their witness and persecute them for their adherence to Jesus and his teachings. The latter has at least come to the fore more clearly in the Lukan context.

Conventional wisdom dictated that one should do harm to one's enemies and good to one's friends,[86] as a course of wisdom some philosophers were already counseling that one should turn one's enemies into friends.[87] The Essenes at Qumran instructed their adherents to love or hate each person according to his or her share in the Council of God or the Vengeance of God.[88] Jesus' admonition to bless those who curse you (cf. Matt 5:44; Rom 12:14) reverses the extended blessing of the godly and cursing of the men of Belial.[89] Striking a person on the cheek was a form of insult—a physical expression of cursing or reviling. Turning the other cheek is an equally dramatic and physical form of non-retaliation that breaks the cycle of violence and rejects the principle of retaliation (cf. Exod 21:24; Lev 24:20; Deut 19:21). The taking of one's outer garment may refer to thievery, but in the context of Luke's attention to how one should respond to one's enemies it probably refers to the act of taking one's outer garment through legal action or as repayment of a debt (see Exod 22:25-27; Deut 24:12-13; Amos 2:8).[90] The Golden Rule can be found in both its positive and its negative forms in various sources, among them Tob 4:15; MS D of Acts 15:29; Did. 1.2; and b. Šabb. 31a (where it is attributed to Hillel). (See Reflections at 6:37-38.)

86. Lysias Pro milite 20.
87. See Joseph A. Fitzmyer, The Gospel According to Luke (I–IX), AB 28 (Garden City, N.Y.: Doubleday, 1981), 637-38; Thucydides 4.19, 1-4; Diogenes Laertius 8.1, 23.
88. 1QS 1.9-11.
89. See 1QS 2.2-17.
90. Fitzmyer, The Gospel According to Luke (I–IX), 638-39.

Luke 6:37-38, Judge Not

NIV

37"Do not judge, and you will not be judged. Do not condemn, and you will not be condemned. Forgive, and you will be forgiven. 38Give, and it will be given to you. A good measure, pressed down, shaken together and running over, will be poured into your lap. For with the measure you use, it will be measured to you."

NRSV

37"Do not judge, and you will not be judged; do not condemn, and you will not be condemned. Forgive, and you will be forgiven; 38give, and it will be given to you. A good measure, pressed down, shaken together, running over, will be put into your lap; for the measure you give will be the measure you get back."

COMMENTARY

The next two verses move beyond the theme of love for one's enemies and counsel non-judgmental generosity. Two prohibitions (do not judge; do not condemn) are followed by two positive commands (forgive; give; cf. Acts 20:35). The consequences are stated with passive verbs (you will not be judged; you will not be condemned; you will be forgiven; it will be given to you), leaving the agent unnamed. The passive construction may indicate divine action (cf. 18:29-30), but it may also affirm that those who are non-violent, merciful, non-judgmental, and generous toward others will indeed be treated in the same way.

The latter part of v. 38 draws images, and perhaps a saying, from the marketplace. The image is that of the sale of grain. The buyer gets his or her money's worth: a full measure, packed down, shaken, and running over. The word for "lap" (κόλπος *kolpos*) literally means one's bosom, chest, or the fold of a garment. In this instance, it probably describes the practice of holding out one's garment or robe, as if to make a basket, and having it filled with grain (Ruth 3:15). Jesus promises that the law of one measure will be invoked—not one measure for buying and one for selling. If the passive again implies divine action, then just as a buyer might specify that the buyer's measure would be used (to ensure that he or she was not cheated), so God will use our measure; the standard of our relationships with others will be the standard God uses in relationship with us. This principle stands in tension with the earlier affirmation that God is merciful, but in both instances the primary interest is the resulting ethic: Be merciful because God is merciful; be generous because God will use the measure of our generosity toward others (or lack thereof) when God judges us.

REFLECTIONS

Jesus' teachings in this section of the sermon concern questions we all face: How do you deal with enemies? Who should you love? The principle of retaliation lies at the very foundation of law and can be traced back to the code of Hammurabi, which guaranteed the victim the right to recompense yet set limits on revenge. As someone has said, however, the end result of the law of an eye for an eye and a tooth for a tooth would be a society in which everyone is blind and toothless! Disciples are not to let selfishness or ill will determine their response to mistreatment. Any limitation on the standard must come from the best interest of the wrongdoer. Taken legalistically, this principle could lead to anarchy, of course, but it presupposes the new quality of relationships that Jesus makes possible. Give and forgive because you have been given and forgiven so much! The command to love one's enemy replaces the concern for limits on whom we treat as neighbors with a concern for inclusiveness: Treat everyone as a neighbor. Such peacemaking partakes of the very character of God. God's love is indiscriminate.

The first and second sections of Jesus' teachings to his followers (6:20-26; 6:27-38) set in place two principles that pose stumbling blocks for most modern Christians: the repudiation of privilege based on wealth and the repudiation of retaliation that spawns violence. These principles are diametrically opposed to the assumptions of the marketplace and the media that shape American culture: The wealthy are privileged, and conflict requires that one show strength through retaliation. Our heroes, therefore, are usually neither poor nor non-violent. As a result, the power of materialism and the quest for possessions have increased dramatically during this century, and violence in our homes, schools, and streets is rampant.

Jesus' alternative is not sheer passivity but aggressive action to undermine hostility and violence. He taught a new attitude toward possessions and persons in need and a new response to hostility. The juxtaposition of the first and second sections of the sermon, which deal with poverty/wealth and hostility respectively also suggests the relationship between the two problems. Oppression of the poor, materialism, and the presumption that problems can be settled by violence and force are all related. Jesus' teachings to his disciples, therefore, call for imaginative, aggressive, but non-violent responses to the problems that have borne such bitter fruit in our own time.

Luke 6:39-49, Parables on the Meaning of Discipleship

NIV

39He also told them this parable: "Can a blind man lead a blind man? Will they not both fall into a pit? 40A student is not above his teacher, but everyone who is fully trained will be like his teacher.

41"Why do you look at the speck of sawdust in your brother's eye and pay no attention to the plank in your own eye? 42How can you say to your brother, 'Brother, let me take the speck out of your eye,' when you yourself fail to see the plank in your own eye? You hypocrite, first take the plank out of your eye, and then you will see clearly to remove the speck from your brother's eye.

43"No good tree bears bad fruit, nor does a bad tree bear good fruit. 44Each tree is recognized by its own fruit. People do not pick figs from thornbushes, or grapes from briers. 45The good man brings good things out of the good stored up in his heart, and the evil man brings evil things out of the evil stored up in his heart. For out of the overflow of his heart his mouth speaks.

46"Why do you call me, 'Lord, Lord,' and do not do what I say? 47I will show you what he is like who comes to me and hears my words and puts them into practice. 48He is like a man building a house, who dug down deep and laid the foundation on rock. When a flood came, the torrent struck that house but could not shake

NRSV

39He also told them a parable: "Can a blind person guide a blind person? Will not both fall into a pit? 40A disciple is not above the teacher, but everyone who is fully qualified will be like the teacher. 41Why do you see the speck in your neighbor's[a] eye, but do not notice the log in your own eye? 42Or how can you say to your neighbor,[b] 'Friend,[b] let me take out the speck in your eye,' when you yourself do not see the log in your own eye? You hypocrite, first take the log out of your own eye, and then you will see clearly to take the speck out of your neighbor's[a] eye.

43"No good tree bears bad fruit, nor again does a bad tree bear good fruit; 44for each tree is known by its own fruit. Figs are not gathered from thorns, nor are grapes picked from a bramble bush. 45The good person out of the good treasure of the heart produces good, and the evil person out of evil treasure produces evil; for it is out of the abundance of the heart that the mouth speaks.

46"Why do you call me 'Lord, Lord,' and do not do what I tell you? 47I will show you what someone is like who comes to me, hears my words, and acts on them. 48That one is like a man building a house, who dug deeply and laid the foundation on rock; when a flood arose, the river burst against that house but could not shake it,

a Gk brother's   b Gk brother

NIV

it, because it was well built. [49]But the one who hears my words and does not put them into practice is like a man who built a house on the ground without a foundation. The moment the torrent struck that house, it collapsed and its destruction was complete."

NRSV

because it had been well built.[a] [49]But the one who hears and does not act is like a man who built a house on the ground without a foundation. When the river burst against it, immediately it fell, and great was the ruin of that house."

[a] Other ancient authorities read *founded upon the rock*

COMMENTARY

The third major section of the sermon is introduced by the Lukan transitional clause "He also told them a parable" (cf. 5:36; 8:4; 12:16; 13:6; 14:7; 15:3; 18:1; 21:29), which is actually followed by a string of four parables (vv. 39-40, 41-42, 43-45, 46-49). It has occasionally been suggested that this section is addressed to teachers of the church, but no such transition is indicated, nor do the parables themselves require such a change of audience or theme. On the other hand, each of these parables probably circulated independently before they were collected in the version of the sermon that underlies both Matthew 5–7 and Luke 6:20-49. Their present context, therefore, influences their interpretation, but each parable and saying retains its own voice, which at times refuses to be confined by its present context.

Nevertheless, in context one can discern the coherence of this section of the sermon. The blind person needs a guide (v. 39), so one blind person cannot lead another. In the language of the appended saying, in order to be a guide, the disciple needs to learn from the teacher (v. 40). The second parable illustrates the same point in grotesque imagery. Before one can help another, that one must attend to his or her own faults—first remove the log from your own eye, then you will be able to take the speck out of your neighbor's eye (vv. 41-42). Our efforts to be good disciples, guides to the blind, or speck-removers for our neighbor require a good heart—integrity of character. Only a good tree bears good fruit (vv. 43-45). Being a good disciple, therefore, requires far more than confession or lip service to the Lord. It requires acting on the Lord's teaching, making it the foundation of one's life (vv. 46-49). The alternative leads to destruction. The final section of the sermon, seen in this light, offers a series of parables that develop the theme of what is required of a disciple.

6:39-40, The Blind Leading the Blind. The proverb that a blind person cannot lead a blind person or else they will both fall into the pit is found elsewhere in Matt 15:14 and *Gospel of Thomas* 34. Jesus began his ministry announcing the recovery of sight for the blind (4:18), and later he will give sight to the blind (7:21-22; 18:35-43; cf. 14:13, 21). If Jesus has concern for blind persons, then literally and metaphorically his disciples should be prepared to lead the blind (cf. Acts 8:31, where the Ethiopian eunuch acknowledges that he needs someone to guide him).

Luke 6:40 effectively sums up Luke's understanding of discipleship: When fully prepared, the disciple will be like the teacher. Parallels to the saying occur in Matt 10:24-25 and John 13:16; 15:20, where it is related to humility and to persecution. Taken with the preceding saying, about leading the blind, the two sayings establish the appropriate status for a disciple; disciples must be better qualified than those they seek to lead, but a disciple can never be greater than the teacher. The appropriate goal is to strive to be like the teacher. The parables that follow in the rest of the sermon and later in the Gospel will define what that calling entails.

6:41-42, The Log in Your Own Eye. The second parable graphically contrasts the disciple's faults with those he or she may find in others. In context it resonates with the admonition not to judge others in the preceding section (vv. 37-38). Taken independently, the parable exposes the common human predilection to point out even the slightest faults in others while being blind to our own, even though they may be much greater (for parallels, see Matt 7:3-5; *Gospel of Thomas* 26; Oxyrhynchus

Papyrus 1.26). Jesus' parables often make a point by exaggeration—the size of the harvest, a camel through the eye of a needle. The term "hypocrite" (ὑποκριτής *hypokritēs*) originally referred to an actor, one who played a role. There is no known comparable term in Hebrew or Aramaic.

6:43-45, Producing Good Fruit. The third parable is also found in a variety of contexts (Matt 7:16-20; 12:31-35; *Gospel of Thomas* 45; 5; Ign. *Eph.* 14.1). In Matthew in particular, this parable is related to the warning concerning false prophets. They will be known by their fruit. The metaphor of fruit for the character of one's deeds is also found in the OT (Jer 17:10; 21:14; cf. Heb 6:7-8). Luke does not relate the parable to the problem of false prophets, however. Instead, he speaks to the truth that what is required of a disciple is not cosmetic alteration, even removing a log from one's eye, but a genuine goodness of heart. Finally, there is a consistency between who one is and what one does, the inner and the outer, the invisible and the visible. The former will inevitably be exposed by the latter. Discipleship, therefore, requires not just good deeds. It requires integrity and a purity of heart such as one sees in Jesus himself.

The basic parable is stated in vv. 43-44, a variation of Matt 7:16-17. The nature of the tree determines the quality of its fruit. Similarly, each plant bears its own kind of fruit; thorns do not bear figs, nor brambles grapes (cf. Jas 3:12). The parable then shifts through two variations. First, the language of trees and fruit is dropped, the corresponding elements of good person and good (deeds) are introduced, and the person becomes a storehouse of good or evil deeds (cf. Matt 13:52). Then, the connection between heart and mouth is introduced at the end of v. 45 (cf. Mark 7:14-23; James 3, esp. vv. 10, 12, 13, 17). What we say is a reflection of who we are—i.e., what is in our heart. Or, as John Nolland put it, summing up the entire parable: "Whether one likes it or not, what one produces is finally a product of what one is."[91]

6:46-49, Building on a Solid Foundation. Luke introduces the fourth parable and the conclusion to the sermon with the question "Why do you call me 'Lord, Lord,' and do not do what I tell you?" The question contrasts right confession with true discipleship, since "Lord" was a common early Christian confession (Rom 10:9; 1 Cor 12:3; Phil 2:11). The question easily leads to the parable of the two builders, which is interpreted as the contrast between those who hear and act and those who hear but do not act. James 1:22 develops the same theme in early Christian teaching: "But be doers of the word, and not merely hearers who deceive themselves." Following the parable of one who looks in the mirror and forgets what he or she looks like, James concludes, "[Be] not hearers who forget but doers who act—they will be blessed in their doing" (1:25). Jesus has been addressed as "Lord" and "Sir" earlier in the Gospel (5:8, 12), but this saying underscores the confessional sense of the title when it occurs later in the Gospel (e.g., 7:6; 9:54, 59, 61).

Matthew 7:21-23 introduces the story of the two builders with a version of the same saying followed by an eschatological interpretation, "On that day many will say to me...." Both the indicative and the interrogative forms of the saying can be found in other sources.[92] The verb for "to do" (ποιέω *poieō*) links the question in v. 46 with the statement in v. 47, which contains three participles in series: the one who comes, hears, and does. Various characters are introduced as ones who come to Jesus (7:7; 8:35, 41, 47). In each instance, an obedient response is possible. Hearing, and more specifically hearing the Word of God, is a recurring theme in Luke (5:1; 8:15, 21; 10:39; 11:28). The references to hearing at the end of the sermon (6:47, 49) tie the end of the sermon to its beginning (6:18, 27). Jesus' mother and brothers are later presented as examples of those who "hear the word of God and do it" (8:21), but in response to a woman who pronounces a blessing on Jesus' mother, Jesus answers, "Blessed rather are those who hear the word of God and obey [do] it!" (11:28). The theme that concludes the sermon, therefore, will continue to be significant later in the Gospel (e.g., 12:43, 47). Indeed, hearing and doing will be important in the next scene (see 7:7-8).

The one who comes, hears, and does is likened to a man who builds his house well. Luke's version of this parable differs from Matthew's (7:24-27) in several respects: (1) Luke does not contrast the two builders as wise and foolish.

---

91. John Nolland, *Luke 1–9:20*, WBC 35A (Dallas: Word, 1989) 309.

92. P Egerton 2.3; *2 Clem.* 3:4; 4:2.

(2) In Luke, the good builder builds on a foundation (something that was unusual in Palestine), while in Matthew the good builder builds on the rock. (3) In Luke, the house is assailed by a flooding river (singular), while in Matthew the threat is rain, floods (plural), and winds.

The third section of the sermon declares the necessity of responding to the teachings of Jesus. Lest the disciple be an example of the blind leading the blind, the disciple will make Jesus his or her model. Disciples will also tend to their own faults before presuming to help others with theirs. A good heart is required of those who would bear good fruit, and obedience to Jesus' words is required of those who would make Jesus their Lord. Moreover, the words of Jesus that are featured in the sermon bless the poor and warn the rich (6:20-26) and exhort his followers to love their enemies and deal generously and non-judgmentally with others (6:27-38). These are the bywords of discipleship.

REFLECTIONS

Once there was a man who took great pride in his automobile. He performed all the routine maintenance on schedule and kept the car clean inside and out. When he could afford to do so, he began to trade cars every couple of years so that he always had a relatively new vehicle. He also traded up, getting a larger, more luxurious car each time. Then he began to trade every year so that he would always have the current model. Eventually, he got to the point where he would buy a new car, drive it home, and leave it in the garage. He refused to use it because he didn't want to put any miles on it or run the risk of getting it scratched. So the new car just sat—pretty, but never used. This could be a parable of the way some people treat their faith, becoming less and less active in church while professing more and more strongly that they are committed Christians.

Jesus knew that it would not be easy for anyone to respond to the call to discipleship. The simple call, "Follow me," meant such a radical change of life. Knowing how difficult it would be, Jesus concluded the sermon with sayings that warn about the urgency of putting discipleship into practice.

1. The first danger threatening discipleship is the inclination to judge others, but how can we help making judgments? What sort of persons would we be if we made no moral judgments? We are constantly faced with the need to make discriminating moral choices. Learning to judge between right and wrong and developing an acute sense of rightness and justice while being able to spot hypocrisy, moral compromises, and oppression reflects a heightened spiritual awareness. What, then, does Jesus mean by this warning not to judge others?

Jesus was talking about a particular kind of judgment. The judgment in view is the inclination to condemn others for their faults and failures. Disciples do not grow better by comparing themselves with someone else. Some of us have gotten so sharp that we can put someone else down with just the quickest flick of the tongue. We are black belts in innuendo and faint praise. Not a speck in our brother's eye escapes our notice. "The Smiths are fine people," we say. "I just don't know why they bought a house in that neighborhood." "Aunt Bea, bless her heart, just never would let Arnold stand on his own feet." "Oh, I love that dress. It's just right for you. Did you find it on sale?" Of course, we would never judge others. Sometimes we merely "speak the truth in love" with a little too much relish.

The warning not to judge and the invitation for the one without sin to cast the first stone are twin sayings that cut the ground from beneath smug superiority. Their sin may not be ours, but ours is just as bad. Judging is the sin of those who are blind to their own faults. It is the obsession of those who seek to make themselves better, not by lifting themselves up, but by bringing others down. It is the mock justice of those who presume to know what others should do. The log in our own eye hardly qualifies us to judge the faults of our brothers and sisters.

Uncommitted Christians masquerading as reliable guides are a serious danger to the church, but the path of wisdom is to let the fruit they bear expose them. We can make two possible responses to these words of Jesus. One is to be aggressive in trying to unmask wolves pretending to be sheep (Matt 7:15). This response leads to suspicion, distrust, and accusations. The other response is to be careful about who we follow, and look again to be sure that we are not misguided ourselves. The calling of the Christian is not to "skin the wolves," but to be obedient and bear good fruit. Judgment belongs to the Lord, who knows our hearts even before the fruit of our lives becomes evident to others.

Deuteronomy counsels that anyone who leads the people to worship other gods is a false prophet (Deut 13:1-3). Similarly, Paul instructed the Corinthians that no one speaking in the Spirit of Christ can say, "Jesus be cursed," and no one can say "Jesus is Lord" except by the Holy Spirit (1 Cor 12:3). But Jesus pointed us even beyond the utterance of a true confession. Only those who do the will of God are actually children of God. This is not a works theology, though. Obedience and righteousness are the tests of true faith, not the means of our salvation.

2. Another of the dangers to discipleship is that of living our lives without a firm foundation. The parable of the two builders vividly draws the contrast between doers of the Word and those who are hearers only. Jesus' teaching was different from that of the scribes and Pharisees because he did not appeal to the authority of his teachers, nor did he dispute fine points in the interpretation of the Law. Instead, he told vivid stories drawn from ordinary life. Everyone had seen houses under construction, and they had also seen houses destroyed by storms.

Luke makes the point graphically. The wise builder "dug deeply and laid the foundation on rock" (6:48). Dig deep and lay the foundation of your life on the Word of God. Keep digging until you get in touch with the revelation of God in the person of Jesus, and then build your life upon that Rock.

How do you put your life back together after a storm? Many have found that faith in God was the only thing that gave them the strength to keep going, renew their hope, and make a new beginning. We do not choose whether we will face severe storms in life; we only get to choose the foundation on which we will stand.

The alternative choice is both simple and disastrous. Hear the words of life, and pay no attention to the teachings of Jesus, and you will be like the man who built with no foundation. The house probably looked wonderful. Neighbors may have talked enviously about how fortunate this man was to have been able to build a new house. The man in Jesus' parable built a new home, but he built it without a foundation.

So there it is. The sermon offers us a vision of life as Christ saw that it could be. Others, too, have shared visions of what life could be and have called us to join them in making their visions a reality. The difference is that Jesus both exposed the inherent nature of human life and called us into a relationship with God, which empowers us to live this life of discipleship. The mystery of discipleship is that it is as much receiving as it is striving.

LUKE 7:1-50, THE MESSIAH GREATER THAN A PROPHET

OVERVIEW

The theme of the next three chapters (7:1–9:50) is the identity of Jesus as the Messiah greater than a prophet. Luke shows that Jesus continues the works of the prophets and fulfills their words. Yet, he is greater than the prophets. The theme is carried along by the interplay be-tween recurring questions about Jesus' identity and repeated testimonies to him until finally Peter confesses him to be the Messiah (9:18-20) and the voice from heaven at the transfiguration de-clares, "This is my Son" (9:28-36).

Luke 7:1-10, Healing the Centurion's Slave

NIV

7 When Jesus had finished saying all this in the hearing of the people, he entered Capernaum. [2]There a centurion's servant, whom his master valued highly, was sick and about to die. [3]The centurion heard of Jesus and sent some elders of the Jews to him, asking him to come and heal his servant. [4]When they came to Jesus, they pleaded earnestly with him, "This man deserves to have you do this, [5]because he loves our nation and has built our synagogue." [6]So Jesus went with them.

He was not far from the house when the centurion sent friends to say to him: "Lord, don't trouble yourself, for I do not deserve to have you come under my roof. [7]That is why I did not even consider myself worthy to come to you. But say the word, and my servant will be healed. [8]For I myself am a man under authority, with soldiers under me. I tell this one, 'Go,' and he goes; and that one, 'Come,' and he comes. I say to my servant, 'Do this,' and he does it."

[9]When Jesus heard this, he was amazed at him, and turning to the crowd following him, he said, "I tell you, I have not found such great faith even in Israel." [10]Then the men who had been sent returned to the house and found the servant well.

NRSV

7 After Jesus[a] had finished all his sayings in the hearing of the people, he entered Capernaum. [2]A centurion there had a slave whom he valued highly, and who was ill and close to death. [3]When he heard about Jesus, he sent some Jewish elders to him, asking him to come and heal his slave. [4]When they came to Jesus, they appealed to him earnestly, saying, "He is worthy of having you do this for him, [5]for he loves our people, and it is he who built our synagogue for us." [6]And Jesus went with them, but when he was not far from the house, the centurion sent friends to say to him, "Lord, do not trouble yourself, for I am not worthy to have you come under my roof; [7]therefore I did not presume to come to you. But only speak the word, and let my servant be healed. [8]For I also am a man set under authority, with soldiers under me; and I say to one, 'Go,' and he goes, and to another, 'Come,' and he comes, and to my slave, 'Do this,' and the slave does it." [9]When Jesus heard this he was amazed at him, and turning to the crowd that followed him, he said, "I tell you, not even in Israel have I found such faith." [10]When those who had been sent returned to the house, they found the slave in good health.

[a] Gk *he*

COMMENTARY

The first story in this new section sets forth themes that will be developed in the coming chapters. Here Luke tells of a Gentile centurion's response of faith in Jesus. Jesus' authority is likened to that of the centurion, and Jesus heals the centurion's slave. The emphasis given to the power of Jesus' word forms a fitting transition from the sermon on discipleship in the previous chapter.

A great deal of attention has been given to the parallels between this story and related stories in the other Gospels. This pericope still falls within what has been called Luke's little interpolation

(Luke 6:20–8:3). Matthew records a close parallel to the story (Matt 8:5-13) in much the same sequence, following the Sermon on the Mount. Matthew's account is simpler and perhaps earlier than Luke's. In Matthew, Jesus speaks directly to the centurion; in contrast, Luke has two delegations to Jesus—the elders and then the servants. On the other hand, Matthew has embellished Jesus' pronouncement recognizing the centurion's faith by the addition of sayings that occur in Luke 13:28-29. Matthew's story also lacks the tension between the elders' testimony to the centurion's worthiness and the centurion's own humility. In

Matt 8:13, Jesus affirms that the slave will be healed: "Go; let it be done for you according to your faith."

The healing of the nobleman's son in John 4:46-54 offers a more distant parallel. In this story also there is an official (though not a centurion) from Capernaum, whose son (not his slave) is ill, who sends a delegation to Jesus (as in Luke, not Matthew). In John, however, the pronouncement is different since it introduces the Johannine concern for the relationship between signs and faith. In both stories, Jesus' word is emphasized, and the healing occurs at a distance.

More tenuous are the parallels between this story and the healing of the Syrophoenician woman's daughter in Mark 7:24-30. Like the Lukan account, however, the story depicts the faith of a Gentile, records an extended dialogue between the Gentile and Jesus, and ends with the healing of a child at a distance. Although the Markan story preserves a separate tradition, it is structurally similar to the story of the healing of the centurion's slave, and the parallels between the stories may have led to their being developed in similar ways during the period of their oral transmission.

When he concluded his words to the disciples, Jesus returned to Capernaum (see 4:23, 31-41; 10:15). The centurion was probably serving Herod Antipas rather than the Romans. Capernaum was a minor trade center and toll station where roads crossed in Galilee. Whereas Matthew records that the boy was paralyzed, Luke describes his condition as a grave illness. The earlier healings in Capernaum provide a background for the centurion's request to Jesus. When he heard about Jesus, the centurion sent a delegation of Jewish elders to Jesus. The elders would have been the "town fathers" or distinguished men of Capernaum, leaders in its synagogue. The action of the centurion is consistent with both the elders' testimony to him and his own declaration of unworthiness. He does not approach Jesus directly, but diplomatically sends the Jewish leaders, who could vouch for the merit of his request. The resulting picture is one of good relations among all parties—the centurion has built a synagogue for the Jews; the Jewish leaders speak well of him; and the centurion is deferential toward Jesus. This story, therefore, provides effective preparation of the reader for the conversion of Cornelius, the God-fearing centurion in Acts 10 (see esp. 10:22), and the link between the two is established by the report that this Gentile was a centurion. The words of the Jewish elders contrast sharply with the accusations of the Jewish assembly later in the Gospel (cf. 23:2).

Jesus started toward the centurion's home (cf. Peter's response in Acts 10:23) but was stopped by a second delegation before he arrived. Structurally, therefore, there are similarities between this story and the healing of Jairus's daughter in Luke 8:40-56, where Jesus is approached by Jairus himself but is stopped on the way to Jairus's house by a delegation reporting that his daughter has died.

The second delegation, friends sent by the centurion, carry a message to Jesus in the centurion's own words (vv. 6b-8). The verb translated "do not trouble" (σκύλλω *skyllō*) occurs again in the message of the delegation from Jairus's house in 8:49. The centurion's words in 7:6, "I am not worthy" (οὐ γὰρ ἱκανός *ou gar hikanos*), contrast sharply with the tribute paid him by the Jewish elders, who testified, "He is worthy" (ἄξιός ἐστιν *axios estin*, 7:4; the Greek words are different but synonymous). The effect is to place the centurion in an even better light. First we are told that he valued his slave highly and was ready to turn to Jesus for help, then that he was worthy, and now his own words have shown him to be humble also, thereby setting up Jesus' praise of his faith in v. 9. More is implicit here, however. The centurion's words may well convey that he was aware that the Pharisees regarded a Gentile's house as unclean and that a Jew would have been defiled by entering a Gentile's home.[93] Moreover, the centurion clarifies that he only expects Jesus to say the word to heal his slave, thereby indicating that he was confident that Jesus could heal at a distance and showing that he acknowledged the power of Jesus' words, a point that Luke has already established for the reader (4:36, 39; 5:13, 24; 6:10). The parallel that the centurion draws between Jesus and his own status is designed to underscore Jesus' authority to command. Just as the centurion acts by commanding his subordinates, he expects no more than that Jesus would do the same.

93. *M. Oholot* 18.7.

155

The point of this story is Jesus' affirmation of the centurion's faith in v. 9, not the report of the healing that concludes the story. Luke's description communicates Jesus' surprise at the Gentile's faith, and his approval as well. Jesus' praise of the centurion's faith contains no judgment on Israel. Instead, it affirms that whereas Jesus might have expected to find an Israelite with faith, here he has found faith in a Gentile. The report of the slave's healing, while subordinated to the importance of Jesus' pronouncement, not only continues to underscore Jesus' role as a healer but also adds to it the confirmation of the centurion's confession that Jesus had the authority merely to command and the slave would be healed. Jesus' authority has, therefore, been elevated by the faith of a respected man of military authority.

REFLECTIONS

The story of the centurion's faith is a brilliant gem in Luke's cluster of scenes from the life of Jesus. Especially when read in a Gentile-Christian context, the scene reflects appealing hues. Because the centurion never actually meets Jesus or speaks with him, in contrast to the Matthean and Johannine parallels, his request is like a prayer mediated to Jesus by others. Thus the story implicitly promises that the Lord hears the prayers of faithful Gentiles and encourages us to believe that when we turn to the Lord in need our requests will be heard also.

At the same time, the centurion serves as a role model for Gentile believers. He is concerned about the well-being of those around him, even his slave. His generosity has extended to the Jewish community as well—he built a synagogue. Although he has not met Jesus, because of what he has heard about Jesus from others he has faith that Jesus can help, and he turns to Jesus with his request. The centurion, therefore, is a model of compassion for weaker persons, goodwill in the midst of divisive tensions between ethnic groups, and faith in Jesus as a result of the testimony of others. He has respect for Jewish sensitivities about entering a Gentile's house, and although he is a man of position and power, he does not want Jesus to be troubled by his problems. Seen in this light, the centurion is one of the unsung and unnoticed heroes of faith in the Gospels.

The other side of the story is the power of Jesus' word. A centurion was a powerful figure, the commander of a military unit of a hundred soldiers, with all the authority of Herod or Rome behind him. With such authority, he was accustomed to doing things by simple command. He ordered soldiers and servants, and his instructions were carried out. His understanding of power serves as a foil to set forth the greater power of Jesus' word. Although readers of the Gospel may never see Jesus or witness his mighty works, where his word is present, there the power that was evident in his works also continues to be present. The Lord we worship is mighty in word, responsive to our needs, and compassionate to heal.

Luke 7:11-17, Raising the Widow's Son

NIV

[11]Soon afterward, Jesus went to a town called Nain, and his disciples and a large crowd went along with him. [12]As he approached the town gate, a dead person was being carried out—the only son of his mother, and she was a widow. And a large crowd from the town was with her.

NRSV

11Soon afterwards[a] he went to a town called Nain, and his disciples and a large crowd went with him. [12]As he approached the gate of the town, a man who had died was being carried out. He was his mother's only son, and she was a

[a]Other ancient authorities read Next day

NIV

13When the Lord saw her, his heart went out to her and he said, "Don't cry."

14Then he went up and touched the coffin, and those carrying it stood still. He said, "Young man, I say to you, get up!" 15The dead man sat up and began to talk, and Jesus gave him back to his mother.

16They were all filled with awe and praised God. "A great prophet has appeared among us," they said. "God has come to help his people." 17This news about Jesus spread throughout Judea*a* and the surrounding country.

a17 Or the land of the Jews

NRSV

widow; and with her was a large crowd from the town. 13When the Lord saw her, he had compassion for her and said to her, "Do not weep." 14Then he came forward and touched the bier, and the bearers stood still. And he said, "Young man, I say to you, rise!" 15The dead man sat up and began to speak, and Jesus*a* gave him to his mother. 16Fear seized all of them; and they glorified God, saying, "A great prophet has risen among us!" and "God has looked favorably on his people!" 17This word about him spread throughout Judea and all the surrounding country.

a Gk he

COMMENTARY

The story of the raising of the widow's son at Nain represents an advance over the healing of the centurion's slave in that healing has escalated to resuscitation. The story also anticipates Jesus' response to John's question: "The dead are raised" (7:22). The primary effect of the story, therefore, is to underscore once more Jesus' work as one like the prophets, mighty in word and deed.

Although there are Greco-Roman accounts of resuscitations,[94] the resuscitations accomplished by Elijah and Elisha (1 Kgs 17:10, 17-24; 2 Kgs 4:18-37) form the background for the raising of the widow's son. When one story follows another well-known story closely, it creates an "echo effect," a reverberation between the two stories, so

that much of the power of the new story comes from its resonance with the old.

The place to begin is by noting the importance of the Elijah-Elisha parallels to this point in Luke. The "spirit and power of Elijah" go before John the Baptist (1:17), and he is called "the prophet of the Most High" (1:76). In his inaugural sermon in Nazareth, Jesus spoke of the work of Elijah and Elisha, citing Elijah's ministry to the widow at Zarephath in particular (4:26). As readers, we have been educated to the importance of Elijah and Elisha for Luke's understanding of John the Baptist and Jesus, but the relationships have not been precisely defined.

The parallels between the two accounts are unmistakable:

94. E.g., Philostratus *Life of Apollonius* 4.45.

1 Kings 17:10, 17-24	*Luke 7:11-17*
"When he came to the gate of the town" (v. 10)	"As he approached the gate of the town"
She was a widow (v. 10)	She was a widow
The widow's son died (vv. 17-18)	The widow's son had died
Elijah cried out to the Lord (vv. 20-21)	He had compassion for her
Elijah stretched himself out over the child three times (v. 21)	Jesus touched the bier and said, "Young man, I say to you, rise"
The life of the child came into him again, and he revived (v. 22)	The dead man sat up and began to speak
Elijah "gave him to his mother" (v. 23)	"and Jesus gave him to his mother"
The woman said, "Now I know that you are a man of God and that the word of the Lord in your mouth is truth" (v. 24)	The crowd said, "A great prophet has risen among us," and "God has looked favorably upon his people"

The similarities in genre, structure, detail, and vocabulary establish the linkage between these stories. Because the similarities between the two stories are so extensive that they must be deliberate, the differences between Luke's narrative and the story of Elijah call for even closer attention. First, one notes that in Luke a crowd is present—actually two crowds, Jesus' followers and the mourners (vv. 11-12). In the previous story, Jesus had instructed the crowd, "I tell you, not even in Israel have I found such faith" (7:9). Now in a story that echoes Elijah's ministry to a non-Israelite (cf. Luke 4:25-26), the crowd, functioning like the chorus in a Greek drama, responds confessing, "A great prophet has risen among us!" (7:16).

Four other distinctive elements in Luke's story call for attention. First, Luke notes that the son was the widow's "only son." Although the term has an important christological function in John (1:14, 18; 3:16, 18), Luke does not use it in this fashion. Instead, Luke uses the term in two other stories, for which there are Markan parallels where the term is not used. Luke heightens the tragedy in each case—it is Jairus's only daughter (Luke 8:42), and the epileptic boy was his father's only son (Luke 9:38).

Second, Luke records Jesus' compassion for the widow. Somewhat surprisingly, however, Luke does not add references to Jesus' compassion to his account but omits all the references from the Markan material he uses (Mark 1:41; 6:34; 8:2; 9:22). The only other occurrences of the verb for "to have compassion" (σπλαγχνίζομαι *splagchnizomai*) that remain are in Jesus' parables (10:33; 15:20). Jesus' reassuring words, "Do not weep," demonstrate his compassion while heightening anticipation for the act he is about to do.

Third, whereas Elijah cried out to God and then stretched himself out over the child three times, the resuscitation is accomplished in Luke by a simple, authoritative command, "Young man, I say to you, rise," again affirming the power of Jesus' word. The contrast between Luke and 1 Kings at this point becomes all the more important when one notes that this is the first time the narrator in Luke has referred to Jesus as "the Lord," a title that has occurred previously in dialogue (5:8, 12; 6:46; 7:6) and will occasionally recur later in the Gospel narrative (e.g., 10:1, 39, 41; 11:39).

Fourth, the crowd's response is distinctive when compared closely with the response of the boy's mother in 1 Kings. In each case the response has two parts: The first affirmation has to do with the identity of Elijah or Jesus. The second affirmation affirms more generally the authenticity of God's work. In Luke, the first affirmation drives home the point that the echoes with the Elijah story have made so clear: "A great prophet has risen among us." The crowd's confession is not all that Luke will want to say about Jesus, but it establishes the important point that Jesus is a prophet who had fulfilled the work of the great prophets of Israel. In coming episodes, Luke will both underscore Jesus' role as a prophet (7:18-23; 9:8, 19; 13:33; 24:19) and affirm that Jesus is greater than both the prophets and John the Baptist (7:24-28; 9:18-20, 28-36). Both John and Jesus continue the work of the prophets, but both are greater than the prophets, and John announces Jesus as the coming one, just as Elijah was expected to announce the coming of the day of the Lord (Mal 4:5). This relationship will be clarified in later scenes.

The second response of the crowd, "God has looked favorably on his people," resonates with earlier affirmations: Zechariah declared, "Blessed be the Lord God of Israel,/ for he has looked favorably on his people and redeemed them" (1:68; cf. 1:78). Later, Acts 15:14 will serve as a counterpoint to this affirmation: "how God first looked favorably on the Gentiles." The raising of the son of the widow of Nain, however, establishes God's favor on Israel first (cf. 4:25-26). The report of this mighty act went throughout all the land of the Jews. (For Luke's use of "Judea" in this manner, see also 4:44; 6:17.)

REFLECTIONS

Death and life are the ultimate polarities of the human condition. Death represents the limit of human autonomy and control over life and poses for everyone a reminder of the frailty and brevity of life. Persons we love pass from our presence, and we can do nothing to prevent their passing.

The widow's only son had died. We do not know their names, his age, or the cause of his death. In the end, none of that matters—only that she had already lost her husband and now she has lost her only child. James says, "Religion that is pure and undefiled before God, the Father, is this: to care for orphans and widows in their distress" (1:27). Had Jesus passed by that funeral procession on the other side when he had the power to stop it, none of his other works would have made much difference. If religion has nothing to say to a grieving widow, it has nothing to say.

Jesus' words to the young man, "Be raised," reverberate with other Gospel words in the presence of death. The angel at Jesus' own tomb will declare that another young man has risen; the disciples will announce, "This Jesus God raised up, and of that all of us are witnesses" (Acts 2:32); and Paul will connect Jesus' resurrection with our own hope for life beyond death: "Christ has been raised from the dead, the first fruits of those who have died" (1 Cor 15:20). The resurrection of Jesus, the one who had compassion on a widow in her grief, provides the basis for the apostle's confident vision of the end: "For the trumpet will sound, and the dead will be raised imperishable" (1 Cor 15:52). The hope of the resurrection, therefore, is not grounded in the fact that the widow's son came back to life but in the fact that the one who had the compassion to bring back the widow's son has himself triumphed over death.

Luke 7:18-23, Signs of the Coming One

NIV

[18]John's disciples told him about all these things. Calling two of them, [19]he sent them to the Lord to ask, "Are you the one who was to come, or should we expect someone else?"

[20]When the men came to Jesus, they said, "John the Baptist sent us to you to ask, 'Are you the one who was to come, or should we expect someone else?'"

[21]At that very time Jesus cured many who had diseases, sicknesses and evil spirits, and gave sight to many who were blind. [22]So he replied to the messengers, "Go back and report to John what you have seen and heard: The blind receive sight, the lame walk, those who have leprosy[a] are cured, the deaf hear, the dead are raised, and the good news is preached to the poor. [23]Blessed is the man who does not fall away on account of me."

[a]22 The Greek word was used for various diseases affecting the skin—not necessarily leprosy.

NRSV

18The disciples of John reported all these things to him. So John summoned two of his disciples [19]and sent them to the Lord to ask, "Are you the one who is to come, or are we to wait for another?" [20]When the men had come to him, they said, "John the Baptist has sent us to you to ask, 'Are you the one who is to come, or are we to wait for another?'" [21]Jesus[a] had just then cured many people of diseases, plagues, and evil spirits, and had given sight to many who were blind. [22]And he answered them, "Go and tell John what you have seen and heard: the blind receive their sight, the lame walk, the lepers[b] are cleansed, the deaf hear, the dead are raised, the poor have good news brought to them. [23]And blessed is anyone who takes no offense at me."

[a]Gk He   [b]The terms leper and leprosy can refer to several diseases

COMMENTARY

The raising of the widow of Nain's son, with its parallels to Elijah's raising of the widow of Zarephath's son and its acclamation of Jesus as a great prophet, has focused sharply on an issue that has surfaced in Luke in the annunciations, the blessings on John and Jesus, John's preaching, and Jesus' sermon in Nazareth: How are John and Jesus related to the prophets? In that light, what is the relationship between John and Jesus, and most important, who is Jesus? The question of Jesus' identity will continue to play a guiding role in the narrative through Luke 9. The issue of the relationship between John and Jesus and their fulfillment of the prophets is the unifying theme of the next three pericopes (7:18-23, 24-30, 31-35), which appear in the same sequence in Matthew (11:2-6, 7-11, 16-19). Was Jesus the fulfillment of the coming of Elijah (Mal 3:1; 4:5), the coming of the Son of Man (Dan 7:13), the prophet like Moses (Deut 18:15, 18), or the Messiah? The first pericope features Jesus' answer to John's question regarding Jesus' identity.

Although Luke reported earlier that John was in prison (3:20), Luke says nothing about John's imprisonment in these verses (contrary to Matt 11:2). Verse 18 describes the setting for John's question. When his disciples report to him what Jesus had been doing—"all these things," i.e., information that we as the readers of the Gospel already know—John calls two of his disciples (a detail not found in Matt 11:2 but probably based on the requirement that there be two witnesses—Deut 19:15; cf. John 1:35).

John's question, "Are you the one who is to come?" is open to multiple interpretations, both of the figure who is expected and of John's reason for asking the question. We may treat the latter first. The report of John's sending for an answer to this question stands in tension with the more prevalent NT portrait of John as a confident witness to Jesus, especially in John (1:29-36; 3:26-30; but also in Matt 3:14-15), which may be an indication of its historicity. Whatever its origin, however, Luke uses the tradition to develop further the theme of Jesus' identity vis-à-vis the prophets and John. In Luke, John has announced that "one who is more powerful than I is coming" (3:16), but he did not identify Jesus as this one, and Luke does not explicitly say that John baptized Jesus (3:21). Thus John's question may be read in various ways: (1) as failure of nerve in which John, in prison, is troubled by uncertainty; (2) as surprise that whereas he had expected a fiery reformer and prophet of judgment, Jesus has come bringing grace and healing; (3) as eager hopefulness that Jesus is indeed the one whose

coming he had announced; or (4) as an effort either to encourage Jesus to make a public announcement of his identity or as a witness to his own disciples. Within the narrative world of Luke, the second and third interpretations work best, because they do not require assuming motives that the story neither requires nor introduces. The tension between the characterization of the coming one as a fiery reformer in John's preaching (3:16-17) and Jesus' response to John (7:22) lends weight to the view that Jesus' ministry took a different course than John expected. What is at issue is how the promises of the OT would be fulfilled. Since Jesus' work in raising the widow's son so closely parallels Elijah's raising of the dead, did that mean that Jesus was Elijah redivivus, the one promised in Malachi (3:1; 4:5)? Mark identified John the Baptist as the fulfillment of the coming of Elijah (9:10-13; 15:35-36), but the Gospel of John seems to reserve that role for Jesus (1:21, 25). In Luke, Jesus continues the work of Elijah, but he is one greater than the prophets. Ironically, if John expects Jesus to be Elijah, he is mistaken—the Gospel has already assigned that role to John himself.

These observations also lead us to greater clarity about the meaning of "the one who is to come" in John's question. Within the Gospel narrative the question echoes John's announcement that "one who is more powerful than I is coming" (3:16). When he came, this one would baptize with the Holy Spirit, clear the threshing floor, gather the wheat, and burn the chaff. That role may well have been linked with the expectation that Elijah would bring judgment (a refiner's fire; Mal 3:2) when he came.

Luke allows the messengers to repeat John's question (v. 20) and then records Jesus' answer both in deeds and in words, something the messengers could see, and something they could hear: "Tell John what you have seen and heard" (v. 22). Luke has reported the healing of the sick and the exorcism of demons previously, but this is the first reference to anointing the eyes of the blind, a sign that fulfills Jesus' announcement in 4:18 and prepares for his response to John.

In v. 22 Jesus offers a list of six prophetic activities. (See Fig. 4.) This compilation of references

Figure 4: Jesus' Works in the Gospel of Luke as Fulfillment of the Prophets

	Elijah/Elisha	Isaiah	Luke
the blind	2 Kgs 6:17	29:18; 35:5; 42:18; 61:1 (LXX)	4:18; 7:21 (cf. 6:39-42) 14:13, 21; 18:35
the lame		35:6	14:13, 21
the lepers	2 Kgs 5:1-14		5:12-16; 17:12-19 (cf. 4:27)
the deaf		29:18; 35:5; 42:18	11:14
the dead	1 Kgs 17:17-24	26:19	7:11-17; 8:40-42, 49-56
the poor	61:1	4:18; 6:20; 14:13, 21; 16:19-31; 18:22; 19:8; 21:1-4	

shows that Luke's portrayal of Jesus' works blends elements from both the Elijah/Elisha cycles and the book of Isaiah. If John expected Elijah redivivus, what Jesus offered was instead a fulfillment of the prophets that concentrated on the healing of the afflicted and the promise of redemption for the poor. Luke has prepared for this scene carefully, as the addition of v. 21 would suggest (cf. Matt 11:3). Prior to this point in the Gospel, each of the six groups has been mentioned except the lame and the deaf, both of which appear in Isa 35:5-6.

The raising of the widow's son established once again Jesus' credentials as a prophet; his answer to John establishes his fulfillment of John's announcement of the coming one. What remains to be established more clearly is Jesus' relationship to John and his identity as one greater than the prophets.

REFLECTIONS

What do you do when Jesus turns out to be someone other than who you thought he was or hoped he would be? John's question, whether Jesus was the Coming One, suggests that the reports John was receiving painted a different picture of Jesus than he had expected. Jesus' final statement in this scene, another beatitude, "Blessed is anyone who takes no offense at me," speaks to all who discover that Jesus is not fulfilling their expectations. Blessed are those who do not reject Jesus, even though he turns out to be someone different from what they had expected, imagined, or hoped he would be.

No biographical issue in human history compares with the effort to understand Jesus. The NT contains not one but four Gospels, four rather different portraits of Jesus. Church councils developed confessions that state his role and identity. Artists have adapted Jesus to various cultures and centuries. Historians and scholars have proposed first one understanding of Jesus then another: a Rationalist who performed no miracles; a liberal who taught the Fatherhood of God and the ethic of love in the human community; the eschatological prophet announcing the end of the world; the existentialist calling for radical obedience and openness to the future; the social reformer; the Galilean peasant—and the parade of portraits goes on. Individual Christians often find that in their own experience Jesus turns out not to be the one they once thought he was as childhood images give way to adolescent expectations and adult disappointments. Typically, each of us shares in John's experience. We think we know who Jesus is, what he is doing, and what he stands for, and then we are forced by experience to revise our understandings: Are you the one, or should we look for another?

In a consumer-oriented age, the question reminds us that other religious options are open to believers. Other religious traditions also claim the authority of revelation and inspired teachings. If the Christian tradition has disappointed us, we tell ourselves that perhaps we should try another.

Jesus' answer first focuses the important issues and then invites a tolerant belief: Don't take offense. The important issue is that through Jesus, God has acted in human experience and relieved the suffering of the poor and the afflicted. In Jesus, God has declared that God is on the side of those who suffer and those who are in need. Color the portrait any way you will, dot the i's and cross the t's of the christological creeds, finally what authenticates any claims for Jesus is that God has acted through Jesus and that through Jesus we see God's commitment to the afflicted, the oppressed, and the impoverished. Those who confess Jesus share in the joy that God has shown that God cares about human suffering, and we share in the call to follow Jesus in ministering to those to whom he mediated God's love. The alternative to taking offense, therefore, is responding to Jesus' call to follow him.

Luke 7:24-30, More Than a Prophet

NIV

²⁴After John's messengers left, Jesus began to speak to the crowd about John: "What did you go out into the desert to see? A reed swayed by the wind? ²⁵If not, what did you go out to see? A man dressed in fine clothes? No, those who wear expensive clothes and indulge in luxury are in palaces. ²⁶But what did you go out to see? A prophet? Yes, I tell you, and more than a prophet. ²⁷This is the one about whom it is written:

"'I will send my messenger ahead of you,
    who will prepare your way before you.'ᵃ

²⁸I tell you, among those born of women there is no one greater than John; yet the one who is least in the kingdom of God is greater than he."

²⁹(All the people, even the tax collectors, when they heard Jesus' words, acknowledged that God's way was right, because they had been baptized by John. ³⁰But the Pharisees and experts in the law rejected God's purpose for themselves, because they had not been baptized by John.)

ᵃ27 Mal. 3:1

NRSV

24When John's messengers had gone, Jesusᵃ began to speak to the crowds about John:ᵇ "What did you go out into the wilderness to look at? A reed shaken by the wind? ²⁵What then did you go out to see? Someoneᶜ dressed in soft robes? Look, those who put on fine clothing and live in luxury are in royal palaces. ²⁶What then did you go out to see? A prophet? Yes, I tell you, and more than a prophet. ²⁷This is the one about whom it is written,

'See, I am sending my messenger ahead of you,
    who will prepare your way before you.'

²⁸I tell you, among those born of women no one is greater than John; yet the least in the kingdom of God is greater than he." ²⁹(And all the people who heard this, including the tax collectors, acknowledged the justice of God,ᵈ because they had been baptized with John's baptism. ³⁰But by refusing to be baptized by him, the Pharisees and the lawyers rejected God's purpose for themselves.)

ᵃGk he   ᵇGk him   ᶜOr Why then did you go out? To see someone   ᵈOr praised God

COMMENTARY

This is the second of the three paragraphs that define the role of John and Jesus. In the preceding unit, Jesus responded to John's expectations regarding Jesus' identity. In this cluster of sayings,

Jesus responds to the crowd's expectations regarding John. In the process the roles of both John and Jesus emerge more clearly.

Verses 24-28 are drawn from Q material, with a close parallel in Matt 11:7-11, whereas vv. 29-30 are a Lukan addition. The first part of v. 24 sets the scene and links the sayings to the preceding scene. Three times Jesus asks the crowd what they went out to see, and each time he suggests an inadequate answer (vv. 24b-25b). The first answer needs no rebuttal, but the inadequacy of the second answer is stated (v. 25c). The third answer (a prophet) is accepted, but its inadequacy is asserted in three stages: first by assertion (v. 26c—"more than a prophet"), then by proof from Scripture (v. 27), and finally by means of a double comparison (with other men and with the least in the kingdom; v. 28). Verses 29-30 are best read as a comment or narrative aside rather than as added sayings by Jesus.

A historical link between these sayings and the previous scene is plausible, though in their present form the sayings reflect the theological influence of the early Christian community and the stair-step parallelism by which Luke has compared Jesus and John from their births, while elevating Jesus over John. The crowds have served alternately as a chorus (7:16) and as an audience (7:9, 11-12). Jesus' address to the crowd here implicitly links them with the crowd that went out to John in the wilderness (3:7, 10). What did they go out to see? Implicitly at least, and by virtue of the references to John in the preceding paragraph, the question asks for a clarification of who John was. The wilderness has been the place where John was in earlier contexts (1:80; 3:2, 4).

The first answer Jesus suggests is "a reed shaken by the wind" (κάλαμον ὑπὸ ἀνέμου σαλευόμενον *kalamon hypo anemou saleuomenon*). Each of the terms in this phrase suggests weakness, vacillation, or fear (cf. 21:25-26; Eph 4:14). One might expect to see reeds blown by the wind in the wilderness, but who would go out to see such a thing? The second answer suggests one who has risen to power and wealth by human standards: "someone dressed in soft robes." In a society in which many had only one garment that they wore every day, fine clothes were a sure sign of wealth (see Jas 2:2; 5:1-2; 1 Pet 3:3). One might go to see a person in fine clothes, but who would go

to the wilderness to find such a spectacle? Luke says nothing about John's clothing, but Mark says he wore the rough camel's hair garment of a prophet (Mark 1:6; cf. 2 Kgs 1:8; Zech 13:4). If they went out to see a prophet, the crowds should not have expected to find someone bearing the marks of worldly success. At this point, Luke embellishes the tradition to drive home the point (cf. Matt 11:8): Those who wear fine clothing and live luxuriously live in palaces—not in the wilderness. John was neither a weak reed nor one compromised by worldly pursuits; he was a true prophet. Hence the third answer. The people had gone to see a prophet, but what they had actually seen was one greater than a prophet. John's role as a prophet has been established (1:17, 76; 3:2). The thrust of this entire unit is conveyed by Jesus' assertion that John was more than a prophet. As confirmation of that assertion, quotations from Scripture follow. The verse is a composite that draws from and resonates with several other significant verses:

Luke 7:27	"See, I am sending my messenger ahead of you, who will prepare your way before you."
Malachi 3:1	"*See, I am sending my messenger to prepare* (MT) *the way before* me."
Exodus 23:20	"*I am going to send an angel in front of* you, to guard you on *the way* and to bring you to the place that I have *prepared*."
Isaiah 40:3	"A voice cries out: 'In the wilderness *prepare the way of the* LORD.'"
Luke 1:17	"With the spirit and power of Elijah he will go before him [the Lord] . . . *to make ready* a people prepared for the Lord."
Luke 1:76	"And you, child, will be called the prophet of the Most High; for you will go before the Lord *to prepare his ways.*"

Luke 3:4   "The voice of one crying out in the wilderness: '*Prepare the way* of the Lord.' "

Jesus' citation of Scripture, therefore, echoes these earlier contexts, both in the OT and earlier in Luke. The effect is to identify not himself but John with the expected messenger of the Lord, who would prepare the way. By implication, therefore, John—not Jesus—is Elijah (Mal 4:5), but Luke does not make this identification explicit, as Matthew does (11:14). Thus John is greater than a prophet, because he is the messenger and forerunner of the Lord. There is no evidence from pre-Christian Jewish sources that Elijah's role was interpreted as the forerunner *for the Messiah*. Rather, that seems to have been an early Christian inference: Since John was the forerunner of Jesus, and Jesus was the Messiah, then John was the forerunner of the Mes-

siah. That understanding, however, is underscored by Luke's presentation of John and by the resonance of this verse with the others listed above. Therefore, the verse shows why John was indeed "more than a prophet."

The verse that follows (v. 28) both offers Jesus' conclusion from the verse of Scripture he has quoted and lifts the characterization of John to a new plane. No one is greater than John—no prophet, no person dressed in soft clothes. On the other hand, John was a forerunner announcing the Messiah, who would inaugurate the coming kingdom. Therefore, as one outside the kingdom, John is less than the least within the kingdom. The effect of this chain of relationships is to elevate both John and Jesus. John was great; Jesus was greater—the same theme Luke developed in the infancy narrative. Near the surface, however, is the reminder that ultimately the only status that matters is one's status with God.

REFLECTIONS

Image, popular appeal, and religious authority often mix in powerful and destructive ways. Televangelists with star-quality appeal every year bilk thousands of gullible believers out of dollars they cannot spare. Cult leaders mix a forceful personality, the assurance of divine authority, and the social pressures of the community to forge an irrational control over the lives of cult members. At times the fascination with guns and sex is mixed in as well. What makes people so vulnerable to such figures? What did they go out to see?

We might reflect on our need for authority figures, the sense of identity that comes from being part of a community or movement, and the influence of culture on our perception of what is religious. These verses force a more personal question on us, however: What did you go out looking for? What is it that you expect to fulfill your spiritual needs? What is the shape of that vacuum or hunger that you are seeking to fill?

Jesus' suggestions of inadequate answers call us to recognize the inadequacy of our efforts to fill that need. If we have turned to human figures or movements, they can be likened to reeds shaken by the wind. If we have turned to charismatic figures with wealth, image, and all the trappings of success, they are nothing more than someone dressed in soft clothes. Are we looking for a prophet? Then what legitimates the prophet?

Look at the relative ranking set up by Jesus' words and the evangelist's comment that follows in vv. 29-30. From the least to the greatest, the figures can be arranged as follows: a reed shaken by the wind, someone in soft robes, a prophet, John—the forerunner, then the least in the kingdom of God, including tax collectors. These are greater even than John because they have acknowledged God's claims on them. By contrast, the Pharisees and lawyers rejected God's purpose for them. This pericope, therefore, moves the reader from searching for figures or movements that will satisfy their spiritual needs to finding and accepting God's justice and God's purposes. The answer is not in our attachment to any movement or human figure, but in our submission to God's claims on us. The two are radically different, and it is important that we recognize the difference and check our personal questing from time to time to be sure that we have not been fooled into substituting one for the other.

To be even the least among those who have submitted to God's sovereignty is to be greater than any of the prophetic figures outside the kingdom, regardless of their appeal or their following.

Luke 7:31-35, Responses to John and Jesus

NIV

[31]"To what, then, can I compare the people of this generation? What are they like? [32]They are like children sitting in the marketplace and calling out to each other:

" 'We played the flute for you,
 and you did not dance;
we sang a dirge,
 and you did not cry.'

[33]For John the Baptist came neither eating bread nor drinking wine, and you say, 'He has a demon.' [34]The Son of Man came eating and drinking, and you say, 'Here is a glutton and a drunkard, a friend of tax collectors and "sinners." ' [35]But wisdom is proved right by all her children."

NRSV

[31]"To what then will I compare the people of this generation, and what are they like? [32]They are like children sitting in the marketplace and calling to one another,

 'We played the flute for you, and you did not
  dance;
 we wailed, and you did not weep.'
[33]For John the Baptist has come eating no bread and drinking no wine, and you say, 'He has a demon'; [34]the Son of Man has come eating and drinking, and you say, 'Look, a glutton and a drunkard, a friend of tax collectors and sinners!' [35]Nevertheless, wisdom is vindicated by all her children."

COMMENTARY

The third unit devoted to clarifying the relationship between John and Jesus responds to the failure of the crowds to take seriously the calls of either John or Jesus. As different as John and Jesus were, the people did not accept either.

This unit is composed of a parable or riddle (vv. 31-32), its interpretation in relation to John and Jesus (vv. 33-34), and a concluding proverb (v. 35). Matthew 11:16-19 preserves a close parallel, confirming that the unit was drawn from Q, where it already had its present structure. The riddle of the children (v. 32) and the accusation against Jesus (v. 34) are nearly verbatim in both accounts. The differences between the two, on the other hand, are slight: (1) Matthew says the children called "to the others," while Luke says they called "each other"; (2) Luke calls John "the Baptist"; (3) Luke adds the terms "bread" and "wine"; and (4) Matthew says that wisdom will

be justified by "her works," while Luke has "all her children."

Scholars have debated how much of this unit should be traced to Jesus' words: (a) the riddle alone, (b) the riddle with its application to John and Jesus, or (c) the whole unit (including v. 35). Although the riddle conceivably may have exposed an adversary's fickleness or obstinance in another setting, the close fit between the riddle and the contrasting character of the ministries of John and Jesus suggests that the riddle and its application were linked from the beginning. Moreover, the character of the accusation against Jesus—that he was "a glutton and a drunkard"—points to the sort of charges brought against Jesus during his ministry rather than in the context of the early church.

The original form of the proverb was probably "Wisdom is vindicated by her children." Matthew changed "children" to "works" (a Matthean theme), while Luke has characteristically added the word for "all," so that v. 35 echoes v. 29. Verses 29 and 35, therefore, frame the riddle and its interpretation and provide clues to Luke's understanding of the unit. Note the repetition of "all" and a form of the verb for "to justify" in the bracketing verses.

The initial question sets the context for the riddle: Jesus will compare "this generation" to the children sitting in the marketplace. First and foremost, therefore, it characterizes those who would not respond—not John or Jesus. The riddle itself is open to various interpretations. Common to all interpretations is the assumption that the first line—the call to dance to the flute—is a challenge for the other children to mimic a festive celebration, such as a wedding, while the call to wail and weep was a challenge for their playmates to mimic the mourners at a funeral. From there, interpretations vary: (1) one group is calling out the first line, and another group of children answers with the second; neither group will play the other's game, and neither group can get the other to play its game. (2) Both lines come from the same group of children; they offered to play two very different games, but the others would not join them in either game. (3) The two lines are actually part of a game of mime; the first group is taunting the second because it has failed to figure out what the first group was miming.

The first interpretation would suggest that the two groups of children represent the followers of John and the followers of Jesus. In disputes between the two groups, neither can persuade the other. If taken in this way, the initial question, which targeted "this generation," would have to be considered a later adaptation of the riddle.

The second interpretation is the most acceptable. Verse 29, as indeed the preceding material, speaks favorably of John. But the ministries of John and Jesus were strikingly different. Whereas John was a prophet announcing judgment and calling for repentance in the wilderness, Jesus announced God's blessing on the poor and called the rich to repent while he ate and drank with the outcasts. The meal settings that were evidently so scandalous but so characteristic of Jesus' ministry (see Commentary on 5:27-32) were the point of contrast. The Pharisees and lawyers (see v. 30) refused to accept either John or Jesus. The lines of the riddle reverse the sequence, since the first line characterizes Jesus and the second John. The point is that those who rejected both John and Jesus could not be pleased; they were like obstinate children who would not join in any game.

The third interpretation, which interprets the riddle as a refrain from the game of mime, takes the meaning in a different direction. John and Jesus have mimed God's call to "this generation," whose members have not understood the mime. Those who were critical of John and Jesus are therefore characterized as children shamed by their failure to understand a simple mime. While this interpretation cannot be ruled out, it does not correlate with the contrast between mourning and dancing (John and Jesus) as forcefully as the second interpretation. In addition, the condemnation comes from what they *would* not do rather than from what they *could* not do.

Even after the basic options for interpreting these verses have been evaluated, difficulties remain: the function of the designations "the Baptist" for John and "the Son of Man" for Jesus, Luke's references to bread and wine, the accusation against Jesus, and the meaning of the concluding proverb. Two of the three occurrences of the title "the Baptist" occur in this chapter, one in the first of the three units on John and Jesus (7:20) and the other here in the third unit (7:33). The third occurrence is in 9:19. The title is traditional, appearing in all three synoptic Gospels, but not in John and not in the infancy material or the description of John's preaching in Luke (chaps. 1–3). The addition of "bread" and "wine" in v. 33 is probably no more than idiomatic; to eat bread and drink wine means no more than to eat and drink (as in Matt 11:18).

The charge against John is that he is a demoniac—a wild man. The title "Son of Man" is used here of Jesus. At least the titular use of the term represents a later addition to the unit. If Jesus used the term in this context, it should be construed as an idiomatic circumlocution for a reference to himself. Alternatively, the title may have replaced an earlier self-reference.

The charge against Jesus echoes Deut 21:20 (see also Prov 23:20). If Luke's readers knew the reference in Deuteronomy—which incidentally occurs just prior to the well-known prescription that if one were hanged on a tree, the corpse should not be left overnight—the interplay between the two texts sets up a powerful irony. In Deuteronomy, the charge "He is a glutton and a drunkard" is leveled at "a stubborn and rebellious son who will not obey his father and mother" (Deut 21:18). The penalty for such stubbornness is extreme: All the men of the town shall stone him to death (Deut 21:21). In Luke, however, Jesus has just castigated "the men of this generation" for their stubborn refusal to heed the calls of either John or Jesus himself. Now he repeats their self-incriminating accusation against him: "Look, a glutton and a drunkard" (Luke 7:34). So who has "rejected God's purpose" for them (v. 30)?

Three terms at the end of this unit also occur in v. 29, a transitional verse composed by Luke himself: "tax collectors" (τελῶναι telōnai), "justify" (δικαιόω dikaioō), and "all" (πᾶς pas). The concluding proverb gives the unit a promising ending. Not all will neglect the call of John and Jesus. Those who are wise will see in their ministries—each of which was offensive in its own way—the evidence of God's redemptive work. Wisdom—which was closely aligned with God's teachings, or with the Spirit—will be vindicated by "all her children"—all who would hear God's prophet and God's Son.

REFLECTIONS

Jesus condemned the people of his generation because they let their expectations prevail over God's call to them. They had a long tradition of interpretation about how God would vindicate them and deliver them from their enemies. The apocalyptic literature of the period contains various descriptions of the coming of God's kingdom and the bounty that would accompany it. Some looked for a political leader like David or the Maccabees. Others looked for an apocalyptic end to the world, and still others for a return to the Garden of Eden. The announcement of the kingdom by John and its dawning in the person of Jesus, however, did not fulfill the expectations that others had for the fulfillment of God's promises. As a result, like children, they sat on the sidelines and refused to join in the game. As different as John and Jesus were, neither satisfied the people of that generation. Because God had not acted as they had expected, they refused to respond to God's call for them to leave the sidelines and join in the fulfillment of God's redemptive purposes for that generation and for generations to come.

This pericope exposes our readiness to criticize and find fault, and our refusal to join in the struggle to bring about God's justice and the celebration of the announcement of good news for the poor and oppressed by forming new communities. One reason for our repeated refusal to respond to the kingdom announcement may be that, like the people of Jesus' generation, we have let our expectations for what God can do and is doing, and our restrictions on what passes for proper church life, prevent us from seeing how God is still at work in our own generation.

For all who seek to heed the words of wisdom and fashion a favorable response to God's call, the twin challenges of this pericope are (1) to recognize the surprising and sometimes even scandalous ways in which God is at work in our time, and (2) to reject the conventional expectations that may otherwise prevent us from responding to God's call to join in the work, struggles, and celebration of the kingdom. Who are we, obstinate children sitting in the marketplace who refuse to play, or the children of wisdom who are ready to play God's game, regardless of whether it is the game we expected?

Luke 7:36-50, Responses of a Pharisee and a Harlot

NIV

³⁶Now one of the Pharisees invited Jesus to have dinner with him, so he went to the Phari-

NRSV

36One of the Pharisees asked Jesus[a] to eat with

[a] Gk him

NIV

see's house and reclined at the table. [37]When a woman who had lived a sinful life in that town learned that Jesus was eating at the Pharisee's house, she brought an alabaster jar of perfume, [38]and as she stood behind him at his feet weeping, she began to wet his feet with her tears. Then she wiped them with her hair, kissed them and poured perfume on them.

[39]When the Pharisee who had invited him saw this, he said to himself, "If this man were a prophet, he would know who is touching him and what kind of woman she is—that she is a sinner."

[40]Jesus answered him, "Simon, I have something to tell you."

"Tell me, teacher," he said.

[41]"Two men owed money to a certain moneylender. One owed him five hundred denarii,[a] and the other fifty. [42]Neither of them had the money to pay him back, so he canceled the debts of both. Now which of them will love him more?"

[43]Simon replied, "I suppose the one who had the bigger debt canceled."

"You have judged correctly," Jesus said.

[44]Then he turned toward the woman and said to Simon, "Do you see this woman? I came into your house. You did not give me any water for my feet, but she wet my feet with her tears and wiped them with her hair. [45]You did not give me a kiss, but this woman, from the time I entered, has not stopped kissing my feet. [46]You did not put oil on my head, but she has poured perfume on my feet. [47]Therefore, I tell you, her many sins have been forgiven—for she loved much. But he who has been forgiven little loves little."

[48]Then Jesus said to her, "Your sins are forgiven."

[49]The other guests began to say among themselves, "Who is this who even forgives sins?"

[50]Jesus said to the woman, "Your faith has saved you; go in peace."

[a]41 A denarius was a coin worth about a day's wages.

NRSV

him, and he went into the Pharisee's house and took his place at the table. [37]And a woman in the city, who was a sinner, having learned that he was eating in the Pharisee's house, brought an alabaster jar of ointment. [38]She stood behind him at his feet, weeping, and began to bathe his feet with her tears and to dry them with her hair. Then she continued kissing his feet and anointing them with the ointment. [39]Now when the Pharisee who had invited him saw it, he said to himself, "If this man were a prophet, he would have known who and what kind of woman this is who is touching him—that she is a sinner." [40]Jesus spoke up and said to him, "Simon, I have something to say to you." "Teacher," he replied, "speak." [41]"A certain creditor had two debtors; one owed five hundred denarii,[a] and the other fifty. [42]When they could not pay, he canceled the debts for both of them. Now which of them will love him more?" [43]Simon answered, "I suppose the one for whom he canceled the greater debt." And Jesus[b] said to him, "You have judged rightly." [44]Then turning toward the woman, he said to Simon, "Do you see this woman? I entered your house; you gave me no water for my feet, but she has bathed my feet with her tears and dried them with her hair. [45]You gave me no kiss, but from the time I came in she has not stopped kissing my feet. [46]You did not anoint my head with oil, but she has anointed my feet with ointment. [47]Therefore, I tell you, her sins, which were many, have been forgiven; hence she has shown great love. But the one to whom little is forgiven, loves little." [48]Then he said to her, "Your sins are forgiven." [49]But those who were at the table with him began to say among themselves, "Who is this who even forgives sins?" [50]And he said to the woman, "Your faith has saved you; go in peace."

[a]The denarius was the usual day's wage for a laborer   [b]Gk *he*

COMMENTARY

All of the units in this chapter have been devoted to portraying Jesus as one greater than a prophet, either by comparison with the OT prophets or by comparison with John. The story of the

Pharisee and a harlot is the culmination of this narrative sequence and is clearly related to what precedes it. The responses of the two characters illustrate the contrasting responses to John in vv. 29-30, and Jesus is eating at a banquet, following the characterization of his ministry in v. 34 as "eating and drinking." Even more to the point, however, this scene demonstrates both that Jesus was a prophet and that he was more than a prophet. When Simon the Pharisee reasons that if Jesus were a prophet he would know the character of the woman who was touching him, Jesus' response shows that he knows both Simon's thoughts and the character of the woman. His response, therefore, confirms that he is a prophet; but when he forgives the woman's sins, he is greater than a prophet. Consequently, this story completes the development of the theme "more than a prophet" and serves as a transition to the vital question that will occupy the coming chapters: "Who is this one?" (see 8:25; 9:9, 18).

The history of this tradition is hard to trace, in part because of the complexity of the parallels in the other Gospels and in part because of the artistry and coherence of the Lukan account. Some relationship with the other stories of the anointing of Jesus is undeniable, but the unity of Luke's account is not easily explained in terms of redaction of the Markan or Johannine parallels. Whereas in the other Gospels the anointing of Jesus takes place in Bethany during the Passover season (Matt 26:6-13; Mark 14:3-9; John 12:1-8), this story is set in Galilee earlier in Jesus' ministry. In Luke's account there is no relation between the anointing and the burial of Jesus (Matt 26:12; Mark 14:8; John 12:7). Nor can it be interpreted as an ironic coronation following Jesus' entry into Jerusalem, as it may be in Matthew and Mark, where the woman anoints Jesus' head. The woman brings an alabaster flask, as in Mark and Matthew, but the ointment is not identified as "pure nard" as in Mark and John. Beyond the tabulation of similarities and differences in setting and detail, however, the Lukan story is distinctive because of its development of the relationship between forgiveness and love, the power with which it evokes the character of the woman and her response to Jesus, and the unity of its various components: the anointing, with Simon's response (vv. 38-39); the riddle, with Simon's response (vv.

40-43); Jesus' response to Simon (vv. 44-47); Jesus' response to the woman (vv. 48, 50); and the response of the other guests (v. 49).

The problems of tradition history are probably best solved by positing two events in the ministry of Jesus that have given rise to these interrelated accounts. Luke preserves the tradition of an event in Galilee in which a harlot approached Jesus at a banquet and wept in gratitude. When her tears fell on Jesus' feet, she let down her hair and wiped away the tears. The parable of the two debtors almost requires such a setting, and it is not easily detached from this context. The Markan account records an event in Bethany at which a woman anoints Jesus' head with pure nard from an alabaster flask. The event is related both to Jesus' coronation and to his burial. In John's account, the home in Bethany has become the home of Mary and Martha, and the occasion and motivation for the act is gratitude for the raising of Lazarus; the woman is Mary of Bethany, not a harlot, and in a clear sign of conflation of the traditions Mary wipes not her tears from Jesus' feet but the expensive ointment. Luke's account, therefore, preserves one of these traditions with relatively few signs of borrowing from the other tradition. The references to the alabaster flask and the anointing probably originated with the other tradition, but their presence in Luke's account probably predates Luke's use of Mark and is not to be explained as Luke's editorial work. The similarity between the identity of the host in Mark (Simon the leper) and in Luke (Simon, a Pharisee) is probably also due to a mingling of details from the two similar stories, but we cannot be sure which has borrowed the name from the other. Beyond these details and the meal setting in each of the accounts, Luke reports an altogether different story.

7:36-37. These verses introduce the setting for the story. One of the Pharisees—who were last mentioned in v. 30 as those who rejected God's purpose for them—invites Jesus to a banquet. Jesus and the harlot each come to the Pharisee's home, Jesus invited, the harlot as one of the uninvited townspeople who would have crowded around the walls inside or the courtyard outside to see the Pharisee and his guests. Such an occasion would have been much more public than a dinner in a private home today, so the presence of uninvited persons would not have been unusual. The woman's past is sufficiently defined by the two brief descriptions: "a woman in the city, who was a sinner." Identifying the woman as a sinner is more important than identifying her specifically as a harlot because the term for "sinner" (ἁμαρτωλός *hamartōlos*) connects with the previous reference to sinners in v. 34, where Jesus is called "a friend of tax collectors and sinners." The introduction to the story, therefore, sets the scene for Jesus' interaction with a Pharisee and a sinner, following references to both groups in the immediately preceding verses. We will not be surprised that the Pharisee takes offense at Jesus while Jesus vindicates the sinner.

7:38. This verse reports the woman's actions. At such a banquet, the guests would have been reclining on pillows, supported by their left arms and eating with their right hands, with their feet away from the mat on which the food would have been spread before them. Thus the woman could easily approach Jesus' feet. The fact that she has brought a jar of ointment shows that she has planned to anoint Jesus—a sign of her love (see v. 47). Small flasks of alabaster or gypsum quarried along the Jordan or imported from Egypt were often used for perfumes.

As the woman stood weeping behind Jesus, she began to wash his feet with her tears. In a spontaneous act, she let down her hair and began to wipe the tears from Jesus' feet and then anointed them with the perfume. The woman's act expresses love and gratitude, but it also violated social conventions. Touching or caressing a man's feet could have sexual overtones, as did letting down her hair, so a woman never let down her hair in public. Moreover, the woman was known to be a sinner. Assuming she was unclean, she would have made Jesus unclean by touching him. The sinner has, therefore, created a scene at the Pharisee's dinner, and he is scandalized. But how will he respond? And how will Jesus respond? In the Pharisee's eyes, the woman's act represents a challenge both to his honor and to Jesus'.

7:39. The reader learns the Pharisee's thoughts. Luke has previously reported interior monologue and Jesus' knowledge of what others were thinking (see 5:21-22; 6:7-8). The Pharisee makes two assumptions that imply two further inferences. First, he assumes the woman is a sinner, as the narrator has reported in v. 37. Second, he assumes that if Jesus were a prophet he would know what sort of woman she was. From these assumptions, both of which appear to have been correct, he draws two false inferences. First, he infers that if Jesus knew what sort of woman was touching him, he would not allow it. Second, he infers that since Jesus has done nothing to stop the woman, he is not a prophet. The Pharisee's assumption, therefore, is expressed as a condition contrary to fact: "If this man were a prophet [which he is not], he would have known who and what kind of woman this is who is touching him [which he did not because he did not stop her]." As readers, we already know that Jesus is more than a prophet and read with delight as Jesus immediately confirms that he not only knows what sort of woman has touched him but what sort of man the Pharisee is as well. Jesus even knows what the Pharisee was thinking at the moment he thought Jesus was not a prophet.

7:40-47. In v. 40 the first dialogue is reported. Jesus calls the Pharisee by name, "Simon," which has not been introduced previously. Jesus addresses the parable to Simon and will speak to the woman later. At banquets and feasts it was common for the host or guests to pose riddles for one another in a contest of wit and wisdom. Jesus poses for Simon a riddle based on the convention of patron-client relationships. If a certain patron had two debtors who could not repay him, one who owed a little and one who owed much, and the patron canceled the debt of each, who would love him more? Since a day laborer earned a denarius per day (Matt 20:2), the scale of the debts is fairly modest, yet sizable enough to be prohibitive for any but the wealthy: 50 denarii and 500 denarii. The only relevant points, however, are the benevolence of the patron and the relative sizes of the two debts.

The answer is so obvious that the Pharisee responds cautiously or with apparent disdain: "I suppose the one for whom he canceled the greater debt." The trap has been sprung. What remains is to connect the Pharisee's answer to his condemnation of the woman's act of love and gratitude. First, Jesus confirms that Simon has given the right answer. Then, after turning toward the woman, Jesus exposes the contrast between Simon's

Figure 5: Coins in the Gospels

By New Testament times coins had been in use in Palestine for over six hundred years. The Jews struck currency of their own from the Persian era (fifth century BCE) until the end of the Bar Kochba revolt (135 CE). The currency circulating at Jesus' time would have been a mixture of various denominations of gold, silver, brass, and bronze coins from all parts of the Roman Empire and beyond.

"They paid him thirty silver coins."

Because they were made of the highest grade of silver, shekels and half-shekels struck at the mint at Tyre were accepted by the Jews as the official standard for payments specified in the Bible. Thus the Greek word *argyria* ("silver"), used to describe the money paid to Judas for betraying Jesus (cf. Exod 21:32; Zech 11:12), is believed to refer to the silver Tyrian shekel, worth approximately four denarii. This same coin is probably what Jesus refers to as a *stater* (Matt 17:27), which Peter used to pay the temple tax for Jesus and himself. The coin shown here, struck in 60/59 BCE, pictures the Phoenician deity Melkart as Heracles; the reverse pictures an eagle and reads "Tyre, Holy and Inviolate." The *didrachma,* or "two drachma" (Matt 17:24), a silver coin used to pay the half-shekel temple tax (Exod 30:13), may refer to a silver half-shekel struck at Tyre, essentially the same design as the shekel but half the weight. Shekels and half-shekels of this type were struck at the mint at Tyre from 126 BCE until about 70 CE.

"Render unto Caesar the things that are Caesar's."

The *denarius,* a Roman silver coin, was the typical day's wage. The coin shown, first issued c. 19 CE, pictures Emperor Tiberius (14–37) and reads "Tiberius Caesar, son of the Deified Augustus and himself Augustus." The reverse shows Livia, mother of Tiberius, represented as Pax, goddess of peace, and reads "High Priest." The denarius is mentioned in Matt 20:2; 22:19; Mark 6:37; 12:15; 14:5; Luke 7:41; 10:35; 20:24; and John 6:7; 12:5.

"What woman having ten drachma. . . ."

The *drachma* (Luke 15:8), a Greek silver coin, was approximate in value to the Roman denarius. The coin shown here, from Parthia, has the bust of Orodes I, the Parthian emperor (57-37 BCE) who briefly drove Herod I from Jerusalem; the reverse shows a seated Arsaces (founder of the Parthian Empire) and reads "King of Kings; Arsaces, Benefactor, Righteous one, God Manifest, Lover of the Greeks."

"Take nothing for the journey except a staff—no bread, no bag, no money [chalkon] in your belts."

The Greek term *chalkon* ("copper"; Mark 6:8) could refer to any midsize copper coin.

"Are not five sparrows sold for two assaria?"

Assarion (Matt 10:29; Luke 12:6) is the designation of various copper coins struck outside of Palestine. In NT times, sixteen assaria equaled one denarius. The obverse of the coin pictured here shows Augustus and reads "Deified Augustus, Father"; the reverse shows an altar between the letters S(ENATVS) C(ONSVLTO), meaning "By the Consent of the Senate," and reads "Providence."

"A poor widow came and put in two lepta, which are worth a quadrans."

The *quadrans* (Mark 12:42) was a small bronze coin; four quadrans normally equalled an assarion, sixty-four a denarius. The coin pictured here was struck in Rome about 5 BCE, during the reign of Augustus. The obverse (not pictured) shows an altar; the reverse contains the legend "Apronius Gallus [the overseer of minting operations], maker of gold, silver, and bronze coins."

A *lepton* (or "thin piece" [Mark 12:42; Luke 21:2]), also called a *perutah* by the Jews, was a small copper coin, the coin of least value in circulation. These coins varied greatly in size and value; normally, two lepta equaled one quadrans. The coin pictured, struck in either 8 or 12 CE, shows a palm tree with clusters (obverse), and a wheat head with the legend "Belonging to Caesar" (reverse).

Photographs and text by Dr. E. Jerry Vardaman

lack of hospitality and the woman's selfless adoration of Jesus. This is the longest stretch of uninterrupted speech in the story. Verses 44-46 contrast the way in which the Pharisee and the woman have treated Jesus, and v. 47 draws the inference from this contrast. In this speech, parts of the story that were not narrated earlier are filled in. As readers we had not been told about the way in which the Pharisee received Jesus into his home. Instead, the story began with its dramatic moment—the woman's scandalous act. Now we learn that when Jesus arrived the Pharisee gave him no water with which to wash his feet, no kiss, no oil for anointing his head. None of these was required, but they were gracious gestures of hospitality attested elsewhere (footwashing: Gen 18:4; 19:2; Judg 19:21; 1 Sam 25:41; John 13:3-5; a kiss of greeting: 2 Sam 15:5; Luke 15:20; 22:47-48; anointing with oil: Pss 23:5; 133:2; Mark 14:3). The effect of Jesus' words is to connect the Pharisee's right answer to Jesus' riddle to his wrong judgment of the woman's anointing of Jesus' feet.

The crux of this story is Jesus' pronouncement in v. 47. Did the woman love because she had been forgiven, or was she forgiven because she loved Jesus? Verse 47 draws together the riddle and the two responses to Jesus, showing that the Pharisee has responded as one who has been forgiven little, while the woman has acted as one who has been forgiven much. The difficulty lies in the causal clause at the end of the first half of v. 47. Some have taken it to mean that the woman was forgiven much because she loved much, but the logic of the riddle, its application to the woman's act, and the parallel with the

second half of v. 47 each dictate that the woman's loving act is evidence that she has been forgiven much. By implication, the woman's preparation in bringing the alabaster flask in the first place suggests that she has experienced acceptance and forgiveness prior to this event. Something more fundamental is implicit here, however. It is not that the Pharisee had less for which to be forgiven than the harlot. Rather, because he did not recognize his need for forgiveness he received less. And she, because she recognized her need and received forgiveness joyfully, received more.

7:48-50. With v. 48, Jesus speaks to the woman for the first time, confirming that her sins have been forgiven. Without such a direct address, the story would remain incomplete and the relationship between the woman and Jesus would have remained unvoiced. When Jesus declares the harlot's sins forgiven, however, the other guests begin to raise the question the Pharisees had raised earlier, but in a slightly different form. At the healing of the paralytic, they asked: "Who is this who is speaking blasphemies? Who can forgive sins but God alone?" (5:21). Now, by combining the first part of the first question with the last part of the second question, the result is a query that suggests that the answer to this divine act lies in Jesus' identity: "Who is this who even forgives sins?" The pursuit of an answer to that question will lead us through the next two chapters of Luke. For the moment, however, Jesus' blessing of the woman remains paramount. Her openness to God's forgiveness and her selfless, loving response are accepted as faith, and forgiveness is equated with salvation. The result is peace, *shalom:* "Your faith has saved you; go in peace."

REFLECTIONS

Unless we see something of ourselves in the character of Simon the Pharisee, we are so blind to our own need that we have failed to hear the story. The soft underbelly of hypocrisy is always vulnerable to the truth, and we are most vulnerable when we are blind to our own faults. Simon thought he was blameless. He "knew" the woman was a sinner, and he assumed she had defiled Jesus. Jesus then exposed the contrast between Simon's distant hospitality and the woman's sincere affection. The contrast was clear, and it left Simon doubly exposed and embarrassed. First a shameful display of affection from a sinful woman occurred in his house. Second, a guest had called attention to the host's lack of hospitality. In the Middle East the importance of honor and shame and the family name can hardly be overestimated.

Does love lead to forgiveness, or is the ability to love the result of being forgiven? The question is not easily answered because the issue can be seen from both perspectives. Jesus accepted the woman's expression of love as a sign that she had been forgiven much. Love is the natural response of the forgiven, but the capacity to love is directly related to the ability to receive grace, forgiveness, and love. Simon's problem was not his conduct but his attitude and self-understanding. Jesus cut through social amenities to Simon's regard for himself and others and his relationship to God. Because Simon thought of himself as pious and righteous, he had no idea what it meant to be forgiven and no awareness of his own need for forgiveness. He loved little because he had experienced so little of God's love. Simon, therefore, represents the position furthest from God. Because Simon did not recognize his need for forgiveness, he excluded himself from God's grace. On the other hand, because the woman knew she was a sinner, she could receive God's forgiveness. Knowing she was a sinner, she could also know what it meant to be forgiven.

If our lives have been changed by an experience of God's grace, we can never get over the fact that we have been forgiven. God's love, experienced in forgiveness, becomes the controlling force in our lives. The gratitude of the forgiven is also the source of new life. Ultimately, that is what salvation is all about. Such gratitude, however, cannot be forced or faked; it requires absolute, transparent humility before God.

The camera recedes from Jesus in the closing verses of this story. The focus is on the reaction of those who were eating at the table with him. They marveled that Jesus dared to pronounce sins forgiven. Only God could forgive sins. No priest, prophet, or rabbi would dare to claim that prerogative. The irony is that Jesus' readiness to forgive the humble and the sinful was one of the clearest evidences that Jesus was more than a prophet. More than any of his miracles or mighty works, Jesus' ability to forgive revealed that he shared the heart and character of God.

LUKE 8:1-21, HEARING AND DOING GOD'S WORD

OVERVIEW

The next section of the Gospel (Luke 8:1-21) contains four units that develop the theme of hearing and doing God's Word. The section opens and closes with references to groups who followed Jesus: the Twelve, a group of women, and his mother and brothers. The effect is to heighten the sense of movement and itinerancy in Jesus' min-istry and to depict models for positive responses to Jesus' announcement of the kingdom. At the center of this section are the parable of the sower, Luke's account of Jesus' explanation of the purpose of the parables, and the interpretation of the parable of the sower. Sayings on what is hidden and what is revealed follow.

Luke 8:1-3, Jesus' Followers: The Women

NIV	NRSV
8 After this, Jesus traveled about from one town and village to another, proclaiming the good news of the kingdom of God. The	**8** Soon afterwards he went on through cities and villages, proclaiming and bringing the good news of the kingdom of God. The twelve were

NIV

Twelve were with him, ²and also some women who had been cured of evil spirits and diseases: Mary (called Magdalene) from whom seven demons had come out; ³Joanna the wife of Cuza, the manager of Herod's household; Susanna; and many others. These women were helping to support them out of their own means.

NRSV

with him, ²as well as some women who had been cured of evil spirits and infirmities: Mary, called Magdalene, from whom seven demons had gone out, ³and Joanna, the wife of Herod's steward Chuza, and Susanna, and many others, who provided for them*a* out of their resources.

*a*Other ancient authorities read *him*

COMMENTARY

Luke 8:1-3 is a Lukan summary that introduces important motifs for both the section that follows and for later sections of Luke and Acts. As the only reference in any of the Gospels to the role of a group of women followers during Jesus' Galilean ministry, it serves as a corrective to the assumption that all of Jesus' followers were men. For raw material, Luke evidently picked up the earlier description of Jesus' itinerant ministry of healing and preaching (Luke 4:40-44); the appointment of the Twelve (with an echo of Mark 3:14); the list or lists of the women who were present at the crucifixion and burial of Jesus; and other traditions regarding the identity, background, and role of the women that are found only in Luke.

The allusions, connections, and foreshadowings contained in this short unit give it an importance in the development of Luke's Gospel that if missed leaves the unit looking like an odd insertion. The summary opens with a favorite Lukan transitional phrase, "And it came to pass" (καὶ ἐγένετο *kai egeneto*), and a term that has special significance in Luke and Acts but is not easily translated. The term rendered "afterwards" (καθεξῆς *kathexēs*) occurs in Luke 1:3; 8:1; Acts 3:24; 11:4; and 18:23, where it indicates sequence, order, and progression, sometimes emphasizing temporal sequence, sometimes geographical progression, and sometimes order or accuracy. Echoing the prologue to the Gospel (1:3), this summary underscores Luke's intention to present an "orderly narrative." The description of Jesus' movement through towns and villages preaching and bringing the good news of the kingdom echoes Luke 4:42-44 and prepares the reader for Jesus' movements in chapters 8 and 9, and more distantly, the long journey section later in the Gospel (9:51–19:44). Some elements of this summary are also taken up

again in Acts 16–17, where Paul "travels" (διοδεύω *diodeuō*]; cf. Luke 8:1; Acts 17:1) from town to town in Macedonia and Greece and converts "not a few of the leading women" (Acts 17:4).

The previous references to the kingdom of God were in Luke 4:43; 6:20; 7:28, but references to the kingdom will become increasingly frequent. Indeed, the section introduced by this summary will feature Jesus' interpretation of the parables of the kingdom (8:10), and in Luke 9:2 Jesus will send the Twelve out to proclaim the kingdom. Therefore, although Luke does not reproduce Mark's statement of Jesus' purpose for appointing the Twelve—"to be with him, and to be sent out to proclaim the message" (Mark 3:14)—Luke 8 and 9 feature this understanding of the role of the Twelve, who are said to be "with him" in Luke 8:1 and "sent" in Luke 9:2.

Characteristically, where Luke mentions a male figure or group, he often links it with a corresponding female figure or group—for example, Zechariah and Elizabeth, Mary and Joseph, Simeon and Anna, in chap. 4 the widow of Zarephath and Naaman the Syrian, in chap. 7 the centurion and the widow of Nain, and in chap. 15 the shepherd and the woman with the coins. The group of women who followed Jesus are given special prominence in Luke by introducing them at this point and alluding to their role when they are introduced again in Luke 23:49 and 23:55 (cf 24:10; Acts 1:14; 13:31).

The syntax of vv. 2-3 is difficult, making unclear whether the final clause of v. 3, "who provided for them out of their means," refers to the group of women in v. 2 or the "many others" in v. 3. Healing and exorcism are referred to together in 4:40-41; 6:18; and 7:21. As with other elements in this summary, the reference to unclean spirits prepares the reader for the exorcism of the Gerasene demoniac (8:26-39) and the boy with convulsions (9:37-43). The introduction of women who had been healed of various diseases foreshadows the healing of the woman with a hemorrhage and the raising of Jairus's daughter (8:40-56).

The only woman healed earlier in Luke was Peter's mother-in-law (4:38-39), but the reader may assume that by this point Jesus has healed many people who have not been singled out individually. There is no previous reference to Mary Magdalene or to the exorcism of demons from her. Magdala, for which she is named, is usually thought to have been located on the west side of the Sea of Galilee, north of Tiberias, and is identified with *Migdalnunaiya,* which means "fish tower." The state of having seven demons would have been far worse than having one (see 11:24-26). Mary Magdalene is also traditionally named first among the women at the cross and the tomb of Jesus (cf. Luke 24:10; Mark 15:40, 47; 16:1; John 20:1-2, 11-18). Joanna follows Mary Magdalene in 24:10, as she does here, but is otherwise unknown. She is identified as the wife of Chuza, Herod's steward, raising the ques-tion of whether a married woman had left her husband to follow Jesus in the company of other women. The reference to Herod prepares the reader for the role of Herod in Luke 9:7-9. Susanna is not mentioned elsewhere in the Gospel records. Although Joanna and Susanna are named after Mary Magdalene, as though in a list of those healed or exorcised by Jesus, presumably some of the women following Jesus had not required heal-ing or exorcism. A sizable group is implied, and these women provided for Jesus and those who followed him. In this respect, their role foreshad-ows that of Mary and Martha in 10:38-42 and the roles of the seven men in Acts 6 and the women who served and assisted Paul in his work. The proper use of one's possessions is a significant theme in Luke (cf. 12:15, 33; 14:33; 19:8).

By means of references that pick up earlier threads of the narrative and prepare for coming scenes, Luke 8:1-3 serves an important role in giving Luke's Gospel "order" (1:3). Before con-tinuing with the larger theme of Jesus' identity as the Christ (9:20), however, Luke will return to the reception of the Word of God, and the expe-rience of the kingdom among Jesus' followers and disciples.

Luke 8:4-15, The Parable of the Seed and the Soil

[4]While a large crowd was gathering and people were coming to Jesus from town after town, he told this parable: [5]"A farmer went out to sow his seed. As he was scattering the seed, some fell along the path; it was trampled on, and the birds of the air ate it up. [6]Some fell on rock, and when it came up, the plants withered because they had no moisture. [7]Other seed fell among thorns, which grew up with it and choked the plants. [8]Still other seed fell on good soil. It came up and yielded a crop, a hundred times more than was sown."

When he said this, he called out, "He who has ears to hear, let him hear."

[9]His disciples asked him what this parable meant. [10]He said, "The knowledge of the secrets of the kingdom of God has been given to you, but to others I speak in parables, so that,

4When a great crowd gathered and people from town after town came to him, he said in a parable: [5]"A sower went out to sow his seed; and as he sowed, some fell on the path and was trampled on, and the birds of the air ate it up. [6]Some fell on the rock; and as it grew up, it withered for lack of moisture. [7]Some fell among thorns, and the thorns grew with it and choked it. [8]Some fell into good soil, and when it grew, it produced a hundredfold." As he said this, he called out, "Let anyone with ears to hear listen!"

9Then his disciples asked him what this parable meant. [10]He said, "To you it has been given to know the secrets[a] of the kingdom of God; but to others I speak[b] in parables, so that

'looking they may not perceive,
    and listening they may not understand.'

[a]Or *mysteries*   [b]Gk lacks *I speak*

NIV

" 'though seeing, they may not see;
though hearing, they may not understand.'[a]

[11]"This is the meaning of the parable: The seed
is the word of God. [12]Those along the path are the
ones who hear, and then the devil comes and takes
away the word from their hearts, so that they may
not believe and be saved. [13]Those on the rock are
the ones who receive the word with joy when they
hear it, but they have no root. They believe for a
while, but in the time of testing they fall away. [14]The
seed that fell among thorns stands for those who
hear, but as they go on their way they are choked
by life's worries, riches and pleasures, and they do
not mature. [15]But the seed on good soil stands for
those with a noble and good heart, who hear the
word, retain it, and by persevering produce a crop."

[a]10 Isaiah 6:9

NRSV

[11]"Now the parable is this: The seed is the
word of God. [12]The ones on the path are those
who have heard; then the devil comes and takes
away the word from their hearts, so that they may
not believe and be saved. [13]The ones on the rock
are those who, when they hear the word, receive
it with joy. But these have no root; they believe
only for a while and in a time of testing fall away.
[14]As for what fell among the thorns, these are the
ones who hear; but as they go on their way, they
are choked by the cares and riches and pleasures
of life, and their fruit does not mature. [15]But as
for that in the good soil, these are the ones who,
when they hear the word, hold it fast in an honest
and good heart, and bear fruit with patient endurance."

COMMENTARY

This section of Luke 8 is devoted to the theme
of hearing the Word of God. The verb for "to
hear" (ἀκούω akouō) is repeated seven times, and
"the word" (ὁ λόγος ho logos) is repeated three
times. This parable has sown its intrigue in the
minds of hearers since its first telling, undoubtedly
by Jesus himself. Is it a parable of the sower, of
the seed, or of the soil? The choice of a title
already tells something of how it is being understood. The inclusion of an interpretation of this
parable in the synoptic Gospels, however, is itself
a recognition that the parable is open to various
interpretations.

Since Luke 6:20, the evangelist has drawn
upon Q and other sources. At this point Luke
returns to the Gospel of Mark and continues
following its sequence. If Luke draws the parable
from Mark, he abbreviates the description of the
setting, the parable, and Jesus' explanation of the
purpose for the parables. Mark's description of
Jesus' teaching from a boat by the sea has already
been used in Luke 5:1-3 to introduce the great
catch of fish. What remains is a statement that
Jesus spoke the parable when a great crowd
gathered around him from the towns (cf. the
similar reference to towns in 8:1). Moreover, in

contrast to Mark 4:1-2, Luke introduces not
"many parables" but this one parable. Mark's
repeated references to Jesus' teaching the crowd
are also gone. Luke retells the parable with a
greater economy of words. In spite of Luke's
emphasis on hearing, the initial injunction to hear
is dropped, as is Mark's extended description of
the rapid germination of the seed that fell on the
rocky soil, the report that the seed that fell among
the thorns did not bear fruit, and the reports of
thirty- and sixtyfold harvests. Breaking this pattern
of abridgment, Luke adds the phrase that the
sower sowed "his seed," thereby shifting attention
from the sower to the seed.

8:4-8. The parable is open to various readings,
depending on how one understands the Galilean
practices of sowing and plowing and how the
report of a hundredfold harvest would have been
understood. The parable is not introduced as a
kingdom parable, but references to the kingdom
of God bracket it in vv. 1 and 9. Why does the
sower sow on the path, the rocks, and the thorns?
Is the sower careless, sowing with confident abandon, or merely following the normal practice?
Joachim Jeremias claimed that the sower was
following the normal practice of sowing first and

then plowing the seed into the ground.[95] Similarly, Jer 4:3 warns, "Do now sow among thorns," and *Jub* 11:11 shows that Jesus drew upon a common metaphor: "Prince Mastema sent ravens and birds to devour the seed which was sown in the earth . . . before they could *plough in the seed* the ravens plucked it from the surface of the ground." K. D. White responded to Jeremias, citing evidence that plowing preceded sowing,[96] and P. B. Payne claimed that whereas plowing normally preceded sowing, in the fall sowing preceded plowing because the ground had already been broken up.[97] Regardless of the sequence of plowing and sowing, one would not deliberately sow on a path, but in broadcast sowing the loss of some seed is inevitable.

A similar debate has arisen over the way the report of a hundredfold harvest would have been received. The average yield was probably around tenfold, calculating the weight of the seed gathered in relation to the weight of the seed sown. A harvest of a hundredfold would have been considered fantastic.[98] Visions of the age to come described a harvest of ten thousandfold,[99] but for a Palestinian farmer a harvest of a hundredfold would have been quite miraculous.[100]

If the sowing is ordinary and the harvest is bountiful, the parable contrasts the end with the beginning and calls for faith that from the ordinary beginnings of Jesus' ministry in Galilee God would bring a bountiful harvest. If the sowing is not meager but a broadcasting of the seed with confident abandon, then the parable calls for hearers to live expansively, confident in God's goodness. If the three unproductive sowings are emphasized (path, rock, thorns), then the parable may speak to the crowds' fawning over Jesus—many will turn away, but some will bear fruit.

Galilean farmers would have smiled knowingly, especially at the mention of the rocky soil. An old Arabic folk tale explains that when Allah created the world he entrusted all the stones to two angels. Each had a full bag. As they flew over Palestine, one of the bags broke, spilling half the stones that were intended for the whole world.[101]

8:9-10. Luke abbreviates and softens the hard-edged statement on the purpose of the parables in Mark 4:10-12, which quotes that judgment on Israel from Isa 6:9-10. This passage is used elsewhere in the NT, in passages not associated with the parables, to explain why Israel rejected the Gospel (John 12:40; Acts 28:26-27). In Mark, Jesus contrasts "those around Jesus" with those who are "outside" (see Mark 3:31-35). Only those around Jesus are able to understand. Those who remain outside cannot enter the kingdom through the parables alone. Luke has discarded Mark's report of Jesus' withdrawal to a private place, identified the interlocutors as the disciples, and focused their question on "this parable." Whereas in Mark Jesus responds that to them "the mystery of the kingdom of God" has been given, in Luke he says that to them has been given "to know the mysteries of the kingdom." The difference is slight but contributes to the softening of Jesus' response in Luke. Instead of distinguishing "those outside" as in Mark, Luke merely contrasts the disciples with the "others." Like Matthew, Luke also draws the sting from the words of judgment from Isa 6:9-10 by omitting the phrase "so that they may not turn again and be forgiven." At each point where Luke differs from Mark, therefore, it softens the effect of this pronouncement: Jesus and the disciples have not withdrawn from the crowd; what is given to the disciples is not the mystery of the kingdom but knowledge of its mysteries; the disciples' counterparts are not "outsiders" but merely the "others"; and the refusal of forgiveness is omitted from the quotation from Isaiah.

The allusion to "mysteries" may have been understood variously by different readers. In the Greco-Roman world, mystery cults drew followers with their assurances of eternal life for those who were initiated into mystery. Such initiation ceremonies seem to have consisted of being shown

95. Joachim Jeremias, *The Parables of Jesus*, rev. ed., trans. S. H. Hooke (New York: Charles Scribner's Sons, 1963) 11-12, esp. n. 3. The following rabbinic references support Jeremias's interpretation: *b. Sabb.* 73b: "In Palestine ploughing comes after sowing"; *Tosefta Berakoth* 7.2: "He sows, ploughs, reaps, binds the sheaves, threshes. . . ."; *m. Sabb.* 7.2: "Sowing, ploughing."

96. K. D. White, "The Parable of the Sower," *JTS* 15 (1964) 300-307.

97. P. B. Payne, "The Order of Sowing and Ploughing in the Parable of the Sower," *NTS* 25 (1978–79) 123-29.

98. Genesis 26:12 and Varro *On Agriculture* 1.193 are sometimes cited to the contrary.

99. See 2 Bar 29:5-8.

100. See further Robert K. McIver, "One Hundred-Fold Yield—Miraculous or Mundane? Matthew 13.8, 23; Mark 4.8, 20; Luke 8.8," *NTS* 40 (1994) 606-8; and for a different view Bernard Brandon Scott, *Hear Then the Parable: A Commentary on the Parables of Jesus* (Minneapolis: Fortress, 1989) 356-58.

101. Peter Rhea Jones, *The Teaching of the Parables* (Nashville: Broadman, 1982) 70.

sacred objects and given secret knowledge. In Jewish tradition, the prophets had been given the mystery of God's redemptive work (Dan 2:28; Amos 3:7). Later, the Essenes at Qumran claimed that the prophets were given only the mysteries, which they did not understand, and that the interpretation of those mysteries was given to the Teacher of Righteousness.[102] With these references may be compared Eph 3:3-6 and 1 Pet 1:10-12.

By characterizing rejection of the Word and ignorance of the mysteries of the kingdom as blindness and deafness, v. 10 connects the parables with the healings of the blind and the deaf, which are demonstrations of Jesus' power to bring not only physical but also metaphorical sight and hearing (see 4:18; 6:39-42; 7:21-22; 18:35-43). Hence, it is all the more significant that the final part of Isa 6:10, with its denial of forgiveness, has been omitted from Luke.

8:11-15. Luke also smoothes the transition from the pronouncement of judgment to the interpretation of the parable, so that the interpretation can be read as part of Jesus' response to the disciples' question. The allegorizing interpretation, which probably originated in the context of the church's preaching of the gospel, explains that the varied responses of acceptance and rejection depend on the soil. The seed is identified as the Word of God, the places where the seed is sown are the different types of hearers, the "birds of the air" (see 9:58; 13:19)

102. 1QpHab 7.4-5, 8.

are the devil, and the thorns are "the cares, and riches and pleasures of life."

Luke has evidently drawn the interpretation from Mark 4:13-20. Careful comparison of the accounts reveals that Luke has removed the obtuseness of the disciples (as he will do elsewhere); inserted an explanation of the devil's effort to prevent hearers from believing and being saved; abridged Mark's emphasis on persecution (Mark 4:17); and added references to the dangers of the "pleasures of life," failure to bear fruit to maturity, and the importance of endurance. The characterization of the devil's purpose as "so that they may not believe and be saved" (8:12), when coupled with the omission of the pronouncement of judgment from v. 10—"so that they may not turn again and be forgiven" (Mark 4:12)—makes it appear that Luke has added the one and omitted the other in order to relieve any implication that Jesus' purpose was to prevent those who heard the parables from believing.

There are various reasons why some do not believe. The seed that falls on the path never has a chance because it is trampled underfoot, and the birds take it away. The seed that falls on the rocky soil germinates but withers from lack of moisture, while the seed that falls among the thorns grows but does not produce fruit. The fruitful ground, in contrast, is distinguished by two qualities: It holds fast to the seed "in an honest and good heart" and bears fruit "with patient endurance."

REFLECTIONS

The parable of the sower (or perhaps better the parable of the seed and the soils) and its interpretation, which already moves in the direction of allegory, serves as a spectrum that separates and tints the responses of various characters in the Gospel with hues that make them recognizable to the reader.

1. The reference to the seed along the path being trodden underfoot is peculiar to Luke, as are the later echoes of the role of the "birds of the air," which suggests that we are justified in reading the parable and its interpretation in its larger narrative context. Who is Luke talking about? On one occasion the crowd that gathered to hear Jesus was large and became unruly, like some persons at contemporary rock concerts and soccer games. The people began to trample one another (12:1). The seed was being trodden underfoot.

The elder brother charged that the father's younger son had devoured their father's living with harlots (15:30), and Jesus warned his disciples about the scribes who devoured widows' houses (20:47). The Word of God apparently can be devoured in many ways. What we do to each other can determine whether we are able to hear God's Word. Our actions can also deprive others of the opportunity to hear.

Although the birds of the air devoured the seed (8:5), they had nests (9:58) and could find shelter in the branches of the mustard tree (13:19). God feeds them. Are we not of more value than they (12:24)?

2. Clear examples of rocky-soil hearers are more difficult to find in Luke. Certainly, Judas Iscariot qualifies as one who hears God's Word, follows for a while, but in crisis betrays Jesus (22:3). The other disciples were also in danger of falling away, but Jesus said to them, "You are those who have stood by me in my trials" (22:28). Growing in discipleship requires that we put down roots that will hold us firm in time of trial or temptation.

3. The third category is characterized by the seed that fell among the thorns. The interpretation of the parable lists three specific thorns that may choke the hearer's life: cares, riches, and the pleasures of life. The cares of life include anxiety and worry. These are experiences common to all of us, but if we allow ourselves to give in to them they consume our lives. While Mary chose to listen to Jesus' teachings, Martha was anxious and troubled about many things (10:41). In other sayings, Jesus charged his followers not to be anxious about what they would say when brought to trial on account of their faith (12:11). He also charged them not to be anxious about what they would eat or wear (12:22). After all, we cannot add an inch to our stature or an hour to the span of our lives by worrying (12:25).

The dangers of wealth is a theme to which Luke returns more than any other Gospel writer. Jesus lamented the plight of the rich; they had received their consolation (6:24). Repeatedly the rich person is a negative example in Jesus' parables (12:16; 14:12; 16:1, 19; 21:1). The rich young ruler is the prime example of one whose wealth crowded the Word from his life (18:23). Again, Jesus lamented: "How hard it is for those who have wealth to enter the kingdom of God!" (18:24).

The pursuit of pleasure can also take a destructive turn. Jesus' teachings associate the cares of life with foolish living and drunkenness. These can weigh down the heart and prove to be a detriment to prayer (21:34; see also 17:27).

4. With a minimum of words, the parable describes what it means to be the good soil. The good soil represents those who (1) hear the word, (2) hold it fast (3) in a good heart, and (4) bring forth fruit (5) with patient endurance. Hearing involves listening, but it also means understanding and being willing to obey. Impressed on the memory of every devout Jew were the words "Hear, O Israel: The LORD is our God, the LORD alone. You shall love the LORD your God with all your heart, and with all your soul, and with all your might" (Deut 6:4-5; Luke 10:27). Hearing the Word of God and responding in obedience were the foundation of Israel's covenant with God. Those who are the good soil also hold fast the Word they have heard. One of the neglected beatitudes says, "Blessed . . . are those who hear the word of God and obey it" (11:28). The temptation to let go of that Word, to accept some other word as the truth by which to live, constantly presses upon those who live in a secular, wealth-oriented, pleasure-seeking society.

Bearing fruit and enduring are the marks of a mature disciple. Again, parallel passages elsewhere in Luke illuminate this verse. Jesus said, "The good person out of the good treasure of the heart produces good" (6:45). Moreover, "By your endurance you will gain your souls" (21:19). Growth is not automatic, bearing fruit may not come easily, and spiritual maturity may require patience. But the harvest can be so magnificent!

In Luke's hands the parable of the seed and the soils has become a call to hold fast and endure. The theological vocabulary of the interpretation reflects the church's situation (the Word of God, the devil, their hearts, believe and be saved, fall away, hold fast, endure). In this context, Luke recognizes that many will reject the Word of God. Hearing requires a strong resolve. Like the fast-germinating seed on the rocky ground and among the thorns, it is easy to make a good beginning, but reaching maturity and bearing fruit require faithfulness and dogged endurance.

Luke 8:16-18, What Is Hidden and What Is Revealed

NIV

16"No one lights a lamp and hides it in a jar or puts it under a bed. Instead, he puts it on a stand, so that those who come in can see the light. 17For there is nothing hidden that will not be disclosed, and nothing concealed that will not be known or brought out into the open. 18Therefore consider carefully how you listen. Whoever has will be given more; whoever does not have, even what he thinks he has will be taken from him."

NRSV

16"No one after lighting a lamp hides it under a jar, or puts it under a bed, but puts it on a lampstand, so that those who enter may see the light. 17For nothing is hidden that will not be disclosed, nor is anything secret that will not become known and come to light. 18Then pay attention to how you listen; for to those who have, more will be given; and from those who do not have, even what they seem to have will be taken away."

COMMENTARY

Luke refashions Mark's handling of the sayings following the interpretation of the parable so that they become a further commentary on the parable of the seeds and the soils. Luke preserves the Markan setting and sequence of these sayings, but omits the transitional formulas ("And he said to them") in Mark 4:21 and 24 so that the sayings flow without any transitional break following the preceding verses. In this way, Luke signals that the sayings—which otherwise might be applied to Jesus' reluctance to take a high profile, or to the warning that all sins will be exposed in the last judgment—should be interpreted in relation to the theme of hearing and doing God's Word.

Luke 8:16-18 consists of three sayings that probably circulated independently but are gathered in this sequence in Mark 4:21-25. Luke omits the parable of the seed growing secretly and Mark's comment on Jesus' use of the parables, but he retains these sayings to underscore the importance of attention to how one hears. The three sayings also appear scattered in other contexts in Luke, suggesting that they also appeared in Q. Luke 8:16, which is most like a parable, also appears in 11:33 (Matt 5:15); v. 17, a proverbial saying that serves as a comment on v. 16, appears in 12:2 (Matt 10:26); and v. 18, which

provides a warning and summary of the foregoing, appears in 19:26 (Matt 25:29).

8:16. Here we have the unusual use of a parable as a commentary on another parable. The parable of the lamp consists of two parts, negative and positive, each of which also has two parts. The observation is drawn from everyday life. When one lights a lamp, one does not cover it with a vessel or put it under a bed. Instead, one puts it on a lampstand so that it may give light. Given Luke's editorial handling of the context, the challenge to the interpreter is to discover how association with the parable of the seeds and the soils controls the meaning of this parable, and then what this parable says about the meaning of the former. The connection would hardly be evident apart from the second and third sayings. Structural parallels may be suggested, however. Just as one sows in order to reap a harvest, so also one lights a lamp in order that it may give light. One does not sow so that the birds may feed on the seed or so that it may be choked by the thorns. Similarly, one does not light a lamp in order to extinguish it under a jar (where the air would be cut off and the smoke would be trapped) or to hide it, ludicrously, under a bed. The purpose for the sowing—God's purpose for the Word—is that it effect change.

8:17. This may well have been a common proverb in a Galilean village: Nothing can be kept secret for very long. Sooner or later, it will get out. Or as one wag put it, a secret is something you tell one person at a time. If related to the theme of God's Word, however, this saying picks up another aspect of the parable. Although the seed sown in the first three locations was fruitless, ultimately the sower reaped a bountiful harvest.

8:18. This verse issues a warning, which is followed by another proverbial saying. Luke omits the saying in Mark 4:24 about receiving the measure you measure out, since this saying was used in Luke 6:38. "Pay attention to how you listen"—this exhortation reminds us that we are not soil; we are persons. We can choose and control how we will respond to God's Word. The hearer has a responsibility for understanding, openness, and making a decisive response. Be careful how you listen.

The last saying in this cluster extends a further warning. The grim patterns of prosperity and poverty dictate in common experience that those who have get more, while those who don't lose even what little they have. If you receive God's Word like the good soil receives the seed, then you gain even greater insight, maturity, and knowledge of God. On the other hand, if you are like the unfruitful soils and God's Word remains barren in your hearing, you will be even worse off than before. The proclamation of the Word, therefore, is a dynamic act that effects change for good or for ill in the hearer—so be careful how you hear it.

REFLECTIONS

Like the interpretation of the parable, the sayings that follow it contain references that in their present context imply a church setting and theological meanings. The one who hears God's Word is likened to a lamp. "Those who come in" (v. 16) may be those who come to the church to hear the gospel. "Those who have" are persons who have already received God's Word, and "those who have not" are outside and choose to remain outside by rejecting God's Word. If that is their response, they are even further from God than they were before. It is not just that the soil affects the seed; in this allegorical interpretation, the seed changes the soil.

The seed is the Word of God (v. 11). Be careful, therefore, how you hear it (v. 18). This interpretation arises from the life of the church. There are always consequences to what we do, especially our responses to God's call to us. Hearing is an active process. God's Word calls for a commitment of life. Those who actually hear God's Word, therefore, burn like a candle. They give light for others, they produce a bountiful harvest, and they will receive an even greater reward. Because the Word is powerful, be careful how you hear it. The very hearing of God's Word can transform us. Moreover, God's Word can have such far-reaching consequences, for blessing or for judgment, that we must always be careful not to consider it casually or hear it only superficially. God's Word demands a radical openness on our part, our most serious and thoughtful consideration, and our most trusting response.

Luke 8:19-21, Jesus' Followers: His Mother and Brothers

NIV	NRSV
[19]Now Jesus' mother and brothers came to see him, but they were not able to get near him because of the crowd. [20]Someone told him, "Your mother and brothers are standing outside, wanting to see you." [21]He replied, "My mother and brothers are those who hear God's word and put it into practice."	19Then his mother and his brothers came to him, but they could not reach him because of the crowd. [20]And he was told, "Your mother and your brothers are standing outside, wanting to see you." [21]But he said to them, "My mother and my brothers are those who hear the word of God and do it."

COMMENTARY

The interpretation of this scene, in which Jesus' mother and his brothers come to him and Jesus responds with a pronouncement regarding the family status of those who hear and do God's Word, is guided by three factors: (1) the context of this scene at the conclusion of Luke 8:1-21; (2) Luke's editing of the Markan form of this scene; and (3) the translation of Jesus' pronouncement in v. 21.

In Mark, the scene occurs earlier, prior to the parable of the sower and its interpretation. There, it contributes to the rising opposition against Jesus. Scribes come down from Jerusalem and declare that Jesus is controlled by Beelzebul. His family comes to him "to restrain him" (Mark 3:31; cf. 3:21), and while the crowd is around Jesus, his family is outside. Jesus responds, first asking who his mother and brothers are, and then announcing the formation of a new family: "Whoever does the will of God is my brother and sister and mother" (Mark 3:35).

By placing Jesus' pronouncement immediately after the interpretation of the parable of the seeds and the soils and the appended sayings, and by altering Jesus' pronouncement so that it echoes "the word of God" from v. 11 and "these are the ones who hear" from v. 15, Luke places the scene in a positive context. It balances the reference to the women who followed Jesus at the beginning of the chapter and the references to the Twelve in v. 1 and his disciples in v. 9. Taken together, these references form a complete set of examples of those who hear the Word of God and do it: the Twelve, the group of women who followed him, the disciples, and finally the family of Jesus.

Luke omits the reference to Jesus' family and their effort to restrain him (Mark 3:20-21). Luke also compresses the scene, omitting any reference to Jesus' sisters, the contrast between the family outside and the crowd seated around Jesus, Jesus' question about who his mother and brothers and

sisters are, and his pronouncement in Mark 3:34 that those seated around him were now his family. The result is that Jesus' rejection of his physical family has been excised from the Gospel story, while leaving his pronouncement in place, granting those who hear and do the Word of God status equal to his family. This positive portrayal of Jesus' family accords well with the role of Mary in the infancy narrative, Luke 11:27-28, and Acts 1:14. Luke says nothing about the family's motive in coming to Jesus and explains their position outside (a note held over from Mark) as being due to the crowd around Jesus.

Jesus' response, which in Mark consists of a question and two statements, is reduced to one statement. Both the question and the first statement, which Luke omits, distance Jesus from his family. The remaining statement, however, is open to various interpretations and translations that range from affirmation of Jesus' family to affirmation of those who hear and do the Word of God, as illustrated by the translations offered in two leading commentaries on Luke:

> "My mother and my brothers, they are the ones who listen to the word of God and act on it."[103]

> "These who hear and do the word of God are a mother and brothers to me."[104]

Although the nouns "mother" (μήτηρ *mētēr*) and "brothers" (ἀδελφοί *adelphoi*) do not have the article, the word order and use of the demonstrative article favor treating "my mother and my brothers" as the subject rather than the predicate. The ambiguity of the saying might be preserved, however, by substituting "these" for "they" in Fitzmyer's translation: "My mother and my brothers, these are the ones who listen to the word of God and act on it."

103. Joseph A. Fitzmyer, *The Gospel According to Luke (I–IX)*, AB 28 (Garden City, N.Y.: Doubleday, 1981) 736.
104. John Nolland, *Luke*, 3 vols., WBC 35A-C (Dallas: Word, 1989–93).

REFLECTIONS

Not to be missed in the debate over the nuance of Jesus' saying and the position of his physical family in Luke and Acts is the function of this scene at the conclusion of Luke 8:1-21. This section develops the theme of hearing and doing God's Word. Various groups have been listed (the women, the crowd, and the disciples), a parable of the seed and its reception by various soils has been told and interpreted, and a series of sayings has warned readers to be careful how they hear God's Word. In the context of this foregoing material, Jesus' pronouncement in v. 21 opens the way for all who hear and act on God's Word to be included in Jesus' family. More important even than familial bonds is the urgency of being receptive and obedient to God's Word. Obedience to that Word also opens the way for a new relationship to the Lord, a kind of spiritual kinship. As Hosea said, we who are no people, by receiving God's Word may become God's people (Hos 2:23; 1 Pet 2:10). No wonder it is urgent to take care how you hear that word.

LUKE 8:22-56, THE POWER OF GOD AT WORK IN JESUS

OVERVIEW

The next section is composed of three stories that demonstrate Jesus' power over nature, demons, illness, and death. The one who brought the Word of God also exercised the power of God (cf. 4:14). The term translated "master" (ἐπιστάτα *epistata*), which occurs in two of the stories (8:24, 45), serves as the recurring element in the titles chosen for the three stories. By so dramatically emphasizing Jesus' power, Luke raises once again the question of Jesus' identity, which binds together 7–9:50—"Who then is this?" (8:25).

Luke 8:22-25, Master over Storms

NIV	NRSV
22One day Jesus said to his disciples, "Let's go over to the other side of the lake." So they got into a boat and set out. 23As they sailed, he fell asleep. A squall came down on the lake, so that the boat was being swamped, and they were in great danger.	22One day he got into a boat with his disciples, and he said to them, "Let us go across to the other side of the lake." So they put out, 23and while they were sailing he fell asleep. A windstorm swept down on the lake, and the boat was filling with water, and they were in danger.
24The disciples went and woke him, saying, "Master, Master, we're going to drown!"	24They went to him and woke him up, shouting, "Master, Master, we are perishing!" And he woke up and rebuked the wind and the raging waves;
He got up and rebuked the wind and the raging waters; the storm subsided, and all was calm. 25"Where is your faith?" he asked his disciples.	they ceased, and there was a calm. 25He said to them, "Where is your faith?" They were afraid and amazed, and said to one another, "Who then
In fear and amazement they asked one another, "Who is this? He commands even the winds and the water, and they obey him."	is this, that he commands even the winds and the water, and they obey him?"

COMMENTARY

The introductory phrase signals a change of setting and the introduction of a new series of related scenes. Luke continues to follow the sequence of the Gospel of Mark (4:35–5:43) and here abridges Mark's account of the stilling of the storm (Mark 4:35-41), omitting the reference to its being late, leaving the crowd, the other boats, the waves hitting the boat, the cushion, the stern, Jesus' words of rebuke, and the disciples' fear. In Luke's hands, the story moves directly through the description of danger, the request for deliverance, and Jesus' command to the winds and the sea to the two questions at its conclusion: Jesus' question, "Where is your faith?" and the disciples' question, "Who then is this . . . ?" The disciples' question about Jesus' identity continues the refrain that began with the scribes (5:21), the disciples of John the Baptist (7:20), and those at the table with him (7:49); it will culminate with Herod's question (9:9).

This is the only sea miracle in Luke, in contrast to Mark and Matthew, which also report Jesus' walking on the water (Matt 14:22-33; Mark 6:45-52; cf. John 6:16-21). It is set at the point of Jesus' crossing to the other side of the Sea of Galilee, where he will encounter Gentiles and exorcise the demons from the Gerasene demoniac. Unlike Mark, however, the symbolism of crisis in moving from Jewish to Gentile regions is not developed in Luke. On the other hand, Paul's command of the storm at sea (Acts 27:9-44) echoes the present account. In the OT the sea is a place of danger; the Hebrews were desert people, not seafarers. Thus declarations of God's power over the sea, which often recalled the exodus, were acclamations of God's power to preserve and protect (e.g., Ps 107:23-25, 28-29; see also Job 9:8; Ps 77:16, 19; Isa 43:2). By stilling the wind and the waves by his word of command, therefore, Jesus does what in the OT God alone could do. The story is an epiphany, a manifestation of Jesus' divine power and identity.

Characteristically, Luke portrays the disciples in a better light than Mark does. Luke does not develop the theme of the disciples' lack of understanding or their hardness of heart, but it is clear that at this point they still do not understand who Jesus is. Luke omits the disciples' sharp question, "Teacher, do you not care that we are perishing?" (Mark 4:38) and Jesus' rebuke to the disciples, "Why are you afraid?" Luke also changes the disciples' address to Jesus from "Teacher" to "Master," a title that Luke uses of Jesus in other miracle stories (5:5; 8:45; 9:33, 49; 17:13).

Although this miracle story is directly related to the stories that will follow it, one should not miss the fact that Jesus' word effects the miracle. The disciples marvel that even the wind and the sea obey him. The effect, therefore, is to underscore once again the theme of the preceding section: hearing and doing God's Word.

REFLECTIONS

Miracle stories offer special challenges for the interpreter. Many believers, for example, will find it difficult to personify winds and waves so that they could be subject to the command of a superior authority. On the other hand, to claim that there was no miracle, only a coincidence of timing and that the wind and the waves subsided when Jesus commanded the storm to cease, does violence to the story and strips it of its wonder and power.

Interpreting the story of Jesus stilling the storm, therefore, calls for the interpreter to use the tools of a poet: imagery, imagination, and subtlety. The story is evocative because it paints a picture of primal power: human beings caught in the grip of the forces of nature. The storm indicates that the sea, a place of danger and chaos, had turned violent. The disciples were being victimized by a force they could not control, and the conditioning of generations of desert-dwelling ancestors would make any Jewish audience recoil at the thought of being caught in a storm at sea.

The sea was a challenge to God's sovereignty. It evoked images of the primordial chaos. God's mighty act of deliverance had led the Israelites through the sea at the exodus, so by telling how Jesus had calmed the sea, early Christians were confessing that Jesus exercised the power of the Lord, which had delivered the Israelites so long ago. What God had done through Moses at the exodus, God was continuing to do through Jesus.

The story leads the reader to two questions, one that probes the nature of the reader's faith and one that leads the reader to consider again the identity of Jesus. The real question is not whether Jesus stilled a storm on the Sea of Galilee but whether the God who delivers people from bondage and from forces beyond their control still acts to deliver those who call on the Lord in desperate circumstances today.

Luke 8:26-39, Master over Demons

NIV	NRSV

NIV

26They sailed to the region of the Gerasenes,*a* which is across the lake from Galilee. 27When Jesus stepped ashore, he was met by a demon-possessed man from the town. For a long time this man had not worn clothes or lived in a house, but had lived in the tombs. 28When he saw Jesus, he cried out and fell at his feet, shouting at the top of his voice, "What do you want with me, Jesus, Son of the Most High God? I beg you, don't torture me!" 29For Jesus had commanded the evil*b* spirit to come out of the man. Many times it had seized him, and though he was chained hand and foot and kept under guard, he had broken his chains and had been driven by the demon into solitary places.

30Jesus asked him, "What is your name?"

"Legion," he replied, because many demons had gone into him. 31And they begged him repeatedly not to order them to go into the Abyss.

32A large herd of pigs was feeding there on the hillside. The demons begged Jesus to let them go into them, and he gave them permission. 33When the demons came out of the man, they went into the pigs, and the herd rushed down the steep bank into the lake and was drowned.

34When those tending the pigs saw what had happened, they ran off and reported this in the town and countryside, 35and the people went out to see what had happened. When they came to Jesus, they found the man from whom the demons had gone out, sitting at Jesus' feet, dressed and in his right mind; and they were afraid. 36Those who had seen it told the people how the demon-possessed man had been cured. 37Then all the people of the region of the Gerasenes asked Jesus to leave them, because they were overcome with fear. So he got into the boat and left.

38The man from whom the demons had gone out begged to go with him, but Jesus sent him away, saying, 39"Return home and tell how much

a26 Some manuscripts Gadarenes; other manuscripts Gergesenes; also in verse 37   b29 Greek unclean

NRSV

26Then they arrived at the country of the Gerasenes,*a* which is opposite Galilee. 27As he stepped out on land, a man of the city who had demons met him. For a long time he had worn*b* no clothes, and he did not live in a house but in the tombs. 28When he saw Jesus, he fell down before him and shouted at the top of his voice, "What have you to do with me, Jesus, Son of the Most High God? I beg you, do not torment me"— 29for Jesus*c* had commanded the unclean spirit to come out of the man. (For many times it had seized him; he was kept under guard and bound with chains and shackles, but he would break the bonds and be driven by the demon into the wilds.) 30Jesus then asked him, "What is your name?" He said, "Legion"; for many demons had entered him. 31They begged him not to order them to go back into the abyss.

32Now there on the hillside a large herd of swine was feeding; and the demons*d* begged Jesus*e* to let them enter these. So he gave them permission. 33Then the demons came out of the man and entered the swine, and the herd rushed down the steep bank into the lake and was drowned.

34When the swineherds saw what had happened, they ran off and told it in the city and in the country. 35Then people came out to see what had happened, and when they came to Jesus, they found the man from whom the demons had gone sitting at the feet of Jesus, clothed and in his right mind. And they were afraid. 36Those who had seen it told them how the one who had been possessed by demons had been healed. 37Then all the people of the surrounding country of the Gerasenes*a* asked Jesus*e* to leave them; for they were seized with great fear. So he got into the boat and returned. 38The man from whom the demons had gone begged that he might be with him; but Jesus*c* sent him away, saying, 39"Return

*aOther ancient authorities read Gadarenes; others, Gergesenes
bOther ancient authorities read a man of the city who had had demons for a long time met him. He wore   cGk he   dGk they
eGk him*

NIV	NRSV
God has done for you." So the man went away and told all over town how much Jesus had done for him.	to your home, and declare how much God has done for you." So he went away, proclaiming throughout the city how much Jesus had done for him.

COMMENTARY

Master over the forces of nature, Jesus now demonstrates that he is also master over demonic spirits. This lengthy and complicated account moves at several levels. It not only demonstrates again the power of Jesus' word but also foreshadows the mission to the Gentile world and describes Jesus' restoration of a deranged person to health and wholeness. In the process, the destructive power of evil is unmasked, and Jesus rises as victor over the devil's deceptions.

The story assumes the sensitivities of Jewish piety. Pigs were unclean and abhorrent (Lev 11:7; Deut 14:8). They were easily associated with Gentile uncleanness. Tombs were also a source of uncleanness, and in Jewish areas they were whitewashed so that one might not come in contact with a tomb accidentally. Demons roamed desolate places seeking refuge, but knowing the name of the demons gave the exorcist control over them. One can imagine the delight with which this story was told in a Jewish-Christian context.

Luke does not say whether the purpose of the sea crossing was to minister to this demoniac, but it is the only incident reported in that area. The location is uncertain and has been debated from an early time, as the manuscript tradition makes clear. Gerasa (Jerash), located thirty miles south of the Sea of Galilee in the Transjordan, was a leading city of the Decapolis. "The country of the Gerasenes" is the reading best supported by the manuscript tradition for Luke, but as Fitzmyer wryly commented, the distance is such that "the stampede of the pigs from Gerasa to the Lake would have made them the most energetic herd in history!"[105] Gadara, lesser known but only six miles from the lake, is named in other manuscripts, and at least since the time of Origen Gergesa, on the shore near Tiberias, has been

proposed. Luke, who draws the story from Mark 5:1-20, adds the clause "which is opposite Galilee," indicating that Jesus and the disciples have crossed to the east side of the lake.

For clarity, the story may be divided into its constituent parts: (1) Jesus' arrival (v. 26); (2) Jesus' encounter with the demoniac and a description of the demoniac's background (vv. 27-31); (3) the destruction of the demons and the swine (vv. 32-33); (4) confirmation of the exorcism by three groups: the swineherds, the people, and "all the people of the surrounding country" (vv. 34-37); and (5) the demoniac's second request and the departure of both Jesus and the demoniac (vv. 38-39). Jesus' command for the demon to come out of the man and the subsequent description of the man's history are both reported after the fact. The latter part of v. 29 is therefore put in parentheses in the NRSV. By means of this device, Luke takes the reader directly to the dramatic moment of the demoniac's initial response to Jesus, even though the later report (v. 29a) stands in some tension with v. 28a.

8:27-31. Luke reduces Mark's initial description of the man's condition and defers further details until v. 29, so the severity of his condition is not underscored until after the initial exchange between Jesus and the demoniac. All we are told at this point is that the man had demons (plural, foreshadowing the name "Legion"), that he wore no clothes (setting up the contrast with v. 35), and that he lived among the tombs rather than in a house.

When he sees Jesus, the demoniac does not "bow down before him" as in Mark 5:6, but falls at Jesus' feet, shouting. His initial question conveys that there can be no accommodation between Jesus and the powers of evil. As a demon with access to the spirit world, the unclean spirit knows Jesus' identity, while ironically the disciples have just been asking, "Who then is this?" Perhaps in an effort to deprive Jesus of his power

---

105. Joseph A. Fitzmyer, *The Gospel According to Luke (I–IX)*, AB 28 (Garden City, N.Y.: Doubleday, 1981) 736.

by revealing his identity, the demon calls out, "Jesus, Son of the Most High God" (v. 28). But rather than abjuring Jesus "by God" (Mark 7), in Luke the spirit begs Jesus not to torment it.

Only now are we told that Jesus had commanded the spirit to come out of the man. Jesus' command is also interpreted as an act of compassion for the man because of all that he had suffered under the power of the demon. Simultaneously, the strength of this demon is dramatized. No one had been able to subdue him before. He even broke chains and shackles.

Jesus first demonstrates his power over the demon by requiring it to divulge its name. "Legion" is a number rather than a name, or at least a name that conveys the number and power of the demons that possessed the man. A Roman legion was composed of five or six thousand men.

Whereas Mark reports that the demons urged Jesus not to send them "out of the country" (Mark 5:10), Luke sets up the action to come by reporting that they pleaded that Jesus not send them "into the abyss" (v. 31). In the thought world of the NT, the abyss was the place where disobedient spirits were imprisoned (Jude 6; 2 Pet 2:4; Rev 9:1-2, 11; 20:1-3).

8:32-33. Now, the herd of swine is introduced. Luke's account is less explicit about the demons' request to enter the swine, but nevertheless it is clear that the demons negotiate their fate and that Jesus allows them to enter the swine. Luke also omits Mark's report that there were two thousand pigs in the herd. The drowning of the swine adds a suggestive twist to the story. No Jewish Christian would have raised questions about the ethics of Jesus' allowing the destruction of the livelihood of the Gentile swineherds. Instead, the fate of the pigs would show that justice had prevailed all around: The man had been delivered from the demons' torment, the unclean herd had been destroyed, the demons had gotten what they wanted, and in the end they had been destroyed along with the pigs. Jesus has outwitted the devil. The demons that wanted most to avoid being sent into the abyss have been drowned in the lake. When it gets its way, evil is always destructive and ultimately self-destructive.

8:34-37. The exorcism is confirmed by witnesses who see the man restored to peace and normalcy. Three groups are mentioned in succes-

sion: the swineherds, the people who came out to see, and finally "all the people of the surrounding country" (v. 37). Three descriptors confirm the exorcism. The man (Luke does not call him a demoniac) was clothed (cf. v. 27), sane, and at the feet of Jesus. As one at the feet of Jesus, the man who had been possessed ranks with the woman who anointed Jesus' feet (7:38), Jairus (8:41), Mary (10:39), and the grateful leper (17:16). The fear of the onlookers acknowledges the numinous power that had worked in their midst. As in other references, Luke reports a universal response: from "all the people" (v. 37). They recognize the mystery and the power of what has taken place, but they cannot make a place for it or accommodate their lives to it. Their response, therefore, is to ask Jesus to leave.

8:38-39. When Jesus got into the boat, the man who had been possessed by the demons asked that he might "be with him" (v. 38). Being "with him" is a phrase Luke has used of Jesus' disciples (8:1; cf. 8:51). This is the man's second request. His first was voiced in protest: "What have you to do with me?" (v. 28). Jesus had delivered him from his torment, and now he wants to "have to do" with Jesus. But Jesus, who has been calling disciples, sends this man to his home—which was in the Decapolis. Thus the beginning of the mission to the Gentiles in Luke and Acts can be traced not just to the work of the apostles but to Jesus' charge to the Gerasene demoniac as well. Mark underscores this commission by reporting that the man began "to preach in the Decapolis" and "all were amazed." Luke, who usually favors such universal responses, omits the final phrase because he wants the story to end with a different emphasis. In place of Mark's description of the Gentiles' response, Luke has a subtle repetition that once again conveys an answer to the disciples' question, "Who then is this that the wind and waves and now the demons obey him?" (see 8:25). Luke, who writes "an orderly narrative" (1:1-4), reports that Jesus instructed the Gerasene demoniac to "relate" or "narrate" "how much God has done for you," and he went proclaiming "how much Jesus had done for him" (v. 39). The story begins and ends, therefore, with confessions whose force may be lost on the characters in the story but is clear to the reader: the confession of the demons, "Jesus,

Son of the Most High God," and the veiled affirmation of the narrator's parallel phrases in which "Jesus" stands in place of "God."

The story of the Gerasene demoniac, therefore,

serves both the theme of the power of Jesus' word in Luke 8 and the larger theme of the disclosure of the identity of Jesus.

REFLECTIONS

In the first century, this story probably had its greatest impact in affirming Jesus' power over demonic spirits, his compassion for a man of the Decapolis, and its foreshadowing of the apostles' victories over the demons and pagan magic (see Acts 8:9-24; 13:6-12; 16:16-18; 19:11-20). In the understanding of many, the world was populated by demons, spirits, nymphs, centaurs, and angels, who controlled natural processes and often took possession of persons or controlled their fate. The demons could enter a person through the ears, nose, or mouth. Amulets, magic, sacrifices, and rituals were needed if one were to have any hope of appeasing or escaping these spiritual powers. Stories of Jesus' power to exorcise demons demonstrated his power and elicited faith.

In our day, we have become far more accustomed to attributing calamities and disorders to the forces of nature or to internal mental or emotional problems. The remedy is not exorcism but counseling or medication. The story of the Gerasene demoniac should now be interpreted so that it speaks a word of assurance and hope to those for whom every day is a battle with depression, fear, anxiety, or compulsive behavior. They will understand what would lead a person to say that his name is "mob" (λεγιών *legiōn*; GNB). With such a response, the man had acknowledged that he no longer had any individual identity. He had lost his name. He had lost his individuality. All that was left was a boiling struggle of conflicting forces. It was as though a Roman legion was at war within him.

How many families are at their wits' end because no one has been able to help them cure or care for a mentally ill loved one? We no longer use chains and shackles but straitjackets, padded cells, injections, tranquilizers, and electric shocks. But still some mentally ill persons are driven "into the wilds" (v. 29). This gospel story affirms that the compassion of Jesus led him to cross a sea to reach such a person and that the power of Jesus' word vanquished the greatest imaginable assembly of demonic powers from this person and restored him to wholeness.

For many whose depression, grief, and fears are not so severe, the story also speaks a word of assurance. Part of the remedy, however, may lie in the commission Jesus gave this man: Tell others "how much God has done for you."

Luke 8:40-56, Master over Sickness and Death

NIV

40Now when Jesus returned, a crowd welcomed him, for they were all expecting him. 41Then a man named Jairus, a ruler of the synagogue, came and fell at Jesus' feet, pleading with him to come to his house 42because his only daughter, a girl of about twelve, was dying.

As Jesus was on his way, the crowds almost crushed him. 43And a woman was there who had been subject to bleeding for twelve years,[a] but no

a43 Many manuscripts *years, and she had spent all she had on doctors*

NRSV

40Now when Jesus returned, the crowd welcomed him, for they were all waiting for him. 41Just then there came a man named Jairus, a leader of the synagogue. He fell at Jesus' feet and begged him to come to his house, 42for he had an only daughter, about twelve years old, who was dying.

As he went, the crowds pressed in on him. 43Now there was a woman who had been suffering from hemorrhages for twelve years; and

NIV

one could heal her. ⁴⁴She came up behind him and touched the edge of his cloak, and immediately her bleeding stopped.

⁴⁵"Who touched me?" Jesus asked.

When they all denied it, Peter said, "Master, the people are crowding and pressing against you."

⁴⁶But Jesus said, "Someone touched me; I know that power has gone out from me."

⁴⁷Then the woman, seeing that she could not go unnoticed, came trembling and fell at his feet. In the presence of all the people, she told why she had touched him and how she had been instantly healed. ⁴⁸Then he said to her, "Daughter, your faith has healed you. Go in peace."

⁴⁹While Jesus was still speaking, someone came from the house of Jairus, the synagogue ruler. "Your daughter is dead," he said. "Don't bother the teacher any more."

⁵⁰Hearing this, Jesus said to Jairus, "Don't be afraid; just believe, and she will be healed."

⁵¹When he arrived at the house of Jairus, he did not let anyone go in with him except Peter, John and James, and the child's father and mother. ⁵²Meanwhile, all the people were wailing and mourning for her. "Stop wailing," Jesus said. "She is not dead but asleep."

⁵³They laughed at him, knowing that she was dead. ⁵⁴But he took her by the hand and said, "My child, get up!" ⁵⁵Her spirit returned, and at once she stood up. Then Jesus told them to give her something to eat. ⁵⁶Her parents were astonished, but he ordered them not to tell anyone what had happened.

NRSV

though she had spent all she had on physicians,ᵃ no one could cure her. ⁴⁴She came up behind him and touched the fringe of his clothes, and immediately her hemorrhage stopped. ⁴⁵Then Jesus asked, "Who touched me?" When all denied it, Peterᵇ said, "Master, the crowds surround you and press in on you." ⁴⁶But Jesus said, "Someone touched me; for I noticed that power had gone out from me." ⁴⁷When the woman saw that she could not remain hidden, she came trembling; and falling down before him, she declared in the presence of all the people why she had touched him, and how she had been immediately healed. ⁴⁸He said to her, "Daughter, your faith has made you well; go in peace."

⁴⁹While he was still speaking, someone came from the leader's house to say, "Your daughter is dead; do not trouble the teacher any longer." ⁵⁰When Jesus heard this, he replied, "Do not fear. Only believe, and she will be saved." ⁵¹When he came to the house, he did not allow anyone to enter with him, except Peter, John, and James, and the child's father and mother. ⁵²They were all weeping and wailing for her; but he said, "Do not weep; for she is not dead but sleeping." ⁵³And they laughed at him, knowing that she was dead. ⁵⁴But he took her by the hand and called out, "Child, get up!" ⁵⁵Her spirit returned, and she got up at once. Then he directed them to give her something to eat. ⁵⁶Her parents were astounded; but he ordered them to tell no one what had happened.

ᵃOther ancient authorities lack *and though she had spent all she had on physicians*   ᵇOther ancient authorities add *and those who were with him*

COMMENTARY

The interlaced miracles of the healing of the woman with the twelve-year-long hemorrhage and the raising of Jairus's twelve-year-old daughter add a further level to the development of the theme of Jesus' power. Jesus' power was demonstrated in his mastery over the elements of nature in the stilling of the storm (8:22-25), then in his mastery over the demonic spirits who tormented the Gerasene demoniac (8:26-39), and now in his mastery over sickness and death

(8:40-56). In two of these stories, the term "Master" (ἐπιστάτα *epistata*) has been used (8:24, 45), and in each Jesus has exercised his power by means of a command (8:24, 29, 54). The two parts of Luke 8, therefore, develop related themes: hearing and doing Jesus' word (8:1-21), and the power of Jesus exercised through his word (8:22-56).

The sandwiching technique—in which the first part of a story is told, then a second story, and then the rest of the first story—is typical of Mark (see Mark 11:12-20; 14:53-72). Luke has drawn the sandwiched miracles from Mark 5:21-43 with no change in their basic structure. Not only are the two stories sandwiched, but also they are related by parallel motifs: "daughter" (θυγάτηρ *thygatēr*; Luke 8:42, 48); twelve years (8:42, 43); "saved/well" (σῴζω *sōzō*; 8:48, 50); less significant parallels in the role of the crowds and the mourners; power leaving Jesus and the spirit returning to Jairus's daughter; and the role of the desire for secrecy in the two stories. Moreover, Luke has shortened the account and improved its style and syntax.

8:40-42. Among the Lukan alterations, the following are the most significant. The introduction to the story is told with greater economy and explains that the crowd gathered because they were "all" waiting for him. The girl is Jairus's only daughter, which invites comparison between the earlier raising of the only son of the widow of Nain (son/mother) and this story of the raising of the only daughter of Jairus, a ruler of the synagogue (daughter/father). In addition, the notice that she was twelve years old is moved from the end of the story to the beginning (v. 42).

8:43-48. Luke softens Mark's comment that the woman with a hemorrhage had suffered much from many physicians and was no better. The NRSV translates the longer reading of v. 43, which contains the clause "and though she had spent all she had on physicians"; but a strong case can be made for following the manuscripts that omit this text, saying only that "no one could cure her." If Luke himself was a physician, his omission of Mark's deprecatory remark is all the more understandable. Luke omits the woman's interior monologue but adds that the woman touched the fringe or tassels of Jesus' garment. Luke also makes Peter the spokesman for the disciples and adds the title "Master," which has been used earlier in Luke (5:5; 8:24). Just as Luke omitted the disciples' harsh address to Jesus in the stilling of the storm ("Do you not care that we are perishing?" [Mark 4:38; Luke 8:24]), so also here Luke omits the disciples' implied rebuke of Jesus, "How can you say, 'Who touched me?'" (Mark 5:31). The report of Jesus' knowledge of what had tran-

spired is deferred until after his question, "Who touched me?" and the report of the woman's knowledge of what had happened is omitted, so that only Jesus has such knowledge. Like the Gerasene demoniac (8:28, 35) and Jairus (8:41), the woman falls at Jesus' feet (8:47), explaining why she had touched him before "all the people" (8:47) and confirming the healing.

8:49-56. Luke's insertion of Jesus' assurance to Jairus, "Only believe, *and she will be saved*" (8:50, italics added) echoes his earlier assurance, "Your faith has made you well" (8:48). Both pronouncements contain forms of the same Greek words, "faith"/"have faith [believe]" (πίστις *pistis*; πίστευσον *pisteuson*) and "has healed"/"will be healed" (σέσωκέν *sesōken*, σωθήσεται *sōthēsetai*). This is the first scene to feature the group of three disciples. Peter, James, and John have a significant role in Mark as those who witness the raising of Jairus's daughter, the transfiguration, and Jesus' agony in Gethsemane. The role of secrecy and epiphanies before these three is not important to Luke, who adds no other scenes in which these three are alone with Jesus and does not single out the group of three in his account of Jesus at Gethsemane. Luke sharpens the exchange between Jesus and the mourners, so that Jesus commands them, "Do not weep," and the narrator explains that the mourners laughed because they knew the child was dead. Luke thereby removes the ambiguity that lingers in Mark regarding whether the child was dead or not. Luke does not report Jesus' movement into the house (or into another part of the house) or his casting out the crowd (cf. Mark 5:40), but moves directly to Jesus' action and the words he spoke. Mark's Aramaic command, "Talitha kumi" ("Little girl, rise"), is translated into Greek. Luke, who typically notes comings and goings at the beginning and end of each scene, reports that "her spirit returned." The command to give the girl something to eat not only underscores Jesus' care for her well-being but also corresponds to Jesus' action in eating fish with his disciples after his resurrection (Luke 24:42-43). The action of eating proves that the person is no ghost, spirit, or angel (see Tob 12:19).

The effect of these editorial modifications is to diminish the role of secrecy while tying the intertwined miracles more closely to the preceding demonstrations of Jesus' power. In Luke, the theological vocabulary of believing and being saved is enhanced by the addition of the promise, "and she will be saved" (v. 50). Little theological content can be attached to faith at this point, but both the woman with the hemorrhage and Jairus demonstrate faith by coming to Jesus in the confidence that he can help them. As a result, Luke shows that Jesus is master not only of the natural order and the demonic powers but master over sickness and death also.

REFLECTIONS

1. In both the story of the Gerasene demoniac and in these miracles Jesus moves toward persons in need with no apparent regard for the laws of ritual purity. The demoniac, who lived among tombs and a herd of pigs, was certainly unclean. The woman with a hemorrhage had lived for twelve years in a state of impurity (Lev 15:25-31), and any contact between her and Jesus would have made him unclean. An entire tractate of the Mishnah is devoted to restrictions regarding menstruants.[106] Similarly, the corpse of Jairus's daughter was unclean, and by taking her hand Jesus would have been defiled. In each case, however, Jesus moved to bring healing, life, and wholeness to the person in need. By implication, if Jesus reached out to an unclean person and a corpse, no such barriers should stand in the way of extending the gospel to Samaritans and Gentiles.

2. Although Luke does not develop the secrecy motif as Mark does, secrecy nevertheless plays an interesting role in these stories. The woman with a hemorrhage sought to keep her condition a secret, confident that even the fringes or tassels of Jesus' garments (see Num 15:38-39) possessed the power to heal her. Because mere contact with Jesus' garment produced healing, the story might have fostered the growth of superstition and magic rather than faith in Jesus (cf. Acts 5:15; 19:11-12, which show that such magic was not unknown in early Christianity). By demanding a personal confrontation with the woman, Jesus was not seeking to shame or embarrass her but to recognize her faith and offer her his blessing. In an interesting contrast, following the resuscitation of Jairus's daughter Jesus ordered her parents not to tell anyone what had happened. The fact that the daughter was alive and well could not be hidden, but the crowd could be left to assume that she had not been dead after all and that she had recovered suddenly. Luke, therefore, portrays Jesus' power to heal and give life, but also records his efforts to stifle reports that would have interpreted Jesus' power as the exercise of magic. The only difference between miracle and magic, however, is whether the act is viewed as being within or outside the bounds of what can be sanctioned.

3. Jesus' claim that the daughter was sleeping and the crowd's jeering response that she was dead call for further reflection on the common euphemism of sleep for death (see John 11:11-15). Jesus' words were not a description of her physical condition but a prediction of her return to life. Because Jesus would take her hand and awaken the little girl, her condition was temporary. Thus the euphemism of sleep for death is a confession of God's promise of life. Luke no doubt understands, on the far side of the resurrection of Jesus, that what Jesus did for Jairus's daughter is a picture of the hope for all believers. Jesus takes the hand of all who trust in his power and says, "Young man, I say to you, rise" (7:14), "Child, get up" (8:54).

---

106. See *m. Niddah.*

LUKE 9:1-50, THE MESSIAH OF GOD AND THE SON OF MAN

OVERVIEW

In Luke 9 the themes and issues that have been developing in the previous two chapters reach a climax. Jesus extends his ministry of healing by sending out the Twelve. When reports of their work reach Herod, he asks, "Who is this about whom I hear such things?" (9:9). This section of the Gospel provides an answer to Herod's question. Jesus is "the Messiah of God" (9:20), but he is also the Son of Man who will be rejected and killed by the religious authorities. Discipleship, therefore, requires a total commitment of one's life. Jesus' identity and role as the Messiah are confirmed and clarified by the events that follow Peter's confession. At the transfiguration, the voice from heaven declares "This is my Son, my Chosen; listen to him!" (9:35). The next day, after casting the demon out of the epileptic boy, Jesus tells of his death a second time. The disciples still have not understood, however, because they debate among themselves as to which of them is the greatest and attempt to prevent others from casting out demons in Jesus' name.

Luke 9:1-17, The Mission of the Twelve and Herod's Question

NIV

9 When Jesus had called the Twelve together, he gave them power and authority to drive out all demons and to cure diseases, ²and he sent them out to preach the kingdom of God and to heal the sick. ³He told them: "Take nothing for the journey—no staff, no bag, no bread, no money, no extra tunic. ⁴Whatever house you enter, stay there until you leave that town. ⁵If people do not welcome you, shake the dust off your feet when you leave their town, as a testimony against them." ⁶So they set out and went from village to village, preaching the gospel and healing people everywhere.

⁷Now Herod the tetrarch heard about all that was going on. And he was perplexed, because some were saying that John had been raised from the dead, ⁸others that Elijah had appeared, and still others that one of the prophets of long ago had come back to life. ⁹But Herod said, "I beheaded John. Who, then, is this I hear such things about?" And he tried to see him.

¹⁰When the apostles returned, they reported to Jesus what they had done. Then he took them with him and they withdrew by themselves to a town called Bethsaida, ¹¹but the crowds learned about it and followed him. He welcomed them

NRSV

9 Then Jesus[a] called the twelve together and gave them power and authority over all demons and to cure diseases, ²and he sent them out to proclaim the kingdom of God and to heal. ³He said to them, "Take nothing for your journey, no staff, nor bag, nor bread, nor money—not even an extra tunic. ⁴Whatever house you enter, stay there, and leave from there. ⁵Wherever they do not welcome you, as you are leaving that town shake the dust off your feet as a testimony against them." ⁶They departed and went through the villages, bringing the good news and curing diseases everywhere.

7Now Herod the ruler[b] heard about all that had taken place, and he was perplexed, because it was said by some that John had been raised from the dead, ⁸by some that Elijah had appeared, and by others that one of the ancient prophets had arisen. ⁹Herod said, "John I beheaded; but who is this about whom I hear such things?" And he tried to see him.

10On their return the apostles told Jesus[c] all they had done. He took them with him and withdrew privately to a city called Bethsaida.

[a] Gk he   [b] Gk tetrarch   [c] Gk him

NIV

and spoke to them about the kingdom of God, and healed those who needed healing.

¹²Late in the afternoon the Twelve came to him and said, "Send the crowd away so they can go to the surrounding villages and countryside and find food and lodging, because we are in a remote place here."

¹³He replied, "You give them something to eat."

They answered, "We have only five loaves of bread and two fish—unless we go and buy food for all this crowd." ¹⁴(About five thousand men were there.)

But he said to his disciples, "Have them sit down in groups of about fifty each." ¹⁵The disciples did so, and everybody sat down. ¹⁶Taking the five loaves and the two fish and looking up to heaven, he gave thanks and broke them. Then he gave them to the disciples to set before the people. ¹⁷They all ate and were satisfied, and the disciples picked up twelve basketfuls of broken pieces that were left over.

NRSV

¹¹When the crowds found out about it, they followed him; and he welcomed them, and spoke to them about the kingdom of God, and healed those who needed to be cured.

12The day was drawing to a close, and the twelve came to him and said, "Send the crowd away, so that they may go into the surrounding villages and countryside, to lodge and get provisions; for we are here in a deserted place." ¹³But he said to them, "You give them something to eat." They said, "We have no more than five loaves and two fish—unless we are to go and buy food for all these people." ¹⁴For there were about five thousand men. And he said to his disciples, "Make them sit down in groups of about fifty each." ¹⁵They did so and made them all sit down. ¹⁶And taking the five loaves and the two fish, he looked up to heaven, and blessed and broke them, and gave them to the disciples to set before the crowd. ¹⁷And all ate and were filled. What was left over was gathered up, twelve baskets of broken pieces.

COMMENTARY

Luke 9 opens with scenes that tie together the issue of Jesus' identity and the spread of the work of the kingdom. Having manifested his power in the series of miracle stories at the end of the previous chapter, Jesus sends his disciples out to preach and heal in the villages. Herod raises the question that others have voiced: "Who is Jesus?" The first answer that is given is a symbolic act: Jesus takes bread and feeds a multitude.

9:1-6, Commissioning the Twelve. 9:1-2. Jesus' instructions to the Twelve parallel Mark 6:6b-13, but Luke has edited his source, adding greater emphasis to the conferral of "power" over "all" the demons (v. 1), and specifying that the Twelve were to heal the sick and preach the kingdom of God (v. 2). Perhaps reflecting his setting in a more affluent social class, Luke records that Jesus forbade the disciples to carry silver coins—not copper coins as in Mark.

Mark 3:14 explains that Jesus called the disciples for two reasons: (1) to be with him and (2) to be sent out. Although Luke omits this

particular statement, he seems to structure this section of the Gospel around these two aspects of discipleship (see 8:1). The disciples have been instructed by Jesus during the sermon in Luke 6:20-49 and by Jesus' sayings and acts of power on other occasions. This is the first of four scenes in which the disciples are commissioned in Luke: (1) sending the Twelve to preach and heal (9:1-6), (2) sending the seventy in pairs (10:1-11), (3) Jesus' preparation of the apostles for their post-Easter mission (22:35-38), and (4) the commissioning of the eleven and the others at the end of the Gospel (24:48-49). A further commissioning follows in Acts 1:6-8.

In contrast to Mark's concentration on the conferral of power over the unclean spirits, Luke's account of the commissioning is more inclusive and more reflective of the character of Jesus' ministry as it has been described to this point. The disciples will have power over all the demons, power to heal the sick, and to preach the kingdom of God. The work of the kingdom requires both preaching and healing (9:2) so that if either is neglected the distinctive nature of the kingdom may be lost.

9:3-5. The second part of this scene—Jesus' instructions to the Twelve—is introduced by a transitional phrase at the beginning of v. 3. The instructions cover three related topics: (1) what they may and may not take with them, (2) how they are to receive hospitality, and (3) their response to rejection. Although the instructions are clear, the rationale and social context for these restrictions have been interpreted variously. Jesus forbade the disciples to take any provisions for their journey—not a traveler's staff (allowed in Mark 6:8) nor a traveler's bag (cf. Mark 6:8; Luke 10:4; 22:35), which might also be interpreted as a beggar's bag nor bread (cf. Mark 6:8) nor silver coins nor two cloaks (cf. Mark 6:8). Various interpretations have been offered for these restrictions. By traveling in this way the disciples will dramatize the urgency of their mission, they will declare their complete dependence on God's provision for their needs, and they will define their solidarity with the poor. Regardless of the precise rationale for these restrictions, they set the pattern for the practice of hospitality in the context of the mission of the early church. The book of Acts, 3 John, and the *Didache* all describe a similar pattern; traveling apostles, prophets, and evangelists depended on the hospitality of other believers wherever they went. For this reason, hospitality was crucial to the conduct of the church's mission (Rom 12:13; Titus 1:8; Heb 13:2; 1 Pet 4:9). The admonition to stay wherever they are received (and therefore not to seek better accommodations) cautioned them against offending their hosts or appearing to be concerned about their own comfort. Jesus' instructions envision the response not just of individuals or families but of whole villages (such as what Paul and his companions experience in Acts 13; 16; 17). If a village refused to receive them, the disciples were to testify against the village by shaking the dust from their feet as they left.

9:6. This verse concludes the commissioning scene, underscoring the disciples' obedience and success, and reiterating the principal features of their mission: preaching the good news and healing the sick. The last word affirms both the power of the disciples who had been commissioned by

Jesus and the universal extent of the kingdom: They were successful "everywhere."

9:7-9, Herod's Question. Although the issue of Jesus' identity is an underlying theme of the entire Gospel, it comes to the fore in this section. Herod has an effective intelligence system. He hears "all that had taken place" and the suggestions that others were offering as to Jesus' identity. In response, Herod rejects the suggestion that it could be John because he has beheaded John: "Who is this about whom I hear such things?" This is the way in which readers of the Gospel learn about John's fate (see earlier 3:19-20; 7:18-23).

Herod's question is the culmination of a series of such questions:

The scribes and Pharisees: "Who is this who is speaking blasphemies?" (5:21).

John the Baptist: "Are you the one who is to come?" (7:19).

Those at table with Jesus: "Who is this who even forgives sins?" (7:49).

The disciples: "Who then is this, that he commands even the winds and the water, and they obey him?" (8:25).

Herod's question, therefore, prepares the reader for the series of answers that the coming scenes will provide. Jesus is "the Messiah of God" (9:20), "the Son of Man" (9:22), and "my Son, my Chosen" (9:35). The effect of this series of questions is not just to set up the answers that are coming, however. The recurring questions about Jesus' identity from different characters who have witnessed different aspects of his work lead the reader to wonder and marvel at the person and work of Jesus. The questions are even more powerful than the lofty titles attributed to Jesus because the answer to the questions is not exhausted by the titles. Jesus is everything the titles confess him to be, but he is more. "Who then is this?"

Luke has edited Mark 6:14-16 in order to create a sharper focus on the issue of Jesus' identity. Whereas Mark presents an extended section at this point describing the arrest and beheading of John, Luke has moved the report of the arrest to 3:19-20 and has Herod merely allude to John's death at this point. Herod is more accurately called tetrarch (cf. 3:1, 19) rather than king, as in Mark 6:14. In addition, Luke's reference to "all that had taken place" is not only more inclusive than Mark's emphasis on Jesus' miracles but also serves to recall for the reader all that has been reported to this point of Jesus' ministry. The reporting of the speculations about Jesus' identity is streamlined, and Herod's response is changed from a rather flat statement to a question that resonates with the earlier questions about Jesus. Luke does not need to have Herod link Jesus with John (as in Mark 6:16) because he has already devoted a series of scenes to establishing the relationship between Jesus and John (see 7:18-35).

The speculations about who Jesus is are significant even if they are not accurate. All of the speculations link Jesus with a prophetic figure, but Luke has already established that whereas Jesus' mighty works were like those of the prophets he was greater than the prophets (see 7:1-35). Elijah was expected to return before "the great and terrible day of the LORD" (Mal 4:5; Sir 48:10), but John has fulfilled the role of Elijah (Luke 1:17). Still, Elijah will play a significant role in the transfiguration account as the representative of the prophets of Israel (see 9:19, 30, 33, 54). Herod's confession that he had beheaded John serves ironically to underscore the truth that God's redemptive work has never been defeated by killing God's prophets. Herod still had John's blood on his hands, yet Jesus' great works were on everyone's lips. The violence of the wicked is no match for God's grace.

Herod's question and his desire to see Jesus foreshadow coming events. Herod might seek to kill Jesus (13:31), but Jesus would not die in Galilee (Herod's territory) but in Jerusalem. When Herod did meet Jesus—after Pilate sent Jesus to him—Herod's desire was fulfilled, but he wanted only to see Jesus perform a sign. If indeed Herod had wanted to kill Jesus (13:31), he further implicates himself by recognizing Jesus' innocence (23:15). Therefore, Herod is a tragic figure; although his desire to meet Jesus is eventually fulfilled, he never grasps the answer to his question.

9:10-17, The Return of the Twelve and the Feeding of the Five Thousand. This passage serves as a bridge between Herod's question and Peter's confession in 9:20. This sequence is created by Luke's "big omission" at Luke 9:17. At this point, Luke omits Mark 6:45–8:26 and moves directly from the feeding to Peter's confession.

None of the Gospels narrates the work accomplished by the Twelve while they are away from Jesus. Mark fills this gap with an extended account of the arrest and execution of John the Baptist. Luke has only the report of Herod's reaction to the reports in vv. 7-9. The summary reference to "all they had done" in v. 10 leaves the reader to imagine works like those performed by Jesus earlier in the Gospel.

The feeding of the five thousand is the only one of Jesus' miracles that is reported in all four Gospels; in Mark and Matthew, there is also a second feeding of four thousand. Luke appears to have depended on Mark 6:30-44 for his account of the feeding, but there are several minor agreements between Matthew and Luke, and Luke has extensively rewritten the account presented in Mark. For reasons that are not entirely clear to us, Luke changes Mark's account of the site of the feeding of the multitude. Whereas Mark says that they went by boat to a wilderness place (Mark 6:32), Luke reports that Jesus led the disciples to Bethsaida. The references to Bethsaida in the omitted material in Mark 6:45 and 8:22 may have influenced Luke's understanding of the tradition. Nevertheless, Luke moves closer to Mark's account by reporting later that they were in a deserted place (see 9:12).

Luke omits the reference to Jesus' compassion and the allusion to the people being like sheep without a shepherd (Num 27:17; 1 Kgs 22:17) in Mark 6:34 and rejects Mark's bland report that Jesus "taught them many things" in favor of a description of Jesus teaching about the kingdom of God and healing the sick. In Luke's account, the feeding is initiated by the disciples. Seeing that evening is coming and that they are in a deserted place, the disciples suggest that Jesus send the crowd away to the villages and countryside so that they could find lodging and food for themselves.

The language of the feeding of the five thousand reverberates with echoes from three other biblical contexts: (1) the feeding of the Israelites in the wilderness; (2) Elisha's feeding of a hundred with twenty loaves (2 Kgs 4:42-44); and (3) the traditional language of the eucharist. Luke does not make the exodus context explicit, as John does, but the provision of bread for a multitude in the wilderness would have evoked powerful associations for all for whom the exodus was a significant event in their religious heritage and

Scriptures. The contacts with Elisha's miraculous feeding are more direct. Elisha does not feed the men himself but instructs another to do so: "Give it to the people and let them eat" (2 Kgs 4:42). The man protests that there will not be enough for such a crowd. Elisha repeats his instructions. After the men had eaten, they "had some left" (2 Kgs 4:44). The collection of the fragments after the feeding of the five thousand probably echoes both 2 Kgs 4:44 and the references to gathering manna in the wilderness (Exod 16:15-21). What is distinctive in the feeding account when compared with these echoes from Moses and the Prophets is the peculiar action of taking the bread, looking up to heaven, blessing the bread, breaking it, and giving it to the disciples. With the exception of looking to heaven, which was the common posture for prayer (Job 22:26-27; Luke 18:13; John 17:1), the other verbs in this series echo the early church's eucharistic formulas (Mark 14:22-23; Luke 22:19; 24:30; 1 Cor 11:23-24). It is also just at this point that Luke's account of the feeding reproduces the language of Mark's account most faithfully (cf. Mark 6:41; Luke 9:16). Luke follows his source closely at this point because it echoes the words that were regularly repeated at the observance of the eucharist.

For early Christian readers, Jesus' actions, described in the sequence of verbs that follow the eucharistic pattern, also have a revelatory function. Just as Jesus' breaking of bread after his death revealed his identity to the two who had accompanied him on the road to Emmaus (24:30-31, 35), so also the echoes of Jesus' distinctive action in taking, blessing, breaking, and giving bread to his followers serves in this scene as an allusion to his identity. By teaching the disciples to meet hunger by giving bread, Jesus' instruction also prepares for the relief efforts described in Acts (4:32-37; 6:1-6; 11:27-30).

The significance of the two fish is not as easily explained as the symbolism of bread. Fish was a staple in Galilean diets and the only meat eaten in great quantities by Jews in the first century. If the accounts of the feeding of the five thousand have been shaped by early Christian worship and reflection on the Hebrew Scriptures, it is possible that the fish would have been understood either as echoes of the prophet's description of Leviathan at the eschatological banquet (4 Ezra 6:49-52; 2 Bar 29:4; *1 Enoch* 6:7-9, 24) or as an allusion to the sign of the fish in early Christian art. Based on an anagram for the Greek word for "fish" (ἰχθύς *ichthys*) the sign of the fish denoted the Christian confession "Jesus Christ is the Son of God, the Savior" (cf. Acts 8:37).

The reference to seating the crowd in groups of fifty has at times been interpreted as imposing some organization on the crowd in fulfillment of the organization of Israel, in imitation of the organization at Qumran, or as the beginning of a zealot revolt. Nevertheless, the text of Luke does not naturally lead one to any of these interpretations.

Luke's report that the multitude who ate "were filled" echoes not only 2 Kgs 4:44 but also Jesus' earlier beatitude in the sermon on the plain: "Blessed are you who are hungry now,/ for you will be filled" (6:21). The feeding of the multitude, therefore, is a sign that the kingdom of God is present in Jesus. The one who feeds the hungry is the one who fulfills the exodus hopes of Israel, the words of Isaiah that announce good news for the poor (4:18), and Jesus' teachings on the kingdom. Luke's placement of the feeding as the bridge between Herod's question and Peter's answer, therefore, exploits the full revelatory power of the feeding tradition.

REFLECTIONS

Luke's account of the sending out of the Twelve, Herod's question, and the feeding of the five thousand present powerful themes for theological reflection. Luke has set the question of Jesus' identity between a commissioning of his followers to preach and heal and the miracle of feeding. Christology and mission are thereby wedded as two sides of the same reality. Jesus' identity is revealed in what he does and what he calls others to do. By the same token, those who desire to see who Jesus is will see him only if they respond to his call to preach the gospel, heal the sick, and feed the hungry. There is still truth in Albert Schweitzer's immortal words at the conclusion of *The Quest of the Historical Jesus:*

He speaks to us the same word: "Follow thou me!" and sets us to the tasks which He has to fulfil for our time. He commands. And to those who obey Him, whether they be wise or simple, He will reveal Himself in the toils, the conflicts, the sufferings which they shall pass through in His fellowship, and, as an ineffable mystery, they shall learn in their own experience Who He is.[107]

Jesus' instructions for the mission are still important, even if few would be tempted to carry a staff today. Jesus' commissioning of the disciples exposes the theological and social core of the mission. First, commitment to the redemptive mission is inseparable from the commitment to be a follower of Jesus. Being sent out is the natural result of being with Jesus. In modern theological terms, missions and evangelism are the natural result of worship and Christian education. The Christian calling never finds its fulfillment in one's own worship, nurture, and piety but always in the extension of God's grace and care to others. Similarly, the Christian mission is rooted in worship, meditation, and study that sustain and empower the disciple. Although the disciples do not yet understand fully who Jesus is, they serve effectively when they respond to Jesus' commissioning, and as a result of their obedience they will eventually see more clearly who Jesus is. Revelation is the companion of experience and the by-product of obedience. The disciples, therefore, will eventually see Jesus as the crucified and risen Lord, while Herod never moves beyond the scandal of political threat, curiosity about the miraculous, and questions of guilt and innocence.

Those who are sent out on mission travel in faith. There is no guarantee of success or safety. The disciple trusts in God's providence and the power of the gospel. Neither can the disciple who brings good news to the poor remain wedded to the system of wealth. The disciple carries no trappings of wealth. Nor will the representatives of God's kingdom seek to climb society's social ladder. Good news for the poor, therefore, can be proclaimed only by those who are willing to take their stand with the poor.

The practice of hospitality gives witness to the power of the gospel to create community. Christians open their doors to one another. Social barriers between rich and poor, native and newcomer are torn down. By receiving outsiders at our table, we declare the power of reconciliation to a fragmented society. Perhaps it is time to revive the practice of evangelical hospitality.

The other side of the sandwich created by the commissioning and feeding scenes reminds us that the preaching of the gospel can never be separated from care for social and physical needs. The early church understood the giving of bread as a sacramental act. The last supper, the institution of the eucharist, was tied to both the meals with the outcasts and the multitudes in Galilee and to the post-resurrection meal scenes at the end of Luke. God's love has been symbolized through the provision of bread ever since the Israelites ate manna in the wilderness and Elisha fed hungry men with "food from the first fruits" (2 Kgs 4:42). The sequence of scenes in Luke suggests the revelatory function of the feeding: Because Jesus fed the multitude, his disciples saw that he was God's anointed one. This conjunction of the feeding of the five thousand and Peter's confession also foreshadows the disciples' recognition of the risen Lord in the breaking of bread at Emmaus. When their companion on the road took bread, blessed it, and gave it to them, they recognized that the risen Lord had been present with them. What do others see when we feed the hungry in the name of Jesus?

---

107. Albert Schweitzer, *The Quest of the Historical Jesus: A Critical Study of Its Progress from Reimarus to Wrede,* trans. W. Montgomery (New York: Macmillan, 1950) 403.

Luke 9:18-27, Peter's Confession and the Demands of Discipleship

NIV

18Once when Jesus was praying in private and his disciples were with him, he asked them, "Who do the crowds say I am?"

19They replied, "Some say John the Baptist; others say Elijah; and still others, that one of the prophets of long ago has come back to life."

20"But what about you?" he asked. "Who do you say I am?"

Peter answered, "The Christ[a] of God."

21Jesus strictly warned them not to tell this to anyone. 22And he said, "The Son of Man must suffer many things and be rejected by the elders, chief priests and teachers of the law, and he must be killed and on the third day be raised to life."

23Then he said to them all: "If anyone would come after me, he must deny himself and take up his cross daily and follow me. 24For whoever wants to save his life will lose it, but whoever loses his life for me will save it. 25What good is it for a man to gain the whole world, and yet lose or forfeit his very self? 26If anyone is ashamed of me and my words, the Son of Man will be ashamed of him when he comes in his glory and in the glory of the Father and of the holy angels. 27I tell you the truth, some who are standing here will not taste death before they see the kingdom of God."

a20 Or Messiah

NRSV

18Once when Jesus[a] was praying alone, with only the disciples near him, he asked them, "Who do the crowds say that I am?" 19They answered, "John the Baptist; but others, Elijah; and still others, that one of the ancient prophets has arisen." 20He said to them, "But who do you say that I am?" Peter answered, "The Messiah[b] of God."

21He sternly ordered and commanded them not to tell anyone, 22saying, "The Son of Man must undergo great suffering, and be rejected by the elders, chief priests, and scribes, and be killed, and on the third day be raised."

23Then he said to them all, "If any want to become my followers, let them deny themselves and take up their cross daily and follow me. 24For those who want to save their life will lose it, and those who lose their life for my sake will save it. 25What does it profit them if they gain the whole world, but lose or forfeit themselves? 26Those who are ashamed of me and of my words, of them the Son of Man will be ashamed when he comes in his glory and the glory of the Father and of the holy angels. 27But truly I tell you, there are some standing here who will not taste death before they see the kingdom of God."

a Gk he   b Or The Christ

COMMENTARY

This section consists of a conversation in three parts between Jesus and the disciples. The first part contains two questions regarding Jesus' identity (vv. 18-20). The first question elicits three answers regarding who the crowds say Jesus is. The second question leads to Peter's confession that Jesus is "the Messiah of God." The second part of the conversation joins Jesus' charge that the disciples tell no one with the first of the passion predictions (vv. 21-22). The third part links the confession of Jesus to teachings on discipleship (vv. 23-27).

After an extended section in Luke that devel-oped the theme of "who then is this" and offered indirect answers by developing Jesus' fulfillment of the prophetic traditions drawn primarily from Isaianic themes, the Elijah-Elisha cycles, and exodus motifs, the disciples offer the first confession of Jesus as the Messiah. The language of Peter's confession echoes earlier declarations embedded in the infancy account, but the second part of the conversation immediately begins to qualify and interpret Peter's confession. Both the confession and the modifications that follow in the remainder of this chapter will have to be considered carefully.

9:18-20, Peter's Confession. Here again, Luke depends on Mark. Luke has moved directly from the feeding of the five thousand, which in Mark occurs in 6:30-44, to Peter's confession (Mark 8:27-30). Various explanations for this omission of Markan material have been suggested (avoiding doublets or omitting accounts of Jesus' work outside of Galilee), but the omitted material is not sufficiently homogeneous to confirm any of these conjectures. The effect of the omission, as was noted in the commentary on the feeding of the five thousand, is to bring the feeding and Peter's confession into direct relation to each other—a fact that may prove significant for defining the meaning of the confession "the Messiah of God."

Three other Lukan modifications of the confession scene give it a distinctive meaning in this context. First, Luke has omitted Mark's designation of the geographical location (Caesarea Philippi) and substitutes instead a designation of the spiritual context of the confession. Rather than locate the confession of Jesus as the Christ at a place named for the Roman emperor and his tetrarch, the confession occurs where Jesus is at prayer to God with his disciples. Prayer is an important theme in Luke because it serves as another way of emphasizing that all Jesus does is a part of God's redemptive plan (see the references to prayer in 3:21; 5:16; 6:12; 11:1; 22:40-41, 44, 46; 23:46). Luke also omits Mark's reference to being "on the way," reserving the introduction of the passion motif until after Peter's confession.

Second, Luke changes Mark's allusion to "people" in Mark 8:27 to "the crowds." The crowds have been a recurring fixture of Luke's account of Jesus' ministry since the end of Luke 4. The crowds press around Jesus. On one occasion Jesus challenged the crowds with the question of John the Baptist's identity: "What did you go out into the wilderness to look at?" (7:24). The crowds are also mentioned three times in the feeding of the five thousand (9:11, 12, 16), so under Luke's editing of the material Jesus' question "Who do the crowds say that I am?" must be understood in direct relation to the previous scene. (In an interesting way, this is parallel to the prominence of the crowd's speculation about Jesus in John 6:22-29.) If the feeding has a revelatory function (at least for Christian readers), have the crowds understood what Jesus has done?

The third Lukan modification that serves an important function in the narrative is the change of "one of the prophets" (Mark 8:28) to "one of the ancient prophets has arisen" (Luke 9:19). The difference between the two phrases is not great, but in Luke the phrase is a verbatim repetition of Luke's earlier summary of Herod's words (9:8). By means of this repetition, the confession scene is tied directly to Herod's question. Peter will give the answer that Herod never finds.

The answers that the disciples give to Jesus' question about the level of the crowd's understanding underscore Jesus' identification with the prophetic tradition: John the Baptist, Elijah, one of the ancient prophets. The crowds have understood that Jesus' mighty works are of the same cloth as those performed and predicted by the prophets: announcing good news for the poor, challenging the rich, giving sight to the blind, healing lepers, and raising the dead. Luke 7 and 8 especially have defined Jesus as one greater than the prophets and greater than John the Baptist. The time has now come to articulate the nature of that "greater than." By means of the succession of two questions regarding Jesus' identity and the emphatic opening of the second question, literally, "But you, who do you say that I am?" Luke telegraphs the fact that the answers the crowds have proposed are inadequate. The disciples, through Peter, now show that they have moved to a higher level of understanding.

Peter's confession, "the Messiah [χριστός *christos*] of God," has been interpreted in various ways, as has the issue of whether it accurately reproduces a pre-Easter confession. The issue of whether the title is to be understood in a prophetic context or a royal, Davidic context is relevant to both of these questions. The reader already knows that Jesus is the Christ from references in Luke 2:11, 26; 3:15; 4:41. Luke has cited the connection between the title "Christ," or the anointed one, and the prophetic tradition by placing Jesus' recitation of Isa 61:1 at the beginning of his ministry, in Nazareth (4:18). It is clear from Luke's repeated description of Jesus as one greater than the prophets that this title cannot signal merely that Jesus was a prophet. He was the eschatological prophet who fulfilled Isa 61:1. The feeding of the five thousand, with its allusions to the exodus, the Moses traditions, and Elisha prepares us to understand this title in context as an indication that Jesus is the fulfillment of these traditions, including the expectation of the coming prophet like Moses (Deut 18:15, 18). Peter's confession also resonates with the predictions of Jesus' fulfillment of the Davidic tradition (Luke 1:32-33).

The angelic prediction at Jesus' birth foreshadows for the reader God's intention for Jesus. He will fulfill God's promises for David and his descendants (2 Sam 7:9-14). The Lukan narrative, therefore, will not allow an easy choice between prophetic and royal contexts for understanding the title "the Messiah of God." Luke has prepared the reader to understand the importance of both traditions. The two are joined and fulfilled in Jesus, but the nature of that fulfillment has yet to be defined, and to that task Luke turns immediately (9:21-50).

9:21-22, Jesus' Death Foretold. Immediately, Peter's confession of Jesus is qualified in three respects: (1) Jesus orders the disciples not to tell anyone; (2) Jesus tells the disciples that he must be killed; and (3) Jesus teaches the disciples what following him will require.

The Greek verb for "rebuke" or "sternly order" (ἐπιτιμάω epitimaō) in v. 21 is a strong word that has been used previously for Jesus' commands to unclean spirits (4:35, 41), fevers (4:39), and the wind and the sea (8:24). These previous occurrences of the term have built the impression that it describes Jesus' response to impersonal or demonic forces that threaten his work as the agent of the kingdom. The force of its use for Jesus' response to the disciples at this point cannot be missed (see further 9:42, 55; 17:3; 18:15, 39; 19:39; 23:40). Similarly, the verb for to "command" (παραγγέλλω parangellō) has a peculiar use in Luke, where it is used almost exclusively for Jesus' commands to those around him that they not tell others what they have seen or heard (see 5:14, a leper; 8:56, Jairus and his wife; cf. 8:29). Although Luke retains the verb epitimaō from Mark 8:30, he shifts the emphasis by making it a participle and making parangellō the principal verb. Luke also omits Jesus' rebuke to Peter following the first of the passion predictions (Mark 8:32-33).

The perplexing problems that the passion prediction presents to the interpreter should not so narrow the focus of our attention that we overlook the fact that it is the third in a closely related sequence of responses to Herod's question regarding the identity of Jesus. First came the three answers proposed by the crowds (9:18-19); then the disciples' answer, voiced by Peter (9:20); and now Jesus' own answer (9:22). Jesus' own answer emphasizes neither fulfillment of the works of the prophets nor his role as a Davidic king but the necessity of his death and resurrection.

Because the title "the Son of Man" has been the subject of intense debate, the interpretation of the passion predictions (see also 9:44b; 18:31-33) has often been controlled by one's estimate of the background, meaning, and titular force of that term rather than by the prediction itself. In context, the saying makes sense only if it is understood that by "the Son of Man" Jesus is referring to himself. This term lacks the royal and political overtones of "Christ," or "the anointed One." Its background is more obscure and, therefore, more open to question and interpretation. On the one hand, it appears in Dan 7:13 as a description of the one who ascends to the Almighty in the last days, and its use in *1 Enoch* and 4 Ezra shows that messianic speculation had embraced the term by the end of the first century CE. On the other hand, its meaning was not clearly defined, and the passion predictions reflect a new development by linking the term with predictions of death and the fulfillment of Isaiah's expectation of a suffering servant.

We make no attempt to settle the difficult issues that control the interpretation of "the Son of Man," but two points are beyond dispute: (1) Luke's Christian readers already understood this title as a reference to Jesus (see 6:5, 22); and (2) the passion prediction, placed immediately following Peter's confession, serves as a sharp corrective to any expectations that Jesus would fulfill expectations of the coming of a descendant of David who would drive out the Gentiles and reestablish the kingdom of Israel (see Psalms of Solomon 17; Acts 1:6). If "the Son of Man" was already understood as a title for a coming heavenly figure at the end of time (as in *1 Enoch* and 4 Ezra), then the passion prediction serves as a double corrective: Jesus will not be a Davidic king, and although he is indeed that expected Son of Man, he will suffer and die—something nowhere predicted of the apocalyptic Son of Man. If "the Son of Man" was not already clearly understood as a title for an apocalyptic figure, then Jesus may be taking a term with vague connotations and attaching it to the Isaianic predictions of a suffering servant rather than to more popular expectations of a political messiah. Jesus was not only greater than the prophets, but also his role—while a fulfillment of the suffering servant passages in Isaiah—would be radically different from current, popular interpretations of the prophetic predictions.

The first point that Jesus underscores regarding his role as the Son of Man is its necessity. God's redemptive will demands it. The term that denotes the necessity, "must" (δεῖ *dei*), occurs 18 times in Luke. The necessity that God's plan of salvation be fulfilled guides the course of events in Luke's "orderly narrative." Jesus must be in his Father's house (2:49), just as later he must preach the kingdom of God (4:43). By the end of the Gospel, Jesus' death and resurrection will be wrapped in divine necessity (24:7, 26, 44). Along the way Jesus teaches that other things also are necessary (see e.g. 11:42; 12:12; 15:32), so that the teachings on discipleship (the *Didache*) are linked by the force of God's will to the necessity of Jesus' death and resurrection (the *kerygma*).

The fact that Jesus must "suffer" (πάσχω *paschō*) does not occur in the second and third passion predictions (9:44*b*; 18:31-33), but it virtually becomes a shorthand reference for Jesus' redemptive death in 17:25; 24:26, 46. As a result of the deaths of faithful martyrs during the Maccabean revolt, the suffering of the righteous was understood to have redemptive significance for Israel: "[the martyrs] having become, as it were, a ransom for the sin of our nation. And through the blood of those devout ones and their death as an atoning sacrifice, divine Providence preserved Israel that previously had been mistreated" (4 Macc 17:21-22).

Similarly, rejection is not mentioned in the second or third passion predictions, but its occurrence in 17:25 and 20:17 shows that it was a significant element of the passion tradition and that it was related to Ps 118:22. On the other hand, whereas the second and third passion predictions declare that Jesus will be "handed over," that motif is absent from the first prediction. The combined group of elders, chief priests, and scribes appears again in 20:1, where they challenge Jesus in the Temple. A similar group, where

the officers of the Temple take the place of the scribes, arrests Jesus on the Mount of Olives. (22:52). The three groups listed in the passion prediction are also absent from the second and third predictions, demonstrating once more that there was no set form for these predictions. The three groups, however, were represented in the Sanhedrin, and they foreshadow the role of that council in Jesus' trial (see 22:66).

The heart of the passion predictions is the declaration that Jesus would be killed (9:22; 18:33; 24:7) and rise or be raised "on the third day" (9:21; 18:33; 24:7, 46). Luke's temporal phrase here is more precise than Mark's "after three days" (Mark 8:31; cf. "on the third day" in Hos 6:2 and 1 Cor 15:4). Jesus' answer to Herod's question effectively explains why Peter's confession of Jesus as the Christ cannot be broadcast publicly and charts the course for the rest of Luke's narrative.

9:23-27, The Demands of Discipleship. The five sayings on discipleship that follow the first passion prediction also serve as an answer to Herod's question regarding Jesus' identity. Lordship and discipleship are always vitally related. By defining what it means to follow Jesus, one defines the nature of Jesus' lordship. Jesus first asked the disciples who the crowds said he was. Then he asked them who they said he was. Jesus' response declaring the necessity of his death was directed to the disciples. The five discipleship sayings, however, are now addressed to "all"— both the disciples and the crowd (see Mark 8:34)—thereby extending the invitation to discipleship to all people.

Luke has drawn the sayings from Mark 8:34–9:1, where the same five sayings occur in the same sequence. As with other sayings of Jesus, Luke follows his source closely, making relatively minor modifications. Luke simplifies Mark's introduction to the sayings in v. 23, adds "daily" (καθ' ἡμέραν *kath hēmeran*) to the demand that the would-be disciples take up the cross and follow Jesus, and omits the phrase "and the gospel" (καὶ τοῦ εὐαγγελίου *kai tou euangeliou*), which occurs in Mark 8:35. Mark 8:37, "Indeed, what can they give in return for their life?" is omitted, perhaps because it adds little to the previous saying (Mark 8:36; Luke 9:25). Luke also omits three other Markan phrases: "in this adulterous and sinful generation" (Mark 8:38), the introduction to the last saying, and "come with power" (Mark 9:1).

9:23. The five sayings draw together a variety of images from various contexts to convey the radical demands of following Jesus. The central image of the first saying is the cross. Although it is not impossible that Jesus may have alluded to death by crucifixion as a graphic metaphor during his ministry—much like his references to a millstone hung around someone's neck (Luke 17:2), one who strains out a gnat but swallows a camel (Matt 23:24), or a camel passing through the eye of a needle (Luke 18:25)—for Luke's readers the image of a cross was unalterably linked with Jesus' death. To follow Jesus means to be ready to lay down one's life just as Jesus did. Luke makes two subtle alterations in the Markan form of the saying: he changes the aorist infinitive of the verb "to come" to a present infinitive, thereby emphasizing its durative, continuing force, and adds the phrase "daily." Thus Luke emphasizes not readiness to die with Jesus in the hour of persecution, but rather that discipleship requires a continuing, daily yielding of one's life to the call to follow Jesus. The first saying contains three imperatives: deny yourself, take up the cross, and follow me. The first two are aorist, but again the third is a present tense: Go on following me.

9:24. The second saying (v. 24) picks up on the motif of laying down one's life by taking up the cross in the first saying. It echoes the exhortations given to soldiers about to enter battle. The first to die will be those who turn and run. The one who seeks to preserve his or her life will lose it, but the one who gives no thought to the preservation of life will keep it. The saying may have had special relevance to Christians facing persecution, but its truth penetrates to the nature of life itself. In the polarity of spending one's life in the pursuits to which Jesus would direct the disciple or indulging only one's own ambitions and interests, true fulfillment is to be found, paradoxically, in the giving up of one's life.

9:25. The third saying moves from the battlefield to the marketplace. The impulse to succeed, to acquire, and to prosper is powerful. In a materialistic culture we are easily seduced by the assumption that security and fulfillment are achieved by means of financial prosperity. This saying cuts the ground from under the preoccu-

pation with material wealth. What have human beings gained, even if they own the whole world, if they lose themselves? This saying reminds us that there are dimensions of life vital to fulfillment and happiness that are not satisfied by financial security or material wealth. The implication left unstated is that each person should seek for those things that bring true fulfillment.

9:26. The fourth saying involves a set of images and contrasts that link our public profession of the lordship of Jesus to his acknowledgment of our discipleship at the end of time. This apocalyptic Son of Man saying promises the future coming of Jesus in glory. Again, it is no doubt colored by the early church's expectations of Jesus' coming as the one who would raise the dead and judge the nations, but for disciples and would-be disciples its force lies in its recognition of the temptation to try to make discipleship a private matter. This saying allows no private discipleship that makes no difference in how one lives. If one denies Jesus, the Son of Man will deny that person. Discipleship requires a public commitment so that the way one lives and what one does may be a witness to others.

9:27. The fifth saying affirms that the hope for the kingdom, drawing on the promise of the coming of the Son of Man in the previous saying, is not a vain one. Difficult as it may be after 2,000 years, the saying promises that the coming of the kingdom is so near that some of those who were alive during Jesus' ministry will live to see it. Each of the synoptic Gospels renders this saying slightly differently. Luke has simply "before they see the kingdom of God" (9:27); Mark has "until they see that the kingdom of God has come with power" (9:1); and Matthew is the most explicit: "before they see the Son of Man coming in his kingdom" (16:28). The variations are semantic, however, not substantial, and the problem is not relieved by explaining one form of the saying but not the others. In all likelihood, the present forms of the saying go back to the apocalyptic expectations of the early church, which made more explicit Jesus' own affirmations of the nearness of the kingdom. Foreshadowings of the coming of the kingdom can be seen in the transfiguration (which follows immediately) and in the events of Pentecost, but these do not in themselves fulfill Jesus' promise of the kingdom.

The fifth saying, therefore, is more properly a kingdom saying rather than a discipleship saying. It is added as the fifth in this sequence of sayings, however, because of its relationship to the warning of Jesus' coming as the Son of Man in the fourth saying.

Taken together, the five sayings supply a further answer to Herod's question. Jesus is the Son of Man who will come in glory at the end of time. Consequently, discipleship to Jesus requires a total commitment of life, taking the cross, giving one's life in obedience to Jesus' direction, forsaking the pursuit of wealth, and living out one's discipleship publicly before others.

REFLECTIONS

At this point in the Gospel, partial answers and proleptic references are giving way to definitive statements of Jesus' identity as the Son of God. Jesus' question to the disciples is an existential query that every reader of the Gospel must answer sooner or later: "Who do you say that I am?" Repeatedly the disciples and others around Jesus had asked one another who Jesus was. Jesus now turns the question back on the disciples. He did not ask who he was but who they believed him to be. Beyond the question of identity is the issue of confession.

Peter gave the best answer he knew, the highest confession he could imagine, but it wasn't enough. On the one hand, it failed to see the struggle and sacrifice that lay before Jesus; on the other hand, it wasn't enough because it failed to recognize the sacrifice and demand that would be required of any who confessed Jesus to be the Christ.

The questions that mean most in life may be the questions of identity and relationship. "Who are you?" "Who is God?" "What does it mean to be a follower of Jesus?" What do our answers to these questions mean for our values, priorities, and commitments? The answers to these questions, however, are not strictly cognitive, rational, or intellectual. They usually emerge from experience and require a commitment of life. We answer these questions by the way we live. Peter may have been partially right about who Jesus was, but he was completely wrong about what following Jesus would mean for him. Jesus was on his way to a cross, not a throne, and those who followed him must be ready to follow him on this road of obedience to God's redemptive will and sacrifice for the salvation of others.

Those who preach a cheap grace or a gospel of health and wealth not only offer false promises, but also they preach a false gospel. Discipleship and lordship are always interrelated. When we offer false assurances and teach a crossless discipleship, we proclaim a distorted christology. On the other hand, when we preach a crucified Christ, the only authentic response is for one to give up all other pursuits that might compromise one's commitment and devote oneself completely to the fulfillment of the kingdom tasks for which Jesus gave his own life. The nature of our discipleship always reflects our understanding of Jesus' lordship.

Discipleship is also a continuing process. That means first that however lofty our understanding or obedient our discipleship, most of us are probably not far from Peter—confessing but failing to grasp the implications of our confession; understanding, but only in part; following Jesus, but maintaining our own aspirations and ambitions also. The present tense verbs of the sayings on discipleship should, therefore, not be overlooked. We might paraphrase: "If you want to continue following me, deny yourself now and take up the cross every day, and keep on following me." What net profit is there if having gained everything you lose your own life?

There are only two impulses in life. One is the impulse to acquire, take, hoard, own, and protect. The other is the impulse to give and to serve. One assumes that each of us can be the Lord of our own lives and that our security and fulfillment depend on our ability to provide for ourselves. The other confesses the sovereignty of God and devotes life to the fulfillment of God's redemptive will in delivering and empowering others, establishing justice and peace, tearing down barriers, reconciling persons, and creating communities. Those who devote themselves to these tasks confess that the true fulfillment of life is to be found in the service of Christ and that our only security is in him.

There is a further truth hidden in the contrasts between the present and the future in the coming Son of Man sayings. In the context of teachings on discipleship, the emphasis is not on the coming Son of Man but on the truth that the way we live in the present determines our relationship to the Lord in the future. We are becoming who we shall be. Who we say Jesus is now determines what he will say of us in the future. How we answer the question "Who do you say that I am?" through our day-to-day discipleship is the only answer that matters—but everything depends on that answer.

Luke 9:28-50, Clarifying Jesus' Messiahship

OVERVIEW

The next five scenes serve to clarify the nature of Jesus' Messiahship, but they also reveal the disciples' lack of understanding. At the transfiguration the voice from heaven announces that Jesus is God's Son, and symbolically Moses and Elijah speak with Jesus about his "exodus" and then depart, leaving only Jesus. Not understanding what he has seen and heard, Peter wants to build three booths. The next day Jesus heals the epileptic boy (whom his disciples could not heal) and forecasts his death a second time (which the disciples do not understand). The last two scenes before Jesus begins his journey to Jerusalem also continue the education of the disciples and show that more teaching will be required.

Luke 9:28-36, The Transfiguration

NIV

[28]About eight days after Jesus said this, he took Peter, John and James with him and went up onto a mountain to pray. [29]As he was praying, the appearance of his face changed, and his clothes became as bright as a flash of lightning. [30]Two men, Moses and Elijah, [31]appeared in glorious splendor, talking with Jesus. They spoke about his departure, which he was about to bring to fulfillment at Jerusalem. [32]Peter and his companions were very sleepy, but when they became fully awake, they saw his glory and the two men standing with him. [33]As the men were leaving Jesus, Peter said to him, "Master, it is good for us to be here. Let us put up three shelters—one for you, one for Moses and one for Elijah." (He did not know what he was saying.)

[34]While he was speaking, a cloud appeared and enveloped them, and they were afraid as they entered the cloud. [35]A voice came from the cloud, saying, "This is my Son, whom I have chosen; listen to him." [36]When the voice had spoken, they found that Jesus was alone. The disciples kept this

NRSV

[28]Now about eight days after these sayings Jesus[a] took with him Peter and John and James, and went up on the mountain to pray. [29]And while he was praying, the appearance of his face changed, and his clothes became dazzling white. [30]Suddenly they saw two men, Moses and Elijah, talking to him. [31]They appeared in glory and were speaking of his departure, which he was about to accomplish at Jerusalem. [32]Now Peter and his companions were weighed down with sleep; but since they had stayed awake,[b] they saw his glory and the two men who stood with him. [33]Just as they were leaving him, Peter said to Jesus, "Master, it is good for us to be here; let us make three dwellings,[c] one for you, one for Moses, and one for Elijah"—not knowing what he said. [34]While he was saying this, a cloud came and overshadowed them; and they were terrified as they entered the cloud. [35]Then from the cloud came a voice that said, "This is my Son, my Chosen;[d]

[a]Gk he   [b]Or but when they were fully awake   [c]Or tents
[d]Other ancient authorities read my Beloved

NIV	NRSV
to themselves, and told no one at that time what they had seen.	listen to him!" [36]When the voice had spoken, Jesus was found alone. And they kept silent and in those days told no one any of the things they had seen.

COMMENTARY

Luke's account of the transfiguration is one of the most elusive and evocative scenes in the Gospel. Interpreters are far from a consensus as to its historical roots. Does the transfiguration report a mysterious event or a vision during the ministry of Jesus? Is it a post-resurrection appearance that has been placed back in the ministry? Or is it entirely the creation of the early church to affirm the church's confession of Jesus as the exalted Lord? Whatever the historical origins of this account, we are on safe ground with two observations that can serve as the starting point for our study of these verses: (1) Luke depends on Mark's account of the transfiguration (9:2-10), and (2) Luke has composed his account of the event with considerable freedom, using images and terms that link this event with other scenes in Luke's account of Jesus' ministry.

The transfiguration scene is actually composed of the following elements: (1) Jesus' withdrawal to the mountain to pray with the three disciples (v. 28), (2) the transfiguration (v. 29), (3) the appearance of Moses and Elijah (vv. 30-33a), (4) Peter's response (v. 33b), (5) the voice from the cloud (vv. 34-35), and (6) the disciples' response. The structure of the scene reveals, therefore, that it moves between revelatory disclosures and responses from the disciples. In this respect, it continues the pattern of this part of the Gospel, where questions have been raised regarding Jesus' identity, answers are offered, and the disciples have been sent out on mission and taught about the meaning of discipleship. The transfiguration, therefore, clarifies Jesus' identity—especially his divine sonship—foreshadows his exaltation to heaven, and continues the training of Jesus' disciples.

Luke's hand is evident in each of the elements of this scene listed above. In the introduction, Luke follows Mark in noting that after some days Jesus took the three disciples and went up on a mountain. As usual, however, the points at which Luke diverges from Mark are revealing. For reasons that are not clear, Luke has changed Mark's interval of six days from Peter's confession to eight days, perhaps as a way of saying "a week later." Luke also lists the names of the disciples in a different order: Peter, John, and James. This group of three disciples has a special role in Mark as the group of disciples who witness the "secret epiphanies" of Jesus: the raising of Jairus's daughter, the transfiguration of Jesus, and Jesus' prayer at Gethsemane. Luke does not mention the special role of these three at Gethsemane and does not single them out in any scenes other than those he derives from Mark. By naming John before James (as in Luke 8:51 also), Luke places Peter and John together, foreshadowing the role of Peter and John later in Luke (22:8) and in Acts (3:1-10; 4:1-22; 8:14-25). Luke has also explained that Jesus' withdrawal to the mountain was for the purpose of prayer. Just as the voice from heaven after Jesus' baptism occurred while Jesus was praying, so also now the transfiguration and the voice from the cloud occur in the context of prayer. The location of the mountain is not given anywhere in the Gospels. Some have thought that it was a part of Mt. Hermon, near Caesarea Philippi, since the transfiguration occurs shortly after Peter's confession there in Mark. On the other hand, since the time of Origen, the mountain has been identified as Mt. Tabor, near Nazareth, but the significance of the location may actually lie more in its parallel with the experience of Moses and Elijah on Mt. Sinai and Mt. Horeb.

The transfiguration itself is narrated briefly. Luke omits Mark's suggestion of a metamorphosis, saying instead that "the appearance of his face changed" while he was praying, and his clothing became "dazzling white" (v. 29). In this way, Luke underscores the power of prayer to mediate the presence of God. Like Moses, who was so radiant when he descended from Mt. Sinai that the Israelites could not look at him, Jesus' appearance confirmed his presence with God. In this context, however, the transfiguration may also be understood as a further disclosure of Jesus' divinity as God's Son, or as a foreshadowing of his resurrection and ascension. The two men who appeared to the disciples at Jesus' ascension were also clad in white robes (Acts 1:10).

Similarly, two men appear talking with Jesus: Moses and Elijah. Although the point has been debated, these two may represent the "Law and the prophets." The two may also have christological significance in that Jesus has demonstrated his mastery over the sea and fed the multitude in the wilderness (fulfilling the pattern of Moses at the exodus) and has multiplied loaves, cleansed lepers, and raised the dead (fulfilling the prophetic works of Elijah and Elisha). Moses and Elijah appear in glory, and later the disciples see Jesus' glory (vv. 31-32). Luke's addition of these two references to glory to Mark's account, which has none, shows that the transfiguration is also a foreshadowing of Jesus' return in glory, fulfilling Jesus' saying in Luke 9:26 (cf. 21:27). The resurrection and ascension, however, are also characterized by Luke as Jesus' entering "into his glory" (24:26; cf. 2 Pet 1:17). Significantly, Moses and Elijah talk with Jesus about "his exodus," which he would fulfill in Jerusalem. Again, events in Jesus' life are interpreted by alluding to events in the history of God's redemption of Israel. The transfiguration, therefore, also serves to confirm the last part of Jesus' passion prediction. The story will not end with Jesus' death; on the third day he will be raised and "enter into his glory."

Peter and the others have been sleeping while Jesus prayed, but rouse themselves in time to witness Jesus' glory, the two speaking with Jesus, and their departure from him. Here sleep functions as the faithless counterpart to watching and praying. At Gethsemane, Jesus will rebuke the disciples: "Why are you sleeping? Get up and pray that you may not come into the time of trial" (22:46).

When Moses and Elijah had withdrawn, Peter responded, suggesting that they build three booths or dwellings there. The term for these structures suggests that Peter saw in the event the fulfillment of Israel's celebration of the wilderness wandering at the Feast of Booths, or Tabernacles, each year.

Again, however, Peter has only partially grasped the significance of the event. He wants to freeze the moment and commemorate the place, but faithfulness will require following Jesus to the cross, not commemorating the place of the transfiguration, which—fittingly—is not named in any of the Gospels.

Clouds also serve in Luke and Acts as in other biblical accounts to manifest and conceal the presence of God (Exod 16:10; 19:9; 24:15-18; 33:9-11). Daniel foresees that the Son of Man will come to the Ancient of Days with the clouds of heaven (Dan 7:13). So, too, Jesus would be taken up in a cloud (Acts 1:9) and return on the clouds (Luke 21:27; cf. 1 Thess 4:17; Rev 1:7; 14:14).

As at Mt. Sinai, a cloud overshadowed them, and God spoke from the cloud (Exod 19:16-20). The voice from the cloud speaks the climactic affirmation of Jesus' identity in this section of the Gospel: "This is my Son, my Chosen; listen to him!" The pronouncement echoes two verses from the OT. Psalm 2:7, "You are my son;/ today I have begotten you," was also echoed at the baptism of Jesus (3:22). Isaiah 42:1, which is one of the servant songs, reads, "Here is my servant, whom I uphold,/ my chosen, in whom my soul delights;/ I have put my spirit upon him;/ he will bring forth justice to the nations." Earlier, at the baptism of Jesus, the voice from heaven had spoken to Jesus alone: "You are my Son, the Beloved; with you I am well pleased" (3:22). Now, the divine voice pronounces the fullest answer to the question of Jesus' identity to this point in the Gospel. Jesus is both the unique son and the chosen Servant in whom God delighted and through whom God would bring salvation to the nations.

The injunction to hear Jesus follows immediately upon Jesus' first passion prediction and his teachings on discipleship. In context, therefore, the injunction endorses both Jesus' interpretation of his death and resurrection and his teachings on discipleship. The command to listen to Jesus may also be related to the role of Moses and Elijah in this scene, because immediately after the voice from the cloud Luke reports that "Jesus was found alone." Moses and Elijah have departed, suggesting perhaps that Jesus has superseded the Law and the prophets. Now the command is "Listen to *him!*"

According to Mark Jesus commanded the disciples to tell no one what they had seen, but in Luke the disciples keep silent about the transfiguration without having to be told. Their silence "in those days" adds a further suggestion that the transfiguration is a proleptic event. It foreshadows Jesus' "exodus," his ascension. It confirms Jesus' forecast of both his death and his resurrection in Jerusalem, so its full meaning would not be apparent until after those events had come to pass.

REFLECTIONS

The account of the transfiguration records the kind of experience that only a privileged few ever had in the entire history of Israel and the early church. Mystics and saints have lived lives of disciplined piety in hopes of attaining such a beatific vision. Others among us—ordinary mortals—have had experiences we could not explain or moments in which we thought we felt God's presence. Who can explain how the divine is present in everyday experience?

Here is a story, though, of the transfiguration of Jesus, the appearance of Moses and Elijah, and an audible voice from a cloud. At times along the way, the future may come clear to us, or we may stop momentarily to survey the distance already traveled and the goal ahead, like a hiker in the woods who climbs a tree to get a clear fix on the peak that lies ahead. There are times for retreat for prayer, meditation, and rest, when the shape of the whole may become clear to us. We may also find that in the midst of the struggle, at a bedside or a graveside, the meaning of the gospel and the nature of God become clear to us in ways that transcend ordinary experience. In the throes of a hard fight for justice, we may discover a purpose or a calling that casts a radiant light over the rest of our lives.

In the transfiguration we, like the disciples, witness such a moment in Jesus' life. The transfiguration is like a composite of the whole Gospel tradition. In one scene we hear echoes of the baptism of Jesus, Jesus' passion predictions, Jesus' fulfillment of the Law and prophets, the death and resurrection of Jesus, and his ascension and future coming. The voice from the cloud, moreover, serves only to underscore the importance of what was happening throughout the ministry of Jesus: The divine voice affirms Jesus' identity as God's Son and instructs the disciples to heed Jesus' teachings. If God were to say nine words to us, what would they be? "This is my Son, the Chosen One; hear Him!" From his baptism to his death, Jesus' experience summed up the whole and allowed him and us to see his path clearly.

The dangers of such experiences, perhaps because they are so rare, are that we may either fail to learn from them as we ought, or we may want to make them the norm and withdraw from the day-to-day struggle that fills most of life. Surprisingly, the transfiguration seems to have little impact on the three disciples. They still do not understand what Jesus told them about his death and resurrection. Peter still denies Jesus, and the others look for an earthly kingdom—a restoration of the kingdom of Israel. Neither do the three refer to this experience in the preaching early in Acts. The Gospel of John does not contain an account of the transfiguration, and the brief reference to it in 2 Pet 1:17-18 is of dubious authorship. The implication, therefore, is that the disciples were not transformed by this "mountaintop" experience.

The disciples wanted to build booths and stay on the mountaintop, but they could not stop time or live on in the radiance of that moment. Discipleship involves following, going on. As much as they were awed by what they had seen, they were not yet ready to be witnesses to Jesus. Only later, after further following, the grief of the cross and the joy of the resurrection, and the coming of the Holy Spirit would they be ready to speak their witness to what God had done in Jesus. Faithfulness is not achieved by freezing a moment but by following on in confidence that God is leading and that what lies ahead is even greater than what we have already experienced.

So what do we say about the quest for visions and revelations in our own time? The transfiguration emphasizes that God has been revealed through Jesus and that the essence of

Jesus' identity and work cannot be understood apart from the cross and resurrection. Only in their light do we ever understand the character of God or the significance of Jesus. At best, therefore, dreams, epiphanies, and visions can give new meaning to the whole of our experience, making the goal clear in the midst of the journey; but they also point us back to the tasks and struggles that give our lives purpose. The view from the overlook may be majestic, but the road beckons, and there will be other vistas and other transforming experiences ahead.

Luke 9:37-43*a*, The Epileptic Boy

NIV

³⁷The next day, when they came down from the mountain, a large crowd met him. ³⁸A man in the crowd called out, "Teacher, I beg you to look at my son, for he is my only child. ³⁹A spirit seizes him and he suddenly screams; it throws him into convulsions so that he foams at the mouth. It scarcely ever leaves him and is destroying him. ⁴⁰I begged your disciples to drive it out, but they could not."

⁴¹"O unbelieving and perverse generation," Jesus replied, "how long shall I stay with you and put up with you? Bring your son here."

⁴²Even while the boy was coming, the demon threw him to the ground in a convulsion. But Jesus rebuked the evil*a* spirit, healed the boy and gave him back to his father. ⁴³And they were all amazed at the greatness of God.

a42 Greek unclean

NRSV

37On the next day, when they had come down from the mountain, a great crowd met him. ³⁸Just then a man from the crowd shouted, "Teacher, I beg you to look at my son; he is my only child. ³⁹Suddenly a spirit seizes him, and all at once he*a* shrieks. It convulses him until he foams at the mouth; it mauls him and will scarcely leave him. ⁴⁰I begged your disciples to cast it out, but they could not." ⁴¹Jesus answered, "You faithless and perverse generation, how much longer must I be with you and bear with you? Bring your son here." ⁴²While he was coming, the demon dashed him to the ground in convulsions. But Jesus rebuked the unclean spirit, healed the boy, and gave him back to his father. ⁴³And all were astounded at the greatness of God.

a Or it

COMMENTARY

No better counterpoint to the transfiguration could be found than the healing of the epileptic boy. Luke again follows the sequence in Mark (9:14-29) but reports it in half as many verses. Without changing the basic structure of the story, Luke omits whole sections of Mark's account: the conversation between Jesus and the disciples as they descend from the mountain, Jesus' initial conversation with the crowd, Mark's extended description of the boy's symptoms, Jesus' second conversation with the father, details of the exorcism, and Jesus' private conversation with the disciples.

In Luke's abbreviated account, v. 37 serves as a transition from the mountain scene to the public

exorcism. As in the healing of the centurion's son and the raising of the only son of the widow of Nain (7:1-17), a great crowd is present. On the mountaintop, God affirmed his Son; now a troubled father asks for help for his only son. The son is the silent victim throughout the story. He never speaks, cannot help himself, and depends on his father's intercession for help. His symptoms are convulsions and foaming at the mouth. Even the disciples, who earlier had cured diseases (9:6), could not help the boy.

Jesus' response is a judgment on this "faithless and perverse generation," which reminds the reader of earlier declarations that God's Son would be rejected by the very people he had been sent to save. The rising conflict can be traced in Jesus' escalating condemnations and laments over "this generation" (see 7:31; 11:29-32, 50-51; 16:8; 17:25; 21:32). Lurking in the background and providing a tragic resonance to Jesus' words is Moses' lament over the faithlessness of Israel (Deut 32:4-6). Earlier Jesus had asked, "To what then will I compare the people of this generation?" (7:31). The echo from the Song of Moses provides a deeply tragic answer to that earlier question.

As in other exorcism accounts in Luke, the power of the demon is demonstrated in a final violent convulsion before submitting to Jesus' power (cf. 4:35). This time the demon does not call out Jesus' identity, as in earlier exorcisms (4:34, 41; 9:28), because now Jesus' identity has been confessed by the disciples and declared by the voice from heaven. Similarly, the response of the crowd is not a question (4:36; 8:25) but praise to God for Jesus' mighty act (cf. 5:25-26; 7:16; 24:53).

REFLECTIONS

One of the puzzling facets of this brief story is the exasperation and anger evident in Jesus' pronouncement in v. 41. It will not do to explain it as a Markan element that is out of place in Luke. The reader may fill the gap in the narrative at this point in various ways. Is Jesus angry with the disciples for their not being able to do anything for the boy, or is he angry at the crowd or at the demon's power over the boy? The repetition of "this generation" sayings in Luke keeps reminding the reader that Jesus will soon be rejected and killed.

In this section of the Gospel, moreover, Luke portrays the disciples in a very poor light. Although the disciples are successful when Jesus sends them out on mission, and although Peter confesses that Jesus is the Christ, they are not yet ready to be witnesses. Jesus orders them to tell no one about him; they don't understand the transfiguration experience; they are not able to help the boy with a demon; and shortly John will try to stop someone who is casting out demons in Jesus' name. The failures of the disciples at this point set the stage for the teachings of Jesus, which will fill the next section of the Gospel. Jesus may lament the faithlessness of "this generation," but he continues to bear with the disciples and eventually dies for all, even those who rejected him.

This brief story also repeats the pattern of blessing that was characteristic of Jesus. He takes what is brought or given to him, blesses it, and gives it back. Jesus restored the leper (5:12-14), the paralytic 5:17-26), and the man with the withered hand (6:6-11). He touched the bier, raised the widow of Nain's son, and "gave him to his mother" (7:15). He took loaves, blessed them, and gave them back (9:16), and now he gives the boy back to his father (9:42). If blessing involves giving back, then faith is demonstrated in what we give to the Lord: "Give, and it will be given to you. A good measure, pressed down, shaken together, running over, will be put into your lap; for the measure you give will be the measure you get back" (6:38). Luke's grasp of this principle explains why the verb "to give" (ἀποδίδωμι apodidōmi) occurs sixty times in Luke—more often than in any other book of the NT except the Gospel of John.

Luke 9:43b-45, The Second Announcement of Jesus' Death

NIV	NRSV
While everyone was marveling at all that Jesus did, he said to his disciples, [44]"Listen carefully to what I am about to tell you: The Son of Man is	While everyone was amazed at all that he was doing, he said to his disciples, [44]"Let these words sink into your ears: The Son of Man is going to

NIV

going to be betrayed into the hands of men." ⁴⁵But they did not understand what this meant. It was hidden from them, so that they did not grasp it, and they were afraid to ask him about it.

NRSV

be betrayed into human hands." ⁴⁵But they did not understand this saying; its meaning was concealed from them, so that they could not perceive it. And they were afraid to ask him about this saying.

COMMENTARY

Sharp juxtapositions lend pathos and power to Luke's brief account of Jesus' second passion prediction. Following immediately after Jesus' mighty work in exorcising the demon in the previous scene, Jesus announces that he will be handed over to men. The crowd praises God for what Jesus has done, but soon enough crowds will call out for Jesus' death. Similarly, throughout this section, the more clearly Jesus' identity is made known, the more the disciples reveal their inability to grasp who he is or what it means to follow him. Earlier in the chapter the three failed to understand the transfiguration, then the disciples could not heal the boy with a demon, and now they do not understand Jesus' prediction. Its meaning was hidden from them, and they were afraid to ask about it. Although Luke typically abbreviates material he takes over from Mark, and here abbreviates the passion prediction (cf. Mark 9:30-32), Luke adds a saying about the gravity of understanding the passion prediction (v. 44a) and expands the report of the disciples' inability to understand (v. 45). By shortening the passion prediction, Luke focuses on Jesus' being handed over and omits any explicit reference to Jesus' death and resurrection. The verb translated to "be handed over" (παραδίδωμι *paradidōmi*) was not a part of the first passion prediction (9:22), and has not occurred previously in Jesus' words to the disciples. It is used to characterize Judas's betrayal of Jesus and Jesus' arrest elsewhere in the Gospel tradition, and so would be readily understood by Christian readers. The effect is to create ironic distance. We as readers understand what Jesus has said, though this term has not been used of Jesus' fate earlier in the Gospel, but the disciples do not understand. Verse 45 is an aside, or comment by the narrator. Not only do the disciples not understand but also the meaning of Jesus' saying is hidden from them—either by God or more likely by Satan (see 8:12; 18:34)—and they are afraid to ask Jesus. Retrospectively, Jesus' exasperation with the disciples as well as the crowd is understandable in light of this verse. Only later will they understand that it was necessary for Jesus to be "handed over" (see 24:7, 20; cf. 24:31, 45).

Luke 9:46-48, Discipleship and Greatness

NIV

⁴⁶An argument started among the disciples as to which of them would be the greatest. ⁴⁷Jesus, knowing their thoughts, took a little child and had him stand beside him. ⁴⁸Then he said to them, "Whoever welcomes this little child in my name welcomes me; and whoever welcomes me welcomes the one who sent me. For he who is least among you all—he is the greatest."

NRSV

46An argument arose among them as to which one of them was the greatest. ⁴⁷But Jesus, aware of their inner thoughts, took a little child and put it by his side, ⁴⁸and said to them, "Whoever welcomes this child in my name welcomes me, and whoever welcomes me welcomes the one who sent me; for the least among all of you is the greatest."

COMMENTARY

Continuing the motif of the failure of the disciples, this scene shows the disciples debating among themselves as to which of them will be the greatest. Their debate underscores their failure to understand Jesus' words about being handed over. Not only do they not understand Jesus' fate, but also they do not understand that as his followers they too will be "handed over" (see 21:12, 16; cf. Acts 8:3; 12:4).

Luke binds this scene to the foregoing by omitting any notice of the passage of time or change of location (cf. Mark 9:33). Luke also characterizes the nature of the dispute among the disciples by calling it an "argument" (or "debate," διαλογισμός *dialogismos*) and repeating the term in the next verses (vv. 46, 47). Indeed, this scene distills into a single event the reversal predicted in the Magnificat (1:51-52). While the disciples "debate" over which of them is the greatest, knowing the thoughts of their hearts, Jesus takes a little child and puts him by his side. The child will be greater than any who argue over their own greatness. The least will be the greatest in God's new order. Debating (διαλογίζομαι *dialogivzomai*) in their hearts" is a trait that Luke assigns to Jesus' opponents, especially the scribes and Pharisees: The people "questioned in their hearts" whether John might be the Messiah (3:15). The Pharisees "questioned" whether Jesus could forgive sins, and Jesus confronts them with the "questions in their hearts" (5:21-22). The scribes and Pharisees disapprove of Jesus' healing of the man with a withered hand on the sabbath, but Jesus knows "what they [are] thinking [τοὺς διαλογισμοὺς αὐτῶν *tous dialogismous autōn*]" (6:8).

Jesus' role, however, will be to reveal "the inner thoughts of many" (2:35; cf. 20:14; 24:38). Indeed, later the disciples will pray to "the one who knows every heart" (see Acts 1:24). The point is clear. By debating among themselves over greatness, the disciples have fallen into the character trait of Jesus' opponents. No stronger censure could be given to the Christian community than to warn it that even its leaders (the disciples) were susceptible to this temptation. In God's realm, however, the child—the least in the community—will be greatest among them. One who receives a child—one who could not bestow any honor or power—receives Jesus, but even more, that one receives the one who sent Jesus. By this succession Jesus cuts the ground from beneath any concern for standing, position, or power among his followers (see 13:30; 18:15-17; 22:24-27; John 13:16, 20).

A rabbinic principle stipulates that "a man's agent is like to himself."[108] The confession of Jesus as one sent by God, which is so important in the Gospel of John, also plays a significant role in Luke (4:18, 43; 10:16). As God's agent, Jesus carried God's authority. But the real scandal for the Christian community in this chain of relationships is Jesus' affirmation that this child is his agent, since the one who receives the child receives Jesus.

108. *M. Berakoth* 5.5.

REFLECTIONS

In the first scene, the disciples' petty quarreling over which of them is the greatest reveals not only that they apparently thought Jesus had come to establish an earthly kingdom in which they would enjoy positions of power but also that they viewed their discipleship as a means of attaining their own aspirations. They had set the agenda for their goals and viewed following Jesus as a convenient or effective means of attaining those goals. Their commitment to Jesus had not changed their underlying aims and ambitions, however. This scene, therefore, demonstrates that discipleship to Jesus means giving up one's own ambitions and taking on in their place the demands of faithfulness to Jesus and aims of the kingdom of God.

Luke 9:49-50, The Unauthorized Exorcist

NIV

NIV

49"Master," said John, "we saw a man driving out demons in your name and we tried to stop him, because he is not one of us."

50"Do not stop him," Jesus said, "for whoever is not against you is for you."

NRSV

49John answered, "Master, we saw someone casting out demons in your name, and we tried to stop him, because he does not follow with us." 50But Jesus said to him, "Do not stop him; for whoever is not against you is for you."

COMMENTARY

The last scene before Jesus turns toward Jerusalem places one of the disciples in a poor light, again establishing the need for further teachings on discipleship. This is the only scene in which the apostle John appears alone in the synoptic Gospels. It is related to the previous scene by catchword linkage—"in my name" (v. 48), "in your name" (v. 49)—and it prepares the reader for the role of James and John in vv. 51-56.

The disciples' concern for position and authority continues. John voices the sentiment that only Jesus' disciples, perhaps only the Twelve, should have the power conferred by Jesus' name. When they saw someone else casting out demons in Jesus' name, John had forbidden him. The irony is that the unauthorized exorcist was doing what recently the disciples had been unable to do (cf. vv. 40-41). Hence, the disciples at this point are unable to cast out demons and are unwilling to allow anyone else to do so.

Later, the disciples would not only cast out demons in Jesus' name (10:17), but in Acts they baptize (3:6; 8:16; 10:48), heal (4:10), teach (4:18; 5:28, 40), and do signs and wonders (4:30) "in the name of Jesus" as well. Hindering is also a significant motif in Acts—so significant that an influential commentary on the book carried as the subtitle "The Early Struggle for an Unhindered Gospel."[109] Taking

his cue from the observation that the last word in the book of Acts is "unhindered" (ἀκωλύτως *akōlytōs*), Frank Stagg interprets the book as a chronicle of the church's effort to surmount the geographical, racial, and political barriers that would have limited the spread of the gospel (see 11:52; 18:16; Acts 8:36; 10:47; 11:17; 28:31).

The issue here is more than just pettiness. Who has the authority to invoke the power of the gospel or act in the Lord's name? The issue can be found in ancient Israel when the unauthorized person prophesied (Num 11:24-30) and would emerge later in Acts (8:14-24; 19:13-16) and in Paul's letters (Phil 1:15-18; 1 Cor 3:5-11).

Jesus' response commands openness and toleration: "Whoever is not against you is for you" (9:50). A parallel saying seems to counsel the opposite: "Whoever is not with me is against me" (11:23), but the two can be reconciled if the former is interpreted as Jesus' counsel for how one should relate to others, and the latter is interpreted as a challenge for each disciple to examine his or her own commitment to Christ. The first welcomes the support of any who will join in; the second warns that only those whose commitment leads them to make a difference are really disciples—"with me." In each case it comes down to the question of who is actually doing the work of the kingdom with Jesus.

109. Frank Stagg, *The Book of Acts: The Early Struggle for an Unhindered Gospel* (Nashville: Broadman, 1955).

REFLECTIONS

John, and we may assume the other disciples as well, looked on relationship to Jesus as one that conferred special privileges and powers. Brokering was the order of the day. Those in the service of a king or governor shared in the sovereign's power. Others had no right to claim the privileges of their exclusive relationship. Jesus, however, conferred no special privileges on his hometown, his family, or his disciples. He was on the way to Jerusalem—to die there—and all that mattered was faithfulness to God's plan for saving sinners, showing mercy, establishing peace and justice, vanquishing the rich, and lifting up the poor. It matters not whether that work is done by insiders or outsiders. Indeed, one's relationship to the kingdom is determined by what one does, not by the privileges of one's position. The temptation is always there, however, for the church to turn from relationships based on faithfulness to exclusive circles based on privilege.

THE JOURNEY TO JERUSALEM

OVERVIEW

In verse 51 Luke reports that Jesus "set his face to go to Jerusalem." This geographical notice marks off the long section that follows, so that from this point until Jesus' arrival at Jerusalem in 19:28 Jesus is on the way, traveling to his "exodus" (see 9:31), the cross and the resurrection. Coincident with this geographical notice, Luke departs from the sequence of scenes in Mark and introduces a lengthy collection of parables, sayings, meal scenes, controversies, and warnings drawn from Q and from Luke's own sources. Having followed Mark (4:1–9:40) since Luke 8:4, Luke leaves Mark aside until Luke 18:15 and then takes up Mark again at Mark 10:13, omitting Mark 9:41–10:12.

Like Mark, Luke's account of Jesus' ministry includes only one journey from Galilee to Jerusalem, where Jesus dies a week later. By expanding the journey into a major section of the Gospel, Luke creates a setting for the Q materials that are not found in Mark. Interpreters have agonized over the anomalies of this central section of the Gospel. Why does Luke introduce the journey motif but make so few references to Jesus' traveling (9:52, 57; 10:38; 13:22; 14:25; 17:11; 18:31, 35)? Why does he give such vague references to Jesus' progress toward Jerusalem: "a village of the Samaritans" (9:52), "a certain village" (10:38), "one town and village after another" (13:22), "the region between Samaria and Galilee" (17:11), "Jericho" (18:35; 19:1), "near Jerusalem" (19:11)? The real difficulty, in addition to the general sparcity of such references, is 17:11, which still locates Jesus—after eight chapters of travel—"between Samaria and Galilee."

Interpreters have also searched for a unifying theme or structure for this section, proposing chiastic structures, lectionary patterns, testamentary forms, structured parable collections, and correspondences with Moses' teaching in Deuteronomy. No consensus has been reached on these matters, however, and since both the formal structure and the thematic coherence of this section are so elusive, we will treat it scene by scene, noting structural and thematic motifs as we go.

LUKE 9:51-56, REJECTION IN SAMARIA

NIV

[51]As the time approached for him to be taken up to heaven, Jesus resolutely set out for Jerusalem. [52]And he sent messengers on ahead, who went into a Samaritan village to get things ready for him; [53]but the people there did not welcome him, because he was heading for Jerusalem. [54]When the disciples James and John saw this, they asked, "Lord, do you want us to call fire

NRSV

[51]When the days drew near for him to be taken up, he set his face to go to Jerusalem. [52]And he sent messengers ahead of him. On their way they entered a village of the Samaritans to make ready for him; [53]but they did not receive him, because his face was set toward Jerusalem. [54]When his disciples James and John saw it, they said, "Lord, do you want us to command fire to

NIV

down from heaven to destroy them*a*?" ⁵⁵But Jesus turned and rebuked them, ⁵⁶and*b* they went to another village.

a54 Some manuscripts them, even as Elijah did   b55,56 Some manuscripts them. And he said, "You do not know what kind of spirit you are of, for the Son of Man did not come to destroy men's lives, but to save them." 56And

NRSV

come down from heaven and consume them?"*a* ⁵⁵But he turned and rebuked them. ⁵⁶Then*b* they went on to another village.

aOther ancient authorities add as Elijah did   bOther ancient authorities read rebuked them, and said, "You do not know what spirit you are of, 56for the Son of Man has not come to destroy the lives of human beings but to save them." Then

COMMENTARY

No sooner has Jesus "set his face to go to Jerusalem" than he meets opposition. As Jesus and his followers start out on their journey, a Samaritan village refuses to receive them. The overtones of this section are set up by its location in the narrative and its allusions to Elijah. In the end, Jesus asserts not only his determination to go to Jerusalem but also the nature of his mission.

Fitzmyer points out that the rejection at the beginning of the travel section corresponds to the rejection at Nazareth at the beginning of Jesus' Galilean ministry (4:16-30).[110] The rejection at the beginning of each of these major sections of the Gospel foreshadows the rejection that lies ahead in Jerusalem.

The Elijah motif serves both to prepare for Jesus' death and ascension and as a foil against which the nature of Jesus' mission can be clarified. The term for the fulfilling of the days of Jesus' ministry in v. 51 is repeated in Acts 2:1, and the reference to Jesus' being taken up echoes not only Acts 1:2, "until the day when he was taken up to heaven," but also the beginning of the account of Elijah's death: "Now when the LORD was about to take Elijah up to heaven by a whirlwind" (2 Kgs 2:1). The term used in v. 51 for Jesus' being "taken up" (ἀνάλημψις *analēmpsis*) is also the noun form of the verb used of Jesus' ascension in Acts 1:11, 22 (ἀναλαμβάνω *analambanō*), suggesting not only Jesus' coming death and resurrection but also the culmination of the story in Jesus' ascension. Just as Elijah set out for Gilgal, so also Jesus sets his face for Jerusalem.

Malachi 3:1 declares that the Lord will send a messenger to prepare the way (see the reference to Elijah in Mal 4:5). The connection can hardly be missed, then, when we are told that Jesus sent

messengers to prepare his way (v. 52). The first reference to Samaria occurs in this scene (cf. 10:33; 17:11, 16), but it foreshadows Philip's work in Samaria in Acts, which results in Peter and John laying hands on the Samaritans. That a Samaritan village should refuse to receive Jewish pilgrims on their way to Jerusalem was not unusual. Later in the first century, a serious incident that led to the removal of Herod Antipas from office began with a massacre of Jewish pilgrims in Samaria.[111] The repetition of "his face was set toward Jerusalem" in v. 53 underscores the importance of this new information.

Just as John erred in hindering the unauthorized exorcist, so now James and John ask Jesus to let them call down fire on the Samaritan village. The request echoes Elijah's answer to the officer sent by the king of Samaria: "If I am a man of God, let fire come down from heaven and consume you and your fifty" (2 Kgs 1:10, 12). Because James and John are called "Sons of Thunder" (Βοανηργές *Boanērges*) in Mark 3:17, it has been suggested either that the nickname was derived from this incident or that the name explains why Luke names these two disciples in this scene. Unfortunately, no connection between this scene and the name given to James and John by Jesus can be verified.

Jesus was not Elijah *redivivus*, however, as the earlier declarations of his identity have made clear, and his mission was not to destroy but to save and to reconcile. Textual variants offer early interpretations of this scene. Some manuscripts add "as Elijah did" at the end of v. 54. Some manuscripts also give words to Jesus' rebuke: "You do not know what spirit

---

110. Joseph A. Fitzmyer, *The Gospel According to Luke (I–IX)*, AB 28 (Garden City, N.Y.: Doubleday, 1981) 827.

111. See Josephus *Antiquities* 20.106-136.

you are of, for the Son of Man has not come to destroy the lives of human beings but to save them."

If not originally part of Luke, these interpretations are not alien to it.

REFLECTIONS

This episode allows us to study the temptation to use violence to achieve right. Does insult entitle one to do injury? Does being right or having a holy cause justify the use of force or violence? Elijah had called down fire on the Samaritans; could not Jesus' followers do the same? Misunderstanding the identity of the one they followed, the disciples mistakenly thought they could achieve his ends by violence. How often have those who claimed to be following Christ repeated the mistake of these early disciples? They had yet to learn that violence begets violence, and that Jesus had come to break the cycle of violence by dying and forgiving rather than by killing and exacting vengeance.

LUKE 9:57-62, THE FAILURE OF THREE WOULD-BE FOLLOWERS

NIV

[57]As they were walking along the road, a man said to him, "I will follow you wherever you go." [58]Jesus replied, "Foxes have holes and birds of the air have nests, but the Son of Man has no place to lay his head."

[59]He said to another man, "Follow me."

But the man replied, "Lord, first let me go and bury my father."

[60]Jesus said to him, "Let the dead bury their own dead, but you go and proclaim the kingdom of God."

[61]Still another said, "I will follow you, Lord; but first let me go back and say good-by to my family."

[62]Jesus replied, "No one who puts his hand to the plow and looks back is fit for service in the kingdom of God."

NRSV

57As they were going along the road, someone said to him, "I will follow you wherever you go." [58]And Jesus said to him, "Foxes have holes, and birds of the air have nests; but the Son of Man has nowhere to lay his head." [59]To another he said, "Follow me." But he said, "Lord, first let me go and bury my father." [60]But Jesus[a] said to him, "Let the dead bury their own dead; but as for you, go and proclaim the kingdom of God." [61]Another said, "I will follow you, Lord; but let me first say farewell to those at my home." [62]Jesus said to him, "No one who puts a hand to the plow and looks back is fit for the kingdom of God."

a Gk *he*

COMMENTARY

Luke's introduction to the journey to Jerusalem continues with a warning of the radical demands of discipleship. The responses of three would-be followers of Jesus show that they have not understood the demands of discipleship and are not prepared to give it the priority that Jesus demands.

The first two sayings are paralleled in Matt 8:19-22. Luke adds a third related saying that is not found elsewhere in the Gospel traditions.

Together the three function to set the call to discipleship above every other duty, whether care for self, care for the dead, or care for family. So stringent is the demand, however, especially in the second saying, that one is tempted to place these sayings in the category of Semitic hyperboles that dramatize a point but are not meant to be taken literally: "If your right eye causes you to sin, tear it out and throw it away" (Matt 5:29 NRSV).

9:57-58. The three would-be followers are similar but not identical cases. The first came with the lofty, enthusiastic promise, "I will follow you wherever you go." The promise is made "as they were going along the road," however, a setting that reminds the alert reader of the journey's tragic destination. Jesus had told his followers that he would be rejected and despised (9:22, 44). He had been in Samaria, and the people there would not receive him (9:53). Would this enthusiastic volunteer really follow him in the face of such rejection?

The first saying establishes two relationships, one explicitly and one implicitly. Explicitly, it contrasts the security of the Son of Man with the condition of animals at the mercy of nature. Even foxes have holes and birds have nests, but the Son of Man has no such home. Implicitly, the saying works on the assumption that the follower will be like the one who is followed: If the Son of Man has no place to lay his head, then neither will those who follow him. Does the would-be follower realize what he has promised?

9:59-60. Jesus then calls another to follow him. This would-be follower asks for permission to "go and bury my father." The duty to bury the dead was binding on all devout Jews. In Jewish folklore, for example, Tobit's piety is demonstrated by his faithfulness in burying the dead (Tob 1:16-20), and his son Tobias takes seriously his duty as an only son to bury his father and mother (Tob 4:3; 6:15). From the sparse context it is not clear whether the father has already died. The one whom Jesus called may have been pledging to follow Jesus as soon as possible. First, however, came the responsibility to care for one's parents for the rest of their lives.

Jesus' response is harsh. It demands that the priority of service to the kingdom be set above every other priority. The saying should probably be understood to mean "Let the spiritually dead bury the physically dead." Others, who had not come alive to the sovereign rule of God, could discharge the duty of burying the dead. Again the saying assumes implicit relationships. Those who have not responded to the call to the kingdom are like the dead, thus let the dead bury the dead. Those who have responded to the call to discipleship are no longer dead. Their concern should be with life and the living: "Go and proclaim the kingdom of God" (9:60).

9:61-62. The third example is similar at points to each of the first two. The third would-be disciple offers to follow Jesus (as did the first) but asks to bid farewell to his family first (a milder version of the request made by the second). Both Jesus' call, "Follow me," and the disciple's response echo 1 Kgs 19:19-21, which records Elijah's call to Elisha. Elisha, who was plowing at the time, responded, "Let me kiss my father and mother, and then I will follow you" (1 Kgs 19:20). The Elijah motif links this scene with earlier scenes with allusions to the expectation of the coming of one like Elijah, most recently 9:28-36 and 9:52-56. Unlike Elijah, however, Jesus will not let the would-be disciple turn aside from the call to follow him even to bid farewell to his family. If one looks back while plowing, the furrow will be crooked. Therefore, building on this element of the story of the call of Elisha, Jesus emphasizes again the unconditional demand of the call to discipleship. On the way to the cross there is no place for rash promises or misunderstandings regarding the cost of following Jesus.

REFLECTIONS

This is the final of four scenes, after Jesus foretells his death for a second time (9:44), that illustrate the disciples' lack of understanding: their quarrel over which of them is the greatest (9:46-48); John's rebuke of the unauthorized exorcist (9:49-50); James and John's offer to call down fire on the Samaritan village (9:52-56); and the false starts of three would-be disciples (9:57-62). Taken together, these four scenes offer a showcase of potential dangers for aspiring disciples. Each scene of discipleship failure also illustrates the connection between the disciples' concept of Jesus and the resulting understanding of discipleship. Every one of us is susceptible to these obstacles to discipleship, but perhaps we can learn from the failures of others. The final scene, which depicts the errors of would-be disciples who do not understand that Jesus is on the road leading to the cross in Jerusalem, challenges us with the radical demands of discipleship. Because faithfulness would require Jesus to lay down his life, the call to discipleship to Jesus inevitably means unconditional commitment to the redemptive work of God for which Jesus gave his life. The disciple will be like the Lord. Therefore, one should not rush into discipleship with glib promises. On the contrary, the radical demands of discipleship require that every potential disciple consider the cost, give Jesus the highest priority in one's life, and, having committed oneself to discipleship, move ahead without looking back.

LUKE 10:1-16, THE COMMISSIONING OF THE SEVENTY(-TWO)

NIV

10 After this the Lord appointed seventy-two[a] others and sent them two by two ahead of him to every town and place where he was about to go. [2]He told them, "The harvest is plentiful, but the workers are few. Ask the Lord of the harvest, therefore, to send out workers into his harvest field. [3]Go! I am sending you out like lambs among wolves. [4]Do not take a purse or bag or sandals; and do not greet anyone on the road.

[5]"When you enter a house, first say, 'Peace to this house.' [6]If a man of peace is there, your peace will rest on him; if not, it will return to you. [7]Stay in that house, eating and drinking whatever they give you, for the worker deserves his wages. Do not move around from house to house.

[8]"When you enter a town and are welcomed, eat what is set before you. [9]Heal the sick who are there and tell them, 'The kingdom of God is near you.' [10]But when you enter a town and are not welcomed, go into its streets and say, [11]'Even the dust of your town that sticks to our feet we wipe off against you. Yet be sure of this: The kingdom of God is near.' [12]I tell you, it will be more bearable on that day for Sodom than for that town.

[13]"Woe to you, Korazin! Woe to you, Bethsaida! For if the miracles that were performed in you had been performed in Tyre and Sidon, they would have repented long ago, sitting in sackcloth and ashes. [14]But it will be more bearable for Tyre and Sidon at the judgment than for you. [15]And you, Capernaum, will you be lifted up to the skies? No, you will go down to the depths.[b]

[16]"He who listens to you listens to me; he who rejects you rejects me; but he who rejects me rejects him who sent me."

[a]1 Some manuscripts *seventy*; also in verse 17
[b]15 Greek *Hades*

NRSV

10 After this the Lord appointed seventy[a] others and sent them on ahead of him in pairs to every town and place where he himself intended to go. [2]He said to them, "The harvest is plentiful, but the laborers are few; therefore ask the Lord of the harvest to send out laborers into his harvest. [3]Go on your way. See, I am sending you out like lambs into the midst of wolves. [4]Carry no purse, no bag, no sandals; and greet no one on the road. [5]Whatever house you enter, first say, 'Peace to this house!' [6]And if anyone is there who shares in peace, your peace will rest on that person; but if not, it will return to you. [7]Remain in the same house, eating and drinking whatever they provide, for the laborer deserves to be paid. Do not move about from house to house. [8]Whenever you enter a town and its people welcome you, eat what is set before you; [9]cure the sick who are there, and say to them, 'The kingdom of God has come near to you.'[b] [10]But whenever you enter a town and they do not welcome you, go out into its streets and say, [11]'Even the dust of your town that clings to our feet, we wipe off in protest against you. Yet know this: the kingdom of God has come near.'[c] [12]I tell you, on that day it will be more tolerable for Sodom than for that town.

[13]"Woe to you, Chorazin! Woe to you, Bethsaida! For if the deeds of power done in you had been done in Tyre and Sidon, they would have repented long ago, sitting in sackcloth and ashes. [14]But at the judgment it will be more tolerable for Tyre and Sidon than for you. [15]And you, Capernaum,

will you be exalted to heaven?

No, you will be brought down to Hades.

[16]"Whoever listens to you listens to me, and whoever rejects you rejects me, and whoever rejects me rejects the one who sent me."

[a]Other ancient authorities read *seventy-two*   [b]Or *is at hand for you*   [c]Or *is at hand*

COMMENTARY

Although the failures of the three would-be disciples in the previous scene might lead the reader to wonder how anyone could become a disciple, this scene records Jesus' commissioning of seventy (or seventy-two). The material is a doublet of the commissioning of the Twelve in 9:1-6 and has parallels in Matt 9:37-38; 10:7-16; and Mark 6:7-13. The commissioning of this larger group of followers, which is not recorded elsewhere in the Gospel records, conveys a sense of growth and movement. As Jesus turns toward Jerusalem, he is still preaching the kingdom of God, but now the kingdom is being preached not just by Jesus and the Twelve. In that sense, this commissioning foreshadows the mission of the early church and establishes the pattern for those who are sent out.

10:1. The manuscript tradition is evenly balanced between those that read "seventy"[112] and those that read "seventy-two."[113] Perhaps more important than resolving the manuscript evidence is the question of the significance of the number. Is it merely a round number for a large group? The significance of the number can probably be traced to the list of nations in Genesis 10, where the Hebrew text lists seventy nations and the Septuagint lists seventy-two. Alternatively, the commissioning may recall Moses' appointment of seventy elders to help him (Exod 24:1; Num 11:16, 24). The *Letter of Aristeas* records that seventy-two translators, six from each of the tribes, completed the translation of the Septuagint in seventy-two days.[114] The most likely interpretation, however, is that the number is related to the biblical number of the nations (Genesis 10), so that the commissioning foreshadows the mission of the church to the nations (see Luke 24:47).

The pattern of sending the disciples out by twos occurs in Mark 6:7 but not in the sending out of the Twelve earlier in Luke (9:1-6). According to the Mosaic Law (Deut 19:15), two witnesses were required for a testimony to be credible. For this reason, and probably because of the rigors of travel in antiquity, the practice of apostles working in pairs is evident in Acts—Peter and John (8:14),

Paul and Barnabas (11:30; 13:1), Barnabas and Mark (15:39), Paul and Silas (15:40). The pattern is not uniform, however, since various persons also work alone (Philip, 8:5, 26; Peter, 10:1-48).

Echoing the reference in Luke 9:52, the seventy(-two) are sent "ahead of him" (lit., "before his face"). Their work, therefore, is to prepare the way for Jesus in each of the villages. In that sense they are forerunners, evangelists who perpetuate the role of John the Baptist, who was beheaded by Herod.

10:2-16. These verses contain the commissioning of these messengers. Actually, although there is no break in the discourse, vv. 2-11 give directions to those who are about to be sent out, v. 12 pronounces a warning on any city that will not accept them, and vv. 13-16 declare woes on Chorazin, Bethsaida, and Capernaum, for which there is a verbatim parallel in Matt 11:20-23a. The situation is more complicated, however, because Luke 10:12 parallels the allusion to Sodom in Matt 10:15, which is repeated in Matt 11:23-24; and Luke 10:16, which concludes the discourse, also concludes the commission in Matt 10:40 (cf. John 13:20). The entire discourse, therefore, appears to have been compiled from individual sayings that are gathered here by catchword linkage and common themes.

10:2-11. Just as the disciples are sent out in pairs, so also the commissioning discourse is structured in paired sayings: two proverbs (vv. 2-3), anticipation of a positive response (vv. 5-9) and a negative response (vv. 10-11), instructions for entering a house (vv. 5-7), instructions for entering a town (vv. 8-9), and the repetition of the message that the kingdom of God has come near (vv. 9, 11).

The prophets of the OT used harvest as a metaphor for eschatological judgment and for the gathering of Israel in the last times (Joel 3:13; Mic 4:11-13). In every culture, harvest season is a time of great urgency. The common day laborer would understand the exhortation to plead with the landowner to bring in more laborers to help with the harvest. In the context of the parable of the sower and the seed earlier (8:4-8), it is now time to gather in the harvest from the soil that has produced a hundredfold.

The wolf was the natural predator of the lamb

112. E.g., ℵ, A, C, L, W, X, Θ, Ψ, $f^{1,13}$.
113. E.g., 𝔓^{75}, B, D, 0181.
114. See *Letter of Aristeas* 39, 50, 307.

(Isa 11:6; 65:25). The metaphor warns the disciples of the opposition they will encounter. Unlike Matthew (10:16), Luke does not give any instruction as to how the disciples should prepare for or respond to the opposition they will encounter, unless the instructions that follow are understood as following from this warning. The instructions to the disciples about what to take parallels the instructions given to the Twelve earlier (9:3-5), but little is actually repeated. The Twelve had been instructed to take nothing—no staff, bag, bread, money, or extra tunic (9:3). The seventy(-two) are told to carry no purse, bag, or sandals and to greet no one along the way. The only common term is the prohibition of carrying a traveler's bag (cf. 22:35-37). The instruction not to greet anyone underscores the need for urgency and singleness of purpose (2 Kgs 4:29; Ps 129:6-8).

The instructions for how the disciples should receive hospitality are greatly expanded from 9:4, which simply commanded that they stay wherever they were received. Here the instruction has two parts, with commentary on each: (1) say, "Peace to this house," and (2) remain in the house where you are received. The pronouncement of peace was a common greeting (1 Sam 25:5-6), but later, after the resurrection, Jesus would greet the disciples, saying, "Peace be with you" (24:36). Similarly, Peter, entering the house of Cornelius, a Gentile, says, "You know the message he sent to the people of Israel, preaching peace by Jesus Christ—he is Lord of all" (Acts 10:36). The promise of peace in the infancy narrative is being realized (see 1:79; 2:14, 29; 19:38). Only a "son of peace" can receive the peace conferred by the greeting, however. To be a "son" was to share the character or quality of the parent (see Luke 5:34; 16:8; 20:34, 36; Acts 4:36). The character of the host is determined by whether the host receives the disciples and their message of the kingdom.

It was universally understood that "The laborer deserves to be paid" (1 Tim 5:18), so the disciple should receive the hospitality, food, and drink provided by the host. Implicit in this command is the removal of all social barriers. In the book of Acts, Peter and Paul will be received in Gentile homes and will eat with Gentiles as part of the mission of the church. Later, because such privilege at times led to abuse, Paul refused to accept the support he could have claimed from the Corinthians (1 Cor 9:4-14; cf. *Did.* 11.3-6; 12.1–

13.3). The injunction not to "move about from house to house" may have been intended to prevent the disciples from seeking better quarters or seeking to prolong their stay.

Three instructions are given regarding the conduct of the mission in each village: (1) Eat what is provided, (2) heal the sick (cf. Matt 10:8), and (3) announce the kingdom. The three facets of the mission encompass the creation of community (table fellowship), care of physical needs, and proclamation of the gospel of the kingdom. The disciples, therefore, were charged to continue the three facets of Jesus' work in Galilee.

Following instructions regarding how they should respond to a positive reception, the disciples are told how they should respond to rejection. The act of shaking off dust from their feet is here given even greater consequence than in 9:5. The disciples were told to go out into the broad streets, street corners, or public squares, shake off the dust from their feet in the traditional act of repudiation, and declare the meaning of their actions. The rejection of their message did nothing to threaten its truth: "The kingdom of God has come near" (v. 11). The repetition of this summary of Jesus' proclamation (see Mark 1:15; Luke 9:2) is just a declaration of the kingdom's eschatological imminence. The disciples declare that the kingdom has come near to those who receive them because of Jesus' works and the disciples' preaching. In their presence, the kingdom has come near.

10:12. This serves as a transition to the second part of this discourse: Jesus' warning to the villages that do not or have not received them. Sodom was the epitome of the wicked, godless city (Gen 19:24-28; Isa 1:9-10). "That day" (Isa 10:20; Jer 30:8; Amos 8:9; Zech 12:3-4) is a reference to "the last days" (Isa 2:2; Jer 23:20; 49:39; Ezek 38:16; Mic 4:1) or "the great and terrible day of the LORD" (Mal 4:5).

10:13-16. Appended to the commissioning of the seventy(-two) in Luke are pronouncements of woes on Chorazin, Bethsaida, and Capernaum. These woes are found in two places in Matthew (10:15 and 11:24), but the duplication is omitted by Luke. The woes are pronouncements of warning, judgment, and lament such as those found in Num 21:29; Isa 10:5; and Jer 13:27, where woes are pronounced on particular cities or regions. Chorazin has often been identified with a town whose ruins lie two and a half miles northwest of Capernaum. Bethsaida is a fishing village (see John 1:44) that lies near where the Jordan flows into the Sea of Galilee. The pronouncement of woe in v. 13 is followed by a double comparison that contrasts the responses of the two towns with the responsiveness of Tyre and Sidon and then compares the judgment coming on each pair of cities. Tyre and Sidon would have been more responsive (see 6:17) than Chorazin and Bethsaida, so the judgment on the latter will be more severe than the judgment on these foreign cities (for condemnations of Tyre and Sidon, see Isa 23:1-18; Ezek 26:1-21; 27:1–28:24). Sackcloth and ashes were traditional signs of mourning or repentance (Esth 4:2-3; Isa 58:5; Dan 9:3; Jonah 3:6).

In the Gospel according to Mark, Capernaum seems to have been the center of Jesus' ministry in Galilee (Mark 1:21; 2:1). From Luke's account, it is clear that Jesus had done mighty works in Capernaum (4:23, 31-41) and that he had returned there on several occasions (cf. 7:1). Although it does not use the woe form, Jesus' pronouncement over Capernaum echoes Isaiah's warning of the downfall of Babylon: "You said in your heart,/ 'I will ascend to heaven;' . . . / But you are brought down to Sheol,/ to the depths of the Pit" (Isa 14:13, 15). In context, these woes are an integral part of the commissioning of the disciples. Following on the instructions for what the disciples are to do when they enter a town,

and what to do when they are rejected, these woes serve to lend further authority to the work of the disciples. If the towns reject them, the towns themselves will be rejected.

The final verse of the commissioning makes this point explicitly but in a more general sense. It confers on the disciples the rights and authorities of a legal agent. See the comments on 9:48, where Jesus indicates that the one who receives him receives the one who sent him. Both sets of sayings develop the principle that the agent carries the authority of the sender, and both develop a chain of three members: the ones whom Jesus sends, Jesus, and the one who sent Jesus.

The motif of hearing plays a significant role in Luke. Hearing means acceptance and obedience. It is related to the Word of God (5:1; 11:28), and those who hear glorify God (7:29). Hearing also requires understanding (8:10) and doing (6:49; 8:21), so one must take care how one hears (8:18). Later in this chapter, Jesus will pronounce a blessing on the disciples because they have heard what prophets and kings desired to hear but did not (10:24).

Similarly, the language of sending and being sent, especially in Jesus' own references to his being sent (Luke 4:18, 43; 9:48), echoes a motif found frequently in the Gospel of John (3:34; 5:36; 6:29).

REFLECTIONS

Luke 10 contains a concentration of sayings that are embarrassing and difficult for the church. The pronouncement of woes on towns and villages is seldom heard from contemporary pulpits, and certainly not from fashionable churches. More revealing, however, is our neglect and discomfort with the commissioning of the seventy(-two). The mission of the church has come to be regarded as something that only a few specially called professionals carry out. One has to be called to be a missioner—one doing the mission of the church. The sending out of the seventy(-two), however, which is peculiar to Luke, reminds us that Jesus sent out not just the Twelve, but perhaps all of his followers. A few churches (such as the Mormons and Jehovah's Witnesses) still send out members on mission, sharing their faith door to door, but most churches have abandoned that practice.

More than ever, therefore, the church must struggle with its understanding of its mission. Having abandoned one traditional form or expression of that mission, has the church abandoned its mission entirely? How does the church articulate its mission today? Can working with and through agencies and institutions substitute for talking with individuals about their response to the gospel? In what ways can the mission of the church be articulated and pursued by the church today? Such questions do not permit easy answers, but the interpretation of these verses for the church is not complete until it leads us to grapple with these issues. The church can neither recreate the itinerary of the earliest days of the Jesus movement in Galilee nor abandon the gospel call to announce the kingdom and devote oneself to kingdom tasks. The expression of the mission of the church in concrete forms and specific activities, however, has changed from generation to generation.

In our own time, the challenges of a shrinking world, ease of travel and communication, multiculturalism, and religious pluralism require us to enter into dialogue regarding what we as American Christians have to offer to people of other cultures and faiths. The development of a world economy and the oppression of Third World countries require that we include in our awareness of the church's mission concerns for the end of economic exploitation of other people, alleviation of disease and hunger, and assurance of basic human rights. It is not that the mission of the church has become unnecessary or impractical, but simply that the changing conditions of the communities in which we live are forcing us to rethink the Gospel's teaching about the mission of those who follow Jesus and to find avenues of obedience that are effective and appropriate for our times as well as faithful to Jesus' teachings.

Jesus' commission to the disciples can serve as a guide for the new models of mission that each generation requires. It contains ten principles. First, it affirms the world's need for the church's mission: "The harvest is plentiful." There is more work to do than laborers to do it. Second, Jesus' commission affirms the importance of prayer in support of the church's mission: "Ask the lord of the harvest." Third, it insists on the active participation of each disciple: "Go on your way." The work of the church is not merely the calling of a select few. Believers can contribute to it in their own way and in the context of their own spiritual journey. Fourth, Jesus' commission warns of the dangers believers will face and provides guidelines: "I am sending you out like lambs into the midst of wolves." By means of this metaphor, Jesus seems to be counseling innocence and sincerity, vulnerability and non-resistance as means of turning aside anger and danger. Fifth, Jesus calls for singularity of purpose: "Greet no one on the road." Sixth, the commission specifies the purpose of the mission: "Say, 'Peace to this house' and 'The kingdom of God has come near to you.' " Disciples declare what God is doing and bring God's peace to whomever receives them. Share table fellowship with whomever receives you. Seventh, the host, not the guest, sets the context for the disciple's witness: "Eat what is set before you." The disciples do not seek to dictate the menu or impose their own cultural background on others. Eighth, Jesus' commission recognizes that the disciples will not always succeed: "[When] they do not welcome you. . . . " Jesus knew that the disciples would meet resistance and rejection some of the time. Ninth, Jesus admonished the disciples to persevere: Shake their dust from your feet. Tenth, and finally, Jesus gives the disciples a word of assurance about the fulfillment of God's redemptive mission: "Know this: the kingdom of God has come near." By principles such as these the church can be guided in every generation. The context, means, and forms of the mission change continually, but its basis in God's redemptive love remains constant.

LUKE 10:17-24, THE RETURN OF THE SEVENTY(-TWO)

NIV

[17]The seventy-two returned with joy and said, "Lord, even the demons submit to us in your name."

NRSV

17The seventy[a] returned with joy, saying, "Lord, in your name even the demons submit to

aOther ancient authorities read seventy-two

NIV

[18]He replied, "I saw Satan fall like lightning from heaven. [19]I have given you authority to trample on snakes and scorpions and to overcome all the power of the enemy; nothing will harm you. [20]However, do not rejoice that the spirits submit to you, but rejoice that your names are written in heaven."

[21]At that time Jesus, full of joy through the Holy Spirit, said, "I praise you, Father, Lord of heaven and earth, because you have hidden these things from the wise and learned, and revealed them to little children. Yes, Father, for this was your good pleasure.

[22]"All things have been committed to me by my Father. No one knows who the Son is except the Father, and no one knows who the Father is except the Son and those to whom the Son chooses to reveal him."

[23]Then he turned to his disciples and said privately, "Blessed are the eyes that see what you see. [24]For I tell you that many prophets and kings wanted to see what you see but did not see it, and to hear what you hear but did not hear it."

NRSV

us!" [18]He said to them, "I watched Satan fall from heaven like a flash of lightning. [19]See, I have given you authority to tread on snakes and scorpions, and over all the power of the enemy; and nothing will hurt you. [20]Nevertheless, do not rejoice at this, that the spirits submit to you, but rejoice that your names are written in heaven."

[21]At that same hour Jesus[a] rejoiced in the Holy Spirit[b] and said, "I thank[c] you, Father, Lord of heaven and earth, because you have hidden these things from the wise and the intelligent and have revealed them to infants; yes, Father, for such was your gracious will.[d] [22]All things have been handed over to me by my Father; and no one knows who the Son is except the Father, or who the Father is except the Son and anyone to whom the Son chooses to reveal him."

[23]Then turning to the disciples, Jesus[a] said to them privately, "Blessed are the eyes that see what you see! [24]For I tell you that many prophets and kings desired to see what you see, but did not see it, and to hear what you hear, but did not hear it."

[a]Gk he   [b]Other authorities read in the spirit   [c]Or praise
[d]Or for so it was well-pleasing in your sight

COMMENTARY

Just as the commissioning of the seventy(-two) has no parallel in the other Gospels, so also there is no parallel report of their return. As with the sending of the Twelve earlier, neither is there any further account of their activities. Following the report of the return, Luke adds Jesus' words of thanksgiving to the Father, which parallel Matt 11:25-27, and a beatitude regarding those who have seen, which parallels the saying in Matt 13:16. When considered together, vv. 17-24 report three clusters of sayings, each of which is preceded by a brief introduction by the narrator (vv. 17, 21, 23). The first section (vv. 17-20) declares the apocalyptic significance of the disciples' mission, the second gives thanks to God for their success (vv. 21-22), and the last picks up the themes of both apocalyptic significance and thanksgiving in a beatitude that reasserts the importance of seeing and hearing (vv. 23-24).

10:17-20. Joy characterizes the experience of the disciples who have obeyed Jesus' mission charge. The joy of the annunciations (1:14; 2:10) of what God was about to do is being realized in the work of disciples empowered by Jesus. The joy of the disciples on mission also foreshadows the joy they would experience at the resurrection (24:41, 52).

Whereas the Twelve had preached and healed (9:6, 10), the success of the seventy(-two) is epitomized in their power over demons. Earlier, the disciples had been unable to help a boy plagued by demons (9:40) and had forbidden another to cast out demons in Jesus' name (9:49). As noted in the comment on 9:49, acting "in Jesus' name" enables the disciples to do various mighty deeds in the early chapters of Acts. Again, therefore, the success of the disciples appears as a proleptic sign of the power they would experience after the resurrection.

Jesus' oracle is couched in the language of a vision: "I saw" (v. 18). Whether we are to read this as the report of an actual vision, or whether it should be understood as simply a metaphorical description of the significance of the apostle's work may be debated. Either way, it sets their work in the context of the expectations that the end times would be marked by a conflict between God and Satan in which Satan would be defeated (see Isa 14:12; John 12:31; Rev 12:7-9). For Satan to be cast out of heaven means that Satan has been defeated, his power broken. Here, the sign of Satan's defeat is the disciples' obedience and success. Their power to liberate others from demons is a sign that the promise of the end time is being realized. The work of the disciples, therefore, has even greater significance than they may have grasped: It signals the coming of God's sovereign reign on earth.

Verse 19 continues the apocalyptic imagery of the previous saying. The language of "giving authority" echoes Luke 9:1, where Jesus gave the disciples authority over the demons, but here Jesus' language is metaphorical, not literal. Serpents and scorpions appear as images for the power of evil in prophetic and apocalyptic writings (serpents, Gen 3:1-14; Num 21:6-9; scorpions, 1 Kgs 12:11, 14; Rev 9:3; serpents and scorpions together, Deut 8:15; Sir 39:30; Luke 11:11-12). Treading on serpents as a sign of divine power and protection echoes Ps 91:13, and though such language seems to have been taken literally by some early Christians (Mark 16:18; Acts 28:3-6), its original purpose was metaphorical. By casting out demons, the disciples had demonstrated their power over Satan; they had trodden on serpents and scorpions. Vanquishing the enemies of God's people was another of the apocalyptic hopes (see 1:71, 74; 19:27; 20:43; Acts 2:35).

Verse 20 picks up several motifs from v. 17, rounding off this unit of sayings: joy/rejoicing, the demons/spirits, are subject, in your name/your names, from heaven/in heaven. This saying points to a higher reason for rejoicing—not just that Satan's power has been broken, but because the disciples' names are now written in the book of life. This image is also found in prophetic and apocalyptic writings (e.g., Exod 32:32-33; Ps 69:28; Dan 12:1; Mal 3:16-17; Phil 4:3; Rev 3:5; 13:8). The proper response to the coming of God's

kingdom is joy, not only for the defeat of evil and the vanquishing of demonic powers but also for the experience of life rightly ordered in God's fellowship.

10:21-22. This is Q material (Matt 11:25-27), but the use of the terms "Father" and "Son" (πατέρ *pater* and υἱός *huios*) has a distinctly Johannine ring (see John 3:35; 13:3; 17:2). A direct literary dependence cannot be established, however, but only a similarity of language and thought. The question of direction of influence can be put as follows: Do these sayings reflect contact between the Q and the Johannine tradition at an early stage, or do these sayings indicate that in the core of sayings from Jesus that circulated in the early church there were sayings that served as a catalyst for the discourses now found in the Gospel of John? The latter is the more commonly accepted explanation. Beyond the parallels with John, it should be noted that these sayings use terms that are seldom or never found elsewhere in Luke and Acts (I thank/praise, Father/Son, hidden, wise, intelligent, infants, and chooses). The vocabulary is distinctly non-Lukan.

In Luke this unit follows the return of the seventy(-two) and continues the note of celebration in vv. 17-20. Verse 21 contains the first reference to the Holy Spirit in the ministry of Jesus (see 3:22; 4:1) and echoes the celebration of the meeting between Mary and Elizabeth (1:41, 47). Jesus' words in v. 21 take the form of a prayer to God, addressed as Father, while v. 21 is instruction apparently addressed to the disciples. The two sayings are bound together by a common vocabulary of antithetical pairs: Father/Son, hidden/revealed, wise and intelligent/infants. Although the two sayings share a common vocabulary, the second statement moves considerably beyond the first. Both the language and the sentiment of v. 21 can be found in Jewish wisdom materials and prayers. God is addressed as "Father" in 3 Macc 6:3, 8, and the expression "Lord of heaven and earth" is found in Gen 14:19, 22; Jdt 9:12; Tob 7:17 [MS B]; and Acts 17:24. Similarly, the expression of praise because God has imparted knowledge is found in the hymn scroll from Qumran: "I give [Thee thanks, O Adonai], for thou hast given me understanding of Thy truth and hast made me know Thy marvellous Mysteries."[115] Close parallels to hiding wisdom from the wise and revealing truth to the simple can be found in 1 Cor 1:18-25 and in Pss 116:6; 119:130; and Isa 29:14. It is God's pleasure to reveal truth and mercy to the simple (see Luke 1:51-52; 2:14). The motifs and sentiment are common to Jewish wisdom literature.

The saying in v. 22, by contrast, is distinctly Christian and christological. That all things have been given to the Son by the Father parallels the claim of the risen Lord in Matt 28:18 and claims made by the Johannine Jesus (John 3:35; 5:21-22; 10:29; 13:3). The Son is the sole revealer because no one knows the Father but the Son (John 1:18; 14:6-7). Rather than the assertion that God reveals wisdom to the simple, as in the previous saying, v. 22 grants to the Son the authority to dispense the revelation of the Father. Accordingly, this verse makes an exclusivistic claim for salvation— here interpreted as knowledge of God—through Jesus as the Son, which may be compared with Rom 10:9 and 1 Cor 12:3, but especially the Johannine text already cited (John 14:6-7). The Pauline texts that make an exclusive claim for salvation through Jesus do not use the language of Father and Son (though this language is not unknown to Paul; Rom 8:15-17). This Q saying, on the other hand, employs the terms for "Father"

and "Son," but the rival to Jesus' authority is not clear, as it is in John, which polemicizes against those who claim to have knowledge of God through Moses and the Law.

10:23-24. The third cluster of sayings is introduced by v. 23, which addresses the ensuing sayings to the disciples. The Matthean parallel is found in Matt 16:16-17. Verse 23 pronounces a blessing on the disciples for what they have seen, and v. 24 offers an explanation of the blessing. The beatitude affirms the privileged position of the disciples, who have witnessed the mighty works of Jesus and the fall of Satan, alluded to earlier (10:18-19). Being an eyewitness of the ministry and resurrection of Jesus would later become a requirement for the one who would be chosen to take Judas's place (Acts 1:21-22). Elsewhere Luke emphasizes the importance of the eyewitnesses for the proclamation of the gospel (1:2; 24:31, 48).

The privileged role of the disciples is emphasized by the explanation in v. 24. Even prophets and kings desire to see and hear what the disciples have seen. The saying contrasts sharply with Jesus' rebuke of the disciples in Mark for what they did not see or hear (Mark 8:18). Jesus is greater than the prophets, and now the disciples see what was denied even to the prophets (cf. Eph 3:4-6; 1 Pet 1:12). The blessing on the disciples for what they have seen follows naturally, therefore, from the lofty claims for Jesus as the Son in the previous sayings.

115. 1QH7:26-27. See A. Dupont-Sommer, *The Essene Writings from Qumran,* trans. G. Vermes (Cleveland: World, 1961) 224.

REFLECTIONS

The three clusters of sayings that follow the return of the seventy(-two) advance both the christology of Luke and its characterization of the disciples. Through the work of the disciples on mission, following Jesus' commission, the power of Satan is broken and demons are cast out. This vision of things to come affirms the victory of those who are faithful to Jesus, regardless of the fearsomeness of those who oppose them.

The sayings also affirm not only that the disciples have power, but also that their names are written in heaven (v. 20), that knowledge of the Father has been revealed to them (v. 22), and that they have seen and heard what even prophets and kings desired to see and hear but could not (vv. 23-24). For this reason, they will later have an important role as witnesses (1:2; 24:48; Acts 1:8).

Similarly, these sayings foreshadow Jesus' ultimate victory over Satan (recall 4:1-13) and extend the characterization of Jesus as God's Son (see 1:35; 2:49; 9:35). All things have been given to Jesus as the Son of God, only the Son knows the Father, and the Son chooses those to whom he reveals the Father. The disciples are blessed, therefore, as persons chosen to receive the revelation through Jesus, to see and to hear.

Seeing and hearing, however, involve both gift and responsiveness. Luke has already emphasized the importance of hearing well (8:9-18). To them has been given to know the secrets of the kingdom, to see and to perceive and to hear and to understand (8:10). They are the good soil, but they must give light with what they have seen and make known what they have heard (8:16-17), and they must be careful how they listen (8:18).

The blessing and the earlier admonitions speak to the gift of election and grace and the responsibility for obedience and faithfulness. The disciples have a high status as witnesses, but that status carries a responsibility for how they carry out their task. Their status is given; they were chosen and called. They were commissioned for their work (10:1-12), and now they are blessed (10:23-24).

These sayings, therefore, develop themes of both christology and discipleship. They affirm election and demand faithfulness, but in the end the words of blessing echo from these verses. Jesus blesses those whom he calls to serve, and they are equipped for their mission by what they have experienced—what they have seen, and what they have heard. That is always the experience of those who serve the Lord.

LUKE 10:25-42, THE LOVE OF GOD AND NEIGHBOR

OVERVIEW

Several themes tie this part of the travel narrative together. Jesus has just affirmed that no one knows the Father but the Son, and now he is challenged to interpret what one must do to have eternal life—life in God's kingdom, the age to come. Jesus has declared that God has hidden wisdom from the wise; now Jesus is questioned by one of the wise—a scribe. Jesus has praised the disciples for what they have seen; now he tells a story in which three men see a man in the ditch, but only the Samaritan stops to help him. Having established the priority of loving God and loving one's neighbor, Jesus tells a story about being a neighbor, and Luke adds a story about a woman who breaks the rules by listening to Jesus' teachings while her sister works in the kitchen. Neither the lawyer nor Martha understands Jesus. The two stories, therefore, illustrate the scandal that radical obedience to Jesus' commands requires.

Luke 10:25-28, The Lawyer's Question

25On one occasion an expert in the law stood up to test Jesus. "Teacher," he asked, "what must I do to inherit eternal life?"

26"What is written in the Law?" he replied. "How do you read it?"

27He answered: " 'Love the Lord your God with all your heart and with all your soul and with all your strength and with all your mind'ᵃ; and, 'Love your neighbor as yourself.'ᵇ"

28"You have answered correctly," Jesus replied. "Do this and you will live."

a27 Deut. 6:5   *b27* Lev. 19:18

25Just then a lawyer stood up to test Jesus.ᵃ "Teacher," he said, "what must I do to inherit eternal life?" 26He said to him, "What is written in the law? What do you read there?" 27He answered, "You shall love the Lord your God with all your heart, and with all your soul, and with all your strength, and with all your mind; and your neighbor as yourself." 28And he said to him, "You have given the right answer; do this, and you will live."

a Gk *him*

COMMENTARY

Although there are other scenes in which Jesus is approached by a lawyer, scribe, or one of the rulers and is asked a question about the commandments or what is required to inherit eternal life (Mark 12:28-34; Matt 22:34-40; Luke 18:18-20; and pars.), only Luke uses this story as the introduction to the parable of the good Samaritan. Luke is distinctive in other aspects as well. Luke has the lawyer ask, "What must I do?" (cf. Mark 12:28; Matt 22:36). Jesus answers with a question of his own: "How do you read?" The command to love the Lord is qualified by four phrases not found elsewhere in exactly that form, and the citation of the command is followed by the assurance, "Do this and you will live."

The setting is not entirely clear. Jesus spoke to the disciples privately in v. 23, but in v. 25 he is addressed by a lawyer. The lawyer's question is readily understandable following Jesus' blessing of the disciples in vv. 23-24 for what they have seen and heard. What if one has not seen and has not heard what the disciples were privileged to see and hear? Is there any hope for them? The lawyer asks the question that all who were not among the eyewitnesses would ask: "But what must *I* do to inherit eternal life?"

The lawyer is testing Jesus. The term "test" or "tempting" (ἐκπειράζω *ekpeirazō*) signals explicitly the challenge to one's honor that is posed by any question. The lawyer, moreover, was recognized as an expert in these matters because in Jewish society there was no distinction between civil law and religious law. The lawyer was an expert in the Scriptures. Jesus had just made outrageously lofty claims for himself. Could he answer a simple question? In Luke, however, the lawyer does not ask which is the greatest command as in Mark and Matthew, but what one must do to "inherit eternal life." Inheritance was the reward promised to those who belonged to the covenant people. God had promised to make them a great people, to bless them, and to give them a land (Gen 12:1-3), but that inheritance had been continually pushed to the future, until now it was associated with the blessings of "the Age to Come" (see Rom 8:17; Eph 1:14; 3:6). That inheritance is here understood as "eternal life" or life in God's kingdom. But was the lawyer testing Jesus to see whether he would give the answer the lawyer expected, or was he testing the one who had claimed to be the Son to see whether he would "choose" to reveal the Father to him (see v. 22)?

Jesus responds to the lawyer's question with one of his own, now a challenge to the lawyer's honor: "Isn't the answer to your question written in the scriptures [and are you not an expert in the scriptures?], how do you read it?" The last part of Jesus' question acknowledges that the matter is not so simple and that it has been debated for generations. How did the lawyer understand what was written? Whereas in Matthew and Mark, Jesus quotes the commands to love God (Deut 6:5) and to love one's neighbor (Lev 19:18), in this story the lawyer quotes these commandments, which had become important in Jewish life. Deuteronomy 6:4-9 was part of the Shema, repeated twice each day, but it had not been linked to Lev 19:18 as it is here. (The closest parallels are in the *Testaments of the Twelve Patriarchs*,[116] but these may be Christian interpolations.[117]) The quotation from (and expansion of) Deut 6:5 includes four qualifying phrases: "heart" (καρδία *kardia*); "soul" (ψυχή *psychē*); "might" (ἰσχύς *ischys*); and a fourth qualifier not found in the Masoretic Text or the LXX, "and with all your mind [διάνοια *dianoia*]." The Gospels use a different Greek word for "strength" or "might" than that found in the Septuagint (δύναμις *dynamis*). Mark 12:30 has the same four qualifiers but reverses the sequence of the last two, whereas Matt 22:37 lists only "heart, soul, and mind."

Whether three or four, the importance of the qualifiers is to plant the flag of God's sovereignty over the whole of one's life. God's claim on us reaches to every area of our experience, to our innermost being (heart); our lives—what gives us our individual identity (soul); our energy, strength, resolve, and resources (might); and our understanding and intellectual capacities (mind). No part of ourselves is to be withheld from God. The

---

116. *T. Issachar* 5:2; *T. Dan* 5:3.
117. See Joseph A. Fitzmyer, *The Gospel According to Luke (X–XXIV)*, AB 28A (Garden City, N.Y.: Doubleday, 1985) 879.

fourth qualifier, though missing from Deut 6:5, was consistent with the teachings of Hillel, who is reputed to have said, "An ignorant man cannot be saintly."[118]

There is no dichotomy between the commands to love God and to love one's neighbor. Indeed, when one loves God, one lives out love for others as well (see 1 John 4:7-21). The phrase "as yourself" implies that love for oneself is also expected. Three loves, therefore, characterize the life of one who is already experiencing a measure of that life that will characterize the age to come: love of God, neighbor, and self. Only in this sequence of priority, however, does each require the others.

The lawyer has read well, but reading is not enough. The Pharisaic elevation of the importance of study of the Torah reached its zenith in the pronouncement of Akiba: "Study of the Law is of higher rank than practising it."[119] In stark contrast, Jesus responds: "Do this, and you will live." Eternal life is found not just in knowing the commandments but in doing them. The answer to the lawyer's question is implicit in the question itself: "What must I *do* to inherit eternal life?" Those who live rightly ordered lives now—living out of their love for God, others, and self—show that they have been touched by the kingdom of God. They will have the capacity to receive the promised inheritance: life in fellowship with God and others in the age to come. (See Reflections at 10:38-42.)

118. M. 'Abot 2.6.

119. *Sifre Deuteronomy* 41 on 11:13; *b. Qiddushin* 40b.

Luke 10:29-37, The Good Samaritan

[29]But he wanted to justify himself, so he asked Jesus, "And who is my neighbor?"

[30]In reply Jesus said: "A man was going down from Jerusalem to Jericho, when he fell into the hands of robbers. They stripped him of his clothes, beat him and went away, leaving him half dead. [31]A priest happened to be going down the same road, and when he saw the man, he passed by on the other side. [32]So too, a Levite, when he came to the place and saw him, passed by on the other side. [33]But a Samaritan, as he traveled, came where the man was; and when he saw him, he took pity on him. [34]He went to him and bandaged his wounds, pouring on oil and wine. Then he put the man on his own donkey, took him to an inn and took care of him. [35]The next day he took out two silver coins[a] and gave them to the innkeeper. 'Look after him,' he said, 'and when I return, I will reimburse you for any extra expense you may have.'

[36]"Which of these three do you think was a neighbor to the man who fell into the hands of robbers?"

[37]The expert in the law replied, "The one who had mercy on him."

Jesus told him, "Go and do likewise."

[a]35 Greek *two denarii*

29But wanting to justify himself, he asked Jesus, "And who is my neighbor?" [30]Jesus replied, "A man was going down from Jerusalem to Jericho, and fell into the hands of robbers, who stripped him, beat him, and went away, leaving him half dead. [31]Now by chance a priest was going down that road; and when he saw him, he passed by on the other side. [32]So likewise a Levite, when he came to the place and saw him, passed by on the other side. [33]But a Samaritan while traveling came near him; and when he saw him, he was moved with pity. [34]He went to him and bandaged his wounds, having poured oil and wine on them. Then he put him on his own animal, brought him to an inn, and took care of him. [35]The next day he took out two denarii,[a] gave them to the innkeeper, and said, 'Take care of him; and when I come back, I will repay you whatever more you spend.' [36]Which of these three, do you think, was a neighbor to the man who fell into the hands of the robbers?" [37]He said, "The one who showed him mercy." Jesus said to him, "Go and do likewise."

[a] The denarius was the usual day's wage for a laborer

COMMENTARY

10:29. In its current setting, the story of the good Samaritan is linked to Jesus' exchange with the lawyer. The lawyer's third response to Jesus is intended as a trap. His original motive was to test Jesus (v. 25), but Jesus had gained the upper hand by forcing the lawyer to answer his own question and then challenging the lawyer to put his answer into practice. Attempting a rally, therefore, the lawyer posed a question that never failed to generate controversy. Like most societies, first-century Judaism was ordered by boundaries with specific rules regarding how Jews should treat Gentiles or Samaritans, how priests should relate to Israelites, how men should treat women, and so on. Because the boundaries allowed for certain groups to establish their positions, power, and privilege, maintaining the boundaries was vital to social order. It was a religious duty. The command to love one's neighbor (Lev 19:18) immediately prompted the lawyer's question, which was understood to define the limits of required neighborliness. Leviticus 19:34, for example, requires that an alien should be treated as a citizen: "Love the alien as yourself."

10:30. The central character in Jesus' story is noticeably undefined. He is not characterized by race, religion, region, or trade. He is merely "a certain man" who by implication could be any one of Jesus' hearers. The phrase "a certain man" (ἄνθρωπός τις *anthrōpos tis*), however, will become a common feature of the Lukan parables (12:16; 14:2, 16; 15:11; 16:1, 19; 19:12; 20:9). Jesus' audience no doubt imagined the man to be Jewish, but Luke's audience may have assumed he was a Gentile. The point is that he is identified only by what happened to him.

The road from Jerusalem to Jericho was notoriously dangerous. It descended nearly 3,300 feet in 17 miles. The road ran through narrow passes at points, and the terrain offered easy hiding for the bandits who terrorized travelers. This unfortunate man had been stripped, beaten, and left for dead. His assailants had left him with nothing to identify his status except his desperate need. The story is told from the point of view of the beaten man, who may be anyone, and the audience may easily identify with this innocent victim of random violence and brutality.

10:31-32. The next words signal hope. "By chance" there was another traveler, one who might come to his aid. Moreover, that traveler is a priest, one who would be expected to help, and he sees the man. The end of the sentence (v. 31) dashes the hope kindled by its beginning; the priest passes by on the other side. No reason is given, but in the end no reason justifies his neglect of the man in need. Could one really argue that pressing duties prevented him from stopping? If a priest on a journey found a corpse, he had a duty to bury it.[120] The Levite's response is described in the same terms. He too saw the man and passed by on the other side. In both cases, their seeing the man renders them culpable.

10:33-35. The story has reached its turning point. By storytelling conventions, the audience can expect that in a series of three, the third character will break the pattern created by the first two. Moreover, the expected sequence would be a priest, a Levite, and then an Israelite.[121] The story would then have an anticlerical edge to it. The ordinary Israelite would do what the priest and Levite would not.

Shattering all expectations, the third traveler is a Samaritan. The story does not pit an Israelite against a priest and a Levite. By making the hero of the story a Samaritan, Jesus challenged the long-standing enmity between Jews and Samaritans. The latter were regarded as unclean people, descendants of the mixed marriages that followed from the Assyrian settlement of people from various regions in the fallen northern kingdom (2 Kgs 17:6, 24). By depicting a Samaritan as the hero of the story, therefore, Jesus, demolished all boundary expectations. Social position—race, religion, or region—count for nothing. The man in the ditch, from whose perspective the story is told, will not discriminate among potential helpers. Anyone who has compassion and stops to help is his neighbor. The question is thereby turned when viewed from the perspective of the one in desperate need. The alteration of the expected sequence

---

120. *M. Nazir* 7.1.
121. *M. Gittin* 5.8; *m. Horayoth* 3.8.

by naming the third character as a Samaritan not only challenges the hearer to examine the stereotype regarding Samaritans, but it also invalidates all stereotypes. Community can no longer be defined or limited by such terms. The three on the road are each identified by social class, but the man in the ditch is not identified by such labels.

Like the first two, the Samaritan sees the man, but seeing him, he has compassion for him. The detailed account of the Samaritan's care for the beaten man stands in sharp contrast to the sparsity of detail in the first part of the story. Count the verbs in v. 34: "He *went* to him and *bandaged* his wounds, having *poured* oil and wine on them. Then he *put* him on his own animal, *brought* him to an inn, and *took care* of him" (italics added). Pouring wine on a wound would help to cleanse it; the oil would keep it soft. The next day the Samaritan goes on with his business, but he leaves two denarii (equivalent to two days' wages) to pay for the beaten man's care at the inn—not a lavish amount, but perhaps enough to provide for him through his recovery. If more is needed, the Samaritan pledges to pay it on his return. By his care for the beaten man, the Samaritan demonstrates that he is a faithful man. The innkeeper will not have to worry about whether he will repay his debt.

10:36-37. Jesus then turns the question back to the lawyer, and the lawyer is caught on the very question with which he intended to impale Jesus. "Which of these three was a neighbor?" The multiple choice question forces such a distasteful answer that the lawyer will not even use the word *Samaritan.* He says instead, "The one who showed him mercy," but ironically his circuitous answer provides an accurate description of a neighbor. Jesus has turned the issue from the boundaries of required neighborliness to the essential nature of neighborliness. Neighbors are defined actively, not passively. As an Arab proverb says, "To have a good neighbor you must be one."

The lawyer had initially asked what he must do to inherit eternal life. Jesus has now answered the question by telling a story about a Samaritan who kept a beaten man from dying. Jesus had steered the lawyer to quote the commandments to love God and love one's neighbor. The first round of the contest between Jesus and the lawyer ended with Jesus' injunction "Do this, and you will live" (v. 28). The second round ends with a similar command: "Go and do likewise" (v. 37). But this time no promise is attached to the command. The duty of neighborliness is an expression of love of God and love of others, and those who show mercy show that they belong among the heirs of the kingdom, but the duty of neighborliness transcends any calculation of reward. The Samaritan could not have expected any reward or repayment for what he did for the beaten man. One who shows mercy in order to gain a reward would, therefore, not truly be doing "likewise."

Jesus' parable, therefore, shatters the stereotypes of social boundaries and class division and renders void any system of religious *quid pro quo.* Neighbors do not recognize social class. Neither is mercy the conduct of a calculating heart, nor eternal life the reward for doing prescribed duties. Eternal life—the life of the age to come—is that quality of life characterized by showing mercy for those in need, regardless of their race, religion, or region—and with no thought of reward. Mercy sees only need and responds with compassion.

The story of the good Samaritan, therefore, gives new meaning to Jesus' blessing on the disciples who had gone out preaching and caring for the sick: "Blessed are the eyes that see what you see!" (10:23). (See Reflections at 10:38-42.)

Luke 10:38-42, Mary and Martha

NIV	NRSV
38As Jesus and his disciples were on their way, he came to a village where a woman named Martha opened her home to him. 39She had a sister called Mary, who sat at the Lord's feet listening to what he said. 40But Martha was distracted by all the preparations that had to be	38Now as they went on their way, he entered a certain village, where a woman named Martha welcomed him into her home. 39She had a sister named Mary, who sat at the Lord's feet and listened to what he was saying. 40But Martha was distracted by her many tasks; so she came to him

NIV

made. She came to him and asked, "Lord, don't you care that my sister has left me to do the work by myself? Tell her to help me!"

[41]"Martha, Martha," the Lord answered, "you are worried and upset about many things, [42]but only one thing is needed.[a] Mary has chosen what is better, and it will not be taken away from her."

[a]42 Some manuscripts *but few things are needed—or only one*

NRSV

and asked, "Lord, do you not care that my sister has left me to do all the work by myself? Tell her then to help me." [41]But the Lord answered her, "Martha, Martha, you are worried and distracted by many things; [42]there is need of only one thing.[a] Mary has chosen the better part, which will not be taken away from her."

[a]Other ancient authorities read *few things are necessary, or only one*

COMMENTARY

The story of Mary and Martha stands in a complementary relationship with the story of the good Samaritan and gains much of its meaning from the tensive relationship between the two stories. The journey motif runs through Luke 10: Jesus sends the seventy(-two) out on mission with instructions for their journey and what to do when they enter a village or a house, and the parable of the good Samaritan is the story of four travelers. The lawyer correctly identified the priority of the commands to love God and love one's neighbor. The story of the good Samaritan then develops the meaning of the command to love one's neighbor, and the story of Mary and Martha highlights the overriding importance of devotion to the Lord's Word as an expression of one's love for God. The story of the good Samaritan features "a certain man" (v. 30), while Martha is introduced as "a certain woman" (v. 38). The good Samaritan exemplifies the disciples' seeing; in a similar way, Mary exemplifies the virtue of hearing (see 10:23-24). Moreover, both the Samaritan and Mary, a woman, represent marginalized persons—unlikely heroes. As a composite, they are model disciples: "those who hear the word of God and do it" (8:21).

10:38. The encounter with Mary and Martha, which takes the form of a pronouncement story featuring Jesus' response to Martha, is set in the context of Jesus' journey to Jerusalem and echoes the journey instructions previously given to the disciples (9:1-6; 10:1-12). The connection between being received and eating is established by 10:8: "Whenever you enter a town and its people welcome you, eat what is set before you." Martha

welcomes Jesus and begins preparing a meal for him (see 19:6-7).

10:39. The complication appears when we are told that Mary, Martha's sister, is sitting at Jesus' feet (in the place of a disciple; see 8:35; Acts 22:3) and listening to his word. Luke has already established a strong link between Jesus' teachings and God's Word (see 5:1; 8:11, 21). The scene resonates positively and negatively with rabbinic lore: "Let thy house be a meeting-house for the Sages and sit amid the dust of their feet and drink in their words with thirst . . . [but] talk not much with womankind."[122] By sitting at Jesus' feet, Mary is acting like a male. She neglects her duty to assist her sister in the preparation of the meal, and by violating a clear social boundary she is bringing shame upon her house.

10:40. Martha's protest is justifiable, but the narrator casts it in a negative light by characterizing Martha as "distracted" by her work (lit., "service," διακονία *diakonia*). Earlier, Jesus spoke of the seed (i.e., the Word of God) that fell among thorns—those who do not receive it because they are preoccupied with "the cares and riches and pleasures of life" (8:14). Martha's distraction places her in this category. Although she is fulfilling the role assigned to her by society, she allows secondary matters to distract her from hearing the Word of God. After all, "One does not live by bread alone" (4:4). Like the disciples, Mary had left everything to follow Jesus (cf. 5:11, 28).

The conjunction of the three words or phrases

122. *M. 'Abot* 1.4-5. See Herbert Danby, ed. and trans., *The Mishnah* (Oxford: Oxford University Press, 1933) 446.

"leaving" (πορεύομαι *poreuomai*), "the word of God" (τὸν λόγον τοῦ θεοῦ *ton logon tou theou*), "to serve" (διακονέω *diakoneō*) will be found again in Acts 6:1-6, where the disciples choose not to leave the ministry of the Word of God to serve tables and instead appoint the seven for this task. In this parallel scene, Jesus allows Mary—a woman—to claim the same role that the disciples later claim for themselves.

10:41-42. Jesus' response to Martha forms the climax of this scene. The repetition of her name, "Martha, Martha," conveys a mild rebuke or lament. Like demons, her cares about fulfilling her duties have thrown her life into disorder. Like thorns, they have prevented her from attending to Jesus' teachings. Like the cares of a husband for his wife, her cares have prevented her from "unhindered devotion to the Lord" (1 Cor 7:32-35). Martha is anxious about many things, but only one thing is needed. This is not a counsel to prepare a simple meal rather than a lavish one, but a reminder that the duty of the love of God and obedience to God's Word take precedence over all other concerns.

Mary, on the other hand, has chosen the "Chosen One" (9:35). While Martha is distracted by "parts" of the meal, Mary chooses "the good part." Disciples often need more discrimination, not more vigorous effort. Martha presumes to tell Jesus what he should do; Mary lets Jesus tell her what she should do. By choosing to attend to Jesus' teachings while laying aside everything else, Mary exemplifies what it means to "love the Lord your God with all your heart, and with all your soul, and with all your strength, and with all your mind" (v. 27). As if to affirm Mary's radical violation of Palestinian social roles, Jesus adds that what she has chosen "will not be taken away from her" (v. 42).

REFLECTIONS

Neither the story of the good Samaritan nor the story of Mary and Martha is complete without the other. Each makes its own point—the Samaritan loves his neighbor, and Mary loves her Lord—but the model for the disciple is found in the juxtaposition of the two. To the lawyer, Jesus says, "Go and do," but he praises Mary for sitting and listening. The life of a disciple requires both.

The power of these two stories consists not just in that they exemplify the great commands of 10:27 but in Jesus' choice of characters to illustrate the love of neighbor and the love of God: a Samaritan and a woman. The social codes and boundaries were clear and inflexible; a Samaritan would not be considered a model of neighborliness, and a woman would not sit with men around the feet of a teacher.[123]

In its own way, the conjunction of the stories about the good Samaritan and the female disciple voice Jesus' protest against the rules and boundaries set by the culture in which he lived. As they develop seeing and hearing as metaphors for the activity of the kingdom, the twin stories also expose the injustice of social barriers that categorize, restrict, and oppress various groups in any society (Samaritans, victims, women). To love God with all one's heart and one's neighbor as oneself meant then and now that one must often reject society's rules in favor of the codes of the kingdom—a society without distinctions and boundaries between its members. The rules of that society are just two—to love God and one's neighbor—but these rules are so radically different from those of the society in which we live that living by them invariably calls us to disregard all else, break the rules, and follow Jesus' example.

123. Bruce J. Malina and Richard L. Rohrbaugh, *A Social-Science Commentary on the Synoptic Gospels* (Minneapolis: Fortress, 1992) 348.

LUKE 11:1-13, INSTRUCTION ON PRAYER

OVERVIEW

While continuing to provide instruction for the early church by reporting Jesus' instruction of his disciples, Luke 11 shifts from the great commandments to love God and love one's neighbor to teachings on prayer. Nevertheless, the teachings on prayer combine themes from the previous chapter: ask of God as a loving father, and forgive others. Three units follow an introductory verse: the Lord's prayer (vv. 2-4), the parable of a shameless neighbor (vv. 5-8), and assurances that God hears our prayers (vv. 9-13).

Luke 11:1-4, The Lord's Prayer

NIV

11 One day Jesus was praying in a certain place. When he finished, one of his disciples said to him, "Lord, teach us to pray, just as John taught his disciples."

²He said to them, "When you pray, say:

" 'Father,*a*
hallowed be your name,
your kingdom come.*b*
³Give us each day our daily bread.
⁴Forgive us our sins,
for we also forgive everyone who sins against us.*c*
And lead us not into temptation.*d* ' "

a2 Some manuscripts Our Father in heaven   b2 Some manuscripts come. May your will be done on earth as it is in heaven.   c4 Greek everyone who is indebted to us   d4 Some manuscripts temptation but deliver us from the evil one

NRSV

11 He was praying in a certain place, and after he had finished, one of his disciples said to him, "Lord, teach us to pray, as John taught his disciples." ²He said to them, "When you pray, say:

Father,*a* hallowed be your name.
Your kingdom come.*b*
³   Give us each day our daily bread.*c*
⁴   And forgive us our sins,
for we ourselves forgive everyone indebted to us.
And do not bring us to the time of trial."*d*

aOther ancient authorities read Our Father in heaven   bA few ancient authorities read Your Holy Spirit come upon us and cleanse us. Other ancient authorities add Your will be done, on earth as in heaven   cOr our bread for tomorrow   dOr us into temptation. Other ancient authorities add but rescue us from the evil one (or from evil)

COMMENTARY

Luke gives more emphasis to Jesus' practice of prayer than do any of the other Gospels, reporting that the Spirit came upon Jesus while he was praying (3:21-22) and that he withdrew to desolate places periodically to pray (5:16). He also prayed before significant turning points in his ministry—e.g., the call of the disciples (6:12-13), Peter's confession (9:18), and the transfiguration (9:28). Later, Luke will report Jesus' prayers at Gethsemane (22:40-42), on the cross (23:34, 46), and at table with his disciples (24:30).

By the first century there were set prayers. A devout Jew would repeat the prayers in the morning and again in the evening. If the situation prohibited reciting these prayers in their entirety, a shorter version could be said. Apparently, John had also taught his disciples a set prayer.

11:1. This verse repeats the introductory phrase of 9:18 with the addition of the phrase "in a certain place." Luke's reference to the unnamed "certain" (τις *tis*) disciple continues the string of references to "a certain lawyer" (10:25), "a certain man" (10:30), "a certain village," and "a certain woman" (10:38). The disciple's question is prompted by Jesus' own practice of prayer.

The model prayer appears in the context of

instructions on prayer in Matthew (6:9-13) and here in Luke. While recognizably the same prayer, there is a greater difference between the two versions than between many other sayings drawn from the Q material—which probably attests to the influence of independent liturgical traditions. The wording of the prayer in Matthew is more polished, and the Matthean version contains seven petitions, whereas the Lukan form contains only five. Neither form of the prayer contains the traditional benediction (see 1 Chr 29:11-13; Matt 6:13; *Did.* 8.2). It is generally agreed that whereas the Matthean wording is more original in places, the Lukan structure is probably closer to the original form of the prayer.

11:2. The Lukan form of the prayer lacks the following elements of the Matthean prayer: "Our . . . who art in heaven. . . . Thy will be done on earth as it is in heaven . . . but deliver us from evil." Stripped of the familiar language of the traditional form of the prayer, the Lukan prayer focuses the reader's attention on its simplicity and the directness of its petitions. Joachim Jeremias's contention that Jesus' use of *Abbā'* (אבא) was without parallel in ancient Jewish prayers has been qualified by others who have pointed to the use of "Father" in Ps 89:26; 3 Macc 6:8 and a fragment from Qumran.[124] The distinctiveness of Jesus' use of the Aramaic *Abbā'* with its connotations of familial intimacy, however, is attested by its place in the memory of the early church (see Mark 14:36; Rom 8:15; Gal 4:6, where the Aramaic term is preserved). Elsewhere in Luke, Jesus also addresses God as Father (10:21; 22:42). The first-person plural "our" (ἡμῶν *hēmōn*) may not be a Matthean addition, but use of the first-person plural later in the Lukan prayer shows that it is still understood as the community prayer of Jesus' disciples. Even in Luke, therefore, the prayer is not an expression of individual piety apart from the life and worship of the community. With the possible exception of 11:13, Luke does not refer to God as being "in heaven," but the phrase is a Matthean favorite. The address "Father" establishes the relationship that makes the rest of the prayer possible.

A person's name, character, and identity were closely related in Semitic thought. To sanctify or make holy is to set apart from the mundane for divine service, or to recognize as being claimed by God. The petition that God's name might be sanctified is double sided. On the one hand, it is a prayer that God would act to establish God's own sovereignty. On the other hand, it voices the longing for the day when all people will revere God. The second petition, therefore, is an extension of the first. If God's name is sanctified, then God's sovereignty and dominion will have been established (Ezek 36:22-23). The preaching of the kingdom of God has been the driving purpose of Jesus' ministry (4:43; 6:20; 8:1; 9:2, 11), and there have been hints of its imminence (9:27; 10:9, 11). Old Testament hopes for the coming of the Day of the Lord (Isa 13:6; Joel 2:1) are therefore recast in the form of a petition that echoes Jesus' announcement of the coming of the kingdom (see 17:20; 22:16, 18).

11:3. Following the twin "thy" petitions come three petitions for our needs: bread, forgiveness, and deliverance. The most debated section of the Lord's Prayer is the petition for bread. Is this a prayer for ordinary bread or the eschatological bread of the messianic banquet (Isa 25:6-8; Luke 6:21; 14:15; 22:29-30)? What is the meaning of the unusual Greek term ἐπιούσιος (*epiousios*), which occurs in only one papyrus outside the NT: "essential," "daily," or "for the morrow"? Luke changes the wording of the prayer at this point by introducing the present tense, which connotes continual giving, and by adding the phrase "each day" (cf. Luke's addition of these words in 9:23; 16:19; 19:47; 22:53). The manna given to the Israelites in the wilderness could not be hoarded, so the Israelites had to rely on God's provision each day (Exod 16:4; Ps 78:24). The interpretation "bread for tomorrow" fits uneasily with Jesus' teachings about anxiety and concern for the future (12:22-31), or with the mission instructions given earlier (9:3). The occurrence of such a rare word (*epiousios*) in both Matthew and Luke shows that it was well fixed in early tradition. The claims for understanding bread in an ordinary sense rather than as a symbol of the messianic age are probably stronger, favoring the interpretation that the petition is that of a peasant who prays that God will supply each day's needs. Understood in this sense, the petition echoes Prov 30:8: "Feed me with the

---

124. Joachim Jeremias, *The Prayers of Jesus* (Philadelphia: Fortress, 1978) 11-65, esp. 60, 62. See also John Nolland, *Luke 9:21–18:34,* WBC 35B (Dallas: Word, 1989) 613; 4Q372 1:16.

food that I need (NRSV)." In Luke, of course, concern for the needs of the poor, the giving of bread, and sharing common meals are distinguishing marks of Jesus' ministry. Genuine prayer, therefore, begins with expressing to God as "Father" our complete dependence on God's mercy for even our most elemental needs (cf. 18:13-14).

11:4. Luke has changed the metaphorical language of Matthew ("debts" [ὀφειλήματα *opheilēmata*]) to theological language, "sins" (ἁμαρτίαι *hamartiai*). Forgiveness was one of the expected blessings of the day of salvation (Jer 31:34; Ezek 36:25-32; Isa 40:2; 55:6-7), and the sixth of the eighteen benedictions was a prayer for forgiveness. The alternation of tenses continues. The aorist was used in the two "thy" petitions, the present in the bread petition, and now the aorist is used in the request for forgiveness and the present in the justifying clause "for we ourselves forgive everyone indebted to us." As surely and desperately as we need bread, we need forgiveness. Jewish teachings, moreover, had already linked the necessity of forgiving others to one's ability to receive forgiveness: "Forgive your neighbor the wrong he has done,/ and then your sins will be pardoned when you pray" (Sir 28:2). One who will not forgive cannot receive forgiveness; mercy flows through the same channel, whether being given or received. There is no *quid pro quo* here; however, the ability to forgive and to be forgiven is part of the same gift. We stand in need not only of daily sustenance but also of continual

forgiveness. We can address these needs to God, however, because we have experienced God as Father.

Interpretation of the final petition again calls for resolution of two issues, one lexical and one theological. Does it speak of "temptation" or "trial"? Would God want to lead us to either temptation or trial? James 1:13-14—which may reflect interpretation of the model prayer, since James has numerous allusions to the Sermon on the Mount—asserts that God tempts no one. The devil tempts us to sin, not God (Rev 3:10). On the other hand, there is a strong biblical tradition of God's testing believers: the testing of Abraham (Gen 22:1), the testing of Job, the righteous one; the testing of the children of Israel in the wilderness (Exod 15:25; Deut 8:2); and Gethsemane, the testing of Jesus (Heb 5:7-8; cf. 12:3-11). In the light of this tradition and the threat of persecution, the model prayer appeals to God as the One who controls all of life for deliverance from any trials that will threaten either our confession of the "thy" petitions ("hallowed be thy name, thy kingdom come, thy will be done") or God's provision of our physical and spiritual needs (the "our" petitions). In this sense, the final petition is a climactic one that underscores our relationship to God as a Father to whom we can appeal for protection from any circumstances that might threaten our lives or our relationship to God. (See Reflections at 11:9-13.)

Luke 11:5-8, The Parable of a Shameless Neighbor

NIV

[5]Then he said to them, "Suppose one of you has a friend, and he goes to him at midnight and says, 'Friend, lend me three loaves of bread, [6]because a friend of mine on a journey has come to me, and I have nothing to set before him.'

[7]"Then the one inside answers, 'Don't bother me. The door is already locked, and my children are with me in bed. I can't get up and give you anything.' [8]I tell you, though he will not get up and give him the bread because he is his friend, yet because of the man's boldness[a] he will get up and give him as much as he needs.

[a]8 Or *persistence*

NRSV

5And he said to them, "Suppose one of you has a friend, and you go to him at midnight and say to him, 'Friend, lend me three loaves of bread; [6]for a friend of mine has arrived, and I have nothing to set before him.' [7]And he answers from within, 'Do not bother me; the door has already been locked, and my children are with me in bed; I cannot get up and give you anything.' [8]I tell you, even though he will not get up and give him anything because he is his friend, at least because of his persistence he will get up and give him whatever he needs.

COMMENTARY

Whereas the Lord's Prayer is followed in Matthew by an admonition to forgive others because if we do not then God will not forgive us, in Luke the Lord's Prayer is followed by assurances that God answers prayer. The assurance is implicit in the parable of vv. 5-8 and explicit in the sayings of vv. 9-13. Both sections employ comparisons and an argument from the lesser to the greater. If we agree that a neighbor or a father will answer a neighbor's or a child's request, then should we not also believe that God answers those who call out to God in need?

The parable assumes the setting of a Galilean village. Houses were simple structures of one or two rooms. Women baked bread in ovens in common courtyards, and so they would know who might have bread left at the end of the day. Hospitality was such a serious duty that any failure to provide for a guest would bring shame on the host.

The parable unfolds in one long question (vv. 5-7) and an answer that drives home the point of the parable (v. 8). Difficulties in interpreting the parable arise at two points: What is the meaning of the Greek term ἀναίδεια (*anaideia*) in v. 8 (translated "persistence" in the NRSV and less satisfactorily as "boldness" in the NIV), and to whom does it apply: the petitioner outside or the sleeper inside? How one resolves these difficulties determines whether the parable encourages persistence on the part of the petitioner or invites confidence because of the assurance that God will answer prayer.

The question, "Which of you?" expects a negative answer: "No one; it would be unthinkable." The repetition of the word for "friend" (φίλος *philos*) four times makes friendship the underlying premise of the parable, but in the end that premise will be displaced by another. The syntax of v. 5 allows some uncertainty regarding whether the hearer is cast in the role of the petitioner or the one petitioned, but the former seems to be the apparent meaning. The parable constructs a web of friendships: the hearer and his or her imagined friend, the one who goes to a friend's house in the middle of the night to ask for bread, and the friend who arrives late as an unexpected guest. The two central characters can be designated as the petitioner and the sleeper. The petitioner has received a guest and is obliged to provide him with a meal. Presumably there was other food in the house, but not the essential ingredient of the meal—bread. The parable then asks whether anyone could imagine a situation in which one would go to a friend in the middle of the night and be told by the neighbor that he could not get up to give his friend the bread the petitioner needed because he and his family were asleep. To get up in the middle of the night, get the bread, and draw the bolt on the door would awaken the whole family. Would a neighbor turn away a friend in the middle of the night and allow him to be shamed because he would not provide hospitality for a guest? Such a thing would be unimaginable in a Galilean village. Proverbs 3:28-29 speaks to a comparable situation: "Do not say to your neighbor, 'Go, and come again,/ tomorrow I will give it'—when you have it with you."

The response in v. 8 not only drives home the point that the sleeper will answer the petitioner's request but explains why such a conclusion is obvious. The Greek term *anaideia* means "shamelessness," but the difficulty in understanding how it applies in this context has led interpreters to translate it as "persistence," a meaning it does not have in any other ancient text. Following the normal meaning of the term, we may understand v. 8 as posing a comparison between the obligations of friendship and those of the honor-shame code. The ambiguous pronouns leave room for debate over whether the petitioner is shameless for begging for food in the middle of the night or whether we are to understand that the sleeper would be shameless for refusing a neighbor's request. Either reading is possible, but the latter is preferable. The situation is unthinkable not because of the petitioner's persistence but because honor demanded that a neighbor get up, awaken his whole family if necessary, and supply his neighbor's need—if not from friendship, then at least to avoid being shamed.

Jesus often drew parables from common experience. Had he perhaps been awakened one memorable night in Nazareth when his father opened the door to a neighbor in need? The parable requires us to compare our expectations of a neighbor with our assumptions about God. If a neighbor would help us, will God be slow to answer an urgent request? The neighbor might have to be roused from sleep, but the psalmist sang: "He who keeps Israel/ will neither slumber nor sleep" (Ps 121:4). We may pray confidently, therefore, not because we trust in our own persistence but because we know that in a time of need God is even more trustworthy than a neighbor. Commenting on this parable and the twin parable of the widow and the unjust judge in Luke 18:1-8, Bishop Richard C. Trench, writing in beautiful Victorian English, concluded, "If churlish man may be won by mere importunity to give, and unjust man to do right, how much more certainly shall the bountiful Lord bestow, and the righteous Lord do justice."[125] (See Reflections at 11:9-13.)

125. Richard C. Trench, *The Parables of Our Lord* (London: Kegan Paul, Trench, Trubner, & Co. Ltd., 1915) 330.

Luke 11:9-13, Assurances That God Hears Our Prayers

NIV

[9]"So I say to you: Ask and it will be given to you; seek and you will find; knock and the door will be opened to you. [10]For everyone who asks receives; he who seeks finds; and to him who knocks, the door will be opened.

[11]"Which of you fathers, if your son asks for[a] a fish, will give him a snake instead? [12]Or if he asks for an egg, will give him a scorpion? [13]If you then, though you are evil, know how to give good gifts to your children, how much more will your Father in heaven give the Holy Spirit to those who ask him!"

[a]11 Some manuscripts *for bread, will give him a stone; or if he asks for*

NRSV

[9]"So I say to you, Ask, and it will be given you; search, and you will find; knock, and the door will be opened for you. [10]For everyone who asks receives, and everyone who searches finds, and for everyone who knocks, the door will be opened. [11]Is there anyone among you who, if your child asks for[a] a fish, will give a snake instead of a fish? [12]Or if the child asks for an egg, will give a scorpion? [13]If you then, who are evil, know how to give good gifts to your children, how much more will the heavenly Father give the Holy Spirit[b] to those who ask him!"

[a]Other ancient authorities add *bread, will give a stone; or if your child asks for*   [b]Other ancient authorities read *the Father give the Holy Spirit from heaven*

COMMENTARY

The sayings that follow develop further the principle that we may pray confidently because we know God's readiness to answer. This unit contains a threefold admonition (vv. 9-10) to pray confidently, using three metaphors (ask, seek, knock), followed by two questions similar to the question in vv. 5-7. The two questions contrast the goodness of a human father with the superior goodness of God. The unit then concludes by underscoring the argument from the lesser to the greater: "how much more will the heavenly Father. . . . "

11:9-10. Just as v. 8 can be read as teaching either persistence or confidence because of God's greater goodness, so also the imperatives of vv. 9-10 can be understood either as encouraging persistence or as suggesting that "such appeal to God will work again and again."[126] The saying in vv. 9-10 has a verbatim parallel in Matt 7:7-8, and it is followed by the same cluster of sayings in both Gospels. The three sayings evoke a spirit and posture that is in keeping with both the Lord's Prayer and the parable in vv. 5-8. Asking in the hope that something will be given to you puts the hearer in the posture of a beggar. Seeking and finding is language common to the quest for wisdom, but it could have wider applications— perhaps even seeking lodging or shelter. Similarly,

126. Nolland, *Luke 9:21–18:34,* 630.

knocking in the hope of being received somewhere again puts the hearer in the posture of the destitute and the homeless.

Key words in the sayings in vv. 9-10 appear again later in Luke (see 11:29; 13:24-25). The three related sayings in vv. 9-10, therefore, draw on a system of metaphors that appear in other Lukan sayings. The assurances given in these sayings assume that the petitioner, the seeker, and the knocker are seeking God's kingdom and are praying in the posture of one who prays the model prayer. To such as these the assurances are given, and at the end of the Gospel Luke signals the fulfillment of these assurances by repeating the verb "to open" (ἀνοίγω *anoigō*) three times in reference to the risen Lord's activities: He opened the eyes of the disciples (24:31), he opened the Scriptures to them (24:32), and he opened their minds (24:45).

11:11-12. Two related sayings concerning the goodness of a father follow. Again the question begins with the typically Lukan phrase "Who among you . . . ?" The question asks the hearer to put himself or herself in the position of a parent whose child asks for a fish or an egg—a request for common food parallel to the petition for bread in the model prayer. What parent would give the child a snake instead of fish or a scorpion instead of an egg? The cruel substitutes may each bear a resemblance to the foodstuff requested. A snake is scaly like a fish, and a scorpion that has rolled into a ball may be mistaken momentarily for an egg. Matthew 7:9-10 renders the same sayings with different pairings—bread/stone, fish/snake—but the point is the same.

11:13. This verse draws the conclusion from the hypothetical questions, just as v. 8 draws the conclusion from the question-shaped parable in vv. 5-7. The conclusion invites the hearer to compare contrasting pairs and reason from the lesser to the greater: You being evil [human fathers]/the [good] heavenly Father; good things/the Holy Spirit. If a human father will give his children good things, then how much more will the heavenly Father give? Therefore, if human fathers give good things, the heavenly Father will give the Holy Spirit—the greatest gift—to those who ask. Matthew draws the more obvious parallel—you being evil/the heavenly Father will give good things—but Luke breaks the parallelism in order to foreshadow the giving of the Holy Spirit and its work in the early church (see Luke 24:49; Acts 1:5, 8; 2:1-4).

REFLECTIONS

As we have seen, Luke 11:1-13 provides a unit of instruction on prayer. The disciples ask Jesus to teach them to pray, but Jesus does not give the disciples magic words to say. Instead, Jesus teaches them about the nature of the one to whom they pray. Luke 11:1-13 begins and ends emphasizing that disciples of Jesus can pray to God as to a heavenly Father. The first word of the model prayer is "Father." The "thy" petitions establish what it means to revere God as Father, while the "our" petitions assure that the Father will provide for the physical and spiritual needs of those who worship him. The concluding and climactic petition asks for protection as from a heavenly Father. The parable of the neighbor in need raises the issue of God's reliability, arguing that if a neighbor will get up in the middle of the night to answer one's need in order to avoid being shamed, how much more can the one who prays count on God's readiness to answer a call for help. The sayings that follow encourage confident and persistent prayer in the knowledge that God's goodness is greater than that of any human father.

When the disciples ask for a lesson on prayer, therefore, Jesus responds with a lesson on the nature of God as Father. The greatest stimuli to prayer are the awareness of our need and absolute dependence on God and our knowledge and experience of the character of God. Only those who know their own need and the love of God as a heavenly Father will be able to pray truly. The sayings in this unit, consequently, speak explicitly of the Fatherhood of God while implicitly casting the one who prays in the position of a beggar or child in need.

The triple sayings in vv. 9-10 seem to offer assurance that ours is a God who gives, opens, and allows us to find. Certainly that is true. The danger comes when we take these sayings as a blank check on which we can write anything our hearts desire. Jesus assured his followers that God answers prayer, but he did not guarantee that they would receive whatever they requested. The assurances that follow the Lord's Prayer assume that those who ask, seek, and knock are asking from their need and for God's will, seeking the kingdom, and knocking at the door as a neighbor in the night. We may be anxious about the necessities of life, but Jesus calls us to a higher pursuit: "Seek his kingdom, and these things shall be yours as well . . . for it is your Father's good pleasure to give you the kingdom" (see 12:31-32). Our praying should be consistent with our seeking. Then, when we pray as Jesus taught us, the assurance that God answers is hardly needed.

Not only does God give, open, and allow us to find God, but God also asks, seeks, and knocks. In the parable of the fig tree, the owner comes seeking fruit but finds none (13:6-7). In another parable the servants wait for their master to come and knock so that they may open the door for him to enter (12:36). Again, Jesus asked in another parable on prayer, "And yet, when the Son of Man comes, will he find faith on earth?" (18:8).

Jesus' teachings on prayer, therefore, require that the one who prays will pray as one aware of desperate self-need before God. Jesus' teachings assure us that prayer is effective not because of our cajoling, or because we have found the right words, but because of God's nature as a Father who loves his own and wants to give to those in need. Both the model prayer and parables elsewhere in the Gospel underscore the related point that prayer is ultimately the worship of God as Father, acknowledging God's holiness and devoting ourselves to the coming of God's kingdom. Where we bring our need to God's love in faith, that is prayer.

LUKE 11:14-36, RESPONSES TO CHARGES OF DEVIANCY

NIV

[14]Jesus was driving out a demon that was mute. When the demon left, the man who had been mute spoke, and the crowd was amazed. [15]But some of them said, "By Beelzebub,[a] the prince of demons, he is driving out demons." [16]Others tested him by asking for a sign from heaven.

[17]Jesus knew their thoughts and said to them: "Any kingdom divided against itself will be ruined, and a house divided against itself will fall. [18]If Satan is divided against himself, how can his kingdom stand? I say this because you claim that I drive out demons by Beelzebub. [19]Now if I drive out demons by Beelzebub, by whom do your followers drive them out? So then, they will be your judges. [20]But if I drive out demons by the finger of God, then the kingdom of God has come to you.

[21]"When a strong man, fully armed, guards his own house, his possessions are safe. [22]But when

a15 Greek *Beezeboul* or *Beelzeboul*; also in verses 18 and 19

NRSV

14Now he was casting out a demon that was mute; when the demon had gone out, the one who had been mute spoke, and the crowds were amazed. [15]But some of them said, "He casts out demons by Beelzebul, the ruler of the demons." [16]Others, to test him, kept demanding from him a sign from heaven. [17]But he knew what they were thinking and said to them, "Every kingdom divided against itself becomes a desert, and house falls on house. [18]If Satan also is divided against himself, how will his kingdom stand?—for you say that I cast out the demons by Beelzebul. [19]Now if I cast out the demons by Beelzebul, by whom do your exorcists[a] cast them out? Therefore they will be your judges. [20]But if it is by the finger of God that I cast out the demons, then the kingdom of God has come to you. [21]When a strong man, fully armed, guards his castle, his property is safe. [22]But when one stronger than he

a Gk *sons*

someone stronger attacks and overpowers him, he takes away the armor in which the man trusted and divides up the spoils.

²³"He who is not with me is against me, and he who does not gather with me, scatters.

²⁴"When an evil*a* spirit comes out of a man, it goes through arid places seeking rest and does not find it. Then it says, 'I will return to the house I left.' ²⁵When it arrives, it finds the house swept clean and put in order. ²⁶Then it goes and takes seven other spirits more wicked than itself, and they go in and live there. And the final condition of that man is worse than the first."

²⁷As Jesus was saying these things, a woman in the crowd called out, "Blessed is the mother who gave you birth and nursed you."

²⁸He replied, "Blessed rather are those who hear the word of God and obey it."

²⁹As the crowds increased, Jesus said, "This is a wicked generation. It asks for a miraculous sign, but none will be given it except the sign of Jonah. ³⁰For as Jonah was a sign to the Ninevites, so also will the Son of Man be to this generation. ³¹The Queen of the South will rise at the judgment with the men of this generation and condemn them; for she came from the ends of the earth to listen to Solomon's wisdom, and now one*b* greater than Solomon is here. ³²The men of Nineveh will stand up at the judgment with this generation and condemn it; for they repented at the preaching of Jonah, and now one greater than Jonah is here.

³³"No one lights a lamp and puts it in a place where it will be hidden, or under a bowl. Instead he puts it on its stand, so that those who come in may see the light. ³⁴Your eye is the lamp of your body. When your eyes are good, your whole body also is full of light. But when they are bad, your body also is full of darkness. ³⁵See to it, then, that the light within you is not darkness. ³⁶Therefore, if your whole body is full of light, and no part of it dark, it will be completely lighted, as when the light of a lamp shines on you."

a24 Greek *unclean*   *b31* Or *something*; also in verse 32

attacks him and overpowers him, he takes away his armor in which he trusted and divides his plunder. ²³Whoever is not with me is against me, and whoever does not gather with me scatters.

²⁴"When the unclean spirit has gone out of a person, it wanders through waterless regions looking for a resting place, but not finding any, it says, 'I will return to my house from which I came.' ²⁵When it comes, it finds it swept and put in order. ²⁶Then it goes and brings seven other spirits more evil than itself, and they enter and live there; and the last state of that person is worse than the first."

²⁷While he was saying this, a woman in the crowd raised her voice and said to him, "Blessed is the womb that bore you and the breasts that nursed you!" ²⁸But he said, "Blessed rather are those who hear the word of God and obey it!"

²⁹When the crowds were increasing, he began to say, "This generation is an evil generation; it asks for a sign, but no sign will be given to it except the sign of Jonah. ³⁰For just as Jonah became a sign to the people of Nineveh, so the Son of Man will be to this generation. ³¹The queen of the South will rise at the judgment with the people of this generation and condemn them, because she came from the ends of the earth to listen to the wisdom of Solomon, and see, something greater than Solomon is here! ³²The people of Nineveh will rise up at the judgment with this generation and condemn it, because they repented at the proclamation of Jonah, and see, something greater than Jonah is here!

³³"No one after lighting a lamp puts it in a cellar,*a* but on the lampstand so that those who enter may see the light. ³⁴Your eye is the lamp of your body. If your eye is healthy, your whole body is full of light; but if it is not healthy, your body is full of darkness. ³⁵Therefore consider whether the light in you is not darkness. ³⁶If then your whole body is full of light, with no part of it in darkness, it will be as full of light as when a lamp gives you light with its rays."

a Other ancient authorities add *or under the bushel basket*

COMMENTARY

Abruptly, the scene shifts and a crowd is present with Jesus. The exorcism of a man who could not speak sets the stage for charges that Jesus casts out demons by the power of Beelzebul and for requests for a sign. Jesus' teachings and mighty works set him apart from every "in" group and broke the stereotypes by which persons were identified in the first century. One way of dealing with the threat that Jesus posed to established groups, norms, and authorities was to discredit him by pinning on him a label of deviancy. This section chronicles the rising hostility and conflict that Jesus encounters. Jesus' answer is composed of several discrete parts: three arguments against the Beelzebul charge (vv. 17-20), the simile of the strong man and the metaphor of gathering and scattering (vv. 21-23), the danger that the unclean spirit may return (vv. 24-26), the response of a woman from the crowd (vv. 27-28), Jesus' answer to the request for a sign (vv. 29-32), and his call for light and health in the whole person (vv. 33-36). In response to the crowd's challenges, Jesus rejects both their charges and the demand for a sign and warns that the removal of evil is not the final solution, since the spirits may return; wholeness and light throughout the body are required. Because Jesus' work represents the vanquishing of Satan and the coming of light and wholeness, it is itself a sign that the kingdom of God is present in Jesus.

11:14, Exorcising the Mute Spirit. The only other reference to the healing of the deaf (or mute) in Luke occurs in 7:22 (cf. 1:22), where it is related to the fulfillment of the prophets. While that connection is not developed here as it is in Matthew, it is nevertheless noteworthy that Jesus meets opposition when he does the mighty works anticipated by the prophets (Isa 35:5; cf. Matt 12:22). When Jesus exorcises the demon, he sets the stage for the charge against him and his response concerning the fate of the demons and those who have been delivered from demons (vv. 24-26).

11:15-16, The Charges Against Jesus. The exorcism generates a controversy dialogue. Although the deaf-mute man speaks, confirming that the miracle has occurred, some in the crowd are more concerned about the threat that such a demonstration of power posed than the healing that the man has experienced. Unable to deny the exorcism, they brand the exorcist as an ally of Beelzebul, "Baal, the Prince." The name *Baalzebub,* which is a deliberate corruption meaning "Lord of the Flies," appears in 2 Kgs 1:2-3, 6, 16. By the first century, however, Beelzebul appears to have been synonymous with Satan. The second response is not found in the parallel material in Matt 11:22-30 or Mark 3:22-27, but echoes Mark 8:11. The narrator's description of the response as arising out of a desire to test Jesus signals that this encounter is like the devil's temptations of Jesus at the beginning of his ministry—the only other place where this verb ("test" or "tempt" [πειράζω *peirazō*]) is used in Luke (4:2; cf. 10:25). Jesus is not allied with Satan; he is being tested just as Satan had tested him earlier (cf. 4:13; 8:13; 11:4; 22:28, 40, 46). Although Jesus has just exorcised a demon and restored the deaf-mute man, some ask for a sign from heaven—something to prove the power or identity of Jesus. The request should probably be understood in the light of the function of signs in confirming the words of prophets in the OT (Deut 13:1-2; 2 Kgs 20:8-11; cf. John 6:30-31). The request for a sign will be answered in vv. 29-32, and the issue of the persecution of the prophets will recur in vv. 47-51. But first, Jesus responds to the charge that he worked by the power of Beelzebul. Regarding the narrator's comment that Jesus knew what they were thinking, see Commentary on 9:47.

11:17-20, Jesus and Beelzebul. Jesus' first response is to insist that those who charged that he was working with Satan did not understand the meaning of the exorcisms; the exorcisms represented a direct assault on Satan's power. If Jesus were Satan's ally, the exorcisms would represent a mutiny, and neither a kingdom nor a house can stand if there is internal dissension.

Jesus' second argument is that if his exorcisms indicate that he works under the power of Satan, then the same would have to be said of other Jewish exorcists: their sons. This argument assumes that there were other exorcists who were esteemed by Jesus' critics (see Mark 9:38; Acts

19:13-14). Josephus writes that he personally saw a certain Eleazar "free men possessed by demons" in the presence of Vespasian and his soldiers.[127] If they believed that other exorcists worked by the power of God, then they should believe the same of Jesus. Otherwise, they were condemning their own exorcists with their condemnation of Jesus.

Jesus' third argument explains the real meaning of his works. If they are not by the power of Satan but indeed by the power of God, then Jesus' works signal that the kingdom of God has come among them. Because the exorcisms show that Satan's power has been broken, they are at the same time evidence that God's reign is being established. The tense of the verb is past (aorist): in Jesus the kingdom has come upon them. The expression "the finger of God" is drawn from the Egyptian magicians' explanation of Moses' signs in Exod 8:19. If Jesus' opponents understood as much as the Egyptian magicians, they would see that Jesus' works were signs that the kingdom had come.

11:21-23, The Simile of the Strong Man. The simile of the strong man is found in a less developed form in Mark 3:27 and Matt 12:29 (cf. Isa 49:24). Luke, however, has developed the image so that the strong man fortifies himself with armor. Rather than the common word for "house," Luke uses a word that can also mean "castle" (αυλή *aulē*). The strong man's goods are safe until one who is even stronger comes and takes away his armor. Then, his armor and the rest of his goods will be divided among the conquerors. By embellishing the image, Luke enhances the meaning of Jesus' works. Seen in the light of this simile, the exorcisms confirm that two kings have clashed. Powerful as Satan is, God had defeated him, seized his armor, and is plundering his possessions.

The saying that concludes this paragraph is the more restrictive form of the saying in 9:50. There Jesus said that one who was not against him was for him; here he says that one who is not for him is against him. (See Commentary on 9:50.) Because one must choose one side or the other (cf. Josh 5:13), each disciple should examine his or her own commitment to Jesus. The latter part of the verse shifts the metaphor; one is either gathering or scattering the sheep. A time of crisis is

no time for indecision; in the struggle to establish God's claims over Satan's there can be no neutrality.

11:24-26, The Return of the Unclean Spirit. This cluster of sayings follows easily from the foregoing interpretations of Jesus' exorcisms. While the exorcisms may be understood as demonstrating that the power of Satan has been broken, decisive action is still needed. Although it has been argued that in this parable the unclean spirit has not been cast out but is just traveling in search of a better dwelling place,[128] the present literary context of the parable suggests that it is an extension of the debate over Jesus' exorcisms and a counterpoint to vv. 21-22. Because there is no middle ground, no room for neutrality (v. 23), the person who has been delivered from the power of the unclean spirit must fill his or her life with the kingdom of God (v. 20) and obedience to the Word of God (v. 28). Otherwise, it will be as though having expelled one demon from a house, that house is set in order only to be inhabited by the original demon and seven others worse than the first.

The waterless places of the desert were thought to be haunted by demons (Lev 16:10; Isa 34:13-14). The language of this parable echoes early Christian warnings about apostasy. Second Peter calls apostates "waterless springs" (2:17): "For if, after they have escaped the defilements of the world through the knowledge of our Lord and Savior Jesus Christ, they are again entangled in them and overpowered, the last state has become worse for them than the first" (2 Pet 2:20).

11:27-28, The Condition of True Blessedness. The introductory phrases of v. 27 tie the next pronouncement to the previous context. Following Jesus' exorcism of the deaf and mute man, the crowds were amazed (v. 14), but some charged that Jesus acted by the power of Beelzebul (v. 15). Now a woman "in the crowd" praises Jesus with a maternal blessing. The blessing is formulated in traditional language (see Gen 49:25). The blessing on Jesus by proclaiming the blessedness of Jesus' mother echoes the benediction of Mary in 1:42, 45, and 48. In effect, the woman's blessing claims that Jesus is so wonderful that he is a blessing to his mother. Jesus does not deny the blessing on his mother but seizes the

---

127. Josephus *Antiquities of the Jews* 8.46.

128. John Nolland, *Luke 9:21–18:34,* WBC 35B (Dallas: Word, 1989) 645-47.

moment to point to the basis for blessing for all disciples: Those who hear God's Word and obey it will be blessed (cf. 8:15, 21).

The particle (μενοῦν *menoun*) used to introduce this beatitude can have various meanings: contradiction ("no, but"), affirmation ("yes, indeed"), or modification ("yes, but"). One from whom a demon has been expelled may be no better off (vv. 24-26), but one who hears the Word of God and obeys it is truly blessed. Another counterpoint is suggested by the repetition of the same verb in different senses in vv. 21 and 28; the strong man who guards his possessions may be defeated and plundered, but the faithful disciple who guards God's Word will be blessed.

11:29-32, The Sign of Jonah. Jesus' debate with the crowd following his exorcism continues but now takes up the second charge. Some said he worked by the power of Beelzebul (11:15), a charge Jesus rebuffed in vv. 17-23. Others called for him to give them a sign (11:16). Jesus' response to this request has parallels in Mark 8:11-12 and more immediately in the Q material also found in Matt 12:38-42. These passages display a variety of responses to the request for a sign:

(1) no sign will be given (Mark 8:11-12);

(2) no sign will be given except the sign of Jonah (Matt 16:4);

(3) no sign will be given except the sign of Jonah, who became a sign to the people of Nineveh (Luke 11:29-30); and

(4) no sign will be given except the sign of Jonah: The Son of Man will be in the heart of the earth for three days and three nights, just as Jonah was in the belly of the sea monster for three days and three nights (Matt 12:39-40).[129]

In both the latter passage in Matthew and here in Luke the saying about Jonah is followed by a comparison with the Queen of the South, but the sequence is reversed. In Matthew the saying about the men of Nineveh (Matt 12:41; Luke 11:32) precedes the saying about the Queen of the South (Matt 12:42; Luke 11:31). The result is that in Luke this cluster of sayings opens and closes with references to Jonah, and Jonah's preaching is interpreted by association with Solomon's wisdom.

The clamor of the crowds recalls their request

for a sign. Jesus' response, however, is not to give them a sign but to underscore his call for them to hear and obey the Word of God (see v. 28). The call for a sign indicates that the crowd has not been receptive to Jesus and his message of the kingdom. Therefore, it justifies the verdict, "This is an evil generation"—indeed, a generation whose iniquity might be compared with that of the people of Nineveh. They were given the sign of Jonah, and none other would be given to the crowd around Jesus.

The question to be answered is, "What was the sign of Jonah?" Matthew (12:39-40) interprets Jonah's three days and nights in the belly of the sea monster as portentous of Jesus' three days in the tomb. Luke, however, says nothing of this early Christian interpretation, saying that Jonah was himself a sign (v. 30) and that the people of Nineveh repented as a result of Jonah's proclamation (v. 32). For Luke the sign of Jonah was his call for repentance, and no other sign would be given to that generation except Jesus' call for them to hear the Word of God and obey it (v. 28).

The Queen of Sheba, or the Queen of the South, journeyed from her kingdom in southwest Arabia to test the reports she had heard of Solomon's wisdom (1 Kgs 10:1-13; 2 Chr 9:1-12). When she had tested Solomon with "hard questions" (1 Kgs 10:1), she was convinced of the wisdom God had given to him and blessed the Lord who had set Solomon on the throne of Israel (1 Kgs 10:9). At the judgment, therefore, she would rise to condemn that wicked generation because they had one who was greater than Solomon, and they did not hear him. Similarly, the people of Nineveh—who were Gentiles!—would add their condemnation because they had repented as a result of Jonah's preaching, but that generation had heard the preaching of one greater than Jonah and yet did not repent. The argument is reminiscent of the warnings to Chorazin and Bethsaida, who did not repent when they saw deeds of power that would have led Tyre and Sidon to repent (10:13-16). Luke has systematically shown that Jesus was greater than any of the prophets (see Commentary on 7:18-35). Jesus was greater than either a prophet (Jonah) or a king (Solomon). They had heard the Messiah (9:20), the Son of God (9:35).

---

129. Joseph A. Fitzmyer, *The Gospel According to Luke Luke (X–XXIV)*, AB 28A (Garden City, N.Y.: Doubleday, 1985) 930.

11:33-36, Giving Light to the Whole Body. A collection of sayings gathered by the catchwords "lamp" and "light" follows. Verse 33 is a doublet of Luke 8:16 (Matt 5:15; cf. Mark 4:21). Verses 34-35 have a parallel in Matt 6:22-23, but v. 36 appears to be a conclusion fashioned by Luke.

The metaphors of light and the lamp are put to different uses in these verses. In context, the lamp in v. 33 may represent Jesus, the one greater than Jonah or Solomon, who has come to give light. That light should not be hidden but set so that it can give light to all who come into the house. The latter phrase may be an allusion to converts—those who come into the early Christian house churches.

Verse 34 takes the metaphor of the lamp in a different direction. The verse has often been misinterpreted, however, because it assumes an ancient understanding of the eye and sight. We know that the eye responds to light from outside the body, but in antiquity the common understanding in both Greco-Roman and Jewish literature was that the eye emitted light and that sight was possible when the light from within met light from outside. The *Testament of Job,* for example, contains the following statement: "My eyes, acting as lamps, looked about" (18.4).[130] Therefore, the eye, that sparkles and flashes, is the lamp of the body. Now the lamp is not Jesus but the light within the disciple. If the eye is clear, pure, and healthy, then it gives sight. Here the physical condition for sight suggests ethical purity and spiritual health. When the eye is clear and gives light, then one can see, and the whole body is filled with light. On the other hand, if the eye is not clear, the whole body remains in the dark. Again, the language suggests not merely a physical but an ethical condition: literally, "but if it is evil"—the same word used in 11:4, 13, 26, 29. Jesus therefore invites that evil generation to consider whether the light in them has become darkness. Verse 36 mixes the metaphors of the two preceding statements. If the body is light (v. 34), then it will be as full of light as when a lamp illumines you (v. 33).

The sayings have been drawn from independent contexts and woven into this controversy scene by the evangelist. In context they remain loosely connected to the preceding exchange, but at least by implication Jesus is the lamp in v. 34. This evil generation, which would have recognized Solomon's wisdom and responded to Jonah's preaching of judgment, does not accept Jesus because its "eye" is evil. The light that Jesus gives should fill the whole body. The point is similar to that made earlier in other ways. It is insufficient merely to exorcise the demons if the space they vacate is not filled with something good. True blessing comes to those who hear the Word of God and obey it. The controversy concludes, therefore, with the insistence that the light Jesus gives to all who enter should fill the whole body.

130. Cited by Dale C. Allison, Jr., "The Eye Is the Lamp of the Body (Matthew 6.22-23=Luke 11.34-36)," *NTS* 33 (1987) 70.

REFLECTIONS

This extended controversy dialogue offers various possibilities for theological reflection and homiletical development. The controversy begins when some in the crowd react to Jesus' exorcism of a deaf and mute person. Jesus was helping a person in need and fulfilling a line from the prophet Isaiah, but still there were those who criticized him for what he did. Many people can identify with the frustrating circumstance of being attacked for doing good (see John 10:32). The hostile reaction to the exorcism reveals further the threat that good poses for those who are not bound to doing good under the sovereignty of God. This confrontation is not petty jealousy or envy but exposes the enmity of Satan to the kingdom of God. Thus the church should never underestimate the level of hostility it may encounter when attempting to carry out its redemptive mission. Jesus named the evil powers for what they were and defined the meaning of his own work—the advent of the kingdom of God (v. 20).

In the struggle between good and evil, change does not come without conflict—not only opposition from others, but internal turmoil. To heal, Jesus had to expel the demon from the man. The images of Beelzebul, divided kingdoms, and overcoming the strong man in his fortress are metaphors of combat. Internally one may expel the demon only to have it return with seven more. What does one do when light has shined into one's soul and the light within is darkness?

In the early chapters of Victor Hugo's *Les Misérables,* Jean Valjean, the ex-convict, steals the bishop's silver. When the police apprehend Valjean and bring him back to the bishop's house, the bishop verifies Valjean's story that the silver was a gift to him and adds that he meant to give the silver candlesticks to him also. The sheer grace of the bishop's act sets off a furious struggle within Jean Valjean that is best described in Hugo's own words:

> Faced with all these things, he reeled like a drunk. . . . Did a voice whisper in his ear that he had just passed through the decisive hour of his destiny, that there was no longer a middle course for him, that if, thereafter, he were not the best of men, he would be the worst, that he must now, so to speak, climb higher than the bishop or fall lower than the convict; that, if he wanted to become good, he must become an angel; that, if he wanted to remain evil, he must become a monster? . . . One thing was certain, though he did not suspect it, that he was no longer the same man, that all was changed in him, that it was no longer in his power to prevent the bishop from having talked to him and having touched him.

An act of grace so changed Jean Valjean's life that he could no longer be the person he had been. One may wonder what became of the deaf-mute man touched by Jesus. Did the demon return or did light fill the man's entire life thereafter? What became of those in the crowd, those who called for a sign, or the woman who called out the blessing on Jesus and his mother? In the end, the text touches the reader so that he or she can no longer be the same.

The controversy poses a range of responses for readers. Some may test it, like those who asked for sign. Some may reject it entirely, like those who charged Jesus with using the power of Beelzebul. To reject the preaching of Jesus, however, is to reject a wisdom greater than Solomon and a prophetic warning more dire than Jonah's. Fortify yourself against grace as you will, but one even stronger has come. No halfway response is permitted. If one merely expels the demon, seven more will return. If one has a good eye, however, the light of Jesus' kingdom will flood one's entire being. True blessedness comes to those who hear the Word of God and obey it (v. 28).

Good preachers paint pictures. Notice the kaleidoscope of images this controversy dialogue spins before the reader: a divided kingdom, demons and exorcists, the finger of God, the strong man's castle and the one who takes his armor, waterless regions, a house swept clean, the womb and breasts that nourish, Jonah and the Ninevites, Solomon and the Queen of Sheba, a lamp and a lampstand, a clear eye and a darkened eye. Who doesn't reel like a drunkard when touched by the grace of such images and metaphors?

LUKE 11:37-54, WOES TO THE PHARISEES AND LAWYERS

NIV

37When Jesus had finished speaking, a Pharisee invited him to eat with him; so he went in and reclined at the table. 38But the Pharisee, noticing that Jesus did not first wash before the meal, was surprised.

NRSV

37While he was speaking, a Pharisee invited him to dine with him; so he went in and took his place at the table. 38The Pharisee was amazed to see that he did not first wash before dinner. 39Then the Lord said to him, "Now you Pharisees

NIV

³⁹Then the Lord said to him, "Now then, you Pharisees clean the outside of the cup and dish, but inside you are full of greed and wickedness. ⁴⁰You foolish people! Did not the one who made the outside make the inside also? ⁴¹But give what is inside *the dish*ᵃ to the poor, and everything will be clean for you.

⁴²"Woe to you Pharisees, because you give God a tenth of your mint, rue and all other kinds of garden herbs, but you neglect justice and the love of God. You should have practiced the latter without leaving the former undone.

⁴³"Woe to you Pharisees, because you love the most important seats in the synagogues and greetings in the marketplaces.

⁴⁴"Woe to you, because you are like unmarked graves, which men walk over without knowing it."

⁴⁵One of the experts in the law answered him, "Teacher, when you say these things, you insult us also."

⁴⁶Jesus replied, "And you experts in the law, woe to you, because you load people down with burdens they can hardly carry, and you yourselves will not lift one finger to help them.

⁴⁷"Woe to you, because you build tombs for the prophets, and it was your forefathers who killed them. ⁴⁸So you testify that you approve of what your forefathers did; they killed the prophets, and you build their tombs. ⁴⁹Because of this, God in his wisdom said, 'I will send them prophets and apostles, some of whom they will kill and others they will persecute.' ⁵⁰Therefore this generation will be held responsible for the blood of all the prophets that has been shed since the beginning of the world, ⁵¹from the blood of Abel to the blood of Zechariah, who was killed between the altar and the sanctuary. Yes, I tell you, this generation will be held responsible for it all.

⁵²"Woe to you experts in the law, because you have taken away the key to knowledge. You yourselves have not entered, and you have hindered those who were entering."

⁵³When Jesus left there, the Pharisees and the teachers of the law began to oppose him fiercely and to besiege him with questions, ⁵⁴waiting to catch him in something he might say.

ᵃ41 Or *what you have*

NRSV

clean the outside of the cup and of the dish, but inside you are full of greed and wickedness. ⁴⁰You fools! Did not the one who made the outside make the inside also? ⁴¹So give for alms those things that are within; and see, everything will be clean for you.

⁴²"But woe to you Pharisees! For you tithe mint and rue and herbs of all kinds, and neglect justice and the love of God; it is these you ought to have practiced, without neglecting the others. ⁴³Woe to you Pharisees! For you love to have the seat of honor in the synagogues and to be greeted with respect in the marketplaces. ⁴⁴Woe to you! For you are like unmarked graves, and people walk over them without realizing it."

⁴⁵One of the lawyers answered him, "Teacher, when you say these things, you insult us too." ⁴⁶And he said, "Woe also to you lawyers! For you load people with burdens hard to bear, and you yourselves do not lift a finger to ease them. ⁴⁷Woe to you! For you build the tombs of the prophets whom your ancestors killed. ⁴⁸So you are witnesses and approve of the deeds of your ancestors; for they killed them, and you build their tombs. ⁴⁹Therefore also the Wisdom of God said, 'I will send them prophets and apostles, some of whom they will kill and persecute,' ⁵⁰so that this generation may be charged with the blood of all the prophets shed since the foundation of the world, ⁵¹from the blood of Abel to the blood of Zechariah, who perished between the altar and the sanctuary. Yes, I tell you, it will be charged against this generation. ⁵²Woe to you lawyers! For you have taken away the key of knowledge; you did not enter yourselves, and you hindered those who were entering."

⁵³When he went outside, the scribes and the Pharisees began to be very hostile toward him and to cross-examine him about many things, ⁵⁴lying in wait for him, to catch him in something he might say.

COMMENTARY

In the next section, the scene shifts to a meal at a Pharisee's home, which becomes the occasion for the pronouncement of three woes against the Pharisees and three woes against the lawyers. The topic of debate changes, but the level of hostility continues to rise. This is the third in the sequence of scenes in Luke in which Jesus debates with Pharisees at a meal or eats in the home of a Pharisee (5:29-32, at Levi's house; 7:36-50, with Simon, the Pharisee; 11:37-54, with a Pharisee; 14:1-24, with a leader of the Pharisees).

The sayings in this scene have parallels in Matthew 23, as will be noted below, but it is difficult to determine the extent of Luke's own contribution to the shaping of these sayings. In general, Luke has collected the sayings in two groups of three, separated those addressed to the lawyers from those addressed to the Pharisees, and deleted references to Jewish concerns that would not have been understood by Gentile-Christian readers.[131] The woes have a double function in Luke. On the one hand, they explain Jesus' conflict with the religious authorities of his day, and on the other hand they serve as a warning to Christian readers not to fall into the same traps of false piety. The woe is an expression of lament that looks to the future judgment. "Alas" for those whose piety is so misdirected that it cloaks greed, corruption, and impurity within.

11:37-41. The stage is set for the confrontation when Jesus takes his place at the table without having washed first (see Mark 7:2, which appears in a section of Mark that is omitted by Luke). The Pharisees observed strict rules regarding ritual cleanness, formed associations called *ḥăbûrôt,* and generally ate only with those who also maintained ritual purity (Mark 7:3-4). By not washing—especially after having performed an exorcism and been in contact with the crowds—Jesus scandalizes his host.

Jesus' initial response has a parallel in Matt 23:25 but lacks the introductory "woe," perhaps in order to create the Lukan scheme of two groups of three woes. The saying starts as though it will condemn the Pharisees for washing

the outside of the cup and the dish while leaving the inside dirty, as is more nearly the case in Matthew. In the second half of the saying, however, Luke abandons the metaphor, saying instead "but inside *you* are full of greed and wickedness." The metaphorical image of the contrast between the condition of the inside and the outside of a cup or vessel continues in Jesus' retort. The Pharisees should realize that God made the whole person, inside and out, and that God is not just concerned with the observance of rituals of purity but with the purity of one's heart. Verse 41 is surprising and probably deliberately cryptic. The NRSV gives a literal translation. Compare the more interpretive translation of the NIV. Does this refer to what is within the cup or what is within the person? If the former, then by giving away the food or drink within the vessel one renders it all clean—a surprising and delightful twist![132] On the other hand, if Jesus challenges the Pharisees to give as alms what is within the person, then the saying requires reflection on how one can give away what is within the person. Or is it that the almsgiving is to be an expression of what is in the person?[133] A person's actions should reflect her or his inner purity. It is probably best to read Jesus' solution as a continuation of the metaphor: Give away the contents of the cup, and it will all be clean. Almsgiving (see 12:33) is the most effective antidote to greed (v. 39).

11:42-44. The first woe continues the contrast between the inner and the outer aspects in the previous saying but adds the contrast between the important and the insignificant. Comparison with the Matthean version of the saying (Matt 23:23) highlights Luke's emphases. Whereas Matthew lists herbs on which the payment of a tithe was required,[134] Luke drops these two from his list and makes the list all inclusive by adding "rue and herbs of all kinds," even though no tithe was required on rue or other herbs that grew wild.[135] Luke also omits Matthew's reference to "the weightier things of the law," which Matthew summarizes as justice, mercy, and faith. In their

131. See Fitzmyer, *The Gospel According to Luke (X–XXIV),* 943.

132. Ibid., 945.
133. John Nolland, *Luke 9:21–18:34,* 664-65.
134. See *m. Maaseroth* 4.5, "dill"; *m. Demai* 2.1, "cummin."
135. See *m. Shebiith* 9.1.

place, however, Luke charges that the Pharisees neglect justice and "the love of God"—concerns that echo the two great commands named in 10:27—love God and your neighbor as yourself. Jesus' criticism of piety that observes external obedience while neglecting justice and the love of God is an echo of Mic 6:8, "And what does the LORD require of you/ but to do justice, and to love kindness,/ and to walk humbly with your God?"

The second woe, which parallels Matt 23:6-7, continues the critique of external piety but lacks the corresponding statement of a corrective act. True piety does not seek praise from others (see Matt 6:1; Mark 12:38-39). Those whose spiritual discipline is concerned with the fulfillment of the corrective statements in vv. 41-42—almsgiving, justice, and the love of God—will not be concerned with occupying the seats of honor in the synagogue or being given special recognition in the marketplace. The love of the thing that brings public applause to oneself (v. 43) is contrary to the love that is directed toward God (v. 42).

The third woe to the Pharisees returns to the contrast between the outer and the inner. Contact with a corpse rendered a person unclean (Lev 21:1-4, 11; Num 19:11-22). Graves had to be marked, therefore, so that persons would not unwittingly defile themselves by contact with them. Matthew's version of this woe refers to the practice of whitewashing tombs so that they would be evident to all who passed by. The Matthean woe then charges that the scribes and Pharisees are like whitewashed tombs, clean on the outside but corrupt within (Matt 23:27-28). Luke's form of the woe makes the same point with a different image. Because the inner corruption of the Pharisees is not visible, others are defiled by their influence.

11:45-52. Three woes to the lawyers follow the three woes to the Pharisees. The lawyers appear elsewhere in Luke (7:30; 10:25; 14:3), usually in combination with a reference to the Pharisees. The implication of the lawyer's response to Jesus is that his condemnation of the Pharisees casts shame on them also—and surely Jesus cannot have intended that they too were guilty of such things. The address to Jesus as "teacher" is a gesture offering Jesus a place among them and inviting Jesus to commend them while condemning the Pharisees. The comment, however, provides the occasion for three woes against the lawyers that parallel and balance the previous woes.

Just as the first woe against the Pharisees condemned them for observing the law regarding the tithing of herbs while neglecting matters of justice and love, so also the first woe against the lawyers condemns them for imposing legal restrictions on others while doing nothing to help them. Rather than a blessing (as it was intended), they have made God's law a burden to the people. Interpreting what is allowed and what is not, therefore, does not exhaust the role of those who are called to interpret God's Word for others.

If the first woe to the lawyers deals with the law, the second deals with the prophets. The lawyers build monuments to the prophets whom their fathers killed. The force of this woe depends on the axiom that the child is like the parent; the sons are like their fathers. They are not really honoring the prophets. Rather, they show themselves to be accomplices in the murders committed by their ancestors. They do not really honor either the prophets of old or the prophets of God in their own time.

The reference to "the wisdom of God" in v. 49 can be interpreted variously: (1) as a quotation from an otherwise unknown source; (2) as a reference to what Wisdom had said or revealed to Jesus; (3) as a self-designation, in which Jesus speaks of himself as "the wisdom of God"; or (4) as a title for Jesus (compare Matthew's use of the first person in Matt 23:34). While "the wisdom of God" is not a title Luke uses for Jesus, the Gospel narrative has indicated that Jesus was filled with wisdom (2:40, 52) and promises that he will give wisdom to his followers (21:15). The Queen of Sheba came to hear Solomon's wisdom (11:31), but now there is one greater than Solomon, and he too can speak the wisdom of God.

Jesus speaks for God: "I will send them prophets and apostles." We may ask whether this pronouncement speaks of the prophets of old whom their ancestors killed, Jesus and John the Baptist, or the apostles whom Jesus would send. Whereas Matthew speaks of "prophets, sages, and scribes," Luke has "prophets and apostles," thereby looking forward to the role of the apostolic martyrs. The force of this pronouncement, therefore, is to link Jesus and the apostles with the prophets whom the lawyers and their ancestors had killed. As a result, Jesus speaks in a veiled way of his own fate and that of his followers. Just as the prophets had been persecuted and killed, so also now those who followed Jesus would be persecuted by the religious authorities, who would not honor the words of God's prophets.

Because that generation had participated in the murder of the prophets (see v. 48), they would be held responsible for the blood of the prophets from the beginning of time (see Jer 7:25-26; Acts 7:52; Rev 18:24). To "seek the blood" is to bring the guilty parties to justice for the blood they have shed (Gen 9:5; Ezek 3:18; Matt 27:24-25). The murders of Abel (Gen 4:8-10) and Zechariah (2 Chr 24:20-22) may be cited here because they were the prototypical murders in Israel's history or because they were the first and the last murders cited in the Hebrew Scriptures. The problem with the latter interpretation is that it is difficult to establish the sequence of the writings or the state of the Hebrew canon in the first century. The place where Zechariah was murdered is described in 2 Chronicles as "in the court of the house of the LORD" (24:21; see "house" [NRSV, "sanctuary"] in Luke 11:51). The coincidence of the name with the reference to the Temple and the altar led some early interpreters to suggest that this Zechariah was the father of John the Baptist.[136]

The third woe condemns those who were ex-perts in the law for possessing the key to the house of knowledge (Prov 9:1), or the way of salvation, and yet they neither used that key to enter the house nor allowed others to enter. The term translated "hinder" (κωλύω *kōlyō*) will play a strategic role in the book of Acts, where it signals the progressive removal of the barriers to the preaching of the gospel to the Gentiles (Acts 8:36; 10:47; 11:17; 28:31).[137] The impulse of the lawyers to hinder, therefore, is an early indication of the resistance that will eventually force the apostles to turn to the Gentiles.

11:53-54. These verses bring this scene to a close by narrating Jesus' departure from the Pharisee's house and the response of the scribes and Pharisees, which is even more hostile than that described in Luke 6:11 (cf. Mark 3:6; 12:13). The verb at the end of v. 53 does not fit easily in this context from what is known of its usage elsewhere, where it means "to teach by dictation" or "to repeat from memory." Thus the NRSV has changed the translation from "to provoke him to speak of many things" to "to cross-examine him about many things." The NIV is again more interpretive: "to besiege him with questions." The meaning is probably an attempt to trap him in his responses, as v. 54 explains. The language is that of hunting prey; they lie in wait for him (cf. Acts 23:21) and set traps in their effort to ensnare him.

---

136. See *Protevangelium of James* 23-24. See also Wilhelm Schnee-melcher, ed., *New Testament Apocrypha,* 2nd ed., ed. and trans. R. McL. Wilson (Louisville: Westminster/John Knox, 1991), 1:436.

137. The role of the term "unhindered" at the end of Acts was first pointed out by Frank Stagg, *The Book of Acts: The Early Struggle for an Unhindered Gospel* (Nashville: Broadman, 1955).

REFLECTIONS

Jesus condemns the Pharisees and the lawyers for various reasons: false piety, attention to minutia while neglecting vital matters, desire for praise from others, making the demands of faithfulness a burden to others, rejecting God's prophets, and possessing the knowledge of God's teachings but neither using it themselves nor helping others to do so. Two dangers lurk here for modern interpreters. The first is to assume that nothing in these woes is relevant to the contemporary church, and the second is to treat them in such a way that they are understood as Jesus' condemnation of Judaism or Jewish religious leaders. The woes are included in the Gospel not merely because they explain Jesus' opposition to the Pharisees and lawyers but as a teaching to disciples and a warning to those who profess to follow him.

The key in interpreting such controversy sayings is to find modern counterparts in the life of the church and the ways in which our own piety is blind to some of the practices and concerns for which Jesus condemned the Pharisees and lawyers. The aphorism of the beam in the eye should guide our reading of these woes. It is all too easy to be critical of others when our own piety is open to criticism. This text is not a club with which to beat the failings out of others but a mirror in which we can see the shortcomings of our own piety.

Another approach to this passage is to reflect on the positive directions that are implicit in the condemnations. What would the passage look like if it were changed from woes to beatitudes? As a blessing on the righteous Pharisees, it would be read: "Blessed are you Pharisees! For you practice justice and the love of God while you pay a tithe on even your smallest sources of income. Blessed are you Pharisees! For you love to give others the seats of honor and greet the lonely and overlooked persons in the marketplace. Blessed are you! For you are like unmarked springs; you bless others without realizing it." Similarly, as blessings on the devout lawyers, it might read: "Blessed also are you lawyers! For you ease the burdens on others and help them carry their loads. Blessed are you! For you honor the prophets and strive to heed their warnings. Because of you there is hope for this generation. Blessed are you lawyers! For you have found the key to knowledge; you have entered yourselves, and you have helped others to find the way also." Now, what would it mean to structure one's life around such positive injunctions?

LUKE 12:1–13:9, READINESS FOR THE COMING JUDGMENT

OVERVIEW

In Luke 12:1–13:9, Jesus instructs his disciples and the crowd to be ready for the coming judgment. The section is composed of sayings and parables that have been drawn together around this theme and introduced by transitional and connective comments at various points through the discourse. The theme of judgment is introduced in the opening verses: "Nothing [is] secret that will not become known" (12:2). If the choice is between public confession that will lead to persecution or refusal to confess the one who will come as the Son of Man in judgment, then one should fear judgment rather than persecution (12:4-12). The parable of the rich fool (12:13-21) exposes the folly of being so preoccupied with

material prosperity that one gives no thought to the security only God can provide. If anxiety over physical needs is what drives one to be preoccupied with gathering material goods, then remember the instruction on prayer: Our Father knows what we need (12:22-34). Like servants waiting on the return of a householder, disciples should be ready for the Lord's coming at an unexpected time (12:35-48). Discipleship inevitably causes division (12:49-53), but even the crowds should interpret the times and settle their accounts (12:54-59). Two further parables warn the reader about the need for repentance and fruitfulness (13:1-9).

Luke 12:1-12, Fear Judgment, Not Persecution

NIV	NRSV
12 Meanwhile, when a crowd of many thousands had gathered, so that they were trampling on one another, Jesus began to speak first to his disciples, saying: "Be on your guard against the	**12** Meanwhile, when the crowd gathered by the thousands, so that they trampled on one another, he began to speak first to his disciples, "Beware of the yeast of the Pharisees, that

NIV

yeast of the Pharisees, which is hypocrisy. ²There is nothing concealed that will not be disclosed, or hidden that will not be made known. ³What you have said in the dark will be heard in the daylight, and what you have whispered in the ear in the inner rooms will be proclaimed from the roofs.

⁴"I tell you, my friends, do not be afraid of those who kill the body and after that can do no more. ⁵But I will show you whom you should fear: Fear him who, after the killing of the body, has power to throw you into hell. Yes, I tell you, fear him. ⁶Are not five sparrows sold for two pennies*? Yet not one of them is forgotten by God. ⁷Indeed, the very hairs of your head are all numbered. Don't be afraid; you are worth more than many sparrows.

⁸"I tell you, whoever acknowledges me before men, the Son of Man will also acknowledge him before the angels of God. ⁹But he who disowns me before men will be disowned before the angels of God. ¹⁰And everyone who speaks a word against the Son of Man will be forgiven, but anyone who blasphemes against the Holy Spirit will not be forgiven.

¹¹"When you are brought before synagogues, rulers and authorities, do not worry about how you will defend yourselves or what you will say, ¹²for the Holy Spirit will teach you at that time what you should say."

a6 Greek two assaria

NRSV

is, their hypocrisy. ²Nothing is covered up that will not be uncovered, and nothing secret that will not become known. ³Therefore whatever you have said in the dark will be heard in the light, and what you have whispered behind closed doors will be proclaimed from the housetops.

⁴"I tell you, my friends, do not fear those who kill the body, and after that can do nothing more. ⁵But I will warn you whom to fear: fear him who, after he has killed, has authority*a* to cast into hell.*b* Yes, I tell you, fear him! ⁶Are not five sparrows sold for two pennies? Yet not one of them is forgotten in God's sight. ⁷But even the hairs of your head are all counted. Do not be afraid; you are of more value than many sparrows.

⁸"And I tell you, everyone who acknowledges me before others, the Son of Man also will acknowledge before the angels of God; ⁹but whoever denies me before others will be denied before the angels of God. ¹⁰And everyone who speaks a word against the Son of Man will be forgiven; but whoever blasphemes against the Holy Spirit will not be forgiven. ¹¹When they bring you before the synagogues, the rulers, and the authorities, do not worry about how*c* you are to defend yourselves or what you are to say; ¹²for the Holy Spirit will teach you at that very hour what you ought to say."

aOr power bGk Gehenna cOther ancient authorities add or what

COMMENTARY

12:1-3. Verse 1 serves as a transition from the woes against the Pharisees and lawyers to the theme of the next section of the travel narrative. When a crowd gathered, apparently listening to Jesus' denunciations of the Pharisees and lawyers, Jesus spoke first to the disciples. The narrator's comment points ahead, however, to the verses in which Jesus will address the crowd also (12:13, 41, 54).

Jesus' warning about the "yeast" of the Pharisees recalls the preceding woes. Here, however, the yeast is identified as their "hypocrisy" (ὑπόκρισις *hypokrisis*). To be a hypocrite originally meant to be an actor, to wear a mask or play a role. The

woes condemned the Pharisees for wearing a mask of piety that concealed their inner corruption. While both Mark 8:15 and Matt 16:5-6 contain versions of this saying, only Luke identifies the Pharisees' yeast as hypocrisy, even though Jesus does not call the Pharisees hypocrites in Luke (see 6:42; 12:56; 13:15). The reference to hypocrisy easily recalls Jesus' charge that the Pharisees wash the outside of the cup but inside are full of greed and wickedness, and that they are like unmarked graves.

Those who love public acclaim and who practice their piety before others so that they will be praised for it are warned that in the coming judgment all secrets will be made public. Then, rather than gain acclaim, they will suffer public shame. Verse 2 contains two paired sayings: What is covered will be uncovered, and what is secret will be known (see 8:17; Mark 4:22; Matt 10:26-27). The effect of these sayings is to remove the possibility that the undeserving will be praised for their feigned virtue. At the judgment everyone's true character will be exposed.

Verse 3 continues the same line of exhortation, dealing now with what is spoken in secret rather than what is hidden from sight. Privacy in the close quarters and simple dwellings of a Galilean village was nearly impossible. The judgment will leave no opportunity for one's public statements to be different from one's private pronouncements. Darkness may give occasion for secrecy, pretension, or wrongdoing, whereas the light—which is commonly associated with the good—exposes the deeds done in darkness. Mixing the language of sight and sound, Jesus warns that what has been said in the dark will be heard in the light. Similarly, what one whispers into the ear of another in privacy will be proclaimed from the housetops so that all may hear. The first sayings on being ready for the judgment, therefore, warn that, because hypocrisy will be exposed, integrity is expected.

12:4-7. The next complex of sayings (vv. 4-7) is loosely bound together by the catchword *fear*. It explains who to fear (vv. 4-5) and who not to fear (vv. 6-7). The verb translated "to fear" (φοβέομαι *phobeomai*) is repeated four times in vv. 4-5, setting up the admonition not to fear in v. 7. The complex begins and ends with commands not to fear (vv. 4, 7). Do not fear those who can kill but have no further power over you. Death should not be one's ultimate fear. The threat of the persecutor is greatly reduced when seen from this perspective. Instead, fear the one who can not only kill but can cast you into hell:—fear God. Only God can cast one into hell, so fear God alone. Here, fear is used in the OT sense of to respect, to reverence, or to obey (Deut 6:2; Josh 24:14; Prov 1:7). First Peter 2:17 seems to grant "fear" a degree of allegiance even higher than "honor" (τιμάω *timaō*): "Honor everyone. Love the family of believers. Fear God. Honor the emperor."

The term *gehenna* (γέεννα *geenna*) does not appear in the metaphorical sense of a fiery place of torment for the wicked prior to the writing of the Gospels. Literally, the term means "the Valley of Hinnom." The location, just south of Jerusalem, had been the site of a pagan high place, the burning of children in child sacrifices, and later the garbage heap of the city where fire burned continually (see Jer 7:29-34; 19:4-13). When later the Jewish views of judgment and torment after death developed to the point that the place of torment was thought of as a fiery abyss, the first metaphorical references to Gehenna outside the NT appear in the *Sibylline Oracles* (1.100-103; 2.283-312) and 4 Ezra (7:36).

Verses 4-5, therefore, contend that the disciples should not fear those who torment them because the most that humans can do is kill the body. Rather, they should reverence God because God can cast persons into eternal torment. Verses 6-7 turn then to assure disciples that there is no need to be afraid of God. One could buy five sparrows (for food) for two copper coins worth only a sixteenth of a denarius each—meaning that the value of a sparrow was only one fortieth of a denarius! Nevertheless, God does not forget even a sparrow (cf. Isa 49:15; Matt 10:29). Again, the argument is from the lesser to the greater; if God does not forget a sparrow, certainly God's providence over those who follow Jesus will not waiver. On the contrary, God's attention to and care for the faithful are so constant that even the hairs of our heads are numbered. Therefore, we should have no fear of God, no uncertainty regarding God's providence, and no doubt as to the value of the individual human life in God's sight.

12:8-12. Luke extends the contrast between fearing persecutors and fearing God by sketching two courtroom scenes, one before human judges and one before the Son of Man. The first two sayings (vv. 8-9) in this cluster affirm that the disciple's confession or denial of Jesus before others will determine the Son of Man's confession or denial of the disciple before the heavenly court. Not only should one not fear possible persecution, therefore, but also if one is intimidated by the threat of arrest or persecution—such as what the disciples experience in the book of Acts—then that person should remember that judgment is determined by whether he or she confesses or denies Jesus now. Do not fear (vv. 4-7). Confess Jesus without fear (vv. 8-9).

Verse 10 is related to the preceding passage by catchword ("the Son of Man") and by motif (speaking, forgiving), and it introduces the Holy Spirit, thereby providing a link with v. 12. The distinction between speaking against the Son of Man and speaking against the Holy Spirit has long puzzled interpreters. This saying regarding the "unpardonable sin" has parallels in Mark 3:28-30 and Matt 12:31-32, but it is important to consider each version of this saying in its own narrative context. Because the theological language and legislative tone of the saying suggest that it is a post-Easter formulation, some commentators have suggested that Luke is distinguishing between those who rejected Jesus during his earthly ministry and those who rejected the preaching of the gospel by the early church. Alternatively, it has been suggested that the saying distinguishes between those who reject the gospel never having professed faith and those who, having embraced the gospel, later commit apostasy. More to the point is the view of those who distinguish here an impulsive, momentary rejection of Jesus, such as Peter's denial of Jesus in the courtyard (Luke 22:54-62), from a persistent, obdurate rejection of God's saving grace through the work of the Holy Spirit. The Lukan context of this saying suggests that it is concerned with those who deny Jesus when faced with persecution. Again, the example of Peter indicates that such denial is forgivable, and he is to be distinguished from those who resist and persistently reject the appeals

of the Holy Spirit. Blasphemy is distinguished from merely "speaking a word against."

In the face of persecution, one should not reject the Holy Spirit, but trust in the Spirit for strength and guidance in time of crisis (vv. 11-12; cf. 21:14-15; Matt 10:19-20; Mark 13:11). The threat of being brought before Jewish and Gentile justice—"the synagogues, the rulers and the authorities"—will be realized in the experiences of the apostles, Stephen, and Paul in the book of Acts. Luke warns believers that because persecution and trial may be expected, each believer should prepare for the crisis with the resolve to confess Jesus openly and publicly and to trust in the power of God through the Holy Spirit to teach them what they should say in that moment. The defense speeches in Acts, therefore, should be viewed as examples of inspired utterances and models for Luke's readers to imitate (see Acts 4:8).

In sum, the cumulative argument of these verses, the first unit in an extended section on preparing for the coming judgment, is that one should not fear earthly judges but the eternal judge. Moreover, one who confesses the Son of Man now will be confessed by the Son of Man at the last judgment. Therefore, believers should be prepared to confess Jesus publicly, trusting in the leadership of the Holy Spirit. If the difficult saying in v. 10 is to be interpreted as allowing forgiveness for those who fail to confess Jesus in such trials (as did even Peter), then v. 10 stands as not only a warning against the unpardonable sin of persistently rejecting the overtures of God's Spirit but also as a word of grace for those who falter under the threat of persecution.

REFLECTIONS

This collection of warnings concerning being prepared for eschatological judgment is hardly one of the most popular sections of this Gospel. In all likelihood it has been avoided by many preachers because of the difficulties it poses; few American Christians are persecuted in the manner envisioned by these verses. Preaching warnings about the last judgment has fallen out of fashion in many churches. And the warning about the unpardonable sin is difficult to interpret and difficult to relate to the Gospel's appeal for repentance and its promise of forgiveness.

1. Overshadowed by these difficulties, however, are elements of these sayings that offer appealing themes for meditation, reflection, and preaching. The first is the imperative of integrity. There is no room for hypocrisy or role-playing in the Christian life. We should be as concerned with inner purity as with outward appearances. How might it change our daily

actions or our relationships to others if we lived by the code that, because nothing is secret now that will not become known, the aim of the Christian is complete honesty and transparency? Integrity demands that there be no place for pretense or deception among believers.

2. These verses contain one of the Bible's most eloquent assurances of God's care and providence for every human being: "His eye is on the sparrow. . . . " In an era in which there is so much anxiety over the uncertainties of life, the Gospel assures us of God's protective care. In a time when rampant violence claims so many lives, the Gospel reminds us of the infinite worth of every human life. God will not forget us; even the hairs of our heads are numbered. When we are thrust beyond the range of our own strength, God will sustain us and guide us through our most trying hours.

3. These exhortations to be prepared for judgment before the Son of Man teach ethical responsibility in a period in which it is all too easy to shirk moral obligations and expect easy pardons. We are accountable to God for the way we live, the way we treat others, and the way we handle both God's teachings and God's gifts. If we refuse God's claim on our lives, then we lose the promise of God's grace toward us. Our actions and words have moral consequences, and integrity demands consistency not only between the inner and the outer person but also between our confessions of faith and our petitions for mercy.

4. The other side of the warning concerning the unpardonable sin is a word of grace that even when we fail under pressure and deny the convictions that sustain us God forgives and restores. Only those who persistently reject God's grace put themselves beyond the reach of God's love and forgiveness.

Luke 12:13-21, Better a Poor Farmer Than a Rich Fool

NIV

13Someone in the crowd said to him, "Teacher, tell my brother to divide the inheritance with me."

14Jesus replied, "Man, who appointed me a judge or an arbiter between you?" 15Then he said to them, "Watch out! Be on your guard against all kinds of greed; a man's life does not consist in the abundance of his possessions."

16And he told them this parable: "The ground of a certain rich man produced a good crop. 17He thought to himself, 'What shall I do? I have no place to store my crops.'

18"Then he said, 'This is what I'll do. I will tear down my barns and build bigger ones, and there I will store all my grain and my goods. 19And I'll say to myself, "You have plenty of good things laid up for many years. Take life easy; eat, drink and be merry."'

20"But God said to him, 'You fool! This very night your life will be demanded from you. Then

NRSV

13Someone in the crowd said to him, "Teacher, tell my brother to divide the family inheritance with me." 14But he said to him, "Friend, who set me to be a judge or arbitrator over you?" 15And he said to them, "Take care! Be on your guard against all kinds of greed; for one's life does not consist in the abundance of possessions." 16Then he told them a parable: "The land of a rich man produced abundantly. 17And he thought to himself, 'What should I do, for I have no place to store my crops?' 18Then he said, 'I will do this: I will pull down my barns and build larger ones, and there I will store all my grain and my goods. 19And I will say to my soul, Soul, you have ample goods laid up for many years; relax, eat, drink, be merry.' 20But God said to him, 'You fool! This very night your life is being demanded of you. And the things you have prepared, whose will they be?' 21So it is with those who store up treasures for themselves but are not rich toward God."

NIV

who will get what you have prepared for yourself?'

²¹"This is how it will be with anyone who stores up things for himself but is not rich toward God."

COMMENTARY

Continuing the theme of this larger section, the next verses shift from confession of Jesus to forsaking the security of material possessions. Those who confess Jesus look to God for their security, not to their own ability to accumulate possessions and lay up wealth for the future.

12:13-15. The crowd was introduced at the beginning of the chapter (v. 1). Now, a man from the crowd approaches Jesus with a request that he serve as the judge in the division of an inheritance. Apparently the man's older brother refused to give him what he felt he was due. The laws of inheritance stipulated that the elder brother would receive a double portion of the inheritance (Deut 21:17). If the father had no sons, his possessions were to be divided among his daughters (Num 27:1-11), but his daughters were then required to marry within their father's tribe so that his possessions would not leave the tribe (Num 36:7-9).

Jesus rejected the role of judge or divider of inheritances, even though Moses had handled a similar request (Exod 2:14; Num 27:1-11). Verse 15 serves as a conclusion to Jesus' response to the man from the crowd and as a transition to the parable that follows. Perhaps for this reason its syntax is difficult. Even so, the meaning is clear. Jesus rejects the man's request because he will not participate in satisfying the greed that he senses had prompted it. Instead of helping the man to get his inheritance, he points the man to a different understanding of life. Life is not to be valued or measured in terms of wealth or possessions. One may gain the whole world and lose one's soul (see 9:25). On the other hand, true blessing comes to those who hear the Word of God and do it (8:21; 11:28).

12:16-21. Just as the lawyer's question in Luke 10 served as an introduction for the parable of the good Samaritan, so also here the man

seeking his inheritance provides the occasion for the parable of the rich fool, which translates the aphorism in Luke 9:25 into parable form. When the parable is introduced as a story about a rich man, a number of associations are triggered. Wealth may be a sign of God's goodness and blessing, but the wisdom tradition is full of warnings about the prudent use of wealth. The psalmist sang the folly of riches:

> Why should I fear in times of trouble,
>   when the iniquity of my persecutors surrounds
>   me,
> those who trust in their wealth
>   and boast of the abundance of their riches?
> (Ps 49:5-6 NRSV)

Similarly, in the closest parallel to this parable, Sirach warns:

> Good things and bad, life and death
>   poverty and wealth, come from the Lord.
> The Lord's gift remains with the devout,
>   and his favor brings lasting success.
> One becomes rich through diligence and
>   self-denial,
>   and the reward allotted to him is this:
> when he says, "I have found rest,
>   and now I shall feast on my goods!"
> he does not know how long it will be
>   until he leaves them to others and dies.
> (Sir 11:14-19 NRSV; cf. 31:5-11; *1 Enoch* 97:8-10)

References earlier in the Gospel to the dangers of wealth and God's reckoning with the rich (see 1:51-53; 6:24; 8:14) have also prepared the reader to expect a reversal of the rich man's good fortune. If his fields have brought forth abundantly, it is a blessing from God that demands both prudence and fidelity in making provisions for the whole community. Abundance requires that one prepare for the famine that will surely follow. Here the model of Joseph's wise response to the seven years of bountiful harvests resonates in the background (see Gen 41:35-36). Instead, the bounty that has come to the rich man pushes him into a quandary and inner uncertainty. Like the rich man in Sir 11:14-19, the rich man muses to himself about what he will do. Here the parable leads the hearer into the man's heart. By means of a soliloquy, we overhear the man's thoughts stripped of pretense or polish for public consumption. The advantage of a soliloquy (a device that occurs frequently in the Lukan parables: 12:45; 15:17; 16:3-4; 18:4-5; 20:13) is that it offers direct and convincing characterization. By exposing the rich man's inner thoughts, Jesus also fulfills the earlier warning that everything secret will become known, whatever is said in private will be broadcast in public (12:2-3). Luke has also reminded the reader repeatedly that the secrets of one's heart are not hidden from God (1:51; 2:35; 3:15; 5:22; 9:47; 16:15; Acts 1:24).

"What will I do?" the man asks himself. Undoubtedly he had prepared for the harvest, but its bounty has exceeded his calculations, and he has no place to store it. The problem is not really posed by the size of the harvest, however, but by his insistence on gathering all of it and storing it up for his own use—as the repetition of "gather" in vv. 17-18 suggests. The thought of giving to persons in need never crosses his mind. Instead, his reverie springs immediately to a solution. He will tear down his barns and build bigger ones. Then he can gather there *all* of his grain and his goods. His plans push confidently into the future tense: "I *will* do this: I *will* pull down my barns and [*will*] build larger ones, and there I *will* store all my grain and my goods. And I *will* say to my soul. . . ." At the same time, his presumption and self-centeredness are reflected in the frequency of the possessive pronoun in his thoughts: my crops, my barns, my grain, my goods, and, finally, my soul. As we shall see, of course, it is not to be.

As quickly as he moves to a solution, he also projects the future he will enjoy: "And I will say to my soul, 'Soul, you have ample goods laid up for many years; relax, eat, drink, be merry.' " Again, his thoughts follow the familiar script of one corrupted by wealth: "I have found rest, and now I shall feast on my goods!" (Sir 11:19); "So now let us do whatever we like; for we have gathered silver, we have filled our treasuries" (*1 Enoch* 97:9). The rich man's dream of eating, drinking, and being merry echoes various references to hedonistic, profligate, Epicurean living (Isa 22:12-14; Tob 7:10-11; 1 Cor 15:32).

The man has shut out everyone else from his life and his thoughts. There is no one else in the story—just the man and his possessions—until God speaks to him. No sooner has he envisioned his future than God speaks to declare what the future actually holds for him. The reversal could not be sharper. God addresses the man as "fool," evoking the familiar reference from the Psalms: "Fools say in their hearts, 'There is no God' " (Ps 14:1). The last words in the man's soliloquy are "be merry" (εὐφραίνω *euphrainō*); the first word in God's speech marks the reversal by alliteration: "fool" (ἄφρων *aphrōn*). Moreover, God's announcement, "this night," sharply contradicts the rich man's presumption of "many years." The rich man had addressed himself (ψυχή *psychē*); now God announces that his "soul" (*psychē*) will be taken from him. Jesus' earlier question rings dramatically: "What does it profit them if they gain the whole world, but lose or forfeit themselves?" (9:25). The verb used here is literally a third-person plural: "they will demand" (ἀπαιτοῦσιν *apaitousin*). The subject is unstated. Probably the verb should be understood as a plural used in place of a divine passive: God will demand the man's soul. But lurking as an alternative is the possibility that the antecedent is none other than the man's goods themselves.[138] His possessions will take his life from him. Then whose will they be? He presumed all along that he could hoard the bounty of the harvest for himself, but now whose will it be?

Verse 21 draws a moral from the story. It is the picture of a man who lays up treasure for himself but is not rich in God's favor. The implication, as in other references to the rich in Luke, is that the two pursuits, or the two conditions, are antithetical and mutually exclusive. Here there is no both/and. Therefore, the story exposes our own inner commitments as clearly as it exposes the thoughts of the rich fool. It holds up a mirror before us and asks us to take a good look at our own inner lives and listen to our own inner voices.

138. See Frank Stagg, *Studies in Luke's Gospel* (Nashville: Convention, 1965) 90-91.

REFLECTIONS

As suggestive as this parable is, it does not specifically answer the crucial question: What was the rich man's folly? Actually, his follies are many and allow the parable to be viewed from several angles of moral reflection.

1. *Preoccupation with Possessions.* Until the voice of God interrupts the fool's reverie, there is nothing in the story but the man and his possessions. His goods and prosperity have become the sole pursuit of his life, until finally the poverty of his abundance is exposed. Thus the parable plunges the hearer into a searching reflection on the meaning of life. We may declare, "Whoever has the most toys when he dies wins," but the parable exposes the emptiness of such a materialistic life-style.

2. *Security in Self-sufficiency.* The parable sketches the figure of a man who does not need anyone else. He can provide for himself, and his provisions will take care of him for many years. He needs the security of the love of neither family nor faithful friends. He does not feel the need of a community of support or the security of God's love. In an extreme case, the parable allows us to see the ultimate extension of the common, prideful inclination to think that we can make it on our own and that we don't need anyone else.

3. *The Grasp of Greed.* Greed is the moral antithesis of generosity. The thought of what he might be able to do for those in need never enters the rich fool's mind. His innermost thoughts reveal that he has no sense of responsibility to use his abundance for the welfare of persons less fortunate than he. Greed has eaten away any compassion he may once have had.

4. *The Hollowness of Hedonism.* The rich fool revels in his prosperity because he envisions that because of it he can "eat, drink, and be merry." His daydream is to spend his future indulging his whims and desires. The greatest good he can imagine is a life of maximizing his own pleasure. Leisure, recreation, freedom from the demands of work—the rich man's vision of the future sounds uncomfortably like one that most of us have for our retirement years. Are we really planning prudently? What gives our life meaning now, and what will give it meaning then?

5. *Practical Atheism.* This is Peter Rhea Jones's provocative term for the rich fool's approach to life.[139] The rich fool may protest that he has always believed in God, but when it comes to managing his life, dealing with possessions and planning for the future, he lives as though there were no God. The parable, therefore, probes our basic commitments. What difference should our faith in God make in the practical matters of life?

A televised interview with a man who had lost his house and all his possessions to a raging brush fire driven by Santa Anna winds in California provides a striking contrast to the rich fool. Recalling that his brother had recently mused that they should be careful not to allow their possessions to possess them, this man who had just seen everything he owned but the shirt on his back go up in smoke announced to the reporter with a note of unexpected triumph: "I am a free man now!"

---

139. For two insightful treatments of this parable, see Peter Rhea Jones, *The Teaching of the Parables* (Nashville: Broadman, 1982) 127-41, esp. 132-33; and Bernard Brandon Scott, *Hear Then the Parable* (Minneapolis: Fortress, 1989) 127-40.

Luke 12:22-34, More Important Things About Which to Be Anxious

NIV

22Then Jesus said to his disciples: "Therefore I tell you, do not worry about your life, what you will eat; or about your body, what you will wear. 23Life is more than food, and the body more than clothes. 24Consider the ravens: They do not sow or reap, they have no storeroom or barn; yet God feeds them. And how much more valuable you are than birds! 25Who of you by worrying can add a single hour to his life*a*? 26Since you cannot do this very little thing, why do you worry about the rest?

27"Consider how the lilies grow. They do not labor or spin. Yet I tell you, not even Solomon in all his splendor was dressed like one of these. 28If that is how God clothes the grass of the field, which is here today, and tomorrow is thrown into the fire, how much more will he clothe you, O you of little faith! 29And do not set your heart on what you will eat or drink; do not worry about it. 30For the pagan world runs after all such things, and your Father knows that you need them. 31But seek his kingdom, and these things will be given to you as well.

32"Do not be afraid, little flock, for your Father has been pleased to give you the kingdom. 33Sell your possessions and give to the poor. Provide purses for yourselves that will not wear out, a treasure in heaven that will not be exhausted, where no thief comes near and no moth destroys. 34For where your treasure is, there your heart will be also."

a25 Or single cubit to his height

NRSV

22He said to his disciples, "Therefore I tell you, do not worry about your life, what you will eat, or about your body, what you will wear. 23For life is more than food, and the body more than clothing. 24Consider the ravens: they neither sow nor reap, they have neither storehouse nor barn, and yet God feeds them. Of how much more value are you than the birds! 25And can any of you by worrying add a single hour to your span of life?*a* 26If then you are not able to do so small a thing as that, why do you worry about the rest? 27Consider the lilies, how they grow: they neither toil nor spin;*b* yet I tell you, even Solomon in all his glory was not clothed like one of these. 28But if God so clothes the grass of the field, which is alive today and tomorrow is thrown into the oven, how much more will he clothe you—you of little faith! 29And do not keep striving for what you are to eat and what you are to drink, and do not keep worrying. 30For it is the nations of the world that strive after all these things, and your Father knows that you need them. 31Instead, strive for his*c* kingdom, and these things will be given to you as well.

32"Do not be afraid, little flock, for it is your Father's good pleasure to give you the kingdom. 33Sell your possessions, and give alms. Make purses for yourselves that do not wear out, an unfailing treasure in heaven, where no thief comes near and no moth destroys. 34For where your treasure is, there your heart will be also."

a Or add a cubit to your stature   *b Other ancient authorities read Consider the lilies; they neither spin nor weave*   *c Other ancient authorities read God's*

COMMENTARY

The parable of the rich fool is followed by a collection of sayings linked by the catchword "worry" (μεριμνάω *merimnaō*). These sayings drive home the lesson of the parable and offer further arguments regarding the futility of worrying over material goods.

12:22-26. The general exhortation in v. 22 sets the theme of this collection of sayings and is linked to the preceding parable both by the causal "therefore" (διὰ τοῦτο *dia touto*) and by the repetition of the key word "self" (ψυχή *psychē*), which played a pivotal role in the parable. Jesus speaks to the basic human anxiety for survival needs: food and clothing. Anxiety is like an itch, however; simply deciding we are not going to think about something does not make it go away. These admonitions speak to the way we live, not just how we feel. The Greek verb for "to be anxious" (*merimnaō*) means also "to take anxious thought." It may also mean "to put forth an effort" or "to strive after." The prohibition against anxiety may, therefore, be interpreted as an encouragement to start making decisions that are not controlled by anxiety.

Two concerns illustrate the command not to be anxious. After introducing the two concerns, this paragraph takes up each matter individually. Verses 24-26 deal with anxiety over food, and vv. 27-28 treat anxiety over clothing. While these are natural and legitimate concerns, real security does not come by simply being concerned about the means of life.

Following the general admonition stated in vv. 22-23, Jesus offers three reasons why his disciples should not allow anxiety to control them. The first is stated in v. 23: "Life is more than food, and the body more than clothing." These words are not intended for persons who do not have enough to eat. One cannot simply say to the starving, "Life is more than food." These words are addressed to persons who have food to eat and clothes to wear and yet spend their lives trying to acquire more and more. Is life not more than the things we spend our lives seeking? The words of Jesus can free us from anxiety over what we have or do not have. They can also refocus our energies on who we are rather than on what we have and on what we are becoming rather than on how we will get ahead.

The second reason for not being anxious is given in v. 24: "Consider the ravens: they neither sow nor reap," but God takes care of them. This reminder calls for renewed trust in God's providence. The argument calls for reasoning from the lesser to the greater. If God cares for the lesser creatures (birds), then will God not also care for you? The passing comment that, unlike human beings, the birds have neither storehouses nor barns subtly reminds the reader that the rich fool's barns offered him no security at all (see v. 18). A vigorous trust in God's ability to care for God's

own will go a long way toward freeing us from the grasp of anxiety.

The third reason is also just good common sense: Being anxious does not solve our problems (vv. 25-26). Verse 25 can be understood in either a spatial or a temporal sense. A cubit was a standard measure, about eighteen inches, or the length of a man's forearm. It could also be used figuratively as a measure of time. Who can add a cubit to his or her stature, or who can add a span (a moment or an hour) to the length of life? Because the argument demands that one see such an extension as a small thing, most interpreters favor the temporal sense. An hour is just a small fraction of the length of one's life, but adding eighteen inches to one's stature would make a considerable difference. Either way, the point is clear: Worry all you will, but you cannot make yourself an inch taller or add a day to the span of your life. Verse 26 clinches the argument. If we cannot do such a small thing by being anxious, why be anxious about other things? Anxiety is ineffective as a means of improving our lot in life.

12:27-32. The challenge to consider the ravens is followed by a call to consider the lilies (probably a general reference to the flowers that grow wild). The birds do not worry about food, and yet they eat. Similarly, the lilies do not worry about clothes, but they are more splendid than even King Solomon.

Solomon's wealth was legendary. First Kings 10:4, 6 reports that the Queen of Sheba was overwhelmed by Solomon's wisdom and wealth. Solomon's wisdom was cited in Luke 11:31; now attention is focused on his wealth (see 1 Kgs 10:4-5, 7, 14-29). The court historian concludes: "Thus King Solomon excelled all the kings of the earth in riches and in wisdom" (1 Kgs 10:23). Wealth greater than Solomon's was unimaginable, yet his splendor was no match for the simple beauty of a lily.

Verse 28 calls for the logic of faith. Reason from the lesser to the greater. If the grass of the fields is splendidly clothed, yet is here today and gone tomorrow, will not God also take care of those who trust God? The sages likened the brevity of human life to the flowering and withering of the grass (Pss 90:5-6; 102:11; 103:15). The expression "you of little faith," which occurs only here in Luke but frequently in Matthew (6:30; 8:26; 14:31; 16:8), invites the reader to look deeper into God's providence. Trust in God's faithfulness relieves one of anxiety over what one will eat or drink.

Verse 30 pits the preoccupation of "the nations of the world" against the promise of God's care of those who trust God as Father. Verses 30-31, 32 combine references to God as Father with references to God's kingdom. The combination evokes echoes of the model prayer and Jesus' teachings on prayer (see 11:2, 11-13). Two further reasons why anxiety cannot control the life of a disciple emerge from these verses: (1) Anxiety reveals a lack of faith in God as heavenly Father, and (2) one whose life is devoted to the pursuit of the kingdom will not be anxious about other things.

Our Father, who provides for the birds and the grass, knows what we need to sustain life. Freed from such mundane concerns, Jesus' disciples are to be concerned, rather, with the things of God's kingdom. On the one hand, disciples should "strive" for the kingdom. On the other hand, they are assured that it is God's purpose to give us the kingdom (cf. vv. 31-32). The two verses neatly balance the indicative and the imperative, promise and command. The disciples, therefore, are assured of both God's care for their needs and the certainty that the kingdom will finally declare God's sovereignty. The references to "God's good pleasure" in Luke express important aspects of Luke's understanding of God's sovereign will and purposes (see 2:14; 3:22; 10:21; 12:32). The church is referred to as a "little flock" elsewhere in Paul's address to the elders at Miletus (Acts 20:28-29) and in 1 Pet 5:2-3.

12:33-34. These verses suggest the antidote to anxiety. What greater denial of a life controlled by anxiety could there be than a devotion to providing for the needs of others? If there are only two basic impulses, either to grasp or to give, then the alternative to anxiety over what we do not possess or control is to release our grasp of that which we do control. The exhortations develop more fully the thought sketched in v. 21. We can lay up treasure on earth or in heaven—but not in both places. The choice must be either/or—either our own advancement or the advancement of the kingdom, either earthly goods or heavenly treasures, either our own concerns or God's. Therefore, Jesus exhorts the disciples to sell their possessions and give alms (see 11:41). Earlier Jesus had instructed the disciples to carry no purse (9:3; 10:4); now he points them to purses that will not wear out and treasure that will not fail. The concern of the rich fool was the preservation of his wealth, but the treasure one lays up in heaven through devotion to the kingdom is unfailing. No thief can steal it, and moths cannot destroy it (see Matt 6:20; 1 Pet 1:4). Thieves may steal our goods, rust may eat away at metals and moths at precious cloth and clothing, but the person whose treasure is in heaven will not be anxious about such things.

Verse 34 declares that there is a connection between one's heart and one's treasure. The aphorism can be interpreted in several ways: The way we handle material goods (1) reveals where our true commitments lie or (2) determines whether we have earthly treasures or treasures in heaven; also (3) where we invest our money determines where our heart will be. All three interpretations expose facets of truth in this aphorism, but the second fits its context best.

Within the larger context of Luke 12:1–13:9, which warns us to be ready for the judgment, the cluster of sayings on anxiety and possessions in vv. 22-34 warns against trying to secure the future by laying up earthly treasure and counsels instead of the wisdom of wholehearted devotion to God's kingdom. True security is to be found not in wealth but in God's providence.

REFLECTIONS

Anxiety must be a by-product of human freedom. At least it seems to be a universal art, cultivated by people in all generations and cultures. Those who do not have enough to live on—to feed, shelter, or clothe themselves—naturally are anxious about how they will live. Those who have opportunities to develop a better life than they now enjoy worry about how they will get ahead. Those who have all they need and more are anxious about maintaining and protecting their wealth. Having more, then, is no solution to anxiety.

Faith in Jesus Christ awakens our consciousness of the spiritual dimensions of life. By so doing, faith allows and even forces us to see our lives from a new perspective. Then we can see that some of the things we have been so concerned about are not all that important. We may also see that we have not given enough attention to important things: family, friends, a more just and peaceful society, or our own personal, intellectual, and spiritual development. When the rat race of materialism threatens to control you, remember Jesus' words; there is more to life.

Followers of Jesus should be the freest persons—free from anxiety, free from the social conventions of materialism, free with their generosity to others. The lives of Jesus' disciples count for more than the pursuit of material wealth. They are devoted to higher things. This cluster of sayings offers both the challenge to center one's life on promoting concerns related to God's kingdom and the extravagant promise of God's providence for those who will do so.

What changes would we make if we were as concerned about God's kingdom as we are about the size of next month's paycheck, the next harvest, or the next step up the career ladder? What value would we give to reconciling broken relationships, sharing the gospel of God's love, and working for peace and justice for the oppressed?

One of Jesus' most difficult words is this: "Sell your possessions, and give alms" (v. 33). As in other parts of the Gospel, this saying contains a tension between two responses to the dangers of wealth and materialism. The first is divestment: "Sell your possessions." The second is generosity in almsgiving. In our culture, the latter has always been easier to consider than the first. Obviously, there are good reasons why divestment should not become the norm for all Christians. On the other hand, this provocative call needs to be considered. Most of us have possessions we do not need. Yet, we hold on to them while other persons are homeless and hungry. Perhaps it is time for churches to hold "discipleship sales," and call on all who will to sell all the goods they do not need in order to give to charities and human services. Such detachment from our materialism would also be a dramatic declaration of the values by which we live.

Luke 12:35-48, Learning Watchfulness from Masters and Slaves

NIV

35"Be dressed ready for service and keep your lamps burning, 36like men waiting for their master to return from a wedding banquet, so that when he comes and knocks they can immediately open the door for him. 37It will be good for those servants whose master finds them watching when he comes. I tell you the truth, he will dress himself to serve, will have them recline at the table and will come and wait on them. 38It will be good for those servants whose master finds them ready, even if he comes in the second or third watch of the night. 39But understand this: If the owner of the house had known at what hour the thief was coming, he would not have let his house be broken into. 40You also must be ready, because the Son of

NRSV

35"Be dressed for action and have your lamps lit; 36be like those who are waiting for their master to return from the wedding banquet, so that they may open the door for him as soon as he comes and knocks. 37Blessed are those slaves whom the master finds alert when he comes; truly I tell you, he will fasten his belt and have them sit down to eat, and he will come and serve them. 38If he comes during the middle of the night, or near dawn, and finds them so, blessed are those slaves.

39"But know this: if the owner of the house had known at what hour the thief was coming, he[a] would not have let his house be broken into. 40You also must be ready, for the Son of Man is coming at an unexpected hour."

[a]Other ancient authorities add *would have watched and*

NIV

Man will come at an hour when you do not expect him."

⁴¹Peter asked, "Lord, are you telling this parable to us, or to everyone?"

⁴²The Lord answered, "Who then is the faithful and wise manager, whom the master puts in charge of his servants to give them their food allowance at the proper time? ⁴³It will be good for that servant whom the master finds doing so when he returns. ⁴⁴I tell you the truth, he will put him in charge of all his possessions. ⁴⁵But suppose the servant says to himself, 'My master is taking a long time in coming,' and he then begins to beat the menservants and maidservants and to eat and drink and get drunk. ⁴⁶The master of that servant will come on a day when he does not expect him and at an hour he is not aware of. He will cut him to pieces and assign him a place with the unbelievers.

⁴⁷"That servant who knows his master's will and does not get ready or does not do what his master wants will be beaten with many blows. ⁴⁸But the one who does not know and does things deserving punishment will be beaten with few blows. From everyone who has been given much, much will be demanded; and from the one who has been entrusted with much, much more will be asked."

NRSV

⁴¹Peter said, "Lord, are you telling this parable for us or for everyone?" ⁴²And the Lord said, "Who then is the faithful and prudent manager whom his master will put in charge of his slaves, to give them their allowance of food at the proper time? ⁴³Blessed is that slave whom his master will find at work when he arrives. ⁴⁴Truly I tell you, he will put that one in charge of all his possessions. ⁴⁵But if that slave says to himself, 'My master is delayed in coming,' and if he begins to beat the other slaves, men and women, and to eat and drink and get drunk, ⁴⁶the master of that slave will come on a day when he does not expect him and at an hour that he does not know, and will cut him in pieces,ᵃ and put him with the unfaithful. ⁴⁷That slave who knew what his master wanted, but did not prepare himself or do what was wanted, will receive a severe beating. ⁴⁸But the one who did not know and did what deserved a beating will receive a light beating. From everyone to whom much has been given, much will be required; and from the one to whom much has been entrusted, even more will be demanded."

ᵃOr *cut him off*

COMMENTARY

The sayings that follow move directly to the theme of the larger unit, 12:1–13:9—watchfulness. The sayings are linked not only by theme but also by the common metaphor of masters and slaves. Although the sayings are parabolic, and Peter refers to the preceding admonitions as "this parable," the allegorical use of the sayings has diminished their parabolic quality to the point that it may be best to view the sayings of this section as a series of related metaphors—lessons on watchfulness drawn from reflections on the roles of masters and slaves.

12:35-40. Verse 35 may be interpreted independently of the sayings that follow. As it stands, it introduces the parable of the returning master in vv. 36-38. Verse 39 speaks of the master's need

for watchfulness against the threat of thieves, and v. 40 draws the lesson of the parables for the audience. When Peter asks to whom the sayings apply, Jesus responds with further warnings that contrast the rewards of faithful and disobedient slaves (vv. 42-48).

Verses 35-40 contain at least the rudiments of two parables: (1) servants awaiting the bridegroom and (2) the householder. The first assures blessing on the faithful; the second warns of judgment on the unprepared. To gird one's loins (which the NRSV translates as "Be dressed for action" and Fitzmyer renders "Keep your aprons on")¹⁴⁰ means literally to draw up the long outer

140. Joseph A. Fitzmyer, *The Gospel According to Luke (X–XXIV),* AB 28A (Garden City, N.Y.: Doubleday, 1985) 983.

garment and tuck it into the sash around one's waist or hips so as to be prepared for vigorous activity. As an exhortation to readiness it appears prominently in the instructions for the celebration of the first Passover (Exod 12:11; cf. 1 Pet 1:13). The lamps in the tabernacle were to be lit with pure oil so that they would burn steadily (Exod 27:20; Lev 24:2). The exhortation to keep your lamps burning and be ready for the master echoes the parable of the wise and foolish maidens in Matt 25:13, but the theme of readiness for the returning master also occurs in Mark 13:33-37. The situation assumed in v. 36 is that the master of the house has gone to his bride's home to be married. His servants await his return so that they may open the door for him when he knocks (see Rev 3:20), but they do not know when he will come.

Verse 37 is a beatitude announcing blessing on those who are watchful. In the parable setting, the danger is that the servants may fall asleep (Mark 13:36). In Luke the disciples occasionally sleep when they should be awake, watching and praying (Luke 9:32; 22:45-46). Watchfulness is marked by prayer, while sleep indicates neglect and unpreparedness.

The promise of the master's generosity toward his servants takes the form of a dramatic reversal of roles. Instead of serving the master, the servants will find that he serves them. Now the master (rather than the servants as in v. 35) will gird his loins and serve the servants (see Luke 17:7-10; John 13:1-17). The master's invitation to the servants to sit at table is an allusion to the great eschatological banquet (see Isa 25:6; Luke 13:29; 14:15-24).

Verse 38 reiterates the beatitudes but adds the need for watchfulness even late into the night. Jewish and Greek practice was to divide the night into three watches, while the Romans marked the passing of the hours from 6:00 P.M. until 6:00 A.M. with four watches (see Mark 13:35). Whichever system Luke assumes, the point is the same. If the master finds his servants ready and watchful, even at a late hour, those servants will be blessed. This exhortation clearly conveys an allegorical allusion to the expected parousia and promises that those who are ready at the Lord's return will be blessed by their Lord. Less clear is the issue of whether the mention of the late watches in the night should be understood as a reference to the delay of the parousia (see 2 Pet 3:3-4, 8-10).

The second parable (v. 39) warns of the alternative. For some the master's coming will be like the approach of a thief in the night (see Mark 3:27; *Gospel of Thomas* 21). This image occurs elsewhere in the NT in reference to the expectation of the parousia (Matt 24:43-44; 1 Thess 5:2; 2 Pet 3:10; Rev 3:3; 16:15). The apocalyptic imagery appropriately yields to a reference to Jesus as the coming Son of Man. Jesus warns his audience, therefore, to be ready. From instructions in earlier contexts, the reader may assume that readiness means trust in God as a heavenly Father, putting away all hypocrisy, handling one's material possessions faithfully, obeying the ethic of the kingdom, and making life a matter of constant prayer.

12:41. Peter's question regarding whether Jesus' "parable" was for the disciples or for everyone, while it does not receive a direct answer from Jesus, raises the question of the extent to which Jesus' answer should be read allegorically in reference to church offices. Both the disciples and the crowd of thousands are introduced in 12:1. In 12:13-14 Jesus responds to a man from the crowd. The sayings introduced in v. 22 are directed to the disciples; therefore, Peter's question in v. 41 asks for clarification regarding the intended audience, but Jesus answers with another parable.

12:42-48. These sayings may be read as either another parable employing the imagery of masters and slaves or an interpretation of the parable of the master returning from his wedding banquet in vv. 36-38. Whether a parable or the interpretation of a parable, this passage addresses in more detail the possibilities for reward and punishment that are presented to the servants by their master's absence. The occasion of the master's wedding banquet drops from view, but still the serving of food is joined in yet another way to the master's return, perhaps as an allusion to the expected messianic banquet (though it is much less explicit here than in v. 37). Luke elevates the position of those in question from slaves (see 12:37; Matt 24:45) to managers, which may also undergird the interpretation that this parable is addressed especially to church leaders, who are represented in the Gospel by Peter and the other disciples. The parable opens with the question that is its chief concern: "Who then is the faithful and prudent manager?" The opportunity for advancement that is held out in the parable is the granting of responsibility for oversight of the regular distribution of food (lit., wheat) to the master's servants. The distribution of food in the early church is of sufficient importance in Acts to raise the question as to whether this parable should be read allegorically as a reference to the selection of someone to serve in a leadership position, like that of the seven appointed to see to the daily distribution of food in Acts 6. The phrase "at the proper time" (ἐν καιρῷ *en kairō*), however, retains eschatological overtones, suggesting that allegorically the appointment is to a position of oversight and responsibility at the eschatological banquet.

Verse 43 reverts to the use of the term "slave" (δοῦλος *doulos*), which continues to appear throughout the rest of this parable (see vv. 45-47). As in the previous parable (v. 37), a beatitude follows. Verse 37 pronounced a blessing on those whom the master finds alert. This time the blessed are those whom the master finds at work. The structural parallelism continues. In v. 37 Jesus says, "Truly [ἀμήν *amēn*] I tell you," and in v. 44 he also follows the beatitude with an assurance "Truly [ἀληθῶς *alēthōs*] I tell you." This time, however, the servant's reward is that he will be put in charge of all the master's possessions—an even greater promotion than was offered in v. 42.

Verse 45 turns to consider the punishment to come for those who are not "faithful and prudent" while the master is away. If the master's absence tempts the servant to say in his heart, "My master is delayed in coming," he will be punished severely (though Luke has established repeatedly that Jesus knows what is in a person's heart—see 2:35; 5:22; 7:39ff.; 9:47; 24:38; Acts 1:24). The reference again seems to be a thinly veiled allusion to those who become faithless because of the delay of the parousia (cf. 2 Pet 3:4; and the use of the verb for "delay" (χρονίζω *chronizō*) in Matt 25:5; Heb 10:37). The servant's disobedience is described in terms appropriate to the narrative world of the parable: beating other slaves, eating, drinking, and getting drunk. Getting drunk, however, is evidence of failure to be ready for the Lord's coming in 1 Thess 5:6-7. Language used by the church to describe the suddenness of the Lord's return reemerges in v. 46; the master will come "on a day when he does not expect him and at an hour that he does not

know." The prophets spoke of the "day of the Lord" (Joel 2:31; Mal 4:5) and NT references speak of the day and hour of the Lord's coming (Mark 13:32; Matt 24:36; Rev. 3:3). The element of unexpectedness echoes the earlier reference in v. 40.

When the master comes, the faithless servant who doubted in his heart will be punished severely. The first punishment is graphic in its violence: He will be cut in two. Fitzmyer comments: "One should not fail to notice, however, how the punishment of the manager, if he abuses his authority, corresponds to the double life that he would be leading."[141] The second punishment again employs theological language and speaks of God's judgment on the faithless; he will be "put with the unfaithful" (cf. "have no part [μέρος *meros*]" in 11:36; John 13:8; 2 Cor 6:15).

Verses 47-48 are composed of two pairs of contrasting statements. The first two (vv. 47-48*a*) may be understood as either a separate parable or as related sayings appended to the preceding parable. Because the sayings relate to the issue of responsibility, they should be read as part of Jesus' answer to Peter's question in v. 41. The first two sayings state the application of the principle, while the last two sayings state the principle itself. Following on the description of the severe punishment of the faithless servant in v. 46, v. 47 declares that the slave who knew what his master required and yet did not do it will receive a severe beating, while the slave who did not know but acted culpably will receive a light beating. The distinction can be found in the OT references to sins committed "with a high hand" and sins of ignorance (Num 15:30; cf. Jam 4:17; 2 Pet 2:21). The two sayings in vv. 47-48*a* differ in that v. 47 concerns refusal to do what is required, while v. 48*a* describes doing what is forbidden—but without the knowledge of what is allowed and what is forbidden. The difficulty in relating the matter to the situation of a slave probably arises because the impetus for the parable is theological, and knowledge of what the master wanted is closely associated with the Mosaic law, which one could violate in either of the ways described in vv. 47-48*a*. Both servants are punished because no

141. Fitzmyer, *The Gospel According to Luke (X–XXIV)*, 986.

violation of the law can be overlooked, but the severity of the punishment will vary.

The two statements in v. 48*b* enunciate the principle of proportional responsibility (cf. 6:37-38; Matt 13:12). The parable of the talents makes a similar point (cf. 16:10-12; 19:26). The passive verb and the third-person plural verb both imply a divine subject—God will seek much from those to whom much has been given. Leaders to whom the church has given responsibility will, therefore, be held to a high standard of expectations.

REFLECTIONS

The parables and sayings of this section once again confront the interpreter with material that is foreign in both its images and its worldview. Our culture is unfamiliar with the wedding practices that are assumed here and the conventions that defined the relationship between masters and slaves, and the apocalyptic expectations of a coming judgment have lost their immediacy and taken on the authority of orthodoxy in the intervening centuries. Thus the question is how to interpret these sayings so that their exhortations are meaningful without either getting bogged down in the historical situation or literalizing their apocalyptic imagery.

The sayings, as we have seen, exhort the listeners to watchfulness, which means living in such a consistently moral and obedient way that we would be ready to give an account to God of how we have lived. There is more here, however. Servants need to be devoted to their tasks, refusing to let distractions, fatigue, or delay divert them from their duties. They must make the fulfillment of what their master has asked them to do their highest obligation and their greatest concern. In this respect, they provide modern readers with a metaphorical measure of complete devotion to Jesus and the kingdom tasks he has given his followers. Their exhortation is to be as faithful to Jesus as devoted slaves were to their masters. Be as concerned with the work of the kingdom as a servant left to watch the door of the master's house until he returns.

The warnings and promises about rewards and punishments remind us that the laws of responsibility and reward apply in our relationship to God just as in other areas of life. Those who are faithful will be given greater privileges and responsibilities, while persons who neglect their responsibilities will have their privileges and responsibilities taken from them. As these sayings are applied especially to Peter and the disciples, they have special relevance for those to whom the church entrusts the responsibilities of leadership. More will be expected from persons who handle sacred matters, interpret God's Word, serve priestly and prophetic functions, and set an example of faith and morality for both church and society.

There is no inconsistency here among responsibility, mercy, and punishment. God's mercy makes allowances for those who do not know what is expected of them. But the most severe punishment is reserved for persons who are entrusted with great responsibilities and who then high-handedly and irresponsibly mistreat others and fail the trust given to them by their Lord. In a time of permissiveness and daily reminders of the pervasiveness of immorality even within the church, these parables can still serve to remind, exhort, and warn Christians of the seriousness of their moral commitments. If much has changed since the first century, some things have changed hardly at all.

Luke 12:49-53, Division Caused by Decision

NIV

49"I have come to bring fire on the earth, and how I wish it were already kindled! 50But I have a baptism to undergo, and how distressed I am until it is completed! 51Do you think I came to bring peace on earth? No, I tell you, but division. 52From now on there will be five in one family divided against each other, three against two and two against three. 53They will be divided, father against son and son against father, mother against daughter and daughter against mother, mother-in-law against daughter-in-law and daughter-in-law against mother-in-law."

NRSV

49"I came to bring fire to the earth, and how I wish it were already kindled! 50I have a baptism with which to be baptized, and what stress I am under until it is completed! 51Do you think that I have come to bring peace to the earth? No, I tell you, but rather division! 52From now on five in one household will be divided, three against two and two against three; 53they will be divided:

father against son
  and son against father,
mother against daughter
  and daughter against mother,
mother-in-law against her daughter-in-law
  and daughter-in-law against mother-in-law."

COMMENTARY

As this extended section of warnings related to the coming judgment moves toward its climax and conclusion, Jesus turns from master-servant sayings to the terrible stress and division that will accompany the coming judgment. Irony and pathos run deep. Jesus has come to bring God's peace, but the work of redemption inevitably brings division also. These verses contain three pronouncements regarding the nature of Jesus' mission (v. 49, "I came"; v. 50, "I have a baptism"; v. 51, "I have come"; cf. the "I" sayings in 4:43; 5:32). Although the kingdom of God is characterized by reconciliation and peace, the announcement of that kingdom is always divisive because it requires decision and commitment.

Jesus claims first that he came "to cast fire upon the earth" (see v. 49). The word order is emphatic and dramatic in Greek: "Fire I came to cast on the earth!" The announcement was foreshadowed by Luke 3:16, where John claims that Jesus will baptize with the Holy Spirit and with fire. In the same context, fire is used as an image of God's judgment (3:9, 17; cf. 12:49; 17:29). Ironically, when the fire comes upon the disciples in Acts, it is not the consuming fire of judgment but the purifying fire of the Holy Spirit. Nevertheless, the crisis of judgment is never far away (see Mal 3:2-3).

A noncanonical saying relates fire to Jesus' mission: "Whoever is near me is near fire; whoever is distant from me is distant from the kingdom" (*Gospel of Thomas* 82). With the coming of the Spirit, the work of the church, and the approach of the kingdom, division and strife would be intensified. Jesus said, "Let it start now!"

Jesus himself would not be spared from the hostility. His "baptism" may be an allusion to his death, as in Mark 10:38, or it may refer more generally to the conflict and distress in which he would be "immersed" as he approached Jerusalem. The closing words of v. 50 can be read to mean "how I am totally governed by this,"[142] "how distressed I am" (NIV), or "what stress I am under" (NRSV). Jesus speaks of the completion of his mission again in 13:32; 18:31; 22:37 (cf. Acts 13:29); in the Gospel of John, which has interesting parallels to Luke, Jesus' dying words are "It is finished" (19:30).

Jesus would be the first casualty of the division that necessarily attends the proclamation of God's Word. Other families would later be divided by faith and unbelief (vv. 52-53), but Jesus would

---

142. Helmut Koester, συνέξω in *Theological Dictionary of the New Testament,* ed. Gerhard Friedrich, trans. and ed. Geoffrey W. Bromiley (Grand Rapids: Eerdmans, 1971) 7:884-85.

suffer the brunt of the opposition and his own family would be pierced by its effects. Compare the words of Simeon: "This child is destined for the falling and the rising of many in Israel, and to be a sign that will be opposed so that the inner thoughts of many will be revealed—and a sword will pierce your own soul too" (2:34-35).

Division would, therefore, precede reconciliation. The announcement of the kingdom would not bring peace—at least not immediately. It would bring division and conflict. Those who commit themselves to Jesus must prepare for the opposition they will face, sometimes even from their own families. The message "peace on earth" is not received without savage conflict (cf. 2:14; 12:51; 19:42; 24:36). Paradoxically, reconciliation is the task of the messianic forerunner (Mal 4:5-6; Luke 1:17), but the eschatological crisis will be marked by tragic divisions. Houses, families, and generations will be divided against one another (cf. Mic 7:6; Mark 10:29; 13:12). The number of five in a family may be related to the litany of division in v. 53, assuming that either the mother and mother-in-law or the daughter and daughter-in-law are the same person. Division between husband and wife is not considered in these Gospel sayings, probably because of Jesus' prohibitions against divorce, but the church would face the problem of separations between believing and unbelieving partners soon enough (1 Cor 7:12-16).

These verses explore the other side of revelation, commitment, and kingdom values. Wherever the Word of God has been heard, division has occurred among the people who heard it (cf. John 7:43; 9:16; 10:19). Peace has a price, too. The absence of conflict is not a present possibility. One can only choose the cause for which to fight and the commitments that are worth holding. As E. Earle Ellis wrote, "The call for decision is a call for 'division.' "[143]

143. E. Earle Ellis, *The Gospel of Luke*, NCB (Greenwood, S.C.: Attic, 1966) 182.

REFLECTIONS

Repeatedly, the warnings about the coming judgment have forced us to examine the implications of our commitments. It is all too easy to make commitments in one area of life as though they did not affect other areas also. Jesus warned that those who make a commitment to him will be persecuted, that a commitment of faith also means that our attitude toward material possessions must change, and that moral responsibilities must be taken with even greater seriousness. Now Jesus warns that persons who make a commitment to him will find their relationships to others, even those closest to them, affected by that commitment. We cannot make a commitment to Jesus Christ as Lord without its affecting the way we relate to friends and to family members. Because our commitment to Christ shapes our values, priorities, goals, and behavior, it also forces us to change old patterns of life, and these changes may precipitate crises in significant relationships.

Some of the most unexpected crises we face come from the opposition of others when we set out to do what we perceive to be the good, moral, and right thing to do. Jesus himself knew how devastating such crises can be, and he warned his followers to be prepared to encounter them also.

Luke 12:54-59, Interpreting the Times and Settling Accounts

NIV

54He said to the crowd: "When you see a cloud rising in the west, immediately you say, 'It's going to rain,' and it does. 55And when the south wind blows, you say, 'It's going to be hot,' and it is. 56Hypocrites! You know how to interpret the appearance of the earth and the sky. How is it that you don't know how to interpret this present time?

57"Why don't you judge for yourselves what is right? 58As you are going with your adversary to the magistrate, try hard to be reconciled to him on the way, or he may drag you off to the judge, and the judge turn you over to the officer, and the officer throw you into prison. 59I tell you, you will not get out until you have paid the last penny.*"

*59 Greek *lepton*

NRSV

54He also said to the crowds, "When you see a cloud rising in the west, you immediately say, 'It is going to rain'; and so it happens. 55And when you see the south wind blowing, you say, 'There will be scorching heat'; and it happens. 56You hypocrites! You know how to interpret the appearance of earth and sky, but why do you not know how to interpret the present time?

57"And why do you not judge for yourselves what is right? 58Thus, when you go with your accuser before a magistrate, on the way make an effort to settle the case,* or you may be dragged before the judge, and the judge hand you over to the officer, and the officer throw you in prison. 59I tell you, you will never get out until you have paid the very last penny."

*Gk *settle with him*

COMMENTARY

The warnings about the coming judgment continue. The closing paragraphs of chap. 12 contain two brief clusters of sayings addressed to the crowds. The first charges the crowds with hypocrisy for not being as observant of the signs of the coming judgment as they are of the weather. The second warns the people to make every effort to settle accounts so that they may be blameless when they are brought to court.

12:54-56. The weather in Judea, Samaria, and Galilee is controlled by the Mediterranean Sea to the west and the desert to the south and southwest. When clouds appeared in the west, rain was coming. When the wind blew from the south or southwest, they were in for scorching heat. The charge of hypocrisy in v. 56 interrupts the flow of thought sharply and unexpectedly. Although the term *hypocrite* appears frequently in Matthew, Luke uses it elsewhere only in 6:42 and 13:15. The reader will recall, however, that this collection of sayings about the coming judgment began with a warning concerning the hypocrisy of the Pharisees (12:1). Again the argument is from the lesser to the greater. If the crowds pay

attention to the slightest sign of change in the weather—even a cloud on the western horizon or a puff of wind from the south—then should they not pay even more attention to "the present time" (καιρός *kairos*) as a sign that the judgment was at hand? (Cf. the textually uncertain saying in Matt 16:2-3.) "The present time" apparently refers to Jesus' works and warnings as signs that the kingdom was at hand and the end near (see 7:22-23; 11:20).

12:57-59. The warnings to the crowd continue without transition, thereby linking v. 57 with the preceding challenge to interpret the signs of "the present time." A further parabolic or metaphorical warning follows. Their situation is as desperate as that of one who is going to court with his accuser. The situation is described first in neutral terms (going with your accuser before a magistrate), but then in ominously threatening terms (being dragged before the judge and thrown into prison). The implication is that their situation is more desperate than they realize. In the light of the context, the point is that they should recognize the urgency of the moment and make every effort to settle with their accuser. Because of exorbitant interest rates, defaults on loans were common, and the situation described here was unfortunately an everyday occurrence. Once at the mercy of the legal system, a debtor had little chance of escape. He would be dragged before the judge, handed over to the officer, and thrown into prison, from which there was no chance of escape. Once in prison, he would not be released until he had paid the last penny of his debt. The term rendered "penny" literally means the last *lepton* (λεπτόν), the smallest copper coin (1/128th of a denarius) in use in Palestine in the first century. The only prudent thing to do, therefore, was to settle with one's accuser before the matter came before the court—even if one was already on the way to court.

REFLECTIONS

To what do we pay close attention, and to what do we turn a blind eye? The images of weather watching and being dragged to court by a creditor invite us to reflect on the contrast between devoted attention and casual neglect in our own lives. What claims our closest attention? Fluctuations in the stock market? Evidence of our social standing? Our grade point average? Opportunities to look good before superiors at work? What things do we watch with the same close attention that a Palestinian farmer paid to changes in the weather?

On the other hand, what areas of life have we so neglected that trouble in those areas may have reached crisis proportions without our knowing it? Our marriage? The well-being of our children or parents? Our own health? What has suffered as a result of our misplaced focus of attention?

Jesus' sayings challenge us to examine the inconsistencies between attention and neglect in our own lives, but the underlying challenge is to consider whether these inconsistencies reveal a pattern of prioritizing the insignificant while jeopardizing the things of greatest value and importance. Have we given as much attention to the health of the church as we have to our golf score? Have we given as much attention to the maintenance of our spiritual disciplines as to the maintenance schedule for our car? Where in the scale of our attention to detail does our devotion to the teachings of our Lord rank?

Luke 13:1-9, A Call for Repentance

NIV

13 Now there were some present at that time who told Jesus about the Galileans whose blood Pilate had mixed with their sacrifices. [2]Jesus answered, "Do you think that these Galileans were worse sinners than all the other Galileans because they suffered this way? [3]I tell you, no! But unless you repent, you too will all perish. [4]Or those eighteen who died when the tower in Siloam fell on them—do you think they were more guilty than all the others living in Jerusalem? [5]I tell you, no! But unless you repent, you too will all perish."

[6]Then he told this parable: "A man had a fig tree, planted in his vineyard, and he went to look for fruit on it, but did not find any. [7]So he said

NRSV

13 At that very time there were some present who told him about the Galileans whose blood Pilate had mingled with their sacrifices. [2]He asked them, "Do you think that because these Galileans suffered in this way they were worse sinners than all other Galileans? [3]No, I tell you; but unless you repent, you will all perish as they did. [4]Or those eighteen who were killed when the tower of Siloam fell on them—do you think that they were worse offenders than all the others living in Jerusalem? [5]No, I tell you; but unless you repent, you will all perish just as they did."

6Then he told this parable: "A man had a fig tree planted in his vineyard; and he came looking for fruit on it and found none. [7]So he said to the

NIV

to the man who took care of the vineyard, 'For three years now I've been coming to look for fruit on this fig tree and haven't found any. Cut it down! Why should it use up the soil?'

⁸"'Sir,' the man replied, 'leave it alone for one more year, and I'll dig around it and fertilize it. ⁹If it bears fruit next year, fine! If not, then cut it down.'"

NRSV

gardener, 'See here! For three years I have come looking for fruit on this fig tree, and still I find none. Cut it down! Why should it be wasting the soil?' ⁸He replied, 'Sir, let it alone for one more year, until I dig around it and put manure on it. ⁹If it bears fruit next year, well and good; but if not, you can cut it down.'"

COMMENTARY

The warnings and admonitions regarding the coming judgment that began with 12:1 reach their conclusion with a sobering call for repentance. Just as the debtor on the way to court in the preceding saying is warned to make every effort at reconciliation, so also Jesus uses the sayings about calamity in 13:1-5 and the parable of the unproductive fig tree in 13:6-9 to make the same point: Repent now, for the time is short.

13:1-5. Verse 1 sets the stage for the sayings that follow. The narrator reports that some of those present, presumably some from the crowd (see 12:1, 13, 54), reported an incident in which Pilate slaughtered a group of Galileans with the result that their blood mingled with that of their sacrifices. No other ancient source reports an event that can be identified with this incident, but Josephus's accounts of Pilate's confrontations with the Jews confirm that such bloodshed was not uncommon: Pilate's troops killed a group of Samaritans climbing Mt. Gerizim;[144] Pilate introduced Roman effigies into Jerusalem, causing a riot and a march on Caesarea;[145] Pilate seized Temple treasury funds in order to build an aqueduct.[146] The response of those who reported this incident to Jesus is not given by the narrator. Did they view Jesus' previous exhortation to seek a reconciliation with an accuser as a political statement? Did they think that because blood had been shed the time for reconciliation had passed?

Jesus adroitly seizes the teachable moment and uses the interruption to drive home his warning

that the coming judgment is inescapable. His response consists of two parallel questions and an identical answer repeated after each question: "Do you think that . . . they were worse sinners/offenders than all the other Galileans/Jerusalemites? No, I tell you; but unless you repent you will all perish as/just as they did." The questions set up the refrain that serves as the punch line to Jesus' warnings concerning the coming judgment.

Jesus' questions assume the popular notion that sin is the cause of calamity (Job 4:7; John 9:2). If God is responsible for everything that happens, and God is a just God, then calamities must be the result of human sinfulness. The fallacy in such logic is the notion that God is the immediate cause of all events, which leaves no room for human freedom or freedom in the created order, and therefore for events that God does not control. Consequently, Jesus' question ignores the immediate causes and the particulars of the situation. We might have expected Jesus to ask whether Pilate had killed these Galileans because they were more zealous rebels than others. Such particulars are irrelevant to Jesus' concern, however. If they died, they must have been sinners (according to the common assumptions). But were they worse sinners than all the other Galileans who were not killed? Jesus exposes the fallacy of such reasoning while at the same time driving home the point that life is uncertain, death is capricious, and judgment is inevitable.

No other ancient source reports the collapse of the Siloam tower. The Pool of Siloam lay in the southern part of Jerusalem, and presumably a tower in the city wall had collapsed, killing eighteen persons. If the deaths of the Galileans was an atrocity, an act of political violence, then the

144. Josephus *Antiquities of the Jews* 18.86-87.
145. Josephus *The Jewish War* 2.169-174; *Antiquities of the Jews* 18.55-59.
146. Josephus *The Jewish War* 2.175-177; *Antiquities of the Jews* 18.60-62. See also Fitzmyer, *The Gospel According to Luke (X–XXIV)*, 1007.

deaths of the Jerusalemites was sheer caprice, the whim of fate. Were these eighteen worse sinners than all the others who lived in Jerusalem at the time?

Jesus answers both questions in the negative. Such a theology is always better in theory than it is in dealing with the tragedies and calamities of life. Nevertheless, these deaths serve as a graphic warning of the coming judgment. Just as these Galileans and Jerusalemites had perished suddenly, so also all of those who heard Jesus would also perish if they did not repent. Jesus is not warning of physical death, of course. Instead, he uses death as a metaphor for the coming judgment. The image is shocking: The need for repentance is urgent.

13:6-9. The parable of the barren fig tree is similar to the stories of unfruitful trees that appear in ancient Near Eastern wisdom literature. The late versions of Ahikar, for example, contain the following story:

> And I spake to Nathan thus: Son, thou hast been to me like a palm-tree which has grown with roots on the bank of the river. When the fruit ripened, it fell into the river. The lord of the tree came to cut it down, and the tree said: Leave me in this place, that in the next year I may bear fruit. The lord of the tree said: Up to this day hast thou been to me useless, in the future thou wilt not become useful.[147]

The differences between this story and Jesus' parable are substantial. In Ahikar, the lord of the tree refuses to allow the tree another year in which to prove itself. In Jesus' parable, the gardener intercedes on behalf of the tree, pleading that it be given another year. Nevertheless, although there is mercy in Jesus' parable, it is still a

147. Ahikar 8.25, Armenian, in R. H. Charles, *Apocrypha and Pseudepigrapha of the Old Testament* (Oxford: Clarendon, 1913), 2:775.

warning of the urgency of repentance. The time until the judgment is extended for just a short time.

The opening of the parable echoes the well-known song of the vineyard in Isaiah 5, in which a man planted a tree in his vineyard. For three years he looked for fruit—time enough for the tree to produce—but found none (cf. Mark 11:13-14). Land was precious, so an unfruitful tree could not be allowed to use resources that could nourish a fruitful one. The man's response is to order the gardener to cut it down, but the gardener intercedes, offering to dig around it and fertilize it. Then, if it did not bear fruit in another year, he would cut it down.

Just as Jesus had asked the crowd to identify with a debtor being hauled to court (12:57-59), so also now he asks them to identify with the fig tree that is given one last chance. The point is the same: The time is short; you have one last chance to put things right before the judgment.

Christian interpreters have been quick to see allegorical meanings in the parable. The fig tree and the vineyard represent Israel, the owner is God, the gardener is Jesus, and the three years refer to the period of Jesus' ministry. None of these allusions is necessary, but the fig tree and the vineyard commonly represent Israel in the OT. The warning is clear even if the parable is taken as a metaphor rather than an allegory; you have but a short time to prepare for the judgment (by heeding the teachings of Jesus throughout this section of the Gospel). If you do not use the time that remains, you will be thrown into prison like the debtor, perish like the Galileans and Jerusalemites, and be cut down like the fig tree. No more forceful series of warnings could be given.

REFLECTIONS

The parable of the fig tree takes us back to an earlier, more agrarian era, but modern readers should not miss the theological payload of this closing section of the warnings in Luke 12:1–13:9. Luke has balanced the warnings of God's judgment with promises of God's mercy. Luke also dismisses the popular, but unworthy, theology of retribution without offering any simplistic answers to atrocities and calamities. If human beings die by the sword, by accident, or by natural disaster, it is not because God has arbitrarily chosen to punish them for their sins while sparing others. God would give even an unfruitful fig tree another chance.

On the other hand, the sudden calamity that claims human lives can serve as a warning of sudden judgment. Is life more precarious or fragile in modern societies, or does it just seem that way? Jesus' warning strikes at our most vulnerable point. Try as we might, none of us can protect ourselves or those we love from every danger: disease, traffic accidents, crime, emotional disorders, or random violence. The bright side of the warnings in Luke 13:1-5 is that Jesus affirms that these calamities are not God's doing. On the other hand, they should stand as graphic reminders that life is fragile, and any of us may stand before our Maker without a moment's notice.

The parable of the fig tree invites us to consider the gift of another year of life as an act of God's mercy. John the Baptist declared that the ax lay at the root, poised to strike (3:9). Any tree that did not bear fruit would be cut down. In Jesus' parable, however, the gardener pleads for and is granted one more year. The year that Jesus proclaimed, moreover, "the year of the Lord's favor" (4:19), would be a year of forgiveness, restoration, and second chances.

What would you do if you had only a year left to live, only a short time in which to make up for wrongs done and opportunities missed? How important that year might be! The lesson of the fig tree is a challenge to live each day as a gift from God. Live each day in such a way that you will have no fear of giving an account for how you have used God's gift.

LUKE 13:10-35, UNEXPECTED REVERSALS BROUGHT BY THE KINGDOM OF GOD

OVERVIEW

The section that follows has a twin in 14:1-35. Just as 13:10-17 reports the healing of a crippled woman on the sabbath, so also 14:1-6 relates Jesus' healing of a man with dropsy on the sabbath. Three parables of the kingdom follow in 13:18-19, 20-21, and 22-30. Similarly, two units of teaching material on humility (14:7-14) and the banquet of the kingdom (14:15-24) follow in Luke 14. Finally, both chapters end with warnings about the fate of Jerusalem (13:31-35) and regarding the cost of discipleship (14:25-35).

Luke 13:10-17, The Stooped Woman

NIV	NRSV
[10]On a Sabbath Jesus was teaching in one of the synagogues, [11]and a woman was there who had been crippled by a spirit for eighteen years. She was bent over and could not straighten up at all. [12]When Jesus saw her, he called her forward and said to her, "Woman, you are set free from your infirmity." [13]Then he put his hands on her, and immediately she straightened up and praised God. [14]Indignant because Jesus had healed on the Sabbath, the synagogue ruler said to the people, "There are six days for work. So come and be healed on those days, not on the Sabbath."	10Now he was teaching in one of the synagogues on the sabbath. [11]And just then there appeared a woman with a spirit that had crippled her for eighteen years. She was bent over and was quite unable to stand up straight. [12]When Jesus saw her, he called her over and said, "Woman, you are set free from your ailment." [13]When he laid his hands on her, immediately she stood up straight and began praising God. [14]But the leader of the synagogue, indignant because Jesus had cured on the sabbath, kept saying to the crowd, "There are six days on which work

NIV

¹⁵The Lord answered him, "You hypocrites! Doesn't each of you on the Sabbath untie his ox or donkey from the stall and lead it out to give it water? ¹⁶Then should not this woman, a daughter of Abraham, whom Satan has kept bound for eighteen long years, be set free on the Sabbath day from what bound her?"

¹⁷When he said this, all his opponents were humiliated, but the people were delighted with all the wonderful things he was doing.

NRSV

ought to be done; come on those days and be cured, and not on the sabbath day." ¹⁵But the Lord answered him and said, "You hypocrites! Does not each of you on the sabbath untie his ox or his donkey from the manger, and lead it away to give it water? ¹⁶And ought not this woman, a daughter of Abraham whom Satan bound for eighteen long years, be set free from this bondage on the sabbath day?" ¹⁷When he said this, all his opponents were put to shame; and the entire crowd was rejoicing at all the wonderful things that he was doing.

COMMENTARY

Luke often balances a scene involving a man with a similar scene about a woman. The parallels between the healing of the stooped woman (13:10-17) and the healing of the man with dropsy (14:1-6) are evident—both occur on the sabbath, both involve controversy with a leader of the synagogue or the Pharisees, both report a pronouncement as well as a healing, and in both Jesus invites his opponents to reason from what they would do for an ox to what they should do for a fellow human being.

For the last time in the Gospel, Jesus enters a synagogue. His teaching activity will continue in later chapters, however (13:22, 26; 19:47; 20:1; 21:37). Healings while Jesus was teaching in a synagogue on the sabbath have been reported in two previous scenes, Luke 4:31-37; 6:6-11. The first established Jesus' authority over the unclean spirits; in the second, Jesus argued that it was right to do good and to save life on the sabbath. In the synagogue scene in chap. 13, Jesus teaches that concern over the suffering of fellow human beings takes precedence over obligations related to keeping the sabbath.

The woman's condition is attributed to "a spirit of weakness." For eighteen years she had been bent over, unable to stand up straight. The number eighteen has probably served as a catchword linking this scene with the report of the eighteen who perished when the tower of Siloam fell (13:4). The term translated "weakness" (ἀσθένεια astheneia) can simply mean "illness" (see 5:15;

8:2; Acts 28:9). It is unclear, therefore, whether her condition is attributed to a demon or simply illness. Nevertheless, several features of the story suggest that the woman's condition may be seen as indicative of her diminished status as a woman; her condition is attributed to "a spirit of weakness," this weakness has left her bent over and unable to stand straight, Jesus addresses her with the general term "Woman," and Jesus answers the leader of the synagogue by contrasting what one would do for an animal with what he has done for the woman. In the end, Jesus confers on the woman a status of dignity: She is a "daughter of Abraham" (see 16:22-31; 19:9). Jesus is in the process of releasing the captive, freeing the oppressed (4:18), and raising up children to Abraham (3:8). As in other scenes in Luke in which Jesus responds to the needs of a woman, this scene points to a new status for women in the kingdom of God.

Jesus releases the woman from her ailment by a pronouncement and the laying on of hands. The physical act again suggests a further significance. The laying on of hands was normally accompanied by prayer and served as an act of blessing. Jesus laid hands on the sick (4:40), but the laying on of hands was also used as a conferral of blessing (Acts 6:6; 8:17-18; 9:12, 17; 13:3; 19:6; 28:8).

The proof of the woman's restoration is immediate. She is able to stand straight, and she praises God—the only proper response to God's redemptive power.

A third character is introduced at this point,

and through the rest of the scene Jesus interacts with the leader of the synagogue rather than the woman. The leader of the synagogue wants to make the issue Jesus' violation of the sabbath, but Jesus returns the focus to the needs and dignity of the woman. Addressing the crowd (which has not been mentioned but assumed), the leader of the synagogue declares that there are six days in which they may come to be healed, but not on the sabbath. His concern is for the sabbath law, and he shows only indignation that the woman has been released from her condition. He construes his role as maintaining proper observance of the sabbath rather than celebrating the release of the woman from her "weakness."

Jesus answers the leader of the synagogue, but like the leader he speaks to the crowd rather than directly to his opponent. Using a principle common among the rabbis, Jesus challenges his opponents to reason from the lesser to the greater. Since the woman is a daughter of Abraham, should they not do more for her than they would do for an animal? If an animal were bound, they would untie it from the manger and lead it to water on the sabbath. Yet here was a woman who had been bound by Satan for eighteen years. Should she not be set free, even on the sabbath? Jesus directly opposed the rabbinic principle that healing on the sabbath was allowed only in critical cases, not for chronic conditions.[148] The leader of the synagogue had cited the necessity of keeping the sabbath, but Jesus counterposed the greater necessity of freeing a human being from whatever crippled, bound, and diminished her.

The response is one of total victory for Jesus. "All his opponents" have been put to shame (see Isa 45:16), and "the entire crowd" rejoiced at "all the wonderful things" Jesus was doing (see Exod 34:10). In the contest of honor and shame, Jesus has been honored and his opponents shamed, but the greatest change has come in the status of the woman. Because of her physical condition, the woman carried shame, but by the end of the story she has been released from her shame and Jesus' opponents have been shamed. Hers is an honorable standing. Just as Zacchaeus will be called a "son of Abraham" (19:9), so this woman is recognized as a daughter of Abraham as well.

148. See *m. Yoma* 8.6.

REFLECTIONS

There is danger in both overreading and underreading. For generations this passage has suffered from underreading. It was taken simply as another of Jesus' healings. No particular significance was attached to the fact that the recipient of Jesus' redemptive healing was a woman. At the risk of overcorrecting and overreading this passage, the preceding interpretation has drawn attention to those features of the story that suggest that it is in fact paradigmatic of Jesus' mediation of the kingdom to women who are demeaned, denied their proper status, and oppressed by religious and social restrictions. The story of the stooped woman is, in fact, the story of many women.

The announcement of good news for women is also a challenge to the religious community, especially its leaders, represented in the story by the leader of the synagogue. If their response is like his, they too will be put to shame. The alternative is to show that one is receptive to the work of the kingdom by joining the crowd in "rejoicing at all the wonderful things that [Jesus] was doing."

The announcement of good news is an invitation to celebration for all who will receive it. But as Jesus' pronouncements in the rest of this chapter and the next will make abundantly clear, whoever does not respond to the invitation and rejoice in the kingdom will eventually be excluded from it.

Luke 13:18-21, The Mustard Seed and the Yeast

NIV

¹⁸Then Jesus asked, "What is the kingdom of God like? What shall I compare it to? ¹⁹It is like a mustard seed, which a man took and planted in his garden. It grew and became a tree, and the birds of the air perched in its branches."

²⁰Again he asked, "What shall I compare the kingdom of God to? ²¹It is like yeast that a woman took and mixed into a large amount[a] of flour until it worked all through the dough."

a21 Greek three satas (probably about 1/2 bushel or 22 liters)

NRSV

18He said therefore, "What is the kingdom of God like? And to what should I compare it? ¹⁹It is like a mustard seed that someone took and sowed in the garden; it grew and became a tree, and the birds of the air made nests in its branches."

20And again he said, "To what should I compare the kingdom of God? ²¹It is like yeast that a woman took and mixed in with[a] three measures of flour until all of it was leavened."

a Gk hid in

COMMENTARY

The next three parables speak of the kingdom of God (vv. 18, 20, 28-29). Again, the reference to a "man" (ἄνθρωπος anthrōpos) in the first parable (v. 19—unfortunately obscured by the NRSV translation, "someone") is balanced by a woman in the second (v. 21).

13:18-19. The parable of the mustard seed has parallels in Mark 4:30-32; Matt 13:31-32; and *Gospel of Thomas* 20. The parable of the leaven is paired with this parable in Matthew, but not in Mark or Thomas, which suggests that it may have originally circulated independently. Each of the Gospels also differs in its description of where the seed was planted (Mark—the ground; Matthew—a field; Luke—a garden; *Gospel of Thomas*—tilled soil). Actually, the Lukan form of the parable reflects little evidence of dependence on any of the parallel forms. Luke's is also the shortest of the canonical versions; it lacks the description of the mustard seed as the smallest of seeds or the mature plant as the largest shrub. The absence of these details is important because, although Luke has set the parable in a section that describes the reversals brought by the kingdom of God, if the parable of the mustard seed is a parable of reversal rather than growth, the reversal is implied simply on the basis of the proverbial smallness of the mustard seed. It has been calculated that it takes 725 to 760 mustard seeds to make a gram, yet the mustard plant grows to a height of eight to nine feet.[149]

Brief as the parable is, it reverberates with echoes from the OT. The prophet found nothing to which he could liken God: "To whom then will you liken God,/ or what likeness compare with him?" (Isa 40:18). But Jesus likens the kingdom to the mustard seed. It is organically present in Jesus' ministry, although its manifestation may be as obscure as the mustard seed is diminutive. Nevertheless, just as the seed certainly grows to a massive bush, so also the kingdom will inevitably come in all its glory. In Nebuchadnezzar's dream, he is represented as a great tree, and "the birds of the air nested in its branches" (Dan 4:12, 21; cf. Ezek 31:5-6). The most important background for the parable, however, is the oracle in Ezek 17:22-23. The reference to the birds nesting in the branches clearly connects the parable of the mustard seed with these prophetic parables. There is a certain irony, however. Rather than describing the kingdom as a great cedar, as did the OT kings and prophets, Jesus describes it as a mustard—hardly the noblest of plants by any reckoning! Jesus' emphasis is, therefore, not on the glory of the future kingdom but on the present sign of its presence. The mustard seed is a parable of the kingdom's beginnings, not its final manifes-

149. See Claus-Hunno Hunzinger, σίναπι, *TDNT,* 7:288-89.

tation.[150] The people expected a mighty cedar, but Jesus' ministry—though accompanied by mighty deeds—was like a mustard seed, merely a promise of the mature plant. Had his opponents read the Scriptures more closely, they might have recognized that they should have been looking for the sprig God had promised to plant rather than a full-grown cedar.[151]

The coming of the birds to nest in the branches of the plant that represents the kingdom of God has often been interpreted as a reference to the inclusion of the Gentiles. In the OT parallels the nesting birds simply underscore the tree's capacity to give peace and security. Nevertheless, Luke's interest in the inclusion of the Gentiles, to which Acts will give attention, is indisputable. In addition, the third parable in this context issues the warning that "people will come from east and west, from north and south, and will eat in the kingdom of God" (v. 29). A secondary allusion to the inclusion of the Gentiles in this detail of the Lukan parable should, therefore, not be ruled out.

13:20-21. The parable of the yeast (vv. 20-21) may have been joined to the parable of the mustard seed, because both emphasize growth or the contrast between small beginnings and great results. The parable of the yeast must be allowed to stand on its own, however, because its point is not exactly the same as that of the mustard seed. (Parallels appear in Matt 13:33; *Gospel of Thomas* 96.) The interpretation of the parable hinges on three issues: (1) the connotations of yeast, (2) the verb "hid" (κρύπτω *kryptō*) and (3) the meaning of the "three measures" of flour.

Yeast is old, fermented dough that is added to a fresh lump of dough in order to start the leavening process in it. Twice Paul quotes or alludes to the proverb "A little yeast leavens the whole batch of dough" (Gal 5:9 NRSV; 1 Cor 5:7); in both instances it is a warning about the permeating effect of evil in the Christian community. Jesus also warned the disciples about the

"yeast of the Pharisees and that of Herod" (Mark 8:15 NIV; see Luke 12:1). Each year at the Passover, moreover, Jewish families followed the prescriptions of Exod 12:15-16 by throwing out all of the leaven from their homes. Thus yeast was used as a metaphor for uncleanness or a corrupting influence.[152]

Luke says that the woman "hid" (ἔκρυψεν *ekrypsen*) rather than "mixed" the yeast in the flour (cf. NIV and NRSV). The verb implies secrecy rather than a normal part of preparing bread for baking. For whatever reason, the woman attempts to hide the yeast in a great quantity of flour. The humor of the situation is readily apparent.

Interpreters have often seen a scriptural allusion in the references to three measures of flour (Gen 18:6), but it may simply mean that the woman attempted to hide the yeast by putting it in a great quantity of flour—far more flour than one would ordinarily use in baking. The three measures would be equivalent to nearly 50 pounds of flour, enough to make bread for 150 people! Many parables have an incongruous or exaggerated element. The large amount of flour accords well with the woman's desire to conceal it, but the result is an enormous amount of leavened dough. Desiring to hide the yeast, the woman put it in flour, but now she has 50 pounds of leavened dough.

The point of the parable is made in a humorous fashion. Like the yeast, the kingdom is powerful and irrepressible. Its enemies may seek to conceal it, but like the yeast it will eventually leaven the whole lump. While the parable of the mustard seed dramatizes the presence of the kingdom in its insignificant beginnings, the parable of the yeast reminds us that even small beginnings are powerful and eventually change the character of the whole. Can one dare to believe that what began with just a handful of followers in Galilee will eventually change the whole world?

150. Ibid., 291.
151. See Peter Rhea Jones, *The Teaching of the Parables* (Nashville: Broadman, 1982) 87.
152. See Bernard Brandon Scott, *Hear Then the Parable* (Minneapolis: Fortress, 1989) 324-25.

REFLECTIONS

Let us tell the story of small beginnings. How could the poor and unschooled receive religious training, especially when there was no public education and many worked six days a week?

In 1780 Robert Raikes started the first Sunday schools. What could God do with a shoemaker in England whose imagination was fired by Captain James Cook's discoveries in the Pacific? William Carey founded the Baptist Society for Propagating the Gospel among the Heathen in 1792 and then went to India as its first missionary. Who can calculate what great things have come from these small beginnings? So what is the kingdom of God like? A mustard seed. Yeast.

Luke 13:22-30, The Narrow Door

NIV

22Then Jesus went through the towns and villages, teaching as he made his way to Jerusalem. 23Someone asked him, "Lord, are only a few people going to be saved?"

He said to them, 24"Make every effort to enter through the narrow door, because many, I tell you, will try to enter and will not be able to. 25Once the owner of the house gets up and closes the door, you will stand outside knocking and pleading, 'Sir, open the door for us.'

"But he will answer, 'I don't know you or where you come from.'

26"Then you will say, 'We ate and drank with you, and you taught in our streets.'

27"But he will reply, 'I don't know you or where you come from. Away from me, all you evildoers!'

28"There will be weeping there, and gnashing of teeth, when you see Abraham, Isaac and Jacob and all the prophets in the kingdom of God, but you yourselves thrown out. 29People will come from east and west and north and south, and will take their places at the feast in the kingdom of God. 30Indeed there are those who are last who will be first, and first who will be last."

NRSV

22Jesus[a] went through one town and village after another, teaching as he made his way to Jerusalem. 23Someone asked him, "Lord, will only a few be saved?" He said to them, 24"Strive to enter through the narrow door; for many, I tell you, will try to enter and will not be able. 25When once the owner of the house has got up and shut the door, and you begin to stand outside and to knock at the door, saying, 'Lord, open to us,' then in reply he will say to you, 'I do not know where you come from.' 26Then you will begin to say, 'We ate and drank with you, and you taught in our streets.' 27But he will say, 'I do not know where you come from; go away from me, all you evildoers!' 28There will be weeping and gnashing of teeth when you see Abraham and Isaac and Jacob and all the prophets in the kingdom of God, and you yourselves thrown out. 29Then people will come from east and west, from north and south, and will eat in the kingdom of God. 30Indeed, some are last who will be first, and some are first who will be last."

[a] Gk He

COMMENTARY

If the beginnings are small but the result is great, will many be saved or just a few? The answer is suitably paradoxical. The door is narrow. The owner of the house will turn away many who assume they are invited, but in the end others will come from far and wide. The reader of these verses catches echoes of various other passages in the Gospels, giving the impression that the whole is constructed from bits and pieces of tradition drawn together by the evangelist. At

points Jesus' response is parabolic, but by the concluding verses the parabolic guise is dropped.

Verse 22 reintroduces the journey motif. The reference to Jerusalem is the first since the beginning of the journey was announced in Luke 9:51. Many interpreters have taken the references to Jerusalem as markers that provide a structure for the journey narrative: (1) 9:51–13:21; (2) 13:22–17:10; (3) 17:11–19:27. Such a structure is of minimal help, however, in identifying the themes and organization of the material in these chapters.

An unidentified interlocutor raises the question to which vv. 24-30 form an answer: "Lord, will only a few be saved?" The answer progresses by means of catchwords. The image of the door is introduced in v. 24, where it is "the narrow door," implicitly contrasted with the broad way (see Matt 7:13-14). The two ways were a common trope in Jewish and early Christian ethical teachings (Jer 21:8; Ps 1:6; 4 Ezra 7:1-9; *Didache* 1-6). Against this familiar background the warning follows: Keep on striving to enter the narrow door. Jesus initially sidesteps the question, offering instead of a direct answer a traditional image that implies that only few will find their way. Then he moves immediately to the exhortation to strive—as an athlete strives to win a race (see 1 Tim 4:10; 6:12; 2 Tim 4:7). Whether one enters depends in part at least on human freedom, one's vigorous effort to reach salvation. Many will try, but few will succeed.

Verse 25 marks the first transition. The narrow door becomes the closed door. The language of this verse evokes echoes of other stories: the neighbor who has closed his door and cannot get up (11:5-7); the exhortation to knock and the door will be opened (11:9); the parable of the foolish virgins who cry, "Lord, open to us" (Matt 25:10-12); and Jesus' warning in the Sermon on the Mount that many would say, "Lord, Lord," but he would send them away (Matt 7:22-23). With all of these allusions in the air, the questioner (and the reader) is shocked to find that he or she has been placed among those who stand outside. This reversal is achieved by means of the direct address "you" in v. 25. A further shock follows when the master of the house responds, "I do not know where you come from" (cf. Matt 25:12). Were those in the crowd Galileans and Judeans? By the end of the story others will come to take their place who did not live in the promised land (see v. 29; cf. 14:15-24).

The image of the door is dropped after v. 25, and as the exchange continues it becomes clear that the master of the house is Jesus himself. Those who stand outside ("you") will then begin to identify themselves by means of their association with Jesus: "We ate and drank with you, and you taught in our streets." (Cf. the response in Matt 7:23, where those outside claim to have prophesied and cast out demons in Jesus' name.) In Luke the emphasis, appropriately, is on table fellowship rather than mighty works. The master's response, "I do not know where you come from," is repeated, but this time it is followed by the condemnation "Go away from me, all you evil-doers" (Ps 6:8).

The image of the eschatological banquet now takes the place of the image of the door. Luke reverses the sequence of the saying in Matt 8:11-12, placing the emphasis on the result for those who are turned away; there will be "weeping and gnashing of teeth." Although this phrase occurs only here in Luke, it is a favorite of Matthew (8:12; 13:42, 50; 22:13; 24:51; 25:30). The trio of patriarchs is named frequently in the OT (cf. Acts 3:13; 7:32), but the phrase "all the prophets" appears to be a Lukan flourish (see 11:50; 24:27; Acts 3:18, 24; 10:43).

One of the unresolved issues regarding this passage is whether those who are gathered into the kingdom from all directions are the children of Israel scattered abroad or the Gentiles. Although the issue cannot be resolved with any certainty in the present context, it is clear that Luke is vitally interested in Israel's rejection of the gospel and the subsequent inclusion of Gentiles. The two foundational reversals of the kingdom are, first, the crucifixion and resurrection of Jesus and, second, the rejection of Jesus by Israel and the subsequent inclusion of the Gentiles. (For references to the ingathering of the elect in the kingdom, see Ps 107:3; Isa 43:5-6.)

The images of the eschatological banquet in Jewish and early Christian writings derive from Isaiah's account of God's triumph and blessing:

> On this mountain the LORD of
>   hosts will make for all peoples
>   a feast of rich food, a feast of well-aged wines,
>   of rich food filled with marrow,
>   of well-aged wines strained clear.
> And he will destroy on this mountain
>   the shroud that is cast over all peoples,
>   the sheet that is spread over all nations;
>   he will swallow up death forever. (Isa 25:6-7 NRSV)

Reflections on the eschatological banquet again lie at the base of Jesus' parable in Luke 14:15-24, which serves structurally as the sequel to the present passage.

This unit of sayings that warn of the reversals

accompanying the coming kingdom ends with the free-floating logion "Some are last who will be first, and some are first who will be last." This saying appears in unrelated contexts in Mark 10:31; Matt 19:30; 20:16. Here it serves to warn those who think they are among the ones who will enter through the narrow door, those who presume to think they are invited to the banquet. When the kingdom comes, many will be surprised. Take care that you are not among those who will be excluded.

REFLECTIONS

Franz Kafka wrote eloquently of the human predicament. His parable "Before the Law" is the story of a man from the country who seeks admission to the Law. When the doorkeeper tells him he may not enter, he looks through the open door, but the doorkeeper warns him that he is just the first of a series of doorkeepers, each one more terrible than the one before. So the man waits for the doorkeeper's permission to enter. For days and then years, the man talks with the doorkeeper, answers his questions, and attempts to bribe him, but with no success. The doorkeeper takes the man's bribes, saying he is only doing so in order that the man will not think he has neglected anything. As the man lies dying, he sees a radiance streaming from the gateway to the Law. Thinking of one question he has not asked, he beckons the doorkeeper and asks him why in all those years no one else has come to that gate. The doorkeeper responds: "No one else could ever be admitted here, since this gate was made only for you. Now I am going to shut it."[153]

Jesus warned his followers that many of them would come to the narrow door seeking admission, only to be turned away by the owner of the house. They would plead with the owner that they had eaten with him and heard him teach, but he would send them away and admit others in their place.

If the door to the Law in Kafka's parable had been made just for that man, why was he not admitted? Jesus' parabolic sayings answer the question "Lord, will only a few be saved?" Jesus answers, in effect, "No, many. But many of you who think you will be admitted will be turned away." Why will they be turned away? By themselves, these sayings do not provide an answer. Jesus says merely, "Strive to enter through the narrow door." Is there any other door? None other is mentioned.

Wherein lies the failure of those who are turned away? It is not because they did not seek to enter. Did they seek to enter by the wrong means? Did they come to the wrong door, when they should have come to the narrow door? Even though they tried to enter, were they unqualified for entry? Did they lack the faith or good works needed for entry? The owner says only, "I do not know where you come from." Yet, others will come from east, west, north, and south—anywhere and everywhere. On the other hand, does the reason for their rejection lie instead with the owner of the house? These questions lead to the heart of the mystery of election and grace, free will and determinism.

Perhaps it is best to allow Jesus' sayings to retain their mystery and ambiguity. Two points remain clear, however: Jesus admonishes his followers to strive to enter by the narrow door, and he warns them that in the end there will be many surprising reversals. Many who think they will enter will not, and others (who are presumed to be excluded from God's fellowship) will take their place. Strive, therefore, as one who dares not presume on God's grace. Strive as though admission to the kingdom depended entirely on your own doing, but know that ultimately it depends on God's grace.

---

153. *Franz Kafka: The Complete Stories*, ed. Nahum N. Glatzer (New York: Schocken Books, 1983) 3-4; cf. Frank Kermode, *The Genesis of Secrecy: On the Interpretation of Narrative* (Cambridge, Mass.: Harvard University Press, 1979) 27.

Luke 13:31-35, Fateful Warnings for Jesus and Jerusalem

NIV

31At that time some Pharisees came to Jesus and said to him, "Leave this place and go somewhere else. Herod wants to kill you."

32He replied, "Go tell that fox, 'I will drive out demons and heal people today and tomorrow, and on the third day I will reach my goal.' 33In any case, I must keep going today and tomorrow and the next day—for surely no prophet can die outside Jerusalem!

34"O Jerusalem, Jerusalem, you who kill the prophets and stone those sent to you, how often I have longed to gather your children together, as a hen gathers her chicks under her wings, but you were not willing! 35Look, your house is left to you desolate. I tell you, you will not see me again until you say, 'Blessed is he who comes in the name of the Lord.'a"

a35 Psalm 118:26

NRSV

31At that very hour some Pharisees came and said to him, "Get away from here, for Herod wants to kill you." 32He said to them, "Go and tell that fox for me,a 'Listen, I am casting out demons and performing cures today and tomorrow, and on the third day I finish my work. 33Yet today, tomorrow, and the next day I must be on my way, because it is impossible for a prophet to be killed outside of Jerusalem.' 34Jerusalem, Jerusalem, the city that kills the prophets and stones those who are sent to it! How often have I desired to gather your children together as a hen gathers her brood under her wings, and you were not willing! 35See, your house is left to you. And I tell you, you will not see me until the time comes whenb you say, 'Blessed is the one who comes in the name of the Lord.'"

a Gk lacks for me   b Other ancient authorities lack the time comes when

COMMENTARY

Following the reference to Jerusalem in v. 22, these verses loom as omens of the fateful events that lie ahead. Jesus' pronouncements serve as oracles that prepare the reader to understand Jesus' death and the fate of Jerusalem. Not surprising, however, these verses also pose a number of exegetical difficulties. Are the Pharisees presented in a positive or negative light? Are they sincerely warning Jesus about Herod's intentions? And what is the meaning of Jesus' declaration, "On the third day I finish my work"?

13:31-33. These verses contain a brief narrative followed by two pronouncements. The effect of these pronouncements is to confirm that Jesus will not die out of season, another of Herod's victims, but that he will finish his divinely appointed mission in Jerusalem. Jesus' approach to Jerusalem, delayed by the extended travel narrative, therefore, takes on further suspense and significance for the reader.

The role of the Pharisees in these verses has served as the linchpin for arguments that Luke presents the Pharisees in a more positive light than do the other Gospels. In references both earlier and later in the Gospel, the Pharisees are presented as religious leaders who oppose Jesus. Luke often characterizes the Pharisees by the questions they raise:

> Then the scribes and the Pharisees began to question, "Who is this who is speaking blasphemies? Who can forgive sins but God alone?" (5:21)

> The Pharisees and their scribes were complaining to his disciples, saying, "Why do you eat and drink with tax collectors and sinners?" (5:30)
> But some of the Pharisees said, "Why are you doing what is not lawful on the sabbath?" (6:2; cf. 6:7)

The narrator in Luke has also characterized the Pharisees as those who "rejected God's purpose for themselves" (7:30), and Jesus denounced the Pharisees in 11:37-44. As a result, the Pharisees began "lying in wait for him, to catch him in something he might say" (11:54). In the immediately preceding reference to the Pharisees, Jesus warned the disciples, "Beware of the yeast of the Pharisees, that is, their hypocrisy" (12:1). In short, nothing prepares the reader to expect that the Pharisees were concerned about Jesus' safety. On the other hand, nothing in the description of the Pharisees' act in v. 31 allows us to posit that they were acting in concert with Herod or that they hoped to convince Jesus to leave Galilee so that they might more easily trap him in Jerusalem.

Herod's desire to kill Jesus, on the other hand, while new information, is readily intelligible in the light of the characterization of Herod to this point in the Gospel. Mary foreshadows God's works, saying, "He has brought down the powerful from their thrones,/ and lifted up the lowly" (1:52). Shortly later, Herod is introduced as the tetrarch of Galilee (3:1). We may expect, therefore, that the story that is about to unfold will pit God's prophet against the wicked king.[154] Luke's infancy narrative draws parallels between John the Baptist and Jesus, and the story of John's life does indeed pit John against Herod. When John spoke against Herod, Herod imprisoned him (3:18-20). Later, the reader abruptly learns of John's fate from Herod himself: "John I beheaded; but who is this about whom I hear such things?" (9:9). Ominously, Herod wanted to see Jesus (9:9).

In response, Jesus asserts that he has nothing to fear from Herod (cf. 23:6-12, 15). Vividly, Jesus characterizes Herod as "that fox" (13:32), a metaphor that paints Herod as sly, cunning, and voraciously destructive. Herod will not hinder Jesus from completing his work, however. He casts out demons and heals the sick—public acts that demonstrate the power of the kingdom of God. The three days declare the continuation and completion of Jesus' work. In v. 33, the three days are explicitly related to Jesus' journey to Jerusalem. Jesus' declaration that he will finish his work may, therefore, refer to either the completion of his journey or his death in Jerusalem.

Jesus *must* be on his way. Ironically, he does not travel to Jerusalem in order to escape death but in order to die there.[155] Luke's series of Jesus'

declarations of divine necessity sketch a profile of God's redemptive purposes:

"Did you not know that I *must* be in my Father's house?" (2:49)

"I *must* proclaim the good news of the kingdom of God to the other cities also; for I was sent for this purpose." (4:43)

"The Son of Man *must* undergo great suffering, and be rejected by the elders, chief priests, and scribes, and be killed, and on the third day be raised." (9:22; cf. 17:25; 24:7, 26)

"Zacchaeus, hurry and come down; for I *must* stay at your house today." (19:5).

"For I tell you, this scripture *must* be fulfilled in me, 'And he was counted among the lawless'; and indeed what is written about me is being fulfilled." (22:37)

Both Jesus' journey to Jerusalem and his death there will be controlled by his faithfulness to God's redemptive purposes, not by Herod.

Jesus journeys to Jerusalem as a prophet obedient to God's direction. His pronouncement that it is not right that a prophet should die outside of Jerusalem foreshadows Stephen's speech in Acts 7 and his death as a Christian martyr. At the end of his defense, Stephen asks, "Which of the prophets did your ancestors not persecute? They killed those who foretold the coming of the Righteous One, and now you have become his betrayers and murderers" (Acts 7:52). Among the prophets killed in Jerusalem were Uriah (Jer 26:20-23), Zechariah (2 Chr 24:20-22), those killed by Manasseh (2 Kgs 21:16; 24:4; cf. Josephus *Antiquities of the Jews* 10.38), and, in later legends, Isaiah.[156]

13:34-35. These verses have a parallel in Matt 23:37-39. Catchwords again link the succession of sayings. The last words of v. 33 become the first words of v. 34: "Jerusalem" and "prophet." References to Jerusalem, therefore, mark the beginning (13:4), middle (13:22), and end of Luke 13. The Wisdom of God spoke of the killing of prophets and apostles in 11:49-51, and the present verses continue in the same idiom. The repeated address "Jerusalem, Jerusalem" is reminiscent of divine addresses in the OT (see Gen 22:11; Exod 3:4; 1 Sam 3:10; see also Acts 9:4).

154. See John A Darr, *On Character Building: The Reader and the Rhetoric of Characterization in Luke–Acts* (Louisville: Westminster/John Knox, 1992) 147-68.

155. See Robert C. Tannehill, *The Narrative Unity of Luke–Acts: A Literary Interpretation*, vol. 1: *The Gospel According to Luke* (Philadelphia: Fortress, 1986) 153.

156. See Mart. Isa 5:1-14. See also Joseph A. Fitzmyer, *The Gospel According to Luke (X–XXIV)*, AB 28A (Garden City, N.Y.: Doubleday, 1985) 1032.

Moses had commanded the stoning of false prophets (Deut 13:10), but at times justice was perverted—as when Naboth (1 Kgs 21:8-14) and Zechariah (2 Chr 24:20-22) were stoned to death. The stage is set, therefore, not only for the death of Jesus but for the stoning of Stephen as well (Acts 7:52, 58).

One of the elements of this passage that is sometimes seen as a difficulty is Jesus' assertion that "often" or "many times" he had sought to gather in the children of Jerusalem when, according to Luke, he went there only once, at the end of his life. Such a saying would fit better in the Gospel of John, in which Jesus travels to Jerusalem on several occasions. On the other hand, Jesus need not have been in Jerusalem himself in order to have desired to gather to him the children of Jerusalem. Jerusalemites had already come to Jesus and rejected him earlier in the Gospel (5:17; 6:17). The metaphor of Jerusalem as a mother and her inhabitants—or all Israel—as children is rooted in the OT (Isa 54:1-8, 13; 62:4-5). The image of a bird mothering her young also appears in various passages (Deut 32:11; Ruth 2:12; Pss 17:8; 36:7; 91:4; Isa 31:5). Jesus, perhaps speaking as the Wisdom of God, has repeatedly offered Israel, God's people, his motherly love and protection, but they would not receive him (cf. John 1:11-12).

The result is that Israel's "house" is forsaken.

This allusion may be taken as a reference to the Temple in Jerusalem, but it should probably be read as a metaphor for Israel, as in Jeremiah's warning, "But if you will not heed these words, I swear by myself, says the LORD, that this house shall become a desolation" (Jer 22:5; cf. 12:7; 1 Kgs 9:7-8). The use of the present tense in the declaration of the verdict presents the future act as already accomplished. Jerusalem would be destroyed, and by the time Luke wrote its destruction had fulfilled Jesus' words.

The end of this discourse is filled with irony. Jesus declares that they will not see him until the time when they will declare, "Blessed is the one who comes in the name of the Lord" (v. 35). These words are part of the processional psalm that was sung by pilgrims entering Jerusalem (Ps 118:26). Jesus looks ahead to his coming as Son of Man at the end time (cf. Acts 3:19-21). Then Jerusalem will hail him as "the one who comes in the name of the Lord," but the judgment will already be confirmed. Ironically, when Jesus arrives in Jerusalem at the end of the Lukan travel narrative, the multitude of disciples chant these words. The chant reminds the reader of who Jesus is and points ahead to Jesus' return as the Son of Man. The city of Jerusalem, however, does not join the disciples in welcoming Jesus as "the one who comes in the name of the Lord" (cf. Luke 23:28-31).

REFLECTIONS

These are fateful words. They clarify in advance both Jesus' fate and that of Jerusalem. Jesus will not be killed by Herod; he will go on to Jerusalem, be killed there as the prophets had been killed, and eventually come again as the Son of Man. Jerusalem will reject Jesus and kill him. Its house, therefore, will be abandoned, and it will not see Jesus until he comes as the Son of Man. The irony and pathos are heavy. Judgment hangs in the air.

Two animal images symbolize the alternatives. On the one side lurks the fox. The Bible consistently depicts evil as dangerous and predatory, nothing one can flirt with without risking one's life. Satan is a serpent (Gen 3:1), and sin lurks at the door (Gen 4:7). The devil prowls around like a lion, looking for someone to devour (1 Pet 5:8). The wolf snatches God's sheep (Matt 7:15; John 10:12). Evil is like a plague of locusts or scorpions from a bottomless pit (Rev 9:1-11). The devil is like "a great red dragon, with seven heads and ten horns" that seeks to devour God's children (see Rev 12:3). As a representative of the powerful who oppress God's people, Herod is depicted as a devouring fox.

The danger to the community of God's people is real and present. God is not only a redeeming God but a protecting, nurturing God as well. To illustrate this facet of God's nature, the Bible turns to mothering images. Jesus likens his desire for Jerusalem, as God's emissary, to that of a mother hen who instinctively draws her young under her wing when danger threatens. Her love is steadfast (Ps 36:7), and we are the apple of her eye (Ps 17:8). A woman cannot forget her nursing child (Isa 49:15; cf. 1 Thess 2:7). How often has she wanted to gather her young to herself? What more tender image could describe God's love?

We live in a menagerie. In the symbolic world of these verses, evil threatens in the form of a fox, and the mother hen laments because her young are exposed but will not accept her protection. What more can the hen do but stand up to the fox and seek to shelter and protect her young? Alas, what will become of the young if they do not accept the shelter of their mother's wing?

LUKE 14:1-24, LESSONS IN KINGDOM ETIQUETTE

OVERVIEW

Someone has said that in Luke "Jesus is either going to a meal, at a meal, or coming from a meal."[157] The meal setting ties together the healing of the man with dropsy (14:1-7), the sayings on humility and hospitality (14:7-14), and the parable of the great banquet (14:15-24). As was noted in the introduction to 13:10-35, Luke 14 bears a structural resemblance to the previous section. The healing of the man with dropsy corresponds to the healing of the stooped woman (13:10-17), the sayings on humility and hospitality and the parable of the great banquet parallel the kingdom parables in 13:18-30, and the warnings regarding the cost of discipleship in 14:25-35 parallel the warnings at the end of chap. 13 (vv. 31-35).

157. Robert J. Karris, *Luke: Artist and Theologian, Luke's Passion Account as Literature* (New York: Paulist, 1985) 47.

Luke 14:1-6, The Man with Dropsy

NIV

14 One Sabbath, when Jesus went to eat in the house of a prominent Pharisee, he was being carefully watched. [2]There in front of him was a man suffering from dropsy. [3]Jesus asked the Pharisees and experts in the law, "Is it lawful to heal on the Sabbath or not?" [4]But they remained silent. So taking hold of the man, he healed him and sent him away.

[5]Then he asked them, "If one of you has a son[a] or an ox that falls into a well on the Sabbath day, will you not immediately pull him out?" [6]And they had nothing to say.

[a]5 Some manuscripts *donkey*

NRSV

14 On one occasion when Jesus[a] was going to the house of a leader of the Pharisees to eat a meal on the sabbath, they were watching him closely. [2]Just then, in front of him, there was a man who had dropsy. [3]And Jesus asked the lawyers and Pharisees, "Is it lawful to cure people on the sabbath, or not?" [4]But they were silent. So Jesus[a] took him and healed him, and sent him away. [5]Then he said to them, "If one of you has a child[b] or an ox that has fallen into a well, will you not immediately pull it out on a sabbath day?" [6]And they could not reply to this.

[a]Gk *he* [b]Other ancient authorities read *a donkey*

COMMENTARY

The invitation to dine at the home of one of the leaders of the Pharisees evokes echoes of Luke 5:29-39; 7:36-50; and 11:37-54. Moreover, this is the third scene describing a healing on the sabbath (6:6-11; 13:10-17). This scene is distinctive in that it takes place at a meal rather than in the synagogue. The issue, however, is still whether the man's need takes precedence over sabbath observance.

Eating was, of course, a significant social occasion. A guest was accepted as an equal, and Jesus might understandably have been watched closely to see whether he would follow the prescribed norms of etiquette, which allowed both guest and host to be honored. A meal with a distinguished guest, such as a prophet or teacher, would also have been an occasion for conversation (as in the Hellenistic symposium) that might be serious or witty or both. The reference to eating a meal (lit., "to eat bread" [φαγεῖν ἄρτον *phagein arton*]) in v. 1 is repeated in v. 15.

The encounter with the man with dropsy starts in exactly the same way as the scene with the stooped woman (καὶ ἰδού *kai idou,* lit. "and behold"; 13:11; 14:2). The narrator does not explain whether the man is another guest or a bystander. Dropsy, or edema—the abnormal accumulation of fluids in the body—is usually a symptom of serious physical problems. Perhaps because this is the third healing on the sabbath in Luke, the scene is abridged. There is no dialogue with the man (as there was with the woman in 13:12) or questioning by the Pharisees (as there was in 6:8; 13:14). Instead, Jesus poses the question of whether one is allowed to heal on the sabbath (cf. Mark 3:4; Matt 12:10; Luke 6:9). The lawyers and Pharisees have been characterized by Luke as those who reject God's purposes (7:30; cf. 10:25; 11:45-54). The question here, the first of two questions Jesus will pose in this scene, is reduced to its simplest, most direct form: "Is it lawful to cure people on the sabbath, or not?" Its simplicity implies an affirmative answer for modern readers—an implication that may not have been assumed by the Pharisees. For the legal prescriptions regarding healing on the sabbath, see the Commentary on 6:6-11. The silence of the lawyers and Pharisees already implies the end of the story; they could not answer Jesus.

The healing is incidental to Jesus' two questions for the lawyers and Pharisees. Consequently, it is reported with no fanfare and no response. Normally, following a healing miracle, some response of awe or praise is reported, either on the part of the one healed (13:13) or on the part of others (5:26). When Jesus cast out an unclean spirit on the sabbath, the people were amazed and said, "What kind of utterance is this?" (4:36). When he healed the man with the withered hand, the scribes and Pharisees "were filled with fury and discussed with one another what they might do to Jesus" (6:11). This time, there is no immediate response. Jesus merely heals the man and sends him away. All interest focuses on Jesus' challenge to the lawyers and Pharisees and their response to Jesus.

Jesus poses a second question for them (v. 5). This question is clearly a version of the question formulated in the healing of the stooped woman: "Does not each of you on the sabbath untie his ox or his donkey from the manger, and lead it away to give it water?" (13:15). The difficulty in the present instance is the textual uncertainty. Although some manuscripts (including א, K, L, Ψ, *f*[1,13]) read "a donkey" here, 𝔓[45], 𝔓[75], (A), B, and the majority of other manuscripts read "a son," which is also preferred because it is considered the more difficult reading. If "a son" is the reading adopted, the reasoning is altered from an argument from the lesser to the greater, as in 13:15, to a reasoning from the urgency of the situation of a child or animal that has fallen into a well to the need of the man with dropsy. Various Jewish groups took different positions on whether one would be allowed to rescue an animal from a ditch on the sabbath, but there was apparently no such argument in the case of a child. The Mosaic law stipulated that one should help an animal in distress, but did not make clear whether this duty should be carried out on the sabbath also (Exod 23:5; Deut 22:4). The Damascus Document takes the more stringent view: "Let no beast be helped to give birth on the Sabbath day; and if it fell into a cistern or into a pit, let it not be lifted out on the Sabbath."[158] On the other hand, the Mishnah, while it forbids delivering the young of cattle on a festival day, allows one to help the dam and allows for summoning a midwife for a woman, delivering a baby, tying up the umbilical cord, and performing circumcision.[159]

158. A. Dupont-Sommer, *The Essene Writings from Qumran*, trans. G. Vermes (Cleveland: World, 1961) 153.
159. *M. Sabb.* 18.3.

The silence of Jesus' opponents concedes to him the victory. The point has been made decisively. Human need takes precedence over sabbath observance. Observance of the sabbath was intended as a gift of rest and restoration. Jesus' healings on the sabbath not only restore the proper priority of meeting human need but also underscore the true meaning of the sabbath itself. The stooped woman could stand straight, and the man with dropsy was cured.

REFLECTIONS

Trying to be good and to do the right thing is never an easy business. The most difficult choices we face are not between right and wrong or good and bad but forced choices between two goods or two bads. How do we determine which is better or worse than the alternative? If one paints the Pharisees as hypocrites maliciously seeking to do away with Jesus, it is easy to side with Jesus over against the Pharisees, but such a reading of this passage is neither true to who the Pharisees were historically nor does it help us to translate this story into a current setting.

The Pharisees were devoutly committed to keeping God's law in every area, to the smallest details of life. Such obedience expressed their devotion to God and recognized God's grace in all of life. The sabbath was a special gift from God that was to be honored by careful observance. Healing on the sabbath was not allowed unless life was in danger. Apparently the man with dropsy was not in imminent danger. Jesus pushed the question of the obligation to meet the needs of a fellow human being, whether critical or not, over the duty of sabbath observance, or more broadly religious observances. The choice was between two goods, but Jesus' act of healing the man pointed to a different standard, and an entirely different vision of God's order for human society. In this story, religious duties are redefined to place priority on meeting the physical needs of fellow human beings. In the next paragraph, by rejecting discriminatory social practices, Jesus redefines the standards by which one gains honor.

Luke 14:7-14, Parables of Humility and Hospitality

NIV

[7]When he noticed how the guests picked the places of honor at the table, he told them this parable: [8]"When someone invites you to a wedding feast, do not take the place of honor, for a person more distinguished than you may have been invited. [9]If so, the host who invited both of you will come and say to you, 'Give this man your seat.' Then, humiliated, you will have to take the least important place. [10]But when you are invited, take the lowest place, so that when your host comes, he will say to you, 'Friend, move up to a better place.' Then you will be honored in the presence of all your fellow guests. [11]For everyone who exalts himself will be

NRSV

[7]When he noticed how the guests chose the places of honor, he told them a parable. [8]"When you are invited by someone to a wedding banquet, do not sit down at the place of honor, in case someone more distinguished than you has been invited by your host; [9]and the host who invited both of you may come and say to you, 'Give this person your place,' and then in disgrace you would start to take the lowest place. [10]But when you are invited, go and sit down at the lowest place, so that when your host comes, he may say to you, 'Friend, move up higher'; then you will be honored in the presence of all who sit at the table with you. [11]For all who exalt themselves will

NIV

humbled, and he who humbles himself will be exalted."

¹²Then Jesus said to his host, "When you give a luncheon or dinner, do not invite your friends, your brothers or relatives, or your rich neighbors; if you do, they may invite you back and so you will be repaid. ¹³But when you give a banquet, invite the poor, the crippled, the lame, the blind, ¹⁴and you will be blessed. Although they cannot repay you, you will be repaid at the resurrection of the righteous."

NRSV

be humbled, and those who humble themselves will be exalted."

12He said also to the one who had invited him, "When you give a luncheon or a dinner, do not invite your friends or your brothers or your relatives or rich neighbors, in case they may invite you in return, and you would be repaid. ¹³But when you give a banquet, invite the poor, the crippled, the lame, and the blind. ¹⁴And you will be blessed, because they cannot repay you, for you will be repaid at the resurrection of the righteous."

COMMENTARY

The meal setting introduced in 14:1 comes to the fore in this section and the next. What follows are parallel exhortations to the guests and to the host. Although the narrator says Jesus told them a parable (v. 7), his words have the form of ethical exhortations and sage advice.

Meals were important social ceremonies. Little was left to chance. As we can see from the Gospel of Luke itself, people noticed where one ate (5:29), with whom one ate (5:30), whether one washed before eating (7:44-46; 11:38), and where one sat to eat. All of these matters determined one's social position. Pliny the Younger recorded a similar criticism of the discriminatory meal practices of his host in one of his letters:

> Some very elegant dishes were served up to himself and a few more of the company; while those which were placed before the rest were cheap and paltry. He had apportioned in small flagons three different sorts of wine; but you are not to suppose it was that the guests might take their choice: on the contrary, that they might not choose at all. One was for himself and me; the next for his friends of lower order (for you must know that he measures out his friendship according to the degrees of quality); and the third for his own freed-men and mine.[160]

The structure of vv. 7-14 provides a framework for the interpretation of these twin "parables." The first section is addressed to the guests (v. 7)

160. Pliny, the Younger *Letters* 2.6, in *Pliny: Letters,* trans. William Melmoth; rev. W. M. L. Hutchinson, LCL (Cambridge, Mass.: Harvard University Press, 1915) 109-11.

and the second to the host (v. 12), but both follow a common pattern.

I. To the guests (vv. 7-11)
  A. "When you are invited . . . do not sit . . . lest. . . ."
  B. "But when you are invited . . . sit . . . so that. . . ."
  C. "Then you will be honored"
  D. Eschatological application (v. 11)
II. To the host (vv. 12-14)
  A. "When you give a dinner . . . do not invite . . . lest. . . ."
  B. "But when you give a banquet . . . invite"
  C. "And you will be blessed"
  D. Eschatological application (v. 14*b*)

14:7-11. Jesus is hardly the model guest. When he notes that they were watching him, he confronts the lawyers and Pharisees (v. 3) and heals a man on the sabbath. When he notes how the guests choose for themselves the places of honor (see 11:43; 20:46), he exposes their maneuvering with direct words drawn from Prov 25:6-7. The ancient sage had counseled:

> Do not put yourself forward in the king's presence
> or stand in the place of the great;
> for it is better to be told, "Come up here,"
> than to be put lower in the presence of a noble. (NRSV)

In vv. 8-10, Jesus appears to sanction the counsel given in Proverbs: Play the game, but play it more shrewdly. Do not be like buffoons who set themselves up for embarrassment. There is a marked contrast in tone between the two potential responses of the host. When the host asks the guest to move down from the place of honor, no term of address, respect, or affection is used. He says merely, "Give this person your place." When the host invites the guest to move up, however, he says, "Friend, move up higher." To be acknowledged as the friend of a powerful or wealthy person was itself a distinct honor (see John 19:12). The polarity is between shame (v. 9) and honor (v. 10).

Honor is not gained by seizing prominence; it must be given by others. But is Jesus merely pointing the Pharisees and lawyers to more prudent and effective ways to gain honor? Two hints are given that Jesus is not merely coaching the guests on how to play the game of gaining public recognition. First, vv. 9-10 mention not a place two or three steps below one's station but "the last place." Christian readers will quickly remember Jesus' adage that the first will be last and the last first (13:30). Second, the word for "honor" (δόξα *doxa*) is usually translated "glory," and it points the hearers beyond the recognition they may receive from the others present to the glory that belongs to God—and that only God can give.

The fact that these hints are significant indicators that Jesus is not merely chiding the guests to play the game more cleverly is confirmed by the eschatological application that follows: "For all who exalt themselves will be humbled, and those who humble themselves will be exalted" (v. 11). The future tense points beyond the immediate situation to the reversal of values that is characteristic of the economy of God's kingdom. Humility is not to be feigned as a strategy for recognition. On the contrary, humility is a quality of life open to persons who know that their worth is not measured by recognition from their peers but by the certainty that God has accepted them.

14:12-14. Now Jesus' words are directed to the host, and they make a related point. Hosts are no more free from the quest for recognition than are guests. The community and sharing of life and bread that takes places at table is too sacred to be perverted for our private advantage. The word for "meal" in v. 12 (ἄριστον *ariston*) designates both the noon meal (a luncheon) and the heavier evening meal (a dinner). Jesus lists four groups one should not invite—precisely those groups most often invited: your friends, your brothers or sisters, your relatives, and your rich neighbors (cf. the list of guests invited to Herod's banquet in Mark 6:21). Balancing this list is another list of four groups who should be invited: the poor, the crippled, the lame, and the blind. Such persons were explicitly forbidden to serve as priests (Lev 21:17-23) and were barred from entry into the Qumran community:

> And let no person smitten with any human impurity whatever enter the Assembly of God. And every person smitten with these impurities, unfit to occupy a place in the midst of the Congregation, and every (person) smitten in his flesh, paralysed in his feet or hands, lame or blind or deaf, or dumb or smitten in his flesh with a blemish visible to the eye, or any aged person that totters and is unable to stand firm in the midst of the Congregation: let these persons not enter.[161]

The contrast between such restrictions and the spirit of Jesus' teachings could hardly be more striking. Jesus does not merely prohibit inviting those in a position to benefit us if our reason for inviting them is to curry their favor. He advises not to invite the powerful or well-to-do because they *might* return the invitation. Instead, we should invite those who have never had such a meal, who could never return the favor, who will never be our superiors. The promise "and you will be blessed" corresponds to the earlier assurance, "then you will be honored." This time, however, it is clear that the matter of blessing and honor has been lifted from the praise of others to praise from God. God is ultimately the only one who can bless us or whose praise matters.

161. 1QSa 2:3-8.

REFLECTIONS

These are liberating words that can free us from the necessity of succeeding in our culture's contests of power and esteem. They free us from over-under relationships and the attitudes and barriers they create, so that we may be free to create human community and enjoy the security of God's grace.

This commentary on ancient meal practices and social stratification makes two points. First, one should cultivate and practice humility, if only because it is a prudent means of avoiding embarrassment. The eschatological application at the end of each of the two sections drives home a deeper meaning. Although the practice of humility is proper and prudent for disciples, the kingdom of God will bring about an even more revolutionary reversal. The very standards and practices of discrimination will be overthrown. The outcasts will be accepted as equals. Those who live by kingdom standards and values now will not only bear witness to the kingdom but also will be rewarded in "the resurrection of the righteous" (v. 14). Righteousness, not social position or the esteem of others, should be our goal. God does not look on the glitter of our guest list. Instead, God looks to see that we have practiced the generosity and inclusiveness of the kingdom in our daily social relationships. One standard offers the reward of social position, the other the reward of God's favor.

The distinctiveness of Jesus' vision of the kingdom was nowhere clearer than in his protest against discriminatory meal practices. Jesus and the Pharisees ate differently. For Jesus, meals were times of celebration and an inclusive fellowship that foreshadowed the inclusiveness of God's kingdom. The last supper, therefore, not only pointed ahead to the eschatological banquet, but also it reflected on Jesus' meals with the disciples, Pharisees, crowds, and outcasts in Galilee. The greatest crisis the early church faced, moreover, was not the delay of the parousia but the burning issue of whom one ate with (see Acts 10:9-16, 28; 15:19-20; Gal 2:11-14). Perhaps it is time we learned new table manners.

Luke 14:15-24, The Parable of the Great Banquet

NIV

15When one of those at the table with him heard this, he said to Jesus, "Blessed is the man who will eat at the feast in the kingdom of God."

16Jesus replied: "A certain man was preparing a great banquet and invited many guests. 17At the time of the banquet he sent his servant to tell those who had been invited, 'Come, for everything is now ready.'

18"But they all alike began to make excuses. The first said, 'I have just bought a field, and I must go and see it. Please excuse me.'

19"Another said, 'I have just bought five yoke of oxen, and I'm on my way to try them out. Please excuse me.'

20"Still another said, 'I just got married, so I can't come.'

21"The servant came back and reported this to his master. Then the owner of the house became angry and ordered his servant, 'Go out quickly into the streets and alleys of the town and bring in the poor, the crippled, the blind and the lame.'

NRSV

15One of the dinner guests, on hearing this, said to him, "Blessed is anyone who will eat bread in the kingdom of God!" 16Then Jesus[a] said to him, "Someone gave a great dinner and invited many. 17At the time for the dinner he sent his slave to say to those who had been invited, 'Come; for everything is ready now.' 18But they all alike began to make excuses. The first said to him, 'I have bought a piece of land, and I must go out and see it; please accept my regrets.' 19Another said, 'I have bought five yoke of oxen, and I am going to try them out; please accept my regrets.' 20Another said, 'I have just been married, and therefore I cannot come.' 21So the slave returned and reported this to his master. Then the owner of the house became angry and said to his slave, 'Go out at once into the streets and lanes of the town and bring in the poor, the crippled, the blind, and the lame.' 22And the slave said, 'Sir, what you ordered has been done, and

[a] Gk he

NIV

[22]" 'Sir,' the servant said, 'what you ordered has been done, but there is still room.'

[23]"Then the master told his servant, 'Go out to the roads and country lanes and make them come in, so that my house will be full. [24]I tell you, not one of those men who were invited will get a taste of my banquet.'"

NRSV

there is still room.' [23]Then the master said to the slave, 'Go out into the roads and lanes, and compel people to come in, so that my house may be filled. [24]For I tell you,[a] none of those who were invited will taste my dinner.'"

[a]The Greek word for *you* here is plural

COMMENTARY

The meal setting described in 14:1 is reintroduced in v. 15. Jesus has addressed his fellow guests in vv. 7-11 and the host in vv. 12-14. Now he responds to one of those reclining with him. The fellow guest has either sensed that Jesus is speaking of the eschatological banquet and joins him in affirming that those who feast at the Lord's table are truly blessed, or else, feeling the embarrassment of the moment, the fellow guest has voiced a common platitude in an effort to ease the situation.

Jesus responds with a parable, one that again features "a certain man" (cf. the parallels in Matt 22:1-10; *Gospel of Thomas* 64). Following a practice in evidence elsewhere (Esth 5:8; 6:14), the man sent out invitations in advance and then sent his servant around to call the guests when everything was ready.

The parable assumes the customs and social stratification of the ancient city. The host is obviously a wealthy person. He can afford to give a banquet, he invites persons who are buying land and oxen, and he has a servant. The practice of the double invitation allowed guests to verify that proper arrangements were being made for the banquet and that the right people would be in attendance. If the right people were not going to be there, then they could decline also. In this case, the man's banquet is snubbed. All the guests politely offer excuses, as if by common assent, claiming that they are unable to come. The first two excuses are absurd, but they serve the social function of declining the host's invitation. No one would buy land without having inspected it first. Nor would anyone buy oxen sight unseen. Both of the first two excuses point to material possessions as hindering them from coming to the banquet (cf. 8:14; 12:13-21).

The third excuse can be read in various ways. It concerns allowing one's family to hinder one's response (cf. 9:59-62; 12:52-53). First, the response of the third guest violates the standard storyteller's device of having the third character in a sequence serve as a reversal of the pattern established by the first two. Jesus thereby underscores the complete rejection of the man's effort to host a banquet. (Cf. the sequence of priest, levite, and Samaritan in the parable of the good Samaritan.) All of the excuses are pretenses. The newlywed man's pretense may be that he is in the midst of his own celebration, that he needs to spend time with his bride, or possibly that as a result of the wedding he has taken on many social debts and cannot afford another at this time. Some interpreters have seen in the third excuse an allusion to the holy war legislation of Deut 20:5-7, which allowed a soldier to be excused from battle if he had built a house but not dedicated it, planted a vineyard but not tasted its fruit, or if he was engaged to a woman but had not married her (cf. Deut 24:5). The situation is not exactly parallel, however, since the invited guest will presumably survive the banquet, whereas he might not survive combat. Since the deuteronomic legislation concerns situations in which one might be exempted from serving in a holy war, the point of contact might be situations in which one could decline God's call. Even so, the newlywed man is not being offered as a legitimate excuse in contrast to the first two—the host has been snubbed, and all the excuses are mere pretenses. Whereas the first two asked to be excused, the third man flatly states that he cannot come.

When the servant reports these outrageous excuses to the owner of the house, the master is justifiably angry. Having been rejected by his social peers, the owner of the house decides to reach out to the only other social groups available to him—the poor and the crippled. By inviting such persons to his banquet, the snubbed host would also be issuing an insult to his family and friends. Their esteem and approval no longer matter to him. He thumbs his nose at the social standards that define their privileged social position. The list of those to whom the servant should extend an invitation is identical to the four groups Jesus had named earlier (14:13), except that the sequence of the last two is reversed. Again, the exalted are being brought down and the lowly are being exalted (1:52-53; cf. 4:18-19; 6:20-25). The servant is sent into the broad streets and the narrow lanes to bring in the outcast from all over the city.

When there is still room, the master sends the servant out a second time. This second invitation matches the two invitations that had been extended to the original guest list. It may also foreshadow the preaching of the gospel first to the Jews and then to the Gentiles (cf. Acts 13:46). The homeless and landless lived outside the city gates, which would have been closed in the evening to keep them away from the homes and holdings of the well-to-do. Their social ostracism was enforced, so the servant might well have had to "compel" them to "come in" where they were normally not allowed.

The master is determined to fill his house so that none of those who had been invited at first could come later. The parable ends with the master's pronouncement. His servant has spoken (vv. 17, 22), the invited guests have spoken (vv. 18-20), and the master has spoken to the servant (vv. 21, 23-24). Only persons who are poor, crippled, blind, and lame, and those out in the roads and lanes remain without a voice. But it is those with no voice, no place, and no social standing who in the end will dine with the master.

Here the point of the whole story comes to light. This parable mirrors the warnings in 13:22-30 in the first half of this extended section on the reversals that will accompany the coming of the kingdom of God. Many of those who presume that they will be included will find themselves excluded, and their places will be taken by the outcasts. The future will not be a continuation of the present but a reversal of its exclusionary and discriminatory social codes. The lawyers and the Pharisees who had been invited to the meal had jockeyed for positions of honor. In Jesus' parable those who are concerned about their honor will exclude themselves from the master's banquet, and their place will be taken by those who exclude no one on the basis on their social standing.

The other versions of the parable interpret it differently. According to Matt 22:1-10, where the allegorical features are much more pronounced, the banquet is given by a king, who then destroys the city that rejected him and invites both the good and the bad to his son's wedding banquet. In Thomas's version (*Gospel of Thomas* 64), the parable ends with the master's announcement that "buyers and sellers shall not come into the places of my Father."

T. W. Manson's observation is worth repeating once more. In the narrative world of this parable, entry into the kingdom depends on neither the master's determination nor human initiative: "The two essential points in His teaching are that no man can enter the Kingdom without the invitation of God, and that no man can remain outside it but by his own deliberate choice."[162]

162. T. W. Manson, *The Sayings of Jesus* (London: SCM, 1957) 130, cited by Fitzmyer, *The Gospel According to Luke (X–XXIV)*, 1054.

REFLECTIONS

Lines from Vachel Lindsay's "General William Booth Enters Heaven" say:

Walking lepers followed, rank on rank,
Lurching bravoes from the ditches dank,
Vermin-eaten saints with mouldy breath,
Unwashed legions from the ways of death.

Such as these would share the feast of which Jesus spoke. None of the guests is kept away by something sinful; they just make excuses. Others would give anything to have the opportunity that these declined.

Excuses are deadly things. They poison the life of the Christian because they block the path to confession and forgiveness and rob faith of its vitality. The most dangerous excuses are those with which we fool ourselves. One of the unrecognized characteristics of excuses is that they accuse as well as excuse because they reveal our true priorities. The excuses we offer reveal the activities and commitments we hold to be of greater importance.

Only those who dare to put aside their excuses can ever know the joy of confession, the peace of forgiveness, or the thrill of living by faith. The Lord is giving a party, and we are all invited!

LUKE 14:25-35, CONDITIONS FOR DISCIPLESHIP

NIV

25Large crowds were traveling with Jesus, and turning to them he said: 26"If anyone comes to me and does not hate his father and mother, his wife and children, his brothers and sisters—yes, even his own life—he cannot be my disciple. 27And anyone who does not carry his cross and follow me cannot be my disciple.

28"Suppose one of you wants to build a tower. Will he not first sit down and estimate the cost to see if he has enough money to complete it? 29For if he lays the foundation and is not able to finish it, everyone who sees it will ridicule him, 30saying, 'This fellow began to build and was not able to finish.'

31"Or suppose a king is about to go to war against another king. Will he not first sit down and consider whether he is able with ten thousand men to oppose the one coming against him with twenty thousand? 32If he is not able, he will send a delegation while the other is still a long way off and will ask for terms of peace. 33In the same way, any of you who does not give up everything he has cannot be my disciple.

34"Salt is good, but if it loses its saltiness, how can it be made salty again? 35It is fit neither for the soil nor for the manure pile; it is thrown out.

"He who has ears to hear, let him hear."

NRSV

25Now large crowds were traveling with him; and he turned and said to them, 26"Whoever comes to me and does not hate father and mother, wife and children, brothers and sisters, yes, and even life itself, cannot be my disciple. 27Whoever does not carry the cross and follow me cannot be my disciple. 28For which of you, intending to build a tower, does not first sit down and estimate the cost, to see whether he has enough to complete it? 29Otherwise, when he has laid a foundation and is not able to finish, all who see it will begin to ridicule him, 30saying, 'This fellow began to build and was not able to finish.' 31Or what king, going out to wage war against another king, will not sit down first and consider whether he is able with ten thousand to oppose the one who comes against him with twenty thousand? 32If he cannot, then, while the other is still far away, he sends a delegation and asks for the terms of peace. 33So therefore, none of you can become my disciple if you do not give up all your possessions.

34"Salt is good; but if salt has lost its taste, how can its saltiness be restored?[a] 35It is fit neither for the soil nor for the manure pile; they throw it away. Let anyone with ears to hear listen!"

[a] Or how can it be used for seasoning?

COMMENTARY

Structurally, these verses parallel Luke 13:31-35, which laments the failure of Jerusalem to respond to Jesus' calls. The conclusion to Luke 14:1-35 now contemplates the danger that many would-be disciples will fail to meet the conditions for true discipleship. Luke returns to the journey motif, leaving behind the meal setting. Because Jesus faces martyrdom in Jerusalem, his followers must be prepared to leave everything behind and make their commitment to Jesus as complete and all-consuming as Jesus' own devotion to his mission.

These sayings are addressed to the large crowds following Jesus. Their intent is to urge persons who are seeking to be disciples to consider first the demands of discipleship. Rather than trying to lure the unsuspecting into unconsidered commitments, Jesus warns the crowd in advance that the way of discipleship will not be easy. Several phrases recur in these verses, giving the section unity and underscoring its dominant emphasis:

> "Whoever comes to me and does not . . . cannot be my disciple" (v. 26)

> "whoever does not . . . cannot be my disciple" (v. 27)

> "So therefore, none of you can become my disciple if you do not . . ." (v. 33)

The three conditions laid down in this sequence of pronouncements concern renouncing family ties that would prevent one from being a disciple, bearing one's cross, and forsaking possessions. Between the second and third conditions, twin parables illustrate the folly of failing to consider the cost of an undertaking: the tower builder (vv. 28-30) and the king going to war (vv. 31-32). In both cases, the parable takes the form of a question that expects the answer, "No one, of course" (cf. 11:5, 11; 14:5; 15:4; 17:7). Verse 33 states the conclusion: Discipleship requires the renunciation of all that we have. Finally, vv. 34-35 warn of the consequences of unworthy discipleship; tasteless salt is not good for anything.

14:26. Because Jesus' ethic of love makes it unthinkable that one should hate his or her own family, v. 26 has always been a difficult saying (cf. Matt 10:37). Two factors help put it into context. First, it is a Semitic hyperbole that exaggerates a contrast so that it can be seen more clearly. "Hate" (μισέω *miseō*) does not mean anger or hostility. It indicates that if there is a conflict, one's response to the demands of discipleship must take precedence over even the most sacred of human relationships (cf. Exod 32:27-29; Deut 33:9; 1 Kgs

19:19-21). There is no duty higher than commitment to Jesus and to being his disciple.

Second, this saying may have had a very practical function in the lives of the first Christians. In the Gospels we see the disciples as an itinerant band. It has been suggested that this portrait reflects the situation of the earliest Christians. Discipleship required a willingness to leave home and family and travel with minimal provisions from village to village in order to proclaim the gospel (cf. 18:29; 10:1-12). Later, in Corinth, the church faced the problems caused by pagan spouses divorcing their believing partners (1 Cor 7:15-16). The addition of "even life itself" at the end of the list of one's family members echoes the sayings about forsaking one's life in Mark 8:35-37 and John 12:25.

14:27. This verse on cross bearing is a version of the saying in Luke 9:23. The saying also evokes again the rejection of Jesus and the suffering that awaits him in Jerusalem. He warns the crowd, therefore, that no one can follow him unless he or she is ready to suffer the same fate Jesus would suffer. In this version of the saying, Jesus speaks not of "taking up" one's cross but of bearing it.

14:28-32. The twin parables that follow might aptly be entitled "Fools at Work and at War." These parables have no parallel in the other Gospels. Jesus draws attention to a simple observation: A prudent person would not begin a project until being sure it can be finished. A man would not lay the foundation for a tower unless he was sure he could finish it. A king would not go to war unless he had enough soldiers to resist the opposing force. By the same token, God has not entered a redemptive process without being prepared to complete it, and Jesus did not set his face for Jerusalem without being prepared to face the sacrifice that would be required of him there. Thus no one should step forward as a disciple without being prepared to forsake everything for the sake of following Jesus.

The two parables move from the lesser to the greater consequence. In the first, the threat is merely that one may be embarrassed before one's neighbors. In the second, the consequence may be defeat at the hands of an enemy. The parable does not advocate building stronger armies; it illustrates the folly of embarking on a venture without being sure one can see it through.

14:33. The parables lead to the third condition (v. 33); they demand that one be ready to give up everything to be a disciple. If you seek to follow Jesus, then understand first that what is required is all you have.

Applying this principle in the area of one's material possessions, as Luke often does, v. 33 concludes with a return to the refrain found in vv. 26-27: "None of you can become my disciple if you do not give up all your possessions." The verb translated "renounce" or "give up" (ἀποτάσσομαι *apotassomai*) literally means "to say farewell to" or "to take leave of." The descriptions of the sharing of goods in the early church in Acts 2:44; 4:32 probably illustrate what Luke understood this demand to mean.

14:34-35. Sayings on salt also appear in Matt 5:13 and Mark 9:49-50. Although Luke uses these aphorisms as the conclusion to this section of warnings, the sayings actually make a different point from the preceding sayings, which were directed to the crowd of would-be disciples. The sayings on salt are more appropriate as warnings to those who are already disciples. The value of salt lies in its salinity. If it loses its saltiness, it cannot be restored. The point of the analogy is that the disciple is defined by his or her relationship to Jesus. If one gives up that relationship, one is like salt that has lost its saltiness.

Real salt cannot lose its flavor, but the complex minerals found around the Dead Sea were not pure salt and could, therefore, become tasteless. The taste, once lost, could not be restored. Jesus observed that this tasteless salt was not even good for fertilizing or killing weeds; "it is fit neither for the soil nor for the manure pile" (14:35). The point seems to be that salt that has lost its saltiness is not even good for menial, alternative uses.

The call for those who have ears to hear is a call to decision. The reversals of the coming kingdom have been dramatically illustrated, the conditions of discipleship have been set forth, and the consequences of rejecting the call to discipleship have been made clear. Now is the time for decision.

REFLECTIONS

Have you ever made a commitment to an organization or committee without first finding out all that would be expected of you? Have you ever gotten caught by purchasing something or joining a book club without first reading all the fine print? Jesus warned would-be followers about the cost of discipleship.

Some churches, preachers, and TV programs present the gospel as though they were selling a used car. They make it sound as easy as possible, as though no real commitment were required. Jesus' call was far different. He was not looking for superficial commitment or a crowd of tagalongs. Instead, he required his followers to be totally committed if they were going to follow at all.

The language of cross bearing has been corrupted by overuse. Bearing a cross has nothing to do with chronic illness, painful physical conditions, or trying family relationships. It is instead what we do voluntarily as a consequence of our commitment to Jesus Christ. Cross bearing requires deliberate sacrifice and exposure to risk and ridicule in order to follow Jesus. This commitment is not just to a way of life, however. It is a commitment to a person. A disciple follows another person and learns a new way of life.

In a sense, no one can know whether he or she will be able to fulfill a commitment to discipleship. Jesus was not asking for a guarantee of complete fidelity in advance, however. If he had, no one would qualify to be a disciple. Through these parables, Jesus was simply calling for each person who would be a disciple to consider in advance what that commitment requires.

Cultural accommodation of the Christian faith has progressed steadily in recent years. As a result, many see no tension between the teachings of Jesus and the common aspirations of middle-class Americans. On the contrary, a complete change of priorities, values, and pursuits is required. Paul wrote that in Christ we become not just nice people but new creations (see 2 Cor 5:17). When Jesus turned and saw the crowd following him, he was not impressed by his own success. He was not interested in the casual, easy acceptance the crowd offered.

The cost of discipleship is paid in many different kinds of currency. For some persons a redirection of time and energy is required, for others a change in personal relationships, a change in vocation, or a commitment of financial resources; but for each person the call to discipleship is all consuming. A complete change in priorities is required of all would-be disciples. No part-time disciples are needed. No partial commitments are accepted.

LUKE 15:1-32, PARABLES OF THE JOY OF RECOVERY AND RETURN

OVERVIEW

Following the unit of sayings on the reversals of the kingdom in Luke 13:10–14:35, Luke presents three parables that have a common theme: the joy of finding what was lost or recovering one who was estranged (the lost sheep, the lost coin, and the lost son). These parables follow easily upon the extended section on the reversals of the kingdom because they respond to the Pharisees' grumbling over Jesus' practice of eating with outcasts.

Although the three parables share a common theme, the first two are paired while the third, which is more elaborate, balances the first two. The first two parables each begin with a question, "which one of you" (τίς ἄνθρωπος ἐξ ὑμῶν *tis anthrōpos ex hymōn;* v. 4), and "what woman" (τίς γυνή *tis gynē;* v. 8). The third parable tells the story of "a certain man" (ἄνθρωπός τις *anthrōpos tis;* v. 11). The pairing of the first two parables is evident not only in their common structure and theme but also in the link between them. Verse 8 introduces the second parable with the term "or" (ἤ *ē*) which conveys the synonymity of the two parables.

The two parables have the same structure: (1) *a question:* What man? What woman? (2) *a story of losing and finding:* if he/she lost/loses one, does not go/seek . . . until he/she finds; (3) *a celebration with friends:* and when he/she has found it, he/she calls together his/her friends and neighbors, saying, "Rejoice with me, for I have found my sheep/the coin which was/I had lost"; (4) *the moral:* Just so, I tell you, there will be/is

joy in heaven/before the angels of God over one sinner who repents.

The common themes that link the parables are evidenced in the repetition of the terms "lost" (ἀπόλλυμι *apollymi*) and "found" (εὑρίσκω *heuriskō*) in the three parables:

I. The lost sheep
"and losing one of them" (v. 4)
"and go after the one that is lost until he finds it?" (v. 4)
"When he has found it" (v. 5)
"I have found my sheep that was lost" (v. 6)

II. The lost coin
"if she loses one of them" (v. 8)
"and search carefully until she finds it" (v. 8)
"When she has found it" (v. 9)
"I have found the coin that I had lost" (v. 9)

III. The lost son
"he was lost and is found" (v. 24)
"he was lost and has been found" (v. 32)

In the parables, what was lost belonged to the owner from the start, but in both stories the owner expends diligent effort to recover the one lost possession.

The theme of joy and celebration also recurs in all three parables: (I) "rejoice/s" (vv. 5-6), "joy" (v. 7); (II) "rejoice" (v. 9), "joy" (v. 10); (III) "celebrate" (vv. 23-24, 29, 32), "rejoice" (v. 32).

Luke 15:1-10, The Lost Sheep and the Lost Coin

NIV

15 Now the tax collectors and "sinners" were all gathering around to hear him. ²But the Pharisees and the teachers of the law muttered, "This man welcomes sinners and eats with them."

³Then Jesus told them this parable: ⁴"Suppose one of you has a hundred sheep and loses one of them. Does he not leave the ninety-nine in the open country and go after the lost sheep until he finds it? ⁵And when he finds it, he joyfully puts it on his shoulders ⁶and goes home. Then he calls his friends and neighbors together and says, 'Rejoice with me; I have found my lost sheep.' ⁷I tell you that in the same way there will be more rejoicing in heaven over one sinner who repents than over ninety-nine righteous persons who do not need to repent.

⁸"Or suppose a woman has ten silver coins*ᵃ* and loses one. Does she not light a lamp, sweep the house and search carefully until she finds it? ⁹And when she finds it, she calls her friends and neighbors together and says, 'Rejoice with me; I have found my lost coin.' ¹⁰In the same way, I tell you, there is rejoicing in the presence of the angels of God over one sinner who repents."

ᵃ8 Greek ten drachmas, *each worth about a day's wages*

NRSV

15 Now all the tax collectors and sinners were coming near to listen to him. ²And the Pharisees and the scribes were grumbling and saying, "This fellow welcomes sinners and eats with them."

3So he told them this parable: ⁴"Which one of you, having a hundred sheep and losing one of them, does not leave the ninety-nine in the wilderness and go after the one that is lost until he finds it? ⁵When he has found it, he lays it on his shoulders and rejoices. ⁶And when he comes home, he calls together his friends and neighbors, saying to them, 'Rejoice with me, for I have found my sheep that was lost.' ⁷Just so, I tell you, there will be more joy in heaven over one sinner who repents than over ninety-nine righteous persons who need no repentance.

8"Or what woman having ten silver coins,*ᵃ* if she loses one of them, does not light a lamp, sweep the house, and search carefully until she finds it? ⁹When she has found it, she calls together her friends and neighbors, saying, 'Rejoice with me, for I have found the coin that I had lost.' ¹⁰Just so, I tell you, there is joy in the presence of the angels of God over one sinner who repents."

ᵃ Gk drachmas, *each worth about a day's wage for a laborer*

COMMENTARY

15:1-2. A new setting is introduced at the beginning of the chapter. In the previous chapter, Jesus had been invited to eat with a leader of the Pharisees (14:1), and the sayings that followed grew out of that setting. Now the Pharisees and scribes "murmur" because Jesus eats with "tax collectors and sinners." The verb for "to murmur" (διαγογγύζω *diagongyzō*) has been used earlier in a similar context (5:30; cf. 19:7), but its more significant overtones arise from its use in the exodus narratives, where the Israelites "murmur" against Moses (Exod 16:7-12). The sound of the Greek verb *diagongyzō* suggests its meaning. For clarification of the role of the "tax collectors" or toll collectors and the scandal of Jesus' table

fellowship with these outcasts, see Commentary on 5:29-32. Those designated as "sinners" by the Pharisees would have included not only persons who broke the moral laws but also those who did not maintain the ritual purity practiced by the Pharisees.

The scandal was that Jesus received such outcasts, shared table fellowship with them, and even played host to them. The God who showed mercy to the apostate Israelites in the wilderness rejoices over the salvation of every lost person like a shepherd who rejoices over the recovery of a lost sheep or a woman who rejoices over the finding of a lost coin. The question posed by the parables is whether we will join in the celebration—but to celebrate with God one must also share in God's mercy.

15:3-7. In the first story, the shepherd leaves the ninety-nine sheep to go and search for the lost one. The *Gospel of Thomas* (107) adds two embellishments: The shepherd tired himself out searching, but the sheep that went astray was the largest of the sheep! Luke and Matthew might aptly have said that the lost one was the smallest (cf. Matt 18:6, 10, 12-13), or "one of the least of these." Matthew says that the sheep "went astray," but Luke brings the story in line with the other two parables in chap. 15 by reporting that the sheep was lost (cf. vv. 8-9, 24, 32).

The parable reflects a Palestinian life setting: "Throughout the biblical period tending flocks, with agriculture, was in Palestine the basis of the economy."[163] In the OT, God is described as Israel's shepherd:

> He will feed his flock like a shepherd;
>   he will gather the lambs in his arms,
> and carry them in his bosom,
>   and gently lead the mother sheep. (Isa 40:11 NRSV)

The image appears most frequently in the Psalms (e.g., 23:1-4; 28:9; 78:52; 80:1; 100:3) and in the post-exilic prophets (Jer 31:10; Ezek 34:11-22; Zech 13:7). By contrast, God is never called a shepherd in the NT, and the image is limited to Jesus' parables. Both in the OT and in Christian literature, the shepherd served as an image of the religious leaders of the people, leaders who at times, like hirelings, did not serve the flock well (Jer 3:15; 23:4; Ezek 34:2, 7; John 10:1-5; Eph 4:11; 1 Pet 5:2). As an image for Christ, the shepherd, carrying or leading the sheep, appears in catacomb art from the third century.

In contrast to the positive image of the shepherd in both the OT and NT writings, shepherds had acquired a bad reputation by the first century as shiftless, thieving, trespassing hirelings. Shepherding was listed among the despised trades by the rabbis, along with camel drivers, sailors, gamblers with dice, dyers, and tax collectors.[164] The Pharisees' estimate of shepherds has a particular force in this context, since Jesus responds to the criticism over his acceptance of tax collectors and

"sinners" by telling a story that casts God in the role of a shepherd.

The conclusion to the parable of the lost sheep reflects its Lukan setting. The calling together of friends and neighbors to celebrate fits the setting of the woman who lost a coin better than it does that of the shepherd (cf. v. 9).

Verse 7 is not part of the parable. Rather, it is Jesus' comment to the Pharisees and scribes regarding the meaning of the parable (cf. v. 10; 14:24). The joy in heaven characterizes God's celebration at the repentance of a sinner—a note that connects the conclusion to the reference to "sinners" in v. 2. By implication, Jesus' actions in accepting sinners and eating with them reflects God's gracious spirit toward those who were held in contempt by the Pharisees and scribes.

The contrast with the ninety-nine righteous persons creates a tension that requires a reversal in the position of Pharisees and scribes and the tax collectors and sinners. On the one hand, the Pharisees and scribes are likened to the ninety-nine who were not in jeopardy. On the other hand, God takes more delight in the return of the tax collectors and sinners than in the others, and because they take offense at Jesus' celebration with the tax collectors and sinners, they show that their spirit is far from God's. The parable poses a double scandal for the Pharisees and scribes; not only are they reminded of the biblical image of God as a shepherd but also God takes more delight in celebrating with a repentant sinner than with the scribes and Pharisees. Their "righteousness" did not make God rejoice. The celebration of the coming of the kingdom was taking place in Jesus' table fellowship with the outcasts, but because their righteousness had become a barrier separating them from the outcasts, they were missing it.

15:8-10. The parable of the lost coin is found only in Luke, where it is a twin of the parable of the lost sheep. This time the parable features not a man with a hundred sheep but a poor woman with ten coins. A drachma was a silver coin worth about a denarius, or a day's wage. Hence, ten drachmas would not have been a great sum of money. The point of the parable would have been lost if the coin had been of great value. Who would not search for a lost fortune? But the parable points to the human reaction to prize what

---

163. Joachim Jeremias, ποιμήν *TDNT,* 6:486.
164. See Joachim Jeremias, *Jerusalem in the Time of Jesus,* trans. F. H. Cave and C. H. Cave (Philadelphia: Fortress, 1969) 304.

Figure 6: Parables in the Synoptic Gospels

Patches and wineskins[1]	Luke 5:36-39	Matt 9:16-17	Mark 2:21-22
The blind leading the blind[2]	Luke 6:39-40	Matt 15:14b	
The log in your own eye[2]	Luke 6:41-42	Matt 7:3-4	
Producing good fruit[2]	Luke 6:43-45	Matt 7:16-20	
The two builders / building on a solid foundation	Luke 6:46-49	Matt 7:24-27	
The riddle of the children	Luke 7:31-35	Matt 11:16-19	
The two debtors	Luke 7:41-43		
The lamp	Luke 8:16	Matt 5:14-1	Mark 4:21-22
Seed and the soil / the sower	Luke 8:4-8	Matt 13:3-8	Mark 4:3-9
The good Samaritan	Luke 10:30-35		
The parable of a shameless neighbor	Luke 11:5-8		
The kingdom divided against itself[3]	Luke 11:17a	Matt 12:25a	Mark 3:24
The house divided against itself[3]	Luke 11:17b	Matt 12:25b	Mark 3:25
The return of the unclean spirit	Luke 11:24-26	Matt 12:43-45	
The rich fool	Luke 12:16-21		
The returning master	Luke 12:36-38		
The thief in the night / the watchful owner	Luke 12:39-40	Matt 24:43-44	
The good and wicked servants	Luke 12:42-46	Matt 24:45-51	[Mark 13:33-37]
Going before a judge	Luke 12:58-59	Matt 5:25-26	
The barren fig tree	Luke 13:6-9	[Matt 21:20-22	Mark 11:20-25]
The mustard seed	Luke 13:18-19	Matt 13:31-32	Mark 4:30-32
The yeast	Luke 13:20-21	Matt 13:33	
The narrow door	Luke 13:24-30		
The choice of places at table	Luke 14:7-11		
The great supper / great banquet	Luke 14:16-24	Matt 22:1-14	
The fool at work	Luke 14:28-30		
The fool at war	Luke 14:31-32		
The lost sheep	Luke 15:3-7	Matt 18:12-14	
The lost coin	Luke 15:8-10		
The prodigal son	Luke 15:11-32		
The dishonest steward	Luke 16:1-9		
The rich man and Lazarus	Luke 16:19-31		
The servant who serves without reward	Luke 17:7-10		
The unjust judge and the persistent widow	Luke 18:1-8		
The Pharisee and the tax collector	Luke 18:9-14		
The talents / the greedy and vengeful king	Luke 19:11-27	Matt 25:14-30	
The wicked tenants / the Lord's vineyard given to others / vineyard tenants	Luke 20:9-18	Matt 21:33-44	Mark 12:1-11
The fig tree in bloom[1]	Luke 21:29-31	Matt 24:32-35	Mark 13:28-29
The weeds		Matt 13:24-30	
The hidden treasure and the pearl		Matt 13:44-46	
The net		Matt 13:47-48	
The owner of a house		Matt 13:52	
What can defile[4]		Matt 15:10-11	Mark 7:14-15
The unmerciful servant		Matt 18:23-35	
The laborers in the vineyard		Matt 20:1-16	
The two sons		Matt 21:28-32	
The bridesmaids		Matt 25:1-13	
The seed growing of itself			Mark 4:26-29
The watchful servants			Mark 13:33-37

[1]Although treated as a saying in Matthew and Mark, this passage is described as "a parable" by Luke.
[2]Although treated as a saying in Matthew, this passage is described as "a parable" by Luke.
[3]Although treated as a saying in Matthew and Luke, this passage is described as "a parable" by Mark.
[4]Described as "a parable" by both Matthew (15:15) and Mark (7:17).

is lost, even if it is of lesser value than what one still possesses. The woman with a small savings or dowry will search tirelessly before accepting the loss of a single coin. Her house is typical of the time, with a dirt floor, a small door, and no window. Three actions characterize her response: She lights a lamp, sweeps the house, and searches carefully. When she finds the coin she rejoices and calls her (female) friends to celebrate with her.

Verse 10, the counterpart of v. 7, applies the parable to the setting described at the beginning of the chapter. The difference is that whereas v. 7 makes reference to God indirectly by saying "in heaven," in v. 10 the indirection takes the form of a reference to "the angels of God." The effect is the same in both cases. There is no contrast with the other nine coins in v. 10 as there is with the ninety-nine in v. 7. The parable focuses even more sharply, therefore, God's joy at the recovery of what had been lost. The ques-

tion of the "righteous persons who need no repentance" is no longer a concern. In this application they have lost their place entirely. The emphasis is on the joy of recovery, not on the need for repentance. The latter is not denied, but in this context emphasis on the need for repentance smacks more of the grudging spirit of the Pharisees and scribes than of the joy of God at those who respond to God's mercy.

In both parables, rejoicing calls for celebration, and the note of celebration may be exaggerated to emphasize the point. Neither sheep nor coins can repent, but the parable aims not at calling the "sinners" to repentance but at calling the "righteous" to join the celebration. Whether one will join the celebration is all-important because it reveals whether one's relationships are based on merit or mercy. Those who find God's mercy offensive cannot celebrate with the angels when a sinner repents. Thus they exclude themselves from God's grace.

REFLECTIONS

The parables that are Jesus' response to the Pharisees' murmuring still have the power to expose the roots of bitterness that dig their way into us whenever we feel that God is too good to others and not good enough to us. Typically, we want mercy for ourselves and justice for others, but the Lukan parables call for us to celebrate with God because God has been merciful not only to us but to others also, even to those we would not otherwise have accepted into our fellowship.

A Jewish story tells of the good fortune of a hardworking farmer. The Lord appeared to this farmer and granted him three wishes, but with the condition that whatever the Lord did for the farmer would be given double to his neighbor. The farmer, scarcely believing his good fortune, wished for a hundred cattle. Immediately he received a hundred cattle, and he was overjoyed until he saw that his neighbor had two hundred. So he wished for a hundred acres of land, and again he was filled with joy until he saw that his neighbor had two hundred acres of land. Rather than celebrating God's goodness, the farmer could not escape feeling jealous and slighted because his neighbor had received more than he. Finally, he stated his third wish: that God would strike him blind in one eye. And God wept.

The parables of the lost sheep and the lost coin expose the grudging spirit that prevents us from receiving God's mercy. Only those who can celebrate God's grace to others can experience that mercy themselves.

Luke 15:11-32, The Prodigal Son, the Waiting Father, and the Elder Brother

NIV	NRSV
[11]Jesus continued: "There was a man who had two sons. [12]The younger one said to his	11Then Jesus[a] said, "There was a man who had two sons. [12]The younger of them said to his [a] Gk *he*

NIV

father, 'Father, give me my share of the estate.' So he divided his property between them.

[13]"Not long after that, the younger son got together all he had, set off for a distant country and there squandered his wealth in wild living. [14]After he had spent everything, there was a severe famine in that whole country, and he began to be in need. [15]So he went and hired himself out to a citizen of that country, who sent him to his fields to feed pigs. [16]He longed to fill his stomach with the pods that the pigs were eating, but no one gave him anything.

[17]"When he came to his senses, he said, 'How many of my father's hired men have food to spare, and here I am starving to death! [18]I will set out and go back to my father and say to him: Father, I have sinned against heaven and against you. [19]I am no longer worthy to be called your son; make me like one of your hired men.' [20]So he got up and went to his father.

"But while he was still a long way off, his father saw him and was filled with compassion for him; he ran to his son, threw his arms around him and kissed him.

[21]"The son said to him, 'Father, I have sinned against heaven and against you. I am no longer worthy to be called your son.[a]'

[22]"But the father said to his servants, 'Quick! Bring the best robe and put it on him. Put a ring on his finger and sandals on his feet. [23]Bring the fattened calf and kill it. Let's have a feast and celebrate. [24]For this son of mine was dead and is alive again; he was lost and is found.' So they began to celebrate.

[25]"Meanwhile, the older son was in the field. When he came near the house, he heard music and dancing. [26]So he called one of the servants and asked him what was going on. [27]'Your brother has come,' he replied, 'and your father has killed the fattened calf because he has him back safe and sound.'

[28]"The older brother became angry and refused to go in. So his father went out and pleaded with him. [29]But he answered his father, 'Look! All these years I've been slaving for you and never disobeyed your orders. Yet you never gave me even a young goat so I could celebrate with my friends.

[a]21 Some early manuscripts son. Make me like one of your hired men.

NRSV

father, 'Father, give me the share of the property that will belong to me.' So he divided his property between them. [13]A few days later the younger son gathered all he had and traveled to a distant country, and there he squandered his property in dissolute living. [14]When he had spent everything, a severe famine took place throughout that country, and he began to be in need. [15]So he went and hired himself out to one of the citizens of that country, who sent him to his fields to feed the pigs. [16]He would gladly have filled himself with[a] the pods that the pigs were eating; and no one gave him anything. [17]But when he came to himself he said, 'How many of my father's hired hands have bread enough and to spare, but here I am dying of hunger! [18]I will get up and go to my father, and I will say to him, "Father, I have sinned against heaven and before you; [19]I am no longer worthy to be called your son; treat me like one of your hired hands."' [20]So he set off and went to his father. But while he was still far off, his father saw him and was filled with compassion; he ran and put his arms around him and kissed him. [21]Then the son said to him, 'Father, I have sinned against heaven and before you; I am no longer worthy to be called your son.'[b] [22]But the father said to his slaves, 'Quickly, bring out a robe—the best one—and put it on him; put a ring on his finger and sandals on his feet. [23]And get the fatted calf and kill it, and let us eat and celebrate; [24]for this son of mine was dead and is alive again; he was lost and is found!' And they began to celebrate.

[25]"Now his elder son was in the field; and when he came and approached the house, he heard music and dancing. [26]He called one of the slaves and asked what was going on. [27]He replied, 'Your brother has come, and your father has killed the fatted calf, because he has got him back safe and sound.' [28]Then he became angry and refused to go in. His father came out and began to plead with him. [29]But he answered his father, 'Listen! For all these years I have been working like a slave for you, and I have never disobeyed your command; yet you have never given me even a young goat so that I might celebrate with my

[a]Other ancient authorities read filled his stomach with
[b]Other ancient authorities add Treat me like one of your hired servants

NIV

[30]But when this son of yours who has squandered your property with prostitutes comes home, you kill the fattened calf for him!'

[31]"'My son,' the father said, 'you are always with me, and everything I have is yours. [32]But we had to celebrate and be glad, because this brother of yours was dead and is alive again; he was lost and is found.'"

NRSV

friends. [30]But when this son of yours came back, who has devoured your property with prostitutes, you killed the fatted calf for him!' [31]Then the father[a] said to him, 'Son, you are always with me, and all that is mine is yours. [32]But we had to celebrate and rejoice, because this brother of yours was dead and has come to life; he was lost and has been found.'"

[a] Gk *he*

COMMENTARY

The name one gives to this parable already telegraphs an understanding of its structure and theme. To call it "The Prodigal Son" is to emphasize the first half of the parable (vv. 11-24) to the neglect of the second half (vv. 25-32). "A Man Had Two Sons" focuses on the father's relationship to the two sons and recognizes that this is "a two-peaked parable," a parable with two stories.[165] "The Compassionate Father and the Angry Brother" compares two ways of receiving the lost.[166] The virtue of the title "The Prodigal Son, the Waiting Father, and the Elder Brother" is that it recognizes the significant role of each of the three characters and calls attention to the shifting point of view in the parable—from the prodigal son (vv. 12-20*a*) to the waiting father (vv. 20*b*-24) and to the elder brother (vv. 25-32). Alternatively, one may regard the parable as having two parts: the father's response to the younger son (vv. 12-24) and the father's response to the older son (vv. 25-32).

If chap. 15 is the center of Luke's gospel of Jesus Christ, then the parable of the prodigal son, the waiting father, and the elder brother is the "paragon of the parables."[167] Drawn from the life experience of family dynamics, with which everyone can identify, it contrasts two responses to the return of the younger brother. In both, the role of the Father is featured.

The opening line (v. 11) identifies the three characters in the story. Significantly, Jesus does not begin this parable with the "or" used to introduce the parable of the lost coin. This parable is not just a third version of the first two in this chapter. It complements and extends them. On the other hand, the force of this parable is more effectively related not only to the introduction in 15:1-2 but also to its relationship to the first two parables than has often been recognized. The theme of the restoration of what was lost but has been found is repeated at the end of both parts of this parable (vv. 24, 32), but whereas this theme was stated by Jesus as an interpretation of the first two parables (vv. 7, 10), in this parable it is voiced by the father. Moreover, whereas the first two parables merely allude to a call for celebration, in this parable the celebration takes place; the elder brother's response to the celebration is vital to the story line of the second part of the parable.

The introduction identifies the siblings as "sons," not as "brothers." It focuses on their relationship to the father, but leaves their relationship to each other open as an issue to be dealt with later. The role of the mother or sisters is not considered. The difficulties posed by the relationship between siblings and their father were rooted deep in Israelite tradition; e.g., Cain and Abel, Ishmael and Isaac (cf. Gal 4:21-30), paradigmatically Jacob and Esau, and later Joseph and his elder brothers. The younger son was favored in the stories of Israel's heritage. Malachi posed the problem succinctly: "Is not Esau Jacob's brother? says the LORD. Yet I have loved Jacob but I have hated Esau; I have made his hill country a desolation and his heritage a desert for jackals" (Mal 1:2-3). The people of Israel were descendants of Jacob, the

165. Bernard Brandon Scott, *Hear Then the Parable* (Minneapolis: Fortress, 1989) 99-100.
166. Peter Rhea Jones, *The Teaching of the Parables* (Nashville: Broadman, 1982) 175.
167. Ibid.

younger brother. How would Jesus' parable treat the conflict between older and younger?

Moreover, Jesus does not introduce this parable with the question he used frequently in other parables, "And which man [or father] among you?" (cf. 11:5, 11; 14:5, 28; 15:4). The audience will identify with the younger son. Identification with the father is closed off at the outset.

Another remarkable feature of this parable is the preponderance of dialogue over narrative in it. The first part includes three speeches by the younger son: his request, an interior monologue, and his confession. The father speaks in both parts, and his words form the climax of both movements. In the second part, the story is carried along by two conversations: the first between the elder son and a servant, and the second between the elder son and the father. Peter Rhea Jones diagrams the parable as follows:

> Part 1 (15:11-24)
>   Request of the Younger Son (v. 12*b*)
>   Interior Monologue Within the Younger Son
>   (vv. 17*b*-19)
>   Confession of the Younger Son (v. 21*b*)
>   Directive of the Father (vv. 22*b*-24)
> Part 2 (15:25-32)
>   Explanation of the Servant (v. 27*b*)
>   Outburst of the Older Son (vv. 29*b*-30)
>   Explanation of the Father (vv. 31*b*-32)[168]

15:11-24. With no further introduction, the younger son asks his father to give him the share of the estate that will eventually come to him. The laws regarding such a transaction are not entirely clear, but it is clear enough that the younger son's demand was both disrespectful and irregular. The granting of the father's goods to a son might occur in case of marriage (Tob 8:21), but no such rationale is given here. He was breaking the family ties and treating his father as though he were already dead. Appropriately, Jesus reports the father's response thus, literally, "So, he divided his life [βίος *bios*] between them." The younger son also gave up any further claim on his father's estate, as he himself acknowledges in v. 19. Sirach, a Jewish sage (c. 190 BCE), counseled against such premature distribution of one's goods:

> To son or wife, to brother or friend,
>   do not give power over yourself, as long
>   as you live;
> and do not give your property to another,
>   in case you change your mind and must
>   ask for it.
> While you are still alive and have breath in
>   you,
>   do not let anyone take your place.
> . . . .
> At the time when you end the days of your
>   life,
>   in the hour of your death, distribute your
>   inheritance. (Sir 33:20-21, 24 NRSV)

Rabbinic judgments protect the rights of the father in the event that he agrees to make an early distribution of his goods:

> If a man assigned his goods to his sons he must write, 'From to-day and after my death.' So R. Judah. R. Jose says: He need not do so. If a man assigned his goods to his son to be his after his death, the father cannot sell them since they are assigned to his son, and the son cannot sell them since they are in the father's possession. If his father sold them, they are sold [only] until he dies; if the son sold them, the buyer has no claim on them until the father dies. The father may pluck up [the crop of a field which he has so assigned] and give to eat to whom he will.[169]

In the parable, the younger son is able to convert his share to cash, but the father retains the ability to dispose of his ring, robe, shoes, and fatted calf. According to the Mosaic law, which may have been designed to protect the rights of the elder brother against favored younger brothers, the elder brother received a double portion of the inheritance (Deut 21:17).

The younger son's actions report his progressive estrangement from his family, mismanagement of his inheritance, and descent into poverty and privation. First, he collects his goods and travels to a "distant country"—a Gentile land! Second, he quickly squanders his inheritance, living fast and loose (cf. Prov 29:3). The noun form of "debauched living" (ασώτως *asōtōs*) occurs three places in the NT: Eph 5:18, where it is related to drunkenness; Titus 1:6, where it is related to rebelliousness; and 1 Pet 4:3, where it sums up Gentile debauchery: "licentiousness, passions, drunkenness, revels, carousing, and lawless idolatry." The famine only hastened his impoverishment.

---

168. Ibid.

169. *B. Bat.* 8.7.

Finally, having renounced his family, he attaches himself to a Gentile, who orders him to feed his pigs. Swine, of course, were an abomination to Jesus' Jewish audience (Lev 11:7; Deut 14:8). The rabbis declared: "None may raise swine anywhere,"[170] and "Cursed be the man who would breed swine, and cursed be the man who would teach his son Grecian Wisdom."[171] So complete was the younger son's fall and so desperate was his need that he desired to be filled with the pods the swine were eating. Still, with neither family nor community, no one gave him anything. Carob pods, common in the Mediterranean area, were used primarily as animal fodder, but human beings ate them in times of famine. Later they came to be known as "St. John's bread" because of stories that John the Baptist ate them in the wilderness. The younger son's destitution was complete. He had reaped the bitter fruit of his foolishness.

The prodigal's return begins in the mire of the swine pen. There he "came to himself." This pregnant phrase leaves much to the reader's imagination. The younger son reclaims his identity. No longer deserving to be called his father's son, he nevertheless resolves to leave the far country and return to his own land and to his father, as Jacob long before had responded to God's call for him to "return to your country and to your kindred" (Gen 32:9). The expression "he came to himself" affirms the human capacity to renounce foolish error and reclaim one's heritage and potential. The son realized that he no longer had any claim on his father's goods, and morally he no longer has the right to be called a son. But if not a son, perhaps his father will allow him to be a servant in his house (cf. John 8:35). That would be far better than the life that now enslaves him. Even his father's servants have more than enough bread to eat while he is dying of hunger.

Verses 17-19 report the younger son's interior monologue and the speech he rehearses for his return. The essence of his return is that he will return *to his father* (see vv. 18, 20). The report that the son has "come to himself" controls all that follows. He is not just seeking to improve his circumstances; he realizes that he has sinned against both God and his father. His speech when he meets his father will consist of four parts: an address, "Father" (cf. v. 12); confession, "I have sinned" (cf. Exod 10:16); contrition, "I am no longer worthy"; and a petition: "treat me like one of your hired hands." For dramatic contrast, compare the interior monologue of the rich fool (12:17-19). As with the parable of the rich fool, the interior monologue here allows the reader to see directly into the heart of the character.

Three steps are involved in the prodigal's return. First, he comes to himself; second, he arises; and, third, he goes to his father. The journey of return begins with coming to himself and ends with going to his father. The prophets of Israel spoke of repentance as returning. Taking the son's act as a portrait of repentance, Joachim Jeremias commented, "Repentance means learning to say 'Abba' again, putting one's whole trust in the heavenly Father, returning to the Father's house and the Father's arms."[172]

Verse 20 reports that the prodigal acts on his resolve: He gets up and returns to his father. Here the point of view shifts from the returning son to the waiting father. No other image has come closer to describing the character of God than the waiting father, peering down the road longing for the son's return, then springing to his feet and running to meet him. In ancient Palestine it was regarded as unbecoming—a loss of dignity—for a grown man to run. Yet the father set aside all concern for propriety and ran. He was moved by compassion, and his joy carried him down the road to his younger son. Perhaps significantly, however, the father does exactly what the elder brother does in the patriarchal narratives: "Esau ran to meet him, and embraced him, and fell on his neck and kissed him" (Gen 33:4). The kiss expressed forgiveness, as when David kissed Absalom (2 Sam 14:33).

The son immediately starts into his rehearsed speech. He calls out "Father" and voices his confession and contrition, now perhaps all the more necessary in the light of his father's joy and embrace. But before the son can ask to be received back as a servant—the fourth part of his speech—the father interrupts him, giving instructions to his servants. He calls for a robe—the first

---

170. See *b. B. Qam.* 82b.
171. See *m. B. Qam.* 7.7. See also Bernard Brandon Scott, *Hear Then the Parable* (Minneapolis: Fortress, 1989) 114.

172. Joachim Jeremias, *New Testament Theology: The Proclamation of Jesus*, trans. John Bowden (New York: Charles Scribner's Sons, 1971) 156.

one, the best one, or possibly the one the son had worn originally. He calls for a ring—although not his signet ring—for his son's finger and calls for sandals for his feet. The father publicly receives the son back into his house. It is a sign to the rest of the village that the boy is to be treated as his son again (cf. Gen 41:42; 1 Macc 6:14-15). He is a freed man, an honored guest, a son. The lavishness of the father's reception is signaled by the order to bring the fatted calf and kill it (Gen 18:7). Meat was not a part of the daily diet and was normally reserved for special festivals. The son's return, however, is an occasion for celebration.

The father's words in v. 24 sum up the significance of the first movement of the story: "This son of mine was dead and is alive again; he was lost and is found!" He was dead because he had broken his relationship with the family, dishonored his father (treating him as though he were dead), left his home, and left his land to live with Gentiles. But his return reestablishes his place as his father's son. Like the sheep and the coin, he was lost but has been found (cf. 19:10). It was time to celebrate (vv. 23-24).

15:25-32. The celebration serves as the impetus for the story's second movement. Verse 25 introduces the elder son for the first time. Once again the point of view shifts, this time to the elder son, coming in from the fields. As he approaches, he hears the celebration, music and dancing. He calls one of the servant boys and asks him what is happening. Ingenuously, the boy answers, "Your brother has come." His father has killed the fatted calf and is celebrating because his son has returned home safely.

Angry, the elder brother refuses to enter the house. Again the plot is characterized by distance, and physical separation signifies alienation. Just as the younger son's intentions were not immediately apparent at the beginning of the story, so also now the reason for the elder son's anger is withheld for dramatic effect. The parallelism continues as the father once again leaves his house and goes out to meet one of his sons. He does not plead with the younger son, but with the elder one.

The conversation between the elder brother and the father forms the climax and focus of the entire parable. The elder brother speaks first, venting his anger (vv. 29-30). His emotion is signaled subtly. Every time the younger brother

has spoken to his father he has always respectfully addressed him as "Father," even in his soliloquy (vv. 12, 18, 21). The elder brother, however, refuses to acknowledge his relationship either to his father or to his brother. First, he abruptly says "Listen!" rather than "Father." Then he likens his role to that of a servant (which, ironically, is what the younger son had been prepared to ask for on his return). Finally he refers to his brother as "this son of yours." As grounds for injustice, he pleads his merit and the younger son's treachery. He has worked long ("all these years"; cf. the laborers' complaint in Matt 20:12) and like a slave. He has been obedient and never disobeyed—a plea reminiscent of Paul's boasts of his achievements as a Pharisee: "as to righteousness under the law, blameless" (Phil 3:6). By contrast, he characterizes his brother's actions with a detail lacking in the earlier report of the prodigal's life in the far country: He "devoured your property ["your life" (*bion*)] with prostitutes" (cf. v. 13; Prov 29:3). Nevertheless, all the younger son has to do is come home, and the father kills the fatted calf; but he has never given the older son so much as a young goat for a party with his friends.

The effect of the father's response is to restore all of the family relationships, defend himself against the charge of injustice toward the elder son, and justify celebrating the younger son's return. Although the elder brother had not addressed him as "Father," the father's first word, "son," predicates all that follows on that relationship. A chiastic statement underscores the closeness of the relationship between them: "*You* are always with *me,* and all that is *mine* is *yours.*" Legally, because the younger son had already received his inheritance, all that was left would come to the elder son. The father also reminds the elder son of his relationship to his brother; "this brother of yours" echoes "this son of yours" in v. 30. If repentance for the prodigal son means learning to say "Father" again, then for the elder son it means learning to say "brother" again (cf. again the reconciliation between Jacob and Esau in Gen 33:3-4).

The celebration was necessary (cf. the affirmation of divine necessity in 2:49; 4:43; 9:22; 17:25; 19:5; 21:9; 22:37; 24:7, 26, 44). In context, surely if one would celebrate the recovery of a sheep or a coin, one could hardly refuse to allow a father to celebrate the recovery of his son. The father's words not only echo vv. 7 and 10, the lesson drawn from the earlier parables, but also repeat his own words in v. 24. Both parts of the parable, therefore, end with the note of celebration, recalling the words of Zephaniah:

> The LORD, your God, is in your midst
> ································
> he will rejoice over you with gladness,
>   he will renew you in his love;
> he will exult over you with loud singing
>   as on a day of festival. (Zeph 3:17 NRSV)

The three parables in this chapter make their point effectively. The position of the Pharisees and scribes who grumbled because Jesus ate with tax collectors and sinners has been unmasked as the self-serving indignation of the elder brother who denied his relationship both to his father and to his brother by his refusal to join in the celebration. In the world of the parable, one cannot be a son without also being a brother.

REFLECTIONS

It is no hyperbole to say that this parable is a gem; all of its facets deserve to be considered. It is no simple simile with a single point but a compressed slice of life with complexity and texture. In the following paragraphs, we will take note of various of the parable's facets, but in preaching the interpreter should probably avoid such a "shotgun" approach and develop only one or two themes for emphasis. Let the parable be one of those beloved texts that always repays a return visit.

Much of the fascination of this parable lies in its ability to resonate with our life experiences: adolescent rebellion; alienation from family; the appeal of the new and foreign; the consequences of foolish living; the warmth of home remembered; the experience of self-encounter, awakening, and repentance; the joy of reunion; the power of forgiveness; the dynamics of "brotherly love" that leads to one brother's departure and the other's indignation; and the contrast between relationships based on merit and relationships based on faithful love.

Unfortunately, we usually learn to demand our rights before we learn to value our relationships. The younger son was acting within his rights, but he was destroying his closest relationships in the process. How many times a week will a parent hear one child say to another, "It's mine. Give it to me"? Children quickly learn to demand their rights, but it often takes much longer for them to learn how to maintain relationships. Governments and law courts defend our civil rights, but how do we learn to defend our civil and familial relationships?

From a distance, the "far country" can be very appealing. Young people leave home for fast living. Spouses move out to form liaisons with exciting new partners. The glow that surrounds the far country is a mirage, however. Home never looks so good as when it is remembered from the far country.

The journey home begins with coming to oneself. That means that the most difficult step is the first one. The younger son had to face himself in the swine pen of his own making before he faced his father on the road. Pride can keep us from admitting our mistakes; self-esteem may require us to take decisive action to set right the things we have done wrong.

Although the opportunity to restore relationships and remedy wrongs begins with coming to oneself, it requires more. We must go to the person we have wronged. Was the younger son just seeking to improve his situation, or was he seeking a reconciliation with his father? The direct confession in his interior monologue confirms the sincerity of his intent. Neither the younger son's pride nor his shame mattered as much as his need to restore his relationship to his father. He did not ask for his filial privileges to be restored. He did not even ask for forgiveness. He merely stated his confession (cf. the attitude of the tax collector in 18:13).

Howard Thurman, who shared his struggles and pilgrimage of spirit as an African American minister and educator in his autobiography, *With Head and Heart,* found that this parable offered a new insight as he reflected on the meaning of the Christian faith in bringing us to ourselves:

> For I believe that Jesus reveals to a man the meaning of what he is in root and essence already. When the prodigal son came to himself, he came to his father. . . .
>
> My mind and spirit churned in a fermentation of doubt and hope. I was convinced there was no more crucial problem for the believer than this—that a way be found by which his religious faith could keep him related to the ground of his security as a person. Thus, to be a Christian, a man would not be required to stretch himself out of shape to conform to the demands of his religious faith; rather, his faith should make it possible for him to *come to himself* whole, in an inclusive and integrated manner, one that would not be possible without this spiritual orientation.[173]

The temptation a parent faces is to allow the child's separation to become reciprocal. If the child separates from the parent, the parent may be tempted to respond in kind. The parable's model of parental love insists, however, that no matter what the son has done he is still the father's son. When no one else would even give the prodigal something to eat, the father runs to him and accepts him back. Love requires no confession and no restitution. The joyful celebration begins as soon as the father recognized the son's profile on the horizon.

Insofar as we may see God's love reflected in the response of the waiting father, the parable reassures all who would confess, "Father, I have sinned against heaven and before you." The father runs to meet his son even before the son can voice his confession, and the father's response is far more receptive than the son had dared even to imagine. The father's celebration conveys the joy in heaven. The picture is one of sheer grace. No penance is required; it is enough that the son has come home.

If this is the picture of God's joy in receiving a sinner coming home, then it can also give assurance of God's love to those who face death wondering how God will receive them. In the end we all return home as sinners, so Jesus' parable invites us to trust that God's goodness and mercy will be at least as great as that of a loving human father.

The elder brother represents all of us who think we can make it on our own, all of us who might be proud of the kind of lives we live. Here is the contrast between those who want to live by justice and merit and those who must ask for grace. The parable shows that those who would live by merit can never know the joy of grace. We cannot share in the Father's grace if we demand that he deal with us according to what we deserve. Sharing in God's grace requires that we join in the celebration when others are recipients of that grace also. Part of the fellowship with Christ is receiving and rejoicing with others who do not deserve our forgiveness or God's grace. Each person is of such value to God, however, that none is excluded from God's grace. Neither should we withhold our forgiveness.

The parable leaves us with the question of whether the elder brother joined the celebration. Did he go in and welcome his brother home, or did he stay outside pouting and feeling wronged? The parable ends there because that is the decision each of us must make. If we go in, we accept grace as the Father's rule for life in the family.

---

173. Howard Thurman, *With Head and Heart: The Autobiography of Howard Thurman* (San Diego: Harcourt Brace Jovanovich, 1979) 115, 120; italics added.

LUKE 16:1-31, RICH MEN AND LOVERS OF MONEY

OVERVIEW

Luke 16 forms a discrete unit that begins and ends with a parable—the dishonest steward and the rich man and Lazarus (vv. 1, 19)—each of which begins with the statement "There was a rich man." Between the two is a collection of sayings that the narrator says were addressed to "the Pharisees, who were lovers of money" (v. 14). The only anomaly in this neat thematic organization is that the sayings in vv. 16-18 deal with the enduring authority of the law and with divorce and remarriage. One explanation for the placement of vv. 16-18 is that this section of Luke's travel narrative has been patterned on Deut 23:15–24:4, which combines sayings on slaves, usury, vows, and restrictions on remarriage.

The warning that one's wealth must be handled wisely has been a recurring theme in the travel narrative. At dinner Jesus denounced the greed of the Pharisees and challenged them to give alms (11:39-41). The rich fool forfeited his soul (12:13-21). The prudent steward was praised (12:42-48), and warnings are given all through chap. 12 regarding how to prepare for the final accounting. The outcasts are called to the great banquet (14:15-24), and the cost of discipleship is high: No one can be Jesus' disciple who will not give up all possessions (14:33). The parable of the dishonest steward is also directly linked to the preceding section, the parable of the prodigal son, in that the title character of both parables "squandered his property" (cf. 15:13; 16:1).

Luke 16:1-13, The Dishonest Steward

NIV

16 Jesus told his disciples: "There was a rich man whose manager was accused of wasting his possessions. ²So he called him in and asked him, 'What is this I hear about you? Give an account of your management, because you cannot be manager any longer.'

³"The manager said to himself, 'What shall I do now? My master is taking away my job. I'm not strong enough to dig, and I'm ashamed to beg— ⁴I know what I'll do so that, when I lose my job here, people will welcome me into their houses.'

⁵"So he called in each one of his master's debtors. He asked the first, 'How much do you owe my master?'

⁶"'Eight hundred gallonsᵃ of olive oil,' he replied.

"The manager told him, 'Take your bill, sit down quickly, and make it four hundred.'

⁷"Then he asked the second, 'And how much do you owe?'

ᵃ6 Greek *one hundred batous* (probably about 3 kiloliters)

NRSV

16 Then Jesusᵃ said to the disciples, "There was a rich man who had a manager, and charges were brought to him that this man was squandering his property. ²So he summoned him and said to him, 'What is this that I hear about you? Give me an accounting of your management, because you cannot be my manager any longer.' ³Then the manager said to himself, 'What will I do, now that my master is taking the position away from me? I am not strong enough to dig, and I am ashamed to beg. ⁴I have decided what to do so that, when I am dismissed as manager, people may welcome me into their homes.' ⁵So, summoning his master's debtors one by one, he asked the first, 'How much do you owe my master?' ⁶He answered, 'A hundred jugs of olive oil.' He said to him, 'Take your bill, sit down quickly, and make it fifty.' ⁷Then he asked another, 'And how much do you owe?' He replied, 'A hundred containers of wheat.' He said to him,

ᵃ Gk *he*

NIV

" 'A thousand bushels[a] of wheat,' he replied.

"He told him, 'Take your bill and make it eight hundred.'

[8]"The master commended the dishonest manager because he had acted shrewdly. For the people of this world are more shrewd in dealing with their own kind than are the people of the light. [9]I tell you, use worldly wealth to gain friends for yourselves, so that when it is gone, you will be welcomed into eternal dwellings.

[10]"Whoever can be trusted with very little can also be trusted with much, and whoever is dishonest with very little will also be dishonest with much. [11]So if you have not been trustworthy in handling worldly wealth, who will trust you with true riches? [12]And if you have not been trustworthy with someone else's property, who will give you property of your own?

[13]"No servant can serve two masters. Either he will hate the one and love the other, or he will be devoted to the one and despise the other. You cannot serve both God and Money."

[a]7 Greek one hundred korous (probably about 35 kiloliters)

NRSV

'Take your bill and make it eighty.' [8]And his master commended the dishonest manager because he had acted shrewdly; for the children of this age are more shrewd in dealing with their own generation than are the children of light. [9]And I tell you, make friends for yourselves by means of dishonest wealth[a] so that when it is gone, they may welcome you into the eternal homes.[b]

[10]"Whoever is faithful in a very little is faithful also in much; and whoever is dishonest in a very little is dishonest also in much. [11]If then you have not been faithful with the dishonest wealth,[a] who will entrust to you the true riches? [12]And if you have not been faithful with what belongs to another, who will give you what is your own? [13]No slave can serve two masters; for a slave will either hate the one and love the other, or be devoted to the one and despise the other. You cannot serve God and wealth."[a]

[a]Gk mammon   [b]Gk tents

COMMENTARY

The narrator signals a change of audience. The following parable is addressed to Jesus' disciples, but the Pharisees do not fade from view for long (cf. 15:1-2; 16:14-15). The sayings that follow the parable in vv. 9-13 continue the interpretation of the parable for disciples.

16:1-2. The story concerns two figures: a rich man and his steward. The rich man may have been an absentee landowner and the steward the manager of his property. The story begins when charges are brought to the rich man that the steward has been "squandering his property." In the present narrative context, the charge echoes the actions of the prodigal son (15:13).

16:3-4. Just as the parable of the rich fool and the parable of the prodigal son feature interior monologues (12:17-19; 15:17-19; cf. 18:4-5), so also the steward's interior speech is a significant turning point in the parable. Like the rich fool (12:17), he asks himself, "What will I do?" His addressing the rich man as "my lord" in v. 3

(κύριος kyrios; "master" in NRSV and NIV) prepares for the recurrence of that term in v. 8, where its meaning has been debated. In distress, the steward considers his options: "To dig (manual labor)? I am not strong enough. To beg? I am too ashamed." Instead, his interior monologue tells us that he has seized on an alternative that will make him welcome in others' homes after he has been dismissed by his master. That course of action is not explained, however, so the reader's suspense and curiosity build while the steward proceeds with his plans.

16:5-7. In response to his imminent crisis, the steward calls in the master's debtors and summarily reduces the debt of each. In the situation presumed by the story, the master has apparently let out his land to tenants, who have agreed to pay him a fixed return in grain or oil. The size of the reduction seems to reflect the arbitrariness of his actions. A debt of a hundred measures of oil is reduced to fifty; a debt of a hundred measures of wheat is reduced to eighty.

The amounts in question underscore the rich man's wealth. The first debtor owes one hundred "baths" (βάτος *batos*) of oil. Since a bath is equivalent to nine gallons, this man owes nine hundred gallons of olive oil. The second debtor owes one hundred "kors" (κόρος *koros*) of grain. Estimates of the size of a kor vary from 6.5 to 10-12 bushels, and even Josephus gives inconsistent reports as to its meaning.[174] Nevertheless, a hundred kors of grain would have been a large amount. The rich man and his debtors were dealing in large commercial interests (cf. Ezra 7:22), therefore, and not in household quantities.

By reducing the amounts of the debts while he is still in the service of the rich man, or at least while the debtors still assume that he is the rich man's steward, he will gain their favor. The rich man will not be able to reverse his actions later without losing face with his debtors, and the steward will have acquired a debt of honor and gratitude from each debtor that will ensure their goodwill toward him in the future.

The chief difficulty in interpreting the parable concerns the steward's action in reducing the debts. Was he dishonestly falsifying the records in order to gain the favor of the debtors, or was he shrewdly sacrificing his own prospect of short-term gains for long-term benefits? The alternatives are these: (1) The steward was cheating the master by reducing the size of the debts; (2) the steward was acting righteously by excluding the interest that had been figured into the debt, interest prohibited by Deut 23:19-20; or (3) the steward reduced the debt due by the amount of his own commission, which had been included in the debt.

Uncertainties abound, cautioning against any confident claims. According to the first two options, the steward's actions cost the master; according to the third, the steward sacrifices his own income. If the first option prevails, the steward's actions are illegal and dishonest. He continues "squandering" his master's goods, as he has been charged. According to the third option, his actions are entirely legal.

The second option is more complicated, and the steward may be seen as showing goodness on behalf of the master to debtors who did not yet know that he had been dismissed. He was removing

the interest that had been imposed, thereby complying with the scriptural prohibition of usury, even though such commercial deals were apparently common. They would praise the master, who then could not easily restore the full amount of the debts. The difficulty with the second alternative is that the 100 percent interest on the oil is excessive even by ancient Near Eastern standards, and the difference between that rate of interest and the 25 percent interest on the wheat is curious. Interpretations vary, therefore, according to one's assessment of the economic conventions of the time.

The simplest solution, and the one that gives the parable the greatest punch, is to take the first alternative: The steward is dishonest, and he continues to squander the master's goods by arbitrarily slashing the amounts owed by his debtors. Accordingly, there is no need to reconcile the difference between the amount the debts are reduced, no need to explain what would amount to 100 percent interest on the oil, and no difficulty in working out the legalities of the steward's actions. If the steward was merely cutting out his own commission on the loans, as proponents of the third option advocate, then wherein did the master stand to gain from these transactions?

The first alternative is to be preferred because the other two require information or assumptions not provided in the parable regarding the amount of interest added to the original debt. On this reading, the force of the parable is evident in v. 8*a*. A dishonest steward—not just a shrewd manager—is praised. Moreover, the master calls the steward "dishonest" (or "unrighteous" [ἀδικία *adikia*]), another point that favors the first interpretation. The steward did not just cancel his own commission or the exorbitant interest charged by the master.

16:8. This verse poses its own difficulties and has led to various proposals by interpreters who have sought to separate the "original" parable from its present context. Did the parable end with v. 7, v. 8*a*, or v. 8? The question hinges on whether one takes "the lord" (*kyrios*; "master" in NRSV and NIV) in v. 8*a* as a reference to Jesus or to the steward's master (see v. 3). If one construes v. 8*a* as a comment on the parable, and takes "master" as a reference to Jesus, then the parable has an abrupt ending. Taking v. 8*a* as the conclusion gives the parable a more satisfactory

174. Josephus *Antiquities of the Jews* 3.321; 15.314.

ending. "The lord" is the steward's master, and the parable has the characteristic unexpected twist. The master praises the steward for his foresighted, shrewd action, regardless of whether his actions are dishonest or merely restore the accounts to their proper amounts. Either way, he casts an aura of honesty and goodness on his master and shrewdly provides for his own future. The debtors are now bound by honor to reciprocate the steward's benevolence. Through the parable, therefore, Jesus admonishes his hearers to cast caution aside, seize the moment of opportunity, and make provisions for their future before God. The kingdom is at hand.

The fact that from the beginning interpreters have struggled to make sense of this parable is evident from the series of interpretations that follows in vv. 8b-13. Verse 8b is an aside or comment on the parable: "For the children of this age [see 20:34] are more shrewd in dealing with their own generation than are the children of light." The terminology is distinctly Semitic, especially the reference to "children of light" (John 12:36; Eph 5:8; 1 Thess 5:5), a term also found frequently in the Dead Sea Scrolls. Here the sons of light are persons who have seen the kingdom dawning in Jesus' works and in his calls for a radical commitment to God's power to deliver people from corruption and oppression. The comment is attached to the conclusion of the parable by catchword linkage, picking up the term "shrewd" from the preceding statement.

16:9. This verse makes a new beginning with the expression "and I tell you," and it clarifies the meaning of the cryptic comment in v. 8b by calling for disciples to be equally shrewd in using their material goods so that when their "unrighteous mammon" fails they will have an eternal home. Understanding the admonition in this way and translating ἐκ (ek) as "instrumental" ("by means of") yields an interpretation that is consistent with Luke's view of material possessions throughout the Gospels. Disciples are not to make friends "of unrighteous mammon" (KJV) but by means of it (NIV; NRSV). The reference to "eternal homes" allegorizes the reference to the debtors' homes in v. 4. The admonition to make friends for yourself is reminiscent of the warning Jesus gave earlier to be reconciled with your accuser, even on the way to court (12:58-59). In context, the parable of the rich man and Lazarus, which follows shortly, gives this warning renewed urgency.

16:10-12. This is a collection of related sayings drawn together both by their relevance to the parable and by catchword linkage. Faithfulness and honesty are not related to wealth and power. One who is faithful over little will be faithful over a large amount. The contrast between little and much is then applied in two ways. First (v. 11), if one has not been faithful over worldly ("dishonest" [ἄδικος adikos]) wealth, how can that person be trusted with true wealth? Second (v. 12), if you have not been faithful over what belongs to another (the worldly wealth God has entrusted to you), then who will give you your own treasure in heaven?

16:13. This forms a conclusion to this unit of parables and related sayings. The verse is a compact unit, formed by (1) an opening assertion; (2) two supporting observations, chiastically arranged; and (3) the conclusion that follows from the argument.

(1) No slave can serve two masters.

(2) for a slave will either hate (a) the one and love (b) the other, or be devoted (b) to the one and despise (a) the other.

(3) You cannot serve God and wealth.

Wealth, which can serve as a means and opportunity for securing one's place in the kingdom if used shrewdly for the sake of others, can also become a master. Materialism enslaves us, but God requires exclusive loyalty. The Shema reminded Israel, "You shall love the LORD your God with all your heart" (Deut 6:5). Since one cannot serve two masters, one cannot be devoted both to acquiring wealth and to serving God. Moreover, the way we use what we have reveals who we serve. The choice of having no master is not an option; we can only choose the Lord we will serve.

Christians are to be faithful whether we deal in little things or vast resources. Whether we are as shrewd as a dishonest steward depends on whether we use our material goods, great or small, to help those in need. Then, when we worship God rather than our wealth, we will find that we truly have "friends in high places."

REFLECTIONS

1. The parable of the dishonest steward challenges its hearers to be as clever and prudent as the steward in ensuring their future. Stories of clever tricksters and wise rogues were popular in Jewish folklore. Jacob was the trickster patriarch who deceived his father, cheated his brother, and then made off with most of his father-in-law's flock. The character of the trickster endures in folklore, as in the following story told by the rabbis:

A man once caught stealing was ordered by the king to be hanged. On the way to the gallows he said to the governor that he knew a wonderful secret and it would be a pity to allow it to die with him and he would like to disclose it to the king. He would put a seed of a pomegranate in the ground and through the secret taught to him by his father he would make it grow and bear fruit ˙overnight. The thief was brought before the king and on the morrow the king, accompanied by the high officers of state, came to the place where the thief was waiting for them. There the thief dug a hole and said, "This seed must only be put in the ground by a man who has never stolen or taken anything which did not belong to him. I being a thief cannot do it." So he turned to the Vizier who, frightened, said that in his younger days he had retained something which did not belong to him. The treasurer said that dealing with such large sums, he might have entered too much or too little and even the king owned that he had kept a necklace of his father's. The thief then said, "You are all mighty and powerful and want nothing and yet you cannot plant the seed, whilst I who have stolen a little because I was starving am to be hanged." The king, pleased with the ruse of the thief, pardoned him.[175]

In this story, as in the parable of the dishonest steward, the central character is accused of stealing and by shrewd actions wins a pardon or commendation from the king/master. The parable does not unmask the dishonesty of the master or expose him to ridicule. Instead, the parable turns on the steward's shrewd response to the urgency of his situation and invites hearers to understand that they are likewise in the midst of a crisis that demands an urgent decision if disaster is to be avoided. Faced with loss of his position, the dishonest steward acted decisively to provide for his future. One who hears the gospel knows that just such a decisive act is required of those who will stake their all on the coming kingdom of God.

2. The figure of the steward has had a significant influence on Christian reflections regarding the believer's relationship to God. A steward could be a chief slave who was put in charge of the master's household or property (cf. Gen 43:16, 19; 44:1, 4; Isa 22:15). Joseph was a steward in Potiphar's house (Gen 39:4-5). In the OT, the earth is the Lord's house (Ps 24:1), and Moses is his steward (Num 12:7; Heb 3:1-6).[176] In Jesus' parables, stewards are expected to invest talents left in their keeping, and when they are faithful they are given even greater responsibilities (Matt 25:14-30; Luke 19:12-27). A steward was expected to be "faithful and prudent" (12:42; the latter is the same term translated "shrewd" in 16:8).

It has been conjectured that Jesus' use of the figure of the steward in his parables led to its use in the early church to describe the duties of Christians and church leaders in particular.[177] Children are put under the care of a guardian or steward (Gal 4:2). The term was also adopted to explain to the Corinthians the role of an apostle (1 Cor 4:1-2). As a steward is responsible for the management of the master's property, so the apostle is entrusted with "God's mysteries" (Matt 13:11; 1 Cor 4:1). Faithfulness is again a steward's highest duty. A bishop is God's steward (Titus 1:7) and must consequently be blameless and above reproach. First Peter 4:10 democratizes the metaphor, regarding all believers as stewards: "Like good stewards of the

---

175. Moses Gaster, *The Exempla of the Rabbis* (London: Asia Publishing, 1924).
176. See Otto Michel, οἰκονόμος *TDNT,* 5:149.
177. Ibid., 151.

manifold grace of God, serve one another with whatever gift each of you has received." It is not surprising, therefore, that the term is used in the patristic writings as well. Ignatius admonished the church under Polycarp's care to "Labour with one another, struggle together, run together, suffer together, rest together, rise up together as God's stewards and assessors and servants. Be pleasing to him in whose ranks you serve, from whom you receive your pay."[178]

The chief duty of a steward is to be faithful—even in small things. Fred Craddock vividly catches the force of the interpretive saying in v. 10:

> Most of us will not this week christen a ship, write a book, end a war, appoint a cabinet, dine with a queen, convert a nation, or be burned at the stake. More likely the week will present no more than a chance to give a cup of water, write a note, visit a nursing home, vote for a county commissioner, teach a Sunday school class, share a meal, tell a child a story, go to choir practice, and feed the neighbor's cat. "Whoever is faithful in a very little is faithful also in much" (v. 10).[179]

178. Ignatius *Polycarp* 6.1-2, in Kirsopp Lake, trans., *The Apostolic Fathers*, LCL (Cambridge, Mass.: Harvard University Press, 1912) 1:275.
179. Fred B. Craddock, *Luke*, Interpretation (Louisville: Westminster/John Knox, 1990) 192.

Luke 16:14-18, Condemnations of the Corrupt at Heart

NIV

[14] The Pharisees, who loved money, heard all this and were sneering at Jesus. [15] He said to them, "You are the ones who justify yourselves in the eyes of men, but God knows your hearts. What is highly valued among men is detestable in God's sight.

[16] "The Law and the Prophets were proclaimed until John. Since that time, the good news of the kingdom of God is being preached, and everyone is forcing his way into it. [17] It is easier for heaven and earth to disappear than for the least stroke of a pen to drop out of the Law.

[18] "Anyone who divorces his wife and marries another woman commits adultery, and the man who marries a divorced woman commits adultery."

NRSV

14 The Pharisees, who were lovers of money, heard all this, and they ridiculed him. [15] So he said to them, "You are those who justify yourselves in the sight of others; but God knows your hearts; for what is prized by human beings is an abomination in the sight of God.

16 "The law and the prophets were in effect until John came; since then the good news of the kingdom of God is proclaimed, and everyone tries to enter it by force.[a] [17] But it is easier for heaven and earth to pass away, than for one stroke of a letter in the law to be dropped.

18 "Anyone who divorces his wife and marries another commits adultery, and whoever marries a woman divorced from her husband commits adultery."

[a] Or *everyone is strongly urged to enter it*

COMMENTARY

Between the two parables in the first and last half of chap. 16, which feature rich men and concern the handling of wealth, stand three brief sayings addressed to "the Pharisees, who were lovers of money" (v. 14). Since the parable of the dishonest steward had been addressed to the disciples, the reintroduction of the Pharisees knits this chapter to Luke 15:1-2. The vilification of the Pharisees as lovers of money who ridiculed Jesus also reflects one dimension of the social situation of the church at the time the Gospel was written. The preceding sayings declare that one cannot serve two masters. The Pharisees are stereotyped as those who seek to serve both God and mammon. Consequently, they are lovers of money.

The three sayings in vv. 14-18 pose two problems for the interpreter: (1) Why were they placed here, since they are not related to the theme of the proper stewardship of possessions that runs through the rest of chap. 16? (2) How should they be understood in the light of other Gospel sayings on the subjects of the law and divorce and remarriage?

Two lines of interpretation have been proposed regarding the rationale for placing the sayings of vv. 14-18 in this context. The first arises from the thesis that the whole of the Lukan travel narrative is patterned on the book of Deuteronomy. This section, it is proposed, is related to Deut 23:19–24:4, which prohibits usury, sets limits on vows and foraging, and restricts remarriage. Although the material in Luke 16:14-18 clearly arises out of debates regarding matters addressed by the law, the difficulties that face this view are the weakness of the larger theory of the relationship between the travel narrative and Deuteronomy and the lack of any specific counterpart in this section of Deuteronomy to the sayings on God's knowledge of human hearts, or the continuing validity of the law and the prophets. The parallel would have been closer if Luke had also included sayings on vows (cf. Matt 5:33-37).

An attractive line of interpretation, proposed by E. Earle Ellis, connects these verses with the parable of the rich man and Lazarus, which follows in vv. 19-31.[180] Ellis observed that vv. 14-15 introduce the first part of the parable, which concerns the rich man's neglect of the poor man; vv. 16-18 in turn foreshadow the reference to the law and the prophets in the second half of the parable.

Although a fully satisfactory explanation of the relationship between these verses and their context may continue to elude us, some progress may be made by taking note of their internal thematic consistency. The verses challenge the Pharisees' presumption that they were righteous. The verb meaning "to justify" (δικαιόω *dikaioō*) in v. 15 continues the chain of words from the same root that occur in vv. 9-11 ("dishonest" [ἀδικία *adikia*]; "unjust" [ἄδικος *adikos*]). Love of money, however, is but one example of unrighteousness that is an abomination to God. The law and the prophets have not been nullified, and the prohibition against divorce serves as an example of the law's continuing validity. Corruption at heart can be seen not only in the love of money (v. 14),

but also in efforts to enter the kingdom by force (v. 16) and in divorce for the purpose of marrying again (v. 18). Taken together, these verses paint a portrait of a person whose life is consumed by greed and lust rather than the desire to serve God. The ruin to which such a perversion of life inevitably leads is then vividly and dramatically etched by the parable of the rich man and Lazarus.

16:14. The terminology used here is rare and without parallel in the other Gospels. "Lovers of money" occurs elsewhere in the NT only in 2 Tim 3:2, where it is included in a list of the evils that will characterize the last days. The verb translated "ridiculed" (ἐκμυκτηρίζω *ekmyktērizō*) occurs elsewhere in the NT only in Luke 23:35, where the leaders scoff at Jesus while he is being crucified. The corrupt at heart cannot tolerate Jesus and will eventually kill him.

16:15. The first of the sayings (v. 15) points out the folly of seeking to justify oneself in the eyes of others. They have no power to acquit. God, however, knows our hearts. The theme of questioning in one's heart and God as the knower of human hearts recurs frequently in Luke and Acts. The narrator reports that the people questioned in their hearts whether John was the Messiah (3:15). Jesus later challenged the Pharisees to explain why they questioned in their hearts (5:22; cf. 9:47). The purity of one's heart determines how one lives and what one says (6:45). One must, therefore, love God with all one's heart (10:27). One serves either God or wealth (16:13), and where one's treasure is determines where one's heart will be (12:34). God is the one to whom all hearts are known (Acts 1:24), so Jesus warns the Pharisees of this fact. There can be no pretense or hypocrisy before God; God knows the true values of each heart.

This saying works by tensive contrasts. "In the sight of others" is opposed to "in the sight of God," and "what is prized" by one is "an abomination" to the other. One element, however, has no corresponding partner: "You justify yourselves." The implication toward which the saying points is the folly of all efforts at self-justification and the necessity of God's justification.

16:16. The requirement that one be justified before God leads to the next saying, which has to do with the role of the law and the prophets. The saying indicates that the ministry of John the

---

180. See E. Earle Ellis, *The Gospel of Luke*, NCB (Grand Rapids: Eerdmans, 1981) 201.

Baptist marks a transition from one era to another, from the period of the law and the prophets to the period of the proclamation of the gospel of the kingdom. The last element of the saying is difficult and has been interpreted and translated both in a middle and a passive sense. Matthew 11:12 offers a parallel to the saying, but both the context and the meaning are quite different in Matthew. Following a saying about the greatness of John (Matt 11:11; cf. Luke 7:28), Jesus declares, "From the days of John the Baptist until now the kingdom of heaven has suffered violence, and the violent take it by force" (NRSV). In Luke, by contrast, the subject is not the kingdom but "everyone" (πᾶς *pas*; a term that Luke uses frequently). Recent translations have preferred the middle sense, "and everyone tries to enter it by force," but following the declaration that the good news is being proclaimed, the passive sense, "and everyone is pressed to enter it," fits the context well and emphasizes the urgency of a positive response to Jesus' announcement of the kingdom.

16:17. This verse affirms that the law continues in effect (cf. Matt 5:18). The announcement of the kingdom by John the Baptist and Jesus does not mean that the law has been nullified. From the birth narratives, Luke has taken pains to show that the work of John and Jesus fulfilled the Scriptures. Luke emphasizes that Moses and the prophets spoke concerning Jesus (24:27) and that all they said was fulfilled by Jesus (24:44). The law and the prophets, therefore, will endure forever, pointing those who discern their meaning to strive to enter the kingdom. So long as the creation endures (and the assumption here is that it will last forever) not one small part of one letter of the law will pass away—not a hook or horn that distinguishes one letter from another. The saying also serves as a fitting introduction to the latter part of the parable of the rich man and Lazarus, where Abraham responds that if the rich man's brothers will not hear Moses and the prophets, neither will they listen if one should rise from the dead (16:31).

16:18. The inclusion of the prohibition of divorce is difficult to explain. At best it may be understood as an illustration of the continuing validity of the law. There has been no slackening of law with the announcement of the kingdom—i.e., divorce is still forbidden.

The prohibitions of divorce in the NT reflect various traditions that illustrate the efforts of the early church to deal with the pastoral application of an absolute prohibition. The Lukan form of the saying may be the most primitive since it lacks the exceptions permitted by Paul and by the Matthean parallels. In 1 Cor 7:10-11, Paul cites Jesus' prohibition of divorce as a traditional logion but turns it to the situation of a wife separating from her husband, which probably reflects the setting in Corinth, where Christian women married to pagan husbands may have been separating from their husbands. Paul adds that if a wife does separate from her husband, she must remain unmarried or else be reconciled to her husband. Similarly, the husband should not divorce his wife. On the other hand, if the unbelieving partner demands the divorce, Paul counsels that it should be allowed. Matthew 5:32; 19:9 both contain the "except" clause: "except in case of πορνεία [*porneia*]," which may be adultery, incest, marriage within forbidden degrees of kinship, or polygamy (cf. Acts 15:20, 29, where the same word is used). Mark 10:10-12 places the prohibition of divorce following a controversy dialogue in which Jesus rejects the provision for divorce in Deut 24:1-4.[181] Moses allowed divorce and remarriage but forbade divorced partners to remarry if the wife had married another man after the divorce. Mark extends the prohibition by forbidding the wife to divorce her husband (as in 1 Cor 7:10-11), a prerogative that was allowed under Roman law but not in Jewish society.

By comparison with these other versions of the prohibition, the primitive nature of the Lukan form is evident. (1) It lacks the "except" clause, which appears to be a Matthean addition. (2) It takes no note of the plight of Christian women married to pagan husbands (as in the mission situation in view in 1 Corinthians 7). (3) It has not been adapted to the provisions in Roman law whereby a woman could divorce her husband (as in Mark 10:10-12). Neither is it set in a controversy dialogue.

In Luke 16:18, only the husband's violation of the marriage union is considered. The husband may not divorce his wife and marry another.

---

181. Cf. the discussion of conditions in which the giving of a certificate of divorce was required in *m. Ketuboth* 7.1-10.

Neither may a man marry a divorced woman. The effect of this double prohibition is to forbid one from divorcing in order to marry another. Strictly speaking, Luke 16:18 does not forbid divorce. It forbids divorcing one's wife in order to marry another woman, and it forbids marriage to a divorced woman (perhaps to forestall the possibility that a woman may provoke a divorce from her husband in order to marry another man). In any case, both parts of the saying declare that it is the man who commits adultery. Adultery was forbidden by the Decalogue (Exod 20:14; Deut 5:18). Moreover, by marrying another woman, the man commits adultery against his wife—not against another man for

violating his property, as in the OT (Lev 18:20; cf. however Mal 2:14-16).

In context, therefore, the sayings in vv. 14-18 progress from the epithet "lovers of money" to the affirmation that "God knows your hearts," and from the declaration that the law and prophets had not been set aside to the pronouncement that a man who divorces and marries another—or marries a woman who divorces her husband— thereby commits adultery. The God to whom all hearts are open requires fidelity in our relationships to God and to our marriage partner. Both greed and lust, so common in human hearts, are an abomination to God.

REFLECTIONS

Does the love of God or the fear of punishment lead us to obey the law and the prophets? These seemingly intrusive and unrelated sayings speak to the condition of the believer's heart. Devotion to God requires us to take a stance toward life that is diametrically opposed to the self-serving of those who quest for more wealth or new sexual relationships.

Each parable that bracket these central verses of Luke 16 warns that we will have to give an accounting of our lives before God. The parable of the dishonest steward commends the steward for his forethought in making provision for his security. Similarly, the parable of the rich man and Lazarus warns of the reversal of fortune that awaits the rich people who hoard their wealth and give no thought to the beggar at their door. The theme of accountability runs through this chapter.

Those who follow Jesus, therefore, are expected to be faithful before God in all aspects of life. As 1 John 4:18 says, "Perfect love casts out fear." Ultimately the motivation for fidelity is not fear of punishment but love of God and love of others with whom we have meaningful relationships (children, parents, friends). Let it be said of us, when it is our turn to give an account before God, "You loved me more than money. Therefore, you did not try to serve both 'God and mammon.' You did not seek to justify yourself before others. You did not use the promise of grace as an opportunity for freedom from the law. Instead, your reverence for God led you also to be faithful in your relationships to others. Your faithfulness to your marriage vows kept you from succumbing to the illusory enticement of an illicit relationship." God loves a faithful person.

Luke 16:19-31, The Rich Man and Lazarus

NIV	NRSV
19"There was a rich man who was dressed in purple and fine linen and lived in luxury every day. 20At his gate was laid a beggar named Lazarus, covered with sores 21and longing to eat what fell from the rich man's table. Even the dogs came and licked his sores.	19"There was a rich man who was dressed in purple and fine linen and who feasted sumptuously every day. 20And at his gate lay a poor man named Lazarus, covered with sores, 21who longed to satisfy his hunger with what fell from the rich man's table; even the dogs would come and lick his sores. 22The poor man died and was carried
22"The time came when the beggar died and	

NIV

the angels carried him to Abraham's side. The rich man also died and was buried. ²³In hell,ᵃ where he was in torment, he looked up and saw Abraham far away, with Lazarus by his side. ²⁴So he called to him, 'Father Abraham, have pity on me and send Lazarus to dip the tip of his finger in water and cool my tongue, because I am in agony in this fire.'

²⁵"But Abraham replied, 'Son, remember that in your lifetime you received your good things, while Lazarus received bad things, but now he is comforted here and you are in agony. ²⁶And besides all this, between us and you a great chasm has been fixed, so that those who want to go from here to you cannot, nor can anyone cross over from there to us.'

²⁷"He answered, 'Then I beg you, father, send Lazarus to my father's house, ²⁸for I have five brothers. Let him warn them, so that they will not also come to this place of torment.'

²⁹"Abraham replied, 'They have Moses and the Prophets; let them listen to them.'

³⁰" 'No, father Abraham,' he said, 'but if someone from the dead goes to them, they will repent.'

³¹"He said to him, 'If they do not listen to Moses and the Prophets, they will not be convinced even if someone rises from the dead.'"

ᵃ23 Greek *Hades*

NRSV

away by the angels to be with Abraham.ᵃ The rich man also died and was buried. ²³In Hades, where he was being tormented, he looked up and saw Abraham far away with Lazarus by his side.ᵇ ²⁴He called out, 'Father Abraham, have mercy on me, and send Lazarus to dip the tip of his finger in water and cool my tongue; for I am in agony in these flames.' ²⁵But Abraham said, 'Child, remember that during your lifetime you received your good things, and Lazarus in like manner evil things; but now he is comforted here, and you are in agony. ²⁶Besides all this, between you and us a great chasm has been fixed, so that those who might want to pass from here to you cannot do so, and no one can cross from there to us.' ²⁷He said, 'Then, father, I beg you to send him to my father's house— ²⁸for I have five brothers— that he may warn them, so that they will not also come into this place of torment.' ²⁹Abraham replied, 'They have Moses and the prophets; they should listen to them.' ³⁰He said, 'No, father Abraham; but if someone goes to them from the dead, they will repent.' ³¹He said to him, 'If they do not listen to Moses and the prophets, neither will they be convinced even if someone rises from the dead.'"

ᵃGk *to Abraham's bosom*   ᵇGk *in his bosom*

COMMENTARY

I have titled this chapter "Rich Men and Lovers of Money" in order to convey its thematic unity. "The Rich Man and Lazarus" pulls the curtain on the fate of the rich man who serves mammon rather than God (16:13). The first part of the parable develops the theme of judgment and reversal stated in vv. 14-15, and the second part develops the affirmation of "the law and the prophets" in vv. 16-18. What the rich man prized during his life is "an abomination in the sight of God" (16:15). Yet, if his five brothers will not hear "Moses and the prophets," neither will they listen if someone rose from the grave.

Not only does this parable cap off the chapter's pronouncement of judgment on the rich, but also in various respects it serves as the capstone of Luke's prophetic critique of wealth. Before the birth of Jesus, Mary declared in her praise of God, "He has brought down the powerful from their thrones,/ and lifted up the lowly" (1:52). Lazarus's exaltation to the bosom of Abraham vividly fulfills John the Baptist's warning that "God is able from these stones to raise up children to Abraham" (3:8), while the rich man's torment fulfills the warning that "the chaff he will burn with unquenchable fire" (3:17). The kingdom of God belongs to the poor and the hungry, but woe to those who are rich and who are full "now" (6:20-26).

16:19-21. 16:19. The parable of the rich

man and Lazarus can be seen as a drama in three acts. In the first act, the rich appear to be rich, and the poor appear to be poor. The first act, however, is a tableau. The characters are introduced, and their way of life is described, but nothing happens. There is no interaction between the rich man and Lazarus. The rich man is not named, but the textual and exegetical tradition of this parable preserves two different efforts to give him a name. Papyrus 75, the oldest Greek manuscript of Luke, adds "by the name of Neues," and later interpretation of the Vulgate misread the Latin term for "rich" (*dives*) as a personal name, Dives. The measure of the man's wealth is illustrated by his conspicuous consumption—his dress and his diet. The rich man wears purple, which may mean that he was a high-ranking official or a member of the royal family. The Romans had set standards regarding who could wear purple and how much purple they could wear. The rich man lived in a house with gates—for privacy or security, for separation from the riffraff of the city. He dressed in fine linen and feasted sumptuously every day. He was "at ease in Zion"; he had everything a person could want. The words that describe his feasting are polyvalent, double-sided. They have kept bad company in Luke, but they can also describe heavenly events. The verb for "to feast" or "to make merry" ($\epsilon \dot{\upsilon}\phi\rho\alpha\acute{\iota}\nu\omega$ *euphrainō*) was first used in the daydreams of the rich fool (12:19), but in the parable of the prodigal son it describes the celebration that reflects the joy in heaven at the recovery of one who was lost (15:23-24, 29, 32). Similarly, the adverb translated "sumptuously" ($\lambda\alpha\mu\pi\rho\tilde{\omega}\varsigma$ *lampros*) is related to the adjective "splendid" ($\lambda\alpha\mu\pi\rho\acute{o}\varsigma$ *lampros*), which describes the robe the soldiers put on Jesus (23:11) and the splendor of the angel that appeared to Cornelius (Acts 10:30). The story will quickly make clear, however, that the glitter of the rich man's life was superficial and transient. It had nothing to do with the eternal glory that surrounds the Lord.

16:20-21. The next verse introduces Lazarus, the only character in any of Jesus' parables who is given a name. The name is part of the characterization, because it comes from Eleazar, which means "God helps," and therefore foreshadows Lazarus's fate. Tragically, no one else helps Lazarus. He is a crippled beggar whose body is covered with running sores. He is "thrown" before the rich man's gate. He would gladly have been "filled" with the soiled bread from the rich man's table. The verb for "to eat" ($\chi o\rho\tau\acute{\alpha}\zeta\omega$ *chortazō*) is commonly used for the feeding of animals rather than humans (Rev 19:21), but it is also used in Luke for the longings of the hungry (see 6:21; 9:17; 15:16). At a feast, bread was used to wipe the grease from one's hands and then was thrown under the table (cf. Mark 7:28). The depth of Lazarus's deprivation is described with one final detail: The dogs (which probably ate the scraps from the rich man's table) lick his sores as they pass by.

Lazarus dies of starvation and disease at the rich man's gate. The first act ends after we have met the two characters. It is a tableau; neither character speaks to the other. Their lives seem to be entirely separate, divided by a table and a gate.

16:22. In the second act, the rich become poor and the poor become rich. The structure is chiastic, hinting that the fates of these two who lived such separate lives in reality intertwine. The rich man was introduced first, as one would expect, and then Lazarus. Now Lazarus's death, which comes as no surprise, is reported first, then the death of the rich man. Dare we ask why Lazarus died? Did he die of starvation while a few feet away the rich man was having one of his daily feasts? Lazarus's death underscores the urgency of Jesus' challenge to the well-to-do: When you give a feast, do not invite your friends and rich neighbors. Instead, invite Lazarus—"the poor, the crippled, the lame, and the blind" (14:13; cf. 14:21, 23). Did Lazarus freeze to death one night outside the house where the rich man slept on linen sheets? Did he die of infected sores while the rich man was enjoying a hot bath and anointing himself with the finest oils? Or did the dogs. . . ?

The parable does not dwell on Lazarus's death. At his death, Lazarus is transported by angels to the bosom of Abraham, which may evoke a comparison with the bodily translations of Enoch (Gen 5:24), Elijah (2 Kgs 2:11), and, according to Jewish legends, Moses.[182] Nothing is said of Lazarus's burial. Again, our imaginations shrink back from attempting to fill the gap in the story. Neglected by others, Lazarus is prized in the sight of God (cf. 16:15).

---

182. See Joachim Jeremias, Μωυσῆς *TDNT,* 4:854-55.

Unexpectedly, we are told that the rich man has died also. Again, do we dare ask why? Did he die of overeating while Lazarus starved? Did the excess food, which the rich man could have given to Lazarus, hasten his own death?

The contrast between the two characters is again drawn with verb usage. While Lazarus is "carried away by angels," the rich man is simply "buried," probably in the purple robes in which he had lived.

16:23-31. The third act is by far the longest and most developed. For the first time, narration gives way to dialogue, with three complete exchanges between the rich man and Abraham. The third act, therefore, is the climax of the story, the focal point of the parable. In the third act, the poor are rich and the rich are poor.

16:23. The bosom of Abraham was regarded as the place of highest bliss. According to Jewish legends of the martyrdom of the mother and her seven sons (2 Maccabees 7), the martyrs were brought to the bosom of Abraham.[183] Interpreters are divided on the issue of whether both the rich man and Lazarus were in Hades (following the older concept of Hades as the place of the dead, both righteous and wicked) or whether only the rich man is in Hades while Lazarus is in paradise (cf. 23:43). Hades was regarded as the place where the dead awaited the final judgment, and by the first century it was thought to be divided into various regions according to people's moral state:

> Rufael, one of the holy angels, who was with me, responded to me; and he said to me, "These beautiful corners (are here) in order that the spirits of the souls of the dead should assemble into them—they are created so that the souls of the children of the people should gather here. They prepared these places in order to put them (i.e. the souls of the people) there until the day of their judgment and the appointed time of the great judgment upon them.... These three have been made in order that the spirits of the dead might be separated. And in the manner in which the souls of the righteous are separated (by) this spring of water with light upon it, in like manner, the sinners are set apart when they die and are buried in the earth and judgment has not been executed upon them in their lifetime." (*1 Enoch 22*)[184]

For the righteous there is a spring of water, which is always associated with paradise in the Jewish and Christian apocalypses. Regardless of whether Lazarus was in Hades or not, Lazarus and Abraham were in sight of the rich man, who was already experiencing the torment that awaited him. Being "in the bosom" of Abraham may imply that Lazarus was the honored guest at the eschatological banquet, feasting while the rich man was in torment. How ironically the table has turned.

To many who heard the parable, this turn of events would have come as a surprise, for it was believed that blessings in this life were a sign of God's favor, while illness, poverty, and hardship were signs of God's displeasure. A just God would not do otherwise. How could a beggar go to heaven? We are not told that Lazarus was a righteous man or that he was a believer, but then the beatitudes in Luke lack the qualifying phrases that Matthew attaches to them.

16:24. Three exchanges between the rich man and Abraham follow. Lazarus, who never asked for anything on earth, never says anything. Abraham now speaks for the beggar who has no voice. In the first exchange, the rich man asks "Father Abraham" to send Lazarus to dip his finger in water to cool his tongue. The request is typical hyperbole. By addressing Abraham as "Father," he may imply that he should be recognized as a "son of Abraham" also (see 13:16; 19:9). Because he knows Lazarus's name, we may wish to assume that the rich man had known of Lazarus's plight and had done nothing. But is that worse than if he had not even known of the suffering of the beggar at his gate? Either way, the rich man still regards Lazarus as being available to serve his personal needs—"Send Lazarus."

16:25-26. Abraham responds, acknowledging the rich man with the address "child." Being a child of Abraham, therefore, is no guarantee that one will dwell with Abraham in paradise. The chiastic sequence in Abraham's response again serves to connect the lives and rewards of the rich man and Lazarus: "Remember...you...good things, and Lazarus...evil things; but now he is comforted here, and you are in agony" (v. 25). Remembering can either be part of one's torment, as here, or part of one's salvation, as in 24:6, 8. In life the beggar got only cast-off goods and was treated shamefully. Now the men's fates

183. See Rudolf Meyer, κόλπος *TDNT*, 3:825.
184. James H. Charlesworth, ed., *The Old Testament Pseudepigrapha* (Garden City, N.Y.: Doubleday, 1983) 1:24-25.

are reversed, fulfilling the beatitudes of Luke 6:20-26. "Now" (cf. the now of the beatitudes, 6:21, 25), the rich man is in torment and Lazarus is in paradise. Clarence Jordan, who retold the parables and other parts of the NT in the idiom of the American Old South, interpreted Abraham's answer insightfully: "Lazarus ain't gonna run no mo' yo' errands, rich man."

The chasm that now separates the rich man and Lazarus confirms the finality of the judgment on the rich man. A similar vision of the place of the dead is described in 4 Ezra 7:36: "Then the pit of torment shall appear, and opposite it shall be the place of rest; and the furnace of Hell shall be disclosed, and opposite it the paradise of delight." Once there was no chasm but indifference and apathy. The rich man could have come to Lazarus at any time. Now, however, the chasm that separates them prevents Lazarus from responding to the rich man's torment with compassion and removes any possibility that the rich man might escape his torment. The rich man has shut himself off from Lazarus, and now no one can reach him.

16:27-28. In the second exchange, the rich man asks that Abraham send Lazarus back to warn the rich man's five brothers. If there is no hope for him, at least he may be able to intervene and spare his brothers. The reference to his extended family as "my father's house" contrasts with his earlier use of "Father Abraham." Admirably, he thinks of someone other than himself for the first time in the story, but he still assumes that Lazarus can be his errand boy.

The word for "torment" (βάσανος *basanos,* v. 28) has an interesting history. It was originally used to describe the testing of coins. The coin would be rubbed or scratched with a hard stone to test its genuineness. Later, the word was applied to torture or the rack by which the truth was extracted from prisoners. In Matthew and Luke it describes the torments of hell.[185]

16:29. Abraham's response to the rich man's second request is that the brothers have Moses and the prophets. Did not Moses say, "Do not be hard-hearted or tight-fisted toward your needy neighbor" (Deut 15:7 NRSV)? And are not the words of Isaiah clear enough?

185. See Johannes Schneider, βάσανος *TDNT,* 1:561-63.

Is not this the fast that I choose:
  to loose the bonds of injustice,
  to undo the thongs of the yoke,
to let the oppressed go free,
  and to break every yoke?
Is it not to share your bread with the hungry,
  and bring the homeless poor into your house;
when you see the naked, to cover them,
  and not to hide yourself from your own kin?
(Isa 58:6-7 NRSV)

The duty of the brothers is expressed with a Greek construction for which there is no English equivalent, a third person imperative: "Let them hear them!" (ἀκουσάτωσαν αὐτῶν *akousatōsan autōn*).

Abraham's appeal to Moses and the prophets as the hope for the rich man's brothers carries the reader back to the verses that precede this parable. Verses 16-17, which are addressed to the "lovers of money" (v. 14), affirm the continuing role of the law and the prophets. The only other references to Moses and the prophets are in the resurrection appearances, where the risen Lord interprets the Scriptures, insists that the Scriptures must be fulfilled, and then opens the disciples' minds to understand the Scriptures (24:27, 44-45; cf. the contrasting command to the disciples at the transfiguration, 9:35).

16:30. This thematic continuity between the parable of the rich man and Lazarus and the end of the Gospel adds an ironic force to the third and final exchange between the rich man and Abraham. The rich man's lament, "No, Father Abraham," conveys his despair that there is little hope that his brothers will heed the Scriptures. For the brothers, repentance requires a complete reversal of their way of life and their regard for the poor at their gates. His last hope for his brothers is that if someone were to go to them from the dead, they would repent.

The call to repent has been lurking silently in the background from the beginning of the chapter. The parable of the prodigal son is a story of repentance. The wisdom of repentance is ironically affirmed in the parable of the dishonest steward, who, though he does not repent of his dishonest dealings, gives thought to his own future. Verses 14-18 call the Pharisees, and all who recognize that they too are lovers of money who seek to serve two masters, to repent and obey the law and the prophets. Now, in the last two verses of the chapter the issue of repentance is stated explicitly. John the Baptist had preached repentance (3:3, 8). Jesus declares that he too has come to call sinners to repentance (5:32). Jesus also pronounced woes on Chorazin and Bethsaida for their failure to repent (10:13). The people of Nineveh repented, but even though one greater than Jonah had come the people of "this generation" had not repented (11:32). Jesus had warned the crowds that unless they repented, they would perish like the Galileans whom Pilate had slaughtered and the Jerusalemites on whom the tower had fallen (13:3, 5). But what joy there is in heaven when even one sinner repents (15:7, 10). No wonder the rich man despaired that his brothers would hear Moses and the prophets and repent.

16:31. Abraham's response, which concludes the parable, adds finality to the urgency of hearing Moses and the prophets. If the brothers will not hear them, then they will not be convinced even if one should rise from the dead. The language echoes the early Christian kerygma, the proclamation of Jesus' resurrection (18:33). Until this point, resurrection has not been mentioned. The rich man's request may be understood as an appeal for Lazarus to appear to his brothers in a dream or a vision (like the appearance of Moses and Elijah at the transfiguration). Abraham's response, however, foreshadows the resurrection of Jesus and the mission of the church in Acts. How could it be that one would rise from the dead, and still some would refuse to repent?

There will be no special dispensation for those who refuse the needs of the wretched at their gate. If they will not hear the Scriptures and be merciful, they show that they have placed themselves beyond the reach of God's mercy.

By the end of the parable, the hearer's point of identification has become clear. The parable is addressed to "lovers of money." At the beginning, hearers or readers may assume that they are expected to identify with the rich man or with Lazarus, but the parable is far more subtle. By the end of the parable we realize that we stand in the place of the brothers, and the question is whether we will hear the Scriptures and repent.

The parable of the rich man and Lazarus also resonates in a peculiar way with the account of the raising of Lazarus in John 11. The parable is the only one of Jesus' parables to feature a named character. Moreover, the common theme of raising a person from the dead and the failure of some to repent even when Lazarus is raised invites speculation about the relationship between the Lukan parable and the Johannine sign. It is doubtful, however, whether either story has been created entirely from the other, since several elements in each one are lacking in the other. There is no counterpart to the rich man or Abraham in John, and Mary and Martha are not identified as Lazarus's sisters in Luke (see 10:38-42). If there is any direct relationship between the two, it is more likely that a previously unnamed character in one of the stories has been given the name "Lazarus" in the other story as a result of resonance between these two passages.

REFLECTIONS

Did the brothers ever get the message? We are not told, for that is the question the parable leaves us to answer. Each of us will write our own ending to the story.

1. Archbishop Richard Trench, writing on this parable more than a century ago, compared the diseases that afflicted the two characters:

The sin of Dives in its root is unbelief: hard-hearted contempt of the poor, luxurious squandering on self, are only the forms which his sin assumes. The seat of the disease is within; these are but the running sores which witness for the inward plague. He who believes not in an invisible world of righteousness and truth and spiritual joy, must place his hope in things which he sees, which he can handle, and taste, and smell. It is not of the essence of the matter, whether he hoards [like the rich fool, 12:16-21] or squanders [like the prodigal son, 15:11-32]: in either case he puts his trust in the world.[186]

---

186. Richard C. Trench, *Notes on the Parables of Our Lord* (London: Kegan Paul, Trench, Trübner, & Co., 1915) 457.

The rich man, therefore, characterizes the life of one who serves mammon because he has no confidence in God (cf. 16:13).

2. At the end of the Gospel, we are told of two whose hearts were "strangely warmed" when the Scriptures were interpreted to them. They were walking on the road to Emmaus. A stranger joined them and began to explain the law and prophets. When evening came, the two insisted that the weary stranger share their table with them. Then, as they shared their bread with the stranger, they recognized their Lord in the stranger. Perhaps if the rich man had tended Lazarus's needs and invited him to share a meal with him, he too would have understood the Scriptures and recognized in him the Lord who had always been a stranger to him.

3. George Buttrick cautioned, however, that important as it is to share food, the parable is about an even deeper and more pervasive attitude of neighborliness toward others: "The story offers no support to the glib assumption that Dives would have fulfilled all duty had he dressed Lazarus' sores and fed his hunger. True charity is more than flinging a coin to a beggar; it is not spasmodic or superficial. Ameliorations such as food and medicine are necessary, but there is a more fundamental neighborliness."[187]

"Fundamental neighborliness," therefore, is the barometer of the soul, an indication of the attitude of one's heart that is prized in the sight of God.

187. George A. Buttrick, *The Parables of Jesus* (New York: Harper and Bros., 1928) 143.

LUKE 17:1-10, THE DEMANDS OF FORGIVENESS AND FAITH

NIV

17 Jesus said to his disciples: "Things that cause people to sin are bound to come, but woe to that person through whom they come. [2]It would be better for him to be thrown into the sea with a millstone tied around his neck than for him to cause one of these little ones to sin. [3]So watch yourselves.

"If your brother sins, rebuke him, and if he repents, forgive him. [4]If he sins against you seven times in a day, and seven times comes back to you and says, 'I repent,' forgive him."

[5]The apostles said to the Lord, "Increase our faith!"

[6]He replied, "If you have faith as small as a mustard seed, you can say to this mulberry tree, 'Be uprooted and planted in the sea,' and it will obey you.

[7]"Suppose one of you had a servant plowing or looking after the sheep. Would he say to the servant when he comes in from the field, 'Come along now and sit down to eat'? [8]Would he not

NRSV

17 Jesus[a] said to his disciples, "Occasions for stumbling are bound to come, but woe to anyone by whom they come! [2]It would be better for you if a millstone were hung around your neck and you were thrown into the sea than for you to cause one of these little ones to stumble. [3]Be on your guard! If another disciple[b] sins, you must rebuke the offender, and if there is repentance, you must forgive. [4]And if the same person sins against you seven times a day, and turns back to you seven times and says, 'I repent,' you must forgive."

[5]The apostles said to the Lord, "Increase our faith!" [6]The Lord replied, "If you had faith the size of a[c] mustard seed, you could say to this mulberry tree, 'Be uprooted and planted in the sea,' and it would obey you.

[7]"Who among you would say to your slave who has just come in from plowing or tending sheep in the field, 'Come here at once and take

[a] Gk *He*   [b] Gk *your brother*   [c] Gk *faith as a grain of*

NIV

rather say, 'Prepare my supper, get yourself ready and wait on me while I eat and drink; after that you may eat and drink'? ⁹Would he thank the servant because he did what he was told to do? ¹⁰So you also, when you have done everything you were told to do, should say, 'We are unworthy servants; we have only done our duty.'"

NRSV

your place at the table'? ⁸Would you not rather say to him, 'Prepare supper for me, put on your apron and serve me while I eat and drink; later you may eat and drink'? ⁹Do you thank the slave for doing what was commanded? ¹⁰So you also, when you have done all that you were ordered to do, say, 'We are worthless slaves; we have done only what we ought to have done!'"

COMMENTARY

This section draws together four units of sayings: a warning against causing others to stumble, a challenge to be forgiving, a call to exercise faith, and a reminder of the duties of discipleship. The change of audience from the Pharisees (16:14-15) back to the disciples in 17:1 (cf. 16:1) signals the beginning of a new section. The repetition of the phrase "into/in the sea" in vv. 2 and 6 helps to stitch these sayings together. It is also possible to see a continuity from the role of Lazarus in the preceding parable to the admonition concerning the otherwise unidentified "little ones" in v. 2.

17:1. Contrary to the smoother NRSV and NIV translations, the Greek employs a double negative in v. 1: literally, "it is impossible for scandals not to come." Here the sense of σκάνδαλον (*skandalon*) is an offense or cause of stumbling. In context it designates anything that causes another to abandon his or her faith or turn away from allegiance to Jesus and his teachings. The inevitability of such offenses, however, does not diminish their gravity. The woe is a cry of grief, literally, "alas for the one by whom they come" (17:1).

17:2. The grotesque metaphor of comparison in v. 2 has parallels in Mark 9:42 and Matt 18:6. Millstones were common in Galilean towns and villages, and several examples of different sizes have been discovered at Capernaum, on the shore of the Sea of Galilee. Once the grain had been separated from the chaff, it was ground between millstones. The lower millstone was an inverted cone. The upper millstone, which fit over the lower, had a funnel shaped opening in the top and a hole through it so that the grain was ground between the stones when it was poured into the

funnel and the top stone was rotated over the lower one. Some of these basalt stones were three or four feet high, so the image readily makes its point. The large stones were rotated by harnessing an ass to a beam of wood that was wedged into a slot in the upper stone. Hence, Matthew and Mark say literally "a mill turned by an ass."[188]

In order for a man to have a millstone "around his neck," his head would have to stick through the hole in the upper stone—a ludicrous and comic image if that is what is meant. Alternatively, and less literally, the stone would have to be tied to one's neck, as is apparently the meaning in Matthew. Either way, the analogy is graphic and effective: There can be no escape from the consequences of blocking, discouraging, or hindering another person's response to God's call.

The "little ones" (μικρός *mikros*) are not defined in this context, but the term probably refers to any person struggling to respond to Jesus' teachings who might be turned aside from this intent by the misguided example or words of a disciple. This pronouncement, therefore, dramatizes the believer's responsibility for the influence of his or her actions and words on others, especially those weaker in faith or those who are looking to the example of the believer as they consider their own response to Jesus. The change of address in v. 1, therefore, is required by the content of the saying that follows. This is a warning that must be addressed to the disciples rather than to the crowd or the Pharisees.

17:3. The next saying also addresses the Chris-

---

188. See Joseph A. Fitzmyer, *The Gospel According to Luke (X–XXIV)*, AB 28A (Garden City, N.Y.: Doubleday, 1985) 1138.

tian community. If your brother or sister sins, rebuke that one (cf. 1 John 5:16). Your fellow disciple's sin may hurt someone else and thus make the believer liable to the terrible consequences of which Jesus has just spoken. One's responsibility to fellow believers is twofold, however. First, confront or rebuke the one who sins. Then, if the person asks for forgiveness, be ready to offer it wholeheartedly.

17:4. Just as the seriousness of becoming an obstacle to another's faith is dramatized by the image of the millstone, so also the necessity of unstinting forgiveness is driven home by the demand that the disciple be prepared to forgive the same person for seven offenses in a single day if that fellow disciple asks for your forgiveness. The responsibility is thereby placed not on the penitent person to demonstrate that his or her repentance is genuine, but on the disciple to demonstrate that he or she is capable of following Jesus' command to forgive one who repents. Jesus' admonition is emphatic, a future tense used as an imperative: "You will forgive him" (v. 4). In Matthew the requirement of forgiveness is extended by a further hyperbole: "Not seven times, but, I tell you, seventy-seven times" or seventy times seven (Matt 18:21-22).

17:5. The disciples respond to Jesus' elevated admonitions to live by a kingdom ethic, repeatedly confronting and forgiving those who sin, with a plea that conveys their surprise, dismay, and sense of inadequacy in the face of such a high standard: "Increase our faith!" References to faith are clustered unevenly in Luke. The term first occurs when Jesus notes the faith of those who brought to him the paralytic (5:20). The recognition of different degrees or levels of faith emerges when Jesus comments that the centurion's faith exceeds any he has found in Israel (7:9). The repeated affirmation of deliverance or salvation, "your faith has saved you" occurs in 7:50 (the woman who anointed Jesus' feet); 8:48 (the woman with a hemorrhage); 17:19 (the grateful leper); and 18:42 (the blind beggar). During the storm at sea, Jesus had challenged the disciples, "Where is your faith?" (8:25; see also 18:8; 22:32). The disciples' plea in this context conveys the recognition that on the one hand faith is a dynamic process and one can grow in faith. On the other hand, the disciples ask that the Lord add to or strengthen their faith, thereby recognizing that faith is not just a matter of their own strength. In both

of these aspects, Luke's concept of faith is similar to Paul's, who writes of righteousness as being revealed "through faith for faith" (Rom 1:17) and declares that we have been saved by grace through faith and that this is not of our own doing (Eph 2:8).

17:6. The reader may expect that Jesus would warmly receive the disciples' request for more faith. Instead, his sharp answer implies that they have not really understood the nature of genuine faith. The saying is difficult both because of its grammatical problems and because it seems to depend on an early form of this logion. In both syntax and imagery the saying is mixed or corrupt. Grammatically, the pronouncement begins like a first-class conditional sentence; the protasis, or "if" clause, assumes the reality of the condition: "Since you have faith. . . . " The apodosis, or "then" clause, however, is that of a second-class condition, or a statement contrary to fact: "you could say . . . and it would obey you [but you cannot and it will not]." The assumptions conveyed by the first part of the sentence, therefore, are denied by the latter part. The disciples say, "Increase our faith," assuming that what they need is more faith, but Jesus' answer declares that they have misunderstood. They assumed that they had faith but would need a greater faith in order to measure up to Jesus' challenge to confront and forgive those who have sinned. Jesus shatters their illusions about faith; they don't even have faith comparable to a tiny mustard seed. If they did, they could command a sycamore tree—a large tree (up to 60 feet high) with deep roots—to be uprooted and planted in the sea. The point is not that they need more faith; rather, they need to understand that faith enables God to work in a person's life in ways that defy ordinary human experience. The saying is not about being able to do miraculous works or spectacular tricks. On the contrary, Jesus assures the disciples that with even a little faith they can live by his teachings on discipleship.

The imagery of the saying is also mixed. Mark and Matthew contain sayings that declare that if the disciples had faith in God they could command a mountain to be taken up and cast into the sea, which may be an allusion to the splitting of the Mount of Olives in Zech 14:4 or the plucking up and planting in Jer 1:10. A mountain may be cast into the sea, and a tree may be planted, but the declaration that a tree would be planted in the sea is apparently the result of a mixing of images drawn from other versions of Jesus' affirmation of the power of faith.

17:7-10. The parable of the servant who serves without reward concludes this section on the demands of faith. In the preceding verses Jesus challenged the disciples to forgive without keeping count of offenses. When the disciples asked that they be given greater faith, Jesus responded that if they had faith even like a mustard seed they could do wondrous things. The parable that follows now affirms that regardless of how much we do, we cannot do more than is expected of us.

The parable assumes the hearer's familiarity with the customs that controlled the lives of slaves in the first century. Like many of Jesus' parables in Luke (11:5, 11; 12:25; 14:28; 15:4) this one begins with the question "Who among you. . . ?" and expects a negative answer, "No one; it would be unthinkable." The parable assumes a small farmer who has one slave who does both the field work and the household chores. The master would never say to the slave, "Come here at once and take your place at the table" (v. 7). Instead, the servant would be expected to start preparing the master's evening meal immediately after coming in from the fields. Only after he had served the master could the servant tend to his own needs. The master would not even thank the servant for doing what was commanded.

Part of the parable's effect is achieved by a shift of point of view and identification from the place of the master to that of the slave. The parable's opening question casts the reader in the role of the master: "Who among you would say to your slave . . . ?" The parable says nothing about what the servant might want or expect. It speaks instead of the master's expectations. But v. 10, which applies the parable to the disciples (v. 1), or apostles (v. 5), reverses the roles. Having accepted the premise that they might expect a slave to do what was expected of him without commendation, the disciples are then challenged to see that they are God's servants and, therefore, even when they do all that is required they have done nothing for which they might expect to be rewarded.

Disciples are thereby challenged to see themselves as servants. Even when the demands seem unrealistic, a servant is only doing what is required and expected. If this is true when the servant is told to prepare the master's evening meal after plowing and tending the sheep all day, then it is also true when the servant is told to forgive a brother seven times in a single day.

The terminology of the parable, while metaphorical, is used by Paul to describe the role of an apostle and the work of a pastor (Rom 1:1; Gal 1:10; Phil 1:1). Plowing (Luke 9:62; 1 Cor 9:10) and shepherding (John 21:16; Acts 20:28; 1 Cor 9:7; 1 Pet 5:2) are also used to describe an apostle's work.[189]

Even when the servant has done all that is required of him, he is still "worthless" or "unworthy" (ἀχρεῖος *achreios*; see Matt 25:30). The thought is similar to Eliphaz's query of Job:

> "Can a mortal be of use to God?
>   Can even the wisest be of service to him?
> Is it any pleasure to the
>   Almighty if you are righteous,
>   or is it gain to him if you make
>   your ways blameless?"
> (Job 22:2-3 NRSV)

What then, if the servant has failed to do everything that was expected?

189. Fitzmyer, *The Gospel According to Luke (X–XXIV)*, 1145.

REFLECTIONS

The parable of the worthless servant is probably no one's favorite, yet it drives us to reexamine our assumptions about our relationship to God. The difficulty is that while the parable makes a significant point about discipleship and humility before God, it casts God in the unappealing role of a slave driver. Even making allowances for the currency of the image in the first century, most of us probably would choose a different metaphor. Our inclination is to think that if we do what we are commanded, we deserve some reward. Particularly do we expect a reward since the standard required for a disciple is so high.

Nevertheless, God owes us nothing for living good, Christian lives. God's favor and blessing are matters of grace—they cannot be earned. Therefore, when we assume that we can deal with God on the basis of what God owes us, we have made a basic mistake. We have rejected grace as the basis of our relationship to God and based that relationship on our own worth and merit. Grace, by definition, is a free gift.

When the parable is read in the context of the earlier verses in this chapter, the point becomes clear. The disciple can do what God requires—through faith—but the disciple can never do more than is required. The preceding verses confirm our need for faith. We cannot meet even the basic demands of discipleship from our own goodness and strength. Only through faith can we protect the little ones and rebuke and forgive as we ought.

These ten verses address three difficulties for disciples: (1) Do not be a hindrance to the discipleship of others. (2) Rebuke those who sin, and forgive all who ask your forgiveness. (3) When you have done all this, do not assume that you have done more than your duty. Faithfulness, forgiveness, and humility are required of those who would be obedient to Jesus. But which is the most difficult part of this teaching unit? Most of us probably will say the first part, the demand that we give no offense, that we rebuke, and that we forgive unceasingly. Certainly, failure in this area is easier to face than the admission that we cannot trust in God's grace toward us.

Such lack of humility, however, is the more dangerous temptation. It prevents us from experiencing the depth of God's love for us. It may also lead us to develop just the kind of self-righteousness and false spiritual superiority that will become an obstacle to the "little one." Spiritual health requires an awareness of both our own sinfulness and God's unlimited love for us.

As Walter Rauschenbush, the great proponent of the social gospel movement earlier in this century, reminded us, sin is never a private matter. What we do or fail to do always has social consequences. He would have applauded the words of John Donne, the Elizabethan poet who penned the following words in his "Hymn to God the Father":

> Wilt thou forgive that sin, by which I've won
> Others to sin, and made my sin their door?
> Wilt thou forgive that sin which I did shun
> A year or two, but wallowed in a score?
> When thou hast done, thou hast not done,
>   For I have more.

Such a prayer of confession acknowledges the sin into which we have led others and the sin that has so stained our lives that we can never be worthy of God's grace.

LUKE 17:11-19, THE HEALING OF THE TEN LEPERS

NIV

[11]Now on his way to Jerusalem, Jesus traveled along the border between Samaria and Galilee. [12]As he was going into a village, ten men who had leprosy[a] met him. They stood at a distance [13]and called out in a loud voice, "Jesus, Master, have pity on us!"

[a]12 The Greek word was used for various diseases affecting the skin—not necessarily leprosy.

NRSV

11On the way to Jerusalem Jesus[a] was going through the region between Samaria and Galilee. [12]As he entered a village, ten lepers[b] approached him. Keeping their distance, [13]they called out, saying, "Jesus, Master, have mercy on us!" [14]When he saw them, he said to them, "Go and show yourselves to the priests." And as they

[a]Gk he   [b]The terms *leper* and *leprosy* can refer to several diseases

NIV

¹⁴When he saw them, he said, "Go, show yourselves to the priests." And as they went, they were cleansed.

¹⁵One of them, when he saw he was healed, came back, praising God in a loud voice. ¹⁶He threw himself at Jesus' feet and thanked him— and he was a Samaritan.

¹⁷Jesus asked, "Were not all ten cleansed? Where are the other nine? ¹⁸Was no one found to return and give praise to God except this foreigner?" ¹⁹Then he said to him, "Rise and go; your faith has made you well."

NRSV

went, they were made clean. ¹⁵Then one of them, when he saw that he was healed, turned back, praising God with a loud voice. ¹⁶He prostrated himself at Jesus'^a feet and thanked him. And he was a Samaritan. ¹⁷Then Jesus asked, "Were not ten made clean? But the other nine, where are they? ¹⁸Was none of them found to return and give praise to God except this foreigner?" ¹⁹Then he said to him, "Get up and go on your way; your faith has made you well."

^aGk *his*

COMMENTARY

A transitional geographical notice and the introduction of new characters mark the beginning of a new unit. The disciples, to whom the preceding sayings were addressed, play no role in this story. Similarly, while the preceding verses emphasize the demands of discipleship, this story turns once again to the theme of God's mercy and salvation. Verse 11 reintroduces the journey motif that was established in 9:51; 13:31-35; and 14:25 and looks ahead to Jesus' entry into Jerusalem (19:28ff.). Verse 11 has also led commentators to observe that Luke seems to have only a vague grasp of Palestinian geography. Traveling from Galilee to Jerusalem, Jesus would have been traveling from north to south. Strictly speaking, there was no "region between Samaria and Galilee." Since Galilee lay above Samaria, Jesus may have traveled near the border between the two regions as he made his way down to the Jordan to skirt around Samaria, as most Jewish travelers did. This geographical note, however vague it is, serves to establish Jesus' proximity to Samaria and hence a setting in which he might meet the Samaritan leper featured in the story.

Recollection of the journey setting is appropriate here because Jesus meets a group of lepers on the road. According to the law, any person with a leprous disease was required to live "outside the camp" (Num 5:2-3) and cry out "Unclean, unclean" whenever anyone approached (Lev 13:45-46). If a leper were fortunate enough to recover, a priest had

to certify that the person was clean before he or she could return to the community (Lev 14:23).

The healing of lepers functions in the Gospel as a sign of the power of God's kingdom. Jesus' programmatic address at Nazareth recalls the healing of Naaman the Syrian (Luke 4:27; 2 Kgs 5:1-14). As in the story of Naaman, the lepers are instructed by "the man of God" to act on his command before there is any evidence that healing has occurred, and the Samaritan will return to offer thanks just as Naaman did (see 2 Kgs 5:15). Jesus' healing of lepers is also reported in Luke 5:12-16, and the connection with the prophets is again implicit in Jesus' response to John in Luke 7:22.

The present story is not a simple healing miracle. It blends elements of a healing miracle and a pronouncement story and resonates with both the healing of Naaman the Syrian and the parable of the good Samaritan. The effect is to extend Luke's portrayal of Jesus' announcement of the kingdom (from Luke 4:18-19). In the immediate context, the lesson of gratitude complements the parable of the unworthy servant in the preceding verses. Discipleship requires doing one's duty, but because of God's mercy, God's servants can never repay the grace they have experienced.

The opening phrase in v. 11 recalls the travel notice in 9:51 and in the Greek repeats some of the constructions found there. Although Jesus encounters the lepers as he enters a village, Luke is careful to note that they stood "at a distance." As the NIV makes clear, Luke identifies the ten not as lepers but as "men who had leprosy" just as earlier he referred to the man who was paralyzed not as a paralytic but as "a man who was paralyzed" (5:18) and called the Gerasene demoniac "a man who had demons" (8:27). The difference is subtle but reflects a humanizing and dignifying recognition of personhood.

The title "master" (ἐπιστάτης *epistatēs*) occurs only in Luke, where it appears repeatedly, but with this one exception always on the lips of Jesus' disciples (5:5; 8:24, 45; 9:33, 45). The rich man pleaded with Abraham for mercy in the parable of the rich man and Lazarus (16:24), and the blind man by the road will address Jesus as "Son of David" and ask for mercy (18:38-39). Literally, the text says that the ten lepers "raised a voice"; they called out in unison. Later, their response to their healing will stand in sharp contrast to their unison at this point. The call for mercy would ordinarily have been a request for alms, but although it has been some time since Luke has reported the spread of news about Jesus' healings (see 4:37; 5:15; 7:17; 8:39), it is possible that the request for mercy should be understood as a request for healing.

The report that Jesus "saw them" (v. 14) would be superfluous if it did not carry the nuance of a further meaning. In the parable of the good Samaritan, the priest, the levite, and the Samaritan each "see" the man in the ditch, but only the Samaritan stops to help him (see 10:31-33); this story follows immediately after Jesus' blessing of the disciples for what their eyes see and their ears hear (10:24; cf. Mark 8:17-18). The reference to Jesus' seeing the lepers also sets up the later notice that "one of them, when he saw that he was healed, turned back" (v. 15). In both cases, seeing means more than just physical sight—it means on the one hand perceiving the opportunity to be merciful toward another, and on the other hand the recognition that God's mercy has touched one's life.

Elisha's response to Naaman was a command, "Go, wash in the Jordan seven times" (2 Kgs 5:10 NRSV). Similarly, Jesus tells the ten lepers, "Go and show yourselves to the priests" (v. 14), echoing Jesus' command in the earlier story of healing a leper (5:14). This time, however, there is no mention of offering the proper sacrifices.

The actual report of the healing is told with a storyteller's flare—literally, "and it happened [that] as they were going they were made clean" (v. 14). The point of the story, however, is not the healing but the response of those who were touched by God's mercy. First we are told that one of them, "seeing that he was healed," returned glorifying God with a loud voice. It is significant that initially he does not return to "thank" Jesus, but glorifies God. His action parallels that of Naaman, who "returned to the man of God" and said, "Now I know that there is no God in all the earth except in Israel" (2 Kgs 5:15). The leper's action also conveys an implicit christology. He recognizes that God has acted through Jesus, and he offers praise to God. Glorifying God is a common response to manifestations of God's saving work in the Gospel of Luke (2:20; 5:25-26; 7:16; 13:13; 18:43; 23:47). The next statement is an extension of this one; the leper fell at the feet of Jesus and thanked him. In earlier contexts, those who have fallen at Jesus' feet have done so to plead for his healing mercy (5:12; 8:41), so the action here stands in contrast to mark the intensity of the leper's gratitude.

Now comes the twist in the story: The leper who returned to give thanks was a Samaritan (v. 16). See the discussion of social boundaries and the relations between Jews and Samaritans in the commentary on the parable of the good Samaritan (10:29-37). Jesus then asks a series of three questions that are not really addressed to the grateful Samaritan but underscore the point of the story. First, "Were not ten made clean?" The question reminds us that the ten were all healed, not just this one. Second, Jesus asks about the other nine—something the reader may not have considered: "Where are they?" What does their failure to return praising God say about them? Were they so caught up in their good fortune that they failed to "see" God's hand in their healing? Two points are underscored by the third question: "Was none of them found to return and give praise to God except this foreigner?" The response of giving glory to God is repeated, and the gratitude of the Samaritan is highlighted by referring to him as "this foreigner." The common disdain for Samaritans stands in sharp contrast to the Samaritan's response to God in this healing narrative. In that sense, this story is a companion piece to the parable of the good Samaritan and the healing of Naaman, who was also a foreigner. The proper response to God's saving mercy, therefore, is not presumption that it is something we deserve (cf. the servant in the preceding parable, vv. 7-10) but untainted gratitude and pure praise of God for God's saving mercy.

This surprisingly subtle story ends with the repetition of Jesus' formula of blessing: "Your faith has saved you" (cf. 7:50; 8:48; 18:42). In this case, the man's faith was not expressed by his request for help but by his gratitude and praise of God. The other nine had been healed, but only this one received Jesus' declaration of salvation. They got what they wanted, but this one received more than he had dreamed of asking for.

REFLECTIONS

The act of seeing plays a vital role in this story. First, Jesus sees the lepers. Then, the one leper sees that he has been healed. Two factors lead us to look more closely at these references to seeing. The first is the role of such references earlier in the Gospel, where Jesus blesses those who see and hear (esp., 10:24). Second, both references to seeing in this story are, strictly speaking, unnecessary to its telling and, therefore, seem to point to a further nuance. "When he saw" the lepers, Jesus saw their need and responded to it, just as the good Samaritan had seen the need of the man in the ditch and responded to it. The central event of the story is not the healing, however, but the response of the one leper "when he saw that he was healed." The repetition of the phrase "when he saw" builds expectation regarding the action that will follow. In this case, "when he saw" actually characterizes not only the recognition that he had been healed but also the recognition that the healing was the work of God that had been effected through Jesus.

The two instances of seeing each represent challenges for the believer. What do we see, and what do we do when we see? The first instance is the recognition of the need of others. Sometimes persons in need simply do not catch our attention. An irritable coworker may be facing a health problem or struggling with a difficult family situation. Who notices an international student far from home and family, or the person separated from family during the holidays? At other times, we simply pass by persons whose lives are a day-to-day struggle for subsistence or for emotional stability. Who sees?

The leper's seeing involved recognition of God's deliverance and grace. Ten were healed, but only one recognized the healing for what it was. Is healing simply the natural process of nature or a sign of God's love? In retrospect, are the opportunities and experiences that prepare one for greater challenges simply chance or evidence of God's providence? Who can fathom the ways in which God works in human experience?

The second question goes to the heart of the story. What do you *do* when you see? Jesus saw need and acted to meet it. When the leper saw healing, he did not just celebrate his good fortune; he returned to praise God and fall on his face before Jesus. Gratitude may be the purest measure of one's character and spiritual condition. The absence of the ability to be grateful reveals self-centeredness or the attitude that I deserve more than I ever get, so I do not need to be grateful.

Did it take a Samaritan—an outcast—to recognize grace for what it was? The grateful person reveals a humility of spirit and a sensitivity to love expressed by others. The grateful person, therefore, regards others' acts of kindness and experiences of God's grace with profound gratitude. Life itself is a gift. Health is a precious gift—the friendship of others and the love of family and special friends are an overwhelming grace to be treasured and guarded with gratitude. What do you see? And what do you do?

This story also challenges us to regard gratitude as an expression of faith. At the end, Jesus says to the Samaritan, "Your faith has made you well." That faith was expressed not primarily in the lepers' collective cry for help but in the Samaritan's individual act of recognition and his cry of grateful praise. Only his "loud voice" of praise matched the lepers' raised voices to call out for help at the beginning of the story.

In what sense, then, is gratitude an expression of faith? Does not gratitude follow from faith? Or is gratitude itself an expression of faith? If gratitude reveals humility of spirit and a sensitivity to the grace of God in one's life, then is there any better measure of faith than wonder and thankfulness before what one perceives as unmerited expressions of love and kindness from God and from others? Are we self-made individuals beholden to no one, or are we blessed daily in ways we seldom perceive, cannot repay, and for which we often fail to be grateful? Here is a barometer of spiritual health: If gratitude is not synonymous with faith, neither response to God is separable from the other. Faith, like gratitude, is our response to the grace of God as we have experienced it. For those who have become aware of God's grace, all of life is infused with a sense of gratitude, and each encounter becomes an opportunity to see and to respond in the spirit of the grateful leper.

LUKE 17:20-37, THE KINGDOM AND ITS COMING

NIV

20Once, having been asked by the Pharisees when the kingdom of God would come, Jesus replied, "The kingdom of God does not come with your careful observation, 21nor will people say, 'Here it is,' or 'There it is,' because the kingdom of God is within[a] you."

22Then he said to his disciples, "The time is coming when you will long to see one of the days of the Son of Man, but you will not see it. 23Men will tell you, 'There he is!' or 'Here he is!' Do not go running off after them. 24For the Son of Man in his day[b] will be like the lightning, which flashes and lights up the sky from one end to the other. 25But first he must suffer many things and be rejected by this generation.

26"Just as it was in the days of Noah, so also will it be in the days of the Son of Man. 27People were eating, drinking, marrying and being given in marriage up to the day Noah entered the ark. Then the flood came and destroyed them all.

28"It was the same in the days of Lot. People were eating and drinking, buying and selling, planting and building. 29But the day Lot left Sodom, fire and sulfur rained down from heaven and destroyed them all.

30"It will be just like this on the day the Son of Man is revealed. 31On that day no one who is on the roof of his house, with his goods inside, should go down to get them. Likewise, no one in the field should go back for anything. 32Remember Lot's wife! 33Whoever tries to keep his life will

[a]21 Or among   [b]24 Some manuscripts do not have in his day.

NRSV

20Once Jesus[a] was asked by the Pharisees when the kingdom of God was coming, and he answered, "The kingdom of God is not coming with things that can be observed; 21nor will they say, 'Look, here it is!' or 'There it is!' For, in fact, the kingdom of God is among[b] you."

22Then he said to the disciples, "The days are coming when you will long to see one of the days of the Son of Man, and you will not see it. 23They will say to you, 'Look there!' or 'Look here!' Do not go, do not set off in pursuit. 24For as the lightning flashes and lights up the sky from one side to the other, so will the Son of Man be in his day.[c] 25But first he must endure much suffering and be rejected by this generation. 26Just as it was in the days of Noah, so too it will be in the days of the Son of Man. 27They were eating and drinking, and marrying and being given in marriage, until the day Noah entered the ark, and the flood came and destroyed all of them. 28Likewise, just as it was in the days of Lot: they were eating and drinking, buying and selling, planting and building, 29but on the day that Lot left Sodom, it rained fire and sulfur from heaven and destroyed all of them 30—it will be like that on the day that the Son of Man is revealed. 31On that day, anyone on the housetop who has belongings in the house must not come down to take them away; and likewise anyone in the field must not turn back. 32Remember Lot's wife! 33Those who try to make their life secure will lose it, but those who lose

[a]Gk he   [b]Or within   [c]Other ancient authorities lack in his day

NIV

lose it, and whoever loses his life will preserve it. [34]I tell you, on that night two people will be in one bed; one will be taken and the other left. [35]Two women will be grinding grain together; one will be taken and the other left.[a]"

[37]"Where, Lord?" they asked.

He replied, "Where there is a dead body, there the vultures will gather."

[a]35 Some manuscripts *left*. 36*Two men will be in the field; one will be taken and the other left.*

NRSV

their life will keep it. [34]I tell you, on that night there will be two in one bed; one will be taken and the other left. [35]There will be two women grinding meal together; one will be taken and the other left."[a] [37]Then they asked him, "Where, Lord?" He said to them, "Where the corpse is, there the vultures will gather."

[a]Other ancient authorities add verse 36, *"Two will be in the field; one will be taken and the other left."*

COMMENTARY

The preceding section dealt with forgiveness, faith, and gratitude—responses to the presence of God in the midst of God's people. The disciples asked that their faith be increased, and they were told that they did not understand the nature of faith (vv. 5-6). This section turns to the nature of the kingdom and warnings to the disciples as they await its coming. The Pharisees ask Jesus about the coming of the kingdom, and Jesus responds that they do not understand the nature of the kingdom.

Parallels in structure and progression of theme serve as a transition from the preceding section to this one. The experience of the leper, seeing his healing and praising God, offers an apt illustration of the affirmation that the kingdom is "among you" (17:21).

17:20-21. For any reader of this part of Luke, the challenge is to discern how the affirmation of the presence of the kingdom in vv. 20-21 can make sense in the light of the attention given to its future coming in vv. 22-37. The pronouncement story in vv. 20-21 begins with a question posed by the Pharisees: When will the kingdom of God come? The reintroduction of the Pharisees and the indefiniteness regarding the connection of this scene with the previous one signal the beginning of a new unit.

These sayings hold the tension between the present reality of the kingdom where Jesus is present and the coming fulfillment of the kingdom when the Son of Man comes. Just as Jesus responded sharply to the disciples earlier, declaring that they did not understand the nature of faith (17:5-6), so also now he rejects the Pharisees' preoccupation with the timing of the kingdom's coming. The Phari-

sees have not understood the nature of the kingdom. Apocalyptic prophets and writers purported to reveal the signs that would precede the cataclysmic coming of God's reign on earth and God's vindication of the faithful Israelites. Jesus cut the ground from beneath any such speculations: "The kingdom of God is not coming with things that can be observed" (v. 20). The Greek term παρατήρησις (*paratērēsis*), translated by the last five words of v. 20 in the NRSV, is used elsewhere to describe the empirical observation of astronomical or physical phenomena—the movements of the planets and signs of illness or changes in the weather. The term occurs nowhere else in the NT, however. The coming of the kingdom is discerned by faith, not by empirical observation.

To the Pharisees' question, Jesus responds with one positive and two negative statements. Not only will the coming of the kingdom not be preceded by observable signs, but also such phenomena will not even accompany the coming of the kingdom. So, when the kingdom does come, others will not say "Here it is" or "There it is." Indeed, the kingdom is already "among you" (v. 21).

The *koine* Greek term ἐντός (*entos*), translated "among" you in the NRSV, occurs elsewhere in the NT only in Matt 23:26, where it designates the inside of a cup. Its meaning in its present context is debated. Does it mean "within you" (NIV)—that is, that the kingdom is an inner condition experienced only by the individual believer? If so, how should one reconcile this affirmation with other sayings that speak of the kingdom as objective and coming (21:31; 22:16,

18)? Moreover, the pronoun for "you" (ὑμεῖς hymeis) is plural—a group or collection of individuals. Does it mean "in the midst of you"—that the kingdom is present among them because Jesus is in their midst? This meaning seems to fit better, but it still does not explain the choice of this unusual term or how the presence of the kingdom in Jesus is to be related to its future manifestation. Other nuances have been proposed: either that the future kingdom has already arrived unobserved or that it is within their grasp if they will only act to seize it.

17:22-37. In addition to the difficulty of choosing the best understanding of v. 21, one must also arrive at some explanation for how Luke understands this assertion to be related to the verses that follow. The next section is closely linked to vv. 20-21, but it contains admonitions for watchfulness because the Son of Man will come suddenly and unexpectedly. The shift of audience from the Pharisees to the disciples signals the beginning of a new section in v. 22, but the catchword links formed by the repetition of " 'Look there!' or 'Look here!' " in v. 23 (cf. v. 21) and the repetition of verbs for "coming" in vv. 20 and 22 tie this new series of pronouncements to the preceding verses. The structural links may mislead a casual reader, however. Verses 22-37 shift from the theme of the presence of the kingdom in their midst to warnings about the suddenness of the coming of the Son of Man. The coming of the Son of Man, however, is not to be equated with the coming of the kingdom of God. The kingdom is already present.

Neither are vv. 22-37 a miscellaneous collection of sayings; rather, they form a carefully structured rhetorical unit that warns of the urgency of decisive action in preparation for the coming of the Son of Man. The leitmotif of the unit is "the day[s] of the Son of Man." This leitmotif echoes the prophetic warnings about the coming "day of the Lord" (Isa 13:6; Ezek 30:1-4; Joel 1:15; 2:1; Amos 5:18; Zeph 1:14-16; Zech 14:1). The expectation of the coming of the Son of Man makes more sense when it

I. Statement of the theme (vv. 22-25)
   A. Warning of the distress that will precede the coming of the Son of Man (v. 22)
   B. The nature of the Son of Man's coming (vv. 23-24)
   C. A passion prediction (v. 25)
II. Arguments from Scripture (vv. 26-30)
   A. First analogy: The days of Noah (vv. 26-27)
      1. Statement of the analogy: "Just as it was in the days of . . . " (v. 26)
      2. Description of life proceeding normally until "the day" (v. 27*a*)
      3. Reference to the cataclysm: "the flood came" (v. 27*b*)
      4. Reminder of the totality of the destruction: "and destroyed all of them" (v. 27*c*)
   B. Second analogy: The days of Lot (vv. 28-29)
      1. Statement of the analogy: "Just as it was in the days of . . . " (v. 28*a*)
      2. Description of life proceeding normally until "the day" (vv. 28*b*-29*a*)
      3. Reference to the cataclysm: "it rained fire and sulfur from heaven" (v. 29*b*)
      4. Reminder of the totality of the destruction: "and destroyed all of them" (v. 29*c*)
   C. The aptness of the analogies (v. 30)
III. Warnings that only decisive action will preserve one's life (vv. 31-35)
   A. "On that day" (vv. 31-33)
      1. Two examples (v. 31):
         a. "anyone on the housetop"
         b. "anyone in the field"
      2. A traditional warning: "Remember Lot's wife" (v. 32)
      3. A traditional saying on losing and keeping one's life (v. 33)
   B. "On that night" (vv. 34-35)
      Two examples:
      1. Two in a bed: one taken, one left
      2. Two grinding meal: one taken, one left
IV. A concluding question and aphorism (v. 37)

is addressed to the disciples than to the Pharisees, of course (see vv. 20, 22).

17:22. The discourse on the coming of the Son of Man begins in v. 22 without any prompting question from the disciples. Jesus simply announces that the days are coming when they will long for the coming of the Son of Man (v. 22). The leitmotif "the days" is repeated twice already in this opening statement. The plural "days" (ἡμέραι *hēmevrai*) is used here to focus attention on the distress that Jesus' followers will experience. Singling out *"one* of the days of the Son of Man" is a way of heightening the disciples' longing for even a taste of deliverance. The force of the opening statement is to warn the disciples of the coming distress. Their suffering or persecution will be so severe that they will long for deliverance, and yet their deliverance will not come.

17:23-24. Some will mistakenly report that the coming is taking place here or there, but the disciples should not be deceived by such apocalyptic hysteria (cf. Mark 13:5-6, 21-23). When the Son of Man comes, he will not appear in just one locale, here or there; it will be like a flash of lightning that is visible everywhere. Luke returns to the theme of the signs and the manner of the coming of the Son of Man in 21:25-36 and in the account of Jesus' ascension, where the disciples ask the Pharisees' question, "Is this the time?" (cf. Luke 17:20; Acts 1:6). The scene ends with the interpreting angels explaining to the disciples, "This Jesus, who has been taken up from you into heaven, will come in the same way as you saw him go into heaven" (Acts 1:11 NRSV). Later in Acts, Stephen "gazed into heaven and saw the glory of God and *Jesus* standing at the right hand of God" and declared, "I see the heavens opened and *the Son of Man* standing at the right hand of God!" (Acts 7:55-56 NRSV, italics added).

17:25. Before Jesus can return as the Son of Man, however, he must endure suffering and rejection. Verse 25, therefore, is an echo of the passion predictions. It anchors this apocalyptic discourse in the context of Jesus' journey to Jerusalem, where he will be arrested and killed (see 9:21-22, 43-44; 18:31-33). In Greek this statement is a verbatim repetition of the first part of 9:22, but there is no mention of the resurrection (cf. also 24:26).

"The Son of Man *must endure much suffering and be rejected* by the elders, chief priests, and scribes . . ." (9:22, author's translation)

"But first he *must endure much suffering and be rejected* by this generation." (17:25, italics added)

Rather, the concern here is to emphasize that the coming glorious Son of Man will be none other than the Son of Man who suffered and died on the cross. The divine imperative ("he must" [δεῖ *dei*]) underscores the fact that the passion also is part of the outworking of God's redemptive will. In Luke, the phrase "this generation" normally appears in warnings of judgment or in condemnations (7:31; 9:41; 11:29-32, 50-51; 16:8; 21:32); "this generation," therefore, is characterized by its wickedness and its failure to respond to Jesus' announcement of the kingdom. In the end, however, the Son of Man will prevail over "this generation" (21:32).

17:26-29. The next section of the discourse presents two analogies to the cataclysmic destruction that lies ahead. The examples of Noah and Lot are cited together in other Jewish and early Christian writings (Wisd 10:4-8; 3 Macc 2:4-5; *T. Naph* 3:4-5; Philo, *De Vita Mos.* 2.10 52-56; 2 Pet 2:5-7).[190] Reminders of the flood and the destruction of Sodom and Gomorrah had become traditional fare in the ethical exhortations of the period. The principal points of comparison in this discourse, however, are the sudden judgment that brings the ordinary activities of life to an end and the impossibility of escaping God's judgment.

Verses 26-29 develop an argument from Scripture that is based on a missing but assumed element. Verse 26 announces the first of the analogies by returning to the leitmotif of the discourse, this time in the plural: "the days of Noah . . . the days of the Son of Man." A general comparison between the events is signaled, but the reader can only guess what the similarities will be. The two analogies entail three points of comparison. First, life will proceed normally prior to the coming of the Son of Man, just as it did in the days of Noah and Lot (vv. 27*a,* 28*a*). Four verbs describe the normal course of life in the days of Noah: eating, drinking, marrying, and being given in marriage. Three pairs of verbs describe the procession of life in the days of Lot:

190. Fitzmyer, *The Gospel According to Luke (X–XXIV),* 1165.

eating and drinking, buying and selling, and planting and building. Eating and drinking—the physical sustenance of life—are common to both lists. The first list then turns to the perpetuation of families (marrying and being given in marriage), while the second list turns to commerce (buying and selling) and labor (planting and building). The lists describe ordinary activities and noticeably refrain from characterizing the wickedness of the antediluvian people or of Sodom and Gomorrah, which is an essential part of each of these biblical stories (see Gen 6:5-7; 18:20–19:23). Second, Jesus briefly describes the cataclysm: "the flood came" (v. 27b), "it rained fire and sulfur from heaven" (v. 29b). In each case, the description is preceded by the leitmotif: "until the day" (v. 27b), "but on the day" (v. 29a). Third, Jesus affirms the totality of the destruction: "and destroyed all of them" (vv. 27c, 29b). These pictures of judgment stand in a series of such warnings in Luke (e.g., 3:17; 6:24-26, 46-49; 10:13-15; 11:29-32; 12:1-3, 49-59; 13:1-9, 34-35).

17:30. This verse draws the rhetorical conclusion from these two biblical precedents: "It will be like that on the day that the Son of Man is revealed." The reference to "this generation" at the conclusion of v. 25, just before the two biblical precedents, and the assumed but unspoken element of each—the wickedness of the people in each case—invite the hearer to recognize the sinfulness of the "days" in which they were living. Life will proceed with apparent normality, but it will include terrible wickedness and rebellion against God. The person who recognizes that wickedness—the missing element in Jesus' precis of these biblical stories—will recognize that "the day" of the Son of Man is imminent.

17:31-33. The imminence of the Son of Man's coming and the absence of any hope of escape for those who are caught unprepared makes decisive action imperative. Only those who seize the present moment to embrace the kingdom will be spared when the Son of Man comes. The urgency of the moment is driven home by further similitudes of disaster that evoke elements of the preceding analogies. As it was in the destruction of Sodom and Gomorrah, when the cataclysm comes, there will not be time for any concern other than the preservation of one's life. Verse 31 draws two pictures from ordinary life. The first assumes the common

flat-topped Palestinian house. Whether on the housetop or in the field, one should make no effort to go into the house to rescue any belongings. Repeatedly, Jesus has warned that having wealth and many possessions is a severe spiritual hindrance (1:53; 6:24; 12:13-21; 16:19-31).

The warning against turning back recalls the fate of Lot's wife, who looked back and was turned into a pillar of salt (Gen 19:26; cf. Luke 9:62). Just at this point, a traditional saying on saving and losing one's life that occurs in other contexts is repeated to underscore the moral of this argument (cf. Matt 10:39; 16:25; Mark 8:35; Luke 9:24; John 12:25). In this context, however, the concern to sustain or preserve one's life should probably be understood as an allusion to v. 31 and the impulse to return to one's house to secure possessions. As in the case of the parable of the rich fool (12:13-21), concern for one's possessions can lead to the loss of one's life. Even if the saying in v. 33 is related to v. 31, the second part of it points to a more general sense. Persons who spend their lives seeking security will ultimately lose their lives, while those who lose their lives (metaphorically) in the pursuit of God's kingdom, bringing release to the captives, sight to the blind, and freedom to the oppressed, will save their lives. Here is the irony of Jesus' gospel for the poor and the outcast.

17:34-35. These verses, along with vv. 32-33, return to the warnings that when the Son of Man comes there will be no time to secure one's life. The phrase "on that night" in v. 34 balances "on that day" at the beginning of v. 31. It may also echo the warning that "the day of the Lord will come like a thief in the night" (1 Thess 5:2 NRSV). Just as v. 31 offers two examples drawn from the activities of ordinary life, such as those cited in vv. 27 and 29, so also v. 34 offers two further examples: two in a bed and two grinding meal. The examples in v. 31 emphasized that there will be time for nothing but decisive action to save one's life. The point of these examples, on the other hand, is to illustrate the judgment that will accompany the coming of the Son of Man.

The pronouns for the two in the bed are both masculine. T. W. Manson, however, argued that "it could not be otherwise if, as is probable, husband and wife are meant. Two persons are together (male *and* female): one (male *or* female) will be taken, and the other (male *or* female) will be left. In each case the masculine gender is inevitable."[191] The two grinding meal (women's work) are women.

In each case, one person is taken and one is left, but we are not told whether the ones taken are carried away for judgment or for deliverance. The analogies of the stories of Noah and Lot imply, however, that those who are taken are spared the judgment that comes upon the rest.

17:37. This rhetorical unit on the coming of the Son of Man concludes with a question and a proverb, both of which are enigmatic. The disciples ask rather obliquely, "Where, Lord?" Apparently the question asks where the Son of Man will come, just as earlier the Pharisees asked when the kingdom was coming (v. 20). The question about place also serves to frame the discourse by picking up one of the motifs from its beginning, where Jesus warned the disciples that they should not be misled by those who say "here" or "there," because the coming of the Son of Man will be a universal or cosmic event—like lightning that flashes across the whole sky (vv. 23-24).

The proverb, though again drawn from ordinary life, is grim. The saying in v. 37, which has a parallel in Matt 24:28, is drawn from Job 39:26-30, which concludes "and where the slain are, there it [the eagle] is" (Job 39:30 NRSV). The eagle was known for its swiftness (Job 9:26; Hab 1:8). The image of the eagle, while drawn from the prophetic and wisdom literature of the OT, may have taken on more specific and immediate connotations in first-century Palestine, since the image of the eagle was carried at the vanguard of every Roman legion; Josephus explains that "it is regarded by them as the symbol of the empire."[192]

Interpretations of the proverb have varied as interpreters have searched for a nuance that fits the context. The proverbial swiftness of the eagle leads to the view that the proverb affirms the swiftness with which the judgment will come, but on this view the proverb would be a response to "When?" and not to "Where?" As a sign, the circling of the vultures may carry a meaning similar to the simile of the lightning flash in v. 24. When the Son of Man comes, his arrival will be evident to everyone. Alternatively, the proverb may point to the inevitability of judgment. Just as the birds of prey gather over a corpse, so also the judgment signaled by the Son of Man will fall upon the wicked. If the latter meaning is chosen, as it is by many interpreters, then Jesus deflects the question "Where?" just as earlier he refuses to say "when" the kingdom will come. The point is that we are to be ready for the coming of the Son of Man because God's judgment will certainly be established.

191. T. W. Manson, *The Sayings of Jesus* (London: SCM, 1957) 146.

192. Josephus *The Jewish War* 3.123.

REFLECTIONS

As a potential text for preaching or personal reflection, this passage starts with two strikes against it: (1) The notion that the kingdom is both present and future is difficult to grasp; and (2) the Gospel's words about the future have been so abused and corrupted by persons who claim to know that the end is coming in our time that they have been all but abandoned by many believers.

1. Jesus deflected questions regarding when the kingdom would come or where the Son of Man would come. He gives the disciples no encouragement to attempt to calculate the times. The pseudo-religious literature so popular today that offers explanations of the signs of the end accomplishes little if anything of positive value. One result is to encourage persons to become preoccupied with an understanding of eschatology that is not unlike a kind of religious science fiction. Such preoccupation has nothing to do with the gospel or the Lord's concern for establishing peace and justice on the earth.

Again, Jesus' refusal to provide us with signs of the end time means that we have no way of gaining the security that predictability provides. The issue of signs, therefore, is quickly translated into a matter of trust. The desire to control drives us to seek knowledge of the future, but the gospel calls instead for trust in God's grace to sustain us both now and in the times to come.

When we keep in balance the present and future aspects of the kingdom, we will not become discouraged. Neither will we lose sight of the priorities and tasks that claim our energies now.

2. Deflecting curiosity about the time or signs of the coming of the kingdom, Jesus declared that the kingdom was already present "among us." Jesus may have deliberately chosen the ambiguity of this way of describing the kingdom. To translate v. 21 as saying "within you" risks overspiritualizing and personalizing the kingdom. The kingdom cannot be a private experience. On the other hand, the kingdom is present among us insofar as the Spirit of Christ is present and the work of redemption is continuing. By refusing to offer a timetable, Jesus turned the disciples' attention to the tasks that lay before them. His task and that of the disciples was to respond with obedience to the call to fulfill their role in God's redemptive work. Before the Son of Man could come in glory, he would die in shame. Before reaching the throne of God, he would endure the throes of death. Many today want to bypass the cross for the glories of the kingdom, but the kingdom in our time will be seen only by those who take the cross as the controlling power of their lives and live for the relief of human suffering and the reconciliation of all persons to one another and to God.

3. From the presence of the kingdom, Jesus turns to the future fulfillment of God's redemptive work in the coming of the Son of Man. The urgency of Jesus' warnings cannot be stressed too strongly. Nothing matters more than the kingdom of God. It dominates the message of Jesus. Thus we can neither push it off to the future nor reduce it to a matter of private piety and experience. The reality of Christ's kingdom claims the lives of his followers totally. The kingdom sets the priorities and guides the decisions that Jesus' disciples make.

4. Jesus' teachings claim that the kingdom of God is already present among us but yet to be fulfilled. Neither aspect can be minimized if we are to be true to his teachings, but how can the two emphases be held in balance? Without the promise that the sovereignty of God will someday be established over all the earth, we would not have the hope that faith requires. Who could trust in the reconciling power of love and self-sacrifice without the promise of the kingdom of God?

On the other hand, if the hope of the kingdom were entirely future, what difference would it make to us now? The coming of the kingdom in the life of Jesus means that the power of the kingdom is already at work among us. We have seen in the ministry of Jesus the beginning of a new community, one that redeems and reconciles. Sin is forgiven and defeated. The broken are made whole. Oppression of the deprived is forbidden, and the powers of this age are challenged by the power at work in Jesus.

The presence of the kingdom, therefore, means that we can already begin to experience the community of the new age in the fellowship of those who are committed to God's reign on earth. The hope of the coming kingdom gives us courage to lead changed lives in the present, yet it will not let us become so heaven bound that we are of no earthly use.

LUKE 18:1–19:27, JESUS' GOSPEL TO THE RICH AND THE POOR

OVERVIEW

Luke 18 turns from Jesus' teachings on the nature of the kingdom and its coming at the end of chap. 17 to a series of scenes that provide depth and contrast to Jesus' teachings regarding the poor and the privileged. The first section contains two parables, each of which contrasts two characters: the unjust judge and the persistent widow (18:1-8) and the Pharisee and the tax collector (18:9-14). The second section contrasts Jesus' teachings regarding the little children and his instructions to the rich ruler (18:15-30). The third section of the chapter contains the third passion prediction (18:31-34). The fourth section unites two scenes that are located in Jericho: Jesus' healing of the blind beggar (18:35-43) and Jesus' encounter with Zacchaeus, the rich tax collector (19:1-10). This extended unit concludes with the parable of the greedy and vengeful king (19:11-27). The contrasts between rich and poor in these two chapters are typically and quintessentially Lukan.

Luke 18:1-8, The Unjust Judge and the Persistent Widow

NIV

18 Then Jesus told his disciples a parable to show them that they should always pray and not give up. [2]He said: "In a certain town there was a judge who neither feared God nor cared about men. [3]And there was a widow in that town who kept coming to him with the plea, 'Grant me justice against my adversary.'

[4]"For some time he refused. But finally he said to himself, 'Even though I don't fear God or care about men, [5]yet because this widow keeps bothering me, I will see that she gets justice, so that she won't eventually wear me out with her coming!'"

[6]And the Lord said, "Listen to what the unjust judge says. [7]And will not God bring about justice for his chosen ones, who cry out to him day and night? Will he keep putting them off? [8]I tell you, he will see that they get justice, and quickly. However, when the Son of Man comes, will he find faith on the earth?"

NRSV

18 Then Jesus[a] told them a parable about their need to pray always and not to lose heart. [2]He said, "In a certain city there was a judge who neither feared God nor had respect for people. [3]In that city there was a widow who kept coming to him and saying, 'Grant me justice against my opponent.' [4]For a while he refused; but later he said to himself, 'Though I have no fear of God and no respect for anyone, [5]yet because this widow keeps bothering me, I will grant her justice, so that she may not wear me out by continually coming.'"[b] [6]And the Lord said, "Listen to what the unjust judge says. [7]And will not God grant justice to his chosen ones who cry to him day and night? Will he delay long in helping them? [8]I tell you, he will quickly grant justice to them. And yet, when the Son of Man comes, will he find faith on earth?"

[a]Gk *he*   [b]Or *so that she may not finally come and slap me in the face*

COMMENTARY

The parable of the judge and the widow serves as a transition between the discourse on the coming of the Son of Man, which precedes it, and the parable of the Pharisee and the tax collector, which follows it. In the preceding discourse, the references to the coming of the Son of Man in vv. 22, 24, and 30 connect with the question at the end of the present unit: "And yet, when the Son of Man comes, will he find faith on earth?" (18:8). The issue of faith, or readiness, is also implied by the references to the days of Noah and Lot and the repeated examples of one taken and one left (vv. 34-35).

Links with the material that follows the parable in its present context are also evident. The parable of the Pharisee and the tax collector in vv. 9-14 concerns prayer and plays on the contrast between the status of the Pharisee and the tax collector, just as the present parable turns on the disparity in power between the judge and the widow.

The force of the parable heavily depends on the social status and religious duties involved in the roles of judges and widows. In ancient Israel, the duty of a judge was to maintain harmonious relations and adjudicate disputes between Israelites. Widows were deprived of the support of a husband, yet they could not inherit their husband's estate, which passed on to the deceased man's sons or brothers, so disputes involving widows and orphans were common (Ps 82:3-4; Jer 5:28-29). Judges were charged with the responsibility of hearing complaints fairly and impartially, a duty that was all the more important because they adjudicated cases without the benefit of a jury. Deuteronomy reports Moses' charge to judges: "Give the members of your community a fair hearing, and judge rightly between one person and another, whether citizen or resident alien. You must not be partial in judging: hear out the small and the great alike; you shall not be intimidated by anyone, for the judgment is God's" (Deut 1:16-17 NRSV). The judge's responsibility within the covenant community, therefore, was to declare God's judgment and establish *shalom* among God's people. Jehoshaphat's charge to the judges of his day included a warning to "let the fear of the LORD be upon you" (2 Chr 19:7). Those who felt wronged by a judge often pleaded for God to intervene and vindicate them (Pss 6:6-10; 82:8). Moreover, Sirach praises divine justice in a passage that has notable parallels with these verses in Luke:

For the Lord is the judge,
    and with him there is no partiality.
He will not show partiality to the poor;
    but he will listen to the prayer
      of one who is wronged.
He will not ignore the
      supplication of the orphan,
    or the widow when she pours out her
      complaint.

· ·

Indeed, the Lord will not delay,
    and like a warrior will not be patient
until he crushes the loins of the unmerciful
    and repays vengeance on the nations.
(Sir 35:15-17, 22-23 NRSV)

The expectation regarding the care of widows was equally clear. Regard for those in need—among whom the widow, the orphan, and the foreigner were classic examples—was grounded in God's mercy on the Israelites when they were in bondage (Deut 24:17-18). God will vindicate the widows and the orphans. Therefore, those who abuse such powerless persons will surely suffer God's judgment (Num 22:22-24; cf. Ps 68:5).

Widows had a place of honor in the early church also. Following the Hebrew Scriptures, James declares that "religion that is pure and undefiled before God, the Father, is this: to care for orphans and widows in their distress, and to keep oneself unstained by the world" (Jas 1:27 NRSV). The Pastoral Epistles document the church's effort to care for its widows and characterize the widow as one whose piety leads her to continual prayer: "The real widow, left alone, has set her hope on God and continues in supplications and prayers night and day" (1 Tim 5:5 NRSV; cf. 5:3-16).

In this light, the prominence of widows in Luke and Acts takes on added significance. Anna, the widow who blessed the infant Jesus, "never left the temple but worshiped there with fasting and prayer night and day" (Luke 2:37). During his address at Nazareth at the outset of his ministry, Jesus recalled Elijah's ministry to the widow in Sidon (4:25-26). Elijah provided her with meal and oil and then revived her son and presented him to her alive (1 Kgs 17:8-24). The commentary on Jesus' raising of the widow of Nain's son in Luke 7:11-17 calls attention to the connections between Luke's account of that event and Elijah's resuscitation of the widow's son.

Later, Luke will record Jesus' condemnation of those who "devour widow's houses" (20:47) and of the widow who put two copper coins in the treasury (21:1-3). On two occasions widows also feature prominently in the book of Acts: the dispute over the distribution of food to the widows of the Hellenists (Acts 6:1-6) and the presence of the widows at the raising of Dorcas (Acts 9:39, 41).

In structure and theme, the parable of the widow and the judge is a twin of the parable of the neighbor in need (11:5-8). Both are used to illustrate the importance of persistent prayer (11:1-4, 9-10; 18:1). Both parables feature a person in need persistently pressing a request, and both parables call for reasoning from the lesser to the greater: If a neighbor or an unjust judge will respond to an urgent or repeated request, then will not God also respond to those who call out in need? Richard C. Trench, Bishop of Dublin, expressed the argument of these parables: "If churlish man may be won by mere importunity to give, and unjust man to do right, how much more certainly shall the bountiful Lord bestow, and the righteous Lord do justice."[193]

193. Richard C. Trench, *Notes on the Parables of Our Lord,* (London: Kegan Paul, Trench, Trübner, & Co., 1915) 326.

Verse 1 serves as an introduction to the parable and instructs the reader to interpret it as a lesson on prayer. The parable itself is related in vv. 2-5. Verse 6 admonishes the hearer to consider the judge's surprising response to the widow. Verse 7 provides interpretation of the parable in different directions by means of two leading questions, and v. 8 answers the second of the questions and leads the reader on to a third one that relates the parable to the preceding discourse on the coming of the Son of Man.

18:1. Jesus' practice of prayer and teachings on prayer form a recurring theme in Luke, and this parable, which is introduced as a parable on prayer, is found only in this Gospel. Luke notes Jesus' withdrawals for periods of prayer in 3:21; 5:16; 6:12; 9:18, 28-29; 22:39-45; 23:34, 46, and he records Jesus' teachings on prayer in 6:28; 11:1-13; 18:9-14; 19:46; 20:47; 22:40, 46. It is not surprising, therefore, that Luke interprets this parable as a call to persistent prayer. Taken by itself, however, the parable may call attention to God's responsiveness to the widow as an exemplar of the poor and oppressed rather than to the widow's persistence in pressing her case. The interpreter may focus on either the widow or the judge, and either focus can foster fruitful reflections.

18:2. The judge is introduced—a certain judge in a certain city. This situation is either hypothetical or deliberately non-specific. All attention is focused on the characterization of this judge, "who neither feared God nor had respect for people." In the light of the requirements and expectations for judges, quoted above, the point is obvious: This judge is completely unfit for his position. The reader can have no confidence that the judge will execute justice or minister compassion. A storyteller may either tell the audience who a certain character is (direct characterization: e.g., Zechariah and Elizabeth "were righteous before God, living blamelessly according to all the commandments and regulations of the Lord," 1:6) or simply show the characters in action and allow the audience to draw their own conclusions (indirect characterization: e.g., the rich man in the parable of Lazarus and the rich man "who was dressed in purple and fine linen and who feasted sumptuously every day" [16:19]). In this case, Jesus provides direct characterization of the judge, and the tension in the parable is created by the

surprise that the judge does not act as we have been led to expect.

To fear God in this context may mean either to reverence God or to live in fear of punishment for violating his office as a judge. Luke and Acts both emphasize fear of God in a sense consistent with the sage's words: "The fear of the LORD is the beginning of knowledge;/ fools despise wisdom and instruction" (Prov 1:7 NRSV). God's mercy comes to those who fear God (Luke 1:50); the shepherds literally "feared a great fear" at the angelic announcement of Jesus' birth (2:9). The disciples and others respond in fear to Jesus' power (8:25, 35; 9:34, 45), and Jesus instructs the disciples not to fear their persecutors but to fear God (12:4-5). Similarly, in Acts those who fear God, like Cornelius and his household (Acts 10:2; cf. 10:22, 35), form a special group. They are recognized for their devotion and their openness to the gospel. This judge, however, neither fears God nor respects people.

18:3. This verse introduces the widow. Her grievance is not described, however, so it is usually assumed that she is calling upon the judge to make a third party give her what is owed to her—a matter of money or property. Neither does the parable tell us why the judge refuses to hear her case. Interpreters have conjectured that the judge may be waiting for a bribe, or that he may be responding to the widow's more powerful adversary, hoping to curry his favor. In either case, the judge's motive is unimportant; his refusal to hear the widow confirms Jesus' characterization of him as one who has no fear of God or regard for others. We may assume that the widow has a legitimate grievance. The judge is her sole hope of securing justice, and persistence is her only recourse.

18:4-5. Now the surprise comes in the judge's soliloquy or interior monologue. Interior monologues are a favorite device in the peculiarly Lukan parables (see the rich fool, 12:17-19; the prodigal son, 15:17-19; the dishonest steward, 16:3-4). We are not actually told that the judge granted the widow's request, only that he decided to do so. The judge's monologue repeats Jesus' characterization of him. It also echoes the words of the neighbor in the parallel parable in Luke 11:5-8, "Do not bother me" (μή μοι κόπους πάρεχε *mē moi kopous pareche*, 11:7; τὸ παρέχειν μοι κόπον *to parechein moi* *kopon,* 18:5). The judge will grant the widow's request for two reasons, but the statement of the second reason may be understood either literally or metaphorically. The language is drawn from the boxing arena. Literally, it means "so that in the end she may not come and strike me under the eye"— that is, slap him or strike him in the face. The expression can also be understood metaphorically to mean "so that she may not wear me out by continually coming." The metaphorical sense is preferred in modern translations.

18:6. The unjust judge, from whom one could hardly expect justice, finally does what is right—if only to keep from being badgered by the persistent widow. The narrator marks a transition at this point by inserting the tag line "and the Lord said." This reference to "the Lord" seems clearly to be a reference to Jesus in contrast to the similar reference in 16:8. The interpretation of the parable begins with the admonition to consider what the unjust judge says. But what is the meaning of this brief story? If one focuses on the unjust judge, the point may be the contrast between the unjust judge and the character of God, who in the texts cited above serves as a just judge over Israel. If even an unjust judge will heed the widow and do what is right, how much more so will God do justice for the poor and oppressed? On the other hand, a lesson on prayer emerges when one considers the widow's persistence in coming to the judge. Here the emphasis may fall either on the importance of praying persistently, earnestly, and without losing heart—the point with which Luke introduces the parable (18:1)—or on the assurance that God will answer those who pray day and night.

18:7. The latter interpretation is suggested by the introduction (v. 1) and by the first of the two questions in v. 7: "And will not God grant justice to his chosen ones who cry to him day and night?" The question confidently assumes an affirmative answer. The phrase "day and night" not only highlights the need for persistent prayer but also resonates with the description of Anna and the pious widows in the Pastoral Epistles who prayed "night and day" (Luke 2:37; 1 Tim 5:5). The verb in the first question (βοάω *boaō*) means "to call," "to shout," or "to cry out." Two characters in Luke "cry out" to Jesus for help, fulfilling the assurance of the first question in v. 7; they are the father of the boy with an unclean spirit

(9:38) and the blind beggar (18:38). The concept of election surfaces in the expression "his chosen ones" (ἐκλεκτός *eklektos*), which occurs only once elsewhere in Luke, and there in reference to Jesus (23:35). The widow now allegorically represents God's elect.

The second of the questions that serve to interpret the parable extends the allegorical interpretation. The verb μακροθυμέω (*makrothymeō*), which usually means "to have patience" or "to be forbearing," is difficult to interpret in this context. The same verb occurs in Sir 35:19 (quoted above). The Septuagint version may be translated, "and the Lord will not tarry, nor will he delay long over them." The Lord has no patience with injustice or oppression but will act speedily to vindicate those who cry out to God in distress. The second question, therefore, suggests the imminence of the Lord's coming to vindicate the elect against their oppressors.

18:8. The first part of v. 8 assures the hearers of a positive response to the two questions posed in v. 7. God will act quickly to vindicate the elect. The third question, in v. 8*b,* shifts the image from the coming of God to vindicate the elect, which was suggested by the judge's decision to grant the widow her request, to the coming of the Son of Man: "And yet, when the Son of Man comes, will he find faith on earth?" The question recalls the references to the coming of the Son of Man in the discourse that precedes the parable (17:22, 24, 30). Thus the parable may function as the conclusion to the previous section or as a transition to the parable of the Pharisee and the tax collector, which follows.

Earlier, the disciples had exclaimed, "Increase our faith!" (17:5), and Jesus had explained to them the power of faith the size of a mustard seed (17:6). Then, Jesus found faith in the Samaritan leper, and Jesus assured him, "Your faith has made you well [saved you]" (17:19). Implicitly the warnings about the judgment at the coming of the Son of Man contrast the vindication of those who have faith with the judgment on those who do not. Now the question is posed directly for the hearer: Will the Son of Man find faith when he comes? From an assurance of God's care for the "little ones" (see 17:2), to a lesson on prayer, to an affirmation of God's vindication of the elect, Luke turns this parable around and around until he spins from it a question regarding faith. In order to answer affirmatively, the reader must be ready to profess a faith like that of the persistent widow who demands justice and the pious widow who prays night and day. When the Son of Man comes, will he find such faith among God's elect (see 7:9)? Will he find faith like a mustard seed (see 17:6)? Will he find that you have a widow's faith?

REFLECTIONS

According to an old dictum, a parable has only one point, but Luke proves that this approach is too restrictive. The parable of the unjust judge and the persistent widow offers opportunities for reflection on the responsibility of the faithful to care for widows, orphans, and strangers in their midst. It affords a striking challenge to any theology to tie God's providence to God's compassion. It serves as a graphic lesson on the importance of prayer and patient endurance, and finally it focuses on the quality and vitality of one's faith.

1. The abstract often lures us to lose sight of the concrete, and specific concerns can fade into pointless generalities. The interpreter should resist the seduction of the parable's introduction (v. 1). Many find it far easier to worry over the health of their prayer life than to be concerned for the well-being of widows. From early in the history of the Judeo-Christian tradition, however, no expression of faithfulness to God is more deeply rooted than the duty to care for widows, orphans, and strangers—the powerless and homeless in our midst. Where had Jesus learned this lesson? Had he been taught it in the synagogue, or had Joseph died when he was a boy, and had he seen his mother's distress as, husbandless, she tried to care for her children and sustain the family? Perhaps this parable was born not just from everyday experience but from a specific childhood memory.

One response to this parable, then, may be to focus sustained attention on the needs of widows within the church as the average age of the American population and of church members rises with the advancing age of the baby-boom generation. What role did widows have in the early church, and how did the church care for their needs? It is time for the church to give renewed attention to this part of the record of the church's faith and practice.

2. There are two characters in this parable, and the unjust judge's failure to fear God or be concerned about the needs of other people establishes him as the antithesis of God's justice and compassion for the oppressed. If even such an arrogant judge will eventually respond to the widow, then how could one doubt that God will vindicate such "little ones" against those who inflict hardship upon them or fail to do what is in their power to ease their plight? The just God does not protect the property interests of the privileged but is compassionate and looks out for those who have no power to leverage privileges from the powerful. The way of the kingdom, therefore, calls for priorities based on compassion.

Once God's compassionate nature has been clearly stated, then the call to pray and not lose heart takes on a different tone. The God to whom we pray is compassionate, ready to respond to the needs of the powerless and oppressed. How does such a God hear our prayers if they are self-centered, concerned only with petty issues, or irrelevant to God's redemptive purposes? To those who are worn out, hard pressed, and lacking in hope, Jesus says to pray night and day. Unlike an unjust judge, God cares about the plight of those who are regarded unimportant by others. To those who have it in their power to relieve the distress of the widow, the orphan, and the stranger but do not, the call to pray night and day is a command to let the priorities of God's compassion reorder the priorities of their lives.

The assurance that God will act to establish justice on earth and vindicate the needs of the disadvantaged is a double-edged word. To the judge it calls for speedy action to turn from false priorities while there is still time, and to the widow it speaks a word of hope. The time is growing short; God will not tarry long.

To each, therefore, the parable of the unjust judge and the persistent widow calls for a reexamination of our faith. Have we turned a deaf ear to those who cry out in need, or have we given up hope that God will hear our calls for help? Faith requires different responses from the widow and the judge. What does faith require of us? Have we the faith of a mustard seed, the faith of a widow?

Luke 18:9-14, The Pharisee and the Tax Collector

NIV

9To some who were confident of their own righteousness and looked down on everybody else, Jesus told this parable: 10"Two men went up to the temple to pray, one a Pharisee and the other a tax collector. 11The Pharisee stood up and prayed about[a] himself: 'God, I thank you that I am not like other men—robbers, evildoers, adulterers—or even like this tax collector. 12I fast twice a week and give a tenth of all I get.'

13"But the tax collector stood at a distance. He would not even look up to heaven, but beat his breast and said, 'God, have mercy on me, a sinner.'

14"I tell you that this man, rather than the other, went home justified before God. For everyone who exalts himself will be humbled, and he who humbles himself will be exalted."

[a]11 Or to

NRSV

9He also told this parable to some who trusted in themselves that they were righteous and regarded others with contempt: 10"Two men went up to the temple to pray, one a Pharisee and the other a tax collector. 11The Pharisee, standing by himself, was praying thus, 'God, I thank you that I am not like other people: thieves, rogues, adulterers, or even like this tax collector. 12I fast twice a week; I give a tenth of all my income.' 13But the tax collector, standing far off, would not even look up to heaven, but was beating his breast and saying, 'God, be merciful to me, a sinner!' 14I tell you, this man went down to his home justified rather than the other; for all who exalt themselves will be humbled, but all who humble themselves will be exalted."

COMMENTARY

The parable of the Pharisee and the tax collector extends the theme of prayer, found in the previous parable. By reading these two parables together, the reader is instructed to pray with the determination of the widow and the humility of the tax collector. Peter Rhea Jones has characterized the complementary themes of the two parables as "the promise of persistent prayer" (18:1-8) and "the peril of presumptuous prayer" (vv. 9-14).[194]

If the preceding parable, with its reference to the coming of the Son of Man (v. 8), is taken as the conclusion of the discourse on the coming of

the kingdom in the previous chapter, then the parable of the Pharisee and the tax collector serves to introduce a new section of the Gospel (18:9-30). In these verses, parallels can be drawn between the figures of the Pharisee and the rich ruler (vv. 18-25) and between the humility of the tax collector and the little children (vv. 15-17).

18:9, 14. The parable is bracketed by interpretive references in vv. 9 and 14. Luke says that Jesus told the parable "to some who trusted in themselves that they were righteous and regarded others with contempt" (v. 9). Both facets of this description anticipate the characterization of the Pharisee in the following verses. One may assume

194. Peter Rhea Jones, *The Teaching of the Parables* (Nashville: Broadman, 1982) 198.

that Jesus was speaking to the Pharisees, as in 15:1-2 (where Pharisees and tax collectors are mentioned together); 16:14-15 (which echoes the characterization of the Pharisee: "You are those who justify yourselves in the sight of others; but God knows your hearts"); and 17:20. While the parable may be intended as a rebuke of the Pharisees in its present context, Luke does not say that Jesus addressed the Pharisees. Moreover, a parable addressed to the Pharisees that placed a Pharisee in an unfavorable light would hardly be subtle—thus the parable probably has a much wider application. Disciples and believers are just as vulnerable to pride and self-righteousness as the Pharisees. Thus, while those who do not recognize their own tendency to play the role of the Pharisee in this parable may assume that Jesus was talking about others, specifically the Pharisees, by the end of the story readers will have to confront the attitude of the Pharisee in their own hearts. The conclusion in v. 14 disallows the limitation of the parable to any one group: "All who exalt themselves will be humbled, but all who humble themselves will be exalted."

Trusting in oneself is obviously a posture of blindness to one's position before God. Like the strong man who trusted in his armor (11:21-22), the religious may trust in their righteousness. Luke takes pains, however, to identify the true basis for righteousness and distinguish it from misplaced pride in obedience to God's commandments. Zechariah and Elizabeth were righteous (1:6). John's role, likewise, was to turn the disobedient to "the wisdom of the righteous" (1:17), of whom Simeon was an appropriate model (2:25). Alongside these models of piety were others whose righteousness was superficial or inadequate. Jesus came, therefore, "to call not the righteous but sinners to repentance" (5:32). The ambivalence continues in other references. The righteous will be raised from the dead (14:14), but there is more joy in heaven over the repentance of one sinner than in the ninety-nine righteous (15:7). Later, Jesus' accusers will feign righteousness (20:20), but the centurion at the cross will pronounce Jesus righteous (23:47), and Joseph of Arimathea will be identified as a righteous man (23:50).

Valuable as the introduction and conclusion may be, they may rob the parable of much of its subtlety and reduce its characters to traits or stereotypes.[195] The parable itself characterizes the Pharisee and the tax collector only indirectly; it does not tell us what to think of them. (On the role of tax collectors, see Commentary on 5:27.) The parabler leaves it to the hearer to decide why one was justified and the other was not.

18:10. Whether coming from north, south, east, or west, people always "went up" to Jerusalem, and the Temple was situated at the highest point in the city, above the Kidron Valley to the east and the older city of David to the south. Praying at the Temple is an underlying motif that runs through Luke and into Acts (see 1:8-10, Zechariah; 2:25-38, Simeon and Anna; 24:53, the disciples; Acts 2:42-47, the first converts; Acts 3:1, Peter and John). Although by this point in the Gospel, the Pharisees are portrayed in a negative light in various earlier passages (e.g., 5:21-22; 6:7; 7:36-50; 11:37-44; 12:1; 15:2; 16:14), the reader is nevertheless expected to recognize the Pharisee as a devout person and the tax collector as a stereotypical sinner.

18:11. Both the position and the prayer of the Pharisee and then of the tax collector are reported, and the reader learns who these two are by the way they pray. The Pharisees separated themselves from others to maintain their purity before God, so this Pharisee takes a position that reflects his identity—standing by himself. Alternatively, the phrase may be interpreted as referring to the Pharisee's prayer rather than his position: "concerning himself he prayed these things." Both prayers begin with a simple, direct address: "God." The Pharisee's prayer, however, continues immediately in the first person. The narrator's initial characterization of the Pharisee as regarding others with contempt (v. 9) is confirmed by his own words. His prayer is one of thanksgiving, but it is a self-serving prayer, thanking God that he is not like other people.[196] By "other people" he means sinners: "thieves, rogues, adulterers, or even like this tax collector." The last member of this list links the two characters of the parable. The Pharisee is aware of the presence of the tax collector in the Temple, but the only link between them is the Pharisee's contempt for the tax collector.

18:12. As the Pharisee's prayer continues, so

195. John Nolland, *Luke 9:21–18:34,* WBC 35B (Dallas: Word, 1989) 878-79.

196. For a contemporary parallel from Qumran, see 1QH 7.34-35.

does his absorption in his own virtue. Fasting and tithing are the proofs of his piety that he offers to God. He fasts twice each week, a practice attested here for the first time (cf. 5:33). The *Didache* (early second century) instructs Christians, "Let not your fasts be with the hypocrites, for they fast on Mondays and Thursdays, but do you fast on Wednesdays and Fridays."[197] (For the prescriptions for fasting in the OT, see Commentary on 5:33.)

Tithing has been referred to earlier also (11:42). Again, there is precedent in the Hebrew Scriptures (e.g., Gen 14:20; Num 18:21-24; Deut 14:22-26; Mal 3:8-10) and prescriptions in the Rabbinic sources.[198] Either to avoid any possibility of neglect or as a work of supererogation, the Pharisee does not just offer a tithe on those foods or animals for which a tithe is specifically required but tithes *all* of his income.

The Pharisee asks nothing of God. He presumes, rather, that he is not a sinner and that his fasting and tithing are ample evidence of his piety. The Pharisee gives no evidence of either humility or contrition before God. By contrast, the tax collector stands "far off," a position that anticipates his confession of unworthiness before God. The common posture for prayer was not with head bowed and hands folded but looking up to God with hands raised (1 Tim 2:8). Indeed, later Christian prayer practices reflect the influence of this parable. Beating one's breast was a sign of remorse or grief.[199] Moreover, there are suggestive parallels between this parable and Luke's description of the responses of the centurion and the bystanders at the death of Jesus, especially the pronouncement of righteousness or innocence and the crowd's response of beating their breasts (see 23:48).

18:13. If the Pharisee asks nothing of God, the tax collector boasts nothing before God. His prayer echoes the opening words of Psalm 51: "Have mercy on me, O God." The crucial addition to the words of Psalm 51, however, is the tax collector's self-designation: "a sinner." Nothing more is reported of the tax collector's prayer. It is complete as it stands, and nothing more needs to be said of his character.

---

197. *Did.* 8.1, in Kirsopp Lake, trans., *The Apostolic Fathers,* LCL (Cambridge, Mass.: Harvard University Press, 1970) 1:321.
198. E.g., *m. Maaseroth* and *m. Maaser Sheni.*

199. See *Joseph and Asenath* 10:15.

REFLECTIONS

Luke has already educated the reader to know how to assess the contrast between the two who went up to the Temple to pray. Early in his ministry, Jesus said, "I have come to call not the righteous but sinners to repentance" (5:32). The parable now contrasts representatives from each of these categories. Jesus' opponents ridiculed him as "a friend of tax collectors and sinners" (7:34), but Jesus responded that "there will be more joy in heaven over one sinner who repents than over ninety-nine righteous persons who need no repentance" (15:7).

Less evident is the reason why the Pharisee's prayer is not accepted. Is it because he presumes he is righteous but is not? Does his lack of humility or his confidence in his own virtue exclude him from God's grace? Does the fact that he has separated himself from others signal that, although he may not realize it, he has separated himself from God as well?

The parable leaves it to the reader to consider the contrast between the two. Verse 14 affirms that the one who presumed he was righteous (v. 9) and not like the unrighteous (v. 11) was not made righteous, while the one who was so acutely aware of his unrighteousness was made righteous. The parable, therefore, is not merely a study in contrasts but ends with a dramatic reversal. The one who said, "I know my transgressions,/ and my sin is ever before me" (Ps 51:3 NRSV) could now rejoice that his petition, "Create in me a clean heart, O God,/ and put a new and *right* spirit within me" (Ps 51:10 NRSV, italics added) had been heard. The proud are brought down, and the lowly are exalted (see 1:52).

The second part of v. 14 moves the lesson of the parable from the particular to the general: "all who exalt themselves will be humbled, but all who humble themselves will be exalted."

This pronouncement is a verbatim repetition of Luke 14:11. In the earlier context, the axiom follows Jesus' admonition to the guests at a banquet to take the lower seats rather than the places of honor. The same scenario has now been played out in God's house. The Pharisee separated himself from the others and boasted of his virtue, while the tax collector stood far off and declared his sinfulness. The Pharisee returned to his home without having been made righteous, but the tax collector was accepted before God.

Both the reversal of the characters in the parable and its echo with the context of Luke 14:11 lead the reader to ponder the relationship between the two characterizations stated in the opening verse (18:9; cf. the judge "who neither feared God nor had respect for people," 18:2). Those who trust in their own righteousness will regard others with contempt, and those who regard others with contempt cannot then bring themselves to rely on God's grace. Therefore, persons who exalt themselves over others and boast of their virtue before God will discover that they have cut themselves off from both, and persons who are aware of their need for grace and forgiveness will not be able to despise other people.

The parable of the Pharisee and the tax collector, contrary to some interpretations, is a two-sided parable. To read it as simply a warning against pride, self-sufficiency, or a relationship with God based on one's own works is to miss the other side of the parable, which connects the Pharisee's posture before God with his contempt for the tax collector. To miss this connection would be tantamount to emulating the Pharisee's blindness to the implications of his attitude toward the tax collector. The nature of grace is paradoxical: It can be received only by those who have learned empathy for others. In that regard, grace partakes of the nature of mercy and forgiveness. Only the merciful can receive mercy, and only those who forgive will be forgiven (6:36-38). The Pharisee had enough religion to be virtuous, but not enough to be humble. As a result, his religion drove him away from the tax collector rather than toward him.[200]

200. See Nolland, *Luke 9:21–18:34,* 877.

Luke 18:15-30, The Little Children and the Rich Ruler

NIV

15People were also bringing babies to Jesus to have him touch them. When the disciples saw this, they rebuked them. 16But Jesus called the children to him and said, "Let the little children come to me, and do not hinder them, for the kingdom of God belongs to such as these. 17I tell you the truth, anyone who will not receive the kingdom of God like a little child will never enter it."

18A certain ruler asked him, "Good teacher, what must I do to inherit eternal life?"

19"Why do you call me good?" Jesus answered. "No one is good—except God alone. 20You know the commandments: 'Do not commit adultery, do not murder, do not steal, do not give false testimony, honor your father and mother.'*a*"

21"All these I have kept since I was a boy," he said.

a20 Exodus 20:12-16; Deut. 5:16-20

NRSV

15People were bringing even infants to him that he might touch them; and when the disciples saw it, they sternly ordered them not to do it. 16But Jesus called for them and said, "Let the little children come to me, and do not stop them; for it is to such as these that the kingdom of God belongs. 17Truly I tell you, whoever does not receive the kingdom of God as a little child will never enter it."

18A certain ruler asked him, "Good Teacher, what must I do to inherit eternal life?" 19Jesus said to him, "Why do you call me good? No one is good but God alone. 20You know the commandments: 'You shall not commit adultery; You shall not murder; You shall not steal; You shall not bear false witness; Honor your father and mother.'" 21He replied, "I have kept all these since my youth." 22When Jesus heard this, he said to him, "There is still one thing lacking. Sell all that you

NIV

²²When Jesus heard this, he said to him, "You still lack one thing. Sell everything you have and give to the poor, and you will have treasure in heaven. Then come, follow me."

²³When he heard this, he became very sad, because he was a man of great wealth. ²⁴Jesus looked at him and said, "How hard it is for the rich to enter the kingdom of God! ²⁵Indeed, it is easier for a camel to go through the eye of a needle than for a rich man to enter the kingdom of God."

²⁶Those who heard this asked, "Who then can be saved?"

²⁷Jesus replied, "What is impossible with men is possible with God."

²⁸Peter said to him, "We have left all we had to follow you!"

²⁹"I tell you the truth," Jesus said to them, "no one who has left home or wife or brothers or parents or children for the sake of the kingdom of God ³⁰will fail to receive many times as much in this age and, in the age to come, eternal life."

NRSV

own and distribute the moneyᵃ to the poor, and you will have treasure in heaven; then come, follow me." ²³But when he heard this, he became sad; for he was very rich. ²⁴Jesus looked at him and said, "How hard it is for those who have wealth to enter the kingdom of God! ²⁵Indeed, it is easier for a camel to go through the eye of a needle than for someone who is rich to enter the kingdom of God."

26Those who heard it said, "Then who can be saved?" ²⁷He replied, "What is impossible for mortals is possible for God."

28Then Peter said, "Look, we have left our homes and followed you." ²⁹And he said to them, "Truly I tell you, there is no one who has left house or wife or brothers or parents or children, for the sake of the kingdom of God, ³⁰who will not get back very much more in this age, and in the age to come eternal life."

ᵃ Gk lacks the money

COMMENTARY

The two preceding sections have featured contrasts between the persistent widow and the unjust judge and between the Pharisee and the tax collector. The little children and the rich ruler do not interact, but taken together they serve to illustrate what the kingdom of God requires.

As the Lukan travel narrative nears its conclusion, Luke again returns to the Markan sequence: Jesus blesses the children (Mark 10:13-16) and calls the rich man (Mark 10:17-22). Throughout this section the theme of the kingdom recurs, focusing the reader's attention on the kingdom's reversals of conventional wisdom and the radical demands that Jesus makes on all who seek to enter the kingdom or gain eternal life.

18:15-17, The Little Children. 18:15. Verses 15-17 are a pronouncement story that features two related sayings, each containing references to "children" (παιδία *paidia,* v. 16; παιδίον *paidion,* v. 17) and the kingdom of God. Although both Mark 10:13 and the two sayings that follow use the term *paidia* for the chil-

dren being brought to Jesus, Luke uses βρέφος *brephos*), a term he uses elsewhere for infants (Luke 1:41, 44; 2:12, 16; Acts 7:19). We are not told why the children were being brought to Jesus. It has been estimated, however, that infant mortality rates ran as high as 30 percent; the terrors of disease, famine, and war claimed 30 percent of those who survived by the age of six and 60 percent by the age of sixteen.[201] Presumably, people were bringing children to Jesus because they had seen or heard that his touch had healed others (6:19). The miracle-working teacher who exercised power over demons, they thought, might bless the children by his touch.

Neither are we told why the disciples sought to stop people from bringing the children to Jesus. We may conjecture that they disregarded the personhood of children, that they wanted to protect Jesus' time for more important activities, or that they were jealous of the children's access to

201. Bruce J. Malina and Richard L. Rohrbaugh, *A Social-Science Commentary on the Synoptic Gospels* (Minneapolis: Fortress, 1992) 383.

Jesus. Whatever their motive, they acted out the role of a famous person's entourage, or a king's court, by shielding Jesus from the people. By doing so, however, they demonstrate that they have again failed to understand the nature of the kingdom. (Cf. Jesus' response to the disciples regarding the "little ones," 17:1-2; the nature of faith, 17:5-6; and the coming of the Son of Man, 17:22-37.)

18:16. Jesus' attention turns directly to the children. He does not say, "Let them bring the little children to me," but "Let the little children come to me." By his words, he gives expression to the gentle, nurturing side of God, which the psalmist sang of in Ps 131:2. Jesus' rebuke, "Do not hinder them," recalls the disciples' misguided censorship of the unauthorized exorcist (9:49-50) and the lawyers' failed stewardship of the key of knowledge (11:52). Whenever people in positions of power hinder others—the outcast, women, the poor, or children—from entering the kingdom (again see 17:2), it is always a mistake. In the book of Acts, "hinder" (κωλύω *kōlyō*) will become a clue to the theme of the gospel's defeat of all who would erect barriers to its being preached to Samaritans (Acts 8:4-8), a eunuch (Acts 8:36), or the Gentiles (Acts 10:47; 11:17; 28:31).[202]

The second half of the saying in v. 16 provides a twist that lifts the incident from being merely a glimpse into Jesus' compassion for the children to a lesson on the nature of the kingdom. The theological motive for receiving children is that "it is to such as these that the kingdom of God belongs" (18:16). Again, the saying leaves the reader to fill the gaps and understand what gives children access to the kingdom: their innocence, their powerlessness, their lack of credentialed virtue such as the Pharisee boasted of in the preceding parable, or their readiness to receive God's love? Who else could be numbered among "such as these"?

18:17. This is the third of six "Amen, I say to you" sayings in Luke (see 4:24; 12:37; 18:29; 21:32; 23:43). "Amen" (ἀμήν *amēn*) was a declaration of affirmation that usually followed a prayer or pronouncement. In the NT only Jesus ever prefaces a saying with this unutterably solemn formula. Whereas v. 16 describes the present

experience of the kingdom, v. 17 looks to the prospect of entering the kingdom in the future.

Verse 17 is a verbatim repetition of Mark 10:15, but it is structurally similar to Matt 18:3 and the Johannine versions of the same saying:

> "Truly I tell you, unless you change and become like children, you will never enter the kingdom of heaven." (Matt 18:3 NRSV)

> "Very truly, I tell you, no one can see the kingdom of God without being born from above." (John 3:3 NRSV)

> "Very truly, I tell you, no one can enter the kingdom of God without being born of water and Spirit." (John 3:5 NRSV)

Each of these sayings is composed of four parts: (1) "Amen" or "Amen, amen," (2) "I say to you," (3) a condition stated negatively, and (4) a warning of exclusion from the kingdom. In each case, the condition involves a reference to children or to birth.

The saying in v. 17 also fits the profile of the nature of the kingdom that Luke sketches for the reader. The kingdom belongs to the poor (6:20), to women—such as the widow of Nain, the woman who anointed Jesus, the woman with the flow of blood, the stooped woman, Mary and Martha, the persistent widow, and the woman who gave all she had—and to the tax collectors, the paralyzed, the Samaritans, and the lepers. The children are now added to this unlikely list. The kingdom is for such neglected, forgotten, or despised persons. Because the kingdom is for such as these, one must become like a child in order to enter the kingdom. Here again, the saying invites the reader to consider what he or she would have to do to "receive the kingdom of God as a little child."

18:18-30, The Rich Ruler. 18:18. Without any notice of a change of time or place, Luke reports a certain ruler's question to Jesus. Is there a connection between the rich ruler and the preceding scene? Had the ruler heard Jesus' pronouncement about the children? How should we read his question, with an emphasis on "I," meaning that if the kingdom belongs to "such as these," what must a ruler do? Or does the emphasis fall on "do" or "inherit" or "eternal life"? The ruler again advances the question of the character of righteousness. In the context of God's covenant with Israel, the question of what one must do to inherit eternal life implicitly raises the much-

202. Frank Stagg, *The Book of Acts: The Early Struggle for an Unhindered Gospel* (Nashville: Broadman, 1955); "The Unhindered Gospel," *Review and Expositor,* 71 (1974) 451-62.

debated question of the relationship among covenant, righteousness, and resurrection.

First-century Jews were divided on the hope of an afterlife. Israelites of earlier centuries believed that the dead went to Sheol, where there was no conscious, individual existence. One lived on, therefore, through descendants and in memory. Consequently, childless persons had no one to care for them in their old age or to remember them after their death. Job in his misery calls on God to "appoint me a set time, and remember me!" (see Job 14:10-14*a*). The first explicit reference to a hope of resurrection from the dead occurs at the end of Daniel in a passage that probably dates from the early second century BCE: "Many of those who sleep in the dust of the earth shall awake, some to everlasting life, and some to shame and everlasting contempt" (Dan 12:2 NRSV). Belief in the resurrection of the dead was, therefore, a relatively recent development. The Sadducees rejected this belief because it was not found in the Torah, but the Pharisees and apparently the Essenes affirmed the hope of resurrection (see Acts 23:8). Still, the nature of the resurrection and the basis for eternal life were vigorously debated. Some inclined toward the Greek notion of the immortality of the soul; some thought of the resuscitation or reconstitution of the physical body; while others spiritualized the notion of resurrection.

The ruler addressed to Jesus a profoundly existential and theological question: "What must I do to inherit eternal life?" The reference to eternal life in v. 30 forms a parenthesis with this question, indicating that all the verses in between contribute to Jesus' response to the ruler. On what basis might one hope for eternal life? Was it sufficient to be born into the covenant people or to be faithful to the requirements of that covenant? The ruler's question assumes that the hope of eternal life depends on what one does or may fail to do: "What must I *do?*" On the other hand, the verb translated "inherit" (κληρονομέω *klēronomeō*) places the ruler's hope in the context of God's promise of an inheritance to the descendants of Abraham, an inheritance that now included the hope of eternal life as a part of God's blessing.

Jairus was identified earlier as a ruler of the synagogue (8:41; cf. 14:1), but the rich ruler in this passage is probably a civil magistrate (see 12:58; 23:13, 35; 24:20). The language of his question suggests that the ruler is a Jewish official.

Only Luke identifies this interlocutor as a ruler, but Luke characterizes him neither as rich—a key element in the exchange that follows but one that is temporarily withheld from the reader—nor as young (see Matt 19:20). The common designation "the rich young ruler," therefore, represents a popular conflation of the synoptic Gospels but is found in none of them.

The ruler prefaces his question with the address "Good teacher." Both John and Jesus have been called "teacher" (διδάσκαλος *didaskalos*; see 3:12; 7:40). The added attribute, "Good teacher," recognizes Jesus' virtue and piety, and hence his ability to speak to the question the ruler has addressed to him. Jesus' credentials did not consist in his discipleship to a great mentor but in the transparent goodness of his own character. Unless the ruler used the address simply as a respectful greeting, it shows great insight on his part.

18:19. Jesus turns the address back on the ruler rather sharply. Instead of being flattered that a ruler would address him in such a way, Jesus seizes the moment to make a theological point, just as he had seized the opportunity afforded by the disciples' effort to turn the children away from him to make a point about the nature of the kingdom. The point of his first response to the ruler is explained in the next sentence: "No one is good but God alone." Far from the church's impulse to venerate Jesus, these words deflect attention from his person to God. God is the source of all goodness, the only one worthy of worship. If a person is good (see 6:45), it is through God's grace; implicitly, if Jesus is to be worshiped, it is because of God's vindication of Jesus through the resurrection.

18:20. The ruler poses the same question that the lawyer posed in Luke 10:25. To the lawyer Jesus responded, "What is written in the law?" Here again, Jesus cites the commandments, four negative and one positive, in what we may designate as his second response to the ruler because it moves to a new topic. Although the list of commandments is found in all three synoptic Gospels, each is different from the others. Luke reverses the Markan sequence of the first two commands and omits the fifth, "You shall not defraud" (Mark 10:19 NRSV). Matthew and Mark follow the sequence in which the commands are given in Exod 20:12-16 and Deut 5:16-20, but

Philo and the B manuscript of the Septuagint contain lists of the commands in the same sequence as Luke.[203] In Exodus and Deuteronomy the command to honor one's father and mother also precedes the other commands.

18:21. Now it is the ruler who rebuffs Jesus. The honor he conferred on Jesus by addressing the question to him and by his honorific address, "Good Teacher" had not elicited an equally honorific response from Jesus. Instead, Jesus had shamed the ruler by questioning his attribution of goodness to Jesus. Moreover, Jesus' answer hardly showed any greater wisdom than might have been expected from a child in the synagogue. Who could not have quoted the commandments back to the ruler? The ruler, therefore, seizes the high ground by affirming that he has kept all of *these* commandments since his youth. Is Jesus able to offer nothing more?

Jesus' responses to the ruler have not been a trap. Instead, his first response points to the exclusive sovereignty of God and his second response to the foundational importance of God's covenant with Israel. Whatever Jesus might say further on the issue of eternal life is based on the continuing validity of these premises. As Luke has repeatedly demonstrated from the first chapter of the Gospel, the new is not a departure from the old but an extension and completion of what God has already been doing in human history.

18:22. "There is still one thing lacking." Jesus' third response to the ruler rivets the reader's attention. The other shoe is about to drop. The focal pronouncement of this scene will follow. That pronouncement contains a rapid series of imperatives without explanation or elaboration: (1) *sell* everything you have; (2) *give* it away to the poor (and you will have treasure in heaven); (3) and *come,* (4) *follow me.* The fourth imperative clarifies the third, while the third adds force to the fourth. The placement of the promise, "and you will have treasure in heaven," is also interesting in that it comes after the commands to sell and give to the poor rather than after the commands to come and follow Jesus. The choice of wording underscores the connection between the promise and the preceding commands, since it implies that the ruler's treasure is now in his possessions rather than in his desire to serve God and God's poor.

The term rendered "treasure" (θησαυρός *thēsauros*) occurs only once in Mark, in the Markan parallel to this verse (Mark 10:21), but four times in Luke and nine times in Matthew. Luke 6:45 links good and evil treasure to the nature of a person's heart. Luke 12:33, in the context of Jesus' instructions to his disciples, provides the basis for the present text. In parallel to the present context, this passage contains an exhortation to sell one's possessions and give alms; the phrase "treasure in heaven," which will result from giving what one has to the poor; and the axiom that one's heart will be where one's treasure is. What Jesus says to the ruler, therefore, is not a new or arbitrary demand imposed only on this man or members of his class; it is an expression of the basic axioms of the kingdom. The children, the widows, the strangers, and the poor have a special place in God's care (see 6:20), so those who would inherit the kingdom must also be committed to their care. Moreover, our priorities and commitments cannot be divided; either we serve God or we pursue wealth (cf. the parable of the rich fool, 12:13-21, and 16:13, "You cannot serve God and wealth").

18:23. The characterization of the ruler as "rich" comes only now, at the end of the scene, where it serves to confirm the appropriateness and force of Jesus' third response to him. In this exchange, Jesus and the ruler have each "heard" the other (see vv. 22-23). The ruler has heard Jesus, but his investment in his possessions prevents him from responding to Jesus' imperatives. He will sacrifice his "treasure in heaven" (eternal life, v. 18) for what he already has. He is a brother to the rich fool, and the reader knows that not only is he sacrificing eternal life, but he will eventually lose his possessions also. He has heard the Word, but here is an example of the seed that is sown among the thorns (8:14). The resonances between Jesus' exchange with the rich ruler and other Lukan passages add richness and texture to the account. Hence, we understand when Luke reports that "he became very sad."

18:24-25. Jesus' fourth response to the rich ruler is a lament followed by an aphorism, both of which feature references to the kingdom of God. The phrase "becoming very sad" in v. 24 is omitted from some of the early manuscripts and may be a duplication of the phrase from v. 23. Without the phrase, however, the transition to

---

203. See Philo *On the Decalogue* 12.51; Joseph A. Fitzmyer, *The Gospel According to Luke (X–XXIV)* (Garden City, N.Y.: Doubleday, 1992) 1199.

Jesus' lament in v. 24 is flat and colorless. The lament is a verbatim repetition of Mark 10:24, but Luke omits the note that it was addressed to the disciples.

The reference to possessions in v. 24 connects this pronouncement with Jesus' other warnings about wealth (6:24; 12:13-21; 16:19-31; 18:18-23). God's love reaches out prejudicially toward the poor because their poverty violates God's intention for human life. Similarly, the rich find it difficult to experience God's sovereignty because their wealth turns them away from people in need and blinds them to their own need of salvation. Wealth easily becomes a pursuit that displaces the priority of serving God and thereby excludes the rich from the opportunity to experience God's grace.

Jesus' lament is prefaced by his observation of the ruler's sadness. Both Jesus and the ruler are sad—and for the same reason: Both realize that the ruler's wealth has hindered him from entering the kingdom. The ruler cannot bring himself to surrender his goods, and Jesus can neither overcome nor ignore the ruler's response. The price of free will is that God cannot force the free to make the right decisions in life. The poignancy of the moment is that the ruler has the spiritual sensitivity to be saddened, but Jesus can do nothing further for him.

The difficulty noted in the lament is heightened and illustrated by the hyperbole in v. 25: "It is easier for a camel to go through the eye of a needle than for someone who is rich to enter the kingdom of God." Interpreters have sought to reduce the incongruity of the image by suggesting that the "eye of a needle" was a narrow gate in the city wall through which a camel could pass only if its load was removed from it, but there is no evidence of such a gate. Origen suggested that with the change of one letter, the Greek word for "camel" (κάμηλος *kamēlos*) would mean "rope" (κάμιλος *kamilos*).[204] The hyperbole of this aphorism is similar, however, to Jesus' warning that one should remove the beam from one's own eye before attempting to remove a speck from another's eye (6:42), or that the scribes and Pharisees "strain out a gnat but swallow a camel" (Matt 23:24 NRSV)—a saying that sets in contrast the smallest insect with the largest animal in Palestine.

204. Ibid., 1204.

18:26-27. The undefined group to whom Jesus spoke these words now responds in amazement. If the rich who have means and power to gain for themselves whatever they want and who have apparently already been blessed by God cannot be saved, then who can? The question misses the reversal to which Jesus' lament and hyperbole point. One cannot infer about the rich and the poor according to traditional standards. The rich do not have more advantages than the poor but less. It is not a matter of human ability but of divine power. Jesus' response to their amazement turns away from the difficulty the rich have in turning to God: God is able to bring salvation to the most obdurate of sinners. Again free will and divine sovereignty are juxtaposed and equally affirmed without relieving the tension between them. While God always calls for a human response of repentance and faithfulness, salvation is always an act of divine initiative and grace. Shortly, the incredulous who ask who can be saved will receive a further answer, when Jesus responds to the blind man by the road, "Your faith has saved you" (18:42). What the rich cannot achieve for themselves apart from God, God can accomplish even with a blind beggar.

18:28-29. Peter responds to Jesus, speaking on behalf of the disciples (cf. 9:20, 33; 12:41). There is a minor textual variant in v. 28. In the parallel in Mark 10:28, Peter says they have left "all" to follow Jesus, a reference that would echo Jesus' instruction for the ruler to sell "all" he had and follow Jesus (Luke 18:22), but Luke—who has a fondness for the term "all"—lacks the word in the preferred version of the text of this verse. The emphatic position of the "we" in Peter's claim conveys the implication that, in contrast to the ruler, Peter and the others have followed Jesus' command and are therefore entitled to their reward. Peter's claim that they have followed Jesus echoes Jesus' call for the ruler to follow him (vv. 22, 28).

Earlier Jesus had warned that no one could be his disciple who did not hate father, mother, wife, children, brothers and sisters, and even his or her own life (14:26). Now Jesus offers a promise of reward to those who have left all to follow him. The saying is one of six "amen, I say to you" sayings in Luke (4:24; 12:37; 18:17, 29; 21:32; 23:43). The conditions of discipleship consist here of a fivefold denial: home, wife, brothers, parents, children. The fivefold denials must be held in context with the commandment to honor one's father and mother, which Jesus cited in v. 20. Mark has a sevenfold list: house, brothers, sisters, mother, father, children, fields (Mark 10:29), so Luke has added the reference to "wife," combined "mother" and "father" as "parents," and omitted the reference to "fields," which might have connected with the role Barnabas's fields play in Acts 4:37. The motivation is also different in Luke: "for the sake of the kingdom of God" rather than "for my sake and the sake of the good news" (Mark 10:29). The repetition of the reference to the kingdom continues the chain of references found in vv. 17, 24-25.

18:30. The rewards of discipleship are both present and future. The pronouncement in v. 30 (par. Mark 10:30) employs expressions that are common in the rabbinic literature: "this age" and "the age to come." The age to come is the time of blessedness when God will vindicate the righteous. In contrast to the Markan parallel, Luke changes the promise of a hundredfold to "very much more" and does not specify the nature of the present rewards that come to the disciples. Instead, by comparison with Mark the emphasis is focused more tightly on the future reward: eternal life.

The last words in this scene return to the theme that was raised by the ruler's question in v. 18, "What must I do to inherit eternal life?" The answer is now complete. Eternal life is promised to those who keep the commandments of God's covenant with Israel (vv. 19-20), sell what they have, give to the poor (v. 22), and leave all to follow Jesus (vv. 22, 28-29). Such a response is impossible for human beings, but entirely possible for God (v. 27). Salvation, therefore, depends on both God's power and our response to God's invitation to faithfulness. Through God's strength, the faithful receive a bountiful reward—the experience of fellowship with God in the present and eternal life in the future.

REFLECTIONS

In his book *Tragic Sense of Life,* Miguel de Unamuno says that he took up his pen to distract his readers for a while from their distractions. The "tragic sense of life" arises from the innate human need to know that there is more to life than this brief span of physical existence on earth. Yearn as we may for such assurance, however, Unamuno contended that we cannot know that there is more to life than our short years here. As a result of our anxiety over our mortality, we spend our lives finding ways to distract ourselves from being preoccupied with what we cannot know. Thus Unamuno wrote to distract us from our distractions and focus our attention on the question of life after death. As an agnostic philosopher, he could find no basis for confident hope of life beyond death. After wrestling with the question at length, he makes a final admonition to the reader to live in such a way that if there is no life after death it will be an injustice![205]

The power of the story of Jesus' encounter with the rich ruler is that it inevitably forces the reader into the role of the ruler. Dancing in our mind's eye are the vivid images of the persistent widow and the unjust judge, the Pharisee and the tax collector. We would never deny a widow her claim. We do not see ourselves in the figure of the judge with no reverence for God or regard for others. That parable ends with a question rather than a command: "When the Son of Man comes, will he find faith on earth?" (18:8). The parable of the Pharisee and the tax collector overturns notions of holiness based on separation and purity. In place of the prevailing system of righteousness, this parable proclaims the imperative of righteousness based on repentance and humility. It ends with a prophetic warning: "All who exalt themselves will be humbled, but all who humble themselves will be exalted" (18:14). The next scene illustrates just this sort of reversal: Jesus rebukes the disciples and receives the children. The scene ends with a warning of the necessity that one who would enter the kingdom must receive it "as

205. Miguel de Unamuno, *Tragic Sense of Life,* trans. J. E. Crawford Flitch (New York: Dover, 1954) 263, 330.

a little child" (18:17). The reader can predict that the ruler will not fare well in his exchange with Jesus. The ruler will be no more attractive as a model for the reader's response to Jesus than is the unjust judge. The difficulty, at least for modern readers of the Gospel, is that we cannot avoid repeating the ruler's response to Jesus. Who will actually "sell all that you own and distribute the money to the poor" (v. 22)? Like the ruler, the reader is forced to recognize the importance we place on the security our possessions give us. The demand is so high that we too are apt to turn away sad, feeling deep internal division, but being unable to do what Jesus commands. The text leaves us with no basis, therefore, for presumption regarding our entitlement to a place in the kingdom of God or to eternal life.

As a result, in the narrative context we are driven to the posture of the tax collector who cries out, "God, be merciful to me, a sinner!" (v. 13). Paradoxically, identification with the ruler whose possessions keep him from the kingdom forces upon the reader the sense of unworthiness that the tax collector expresses. The demand for humility, repentance, divestiture of wealth and rival allegiances, care for the poor, and complete dependence on the mercy of God is not compromised in the least. The hope of mercy is never an excuse for failure to obey. Jesus' words recognize that salvation depends on the power of God (v. 27).

If full obedience remains beyond our grasp, at least the mix is right: the call to care for the poor; the models offered by the widow, the tax collector, and the children; and the twin insistence that we call on God for mercy and remember that what is impossible for us is still possible for God. In the creative blending of these emphases, Luke calls those who would heed Jesus' call not to live in such a way that if there is nothing beyond this life it will be an injustice, but to live so that the widows will receive justice, the children blessing, and the poor sustenance. If we can learn to humble ourselves so that the humble may be exalted, then before God the camel may yet make it through the eye of the needle.

Luke 18:31-34, The Third Passion Prediction

NIV

31Jesus took the Twelve aside and told them, "We are going up to Jerusalem, and everything that is written by the prophets about the Son of Man will be fulfilled. 32He will be handed over to the Gentiles. They will mock him, insult him, spit on him, flog him and kill him. 33On the third day he will rise again."

34The disciples did not understand any of this. Its meaning was hidden from them, and they did not know what he was talking about.

NRSV

31Then he took the twelve aside and said to them, "See, we are going up to Jerusalem, and everything that is written about the Son of Man by the prophets will be accomplished. 32For he will be handed over to the Gentiles; and he will be mocked and insulted and spat upon. 33After they have flogged him, they will kill him, and on the third day he will rise again." 34But they understood nothing about all these things; in fact, what he said was hidden from them, and they did not grasp what was said.

COMMENTARY

After a long interval that is the result of Luke's extended travel narrative, Jesus voices the third of the passion predictions regarding his fate as the Son of Man. Other allusions to what awaits him in Jerusalem appear in 12:50; 13:32-34; and 17:25, but the parallels to the first two Markan passion predictions (Mark 8:31; 9:31) occur in Luke 9:22, and 44-45. This third prediction is by far the most detailed, anticipating and foreshadowing the passion narrative, which will soon unfold.

18:31. Not to be missed in the discussion of the passion prediction is the way in which Luke makes this pronouncement a scene to prepare the reader for the lack of understanding on the part of the Twelve. The opening of their minds to understand the death and resurrection of Jesus will be an important feature of the last chapter of the Gospel (see 24:45-46). Luke omits Mark's scene-setting comment that they were on the road going up to Jerusalem because it merely repeats the first part of the pronouncement in v. 31. By reporting that Jesus took the Twelve aside, Luke alerts the reader to the importance of the pronouncement that will follow. This is private instruction to the Twelve.

Jesus reasserts that Jerusalem is the goal of their journey (see 9:51, 53; 13:22, 33-34; 17:11; on "going up," see Commentary on 18:10). The passion prediction in Luke 18:31 may be patterned after the Markan prediction in Mark 10:32-34, but it includes some features not found in the Markan account and omits others that are found there. Specifically, Luke adds the emphasis on the fulfillment of Scripture, which will feature prominently in the crucifixion and resurrection of Jesus (see 22:37; 24:44, 46). Jesus' allusion to Scripture's being "completed" or "finished" picks up his earlier veiled reference, "and on the third day I finish my work" (13:32), and both of these pronouncements will later find an echo when Jesus says that "this scripture must be fulfilled [lit., finished] in me" (22:37). Luke does not specify which passages or which prophets he has in mind. It is enough to affirm that all that happened to Jesus was a fulfillment of the prophets. Jesus refers to himself here with the cryptic self-designation "Son of Man," just as he does in the earlier passion predictions (9:22, 44; see the discussion of this title in Commentary on 5:24).

18:32-33. Mark's version of the passion prediction says that the Son of Man will be handed over "to the chief priests and the scribes, and they will condemn him to death" (Mark 10:33 NRSV), but Luke says nothing here about the role of the Jewish religious leaders in the death of Jesus. Instead, Luke moves directly to the role of the Gentiles, who will mock, beat, and kill Jesus. The details of the prediction set it up as a foreshadowing of coming events. Even the first-time reader now knows what is coming and participates helplessly as the narrative moves inexorably toward Jesus' death. The table below reveals the correlation among these verses, the third passion prediction in Mark, and the coming action. References in which there is a corresponding action but no verbal parallel appear in parentheses. Judas hands Jesus over to the authorities. The Jewish leaders then take Jesus to Pilate, who hands him over to be crucified. Several themes run through the references to the Gentiles in Luke. Jesus will fulfill the prophecy of "light for revelation to the Gentiles" (2:32), but "Jerusalem will be trampled on by the Gentiles, until the times of the Gentiles are fulfilled" (21:24). Disciples will not lord it over one another as the rulers of the Gentiles do (22:25). Instead, Jesus commissions the disciples to preach repentance to all nations (24:47).

While this third passion prediction anticipates the mockery of Jesus, which is repeated three times, other terms are used to describe the insulting or reviling of Jesus, and there is no mention of spitting in the Lukan passion narrative. Similarly, Pilate proposes to have Jesus beaten and released (23:22), but the flogging is not recorded

Luke 18:32-33	Mark 10:33-34	Lukan Passion Narrative
handed over	Mark 10:33	22:4, 6, 21, 22, 48; 23:25; 24:7, 20
to Gentiles	Mark 10:33	(23:1, 25)
mocked	Mark 10:34	22:63; 23:11, 36
insulted		(22:65; 23:11)
spat upon	Mark 10:34	only in Matthew and Mark
flogged	Mark 10:34	only in John 19:1; cf. Luke 23:22
killed	Mark 10:34	see 20:14-15; Acts 3:15
the third day	Mark 10:34	24:7, 21, 46
rise again	Mark 10:34	24:7, 46

in Luke (cf. Matt 27:26; Mark 15:15, where "scourge" [φραγελλόω *phragelloō*] occurs; and John 19:1, which has the only other occurrence of "scourge" [μαστιγόω *mastigoō*]). Striking, insulting, and spitting all occur in the words of the servant of the Lord in Isa 50:6, which very likely accounts for their presence in the passion predictions. Elements of traditional accounts of the crucifixion, therefore, are mixed in the passion predictions and in the passion narratives themselves so that the various elements of this passion prediction are not all fulfilled in the action that follows.

Luke changes Mark's "after three days" (Mark 10:34) to "on the third day," but retains the intransitive use of the term used to translate "he will rise again" (ἀνίστημι *anistēmi*). The fulfillment of Jesus' words is underscored not only by the repetition of some of these specific verbs but also by the angelic reminder of the passion predictions in 24:7, the ironic statement by the two on the road to Emmaus that it was now the third day (24:21), and the risen Lord's own allusions in 24:26, 44-46.

18:34. Like the parents of the twelve-year-old Jesus in the Temple, the disciples do not understand what Jesus has just said to them (see 2:50). Similarly, "the things that make for peace" were hidden from those in Jerusalem (19:42). Earlier Jesus warned—but perhaps there is a promise here too—that nothing is now hidden that will not come to light (8:17), and in the next scene, as though a metaphorical fulfillment of this promise, Jesus will give sight to a blind man (18:35-43). The plot functions of these scenes will become evident to the reader in the last chapter of the Gospel, when the meaning of these events is revealed to the disciples: "Then their eyes were opened" (24:31), and "Then he opened their minds to understand the scriptures" (24:45). Sometimes truth has a time lock. Even new wine cannot be drunk before its time!

REFLECTIONS

The third passion prediction is a painful passage. It is loaded with the language of violence: mocking, insulting, spitting, flogging, killing. Each verb is a station for meditation on the *Via Dolorosa*. The way of the cross in Luke illustrates Jesus' superhuman ability to absorb hostility. The hostility toward God's redemptive work in Jesus was prophesied in the infancy narrative and began with the arrest of John the Baptist and the attempted stoning of Jesus at Nazareth. Soon it will erupt in an orgy of violence that will leave Jesus beaten and hanged until dead.

The capacity to absorb hostility, however, is one of the secrets of God's redemptive work. Violence always breeds more violence. Insult is met with insult, spit with spit, blows with blows, and killing with more killing. When those called of God to be his people absorb insult, hostility, and violence without returning it, three things happen: They grow spiritually, the level of violence is reduced, and the violent are transformed by the witness of love. The overcoming of hostility is never easy, however. The provision of forgiveness through the death of Jesus was achieved at infinite cost, and those who pray "Thy kingdom come" must be ready to bear the cost of being a child of the kingdom. Otherwise, how shall God's kingdom come? The pain of the work of the kingdom is not God's arbitrary choice. We cannot blame God of capriciously making it so difficult for good to triumph. Suffering is necessary, and Jesus suffered not because God chose to make it that way but because suffering love and obedience to the call of the kingdom are the only effective means for ending the spiral of violence that grips the violent.

The passion prediction's language of violence, therefore, is not only a call to meditation on the cost of the suffering that Jesus bore for us, but it is also a sobering reminder that when we return violence we add to that suffering. Our calling, on the other hand, is to "take up the cross daily" (9:23) and follow Jesus. When angry persons hurl insults and when those who have been hurt seek to hurt others, who will be for them a witness to the love of the crucified Christ? The church meets to worship the Christ, to bind up wounds, to encourage one another to keep the faith, and to go back into the places where otherwise hostility would destroy human life unchallenged. The experience of the church is that the experience of Christ is our experience also. From this perspective, the passion prediction could just as well be plural rather than singular. All who seek to follow Jesus will find that they are called to absorb hostility in his name. They will be betrayed, insulted, beaten, and at times even killed. But the violence will not triumph. The resurrection of Jesus is God's affirmation that violence will not have the last word. In the end, God's redemptive love will prevail. That is the gospel.

Luke 18:35-43, The Blind Beggar

NIV

35As Jesus approached Jericho, a blind man was sitting by the roadside begging. 36When he heard the crowd going by, he asked what was happening. 37They told him, "Jesus of Nazareth is passing by."

38He called out, "Jesus, Son of David, have mercy on me!"

39Those who led the way rebuked him and told him to be quiet, but he shouted all the more, "Son of David, have mercy on me!"

40Jesus stopped and ordered the man to be brought to him. When he came near, Jesus asked him, 41"What do you want me to do for you?"

"Lord, I want to see," he replied.

42Jesus said to him, "Receive your sight; your faith has healed you." 43Immediately he received his sight and followed Jesus, praising God. When all the people saw it, they also praised God.

NRSV

35As he approached Jericho, a blind man was sitting by the roadside begging. 36When he heard a crowd going by, he asked what was happening. 37They told him, "Jesus of Nazareth[a] is passing by." 38Then he shouted, "Jesus, Son of David, have mercy on me!" 39Those who were in front sternly ordered him to be quiet; but he shouted even more loudly, "Son of David, have mercy on me!" 40Jesus stood still and ordered the man to be brought to him; and when he came near, he asked him, 41"What do you want me to do for you?" He said, "Lord, let me see again." 42Jesus said to him, "Receive your sight; your faith has saved you." 43Immediately he regained his sight and followed him, glorifying God; and all the people, when they saw it, praised God.

[a] Gk the Nazorean

COMMENTARY

Jericho and Bethany are the staging areas for Jesus' entry into Jerusalem. The events that occur in these places set the context and the themes for his arrival in the holy city. In Jericho, Jesus heals the blind man who acclaims him as the son of David. He continues his ministry to the tax collectors by bringing salvation to a chief tax collector, Zacchaeus, and tells the parable of the "talents" (μνᾶ mna). Then he sends two of the disciples to secure a colt for his entry into Jerusalem. These scenes prepare the reader for Jesus' arrival and the disciples' shouts of "Blessed is the king who comes in the name of the Lord!" (19:38).

Luke's account of the healing of the blind man follows Mark's account (10:46-52) closely and has only a few points of contact with Matthew's two accounts of the healings of two blind men (Matt 9:27-31; 20:29-34). In Mark, the healing accounts seem to function metaphorically to demonstrate Jesus' ability to bring understanding to the disciples just as he brings sight to the blind (see Mark 8:22-26; 10:46-52). The first of the Markan healing stories precedes the confession of Peter at Caesarea Philippi, and the second follows the request of James and John for places of honor in the kingdom. Luke omits that scene (Mark 10:35-35) and moves instead directly from the third passion prediction to the healing of the blind man. Significant linkages still connect the scene with the foregoing material in Luke, however. Although Luke regularly portrays the disciples in a more positive light than does Mark, Luke adds the explanation of the disciples' inability to understand (see 18:34). This explanation may well be Luke's substitute for the longer demonstration of the disciples' obduracy in Mark 10:35-45. Significantly, Luke states that these things were "hidden from them." Now he relates Jesus' ability to enable even a blind man to see.

Other linkages with the foregoing material can be seen in the parallel between the disciples' act of preventing the children from coming to Jesus (18:15) and the response of "those who were in front" (which may be a reference to the disciples) who ordered the blind beggar to be silent. In both contexts, the verb is the same; they "sternly ordered" (ἐπιτιμάω *epitimaō*; cf. 18:15, 39), and in both cases they act to stop powerless, marginalized persons from coming to Jesus. In the end, the blind man follows Jesus, something the rich ruler was unable to do, but then, as John Nolland has observed, the blind man had nothing to leave behind (cf. 18:22, 28, 43).[206] The blind beggar, therefore, is an antitype of both the disciples and the rich ruler. He gains his sight (which the disciples will not do until after the resurrection; see 24:31: "Then their eyes were opened") and follows Jesus (which the rich ruler was unable to do).

Jesus' healing of the blind man also fulfills part of the program for his ministry, drawn from Isaiah and announced at Nazareth:

"He has sent me to proclaim
   release to the captives
and recovery of sight to the blind,
   to let the oppressed go free." (4:18)

Although Luke 7:21-22 alludes to other healings, this is the only account of the healing of a blind man in Luke. The stage has been carefully set, therefore, by preceding references so that the reader may hear the overtones of Luke's account of the healing of this blind beggar.

18:35. This verse sets the stage and introduces a new character. Whereas Mark relates the event as Jesus is leaving Jericho, in Luke, Jesus is just arriving at Jericho, a change that Luke may have made in order to place the healing of the blind man before Jesus' meeting with Zacchaeus in Jericho (see 19:1). Earlier Jesus had told a parable about a priest and a Levite who would not stop for a man beside the road because they were on

their way to Jerusalem. The beaten man had been on his way to Jericho (10:30). Now Jesus—on his way to Jerusalem—stops for a man beside the road in Jericho. Earlier Jesus had told the parable of the man who ordered his servant to go out into the streets and lanes and bring in "the poor, the crippled, the blind, and the lame" (14:21). Now Jesus will order his followers to bring the blind man to him. The dishonest steward was too ashamed to beg (see 16:3), but the blind man had no choice.

18:36-37. Luke omits Mark's report that the blind man was named Bartimaeus and revises Mark's account to introduce the crowd in v. 36. The effect of Luke's editing is to concentrate more attention on the designation of Jesus as "the Nazorean" (ὁ Ναζωραῖος *ho Nazōraios*; v. 37). "Nazarene" (Ναζαρηνός *Nazarēnos*) occurs in Mark 1:24; 10:47; 14:67; 16:6 and elsewhere in Luke (4:34; 24:19), and the more Semitic "Nazorean" appears in Matthew (2:23; 26:71), in this passage in Luke, in John (18:5, 7; 19:19), and several times in Acts. Both forms of the word refer to a person from Nazareth, but it has often been suspected that here and elsewhere (e.g., Matt 2:23) the term has a further connotation. The Hebrew word for "Nazirite" (נזיר *nāzîr*), one who had taken a vow of consecration, is similar. The use of the term in Luke, especially, may evoke echoes of the parallels that Luke draws between the births of Jesus and Samuel, the Nazirite (see 1 Sam 2:1-10, 26; Luke 1:46-55; 2:52).[207] More distant is the association with Isa 11:1, which promises a "shoot" (נצר *nēṣer*) "from the stump of Jesse."

18:38-39. Why did the blind man call Jesus "son of David"? Did he see what the sighted persons around him could not see? Was the association communicated by the title "Nazorean"? Was a healer understood to be a son of David, or is the term purely political? In its literary context, which furnishes the most plausible explanation, Luke's use of the word resonates with his notice that Joseph was from the house of David (1:27; cf. 1:69; 3:31) and the promise at Jesus' birth that "the Lord God will give to him the throne of his ancestor David. He will reign over the house of Jacob forever, and of his kingdom there will be no end" (1:32-33). The blind man's

206. John Nolland, *Luke 18:35–24:53*, WBC 35B (Dallas: Word, 1989) 901-2.

207. Raymond E. Brown, *The Birth of the Messiah: A Commentary on the Infancy Narrative in Matthew and Luke* (New York: Doubleday, 1977) 210-11.

use of this title also prepares the reader for the royal overtones of Jesus' entry into Jerusalem and the debate over the designation "Son of David" in 20:41-44.

At the beginning of Luke 18, Jesus promised that God will "grant justice to his chosen ones who cry to him day and night" (18:7; cf. 9:38). Now the blind beggar cries out to Jesus, "Have mercy on me!" It is the same as the desperate plea of the rich man to Abraham (16:24) and the ten lepers (17:13). Just as the disciples had sought to stop those who were bringing the children to Jesus, so also those who went before Jesus ordered the beggar to be silent. Their efforts only provoked the man to "cry out" more insistently. The verb that Luke uses here (κράζω *krazō*) was used earlier to describe the deranged cries of the demon possessed (see 4:41; 9:39). In a reversal of the action of this scene, when the Pharisees later challenge Jesus to order his disciples to be silent, he uses this same verb when he replies "I tell you, if these were silent, the stones would shout out" (19:40).

18:40-42. At Jesus' command, the blind beggar is brought to him. Jesus' question, "What do you want me to do for you?" ironically is verbatim the question with which Jesus responds to James and John in the Markan scene that Luke has omitted (see Mark 10:36, 51). The man's response is that of a beggar, literally, "Lord, that I may see again" (18:41). Jesus' response is equally direct: "See again!" There is no indication of touching, washing, or any other means of healing. Neither is there any indication that Jesus violated the sabbath by performing this healing. Instead, its thematic value lies in another direction. This scene and the next conclude Jesus' ministry to the outcasts, the oppressed, and the overlooked on his journey to Jerusalem. The giving of sight also marks Jesus' fulfillment of the program he set

forth at the outset of his ministry (4:18), and in the immediate context demonstrates the power of God to save those who call out for mercy—like the tax collector who prayed, "God, be merciful to me, a sinner!" (18:13). Jesus then responds: "Your faith has saved you" (cf. 7:50; 8:48; 17:19). What is impossible for human beings is possible for God (18:27). Just as Jesus' response to his pleas for help was twofold, sight and salvation, so also Luke's report of the effect of Jesus' words is twofold. Immediately, the man regained his sight and began to follow Jesus. By following Jesus, the beggar has joined the company of Jesus' disciples on the way to Jerusalem. Others left everything to follow Jesus (see 5:11, 28); this man gained what he wanted most.

18:43. Calling others to follow him was not the ultimate purpose of Jesus' ministry, however. That purpose is signaled by Luke's further description of the blind beggar's response. He followed Jesus, "glorifying God," and all the people "praised God." Both notices contribute to the doxological theme in Luke. Jesus healed by the power of God; the Spirit of the Lord was upon him (4:18), and "the power of the Lord was with him to heal" (5:17). Therefore, the response of the beggar and the crowd, like that of the Samaritan leper who praised God (17:15), not only recognizes that Jesus acted by the power of God but also fulfills his mission to announce God's kingship on earth. The pattern of all the people's praising God because of healing through the mercy of Jesus is itself a vision of the nature of the kingdom. How different this response is from that of the scribes and Pharisees, who were filled with fury when Jesus healed the man with the withered hand (6:11). They discussed what they might do to Jesus; the reader has just been reminded (18:31-34) that the response of the crowd in Jerusalem will be tragically different from the response of this praising crowd.

REFLECTIONS

Miracle stories pose a challenge to readers who harbor doubts about even Jesus' ability to give sight to a blind man simply by commanding him to see again. Some might suggest that persons cured of paralysis (see 5:24-25) actually suffered from psychosomatic disorders, but such a suggestion not only becomes less plausible in the case of blindness but misses the point of the story entirely as well. The healing of the blind man carries important theological freight. It affirms that Jesus acted by the power of God. It declares God's mercy on those who have been damaged or incapacitated by life and by human society and evokes again Jesus' identity as the Son of David. It illustrates the power of pleas for God's mercy and assures us of God's readiness to respond to us when we cry out for mercy. Finally, both the recovery of sight and the people's response of praise to God give us a glimpse of the nature of the kingdom Jesus announced.

The Gospel accounts of the healing of blind men generally play on the recovery of sight as symbolic of Jesus' ability to grant insight and faith sufficient for any challenge. When the blind man in Mark 8 sees but not clearly—just before Peter confesses Jesus' messiahship but fails to understand the suffering that lies ahead—Jesus touches the man's eyes a second time, and he sees clearly. The blind Bartimaeus of Mark 10 gains his sight and follows Jesus on the road to his suffering in Jerusalem. Similarly, the blind man in John 9 comes to faith, while the Pharisees who can see have their blindness exposed.

Luke 19:1-10, Zacchaeus, a Son of Abraham

NIV

19 Jesus entered Jericho and was passing through. [2]A man was there by the name of Zacchaeus; he was a chief tax collector and was wealthy. [3]He wanted to see who Jesus was, but being a short man he could not, because of the crowd. [4]So he ran ahead and climbed a sycamore-fig tree to see him, since Jesus was coming that way.

[5]When Jesus reached the spot, he looked up and said to him, "Zacchaeus, come down immediately. I must stay at your house today." [6]So he came down at once and welcomed him gladly.

[7]All the people saw this and began to mutter, "He has gone to be the guest of a 'sinner.'"

[8]But Zacchaeus stood up and said to the Lord, "Look, Lord! Here and now I give half of my possessions to the poor, and if I have cheated anybody out of anything, I will pay back four times the amount."

[9]Jesus said to him, "Today salvation has come to this house, because this man, too, is a son of Abraham. [10]For the Son of Man came to seek and to save what was lost."

NRSV

19 He entered Jericho and was passing through it. [2]A man was there named Zacchaeus; he was a chief tax collector and was rich. [3]He was trying to see who Jesus was, but on account of the crowd he could not, because he was short in stature. [4]So he ran ahead and climbed a sycamore tree to see him, because he was going to pass that way. [5]When Jesus came to the place, he looked up and said to him, "Zacchaeus, hurry and come down; for I must stay at your house today." [6]So he hurried down and was happy to welcome him. [7]All who saw it began to grumble and said, "He has gone to be the guest of one who is a sinner." [8]Zacchaeus stood there and said to the Lord, "Look, half of my possessions, Lord, I will give to the poor; and if I have defrauded anyone of anything, I will pay back four times as much." [9]Then Jesus said to him, "Today salvation has come to this house, because he too is a son of Abraham. [10]For the Son of Man came to seek out and to save the lost."

COMMENTARY

Luke's account of Jesus entering the house of Zacchaeus stands fittingly as the last of Jesus' encounters with outcasts before his entry into Jerusalem. Earlier, Jesus was mocked as "a friend of tax collectors and sinners" (7:34; see also 5:27-32; 7:29; 15:1-2; 18:9-14). In Luke, the tax collectors function as the prototypical outcasts—those whom Jesus befriends. Roman officials con-tracted with local entrepreneurs to collect the prescribed indirect taxes, tolls, tariffs, and customs fees in a given area. These entrepreneurs, the "chief tax collectors," were required to pay the contract in advance. They would then employ others to collect the taxes with the hope that the amount collected would yield a profit. The sys-tem, not surprising, was open to abuse, and Jews who collected taxes for the Romans were assumed to be dishonest and were hated by other Jews for their complicity with the Gentile oppressors.

Jesus' meeting with Zacchaeus artfully picks up threads of the narrative in the previous chapter. The parable of the Pharisee and the tax collector (18:9-14) turns on the question of righteousness. Jesus declared that "all who humble themselves will be exalted" (18:14), and Zacchaeus cast aside all regard for his own dignity by climbing a tree in order to see Jesus. Jesus challenged the rich ruler to sell all he had and give it to the poor (18:22), but he went away sad. Joyfully, Zacchaeus responds to Jesus' declaration that he would stay at Zacchaeus's house by promising to sell half of his possessions and give the proceeds to the poor. The difference between half and all is not the issue. Rather, it is Zacchaeus's eagerness to do what is right for the poor. Thus the salvation of Zacchaeus is told in the form of a miracle story. Jesus demonstrated the power of God at work in the announcement of the kingdom: "How hard it is for those who have wealth to enter the kingdom of God!" (18:24). Finally, the story of Zacchaeus is coupled with the healing of the blind beggar—both occur as Jesus is passing through Jericho; the blind man wanted to see, and Zacchaeus wanted to see Jesus; in both stories the crowd serves as an impediment to the one who desires to see; in both the verb for "stood" (ἵστημι *istēmi*) marks a dramatic turn in the story (18:40; 19:8); joy or the praise of God accompanies the "healing" (18:43; 19:6); and in both the effect is immediate ("immediately," 18:43; "today," 19:9). In the first story, Jesus is called "Son of David" (18:39); in the latter he refers to himself as "the Son of Man" (19:10).

19:1-2. Whereas the healing of the blind man occurred as Jesus approached Jericho (18:35; cf. Mark 10:46), the encounter with Zacchaeus takes place while Jesus is passing through the town. Zacchaeus's name is introduced by means of an idiom also found in Luke 1:5; 10:38; 16:20; 23:50; and 24:18, and the new character is introduced in stages: a man, named Zacchaeus, a chief tax collector—rich. The emphasis falls heavily on the last word. The rich have not fared well in Luke. Jesus pronounced woes on the rich (6:24). God called the rich farmer a fool (12:16, 20)

and required his soul of him. The rich man went to Hades while Lazarus went to the bosom of Abraham (16:19-31), and Jesus observed how hard it is for the rich to enter the kingdom of God (18:23, 25). The reader may, therefore, initially expect that Jesus is about to meet a person on whom he will pronounce a severe judgment or one whose dishonesty will be dramatically exposed.

19:3-4. On the contrary, this rich man plays the role of the blind man in the previous scene. He desires to see Jesus, but cannot because of the crowd. Zacchaeus was small of stature, so he could neither push his way through the crowd nor see over those in front. Clever and with singular purpose, Zacchaeus ran ahead and climbed a sycamore tree. In doing so, however, he exposed himself to ridicule on two counts. It was considered undignified for a grown man to run, and a man of his importance would certainly not climb a tree. The reader who is attuned to the social codes of the day can imagine the glee of the crowd at seeing the little tax collector running and climbing a tree because he could not get through the crowd.

A sycamore (or sycomore, *Ficus sycomorus*) was a large evergreen tree with large, low branches that would have been ideal for Zacchaeus's purposes. The sycamore produced an inferior type of fig that was consumed by the poor (see Amos 7:14).[208]

19:5-6. The sense of movement is conveyed repeatedly in the two Jericho stories, with recurring references to approaching, going by, passing by, following, entering, passing through, and passing that way. Jesus moves with an entourage of disciples and onlookers around him as he makes his way with intensifying urgency toward Jerusalem and the fate that awaits him there. Zacchaeus's excitement over Jesus' coming is conveyed by his running. Jesus signals the urgency of the kingdom proclamation by commanding Zacchaeus to hurry and come down from the tree. Then, Zacchaeus's receptiveness to Jesus is again conveyed by the report that he "hurried down" and welcomed Jesus, "rejoicing" (χαίρων *chairōn*; cf. the less satisfactory translations in the NRSV and the NIV).

208. See Bruce J. Malina and Richard L. Rohrbaugh, *A Social-Science Commentary on the Synoptic Gospels* (Minneapolis: Fortress, 1992) 386.

In this scene Jesus fulfills the pattern of household evangelism to which he commissioned the disciples earlier (10:5-6). The declarative nature of Jesus' pronouncement is signaled both by the emphatic, initial position of "today"—"Today I must stay in your house" (author's trans.) and by the verb for "must" (δεῖ *dei*), which can be used as a divine imperative—"I must stay at your house."

By staying at Zacchaeus's house, Jesus was again crossing the barrier of ritual purity. A tax collector would regularly be rendered unclean by entering houses and inspecting goods. By entering Zacchaeus's house, Jesus was also acknowledging the chief tax collector's dignity and standing in the community. Jesus, who was being followed by the crowds, would have brought honor to whatever house he entered. Therefore, he conferred a special honor on Zacchaeus by offering to receive hospitality from him. Today, inviting oneself to someone else's home would be a violation of etiquette even for a celebrity. In this case, however, Jesus offered Zacchaeus, who merely wanted to see Jesus, an opportunity to be recognized prominently before the whole community. Jesus was exalting a man who had "stooped" to running and climbing a tree.

19:7. The reactions of both Zacchaeus and the crowd echo the theme of the parables in Luke 15. In Luke 15:1-2, the Pharisees and the scribes were "grumbling" (διαγογγύζω *diagongyzō*) and saying, "This fellow welcomes sinners and eats with them." Jesus responded by telling parables that emphasize the rejoicing that occurs when one that was lost is found (15:5-7, 9-10, 23-24, 32). Here, all who saw what had happened grumbled, while Zacchaeus rejoiced. The blind man had desired to see (18:41), and Zacchaeus had desired to see Jesus (19:3). Now the crowd sees Jesus doing the work of the kingdom, and they grumble. Jesus had declared, "Blessed are the eyes that see what you see!" (10:23), but here are eyes that see but do not see (8:10). All they can see is their predetermined judgment that Zacchaeus is a sinner (19:7).

19:8. The interpretive crux of this story appears in Zacchaeus's declaration in v. 8. The pronouncement is introduced by the report that Zacchaeus "stood up" (*isttēmi*; cf. 18:40). Traditionally, this verse has been read as an indication of the genuineness of Zacchaeus's repentance. Henceforth, he will sell half his possessions and give to the poor, and if he has wronged any, he will repay them four times over. More recently, several interpreters have read this vow as Zacchaeus's protest of the injustice of the crowd's assumption that he is a sinner; he regularly sells half of his goods and gives the proceeds to the poor, and if he has wronged anyone he repays them four times over.[209] The verbs used here are present tense as in the RSV, not future as in the NRSV. Nor are the NIV's "here and now" in the Greek text. The choice between the two interpretations is difficult, however. There is no other indication of Zacchaeus's repentance. Moreover, although the verbs in question are clearly present tense, they may report either Zacchaeus's customary actions or his resolve henceforth to rectify his past injustices. Nevertheless, the latter part of v. 8 tips the interpreter's scales in favor of the traditional reading. Zacchaeus is not protesting his customary action to the disbelieving crowd. Instead, he is freely declaring his resolve to make amends for his past wrongs as a result of the honor that Jesus has bestowed on him. Zacchaeus does not envision the possibility of defrauding others in the future, nor does he regularly defraud others and repay them. Rather, Zacchaeus vows to repay all those whom he has defrauded in the past (and by implication to take care not to defraud anyone else in the future).

Zacchaeus's pledge conforms to both OT laws of restitution and the standard advanced by John the Baptist. Old Testament laws varied, so Zacchaeus offered to follow the most stringent standards. According to Lev 6:5, "you shall repay the principal amount and shall add one-fifth to it. You shall pay it to its owner when you realize your guilt" (NRSV; cf. Num 5:7). If a stolen animal was found alive in the thief's possession, the thief was required to pay double (Exod 22:4). If the stolen animal was slaughtered or sold, the thief was required to pay fivefold for an ox and fourfold for a sheep (Exod 22:1; 2 Sam 12:6). On the other hand, according to later rabbinic interpretation, if a man confessed his guilt, he was not

---

209. The former interpretation is favored by I. Howard Marshall, *The Gospel of Luke*, NIGTC (Grand Rapids: Eerdmans, 1978) 697-98; John Nolland, *Luke 18:35–24:53*, WBC 35C (Dallas: Word, 1993) 906. For the latter interpretation, see Joseph A. Fitzmyer, *The Gospel According to Luke (X–XXIV)*, AB 28A (Garden City, N.Y.: Doubleday, 1985) 1220-22; Malina and Rohrbaugh, *A Social-Science Commentary on the Synoptic Gospels,* 387.

required to pay double, fourfold, or fivefold restitution.[210] Zacchaeus, by contrast, volunteered to repay fourfold.[211]

Similarly, Zacchaeus's pledge conforms to the standards set by John the Baptist: "Whoever has two coats must share with anyone who has none" (3:11)—half of his possessions. Tax collectors should collect no more than the amount prescribed for them (3:13), and soldiers were not to extort money from anyone by threat or false accusation (3:14).

19:9. Jesus responds, confirming Zacchaeus's status as a "son of Abraham," just as he had pronounced the woman freed from her stooped condition a "daughter of Abraham" (13:16). John the Baptist had warned the crowds to bear fruits worthy of repentance and not even to consider saying "we have Abraham as our ancestor" (3:8). Zacchaeus, however, bore fruits worthy of repentance, and Jesus declared that he was a true son of Abraham. Again, it is more likely that Jesus is confirming the change that has occurred in Zacchaeus than that he is defending Zacchaeus as an exemplary rich man. A camel could not pass through the eye of a needle, but God could lead a rich man into the kingdom of God (see 18:25-26), and God could raise up children of Abraham from stones (3:8)—or even from among tax collectors. Zechariah's prophecy has been fulfilled by John, but even more by Jesus; Jesus has become a "horn of salvation" (see 1:69), and he has given "knowledge of salvation to his people" (1:77).

19:10. The hero of the story is Jesus, not Zacchaeus. The last line appropriately returns to the issue of what this scene has revealed about Jesus: "the Son of Man came to seek out and to save the lost." In Ezek 34:16, the Lord declares, "I will seek the lost, and I will bring back the strayed" (NRSV). Again Luke reminds his readers that Jesus fulfills Moses and the prophets (see 24:27, 44). The pattern of his ministry among the lost points to his true identity.

The saying in Luke 19:10 stands midway along the trajectory of related sayings in the NT. In Mark 2:17 and Matt 9:13 Jesus says, "I have come to call not the righteous but sinners." Luke 5:32 adds a further phrase: "I have come to call not the righteous but sinners *to repentance.*" Luke 19:10 adds the title "Son of Man," and gives evidence of reflection on Ezek 34:16 with its use of "seek," the doubling of the verb "to seek and save," and by dropping the tensive "not the righteous but. . . ." The allusion to this saying in 1 Tim 1:15 reflects the complete transformation of the saying from its original tensive form to that of a traditional christological axiom: "Christ Jesus came into the world to save sinners." Here there is no rejection of the "righteous," who might be understood as Christians rather than Pharisees, and Paul (at least the Paul of the Pastoral Epistles) hastens to add, "And I am the foremost of sinners."

The story of Zacchaeus is a tale of unexpected twists and reversals. A chief tax collector embarrasses himself by running and climbing a tree, but Jesus' ministry to the outcast and despised reaches the rich as well as the poor, tax collectors as well as harlots. Jesus has sought out and saved one who was lost. In response to Jesus' bestowal of favor, unexpected and unmerited, the rich tax collector joyfully pledged to bear "fruits worthy of repentance" (3:8). Zacchaeus thought he was seeking to see Jesus (19:3), but in reality Jesus was seeking Zacchaeus (19:10). Thus salvation can come even to the house of tax collector. Zacchaeus just wanted to see Jesus, but like Simeon, by the end of the story he could say to God, "My eyes have seen your salvation" (2:30).

---

210. See *m. Kethub.* 3.9.
211. See Charles H. Talbert, *Reading Luke* (New York: Crossroad, 1982) 176.

REFLECTIONS

1. In an era of overwhelming problems, the believing community can read the story of Zacchaeus as a potent antidote to pessimism. What do you say to those who live under the burden of deadening defeat and deflated dreams? "We can't do anything about it." "Some people will never change." "Nothing exciting ever happens to me."

The Gospel of Mark uses the word for "today" (σήμερον *sēmeron*) only one time (Mark 14:30). Luke uses the term eleven times, often emphatically. The angelic chorus announces gladly, "To you is born *this day* in the city of David a Savior, who is the Messiah, the Lord" (2:11, italics added). In Nazareth, Jesus explains, "Today this scripture has been fulfilled in your hearing" (4:21). When Jesus heals the paralytic, the onlookers glorify God, "We have seen strange things today" (5:26). And to the thief on the cross, Jesus promises, "Truly I tell you, today you will be with me in Paradise" (23:43). The good news Luke declares is the proclamation that God is doing a great thing *today!* This is the time of deliverance and redemption. This is the time to open our eyes and see what God is doing all around us. When even one person is offered forgiveness, hears a word of affirmation, clings to hope that life can be different, or resolves to live by a new set of values in the future, there the kingdom of God is at work.

2. Another of the impediments to the progress of the kingdom is the enslaving prejudice that we know who people are and that they cannot change. In the wisdom of his years, a sophomore writes off a person who has disappointed him and let him down, a pastor gives up on a "dead" congregation, a coach assumes a player cannot make the team in spite of her desire to play, or an employer pigeonholes an employee on their first meeting. Over and over again, we hear the whisper of the crowd: "He's a rich tax collector."

Yet Jesus stopped for a single person. "Today" came for Zacchaeus because he wanted to see so badly that he ran and climbed a sycamore. Today can be filled with joy because God is still at work bringing the kingdom and because words of grace can still be spoken and forgiveness can still be experienced. What outrageous good news—a camel passed through the eye of a needle!

Luke 19:11-27, The Parable of the Greedy and Vengeful King

NIV

[11]While they were listening to this, he went on to tell them a parable, because he was near Jerusalem and the people thought that the kingdom of God was going to appear at once. [12]He said: "A man of noble birth went to a distant country to have himself appointed king and then to return. [13]So he called ten of his servants and gave them ten minas.[a] 'Put this money to work,' he said, 'until I come back.'

[14]"But his subjects hated him and sent a delegation after him to say, 'We don't want this man to be our king.'

[15]"He was made king, however, and returned home. Then he sent for the servants to whom he had given the money, in order to find out what they had gained with it.

[16]"The first one came and said, 'Sir, your mina has earned ten more.'

[17]"'Well done, my good servant!' his master replied. 'Because you have been trustworthy in a very small matter, take charge of ten cities.'

[a]13 A mina was about three months' wages.

NRSV

11As they were listening to this, he went on to tell a parable, because he was near Jerusalem, and because they supposed that the kingdom of God was to appear immediately. [12]So he said, "A nobleman went to a distant country to get royal power for himself and then return. [13]He summoned ten of his slaves, and gave them ten pounds,[a] and said to them, 'Do business with these until I come back.' [14]But the citizens of his country hated him and sent a delegation after him, saying, 'We do not want this man to rule over us.' [15]When he returned, having received royal power, he ordered these slaves, to whom he had given the money, to be summoned so that he might find out what they had gained by trading. [16]The first came forward and said, 'Lord, your pound has made ten more pounds.' [17]He said to him, 'Well done, good slave! Because you have been trustworthy in a very small thing, take charge of ten cities.' [18]Then the second came, saying, 'Lord, your pound has made five pounds.'

[a]The mina, rendered here by *pound,* was about three months' wages for a laborer

NIV

18"The second came and said, 'Sir, your mina has earned five more.'

19"His master answered, 'You take charge of five cities.'

20"Then another servant came and said, 'Sir, here is your mina; I have kept it laid away in a piece of cloth. 21I was afraid of you, because you are a hard man. You take out what you did not put in and reap what you did not sow.'

22"His master replied, 'I will judge you by your own words, you wicked servant! You knew, did you, that I am a hard man, taking out what I did not put in, and reaping what I did not sow? 23Why then didn't you put my money on deposit, so that when I came back, I could have collected it with interest?'

24"Then he said to those standing by, 'Take his mina away from him and give it to the one who has ten minas.'

25" 'Sir,' they said, 'he already has ten!'

26"He replied, 'I tell you that to everyone who has, more will be given, but as for the one who has nothing, even what he has will be taken away. 27But those enemies of mine who did not want me to be king over them—bring them here and kill them in front of me.'"

NRSV

19He said to him, 'And you, rule over five cities.' 20Then the other came, saying, 'Lord, here is your pound. I wrapped it up in a piece of cloth, 21for I was afraid of you, because you are a harsh man; you take what you did not deposit, and reap what you did not sow.' 22He said to him, 'I will judge you by your own words, you wicked slave! You knew, did you, that I was a harsh man, taking what I did not deposit and reaping what I did not sow? 23Why then did you not put my money into the bank? Then when I returned, I could have collected it with interest.' 24He said to the bystanders, 'Take the pound from him and give it to the one who has ten pounds.' 25(And they said to him, 'Lord, he has ten pounds!') 26I tell you, to all those who have, more will be given; but from those who have nothing, even what they have will be taken away. 27But as for these enemies of mine who did not want me to be king over them—bring them here and slaughter them in my presence.'"

COMMENTARY

Although this parable is related to the parable of the talents in Matt 25:14-30, its distinctive features and its context in Luke make it an entirely different story. The Matthean parable is about the stewardship of what is entrusted to a disciple. The Lukan parable, however, contrasts the coming of the kingdom of God with the typical pattern of the establishment of a political kingdom. Thus the greedy and vengeful king of this parable serves as an antitype for Jesus as he enters Jerusalem as "the king who comes in the name of the Lord" (19:38).

In the Matthean parable of the talents, the master is not a king, nor is the reason for his journey explained. He entrusts his property to three servants, giving them five talents, two talents, and one talent respectively. A talent was a great deal of money, the equivalent of 6,000

denarii, or at a denarius a day, for 300 days a year, 20 years' income for a common laborer. The first two servants double the amount entrusted to them; the last buries his talent in the ground. When the master returns and calls the servants to give an account, the first two are praised while the last is called a "wicked and lazy slave" (Matt 25:26). Because he did not at least invest it with bankers, the talent is taken from him and given to the one with ten talents. In Matthew the parable follows immediately after Jesus' warning, "Keep awake therefore, for you know neither the day nor the hour" (Matt 25:13 NRSV) and is in turn followed by the parable of the sheep and the goats in Matt 25:31-46. In this context, therefore, the parable of the talents serves as a warning for disciples to work diligently because they will be called to give an account of what has been given to them—and they do not know when the judgment may come.

In Luke, the parable follows Jesus' declaration to Zacchaeus that "today salvation has come . . ." (19:9) and comes just before Jesus' entry into Jerusalem. It contributes to the kingship motif of this section of the Gospel (cf. 21:12; 22:25; 23:2-3, 37-38). Jesus has been hailed as "son of David" (18:38) and will be greeted as a king when he enters Jerusalem (19:38). The parable features not just a master but also one who went on a journey to be appointed king. "A certain man" (a favorite Lukan expression) travels to a "distant country" (19:12), and the Lukan reader knows that nothing good happens in a "distant country" (cf. 15:13). The man summons ten servants and gives each of them one pound—one mina. A mina was only one sixtieth of a talent, worth 100 denarii—a very small amount for a king, but a lot for a servant. The citizens of his country send a delegation to protest his appointment as king. Upon his return, the king settles matters with his servants. One servant has made ten pounds, and the king gives him ten cities. The second had made five pounds, so the king gives him five cities. The third returns the pound he had wrapped in a piece of cloth, saying he knew the king to be a harsh man. The king replies that the man has judged himself by his own words, takes the pound from him, and gives it to the servant who had ten pounds. When the bystanders protest, the king replies that more will be given to those who have and that from those who have nothing, even the little they have will be taken away. As a final act of vengeance, the king commands that those who had opposed him be brought and slaughtered before him.

This parable cannot have the same meaning as the Matthean parable of the talents. It features not a lesson on responsibility and stewardship but a portrait of greed and vengeance. The king is acquisitive. He seeks a royal title and expects others to multiply his property five and tenfold. Readers in an entrepreneurial society will not immediately recognize the social codes invoked by this parable. Our society functions with an economics of unlimited goods. The American dream affirms that anyone who is sufficiently ambitious, industrious, clever, or fortunate can start from nothing and become fabulously wealthy. In the process, he or she may even create

jobs for others. First-century Mediterranean culture, in contrast, functioned with an economics of limited goods. There was only so much wealth or property to go around, so if anyone acquired more property, others lost it. This king was greedy and acquisitive, seeking power and taking property. A peasant audience would identify with the fear of the third servant and the bystanders' protest of this redistribution of wealth. The protest only leads the king to call for the fulfillment of the common proverb that "the rich get richer and the poor get poorer." If a chief tax collector was hated and condemned as a sinner, how much more this greedy king!

The parable, consequently, employs what we may call a cultural type scene.[212] A type scene incorporates such familiar elements that the audience recognizes the pattern and anticipates the outcome. The storyteller's art, therefore, is evident in the subtle variations and departures from the pattern. The cultural type scene employed by this parable consists of three elements, all of which are distinctive to the Lukan parable form: (1) A throne claimant travels to a distant country to secure the title "king"; (2) the citizens of his country send a delegation to oppose the conferral of royal power on him; and (3) when the throne claimant returns, he rewards those who have served him well and slaughters his enemies.

The currency of this cultural type scene is clearly documented by Josephus. At various times a ruler had traveled to Rome to seek the title "king." First, following the death of his brother Phasel, Herod traveled to Alexandria, where he was received by Cleopatra. From there he sailed to Rome to seek aid from Antony. Earlier, a delegation of Jews had brought accusations against Phasel and Herod.[213] Because of his gratitude for the hospitality of Antipater (Herod's father), aversion to Antigonus (Herod's opponent), and concern to repulse the Parthians, Antony led the Roman senate to declare Herod King of Judea in 40 BCE, although he did not gain control of the region until 37 BCE.[214] Herod proceeded to estab-

---

212. The term *cultural type scene* was suggested to me by my colleague Mikeal Parsons. For the use of type scenes in biblical literature, see Robert Alter, *The Art of Biblical Narrative* (New York: Basic Books, 1981) 47-62. In this instance, the type scene does not draw from a common literary pattern but a pattern created by recurring events in the contemporary cultural context.

213. Josephus *Antiquities of the Jews* 14.302.

214. Josephus *The Jewish War* 1.279-85.

lish his control over his unruly kingdom by putting his adversaries to the sword. When the followers of Antigonus sought refuge in the caves of Galilee, Herod lowered men in baskets over the side of the cliff and burned the rebels out.[215] Josephus sums up Herod's reprisals in Jerusalem as follows: "King Herod, discriminating between the two classes of the city population, by the award of honours attached more closely to himself those who had espoused his cause, while he exterminated the partisans of Antigonus."[216]

A generation later Archelaus and Antipas, Herod's sons, each sought control over Judea. The events that followed parallel the action of the parable so closely that they probably inspired this version of the parable. Archelaus and Antipas each traveled to Rome to appeal to Caesar. After Archelaus departed from Judea, the Jews revolted—"the whole nation became unruly."[217] A Jewish delegation opposed Archelaus because of his ruthless cruelty and greed: "He had indeed reduced the entire nation to helpless poverty after taking it over in as flourishing a condition as few ever know, and he was wont to kill members of the nobility upon absurd pretexts and then take their property for himself."[218] Among other atrocities, Archelaus had slaughtered 3,000 of his countrymen in the Temple precinct. After hearing both sides, Caesar appointed Archelaus tetrarch of Judea and Idumea and split the remainder of Herod the Great's kingdom between Archelaus's brothers, Antipas and Philip.[219] Eventually, the Romans deposed Archelaus because of his excessive cruelty.

Some years later, after Jesus' death but before the Gospel was written, Agrippa was made king of part of Herod's kingdom. Herodias prompted Herod Antipas to request the title of king also, saying, "Come, let us go to Rome; let us spare neither pains nor expense of silver and gold, since there is no better use for which we might hoard them than to expend them on the acquisition of a kingdom."[220] Agrippa, however, sent emissaries to oppose Antipas's petition. As a result, instead of extending Antipas's powers, the emperor deposed him and banished both Antipas and Herodias to Lyons in Gaul.[221] These examples confirm that a story of an ambitious ruler's departing to seek the title king, opposition by his countrymen, and then brutal reprisals against his enemies would have been readily understood by both the crowds in Jericho and by Luke's first readers.

The parable's use of this cultural type scene rules out any possibility of interpreting the parable as an allegory in which the king represents either God or Jesus. On the contrary, placed just before Jesus' entry into Jerusalem, the parable establishes the common pattern of kingship so that the distinctive features of Jesus' kingship (and the kingdom of God) can stand in relief against the common pattern of kingship. In scenes following Jesus' arrival in Jerusalem, he will warn his disciples that they will be brought before kings and governors (21:12), but they should not be afraid. The kings of the Gentiles lord it over them, and those in authority are called benefactors, but it shall not be so among Jesus' followers (22:25-26). A delegation brought Jesus to Pilate and accused him of perverting the nation (23:1-3), and Jesus died under the inscription, "This is the King of the Jews" (23:38). Thus the greedy and vengeful king in the parable, who conforms to the contemporary pattern of kingship, serves as the antitype for Jesus' kingship.

The parable underscores not the similarity between the king's servants and the followers of Jesus but the contrast between such a king and the kingdom of God. The king condemns the third servant as wicked (19:22), but Luke introduced the Gospel with a reference to "King Herod of Judea" (1:5) and alluded to the wicked things Herod had done (3:19). The reversal is subtle but unmistakable. When the wicked king rewards servants for their acquisition of property and condemns the third servant as wicked, the reader knows that the servant and the bystanders who protest his punishment are not wicked but righteous.

On the other hand, Jesus too has been on a journey, and he is on his way to Jerusalem where he will be hailed as a king. He will confront the authorities in the Temple and condemn the scribes who "devour widows' houses" (20:47). He will praise the widow who gives two copper coins

215. Josephus *The Jewish War* 1.307-16; *Antiquities of the Jews* 14.423-33.

216. Josephus *The Jewish War* 1.358.

217. Josephus *The Jewish War* 2.15, 18; *Antiquities of the Jews* 17.224, 250.

218. Josephus *The Jewish War* 2.80; *Antiquities of the Jews* 17.299, 304, 307.

219. Josephus *Antiquities of the Jews* 17.237, 313, 317-18; *The Jewish War* 2.89, 93-94.

220. Josephus *Antiquities of the Jews* 18.244.

221. Josephus *Antiquities of the Jews* 18.240-56; *The Jewish War* 2.181-83.

(21:1-4) and announce the imminent destruction of the city (21:20-24).

The parable, therefore, invites reflection on what it means to claim Jesus as "the king who comes in the name of the Lord" (19:38). The norm of royal retribution applies: Every king rewards those who serve him well and punishes his enemies. But in Jesus' kingdom the standards for reward and punishment are reversed. The enemies of the kingdom of God will be punished no less severely than if they had opposed one of the Herods, but in God's kingdom the greedy will be driven out of the Temple and the generous will be rewarded. If we can learn a lesson from a dishonest steward (see 16:1-8), then we can also learn from the story of a vengeful and greedy king.

The parable of the vengeful king graphically reminds the crowds in Jericho that the kingdom has not yet come (see 19:11). The protest of the bystanders is a call for justice, an encouragement for those who are committed to God's kingdom to join the bystanders in opposing the wicked king.

REFLECTIONS

This is a difficult parable and is made more difficult because we are accustomed to reading it as having the same sense as the parable of the talents in Matthew. Luke's parable contains elements of both the parable of the talents and the story of a king's vengeance on those who oppose him. It will not do to disregard either story as a corruption of an earlier parable or as a later redaction. The interpreter must deal with the text at hand and understand it in its present literary context.

The parable creates dissonance because it invites reflection on Jesus' role as a king, when kings were uniformly corrupt, greedy, and violent. Jesus' disciples can neither follow such a king nor understand their role as that of stewards or slaves of such a king. The value system of Jesus' kingdom is diametrically opposed to that of the kingdom in this parable. On the other hand, the law of retribution still applies, for those who serve God faithfully will be rewarded, and those who resist God's kingly rule will perish.

The kingdom will not appear immediately (19:11). Disciples, therefore, are called to be trustworthy while they wait for the coming of the king. They are to advance the king's interests, but rather than contributing to greed and the oppression of the poor by adding to the wealth of the wealthy, they will find it necessary to echo the protest of the bystanders. Read in this way, the parable calls for faithful allegiance to a king whose kingdom is opposed to the quests of earthly kings for vengeance and profit at the expense of the poor.

What should we say, for example, when those who have access to medical care protest the expense of providing medical care for those who have none? "Lord, they already have. . . . "? What should we say when municipalities channel funds for road repair, police protection, or school equipment to well-to-do neighborhoods while neglecting the needs in other areas? "Lord, they already have. . . . "? What should we say when regressive taxes are proposed that protect the assets of the wealthy at the expense of the poor? "Lord . . . "?

JESUS' MINISTRY IN JERUSALEM

OVERVIEW

The next major section of the Gospel features Jesus teaching in the Temple. It opens with Jesus' entry into Jerusalem (19:28-40) and his weeping over the city (19:41-44) and cleansing the Temple so that it may serve as the site for his messianic teaching (19:45-47). Luke distinguishes the people, who hear Jesus gladly, from their leaders, who seek to trap him with their questions in 20:1-40. Following Jesus' explanation about the Davidic sonship of the Messiah (20:41-44), his denunciation of the scribes (20:45-47), and his commendation of the widow (21:1-4), his teaching turns toward coming events. Jesus foretells the destruction of the Temple, the persecution of his followers, the destruction of Jerusalem, and the coming of the Son of Man in 21:5-36. A Lukan summary statement (21:37-38) regarding Jesus' teaching in the Temple balances a similar statement in 19:45-47 and provides a sense of closure for this section of the Gospel.

LUKE 19:28-40, THE ENTRANCE PROCESSION OF THE KING

NIV

28After Jesus had said this, he went on ahead, going up to Jerusalem. 29As he approached Bethphage and Bethany at the hill called the Mount of Olives, he sent two of his disciples, saying to them, 30"Go to the village ahead of you, and as you enter it, you will find a colt tied there, which no one has ever ridden. Untie it and bring it here. 31If anyone asks you, 'Why are you untying it?' tell him, 'The Lord needs it.'"

32Those who were sent ahead went and found it just as he had told them. 33As they were untying the colt, its owners asked them, "Why are you untying the colt?"

34They replied, "The Lord needs it."

35They brought it to Jesus, threw their cloaks on the colt and put Jesus on it. 36As he went along, people spread their cloaks on the road.

37When he came near the place where the road goes down the Mount of Olives, the whole crowd of disciples began joyfully to praise God

NRSV

28After he had said this, he went on ahead, going up to Jerusalem.

29When he had come near Bethphage and Bethany, at the place called the Mount of Olives, he sent two of the disciples, 30saying, "Go into the village ahead of you, and as you enter it you will find tied there a colt that has never been ridden. Untie it and bring it here. 31If anyone asks you, 'Why are you untying it?' just say this, 'The Lord needs it.'" 32So those who were sent departed and found it as he had told them. 33As they were untying the colt, its owners asked them, "Why are you untying the colt?" 34They said, "The Lord needs it." 35Then they brought it to Jesus; and after throwing their cloaks on the colt, they set Jesus on it. 36As he rode along, people kept spreading their cloaks on the road. 37As he was now approaching the path down from the Mount of Olives, the whole multitude of the disciples began to praise God joyfully with a loud

NIV

in loud voices for all the miracles they had seen:

³⁸"Blessed is the king who comes in the name of
    the Lord!"ᵃ

"Peace in heaven and glory in the highest!"

³⁹Some of the Pharisees in the crowd said to
Jesus, "Teacher, rebuke your disciples!"

⁴⁰"I tell you," he replied, "if they keep quiet,
the stones will cry out."

ᵃ38 Psalm 118:26

NRSV

voice for all the deeds of power that they had
seen, ³⁸saying,

    "Blessed is the king
        who comes in the name of the Lord!
    Peace in heaven,
        and glory in the highest heaven!"

³⁹Some of the Pharisees in the crowd said to him,
"Teacher, order your disciples to stop." ⁴⁰He answered, "I tell you, if these were silent, the stones
would shout out."

COMMENTARY

The announcement of Jesus' arrival in the vicinity of Jerusalem brings Luke's long travel narrative (9:51–19:27) to a close. Jesus' approach to
Jerusalem was signaled by the third passion prediction (18:31-34), two scenes in Jericho (18:35-
43; 19:1-10), and the parable of the greedy and
vengeful king (19:11-27). Jesus told the parable
"because he was near Jerusalem, and because they
supposed that the kingdom of God was to appear
immediately" (19:11), and 19:28 again reports his
movement toward Jerusalem. Whereas the story
of Jesus' encounter with Lazarus and the parable
that follows it have been inserted in the Markan
outline, Luke takes up Mark again at this point,
adapting Mark's account for his own purposes.

The theme of Jesus' kingship has also been established by use of the title "Son of David" (18:38-39)
and by the use of the cultural type scene of a throne
claimant in the parable of the greedy and vengeful
king. Luke's account of Jesus' entry into the city
continues the theme of royalty. At its high point,
Jesus is hailed "king," a title that Luke adds to the
quotation of Ps 118:26.

Entrance processions were a familiar ceremony in
the first century. Numerous kings and conquering
generals had entered Jerusalem over the years. Although the welcoming ceremony of a conqueror and
the celebration of the return of a victorious general
can be distinguished from each other, they share similar
features. Paul Brooks Duff has summarized the characteristic pattern of an entrance procession as follows:

In such Greco-Roman entrance processions we
have seen the following elements: (1) The con-

queror/ruler is escorted into the city by the citizenry
or the army of the conqueror. (2) The procession is
accompanied by hymns and/or acclamations. (3)
The Roman triumph has shown us that various
elements in the procession . . . symbolically depict
the authority of the ruler. (4) The entrance is
followed by a ritual of appropriation, such as sacrifice, which takes place in the temple, whereby the
ruler symbolically appropriates the city.²²²

As examples of this pattern, Duff cites Josephus's
account of Alexander the Great's entrance into
Jerusalem and Plutarch's description of Antony's
entry into Ephesus:

Then all the Jews together greeted Alexander
with one voice and surrounded him . . . [then]
he gave his hand to the high priest and, with
the Jews running beside him, entered the city.
Then he went up to the temple where he
sacrificed to God under the direction of the high
priest.²²³

When Antony made his entrance into Ephesus,
women arrayed like Baccanals, and men and
boys like satyrs and Pans, led the way before
him, and the city was full of ivy and thyrsus-
wands and harps and pipes and flutes, the people
hailing him as Dionysius Giver of Joy and Be-
neficent. For he was such undoubtedly, to
some.²²⁴

222. Paul Brooks Duff, "The March of the Divine Warrior and the
Advent of the Greco-Roman King: Mark's Account of Jesus' Entry into
Jerusalem," *JBL* 111 (1992) 66. A similar pattern has been observed by
David R. Catchpole, "The 'Triumphal' Entry," in *Jesus and the Politics of
His Day,* ed. Ernst Bammel and C. F. D. Moule (Cambridge: Cambridge
University Press, 1984) 319-21.
223. Josephus, *Antiquities of the Jews,* 11.332-36, trans. Ralph Mar-
cus, LCL (Cambridge, Mass.: Harvard University Press, 1937) 475, 477.
224. Plutarch, *Antonius,* 24.3-4, trans. Bernadotte Perrin, LCL (Cambridge, Mass.: Harvard University Press, 1920) 187-89.

In significant respects, Luke's account of Jesus' entry into Jerusalem conforms to the pattern identified above. (1) Jesus is escorted into Jerusalem by people who spread their cloaks on the road (v. 36) and by "the whole multitude of the disciples" (v. 37). (2) The procession is accompanied by hymns of acclamation, in this case a verse from the Hallel psalms (Ps 118:26). (3) Various elements of the procession depict the authority of Jesus; Jesus' divine knowledge is illustrated by his commanding the disciples to bring the colt, the spreading of cloaks on the road, praise of God for Jesus' "deeds of power," and praise of Jesus as the bringer of peace and glory in heaven. (4) Jesus' appropriation of the city is accomplished by his prophetic act of weeping over the city, his oracle of destruction, his entry into the Temple as God's emissary, and the act of driving out the merchants from the Temple area. Like the parable of the greedy and vengeful king, therefore, Luke's account of Jesus' entry into Jerusalem makes use of a well-established type scene. Once more, the nuances of Luke's account will be found in the details and distinctive elements of the story.

Jesus' approach to the city is emphasized by the repeated use of the verb for "to draw near" (ἐγγίζω *engizō*) in this part of the narrative (see 19:11, 29, 37, 41). Bethphage and Bethany were villages on the Mount of Olives. Bethphage means "house of unripe figs," but Bethany may mean "House of Ananiah," "house of the poor," or "house of dates." The specification that Jesus and his followers were on the Mount of Olives may connect with the reference to the Mount of Olives in Zechariah: "On that day his feet shall stand on the Mount of Olives, which lies before Jerusalem on the east. . . . Then the LORD my God will come, and all the holy ones with him" (Zech 14:4-5 NRSV).

Jesus' preparation for the entrance procession—sending two disciples to bring a donkey on which he can ride—is reported in unusual detail in six verses. The meaning of this event lies in what it contributes to the characterization of Jesus, which is conveyed in part by reflection on Zech 9:9-10 (NRSV):

> Rejoice greatly, O daughter Zion!
>   Shout aloud, O daughter Jerusalem!
> Lo, your king comes to you;
>   triumphant and victorious is he,
> humble and riding on a donkey,
>   on a colt, the foal of a donkey.

> He will cut off the chariot from Ephraim
>   and the war horse from Jerusalem;
> and the battle bow shall be cut off,
>   and he shall command peace to the nations;
> his dominion shall be from sea to sea,
>   and from the River to the ends of the earth.

Matthew 21:5 quotes Zech 9:9, but even without the quotation, it is clear that reflection on this verse has colored this account. Both passages identify the animal as "a young donkey" (πῶλος *pōlos*). Balancing Jesus' burial in a new tomb at the end of the passion narrative (Luke 23:53) is the report that Jesus enters Jerusalem on a donkey on which no one has previously sat—another detail that links the reported action with this OT reference. The choice of a donkey rather than a horse probably signals Jesus' humility. In contrast to a typical processional entrance, Jesus rides a donkey rather than a war horse. He will also be hailed as the bringer of peace. More tenuously, early in Acts Jesus commissions the disciples to be his witnesses "to the end of the earth" (Acts 1:8 NRSV; cf. Isa 49:6; Acts 13:47. The Greek of Zech 9:10 LXX, however, is different from the Greek phrase in these verses).

The carefully orchestrated securing of the donkey is probably meant to convey Jesus' foreknowledge of these events. Rationalizing explanations suggesting that Jesus had previously arranged for the use of the donkey might explain Jesus' ability to tell the disciples where the donkey would be tied, but hardly do justice to the instruction he gives the disciples regarding what they are to say when they are challenged by its owners. Again, the detail and the repetition of the declaration "The Lord needs it" suggest that these words convey a christological affirmation. The events are unfolding according to God's foreordained redemptive purposes—as will all that follows. They fulfill the Scriptures, and they point to Jesus' messianic identity—the donkey is tied as in Gen 49:11, which follows the declaration that "the scepter shall not depart from Judah,/ nor the ruler's staff from between his feet,/ until tribute comes to him;/ and the obedience of the peoples is his" (Gen 49:10 NRSV); and Jesus rides on a donkey, just as Solomon did before he was crowned king (see 1 Kgs 1:33-37). The spreading of garments before Jesus' path was another sign of acclamation (2 Kgs 9:13),[225] but Luke omits the reference to gathering leafy branches from the fields (see Mark 11:8).

225. See also Josephus *Antiquities of the Jews* 9.111.

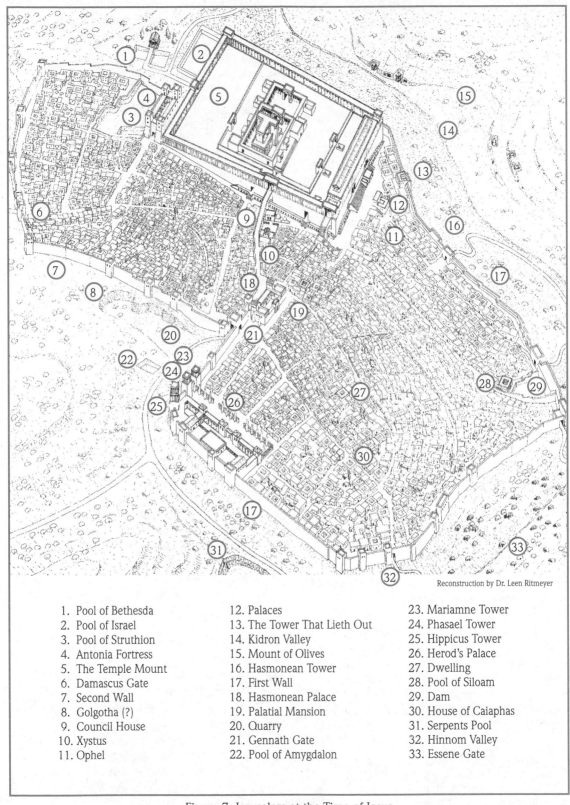

1. Pool of Bethesda	12. Palaces	23. Mariamne Tower
2. Pool of Israel	13. The Tower That Lieth Out	24. Phasael Tower
3. Pool of Struthion	14. Kidron Valley	25. Hippicus Tower
4. Antonia Fortress	15. Mount of Olives	26. Herod's Palace
5. The Temple Mount	16. Hasmonean Tower	27. Dwelling
6. Damascus Gate	17. First Wall	28. Pool of Siloam
7. Second Wall	18. Hasmonean Palace	29. Dam
8. Golgotha (?)	19. Palatial Mansion	30. House of Caiaphas
9. Council House	20. Quarry	31. Serpents Pool
10. Xystus	21. Gennath Gate	32. Hinnom Valley
11. Ophel	22. Pool of Amygdalon	33. Essene Gate

Reconstruction by Dr. Leen Ritmeyer

Figure 7: Jerusalem at the Time of Jesus

The presence of the multitude of disciples evokes echoes of the "multitude of the heavenly host" at the birth of Jesus (2:13), the multitude of the people Jesus taught in Galilee (6:17), the multitude from the region of Gerasa (8:37), and the multitude that will take Jesus to Pilate and follow him to the place of crucifixion (23:1, 27). Joy and the praise of God often accompany the great events of God's salvation in Luke. The multitude of the heavenly host and then the shepherds praised God at the birth of Jesus (2:13, 20), and the disciples' praise in this context serves as an antiphonal response to the heavenly chorus. The crowd following Jesus through Jericho had responded with praise to Jesus' healing of the blind man (18:43), and the Gospel will end with the disciples praising God in the Temple (24:53). Praise is, therefore, the natural response of gratitude and awe from those who have witnessed God's redemptive power at work. Unlike Mark, however, the crowd does not hail Jesus' arrival with "Hosannas" (cf. Mark 11:9-10).

The kingship motif that is implicit in the details of the processional entrance to this point becomes explicit in the praise of the multitude:

> "*Blessed* is the king
> who comes in the name of the Lord!
> Peace in heaven,
> and glory in the highest heaven!" (Luke 19:38)

The verse is drawn from one of the Hallel psalms (Ps 118:26), which was used to welcome pilgrims coming to Jerusalem for the pilgrimage festivals. Luke, however, has added both the royal title "the king" and the last couplet. The insertion of the title contributes significantly to the kingship motif developed by the acclamation of Jesus as the "Son of David" in Jericho (18:38-39), the parable of the greedy and vengeful king (19:11-27), and by the overtones of the entrance procession. The last couplet echoes the words of the heavenly host at Jesus' birth (2:14). Now, Jesus is hailed as the bringer of "peace in heaven" and "glory in the highest heaven." Jesus' reign as king will bring shalom on the earth and glory to God.

The first sign of opposition to Jesus in Jerusalem arises in the response of the Pharisees to the spectacle of Jesus' approach to the city. They order Jesus to rebuke his disciples—and thereby reject their accolades. Jesus, however, responds with an allusion to Habakkuk's words of judgment:

> "Alas for you who get evil gain for your houses,
> setting your nest on high
> to be safe from the reach of harm!"
> You have devised shame for your house
> by cutting off many peoples;
> you have forfeited your life.
> The very stones will cry out from the wall,
> and the plaster will respond from the woodwork."
> (Hab 2:9-11 NRSV)

Jesus' response also echoes John the Baptist's warning that "God is able from these stones to raise up children to Abraham" (3:8) and prepares the reader for the full import of Jesus' announcement that "they will not leave within you one stone upon another; because you did not recognize the time of your visitation from God" (19:44). This ominous warning is all the more devastating because this is the last reference to the Pharisees in Luke. They have consistently opposed Jesus. Now they are silenced and pass from the scene. If the people did not cry out in praise, God could raise up another people to fulfill God's purposes—even from the stones.

Old Testament allusions inform each section of this narrative.

The Place	the Mount of Olives	Zech 14:4
The Preparation	securing the donkey	Gen 49:10-11
The Procession	riding on the donkey	Zech 9:9-10
		1 Kgs 1:33-37
	garments strewn	2 Kgs 9:13
The Proclamation	the Hallel	Ps 118:26
The Pharisees' Response	the stones	Hab 2:11

Part of Luke's art as an evangelist and storyteller is evident in his use of OT allusions and quotations as commentary on the significance of the events being narrated. Why was Jesus' entrance procession different from that of other pilgrims arriving in Jerusalem for the Passover? His entrance followed the pattern of the ceremony for welcoming a conquering king, but the allusions to Scripture confirm that Jesus comes to bring peace. Like the parable of the greedy and vengeful king (19:11-27), therefore, Jesus' entry into Jerusalem serves to confirm his kingship while setting Jesus apart from any earthly king.

REFLECTIONS

For many of us, the excitement of a parade is a secondhand, vicarious experience. We go to parades to watch others, especially children, enjoying the parade, but Jesus' entry into Jerusalem stirs emotions that should not be denied. It was a moment filled with possibility. The thought of what might be exhilarated all who followed Jesus. Might this be the king who would deliver them from the Romans? Might this be the Messiah who would usher in the blessing of the age to come and the return of all the children of God who had been scattered abroad? This was the moment on which the wheel of history would turn. Either God's kingdom would be established on earth, or the people's hope would be forever shattered.

Entrance processions were a familiar ceremony in the first century. Many anointed kings and conquering generals had entered Jerusalem over the years, but never had they seen a king like this one. The triumphal entry, staged on a donkey, is a prophetic sign, an acted-out parable. In the Gospels, something is always out of place—the rich fool dies; the neighbor is a Samaritan; the publican goes down from the Temple justified—and now the king enters the city riding on a borrowed donkey.

Jesus was a king, but no ordinary one—the king of fishermen, tax collectors, Samaritans, harlots, blind men, demoniacs, and cripples. Those who followed Jesus were a ragtag bunch, pathetically unfit for the grand hopes that danced in their imaginations. There were women who now leaped with joy, a Samaritan leper with a heart full of gratitude, a crippled woman who had been unable to stand straight with dignity for eighteen years, and a blind man who had followed Jesus all the way from Jericho.

The cloaks thrown on the road that day were not expensive garments but tattered shawls and dusty, sweat-stained rags. Jesus was the king of the oppressed and suffering. He shared their hardships, relieved their suffering, accepted them when others deemed them unacceptable, gave them hope, and embodied God's love for them. Now they came to march with him into the holy city. Only a few days later, on their way home, they would say to one another, "But we had hoped that he was the one to redeem Israel" (24:21).

Jesus' entry into Jerusalem was a moment filled with fragile possibility. Their last hope was riding on that borrowed donkey. Oh, what might have been! Everything was just right—if only Jesus had seized the moment; if only the people of Jerusalem had responded as they should have; if only God had fulfilled the dreams of those who followed Jesus. Life is filled with moments of what might have been—moments when everything seems right, but then it just doesn't work out as we had hoped. It can be so hard to go on believing in God when life doesn't give us what matters so dearly to us, but there is always a danger when we attempt to chart the course for what God will do. God was about to do something powerful and wonderful—but that day the disciples were not looking for a different kind of king. Their imaginations anticipated a far more limited kind of kingdom, but God had a different way.

It is so easy to project false images of the Lord we worship, to make for ourselves a king whom we can worship rather than to worship the Christ as our king. We construct cults to the god who is always on our side and looks after our interests rather than those of our adversaries and enemies. We desire a God who promises health and prosperity, and so we join the train of those whose worship is false because they do not know that the kingdom of God belongs to a different kind of king.

Lord John Culpepper was witness to a dramatic turn of events in English history. He was a member of the privy council of King Charles I, who was executed in 1649, apparently contrary to the law and the will of the Parliament. John Culpepper was entrusted with the safety of Charles II and accompanied him into exile during twelve years of Oliver Cromwell's reforms, experiments, excesses, and bloodshed. Then, in 1660, six weeks before John

Culpepper's death, Charles II returned from exile. The cry "Habemus rei! We have a king!" rose from the people. Sir Winston Churchill wrote in his *History of the English Speaking Peoples*: "It was most plainly the wish of the people that the King should 'enjoy his own again.' This simple phrase sprung from the heart of the common folk. . . . It was carried . . . on the wings of a joyous melody from village to village and manor to manor." On May 25, 1660, Charles II landed at Dover and was escorted in triumphal procession to London. Churchill described the scene: "All classes crowded to welcome the King home to his own. They cheered and wept in uncontrollable emotion. They felt themselves delivered from a nightmare. They now dreamed they had entered a Golden Age. . . . It was England's supreme day of joy."[226]

Do we yearn, deep in our souls, for a king—for a different kind of king? The king of sinners and outcasts, the poor and the oppressed, calls us to join the worship of the one who "has brought down the powerful from their thrones,/ and lifted up the lowly . . . filled the hungry with good things,/ and sent the rich away empty" (1:52-53), the God who "has looked favorably on his people and redeemed them" (1:68), the God who gives "light to those who sit in darkness and in the shadow of death," the God who will "guide our feet into the way of peace" (1:79).

Do we long for the day when "the King enjoys his own again"? Here is the Messiah who gives hope to all who serve him, no matter how lowly. This is a parade at which all of us should cheer and weep. No secondhand joy here! The Messiah is coming! Don't let the parade pass you by. Cast your cloaks before him and let him who has no other hope and no other Lord cast the first cloak!

226. Winston S. Churchill, *A History of the English Speaking Peoples,* vol. 2, *The New World* (New York: Dodd, Mead, 1956) 325-28.

LUKE 19:41-46, JESUS WEEPS OVER THE CITY AND DRIVES THE MERCHANTS FROM THE TEMPLE

NIV

[41]As he approached Jerusalem and saw the city, he wept over it [42]and said, "If you, even you, had only known on this day what would bring you peace—but now it is hidden from your eyes. [43]The days will come upon you when your enemies will build an embankment against you and encircle you and hem you in on every side. [44]They will dash you to the ground, you and the children within your walls. They will not leave one stone on another, because you did not recognize the time of God's coming to you."

[45]Then he entered the temple area and began driving out those who were selling. [46]"It is written," he said to them, " 'My house will be a house of prayer'[a]; but you have made it 'a den of robbers.'[b]"

[a]46 Isaiah 56:7   [b]46 Jer. 7:11

NRSV

[41]As he came near and saw the city, he wept over it, [42]saying, "If you, even you, had only recognized on this day the things that make for peace! But now they are hidden from your eyes. [43]Indeed, the days will come upon you, when your enemies will set up ramparts around you and surround you, and hem you in on every side. [44]They will crush you to the ground, you and your children within you, and they will not leave within you one stone upon another; because you did not recognize the time of your visitation from God."[a]

[45]Then he entered the temple and began to drive out those who were selling things there; [46]and he said, "It is written,

'My house shall be a house of prayer';

   but you have made it a den of robbers."

[a]Gk lacks *from God*

COMMENTARY

Following the pattern of ancient accounts of entrance processions cited above, the entrance procession typically culminated with the distinguished personage entering the Temple and offering a sacrifice, thereby declaring his appropriation of the city. Once again, the Gospel account of Jesus' entry into Jerusalem follows the common pattern but also departs from it in significant ways. First, Jesus stops and pronounces an oracle over the city, then he enters the Temple, drives out the merchants, and declares that Scripture has been fulfilled. Both pronouncements declare God's sovereignty over the city of Jerusalem and its Temple, and both point ahead to the destruction of the city during the war of 66–70 CE. In order to grasp the nuances of Luke's account of these events, one must read it with multiple horizons in focus: the ancient pattern of entrance processions, the OT pronouncements of judgment on Jerusalem and the Temple, and the accounts in Josephus of the destruction of Jerusalem in 70 CE. Luke marshaled all of these resources, and each is reflected in his account of these events.

19:41-44, Jesus Weeps over Jerusalem. Seeing and perceiving are significant motifs in this Gospel. At Jesus' approach to the city, the crowd of disciples praised God, "for all the deeds of power that they had seen" (19:37). Now Jesus weeps because they have not recognized the things that make for peace (v. 42). The oracle begins and ends with references to "knowing" or "recognition" (γινώσκω *ginōskō*; 19:42, 44). Echoes of Luke's emphasis on "today" as the time of fulfillment (see Commentary on Luke 19:5, 9) may be overheard in the emphatic references to "this day," "but now," and "the time of your visitation from God." Because Jerusalem did not respond to Jesus' declaration of the kingdom and God's work of salvation in that city, it would soon be destroyed. The events of "the days [that] will come upon you" are directly related to what they failed to recognize on "this day."

Jesus' weeping over the city also evokes echoes of his earlier lament in Luke 13:34-35. There Jesus declared that he had often desired to gather the people as a hen gathers her brood under her wings, but the people were not willing. The lament ended, "And I tell you, you will not see me until the time comes when you say, 'Blessed is the one who comes in the name of the Lord!' "—the words chanted as Jesus approached the city. Later, Jesus will admonish the "daughters of Jerusalem" not to weep for him but to weep for themselves and their children (23:28-31)—a warning that echoes the dire prediction in the present context that "they will crush you to the ground, you and your children within you" (19:44). Jesus' lament over Jerusalem, therefore, is part of the theme of lament over Israel's failure that runs through Luke and Acts (cf. Luke's use of the Isaianic judgment oracle in Acts 28:24-28). The wonder and joy of God's redemptive work are also accompanied by lament for those who will not respond to God's declaration of salvation.

The word *Jerusalem* contains a reference to "peace" (εἰρήνη *eirēnē*), but the city failed to recognize the things that make for peace.[227] The psalmist had exhorted, "Pray for the peace of Jerusalem" (Ps 122:6 NRSV), but the people of Jerusalem did not recognize the things that made for peace. Jeremiah was the weeping prophet (Jer 9:1; 13:17; 14:17), remembered for his laments over Jerusalem (Jer 11:18–20:18), and these too are echoed by Jesus' lament. Jeremiah warned that the Lord would punish Jerusalem because its brokenness was not healed by leaders who glibly promised, " 'Peace, peace,' when there is no peace" (Jer 6:14 NRSV; cf. 10:15). The dashing of children against the rocks is an allusion to Ps 137:9; Nah 3:10; and Hos 13:16—but the vengeance Israel had looked forward to reaping on Babylon, Nineveh, and Samaria will be suffered by Jerusalem instead. The prophets had warned of sieges against Jerusalem at various times in the past (Isa 29:3; Ezek 4:1-3) and had foreseen its destruction (Jer 26:18; Mic 3:12).

Against this backdrop, Josephus's account of the destruction of Jerusalem resonates with a fascinating horror. When the Romans constructed earthworks and walls around the city to choke it off, the famine became so severe people seized food even from their own family, and "children were

---

227. See Joseph A. Fitzmyer, *The Gospel According to Luke (X–XXIV)*, AB 28A (Garden City, N.Y.: Doubleday, 1985) 1256.

actually lifted up with the fragments to which they clung and dashed to the ground."[228] An incident of infant cannibalism horrified the dying city.[229] Later, after the city had fallen, Titus, the Roman general, marveled at the strength of its fortifications and said, "God indeed has been with us in the war. God it was who brought down the Jews from these strongholds."[230] Finally, the city's destruction was complete; the city was leveled— "they will not leave within you one stone upon another" (Luke 19:44). Josephus describes the scene as follows:

> Caesar ordered the whole city and the temple to be razed to the ground, leaving only the loftiest of the towers, Phasael, Hippicus, and Mariamne, and the portion of the wall enclosing the city on the west: the latter as an encampment for the garrison that was to remain, and the towers to indicate to posterity the nature of the city and of the strong defences which had yet yielded to Roman prowess. All the rest of the wall encompassing the city was so completely levelled to the ground as to leave future visitors to the spot no ground for believing that it had ever been inhabited.[231]

The savagery and destruction that lay ahead, therefore, lent an overwhelming pathos to Jesus' entry into the city. He had been hailed as their king, but they had not recognized "the things that make for peace" (19:42).

19:45-46, The Cleansing of the Temple. The distinctiveness of Luke's account of the cleansing of the Temple stands out more clearly when it is compared with Mark. In Mark's account, Jesus enters the city and the Temple, then withdraws for the night to Bethany. The next day he curses the fig tree, then drives the merchants and money changers out of the Temple. As a result of Jesus' action in the Temple, the authorities look for a way to kill him, but they are afraid of the crowd. In the evening, Jesus again withdraws from the city, and the next morning the fig tree is found withered away.

In contrast, Luke has Jesus proceed directly to the Temple (cf. Mal 3:1). The cleansing of the Temple is greatly abbreviated, omitting Mark's references to those who were buying, overturning

the tables, selling doves, and forbidding anyone to carry anything through the Temple. Moreover, in Luke there is no withdrawal from the city or the Temple: "Every day he was teaching in the temple" (19:47). The differences also point to a difference in the significance of Jesus' action in the Temple. In Mark the false witnesses at Jesus' trial report that he had said he would destroy the Temple and build another not made with hands (Mark 14:58). The mockers at the cross taunt Jesus with these words (Mark 15:29), but the saying never appears in Luke. The cumulative effect of these differences is that while Jesus' action in Mark is part of his prophetic announcement of the destruction of the Temple, Luke has muted this emphasis. Instead, the cleansing of the Temple in Luke prepares his "father's house" (2:49) to serve as the site for Jesus' teaching in the following section (19:47–21:38).

Still, Luke knows of the coming destruction of the Temple. When Jesus wept over the city in the preceding verses, he warned of its destruction (19:41-44; cf. 21:5-6, 20-24). At Jesus' death, Luke retains the report of the rending of the veil in the Temple (23:45), and later Stephen declares that "the Most High does not dwell in houses made with human hands" (Acts 7:48 NRSV).

In spite of the differences between Mark and Luke, what remains of the account follows the Markan text closely. In keeping with the pattern of ancient entrance processions (see Commentary on 19:28-40), Jesus goes directly to the Temple. There, he does not offer a sacrifice as his means of appropriating the city but protests the corruption of the Temple by driving out the merchants (thereby fulfilling Zech 14:21) and by quoting two phrases from Scripture. Luke's abridgment of Jesus' action in the Temple thereby turns it into a pronouncement story, focusing attention on his words in the Temple and the fulfillment of Scripture.

Luke 19:46 cites memorable phrases from two significant passages from the prophets: " 'My house shall be a house of prayer [cf. Isa 56:7]'; but you have made it a den of robbers [cf. Jer 7:11]." The latter has probably been associated with the former because it too refers to what the Temple will be called: "Has this house, which is called by my name, become a den of robbers in your sight?" (Jer 7:11 NRSV). In each case, moreover, the context of the quoted phrase suggests

228. Josephus *The Jewish War* 5.433.
229. Ibid., 6.205-13.
230. Ibid., 6.411.
231. Josephus, *The Jewish War*, 7.14, trans. H. St. J. Thackeray, LCL (Cambridge, Mass.: Harvard University Press, 1928) 505.

important nuances of Jesus' action in the Temple. One of the puzzling aspects of Luke's handling of this tradition is the omission of the phrase "for all peoples" (Isa 56:7; Mark 11:17). Luke no less than Mark has the Gentile mission in view, but in Acts the gospel spreads from Jerusalem to the ends of the earth (Acts 1:8). People from all nations are drawn to the Temple at Pentecost (see Acts 2:9-11), but the Temple is displaced following Stephen's speech, and believers meet in homes. The work of gathering outcasts from Israel and from the Gentiles will continue, however, just as Isaiah had foreseen (see Isa 56:8).

Similarly, the context of the phrase "den of robbers" in Jeremiah's famous sermon in the Temple furnishes significant commentary on Jesus' action in the Temple. The God of Israel appeals to the people, "Amend your ways and your doings, and let me dwell with you in this place" (Jer 7:3 NRSV). But the prophet warned them not to trust the claim "This is the temple of the LORD" (Jer 7:4 NRSV), with the implication that they were safe in the Temple. God would dwell among them only if they amended their ways (see Jer 7:5-6). On the contrary, the people committed violence against one another and idolatry with other gods and then sought refuge in the Temple, like bandits hiding out in caves while planning their next crimes. They had made the Temple "a den of robbers" (Jer 7:11). As a result, the prophet warned the people that God would destroy their Temple and cast them out (see Jer 7:12).

The phrases from the prophets neatly evoke the significance of Jesus' cleansing of the Temple. It was an act that in the Lukan context has several implications. Jesus was continuing in Jerusalem his declaration of the coming of the kingdom, just as he had in Galilee—gathering the outcasts. He challenged the people and the Temple authorities with corrupting the Temple and not bearing "the fruits worthy of repentance" (Luke 3:8). Therefore, the Temple would be displaced and destroyed. Jesus' act in the Temple was a prophetic warning, but the prophetic warnings had gone unheeded in the past. The cleansing of the Temple, as a result, declared Jesus' appropriation of his Father's house and signaled the continuation of his ministry to outcasts and the coming confrontation with the religious leaders in Jerusalem. It foreshadowed both Jesus' claim on the Temple and the people of God and the eventual displacement and destruction of the Temple.

REFLECTIONS

The related scenes of Jesus weeping over the city and driving out the merchants from the Temple speak poignantly of God's judgment on human sinfulness. These are passages heavy with pathos and tragedy. Jesus weeps, laments, and sounds warnings that fall on deaf ears. The air of hopefulness that surrounded the entrance procession quickly fades in these two scenes.

The messianic lament over Jerusalem starkly juxtaposes the imperative of recognizing "the things that make for peace" and the consequences of war—women and children dashed to the ground and total destruction of the city, not one stone left upon another. The scope of war is even more terrible now than then, and graphic reminders of tragic and devastating violence bombard our senses on daily news casts. How must the Messiah weep at Buchenwald and Nagasaki, the killing fields of Cambodia, and the devastation of Rwanda: "If you, even you, had only recognized on this day the things that make for peace!" (19:41).

What are "the things that make for peace"? In the narrative world of the Gospel, the redemptive God of Israel sends prophets and God's Son "to guide our feet into the way of peace" (1:79) and to bring peace on earth (2:14). The bringing of peace begins with a call for repentance, for sharing coats, for making taxation just, and for ending military oppression (3:10-14). The coming of God's kingdom on earth means good news for the poor, a place at the table for the outcasts, sight for the blind, an end to the subjugation of women, the responsible handling of wealth and property, and a reevaluation of what constitutes piety and holiness.

The vision of such a community on earth should beckon us as strongly as the specter of the consequences of neglecting the things that make for peace horrifies and repels us. Here, in two short scenes the two ways are set before us: repentance and peace on one side, and disobedience and destruction on the other. If we can read these scenes and be unmoved, cynical about the possibility of peace on the one hand or complacent in the face of destruction on the other, it should challenge us to ask whether we have given up hope in the power of God to bring wholeness to our humanity and our human community, or whether we have forgotten the lessons of Israel's suffering, exile, and destruction in the past. Only an impotent theology affirms a God of love who cannot bring peace and will not punish disobedience. Whatever we make of God's justice and retribution, experience should teach us the tragic consequences of our sinfulness. Go to Shiloh, to Bataan or Guadalcanal, to Hiroshima or Coventry, to Anzio or Gettysburg, Omaha Beach or the nameless sites of the Tet offensive. The Messiah's lament echoes in each of these places and hundreds and hundreds more: "If you, even you, had only recognized on this day the things that make for peace!"

LUKE 19:47–21:38, JESUS' TEACHINGS IN THE TEMPLE

OVERVIEW

The next two chapters of the Gospel contain an extended section devoted to Jesus' teachings in the Temple. Luke 19:47-48 functions as an introduction to this section, just as the summary verses in Luke 4:14-15 introduced Jesus' ministry in Galilee. The earlier summary ends with the statement that "he began to teach in their synagogues and was praised by everyone" (4:15). Here, in contrast, "he was teaching in the temple . . . and the leaders of the people kept looking for a way to kill him" (19:47). Luke 20:1–21:38 is devoted to Jesus' teachings in the Temple. Throughout this section Luke follows Mark, omitting only Mark 12:28-34, which Luke used earlier (10:25-28).

In the first six scenes (20:1-8, 9-19, 20-26, 27-40, 41-44, 45-47) Jesus confronts the authorities, answering their questions, correcting their teachings, and denouncing their corrupt leadership of the people. Jesus' praise of the widow's offering (21:1-4) is also set in the Temple context, following the condemnation of the scribes for "devouring widows' houses" (20:47). The last three sections (21:5-19, 20-24, 25-36) warn the disciples of coming events: wars and persecutions, the destruction of Jerusalem, and the coming of the Son of Man. Luke 21:37-38 then concludes this section of confrontations and teachings in the Temple by restating many of the elements of its introduction.

Luke 19:47-48, The Beginning of Jesus' Teaching in the Temple

NIV	NRSV
47Every day he was teaching at the temple. But the chief priests, the teachers of the law and the leaders among the people were trying to kill him. 48Yet they could not find any way to do it, because all the people hung on his words.	47Every day he was teaching in the temple. The chief priests, the scribes, and the leaders of the people kept looking for a way to kill him; 48but they did not find anything they could do, for all the people were spellbound by what they heard.

COMMENTARY

The ministry in Jerusalem, as the repeated passion predictions have made clear, will end in Jesus' death. Appropriately, therefore, this extended section of teachings in the Temple concludes with the statement that "every day he was teaching in the temple. . . . And all the people would get up early in the morning to listen to him in the temple" (21:37-38). In the very next paragraph, Luke tells us that the "chief priests and the scribes were looking for a way to put Jesus to death, for they were afraid of the people" (22:2).

Both at the beginning and at the end of this section, therefore, Luke specifies the setting (the Temple), Jesus' activity (teaching), its duration (every day), and the fate that lay ahead (his death). Both introduction and conclusion also distinguish the leaders of the people, who are intent on killing Jesus, from the people, who "were spellbound by what they heard" (19:48). The introduction includes a list that occurs nowhere else in the Gospel: "the chief priests, the scribes, and the leaders of the people." This list, however, is reminiscent of the authorities named in the passion prediction in Luke 9:22, "the elders, chief priests, and scribes."

The high priest exercised leadership over the Sanhedrin and officiated in the Temple on certain occasions. In particular, he presided over the sin offerings on the Day of Atonement, when he entered into the Holy of Holies to secure atonement for the people of Israel. The plural "chief priests" occurs frequently in the Gospels and Acts and twice in Hebrews. This title seems to refer to priests who had prominent positions of responsibility over other priests. Some historians contend that it designates the high priests, former high priests, and members of the aristocratic families from which the high priests were selected (e.g., Acts 4:6). Priests from such families were no doubt given positions of influence. The captain of the Temple, who was responsible for oversight of the temple ceremonies, was the head of the chief priests, who included leaders of the weekly and daily courses of priests and the temple treasurers.

The chief priests appear repeatedly in the next four chapters of Luke.

In the exchanges that follow, various groups of authorities confront Jesus in the Temple: (1) the chief priests, the scribes, and the elders (20:1); (2) the scribes and chief priests (20:19); (3) some Sadducees (20:27); (4) the scribes (20:46). Various groups of religious leaders are also named in the arrest and trial of Jesus (22:2, 52, 66; 23:10, 13, 35; 24:20). Interestingly enough, the Pharisees are not named in any of these lists, having made their last appearance in the Gospel in 19:39, and the phrase "the leaders of the people" occurs only in 19:47. This phrase is both inclusive of the various groups of leaders and explicitly sets the leaders in opposition to the people, who early in the Gospel are named as the object of God's redemptive intent (e.g., 1:68, 77). After relatively frequent references to "the people" (ὁ λαός *ho laos*) early in the Gospel, there are only two such references during the travel narrative (11:53; 18:43), and the last already anticipates the role of the people in the Jerusalem ministry and the passion narrative. Jesus teaches the people (20:1, 9, 45; 21:38; 23:5), and the leaders hesitate to seize Jesus because of their fear of the people (20:6, 19, 26; 22:2). Only in Luke 23:13, where Pilate calls together the leaders and the people, do the two groups appear together, and there Jesus is charged with "perverting the people" (23:14). Finally, the people will follow Jesus to the place of crucifixion (23:27) and watch as the leaders mock him (23:35). In Luke, however, the chief priests and leaders (24:20) hand Jesus over to be crucified—not the people. The introduction to Jesus' teachings in the Temple, therefore, sets up the opposition between these two groups in Jerusalem and prepares the reader to see that the onus of Jesus' death lay primarily with the leaders of the people.

Earlier predictions of Jesus' death and reports of the leaders' desire to kill him have been reported in Luke 6:11; 9:22, 44; 11:53-54; 12:50; 13:32-34; 17:25; and 18:31-33. From this point on, the action builds to the fulfillment of their violent intentions.

Luke 20:1-8, The Question of Jesus' Authority

NIV

20 One day as he was teaching the people in the temple courts and preaching the gospel, the chief priests and the teachers of the law, together with the elders, came up to him. ²"Tell us by what authority you are doing these things," they said. "Who gave you this authority?"

³He replied, "I will also ask you a question. Tell me, ⁴John's baptism—was it from heaven, or from men?"

⁵They discussed it among themselves and said, "If we say, 'From heaven,' he will ask, 'Why didn't you believe him?' ⁶But if we say, 'From men,' all the people will stone us, because they are persuaded that John was a prophet."

⁷So they answered, "We don't know where it was from."

⁸Jesus said, "Neither will I tell you by what authority I am doing these things."

NRSV

20 One day, as he was teaching the people in the temple and telling the good news, the chief priests and the scribes came with the elders ²and said to him, "Tell us, by what authority are you doing these things? Who is it who gave you this authority?" ³He answered them, "I will also ask you a question, and you tell me: ⁴Did the baptism of John come from heaven, or was it of human origin?" ⁵They discussed it with one another, saying, "If we say, 'From heaven,' he will say, 'Why did you not believe him?' ⁶But if we say, 'Of human origin,' all the people will stone us; for they are convinced that John was a prophet." ⁷So they answered that they did not know where it came from. ⁸Then Jesus said to them, "Neither will I tell you by what authority I am doing these things."

COMMENTARY

The first group to confront Jesus is composed of the chief priests, the scribes, and the elders (cf. 9:22). The chief priests and the scribes were the first two groups named in 19:47. Priests were divided into twenty-four groups that served in the Temple on a rotating basis. The chief priests supervised the Temple activities. Together with the scribes, they assigned duties and instructed the priests in the performance of their tasks. The scribes were trained in the law and in legal matters. The elders were the heads of the leading families of Jerusalem. Representatives from each of these groups composed the Sanhedrin, and together the chief priests, scribes, and elders were the guardians of tradition.[232]

20:1-2. The setting for the confrontation is Jesus' teaching and preaching in the Temple, and the first question challenges his authority to "do these things." The reference could be broadly construed to include his entry into Jerusalem and driving out the merchants, but following the references to teaching in 19:47 and 20:1, it probably

concerns Jesus' authority to teach. One of the places Luke has redacted the Markan account of this scene most heavily is the introduction, where Luke has added references to Jesus' teaching and preaching the good news. For Luke's use of the latter (εὐαγγελίζεσθαι *euangelizesthai*), see 1:19; 2:10; 3:18; 4:18, 43; 7:22; 8:1; 9:6; and 16:16.

The authority of the chief priests was hereditary, the scribes' authority lay in their education and expertise, and the elders' was social and economic. The authority of these groups was clear. What was Jesus' authority? Early in the first century, rabbis may not yet have been formally ordained or authorized to teach, but it would have been common for one to establish his authority by citing the tradition of his teachers. Paul, for example, could say that he was "brought up in this city at the feet of Gamaliel, educated strictly according to our ancestral law" (Acts 22:3 NRSV; cf. Phil 3:4-6). In Acts, the authorities challenge the apostles: "By what power or by what name did you do this?" (Acts 4:7 NRSV).

Those whose authority is clear have challenged

232. See further Joachim Jeremias, *Jerusalem in the Time of Jesus*, trans. F. H. and C. H. Cave (Philadelphia: Fortress, 1969) 160-82, 222-45.

someone who has acted with authority but whose source of authority is not clear. The question, therefore, is a challenge to the basis of Jesus' entire message and ministry. If he cannot state his authority, he will lose credibility and expose himself to the judgment of the authorities. The question constitutes a serious challenge to Jesus' honor, but one that involves little risk to the authorities.

20:3-4. When Jesus responds to the authorities' question with one of his own, he turns the challenge into a contest of wits. Jesus was baptized by John the Baptist, and the reader knows of Jesus' connection with John from even before their births. Hence, the question of John's authority is relevant to the issue. Jesus frames the question in terms of human or divine authority: "Did the baptism of John come from heaven, or was it of human origin?" The emphasis on tradition implicit in the question has also been altered to a question of origin—which again has an additional nuance for readers, who are familiar with the birth accounts.

20:5-7. The authorities are hung on the horns of the alternatives posed by Jesus' question. The basis for their dilemma is John's following among "the people" (ὁ λαός *ho laos*)—a term added to the account by Luke, and one that has particular importance in this Gospel (see Commentary on 19:47-48). Thus this scene serves to clarify further the division between the people (Israel, God's people) and their leaders. John's following was established at various points earlier in the narrative (1:14; 3:15, 21; 7:24). We recall that the angel messenger had declared that John would "turn many of the people of Israel to the Lord their God" (1:16). The reader may also recall Luke's comment that "by refusing to be baptized by him, the Pharisees and the lawyers rejected God's purpose for themselves" (7:30). The people, on the other hand, held John to be a prophet (cf. 1:76; 7:26).

The question places the authorities over against Jesus and the people. If they answer "from heaven," then they leave themselves open to the charge of rejecting God's prophet. If they say "of human origin," they risk violent opposition from those who were convinced that John was a prophet. The question, therefore, aligns Jesus with the people in its implicit acceptance of John's divine authority and exposes the authorities' opposition to God's prophets. As a result, the reader may hear echoes of Jesus' lament, "Jerusalem, Jerusalem, the city that kills the prophets and stones those who are sent to it!" (13:34).

The authorities attempt to cut their losses by refusing to answer the question. Their refusal to answer, however, is an admission that they have lost the contest of wits. They have lost face and incurred shame, but that was preferable to either of the alternatives allowed by the question. They say that they do not know, but their admission of ignorance incurs shame—a loss of honor. For the reader of Luke, who has been privy to the deliberations of the authorities, their response serves to discredit the leaders as religious authorities. Who could hope for truth or justice from those who did not recognize God's prophets but chose rather the path of expediency?

20:8. Jesus interprets their answer as a refusal to give an answer. Consequently, he can refuse to answer the authorities. Because they would not answer his question, he was relieved of any obligation to answer theirs. The last line of the scene takes us back to the authorities' question. Jesus' response leaves the clear implication that he, in fact, has authority. Moreover, the alternatives he poses to the authorities imply that his teaching is "from heaven"—it carries God's authority.

REFLECTIONS

The function of the question of Jesus' authority is both christological and polemical. It serves to undergird Jesus' divine authority while exposing the opposition of the leaders of the people to those who were authorized by God. Therefore, the question focuses the issue of the authority of Jesus' announcement of the kingdom and the teachings in this immediate context: the parable of the greedy and vengeful king, Jesus' lament over Jerusalem, and his pronouncements regarding the Temple.

The question of religious authority is one of the burning issues of our time. How does one resolve theological or ethical issues? What relative weight have Scripture, tradition, reason, and experience? Denominations split over such issues. Moreover, in a society marked by increasing religious pluralism, by what authority does one maintain religious convictions in the face of civil pressure, secularism, or the convictions of persons of other religious traditions?

Before we jump too quickly to identify with Jesus in his conflict with the religious authorities of his day, perhaps we should note that the leaders were only doing their duty. Jesus had come into the Temple hailed by his followers as a king, disrupted normal activities in the Temple, and announced its destruction. For the security of the people and the Temple if for no other reason, the religious authorities had a responsibility to investigate Jesus.

What are the leaders of Christian denominations to do when preachers or evangelists with questionable credentials, background, and theology create excitement and gather a following outside the established programs of the church? What are religious leaders to do when government authorities either sponsor unjust legislation or block programs that would contribute to justice, peace, and the well-being of those who cannot fend for themselves? Such issues are seldom simple.

Religious leaders carry a double responsibility, twin tasks that may at times come in conflict. Those who are ordained or minister in a given tradition represent both God and their respective confessions. They are responsible both for maintaining the distinctive teachings and practices of that tradition and for correcting them when they fail to advance God's redemptive work. But what does one do when the teachings or traditions of the church fail to conform to the minister's convictions regarding God's purposes? How does one know where one's responsibility lies? Again, such issues are seldom simple or one sided.

The failure of the religious leaders who confronted Jesus was not in raising the question of Jesus' authority but in being more concerned about their position and honor than about discerning what distinguished those who were doing God's redemptive work among the people. Beyond the issue of authority is the call to respond to the promptings of God's Spirit to recognize and commit oneself to the work of the kingdom wherever and in whatever form one meets it.

Luke 20:9-19, The Parable of the Wicked Tenants

NIV

9He went on to tell the people this parable: "A man planted a vineyard, rented it to some farmers and went away for a long time. 10At harvest time he sent a servant to the tenants so they would give him some of the fruit of the vineyard. But the tenants beat him and sent him away empty-handed. 11He sent another servant, but that one also they beat and treated shamefully and sent away empty-handed. 12He sent still a third, and they wounded him and threw him out.

13"Then the owner of the vineyard said, 'What shall I do? I will send my son, whom I love; perhaps they will respect him.'

14"But when the tenants saw him, they talked the matter over. 'This is the heir,' they said. 'Let's kill him, and the inheritance will be ours.' 15So they threw him out of the vineyard and killed him.

NRSV

9He began to tell the people this parable: "A man planted a vineyard, and leased it to tenants, and went to another country for a long time. 10When the season came, he sent a slave to the tenants in order that they might give him his share of the produce of the vineyard; but the tenants beat him and sent him away empty-handed. 11Next he sent another slave; that one also they beat and insulted and sent away empty-handed. 12And he sent still a third; this one also they wounded and threw out. 13Then the owner of the vineyard said, 'What shall I do? I will send my beloved son; perhaps they will respect him.' 14But when the tenants saw him, they discussed it among themselves and said, 'This is the heir; let us kill him so that the inheritance may be ours.' 15So they threw him out of the vineyard and killed him. What then will the owner of the vineyard

NIV

"What then will the owner of the vineyard do to them? [16]He will come and kill those tenants and give the vineyard to others."

When the people heard this, they said, "May this never be!"

[17]Jesus looked directly at them and asked, "Then what is the meaning of that which is written:

" 'The stone the builders rejected
    has become the capstone[a][b]?

[18]Everyone who falls on that stone will be broken to pieces, but he on whom it falls will be crushed."

[19]The teachers of the law and the chief priests looked for a way to arrest him immediately, because they knew he had spoken this parable against them. But they were afraid of the people.

a17 Or *cornerstone*   *b17* Psalm 118:22

NRSV

do to them? [16]He will come and destroy those tenants and give the vineyard to others." When they heard this, they said, "Heaven forbid!" [17]But he looked at them and said, "What then does this text mean:

'The stone that the builders rejected
    has become the cornerstone'?[a]

[18]Everyone who falls on that stone will be broken to pieces; and it will crush anyone on whom it falls." [19]When the scribes and chief priests realized that he had told this parable against them, they wanted to lay hands on him at that very hour, but they feared the people.

a Or *keystone*

COMMENTARY

According to Luke, Jesus told the parable of the wicked tenants to the people (20:9), but he told the parable "against" the scribes and the chief priests (20:19). Interestingly, in both verses the same preposition is used, and the phrase is very nearly the same. Luke thereby uses the parable to intensify the opposition between the people—who are mentioned both in Luke's introduction to the parable and in his concluding comment (20:9, 19)—and their leaders. The parable also augments the negative characterization of the leaders of the people. In this way, the parable serves as commentary on the characters and plot of the unfolding narrative of Jesus' death. It is possible that the parable originated in a non-allegorical form, perhaps closer to that found in the *Gospel of Thomas* 65, but that early version has long since been overlaid by allegorical interpretation that relates the story of the wicked tenants to the authorities' role in Jesus' death.

20:9. Luke depends on Mark (12:1-2) but retells the parable, adding, deleting, and revising phrases. In Mark the parable begins with clear echoes of the song of the vineyard in Isaiah 5:

Mark 12	Isaiah 5
A man planted a vineyard, put a fence around it, dug a pit for the wine press, and built a watchtower;	He dug it and cleared it of stones, and planted it with choice vines; he built a watchtower in the midst of it, and hewed out a wine vat in it;

Luke retains only the statement "A man planted a vineyard," but even this brief statement repeats the words "planted a vineyard" (ἐφύτευσεν ἀμπελῶνα *ephyteusen ampelōna*) verbatim from Isa 5:2 LXX and is sufficient to evoke echoes of this familiar text. In the song of the vineyard, the vineyard serves as a symbol for Israel, as it does in other scriptural contexts (Ps 80:8-13; Isa 27:2-6; Jer 2:21; Hos 10:1; Ezek 19:10-14).

The practice of absentee landlords' leasing vineyards or olive groves to tenants dates back at least to the period of the Ptolemies (3rd cent. BCE) and continued through the Roman period. In Luke, the story of a certain man who went on a journey resonates with the parable of the greedy and vengeful king in the previous chapter (19:11-27). In this story, however, it is the tenants who are greedy and vengeful. Luke adds the note that the owner was gone "for a long time" (20:9)—long enough for the tenants to grow rebellious and desire to keep all the produce of the vineyard for themselves. According to levitical law, the owner was forbidden from making a profit on the vineyard for five years (Lev 19:23-25).

20:10-12. According to the version of the parable in *Thomas,* the owner sends two servants and then his son. In Mark he sends three servants, then many others (12:5; cf. Matt 21:36), and then his son. In Luke, however, the owner sends three servants (20:12) before sending his son. The first they beat and send away empty-handed; the second they beat and insult and send away empty-handed; and the third they wound and throw out. The verb for "to beat" (δέρω *derō*) will recur in Luke's account of the abuse of Jesus (cf. 22:63). Luke employed the storyteller's sequence of threes in the parable of the good Samaritan (10:29-37), but here the turning point comes after the third servant has been rejected.

20:13. The actions of the owner are interpreted in *Thomas,* where the owner responds to the rejection of the first servant by saying, "Perhaps he did not know them."[233] The canonical Gospels offer no such explanation or justification of the owner's actions. Luke, however, gives the reader an inside view by reporting the vineyard owner's soliloquy after the rejection of the third servant: "Then the owner of the vineyard said, 'What shall I do? I will send my beloved son; perhaps they will respect him' " (20:13). Soliloquies are common in the distinctively Lukan parables (see 12:17, 45; 15:17; 16:3-4; 18:4-5; 20:13), but this soliloquy also echoes the song of the vineyard, where the owner says, "what yet will I do?" (τί ποιήσω; *ti poiēsō,* Isa 5:4-5 LXX). Like the rich fool and the dishonest steward, the vineyard owner asks, "What will I do?" (cf. 12:17; 16:3-4) and then decides on a course of action.

The vineyard owner's decision to send his "beloved son" echoes the references to Jesus as the "beloved son" at Jesus' baptism (3:22) and "chosen son" at the transfiguration (9:35, where "beloved" is a textual variant). The reader cannot escape the meaning of this allusion. The prophets of God were stoned and killed (13:34). John was the greatest of the prophets (7:28), but he too was rejected and killed, and now Jesus faces death

in Jerusalem. The vineyard owner hopes that the tenants will respect his son, but the unjust judge neither feared God nor had respect for people (18:2, 4).

20:14. On the story level, the tenants see an opportunity to secure the vineyard for themselves. If the owner died with no heir, they as the tenants might have a claim to the vineyard. Just as the chief priests, scribes, and elders debated among themselves regarding how they should answer Jesus' question about the authority of John's baptism (20:5), so also the wicked tenants now debate among themselves regarding what they should do with the vineyard owner's son (20:14). The real significance of their debate over what to do, however, lies in the importance of inheritance in the language of the Scriptures. That context is evoked early in Luke, when at the annunciation the angel declares that Jesus "will be called the Son of the Most High, and the Lord God will give to him the throne of his ancestor David. He will reign over the house of Jacob forever" (1:32-33). Isaac was the child of the covenant, Abraham's beloved son, his heir (Gen 22:2; cf. Gen 12:1-3). Israel itself was God's beloved son (Isa 42:1; Jer 31:20), but the NT writers show that there was considerable reflection in the early church on the shifts that had occurred in the Christian understanding of the church's role as the heirs of God's promises to Israel (see Rom 8:14-17; Gal 3:29–4:7; Eph 1:11, 14; 3:6). In this context, one receives the inheritance not by killing the son but by having faith in God's Son.

20:15-16a. The misguided plot of the wicked tenants leads to violence and then to the loss of the vineyard. Foreshadowing the crucifixion of Jesus, the antagonists of the parable cast the son out of the vineyard and kill him. Later, Pilate will hand Jesus over to the chief priests, the leaders, and the people, and they will lead Jesus out of the city, to the place set aside for crucifixions (see esp. 23:26, 32-33). Through the parable, therefore, Jesus' death is set in the twin contexts of the deaths of the prophets before him and the redemptive hope of God, represented by the image of the vineyard owner, who says, "Perhaps they will respect him" (20:13).

The wicked tenants do not determine the outcome of the story, contrary to what they had assumed. They cannot secure the vineyard for

---

233. A. Guillaumont et al., trans., *The Gospel According to Thomas* (New York: Harper & Row, 1959) 39.

themselves by killing the heir. The vineyard still belongs to the owner, and he will determine what will become of it—not the wicked tenants. Earlier, the owner had pondered, "What shall I do?" (v. 13). Now the narrator of the parable poses a more pointed question to the audience: "What then will the owner of the vineyard do to them?" The owner had a decision to make: He sent his beloved son. The tenants had a decision to make: They killed him. Now the audience is drawn into the parable: What will the vineyard owner do in response to the murder of his beloved son? Polemically, the question reminds the audience that the owner still holds the initiative for determining the ending of the story. Historically considered, Jesus invites the audience, which includes the scribes and chief priests, to consider what God will do with them for their failed stewardship over Israel. Theologically, the question invites the reader to consider what God might have done in response to the crucifixion, and thereby to see more clearly the depth of God's commitment to the redemption of his vineyard.

The narrator of the parable supplies the threefold answer with future tense verbs. Here the narrative future of the parable coincides with the future of the story world of the Gospel (what will become of the scribes and chief priests). The reader, however, may consider the parable from the vantage point of a later time, when what the owner resolves has already begun to occur. The owner (1) will come, (2) will destroy the wicked tenants, and (3) will give the vineyard to others. The coming of the owner resonates with OT prophecies of the Lord's coming (e.g., Mal 3:1; 4:1-6), Jesus' arrival in Jerusalem and entry into the Temple, and the church's expectation of the coming of the risen Lord and the Son of Man in the near future (see 21:25-36).

The destruction of the wicked tenants and the giving of the vineyard to others symbolically but graphically predicts the destruction of Jerusalem and the Temple and the passing of the mantle of leadership from Israel's religious leaders to the leaders of the church—which in Acts begins with the apostles and progresses to the seven Hellenists, Paul, and then the elders of the Gentile churches.

20:16b-19. The focus of attention now shifts from the parable to two responses. First, the Gospel narrator reports that those who

heard it responded with a forceful exclamation, μὴ γένοιτο *mē genoito* ("Heaven forbid!" NRSV; "May this never be!" NIV). Paul uses this prohibition frequently (e.g., Rom 3:4, 6, 31; 6:2, 15; 7:7, 13), but it occurs only here in the Gospels and Acts. The reference to those who heard the parable recalls the introductory statement that Jesus told the parable to "the people" (v. 9).

Responding to the people, Jesus provides his own comment on the parable in the form of a question about the meaning of Ps 118:22, a verse from one of the Hallel (praise or festival) psalms. The verse poses an allegorical riddle for the hearers. What is the meaning of the irony that "The stone that the builders rejected has become the cornerstone"? Because the verse appears in other NT contexts, it is clear that it was used by the early church as a scriptural proof of the crucified Christ (cf. Acts 4:11; 1 Pet 2:7). A cornerstone set the angle of two walls and bore the weight of both walls at the corner. In its NT usage it may also have a temporal significance. The church would be built on the cornerstone that was set for it (see Isa 28:16; Matt 16:18; 1 Cor 3:11; 10:4; Eph 2:20; 1 Pet 2:6). Luke has prepared the reader for this riddle by using the verb "rejected" (ἀποδοκιμάζω *apodokimazo*) in two earlier contexts, which warn that the Son of Man must be rejected by "the elders, chief priests and scribes" (9:22) and by "this generation" (17:25).

Verse 18 extends the stone metaphor to encompass the judgment that the parable pictured as taking the vineyard away from the tenants and giving it to others. Irony gives way to paradox. If one strikes the stone, one will be shattered; if the stone falls on any, they will be crushed. Both parts of this verse echo scriptural references (cf. Isa 8:13-14). The prophetic words of Simeon are being fulfilled: "This child is destined for the falling and the rising of many in Israel" (2:34). Once again the inhabitants of Jerusalem encounter the Lord's work as a stumbling stone.

The last half of Luke 20:18 alludes to Daniel's interpretation of Nebuchadnezzar's dream. A stone cut from the mountain, not by human hands, struck the great statue and broke it in pieces (Dan 2:34). The dream, Daniel said, was a portent of the kingdom that would crush all other kingdoms (Dan 2:44). By joining allusions to a vineyard, a cornerstone, a stumbling stone, and a crushing stone,

Luke's successive references construct a powerful allegorical interpretation of Jesus' confrontation with the authorities in Jerusalem.

The allusions to rejection and judgment are followed by the reappearance of the scribes and chief priests, who were introduced at the beginning of this section (19:47; 20:1). Their reappearance at this point forms a neat *inclusio*—the end of the section returns to its beginning. Again, they oppose both Jesus and "the people." The meaning of the parable is confirmed for the reader by means of the narrator's comment that "the scribes and chief priests realized that he had told this parable against them" (v. 19). The response of the people had been "Heaven forbid!" The response of the religious leaders is a desire to seize Jesus "that very hour," but they are prevented from doing so because "they feared the people" (v. 19; cf. 22:2). Both of these motifs, the hour and fear, have distinctive though different roles in the Gospel of John. In that Gospel, Jesus cannot be seized until his hour has come (see John 2:4; 7:30; 8:20; 12:27; 13:1). Similarly, the authorities would not confess Jesus "for fear that they would be put out of the synagogue" (John 12:42 NRSV), while others hide from "fear of the Jews" (John 7:13; 19:38; 20:19—and in these instances "the Jews" seems to refer to the religious authorities in Jerusalem).

REFLECTIONS

Although the parable of the wicked tenants is cast in the context of the chief priests' and scribes' rejection of Jesus, it resonates with Isaiah's song of the vineyard and hauntingly depicts self-serving rebellion against God's sovereignty. The essence of sin is humanity's failure to take its place in covenant with God. Human beings alternately overreach and underachieve what God intends them to be. In this story, the tenants who have been given charge of the vineyard reject the owner's authority and plot to take it from him.

Like most biblical texts, this one can be read in various ways. I propose that we read it in four ways: (a) historically, within the context of the whole biblical story; (b) narratively, within the context of the Gospel story; (c) theologically, within the context of God's self-revelation; and (d) existentially, within the context of our own experience.

1. This is a parable with a long memory. It remembers where it has been, what God has done through the centuries, and how God's people have responded. Consequently, it sets Jesus' ministry in the context of the history of Israel and the rejection of the prophets. As we read this part of the Gospel, therefore, we see Jesus' ministry against the dramatic backdrop of centuries of God's efforts to call, reform, and renew Israel. The life of Jesus is not adequately understood in isolation; it is the culmination of God's redemptive efforts toward those who have rejected the messengers of judgment and grace in the past.

2. The story of the vineyard is not merely an allegory about the history of Israel, however. It is also a mirror in which we can see our own repeated rejections of God's grace. How often, by word or circumstance, have we been called to respond to God's claim on our lives and responded instead with calculations spawned by our own ambitions? The parable, therefore, calls us to identify not with the owner or his son but with the wicked tenants. It requires a double sense of identification, however. First, we identify with "the others" to whom the vineyard will be entrusted. Then, we hear the implicit warning that the new tenants not become as wicked as the first tenants. The parable's effect, therefore, is double-sided: (1) It reminds us of our stewardship of the vineyard God has given us, and (2) it conveys a prophetic warning that we not follow other false leaders by seeking selfish ends rather than rendering to God the fruit of the vineyard entrusted to us.

The sinful impulse is insidiously dynamic. The tenants did not start out to take the vineyard from its owner; they only wanted to keep its produce for themselves. They did not set out to commit murder; the first servant they only beat and sent away empty-handed. Once committed to this path, however, they were led to its consequences. Wanting to keep all the produce for themselves, they ended up losing the vineyard. Sin is not only dynamic, but it is also inherently destructive. Greed leads to rebellion, which is expressed in violence, which escalates to murder, which results in loss of the vineyard. James said it in more theological language: "But one is tempted by one's own desire, being lured and enticed by it; then, when that desire has conceived, it gives birth to sin, and that sin, when it is fully grown, gives birth to death" (Jas 1:14-15 NRSV).

3. Privilege and responsibility, grace and stewardship are inescapably joined. The link between the tenants and the religious leaders was their special role and the responsibilities it carried with it. God never demands responsibility without conferring privilege, but to desire privilege without its accompanying responsibilities is a sign of immaturity and self-centeredness. When the tissue that binds responsibility and privilege is torn, the whole fabric of community will soon be destroyed. What does the parable have to say to a society in which greed is often given free reign with no consideration for its consequences in the lives of others?

4. The parable also graphically portrays the consequences of greed, rebellion, and irresponsibility. The vineyard is taken away from the tenants and given to others. Does the flame of spiritual response in the Third World and the decline of Christianity in Europe signal the passing of the vineyard to others once again?[234]

5. Also there is the paradoxical image that the stone that can serve as a cornerstone can also be a stumbling block. What was rejected can be chosen, and what can build can also destroy. The rejected Christ was then risen. Grace rejected becomes condemnation.

6. Similarly, the parable clarifies that God is sovereign and God will prevail, not human sinfulness. The tenants thought they could determine the course of events and seize the vineyard, but the owner retained the prerogative to give the vineyard to others. God's purposes will not be defeated.

Hear, then, the parable. We are the tenants, and we are the others to whom the vineyard has been given. We have received as a free gift the vineyard that others would have killed for. By God's grace, the vineyard is twice given. So let us not close the story by calling it "the parable of the wicked tenants." Let's leave it open by calling it "the parable of the twice-given vineyard." Because we know the gospel story and have experienced it in our own lives, we know God's love and God's boundless grace. But now come the final questions: If we are the others to whom the vineyard has been given, what will we do with it? Will we be any more responsive to God's purposes than the first tenants were? If so, what does obedience require of us?

234. Fred B. Craddock, *Luke,* Interpretation (Louisville: Westminster/John Knox, 1990) 234.

Luke 20:20-26, The Question About Paying Taxes

NIV

[20]Keeping a close watch on him, they sent spies, who pretended to be honest. They hoped to catch Jesus in something he said so that they might hand him over to the power and authority of the governor. [21]So the spies questioned him: "Teacher, we know that you speak and teach what is right, and that you do not show partiality but teach the way of God in accordance with the

NRSV

20So they watched him and sent spies who pretended to be honest, in order to trap him by what he said, so as to hand him over to the jurisdiction and authority of the governor. [21]So they asked him, "Teacher, we know that you are right in what you say and teach, and you show deference to no one, but teach the way of God in accordance with truth. [22]Is it lawful for us to

NIV

truth. ²²Is it right for us to pay taxes to Caesar or not?"

²³He saw through their duplicity and said to them, ²⁴"Show me a denarius. Whose portrait and inscription are on it?"

²⁵"Caesar's," they replied.

He said to them, "Then give to Caesar what is Caesar's, and to God what is God's."

²⁶They were unable to trap him in what he had said there in public. And astonished by his answer, they became silent.

NRSV

pay taxes to the emperor, or not?" ²³But he perceived their craftiness and said to them, ²⁴"Show me a denarius. Whose head and whose title does it bear?" They said, "The emperor's." ²⁵He said to them, "Then give to the emperor the things that are the emperor's, and to God the things that are God's." ²⁶And they were not able in the presence of the people to trap him by what he said; and being amazed by his answer, they became silent.

COMMENTARY

The authorities' efforts to trap Jesus continue. Deceptively, they send spies to try to get Jesus to make a pronouncement on a politically sensitive issue so that they can report him to the governor. The religious leaders will charge Jesus with "forbidding us to pay taxes to the emperor" (23:2), but the present passage alerts the reader that it is a false charge. Ancient sources contain several versions of this story, but none of the non-canonical accounts is earlier than Luke.[235]

Luke continues to follow Mark, but alters the introduction to this controversy story by omitting Mark's reference to the Pharisees and Herodians, which would be extraneous in Luke. The result is that Jesus deals with emissaries who are sent to him and responds to a question of what should be given to Caesar. Both the sending and the issue of giving what is due link this exchange with the preceding parable. The question of paying taxes exposes the underlying question regarding one's obligations to the Roman authorities. In the volatile environment of first-century Judea, any answer Jesus might give would be scrutinized for evidence of either capitulation to the Romans or rebellion against them. On the one hand, Jesus might lose the support of the people; on the other hand, he might expose himself to charges of insurrection. Jesus' answer, however, unlike the authorities' earlier response to his question about John's baptism, shows that he is not guided by political expediency.

20:20-21. The narrator informs the reader of the scribes' and chief priests' deception: (1) They sent spies; (2) the spies pretended to be honest (see 16:15); (3) their real purpose was "to trap him by what he said"; and (4) their ultimate plan was "to hand him over to the jurisdiction and authority of the governor." The reader, then, is immediately able to see through the spies' malicious flattery. Ironically, though, what they say about Jesus is true, while what they say about themselves is false or they condemn themselves with their own words. If they know that Jesus is right in what he says and teaches, they should accept his teachings. Jesus' answer to their trapping question will confirm that he shows deference to no one. Literally, the idiom says that Jesus does not "receive faces" (οὐ λαμβάνεις πρόσωπον *ou lambaneis prosōpon*); he makes no distinction between persons (cf. Acts 10:34; Jas 2:1). The empty praise of the spies is not only true but also resonates powerfully with the Hebrew Scriptures. Had not Moses said: "So now, O Israel, what does the LORD your God require of you? Only to fear the LORD your God, to walk in all his ways" (Deut 10:12 NRSV).

20:22. Perhaps hoping that "pride goeth before . . . a fall" (Prov 16:18 KJV), the spies spring their trap immediately after their words of praise. Their question already places the issue of taxation in a religious context: "Is it lawful. . . ?" For all its political bristles, the question is at base a religious one, a matter of interpretation of the law. The lure entices Jesus to appeal to the authority

235. See Egerton Papyrus 2, frg. 2r; *Gospel of Thomas* 100; and Justin Martyr *Apology* 1.17.2. For the evidence that none of these accounts is earlier than Luke, see Joseph A. Fitzmyer, *The Gospel According to Luke (X–XXIV),* AB 28A (Garden City, N.Y.: Doubleday, 1985) 1290-91.

of the Law of Moses to decree that paying taxes was illegal. In its present context, the question invites Jesus to counsel the people to act as the wicked tenants of the preceding parable and refuse to give the emperor his due (cf. 20:10, 22; both contain the verb "to give" [δίδωμι *didōmi*]). Luke chooses a general word for "taxes" or "tribute" (φόρος *phoros*) rather than the Latin loan word "census" or "head tax" (κῆνσος *kēnsos*) found in Mark 12:14. Significantly, it is the same word that will be used in the false charge against Jesus in 23:2.

20:23-24. Jesus catches the wise in their craftiness and deceitful scheming (cf. 1 Cor 3:19; Eph 4:14). His trap is even more sly. He asks for a denarius, a common coin, a laborer's daily wage. The silver denarius bore the image of Tiberius and the inscription "Tiberius Caesar, son of the divine Augustus, Augustus."[236] Evidently, Jesus' opponents themselves carried Roman coins. Jesus further forces his interrogators into an uncomfortable position by asking whose image and inscription were on the coin. Not only are they forced to answer a question that any child could answer, but the spies are also forced to pronounce the name "Caesar."

20:25. From their simple and obviously correct answer, Jesus forms his response—with the implication that it should be equally simple and obvious. If the coin bears Caesar's image, then it

236. Fitzmyer, *The Gospel According to Luke (X–XXIV)*, 1296.

belongs to Caesar, so give it to Caesar. But give to God whatever belongs to God. If what belongs to Caesar bears his image, then whatever belongs to God bears God's image as well. Human beings, made in the image and likeness of God, belong exclusively to God. Pay taxes to Caesar, but give your highest loyalty to God. Jesus' answer cleverly avoids the spies' trap while calling the people to be faithful to God in all things. By affirming that the people should pay taxes, Jesus refuses to support violent rebellion against Rome. On the other hand, the effect of his response is not to create an arena of life that is exempt from God's authority but to reserve for God a level of fidelity that supersedes any other obligation.

20:26. This verse provides closure for the scene. The spies acting for the religious authorities had set out to trap Jesus in his words, but they have failed to do so (cf. 20:20, 26, the beginning and end of the scene). They fail "in the presence of the people" (see Commentary on 19:47-48 and 20:1 regarding the opposition between the leaders and the people). Thus later the people should be able to recognize that the charge against Jesus is false (23:1-2). The spies' amazement at Jesus' answer reminds the reader of earlier reports of amazement at Jesus' mighty works (8:25; 9:43; 11:14) and at his teachings (4:22). Failing to trap Jesus in his words, his opponents are reduced to silence.

REFLECTIONS

Jesus' pronouncement to "render to Caesar the things that are Caesar's, and to God the things that are God's" is a response to a trap question about paying taxes. While affirming the payment of taxes, Jesus holds out the further, more encompassing imperative of serving God. The pronouncement is not a nuanced treatise on church-state relations or on the civil duties of the Christian. Rather, it is an aphorism that teases the mind to remember that one's duty to God exceeds all other duties. The determination of what should be given to Caesar and what should be reserved for God must be worked out in every particular situation.

Nevertheless, given the tensive and open-ended character of the aphorism and the paucity of other pronouncements from Jesus on the subject, this statement has often served as the authority for various political views. Its primary force, however, is to warn against rendering to Caesar what one should rightfully give only to God. This means that patriotism should never assume the fervor, or make the absolute claims of, religion. Then as now, however, the lines between the two were often blurred. Both demanded loyalty, both made laws that regulated life, both had festivals, both had their heroes, and both were supported by a cult. The power of civil religion is evident today especially in times of international conflict, when political leaders proclaim that *our* cause is *God's* cause. God is on our side. The United States Constitution is given the authority of scripture by Americans. The monuments in Washington,

D.C.—the Lincoln Memorial, the Washington Monument, and the Jefferson Memorial—serve as the cult's shrines, embodying its sacred history, and the Congress and president assume priestly roles. Whereas Jesus held forth the kingdom of God as the highest ideal for human society, the American ideal is democracy and the Union of the States: "One nation, under God, with liberty and justice for all."

Noble as national ideals may be, there is the danger of rendering the things of God to Caesar or expecting God to look after Caesar's affairs. What message do we send when Christian churches celebrate the Fourth of July with flag and color guard in the sanctuary? What is the difference between the roles of the church and the state in educating or legislating morality, enhancing the quality of life, and attaining Christian ideals and values? Jesus' pronouncement affirms at a minimum that while the state has a rightful place, God's claims surpass one's obligations to the state (see Rom 13:1-7; 1 Pet 2:13-17). Christians, therefore, are not to confuse the two or misplace their ultimate trust and commitments.

Luke 20:27-40, The Question About the Resurrection

NIV

27Some of the Sadducees, who say there is no resurrection, came to Jesus with a question. 28"Teacher," they said, "Moses wrote for us that if a man's brother dies and leaves a wife but no children, the man must marry the widow and have children for his brother. 29Now there were seven brothers. The first one married a woman and died childless. 30The second 31and then the third married her, and in the same way the seven died, leaving no children. 32Finally, the woman died too. 33Now then, at the resurrection whose wife will she be, since the seven were married to her?"

34Jesus replied, "The people of this age marry and are given in marriage. 35But those who are considered worthy of taking part in that age and in the resurrection from the dead will neither marry nor be given in marriage, 36and they can no longer die; for they are like the angels. They are God's children, since they are children of the resurrection. 37But in the account of the bush, even Moses showed that the dead rise, for he calls the Lord 'the God of Abraham, and the God of Isaac, and the God of Jacob.'[a] 38He is not the God of the dead, but of the living, for to him all are alive."

39Some of the teachers of the law responded, "Well said, teacher!" 40And no one dared to ask him any more questions.

[a]37 Exodus 3:6

NRSV

27Some Sadducees, those who say there is no resurrection, came to him 28and asked him a question, "Teacher, Moses wrote for us that if a man's brother dies, leaving a wife but no children, the man[a] shall marry the widow and raise up children for his brother. 29Now there were seven brothers; the first married, and died childless; 30then the second 31and the third married her, and so in the same way all seven died childless. 32Finally the woman also died. 33In the resurrection, therefore, whose wife will the woman be? For the seven had married her."

34Jesus said to them, "Those who belong to this age marry and are given in marriage; 35but those who are considered worthy of a place in that age and in the resurrection from the dead neither marry nor are given in marriage. 36Indeed they cannot die anymore, because they are like angels and are children of God, being children of the resurrection. 37And the fact that the dead are raised Moses himself showed, in the story about the bush, where he speaks of the Lord as the God of Abraham, the God of Isaac, and the God of Jacob. 38Now he is God not of the dead, but of the living; for to him all of them are alive." 39Then some of the scribes answered, "Teacher, you have spoken well." 40For they no longer dared to ask him another question.

[a] Gk his brother

COMMENTARY

The Sadducees' challenge to Jesus is unusual for several reasons. This is the only place where the Sadducees appear in the Gospel of Luke, there is no explicit reference to an attempt to trap Jesus, and their question does not concern Jesus but an issue on which the Sadducees and the Pharisees disagreed. Once again, however, Jesus' wit and insight silence the interlocutors.

20:27-33. The Sadducees were a Jewish group that was closely aligned with the aristocratic and priestly classes. Because they left no writings, little is known about them; our only knowledge of the Sadducees comes from references in Josephus,[237] in the NT (esp. Matthew and Acts), and later rabbinic writings. The name goes back to Zadok, the high priest at the time of David and Solomon. Nevertheless, the earliest reference to the Sadducees in Josephus describes their activity during the time of John Hyrcanus (135–104 BCE). In contrast to the Pharisees, the Sadducees rejected the authority of oral tradition, denied the belief in resurrection and angels, and emphasized free will over determinism. Their views on the authority of the prophetic writings, their openness to Hellenism, and the nature of their relationship to the priests are all debated.

The Sadducees appear in Luke as a group aligned with the chief priests, scribes, and leaders of the people. Luke introduces the Sadducees to his readers as a group who say there is no resurrection, presumably because Gentile Christians would not have known of this group. The one piece of information that Luke supplies enables the reader to see that their question is designed to reduce belief in resurrection to the point of absurdity. The first clear reference to belief in the resurrection of the dead appears in Dan 12:2. By the first century, the resurrection was affirmed by the Pharisees and apparently also the Essenes. In some Jewish writings the Hellenistic belief in the immortality of the soul also appears (Wis 3:4; 8:13; 15:3; 4 Macc 14:5).

The Sadducees' question assumes the practice of levirate marriage. Prior to belief in resurrection, the Israelites believed that one lived on in one's descendants and in their memory. Hence, if a man died without children, his brother was obligated to take his wife and have children by her. The provision of children in this way also ensured the perpetuation of property within the immediate family and security for the brother's widow. Levirate marriage, a term that derives from the Latin, *levir,* "brother-in-law," is attested in Ugarit, Middle Assyrian, and Hittite law codes.[238] Deuteronomy 25:5-10 provides that the widow shall not marry a stranger. Rather, the deceased's brother "shall go in to her, taking her in marriage, and performing the duty of a husband's brother to her" (Deut 25:5 NRSV; cf. Gen 38:8; Lev 18:16; Ruth 3:9, 12-13). If the man refuses to take his brother's widow, she shall summon the elders, pull his sandal off his foot, and spit in his face (Deut 25:9), thereby demonstrating that she is free from any further obligation to her husband's family. Thereafter, his house would be known as "the house of him whose sandal was pulled off" (Deut 25:10 NRSV).

The summary of Deut 25:5 in Luke 20:28 follows Mark 12:19 (with editorial changes) but only paraphrases the OT text. The last clause, "and raise up children for his brother," comes from Gen 38:8. The Sadducees extend the situation to the point of ridicule. What if there were seven brothers and each in turn died and took the woman as wife, but none could give her children? In the resurrection whose wife would she be?

20:34-36. Luke eliminates Jesus' rebuke of the Sadducees, found in Mark 12:24. Instead, Jesus begins immediately to teach the Sadducees. The role of marriage and childbearing for Christians was a matter of dispute in some circles (see Luke 2:36-37; 1 Cor 7:1-16; 1 Tim 2:15; 5:3-16), and Luke's account of Jesus' exchange with the Sadducees may have been influenced by these debates. The dictum that "those who belong to this age marry and are given in marriage; but those who are considered worthy of a place in that age and in the resurrection from the dead neither marry nor are given in marriage" (Luke 20:34-35) is an extension of Mark 12:25a: "For when they rise from the dead, they neither marry nor are given

---

237. See Josephus *The Jewish War* 2.165-66; *Antiquities of the Jews* 13.293, 297-98; 18.16-17.

238. See Victor P. Hamilton, "Marriage," *Anchor Bible Dictionary* (New York: Doubleday, 1992) 4:567.

in marriage" (NRSV). In Luke the point of equality with the angels is not that those who are raised do not marry but that they do not die (cf. Mark 12:25; Luke 20:36). The logic may be that since those who are raised do not die, neither is there any need to marry and raise up children. Because they are "sons of the resurrection" (a Semitic construction), they are also "sons of God." In the Hebrew Scriptures angels are called "sons of God" (see esp. Gen 6:1-4, where the "sons of God" have children by human women, and as a result God decrees, "My spirit shall not abide in mortals forever, for they are flesh.").

20:37-38. Having dismissed the basis for the Sadducees' question by explaining that life in the resurrection will not simply be a continuation of life as we now know it, Jesus turns to the root of their question: the doctrine of the resurrection of the dead. By means of midrashic argument, Jesus grounds the teaching of resurrection in the writings accepted by the Sadducees themselves—the Law of Moses. He calls their attention to the familiar story of the burning bush. Rather than quoting the words of the Lord (as Mark does), Luke cites Moses' report of the words: "He speaks of the Lord as the God of Abraham, the God of Isaac, and the God of Jacob" (v. 37). The logic of the argument hinges on the axiom that God is "God not of the dead, but of the living"; therefore, the patriarchs must be in some sense alive to God or in God. The verse may be a deliberate allusion to 4

Macc 7:19 (or a similar tradition), which appears in an encomium to Eleazar, the faithful priest who chose death rather than compromise his faith (2 Macc 6:18-31): "They believe that they, like our patriarchs Abraham and Isaac and Jacob, do not die to God, but live to God" (4 Macc 7:19 NRSV). Even if Luke 20:38 alludes to this reference, the emphasis in Luke is clearly on resurrection, not immortality. In both 4 Maccabees and Luke, God remains the source of life for the faithful.

20:39-40. Luke adds a fitting conclusion to this exchange, omitting Jesus' rebuke "you are quite wrong" (Mark 12:27). Instead, some of the scribes (who presumably affirmed the resurrection) declare, "Teacher, you have spoken well" (Luke 20:39). The title of respect, "teacher," recalls the Sadducees' address to Jesus as teacher at the beginning of the scene (v. 28) and continues the emphasis on Jesus' role as teacher in the Temple (see 19:47; 20:1, 21, 28).

The scene concludes with the narrator's report that "they" no longer dared to ask Jesus anything. The pronoun is ambiguous, probably referring to the Sadducees—who disappear from the narrative at this point—but the immediate antecedent would be the scribes. Regardless, Jesus has once again turned away a group of leaders of the people, bested them in a contest of wits, and declared the faithfulness of God.

REFLECTIONS

Jesus' words on the nature of life after death are at once intriguing, reassuring, and disturbing. The question is as old and as timeless as the struggles of Job, who asked, "If mortals die, will they live again?" (Job 14:14 NRSV). Recall the Spanish philosopher Miguel de Unamuno's quest to know whether there is life beyond death (see Reflections above). It is the question we cannot dismiss but cannot answer from reason or experience alone. Is there life beyond death, and if so what will it be like?

Because Jesus said so little about the subject—a parable about Lazarus and the rich man, a word to the thief on the cross—this pronouncement is all the more important. Critical questions remain. To what extent have the words attributed to Jesus been shaped or altered by early Christian debates about marriage, sex, and childbearing? At the least, Luke differs from Matthew and Mark in his account of the words of Jesus (Luke 20:34-36). Luke has evidently introduced deliberate changes from Mark at this point, and his editing heightens the contrast between the place of marriage in this life and in the resurrection.

For those who have lived through violent, abusive marriages, the pronouncement that in the resurrection we will neither marry nor be given in marriage may come as liberating good news. On the other hand, those who have enjoyed lifelong intimacy and companionship in marriage may well object that God has invested so much in establishing faithful, loving, and fulfilling relationships in this life that it is unthinkable that such relationships would be terminated in the resurrection. One approach to interpreting this saying is to recognize that it is set in a time when marriage was viewed primarily as an arrangement of a man's rights to a woman and a woman's right to male support. In heaven there will be no need for such arrangements. Leaving aside the physical side of love and marriage (which belongs to the flesh), there will be no need to restrict love, intimacy, or companionship to a monogamous relationship.[239]

Sometimes it is best to recognize the mystery of the unknown and the limitations of our understanding. A child cannot grasp either the complexities or the pleasures of adulthood. What child finds a quiet evening on the back porch talking and watching the sun set more enjoyable than running to catch fireflies or playing hide and seek in the dusk? "When I became an adult, I put an end to childish ways. For now we see in a mirror, dimly" (1 Cor 13:11-12 NRSV).

Jesus' words can thus be approached from a positive side. The God who created human life, including the institution of marriage, has also provided for life after death for those who have cultivated the capacity to respond to God's love. The biblical teaching is that life comes from God. There is nothing in or of the human being that is naturally or inherently immortal. If there is life beyond death, it is God's gift to those who have accepted God's love and entered into relationship with God in this life: They "are children of God, being children of the resurrection" (20:36).

239. See John Nolland, *Luke 18:35–24:53,* WBC 35C (Dallas: Word, 1993) 968.

Luke 20:41-44, The Question About David's Son

NIV

⁴¹Then Jesus said to them, "How is it that they say the Christ[a] is the Son of David? ⁴²David himself declares in the Book of Psalms:

"'The Lord said to my Lord:
   "Sit at my right hand
⁴³until I make your enemies
   a footstool for your feet."'[b]

⁴⁴David calls him 'Lord.' How then can he be his son?"

a41 Or *Messiah*   b43 Psalm 110:1

NRSV

⁴¹Then he said to them, "How can they say that the Messiah[a] is David's son? ⁴²For David himself says in the book of Psalms,

   'The Lord said to my Lord,
   "Sit at my right hand,
⁴³   until I make your enemies your footstool."'
⁴⁴David thus calls him Lord; so how can he be his son?"

aOr *the Christ*

COMMENTARY

Luke omits the question about the greatest commandment (Mark 12:28-34) because this pericope has been used in Luke 10:25-28. Luke also omits any reference here to the setting of Jesus' question about David's son (Mark 12:35) or the group to whom he addressed the question (Matt 22:41). Instead, Luke allows the unit to nestle in the larger context of Jesus' teaching in the Temple and his confrontations with the chief priests, scribes, and leaders of the people. Since they will not ask him any further questions (see 20:26, 40), he puts a question to them.

The unit consists of (1) a question: "How can they say that the Messiah is David's son?"; (2) the basis for the question, stated in the form of a quotation from Scripture (Ps 110:1); (3) a conclusion drawn from the quotation: "David thus calls him Lord"; and (4) a restatement of the question: "So how can he be his son?" The whole unit is constructed to undermine either the argument that the Messiah is the son of David or the assumptions about the role of the Messiah that accompany that designation. The middle parts of the unit, the quotation and the conclusion drawn from it, undermine any implication that the Messiah is only David's son.

The Davidic sonship of Jesus is well established in the NT. An early confession embedded in the opening of Paul's Letter to the Romans declares that Jesus "was descended from David according to the flesh and was declared to be Son of God with power according to the spirit of holiness by resurrection from the dead" (Rom 1:3-4 NRSV). Accordingly, the genealogies and birth narratives in both Matthew (1:1, 6, 17, 20) and Luke (1:27, 32, 69; 2:4, 11; 3:31) emphasize Jesus' claim to descent from David through Joseph. The Gospel of John also reflects awareness of the same tradition (John 7:42).

Luke preserves the tradition because of its christological significance, but it is difficult to determine whether the questions are directed at critics who denied Jesus' physical lineage or at those who drew erroneous conclusions from it by attaching certain messianic expectations to "the son of David." As with other controversy stories, Jesus' answer may have functioned differently in different settings (Jesus' ministry, early Christian tradition, or the Lukan setting). In the birth narratives, Luke alludes to the Davidic covenant in 2 Sam 7:8-16 (see Luke 1:32-33). Other references confirm that the expectation of a future Davidic king was eventually given messianic sig-nificance (see Isa 9:6-7; 11:1-5; Jer 23:5; 30:9; Ps Sol 17:21; 1QS 9:11). The Davidic king would reestablish the kingdom of David and drive the Gentiles out of Israel (see Ps Sol 17; cf. Acts 1:6). Jesus' fulfillment of expectations for the Davidic Messiah is developed in Acts 2:25-36. On the other hand, there is no evidence that Psalm 110 was related to expectations of a Davidic Messiah in pre-Christian Judaism.[240]

Just as Jesus had appealed to Moses (the Torah) for evidence of the resurrection (see 20:37), so also now he appeals to David (to whom the Psalms were attributed) for proof that the Messiah is greater than David; David himself addresses this one as "my lord." The argument from Scripture thereby makes the point that the Messiah is not merely David's son, with the implication that the role of the Messiah should not be narrowly understood as that of a nationalist liberator or one who would reestablish the kingdom of David. Whether "son of David" is used here in a titular sense or is associated with authority to heal or to exorcise is uncertain.

In its current Lukan context, this unit represents a further clarification of Jesus' kingship, following his entry into Jerusalem (see 18:38, where Jesus is addressed as "Son of David"; and 19:28-40). Jesus is the expected son of David, but he is more, just as earlier Luke shows that he is more than a prophet. As son of David, however, he will sit at the right hand of God—and in context his enemies can only be those who are seeking to trap him and kill him, as the earlier passion predictions have made clear.

240. Joseph A. Fitzmyer, *The Gospel According to Luke (X–XXIV)*, AB 28A (Garden City, N.Y.: Doubleday, 1985) 1311.

REFLECTIONS

Interpretation of this unit is all the more difficult because it appears to be an argument without a context, a pronouncement whose original setting has been lost. Nevertheless, enough remains for us to see that it is a warning not to limit Jesus' role to traditional categories. Eduard Schweizer has summarized the NT's interpretation of Jesus under the rubric "the man who fits no formula." A whole array of titles and messianic references is used of Jesus: the Word, the lamb of God, the Son of God, the Son of Man, King of Israel, the prophet like Moses, and high priest after the order of Melchizedek, to name but a few. As the early Christians sought to explain Jesus' identity and role, they turned to one after another of the traditional terms and expectations. They mined their Scriptures for the light they might shed on the risen Lord and found a wealth of references, each of which clarifies aspects of who

Jesus was and what he did, but no one of the titles fully encompasses his identity. In each case, he is that and more. Schweizer, therefore, contends: "By his very act of avoiding all common labels, Jesus keeps free the heart of the man who encounters him. He wants to enter into this heart himself, in all the reality of what he does and says, not as an image already formed before he himself has a chance to encounter the person."[241]

If no formula, title, or creed can fully or finally describe Jesus, then the church must continually guard against absolutizing its creeds or limiting Jesus to traditional categories. Creeds should be seen as minimal and provisional statements. Jesus is the Lord who transcended the traditional and continues to do so in each generation. Just as every believer learns to be open to new ways of experiencing and expressing Jesus' lordship, so also the church is most faithful to the faith received when it is continually searching for new understandings of the one who opposed those who would limit him to one traditional role. This is christology by addition, not subtraction. He was both David's son and the one whom David called "my Lord."

241. Eduard Schweizer, *Jesus,* trans. David E. Green (Richmond: John Knox, 1971) 22.

Luke 20:45-47, The Denunciation of the Scribes

NIV

45While all the people were listening, Jesus said to his disciples, 46"Beware of the teachers of the law. They like to walk around in flowing robes and love to be greeted in the marketplaces and have the most important seats in the synagogues and the places of honor at banquets. 47They devour widows' houses and for a show make lengthy prayers. Such men will be punished most severely."

NRSV

45In the hearing of all the people he said to the[a] disciples, 46"Beware of the scribes, who like to walk around in long robes, and love to be greeted with respect in the marketplaces, and to have the best seats in the synagogues and places of honor at banquets. 47They devour widows' houses and for the sake of appearance say long prayers. They will receive the greater condemnation."

[a]Other ancient authorities read *his*

COMMENTARY

Jesus' teaching in the Temple continues but now takes the form of a condemnation of the scribes that is reminiscent of the sharp and categorical condemnations leveled by the prophets. Earlier in this chapter Jesus answered the scribes' questions about his authority (20:1-8) and likened them to the wicked tenants (20:9-19). Once again, Luke takes care to maintain the distinction between the people and the religious leaders. He does so here by reporting that he addressed his condemnation of the scribes to his disciples "in the hearing of all the people" (20:45). Thus he omits Mark's reference to "a large crowd" (Mark 12:37*b*), introducing in its place the typically Lukan "all the people." The condemnation is addressed to

Jesus' disciples, who have not appeared in the narrative since 19:39. Those who would follow Jesus should guard against the temptation to be like the scribes.

One of the difficulties of this passage is that it appears to pronounce a blanket condemnation on the scribes when Luke has previously portrayed them in a positive light (20:39). The scribes first enter the narrative in references where they are associated with the Pharisees as those who condemn Jesus as a blasphemer (5:21), complain that he eats with tax collectors and sinners (5:30, "their scribes"), and watch to see whether Jesus will heal on the sabbath (6:7). The first reference to the scribes apart from the Pharisees forecasts their role in the death of Jesus; in 9:22 they are named with the elders and chief priests. The next two references again link the scribes with the Pharisees and note their hostility toward Jesus (11:53; 15:2). Once Jesus reaches Jerusalem, there are no further references to the Pharisees (the last occurrence is in 19:39). Hereafter, the scribes are listed with the chief priests as leaders of the people (19:47; 20:1, 19; 22:2, 66; 23:10). They appear alone only in 20:39, 46, so 20:39 is the only place in Luke where the scribes do not appear in a negative light, and there they simply commend Jesus' rebuttal of the Sadducees. There is no need, then, to attempt to ameliorate Jesus' blanket condemnation of the scribes in the present context. Reading the Greek as a restricted clause forces the syntax unnecessarily. The NRSV and NIV translations are, therefore, preferable to Nolland's rendering: "Beware of those scribes who want to walk about in fine garb."[242]

Jesus condemns the scribes on three counts: their desire for public recognition, their exploitation of widows, and their pretense of piety while praying. Jesus also gives three examples of their desire for public recognition: They like to walk around in long, ornate robes that convey their social position; they seek the deferential greetings by which others recognize their superior learning and the authority it gives them; and they enjoy having the best seats in the synagogues and at dinners. Social custom accorded them all of these privileges. It is not clear that Jesus condemns the privileges given to the scribes, though that is a question worth pondering. Instead, he condemns the love of privilege that makes that privilege the object of the scribes' life-style. Rather than seeking to reverence God in all that they do—"to do justice, and to love kindness, and to walk humbly with your God?" (Mic 6:8)—the scribes seek the public recognition of others. Jesus has previously castigated the guests at a banquet for seeking the places of honor (14:7-14), and he denounced the Pharisees because they loved "to have the seat of honor in the synagogues and to be greeted with respect in the marketplaces" (11:43 NRSV). In the synagogue, the best seats were in the front, facing the assembly, seats normally reserved for the elders and those with the greatest learning.

The reference to the scribes' conduct at dinners leads to the metaphorical reference to eating. They covet the seats of honor at a dinner, but they eat up widows' houses. Jesus may have had in mind a variety of means of extortion or deceit. Fitzmyer lists six possibilities: (1) Scribes accepted payment for legal aid to widows, even though such payment was forbidden. (2) Scribes cheated widows of what was rightly theirs. (3) Scribes sponged off the hospitality of these women of limited means. (4) Scribes mismanaged the property of widows, like Anna, who had dedicated themselves to the service of the Temple. (5) Scribes took large sums of money from credulous old women as a reward from prolonged prayer that they professed to make on the women's behalf. (6) Scribes took the houses as pledges for debts that could not be paid.[243]

The various suggestions at least confirm that the scribes had a number of ways in which they could defraud widows of their livelihood. No specific means of deceit is indicated, however. The point is that the scribes misused their position and prestige to prey upon the very members of society they were charged with protecting. For the social position of widows and the special consideration that is extended to widows in the Hebrew Scriptures, see Commentary on 18:1-8.

The third charge makes their hypocrisy sacrilege. Not only are the scribes pretentious, and not only do they take advantage of those they are charged with protecting, but also they do not even quail at using prayer as a pretense for piety. Perhaps to the chagrin of some, Jesus is not condemning long prayers (though see Matt 6:5, 7-8); he is condemning any prayer that is offered to influence others rather than as a sincere and humble petition for God's mercy (cf. 18:9-14).

The closing statement of this unit is chillingly direct: "They will receive the greater condemnation" (20:47). A sliding scale of rewards and punishments was suggested earlier (see 12:48). Having found the scribes guilty of using their privileged position merely for their own gain and violating the trust placed in them, Jesus warns of the severity of the sentence. Because they are among the privileged who have received much, held great trust, and been given great opportunities, "they will receive the greater condemnation."

242. John Nolland, *Luke 18:35–24:53,* WBC 35C (Dallas: Word, 1993) 975.

243. Joseph A. Fitzmyer, *The Gospel According to Luke (X–XXIV),* AB 28A (Garden City, N.Y.: Doubleday, 1985) 1318.

REFLECTIONS

Jesus' warning to the disciples speaks especially to temptations facing the clergy, but it also warns of dangers of hypocrisy and pretentiousness to which none are immune. In T. S. Eliot's classic drama about the death of Thomas à Becket, *Murder in the Cathedral,* the fourth tempter coaxes Thomas to remain steadfast in his resistance to the king and accept his martyrdom, knowing that it will lead to a far greater glory than even a king could hope for. He would be remembered as a saint and dwell forever in the presence of God. In the end, however, Eliot's Becket responds, "The last temptation is the greatest treason: To do the right deed for the wrong reason." The scribes went further, taking advantage of widows. So Jesus exposes two dangers in the quest of virtue: (1) doing good out of ulterior motives, and (2) doing wrong with the power or privilege accorded to those appointed to do good.

1. Televangelists and media ministers are the most easily recognizable contemporary counterparts to the scribes who pray on widows' houses. With their weekly appeals for generous support so that their programs can continue, religious charlatans have defrauded many widows of their limited means. Others, too, must guard against the same treachery. The elderly may welcome opportunities to ensure that their means will continue to be used for good purposes after they are gone, but development officers for universities, hospitals, and charities, and even family members, must be especially careful that they are not guilty of taking advantage of such goodwill for the wrong reasons and the wrong ends.

2. Jesus' warning about those who take advantage of widows applies even more broadly, however. The role of a priest, minister, or Christian friend carries with it opportunities for intimate relationships with persons needing help at moments when they are particularly vulnerable. A caring relationship or a caring profession should never become the occasion for meeting one's own needs or satisfying one's lusts in the pretense that it is helping the other person.

3. The devouring of widows' houses is a repulsive violation of trust, but loving to wear the long robes and have the seats of honor is the more insidious failing that leads the virtuous Christian or the religious professional to believe that he or she really is better, more important, or less vulnerable to temptation than others. Day to day, we may not be tempted to steal from widows in the ruse that their means are needed for a worthy cause, but who does not enjoy being recognized by others for the good that we do? How easy it is to develop a need for that recognition once we have tasted it and to begin to calculate and to act in ways that will attract the approval and applause of others.

Public prayer is difficult for precisely this reason. When is a person talking to God, and when is the prayer a performance before others? Prayer should be considered, thoughtful, and at times eloquent—the issue here is one's motive and the object of prayer, not the form of the prayer. Moreover, public prayer is not just baring one's soul before God in public, but leading others in prayer, so one needs to give thought to how the prayer will assist others to join in confession, thanksgiving, and petition to God. The issue here is not whether one who leads in public prayer will give thought to how others will hear the prayer. Again, the issue is motive.

Virtue, piety, and doing good should not become guilt-ridden odysseys of second-guessing and self-condemnation in case one has erred. On the contrary, they should be the spontaneous and joyful expression of one's truest self. Jesus' warning, therefore, should not cause us to doubt and question the motive of our every action. Rather, it declares that those who pervert piety and do not care about the consequences of their hypocrisy and injustice will surely be punished. Those who are the purest in heart are persons who give no thought to the good they are doing or to any recognition they might receive from it. They do good for its own sake because they would not consider doing anything else, and it is so natural to them that they keep no account of the good they have done: "Blessed are the pure in heart" (Matt 5:8 NRSV).

Luke 21:1-4, The Widow's Offering

NIV

21 As he looked up, Jesus saw the rich putting their gifts into the temple treasury. ²He also saw a poor widow put in two very small copper coins.^a ³"I tell you the truth," he said, "this poor widow has put in more than all the others. ⁴All these people gave their gifts out of their wealth; but she out of her poverty put in all she had to live on."

^a2 Greek *two lepta*

NRSV

21 He looked up and saw rich people putting their gifts into the treasury; ²he also saw a poor widow put in two small copper coins. ³He said, "Truly I tell you, this poor widow has put in more than all of them; ⁴for all of them have contributed out of their abundance, but she out of her poverty has put in all she had to live on."

COMMENTARY

Jesus' comment on the widow's offering follows immediately after his condemnation of the scribes: "they devour widow's houses" (20:45). The device of catchword linkage, by which originally independent units are connected because they share a prominent term, is a memory device found commonly in oral materials and in various NT passages (see, e.g., Mark 9:47-50; Jas 1:1-8). The question is whether this linking of the two sayings makes any difference in the meaning of Jesus' comment on the widow's offering. Does Jesus praise the widow for her generosity or lament that in giving all she had she has become a victim of the Temple system?

There is only a minimal shift between Jesus' denunciation of the scribes and his comment on the widow's offering. Luke omits most of Mark's introduction to the latter (see Mark 12:41). The report that Jesus "looked up and saw" shifts the reader's attention to a new set of characters without separating the two scenes geographically or temporally. Two new sets of characters are introduced: the rich contributors and a poor widow. Both engage in the same action—putting their gifts into the treasury—so the contrast between them is not apparent at the outset.

Josephus reports that the treasury was located in the court of the women.[244] There were thirteen receptacles or Shofar-chests in the Temple, probably so called because they were trumpet shaped.[245] Each of the chests was labeled for a different type of offering.

Luke describes the widow as needy in v. 2 and poor in v. 3. By this point, the reader understands that Luke has a special regard for widows, in keeping with the OT instructions to care for widows and consistent with the early church's support of widows (see Acts 6:1-6; 1 Tim 5:3-16). For earlier references to widows in Luke, see the comments on Anna (2:36-38), the widow at Zarephath (4:25-26), the widow at Nain (7:11-17), the parable of the widow and the unjust judge (18:1-8), and the widows on whom the scribes preyed (20:47). The reader understands that the widow is cast in a positive light, either as one of simple, genuine piety or as one for whom the righteous should have special care.

Whereas the size or amount of the gifts of the rich is not specified, the narrator reports that the widow put in two lepta, the smallest copper coins then in use (see 12:59). Calculating that a lepta was

244. See Josephus *The Jewish War* 5.200; cf. John 8:20.
245. See *m. Shekalim* 6.5.

worth one-half a Roman quadrans, it would have taken 128 lepta to make a denarius, a day's wage.[246] Two lepta were nearly worthless—an inconsequential gift by any ordinary standard. (See Fig. 5, "Coins in the Gospels," 171.)

In a twist reminiscent of Jesus' parables, Jesus declares that the poor widow had put in more than any of the rich people. Verse 1 introduced the rich, v. 2 the poor widow, and Jesus' pronouncement in v. 3 characterizes the one in terms of the other. How could two lepta be more than any of the other gifts? Verse 4 supplies the rationale for the surprising and seemingly ridiculous statement in v. 3.

Verse 4 characterizes first the gift of the rich: They contributed "out of their abundance." Then it characterizes the widow's gift in contrast: "but she out of her poverty." But there is a second contrast (more clearly seen in the Greek and the NIV than in the NRSV): The rich put in "gifts," but the widow put in "all she had to live on." This brief unit, therefore, contrasts the widow and the rich three times: first in the introduction of the characters (vv. 1-2), then in Jesus' comparison of their gifts (v. 3), and finally in his explanation (v. 4).

Jesus' praise of the widow's small gift over the larger gifts of the rich is not unique; it has parallels in Greek and Jewish literature. Josephus, for example, interprets Samuel's rebuke to Saul in 1 Sam 15:22 as follows:

> And from such as submit not nor offer the true worship that alone is acceptable to God, even though they sacrifice many fat victims, even though they present to Him sumptuous offerings wrought of silver and gold, yet does He not receive these gifts graciously, but rejects them and regards them as tokens of iniquity rather than as piety. But they who are mindful of this one thing alone, to wit what God has spoken and commanded, and who choose rather to die than to transgress aught thereof, in them does

He rejoice; from them He requires no sacrifice, or should they offer any, however modest, more gladly does He welcome this homage from poverty than that of the wealthiest.[247]

We return, therefore, to the problem posed by the narrative context of this scene. How could Jesus praise the act of a widow who put all that she had to live on into the Temple treasury after having just pronounced judgment on the scribes for devouring widows' houses? On the other hand, the surprising twist in v. 3 is characteristic of Jesus and gives every appearance of holding up the widow for her exemplary piety. Moreover, the contrast between God's favor on the gifts of the pure of heart, however small the gifts, is clearly established by Josephus. For this reason, while Jesus' comment on the widow's offering has traditionally been interpreted as praise, some interpreters have recently concluded that it is a lament.[248] The Temple system, no less than the scribes, has rendered the widow destitute.

The best solution is probably to honor Luke's characterization of widows as pious, to recognize that there is no condemnation of the Temple system explicit or implicit in 21:1-4, to recognize also that v. 3 is the heart of the unit rather than v. 4, and to accept Jesus' words as praise rather than lament. Interpreting the scene in this way reinforces the treachery of the scribes who prey upon such widows. The scribes take even the widows' houses, but the widows give even their last two lepta to the Lord.

Jesus by no means condones any religious appeal that renders widows destitute. But neither does he lament the widow's selfless giving.

---

246. See John W. Betlyon, "Coinage," *Anchor Bible Dictionary* (New York: Doubleday, 1992) 1:1086; Helmut Koester, *Introduction to the New Testament* (Philadelphia: Fortress, 1982) 1:90.

247. Josephus, *Jewish Antiquities,* 6:148-49, trans. H. St. J. Thackeray and Ralph Marcus, LCL (Cambridge, Mass.: Harvard University Press, 1934) 241.

248. See A. G. Wright, "The Widow's Mites: Praise or Lament?—A Matter of Context," *CBQ* 44 (1982) 256-65, followed by Fitzmyer, *The Gospel According to Luke (X–XXIV),* 1321.

REFLECTIONS

Jesus' praise of the widow issues a challenge for those who would be his disciples (see 20:45). The most obvious challenge is to give with the complete devotion and selflessness that marked the widow's gift. Seek first the kingdom and do not be anxious (cf. 12:22-31). Beyond the obvious, however, Jesus' example teaches his disciples that part of seeking the kingdom requires vindicating the poor, the widows, and the orphans. Jesus recognized their inherent worth and called on the community to care for the weakest and neediest in their midst. He recognized that those who were often sustained by the gifts of others could themselves give gifts of great value. Without knowing it, the widow gave others a timeless example of selfless devotion to God.

This brief scene exposes for self-examination the private side of all our acts of religious devotion. Why do we do what we do for others and for God? By what measures do we calculate our actions? By what standards do we judge ourselves and others?

Small gifts are easily overlooked. Who stops to notice the secretary who puts out mints on the desk for those who pass through the office? Who appreciates the thoughtfulness of a coworker who sends colleagues notes on their birthdays? Does it matter that some adults regularly work in the nursery so that others can participate in the worship service? Does it make any difference that some teachers stay after school to work with children who are having difficulty in class? The first observation that might be made about this scene is that Jesus noticed one of the neglected. He recognized the importance of the small gift that might so easily be overlooked.

By singling out the widow as exemplary, Jesus also rejected the insidious presumption that those who gave the great gifts were more important or better than the one whose gift was small because her means were limited. In a society in which wealth is the measure of success and happiness, the wealthy are esteemed and given special treatment, while the poor are judged as failures who could have done better if they had tried. A person's value or worth as a human being is, therefore, measured by the evidence of his or her prosperity. Just as in the parables, Jesus' pronouncement reverses the norms and standards by which we are accustomed to living. He turns our world's standards on their head. A widow or a homeless person's gift to God or to others may be more important than the gifts of the wealthy.

Luke 21:5-19, The Coming Wars and Persecutions

NIV

[5]Some of his disciples were remarking about how the temple was adorned with beautiful stones and with gifts dedicated to God. But Jesus said, [6]"As for what you see here, the time will come when not one stone will be left on another; every one of them will be thrown down."

[7]"Teacher," they asked, "when will these things happen? And what will be the sign that they are about to take place?"

[8]He replied: "Watch out that you are not deceived. For many will come in my name, claiming, 'I am he,' and, 'The time is near.' Do not follow them. [9]When you hear of wars and revolutions, do not be frightened. These things must happen first, but the end will not come right away."

[10]Then he said to them: "Nation will rise against nation, and kingdom against kingdom. [11]There will be great earthquakes, famines and

NRSV

[5]When some were speaking about the temple, how it was adorned with beautiful stones and gifts dedicated to God, he said, [6]"As for these things that you see, the days will come when not one stone will be left upon another; all will be thrown down."

[7]They asked him, "Teacher, when will this be, and what will be the sign that this is about to take place?" [8]And he said, "Beware that you are not led astray; for many will come in my name and say, 'I am he!'[a] and, 'The time is near!'[b] Do not go after them.

[9]"When you hear of wars and insurrections, do not be terrified; for these things must take place first, but the end will not follow immediately." [10]Then he said to them, "Nation will rise against nation, and kingdom against kingdom;

[a]Gk I am   [b]Or at hand

pestilences in various places, and fearful events and great signs from heaven.

12"But before all this, they will lay hands on you and persecute you. They will deliver you to synagogues and prisons, and you will be brought before kings and governors, and all on account of my name. 13This will result in your being witnesses to them. 14But make up your mind not to worry beforehand how you will defend yourselves. 15For I will give you words and wisdom that none of your adversaries will be able to resist or contradict. 16You will be betrayed even by parents, brothers, relatives and friends, and they will put some of you to death. 17All men will hate you because of me. 18But not a hair of your head will perish. 19By standing firm you will gain life.

11there will be great earthquakes, and in various places famines and plagues; and there will be dreadful portents and great signs from heaven.

12"But before all this occurs, they will arrest you and persecute you; they will hand you over to synagogues and prisons, and you will be brought before kings and governors because of my name. 13This will give you an opportunity to testify. 14So make up your minds not to prepare your defense in advance; 15for I will give you words[a] and a wisdom that none of your opponents will be able to withstand or contradict. 16You will be betrayed even by parents and brothers, by relatives and friends; and they will put some of you to death. 17You will be hated by all because of my name. 18But not a hair of your head will perish. 19By your endurance you will gain your souls.

[a] Gk a mouth

COMMENTARY

Jesus' confrontation with the authorities in the Temple (which began back at 19:47) now shifts to the future tense. The second half of the extended section 19:47–21:38 concerns the coming persecutions and the destruction of the Temple (21:5-19), the destruction of Jerusalem (21:20-24), and the coming of the Son of Man (21:25-36).

Jesus' warning of wars and persecutions seems to be drawn from Mark 13:1-13, but if so, Luke has exercised more freedom than usual in recasting, editing, and paraphrasing his source. Among the most significant differences between Mark and Luke in this section are that (1) Luke has omitted the reference to the disciples in Mark 13:1 and the list of four disciples in Mark 13:3; (2) Luke structures a series of three imperatives in vv. 8-9: "do not be led astray" (μὴ πλανηθῆτε mē planēthēte), "do not go" (μὴ πορευθῆτε mē poreuthēte), and "do not be terrified" (μὴ πτοηθῆτε mē ptoēthēte); (3) Luke changes Mark's "but the end is still to come" (Mark 13:7) to "but the end will not follow immediately" (21:9); (4) the list of signs in v. 11 is expanded so that it anticipates the apocalyptic signs of the coming of the Son of Man in 21:25-36; (5) the reference to prisons in 21:12 foreshadows the imprisonments of Peter and Paul in Acts;

(6) Luke omits Mark's declaration that "the good news must first be proclaimed to all nations" (Mark 13:10 NRSV); (7) Luke omits the reference to the Holy Spirit in Mark 13:11—Jesus himself will give them what they are to say; and (8) Luke adds the proverbial assurance that not a hair will be lost from their heads (21:18; cf. 12:7).

21:5. In contrast to Mark, where the disciples are mentioned and then named, Luke does not identify Jesus' interlocutors. The most recent reference to the disciples was in 19:45, and whereas Mark says that Jesus went out of the Temple (Mark 13:1), Luke omits the reference, leaving Jesus in the Temple while he tells of its destruction (see 21:1, 37). The unidentified "some," Luke says, were speaking "about the Temple," admiring its beautiful stones and adornments. Josephus is even more lavish in his descriptions of the beauty of the Temple:

> The sacred edifice itself, the holy temple, in the central position, was approached by a flight of twelve steps. The façade was of equal height and breadth, each being a hundred cubits; but the building behind was narrower by forty cubits, for in front it had as it were shoulders extending twenty cubits on either side. The first gate was seventy cubits high and twenty-five broad and

had no doors, displaying unexcluded the void expanse of heaven; the entire face was covered with gold, and through it the first edifice was visible to a spectator without in all its grandeur and the surroundings of the inner gate all gleaming with gold fell beneath his eye. . . .

The exterior of the building wanted nothing that could astound either mind or eye. For, being covered on all sides with massive plates of gold, the sun was no sooner up than it radiated so fiery a flash that persons straining to look at it were compelled to avert their eyes, as from the solar rays.[249]

Even the outer walls of the Temple were constructed with large stones, carefully squared off and finished with a border around each exposed edge.[250] The votive offerings included lavish gifts of ornate adornments and sacred vessels (cf. 2 Macc 9:16).

21:6. Jesus quickly reminds those who are so taken by the grandeur of the Temple that "not one stone will be left upon another" (21:6). The phrase echoes his earlier warning of the destruction of the Temple (19:44). The statement now serves as the controlling theme or keynote for the rest of the discourse. The introductory expression, "the days will come," prompts the question regarding when these things will be (21:7) and the various temporal references that follow: e.g., "when you hear" (v. 9), "but before all this occurs" (21:12), and "when you see" (21:20).

21:7. The anonymous interlocutors address Jesus as "teacher." This is the eleventh and last time Jesus is so addressed in Luke, and in none of the previous ten occurrences of this title is it used by the disciples. Luke reserves it exclusively for non-disciples; Pharisees, lawyers, persons from the crowd, the rich ruler, Sadducees, and scribes all call Jesus "teacher," but the disciples never do. Hence, the assumption may be warranted that whereas in Mark Jesus responds to his disciples, Luke portrays his interlocutors as the scribes (20:39) or "the people" (20:45) in the Temple. Jesus has said nothing about a "sign" of the approach of the Temple's destruction, but his interlocutors assume there must be one. The OT prophets had identified signs that would signal that the destruction or deliverance of Jerusalem was imminent (2 Kgs 19:29-31/Isa 37:30-32;

Isa 7:11-16). Earlier Jesus had said that no sign would be given except the sign of Jonah (11:29), but later he will indeed enumerate signs preceding the coming of the Son of Man (21:11, 25).

Josephus reports that preceding the destruction of the Temple, there were various signs to warn the people of its destruction, but they chose instead to trust in the false prophets who reassured them: "Thus it was that the wretched people were deluded at that time by charlatans and pretended messengers of the deity; while they neither heeded nor believed in the manifest portents that foretold the coming destruction. . . . Reflecting on these things one will find that God has a care for men, and by all kinds of premonitory signs shows His people the way of salvation."[251] Among Josephus's accounts of the signs that he claims occurred at this time, one finds the following: A star resembling a sword stood over the city; a comet continued for a year; a light as bright as day shone around the altar for half an hour; a cow gave birth to a lamb in the Temple; the great brass gate of the inner court swung open of its own accord; chariots appeared in the air and armed battalions hurtled through the clouds; and one Jesus, son of Ananias, stood up in the Temple and pronounced woes on Jerusalem.[252]

21:8-9. Rather than describe the signs that would precede and confirm the destruction he foresaw, Jesus issued a series of three warnings. Explanations follow the first and third warnings ("for . . . "), while the second warning grows out of the first explanation:

"Beware that you are not led astray [μὴ πλανηθῆτε *mē planēthēte*]; for many will come in my name and say, 'I am he!' [ἐγώ εἰμι *egō eimi*] and, 'The time is near!' Do not go after them [μὴ πορευθῆτε *mē poreuthēte*]. When you hear of wars and insurrections, do not be terrified [μὴ πτοηθῆτε *mē ptoēthēte*]; for these things must take place first, but the end will not follow immediately." (21:8)

This is the only occurrence of the verb "to lead astray" (πλανάω *planaō*) in Luke and Acts, but it occurs eight times in Matthew and four times in Mark. Its meaning encompasses being led to sin, being taught false teachings, and being deceived regarding apocalyptic events (John 7:12, 47; 1 Cor

249. Josephus, *The Jewish War*, 5:207-208, 222, trans. H. St. J. Thackeray, LCL (Cambridge, Mass.: Harvard University Press, 1928) 263, 269.

250. See Josephus *The Jewish War* 5.174-175.

251. Josephus, *The Jewish War*, 6.288, 310, trans. H. St. J. Thackeray, LCL (Cambridge, Mass.: Harvard University Press, 1928) 459-61, 467.

252. Ibid., 6.289-309.

6:9; 15:33; Gal 6:7). Often in the NT deception is characterized as the work of false prophets (Matt 24:11; Mark 13:22; cf. 1 John 2:26; 3:7; 4:1). The claim "I am he!" is couched in the revelatory formula *egō eimi,* which appears in the Gospel of John on the lips of Jesus at least four times in the absolute sense (John 8:24, 28, 58; 13:19) and as many as five other times (John 4:26; 6:20; 18:5, 6, 8) with echoes of this sense (see also Mark 13:6; 14:62). In this context it probably represents a messianic claim, "I am the Christ" (cf. Matt 24:5). The references to various false prophets at this time confirm the necessity of Jesus' warning (cf. Acts 5:36-37).[253]

The warning not to go out to the false prophets is a doublet of Luke 17:23. The other claim of the false prophets will be that "the time is near" (cf. Matt 3:2; 4:17; Mark 1:15; Luke 10:9, 11; 19:11; Rev 1:3). The announcement may be an allusion to Dan 7:22. Wars and uprisings were always times of terror. Consequently, they are often mentioned as signs of apocalyptic events (Dan 11:25, 44; Rev 6:1-8; 9:7-11). Jesus instructs his followers not to be terrified by these developments. In God's providence they are necessary, and moreover they do not signal that the end is near. In this context "the end" refers primarily to the time of the destruction of the Temple (see 21:6-7), but the Lukan eschatological discourse does not distinguish very clearly the relation of the destruction of Jerusalem from the time of the coming of the Son of Man (see 21:25).

21:10-11. This develops further the warning of coming wars and insurrections, "nation will rise against nation, and kingdom against kingdom" (cf. 2 Chr 15:6; Isa 19:2). Earthquakes (Ezek 38:19; Matt 27:54; 28:2; Rev 6:12; 8:5; 11:13, 19; 16:18), famines (Luke 4:25; Acts 11:28; Rom 8:35; Rev 6:8; 18:8), and plagues also appear as typical signs of apocalyptic events. The phrase "famines and plagues" is pleasantly alliterative in Greek (λιμοὶ καὶ λοιμοί *limoi kai loimoi*) and occurs in various non-biblical sources.[254] The allusion to "dreadful portents and great signs from heaven" in v. 11 prepares the reader for the detailed description of these events in vv. 25-26, at the time of the coming of the Son of Man, but

they are also reminiscent of Josephus's description of the signs and portents that accompanied the destruction of Jerusalem (see above).

21:12-19. These verses represent a parenthesis in this eschatological discourse that speaks directly to the fate of the disciples. As such, it foreshadows the arrests and trials that will be reported in the book of Acts. The main point of the paragraph is to prepare the disciples for these trials by exhorting them to regard trials as occasions for bearing witness.

The initial phrase of v. 12, "But before all this occurs," serves to separate the trials of the disciples from the destruction of Jerusalem, pushing the apocalyptic events further into the future. The succession of verbs that follows lends the exhortation something of the character of a covenant. First, it speaks of what "they" will do (v. 12), then what "you" should do (vv. 13-14), and then what "I" will do (v. 15). Verses 16-19 append a series of traditional exhortations regarding betrayal by family members, persecution on account of Jesus' name, God's providence over the faithful, and the need for endurance.

The four verbs in v. 12 outline the fearsome persecution that will engulf the disciples: "arrest" (ἐπιβάλλω *epiballō* [literally, "lay hands on you"), "persecute" (διώκω *diōkō*), "hand (παραδίδωμι *paradidōmi*) you over," and "bring (ἀπάγω *apagō*) you before kings and governors." The first two are finite verbs; the latter two are participles. The English verb "arrest" is really a translation of the idiom "to lay hands on," which also occurs in Luke 20:19 in reference to the arrest of Jesus and repeatedly in Acts in references to the arrests of the disciples (4:3; 5:18; 12:1; 21:27). Similarly, the reference to persecution foreshadows one of the leading motifs of the plot of Acts (8:3; 12:4), where Saul is chief persecutor of the church (see Acts 7:52; 9:4-5; 22:4, 7-8; 26:11, 14-15). Luke adds "and prisons" to Mark's warning that the disciples would be handed over to synagogues, perhaps signaling that the disciples would experience persecution from both Jewish and Gentile officials. Accounts of persecution and exclusion from the synagogues are found so frequently in Acts that it is another of the book's major motifs (Acts 6:9; 9:2; 13:44-51; 17:1-5, 10-13; 18:4-7; 19:8-9; 22:19; 26:11). As the place where the apostles preach, the synagogue also

---

253. See also Josephus *Antiquities of the Jews* 20.97-99; 20.169-172; *The Jewish War* 6.285-288.

254. See Fitzmyer, *The Gospel According to Luke (X–XXIV),* 1337.

becomes the site of opposition and rejection. John the Baptist was locked in prison (Luke 3:20), and Peter vows that he is ready to go with Jesus to prison (Luke 22:33), but the time of his imprisonments comes later (Acts 5:18-19, 22, 25; 12:4-11, 17). Similarly, Paul and Silas are imprisoned (Acts 16:23-40), as are those whom Saul persecuted (Acts 8:3; 22:4; 26:10).

The pattern of providing a program for Acts through Jesus' predictions continues in the references to kings (Herod, Acts 12:1; Agrippa, Acts 25:13-14, 24, 26; 26:2, 27) and governors (Felix, Acts 23:24, 26, 33; 24:1, 10; and Festus, Acts 26:30). Jesus has already warned his followers that they will be reviled and persecuted (6:22; 12:4-12), using some of the same language that appears in the present context. In 6:22, the warning is that they will be persecuted "on account of the Son of Man"; here the persecution will arise "because of my name" (21:12). In the early chapters of the book of Acts, the disciples do a variety of wonderful things "in the name of Jesus": baptize (2:38), heal (3:6; 4:10), teach (4:18; 5:28), and do signs and wonders (4:30). They are also charged not to teach in Jesus' name (4:18; 5:28), and they are flogged and suffer dishonor on account of Jesus' name (5:40-41; 9:16).

The arrests and persecution of the disciples will become occasions for them to give testimony.[255] Luke omits the Markan language of Mark 13:10, "and the good news must first be proclaimed to all nations," but the pattern of fulfillment of these predictions in Acts continues. Peter and John are arrested and bear witness to the council (4:8-12, 19-20), then Peter and the apostles (5:29-32), Stephen (7:2-53), Paul, and Silas (16:25-39), and on various other occasions Paul is arrested and testifies (22:1-21; 23:1-6; 24:10-21; 26:2-29).

The persecution of the disciples, however, does not exceed what Jesus himself experiences. He, too, is about to be arrested and brought before Pilate and Herod. Luke further strengthens the connection between Jesus and the persecution of the disciples by substituting the promise that Jesus himself will give the disciples what they are to say for the Markan assurance that the Holy Spirit will speak for them (Mark 13:11; cf. Luke 12:11-

12). The fulfillment in Acts of Jesus' promise that he will give his disciples the words they should speak is particularly striking in the following vv.:

One night the Lord said to Paul in a vision, "Do not be afraid, but speak and do not be silent; for I am with you, and no one will lay a hand on you to harm you, for there are many in this city who are my people." (Acts 18:9-10 NRSV)

That night the Lord stood near him and said, "Keep up your courage! For just as you have testified for me in Jerusalem, so you must bear witness also in Rome." (Acts 23:11 NRSV)

Likewise, Jesus promises that they will have a wisdom that none of their opponents can resist, but in Acts explicit references to wisdom are limited to the descriptions of the Seven (6:3), Joseph (7:10), Moses (7:22), and Stephen, of whom the narrator reports, "They could not withstand the wisdom and the Spirit with which he spoke" (6:10 NRSV). The magician Elymas tried to withstand Paul, but Elymas's magic was quickly defeated (Acts 13:8-12). The preaching of Jesus prevails, therefore, in spite of those who speak against it (see Acts 13:45; 28:19, 22).

As we have seen, virtually every detail of vv. 12-15 foreshadows the work of the disciples in the book of Acts. Jesus' prophecy first sets up expectations for the reader and opens gaps to be filled in the narrative. Then the fulfillment of these predictions serves to confirm both Jesus' sovereign authority and the divine necessity of the persecutions experienced by the early Christians.

Verses 16-19 add predictions and assurances that appear to be drawn from common tradition. Parts of these verses appear elsewhere in Luke, but they are not as closely related to the program for Acts as the preceding verses are. The prediction of betrayal by family members echoes the earlier warnings of 12:53, which drew from Mic 7:6 (see also Luke 18:29). In this context, however, the connection with the OT is muted. Jesus himself will be betrayed by a friend—Judas—and put to death, so again he experiences the full measure of the trials that are about to fall upon his followers.

Betrayals by family members and friends are notably absent from the ordeals of the disciples described in Acts, but the prediction that some will be put to death (21:16) is fulfilled in the martyrdoms of Stephen (7:54-60), James the son of Zebedee (12:1-2), and, we may presume, Paul

---

255. Regarding the theme of witness in Luke and Acts, see Marion L. Soards, *The Speeches in Acts: Their Content, Context, and Concerns* (Louisville: Westminster/John Knox, 1994) 192-200.

(Acts 20:24-25, 29; 21:11-13). Verse 17, the prediction that the disciples will be hated by all because of Jesus' name, repeats Mark 13:13 verbatim, whereas Luke has consistently rewritten the material from Mark 13:9-13 in this paragraph. The verb for "hate" (μισέω *miseō*) does not appear in Acts, but parallels to the present verse do appear earlier in Luke (1:71; 6:22, 27).

Verse 18, "But not a hair of your head will perish," is an assurance of divine protection that occurs in various places in the OT (1 Sam 14:45; 2 Sam 14:11; 1 Kgs 1:52).[256] In this context, it extends the earlier assurance, "But even the hairs of your head are all counted" (12:7), and in Acts it is the assurance that Paul gives to the soldiers: "for none of you will lose a hair from your heads" (Acts 27:34 NRSV).

The predictions of this paragraph all have a didactic or hortatory purpose. The reason for warning the disciples about the coming trials is so that they may be prepared to endure them faithfully. James exhorts early Christians to face trials with joy, knowing that "the testing of your faith produces endurance . . . let endurance have its full effect, so that you may be mature and complete, lacking in nothing" (Jas 1:3-4 NRSV). Similarly, the good soil bears fruit "with patient endurance" (8:15), but endurance does not mean passive waiting; it is more akin to perseverance than to patience.

The paragraph concludes with Luke's last lesson on how to save one's life. Those who seek to save their lives will lose them, but saving one's life comes from losing it for Jesus' sake (9:24; 17:33). Consequently, one must love God with all one's life (10:27). The rich fool reassured his soul that he had all he could possibly need, but God intervened, saying, "This very night your life is being demanded of you" (12:20). On the contrary, Jesus assured his disciples, "Do not worry about your life. . . . For life is more than food, and the body more than clothing" (12:22-23). But one cannot value even life itself above following Jesus (14:26). Such discipleship will require endurance, but the result is that one gains life.

256. See Joseph A. Fitzmyer, *The Gospel According to Luke (X–XXIV)*, AB 28A (Garden City, N.Y.: Doubleday, 1985) 1341.

REFLECTIONS

The first section of Jesus' response to the questions regarding the destruction of the Temple contains both a warning of the wars, earthquakes, famines, and plagues that will come and a warning to the disciples of the persecutions they must endure. Jesus' words about the future command a special fascination for those in every generation who seek signs of the end times. In times of great danger, stress, and hardship it is natural for persons and communities of faith to turn to God and to the future for hope, for the promise of deliverance. The power and pathos of the great spirituals are born of suffering and oppression. But for those who have the means to relieve suffering and oppression, idle preoccupation with prophecies of the end of time is surely a perversion of the gospel. The force of Jesus' warning in vv. 7-11 is that the disciples should not be misled by the false prophets who will come claiming a messianic authority and saying that the time is near. Such claims are the words of charlatans who prey upon the gullible.

In our day, too, there is a plague of pseudo-religious prophets claiming that the end is at hand. Pastors and teachers will need to distinguish biblical teachings and sound biblical interpretation from the sensational claims carried by the media and popular religious best-sellers. Jesus did not call his disciples to be prophets but to disregard the false prophets; do not be led astray, and do not go after them (see v. 8).

The gospel offers not a way of predicting the end of the world but the spiritual resources to cope with adversity and hardship. In times of distress, "do not be terrified" (v. 9). On the other hand, following Jesus always exposes the faithful to opposition from the authorities. If in every generation there are those whose religion is simply a form of escapism into the fantasy of futurism, every generation has also had its courageous and prophetic visionaries who devoted themselves completely to Jesus' call to create community, oppose injustice, work for peace, and make a place for the excluded. Every generation, therefore, is called back to the teachings of Jesus by the examples of those who have suffered persecution and hardship because they dared to strive to live out Jesus' call for a community that transcends social barriers, that cares for its least privileged, and that confronts abuses of power and wealth. These verses allow us to examine two visions of what it means to follow Jesus. One is focused on prophecies of the future and makes no difference in how one lives in the here and now. The other calls for such a commitment of life that those who dare to embrace it will find themselves persecuted by authorities.

As a parenthesis within the discourse on the destruction of the Temple and the destruction of Jerusalem, vv. 12-19 both warn the disciples of the ordeals that lie ahead and offer assurances. They will be arrested, persecuted, and brought to trial, but Jesus himself will give them the words they are to speak and a wisdom that their opponents cannot withstand. Therefore, they are not to prepare their defense in advance (v. 14) but endure the coming trials (v. 19).

The severity of the persecution is balanced by the certainty of God's protection in a paradoxical fashion: "They will put some of you to death" (v. 16), "but not a hair of your head will perish" (v. 18). In Acts, the deaths of the martyrs confirm the wickedness of those who oppose the apostles, but God's faithfulness remains beyond question. It is demonstrated repeatedly through the empowerment of the disciples' witness, wondrous deliverances, and repeated triumphs over those who oppose their message. Nevertheless, the dangers and hardships for the faithful are real indeed. Truth is tested and faith is confirmed not in idle speculation but in the crucible of adversity. Those who wish to find a more vibrant religious experience, therefore, should look not for signs of the future but for signals that it is time to live by Jesus' call for obedience here and now.

Luke 21:20-24, The Destruction of Jerusalem Foretold

NIV

20"When you see Jerusalem being surrounded by armies, you will know that its desolation is near. 21Then let those who are in Judea flee to the mountains, let those in the city get out, and let those in the country not enter the city. 22For this is the time of punishment in fulfillment of all that has been written. 23How dreadful it will be in those days for pregnant women and nursing mothers! There will be great distress in the land and wrath against this people. 24They will fall by the sword and will be taken as prisoners to all the nations. Jerusalem will be trampled on by the Gentiles until the times of the Gentiles are fulfilled."

NRSV

20"When you see Jerusalem surrounded by armies, then know that its desolation has come near.[a] 21Then those in Judea must flee to the mountains, and those inside the city must leave it, and those out in the country must not enter it; 22for these are days of vengeance, as a fulfillment of all that is written. 23Woe to those who are pregnant and to those who are nursing infants in those days! For there will be great distress on the earth and wrath against this people; 24they will fall by the edge of the sword and be taken away as captives among all nations; and Jerusalem will be trampled on by the Gentiles, until the times of the Gentiles are fulfilled."

[a]Or is at hand

COMMENTARY

After the parenthesis in vv. 12-19 on the persecution of the disciples, the discourse returns to the signs that the destruction of Jerusalem is at hand. Verse 9 warned that the disciples would hear of wars and insurrections, but they would not be a sign of the end. Verse 20, by contrast, says that when they see Jerusalem surrounded by armies, they will know that the time of its destruction has come. Verses 20-24, therefore, resume the answer to the questions raised in v. 7 and relate directly to vv. 9-11.

The interpreter of these verses must work continually in four contexts: (1) allusions and oracles concerning the fate of Jerusalem that Luke has placed earlier in the Gospel in preparation for this discourse; (2) Mark 13:14-20, which served as a source for Luke, but that Luke has extensively rewritten; (3) warnings from the writings of the OT prophets of the destruction of Jerusalem, which Luke has mined for their biblical language; and (4) Josephus's accounts of the siege of Jerusalem, which Luke would not have read but that may tell us the kinds of things Luke may have known about these events. The following interpretation is informed by all four of these perspectives.

21:20. The first phrase echoes v. 9, "When you hear." The same phrase is found at the beginning of Mark 13:14, which is similar in content, but Luke has omitted Mark's reference to "the abomination of desolation" (cf. Dan 9:27; 12:11), retaining only the word "desolation" (ἐρήμωσις *erēmōsis*), which occurs elsewhere in the NT only in the Matthean and Markan parallels where one finds this phrase from Daniel. The word translated "armies" (στρατόπεδον *stratopedon*) literally means "camps," and Josephus uses the same term repeatedly in his description of the advance on Jerusalem and the siege of the city. First, Vespasian placed camps at Jericho and at Adida, surrounding the city "on all sides" so that "all egress from Jerusalem was cut off" by "the army which hemmed in the city from every side."[257] Later, he describes how Titus placed three camps comprising four Roman legions around the city.[258] Earlier, when Jesus wept over Jerusalem, he warned that "the days will come upon you, when your enemies will set up ramparts around you and surround you, and hem you in on every side" (19:43). The city surrounded would be the sign of its "desolation," a term that Jeremiah also used to describe the destruction of Jerusalem (Jer 44:6, 22). Her house would be abandoned (Luke 13:35). If the false prophets claimed that the end of time was near, they were

wrong; the armies would confirm that the desolation of Jerusalem was at hand (cf. 21:8, 20). On the other hand, if they did not distinguish the end of time from the destruction of the Temple, their warnings were premature and ill-founded.

21:21-22. Once the city was surrounded, the Judeans should flee to the mountains, and its inhabitants should make every effort to flee before the final assault. As it happened, the attack on the city was delayed by news of the death of Nero.[259] The call to come out of the city echoes the words of Jeremiah: "See, I am setting before you the way of life and the way of death. Those who stay in this city shall die by the sword, by famine, and by pestilence; but those who go out and surrender to the Chaldeans who are besieging you shall live" (Jer 21:8-9 NRSV; cf. 51:45; Rev 18:4).

The expression "the days of vengeance" occurs in Hos 9:7, but it may be derived more immediately from Jer 51:6.[260] Again, we may compare the vision of the fall of Babylon in Revelation 18, which draws on Jeremiah, confirming that the passage was known by Christian writers. More proximately, Jesus assured his followers that God would avenge those who cried out for justice (18:7-8). Paradoxically, Luke uses the phrase "all that is written" to refer to the fulfillment of the Scriptures in reference to both Jesus' death and the destruction of Jerusalem (see 18:31; 21:22; 24:44). Jesus had lamented the fate of Jerusalem (13:34-35; 19:41-44), but "the time of [her] visitation" would pass (19:44), and the "days of vengeance" (21:22) were coming.

21:23. Mark's warning (13:15-16) that those on the rooftops should not come down and those in the fields should not turn back to retrieve their belongings is omitted, probably because it was used earlier in Luke 17:31. Expectant and nursing mothers will be especially vulnerable (cf. 23:28-29). Alas for them! Josephus records the grim story of a mother so wracked by famine that she tore her child from her breast and roasted it for food.[261]

Luke also omits Mark's call to pray that the end of siege might not be in winter (Mark 13:18). Actually, the assault on the city lasted from April until August, but even assuming that Luke knew

257. Josephus *The Jewish War* 4.486-490.
258. Ibid., 5:67-70.
259. Ibid., 4.491, 497-98, 502.
260. See John Nolland, *Luke 18:35–24:53,* WBC 35C (Dallas: Word, 1993) 1001.
261. Josephus *The Jewish War* 6.201-13.

this his reasons for omitting Mark 13:18 are not self-evident.[262]

Perhaps again separating the destruction of Jerusalem from "the end" or the coming of the Son of Man, Luke alters Mark 13:19 with its reference to Dan 12:1. "The earth" (ἡ γῆ *hē gē*) might better be rendered "the land" here, since the reference seems to be to Judea rather than to the whole earth, as in v. 25. God's wrath is here expressed against "this people" because they do not receive the salvation that God has prepared for them (cf. 2:34).

21:24. Verse 24 echoes the warnings of prophets through the centuries as it forecasts the complete destruction of Jerusalem. The manifestations of defeat and destruction are described. (1) They will fall by the sword. The phrase "the edge of the sword" occurs in Jer 21:7; Sir 28:18. (2) They will be taken away as captives (Deut 28:64; Ezra 9:7; Ezek 32:9). (3) They will be trampled on by the Gentiles (Dan 8:13; Zech 12:3 LXX; Rev 11:2). The last phrase of v. 24, "until the times of the Gentiles are fulfilled," means until the Gentiles have exercised their complete domination or until the period allotted to them for the punishment of Israel is complete. God's promise of a limit to the period of Israel's oppression by

the Gentiles can also be found in the Scriptures (Tob 14:5; Dan 12:7; Rom 11:25), so it has been suggested that the phrase refers to the time when God's judgment upon the Gentiles is fulfilled.[263] The former interpretation best fits the description of utter defeat that is painted here. Jerusalem will be destroyed with great shame and suffering, just as the prophets warned.

The events of the fall of Jerusalem in 70 CE were no less catastrophic. Elderly and infirm persons were slain; the rest taken captive, and many of those who wished to plunder the city were repelled by the stench of the bodies.[264] The emperor then ordered that the whole city be razed, leaving only the towers of Herod's palace to remind visitors of the city's former strength and glory.[265] Even Titus himself, the general who had commanded the assault, lamented the fate of the city: "On his way he visited Jerusalem, and contrasting the sorry scene of desolation before his eyes with the former splendour of the city, and calling to mind the grandeur of its ruined buildings and their pristine beauty, he commiserated its destruction."[266]

262. Nolland, *Luke 18:35–24:53*, 1002.

263. Ibid., 1002-4.
264. Josephus *The Jewish War* 6.415, 431.
265. Ibid., 7.1-4.
266. Josephus, *The Jewish War*, 7.112, trans. H. St. J. Thackeray, LCL (Cambridge, Mass.: Harvard University Press, 1928) 539.

REFLECTIONS

Biblical forecasts of destruction, suffering, and the loss of human life have only one purpose: to call God's people to repentance. In the case of Jesus' prophetic lament over the destruction of Jerusalem, the overlay of temporal perspectives adds to its rhetorical force. In all likelihood, Luke and his readers knew that the destruction of the city had already occurred, just as Jesus said it would. Luke's rendition of Jesus' prophetic words draws on the words of Israel's prophets and reflects the events that actually occurred. Echoes of familiar warnings and flashes of scenes from the assault on the city underscore the fateful warning. It would and did happen just as Jesus and the prophets had said it would.

The fulfillment of Jesus' warning so recently and so fully serves also to drive home Luke's description of Jesus as one greater than a prophet who fulfilled the prophets and "all that is written" (v. 22). Jesus' words are devoid of any joy of triumph or vindication. Consistently, Jesus laments the fate toward which the city is rushing headlong (cf. 13:34; 19:41-44). There is no place here for anti-Jewish sentiment, no place for the triumphalism that so often cheapens and perverts Christian teachings regarding the future. Even the Roman general lamented the tragedy of Jerusalem's destruction. Can a Christian do less when warnings of judgment come to pass?

"When you see Jerusalem surrounded by armies, then know that its desolation has come near" (v. 20). When nations unleash their military might against other nations, the result is inevitable: desolation and horrors that repulse the human mind. Jesus counsels the disciples to join neither the Romans nor the resistance but to flee. They have no place in this conflict.

Alas for the mothers and their infants. Civilian casualties—now spoken of as "collateral losses"—often outnumber those of the enemy forces.

The danger of reading Jesus' words as a warning about an isolated event in antiquity or merely as a forecast of the deserved fate of Jerusalem robs the text of meaning or relevance for today's readers. On the contrary, Jesus laments the fate of those who have consistently rejected God's prophets and God's call for repentance from a way of life that leads to a breakdown of justice, order, and peace. Jesus' confrontations with the leaders of the people in Luke 20 are directly connected with his forecast of the city's destruction. The leaders were like the stewards who wanted to keep the produce of the vineyard for themselves; they killed the owner's son and eventually lost the vineyard (20:9-19). Give Caesar his due—maintain civil order—but live all of life as befits those made in God's image (20:20-26). Otherwise, oppression and anarchy will beget violence with all its savage consequences. Let us calculate the times and the seasons, but let us look to the rising incidence of violence, especially in areas of deprivation and poverty—neighborhoods surrounded by armed gangs. What sort of response do these signs of the times call forth from the Christian community? Movies about what life will be like in the future in metropolitan areas regularly depict a society overcome by violence and polarized between warring factions. In its own way, this secular vision of the future serves as a prophetic warning, but unlike the Hollywood script, the biblical vision offers no hope that violence can be redemptive. There is no salvation at the hands of a violent hero of superhuman strength and ability in combat. The only hope that Jesus offers is the call to repent, the call of obedience to his gospel for the poor and the outcast, and his assurance that "by your endurance you will gain your souls" (v. 19).

Luke 21:25-36, The Coming of the Son of Man Foretold

NIV

25"There will be signs in the sun, moon and stars. On the earth, nations will be in anguish and perplexity at the roaring and tossing of the sea. 26Men will faint from terror, apprehensive of what is coming on the world, for the heavenly bodies will be shaken. 27At that time they will see the Son of Man coming in a cloud with power and great glory. 28When these things begin to take place, stand up and lift up your heads, because your redemption is drawing near."

29He told them this parable: "Look at the fig tree and all the trees. 30When they sprout leaves, you can see for yourselves and know that summer is near. 31Even so, when you see these things happening, you know that the kingdom of God is near.

32"I tell you the truth, this generation^a will certainly not pass away until all these things have happened. 33Heaven and earth will pass away, but my words will never pass away.

34"Be careful, or your hearts will be weighed down with dissipation, drunkenness and the anxi-

^{a}32 Or race

NRSV

25"There will be signs in the sun, the moon, and the stars, and on the earth distress among nations confused by the roaring of the sea and the waves. 26People will faint from fear and foreboding of what is coming upon the world, for the powers of the heavens will be shaken. 27Then they will see 'the Son of Man coming in a cloud' with power and great glory. 28Now when these things begin to take place, stand up and raise your heads, because your redemption is drawing near."

29Then he told them a parable: "Look at the fig tree and all the trees; 30as soon as they sprout leaves you can see for yourselves and know that summer is already near. 31So also, when you see these things taking place, you know that the kingdom of God is near. 32Truly I tell you, this generation will not pass away until all things have taken place. 33Heaven and earth will pass away, but my words will not pass away.

34"Be on guard so that your hearts are not weighed down with dissipation and drunkenness and the worries of this life, and that day does not

NIV

eties of life, and that day will close on you unexpectedly like a trap. [35]For it will come upon all those who live on the face of the whole earth. [36]Be always on the watch, and pray that you may be able to escape all that is about to happen, and that you may be able to stand before the Son of Man."

NRSV

catch you unexpectedly, [35]like a trap. For it will come upon all who live on the face of the whole earth. [36]Be alert at all times, praying that you may have the strength to escape all these things that will take place, and to stand before the Son of Man."

COMMENTARY

21:25. Although the apocalyptic discourse in Luke generally follows the order of the discourse in Mark 13, Luke has omitted the Markan assurance that the Lord has cut short the days (Mark 13:20), and the repetition of the warning about the false prophets (Mark 13:21-23; cf. Luke 21:8). Instead, the reference to the fulfillment of "the times of the Gentiles" (v. 24) leads directly to the forecast of the signs that will mark the coming of the Son of Man. Here we may detect an escalation of the signs that precede earlier events (cf. vv. 10-11). No longer is it a question of the meaning of wars, earthquakes, famines, or persecutions. The "great signs from heaven" (v. 11) are now specified. Note the repetition of the word for "signs" (σημεῖα *sēmeia*) in vv. 11 and 25, which links these turning points in the discourse with the initial question in v. 7, where the singular "sign" occurs (σημεῖον *sēmeion*).

These cosmic signs will be unmistakable: "signs in the sun, the moon, and the stars" and distress among the nations on earth (v. 25). Luke omits Mark's introductory phrase, "But in those days, after that suffering" (Mark 13:24 NRSV), but it is not clear that by doing so he is distinguishing or separating the time of the coming of the Son of Man from the destruction of Jerusalem.[267] One follows after the other.

The cosmic signs that will precede the coming of the Son of Man echo and fulfill the oracles of the prophets (see Isa 13:10; Ezek 32:7; Joel 2:30-31). Similarly, the terrors on land and sea were described by the prophets (see Ps 46:2-3; Hag 2:6; Wis 5:22; cf. Isa 24:19 LXX, where the term "distress" [ἀπορία *aporia*] occurs, as in Luke 21:25).[268]

The signs that will precede the coming of the Son of Man, therefore, are not only unmistakable, cosmic signs but signs that fulfill the Scriptures as well. The reference to "the nations" (τὸ ἔθνος *to ethnos*), a term that does not appear in this selection of verses most closely related to the signs in Luke 21:25, ties the warning of the signs of the coming of the Son of Man to the references to "the nations" in the preceding verses (see vv. 10, 24).

21:26-27. Verse 26*a* has no parallel in Mark. Neither is it drawn from an OT reference. The description of people fainting from fear and foreboding serves effectively, however, to heighten suspense and curiosity while the reader waits to hear what is coming. To what are these terrible portents a prelude? What is "coming upon the world" (v. 26)? The final clause of v. 26, "the powers of the heavens will be shaken," reflects the language of Hag 2:6, 21 and Isa 34:4.

Once all of these signs have come to pass, signaling "the end" that is at hand (cf. v. 9), then those who have been terrified, fainting "from fear and foreboding" (v. 26) will see "the Son of Man coming in a cloud" (v. 27). This description of the coming of the Son of Man is drawn from Dan 7:13: "I looked, and there before me was one like a son of man, coming with the clouds of heaven" (NIV). Jesus has referred earlier to the future, coming Son of Man, but this is the first time that the Son of Man has been described in the language of Daniel, "in a cloud."[269] The reference to the cloud also sets up the link between the ascension of the risen Lord and the coming of the Son of Man (Acts 1:9-11). References to the coming of the Son of Man earlier in Luke

267. Contra Fitzmyer, *The Gospel According to Luke (X–XXIV)*, 1348.
268. Translation by Fitzmyer, ibid., 1349.

269. See John Nolland, *Luke 18:35–24:53*, WBC 35C (Dallas: Word, 1993) 1006.

have warned that he will be ashamed of those who are ashamed of Jesus now (9:26), but will confess those who confess him now (12:8). The Son of Man will come at an unexpected hour (12:40). His coming is compared to flashes of lightning that light up the whole sky (17:24), and there will be cataclysmic destruction, as in the days of Noah and Lot (17:26-30), but will he find faith on earth (18:8)?

21:28. While others faint with fear and foreboding at the coming of the Son of Man, the disciples are instructed to "stand up and raise your heads, because your redemption is drawing near." Luke omits Mark's description of the angels gathering the elect (Mark 13:27). The focus remains on the significance of the coming of the Son of Man and the way the disciples are to receive him. For the disciples, his coming means an end to the persecutions and terrors that have been described earlier. Whereas the Son of Man will come to judge the wicked, his coming means deliverance for the faithful. The term "redemption" (ἀπολύτρωσις *apolytrōsis*) occurs only here in Luke and Acts, but seven times in the Pauline writings and twice in Hebrews.

21:29-33. The "drawing near" of their redemption leads to a lesson on the approach of the kingdom (21:31; cf. the conjunction of "drawing near" and the kingdom in Luke 10:9, 11). Not to be missed in this context is the connection between heavenly portents and the fig tree in Isa 34:4, whose influence was noted in the formation of vv. 25-26. Verse 29 introduces Jesus' last parable. The parable reproduces Mark 13:28-31 closely, but Luke omits Mark 13:32, Jesus' claim that he did not know the time of the end. The parable itself is given in vv. 29-30. Verse 31 explains the meaning of the parable in this context, and vv. 32-33 append related sayings that have been attracted and attached by catchword linkage ("taking place," vv. 31-32; "pass away," vv. 32-33).

The fig tree is often used as a metaphor for the peace and prosperity of Israel in the OT (Deut 8:7-8; Hos 9:10; Mic 4:4). It has been suggested, therefore, that the reference to the fig tree "and all the trees" in this context, immediately after the discussion of the destruction of Jerusalem and the fate of the nations (esp. 21:24-26), is not a stray detail that diffuses the parable but a reference signaling that the fig tree and all the trees should be understood in reference to Israel and all the nations.[270]

270. See ibid., 1008-9, where Nolland credits G. W. H. Lampe for this suggestion.

Although Luke follows Mark's wording for most of the parable, three differences are significant. First, Luke introduces the phrase "and all the trees" (v. 29), then he rewrites the beginning of the parable, adding "you can see for yourselves" (v. 30), and later adds the reference to the kingdom of God (v. 31). The first change, which is often overlooked, is significant because it establishes the verb sequence "see and know" followed by "near" (v. 30). The same sequence occurs in v. 20, "When you *see* Jerusalem surrounded by armies, then *know* that its desolation has come near." Similarly, when you see the trees sprouting leaves, "know that summer is already near" (v. 30). This pattern underlies the whole discourse, which begins, "As for these things that you see" in v. 6. Jesus has interpreted what they will see and what the signs will mean.

One of the peculiarities of this parable is that the coming of the end and the judgment of the Son of Man more naturally evoke the time of harvest rather than summer. Why, then, does the parable say that summer is already near? As an explanation, interpreters have turned to the riddle of the basket of summer fruit in Amos 8:1-2. The Lord asks, "Amos, what do you *see*?" Amos answers, "a basket of summer fruit [קַיִץ *qayiṣ*]," and the Lord says, "The end [קֵץ *qēṣ*] has come upon my people Israel." The parable of the trees in Luke makes the same point: The end is near; see the signs and know their meaning.

Mark's parallel to v. 31 is at best ambiguous since it lacks a noun or pronoun to specify who or what is near (see Mark 13:29). Luke fills the gap and removes the ambiguity by inserting a reference to the kingdom of God. One might have expected a reference to the Son of Man, as in vv. 27 and 36, but instead the coming of the Son of Man and the coming of the kingdom of God are brought into juxtaposition by this reference. "These things" in v. 31 must include the coming of the Son of Man, forecast in vv. 27-28. The coming of the Son of Man, therefore, will itself be a sign that God's kingdom is at hand (cf. the claims of the false prophets in v. 8). Those who had supposed that the kingdom of God would come immediately (19:11) were mistaken.

Two sayings are appended to the parable and its interpretation, and together they distinguish that which is passing away from that which will not pass away. The first saying begins with the revelatory formula "Truly [ἀμήν *amēn*] I say to you, . . . " which occurs six times in Luke (4:24; 12:37; 18:17, 29; 21:32; 23:43). This generation will not pass away until all things come to pass (v. 32). Because the natural and literal sense of this verse has been contradicted by history, interpreters have often sought for other meanings of either "this generation" (Israel, the wicked, humanity, or the generation of the end times) or "all things" (the persecutions and the destruction of Jerusalem), but none of the alternatives carries any conviction or arises out of the natural sense of the text. Like the prophets, both Jesus and Luke probably expected the end to come before the end of their generation, but the continuation of history does nothing to invalidate the warning of the judgment of the wicked or the assurance of the redemption of the faithful.

The signs that precede the coming of the Son of Man will involve cataclysmic events in the heavens and on earth (see v. 25). Jesus now assures the disciples that although "heaven and earth will pass away," his words will not pass away (v. 33). The pronouncement is an assurance. The crowd at Nazareth was amazed at Jesus' words (4:22), and in Capernaum they were astounded because he spoke with authority (4:32). On various occasions, Luke has reported that Jesus spoke "the word of God" (5:1), and Jesus has warned them of the consequences of hearing the Word and failing to do it (6:47-49). Now the words of Jesus are given a status reminiscent of that claimed for the Word of the Lord by the OT prophets: "The grass withers, the flower fades;/ but the word of our God will stand forever" (Isa 40:8 NRSV; cf. Ps 119:89, 160). Indeed, earlier in Luke, Jesus declared the enduring authority of the law in similar terms: "It is easier for heaven and earth to pass away, than for one stroke of a letter in the law to be dropped" (16:17).

21:34-36. At the conclusion of the eschatological discourse, Luke omits the simile of the man going on a journey (Mark 13:33-37), perhaps because elements of it have already been used in Luke 12:42-47 and 19:11-27. In its place Luke composes an exhortation that emphasizes watchfulness and prayer and that warns against drunkenness and dissipation. The unit begins with a warning (v. 34) that is then related to the eschato-

logical events that have just been forecast. Verse 35 supplies a rationale for the warning, and v. 36 offers both a general exhortation ("Be alert") and a specific one ("Pray").

The language of this unit is drawn from both OT and early Christian ethical exhortations. Jesus has warned the disciples to be on their guard on three other occasions (12:1; 17:3; 20:46), but the warning "Be on guard" (προσέχετε *prosechete*) occurs in Luke only where Jesus is addressing his disciples. Here they are warned not to let their hearts be "weighed down." The only other occurrence of this term in Luke is in 9:32, the account of the transfiguration, where Peter and the others are "weighed down with sleep." Nevertheless, because they remained awake, they witnessed Jesus' glory. Here Jesus warns the disciples to be on guard against (1) dissipation, (2) drunkenness, and (3) the worries of this life. The term "dissipation" (κραιπάλη *kraipalē*) occurs only here in the NT. Robertson discovered that it is "a rather late word, common in medical writers for the nausea that follows a debauch."[271] Although there are various injunctions against drunkenness in the NT (Eph 5:18), the term used here occurs elsewhere only in Rom 13:13 and Gal 5:21. The servant who gets drunk, however, will be surprised by the return of his or her master (12:45-46). The warning about "the worries of this life" reminds the reader of the earlier warnings about worry and anxiety (10:41; 12:22-31), especially the interpretation of the parable of the sower, in which Jesus warns that seed that falls among the thorns is "choked by the cares and riches and pleasures of life" (8:14). In both of these contexts, the warning against the cares of life is that they may prevent one from obeying Jesus' word (cf. the reference to Jesus' words in 21:33).

The warning is further related to the eschatological context by the reference to "that day," which refers to the day of the coming of the Son of Man (21:27). Luke has used similar constructions with an eschatological sense previously: "on that day" (10:12; 17:31; cf. 12:46); "in those days" (5:35; 21:23); and "the days are coming" (17:22; 21:6). The danger is that if the disciples allow their hearts to be weighed down by worldly distractions, the coming of the day will catch them the way a trap catches an animal

271. A. T. Robertson, *Word Pictures in the New Testament,* vol 2: *The Gospel According to Luke* (New York: Richard R. Smith, 1930) 262.

unawares (Isa 24:17; 1 Tim 3:7; 6:9; 2 Tim 2:26; cf. Jas 1:14). The claim that the day will come suddenly echoes the exhortation found in 1 Thess 5:2-3. Verse 35 was probably formulated as a result of reflection on Isa 24:17, which contains references to both "the trap" and the inhabitants of the earth (cf. Jer 25:29; Acts 17:26, which contain only the latter). The adjective for "all" ($\pi\hat{\alpha}\varsigma$ *pas*), a Lukan favorite, here emphasizes the universal scope of God's sovereignty.

Verse 36 introduces a positive exhortation. The opposite of sleep and dissipation is vigilance and prayer. Note the contrast between these two both at the transfiguration (9:32) and at Gethsemane (22:40, 45-46). Indeed, the disciples' experience at Gethsemane appears to be a parable of the consequences of failure to heed this exhortation. They sleep because they cannot "watch and pray" in the hour of trial. The verb used here for "pray" ($\delta\acute{\epsilon}o\mu\alpha\iota$ *deomai*) is a Lukan

favorite, occurring eight times in Luke, seven times in Acts, and only seven times in the rest of the NT.

Verse 36 provides an apt conclusion for the eschatological discourse by enjoining the disciples to pray at all times so that they might have the strength to escape "all these things," a phrase that evokes the opening question of the discourse, "What will be the sign that this [lit. "these things"] is about to take place?" (21:7) and v. 12, "Before all this occurs. . . . " By the end of the discourse, "all these things" includes the errors of the false prophets (vv. 8-11), the persecution and trials the disciples will experience (vv. 12-19), the terrors of the destruction of Jerusalem (vv. 20-24), and the cataclysm of the coming of the Son of Man (vv. 25-28). The only way to escape these events and be ready to stand before the Son of Man (cf. vv. 27, 36) is to be strengthened by constant prayer.

REFLECTIONS

Preaching on the Second Coming, the coming of the Son of Man, has fallen into disrepute in many churches. It is one of those themes that has been given over to churches that advertise their emphasis on Bible prophecy. Yet, the coming of the Son of Man is one of the important themes of Jesus' teaching. A whole category of "Son of Man" sayings deals with this subject, each of the synoptic Gospels features an eschatological discourse parallel to Luke 21 (Mark 13; Matthew 24), and it is one of the few subjects of Jesus' teachings that also occupies a significant place in the Pauline epistles (e.g., 1 Corinthians 15; 1 Thessalonians 4; 2 Thessalonians), the Petrine epistles (2 Peter 3), and Revelation (19).

1. One of the inescapable facts of life is that every life comes to an end, and the end of life lends urgency and significance to each new day. For those who have no faith and no knowledge of God, death stands as a final denial of life. All that we may attempt or do is eventually swept away by time. Wisdom of Solomon's description of life as the ungodly see it is particularly haunting:

Short and sorrowful is our life,
and there is no remedy when a life comes to its end,
and no one has been known to return from Hades.
For we were born by mere chance,
and hereafter we shall be as though we had never been,
for the breath in our nostrils is smoke,
and reason is a spark kindled by the beating of our hearts;
when it is extinguished, the body will turn to ashes,
and the spirit will dissolve like empty air.
Our name will be forgotten in time,
and no one will remember our works;
our life will pass away like the traces of a cloud,
and be scattered like mist
that is chased by the rays of the sun

and overcome by its heat.
For our alloted time is the passing of a shadow,
and there is no return from our death,
because it is sealed up and no one turns back.
(Wis 2:1-5 NRSV)

The ungodly, therefore, resolve to make the most of every moment with no respect for others.

On the other hand, the Gospel teaches that beyond the end of time stands the Lord, who has come among us in the person of Jesus. Those whose lives are lived under Jesus' Lordship can live expectantly, filling each day with activity that is meaningful because of its divine mandate and its contribution to the fulfillment of God's purposes for human life. Similarly, the end of time or the end of life holds no terror for those who know God's love because they know the one who determines the reality that lies beyond what we can know here and now. Thus those who know Christ as the Son of God can approach the end with heads raised high, knowing that their redemption is near (21:28).

2. These verses also provide encouragement for the faithful when the very foundation of life seems to be shaken. What do you do when others grow faint "from fear and foreboding" and "the powers of the heavens" are shaken (21:26)? These cosmological terms can aptly evoke the distress that we feel during the most anxious, trying, and dangerous experiences of life. What gives you direction when tornadoes strike, loved ones are imperiled, your livelihood is jeopardized, and the future is dark? Reading Jesus' words on the coming of the Son of Man as a reflection of the God-ordered world in which we live, the reader finds the assurance that in the worst of times the Son of Man is near at hand, coming "with power and great glory" (21:27). The message of the eschatological discourse, therefore, needs to be proclaimed in every time because it is one of hope: "Your redemption is drawing near" (21:28). God's Word will never pass away (21:33). The other side of this assurance is the exhortation not to debase life through dissipation or worry but to pray, depending on God for strength to meet life's challenges.

Luke 21:37-38, The Conclusion of Jesus' Teaching in the Temple

NIV

³⁷Each day Jesus was teaching at the temple, and each evening he went out to spend the night on the hill called the Mount of Olives, ³⁸and all the people came early in the morning to hear him at the temple.

NRSV

37Every day he was teaching in the temple, and at night he would go out and spend the night on the Mount of Olives, as it was called. ³⁸And all the people would get up early in the morning to listen to him in the temple.

COMMENTARY

At the end of this section Luke appends a summary statement that recalls his summary statements elsewhere in the Gospel (2:40, 52; 4:14-15, 31-32, 44; 6:17-19) and in Acts (2:42-47; 4:32-37; 5:12-16; 6:7). This concluding summary balances the summary statement at the beginning of Jesus' teachings in the Temple (19:47-48), repeating the opening almost verbatim, "every day

he was teaching in the temple" (19:47; cf. 20:1; 21:37). The key elements are repeated: activity—teaching; location—the temple; audience—the people; response—listening. The eagerness of the people, which is here characterized by the report that they "would get up early in the morning to listen to him" balances the earlier statement that "all the people were spellbound by what they heard" (19:48). Noticeable by their absence from the summary are Jesus' opponents, the authorities who were silenced by his wisdom but who will return in the next section (see 22:2-6).

The added details in the summary statement include a description of his spending the night on the Mount of Olives. The location was introduced for the first time at Jesus' approach to Jerusalem (19:29, 37) and will play a significant role later as the site of Gethsemane (22:39) and the ascension (Acts 1:12). The verb used in "to spend the night" (αὐλίζομαι *aulizomai*) may mean either that he spent the night in the open or that he found lodging for the night. In favor of the former, one may cite the reports of the number of pilgrims to Jerusalem, and at Gethsemane Jesus and the disciples have retreated to an open place (see "the place," 22:40) for the night, "as was his custom" (22:39).[272] The summary concludes by reiterating its primary theme: The "people" (λαός *laos*) were listening to Jesus in the Temple.

272. See Joachim Jeremias, *Jerusalem in the Time of Jesus,* trans. F. H. and C. H. Cave (Philadelphia: Fortress, 1969) 61. Because he harmonizes Luke with the other Gospels, Jeremias concludes that "Luke was ignorant of the local geography, and has mistaken the place where Jesus was arrested, i.e. Gethsemane, for the usual nightly lodging place."

THE PASSION AND RESURRECTION NARRATIVES

OVERVIEW

The last section of the Gospel chronicles its climactic events. In each scene the Gospel continues to proclaim and interpret the identity of Jesus and his fulfillment of God's redemptive purposes. Luke's skill as a literary artist and his grasp of the theological significance of these events are evident throughout. Some of the most moving and memorable scenes in the Gospel appear in the following sections: Jesus at the table with the disciples, Jesus praying on the Mount of Olives, Peter's denials, Jesus' words from the cross, the death of Jesus, and the story of the two disciples on the road to Emmaus. Each is a work of art, a Gospel in miniature.

At the outset of the passion narrative, it is good to take stock of what the reader has already been told about the coming events. At the birth of Jesus, Gabriel announced that Jesus would "reign over the house of Jacob forever" (1:33), but a darker allusion appears in the words of Simeon, spoken to Mary: "and a sword will pierce your own soul too" (2:35). After the temptation of Jesus, the devil "departed from him until an opportune time" (4:13). In later references, the devil snatches some of the seed that is sown (8:12), but Jesus' victory over Satan is also reported (10:18; 11:18; 13:16). With the beginning of the passion narrative, Satan's assault on Jesus intensifies (see 22:3, 31).

LUKE 22:1-13, PREPARATIONS FOR PASSOVER

NIV

22 Now the Feast of Unleavened Bread, called the Passover, was approaching, [2]and the chief priests and the teachers of the law were looking for some way to get rid of Jesus, for they were afraid of the people. [3]Then Satan entered Judas, called Iscariot, one of the Twelve. [4]And Judas went to the chief priests and the officers of the temple guard and discussed with them how he might betray Jesus. [5]They were delighted and agreed to give him money. [6]He consented, and watched for an opportunity to hand Jesus over to them when no crowd was present.

[7]Then came the day of Unleavened Bread on which the Passover lamb had to be sacrificed.

NRSV

22 Now the festival of Unleavened Bread, which is called the Passover, was near. [2]The chief priests and the scribes were looking for a way to put Jesus[a] to death, for they were afraid of the people.

[3]Then Satan entered into Judas called Iscariot, who was one of the twelve; [4]he went away and conferred with the chief priests and officers of the temple police about how he might betray him to them. [5]They were greatly pleased and agreed to give him money. [6]So he consented and began to look for an opportunity to betray him to them when no crowd was present.

[7]Then came the day of Unleavened Bread, on

[a]Gk *him*

NIV

⁸Jesus sent Peter and John, saying, "Go and make preparations for us to eat the Passover."

⁹"Where do you want us to prepare for it?" they asked.

¹⁰He replied, "As you enter the city, a man carrying a jar of water will meet you. Follow him to the house that he enters, ¹¹and say to the owner of the house, 'The Teacher asks: Where is the guest room, where I may eat the Passover with my disciples?' ¹²He will show you a large upper room, all furnished. Make preparations there."

¹³They left and found things just as Jesus had told them. So they prepared the Passover.

NRSV

which the Passover lamb had to be sacrificed. ⁸So Jesus^a sent Peter and John, saying, "Go and prepare the Passover meal for us that we may eat it." ⁹They asked him, "Where do you want us to make preparations for it?" ¹⁰"Listen," he said to them, "when you have entered the city, a man carrying a jar of water will meet you; follow him into the house he enters ¹¹and say to the owner of the house, 'The teacher asks you, "Where is the guest room, where I may eat the Passover with my disciples?"' ¹²He will show you a large room upstairs, already furnished. Make preparations for us there." ¹³So they went and found everything as he had told them; and they prepared the Passover meal.

b Gk *he*

COMMENTARY

The passion predictions and references to the fate that awaits Jesus in Jerusalem have made it clear that Jesus will be killed by the authorities and rise again (see 9:22, 44; 12:50; 13:33-34; 17:25; 18:31-33). Jesus, as the Son of Man, will be "betrayed" (lit., "handed over" [παραδίδωμι *paradidōmi*], 9:44)—a foreshadowing of Judas's role in the plot to kill Jesus. The first passion prediction specified that Jesus would be rejected by "the elders, chief priests, and scribes" (9:22), and the most recent prediction indicated that Jesus would be handed over to "the Gentiles" (18:32). The opposition of "the chief priests, the scribes, and the leaders of the people" was noted at the beginning and at various points throughout the section devoted to Jesus' teaching in the Temple (19:47-48; 20:1, 19). Conspicuously, Jesus' opponents were not mentioned in the summary at the conclusion of this section (see 21:37-38).

Earlier, in the list of the Twelve, Judas was introduced as the one "who became a traitor" (6:16). The reintroduction of Jesus' opponents, the reappearance of Satan in the narrative, and the reintroduction of Judas confirm for the reader that the plot leading to Jesus' death will move swiftly from this point on.

22:1-2. The time is set in the introductory phrase by a reference that links two Jewish festivals that celebrate God's deliverance of Israel from bondage in Egypt: the Festival of Unleavened Bread and the Passover (22:1). All leaven was ceremonially removed from the house, and the Passover lamb was slaughtered on Nisan 14 and eaten that evening (Exod 12:6-8). That evening also marked the beginning of the festival of Unleavened Bread (Exod 12:18; Lev 23:5-6; Num 28:16-17; Deut 16:1-8). For the next seven days, the Israelites ate unleavened bread (Exod 13:6-7).

Verse 2 reintroduces Jesus' opponents, the chief priests and scribes who were characterized in the earlier section (19:47; 20:1, 19, 46-47). Their intent is now made clear; they were "looking for a way to put Jesus to death." The last part of the verse states the complication that will be resolved by the complicity of Judas in the plot against Jesus: "They were afraid of the people." The "people" (λαός *laos*) praised God at Jesus' entry into Jerusalem (18:43). They were "spellbound" by Jesus' teachings and rose early each day to hear him (19:48; 21:38) as he taught them in the Temple (20:1, 9). The chief priests and scribes refused to claim that John's authority was of human origin for fear that the people would stone them (20:6). Jesus was openly critical of the scribes "in the hearing of all the people" (20:45). Now, the report that the chief priests and scribes feared the people echoes the narrator's assessment of the situation at the end of the parable of the wicked tenants (cf.

20:19; 22:2). Luke has carefully developed the difficulty faced by the authorities. They could not simply arrest Jesus while he was teaching in the Temple. They had to find some way of seizing him when "the people" were not present.

22:3-6. Luke omits the account of the anointing of Jesus that Mark places between the beginning of the passion narrative and Judas's agreement to betray Jesus. The omission is usually explained as consistent with Luke's effort to avoid duplicate scenes (cf. Luke 7:36-50; Mark 14:3-9). The report that Satan entered Judas signals an ominous escalation in the plot against Jesus. He had silenced the authorities who confronted him in the Temple, but now Satan reappears for the first time since the temptation scene (cf. 10:18; 11:18; 13:16). Verse 2 echoes John 13:27 almost verbatim, though Luke is distinctive in reporting Satan's entry into Judas prior to the last supper.

Judas is identified in various ways in the Gospels. "Judas the Iscariot" (Matt 10:4; John 12:4); "Judas Iscariot" (Matt 26:14); "Judas of Iscariot" (Mark 3:19; 14:10; Luke 6:16); "Judas, the one called Iscariot" (Luke 22:3); "Judas, son of Simon of Iscariot" (John 6:71; 13:26); and "Judas, son of Simon the Iscariot" (John 13:2). "Iscariot" probably derives from the Hebrew construction that means "man of Kerioth," a town in southern Judea. Although the second identifying phrase, "one of the Twelve," appears only here in the NT, the numbers of groups and crowds are cited often in Acts (4:4; 5:36; 6:7; 11:21; 16:5).

The result of Satan's entry into Judas is manifested immediately as Judas goes to speak with Jesus' opponents, the chief priests and officers of the Temple. The latter appear only here and in 22:52 in Luke, but frequently in Acts (4:1; 5:24-26; 16:20-22, 35-38). Their duties are not described, but apparently they were responsible for order and oversight of Temple activities. The act of handing Jesus over to the authorities has been alluded to earlier in the passion predictions (9:44; 18:32; 20:20), but it will now become the single act that characterizes Judas (see 22:6, 21-22, 48). Hereafter, Judas will be known as "the betrayer," or more literally, "the one who is handing me over" (22:21). Judas conspires with the authorities. Satan leads him to them; they do not come to Judas. Nevertheless, Judas's motives are never explored in Luke. The authorities agree to give him silver, but Luke does not specify thirty pieces of silver (see Matt 26:15; cf. Zech 11:12). In exchange, Judas agrees to seek a time when he can deliver Jesus into their hands away from the crowd. By reporting Judas's deal with the authorities at this point, Luke adds suspense to the passion narrative. Even for those who know the story, tension mounts as Jesus moves toward his arrest and then on to the trial and the cross.

22:7-13. The sending of two disciples to make preparations for the Passover meal is reminiscent of the sending of two disciples to make preparations for Jesus' entry into Jerusalem in 19:29-35. In this context the preparation provides a transition from the announcement of the time for the Passover celebration (22:1, 7) and the last supper. Luke's reference to "the day of Unleavened Bread" is not as accurate technically as Mark's "the first day of Unleavened bread" (Mark 14:12 NRSV), since it was a weeklong festival (see 22:1). On Nisan 14 all of the leavened bread was removed from the house in preparation for the start of the celebration that evening, the beginning of Nisan 15. The Passover lamb was slaughtered on Nisan 14. In the first century, the Passover lambs were slaughtered in the Temple forecourt and then roasted and eaten in private homes. According to the chronology followed by the synoptic Gospels, therefore, the institution of the Lord's supper coincided with the Passover meal. According to John, however, the Jewish authorities had not yet eaten the Passover meal at the time of Jesus' trial (John 18:28), so the death of Jesus coincides with the time of the slaughter of the Passover lambs (John 19:31; cf. Exod 12:5-9). Both accounts agree that Jesus' death took place during the Passover observances, and both chronologies serve theological interests, the one linking the Lord's Supper to the Passover meal and the other identifying Jesus as the Passover lamb.

Luke follows Mark 14:12-17 closely through most of this scene. The major difference between Luke and his source is that Luke identifies the two unnamed disciples in Mark as the two disciples who will emerge as the leading apostles in the early chapters of Acts (1:13; 3:1-4; 4:13, 19; 8:14). Peter and John appear together with James in scenes drawn from Mark (Jairus's daughter, Luke 8:51; the transfiguration, Luke 9:28), but "the inner three" are not featured in any distinctively Lukan material, and this is the only place where only Peter and John are named.[273] One may also observe that in the Gospel of John, Peter and the Beloved Disciple (who is not identified as John in the Gospel but has been so identified by later tradition) appear together frequently in the passion narrative (John 13:23-24; 20:2-10; 21:2, 7, 20). At a minimum, it appears that the naming of the disciples in this context foreshadows their role as leaders among the apostles. Significantly, it also portrays them as "waiting tables"—an activity that will emerge as an issue of controversy in Acts 6. The question of greatness will emerge explicitly in 22:24-27.

Luke's editing of the scene also allows Jesus to initiate the action. Rather than being asked about preparations for the Passover meal (as in Mark), Jesus sends the two and then they ask where they are to prepare the meal. The question of where this is to take place dominates the rest of this unit. Luke leaves unresolved the ambiguity in Mark regarding whether Jesus had made arrangements for the location privately or whether the mission of the disciples confirms Jesus' foreknowledge as it unfolds. Whereas the argument for Jesus' foreknowledge is stronger in relation to the preparation for the entry into Jerusalem, here the aura of secrecy and the previous disclosure of the plot to arrest Jesus may serve as a rationale for why Jesus would make arrangements that were kept from the disciples.

The disciples will meet two different people. First, they will be met by a person carrying a jar of water. The "person" (ἄνθρωπος *anthrōpos*) may have been either male or female, but presumably Jesus is speaking of a man. Carrying water was normally women's work (John 4), so being met by a man carrying water would have been unusual. The man will lead them to a house where they are to say to the owner, "The teacher asks you, 'Where is the guest room, where I may eat the Passover with my disciples?' " (22:11). The guest room was a large upstairs room. Again, the request may be explained either as an allusion to the prearranged plans or as a request to one of Jesus' followers in Jerusalem. The making of the arrangements is more important to the narrative, however, than is the issue of Jesus' foreknowledge or previous arrangements. Either way, Jesus maintains complete control of the events. He will eat the Passover meal with his disciples without interference from those who seek to arrest him. When the disciples go into the city, they find everything as Jesus had told them, and they make preparations for the Passover meal, presumably by securing a lamb and roasting it.

273. On the references to Peter and John in the Synoptics and Acts, see R. Alan Culpepper, *John, the Son of Zebedee: The Life of a Legend* (Columbia, S.C.: University of South Carolina Press, 1994) 28-51.

REFLECTIONS

This section of the Gospel is deeply troubling because it presumes a worldview that is foreign to most modern readers. Is the devil a force or a being that can enter into persons and take control of their actions? Does that mean that Judas was not really responsible for betraying Jesus? Could Jesus have known the movements of a stranger carrying water and the availability of a room in a house he had never visited? If so, in what sense was he really human? The story line itself creates difficulties for the credibility of the story—at least for modern readers.

At an even further level this section is disturbing because it portrays a vision of life in which human beings are mere pawns of spiritual forces they can neither control nor understand. Judas is controlled by the devil, the man carrying water and the owner of the house are presumably playing roles in a great spiritual drama without any awareness of the significance of what they are doing, and the disciples, doing as they were instructed, find things just as Jesus said they would be.

Disturbing as such reflections may be, they raise ultimate issues. Is freedom an illusion? The modern assumption is that human beings are totally free to act as they choose within the matrix of their genetics, social conditioning, historical context, and strength of will. We are far from sharing the ancient notions of determinism or the Essene notion of the allotment of shares of the spirits of good and evil to each individual. We do not explain our actions as the result of conflict of the *yēṣer hāra'* (יצר הרע "the evil inclination") and the *yēṣer hattôb* (יצר הטוב "the good inclination") within us. But does our assumption of free will also carry with it a denial of the potency of spiritual beings? We have dismissed angels and demons to the fringes of piety and experience. Have we also diminished God and Satan to the roles of spectators or aloof powers rather than principals and participants in the contest between good and evil in human experience?

One of the reasons why these verses are disturbing is that the roles of the characters resonate with our own occasional sense of being pawns in something greater than that part of life that we can understand or control. We are aware of our finitude, the limitations of our powers and our years. Life often appears as though it is controlled by powers beyond our realm of comprehension. Is it possible that in these events at the fulcrum of human history we see the contest between the forces of good and evil exposed more clearly than we do in the ordinary course of life? Or is this part of the gospel story merely an expression of the ancient superstitious worldview?

We will no doubt continue to wrestle with the intellectual issues. As it resonates with our own sense of finitude, however, this passage also calls us to wonder and have awe at God's determination not to abandon humanity to the forces of evil but to carry out a plan for the salvation of all who place their hope in God. These verses are just one small part of a much larger story, of course, but that story offers to all the assurance that if we do not control the forces whose power we experience, we can live in the faith and hope that God's power is greater and that God's love is revealed in the dark events that unfolded at Jesus' death.

LUKE 22:14-20, THE LAST SUPPER

NIV

14When the hour came, Jesus and his apostles reclined at the table. 15And he said to them, "I have eagerly desired to eat this Passover with you before I suffer. 16For I tell you, I will not eat it again until it finds fulfillment in the kingdom of God."

17After taking the cup, he gave thanks and said, "Take this and divide it among you. 18For I tell you I will not drink again of the fruit of the vine until the kingdom of God comes."

19And he took bread, gave thanks and broke it, and gave it to them, saying, "This is my body given for you; do this in remembrance of me."

20In the same way, after the supper he took the cup, saying, "This cup is the new covenant in my blood, which is poured out for you."

NRSV

14When the hour came, he took his place at the table, and the apostles with him. 15He said to them, "I have eagerly desired to eat this Passover with you before I suffer; 16for I tell you, I will not eat it[a] until it is fulfilled in the kingdom of God." 17Then he took a cup, and after giving thanks he said, "Take this and divide it among yourselves; 18for I tell you that from now on I will not drink of the fruit of the vine until the kingdom of God comes." 19Then he took a loaf of bread, and when he had given thanks, he broke it and gave it to them, saying, "This is my body, which is given for you. Do this in remembrance of me." 20And he did the same with the cup after supper, saying, "This cup that is poured out for you is the new covenant in my blood."[b]

[a]Other ancient authorities read *never eat it again*   [b]Other ancient authorities lack, in whole or in part, verses 19b-20 (*which is given . . . in my blood*)

COMMENTARY

Because of its differences from Matthew and Mark, Luke's account of the last supper presents notorious difficulties for the interpreter. Foremost among the peculiarities of Luke's account is the giving of the cup before the bread (v. 17), and then the giving of a second cup after the bread (v. 20). Verses 15-17, which include the account of the first cup, have no parallel in the other Gospels. Luke also moves Jesus' declaration that he will not drink again of the fruit of the vine until the kingdom of God comes, placing it before the giving of the bread and the cup rather than after, as in Mark 14:25. Upon close examination, it is also evident that the words of institution in Luke parallel the tradition known to Paul (1 Cor 11:24-25) more closely than the Markan tradition (Mark 14:22-24).

Not surprisingly, the early scribes noticed these difficulties and sought to alleviate them by altering the text. Even after certain texts (such as Luke) were regarded as sacred, the form of the text remained somewhat fluid and open to emendation. Then, after the form of the text was fixed, difficulties had to be resolved by interpretation. The short version, preserved in D and some manuscripts of the Old Latin version, contains only vv. 17-19a, through "this is my body." The long version (preserved in $\mathfrak{P}^{75}$, א, A, B, and other important manuscripts and ancient versions) contains all of vv. 17-20. Although the short text was championed by Westcott and Hort as one of the Western non-interpolations, the long text has subsequently regained its standing in critical editions of the Greek text. Nevertheless, it remains a difficult and debated textual problem.

According to the synoptic Gospels, the last supper was a Passover meal. Luke, for example, has said that Jesus gave explicit instructions to prepare the Passover (22:7-8, 11, 13). By contrast, the Gospel of John has the last supper twenty-four hours earlier (see John 18:28; 19:31). Thus the Passover setting may hold some clues to Luke's distinctive account of the giving of two cups. According to the earliest prescriptions regarding the Passover meal, it required four cups of wine.[274] Joachim Jeremias has reconstructed the ceremony as follows:

A. Preliminary Course:

Word of dedication (blessing of the feast day and of the cup) spoken by the *paterfamilias* over *the first cup*.

Preliminary dish, consisting among other things of green herbs, bitter herbs and a sauce made of fruit purée.

The meal proper is served but not yet eaten; the second cup is mixed and put in its place but not yet drunk.

B. Passover Liturgy:

Passover *haggadah* by the *paterfamilias* (in Aramaic): Here the son asks, "Why is this night different from other nights?" and the father explains, beginning with "A wandering Aramean was my father. . . ."

First part of the passover Hallel (Psalms 113–118), to the end of Psalm 113 or the end of Psalm 114.

Drinking of *the second cup* (*haggadah* cup).

C. Main Meal:

Grace spoken by the *paterfamilias* over the unleavened bread.

Meal, consisting of passover lamb, unleavened bread, bitter herbs, with fruit purée and wine.

Grace over *the third cup* (cup of blessing).

D. Conclusion:

Second part of the passover Hallel (in Hebrew).

Praise over *the fourth cup*.[275]

This reconstruction of the Passover meal has important implications for Luke's account of the last supper because it helps us to make sense of the two cups.

22:14. The hour for the eating of the Passover meal was set at sundown on Nisan 14. In the Gospel of John (cf. Luke 22:53) "the hour" is an allusion to the time of Jesus' death, but in 22:14 it lacks such overtones, setting only the time for the ceremonial meal. Jesus and his disciples reclined rather than sat for the meal, which Jeremias argued further confirms that it was a special occasion.[276]

22:15-18. The meaning of v. 15 is debated. The question is whether Jesus ate the Passover meal with his disciples or whether he abstained, vowing that he would not eat again until the kingdom of God was fulfilled. Jeremias argued for the latter, but most commentators have understood the verse as a statement of how intensely Jesus looked forward to eating this meal with his disciples. Jesus makes a vow in vv. 16 and 18. While it is true that the word "again" (implying

274. See *m. Pesahim* 10.1-9.

275. Adapted from Joachim Jeremias, *The Eucharistic Words of Jesus,* trans. Norman Perrin (Philadelphia: Fortress, 1966) 85-86.
276. Ibid., 48-49.

that Jesus was eating with his disciples) does not appear in v. 16, nevertheless, it is probably to be read as looking to the future: "Henceforth I will not eat. . . . " The phrase "from now on" in v. 18 is omitted from some manuscripts, but again should probably be retained. The pronouncement retains a strongly Semitic idiom, literally "with desire I have desired."

When Jesus says, " . . . before I suffer," the words are a veiled reference to his death. The Greek verb for "to suffer" (πάσχω *paschō*) is nearly the same as the word for "Passover" (πάσχα *pascha*). Moreover, in early Christian usage, Jesus himself became the Passover: "For our paschal lamb, Christ, has been sacrificed" (1 Cor 5:7). The pronouncement also resounds with echoes of the earlier passion predictions in which Jesus spoke of what he was about to "suffer" (9:22; 17:25). Later, the risen Lord will admonish the disciples, "Thus it is written, that the Messiah is to suffer and to rise from the dead on the third day" (24:46; cf. 24:26).

Codex Bezae (D) and several other ancient manuscripts read "never again" in v. 16, which seems to be the proper sense even if it is not the earliest text. Jesus' vow speaks of the Passover lamb, pointing to its metaphorical meaning (his own death): "I will not eat it [again] until it is fulfilled in the kingdom of God." In their own way, these words transform the meaning of the supper just as forcefully as the traditional words of institution. The Passover lamb foreshadowed Jesus' own sacrificial death for the deliverance of the people of God. His death, therefore, would be a fulfillment of the Passover. The expected eschatological banquet will celebrate this fulfillment.

The cup in v. 17 must be one of the early cups of the Passover meal, since a second cup, "after the meal," will be interpreted in v. 20. Because Jesus' words about eating the Passover may imply that the meal has already been served, the cup in v. 17 fits into the order best if it is the second cup. The uncertainties regarding the practice of the Passover celebration, its interpretation in early Christian tradition, and Luke's knowledge of these matters prevent us from doing more than noting how Luke's account of the last supper *might* be correlated with what is known of the Passover meal.

The succession of verbal forms is typical of eucharistic language: "having received . . . having blessed [he said] take and divide." The formula of blessing and distributing is followed by another vow that underscores the eschatological significance of the observance. The meal that had been a celebration of God's deliverance of Israel in the past will henceforth point toward the fulfillment of God's redemptive work in the kingdom. Verse 18, therefore, closely parallels v. 16. The expression "the fruit of the vine" is used in a traditional blessing over wine.[277]

The short text, which omits the second cup (v. 20), results in placing the cup before the bread, the reverse of the sequence found in Matthew and Mark. The cup precedes the bread, however, in 1 Cor 10:16 and in *Did.* 9.2-4. On the other hand, the long text preserves the traditional sequence (the bread then the cup) in vv. 19-20. The result may be the product of combining two early eucharistic traditions: the paschal lamb then the cup; the bread then the cup.[278]

The phrase "from now on" is omitted from some manuscripts, but on balance the evidence favors retaining it. The meaning of Jesus' second vow is similar to that of the previous one (v. 16), but different from it. Both verses link the elements of the Passover meal with the kingdom of God, but whereas v. 16 speaks of fulfillment of the paschal lamb *in* the kingdom, v. 18 looks ahead to coming of the kingdom of God. The irony is that the kingdom of God will not come soon, but Jesus will not drink wine again before he dies (cf. 23:36).

22:19-20. Whereas vv. 16-18 offer Jesus' pronouncements over the lamb and the cup, vv. 19-20 contain his blessing of the bread and the cup. In the sequence of the bread then the cup, Luke agrees with Mark, but the language of the blessings is much closer to the tradition preserved by Paul in 1 Cor 11:24-25.

---

277. See *m. Berakoth* 6.1. The phrase also appears in the OT (Deut 22:9 LXX; Isa 32:12; cf. Mark 14:25).
278. John Nolland, *Luke 18:35–24:53*, WBC 35C (Dallas: Word, 1993) 1051.

Luke 22:19-20[279]	Mark 14:22-24	1 Corinthians 11:23-25
Then he took a loaf of bread, and when he had given thanks, he broke it and gave it to them, saying, "This is my body, which is given for you. Do this in remembrance of me." And he did the same with the cup after supper, saying, "This cup that is poured out for you is the new covenant in my blood."	While they were eating, *he took a loaf of bread,* and after blessing it *he broke it, gave it to them,* and said, "Take; *this is my body.*" Then he took a cup, and after giving thanks he gave it to them, and all of them drank from it. He said to them, *"This is my blood of the covenant, which is poured out for* many."	The Lord Jesus on the night when he was betrayed *took a loaf of bread, and when he had given thanks, he broke it and said, "This is my body that is for you. Do this in remembrance of me." In the same way he took the cup also, after supper, saying, "This cup is the new covenant in my blood.* Do this, as often as you drink it, in remembrance of me."

279. Scripture quotations are from the NRSV; italics added.

John has no words of institution, and Matthew follows Mark closely but not verbatim. What emerges from this survey, therefore, is that no two of the four canonical versions of the words of institution agree exactly. The tradition was flexible. Luke agrees with Mark in preserving the sequence of four verbs (including "gave" [δίδωμι *didōmi*]) at the beginning, and the concluding clause of the blessing over the cup, "that is poured out for you/many." On the other hand, Luke agrees with Paul in the verb for "to bless" (εὐχαριστέω *eucharisteō*), the additional clause, "which is [given] for you"; the exhortation "do this in remembrance of me" (though Paul repeats the injunction after the cup also); the adverbial phrase "in the same way"; the temporal phrase "after the supper"; and with minor variations the blessing over the cup, including the specification *"new* covenant."

The use of the term for "bread" (ἄρτος *artos*) does not contribute significantly to the debate over whether the last supper was the Passover meal because the term is also used in the Septuagint for "unleavened bread," which was eaten at Passover (Exod 29:2; Lev 2:4; 8:26; Num 6:19). Just as the head of the family interpreted the bread by reference to "the bread of affliction" (Deut 16:3),[280] so also Jesus interpreted the bread he gave to his disciples, but this time identifying the bread with himself—his suffering for them. Jesus' blessing over the bread, therefore, affirms that his death will have a vicarious, sacrificial significance. He gives himself for them. The ob-

280. Joseph A. Fitzmyer, *The Gospel According to Luke (X–XXIV)*, AB 28A (Garden City, N.Y.: Doubleday, 1985) 1399.

servance of the Lord's supper is consequently a commemorative meal, a meal of remembrance of Jesus' death and expectation of its fulfillment in the kingdom of God. As a communal observance, it links the church in any generation with both its origins and the fulfillment of God's promise of redemption. Just as the Passover was observed "so that all the days of your life you may remember the day of your departure from the land of Egypt" (Deut 16:3 NRSV), so also the Lord's supper would be observed "in remembrance of me." The farewell commissioning contained in these words is greatly expanded in a different form in John's farewell discourse (John 13–17).

The observance of "the blood of the covenant" goes back to the ceremony described in Exod 24:8. An allusion to this ceremony also appears in the opening of 1 Peter, which describes the believers as "chosen and destined by God the Father and sanctified by the Spirit to be obedient to Jesus Christ and to be sprinkled with his blood" (1 Pet 1:2 NRSV). By designating the cup as "the new covenant in my blood," Jesus was also evoking the prophetic promise of a new covenant. Jeremiah wrote, "The days are surely coming, says the LORD, when I will make a new covenant with the house of Israel and the house of Judah. . . . I will put my law within them, and I will write it on their hearts" (Jer 31:31, 33 NRSV). The author of Hebrews interprets at length the significance of both the new covenant (Heb 8:6-13) and the fact that it was constituted with Jesus' own blood (Heb 9:13-14, 18-22).

The concluding affirmation of the vicarious significance of the cup in v. 20 balances the earlier statement after the bread; the bread is the body "which is given for you" (v. 19), and the cup is the new covenant in his blood "that is poured out for you" (v. 20). The parallel to Luke 22:19 in 1 Cor 11:24 lacks the participle "given," and there is no parallel in 1 Corinthians to the latter clause. Mark lacks the former but contains a broader version of the latter: "which is poured out for many" (Mark 14:24). Thus Luke has apparently constructed the balanced parallelism of the repeated clauses, using the second person plural "you" in both.

The pouring out of blood in the OT is often an allusion to death (Gen 9:6; Isa 59:7; Ezek 18:10; cf. Luke 11:50). The reference to pouring out may also be an echo of Isa 53:12, but if so the echo is stronger in Mark than in Luke, because Mark couples the reference to pouring out with "many," as in Isa 53:12 (cf. Mark 10:45).

REFLECTIONS

No other ceremony or act of worship has moved the church through the centuries as much as following Jesus' command to eat the bread and drink the cup of the new covenant. Again we stand in the presence of mystery and wonder. One approach to the observance's surplus of meaning is to consider the ways in which it creates community—with the outcast, with the Jewish people, with other believers, and with the Lord.

The act of eating together cemented Jesus' fellowship with his disciples, the crowds, and the outcasts in Galilee on various occasions, and Luke more than any other Gospel emphasizes the meal scenes of Jesus' ministry. By eating with the outcasts, Jesus had tangibly demonstrated his solidarity with them. He had received from them and given to them, he had publicly crossed the social barriers that divided the righteous from the outcasts, and he had physically embodied the love of God for the despised.

Instituted at the time of the Passover meal, the Lord's Supper also embraces and fulfills the celebration of God's act in delivering the Israelites from Egypt. When we eat the bread and drink the cup, we declare that the Lord whom we worship is also the God committed to the deliverance of the people of Israel from oppression by non-Israelites. Fulfillment in Christ of the ancient deliverance at the exodus should, therefore, never be taken to diminish the Christian church's common heritage with the Jewish people.

Because of the significance of meals in Jesus' ministry and the experience of the early church, fasting has never been as significant a part of the Christian experience as eating together has been. At first, the Lord's Supper was observed in connection with a fellowship meal. The risen Lord becomes known to the early disciples in the breaking of bread (24:30-31). The early Christians broke bread at home (Acts 2:46), and problems arose when the meal did not express the oneness and fellowship of the church (1 Cor 11:17-22). Following the supper in Luke, Jesus reminds the disciples that they are to serve one another. The supper further binds the disciples together because it is an assurance of God's providence in times of testing. Whenever the church is persecuted, it can remember that it was born out of the steadfastness of God's love in a time of desperate trial.

The supper, therefore, relates the community of believers physically and spiritually to the Lord, who laid down his life that they might live. It is a commemoration of the life and death of Jesus, a celebration of his real and spiritual presence now, and an affirmation of the hope that we shall eat and drink with him in the kingdom of God.

The experience of the supper, therefore, spans the breadth of God's love; the depth of Jesus' sufferings; and the past, present, and future of God's mighty acts. The challenge for the believer is not that we grasp the full potential of its meaning but that we open ourselves to the full extent of its power to change us and create intimacy among the worshiper and outcasts, our Jewish heritage, other believers, and the Lord whom we worship. What, then, shall we do after we eat together?

LUKE 22:21-38, THE LUKAN FAREWELL DISCOURSE

OVERVIEW

Luke alone among the Synoptics reports a discourse at the table following the meal. This Lukan discourse is a compilation of four units: (1) Jesus' announcement of his betrayal (22:21-23); (2) Jesus' response to the disciples' debate over greatness (22:24-30); (3) Jesus' prediction of Peter's denial of him (22:31-34); and (4) Jesus' call for purse, bag, and sword (22:35-38). The material for this discourse is drawn variously from Mark, Q, and L, but the result is clearly Luke's own.

Luke 22:21-23, Jesus' Announcement of His Betrayal

NIV	NRSV
²¹But the hand of him who is going to betray me is with mine on the table. ²²The Son of Man will go as it has been decreed, but woe to that man who betrays him." ²³They began to question among themselves which of them it might be who would do this.	²¹But see, the one who betrays me is with me, and his hand is on the table. ²²For the Son of Man is going as it has been determined, but woe to that one by whom he is betrayed!" ²³Then they began to ask one another which one of them could be who would do this.

COMMENTARY

Breaking the intimate mood of Jesus' pledge to give his body and blood for his disciples, Jesus declares that he will be betrayed by one who has eaten with him. The announcement transposes the material from Mark 14:18-21 from before the giving of the bread and the cup until after the meal. The effect is a dramatic refocusing of the plot to kill Jesus. At the beginning of the chapter the reader was told that the chief priests and scribes were looking for a way to put Jesus to death, and then that Satan entered Judas, who made a pact with the authorities. Therefore, while Jesus does not identify Judas by name, the readers know of whom he is speaking.

Betrayal has been an element of Jesus' passion predictions (9:44; 18:32; 20:20), and we have been told that Judas was seeking an opportune time to betray Jesus (22:4, 6). The nearness of the betrayer (at the table) and Jesus' use of the present participle in "the one who betrays me" both suggest that the time of the fulfillment of Jesus' warnings is at hand.

Verse 22 addresses the paradox of divine foreknowledge and human freedom. Jesus' death is a part of God's redemptive plan, and Judas's betrayal has a place in that plan. Nevertheless, God is not responsible for Judas's act, nor does its redemptive result lessen Judas's culpability. Here divine intent and human freedom cooperate independently. Jesus is betrayed by a trusted disciple.

Jesus' use of the explicative "but" (πλήν *plēn,* a more intensive adversative particle than δέ *de*) in vv. 21-22 signals the intensity of the moment. The closest parallel between the Markan and Lukan accounts of this unit occurs in v. 22, which reproduces words and phrases from Mark 14:21. Luke's hand is still visible in the editing, however. Both Mark and Luke use the circumlocution "the Son of Man," but in Luke the verb for "going" (πορεύομαι *poreuomai*) is different, and the cause is different. Luke ties Jesus' death to God's redemptive plan ("as it has been determined") rather than to the fulfillment of Scripture ("as it is written of him") as in Mark 14:21. Luke appeals again to God's redemptive plan, abridging the woe pronounced over the betrayer and omitting the second reference to the Son of Man and the statement that it would have been better if he had not been born. The force of the woe remains, however.

While the readers know that Jesus was speaking of Judas, the disciples do not know. Each Gospel handles the disciples' response differently. In Mark it comes earlier. The disciples are grieved and ask one by one, "Is it I?" (see Mark 14:19). In Matthew, Judas says, "Surely not I, Rabbi?" (Matt 26:25 NRSV). John reports that the disciples looked at one another (John 13:22). According to Luke, the disciples ask one another which one of them could do this.

REFLECTIONS

Judas's betrayal of Jesus has been fertile ground for theological reflection on human sinfulness, free will and determinism, and the recognition that each of us is capable of betraying ourselves and others in ways we would hardly believe. The setting of Jesus' announcement thrusts the issue into the heart of the church's observance of the Lord's supper. We cannot partake of the bread and cup in smugness that we would never betray Jesus as Judas did. Again, Jesus' announcement that "his hand is on the table" reminds his followers that participation in the supper does not protect one from sin or treachery in some magical way.

Love makes betrayal all the more devastating. Jesus was not delivered to his enemies by one of the chief priests, or even by one of the people who has come to the Temple to hear him teach. He was betrayed by a friend to whom he had just pledged his body and blood. Judas's betrayal, then, is as tragic as any scene in Greek drama.

So powerful is its effect that each of the evangelists telegraphs a response his readers might imitate by reporting how the disciples received Jesus' announcement. The differences in the accounts provide a telling reflection of human nature. Do we respond by assuming that we could not do such a thing, so it must be one of the others (John 13:22), or by recognizing that each of us is capable of betraying those who have loved and trusted us (Mark 14:19)?

Luke categorically declares that Judas's action cannot be excused by appeal to God's foreknowledge or plan for redemption. Judas is not passively playing out a role assigned to him. On the contrary, God has taken Judas's treachery and all the other events that led up to Jesus' death and brought from them a positive and redemptive effect. We may speculate that had Judas's and Jesus' enemies made other decisions, the course of events might have been different, but the redemptive effect would have been the same.

Judas may not have had a chance to see the treachery of his act played out before him and to reconsider it, but everyone who reads the Gospel and everyone who sits at Jesus' table and hears the story while receiving the bread and cup has the chance to recognize his or her own capacity for sin in Judas's treachery and to choose faithfulness instead. Our response, therefore, should be to hear the story again and recognize that we, too, are capable of betrayal. We, too, assume that we are superior to others or that whatever others might do we would not deny Jesus. Luke's account of Jesus' discourse at the table is not for those who are afraid to confront their own capacity to sin, but it does speak redemptively to all who are ready to acknowledge their sinfulness and make a new covenant with God.

Luke 22:24-30, The Disciples' Debate over Greatness

NIV

²⁴Also a dispute arose among them as to which of them was considered to be greatest. ²⁵Jesus said to them, "The kings of the Gentiles lord it over them; and those who exercise authority over them call themselves Benefactors. ²⁶But you are not to be like that. Instead, the greatest among you should be like the youngest, and the one who rules like the one who serves. ²⁷For who is greater, the one who is at the table or the one who serves? Is it not the one who is at the table? But I am among you as one who serves. ²⁸You are those who have stood by me in my trials. ²⁹And I confer on you a kingdom, just as my Father conferred one on me, ³⁰so that you may eat and drink at my table in my kingdom and sit on thrones, judging the twelve tribes of Israel."

NRSV

²⁴A dispute also arose among them as to which one of them was to be regarded as the greatest. ²⁵But he said to them, "The kings of the Gentiles lord it over them; and those in authority over them are called benefactors. ²⁶But not so with you; rather the greatest among you must become like the youngest, and the leader like one who serves. ²⁷For who is greater, the one who is at the table or the one who serves? Is it not the one at the table? But I am among you as one who serves.

²⁸"You are those who have stood by me in my trials; ²⁹and I confer on you, just as my Father has conferred on me, a kingdom, ³⁰so that you may eat and drink at my table in my kingdom, and you will sit on thrones judging the twelve tribes of Israel."

COMMENTARY

The Lukan discourse at the table continues with Jesus' response to the disciples' debate over greatness. The announcement that one of them will betray Jesus spurs a debate among the disciples regarding their rank in relation to one another. The accusing attitude implied by v. 23, which reports that they began to ask one another which of them could do such a thing, is the other side of the concern over status and greatness. Those who are out of touch with their capacity to betray close relationships may also be out of touch with their status in relation to others. Both the denial that one could betray and the presumption that one is greater than others reflect a lack of awareness of one's own identity and place in community. The term for "dispute" in v. 24 (φιλονεικία *philoneikia*) literally means "love of strife."

Jesus' response to the disciples in vv. 25-30 establishes their place in the kingdom both in the present and in the future. Their identity and their relationship to one another are determined by two new realities: the standards of the kingdom and Jesus' own example (vv. 25-27). Similarly, their faithfulness now will guarantee a reward that is greater than the greatness they imagine for themselves (vv. 28-30). True greatness is to be found in faithfulness to Jesus, not in trying to exalt oneself over others.

22:25-27. Jesus begins his response with an appeal to the exercise of authority by Gentile kings. As members of an occupied and oppressed country, the disciples would have an immediate antipathy for the Gentiles' oppressive exercise of power. They established their own position by subjugating and subordinating others. Gentile kings and princes were called "Benefactor" by their subordinates. The title evokes the contemporary system of patronage with its clear class distinctions and the hoarding of wealth among the powerful. In this context, there is a tinge of irony to the term. Literally, a benefactor was a worker or doer of good. The Gentile lords were called good, when the harsh experience of those they oppressed showed that they were not. Gifts, benefactions, and benevolences mean little to the oppressed who desire nothing so much as freedom from their oppression. Worse, they are often a charade in which the oppressed are forced to praise the generosity of their oppressors. It shall not be so, Jesus declared, in the community of the kingdom.

On the contrary, in the kingdom the standards of the Gentiles are turned on their head. The great among them should take the position of a youth, and the leader should become like a servant. The logic of Jesus' argument is delightful but almost devious. The disciples who wanted to establish their superiority over their fellow disciples are now challenged to abandon the ways of the Gentile overlords whom they detested. To do so, however, they also had to give up their quest to establish their greatness over others.

Commentators have called attention to the hints of ecclesiastical language in this passage. While it records Jesus' words to his disciples following the last supper, Luke also intends for it to be overheard by believers and church leaders in his own time. Verse 26 uses three terms that have connections with the emerging structure of church offices: "the younger" (ὁ νεώτερος *ho neōteros*), "the leader" (ὁ ἡγούμενος *ho hēgoumenos*), and "the one who serves" (ὁ διακονῶν *ho diakonōn*). The only other place "the younger" appears in Luke is in reference to the prodigal son (15:12-13), but in Acts 5:6 it designates those in the church who come to remove the body of Ananias. There it is used interchangeably with "the young men" (οἱ νεανίσκοι *hoi neaniskoi,* Acts 5:10), which also appears in other significant contexts (Mark 14:51; 16:5; Acts 2:17; 23:18, 22; 1 John 2:13-14). "Younger men" (νεώτεροι *neōteroi*) occurs in some of the later epistles that deal explicitly with rank and offices in the church (1 Tim 5:1; Titus 2:6; 1 Pet 5:5). Acts (15:22; cf. 7:10; 14:12) and Hebrews (13:7, 17, 24) both refer to the role of church "leaders" (ἡγούμενοι *hēgoumenoi*), and the verb for "to serve" (διακονέω *diakoneō*) and the noun for "servant" (διάκονος *diakonos*) evolved, referring originally to any serving, then to ministry in the church, and then to the role of ministers or deacons (see, e.g., Luke 10:40; John 12:2, 26; Acts 6:2; Rom 16:1; 1 Cor 3:5; 1 Tim 3:8, 12; 1 Pet 4:10-11). A survey of the NT passages in which these terms appear confirms that they carried overtones of roles within the Christian communities. Jesus' words to the disciples in which these terms are used as metaphors inevitably created connections between the gospel story and the life situation of

the later church, particularly as it gathered to observe the Lord's supper.

Verse 27 moves the argument a step further by introducing the example of Jesus' own life—a fitting comment in a farewell discourse. Common sense dictates that one who reclines at table is greater than the one who serves, yet Jesus points to his own life: He is in the midst of them as one who serves. As the leader, Jesus' superiority was assumed, but his pattern of life did not exploit the privileges he could have expected. Again, the disciples are presented with a forced choice: either deny Jesus' greatness or accept his example of what constitutes true greatness.

These verses have a parallel in Mark 10:42-45, but source critics debate whether Luke has derived this unit from Mark or from another source. The only verbal parallels are between vv. 25-26*a* and Mark 10:42-43. There is no parallel in Mark to Luke 22:27, nor is there a parallel to Mark 10:45 in Luke, but similarities between the two verses have been noted and the possibility of a common origin cannot be discounted. The parallel between Jesus' reference to himself as one who serves in Luke and Jesus' example of service in the Johannine foot washing should also be noted.

Earlier, Jesus' parable of the master who finds his servants alert and ready promises that he will serve them. The allusion is to the promise of the great eschatological banquet (see also 13:28-29; 14:15-24; 16:19, 23-24; 22:16, 18). The connection between the language of v. 27 and earlier references to the eschatological banquet prepare the reader for the more explicit eschatological references in vv. 28-30.

If the first reason to abandon self-serving quests for status through power is that such striving is contrary to the example of Jesus' own life and the way power will be used in the kingdom of God, the second reason is that those who are faithful to Jesus now will receive a reward that is greater than what they now seek.

22:28-30. These verses have no parallel in Mark, and only the latter part of v. 30 resembles Matt 16:28. Having chided the disciples about their quarreling over greatness, Jesus now praises them as those who have stood by him in his trials. Luke has characterized Jesus' temptations as "trials" (πειρασμός *peirasmos*; 4:13). The disciples' faith in Luke—in contrast to the portrayal of the disciples in Mark, one might argue—is not like that of the seed that falls on the rocky ground and then withers "in a time of testing [i.e. trial]" (8:13). The disciples are to pray that God may not lead them into temptation (trials, 11:4), and they are to pray so that they may not experience trials (22:40, 46). The disciples have stood by Jesus in his trials, Luke mutes the defection of the disciples recorded in Mark, and the disciples will again stand faithful during the trials recorded in the book of Acts.

Jesus, therefore, confers on them a kingdom. Entry into this kingdom, however, comes through faithfulness in the midst of opposition, strife, and temptation. The reward promised for the disciples is based on the Father's vindication of Jesus. The argument echoes a typically Johannine formulation: "As the Father . . . me, so I . . . you" (see John 15:9; 17:21; 20:21). The first part of the formula occurs in various other places in John, and adaptations of it also occur in the Johannine Epistles. The Johannine Jesus promises that the disciples will be hated and persecuted, just as Jesus was persecuted (John 15:18–16:4)—much as in Luke Jesus has warned the disciples of the trials that await them (21:12-19).

At the annunciation of Jesus' birth, the angel revealed that "the Lord God will give to him the throne of his ancestor David. He will reign over the house of Jacob forever, and of his kingdom there will be no end" (1:32-33). The motif of Jesus' kingship resurfaces later, in the account of his entry into Jerusalem. Now, Jesus promises to confer a kingdom on his disciples.

In fulfillment of this promise, they will "eat and drink" at his table in his kingdom, and they will "sit on thrones judging the twelve tribes of Israel" (v. 30). The combination of eating and drinking is characteristic of Luke; the two verbs occur together fourteen times. Jesus "eats and drinks" with tax collectors and sinners (5:30). Whereas John's disciples fasted, Jesus' disciples ate and drank (5:33; cf. 7:33-34). Eating and drinking also characterize the hospitality the disciples experience as they follow Jesus' commission (10:7). Earlier, Jesus told them not to worry about what they would eat and drink (12:29); now they are told that they will eat and drink at his table. Eating and drinking with Jesus, however, are no guarantee of future rewards (13:26)—that promise is based on faithfulness to Jesus in times of trial. Whereas others may eat and drink now, unaware of the urgency of faithfulness (12:19, 45; 17:27-28), the disciples will endure trials now knowing that they will again share in Jesus' table because of their faithful endurance. This hope of sharing in the great eschatological banquet is, of course, grounded in the ancient lore of Israel (Isa 25:6; Rev 19:9).

The promise that the disciples will sit on thrones and judge the twelve tribes of Israel has a parallel in Matt 19:28. The promise does not express judgment against Israel or the Jews. On the contrary, it looks ahead to the fulfillment of Israel's hopes in a reconstituted Israel (cf. Ps 122:4-5). The verb for "to judge" (κρίνω *krinō*) here carries the sense of "ruling."[281] The election of Matthias (Acts 1:15-26) may, therefore, have been necessary as a sign of the restoration of all twelve tribes of Israel. Such positive indications of the role of Israel should not be overlooked in the midst of the litany of references in Luke and Acts to Israel's failure to recognize the Christ and his disciples. God's purposes will yet be fulfilled.

281. Joseph A. Fitzmyer, *The Gospel According to Luke (X–XXIV)*, AB 28A (Garden City, N.Y.: Doubleday, 1985) 1419.

REFLECTIONS

In this context, Luke gives a lesson on humility and serving others, similar to John's recounting of the foot washing at this point. The story also tells a tale of two betrayals. Judas and Peter are examples of the first form of betrayal. Judas, of course, made a pact to deliver Jesus to his enemies. Peter's betrayal was more subtle—therefore, more of an example for other would-be followers. When the chips were down, he denied that he was one of Jesus' disciples. The second form of betrayal is represented by those who were debating which of them would be greatest in the kingdom. Seeking our own advantage and status over the interests of others is a rejection of the ways of the kingdom and a return to the ways of "the Gentiles," who seek status and power over others. The kingdom overturns the assumptions of the Gentiles, those who hold and wield power in this world, and Jesus calls for faithfulness to a new vision of community in which the least are exalted and the greatest are those who serve others.

In a time of crisis or stress, however, there is always the temptation to deny the ways of the kingdom and return to the familiar patterns of the exercise of power. When there is dissension in the community, when there is threat from an external source, or when there are problems in meeting the budget, how do we operate: on the basis of authority or out of servanthood?

Perhaps it is important that the story leaves us no good role models, no characters with whom to identify—only the promise of true greatness if we remain faithful to Jesus and to his kingdom, even when the chips are down.

Luke 22:31-34, Jesus' Prediction of Peter's Denial

NIV

31"Simon, Simon, Satan has asked to sift you[a] as wheat. 32But I have prayed for you, Simon, that your faith may not fail. And when you have turned back, strengthen your brothers."

33But he replied, "Lord, I am ready to go with you to prison and to death."

34Jesus answered, "I tell you, Peter, before the rooster crows today, you will deny three times that you know me."

a31 The Greek is plural.

NRSV

31"Simon, Simon, listen! Satan has demanded[a] to sift all of you like wheat, 32but I have prayed for you that your own faith may not fail; and you, when once you have turned back, strengthen your brothers." 33And he said to him, "Lord, I am ready to go with you to prison and to death!" 34Jesus[b] said, "I tell you, Peter, the cock will not crow this day, until you have denied three times that you know me."

a Or has obtained permission   b Gk He

COMMENTARY

Our sense of the intensity of the conflict continues to grow with Jesus' warning that Peter, too, will deny him. This warning follows naturally the promise of reward for all who stand with Jesus during his trials (v. 28). The series of warnings given in this chapter is relentless. The authorities plot Jesus' death (v. 2); Satan enters Judas, and he makes a pact with the authorities (vv. 3-4). Then Jesus speaks of the new covenant in his blood (v. 20) and warns the disciples that one of them will betray him (v. 21). They ask which of them could do such a thing, but Jesus points out that by seeking greatness they have already taken the side of the kings and those in authority (v. 25). There are other forms of betrayal, however, and now Satan is seeking to test Simon Peter.

22:31. Luke follows a fairly regular pattern in his use of the names "Simon" and "Peter." The narrator uses the name Simon up to the call of Peter

to discipleship (4:38; 5:3-5, 10). At Simon's call, Jesus gives him the name "Peter" (5:8; 6:14), and Luke uses the name consistently up to this point (8:45, 51; 9:20, 28, 32-33; 12:41; 18:28; 22:8). Here Luke breaks the pattern, and in Jesus' only addresses to Peter he calls him "Simon, Simon" in v. 31 and "Peter" in v. 34. The repetition of the name is reminiscent of the voice to Saul on the road to Damascus (Acts 9:4). The name "Simon" will again be used in the report that the Lord had risen and appeared to "Simon" (24:34).

Satan's seeking to sift Simon is consistent with the story of Satan's request to test Job's faith (Job 1–2). The implication is that Satan has requested or demanded of God permission to test Peter's steadfastness. Judas has failed; now will Peter fare any better? The image of sifting is drawn from daily life. Flour was poured onto a screen or mesh, which was then shaken vigorously. The fine flour sifted through, while the impurities were trapped and exposed on the mesh (cf. Amos 9:9). Peter will be shaken by the events that are about to unfold, but these events involved more than ordinary human failings. They are Satan's attack on Jesus, the work of the kingdom, and the resolve of Jesus' followers. In this paradigmatic moment, we see Satan's work clearly for what it is (see 2 Cor 2:11).

22:32. Jesus will not yield Peter to Satan, however. Jesus has prayed for him. If we ask why Jesus did not do the same for Judas (a question that is extraneous to the text), a partial answer may be constructed from Jesus' claim that he has prayed "that your own faith may not fail" (v. 32). The outcome is a result of both the strength of Peter's faith and the effectiveness of Jesus' prayer. In a sense, Luke reports a trial scene or a contest over Peter. Satan and Jesus have both asked for him. Satan stands as the prosecuting attorney, the tester, while Jesus serves as Peter's advocate and defense (cf. Jesus' promise of the Paraclete in John).[282]

Jesus' initial prediction slides over the moment of Peter's denials and looks to his return and his role in strengthening his "brothers." Jesus' concern for Peter will be borne out further in an appearance to Peter (24:34), and in Acts Peter will emerge as the leader of the disciples, who on various occasions exhorts and encourages "the brethren" (Acts 1:15-16; 2:29; 3:17; 11:12; 15:7).

22:33. Jesus' initial silence about Peter's actual denials serves as an opening for Peter to assert his readiness to follow Jesus to prison or even to death. Acts records Peter's later imprisonments and the threat of death (Acts 4:3; 5:18; 12:3-17).

The Gospel of John makes explicit that Peter will indeed be arrested and put to death, but not yet (John 13:36-38; 21:18). As in the Gospel of John, the scene occurs in the room where they have eaten, not on the Mount of Olives, and Peter does not assert that he will not deny Jesus even if all the others fall away. Instead, he affirms his readiness for the trials about which Jesus has warned them (see 21:12-19; 22:28). Peter understands that Jesus is about to be arrested and put to death, but he overestimates his own ability to be faithful in the face of the coming events.

22:34. Jesus' second statement to Peter in this paragraph is devastating: The cock will not crow before Peter has denied three times that he knows Jesus. Jesus says "today," even though it is the evening before, because the day was counted from sunset to sunset. Before that night was over and the sun dawned again, Peter, who claimed to be ready to die with Jesus, would deny that he even knew him. Luke departs from Mark here by dropping the reference to the cock's crowing a second time (Mark 14:30), by adding the specification that Peter would deny *knowing* Jesus, and by allowing Jesus to have the last word, not Peter (see Mark 14:31). Later Jewish tradition prohibited the raising of chickens in Jerusalem,[283] but it is not clear that this prohibition was in force early in the first century.

The coming crisis will not leave any of the disciples untouched. Judas will betray Jesus, all will be tested, and Peter—who will emerge as the leader of the apostles—will deny that he knows Jesus.

---

282. Fitzmyer, *The Gospel According to Luke (X–XXIV)*, 1425.

283. See *m. Bab. Qam.* 7.7.

REFLECTIONS

The experience of Peter provides hope for all who feel inadequate for the trials they face. If fidelity to Christ were a matter of one's own strength, virtue would be a matter of the success of the fittest. No such Darwinian principle is operative here. Again, the way of the kingdom is not like that of natural processes. Jesus intercedes for Peter, and though Peter denies Jesus, ultimately his faith does not fail. Repentance and seeking forgiveness, even for a grievous failure, are themselves signs of faith.

Not to be missed is the future that Jesus charts for one who has failed. As in the Gospel of John, where Jesus three times charges Peter to "feed my sheep" or some variation thereof, in Luke 22:32 Jesus instructs Peter to "strengthen your brothers." There will be no restoration scene in Luke (cf. 24:34). In a sense none is needed, because this verse looks ahead to Peter's restoration and future service. In the kingdom (and the church) the requirement is not that one never have failed but that one has "turned back"; "once you have turned back, strengthen your brothers."

As Jesus predicts Peter's denials, he affirms that his role has been to pray that Peter's faith may not fail. Peter's role will be to turn back and having turned back to strengthen the others who will face similar trials. As a model for Christian discipleship, this passage assumes that we will not always prove faithful. We will fail despite our best intentions and the Lord's intercession, but the passage is open ended. The end of the story has yet to be written. What do we do with our failures? Do we let them stand as the final verdict on us, or do we turn back from them and use them to strengthen our resolve in the future and help those who face trials that we now know from the inside out? Peter is the model disciple, not because he never failed, but because he turned back.

Luke 22:35-38, Jesus' Call for Purse, Bag, and Sword

NIV

³⁵Then Jesus asked them, "When I sent you without purse, bag or sandals, did you lack anything?"

"Nothing," they answered.

³⁶He said to them, "But now if you have a purse, take it, and also a bag; and if you don't have a sword, sell your cloak and buy one. ³⁷It is written: 'And he was numbered with the transgressors'[a]; and I tell you that this must be fulfilled in me. Yes, what is written about me is reaching its fulfillment."

³⁸The disciples said, "See, Lord, here are two swords."

"That is enough," he replied.

a37 Isaiah 53:12

NRSV

35He said to them, "When I sent you out without a purse, bag, or sandals, did you lack anything?" They said, "No, not a thing." ³⁶He said to them, "But now, the one who has a purse must take it, and likewise a bag. And the one who has no sword must sell his cloak and buy one. ³⁷For I tell you, this scripture must be fulfilled in me, 'And he was counted among the lawless'; and indeed what is written about me is being fulfilled." ³⁸They said, "Lord, look, here are two swords." He replied, "It is enough."

COMMENTARY

The fourth and final exchange of Luke's farewell discourse is the most enigmatic. Although it has no parallel in the other Gospels, this unit follows naturally after Jesus' warnings that one of the disciples would betray him, that greatness will come to those who stand by him in his trials, and that even Peter will deny him. So severe will be the "sifting" that is coming upon the disciples that the previous assurances of God's protection can no longer be assumed. Jesus' arrest and crucifixion will usher in a new period in which the disciples will face similar persecution. Verses 35-38 serve, therefore, as a warning to the disciples (and the early church) to be prepared for the dangers they will face.

Jesus reminds the disciples of their experience when he sent them out on mission. Jesus' question actually refers more precisely to the instruction he gave to the seventy(-two) in Luke 10:4 than to the commissioning of the Twelve in Luke 9:3. In the former place, Jesus told those who were being sent out to "carry no purse, no bag, no sandals." Did they lack anything? No, the disciples recall, "not a thing." Jesus had assured them of providential protection and benevolent hospitality, and even journeying without provisions or protection they had lacked nothing.

Verse 36 signals a radical change: "But now. . . ." Satan's renewed attacks on Jesus and his disciples, the intensified opposition of the chief priests and scribes, and the coming destruction of Jerusalem and persecution of the followers of Jesus (21:7-24) will all follow. Now they will need to provide for themselves. The syntax of v. 36 allows it to be translated in various ways. Rather than taking "the one who has" and "the one who has not" in an absolute sense as references to the "haves" and the "have nots," it is better to translate the verse as the NRSV, the NIV, and most other translations do. Anyone who has a purse or a bag should take it. Nothing is said about sandals. Instead, a new third element is introduced. Anyone who does not have a sword should sell his or her cloak and buy one; the sword was evidently standard equipment for a traveler.

The instruction to buy a sword has prompted a great deal of discussion among commentators. As a basic principle, interpreters should take care not to pile up assumptions or take an obscure reference as evidence for something that is not supported by other references in the Gospel. The immediate context is a change in instructions for the disciples as they carry out their mission. Just as they will need a purse, bag, or sandals, so also they will need a sword. Jesus is not preparing to launch an armed revolt, however; there is no evidence of Zealot sentiment in his teachings. Neither is Jesus instructing the disciples to take arms to prevent his arrest. The sword carried by a traveler was for self-defense.

Readers have often made the same mistake that the disciples make in the story. They have thought that Jesus was condoning their instinct to fight, to advance the cause of the kingdom by taking up arms. Jesus explains his instructions by appealing not to the holy war commands of the OT but instead to a phrase from the suffering servant texts in Isaiah: "because he poured out himself to death,/ and *was numbered with the transgressors*" (Isa 53:12 NRSV, italics added). Jesus is talking about the persecution that comes upon those who choose the way of self-sacrifice, not the provisions of those who plot to take the lives of others. Throughout the Gospel, Luke has returned to the theme of the fulfillment of Scripture in the events of Jesus' life (see 2:23; 7:27; 18:31; 19:46; 20:17; 21:22; 24:44, 46). Isaiah 53:12 will be graphically fulfilled when Jesus is crucified between two criminals (23:32). The principle underlying Jesus' point is stated elsewhere: The disciple will be like the teacher (6:40), so "you will be hated by all because of my name" (21:17). Jesus warns the disciples to be ready for persecution, not revolution.

The end of v. 37 can again be read variously as "what is written about me is being fulfilled" (NRSV), or "all that concerns me comes now to its end."[284] The latter reproduces the Greek literally; the former picks up on the preceding quotation of Scripture.

Just as earlier the disciples showed that they did not understand about true greatness (vv. 24-27), so also now they show that they do not understand Jesus' call for redemptive self-sacrifice. They hear not his appeal to the suffering servant passage but his call to buy a sword. Two of them apparently already have swords. Jesus' reply is ironic and dismissive: "It is enough." The disciples have not understood, and perhaps could not then understand. Jesus would not try further to prepare them for the coming crisis. His comment is not only a reply to their eager production of two swords, but it also brings the discourse to a close and prepares for the change of scene in the next verse.

284. Fitzmyer, *The Gospel According to Luke (X–XXIV)*, 1428.

REFLECTIONS

Verse 36 presents a command from the Lord, but there is no evidence that the early church ever followed it. If the disciples originally took literally Jesus' command to buy a sword, his final comment, "It is enough," discouraged them from ever seeking to arm themselves. There is no mention anywhere in Acts that the disciples ever took swords with them when they traveled, even when they traveled in dangerous areas.

The sword is the weapon of the Gentiles (21:24); it is the weapon of the minions of Satan, "the power of darkness" that comes out to arrest Jesus (22:52-53). When his disciples wield the sword, Jesus says, "No more of this," and heals the one who was struck (22:50-51). For further reflections on the role of the sword in the NT, we may note that James the brother of John was killed with a sword (Acts 12:2), and the horseman who takes peace from the earth carries a sword (Rev 6:4). According to the Gospel of John, Jesus himself was pierced with a spear (19:34), so when the Lamb of God appears in Revelation riding on a white horse, his robe has been dipped in blood, apparently his own (Rev 19:13), and his sword is the word that comes from his mouth (Rev 19:15). The Lord would not take the sword by its handle; instead he was pierced by its point. It was not his weapon but that of Satan, and one who chooses to fight with Satan's weapons has already lost:

> If you kill with the sword,
>   with the sword you must be killed.
> Here is a call for the endurance and faith of the saints.
> (Rev 13:10 NRSV)

LUKE 22:39-46, PRAYING FOR STRENGTH AND DELIVERANCE

NIV

³⁹Jesus went out as usual to the Mount of Olives, and his disciples followed him. ⁴⁰On reaching the place, he said to them, "Pray that you will not fall into temptation." ⁴¹He withdrew about a stone's throw beyond them, knelt down and prayed, ⁴²"Father, if you are willing, take this cup from me; yet not my will, but yours be done." ⁴³An angel from heaven appeared to him and strengthened him. ⁴⁴And being in anguish, he prayed more earnestly, and his sweat was like drops of blood falling to the ground.ᵃ

⁴⁵When he rose from prayer and went back to the disciples, he found them asleep, exhausted from sorrow. ⁴⁶"Why are you sleeping?" he asked them. "Get up and pray so that you will not fall into temptation."

ᵃ44 Some early manuscripts do not have verses 43 and 44.

NRSV

39He came out and went, as was his custom, to the Mount of Olives; and the disciples followed him. ⁴⁰When he reached the place, he said to them, "Pray that you may not come into the time of trial."ᵃ ⁴¹Then he withdrew from them about a stone's throw, knelt down, and prayed, ⁴²"Father, if you are willing, remove this cup from me; yet, not my will but yours be done." [[⁴³Then an angel from heaven appeared to him and gave him strength. ⁴⁴In his anguish he prayed more earnestly, and his sweat became like great drops of blood falling down on the ground.]]ᵇ ⁴⁵When he got up from prayer, he came to the disciples and found them sleeping because of grief, ⁴⁶and he said to them, "Why are you sleeping? Get up and pray that you may not come into the time of trial."ᶜ

ᵃOr into temptation   ᵇOther ancient authorities lack verses 43 and 44   ᶜOr into temptation

COMMENTARY

After the discourse around the table, Jesus leads the disciples out to the Mount of Olives. This unit challenges us to read Luke without introducing motifs from the other Gospel accounts. It also offers an interesting example of the way in which structure, plot, and textual criticism are interrelated.

All who know the gospel story are familiar with Jesus' prayer in the Garden of Gethsemane. In the Gospel of John, however, Jesus does not pray in the garden, and no NT document reports that Jesus went to the Garden of Gethsemane. Matthew and Mark say he went to Gethsemane, and John says he went to a garden; hence, tradition speaks of "the Garden of Gethsemane." But Luke has neither a garden nor Gethsemane—Jesus went out to the Mount of Olives, "as was his custom" (cf. 21:37). This difference alone alerts the reader to respect the distinctiveness of Luke's version of this part of the story.

Part of that distinctiveness is conveyed by the relationship between the plot and the structure of this unit. Various interpreters have noted that the story employs a chiastic structure:[285]

A He said to them, "Pray that you may not come into the time of trial" (NRSV; "into temptation," NIV)
 B Then he withdrew from them
  C knelt down, and prayed
   D "Father, if you are willing, remove this cup from me; yet, not my will but yours be done"
  C' When he got up from prayer
 B' he came to the disciples and found them sleeping because of grief
A' and he said to them, "Why are you sleeping? Get up and pray that you may not come into the time of trial." (NRSV; "into temptation," NIV)

As this scheme illustrates, after the introductory verse (39-40a), the rest of the story follows a chiastic structure if the textual variant (vv. 43-44) is left out. Structure alone is not a sufficient basis for deciding the merits of the textual variant, but in this case it is one factor in the argument. Clearly, Jesus' admonition to the disciples, "Pray that you may not enter into the time of trial [temptation]," forms an *inclusio,* marking the beginning and end of the unit. When we compare Luke with Mark, we find that Jesus' admonition to the disciples appears only once in Mark, at the end but not at the beginning of the story. Luke, therefore, or the pre-Lukan tradition, has created the chiasm and the inclusio, part of which is constructed by repeating this echo of the model prayer, "that you may not come into the time of trial." The words of Jesus' prayer (v. 42) stand at the center of the structure. Accordingly, one may either emphasize the beginning and end of the unit (Jesus and the disciples) or the center (Jesus

and the Father). Both develop significant plot lines in the larger structure of the Gospel.

Upon examination of the chiastic structure, another clue to the plot of the story becomes evident. Nothing in the first part corresponds to the references to sleep in the second part. Jesus warns the disciples to pray that they might be delivered, but they fall asleep. Therefore, the unit contains two related plots that take place "a stone's throw" apart: Jesus prays for deliverance, if it be the Father's will; and Jesus instructs the disciples to pray that they may be delivered. Both petitions fail. It will not be the Father's will to remove the cup of suffering from Jesus, and the disciples fall asleep—they will not be spared either.

Luke's report that Jesus went out to the Mount of Olives "as was his custom" picks up the reference to the Mount of Olives in 21:37 and explains how Judas knew where they would be. Luke omits Mark 14:26-31, which contains the forecast of Peter's denial, because that prediction is placed back in the discourse at the table (vv. 31-34). Mark uses the Gethsemane scene to reveal the final failure of the disciples to follow Jesus. Mark also features the "inner three" (Peter, James, and John), who are named as a group at the raising of Jairus's daughter and the transfiguration in Luke (8:51; 9:28), but not here. Three times Jesus tells the disciples to watch and pray in Mark; then three times he finds them asleep. When Jesus is arrested, they flee. Luke softens the failure of the disciples by having Jesus return to find them sleeping only once rather than three times and by adding the peculiar explanatory phrase "because of grief," in v. 45. Correspondingly, Luke also adds the statement that "the disciples followed him" (v. 39), just as they had been called to do (see 5:11, 27-28; 9:23, 57, 59, 61; 18:22, 28, 43).

The importance of prayer is another prevalent theme in the Gospel of Luke. Jesus has prayed at many of the key moments of his ministry: his baptism (3:21), early in his ministry (5:16), before appointing the disciples (6:12), before Peter's confession (9:18), on the mount of transfiguration (9:28-29), before teaching his disciples about prayer (11:1-2), and while teaching the disciples (18:1). Jesus also declared that the Temple should be "a house of prayer" (19:46). In the end, Jesus dies praying (23:34, 46), and as the risen Lord, he is recognized when he prays (24:30-31). It is

285. John Nolland, *Luke 18:35–24:53,* WBC 35C (Dallas: Word, 1993) 1081, cites Ehrman and Plunkett, Galizzi, and Stanley. Raymond E. Brown, *The Death of the Messiah* (New York: Doubleday, 1994) 1:182-83, however, dismisses the chiastic structure as incidental.

entirely appropriate in Luke, therefore, that Jesus should withdraw from the disciples to pray before facing the events that lead to his death.

In Luke's account, as we have seen, Jesus twice exhorts the disciples to pray "that you may not come into the time of trial." The phrase is subject to two differing interpretations because the word πειρασμός (peirasmos) can mean either "trial" or "temptation." Accordingly, Jesus may instruct them to pray that they would be delivered from the trial that lay ahead or from the temptation to succumb to evil in the midst of adversity. The phrase itself echoes the closing petition of Luke's form of the model prayer (11:4).

The primary subject of this scene is Jesus' prayer as he prepares for his impending death. Jesus' prayers here and on the cross in Luke establish Jesus as the model for the Christian martyr. The prayer also demonstrates that Jesus did not seek or will his death. His desire to avoid death indirectly underscores Jesus' real humanity. He would choose some other course were it not for his greater devotion to the Father's redemptive purpose for his life.

The idiom for "kneeling" (θεὶς τὰ γόνατα theis ta gonata), literally "placing the knees," that is used here is also found in Acts 7:60; 9:40; 20:36; 21:5. Luke omits the distinctive Aramaic term 'Abbā', which is found in Mark 14:36, using instead the vocative of "Father" (πάτερ pater). Moreover, whereas in Mark Jesus petitions, "For you all things are possible; remove this cup from me," Luke omits the first statement and prefaces the petition with the concession "If you will." Just as Jesus' conflict with the disciples is softened in Luke, so also is his petition to the Father. Almost as in John, the Lukan Jesus is completely devoted to doing what the Father has given him to do. "The cup" (ποτήριον potērion) is a metaphorical reference to the suffering that lies ahead for him. In the OT "the cup" is often associated with God's wrath (Ps 75:8; Isa 51:17, 22; Jer 25:15; 49:12; Lam 4:21). In the *Martyrdom of Polycarp* (14.2) and the *Martyrdom of Isaiah* (5:13) the cup is a metaphor for martyrdom. In the latter reference, the prophet says, "Only for me has God mixed this cup."[286]

Verses 43-44 are omitted in 𝔓[75], ℵ[1], A, B, and other ancient manuscripts, including apparently 𝔓[69]. In addition, the insertion of these verses disrupts the chiastic structure sketched earlier and injects an emphasis on Jesus' emotion that has been distinctly absent from the scene. It appears, therefore, that these verses are an early gloss on the text that heightens Jesus' agony (contrary to the softening noted above) and emphasizes the immediate efficacy of prayer for strength in a time of crisis.

Some of the language of this insertion, however, is at home in Luke. The expression "an angel appeared to him" is also found in 1:11, and the phrase "from heaven" in 17:29 and 21:11. The verb for "to strengthen" (ἐνισχύω enischyō) is found elsewhere in the NT only in Acts 9:19, and "to pray earnestly" (ἐκτενέστερον προσεύξομαι ektenesteron proseuchomai) has a close parallel in Acts 12:5. The phrase "in anguish" (ἐν ἀγωνίᾳ en agōnia) does not occur elsewhere in Luke or Acts, and "sweat" (ἱδρώς hidrōs) and "drops" (θρόμβοι thromboi) do not occur elsewhere in the NT.[287] The latter phrase does not mean that Jesus sweated blood, but that his perspiration was as heavy as drops of blood. Justin Martyr (c. 150), the earliest source to cite this tradition, understands it in this way: "For in the memoirs which I say were drawn up by His apostles and those who followed them, [it is recorded] that His sweat fell down like drops of blood while he was praying and saying, 'If it be possible, let this cup pass.' "[288] The elements of these two verses have parallels in the OT and the Apocrypha: angelic strengthening of the faithful (Dan 10:13, 18) and the blood and sweat of a righteous sufferer (Eleazar in 4 Macc 6:6, 11; 7:8).

The subplot of this story revolves around Jesus' instruction to the disciples to pray and their failure to do so. As our analysis of the structure of the passage revealed, the references to sleep have no parallel in the corresponding verses in the first half of the chiasm. Luke softens the judgment on the disciples by commenting that they were sleeping "because of grief," but commentators have generally noted that the explanation seems

---

286. See Brown, *The Death of the Messiah*, 1:169.

287. Joseph A. Fitzmyer, *The Gospel According to Luke (X–XXIV)*, AB 28A (Garden City, N.Y.: Doubleday, 1985) 1444.

288. Justin Martyr, *Dialogue with Trypho*, 103.5, in Alexander Roberts and James Donaldson, eds., *The Ante-Nicene Fathers* (Grand Rapids: Eerdmans, 1985) 1:251.

strained. Again, Jesus repeats his command, "Get up and pray that you may not come into the time of trial." The rhetorical effect is to exhort readers to imitate the example of Jesus rather than the example of the disciples. In the end, Jesus has fortified himself through prayer for the suffering that lies before him, assuring himself that it is the Father's will, whereas the disciples have failed to do so. Their sleep is evidence of their failure to be vigilant and pray in a time of trial.

As at the annunciation of John the Baptist's birth, Jesus' baptism, and the transfiguration, therefore, at least with the inclusion of vv. 43-44,

Jesus' prayer is followed by a heavenly apparition (see 1:8-12; 3:21-22; 9:28-32). Likewise, as at the transfiguration, the disciples are overcome by sleep while Jesus prays. In this context, Jesus' earlier words of exhortation to the disciples take on added meaning: "Be alert at all times, praying that you may have the strength to escape all these things that will take place, and to stand before the Son of Man" (21:36). Thus Jesus' example and the failure of the disciples on the Mount of Olives serve as specific illustrations for the church of the importance of faithfulness and prayer in times of crisis.

REFLECTIONS

Prayer and devotion at times of physical and spiritual crisis have left a long trail of powerful effects in Christian history. The death of a friend, a narrow escape from lightning, and anxiety over his soul's salvation led the young Martin Luther to feverish prayer and a driven search for assurance of his salvation. On May 24, 1738, John Wesley heard Luther's preface to his *Commentary on Romans* read at the meeting of an Anglican society in Aldersgate Street, London, and later reported, "I felt my heart strangely warmed."[289]

The book of Acts itself records the disciples' experience of the power of the Spirit at Pentecost after they followed Jesus' instructions and devoted themselves to prayer (Acts 1:14). At the hour of prayer, Peter and John healed the lame man in the Temple (Acts 3:1). After the arrest and release of these two disciples, the church again prayed and was filled with the Holy Spirit and spoke the Word of God boldly (Acts 4:31). And so on many other occasions in Acts.

However, prayer in times of crisis or need is hollow unless it is an extension of a reverence for God in which we express thanks daily for God's providence in our lives, open ourselves to God's presence, and intercede for others. Apart from the daily practice of prayer, the injunction to pray for help in times of distress reduces prayer to another kind of insurance policy—in time of need, or when there is no other resource, pray.

Prayer is a matter of neither desperation nor luck. It is one of the ways in which believers respond to the presence of God each day and seek direction from God. In truth, the injunction to pray that we might be delivered from temptation or trial is part of the larger tapestry of devotion to God. A balanced interpretation of the injunction would not deny the efficacy of "fox hole" prayer but might say, "Pray without ceasing so that you may be open to God's power and sensitive to God's Spirit in times of crisis." Jesus' instructions to the disciples on the Mount of Olives not only echo the Lord's Prayer, then—he assumes its regular practice.

289. Williston Walker, *A History of the Christian Church,* rev. ed. (New York: Charles Scribner's Sons, 1959) 459.

LUKE 22:47-53, THE ARREST OF JESUS

NIV	NRSV
⁴⁷While he was still speaking a crowd came up, and the man who was called Judas, one of the	47While he was still speaking, suddenly a crowd came, and the one called Judas, one of the

NIV

Twelve, was leading them. He approached Jesus to kiss him, [48]but Jesus asked him, "Judas, are you betraying the Son of Man with a kiss?"

[49]When Jesus' followers saw what was going to happen, they said, "Lord, should we strike with our swords?" [50]And one of them struck the servant of the high priest, cutting off his right ear.

[51]But Jesus answered, "No more of this!" And he touched the man's ear and healed him.

[52]Then Jesus said to the chief priests, the officers of the temple guard, and the elders, who had come for him, "Am I leading a rebellion, that you have come with swords and clubs? [53]Every day I was with you in the temple courts, and you did not lay a hand on me. But this is your hour—when darkness reigns."

NRSV

twelve, was leading them. He approached Jesus to kiss him; [48]but Jesus said to him, "Judas, is it with a kiss that you are betraying the Son of Man?" [49]When those who were around him saw what was coming, they asked, "Lord, should we strike with the sword?" [50]Then one of them struck the slave of the high priest and cut off his right ear. [51]But Jesus said, "No more of this!" And he touched his ear and healed him. [52]Then Jesus said to the chief priests, the officers of the temple police, and the elders who had come for him, "Have you come out with swords and clubs as if I were a bandit? [53]When I was with you day after day in the temple, you did not lay hands on me. But this is your hour, and the power of darkness!"

COMMENTARY

"The time of trial" (v. 46) begins while Jesus is still speaking. The arrest of Jesus in Luke unfolds in an abridged version of the story in Mark, but one with several Johannine parallels. Luke omits Mark's description of the weapons, the initial description of the crowd, the report of the agreed upon sign, and Judas's words to his co-conspirators (Mark 14:43-44). Mark also omits Judas's words to Jesus and the report that he kissed Jesus (Mark 14:45), defers the capture of Jesus to the end of the scene (cf. Mark 14:46), and omits the flight of the disciples (Mark 14:50). In spite of the brevity of his account, Luke adds details that have Johannine parallels: Jesus is in control of the entire scene; the disciple cuts off the servant's right ear (John 18:10); Jesus speaks of the significance of the "hour" and "the power of darkness" (Luke 22:53); and in John there is no flight of the disciples.[290]

22:47. Luke's streamlined account of Jesus' arrest emphasizes Jesus' response to Judas, his response to violence perpetrated by his followers, and his response to the "trial" that has overtaken him. Luke makes note first of the arrival of the crowd, then the presence of Judas leading them. The departure of Judas from the group of disciples

was not recorded earlier, but must be conjectured. The naming of Judas here recalls Luke 22:3-6, where Judas was introduced as one of the Twelve, and where under the influence of Satan he made a pact with the chief priests and officers of the Temple. The attentive reader, therefore, already has clues that Judas is about to "betray him to them" (see 22:6).

22:48. When Judas came near to Jesus to kiss him, Jesus rebuffed him: "Judas, is it with a kiss that you are betraying the Son of Man?" (v. 48). The question is found only in Luke among the Gospels, and its language recalls earlier references: a kiss as a greeting (7:45, but see Prov 27:6), the Son of Man (see esp. 9:22, 44; 18:31-32; 22:22), and "betray" (9:44; 18:32; 22:4, 6, 21-22). The event that Jesus has predicted repeatedly is now coming to pass. Luke does not indicate that the kiss was a prearranged signal, and it need not have been. Judas's approach to Jesus would have been self-evident to his co-conspirators. Neither is it clear whether Judas actually kissed Jesus. All attention is focused on the fulfillment of Judas's role as the betrayer.

22:49-51. Earlier, the disciples had taken Jesus' instructions to buy a sword literally, and Jesus had responded with resignation, "It is enough" (22:38). Now, "those who were around him"—presumably the disciples—ask whether they

290. See John Nolland, *Luke 18:35–24:53,* WBC 35C (Dallas: Word, 1993) 1086.

should wield the sword. Again, the question is peculiar to Luke. One of them, here unnamed (cf. John 18:10), strikes the servant of the high priest and cuts off his right ear; only Luke and John specify that it was the right ear. Striking the servant of the high priest would have been an affront to the high priest himself. Jesus' response is immediate: "No more of this!" The kingdom is not advanced by violence, so the sword has no place in the church's arsenal (cf. Eph 6:17; Rev 13:10). Healing was characteristic of Jesus' ministry, especially in Luke, where the verb "to heal" (ἰάομαι iaomai) is used more frequently than in any other book of the NT (11 times). Luke reports that "the power of the Lord was with him to heal" (5:17), and Jesus had sent the disciples out "to proclaim the kingdom of God and to heal" (9:2). Touching is associated with healing in 5:13 and 8:43-48, and with blessing in 18:15. Even in the midst of his "trial," therefore, Jesus continues to carry out his redemptive mission, teaching the disciples and healing a man whom they had injured.

22:52-53a. Having addressed Judas and then his disciples, Jesus turns to the three groups represented in the arresting party: the chief priests, the officers of the Temple, and the elders. The listing of these groups recalls the groups of the authorities who opposed Jesus in the Temple (19:47; 20:1, 19) and who were looking for an opportunity to kill him (19:47; 22:2). Here the scribes have been dropped from the list and the officers of the Temple have been added (as in 22:4). Jesus' question to the authorities is drawn from Mark 14:48-49 (cf. John 18:3). It underlines the incongruity of the situation. Were the chief priests and elders carrying swords and clubs, as were the officers of the Temple? Did they really think that Jesus would respond with armed resistance? By their own actions, paradoxically, they themselves were fulfilling the words of Isa 53:12: "And [he] was numbered with the transgressors." Perhaps they feared his followers, one of whom did indeed draw his sword. The reference to Jesus' teaching in the Temple recalls the period of teaching reported in 19:47–21:38, where at

both the beginning and the end of this unit we were told that "every day he was teaching in the temple." Why had they not seized him then? It was not because he was a *lēstēs* (λῃστής), a "brigand," a "bandit," or a "violent man." It was because they feared the people (19:48; 20:19; 22:2). They could not trap Jesus with an incriminating answer in the presence of the people (20:26), so they had arranged an opportunity to seize him "when there was no crowd present" (22:6). The crowd that night was on their side (see 22:47). Their weapons were unnecessary. Jesus had rebuked the disciple who had thought that armed resistance was the answer.

Judas had sought to kiss Jesus while betraying him. Jesus had touched the servant of the high priest to heal him. Now the authorities sought to lay their hands on Jesus to arrest him (cf. 20:19; 22:53). How many different intentions can be conveyed by a touch!

22:53b. The time of Jesus' "trial" had begun. It was their time, their "hour, and the power of darkness" (v. 53). Luke uses references to the hour to characterize various events or periods in Jesus' ministry: the hour of incense offering (1:10), the time when Jesus healed many (7:21), a time when Jesus rejoiced (10:21), the hour of the disciples' trials (12:12), the hour when the thief comes or the Son of Man comes (12:39-40, 46), the hour when the Pharisees warned Jesus about Herod (13:31), the time when the authorities desired to arrest him (20:19), and then the hour of the Passover meal (22:14). Darkness has been used metaphorically in 1:79 and 11:35 (cf. 23:44). Likewise, the power of darkness can be contrasted with the "power" (ἐξουσία exousia) that Jesus claimed (4:32, 36; 5:24; 9:1; 10:19; 20:8). Brown observes, regarding the hour and authority of Jesus and the hour and authority of the devil: "The devil, who after testing Jesus at the beginning of the ministry [4:13] left him until 'an opportune time [καιρός kairos],' has at last his hour."[291]

---

291. Brown, *The Death of the Messiah*, 293.

REFLECTIONS

1. The didactic overtones of this scene are not as strong as those of the previous one. The clearest concern is again to reject violence as the means of accomplishing God's purposes. The foil for Jesus is the disciple who in the face of immediate threat and the treachery of Judas unsheathes his sword to defend his master. Jesus' last instruction to his disciples before his arrest, therefore, is "No more of this!" No more retaliation, no more bloodshed, no more rule by might, no more victimization of others. Even if the immediate goal is achieved by taking the sword, the ultimate goal is lost. The disciples' first compromise is to resist Satan's minions by fighting with Satan's weapons. But when they do so they have already betrayed their cause.

2. More broadly, the betrayal and arrest of Jesus point to the failure of the disciples. The steadfastness of Jesus and the impulsive act of the disciple (following the question of the others in v. 49), paint a picture of clear contrasts. Even when those closest to him fail him in the hour of his greatest trial, Jesus is firm in his conviction and purpose. Even when all about him are losing their heads, Jesus never waivers.

Lest we be too hard on the disciples, however, we should also recognize their frustration. Not only Jesus but they too had been betrayed by one of their own. Jesus knew of Judas's treachery in advance, but the disciples were caught by surprise. Their intent was to defend Jesus, but there was really no way they could do so. The alliance of civil and religious authorities controlled the situation. What do we do when our intent is good but there are no good means at hand by which we can accomplish it? The disciples failed because they allowed frustration and fear to lead them to violence. Jesus met the crisis with the recognition that this was the hour of the power of darkness. There would be other hours, when the power of good would be victorious—Easter Sunday was coming. In this instance, faithfulness called for surrender and self-sacrifice in the steadfast confidence that the end of the story has not yet been reached.

3. At a deeper level, the story presents us with the paradox of human intention and divine purpose. The disciples were frustrated and failed because they were not able to deliver Jesus from his adversaries. The implication of Jesus' passion predictions and his prayer in the previous scene, however, is that God did not will for Jesus to be delivered from those who were seeking his life. Hence, to have defended Jesus successfully would have meant that God's will for these events would not have been realized. Deliverance is achieved by failure, victory by dying rather than killing, redemption by self-sacrifice rather than by conquest, life through death. Consequently, the events at Jesus' arrest are part and parcel of the paradox of the Christian gospel: that the lost are saved by the death of Jesus.

LUKE 22:54-62, DENIALS IN THE COURTYARD

NIV

54Then seizing him, they led him away and took him into the house of the high priest. Peter followed at a distance. 55But when they had kindled a fire in the middle of the courtyard and had sat down together, Peter sat down with them. 56A servant girl saw him seated there in the firelight. She looked closely at him and said, "This man was with him."

NRSV

54Then they seized him and led him away, bringing him into the high priest's house. But Peter was following at a distance. 55When they had kindled a fire in the middle of the courtyard and sat down together, Peter sat among them. 56Then a servant-girl, seeing him in the firelight, stared at him and said, "This man also was with

NIV

⁵⁷But he denied it. "Woman, I don't know him," he said.

⁵⁸A little later someone else saw him and said, "You also are one of them."

"Man, I am not!" Peter replied.

⁵⁹About an hour later another asserted, "Certainly this fellow was with him, for he is a Galilean."

⁶⁰Peter replied, "Man, I don't know what you're talking about!" Just as he was speaking, the rooster crowed. ⁶¹The Lord turned and looked straight at Peter. Then Peter remembered the word the Lord had spoken to him: "Before the rooster crows today, you will disown me three times." ⁶²And he went outside and wept bitterly.

NRSV

him." ⁵⁷But he denied it, saying, "Woman, I do not know him." ⁵⁸A little later someone else, on seeing him, said, "You also are one of them." But Peter said, "Man, I am not!" ⁵⁹Then about an hour later still another kept insisting, "Surely this man also was with him; for he is a Galilean." ⁶⁰But Peter said, "Man, I do not know what you are talking about!" At that moment, while he was still speaking, the cock crowed. ⁶¹The Lord turned and looked at Peter. Then Peter remembered the word of the Lord, how he had said to him, "Before the cock crows today, you will deny me three times." ⁶²And he went out and wept bitterly.

COMMENTARY

The arrest of Jesus introduces three related scenes: Peter's denials of Jesus (vv. 54-62); the mocking of Jesus (vv. 63-65); and the trial before the religious authorities (vv. 66-71). The story of Peter in the courtyard denying Jesus three times is distinctive because for eight verses of the passion narrative the Gospel focuses not on Jesus but on Peter. Three times Peter denies that he knows Jesus, then the cock crows, and Peter remembers that Jesus had told him that he would deny Jesus (22:31-34).

Although all four Gospels record the story of Peter's denials, Luke's account is unique in the following respects: (1) *sequence:* the three denials take place immediately after Peter enters the courtyard and before the mocking and interrogation of Jesus by the authorities; (2) *structure:* Luke does not use a sandwiching technique as do the other Gospels, (a) introducing Peter, (b) reporting the trial, and (a') relating Peter's denials; (3) *style:* Luke writes freely—the only verbal parallels are those that might be expected in any retelling of the story; and (4) *detail:* the servant girl is seated at the fire (where she can see Peter clearly); Peter prefaces each denial with an address, "woman" the first time and "man" the second and third times; about an hour elapses between the second and third denials; and when the cock crows, Jesus turns and makes eye contact with Peter. Unlike Mark, in Luke Peter is accused by three different

people (the servant girl and two men), and the cock crows only once, not twice.

The hour and the power of darkness (v. 53) overtake Peter also. Jesus warned Peter that Satan had demanded to sift him like wheat (22:31). Peter follows Jesus, as he had pledged he would (see 22:33, 54), but in the end he denies Jesus, just as Jesus had predicted as well. The events take place in darkness, before the trial. Jesus is led to the house of the high priest, where Jesus is evidently held in the courtyard until daybreak (v. 66). Peter's movements foreshadow his denials: He follows Jesus, but at a distance, and when the captors build a fire, Peter sits with them. The servant girl sees Peter in the firelight and peers at him closely. Presumably she had seen Peter with Jesus either at the arrest or earlier in the Temple. The accusations are that Peter was with Jesus or that he was "one of them"—guilt by association. The third time an added reason for suspicion is leveled against Peter: Either his dress or his accent gives him away as a Galilean. Each time, Peter denies that he knows Jesus: "Woman, I do not know him" (v. 57); "Man, I am not" (v. 58); "Man, I do not know what you are talking about!" (v. 60).

Following the threefold denials, Luke records a double dénouement. First, the cock crows, and then Jesus looks at Peter. The end of the story comes as suddenly as a trap closing around its victim. Luke here uses the term "suddenly" (παραχρῆμα *parachrēma*; NRSV, "at that moment"). The same term is used nine other times in the Gospel and six times in Acts (elsewhere in the NT it occurs only twice in Matthew). Luke has also used the clause "while he was still speaking" earlier to mark sudden developments (8:49; 22:47). The use of the aorist participle of the verb "to turn" (στρέφω *strephō*) is another typically Lukan narrative device (7:9, 44; 9:55; 10:22-23; 14:25; 22:61; 23:28).

Three verbs characterize Peter's response: he "remembered" (ὑπομιμνήσκω *hypomimnēskō*), he "went" out (ἐξέρχομαι *exerchomai*), and he "wept" (κλαίω *klaiō*) bitterly. Although Jesus' words in v. 61 are recalled as a direct quotation, they reproduce only the substance of 22:34 rather than repeating it verbatim. In Luke it is the combination of the cockcrow and the Lord's look that causes Peter to remember. Verse 62 is a verbatim parallel to Matt 26:75, which has suggested to some interpreters that Luke had a second account of the event. Because Luke has repeatedly taken the edge off of Mark's portrayal of their failure to understand or follow Jesus, it is not surprising that this story should end with Peter's bitter remorse. Peter's tears indicate that Jesus' prayers have been answered. Not only did Peter deny Jesus, as he had said Peter would, but also Peter's turning was announced earlier (22:32). At Jesus' calling of Peter to discipleship, Peter had warned Jesus that he was "a sinful man" (5:8), but Jesus' commission for Peter overrode Peter's confession: "From now on you will be catching people" (5:10). Peter, therefore, fulfills both his own self-assessment and Jesus' calling for him. At this point in Luke-Acts, the first has been fulfilled, and evidence of the eventual fulfillment of the second has been provided in the mission accounts in Luke 9–10. The one who failed will fish again. Readers familiar with the Gospel of John will remember that the story of the miraculous catch of fish, which in Luke marks the calling of Peter to discipleship, occurs in John 21 as a post-resurrection appearance scene in which Peter is restored to discipleship and commissioned to "feed my sheep."

REFLECTIONS

Failure comes in many forms, but we never fail our Lord without failing ourselves, and when we fail ourselves in some sense we always fail our Lord, because God calls us to be our best selves and reach our highest personal and spiritual potential. Peter succumbed to one of the most basic of human instincts—self-preservation. On our scale of needs, survival, physical safety, and security rank as the most basic. Self-esteem, loyalty to others, and faithfulness to our commitments come much later. The call to faith, as Peter learned from painful experience, can at times call us to reverse the natural order of our hierarchy of needs and attend to higher callings rather than to instinctual impulses.

Failure can come in many guises. Judas plotted to betray Jesus and then shamelessly approached him to kiss him. Whatever Judas's motivation, his act was calculated and premeditated. He planned his act of betrayal. Peter, by contrast, was trying to follow Jesus (see v. 54). Although repeated three times, his act was not premeditated but spontaneous. Like the disciple who lashed out with his sword to prevent Jesus' arrest (identified as Peter in John 18:10), Peter's response to the moment was unplanned. Had he given more thought to what his commitments and intentions would have meant for him in that moment, he might have acted differently. But who can anticipate such eventualities?

Peter feared exposure. His life may have been at stake. Guilt by association may have been guilt enough. He would either be guilty in the eyes of the authorities or guilty in the eyes of his Lord. His actions showed that his fear of the authorities dominated, but his failure and remorse stand as a lesson for others who face trials as real and dangerous as Peter's. In Luke's hands, therefore, the story of Peter's denials is a lesson in discipleship: Be prepared for the hour of testing so that you may not fail as Peter did. Peter, who was ready to go with Jesus to prison and to death (22:33), fails before the trial begins.

Until the end of the story, nothing is reported of the characters' inner feelings. Even then, nothing is said about Jesus' response. We are simply told that he looked at Peter. What is conveyed in a look? Criticism, condemnation, or compassion? Jesus could take no pleasure in the fulfillment of his warning to Peter, and even if Jesus' look conveyed compassion rather than judgment, it could scarcely have been much comfort to Peter at that moment.

The reader's position is clear. In this story anyone who has any degree of self-understanding will see himself or herself in Peter's failure. How easy it is to slip, to fail our best intentions and our truest commitments. How quickly we can betray and hurt the persons we love. In such situations we can do no better than follow Peter's response. He recognized that he had failed and made his way down the road of remorse and repentance, which would lead to his restoration.

LUKE 22:63-65, THE CHALLENGE TO PROPHESY

NIV

[63]The men who were guarding Jesus began mocking and beating him. [64]They blindfolded him and demanded, "Prophesy! Who hit you?" [65]And they said many other insulting things to him.

NRSV

63Now the men who were holding Jesus began to mock him and beat him; [64]they also blindfolded him and kept asking him, "Prophesy! Who is it that struck you?" [65]They kept heaping many other insults on him.

COMMENTARY

Ironically, immediately after the fulfillment of Jesus' prophecy that Peter would deny him three times, his captors begin to mock and torment him by challenging him to prophesy. In contrast to the order in Mark, in Luke this mockery of Jesus occurs after Peter's denials and before the trial, which occurs in the morning rather than during the night. Those involved are identified only obliquely as "the men who were holding Jesus." Luke may intend that they were servants or soldiers or that they were a group of the authorities listed in v. 52.

The verbs used in this brief scene tie it to the passion predictions and other significant contexts in the Gospel. First, the men's cruel game is characterized as mockery. In one of the passion predictions, Jesus had warned that he would be handed over to Gentiles, mocked, insulted, and spat upon (18:32). The present scene is the first of three occasions in the Lukan passion narrative in which this prediction will be fulfilled. Jesus is mocked before the Jewish trial (22:63), before Herod and his soldiers (23:11), and before the soldiers at the cross (23:36). Here was a king who

had counted the cost, and still he was mocked (cf. 14:29).

Luke uses the verb "to beat" ($\delta \acute{\epsilon} \rho \omega$ *derō*) five times, more often than any other book of the NT. Two of the other references occur in the parable of the wicked tenants who beat the servants sent by the owner of the vineyard (20:10-11; cf. 12:47-48). The scribes and chief priests realized that Jesus had told this parable about them, but now they have begun to enact their part without realizing it.

The vicious game of blind man's buff continues with the men blindfolding Jesus and taunting him, "Prophesy!" The taunt is a bitter irony. Luke has established Jesus as one greater than a prophet. At the annunciations, the angel promised that John would fulfill the role of Elijah (1:17), but Jesus would be greater. Concentrated attention is given to clarifying the relationship between Jesus and John in Luke 7, and again Jesus is hailed as one greater than a prophet (7:18-35). Jesus had given repeated predictions of the events of his passion, and they were unfolding as he had said they would. Jerusalem was about to kill another prophet (13:34; cf. 24:19). Jesus had told his disciples that one of them would betray him and that Peter would deny him, and Luke has just related the fulfillment of those predictions; even the men's act of mockery had been predicted.

The final verb of note in these verses is the one Luke uses in v. 65 to characterize the whole scene of the mockery: for him it is blasphemy. Moreover, while they blaspheme, Jesus says noth-ing at all. He is deprived even of his voice in this scene. Earlier, Jesus had warned that those who blaspheme against the Holy Spirit will not be forgiven (12:10). Now Luke characterizes the acts of those who mock Jesus and the taunt of the criminal on the cross (23:39) as blasphemy. At its root, blasphemy is the act of scorning the sacred. Who would dare to taunt God or challenge the Lord to prophesy?

REFLECTIONS

The story of Jesus blindfolded in a dark courtyard surrounded by his captors, who make sport of him, is as hard for us to relate to as are the accounts of senseless violence that are reported daily. Parents abuse their children, children kill other children, gang members live and die by violence, and deranged gunmen kill indiscriminately. Who can understand such violence? Yet, the Gospel affirms that Jesus himself suffered from the impulse of fallen humanity to take advantage of the powerless and to exploit the victim.

Jesus died a redemptive death. His solution to the problem of violence was not to attempt to overcome it with more violence but to absorb it in suffering love. Perhaps only one who is divine can redeem the violent in this way, but from time to time spiritual leaders have succeeded in following Jesus' example in the exercise of redemptive non-violence. Jesus not only suffered for us but he also suffered to teach us how to overcome the violent and corruptive impulses within us and within our society. This, too, was a part of Jesus' proclamation of the coming of kingdom.

LUKE 22:66-71, JESUS BEFORE THE SANHEDRIN

NIV

66At daybreak the council of the elders of the people, both the chief priests and teachers of the law, met together, and Jesus was led before them. 67"If you are the Christ,[a]" they said, "tell us."

Jesus answered, "If I tell you, you will not believe me, 68and if I asked you, you would not answer. 69But from now on, the Son of Man will be seated at the right hand of the mighty God."

70They all asked, "Are you then the Son of God?"

He replied, "You are right in saying I am."

71Then they said, "Why do we need any more testimony? We have heard it from his own lips."

a67 Or Messiah

NRSV

66When day came, the assembly of the elders of the people, both chief priests and scribes, gathered together, and they brought him to their council. 67They said, "If you are the Messiah,[a] tell us." He replied, "If I tell you, you will not believe; 68and if I question you, you will not answer. 69But from now on the Son of Man will be seated at the right hand of the power of God." 70All of them asked, "Are you, then, the Son of God?" He said to them, "You say that I am." 71Then they said, "What further testimony do we need? We have heard it ourselves from his own lips!"

aOr the Christ

COMMENTARY

In Luke's arrangement, Jesus' appearance before the Sanhedrin comes third in the sequence of scenes, following the denials by Peter and the mockery in the courtyard. The proceedings have less of the air of a formal trial in Luke than in Mark. There are no other witnesses, no recitation of the saying about the destruction of the Temple, and no formal verdict. It appears, therefore, to be a hearing to prepare charges against Jesus for the Roman court rather than a formal trial. After the council is assembled and Jesus is brought to it, they ask Jesus two christological questions, the first involving the title "Christ" (Messiah), and the second "the Son of God." Both titles are important in the other Gospels. At least, according to some manuscripts, Mark opens with the line, "The beginning of the good news of Jesus Christ, the Son of God" (Mark 1:1 NRSV), and John 20 concludes with a statement of the Gospel's purpose that again uses the two titles: "But these are written so that you may come to believe that Jesus is the Messiah, the Son of God" (John 20:31 NRSV; cf. 11:27).

22:66. In Luke and Acts, the council convenes early in the morning (see Acts 4:3; 5:21-22). The assembled group is composed of the elders, chief priests, and scribes. Luke has recorded the maneuverings of the chief priests and scribes in several earlier passages (19:47; 20:1, 19; 22:2). The elders have appeared earlier in 20:1 and 22:52, but here it is the council or assembly of the elders (cf. Acts 22:5). Jesus is not interrogated by the chief priest (as in Mark 14:61) but by the indefinite "they."

22:67a. The stratagem of the council seems to be to goad Jesus into incriminating himself. Luke's interests, of course, are christological, so both questions involve titles that have already been clearly established for the reader. First, they challenge Jesus to tell them if he is the Messiah. In popular expectations, the Messiah would have been a royal figure who would deliver Israel from foreign oppressors. Such a confession, then, might have been useful before the Roman court. At his birth, Jesus was announced as the Christ (2:11, 26), and the demons knew that he was the Christ (4:41). Later, Peter confessed that Jesus was the

Christ (9:20), but Jesus had ordered the disciples not to tell anyone. The royal overtones of the title are again evident in the questions regarding the relationship of the Christ to David (20:41-44).

22:67b-68. Jesus' answer is evasive and noncommittal. In that context, he can neither affirm nor deny the title. Instead, he points to the obduracy of the council. They have put the question to him, but they would not accept his answer if he were to respond forthrightly. Neither would they answer him if he questioned them—as he had done when they confronted him in the Temple and they refused to answer (see 20:5-8, 26, 40).

22:69. Jesus himself introduces a third title, just as earlier he had deflected Peter's confession that Jesus was the Christ by teaching them about the Son of Man (see 9:20-22). Now what he had said about the Son of Man was in the process of coming to pass—he was being rejected by the elders, the chief priests, and the scribes—the same three groups of whom he had spoken on that occasion (cf. 9:22; 22:66). As Jesus looks ahead, he affirms that the Son of Man will be seated "at the right hand of the power of God." This declaration evokes the well-known references in Dan 7:13, "one like a son of man" (NIV) coming to "the Ancient One," and Ps 110:1, seated at the "right hand."

22:70. From this affirmation, the council draws the conclusion that Jesus is claiming to be the Son of God. Again, they seek incriminating words from Jesus by challenging him to claim this title. The title "Son of God" is not used frequently in Luke and has not appeared in the text since chap. 9. This reference, however, is the climactic one that demonstrates why the title could not be used openly. At the annunciation, Jesus was designated the Son of God (1:35), and his identity was confirmed by the voice from heaven at his baptism (3:22) and at the transfiguration (9:35). Although the devil tempted Jesus to prove his power as the Son of God (4:3, 9) and the demons proclaimed his identity (4:41; 8:28), no one confesses Jesus as the Son of God in Luke. Ironically, the council infers correctly that what Jesus has said about the Son of Man means that he is—or at least understands that he is—the Son of God, but they will not accept their own conclusion.

Jesus offers an equivocal response: "You say that I am." He neither denies their deduction nor openly affirms it. The formula "I am" (ἐγώ εἰμι *egō eimi*) is used in the Gospel of John in an absolute sense that echoes the divine name revealed to Moses at the burning bush (Exod 3:14). The Lukan use of "I am" does not have such overtones (21:8; 24:39). Nevertheless, when Jesus replies, "You say that I am," the reader may recall that Peter denied Jesus, saying, "I am not" (22:58).

22:71. The conclusion of the hearing before the council underscores the weakness of their case against Jesus. All they have is Jesus' equivocal acceptance of their unbelieving confession that he is the Son of God. They said that they did not need any other testimony (cf. the false witnesses in Mark 14:57-59). Instead, the disciples would be the witnesses "of these things" (24:48; Acts 1:8).

REFLECTIONS

Once again, these verses declare who Jesus is. Three titles are used: the Messiah, the Son of Man, and the Son of God. Yet, even though the authorities heard Jesus' testimony from his own lips, they would not believe. Later, we will hear that at least one member of the council was receptive (Joseph of Arimathea, 23:50-51), but the opposition to Jesus forces on us the question of why some reject God's self-disclosure. Here is the "heart of darkness," the irredeemable refusal to respond to God's mercy and God's unwavering commitment to human freedom. God grants us freedom even to reject God's own love and mercy. The Son of God would lay down his life to redeem those who opposed him, but God would not refuse them the freedom to oppose him. What love is this that will neither cease to love nor overrule our freedom to reject that love?

The one who was mocked and beaten, moreover, is also the one who will sit "at the right hand of the power of God" (v. 69). The paradox of love and freedom is matched by that of humiliation and exaltation. The sovereign Lord is also the one who was blindfolded and beaten. The juxtaposition of the mocking of Jesus and the questioning of his messiahship foreshadows that Jesus will, indeed, triumph in spite of those who sought to kill him. The Lord we worship has identified with the rejected and despised.

LUKE 23:1-25, JESUS' TRIAL BEFORE PILATE

NIV

23 Then the whole assembly rose and led him off to Pilate. ²And they began to accuse him, saying, "We have found this man subverting our nation. He opposes payment of taxes to Caesar and claims to be Christ,[a] a king."

³So Pilate asked Jesus, "Are you the king of the Jews?"

"Yes, it is as you say," Jesus replied.

⁴Then Pilate announced to the chief priests and the crowd, "I find no basis for a charge against this man."

⁵But they insisted, "He stirs up the people all over Judea[b] by his teaching. He started in Galilee and has come all the way here."

a2 Or *Messiah*; also in verses 35 and 39   b5 Or *over the land of the Jews*

NRSV

23 Then the assembly rose as a body and brought Jesus[a] before Pilate. ²They began to accuse him, saying, "We found this man perverting our nation, forbidding us to pay taxes to the emperor, and saying that he himself is the Messiah, a king."[b] ³Then Pilate asked him, "Are you the king of the Jews?" He answered, "You say so." ⁴Then Pilate said to the chief priests and the crowds, "I find no basis for an accusation against this man." ⁵But they were insistent and said, "He stirs up the people by teaching throughout all Judea, from Galilee where he began even to this place."

a Gk *him*   b Or *is an anointed king*

NIV

⁶On hearing this, Pilate asked if the man was a Galilean. ⁷When he learned that Jesus was under Herod's jurisdiction, he sent him to Herod, who was also in Jerusalem at that time.

⁸When Herod saw Jesus, he was greatly pleased, because for a long time he had been wanting to see him. From what he had heard about him, he hoped to see him perform some miracle. ⁹He plied him with many questions, but Jesus gave him no answer. ¹⁰The chief priests and the teachers of the law were standing there, vehemently accusing him. ¹¹Then Herod and his soldiers ridiculed and mocked him. Dressing him in an elegant robe, they sent him back to Pilate. ¹²That day Herod and Pilate became friends—before this they had been enemies.

¹³Pilate called together the chief priests, the rulers and the people, ¹⁴and said to them, "You brought me this man as one who was inciting the people to rebellion. I have examined him in your presence and have found no basis for your charges against him. ¹⁵Neither has Herod, for he sent him back to us; as you can see, he has done nothing to deserve death. ¹⁶Therefore, I will punish him and then release him.ᵃ"

¹⁸With one voice they cried out, "Away with this man! Release Barabbas to us!" ¹⁹(Barabbas had been thrown into prison for an insurrection in the city, and for murder.)

²⁰Wanting to release Jesus, Pilate appealed to them again. ²¹But they kept shouting, "Crucify him! Crucify him!"

²²For the third time he spoke to them: "Why? What crime has this man committed? I have found in him no grounds for the death penalty. Therefore I will have him punished and then release him."

²³But with loud shouts they insistently demanded that he be crucified, and their shouts prevailed. ²⁴So Pilate decided to grant their demand. ²⁵He released the man who had been thrown into prison for insurrection and murder, the one they asked for, and surrendered Jesus to their will.

ᵃ16 Some manuscripts him." ¹⁷Now he was obliged to release one man to them at the Feast.

NRSV

6When Pilate heard this, he asked whether the man was a Galilean. 7And when he learned that he was under Herod's jurisdiction, he sent him off to Herod, who was himself in Jerusalem at that time. 8When Herod saw Jesus, he was very glad, for he had been wanting to see him for a long time, because he had heard about him and was hoping to see him perform some sign. 9He questioned him at some length, but Jesusᵃ gave him no answer. 10The chief priests and the scribes stood by, vehemently accusing him. 11Even Herod with his soldiers treated him with contempt and mocked him; then he put an elegant robe on him, and sent him back to Pilate. 12That same day Herod and Pilate became friends with each other; before this they had been enemies.

13Pilate then called together the chief priests, the leaders, and the people, 14and said to them, "You brought me this man as one who was perverting the people; and here I have examined him in your presence and have not found this man guilty of any of your charges against him. 15Neither has Herod, for he sent him back to us. Indeed, he has done nothing to deserve death. 16I will therefore have him flogged and release him."ᵇ

18Then they all shouted out together, "Away with this fellow! Release Barabbas for us!" 19(This was a man who had been put in prison for an insurrection that had taken place in the city, and for murder.) 20Pilate, wanting to release Jesus, addressed them again; 21but they kept shouting, "Crucify, crucify him!" 22A third time he said to them, "Why, what evil has he done? I have found in him no ground for the sentence of death; I will therefore have him flogged and then release him." 23But they kept urgently demanding with loud shouts that he should be crucified; and their voices prevailed. 24So Pilate gave his verdict that their demand should be granted. 25He released the man they asked for, the one who had been put in prison for insurrection and murder, and he handed Jesus over as they wished.

ᵃ Gk he   ᵇ Here, or after verse 19, other ancient authorities add verse 17, *Now he was obliged to release someone for them at the festival*

COMMENTARY

The maneuverings of the religious authorities to put Jesus to death now move to a second stage as they deliver Jesus to Pilate and press Pilate for a guilty verdict. The drama takes place in five scenes: (1) Pilate's first declaration of Jesus' innocence (23:1-5); (2) Jesus' appearance before Herod (23:6-12); (3) Pilate's second declaration of Jesus' innocence (23:13-16); (4) Pilate's third declaration of Jesus' innocence (23:18-22); and (5) Pilate's capitulation to the crowd (23:23-25). Jesus has been "rejected by the elders, chief priests, and scribes" (9:22) and is now handed over to "human hands" (9:44), indeed "to the Gentiles" (18:32). The effect of this five-part episode is to show that Jesus was innocent of the political charges brought against him. Less explicit but no less important is the sub-theme that God's redemptive purposes are being accomplished in spite of the travesty of Jesus' trial. The events of Jesus' betrayal and death are unfolding just as Jesus had predicted.

23:1-5, Pilate's First Declaration of Jesus' Innocence. The first verse marks the transition from the previous scene to the trial before Pilate. Notable is Luke's comment that the whole Sanhedrin, acting as a body, delivered Jesus to Pilate.

Luke has noted on earlier occasions that the scribes and Pharisees were looking for charges they could bring against Jesus (6:7; 11:54); now they accuse him of sedition. Whereas the interrogation before the Sanhedrin had primarily concerned religious matters, specifically Jesus' messiahship, the charges reported to Pilate are political. Although v. 2 may be read as containing three separate charges (perverting the nation, forbidding the payment of taxes, and proclaiming himself to be a king), the latter two charges probably define and substantiate the first. Jesus is, therefore, accused of sedition, the proof of which is his teaching regarding the payment of taxes and his statements regarding his messiahship.

From the beginning of the Gospel, Luke interpreted God's work in John the Baptist and Jesus as fulfillment of the divine purposes for Israel. John was sent to "turn many of the people of Israel to the Lord their God" (1:16), and in Jesus the God of Israel had raised up a mighty savior in the house of David (1:68-69). Simeon, who

had been looking for "the consolation of Israel" (2:25), recognized that Jesus was the one sent to fulfill the promise of "glory to your people Israel" (2:32). Even at the last supper, Jesus had promised the disciples that they would "sit on thrones judging the twelve tribes of Israel" (22:30). Jesus' accusers were right in seeing that Jesus' work had implications for the nation of Israel, but what was in fact redemption they saw as perversion.

Moreover, Luke has also prepared the reader to see that the two substantiating charges are false. When the scribes and chief priests had asked Jesus whether they should pay taxes, he had affirmed that they should do so (20:25). The relationship between the terms "Messiah" (χριστός *christos*) and "king" (βασιλεύς *basileus*) at the end of v. 2 is sufficiently ambiguous that various translations are possible: "the Messiah, a king" (NRSV), "Christ, a king" (NIV), or "an anointed king" (Fitzmyer). At his birth, Jesus was announced by the heavenly chorus as "a Savior, who is the Messiah, the Lord" (2:11; cf. 2:26; 4:41). The title "king" is not ascribed to Jesus until he approaches Jerusalem. Then, he tells a story about a grasping, worldly king (19:11-27), following which his disciples hail him, corresponding to the angelic chorus at his birth with the words:

"Blessed is the king
who comes in the name of the Lord!
Peace in heaven,
and glory in the highest heaven!" (19:38)

Thereafter, Jesus responds to the political overtones of the expectation of a messiah who would be "David's son" (cf. 1:32-33) by citing Ps 110:1 (see 20:41-44). To his disciples he had explicitly renounced the ways of "the kings of the Gentiles" (22:25-27). Unlike such kings, Jesus worked among them "as one who serves" (22:27). As Luke tells it, when the Sanhedrin interrogated Jesus about his messiahship (22:67), therefore, they were looking for grounds to charge him with treason. They had failed to see that Jesus was the promised "savior," not a political schemer.

Roman justice had no trial by jury, and since Jesus was not a Roman citizen, Pilate was free to handle the proceedings in any way he wished. There was no attorney for the defense; the judge interrogated the accused, the accuser, and the witnesses and then determined guilt or innocence and mandated any punishment he deemed appropriate. Picking up the charge brought by the religious authorities, Pilate asked Jesus, "Are you the king of the Jews?" (23:3), echoing Mark 15:2. Jesus' answer is as equivocal as his answer to the Sanhedrin had been (cf. 22:70): "You say so" (v. 3). Still, it should probably not be read as a question.[292] Immediately, Pilate announces to the chief priests (i.e., the Sanhedrin) and the crowd that he finds Jesus innocent of any crime (cf. John 18:38).

The response of the chief priests (and evidently the crowd) is to repeat the general charge against Jesus in such a way that it summarizes Luke's account of Jesus' ministry: He has stirred up the people by his teaching. Jesus has taught in Galilee (4:15, 31; 5:3, 17; 6:6), in the villages (12:12; 13:10, 22), and in the Temple (19:47; 20:1; 21:37). Luke uses the term *Judea* here in the general sense found earlier in 4:44; throughout all the lands of the Jews, from Galilee to Jerusalem, Jesus has been spreading his teaching and arousing "the people" (ὁ λαός *ho laos*). Again, the people stand in a more positive light than do the chief priests and their associates. The role of the crowd at the trial before Pilate, therefore, is uncertain.

23:6-12, Jesus' Appearance Before Herod. Luke is the only Gospel to report this scene. When the chief priests inform Pilate that Jesus is from Galilee, Pilate seizes an opportunity to refer the case to Herod, who was in Jerusalem for the Passover (some see here an allusion to Ps 2:1-2). Herod hopes to see Jesus do a sign, but in the end sends Jesus back to Pilate for judgment.

Verses 6-7 describe the transfer of Jesus to Herod. The reference to "Galilean" in v. 6 picks up the allusion to Galilee in the previous verse. Peter and the other disciples are identified elsewhere in Luke and Acts as Galileans (Luke 22:59; Acts 1:11; 2:7). Verse 7 is actually an "inside view," the narrator's description of Pilate's mental process. Even though the complaint was brought in Jerusalem, Pilate sends Jesus to Herod because Jesus is from his jurisdiction. Pilate may have decided upon this course of action in an effort to

show deference to Herod and thereby repair the breach in their relationship, reported in v. 12; but it is more likely that Pilate simply hoped that Herod would act on the matter and thereby relieve Pilate of any responsibility for the case.

The temporal references in vv. 7 and 12 ("at that time"; "that same day") not only balance one another, but also underscore the historic significance of the events that were happening, of which neither Pilate nor Herod had any awareness. For Luke it was more than merely the time of the Passover festival.

Although Luke does not say so, one may conjecture that Pilate was staying in the Antonian Fortress and Herod nearby in the residence built by his father, Herod the Great. The narrator again informs us of Herod's great joy at seeing Jesus and the reason for it: Herod had long wanted to meet Jesus and see him do a "sign" (σημεῖον *sēmeion*, here used in the sense of a mighty act, something wondrous). Reports of Jesus' healings and exorcisms had spread around Galilee (4:14, 37; 5:17; 7:17), and when Herod heard the reports of what Jesus and his disciples were doing, he desired to see Jesus (9:7-9). His desire to see a sign was not a request that Jesus do something to confirm the truth of his teachings (cf. 11:16, 29). He was merely curious about the rumors he had heard and hoped that he might see something spectacular. Although Herod questioned Jesus at length, Jesus remained silent, thereby fulfilling Isa 53:7 (cf. Matt 27:12; Mark 14:61; 15:5). The scribes and Pharisees who led Jesus to Pilate apparently followed him to Herod, where they continued to accuse Jesus (cf. 22:66; 23:2, 4).

Jesus' silence is an affront to Herod, which he answers by allowing his soldiers to make sport of Jesus. Their mockery is directly related to the charges brought by the chief priests and scribes—namely, that Jesus makes himself a king (cf. 23:2-3). Thus Herod and his soldiers dress Jesus in an elegant robe and taunt him. Luke reports their derision with three participles: *treated* him with contempt, *mocked* him, and *put* a robe on him. Once again, the actions of Jesus' adversaries fulfill his own prophecies (cf. 9:22; 18:32; 22:63; 23:36).

Three aspects of Luke's narration bring closure to the scene. First, Herod sends Jesus back to Pilate (v. 11); compare the nearly identical language in v. 7, where Pilate sends Jesus to Herod.

292. Joseph A. Fitzmyer, *The Gospel According to Luke (X–XXIV)*, AB 28A (Garden City, N.Y.: Doubleday, 1985) 1475; contra John Nolland, *Luke 18:35–24:53*, WBC 35C (Dallas: Word, 1993) 1118.

Second, Luke comments on the day(s) in which these events occurred (v. 12); compare the phrase "at that time" in v. 7. Third, Luke reports that Herod and Pilate, who had previously been adversaries, became friends as a result of these events. Fitzmyer calls v. 12 "one more of Luke's inconsequential explicative notes" and cites Luke 1:66; 2:50; 3:15; 8:29; 9:14; 12:1; 16:14; and 20:20 to illustrate the pattern.[293] Even in this list, however, v. 12 is distinctive in that it introduces peripheral historical data that is not found elsewhere. Ironically, the events leading to Jesus' death already signal its reconciling effect, but Herod and Pilate are reconciled to each other, not to God (cf. Acts 4:27). Their reconciliation, therefore, is as hollow as Herod's worship of Jesus as king had been.

23:13-16, Pilate's Second Declaration of Jesus' Innocence. When Herod sends Jesus back to Pilate, Pilate assembles the leaders and the people, pronounces Jesus innocent for a second time, and then resolves to flog Jesus and release him.

The scene unfolds with greater subtlety than is at first apparent. The division of the larger unit into these smaller sub-units (vv. 13-16, 18-22) neatly separates Pilate's second and third pronouncements of Jesus' innocence, but the story is all of one piece. The first hint of subtlety appears with the designation of those whom Pilate summons: the chief priests, the leaders, and the people. The chief priests have been active throughout the arrest and trial of Jesus (22:52, 66; 23:4, 10). The "leaders" have been mentioned previously only in 14:1 (cf. 18:18; 23:35; 24:20). The mention of "the people" is what attracts our attention, however. Previously, the people have supported Jesus (see 19:47-48; 20:1, 6, 19; 21:38). Moreover, when the assembly of the leaders brought Jesus to Pilate, they had accused him of "perverting our nation" (23:2) and then of stirring up "the people" (23:5). Now, when Pilate recalls their charge against Jesus, he says, "You brought me this man as one who was *perverting the people*" (v. 14, italics added). Verses 2 and 14 use different verbs (διαστρέφω *diastrephō*, v. 2; ἀποστρέφω *apostrephō*, v. 14), but the meaning is synonymous ("perverting"). Therefore, whereas the religious

leaders use the more political designation "our nation" (τὸ ἔθνος ἡμῶν *to ethnos hēmōn*) when speaking to Pilate, he uses the more religious term *laos* (i.e. "people of God"), when addressing the chief priests. Calling together the people along with the leaders allows for the possibility that the people may now either controvert or confirm the charge that the chief priests have brought against Jesus. Will they defend Jesus as the chief priests had feared earlier (see 22:2), or will they confirm the allegations against him? When the people join the leaders in crying out "Away with this fellow!" (v. 18), it becomes clear that the chief priests, in fact, are the ones who have "perverted the people."[294]

Pilate continues to review the proceedings to this point. He has already examined Jesus and pronounced him innocent (no further interrogation is necessary, therefore—see v. 4). Moreover, he had sent Jesus to Herod, who has returned Jesus to him—an action that means that Herod did not find Jesus guilty either. Consequently, Jesus has been tried by two judges independently, and each has declared that he is innocent, fulfilling the law of two witnesses (Deut 19:15). Pilate repeats his verdict: "He has done nothing to deserve death."

The emphasis on Jesus' innocence in this scene needs to be placed in its larger context. First, it is an important part of Luke's passion narrative. Luke's report of the charge against Jesus in 23:2 and the earlier account of Jesus' teaching on the payment of taxes prepares the reader to see immediately that the charges against Jesus are false. Then, Jesus is declared innocent by both Pilate and, at least by implication, Herod. Later, the thief on the cross will defend Jesus' innocence (23:41), and the centurion will confirm, "Certainly this man was innocent" (23:47). Later, the innocence of the apostles and Paul will be emphasized repeatedly in Acts (4:15-22; 18:12-17; 19:37-40; 24:22-23; 25:25; 26:31-32), demonstrating that Luke is concerned from beginning to end to demonstrate that the early Christians are innocent under Roman law. Whether Luke intends for his record to be used to convince Roman authorities of the innocence of Christians or to assure believers that they have nothing to fear from the Roman authorities is less clear.

293. Fitzmyer, *The Gospel According to Luke (X–XXIV)*, 1482.

294. See Nolland, *Luke 18:35–24:53*, 1128.

Verse 16 is puzzling, but it is probably the first indication that Pilate will eventually accede to the desires of the chief priests and leaders of the people. Flogging was a severe punishment, not a mild chastisement. Pilate's words, as reported by Luke, contain an appalling euphemism. When read with the meaning that the verb παιδεύω (paideuō) has in other contexts, Pilate resolves that he will "instruct," or "discipline" Jesus (cf. Heb 5:8). Flogging was a severe penalty exacted after the condemnation of one who was guilty. Nevertheless, Pilate, having declared Jesus innocent, now decides to have him flogged. We may surmise that the flogging was an effort to appease Jesus' accusers (as apparently also in John 19:1). Luke never reports that the flogging was carried out, however.[295]

23:17. Verse 17 is omitted in most modern critical editions and translations. The manuscript evidence is divided, and the verse appears to be a later effort to smooth out the text by alluding to the practice of releasing a prisoner at Passover (thereby harmonizing Luke with Mark 15:6; Matt 27:15; and John 18:39). Verse 17 is not necessary to the flow of the story, but it does explain the crowd's call for the release of Barabbas in v. 18. While v. 17 is textually dubious, and there is no reference to the practice outside of the Gospels, the contention that the crowd could appeal for the release of a prisoner during a festival is credible in this context.[296]

23:18-22, Pilate's Third Declaration of Jesus' Innocence. When the assembled crowd cries out in unison against Pilate's plan and calls for the release of Barabbas, Pilate addresses them for the third time (see vv. 4, 13-14) and for the third time affirms Jesus' innocence. This scene reproduces many of the details of Mark 15:6-14, but both the order and the language of Luke's account differ from Mark. Luke's account is also briefer than Mark's, omitting, for example, Mark's claim that the chief priests stirred up the crowd to call for Barabbas rather than Jesus.

The main difficulties posed for the interpreter of this section involve the release of Barabbas. What is the relationship between Pilate's declaration of Jesus' innocence, his hope to release Jesus, and the crowd's call for the release of Barabbas? The question of the textual uncertainty of v. 17 aside, does Luke presume the practice of releasing a prisoner at the Passover? If so, does Pilate hope to release Jesus because he is innocent or because by doing so Pilate can avoid releasing Barabbas, who was guilty of insurrection and murder?

Having introduced the people in v. 13, Luke does not further explain their sudden collusion with the chief priests and leaders in calling for the death of Jesus (v. 18), as does Mark (15:11), who explicitly blames the chief priests for inciting the crowd. Nevertheless, it is clear that the chief priests have played a leading role in the process of discrediting Jesus. It is they, in the end, who have "perverted the nation."

Further ironies reside in the people's call for the release of Barabbas. Luke comments in v. 19 that Barabbas was guilty of insurrection. The council had brought Jesus to Pilate on political charges, but they end up calling for the release of one who was guilty of the very crime they had attempted to pin on Jesus. Once again, Luke demonstrates Jesus' innocence by the way he tells the story. Moreover, in rejecting Jesus, the true "son of the Father," the crowd calls for the release of one whose name means "son of the father" (בר־אבא Bar'abbā') but whose actions reflect a very different character. Anyone who remembers Luke's references to Jesus as the Son of God (1:32, 35; 3:22; 4:41; 9:35; 10:22) and Jesus' prayers to God as "Father" (2:49; 11:2; 22:42; cf. 23:34, 46) will not miss the irony here.

Earlier Jesus had predicted his death, and Luke reported that the authorities were looking for a way to put Jesus to death (22:2), but crucifixion appears for the first time in the Gospel in v. 21, in the crowd's insistent cry, "Crucify, crucify him!" Crucifixion was a gruesome form of execution, favored by the Romans and known to have been practiced also by the Hasmonean rulers in Palestine during the previous century. Josephus, for example, reports that Alexander Jannaeus crucified 800 persons.[297]

For the third time, as Luke reminds us (v. 22), Pilate declares Jesus innocent (vv. 4, 14-15, 22).

295. See Joseph A. Fitzmyer, *The Gospel According to Luke (X–XXIV)*, 1484.

296. See Nolland, *Luke 18:35–24:53*, 1130; Brown, *The Death of the Messiah*, 1:814-20.

297. Josephus *Antiquities of the Jews* 13.380; *The Jewish War* 1.97. For a full account of the references to crucifixion in antiquity, see Martin Hengel, *Crucifixion*, trans. John Bowden (Philadelphia: Fortress, 1977).

Three times Pilate addresses the crowd, three times he proclaims Jesus' innocence, and three times Luke reports Pilate's intention to release Jesus (vv. 16, 20, 22). In the end, however, he will release another man and allow Jesus to be put to death. Pilate's second declaration that he will have Jesus flogged uses the same euphemism ("disciplined") as the first (see v. 16). Pilate's last words in the Gospel are his hollow declaration that he will release Jesus.

23:23-25. Pilate's Capitulation to the Crowd. Verses 23-25 contain no direct discourse. They are instead the narrator's report of the outcome of Jesus' trial. The crowd kept pressing Pilate with loud cries to crucify Jesus (v. 23). Thus Pilate capitulated to their demand (v. 24) and handed Jesus over "as they wished" (v. 25). Each of these three verses underscores the crowd's responsibility for reversing Pilate's initial decision (cf. Acts 3:13-15). After three times vowing to release Jesus, Pilate releases Barabbas instead. Luke's final words in this scene, however, concern not Pilate (as in Mark 15:15), but the crowd. Pilate merely did "as they wished" (v. 25).[298]

298. Fitzmyer, *The Gospel According to Luke (X–XXIV)*, 1492.

REFLECTIONS

Reading of the arrest and trial of Jesus is like watching film footage of John F. Kennedy's motorcade winding its way through Dallas toward the fateful moments that are seared into the memories of all Americans who were touched by the events of that day in 1963. Or it is like watching film footage of the explosion of the *Challenger* space shuttle in 1986. We know what is coming, but suspense, dread, and awe build as we rehearse the events we have no power to undo.

1. From the beginning, efforts have been made to pin the blame for the death of Jesus on the Jewish leaders rather than the Romans. Luke, as we have seen, repeatedly emphasizes that Pilate declared Jesus innocent. It may have been important for the life and witness of the church late in the first century to clarify that Jesus and those who followed him were innocent under Roman law. During the Middle Ages and in more recent memory, however, assigning blame for the death of Jesus to the Jewish leaders has led to terrible atrocities against Jews. How bitterly ironic that a Gospel that emphasizes Jesus' inclusive love should be used as a weapon against persons of another religious tradition. Christian teachers and preachers have a moral responsibility, therefore, to prevent further distortions of the gospel. To read or teach the Gospel accounts of the death of Jesus without making it clear that they can easily mislead some readers into transferring hostility from the Jewish religious leaders of Jesus' day to individuals and groups today is to run the risk of perverting the gospel and allowing it to be used in a way that would be directly antithetical to Jesus' teachings. The response that these accounts should elicit is not hostility toward others but reflection that any one of us might have done the same thing had we been there. The disciples, Jesus' closest followers, did nothing to stop the events. Judas collaborated with the authorities. Peter denied Jesus, and before the end of the trial there is no longer any distinction between the leaders and the people—all are shouting, "Crucify him!"

2. On a more personal level, much of the drama of the trial narrative arises from our awareness that in this scene both Jesus and Pilate are facing the ultimate test of their convictions. Each will be marked for the duration of human memory by how he responds to this test of character. Throughout the trial, Jesus maintains composure before his accusers, while Pilate tries one ploy and then another to extricate himself from the situation: Pilate pronounces Jesus innocent, but he cannot make his verdict stick; he sends Jesus to Herod, but Herod will not resolve the crisis for him; he has Jesus beaten, but the crowd is not satisfied; he offers to release a prisoner, but they call for the release of Barabbas instead. Jesus has entered into his trial (see 22:28) confident in God's purpose, steeled by prayer, and sustained by the Spirit.

The Gospel accounts of the trial of Jesus, ironically, show that while Jesus was at cross purposes with Pilate, others are on trial in a deeper sense. Who is guilty of perverting the people? Will the people follow their misguided leaders? Will Pilate allow himself to be maneuvered into condemning an innocent man? And where are Jesus' disciples during the trial?

The trial has a way of exposing the forces, commitments, and loyalties that we hold most dear. When the chips are down, can Jesus count on us, or will we move instead to secure our dreams of power, our cherished social positions, our desire to fulfill our personal plans untroubled by Jesus' call to kingdom purposes? It is not a question of whether we will follow Jesus when the going is easy. The trial of Jesus forces the uncomfortable question: Can Jesus count on me? How willing are you to follow when following becomes costly?

LUKE 23:26-56, THE CRUCIFIXION, DEATH, AND BURIAL OF JESUS

OVERVIEW

Luke's account of the events surrounding the death of Jesus unfolds in a series of five scenes. Simon of Cyrene is compelled to carry Jesus' cross, and Jesus warns the "daughters of Jerusalem" about the terrors that are to come (vv. 26-31). The actual crucifixion is reported with attention to the place, to the two who were crucified with Jesus, to the dividing of his garments, to the mockery of Jesus, and to the inscription over him (vv. 32-38). Verses 39-43 relate Jesus' conversation with the penitent thief. From

noon until three in the afternoon there was darkness, but when the centurion heard Jesus' dying prayer, he too affirmed Jesus' innocence while the crowds beat their breasts (vv. 44-49). Verses 50-56 conclude the series of scenes with an account of Joseph of Arimathea's role in the burial of Jesus and the women's preparations for the anointing of his body. As we will see below, the details of each of these scenes provide important insights into Luke's interpretation of the meaning of Jesus' death.

Luke 23:26-32, Simon of Cyrene and the "Daughters of Jerusalem"

NIV

26As they led him away, they seized Simon from Cyrene, who was on his way in from the country, and put the cross on him and made him carry it behind Jesus. 27A large number of people followed him, including women who mourned and wailed for him. 28Jesus turned and said to them, "Daughters of Jerusalem, do not weep for me; weep for yourselves and for your children. 29For the time will come when you will say, 'Blessed are the barren women, the wombs that never bore and the breasts that never nursed!' 30Then

NRSV

26As they led him away, they seized a man, Simon of Cyrene, who was coming from the country, and they laid the cross on him, and made him carry it behind Jesus. 27A great number of the people followed him, and among them were women who were beating their breasts and wailing for him. 28But Jesus turned to them and said, "Daughters of Jerusalem, do not weep for me, but weep for yourselves and for your children. 29For the days are surely coming when they will say, 'Blessed are the barren, and the wombs that never

NIV

"'they will say to the mountains, "Fall on us!" and to the hills, "Cover us!"'ᵃ

³¹For if men do these things when the tree is green, what will happen when it is dry?"

³²Two other men, both criminals, were also led out with him to be executed.

ᵃ30 Hosea 10:8

NRSV

bore, and the breasts that never nursed.' ³⁰Then they will begin to say to the mountains, 'Fall on us'; and to the hills, 'Cover us.' ³¹For if they do this when the wood is green, what will happen when it is dry?"

32Two others also, who were criminals, were led away to be put to death with him.

COMMENTARY

Verses 26-32 describe the events that occurred on the way to the place of crucifixion. The unit begins and ends with references to Jesus and the two criminals being led away (vv. 26, 32). The scene features three figures or groups who are sympathetic to Jesus (Simon of Cyrene; a great number of the people, including women from Jerusalem; and finally the two criminals crucified with Jesus), just as the verses following Jesus' death also feature three groups: the centurion, the crowds, and Jesus' acquaintances, including the women from Galilee.[299] Mark records the role of Simon of Cyrene (Mark 15:21), but the rest of the scene is unique to Luke. In its Lukan context, it serves to characterize further the role of the people and the coming judgment upon the people in the destruction of Jerusalem.

23:26. Those who led Jesus away are identified only by the third person plural form of the verb (i.e, "they"). Technically, the execution took place under Roman authority, but Luke allows this verse to follow directly after the note that Pilate handed Jesus over to "their will," thereby emphasizing once more the role of the chief priests, the leaders, and the people (v. 13). Crucifixions normally took place outside the city but near a major road leading into it so that passersby could witness the punishment of the criminals. Since Herod Agrippa built the third wall on the north side of the city, however, the traditional site of the crucifixion has been inside the city.

Simon of Cyrene is not mentioned in any other scene in the Gospels, nor elsewhere in the New Testament. Normally, the condemned man was

forced to carry the crossbeam to the place of execution. Consequently, interpreters often conjecture that Jesus must have been so weakened by the beating (which Luke does not describe) that he was unable to carry the cross. The soldiers, therefore, conscripted a passerby, Simon, to carry Jesus' cross. There is no evidence that Simon was a disciple, but by bearing the cross he enacts the role of a disciple (see 9:23; 14:27). Luke does not explain why Simon was "coming from the country"; the reference may either mean that he was a traveler coming into Jerusalem or that he had been working in the field. Why he would have been working in the field on the Passover (according to the chronology of the synoptic Gospels) is not explained, but neither is it certain that Simon was a Jew. Cyrene was the capital of Cyrenaica, which lay on the coast of North Africa, where today Libya is located. The population of Cyrene was mixed, but included Jews.[300] Presumably, therefore, Simon was a Jew from the diaspora.

23:27-31. Using one of his favorite constructions, Luke records that "a great number of the people," among them women, were following Jesus. The women exemplify the response of the people, who will appear again in v. 35, at the cross. "The people" who had recently joined in calling for Jesus' crucifixion (vv. 18, 21) now begin to lament the tragedy of his death. Acting out traditional expressions of lament, the women were beating their breasts and wailing (cf. Zech 12:10; Jer 9:19).[301]

The wailing of the women serves as the setting for Jesus' last lament over the city of Jerusalem.

299. Raymond E. Brown, *The Death of the Messiah* (New York: Doubleday, 1994) 905, 918.

300. See Josephus *Against Apion* 2.44.
301. See also Josephus *Antiquities of the Jews* 6.377.

It is composed of four sayings: (1) "Weep for yourselves and for your children" (v. 28); (2) "Blessed are the barren" (v. 29); (3) "Then they will begin to say to the mountains, 'Fall on us' " (v. 30); (4) "For if they do this when the wood is green . . . " (v. 31). Each saying must be examined individually, but as a unit they form Jesus' last words concerning the fate of Jerusalem.

Earlier Jesus had spoken of Jerusalem's role in killing the prophets (11:49-50; 13:34-35). Jesus had wept over Jerusalem (19:41-44); now the "Daughters of Jerusalem" (Cant 2:7; 5:16) weep over the coming judgment upon the city. In his earlier warnings of the coming destruction of Jerusalem, Jesus had lamented in particular the suffering of the women and children (see 19:41-44; 21:20-24), which is again the focus of his lament. *Gospel of Thomas* 79 contains a close parallel to this saying, which places it in the context of the saying preserved in Luke 11:27-28.

> A woman from the multitude said to Him: Blessed is the womb which bore Thee and the breasts which nourished Thee. He said to [her]: Blessed are those who have heard the word of the Father (and) have kept it in truth. For there will be days when you will say: Blessed is the womb which has not conceived and the breasts which have not suckled.[302]

It is difficult to determine, however, whether *Thomas* preserves a unit of tradition that Luke has divided or unites sayings that were similar but originally separate, as in Luke. Regardless, the force of the saying is clear: The coming judgment will be so terrible that childless persons (a great misfortune; see 1:7) will be considered fortunate. The thought is the same as Jesus' lament in 21:23: "Woe to those who are pregnant and to those who are nursing infants in those days!"

Apocalyptic imagery appears again in v. 30 to describe how terrible it will be for those on whom God's judgment will fall in the coming days. Luke has adapted the image from Hosea 10:8, but it appears also in Revelation 6:16.

Jesus' fourth statement to the daughters of Jerusalem invites them to reason from the lesser judgment to the greater, as in 1 Pet 4:17: "If it begins with us, what will be the end for those who do not obey the gospel of God?" (NRSV). The image of green wood and dry wood occurs in Ezek 17:24; 20:47, where it is connected with burning. In Luke, the saying is open to various interpretations, depending on whether one understands the agent of the destruction to be God, the Romans, or human beings in general. In Jesus' earlier warnings about the fate of Jerusalem, it is clear that the Romans will be the agents of destruction (19:41-44; 21:20-24). The destruction, however, is to be understood as God's judgment on the city for its role in killing the prophets and rejecting their appeals for repentance. In the present context, therefore, the same connection between the Romans and God's judgment may be assumed. As terrible as are the events over which the daughters of Jerusalem lament now (the green wood, Jesus' death), the days to come (the dry wood, the destruction of Jerusalem) will be far worse. Jesus' death, ironically, is a sign of the coming destruction of the city, which so shortly before had hailed his arrival with shouts of "Blessed is the king who comes in the name of the Lord!" (19:38).

23:32. Luke draws this scene to a close by reporting that they also led two others out to be crucified. Mark (15:27) does not introduce the two crucified with Jesus until after Jesus has been crucified. On the one hand, the introduction of the two at this point may serve to underscore the fulfillment of 22:37, "and he was counted among the lawless [ἄνομος *anomos*]" (see Isa 53:12), but the designation used here is different, "criminal" [κακοῦργος *kakourgos*]. On the other hand, the introduction of the two at this point prepares the reader for the expanded role they will play in Luke's crucifixion scene (vv. 39-43). Some of the early manuscripts alter the word order so that one could not read v. 32 to mean "two other criminals" and infer that Jesus was a wrongdoer (contrary to the repeated pronouncements of his innocence).[303] One of the Old Latin manuscripts supplies names for the two crucified with Jesus: Joathas and Maggatras.

---

302. A. Guillaumont et al., trans., *The Gospel According to Thomas* (New York: Harper & Row, 1959) 43-45.

303. On these matters, see Brown, *The Death of the Messiah*, 927-28.

REFLECTIONS

No one likes to be reminded of his or her worst moments—times when they hurt someone else, stole something, denied everything they believe, or betrayed a friend. The passion narrative is filled with such painful memories. It continually confronts us with the underside of human sinfulness and its awful consequences. The innocent suffer (Jesus, the women, and their children), and terrible as were the events of the day of Jesus' crucifixion, greater suffering lay ahead.

The lament over tragic violence and suffering is an important element of Luke's passion narrative. God could not spare Jesus from the cross, and Jesus could not spare Jerusalem the destruction that lay ahead. Instead, Jesus joined with the women who were wailing for him, lamenting their suffering. Here is a moving aspect of the meaning of Jesus' death. Jesus had warned the crowds and his disciples of what was coming—both for him and for Jerusalem. He had called for repentance and wept for the city. When his pleas were not heeded, however, he joined himself to the plight of those who suffer the ravages of violence, dying with criminals on a cross.

We may rail against God for the tragedy, suffering, and loss that we experience, but God did not turn away from our plight or miraculously deliver Jesus from his suffering. Knowing that he could not stop the judgment that Israel (indeed, humanity) had brought upon itself, Jesus went to the cross lamenting that although he was about to die he could not deliver Jerusalem from its fate.

The lament, like the passion narrative itself, is a call for us to see that our only hope is to trust in God's faithfulness. Apart from repentance and commitment to the kingdom of God there is no hope for an end to violence and suffering. The suffering of the innocent—the death of Jesus and the suffering of the women and the children—is an indictment of the institutions and means of human vindictiveness and a call to turn from our sinful inclinations and accept the new order of God's mercy. Otherwise, "if they do this when the wood is green, what will happen when it is dry?" (v. 31).

Luke 23:33-38, The Crucifixion and Mocking of Jesus

NIV

[33]When they came to the place called the Skull, there they crucified him, along with the criminals—one on his right, the other on his left. [34]Jesus said, "Father, forgive them, for they do not know what they are doing."[a] And they divided up his clothes by casting lots.

[35]The people stood watching, and the rulers even sneered at him. They said, "He saved others; let him save himself if he is the Christ of God, the Chosen One."

[36]The soldiers also came up and mocked him. They offered him wine vinegar [37]and said, "If you are the king of the Jews, save yourself."

[38]There was a written notice above him, which read: THIS IS THE KING OF THE JEWS.

[a]34 Some early manuscripts do not have this sentence.

NRSV

[33]When they came to the place that is called The Skull, they crucified Jesus[a] there with the criminals, one on his right and one on his left. [[[34]Then Jesus said, "Father, forgive them; for they do not know what they are doing."]][b] And they cast lots to divide his clothing. [35]And the people stood by, watching; but the leaders scoffed at him, saying, "He saved others; let him save himself if he is the Messiah[c] of God, his chosen one!" [36]The soldiers also mocked him, coming up and offering him sour wine, [37]and saying, "If you are the King of the Jews, save yourself!" [38]There was also an inscription over him,[d] "This is the King of the Jews."

[a]Gk him   [b]Other ancient authorities lack the sentence Then Jesus . . . what they are doing   [c]Or the Christ   [d]Other ancient authorities add written in Greek and Latin and Hebrew (that is, Aramaic)

COMMENTARY

Because crucifixion was a common and shameful form of execution, the challenge facing the Gospel writers was to make clear to the readers the distinctive significance of Jesus' crucifixion. Because Luke is not composing an essay but "an orderly account" (1:3), the details of the narrative itself must convey Luke's understanding of Jesus' death. For this purpose, he makes full use of the roles of the various characters in the story, the structure of three mockings, repeated allusions to the Scriptures, selected christological titles, the mysterious phenomena that accompany the death of Jesus, the ironic truth of the taunts hurled at Jesus, and Jesus' three pronouncements from the cross.

This section properly extends through v. 43, but it is so full of significant details that Jesus' conversation with the penitent thief is best treated separately. In the previous scene (vv. 26-32), on the way to the place of crucifixion, Luke describes the roles of Simon of Cyrene, the women, and the two wrongdoers crucified with Jesus. Following the crucifixion and Jesus' prayer for his tormentors, Luke records the taunting of Jesus by three groups using three different verbs: the leaders "scoffed" (v. 35, ἐκμυκτηρίζω *ekmyktērizō*), the soldiers "mocked" (v. 35, ἐμπαίζω *empaizō*), and one of the criminals "derided" him (v. 39, βλασφημέω *blasphēmeō*). All three taunts focus on the saving significance of Jesus' death: "He saved others; let him save himself" (v. 35), "save yourself" (v. 37), and "save yourself and us" (v. 39). The christological significance of the scene becomes apparent in Luke's use of the titles for Jesus: "the Messiah [of God]" (vv. 35, 39), "the Chosen One" (v. 35), and "the King of the Jews" (vv. 37, 38).

Further reflections on the significance of the events surrounding Jesus' death come to the fore when one notes the number of allusions to the OT that occur in these verses. Psalm 22:18 is quoted, describing the casting of lots for Jesus' garments (v. 34). The reference to the people's looking on and the mocking of Jesus may be a tribute to reflection on Ps 22:7. The title "the Chosen One" comes from Isa 42:1, and Luke uses the same term as Ps 69:21 (68:22 LXX) for the "sour wine" (ὄξος *oxos*, v. 36). Taken together, these allusions suggest early and intensive reflec-tion on the ways in which the death of Jesus fulfilled the Scriptures of Israel.

Luke's handling of this scene is further highlighted when one notes the features of the Markan account that Luke has omitted and contrasts them with the elements that he has added that do not appear in Mark. Luke omits the Aramaic name "Golgotha" (Mark 15:22), the initial offer of wine mixed with myrrh (15:23), Mark's note that it was the third hour (15:25), the description of the passersby shaking their heads (15:29; cf. Ps 22:7), the accusation that Jesus said he would destroy the Temple (15:29), and the mocked confession of Jesus as "the King of Israel" (15:32). On the other hand, the following items are distinctively Lukan: the description of the other two as criminals, Jesus' prayer for his tormentors (if v. 34*a* is authentic; see Commentary below), the title "his chosen one," and the distinction between "the people" and those who mocked Jesus.[304]

23:33. Luke departs from the other Gospels in calling the place where Jesus was crucified simply "The Skull" (not Golgotha, as in Mark 15:22, or "the Place of the Skull," as in John 19:17). The name probably reflects the shape or other features of the hill on which Jesus and the others were crucified. Luke, like the other Gospel writers, is remarkably brief in his description of the crucifixion, providing no details regarding the shape of the cross, its size, or the manner in which Jesus was affixed on it.[305] Although crucifixion was widespread in antiquity, there are few detailed descriptions of it. In one account, Seneca wrote, "I see crosses there, not just of one kind but made in many different ways: some have their victims with head down to the ground; some impale their private parts; others stretch out their arms on the gibbet."[306] Luke does not record the stripping of the fine garments that were put on Jesus during the earlier mockery or the restoration of his own garments. When Jesus was crucified,

---

304. See Joseph A. Fitzmyer, *The Gospel According to Luke (X–XXIV)*, AB 28A (Garden City, N.Y.: Doubleday, 1985) 1500.

305. For a full discussion of these matters, see Brown, *The Death of the Messiah*, 945-52.

306. Seneca, *Dialogue* 6 (*De consolatione ad Marciam*) 20.3; quoted by Hengel, *Crucifixion*, 25.

however, the soldiers stripped him of his garments and cast lots to see who would take them. Whether Jesus was crucified naked or with a loin cloth out of deference to Jewish sensitivities is debated. Again, nothing is said of the charges against the two crucified with Jesus, their names, or their garments. Jesus' conversation with the penitent thief, however, will be one of the distinctive features of Luke's account of the events at the cross.

23:34a. In Luke's account, the first thing the crucified Jesus does is pray for those who have crucified him. Several difficult issues surround v. 34a. Who was Jesus praying for? Was the verse composed by Luke or inserted by a later scribe? If composed by Luke, why was it omitted in many early manuscripts?

Although the presence of v. 34a makes the change of subject to the soldiers in the latter part of the verse rough, it fits well following the report of the crucifixion in the previous verse. The setting raises the question of who Jesus was praying for: the Romans, the Jewish leaders, or both? The immediate context of the prayer requires that Jesus was praying for the soldiers who carried out the execution—they are the easiest to fit under the category of ignorance of what they were doing. Throughout, however, Luke has emphasized the role of the Jewish leaders (22:1-6, 52, 66; 23:4, 10, 13), and in the end the people are swayed to join in calling for Jesus' death (23:18). Moreover, through the speeches in Acts, Luke repeatedly maintains that the Jewish leaders acted out of ignorance (e.g., Acts 3:17; cf. 13:27). Thus Jesus' prayer should be understood as asking forgiveness for all who were involved in his death.

The prayer is consistent with both Luke's characterization of Jesus and Luke's style. Jesus has prayed to God as "Father" repeatedly in Luke (10:21; 11:2; 22:42; 23:46), and Jesus has taught his followers to forgive (5:20-24; 6:27-29; 7:47-49; 17:3-4). Indeed, Jesus' prayer here echoes the petition for forgiveness in the model prayer (11:4). It is more likely that Jesus died a model death, praying for those who were killing him—and this motif was repeated in the death of Stephen (Acts 7:60), the first Christian martyr—than that a scribe later composed the prayer for Jesus imitating Luke's style and theme.

The manuscript evidence is divided, but taken alone it would favor regarding the prayer as a later gloss. The prayer is found in ℵ*, ℵ², A, C, and D², among others, but it is omitted in 𝔓⁷⁵, ℵ¹, B, D*, W, and Θ, among others. The omission of Jesus' prayer for forgiveness in these manuscripts raises the question of why anyone would omit the prayer if it were originally part of the Gospel. Although the evidence does not permit us to say that any scribe did omit the verse for one of the following reasons, several plausible reasons have been suggested. (1) Tension between Christians and Jews led Christian scribes to delete Jesus' prayer for forgiveness of the Jewish leaders. (2) Scribes may have deleted the prayer after the destruction of Jerusalem so that it would not appear that his prayer had not been answered. (3) Scribes may have found the prayer (with its presumption of ignorance) morally unjustifiable. In sum, therefore, the evidence favors accepting the prayer as authentic; while the manuscript evidence is divided (and inclines toward its omission), the prayer fits Luke's style, the Lukan emphasis on forgiveness, and Luke's presentation of Jesus' death as a model for Christian martyrs; and plausible reasons can be advanced for the omission of the prayer by later scribes.[307]

23:34b. In Luke, the division of Jesus' garments provides a counterpoint to his prayer for forgiveness. The soldiers go about their grim business unaware of what was actually transpiring, but nevertheless fulfilling the Scriptures (Ps 22:18). Earlier, a woman in the crowd had desired to touch even the hem of Jesus' garment (8:44), and when he entered Jerusalem, his followers had thrown their garments on the colt and on the road for him (19:35-36). Now, the soldiers take his last earthly possessions.

23:35-38. The people, who appear here for the last time (cf. 24:19), stand by watching. Contrary to Mark (15:29), Luke does not say that the passersby took part in the mocking of Jesus, and "the people" do not join their leaders in taunting Jesus. Instead, the threefold scene of mockery is carried out by the leaders (v. 35), the soldiers (vv. 36-37), and one of the criminals crucified with Jesus (v. 39). The leaders ridiculed Jesus (lit. the verb *ekmyktērizō* means something

---

307. See Brown, *The Death of the Messiah,* 971-81.

like "looked down their noses" or "thumbed their noses" at Jesus); the soldiers "mocked" Jesus (*enpaizō*; Robertson suggests "acted like boys"),[308] and escalating the seriousness of the offense the criminal "blasphemed." In each instance, they mock Jesus as the Savior (see vv. 35, 37, 39).

Through the irony of these taunts, Luke underscores both Jesus' real identity and the true meaning of his death. Jesus was hailed as the Savior at his birth (2:11); as the Son of Man, he had come to seek and to save the lost (19:10). But just as he had taught that those who lost their lives for his sake would save them (9:24), so now he must lose his life so that they might be saved. Jesus' death did not contradict the christological claims; it confirmed them. For him to have saved himself would have been a denial of his salvific role in the purposes of God. In addition to references to saving, the taunts evoke titles for Jesus that Luke has already certified earlier in the Gospel. He is the Messiah or Christ (vv. 35, 39). The title "Christ" (or "Messiah") is coupled with the title "Savior" at Jesus' birth (2:11). Simeon recognized the Christ child (2:26), the people questioned whether John the Baptist might be the Messiah (3:15), but the demons knew that he was the Messiah (4:41). Later, Peter confessed that Jesus was "the Messiah of God" (9:20), while Jesus' accusers questioned and then condemned him as the Christ (20:41; 22:67; 23:2; cf. 24:26, 46).

He is God's "chosen one" (v. 35; cf. Isa 42:1). This title appears in a related form earlier at the

308. A. T. Robertson, *Word Pictures in the New Testament,* vol. 2: *The Gospel According to Luke* (New York: Richard R. Smith, 1930) 285.

transfiguration (9:35; cf. 18:7). He is also "the king of the Jews" (vv. 37-38). The title occurs both in the soldiers' taunt and in the inscription over Jesus. Again, Luke has prepared the reader to understand its significance. At the annunciation the angel declared that Jesus would receive "the throne of his ancestor David . . . and of his kingdom there will be no end" (1:32-33). Then, when Jesus entered Jerusalem, the multitude chanted, "Blessed is the king who comes in the name of the Lord!" (19:38), but the title of praise had become a charge of treason (23:2-3) and finally a term of derision (vv. 37-38). In Luke's hands, the mockery of the title is underscored by linking it with the soldiers' taunts and by adding "this one" to the inscription: "This is the King of the Jews" (v. 38). The soldiers' derision echoes the devil's challenge to Jesus at the beginning of his ministry: "If you are the Son of God . . . " (see 4:3, 9). The irony and pathos of Jesus' death are that those who mock him declare his messianic identity and the salvific significance of his death but do not grasp the truth they speak.

In addition to the verbal taunt, the mockery by the soldiers includes offering Jesus sour wine to drink—perhaps a burlesque of offering a king the best wine. Again, the action, unknown to them, fulfills Scripture (Ps 69:21), as each of the evangelists makes clear in one form or another. Both what is said and what is done at the cross, therefore, confirm the truth of Luke's claims about the one who is crucified: He is the Christ, the king of the Jews, the Savior.

REFLECTIONS

By breaking the unit at v. 38, the reader is able to end this section with the christological confession articulated in the inscription above Jesus: "This is the king of the Jews." So filled with pathos is the death of Jesus that one must respond with either derision or confession. Luke's account of the crucifixion itself contains no meaningless details. Every element of the story serves to declare Jesus' identity as the Messiah, the significance of his death for the salvation of the world, or the fulfillment of Scripture in the events of this scene. The christological focus of the passion narratives is as inherently right as it is restrained. We are spared graphic accounts of Jesus' agony and the details of his appearance. Instead, the passion narratives make the point that the death of Jesus is salvifically important not because of how much he suffered but because of who he was and how his death was connected to both his life and the redemptive acts of God in the history of Israel. For this reason, the allusions to Scripture and to scenes earlier in the Gospel convey the themes by which we can make sense of the event. W. J. Ong observed, "Without themes, there would be no way to deal with event."[309] We can scarcely do better when interpreting the crucifixion of Jesus in Luke, therefore, than to follow Luke's lead in portraying Jesus as the Christ, God's chosen one, whose death fulfilled the Scriptures and brought salvation to the lost.

With bitter irony, the Lukan Jesus is one who brings good news to the poor, but at his death the people watch, the soldiers mock, and one of the criminals beside him blasphemes. God's vindication of Jesus through the resurrection will mean God's validation of Jesus' message. In the interim, however, Jesus is "numbered with the transgressors" and bears "the sin of many" (Isa 53:12).

Luke does not defend any particular theory of the atonement. The traditional theories generally fall into one of the following categories: sacrifice, ransom, or moral influence. Luke never calls Jesus "the Lamb of God who takes away the sin of the world" (John 1:29 NRSV; cf. John 1:36; Acts 8:32). Neither does the Lukan Jesus say "the Son of Man came . . . to give his life a ransom for many" (Mark 10:45 NRSV). At most, the two on the road to Emmaus report, "We had hoped that he was the one to redeem Israel" (24:21; cf. 1:68; 2:38). No proof text suffices in these matters, but the absence of even such references as one finds in the other Gospels underscores the extent to which Luke relies on the account of Jesus' death to carry the message of its significance. How one chooses to explain it, after all, is quite secondary to the confession that Jesus is the Christ, our Savior.

309. Walter J. Ong, *Interfaces of the Word: Studies in the Evolution of Consciousness and Culture* (Ithaca, N.Y.: Cornell University Press, 1977) 74.

Luke 23:39-43, The Assurance of Salvation

<table>
<tr><td>

NIV

39One of the criminals who hung there hurled insults at him: "Aren't you the Christ? Save yourself and us!"

40But the other criminal rebuked him. "Don't you fear God," he said, "since you are under the same sentence? 41We are punished justly, for we are getting what our deeds deserve. But this man has done nothing wrong."

42Then he said, "Jesus, remember me when you come into your kingdom.*a*"

43Jesus answered him, "I tell you the truth, today you will be with me in paradise."

a42 Some manuscripts come with your kingly power

</td><td>

NRSV

39One of the criminals who were hanged there kept deriding*a* him and saying, "Are you not the Messiah?*b* Save yourself and us!" 40But the other rebuked him, saying, "Do you not fear God, since you are under the same sentence of condemnation? 41And we indeed have been condemned justly, for we are getting what we deserve for our deeds, but this man has done nothing wrong." 42Then he said, "Jesus, remember me when you come into*c* your kingdom." 43He replied, "Truly I tell you, today you will be with me in Paradise."

*a*Or *blaspheming*   *b*Or *the Christ*   *c*Other ancient authorities read *in*

</td></tr>
</table>

COMMENTARY

When one of the criminals crucified with Jesus joins in the mocking, the other criminal rebukes him, maintaining that Jesus has done nothing wrong. Jesus responds, assuring the "penitent thief" that he would be with Jesus in paradise.

Luke's is the only Gospel to record the words of the men crucified with Jesus or to report a conversation among the three dying men. Mark 15:32 says only that those who were crucified with Jesus taunted him also. Whatever the origin of this tradition, it contributes to prominent Lukan themes. The taunt in v. 39 is the third in the series and again derides Jesus as the Savior (see Commentary on vv. 35-38). This scene further pictures Jesus dying among the outcasts, with whom he spent much of his ministry. In his rebuke of the other, the criminal adds his own affirmation of Jesus' innocence. Earlier, Pilate and Herod had pronounced Jesus innocent, and later the centurion will echo the same judgment. Jesus' defender asks to be remembered when Jesus comes into his kingdom, a request that may have arisen solely from the inscription over Jesus, but it also effectively reminds the reader of Jesus' earlier declarations of the coming of the kingdom of God. Fittingly, as he is dying, Jesus extends mercy to one of the wretched, whose fate he shares.

23:39. This introduces the taunt from "one of the criminals who were hanged there." The verb recurs in Acts in descriptions of the death of Jesus, "whom you had killed by hanging him on a tree" (Acts 5:30 NRSV; see also 10:39). This one derided (lit. "blasphemed" [βλασφημέω *blasphēmeō*]) Jesus. Both criminals ask for salvation, the first in mocking sarcasm, the second in an understated echo of Semitic voices from the past: "Remember me." The one is heard, while the other dies in bitter cynicism a few feet from the Savior, who could have extended him mercy.

23:40-41. "The penitent thief" is a term of convenience that is more specific than Luke's description of him. His crime is never specified, and his penitence is conveyed only by his acknowledgment of their guilt and Jesus' innocence and by his request that Jesus remember him. The verb for "to rebuke" (ἐπιτιμάω *epitimaō*) occurs twelve times in Luke, and usually it is Jesus who does the rebuking (cf. 18:15, 39). Nevertheless, the penitent thief's words fulfill Jesus' instructions to his disciples: "If your brother sins, rebuke him, and if he repents, forgive him" (17:3). His rebuke reminds the other criminal that he, too, has been condemned to die and will soon be facing God's judgment (cf. 12:5). They were getting what they deserved, but Jesus had done nothing wrong (lit., nothing "out of place" [ἄτοπος *atopos*]). They had been judged "rightly" (δικαίως *dikaiōs*, v. 41), but Jesus was "righteous" (δίκαιος *dikaios*, v. 47).

23:42. The criminal addresses Jesus by name. His request that Jesus remember him echoes the plaintive cries of those in need and those dying in centuries past. Interpreting the dream of the Pharaoh's chief cupbearer, Joseph predicted that his fellow prisoner would be released in three days

and requested, "Remember me when it is well with you" (Gen 40:14 NRSV). Hannah prayed to God, "Remember me" (1 Sam 1:11), as did Nehemiah (5:19; 13:31), Job (14:13), the psalmist (25:7; 106:4), and Jeremiah (15:15). The criminal's request is not that Jesus remember him when he comes in the parousia ("in his kingdom") but when he is delivered from his suffering and comes "into his kingdom" (cf. 24:26).

23:43. Jesus replied, granting the man more than he had asked for. The pronouncement is the sixth of the "Amen, I say to you" sayings in Luke, and the only one addressed to one person (cf. 4:24; 12:37; 18:17, 29; 21:32). It is also the last of the emphatic "today" pronouncements in Luke (e.g., 4:21; 19:9). Like the poor, the crippled, the blind, and the lame in Jesus' parable of the great banquet (14:21), the criminal would feast with Jesus that day in paradise. Like the wretched Lazarus who died at the rich man's gate (16:19-31), he would experience the blessing of God's mercy.

"Paradise" (παράδεισος *paradeisos*) originally meant a garden, then in the Septuagint it is used of the Garden of Eden (Gen 2:8). In later Jewish apocalyptic literature, where the end is often a return to the beginning, it designates the place of the blessed, which for those who lived in a hot, arid climate is often represented as a place with a stream and lush vegetation (see Rev 2:7).[310] Paul wrote that he knew a person "who fourteen years ago was caught up to the third heaven . . . into Paradise and heard things that are not to be told, that no mortal is permitted to repeat" (2 Cor 12:2, 4 NRSV). One of the later apocalypses, *2 Enoch,* lacking Paul's restraint, contains the following description of Paradise: "They brought me up to the third heaven. And they placed me in the midst of Paradise. And that place has an appearance of pleasantness that has never been seen. Every tree was in full flower. Every fruit was ripe, every food was in yield profusely; every fragrance was pleasant. And the four rivers were flowing past with gentle movement, and with every kind of garden producing every kind of good food. And the tree of life is in that place, under which the LORD takes a rest when the LORD takes a walk in Paradise. And that tree is indescribable for pleasantness of fragrance."[311]

310. See also *T. Levi* 18:10-11; *Ps Sol* 14:3; and *1 Enoch* 61:12.
311. *2 Enoch* 8:1-3, in James H. Charlesworth, ed., *The Old Testament Pseudepigrapha* (Garden City, N.Y.: Doubleday, 1983) 1:115.

REFLECTIONS

Paul wrote: "If for this life only we have hoped in Christ, we are of all people most to be pitied" (1 Cor 15:19 NRSV). The Gospels reflect keen theological acumen, therefore, in connecting Jesus' death with the promise of life to those who trust in him. Matthew inserts the legendary story that "the tombs also were opened, and many bodies of the saints who had fallen asleep were raised. After his resurrection they came out of the tombs and entered the holy city and appeared to many" (Matt 27:52-53 NRSV). The Gospel of John, which emphasizes the present fulfillment of future hopes, records that before his death Jesus approached the tomb of Lazarus and called him back to life (John 11:38-44), doing for one he loved a sign of what he would do for all "his own." The promise to the dying criminal, therefore, is Luke's way of making the same point. Others taunted Jesus, mocking him with challenges to save himself and others, so with fitting irony his last words to another human being are an assurance of salvation. Jesus began his ministry proclaiming "good news to the poor" and "release to the captives" (4:18), and he ends it extending an assurance of blessing to one of the wretched.

Here is good news not just for the "sweet by and by," or even for "the year of the Lord's favor" (4:19), but for "today" (23:43). The second of the words from the cross in Luke should move every reader to recognize that we, too, stand in need of God's mercy ("Do you not fear God?") and ask that God might remember us. As with so many other scenes from the Gospel, this one is a Gospel in miniature: Jesus, the dying Savior among the wretched; one who taunts him cynically and thereby rejects his mercy; and one who receives salvation because he looks forward to the kingdom of God. Thus the story invites the same response as the Gospel as a whole: Turn to the Lord for mercy and then spread the good news of God's kingdom among the poor by doing for them as Jesus did during his ministry.

In what do you trust? The rich fool thought he had provided for himself for years to come, but God said, "This night . . . " (12:20). The dying criminal knew that he had no one else to whom he could appeal, and Jesus said to him, "Today. . . . "

Luke 23:44-49, The Events Surrounding Jesus' Death

NIV

[44] It was now about the sixth hour, and darkness came over the whole land until the ninth hour, [45] for the sun stopped shining. And the curtain of the temple was torn in two. [46] Jesus called out with a loud voice, "Father, into your hands I commit my spirit." When he had said this, he breathed his last.

[47] The centurion, seeing what had happened, praised God and said, "Surely this was a righteous man." [48] When all the people who had gathered to witness this sight saw what took place, they beat their breasts and went away. [49] But all those who knew him, including the women who had followed him from Galilee, stood at a distance, watching these things.

NRSV

[44] It was now about noon, and darkness came over the whole land[a] until three in the afternoon, [45] while the sun's light failed;[b] and the curtain of the temple was torn in two. [46] Then Jesus, crying with a loud voice, said, "Father, into your hands I commend my spirit." Having said this, he breathed his last. [47] When the centurion saw what had taken place, he praised God and said, "Certainly this man was innocent."[c] [48] And when all the crowds who had gathered there for this spectacle saw what had taken place, they returned home, beating their breasts. [49] But all his acquaintances, including the women who had followed him from Galilee, stood at a distance, watching these things.

[a] Or earth [b] Or the sun was eclipsed. Other ancient authorities read the sun was darkened [c] Or righteous

COMMENTARY

These verses are in many respects the heart of the Gospel. They are both chronologically and thematically the culmination of Jesus' life. To interpret the significance of Jesus' death, Luke reports a series of numinous events (vv. 44-45), then Jesus' last words (v. 46), and then the response of those who witnessed Jesus' death (vv. 47-49). Luke seems to be following Mark's account at this point, but rearranges, alters, and adds elements to convey his own understanding. Each element of Luke's account, therefore, merits close study.

23:44-45. Following Mark 15:33, Luke reports that there was darkness over "the whole land" from noon until three in the afternoon. Luke has omitted Mark's first temporal reference, the crucifixion of Jesus at the "third hour" (9:00 A.M.; Mark 15:25), thereby leaving undefined the length of time between the crucifixion and Jesus' death but conveying the impression of a shorter period than in Mark.

Luke's statement that the sun's light "failed" (ἐκλείπω *ekleipō*; v. 45) has at times led to the speculation that there was a solar eclipse, but an eclipse would have been impossible at Passover, when there was a full moon. Thus some commentators have attributed the darkness to a dust storm or, more plausibly, suggested that Luke has linked Jesus' death with the memory of an eclipse at about that time in history.[312] Beyond a possible explanation of the darkness, one has to ask what it might have meant to Luke. In the OT the darkening of the sun was a sign of judgment associated with "the day of the Lord" (Isa 13:9-10; 50:2-3; Jer 15:6-9; Lam 3:1-2; Amos 5:18, 20; Joel 2:2, 10, 31; 3:15; Zeph 1:15). Darkness will come upon the false prophets and rulers of Israel (Mic 3:6). The closest parallel to the darkness in the passion narratives, however, is Amos 8:9. Gentile readers would also understand the darkness as a cosmic sign that often accompanied the death of great men and kings:

> The Sun will give you signs. Who dare say the Sun false? Nay, he oft warns us that dark uprisings threaten, that treachery and hidden wars are upswelling. Nay, he had pity on Rome,

when, after Caesar sank from sight, he veiled his shining face in dusky gloom, and a godless age feared everlasting night.[313]

Josephus, moreover, records that the battles following the death of Julius Caesar were the struggles of "mankind in common" against "unlawful acts against the gods, from which we believe the very sun turned away."[314] In the Lukan context still other meanings are possible. Jesus had said at his arrest that it was the hour "and the power of darkness" (22:53). The coming of the Son of Man, however, would also be foreshadowed by "signs in the sun, the moon, and the stars" (21:25).

Luke further describes the darkness as covering "the whole land," just as the birth of Jesus had occurred when Emperor Augustus had decreed that "all the world" should be registered (2:1). Later, the witnesses to Jesus' death and resurrection would carry the gospel "to the ends of the earth" (Acts 1:8). The darkness over the land in Luke, therefore, may be understood as a cosmic sign of the significance of Jesus' death for all the world, an omen of God's judgment on the leaders of Israel, and a tribute to the death of "the king of the Jews."

Luke brings forward the rending of the veil in the Temple (which Mark reports only after Jesus' death), thereby linking it with the darkness. Luke also says that the veil was (literally) torn "in the middle" (μέσος *mesos*) rather than "from top to bottom" (Mark 15:38). The use of the passive voice may imply that this was God's action. The reader of the Gospel will understand that God has vindicated Jesus' judgment on the Temple (see 19:45-46; 21:5-6). It has been argued that Luke has deliberately linked the rending of the veil to Jesus' commending his spirit into the hands of God so that the reader can imagine that the veil is rent in order for Jesus to make his "exodus" to the Father, but this interpretation is overly subtle. Nevertheless, the rending of the veil probably carries a more positive sense than in Mark. Arguments over a symbolism that is based on identi-

---

312. See Brown, *The Death of the Messiah*, 1041-42.

313. Virgil, *Georgics*, 1.463-64, in *Virgil*, trans. H. Rushton Fairclough, LCL (Cambridge, Mass.: Harvard University Press, 1978) 1:113.

314. Josephus, *Antiquities of the Jews*, 14.309, in *Josephus*, trans. Ralph Marcus, LCL (Cambridge, Mass.: Harvard University Press, 1943) 7:613.

fying the location of the veil either in the forecourt or in the sanctuary finally prove unconvincing, because none of the evangelists specifies the location of the veil or gives any indication that he knows of more than one (see 1:9). Gentile readers could certainly not be expected to grasp such nuances.

The rending of the veil in Luke, however, may well be a divine validation of Jesus' act of cleansing the Temple so that it could serve as the place for his teaching (see 19:45-48). Accordingly, the rending of the veil may mean that all now have access to the presence of God, or as the author of Ephesians put it, "the dividing wall of hostility" (see Eph 2:14-15) has been torn down so that all may now approach God on an equal basis through the death of Jesus. The death of Jesus, with the rending of the veil in the Temple, therefore, prepares the way for the gospel to be preached "openly and unhindered" (see Acts 28:31).

23:46. Luke also changes the inarticulate "loud cry" in Mark 15:37 into a prayer of consecration: "Father, into your hands I commend my spirit." The prayer is a quotation of Ps 31:5. Handed over "into the hands of men" (9:44), Jesus now commends himself to the hands of God (cf. 1:71, 74). Fittingly, in Luke Jesus does not die with a cry of abandonment but with full confidence in the One whom he addressed as "Father" (cf. 10:21-22; 11:2, 13; 12:30, 32; 22:42; 23:34). Prayer has been the leitmotif of Jesus' ministry, most recently on the Mount of Olives the night before he died (22:42) and in his prayer for forgiveness for those who "do not know what they are doing" (23:34). And what Jesus said in the darkness would be proclaimed from the housetops (see 12:3). Jesus' serenity in the face of death becomes a model for Stephen, the first Christian martyr, who at his death also prays, "Lord Jesus, receive my spirit" (Acts 7:59 NIV).

Luke records Jesus' death simply: "He breathed his last" (ἐκπνέω *ekpneō*). Whereas Mark prefaces this statement with a loud cry, Luke has moved the reference to the "loud voice" so that it introduces Jesus' dying prayer. In this way the death of Jesus in Luke is more peaceful; there is no hint of a loud cry of anguish as he dies, only his complete trust in the Father, into whose hands he commits his spirit.

23:47-49. Just as Luke has constructed the narrative of the crucifixion so that there are three sympathetic witnesses before Jesus' death (Simon of Cyrene, a large number of the people, and the two criminals), so also following Jesus' death there are three sympathetic witnesses (the centurion, "all the crowds," and "all his acquaintances").[315] Luke's craftsmanship, always subtle, is clearly evident.

In Mark's account, the confession of the centurion (15:39) is the christological high point of the Gospel. As a result of Mark's treatment of the theme of "the messianic secret," no one around Jesus knows his true identity except the demons, and no one confesses that Jesus is the Son of God until Jesus has died. The reader is told in the opening line of Mark that Jesus is "the Christ, the Son of God" (Mark 1:1, though the last phrase is missing in some MSS). The voice from heaven identifies Jesus as the beloved son (Mark 1:11; 9:7), and the demons attempt to make him known (Mark 1:24; 3:11; 5:7), but no one confesses that Jesus is the Son of God until after his death (cf. Mark 14:62). The climax of the first half of the Gospel occurs with Peter's confession that Jesus is the Christ (Mark 8:29), and the climax of the second half occurs when the centurion confesses that he is the Son of God (Mark 15:39).

Luke has other designs in mind, however. The key word of the centurion's response (δίκαιος *dikaios*) may be translated either "innocent" (NRSV) or "just" (NIV, "a righteous man"). The term comes from a legal context and can certainly mean "innocent," but its meaning elsewhere in Luke (see, e.g., 2:25, "righteous and devout," or 23:50, "good and righteous") and Acts (where it is also used as a title: "the Holy and Righteous One," 3:14; cf. 7:52) is not limited to innocence. It also conveys a positive sense: "just," "righteous."

The confession of the centurion is not the christological climax of the Gospel but the last in the series of pronouncements of Jesus' innocence. Pilate pronounces Jesus innocent three times (23:4, 14, 22), Pilate reports that Herod also found him innocent (23:15), and the criminal on the cross affirms his innocence (23:41). Now the centurion, having witnessed the manner of Jesus' death—and perhaps the darkness, Jesus' prayers, and Jesus' conversation with the criminal—also affirms Jesus' innocence. But more, he affirms that the one who died praying to God was "just."

315. See Brown, *The Death of the Messiah*, 2:1160.

Luke prefaces the centurion's response by saying that he "praised God" (δοξάζω *doxazō*). Throughout the Gospel, Luke has characterized the result of Jesus' life as leading others to glorify God. At Bethlehem the shepherds responded to the birth of Jesus by glorifying God (2:20). When Jesus taught in the synagogues in Galilee, the people glorified God (4:15). Then it was the paralyzed man whom Jesus healed and those who witnessed the healing (5:25-26), those who witnessed his raising of the widow at Nain's son (7:16), the crippled woman (13:13), the Samaritan leper (17:15), and the blind man in Jericho (18:43). So significant in Luke is the response of praising God for wondrous deeds of redemption that the Gospel itself will end with this response (24:53, though with the verb "to bless" (εὐλογέω *eulogeō*). The centurion is but the first of many—Jews (4:21; 11:18; 21:20) and Gentiles (Acts 13:48)—who will respond to the gospel by glorifying God.

The second response Luke describes is that of "all the crowds" who were standing by. The crowds here continue the response of the people (see 23:5, 13, 27, 35). This is the last reference to the crowds in Luke. They have been "watching" the spectacle of the crucifixion (as in v. 35). Luke's phrase "what had taken place" (v. 48) echoes the similar reference in v. 47. The crowds also had seen what the centurion saw. Their response is one of mourning and self-condemnation. The response of "beating their breasts" echoes the posture of the tax collector in the parable of the Pharisee and the tax collector. The tax collector "standing far off" would not look to heaven, but "beat his breast," saying, "God, be merciful to me, a sinner!" (18:13). The crowd says nothing, but their actions speak for them. The sequence of the responses to Jesus' death in Luke is instructive—and profoundly right. First,

the identity of Jesus is recognized, then the people respond in an act of contrition or a plea for mercy. What else can sinners do when they recognize the meaning of Jesus' death but humble themselves before God and ask for mercy?

The third response comes from "all his acquaintances, including the women who had followed him from Galilee" (v. 49). The reference to "all" is a Lukan signature, as we have noted throughout Luke (cf. v. 48). The acquaintances are not further identified. They may have included the eleven disciples, but Luke does not say so. More likely, it is intended as a general reference to relatives and/or to the larger group of disciples and followers, such as the seventy(-two) from 10:1ff. and those who would soon be numbered among the 120 in Acts 1:15. They stood "at a distance" (cf. 18:13). The group included the women who had followed him from Galilee (some of whom were named in 8:2-3). Perhaps because they are named there, Luke does not name them here (cf. Mark 15:40-41; Luke 23:55; 24:10). They, too, were "watching these things"—which qualifies them as witnesses (cf. 24:46-48; Acts 1:22). The responses of the three sympathetic observers occur in diminishing order: The centurion sees and speaks; the crowds see and beat their breasts; and the acquaintances see—neither their words nor their actions are recorded, perhaps because no further description of the sympathetic or confessing responses is needed. The spectacle of Jesus' death is over, but the events at the cross have clearly revealed his identity as the Savior and the meaning of his death. Moreover, the story will not end at the cross. First, we may recall that only the first part of the passion predictions has been fulfilled. And, second, there were persons standing there who had seen these things. Their story, too, would have to be told.

REFLECTIONS

Sometime during the seventh or ninth century, St. Angus came to Balquidder, a beautiful valley surrounded by forested hills in the Scottish highlands. Moved by its beauty, he said it was "a thin place"—a place where the separation between heaven and earth was very thin—so he built a church there that has survived to this day.

The death of Jesus is "a thin place." Indeed, the heavens become dark, and on earth the veil in the Temple is rent. So thin is the separation that Jesus talks to God from the cross, and those who hear his prayers are moved to confession and contrition. The one who was hailed by a chorus of angels at his birth and was designated by an angel visitant as the Son of God commits his spirit to God as he dies. The holy one dies a common criminal's death and speaks of Paradise to the criminal beside him.

Each of the Gospels presents the death of Jesus in a different way, as is evident from the observation that only the cry of dereliction appears in two Gospels (Matthew and Mark). Six "words" of Jesus from the cross appear in the other three Gospels, and none in more than one Gospel. Mark depicts Jesus dying in agony and abandonment. In Mark we see the depth of Jesus' suffering. Matthew follows Mark closely but adds a description of the opening of the tombs and the resurrection of the saints. In Matthew we see that the death of Jesus leads to life for all who trust in God. John portrays the cross as ironic exaltation. Jesus is "lifted up" in mock coronation as the King of the Jews as he returns to the Father. The giver of living water thirsts as he dies. In John we see the Logos completing his mission of revelation and the lamb of God taking away the sin of the world.

The divergent colors that the evangelists use to paint the crucifixion scene call us to read each one individually and appreciatively. In Luke we stand with the crowd of the people watching while Jesus is crucified by those who taunt him with mocked pleas that he save himself and others. Jesus' death, therefore, confirms who he has been throughout his ministry. The authorities pronounce him innocent. The taunts derisively hail him as the Messiah, God's chosen one, and the King of the Jews, but Jesus prays for forgiveness for those who have rejected and crucified him. He assures the penitent criminal of blessing in Paradise and dies with the prayer of one who trusts God even in death. Jesus has faithfully undertaken the work of redemption—lifting up the lowly (1:52) and preaching good news to the poor (4:18)—and it has cost him his life. Ironically, though, his death also signals the inevitability of the completion of the other side of the redemption of the humble—judgment upon the proud and bringing down "the powerful from their thrones" (1:52).

The people leave "The Skull" beating their breasts. How terrible that God has sent "the Savior," and we rejected him and crucified him on a hill outside the city. At his death, even a hardened soldier was moved to confess that he was just. If we have rejected the Savior, God's only son, what hope is there? "What then will the owner of the vineyard do to them?" (20:15). Perhaps it is good not to dispel the darkness of the death of Jesus too quickly. We naturally move on to wonder at the love of God revealed in the death of Jesus or to translate its meaning into sacrificial terms (which are not clearly invoked in Luke) or to press on to the next chapter—to the resurrection. But part of the power of the gospel is that it calls us to tarry at the cross and then return home beating our breasts with those whose hopes seemed to have died there. Only by witnessing the darkness of his death and the despair of the loss of hope can we fully appreciate the joy of the resurrection. God's purposes for Jesus, the Savior, however, will not be defeated by the power of darkness. Jesus came "to give light to those who sit in darkness and in the shadow of death" (1:79). So those who see the light in the darkness can join those at the cross who confessed Jesus, beat their breasts in grief and contrition, and then went away to serve as witnesses that they had been at the "thin place" where the design of the God of the heavens was revealed on earth.

Through the centuries, human beings have looked for "thin places" in many ways. Some have climbed mountaintops; others have meticulously observed cultic rituals; some have searched religious lores; and others have looked within through prayer and meditation. Where is God to be found in human experience? Where can we see God revealed through the veil that surrounds us? Who would have thought that "The Skull" would be the "thin place"? At such a place we can only confess our wretched unworthiness of such love as this.

Luke 23:50-56, The Burial of Jesus

NIV

⁵⁰Now there was a man named Joseph, a member of the Council, a good and upright man, ⁵¹who had not consented to their decision and action. He came from the Judean town of Arimathea and he was waiting for the kingdom of God. ⁵²Going to Pilate, he asked for Jesus' body. ⁵³Then he took it down, wrapped it in linen cloth and placed it in a tomb cut in the rock, one in which no one had yet been laid. ⁵⁴It was Preparation Day, and the Sabbath was about to begin.

⁵⁵The women who had come with Jesus from Galilee followed Joseph and saw the tomb and how his body was laid in it. ⁵⁶Then they went home and prepared spices and perfumes. But they rested on the Sabbath in obedience to the commandment.

NRSV

50Now there was a good and righteous man named Joseph, who, though a member of the council, ⁵¹had not agreed to their plan and action. He came from the Jewish town of Arimathea, and he was waiting expectantly for the kingdom of God. ⁵²This man went to Pilate and asked for the body of Jesus. ⁵³Then he took it down, wrapped it in a linen cloth, and laid it in a rock-hewn tomb where no one had ever been laid. ⁵⁴It was the day of Preparation, and the sabbath was beginning.ᵃ ⁵⁵The women who had come with him from Galilee followed, and they saw the tomb and how his body was laid. ⁵⁶Then they returned, and prepared spices and ointments.

On the sabbath they rested according to the commandment.

ᵃ Gk was dawning

COMMENTARY

The burial of Jesus provides closure to the account of the trial and crucifixion of Jesus and serves as a transition to the resurrection of Jesus in the next chapter. Brief as it is—and Luke has abridged Mark's account—the report of the burial of Jesus is not without significance or artistry.

23:50. The introduction of Joseph of Arimathea reminds the reader of the devout Jews who played prominent roles in the infancy narrative. Using a formula reminiscent of the Septuagint, Luke introduces "a good and righteous man named Joseph." Luke extols the character of Joseph rather than his social position—fittingly, since Luke has typically portrayed the difficulties the rich have in receiving the kingdom. Although Joseph is a member of the Sanhedrin, he is a "good man," who will bring forth good things out of his treasure (6:45); he is good soil in which the kingdom of God may grow (8:8, 15). The term for "just," which was used by the centurion of Jesus (v. 47) is now used of Joseph. Zechariah, Elizabeth (1:6), and Simeon (2:25) were described as "just" or "righteous." In contrast to the hostile response of the chief priests and leaders of the

people, therefore, pious representatives of the heritage of Israel receive Jesus at his birth and care for his body at his death.

23:51. In order to make the point that Joseph was a just man, however, Luke clarifies that, although he had said earlier that "the assembly rose as a body and brought Jesus before Pilate" (23:1) and later that "they all shouted together, 'Away with this fellow!'" (23:18), Joseph had not joined in their plan or supported the crucifixion. Instead, the man from Arimathea was looking for the kingdom of God, just as Simeon was "looking forward to the redemption of Jerusalem" (see 2:25; cf. 2:38). Joseph was from (literally) "a city of the Jews" (v. 51). Except in the references to "the king of the Jews," the term "Jews" (Ἰουδαῖος *Ioudaios*) does not appear elsewhere in Luke except in 7:3, in a reference to elders of the Jews.

23:52. Luke, who is fond of symmetry and balanced pairs, records that at Jesus' burial there was a man from a city of the Jews and women from Galilee. Earlier, Luke has featured the roles of Zechariah and Elizabeth, Joseph and Mary, Simeon and Anna, the centurion and the widow at

Nain, Simon the Pharisee and the woman of the city, the man with dropsy and the bent woman, and other male-female pairs. Joseph and the women have significant roles. Joseph secures from Pilate permission to bury the body of Jesus; the necessity of securing permission from Pilate confirms that the Romans were in charge of the execution. The Romans did not usually allow executed persons to be taken by their family or supporters for a decent burial. In this case, however, the request came not from Jesus' family or his disciples, but from a member of the council that had brought Jesus to Pilate, who himself had never been convinced of Jesus' guilt. There was little reason to think that the people would make a martyr of this one.[316]

23:53-54. According to Luke, Joseph took Jesus' body down from the cross himself (cf. Matt 27:58 where Pilate orders the body taken down) and wrapped it in fine linen. Luke omits Mark's reference to Joseph's purchasing the linen cloth. Joseph then places the body in a tomb hewn out of the rock (cf. John 19:41). Having entered Jerusalem on a donkey on which no one had ever sat (19:30), he is buried in a tomb in which no one has ever been laid (cf. John 19:41). Nothing is said about spices or anointing the body, perhaps because the approach of the sabbath left little time for the burial. Luke defers the reference to the time from the beginning of the burial report (as it is in Mark 15:42) to the end of it, where it

confirms that the burial was completed before sundown (cf. Deut 21:22-23), and in that case before the beginning of the sabbath.[317]

23:55-56. The women who had followed Jesus from Galilee were witnesses to these events. The women, who were mentioned at the cross (23:49), will return to anoint the body on the first day of the week (24:1). Unlike Mark, who includes lists of names of the women at the cross, the burial of Jesus, and the empty tomb (Mark 15:40, 47; 16:1), Luke lists the names only once, in 24:10. The specific report that the women saw the tomb and the way Jesus was laid in it may have served as an apologetic motif, confirming that the burial occurred and that the women did not later go to the wrong tomb (cf. Matt 27:61-66; Mark 15:47; 1 Cor 15:4). They apparently also saw that Joseph did not anoint the body, perhaps because of the lateness of the hour. Having provided for Jesus during his life (8:2-3), the women now return to prepare spices, probably scented oils, for anointing his body in death. Luke underscores, nevertheless, that the women rested on the sabbath, keeping the law. Given the situation, therefore, everything about Jesus' burial was done properly: A good and righteous man, a member of the Sanhedrin, secured permission from Pilate and buried the body; it was wrapped in linen and laid in a new tomb hewn from the rock; the burial was witnessed by the women, who then prepared to anoint it; the burial was completed before sundown; and the women rested on the sabbath. It was a burial fit for a just man.

316. For a full discussion of the factors involved in the release of Jesus' body, see John Nolland, *Luke 18:35–24:53*, WBC 35C (Dallas: Word, 1993) 1164.

317. See also *m. Sanh* 6.5. Cf. *m. Sabb.* 23.4-5.

REFLECTIONS

Although funerals are part of the ministry of the church, and burials perhaps are the most ancient of religious ceremonies, the NT is surprisingly silent about the ritual of burial. John the Baptist's disciples took his body and buried it (Mark 6:29), and "devout men buried Stephen and made loud lamentation over him" (Acts 8:2 NRSV). But who buried James the brother of John (Acts 12:2)? We know much more about Jesus' burial than about the burial of anyone else in the NT.

Moreover, although the burial is recorded only briefly, the taking down of the body from the cross is one of the scenes that dominates Christian art. Joseph of Arimathea, therefore, has had a disproportionately large place in Christian art. Why do we find this interlude between the crucifixion and the discovery of the empty tomb so fascinating?

Joseph of Arimathea is a minor character in the Gospels, but one whose name will be remembered throughout history for one decent act. Was he moved by a raging sense of injustice at the death of Jesus (23:51), by devotion to the Lord he had feared to confess openly (John 19:38)? Or was he simply moved to do a decent and compassionate thing? We may never know, but how could he have ever known that, even though he was a man of some distinction in his own time, he would be remembered for all time for this one compassionate act? It would not be a bad thing to be remembered as one who did something good and decent.

Jesus was not buried in the manner of "the kings of the Gentiles" (cf. 22:25). In the kingdom of God, a state funeral is a much simpler affair. But Jesus was buried by a good and righteous man, and things were done properly. For one who lived and died among the outcasts, it was appropriate. If the NT does not offer much guidance regarding how a funeral should be conducted, therefore, what guidance the account of Jesus' burial offers goes to the heart of the matter. Jesus' funeral fittingly reflected his life, and those who buried him acted with compassion, caring for the body, cherishing the memory of his life, and honoring God in the process.

LUKE 24:1-53, THE RESURRECTION NARRATIVES

OVERVIEW

The final section of the Gospel contains the discovery of the empty tomb (24:1-12), the appearance to the two disciples on the road to Emmaus (24:13-35), and the appearance to the eleven back in Jerusalem (24:36-53). The latter ends with the departure of Jesus (24:50-53). This chapter fulfills some vital functions. Most obviously, it proclaims the resurrection of Jesus. Beyond the obvious, however, it also relates the resurrection to the proclamation of the church, declares that the events of the crucifixion and resurrection fulfilled the Scriptures, establishes that the presence of the risen Lord will be found in the study of Scripture and the sharing of bread, commissions the disciples for their mission in the book of Acts, and brings closure to the Gospel through the report of Jesus' departure.

The resurrection narratives pose some of the most difficult problems for historical reconstruction. The earliest references to the resurrection occur in confessional passages in Paul's letters (Rom 1:3-4; 1 Cor 15:3-5; Phil 2:6-11; Col 1:15-20) and in the core of the early kerygma (Acts 2:23-24; cf. 2:32; 3:15; 4:10; 10:40; 13:30, 37). In the Gospels, Acts, and Paul's letters we find brief *reports* of appearances: to Peter and then to the Twelve (1 Cor 15:3-5; cf. Mark 16:7), to Peter (Luke 24:34), to the apostles (Acts 1:3), to those chosen to be witnesses (Acts 10:40-41), and to those who came with Jesus from Galilee (Acts 13:31). In the Gospels we also find accounts of the discovery of the empty tomb by the women, and accounts of appearances to the disciples. Mark contains no appearances but forecasts an appearance in Galilee, which Matthew then reports. Luke and Acts contain appearances to the disciples in and around Jerusalem. Only John contains appearances both in Jerusalem (John 20) and in Galilee (John 21), and it has often been proposed that John 21 was added to the Gospel at one of the later stages of its composition. If that is the case, then one of the notable parallels between Luke and John is that, in contrast to the tradition known to Mark and Matthew, they report appearances to the disciples in Jerusalem. The traditions of the discovery of the empty tomb by the women probably derived from Jerusalem, whereas the appearances to the disciples represent various local traditions. The empty tomb and appearance traditions were probably originally separate, but the Gospels reflect efforts to link them together. Matthew and John report appearances to the women at the tomb (Matt 28:9-10; John 20:14-18), and Luke reports that Peter (24:12) and others (24:24) subsequently went to the tomb to confirm the women's report. Peter's visit to the tomb is also reported by John, who adds that the Beloved Disciple ran with Peter (John 20:3-10; see Commentary on v. 12). Although it is difficult to trace the growth of the tradition in detail, an extended process of development is nevertheless evident. Luke's distinctive treatment of these traditions will emerge in the commentary that follows.

Luke 24:1-12, The Discovery of the Empty Tomb

24 On the first day of the week, very early in the morning, the women took the spices they had prepared and went to the tomb. [2]They found the stone rolled away from the tomb, [3]but when they entered, they did not find the body of the Lord Jesus. [4]While they were wondering about this, suddenly two men in clothes that gleamed like lightning stood beside them. [5]In their fright the women bowed down with their faces to the ground, but the men said to them, "Why do you look for the living among the dead? [6]He is not here; he has risen! Remember how he told you, while he was still with you in Galilee: [7]'The Son of Man must be delivered into the hands of sinful men, be crucified and on the third day be raised again.'" [8]Then they remembered his words.

[9]When they came back from the tomb, they told all these things to the Eleven and to all the others. [10]It was Mary Magdalene, Joanna, Mary the mother of James, and the others with them who told this to the apostles. [11]But they did not believe the women, because their words seemed to them like nonsense. [12]Peter, however, got up and ran to the tomb. Bending over, he saw the strips of linen lying by themselves, and he went away, wondering to himself what had happened.

24 But on the first day of the week, at early dawn, they came to the tomb, taking the spices that they had prepared. [2]They found the stone rolled away from the tomb, [3]but when they went in, they did not find the body.[a] [4]While they were perplexed about this, suddenly two men in dazzling clothes stood beside them. [5]The women[b] were terrified and bowed their faces to the ground, but the men[c] said to them, "Why do you look for the living among the dead? He is not here, but has risen.[d] [6]Remember how he told you, while he was still in Galilee, [7]that the Son of Man must be handed over to sinners, and be crucified, and on the third day rise again." [8]Then they remembered his words, [9]and returning from the tomb, they told all this to the eleven and to all the rest. [10]Now it was Mary Magdalene, Joanna, Mary the mother of James, and the other women with them who told this to the apostles. [11]But these words seemed to them an idle tale, and they did not believe them. [12]But Peter got up and ran to the tomb; stooping and looking in, he saw the linen cloths by themselves; then he went home, amazed at what had happened.[e]

[a]Other ancient authorities add *of the Lord Jesus* [b]Gk *They* [c]Gk *but they* [d]Other ancient authorities lack *He is not here, but has risen* [e]Other ancient authorities lack verse 12

COMMENTARY

All four Gospels report the discovery of the empty tomb, so there is much greater accord regarding the empty tomb tradition than regarding the various appearances. Nevertheless, each Gospel's account of the discovery of the empty tomb contains features unique to that Gospel. In Mark the women tell no one. Matthew continues the heightening of the miraculous that was evident in his account of the phenomena that accompanied Jesus' death by reporting that the women witnessed the opening of the tomb and that later Jesus appeared to the women as they left the tomb. John relates that Mary Magdalene went to the tomb alone and reported what she had seen to the disciples. When Peter and the Beloved Disciple ran to the tomb, the Beloved Disciple "saw and believed" (John 20:8), so the angelic appearance at the tomb is deferred until later in the account (20:11-13) and altered in form. Luke's account, as we shall see, is distinctive primarily in the angelic announcement (vv. 5-7) and in Peter's role in confirming the women's report (v. 12).

24:1-3. Luke moves from the burial of Jesus to the discovery of the empty tomb with scarcely a break. The first verse is transitional, a coming to the tomb corresponding to the returning from the tomb in 23:56a. Like the other Gospels, Luke reports that the women went to the tomb early on the first day of the week but adds that the women brought the spices they had prepared earlier (cf. v. 2; 23:56). The women are not named (in contrast to Mark 16:1). Indeed, they are referred to only by the third person plural verb, which connects the beginning of this scene even more closely with the previous one.

The women's intent is to anoint the body, presumably because Joseph of Arimathea had not done so and the beginning of the sabbath had precluded them from completing a proper burial without violating the sabbath. Verses 2-3 report what they found—and what they did not find. They found the stone rolled away from the tomb, but they did not find the body. Luke's work in abbreviating Mark's account is evident in that Luke has not previously mentioned the stone, whereas Mark related that the tomb was sealed with a stone and that the women had worried about how they would roll it away (see Mark 15:46; 16:3). Similarly, whereas Luke abbreviates, Matthew embroiders at this point: "And suddenly there was a great earthquake; for an angel of the Lord, descending from heaven, came and rolled back the stone and sat on it" (Matt 28:2 NRSV). Matthew, therefore, takes a half step toward reporting the actual resurrection and the departure of Jesus from the tomb, such as we find in the *Gospel of Peter* 35-42. Matthew continues by reporting the effect of these events on the guards at the tomb—another secondary feature found only in Matthew. The title "Lord Jesus" is a confessional reference that does not appear elsewhere in Luke, but occurs frequently in Acts and the Epistles.

24:4. In Matthew the angel appeared and rolled back the stone while the women were outside. In Mark the women see a young man when they enter the tomb, but in Luke they enter the tomb and find the body missing before the angel appears (as in John). The appearance of the two men "in dazzling clothes" occurs in Luke as a response to the women's lack of understanding regarding what they were seeing. Again as in John, there are two angelic figures, apparently to fulfill the requirement of two witnesses (Deut 19:15). Luke does not call the figures angels, but conveys their identity by describing their apparel as "radiant," "dazzling," or "gleaming"—a term that Luke uses to describe lightning in 17:24 (cf. Acts 10:30). The appearance of the two heavenly figures at the empty tomb in Luke links the scene to the other scenes at which two figures appear: the transfiguration and the ascension

(9:30; Acts 1:10). The messengers from the heavenly realm will report that Jesus has been raised from the dead.

24:5-6. The appearance of the angels follows a pattern similar to that of the angelophanies and theophanies in the OT (Judg 6:12-24; 13:2-23; cf. 2 Macc 3:26-28) or the appearances of Gabriel in Luke 1 (vv. 13-20, 36-38). The women are terrified (cf. 1:12; 24:37) and turn their faces to the ground, but in this instance no reassurance is given. The angels proceed to deliver the Easter announcement, which is the center of the empty tomb tradition. In Mark 16:6-7 the angelic announcement that interprets the meaning of the empty tomb follows closely the pattern of the early kerygma in 1 Cor 15:3-5.

The early confession in 1 Corinthians 15 follows a fourfold pattern: died, buried, raised, appeared. Accordingly, Mark sets the action on the third day after Jesus' death. The "young man" at the tomb calls attention to the place where they laid Jesus' body (perhaps preserving part of an ancient liturgy at the tomb), announces that he has been raised, and promises that Jesus will appear to Peter and the Twelve in Galilee. The angelic announcement, therefore, relates the early kerygma in a narrative form.

Luke has modified the Markan angelic announcement by omitting the words of reassurance ("Do not be alarmed"), changing the object of the women's search from "Jesus of Nazareth" to "the living among the dead," dropping the reference to the crucifixion and the invitation to see the place where he was laid, and substituting a reminder of the passion predictions for the promise of an appearance to Peter and the Twelve in Galilee. The common core of the announcements in Mark and Luke is simply the declaration "he is not here but has risen" (v. 5); this declaration is omitted in D (see the discussion of the Western non-interpolations below at v. 12). The verb for "to rise" (ἠγέρθη *ēgerthē*) should probably be read as a passive, "He has been raised," so that it preserves the sense that God raised Jesus from the dead, as in the early preaching (Acts 3:15; 4:10). The invitation to see the place where Jesus was laid has been omitted because Luke reported earlier that the women entered the tomb but did not find the body (v. 3).

24:7-8. In place of the simple reference to the crucifixion in Mark, Luke repeats the passion predictions. The reference to Galilee assumes a new focus. Rather than the place of the coming appearance of the risen Lord, it is the place where Jesus foretold his death. The explanation for this change may be that Luke has no place in his geographical scheme for appearances in Galilee. Instead, Jesus journeys from Galilee to Jerusalem, where he is crucified and raised. After he ascends, the disciples remain in Jerusalem until they are empowered by the Holy Spirit for their work as witnesses "in Jerusalem, in all Judea and Samaria, and to the ends of the earth" (Acts 1:8 NRSV). Luke, therefore, reports no appearances in Galilee, and the angel at the tomb, instead of commissioning the women to go and tell the disciples to go to Galilee, merely reminds them of what Jesus had told them while they were in Galilee. It is even possible that Luke has taken the story of the miraculous catch of fish and used it as Peter's call to discipleship (Luke 5:1-10) rather than as an appearance story, as it is in John 21:1-14, in order to avoid having an appearance in Galilee.

The passion prediction recalled in v. 7 is not exactly like any other in the Gospel but reproduces elements of the previous passion predictions.

> "The Son of Man must be handed over to sinners, and be crucified, and on the third day rise again." (24:7, italics added)

> "The Son of Man must undergo great suffering, and be rejected by the elders, chief priests, and scribes, and be killed, and on the third day be raised." (9:22, italics added)

> "The Son of Man is going to be betrayed into human hands." (9:44, italics added)

> "For he [the Son of Man] will be handed over to the Gentiles; and he will be mocked and insulted and spat upon. After they have flogged him, they will kill him, and on the third day he will rise again." (18:32-33, italics added)

All four formulations employ the title "the Son of Man." Luke 24:7 parallels 9:22 in that it uses the imperative of divine necessity, "must." The verb for "to be handed over" or "betrayed" (παραδίδωμι paradidōmi) occurs in 9:44; 18:32-33; and 24:7, but each reports the group(s) to whom Jesus is betrayed differently. There is also great variation in the description of the torment and death of Jesus, but with the exception of 9:44 each of the other three predictions forecasts the resurrection of Jesus on the third day. The formulation of these

two variable elements in 24:8 is probably significant. Jesus is crucified by sinners. The verb "to crucify" (σταυρόω stauroō) did not occur in any of the passion predictions. Indeed, it does not occur in Luke prior to the crowd's cry of "Crucify, crucify him!" (23:21). Moreover, in retrospect, the claim that Jesus was crucified by sinners links his death, which was accompanied by taunts of Jesus as the Savior, with Jesus' claim that he had come to call sinners to repentance (5:32) and to seek and to save the lost (19:10).

The phrase "on the third day" occurs not only in the passion predictions but also in 1 Cor 15:4. In each instance, it is related to the resurrection rather than to the discovery of the empty tomb or the first appearance. At best we can count only one full day and parts of two others, which leads us to question whether "the third day" had some meaning beyond merely historical recollection. Various OT passages speak of significant events on the third day: Earth was created on the third day (Gen 1:9-13); the Lord appeared to the people at Sinai to make a covenant with Israel on the third day (Exod 19:11, 16-25); Jonah was delivered from the belly of the fish on the third day (Jonah 1:17); and Hos 6:2 says: "After two days he will revive us;/ on the third day he will raise us up,/ that we may live before him" (NRSV). Significant as these OT references are, however, it is unlikely that they generated the tradition of the resurrection on the third day. It is much more likely that, given the report that the tomb was discovered empty on the third day, the early Christians found good reason to declare that this too had been "according to the scriptures" (1 Cor 15:4).

24:9. Whereas in Mark the women go and tell no one because they were afraid, even though they were instructed to tell the disciples and Peter, in Luke the women are not told to go and tell the disciples, but they do so. Luke has used the verb "to return" (ὑποστρέφω hypostrephō) earlier in 23:48, 56, and it will recur in 24:33, 52. The women tell the eleven (the Twelve minus Judas), and "all the rest," "all these things" (v. 9). In these phrases we see both Luke's fondness for the generalizing "all" and his understanding that from the beginning more persons than just the Twelve followed Jesus (see 8:1-3; 10:1, 17; 19:37; 23:49; Acts 1:15, 21-22).

24:10-11. The women, whose names were

not reported at the crucifixion or at the beginning of the empty tomb story, are now listed. As Fig. 8 shows, Luke's list owes something to the Markan lists, but since they vary Luke has acknowledged that there were others besides those whom he has listed.

Figure 8: Women at the Crucifixion or the Tomb of Jesus

At the crucifixion

Matt 27:55	Mark 15:40	Luke 23:49	John 19:25
many women	Mary Magdalene	the women who had	the mother of Jesus
Mary Magdalene	Mary the mother of	followed Jesus	Jesus' mother's sister
Mary the mother of	James and Joses	from Galilee	Mary the wife of Clopas
James and Joseph	Salome		Mary Magdalene
the mother of the	many other women		
sons of Zebedee			

At the burial of Jesus

Matt 27:61	Mark 15:47	Luke 23:55	
Mary Magdalene	Mary Magdalene	the women who had	
the other Mary	Mary the mother of	followed Jesus	
	Joses	from Galilee	

At the tomb on Sunday morning

Matt 28:1	Mark 16:1	Luke 24:10	John 20:1
Mary Magdalene	Mary Magdalene	Mary Magdalene	Mary Magdalene
the other Mary	Mary the mother of	Joanna	
	James	Mary the mother of	
	Salome	James	
		the other women	

Mary Magdalene and Joanna were both listed among the women who followed Jesus in Galilee (see 8:2-3). The women's report should have been credible because (1) they were relating events of which they had firsthand experience, (2) there were several witnesses, and (3) their character has been established by the reports of their selfless service to Jesus and his disciples (8:2-3; 23:49). Nevertheless, the others do not accept their testimony. That testimony would have included not only the report that the tomb was empty (as in John 20:2) but also the angelic announcement of the resurrection. The motif of doubt is one that recurs in each of the resurrection accounts (Matt 28:17; John 20:24-29; and the longer ending of Mark, 16:9-20). The report of the disciples' refusal to believe sets up the plot of how they will come to accept the Easter news.

24:12. This verse is not part of the text in D and some of the Old Latin manuscripts. Since D is a leading exemplar of the Western manuscript tradition that often includes words and phrases not found in other manuscripts, the omission of this verse represents an anomaly over which textual criticism is divided. Westcott and Hort grouped v. 12 with eight other passages that they called "Western non-interpolations" rather than concede that there are interpolations in the so-called neutral textual tradition.[318] The Western non-interpolations are found in Matt 27:49 and Luke 22:19b-20; 24:3, 6, 12, 36, 40, and 51-52. Although Westcott

318. B. F. Westcott and F. J. A. Hort, *The Greek New Testament in the Original Greek,* 1881.

and Hort omitted the words, phrases, or verses in question in these nine passages preferring the shorter text, the discovery of 𝔓⁷⁵, which dates from 175–225 CE and includes the Western non-interpolations, has led the editorial boards of the critical editions of the Greek NT and translation committees (including the NRSV and the NIV) to include the Western non-interpolations as part of the text, though usually with a note indicating that they are missing from some ancient manuscripts. The Western non-interpolations are also now usually evaluated individually on their own merits rather than as a group. The three Western non-interpolations in the account of the discovery of the empty tomb are the words "of the Lord Jesus" in v. 3, "he is not here, but has risen" in v. 6, and all of v. 12. To these might be added "sinful" in v. 7 and "from the tomb" in v. 9, which are also omitted in D and the Old Italian manuscripts. In each case, the addition of the variant readings is easier to explain than their omission, even though the weight of the manuscript tradition is clearly on the side of their inclusion.

In the case of v. 12, the issue is further complicated by two factors: (1) the report that Peter ran to the tomb, looked in, and saw the grave cloths has a parallel in John 20:3-10, where Peter and the Beloved Disciple run to the tomb; and (2) v. 24, which is present in all manuscripts, says that some of the disciples ran to the tomb. Much of the weight of a decision over the authenticity of v. 12, therefore, rests on two issues: (1) whether one is more disposed toward the strength of 𝔓⁷⁵, ℵ, B, and the other manuscripts that include the verse, or the principle that generally favors the shorter reading on the grounds that it is easier to explain an addition to the text than an omission; and (2) whether one is more disposed to see v. 12 as another instance of Lukan material that draws from tradition also known to John or to regard it as a later gloss added by a scribe familiar with John. Similar considerations apply, however, to the presence of the Beloved Disciple in John 20:3-10 and the absence of that disciple from Luke 24:12—it is easier to assume that John has inserted the Beloved Disciple into tradition that did not originally mention him than to assume that a scribe who added v. 12 to Luke 24 omitted the Beloved Disciple in the process. The Beloved Disciple and Peter are often found together in the latter chapters of John, and it has often been observed that John has apparently inserted the Beloved Disciple into traditions that did not originally contain references to that disciple. Following the majority of recent critical editions and translations, we will treat v. 12 as part of the text but recognize that its authenticity is far from certain.

Even if v. 12 is authentic, the similarity between it and John 20:3-10 is such that some interchange between the two passages in the textual tradition was inevitable. Given the best attested readings of v. 12, the parallels are:

Luke 24:12	John 20:3-10
But *Peter* got up	Then *Peter*
	and the other disciple set out
and ran to *the tomb*;	and went toward *the tomb*
	. . . . *He* [the Beloved Disciple]
stooping and looking in,	*bent down to look in*
he saw the linen cloths	*and saw the linen wrappings*
[παρακύψας βλέπει τὰ ὀθόνια	[παρακύψας βλέπει . . . τὰ ὀθόνια
parakypsas blepei ta othonia]	*parakypsas blepei ta othonia*]
by themselves;	lying there . . . and the cloth
	that had been on Jesus' head,
	. . . rolled up in a place by itself.
then he *went home,*	Then the disciples *returned to*
	their homes.
amazed at what had happened.	

From these parallels, it appears that John has embellished a tradition known to Luke by placing the Beloved Disciple with Peter at the empty tomb and attributing to the Beloved Disciple the honor of being the first to believe in the resurrection of Jesus (John 20:8).

The word used for the linen cloth(s) in v. 12 is ὀθόνη (othonē), whereas in 23:53 Luke used the term σινδών (sindōn). The difference is curious but probably not significant. The wrapping of bodies in strips of cloth, mummy style, was not practiced in Palestine in the first century, so in both verses the evident meaning is that the body had been wrapped in a linen cloth, or perhaps several linen cloths, and laid in the tomb. Peter saw only the cloth(s)—no body.

In Luke, Peter's amazement at the empty tomb serves to heighten the suspense. The tomb is empty, but the disciples do not believe the women's report. How, then, would they believe in the resurrection? Verse 12 makes it clear that the empty tomb alone did not lead to the Easter faith. Instead, faith was based on the post-resurrection appearances—personal encounters with the risen Lord, such as those that follow in the rest of the chapter.

REFLECTIONS

1. Repeatedly, we have seen how Luke represents the gospel in each episode or scene in the Gospel. If the whole is too big to wrap our minds around, Luke serves up miniatures, bite-sized chunks. It is no exaggeration, however, to claim that the discovery of the empty tomb is the heart of the matter for the Christian faith. Paul's words echo somewhere on the edge of our consciousness: "If Christ has not been raised, then our proclamation has been in vain and your faith has been in vain . . . we are of all people most to be pitied" (1 Cor 15:14, 19 NRSV). The NT never suggests that the death of Jesus would have been adequate for salvation apart from Jesus' resurrection. The two are fused so that neither can be considered apart from the other. It is not just that someone was raised from the dead but that God raised Jesus from the dead, and it is not just that someone was crucified but that the one who was crucified had proclaimed the kingdom and that his death was redemptive. The resurrection of Jesus is God's response to Jesus' death, God's vindication of Jesus, and God's validation of Jesus' preaching of the kingdom to the poor, the outcast, and the penitent. In Luke, the matter is expressed not just in twelve verses, but in five words in Greek: "He is not here; he is risen."

2. How often do we spend Easter looking for Jesus in the wrong places? The religious establishment shunted Jesus aside and thought it was safe to go on with religion as usual—services, sacrifices, debates over the law, and alms for the poor. No longer would they have to contend with those who looked forward to the coming of a kingdom whose rules for admission and the boundaries of whose fellowship they did not control. No longer would they have to debate what to do about a prophet who ate with tax collectors and rebuked those who gave fine dinners for their respectable friends. Jesus can never be confined to the traditional, the safe, and the predictable, however. Inherent in the expectation of a kingdom that has not yet come is the continual discovery of new aspects of what Jesus requires of those who follow him. The women were dutifully serving Jesus in the best way they knew. They had prepared spices to anoint his body and had gone to the tomb early to finish the burial, only to be met with the challenge, "Why do you look for the living among the dead?" In what ways do we continue to look for the living Lord among the dead? Jesus was not in the tomb. He would be found instead out among the grieving, among his disciples, and later in a Samaritan village and the households of a Gentile centurion and a Philippian jailer. "Why do you look for the living among the dead?"

3. Part of understanding the Easter event requires an enlightenment of memory: "Remember how he told you. . . . " In the crises of life, and whenever we lay a loved one in the grave, the loss can obliterate all the rest of life from our awareness and sever the connections between us and the past. Remembering God's presence in the past, therefore, can give us resources for dealing with the present. God had vindicated Jesus—remember Galilee. Remember what Jesus had done and what he had taught. Remember the meals in Jesus' fellowship, his healings and his parables, the bent woman and the ten lepers. Would you understand the meaning of the empty tomb? Remember Galilee.

4. In the midst of tending to the necessary chores, especially the things that need to be done in the hard times, the women were met by the unexpected experience of God's grace. Sometimes faith means going on and tending to the necessary chores. Prepare the spices, go to the tomb, tell the others, even when they think it an idle tale. Be faithful in the tasks that are ours and do the necessary tasks, for in them we, too, may be bearers of the good news of the day: "He is not here, but has risen!"

5. The defining conviction of the Christian hope is that because Jesus was raised from the dead the grave is not the final reality of human experience. The age-old question of the philosophers, "If a man dies, will he live again?" (Job 14:14 NIV), has now been answered. The tomb is empty. It is not surprising, therefore, that the empty-tomb account has often been the touchstone of debate over the validity of the Christian gospel. Rationalist interpretations were rejected from the very beginning: Jesus was really dead—he did not "swoon"; the women saw where he was laid—they did not go to the wrong tomb; in Matthew, a guard was posted at the tomb—no one moved the body; and in Luke and John some of the disciples confirmed the women's report.

Such apologetics raise the question, "Does our faith rest ultimately on the location of a stone or the position of a linen cloth?" The question is closely tied to the meaning of resurrection. When Jesus was raised, he did not return to normal human life. He did not live another thirty years and die again. He appeared and disappeared at will, moving in and out of human perception of his presence. Through the resurrection, Jesus moved into the existence of eternity, the life of the future, from which he would bring the kingdom to fulfillment and come again. What, then, are the tangible evidences of resurrection in our present experience? Do they consist in the physical remains of the tomb, or in Jesus' continuing presence in the lives of those who hope for his kingdom?

One way to reflect on the nature of the resurrection and the meaning of the empty tomb is to ask what we might see if Jesus' tomb had been equipped with a twentieth-century bank surveillance camera that weekend. Would the tape show Jesus waking up, taking off the wrappings, folding them and laying them to one side, pushing back the stone, and walking out of the tomb? Or would the image on the film have been obliterated by a flash of light from a great energy source, and then reveal the grave wrappings lying there limp and empty? Or perhaps there would be no blinding light, simply the disappearance of the body in a moment of time. If so, how and why was the stone moved aside? Was it to let Jesus out or to let the women in?

While the Gospels all affirm that the tomb was empty, they point beyond it to the post-resurrection appearances. For all the importance of the historical data, the Gospels ground our faith not on the stone and the linen cloths but on the presence of the risen Lord in human experience. Typically, it is not the persuasive power of the empty tomb but a personal encounter with the risen Lord that leads to faith. It was that way for Peter and Thomas and the other disciples and for Paul, and it is still that way. We make a pilgrimage in search of the empty tomb—whether literally or in memory—not in order to run a conclusive laboratory test on the evidence for the resurrection but because we have found it to be so in our own experience. As we reflect on the meaning of the empty tomb, therefore, we can hardly do better than to explore the meaning of the Easter declaration of the interpreting angels: "Why do you look for the living among the dead? He is not here, but has risen. Remember. . . . "

Luke 24:13-35, The Appearance on the Road to Emmaus

NIV

¹³Now that same day two of them were going to a village called Emmaus, about seven miles*a* from Jerusalem. ¹⁴They were talking with each other about everything that had happened. ¹⁵As they talked and discussed these things with each other, Jesus himself came up and walked along with them; ¹⁶but they were kept from recognizing him.

¹⁷He asked them, "What are you discussing together as you walk along?"

They stood still, their faces downcast. ¹⁸One of them, named Cleopas, asked him, "Are you only a visitor to Jerusalem and do not know the things that have happened there in these days?"

¹⁹"What things?" he asked.

"About Jesus of Nazareth," they replied. "He was a prophet, powerful in word and deed before God and all the people. ²⁰The chief priests and our rulers handed him over to be sentenced to death, and they crucified him; ²¹but we had hoped that he was the one who was going to redeem Israel. And what is more, it is the third day since all this took place. ²²In addition, some of our women amazed us. They went to the tomb early this morning ²³but didn't find his body. They came and told us that they had seen a vision of angels, who said he was alive. ²⁴Then some of our companions went to the tomb and found it just as the women had said, but him they did not see."

²⁵He said to them, "How foolish you are, and how slow of heart to believe all that the prophets have spoken! ²⁶Did not the Christ*b* have to suffer these things and then enter his glory?" ²⁷And beginning with Moses and all the Prophets, he explained to them what was said in all the Scriptures concerning himself.

²⁸As they approached the village to which they were going, Jesus acted as if he were going farther. ²⁹But they urged him strongly, "Stay with us, for it is nearly evening; the day is almost over." So he went in to stay with them.

³⁰When he was at the table with them, he took bread, gave thanks, broke it and began to give it to them. ³¹Then their eyes were opened and they

a13 Greek sixty stadia (about 11 kilometers)   b26 Or Messiah; also in verse 46

NRSV

13Now on that same day two of them were going to a village called Emmaus, about seven miles*a* from Jerusalem, ¹⁴and talking with each other about all these things that had happened. ¹⁵While they were talking and discussing, Jesus himself came near and went with them, ¹⁶but their eyes were kept from recognizing him. ¹⁷And he said to them, "What are you discussing with each other while you walk along?" They stood still, looking sad.*b* ¹⁸Then one of them, whose name was Cleopas, answered him, "Are you the only stranger in Jerusalem who does not know the things that have taken place there in these days?" ¹⁹He asked them, "What things?" They replied, "The things about Jesus of Nazareth,*c* who was a prophet mighty in deed and word before God and all the people, ²⁰and how our chief priests and leaders handed him over to be condemned to death and crucified him. ²¹But we had hoped that he was the one to redeem Israel.*d* Yes, and besides all this, it is now the third day since these things took place. ²²Moreover, some women of our group astounded us. They were at the tomb early this morning, ²³and when they did not find his body there, they came back and told us that they had indeed seen a vision of angels who said that he was alive. ²⁴Some of those who were with us went to the tomb and found it just as the women had said; but they did not see him." ²⁵Then he said to them, "Oh, how foolish you are, and how slow of heart to believe all that the prophets have declared! ²⁶Was it not necessary that the Messiah*e* should suffer these things and then enter into his glory?" ²⁷Then beginning with Moses and all the prophets, he interpreted to them the things about himself in all the scriptures.

28As they came near the village to which they were going, he walked ahead as if he were going on. ²⁹But they urged him strongly, saying, "Stay with us, because it is almost evening and the day is now nearly over." So he went in to stay with them. ³⁰When he was at the table with them, he

a Gk sixty stadia; other ancient authorities read a hundred sixty stadia
b Other ancient authorities read walk along, looking sad?"
c Other ancient authorities read Jesus the Nazorean   d Or to set Israel free   e Or the Christ

recognized him, and he disappeared from their sight. [32]They asked each other, "Were not our hearts burning within us while he talked with us on the road and opened the Scriptures to us?"

[33]They got up and returned at once to Jerusalem. There they found the Eleven and those with them, assembled together [34]and saying, "It is true! The Lord has risen and has appeared to Simon." [35]Then the two told what had happened on the way, and how Jesus was recognized by them when he broke the bread.

took bread, blessed and broke it, and gave it to them. [31]Then their eyes were opened, and they recognized him; and he vanished from their sight. [32]They said to each other, "Were not our hearts burning within us[a] while he was talking to us on the road, while he was opening the scriptures to us?" [33]That same hour they got up and returned to Jerusalem; and they found the eleven and their companions gathered together. [34]They were saying, "The Lord has risen indeed, and he has appeared to Simon!" [35]Then they told what had happened on the road, and how he had been made known to them in the breaking of the bread.

[a]Other ancient authorities lack *within us*

COMMENTARY

The story of the appearance to the two disciples on the road to Emmaus is arguably the most developed and the most beautiful of the appearance stories. Its plot revolves around the failure of the two disciples to recognize their fellow traveler. The suspense builds until the moment when the two recognize the risen Lord and he disappears from their presence. The origins of the story are debated and difficult to reconstruct, but the raw materials are easier to identify: (1) early tradition, such as may lie behind Mark 16:12-13, unless the longer ending of Mark draws upon Luke: "After this he appeared in another form to two of them, as they were walking into the country. And they went back and told the rest, but they did not believe them" (NRSV; other indicators of early tradition have been found in the names "Emmaus" and "Cleopas"); (2) the development of the kerygma (e.g., 1 Cor 15:3-5) into narrative: died, buried, raised, and appeared, "according to the scriptures"; (3) the story form of the OT theophanies and angelophanies, in which humans occasionally "entertained angels unawares" (Heb 13:2 RSV); (4) Lukan interests: Jesus as prophet, hope for the redemption of Israel, the fulfillment of Scripture, and the importance of table fellowship; and (5) a central theme: how people who have not seen the risen Lord can come to know him.

Three sites are candidates for the location of Emmaus. The best manuscript tradition says that Emmaus was located sixty stadia from Jerusalem.

A stadium was 600 Roman feet, so sixty stadia would be about 7.5 miles. Other manuscripts read 160 stadia, or 19.5 miles. The longer distance accords with the erroneous tradition of the pilgrims from the fourth century that identified the site as Emmaus-Nicopolis. Three alternative sites lie closer to Jerusalem (el-Qubeibeh, favored by the Crusaders, but there is no evidence that it existed in the first century; Abu Ghosh; and Qaloniyeh), but there is no consensus as to which if any of these was the site of Emmaus.[319]

Both the Greco-Roman literature and the OT contain stories of appearances to heroes, angels, or gods, sometimes incognito and sometimes to travelers. The tradition of entertaining "angels unawares" (Heb 13:2) derives from the experience of Abraham in Genesis 18, when the Lord visited him at the oaks of Mamre in the form of three travelers. In Exodus 3 the Lord speaks to Moses from a burning bush, but at first Moses does not know who is speaking to him. The form is more developed in Judges, where the angel of the Lord appears to Gideon (Judg 6:11-24), commissions Gideon, and Gideon brings food, which is then consumed by fire. When Gideon realizes that he has seen an angel, he is afraid that he will

319. James F. Strange, "Emmaus," *Anchor Bible Dictionary* (New York: Doubleday, 1992) 2:497-98; Joseph A. Fitzmyer, *The Gospel According to Luke (X–XXIV)*, AB 28A (Garden City, N.Y.: Doubleday, 1985) 1561-62.

die, but the angel reassures him. In Judges 13 the angel of the Lord appears to Manoah and announces the birth of Samson. Manoah and his wife offer to kill a kid and prepare a feast, but they are told to offer a sacrifice. When they do so, the angel ascends in the flame. Like Gideon, Manoah fears that he will die when he realizes that he has seen an angel. In the book of Tobit, Raphael appears to Tobias and accompanies him on his journey. In the end, Raphael identifies himself and tells Tobit and Tobias that all this time they were just seeing a vision; Raphael reminds them that they had not seen him eat anything (Tob 12:19). Raphael then announces that he is ascending, and when they look up he is gone. In each of these stories, an angel appears. Often the angel is not recognized immediately, a promise or commissioning is given, sometimes eating and drinking are mentioned or are conspicuously absent, and when the identity of the one who has appeared is known, the humans express fear, awe, or reverence.

Similarly, in Greco-Roman accounts appearances of supernatural beings occasionally involve travelers. Plutarch records that a colonist from Alba, Julius Proculus, swore that "as he was travelling on the road, he had seen Romulus coming to meet him, fair and stately to the eye as never before," and that Romulus told him that the gods had allowed him to return to found "a city destined to be the greatest on earth for empire and glory" and then to return to heaven. Plutarch comments that the story is similar to the fables the Greeks tell about Aristeas, for after his death "certain travellers returning from abroad said they had met Aristeas journeying towards Croton."[320] Diogenes Laertius tells the story of how Empedocles disappeared after a feast, and someone said they had heard a voice from heaven calling Empedocles and then saw a light in the heavens.[321] Gentile Christians who knew both the Scriptures and the legends of their cultures, therefore, would readily recognize the genre and repertoire of the Emmaus story.

When the Lord appears to Thomas in the Gospel of John, he pronounces a final beatitude on all who would believe without having seen. Luke addresses a similar issue: How, especially in view of the ascension that he will report, can later believers experience the presence of the risen Lord? Would it not have been far better to have been among the first witnesses who actually saw him? The Emmaus story responds by showing that the presence of the Lord is known in experiences that transcend the events of the resurrection appearances. Fitzmyer divides the story into four parts: (1) the meeting (vv. 13-16), (2) the conversation in route (vv. 17-27), (3) the Emmaus meal (vv. 28-32), and (4) the return to Jerusalem (vv. 33-35).[322]

24:13-16, The Meeting. The opening words shift the scene from Peter, who had gone home amazed at what he had seen, to two others, who were apparently also returning home after having traveled to Jerusalem for Passover. Verses 13-16 are all initial exposition by the narrator, setting the time and place and introducing the characters and the plot complication. The dialogue does not begin until v. 17. Luke reports that it is "the same day." Indeed, all of Luke 24 takes place on the same day, the first day of the week, even though it stretches the limits of credulity by having the two disciples travel to Emmaus and back (certainly not 20 miles each way!), and then experience another appearance and meal scene with the risen Lord before going out to the Mount of Olives (at night?), where the Lord departs from them, and the disciples return to Jerusalem. The two are not identified in v. 13 beyond the connection of the pronoun in the phrase "of them" with the reference to the apostles in v. 10. Later we will learn that one of them is named Cleopas (v. 18) and that they knew "the eleven and their companions" (v. 33). We may presume, therefore, that the two were among the extended group of Jesus' followers in Jerusalem (cf. Luke 23:49; Acts 1:15, 21-22).

The proposed sites for Emmaus lie along a road that runs generally northwest from Jerusalem. As they walked, they were discussing "all these things that had happened" (v. 14). With this phrase Luke recalls the events of the passion narrative to this point. The plot complication is introduced in vv. 15-16 along with a hint of irony. Not only are the eyes of the two kept from recognizing Jesus (prevented by God, as may be suggested by the passive voice?), but also they are discussing the things that had happened to Jesus when Jesus himself approaches them. The report

320. Plutarch, *Romulus,* 28.1-4, in Bernadotte Perrin, trans., *Plutarch's Lives,* LCL (Cambridge, Mass.: Harvard University Press, 1914) 1:177-79.

321. Diogenes Laertuis *Lives of Eminent Philosophers* 8.67-68.

322. Fitzmyer, *The Gospel According to Luke (X–XXIV),* 1559.

that they do not recognize him raises the question of when and how the disciples will recognize Jesus (cf. Tob 5:4). It also establishes the basis for the irony in the ensuing conversation because now the reader knows something that the two travelers do not know. The verb translated "to recognize" or "to perceive" (ἐπιγινώσκω *epiginōskō*) is one Luke uses frequently (1:4, 22; 5:22; 7:37; 23:7), and its use here will be balanced by the report in v. 31 that the disciples' eyes were opened and they recognized him.

24:17-27, The Conversation En Route. Jesus initiates the conversation by asking the two what they have been talking about as they walked. The question is a picturesque one: literally, "What are these words that you have been pitching back and forth to each other?" Jesus' question stops them in their tracks, and they stand looking sad, downcast, or gloomy (the same term is used in Matt 6:16 [σκυθρωπός *skythrōpos*]).

24:18. The narrator provides further information by reporting that one of the disciples was named Cleopas. Providing the name adds authority and credibility to the story. The name is close to the Clopas of John 19:25, but there is no basis for identifying the two as the same person. Cleopas responds with a question that can be read variously:

"Are you the only stranger in Jerusalem who does not know . . . ?" (NRSV)

"Are you only a visitor to Jerusalem and do not know . . . ?" (NIV)

"Are you sojourning alone in Jerusalem and have not learned . . . ?"[323]

The reference to the things that have taken place again recalls the events of the passion narrative (cf. "all these things that had happened" in v. 14).

The irony is that whereas the question assumes Jesus is the only one who does not know of these earth-shattering events, he is the only one who does know the meaning of all that has happened. In classical irony the ignorance of the "know it all" character (ἀλαζών *alazōn*) is exposed by the character who feigns ignorance (εἴρων *eirōn*).[324] The two disciples assume they know much more about what has happened than does the stranger who has joined them. Jesus plays the *eirōn*: "What things?" (ποῖα; *poia?*).

323. Fitzmyer suggests this as a literal translation. See ibid., 2:1564.
324. Aristotle *Nicomachean Ethics* 4.7.

24:19-24. Jesus' short response (which is only one word in Greek) is followed by a response that stretches across six verses (112 words in Greek) that summarize the events that have transpired and reveal that the two disciples do not understand what has occurred. Just as Luke's account of the trial and death of Jesus was tightly focused on christological issues, so also is Cleopas's summary of these events. In effect, he responds with a christological confession and a summary of the Lukan passion narrative, each element of which is revealing. Cleopas calls Jesus "the Nazarene" (as in 4:34), which is usually translated "of Nazareth." He was (literally) "a man, a prophet mighty in work and word." Jesus' identity as a prophet, but one greater than the prophets, was the theme of much of Luke 7. The confession of Jesus as prophet also evokes earlier confessions (7:16; 9:8, 19) and self-references (4:24; 13:33). For Luke the confession "prophet" is correct but not as high a confession as Christ, Lord, Son of Man, or Son of God. Moses was "powerful in his words and deeds" (Acts 7:22), and Apollos was (literally) "powerful in the scriptures" (Acts 18:24). The preposition "before" or "in the presence of" (ἐναντίον *enantion*) appears three times in the Gospel: Zechariah and Elizabeth were "righteous [δίκαιοι *dikaioi*] before God" (1:6), the scribes and chief priests were not able to trap Jesus in his words "in the presence of the people" (20:26), and now Jesus is confessed as mighty in deed and word "before God and all the people."

Verse 19 is the last reference to "the people" (ὁ λαός *ho laos*) in Luke. Overlooking their temporary complicity in calling for Jesus' crucifixion (23:18-21), Cleopas's summary of the preceding events characterizes the response of "the people" as a positive one in contrast to the role of "the chief priests and leaders" who handed Jesus over to be crucified. Luke has ensured that Cleopas's report of the events accurately summarizes the passion narrative. The role of the chief priests in the death of Jesus is forecast in Luke 9:22 and detailed in Luke 19:47; 20:1, 19; 22:2, 4, 50, 52, 54, 66; 23:4, 10, 13. Similarly, the leaders are associated with the chief priests in 23:13 and distinguished from the people in 23:35 (cf. 19:47; 20:1). Along with the chief priests, Luke has mentioned the scribes, the elders, and the "first ones." Here "the leaders" is an inclusive reference to the groups named earlier. Their role was to hand Jesus over (cf. v. 7) to Pilate and press him for Jesus' condemnation (see 23:1-2, 13-25). Although, strictly speaking, the Romans crucified Jesus, Luke has Cleopas lay the blame for it at the feet of the chief priests and leaders (see 23:25-26).

Verse 20 completes the report of Jesus' trial and death. Cleopas turns next to the response of the disciples and the report of the women. Jesus had kindled hope in the disciples. At the birth of John the Baptist, Zechariah prophesied that the Lord God of Israel had "looked favorably on his people and redeemed them" (1:68). Simeon had spent his life "looking forward to the consolation of Israel" (2:25), and Anna was a witness "to all who were looking for the redemption of Jerusalem" (2:38). By speaking of Jesus as the hoped-for Redeemer of Israel, Cleopas echoes the words of Isaiah (41:14; 43:14). They had hoped that the promises of the Scriptures were about to be fulfilled (a point that will be important in vv. 26-27, 32, 44-47). Again, Cleopas is a victim of irony; they had hoped that Jesus would fulfill the Scriptures, but they saw his death—which was indeed the fulfillment—as only the frustration of their hope. The reference to "the third day" resonates with the passion predictions in 9:22; 18:33; and 24:7 (cf. 24:46). No Christian reader would miss the irony of Cleopas's lament that it was now "the third day"—the day that Christians would forever celebrate with joy.

Cleopas summarizes the discovery of the empty tomb (vv. 1-2) in vv. 22-24. "Some women" appropriately refers to the women in the open-ended list in v. 10. The time of their visit to the tomb corresponds with the temporal reference in v. 1 (ὄρθρου βαθέως orthrou batheōs, v. 1; ὀρθριναί orthrinai, v. 22). The report that they did not find the body repeats the account of v. 3 verbatim. The appearance of the interpreting angels, however, is recast as an item of lesser credibility. In accord with the earlier report that the women's words "seemed to them an idle tale" (v. 11), instead of saying that the women did not find the body but saw two angels who told them that Jesus had been raised, Cleopas reports that the women came back and said that they had seen a vision of angels who said that he was alive. Earlier the word "vision" (ὀπτασία optasia) had not been used (see v. 4), nor were the two explicitly called "angels." Verse 24 reports that some of the disciples had gone to the tomb to verify the women's report.[325] Cleopas concludes his report with an emphatic statement, "But him they did not see." The failure to see the risen Lord created confusion regarding the meaning of the empty tomb. Again there is irony: The two were confused because Peter had not seen Jesus, but now they have seen the risen Lord and still they do not understand.

24:25-27. Jesus brings the sad irony to an end and begins the process of revealing himself and the meaning of the resurrection to the disciples. The revelation of the Easter reality begins with the fulfillment of the Scriptures, just as the Gospel opened with emphasis on this theme in the first chapter. Those who do not see this fulfillment are "foolish" and "slow of heart to believe" (v. 25). Luke's fondness for the encompassing "all" is evident again in "all that the prophets have declared" (v. 25) and "all the prophets" (v. 27; cf. 11:50; 13:28).

The suffering of the Messiah was necessary in God's providential plan for the redemption of Israel and the salvation of sinners. It was necessary that Jesus be about his Father's business (2:49), and for the kingdom of God to be preached (4:43). It was necessary to set the crippled woman free from her bondage (13:16) and for Jesus to stay with Zacchaeus (19:5). Above all, it was necessary for Jesus to go to Jerusalem (13:33) and there to suffer and die (9:22; 17:25). It was necessary that the Scriptures be fulfilled in Jesus (22:37; 24:44). The fulfillment, however, consisted not only in Jesus' suffering but also in his entering "into his glory" (v. 26). One may understand either the resurrection or the ascension as Jesus' entry into his glory. The other evangelists did not separate the two. John treats the cross as already part of Jesus' exaltation (but see John 20:17). Luke separates the ascension from the resurrection, but the ascension may simply make clear and visible what is already implicit in the resurrection of Jesus. The language of entering into his glory is anticipated by earlier references to Jesus' "exodus" (9:31), the revelation of Jesus' glory in the transfiguration (9:32), and the penitent thief's antici-

---

325. If v. 12 is accepted (see Commentary on v. 12), v. 24 summarizes Peter's visit to the tomb. If v. 12 is not authentic, then v. 24 is the only part of Cleopas's story that has no antecedent earlier in Luke. This point alone would argue for the inclusion of v. 12. The only difference is that v. 24 is plural and anonymous, whereas v. 12 names Peter as the one who ran to the tomb. Interestingly, John reports that two of the disciples went to the tomb (Peter and the Beloved Disciple).

pation of Jesus' entry into his kingdom (23:42). The glory of the Lord shone at Jesus' birth (2:9, 14). The Son of Man will come in glory (9:26; 21:27). The disciples had chanted "glory in the highest" while Jesus rode into Jerusalem (19:38). Now, their hopes were being fulfilled even beyond what they knew to hope for.

Just as Luke introduced the conversation on the road to Emmaus with a summary reference to the conversation between the two disciples before Jesus joined them, so also he brings it to a close by shifting from dialogue to a summary of the rest of the conversation. The summary continues the emphasis on the importance of the fulfillment of Scripture in all that had happened. "Moses and all the prophets" (cf. 16:29, 31) designates the Scriptures at that time without entering into debate about which books were scriptural and which were not. In v. 44 the psalms are included. At the transfiguration, Moses and Elijah (the prophet) appeared to Jesus in his glory (9:30) and spoke of his departure; now the risen Lord appears and explains how his suffering and entry into glory fulfilled Moses and the prophets (cf. Acts 17:2-3). The suffering servant passages in Isaiah (e.g., 52:13–53:12) were mined repeatedly by the church for scriptural warrant for the suffering of Jesus. The christological interpretation of the OT, as practiced by the early church, therefore, is authorized by the risen Lord himself. Those who do not accept the proclamation of the gospel, consequently, are foolish and "slow of heart to believe." Christ is the fulfillment to which all Scripture points.

24:28-32, The Meal at Emmaus. The meal scene at Emmaus is one of the most evocative of the Gospel scenes. It is the *anagnorisis*—the recognition scene in classical drama. The *anagnorisis* often involves recognition of someone to whose identity one was previously blind. Aristotle—whose works are the foundation for poetics, rhetoric, and literary theory—wrote that "recognition is, as its name indicates, a change from ignorance to knowledge, tending either to affection or to enmity; it determines in the direction of good or ill fortune the fates of the people involved." Recognition may be based on visible signs, memory, or reasoning, but the best kind is "that which arises from the actions alone."[326]

326. Aristotle *Poetics* 1452a, 1454b-55a, in D. A. Russell and M. Winterbottom, eds., *Ancient Literary Criticism: The Principal Texts in New Translations* (Oxford: Clarendon Press, 1972).

Aristotle would have been pleased with the recognition scene of the Emmaus story.

Narration dominates. Having summarized the risen Lord's discourse in vv. 25-27, the narrator guides the reader through this scene, yielding the floor to the characters only in vv. 29 and 32. In these verses the two disciples speak, but no further words of the risen Lord are reported. At most, we are told that he blessed the bread. The scene is almost a mime, therefore, in which the unknown fellow traveler is recognized by his actions.

24:28. Jesus' first action is probably significant both thematically and theologically. He "walked ahead as if he were going on." On the surface it is a gesture of social deference and polish. It implies that Jesus was not really going further but that he would not impose on the disciples to offer him hospitality. In Near Eastern customs, the guest was obligated to turn down such an invitation until it was vigorously repeated (see Gen 19:2-3). Theologically, Jesus' action demonstrates that he never forces himself upon others. Faith must always be a spontaneous, voluntary response to God's grace. Thematically, the action is suggestive, because all the way through the Gospel Jesus has been going further. When the people at Nazareth rejected him, Jesus "passed through the midst of them and went on his way" (4:30). When the crowds wanted to prevent Jesus from leaving them, he responded, "I must proclaim the good news of the kingdom of God to the other cities also" (4:43). He preached in synagogues and withdrew to desert places to pray (4:44; 5:16). In Galilee he was constantly on the move, and from Luke 9:51 until 19:44 he is on the way to Jerusalem. The Lukan Jesus, therefore, was always going further, and in the book of Acts the gospel of Jesus will spread "to the ends of the earth."

24:29. It is evening by the time they reach their destination, so the two urge Jesus to stay with them (cf. Judg 19:9). Thus Jesus was modeling the kind of ministry to a household in which he had instructed his disciples (see 10:7, "Remain in the same house, eating and drinking whatever they provide"; cf. 9:4). Just as earlier Jesus had received hospitality from Zacchaeus, so also now he accepts the hospitality of the two with whom he had traveled; the Savior had come to another house (cf. 19:5, 9).

24:30-32. Immediately the scene shifts to the table for the evening meal. Christian readers may be reminded of Rev 3:20, "Listen! I am standing at the door, knocking; if you hear my voice and open the door, I will come in to you and eat with you, and you with me." The meal is not mentioned in Mark 16:12-13, but Mark 16:14 reports an appearance to the eleven "as they were sitting at the table," which may be a conflation of the Emmaus meal and the subsequent appearance to the eleven (cf. Luke 24:33, 36, 41-43). In the later scene in Luke, Jesus' eating has an apologetic purpose, but at Emmaus Jesus' actions recall the pattern of earlier meal scenes. The guest becomes the host. Jesus takes the bread, blesses it, breaks it, and gives it to them. The four verbs are Jesus' signature, which the disciples (or at least the readers) may remember from the feeding of the five thousand (9:16) and the last supper (22:19).

The liturgical language reports the action by which the *anagnorisis* occurred; it does not mean that Jesus celebrated the eucharist in Emmaus but that every meal has the potential of being an event in which hospitality and table fellowship can become sacred occasions. The eucharistic language further implies that the church experiences the continuing presence of the risen Lord when it gathers at the Lord's table. The two had not recognized the risen Lord when he appeared to them, but at the table they saw who he was. Later believers may not have the opportunity to experience an appearance, but they can see him clearly in Moses and the prophets and know that he is present when they share their bread with a stranger or gather for the Lord's supper. The appearance experience, therefore, is no spiritual Camelot locked in the past but a sign of the ways in which the risen Lord continues to be present with his disciples.[327]

The *anagnorisis* is reported as the opening of the two disciples' eyes. This motif is also present in the OT, where the Lord opens the eyes of Elisha's servant to see the horses and chariots surrounding the prophet (2 Kgs 6:17, 20). Earlier Luke said that "their eyes were kept from recognizing him" (v. 16). Now, "their eyes were opened, and they recognized him" (v. 31), resolving the plot and closing the gap opened by the narrator in v. 16. Immediately, Jesus vanishes from their sight. Luke plays on the verbs "to interpret" (διερμηνεύω *diermēneuō*) and "to

open" (διανοίγω *dianoigō*). Jesus opened the Scriptures (vv. 27, 32; cf. Acts 17:3), he opened their eyes (v. 31), and later he will open their minds (v. 45). This is the heart of Luke's hermeneutics: "After investigating everything carefully from the very first" (1:3), Luke has found that he recognizes "the truth concerning the things about which you have been instructed" when memory of the actions and teachings of Jesus' ministry is enlightened by the Scriptures and reenacted in the hospitality and table fellowship of the community of believers. Although Luke never formulates his hermeneutic as clearly as John does, the two are again strikingly similar:

> "After he was raised from the dead, his disciples remembered that he had said this; and they believed the scripture and the word that Jesus had spoken." (John 2:22 NRSV)

> "His disciples did not understand these things at first; but when Jesus was glorified, then they remembered that these things had been written of him and had been done to him." (John 12:16 NRSV; cf. 20:9)

No sooner do the disciples recognize the Lord than he vanishes from them (cf. Judg 6:21; 2 Macc 3:34; Tob 12:21; Acts 1:9; 8:39). The scene ends with the disciples recalling how their hearts "burned" within them while Jesus was talking with them and interpreting the Scriptures to them. The Emmaus story, therefore, sets before the reader two sorts of responses: One may either be "slow of heart to believe" (v. 25) or know the joy of those whose hearts burn within them. The burning hearts were the result of both Jesus' words and the interpretation of Scripture (see v. 32). Earlier, Jesus had said that he had come to bring fire to the earth (12:49-50); now the fire has been kindled (cf. Jer 20:9; Acts 2:3).

24:33-35, The Return to Jerusalem. The final movement of the Emmaus story returns the two disciples to Jerusalem and serves as a transition to the appearance there. Jerusalem is the focus of Luke's geographical scheme throughout Luke and Acts. The Gospel begins and ends in Jerusalem, and the journey to Jerusalem dominates the record of Jesus' ministry. In Acts the mission of the church begins in Jerusalem, and Paul returns there at regular intervals.

The disciples set out immediately, that very hour, even though by Luke's reckoning the day

---

327. See Fred B. Craddock, *Luke,* Interpretation (Louisville: Westminster/John Knox, 1990) 287.

was nearly over when they arrived in Emmaus (see v. 29). By means of this temporal notice, all of the appearances recorded in Luke 24 will occur on the first day of the week—the day early Christians met for worship. The noting of departures and returns is part of Luke's "orderly account" (cf. 23:48, 56; 24:9, 52). Whereas Luke devotes vv. 13-28 to the journey to Emmaus, the return journey is reported in half a verse.

When the two arrive in Jerusalem, they find "the eleven and their companions" (cf. v. 9) gathered together. Before they can relate the appearance on the road to Emmaus, however, the others tell them, "The Lord has risen [ἠγέρθη *egerthē*] indeed, and he has appeared [ὤφθη *ōphthē*] to Simon" (v. 34). The language is formal and liturgical, echoing 1 Cor 15:4, "and that he was raised [ἐγήγερται *egēgertai*] on the third day in accordance with the scriptures, and that he appeared [*ōphthē*] to Cephas, then to the twelve" (NRSV). The parallel is further evidence of the influence of the early kerygma in the formation of the appearance narratives. "Cephas" never occurs in Luke or Acts. Luke has used the name "Simon" earlier in 4:38; 5:1-10; 6:14; and 22:31. Its use here is usually attributed to pre-Lukan tradition. By means of the device of having the eleven report the appearance to Simon Peter before the two tell of their experience, Luke preserves the tradition that the first appearance was to Peter (cf. Mark 16:7; 1 Cor 15:5). However, the NT contains no account of this appearance. The closest thing to an account of an appearance to Peter is the Johannine account of the miraculous catch of fish and the reconciliation and commissioning of Peter, which followed (John 21:1-19). Luke either knew of no such account or has transposed it into the call of Peter to discipleship in Luke 5:1-10—possibly because the appearance took place in Galilee (following Mark, Matthew, and John 21), and Luke has no place in his geographical scheme for an appearance in Galilee. The report of the appearance to Peter also authorizes his role as the leader of the apostles early in Acts and prepares for the appearance to the eleven that follows (cf. Matt 28:16-20; John 20:19-29; 1 Cor 15:4-5).

Only after they hear of the appearance to Peter do the two get a chance to share their experience of "what happened on the road" (i.e., the opening of the Scriptures; vv. 27, 32) and "how he had been made known to them in the breaking of the bread." The latter phrase comes to designate the church's fellowship meal and the observance of the Lord's Supper in Acts 2:42. The Lord's Supper was probably originally celebrated in the context of a fellowship meal, as 1 Cor 11:17-26 implies. Verse 35, therefore, neatly provides closure by recapping the two main parts of the Emmaus story (the conversation and the meal) and reiterating its main theme: The risen Lord was made known to them in the interpretation of Scripture and "the breaking of the bread."

REFLECTIONS

The Emmaus story is so full of wonderful material for theological reflection, preaching, and discussion that the natural temptation is to try to deal with too much at one time. By a strange axiom of perception, one fresh insight well developed always seems more significant than a list of ten or twelve possible meanings, however perceptive or relevant they may be. The Emmaus story, therefore, is a rich mine to which one should return again and again, bringing out one cartload of ore at a time.

Although this text should not be read only at Easter each year, it is obviously relevant to that season. Each year at Easter we face the same question: how to approach the meaning of the Easter experience. It is at once more than we can comprehend and so familiar that we constantly search for a new angle of vision. We may well find ourselves in the position of the travelers at the opening of the story, discussing these things as we walk, trying to discern the meaning of what has happened in the Gospel story and in our own experience. Is there any persuasive reason to believe that Jesus really was raised from the dead or that God is present in the turbulence of our lives?

1. Emmaus was a little-noted town. Luke doesn't say why the two disciples were going there.

They may have been going home, going there on business, or just going there to get away from the terrible things they had witnessed in Jerusalem. Frederick Buechner interprets Emmaus as

> the place we go to in order to escape—a bar, a movie, wherever it is we throw up our hands and say, "Let the whole damned thing go hang. It makes no difference anyway." . . . Emmaus may be buying a new suit or a new car or smoking more cigarettes than you really want, or reading a second-rate novel or even writing one. Emmaus may be going to church on Sunday. Emmaus is whatever we do or wherever we go to make ourselves forget that the world holds nothing sacred: that even the wisest and bravest and loveliest decay and die; that even the noblest ideas that men have had—ideas about love and freedom and justice—have always in time been twisted out of shape by selfish men for selfish ends.[328]

The risen Lord meets us on the road to our Emmauses, in the ordinary places and experiences of our lives, and in the places to which we retreat when life is too much for us. The story warns us, however, that the Lord may come to us in unfamiliar guises, when we least expect him.

2. Cleopas and his companion discovered at the table that their traveling companion was the Lord himself. They had not planned it as a sacred moment, but in the act of sharing their bread with a stranger they recognized the risen Lord in the fellow traveler. In a fascinating way, the Emmaus story is the counterpart to the parable of the rich man and Lazarus. In that parable, the rich man feasts daily but never notices the beggar at his gate or shares his bread with him. From Hades he pleads with Abraham to send Lazarus back to warn his brothers, but Abraham responds, "They have Moses and the prophets," and when the rich man persists, Abraham's final word is, "If they do not listen to Moses and the prophets, neither will they be convinced even if someone rises from the dead" (16:31). Here again is a story that involves Moses and the prophets and resurrection from the dead, and a story that pivots at the table. The difference between them is what happens at the table. Cleopas and his companion share their table with a stranger and discover that they have been in the presence of the Lord. The rich man took no notice of the beggar until he was in torment in Hades. Fantasize for a moment. What might the rich man have discovered if he had shared his bread with Lazarus?[329]

3. One of the tantalizing elements of the story is the report that as soon as the two disciples recognized the risen Lord he disappeared from their sight. God's presence is always elusive, fleeting, dancing at the edge of our awareness and perception. If we are honest, we must confess that it is never constant, steady, or predictable. The nuns in *The Sound of Music* sing, "How can you catch a moonbeam in your hand, how do you hold a wave upon the sand?" The mystery of transcendence is always transitory. God's faithful perceive God's presence in fleeting moments, and then the mundane closes in again.

For this reason, we learn to treasure religious experiences in retrospect. The two in Emmaus exclaim, "Did not our hearts burn within us?" Like Moses, we usually see only the back side of God as God passes by us (Exod 33:23). With Job we confess, "Look, he passes by me, and I do not see him;/ he moves on, but I do not perceive him" (Job 9:11 NRSV). One of the secrets of a vigorous spirituality and a confident faith, therefore, is learning to appreciate the importance of meeting God in the past as well as in the present. Luke guides us in this spiritual discipline: "Remember how he told you, while he was still in Galilee. . . . Then they remembered his words" (24:6, 8).

4. The experience of the presence of God is not a private gift. It is never for us alone. Neither in the discovery of the empty tomb nor in the discovery of the identity of the fellow traveler is there the familiar command to go and tell that is typical of other resurrection appearance scenes. Nevertheless, in both the recipients of the revelation immediately and

---

328. Frederick Buechner, *The Magnificent Defeat* (New York: Seabury, 1966) 85-86.
329. This line of interpretation derives from Eugene S. Wehrli, "Luke 16:19-31," *Int.* 31 (1977) 280.

spontaneously return from the liminal tomb and table to share their experience joyfully with others: "He is risen" (v. 5); "He is alive" (v. 23); "The Lord has risen indeed" (vv. 34-35). These words may seem an idle tale to others, but to those who have witnessed God's transcendent presence in their lives at a tomb, on a lonely road, or in hospitality extended to a fellow traveler, they are a transforming reality.

5. Easter is not over at sundown Easter Sunday. It stretches into the rest of our lives. The women could not call back the angels, and the two disciples might never meet the stranger again, but it would not matter. Life would never again be the same. Luke's Gospel sparkles with theological insight when it stretches Easter day into the series of experiences that happened thereafter. All the rest of the story will be an extension of the Easter reality: The Lord is risen and he comes back to meet us on the road to Emmaus. Through the study of Scripture, we find our hearts "strangely warmed,"[330] and we recognize him in "the breaking of the bread." How can we not go and tell?

---

330. The phrase comes from John Wesley's account of his conversion while he listened to a reading of Luther's preface to the *Commentary on Romans*. See Williston Walker, *A History of the Christian Church*, rev. ed. (New York: Charles Scribner's Sons, 1959) 459.

Luke 24:36-53, The Appearance to the Eleven, Commissioning of the Disciples, and Jesus' Departure

NIV

36While they were still talking about this, Jesus himself stood among them and said to them, "Peace be with you."

37They were startled and frightened, thinking they saw a ghost. 38He said to them, "Why are you troubled, and why do doubts rise in your minds? 39Look at my hands and my feet. It is I myself! Touch me and see; a ghost does not have flesh and bones, as you see I have."

40When he had said this, he showed them his hands and feet. 41And while they still did not believe it because of joy and amazement, he asked them, "Do you have anything here to eat?" 42They gave him a piece of broiled fish, 43and he took it and ate it in their presence.

44He said to them, "This is what I told you while I was still with you: Everything must be fulfilled that is written about me in the Law of Moses, the Prophets and the Psalms."

45Then he opened their minds so they could understand the Scriptures. 46He told them, "This is what is written: The Christ will suffer and rise from the dead on the third day, 47and repentance and forgiveness of sins will be preached in his name to all nations, beginning at Jerusalem. 48You are witnesses of these things. 49I am going to send you what my Father has promised; but stay

NRSV

36While they were talking about this, Jesus himself stood among them and said to them, "Peace be with you."[a] 37They were startled and terrified, and thought that they were seeing a ghost. 38He said to them, "Why are you frightened, and why do doubts arise in your hearts? 39Look at my hands and my feet; see that it is I myself. Touch me and see; for a ghost does not have flesh and bones as you see that I have." 40And when he had said this, he showed them his hands and his feet.[b] 41While in their joy they were disbelieving and still wondering, he said to them, "Have you anything here to eat?" 42They gave him a piece of broiled fish, 43and he took it and ate in their presence.

44Then he said to them, "These are my words that I spoke to you while I was still with you—that everything written about me in the law of Moses, the prophets, and the psalms must be fulfilled." 45Then he opened their minds to understand the scriptures, 46and he said to them, "Thus it is written, that the Messiah[c] is to suffer and to rise from the dead on the third day, 47and that repentance and forgiveness of sins is to be proclaimed in his name to all nations, beginning from

---

*a*Other ancient authorities lack *and said to them, "Peace be with you."* *b*Other ancient authorities lack verse 40 *c*Or *the Christ*

NIV

in the city until you have been clothed with power from on high."

⁵⁰When he had led them out to the vicinity of Bethany, he lifted up his hands and blessed them. ⁵¹While he was blessing them, he left them and was taken up into heaven. ⁵²Then they worshiped him and returned to Jerusalem with great joy. ⁵³And they stayed continually at the temple, praising God.

NRSV

Jerusalem. ⁴⁸You are witnesses*a* of these things. ⁴⁹And see, I am sending upon you what my Father promised; so stay here in the city until you have been clothed with power from on high."

50Then he led them out as far as Bethany, and, lifting up his hands, he blessed them. ⁵¹While he was blessing them, he withdrew from them and was carried up into heaven.*b* ⁵²And they worshiped him, and*c* returned to Jerusalem with great joy; ⁵³and they were continually in the temple blessing God.*d*

*a*Or *nations. Beginning from Jerusalem* ⁴⁸*you are witnesses*
*b*Other ancient authorities lack *and was carried up into heaven*
*c*Other ancient authorities lack *worshiped him, and*
*d*Other ancient authorities add *Amen*

COMMENTARY

Just as the kerygmatic tradition known to Paul reported an appearance to Peter followed by an appearance to the eleven, so also Luke follows the report of the appearance to Simon Peter (v. 34) with an appearance to the whole group of the disciples (see v. 33). The account of this appearance falls easily into three parts: (1) proofs of the resurrection (vv. 36-43); (2) interpretation of Scripture and the commissioning of the disciples (vv. 44-49); and (3) the departure of Jesus (vv. 50-53). Verses 36-53 form a unit, however, in that they record an appearance with its own plot and resolution, from appearance to departure. Appearances to the eleven are forecast in Mark 16:7 and reported in Matt 28:16-20 and John 20:19-29. As we shall note, Luke's account, while not found elsewhere, has distinct parallels with these other accounts, especially John 20:19-29.

The repetition of motifs found earlier in the Emmaus story invites close comparisons. Both stories feature an appearance in which there is a failure to recognize or believe, the interpretation of Scripture, eating, the opening of eyes or minds, and the departure of Jesus and return of the disciples. Distinctive in the appearance to the eleven are (1) the apologetic development of the doubt motif, (2) the physical proofs of the resurrection, (3) the commissioning of the disciples, and (4) the ascension of Jesus.

24:36-43, Proofs of the Resurrection. The plot complication for the story of the appearance to the two on the road to Emmaus was given in v. 16: "but their eyes were kept from recognizing him." The plot complication for the appearance to the eleven, in contrast, is the doubt and fear reported in vv. 37-38. The issue, therefore, is how the disciples will be led from fear and doubt to worship. The developments in the appearance story resolve this complication satisfactorily, while leaving the story open for its sequel in the book of Acts.

A number of parallels between Luke 24:36-43 and John 20:19-29 (and also John 21:1-14) suggest that both evangelists are independently developing material drawn from common early tradition. Among these parallels we may cite the following:

> Jesus "stood among them" and said "Peace be with you" (Luke 24:36; John 20:19);
> Jesus showed them his hands and feet (Luke) or his hands and side (John) and invited them (Luke) or Thomas (John) to touch him;
> the disciples (Luke) or Thomas (John) doubted;
> Jesus asked if they had anything to eat (Luke 24:41; John 21:5) and then ate fish (Luke 24:42; John 21:9, 12, 15);
> Jesus commissioned the disciples; and
> Jesus breathed the Holy Spirit into them (John) or promised that they would be "clothed with power from on high" (Luke).

Two of the parallels occur in Western non-interpolations (24:36*b*, 40), but even if these were omitted (following D) the remaining parallels are sufficient to establish some relationship between these appearance accounts. As numerous as these parallels are, however, each evangelist develops the appearance stories for his own purposes in the context of his own Gospel, and the redactional elements of each are missing in the other, pointing to the conclusion that they have both used early tradition rather than that one Gospel depends directly on the other.

24:36. The report that Jesus "stood" among them echoes the language of OT angelophanies (Gen 18:2; 1 Chr 21:15-16; Dan 8:15; 12:5; Tob 5:4; cf. Num 22:22-24; Luke 1:11; Acts 10:30).[331] Similarly, Jesus' greeting "Peace be with you," while it was the common Semitic greeting (שלום עליכם *šālôm ʿălêkem*), also follows the pattern of Jesus' instruction to speak "Peace" to whatever house one enters (10:5-6).

24:37-38. The disciples react in the manner typical of angelophanies: They were "startled and terrified" (cf. v. 5). Luke adds that they thought they were seeing a ghost or a spirit (cf. 1 Sam 28:13-14). By thinking that the risen Lord was a spirit, the disciples may have either misunderstood the nature of the resurrection or thought that a spirit (not Jesus) was deceiving them. Either way, the complication sets up the need to clarify the nature of the resurrection and confirm its reality. The disciples say nothing. The first part of Jesus' response further characterizes their reaction as fear and doubt. Like Zechariah, they were "frightened" (cf. 1:12). More important for the plot of the story, the question "Why do doubts arise in your hearts?" characterizes the response of unbelief elsewhere in Luke (5:22; cf. 2:35; 3:15; 9:47).

24:39-43. The doubt motif recurs in various appearance stories. Matthew says, "When they saw him, they worshiped him; but some doubted" (28:17 NRSV). John allows Thomas to characterize the response of doubt (20:24-29), and the longer ending of Mark develops the motif (Mark 16:11, 13-14). In the ensuing verses in Luke, Jesus offers two proofs: first, his hands and feet, and then he eats in front of them. Both actions verify that he is not an apparition but that he has indeed risen from the grave. The appearance in Matthew and the appearance to Paul in Acts may

be interpreted as visions or appearances of the heavenly Lord. The appearances in John are more physical; he tells Mary not to hold him and Thomas to touch him, then walks and eats with the disciples in John 21. The proofs in these verses, however, insist on the reality of the physical body of the risen Lord in a way not found in the other appearances, and perhaps for this reason Luke also includes the account of the ascension after a period of forty days of appearances (not found elsewhere in the NT) in order to remove the risen Lord and distinguish the appearances from the later experiences of the church in Acts.

The first proof is the invitation to examine his hands and feet. John 20:20, 25, and 27 speak of Jesus' hands and side, no doubt because John records the piercing of Jesus' side with a spear (John 19:34). There is no mention in Luke of the nail prints, as in John 20, and the account of the crucifixion in Luke 23 makes no mention of nails. One may either assume that nail prints are meant or understand that the risen Lord was inviting the disciples to examine those parts of his body that were not covered by his clothing, to verify that he was solid flesh and not an apparition.[332] The invitation to touch him recalls the invitation to Thomas (John 20:27) and 1 John 1:1, but neither here nor in John 20 does anyone touch him. Nevertheless, a spirit would not be substantial and tangible; it is not "flesh and bones" (v. 39). In 1 Corinthians 15, by contrast, Paul carefully avoids speaking of the "flesh" (σάρξ *sarx*) when describing the resurrected body (cf. 1 Cor 15:44).

Verse 40, although it is a Western non-interpolation, merely completes the thought of the preceding verses. It adds nothing new. The first proof is not sufficient. Even when Jesus showed them his hands and feet, "they still did not believe it because of joy and amazement" (v. 41). The narrator's comment here is reminiscent of the earlier comment that the disciples were "sleeping because of grief" (22:45).

The second proof is the confirmation that Jesus is not a spirit because he eats in front of them. The OT angelophanies record that Abraham ate with the angel of the Lord (Gen 18:8; 19:3). In Judges when food is presented to the angel it is consumed in fire and the angel disappears in the

---

331. See John Nolland, *Luke 18:35–24:53*, WBC 35C (Dallas: Word, 1993) 1212.

332. See ibid., 1213.

fire (Judg 6:19-21; 13:19-20), and in Tobit the fact that Tobias never sees Raguel eat or drink is offered as proof that what they had seen was a vision (Tob 12:19). Accordingly, the risen Lord's act of eating broiled fish is offered here as proof that he is not a spirit (v. 37). The reference to fish, especially following the reference to bread at the table in Emmaus, recalls the loaves and the fish at the feeding of the five thousand (9:10-17; cf. John 21:9). The meal here, however, serves an apologetic purpose, whereas earlier it had eucharistic overtones. In Luke 8:55, when Jesus raises the daughter of Jairus, he instructs her parents to give her something to eat. The verb used in Acts 1:4 means literally to "take salt with" or "to eat with," and Acts 10:41 distinguishes the eyewitnesses to the resurrection as those who "ate and drank with him after he rose from the dead." So significant is the apologetic interest of this scene that whereas in other accounts it is the appearance of the Lord that leads to faith, here it is the proofs that lead the disciples to believe.[333] Presumably, the proofs are intended to contribute further to the reader's "certainty of the things you have been taught" (1:4), but there is no report at this point that the disciples believed or worshiped him (see v. 52).

24:44-49, Interpretation of Scripture and the Commissioning of the Disciples. The second part of the appearance to the eleven and the others looks both backward and forward. It serves both to bring closure by recapping major themes of the Gospel and to set the stage for the coming of the Spirit and the work of the disciples as witnesses in the book of Acts. Verses 44-46 return to the theme of the necessity of Jesus' death and the fulfillment of Scripture, while in vv. 47-49 Jesus commissions the disciples, promises their empowerment from on high, and outlines the mission that lies ahead.

The fulfillment of Scripture is tied to the resurrection in the early kerygma (1 Cor 15:3-5), John's account of the discovery of the empty tomb (John 20:9), and less explicitly in the allusions to Daniel 7 and the Emmanuel theme in the Great Commission at the end of Matthew. Luke, however, emphasizes the fulfillment of Scripture in the resurrection appearances more than does any other NT writer. The theme has already surfaced in vv. 25-27

and 32. Now, in his last words to the disciples in the Gospel, Jesus returns to this central theme.

Whereas v. 26 emphasized the necessity of Jesus' death and resurrection, and v. 32 the power of Scripture to set hearts on fire, vv. 44-46 introduce a new set of perspectives on Scripture. First, the risen Lord reminds the disciples that he had told them these things while he was still with them. Note that this retrospective reference gives to the resurrection appearance an air of liminality; he has appeared to them, but he is no longer with them. The reader recalls the passion predictions (9:22, 44; 13:33; 17:25; 18:31-33). Of particular importance are Jesus' words in 18:31, "Everything that is written about the Son of Man by the prophets will be accomplished," and 22:37, "This scripture must be fulfilled in me, 'And he was counted among the lawless'; and indeed what is written about me is being fulfilled." In these references, the passion predictions are related to the fulfillment of Scripture. Luke uses the encompassing "all" that he is so fond of ("everything written about me") and lists not only Moses and the prophets (as in 16:29, 31; and 24:27), but also the Psalms, anticipating the three-part canon of the Hebrew Scriptures (the Torah, the Prophets, and the Writings). It was necessary, in God's providence, that the Scriptures be fulfilled in this way (see 24:7, 26). Indeed, Luke has devoted the entire Gospel to "the things that have been fulfilled among us" (1:1).

Earlier Luke reported that the risen Lord had "opened" the eyes of the two disciples in Emmaus (v. 31) and "opened" the Scriptures to them (v. 32). Now he uses the same verb (διανοίγω *dianoigō*) in v. 45: "Then he opened their minds to understand the scriptures." The message of the Scriptures is not self-evident; one's mind must be opened to it, and they are rightly understood only in the light of Jesus' death and resurrection.

In vv. 46-47, Luke gathers under the authority of Scripture not only the death and resurrection of Jesus (as in vv. 25-27) but also the mission to all nations. Luke does not cite specific passages for each item in these verses. If prooftexts are sought, one could cite the suffering servant passages in Isaiah for confirmation that the Messiah had to suffer (Isa 52:13–53:12), Hos 6:2 for the resurrection on the third day (see Commentary on 24:7), and Isa 49:6 for the preaching of repentance to all nations (cf. Luke 2:31-32; Acts 13:47). Beyond

---

333. See further Ignatius *Smyrnaeans* 3.1-3.

specific texts, however, the point is that all of these events should be understood as fulfilling Scripture—the record of God's redemptive acts.

The new element in this list is the preaching of repentance in Jesus' name to all the nations. A commissioning is a regular feature of the appearance accounts, and each evangelist has tailored the words of the commissioning to reflect the themes of his Gospel.[334] Paul related his call to be an "apostle to the Gentiles" to the Lord's appearance to him on the road to Damascus (Acts 22:21; 26:22-23; Gal 1:15-16). The commissionings in the various appearance scenes can easily be compared in the following list of passages.

"Go therefore and make disciples of all nations, baptizing them in the name of the Father and of the Son and of the Holy Spirit, and teaching them to obey everything that I have commanded you." (Matt 28:19-20 NRSV)

"As the Father has sent me, so I send you." (John 20:21 NRSV)

"Go into all the world and proclaim the good news to the whole creation." (Mark 16:15 NRSV)

"But you will receive power when the Holy Spirit has come upon you; and you will be my witnesses in Jerusalem, in all Judea and Samaria, and to the ends of the earth." (Acts 1:8 NRSV)

To these one might add the commissions given to Mary Magdalene (John 20:17) and to Peter (John 21:15-17; cf. Luke 5:10 and Matt 16:18-19, which some interpreters relate to the appearance scenes). Matthew emphasizes making disciples and keeping Jesus' teachings. The longer ending of Mark picks up the emphasis on preaching "the gospel" in Mark 1:15 and 13:10, and John uses the distinctive Johannine idiom of the Father sending the Son.

The mission of the church in Acts is tied to the fulfillment of Scripture, and it is a continuation of the same divine necessity that guided Jesus through his death and resurrection. John the Baptist had preached a baptism of repentance for the forgiveness of sins (3:3), and Jesus had preached good news to the captives (4:18) and the coming of the acceptable year of the Lord (4:19). He had preached the coming of the kingdom in their

synagogues (4:44; 8:1) and sent the disciples to do the same (9:2). Earlier in Luke, Jesus commissioned the disciples to act in the power of his name (9:48-49; 10:17; 21:8, 12, 17). Accordingly, in the book of Acts the apostles baptize "in the name of Jesus" (2:38; 8:16; 10:48; 19:5), heal (3:6; 4:10), teach (4:18; 5:28, 40), do signs and wonders (4:30), and suffer because of his name (5:41). In a distinct echo of Luke 24:47, Philip proclaims the good news of the kingdom of God in Jesus' name to the Samaritans (Acts 8:12). In the Gospel, Jesus continued John the Baptist's preaching of repentance and the forgiveness of sin (1:77; 3:3, 8; 5:32), and the disciples will continue this work in Acts (2:38; 5:31; 10:43; 11:18; 13:38; 20:21; 26:18-20).

The mission will begin in Jerusalem and extend to all nations (v. 47). Jerusalem has been the center and focus of the Gospel from its beginning. The annunciation of the birth of John occurred in Jerusalem, as did the presentation of Jesus in the Temple. Jesus tarried in Jerusalem while his family returned to Nazareth (2:41-51). Some of the crowds that followed Jesus came from Jerusalem (5:17; 6:17), and from the time that Jesus "sets his face" to go to Jerusalem (9:51, 53) it is the focus of his ministry to Israel, his cleansing of the Temple, and his death, resurrection, and appearances. A prophet could not perish outside of Jerusalem (13:34-34), and Jesus wept over the city when he saw it (19:41-44). The commission given the disciples in Acts 1:8 repeats the mandate that the mission begin in Jerusalem. There they will receive the power of the Spirit (Acts 2:1-12), and they remain there until they have filled the city with their teaching (Acts 5:28). In the faithfulness of God, the forgiveness of sins will be preached to Israel first, then to the Gentiles. At Pentecost, however, the disciples will preach to "devout Jews from every nation under heaven" (Acts 2:5 NRSV). Paul was chosen to "bring my name before Gentiles and kings and before the people of Israel" (Acts 9:15 NRSV). One of the great breakthroughs in the mission of the church comes when Peter understands that "God shows no partiality, but in every nation anyone who fears him and does what is right is acceptable to him" (Acts 10:34-35 NRSV). The Holy Spirit is conferred even upon Gentiles (Acts 10:45), so the rest of the book of Acts records the mission to

---

334. See Joseph A. Fitzmyer, *The Gospel According to Luke (X–XXIV)*, AB 28A (Garden City, N.Y.: Doubleday, 1985) 1578-79.

the Gentiles until the gospel is preached "openly and unhindered" in Rome, the center of the Gentile world (cf. Acts 28:28, 31).

The concept of "witness" develops in the course of the NT writings from the role of an eyewitness, to one who can testify to the gospel, to one who dies for the sake of the gospel (a "martyr" [μάρτυς *martys*]). Luke 24:48 links the first two senses. The disciples "are fitted because from experience they can bear witness to the factuality of the suffering and resurrection of Jesus, and also because they have grasped in faith the significance of Jesus, and can thus attest it. They discharge the task by proclaiming both the facts and their significance as they have grasped this in faith."[335] By the time we come to Paul (Acts 22:15), the sense has already shifted from the eyewitness role to the role of one who can testify to the significance of Jesus. Paul can bear a confessing witness, but he was not an eyewitness to the events of Jesus' ministry (Acts 1:22). The special Lukan use of "witness," which combines both senses, can also be found in Acts, where it is applied to the work of the apostles (Acts 1:8, 22; 2:32; 3:15; 5:32; 10:39, 41; 13:31).

Jesus' last statement to the disciples is an assurance that he will send "what my Father promised" upon them and that they will be "clothed with power from on high" (v. 49). The assurance is notable for its ambiguity; it does not explicitly refer to the Holy Spirit. This part of the commission to the disciples will be repeated almost verbatim in Acts 1:4, but there it is followed by a clarifying comment: "You will be baptized with the Holy Spirit not many days from now" (Acts 1:5 NRSV).

The language of sending recurs frequently in Luke, almost in a Johannine sense. Jesus himself was sent (4:18, 43; 9:48; 10:16), and he sent the disciples (9:2, 52; 10:1, 3; 22:35). Now he promises to send what the Father promised (cf. John 14:16, 26; 15:26). There is no previous reference to "what my Father promised" in Luke, but various references to the Spirit, especially at the beginning of the Gospel (cf. 1:15, 35, 41, 67; 2:25-26; 3:16, 22; 4:1; 10:21). The closest antecedent to Jesus' assurance in v. 49 is the earlier assurance, "How much more will the heavenly Father give the Holy Spirit to those who ask him!" (11:13).

335. H. Strathmann, μάρτυς *TDNT,* 4:492-93.

The metaphor of being clothed was used in early baptismal contexts (Gal 3:27; cf. 1 Cor 15:53-54; Eph 4:24; 6:11, 14; Col 3:10-12). "Power" (δύναμις *dynamis*) has attended Jesus' work throughout the Gospel (1:35; 4:14, 36; 5:17; 6:19; 8:46; 19:37). The Son of Man will be seated "at the right hand of the power of God" (22:69) and come again with power and glory (21:27), but now the risen Lord promises to confer that power on the disciples (cf. 9:1). Similarly, the reference to "on high" echoes language from the beginning of the Gospel (1:35), "the dawn from on high will break upon us" (1:78), and "Glory to God in the highest heaven" (2:14; cf. 19:38). The conferring of the Spirit from on high will also fulfill the Scriptures (see Isa 32:15; Joel 2:28). There will be plenty of work for the disciples to do, but for now their instructions are to stay in Jerusalem ("sit still") and wait for the fulfillment of the Lord's promises.

24:50-53, The Departure of Jesus. In the third part of Jesus' appearance to the eleven, Jesus leads the disciples out to Bethany, and as he blesses them he is carried into heaven. The disciples return to Jerusalem and praise God in the Temple.

Luke's is the only Gospel that chronicles the departure of Jesus. Matthew could hardly end with the ascension, since the last words of the Gospel are "And remember, I am with you always, to the end of the age" (Matt 28:20 NRSV). Paul writes of the exaltation of Jesus (Phil 2:9; cf. 1 Tim 3:16; 1 Pet 3:22), but Mark and Matthew may not have distinguished the resurrection from the exaltation. While John does not record an ascension, and indeed speaks of the crucifixion as Jesus' being "lifted up" (John 3:14; 8:28; 12:32), in John 20:17 Jesus says to Mary Magdalene, "Do not hold on to me, because I have not yet ascended to the Father. But go to my brothers and say to them, 'I am ascending to my Father and your Father'" (NRSV).

Luke records not one but two ascensions, one on Easter day (24:51; Acts 1:1-2) and one after forty days (Acts 1:9-11). The ascension both closes the period of Jesus' ministry and opens the period of the church's mission, so both accounts are appropriate. Perhaps in an effort to relieve an apparent inconsistency between the ending of Luke and the beginning of Acts, however, D omits "and was carried up into heaven" (v. 51) and the response "they worshiped him" (v. 52). Most recent translations and critical editions of the NT favor the longer reading on the basis of both internal considerations and the manuscript evidence.[336]

Following the pattern of other biblical departure scenes (Genesis 49–50; Deuteronomy 33–34), Luke concludes both the appearance to the eleven and the Gospel with (1) a blessing, (2) the departure, (3) a response from the witnesses, and (4) an act of obedience.[337] Jesus, like Enoch (Gen 5:24) and Elijah (2 Kgs 2:11), and according to apocryphal tradition Ezra (2 Esdr 14:9) and Moses (*As. Mos.* 10:12), is taken up into heaven.[338] The ascent of heroes and immortals into heaven is also found in Greco-Roman literature: e.g., the nobles exhort the people to revere Romulus, "since he had been caught up into heaven, and was to be a benevolent god for them instead of a good king."[339]

The closest parallels to Luke's account of the blessing are found in Lev 9:22 and Sir 50:20-21. Aaron "lifted his hands toward the people and blessed them" (Lev 9:22 NRSV). In Sir 50:20-21, at the conclusion of a section on the heroes of faith, Simon the high priest

> raised his hands
> over the whole congregation of Israelites,
> to pronounce the blessing of the
> Lord with his lips,
> and to glory in his name;
> and they bowed down in worship a second time,
> to receive the blessing from the Most High. (NRSV)

Similarly, Jesus raises his hands, blesses the disciples, and they worship him.

The ascension of Jesus also provides closure for the Gospel. The Gospel ends where it began, in the Temple, and Jesus supplies the blessing Zechariah could not pronounce (1:22). Midway through the Gospel, Jesus leaves Galilee and turns toward Jerusalem "when the days drew near for him to be taken up" (9:51). The "departure, which he was about to accomplish in Jerusalem," and toward which the Gospel has been moving since 9:31, is here accomplished. The people who waited in the Temple early in the Gospel (Zechariah, serving before God, 1:8; the assembly of the people, 1:10; Simeon, who "praised God" in the Temple, 2:25; and Anna, who "never left the Temple," 2:37) are replaced at the conclusion by the disciples. Blessing is a recurring motif in Luke, especially in the first two chapters and the last chapter (1:28, 42, 64; 2:28, 34; 24:30, 50-51, 53).

The appearance to the eleven began with the note that the disciples were terrified and thought they were seeing a ghost. Now, after the two proofs, the instruction from Scripture, the commission, Jesus' parting blessing, and his ascension, the disciples worship him (cf. Matt 28:17). The report that they worshiped him, therefore, brings resolution and closure to this second appearance scene. It also points the reader to the only appropriate response to the reading of the Gospel.

The movement of the Gospel is characterized by turning and returning (e.g., 1:56; 2:20, 43, 45; 24:9, 33), so appropriately Luke marks the final return in the closing verses when the disciples return to Jerusalem, where they will remain throughout the early chapters of Acts. By returning to Jerusalem, the disciples demonstrate their obedience to Jesus' command in v. 49.

The joy that was announced at the births of John and Jesus (1:14; 2:10) and anticipated in the ministry of Jesus (8:13; 10:17; 15:7, 10) is now finally fulfilled (cf. 24:41). Blessing is the presiding motif of the close of the Gospel. Those who have been blessed can scarcely do anything other than return the blessing (the verb used in vv. 50-51 is repeated in v. 53). God has provided a savior, and those who are not "slow of heart to believe" (24:25) but whose eyes and minds have been opened by the resurrection of Jesus and the interpretation of Scripture will follow the lead of the disciples and praise God continually.

---

336. For a full discussion of the issues, see Bruce M. Metzger, *A Textual Commentary on the Greek New Testament* (New York: United Bible Societies, 1971) 189-90 (in favor of the longer text); and Mikeal C. Parsons, *The Departure of Jesus in Luke-Acts: The Ascension Narratives in Context,* JSNTSup 21 (Sheffield: Sheffield Academic Press, 1987) 29-52 (in favor of the shorter text).
337. See Parsons, *The Departure of Jesus,* 56-57.
338. See Fitzmyer, *The Gospel According to Luke (X–XXIV),* 1588.
339. Plutarch *Lives* 1:177.17; *Romulus* 27.8.

REFLECTIONS

Literary theorists speak of a "primacy effect," the influence of the opening of a story in shaping the reader's expectations, and a "recency effect," the impact of the end of the story on the reader's memory and perception of the whole. The end of the Gospel exerts a powerful influence on our understanding of Luke's themes and theology. The appearance to the eleven guides the reader in a meditation with three movements: the proofs of the resurrection, Jesus' commission to his disciples, and the parting blessing.

As proofs of the resurrection, Jesus shows the disciples his hands and feet and eats in front of them. Simple as these proofs may be, the preaching of the resurrection reaches back to the word and experience of eyewitnesses. Once there were those who could say, "We saw him." The preaching of the gospel does not rest on fiction or fantasy but on the experience of the apostles. Ultimately, it is their story and the story of the women who went to the tomb.

Again, however, we may ask what place have "proofs" of the resurrection. The witness of the NT makes the proclamation of the resurrection credible. Something changed the disciples and sustained them through the trials they experienced. Their preaching, moreover, centered not on the teachings of Jesus but on his death and resurrection. Nevertheless, the resurrection is not a datum subject to empirical proof or rational verification. The experience of the presence of the risen Lord led the disciples to see that he had been raised, and the experience of the individual believer and the community of believers is still the foundation of faith. Where the Lord's physical hands and feet are no longer present, the ministry of the hands of countless saints in simple and sincere ministries continues to bear witness to the Lord's living presence. Although he may not appear in our midst to eat broiled fish, his presence is tangible in soup kitchens, around the kitchen table, and around the altar table. We see him "in the breaking of bread." As in the first century so now the most convincing proof of the resurrection is the daily testimony of the faithful that the Christ still lives and the work of his kingdom continues.

For this reason, the movement from proofs to commissioning is natural. In a surprising way, the appearances of the risen Lord in the Gospels and Acts authorize much that is integral to the life of the church: the preaching of the gospel, the interpretation of Scripture, the teachings of Jesus, the Lord's Supper, responses to doubt, the presence of the Lord with gathered believers on the first day of the week, baptism in Jesus' name, and (in Matthew) even the doctrine of the Trinity. At their core, the appearances report the manifestation of the risen Lord to believers and their sense that he had sent them to share the good news of the resurrection of the one who had preached the coming of the kingdom among us. The believer who affirms that the Lord is risen, therefore, should consider next what it is that the Lord has sent him or her to do. The uniqueness of the Easter message is that it invariably changes the lives of those who find themselves touched by it.

Jesus blessed the disciples he had sent out on mission. The Gospel, therefore, ends by elevating three of the most characteristic of God's actions. God has been experienced by the community of faith as the One who saves, sends, and blesses. God is our redeemer, and God has blessed us. There are no more ancient or fundamental confessions in the Jewish and Christian traditions. And those who have been saved and blessed know themselves to be sent to save and bless others in God's name. Unfortunately, in some traditions so much attention has been given to the importance of redemption and salvation that attention to God's work in blessing has been overlooked or given over to groups that sometimes focus too narrowly and superficially on this aspect of the community's experience of God. A healthy and biblical spirituality and worship require an appropriate balance among the preaching of God as Redeemer and Savior, the experience of God's blessing, and obedience to the commission to proclaim God's name to all the nations.

The final words of the Gospel lead us to an appropriate response to the gospel of the one who saves, sends, and blesses us. The disciples received Jesus' blessing with great joy, they worshiped him and praised God, and they began immediately to do what he had instructed them to do. Here, then, is the completion of the gospel drama, the narration of what God has done for us, the challenge of Jesus' teachings, and the model of those who made a faithful and joyful response.

Joy is the natural by-product of blessing. May it always be God's gift to those who study God's Word and seek God's kingdom.

THE GOSPEL OF JOHN

INTRODUCTION, COMMENTARY, AND REFLECTIONS
BY
GAIL R. O'DAY

THE GOSPEL OF
JOHN

INTRODUCTION

On even the most cursory reading of the four Gospels, it is apparent that the story of Jesus in the Gospel of John differs from that found in the other three Gospels in significant ways. In the synoptic Gospels, Jesus' ministry is a one-year Galilean ministry; he leaves Galilee to go to Judea and Jerusalem only once, in the final journey that culminates in his death. John recounts a three-year ministry; three different Passover feasts are celebrated in the course of Jesus' ministry (2:13; 6:4; 11:55), as opposed to the one Passover celebrated during Jesus' final days in the Synoptics. Moreover, in John, Jesus' ministry alternates between Galilee and Jerusalem. He makes three trips from Galilee to Jerusalem in the course of his ministry (2:13; 5:1; 7:10), and, indeed, most of his ministry is concentrated in Judea and Jerusalem. The chronology of Jesus' trial and crucifixion is also different in John. All the Gospels agree that Jesus was crucified on a Friday, but in the synoptic Gospels that Friday is the first day of Passover and in John it is the Day of Preparation for the Passover (18:28; 19:14).

The Johannine Jesus uses some short parables and proverbs (e.g., 4:36-37; 8:35; 10:1-5; 12:24; 16:21), but there are no parables that begin, "The kingdom of God is like . . ." in John. There are few compact narrative units that make up much of the story of Jesus in the Synoptics,[1] and little of the ethical teaching material found in the other Gospels. Instead, the Gospel of John is characterized by a literary style that interweaves narrative, dialogue, and discourse to create lengthy drama-like scenes (e.g., 4:4-42; 6:1-69; 9:1–10:21;

---

1. See Robert C. Tannehill, "The Gospels and Narrative Literature," in *The New Interpreter's Bible* (Nashville: Abingdon, 1995) 8:56-70.

11:1-44). The centerpiece of Jesus' teaching in John is the Farewell Discourse and Prayer (John 14–17), a speech of unparalleled length compared with any in the other Gospels. The common scholarly nomenclature through which the Gospels are identified underscores the distinctiveness of John—Matthew, Mark, and Luke are grouped together as the synoptic (literally, "seen together") Gospels, whereas John is isolated as the "Fourth Gospel."

The liturgical life of the church heightens the sense of a divide between John and the Synoptics. Within the church's three-year lectionary cycle, each of the synoptic Gospels has its own year—Matthew (Year A), Mark (Year B), Luke (Year C)—but there is no year for John. The lectionary thus seems to reinforce for clergy and laity alike that John is somehow both different from the other Gospels and perhaps not as essential to the church's reflection on Jesus. Because John is not heard as often in the preaching of the church, John remains a strange and less familiar voice.

Yet if one studies the lectionary cycle carefully, looking not simply at the broad strokes of the three-year cycle but at the texts assigned to particular liturgical seasons, a different picture of the distinctiveness of the Johannine voice emerges. In each of the lectionary cycles, texts from John are read during the Christmas, Lenten, and Easter seasons. For example, the Christmas Day Gospel in each of the three lectionaries is John 1:1-18. Readings from John 3, 4, 9, and 11 form the heart of the Lenten lectionary in Year A, and the Gospel lessons during the Sundays of Easter in each of the three years are drawn from John. The fact that the church turns to readings from John to guide it through each of the critical turning points in its liturgical life—the celebration of the birth of Jesus, the preparation for Jesus' death, and the joy of Easter—highlights another distinctive quality of the Gospel of John.

Story and theological interpretation are inseparably intertwined in John. The "I am" sayings that are a trait of Jesus' speech in John; the Gospel's rich metaphors and images; the poetic language of the Prologue; the theological reflections of the Farewell Discourse; Jesus' repeated statements about his unity with the One who sent him into the world, the One who loves him; the repeated identification of God as Jesus' Father—all ask the reader to ponder who Jesus is and who God is.

The Gospel's various literary techniques have a common theological goal: to open up the world of the Gospel story to the world of the reader's own experience. Because the questions Jesus asks his conversation partners become questions for the reader, the Gospel's dialogues and conversations seem to draw the reader into the stories as a participant. The Gospel makes frequent use of irony and symbolism, literary devices that ask the reader to discover the deeper meaning of an expression. At times, the Gospel narrator comments directly on a story to ensure that the reader is grasping its significance (e.g., 7:39; 8:27; 11:51-52; 12:33; 18:32; 19:35). The confessional language of the Prologue, which affirms, "We have beheld his glory" (1:14), blurs the line between storyteller and reader, as it invites the reader to join in its affirmation. The Gospel of John opens up the story of Jesus to the reading community's own experience so that readers can discover the presence of God in Jesus for themselves.

This commentary combines attention to the social and historical world of John with attention to its narrative and theological world. In this regard, this commentary takes its cues from the Gospel of John itself, because John draws no lines between history and interpretation, story and theology. To try to separate what happened in the life of Jesus from its meaning is a false pursuit for this Gospel. That claim does not minimize or dismiss the possible historical value of the account of Jesus' life and ministry in John, but instead recognizes that, for John, the value of the events of Jesus' life and ministry lies in their theological significance—what they reveal about God—and not in the events in and of themselves. In order to understand *what* John says about Jesus and God, then, one must attend carefully to *how* he tells his story. The literary style of this Gospel works in partnership with its theology to invite the reader into a new world shaped by the revelation of God in Jesus.

This commentary, therefore, pays close attention to both the details of the Gospel's literary style and form and the particulars of its theological claims. The goal of the commentary is to enable the Johannine voice to be heard on its own terms, to enable its portrait of Jesus, God, and the life of faith to emerge more fully for the reader. The Johannine theological vision often differs from what many Christians assume to be normative for Christian faith. For example, the Johannine treatment of the eucharist, lodged in the metaphorical discourse of John 6, is radically different from the accounts of the last supper in the Synoptics (Mark 14:22-25 and par.) or the words of institution recorded in 1 Cor 11:23-26. The Johannine understanding of sin (see Reflections on John 9) and the death of Jesus (see Reflections on John 12:20-36; 19:16-42) also brings an important alternative voice to conversations about sin, salvation, and atonement.

THE THEOLOGICAL WORLD OF JOHN

To understand the theological world of John, one must begin by recognizing the centrality of the incarnation to the Gospel. The theological significance of the incarnation is cogently expressed in two lines from the Prologue: "In the beginning was the Word, and the Word was with God and the Word was God" (1:1) and "the Word became flesh and lived among us" (1:14). These two claims are the foundation on which the rest of the Gospel is built: Jesus is the incarnate Word of God. That is, as 1:18 makes clear, Jesus provides access to God in ways never before possible, because Jesus' revelation of God derives from the most intimate relation with God. Jesus provides unique and unprecedented access to God because Jesus shares in God's character and identity; that is what 1:1 draws to the reader's attention. Yet, it is as the Word made flesh that Jesus brings God fully to the world (1:14). Jesus' revelation of God is thus not simply that Jesus speaks God's words and does God's works, although that is part of it (e.g., 5:19-20, 30; 10:25, 37-38; 12:48-49). It is, rather, that Jesus *is* God's Word. No line can be drawn between what Jesus says and what he does, between his identity and mission in the world. Jesus' words and works, his life and death, form an indissoluble whole that provides full and fresh access to God.

Theology and Christology. The pivotal role of the incarnation in John helps to clarify the relationship between theology and christology in the Gospel. The ultimate concern of this Gospel is with God. The good news is the revelation of *God* in Jesus. To focus exclusively on Jesus, as is often the case when verses from John are taken out of context in the contemporary church, is to miss the Gospel's central claim. What Jesus reveals about God comes through what Jesus reveals about himself. Christology redefines theology—that is, Jesus decisively changes how one talks about and knows God—but christology does not replace theology.

The interrelationship of theology and christology in John is clearly seen in the way to which God is referred. God is referred to as "the one who sent me [Jesus]" (e.g., 4:34; 5:38; 8:29) and as "the Father" (e.g., 5:17; 6:45; 14:16). Both of these ways of speaking of God highlight God's relationship with Jesus. "The one who sent Jesus" identifies God as the one from whom Jesus' mission in the world originates (e.g., 3:17). This identification of God points to the union of God's and Jesus' work in the world. By speaking of God as Father and Jesus as Son, John calls attention to the love and familial intimacy between them. Indeed, this familial intimacy is one of the central theological metaphors of the Gospel. At 1:12-13, for example, the Gospel notes that all who receive Jesus and believe in him become "children of God."

The use of father language for God is a painful issue for many women in the contemporary church because of the burden of patriarchy it frequently carries. Many women rightly note that an exclusive use of father language for God both flattens the richness of biblical images for God that sends disturbing messages about systems of power and authority. Yet the Gospel of John is an acute reminder that the elimination of father language is not the solution to this issue. "Father" is an essential name for God in John, and it is impossible to eliminate or even change the Father/Son language of this Gospel without seriously altering the Gospel's theological vision. The church's task, therefore, is to move beyond the assumption that *Father* is a generic synonym for "God." The Fourth Gospel itself argues against that claim, since God is identified as "the one who sends" with the same frequency as God is identified as "Father." The theological and pastoral task is to discover what the particulars of Father/Son language in John contribute to a fuller understanding of God, Jesus, and the Christian life. John does not use Father/Son language to reinforce the claims of patriarchy. Rather, he uses it to highlight the theological possibilities of intimacy and love that rest at the heart of God.[2]

Eccesiology. All of the Gospel's other theological concerns derive from its theology of the incarnation. For example, its eccesiology—its understanding of the life of the faith community—is expressed succinctly in Jesus' commandment of John 13:34-35: "Just as I have loved you, you also should love one another. By this everyone will know that you are my disciples, if you have love for one another." The full expression of Jesus' love is the gift of his life (see 10:11, 14, 17-18; 15:12-15), the crowning moment of the incarnation (19:30).

2. See Gail R. O'Day, "John," in *The Women's Bible Commentary,* ed. Carol A. Newsom and Sharon H. Ringe (Louisville: Westminster/John Knox, 1992) 303-4.

For us to love one another as Jesus loves, then, is to live out the love of the incarnation, to show in one's own life the fullness of love that unites God and Jesus. The commandment to love as Jesus loves takes on added urgency in a community for which persecution and martyrdom were a social reality (cf. 16:2-3). John's image of the faith community, then, derives from his understanding of the relationship between God and Jesus.

Pneumatology. John's pneumatology, his understanding of the Spirit, also derives from his understanding of the relationship between God and Jesus. Jesus' death marked the end of the incarnation. If the revelation of God is lodged decisively in the incarnation, what happens after Jesus has died? Is the revelation of God so temporally bound that it is available only to those who knew the historical Jesus? The Paraclete is the Fourth Evangelist's solution to this theological dilemma. "Paraclete" is the transliteration of the Greek noun παράκλητος (*parakletos*), the noun the Fourth Evangelist uses to speak of the Spirit. This noun has many meanings—for example, "the one who exhorts," "the one who comforts," "the one who helps"—all of which the Gospel seems to employ in its discussion of the identity and function of the Spirit in the life of the faith community (see Commentary on John 14–16). The Spirit/Paraclete will remain in the community after Jesus' death and return to God ("And I will ask the Father, and he will give you another Paraclete, to be with you forever" [14:16; see also 14:26]). The Spirit/Paraclete will continue the revelation of God begun in the incarnation, "He will glorify me because he will take what is mine and declare it to you" (16:14; see also 14:26; 16:13, 15). The Spirit thus makes it possible for succeeding generations of believers to come to know the God revealed in Jesus.

Eschatology. John's eschatology is also shaped by his understanding of the incarnation. Because God is fully revealed in Jesus, Jesus' advent into the world brings the world to a moment of crisis and decision (e.g., 3:16-21). One does not have to wait for a future revealing of the fullness of God's glory and God's will for the world or for eternal life to be bestowed. Both are available now in Jesus: "Very truly, I tell you, anyone who hears my word and believes him who sent me has eternal life, and does not come under judgment, but has passed from death to life" (5:24); "And this is eternal life, that they may know you, the only true God, and Jesus Christ whom you have sent. I glorified you on earth by finishing the work that you gave me to do" (17:3-4). In Jesus' death, resurrection, and ascension, his "hour," the world is judged. Jesus' death, the full expression of his love, judges the world because it reveals the character of God (e.g., 14:31; 17:24). Jesus' victory over death judges the world because it reveals the impotence of the ruler of the world (e.g., 12:31; 14:30; 16:11). Jesus' ascension judges the world because when he is reunited with God "with the glory that I had in your presence before the world existed" (17:5), his work is completed (e.g., 16:10).

The theological intensity of this Gospel can be discouraging to many readers. In the middle of yet another complex theological statement in the Farewell Discourse, one may long for one of the short, pithy narratives of the synoptic Gospels. Yet the theological intensity of this Gospel is its genius. The Fourth Evangelist held his faith deeply, and he clearly wanted his readers to share his passion for life shaped by the incarnation. He weaves together narrative and theology in an attempt to open up the wonder and mystery of the incarnation as fully as possible, so that the Gospel readers can know themselves to be the recipients of Jesus' gifts. The Fourth Evangelist loved God and Jesus deeply, and he invites his readers to share that love.

As a preliminary step in orienting the reader to the distinctive Johannine narrative and theological voice, it is important to review issues that illumine the historical setting of this document within first-century Judaism and the later life of the church.[3]

AUTHORSHIP

Like all the other Gospels, John is an anonymously written document; its traditional title, "The Gospel According to John," first appears as the heading of second-century CE manuscripts. The "John" of this title is presumably John, the son of Zebedee, thus according apostolic authorship to the Gospel. The authorship of the Fourth Gospel was a subject of much debate in the second and third centuries. Christian Gnostics (e.g., Valentinus and Heracleon) who were drawn to the Fourth Gospel claimed apostolic authorship as a way of giving apostolic grounding to their faith perspectives. The opponents of Gnosticism, especially Irenaeus, the bishop of Lyons (c. 130–200 CE), claimed apostolic authorship as a way of refuting gnostic claims. Christian Gnostics drew on a wide spectrum of early Christian documents as sources and expressions of their theology and christology (for example, the *Gospel of Thomas*).[4] In *Against Heresies,* Irenaeus points to the apostolic authorship of Matthew, Mark, Luke, and John and insists on the authority of these four Gospels alone in his attempt to delegitimate the gnostic Gospels and other writings. This apologetic setting must always be kept in mind when one weighs the issue of apostolic authorship.

Beginning in the mid-second century, church theologians identified John, the son of Zebedee, with "the disciple whom Jesus loved," as this quotation from Irenaeus shows: "Afterwards John, the disciple of the Lord, who also had leaned upon his breast, himself published his Gospel, while he was living at Ephesus in Asia."[5] Despite Irenaeus's identification, there is no clear internal Fourth Gospel evidence to support linking John, the son of Zebedee, with the beloved disciple; the tradition of the apostolic authorship of the Gospel began to erode in the nineteenth century. The "disciple whom Jesus loved" is always identified by his relationship with Jesus, never by name. There is one passing reference to "the sons of Zebedee" at 21:2, the introduction to a scene in which the beloved disciple appears, but this verse also contains a reference to "two others of his disciples," so that no clear identification is possible.

The identification of John, the son of Zebedee, with the beloved disciple can be

3. For a thorough overview of the historical and religious setting of the Gospel of John, see D. Moody Smith, *The Theology of the Gospel of John* (Cambridge: Cambridge University Press, 1995) 1-74.
4. See James M. Robinson, ed., *The Nag Hammadi Library in English,* 3rd ed. (San Francisco: Harper & Row, 1988).
5. Irenaeus *Against Heresies* III.11.2.

conjecture at best and is based largely on the desire to ascribe apostolic authorship to this Gospel. Yet this very understanding of apostolic authority runs counter to the Fourth Gospel's understanding of discipleship. The Twelve have a very minimal role in this Gospel (they are mentioned explicitly only at 6:69, 71; 20:24). Therefore, it is not necessary to postulate that the beloved disciple was one of the Twelve in order for him to have had authority within his community.

In addition to the Gospel, four other NT books are associated with the name "John": 1, 2, and 3 John, and the Revelation to John. Like the Gospel, the three epistles are anonymous documents; their attribution to John the apostle derives from the manuscript tradition of the early church. The author of Revelation, by contrast, identifies himself as "John" at Rev 1:1, 4, 9; 22:8.

Although the tradition labeled the epistles and the Gospel as having been written by the same author, the internal evidence does not support that conclusion. The three epistles (particularly 1 John; 2 and 3 John are too brief to enable much comparison) do share some pivotal theological language and concepts with the Gospel of John (e.g., the commandment to love one another; the image of the faith community as children; light; life), but there are also many important differences. For example, the role of the Spirit/Paraclete, so pivotal to the picture of the life of the community in John (e.g., 16:8-11), has no similar role in 1 John, which is singularly concerned with community life. The understanding of sin and atonement (e.g., 1 John 1:7; 2:2; 4:10) is also quite different from that found in the Gospel. Most important, the situations addressed by the Gospel and 1 John are quite different. Whereas the Gospel is oriented toward the community's conflict with synagogal Judaism (see below), the epistle is primarily concerned with intra-Christian conflicts. The opponents with whom the author of 1 John debates are members of the Christian community (or have been).

It is, therefore, widely held that the epistles originated within the same faith community that produced the Gospel, but not from the same author at the same time. Much of the conflict to which 1 John is addressed seems to be generated by disagreement over the interpretation of the theology contained in the Gospel (e.g., the reality of the incarnation, 1 John 4:2-3; 5:6). This suggests that the epistles came from a later stage in the community's life.[6]

It is unlikely that the "John" of Revelation is the apostle John, the son of Zebedee, or the author of the Gospel or the Johannine epistles. He does not claim that identity for himself, but records that he was persecuted and imprisoned on Patmos for his faith (1:9; note also his reference to the "twelve apostles of the Lamb" at 21:14). The differences between the Gospel and Revelation are quite striking, beginning with the thoroughgoing apocalypticism that shapes Revelation. Yet behind these striking differences, the two books nonetheless contain some distinctive theological and imagistic echoes; Rev 19:3, like John 1:1, refers to Jesus as the Word of God; Jesus' gift of living water appears in both (John

6. For the view that the epistles precede the Gospel, see Charles Talbert, *Reading John: A Literary and Theological Commentary on the Fourth Gospel and the Johannine Epistles* (New York: Crossroad, 1992).

4:13-14; 7:37-38; cf. 6:35; Rev 22:17). The invective toward "those who say that they are Jews" in Rev 2:9 is very similar to the language of John 8:44-47. These echoes suggest that the Gospel and Revelation may have originated within communities that shared some traditions about Jesus.

The key to any discussion of authorship of the Gospel is the Gospel's own evidence about the relationship between the beloved disciple and the author of the Fourth Gospel. The "disciple whom Jesus loved" first appears at 13:23 and plays a prominent role in the last chapters of the Gospel (19:26-27; 20:3-10; 21:1-14, 20-24; see also 19:35). It is difficult to imagine that the author of the Gospel, who is so insistent on maintaining the anonymity of the disciple, would nonetheless refer to himself as "the disciple whom Jesus loved." More important, there are two verses that explicitly distinguish the witness of the beloved disciple from the work of the author. Both 19:35 and 21:24 use a third-person pronoun to refer to the beloved disciple and his testimony and stress that this testimony is true. John 21:24 is especially important in this regard, "This is the disciple who is testifying to these things and has written them, and we know that his testimony is true." The author of the Gospel thus claims eyewitness authority for the accounts in the Gospel, but points to another, the beloved disciple, as the source of that witness. The beloved disciple, therefore, is not the author of the Gospel, but is presented as the authorizing voice of the traditions that are recounted in the Gospel.

The identity of the beloved disciple was probably known to the first readers of the Gospel. That is, he is not a fictional creation,[7] but a historical figure who played an important role as an eyewitness link to Jesus for the community out of which the Gospel arose (note the concern about his death in 21:20-24). That identity is no longer recoverable for contemporary readers, who must rest content with the information the Gospel supplies about this disciple. Yet the beloved disciple's significance is not limited to his role as eyewitness. Because he is never named and is instead always portrayed as the recipient of Jesus' love, this disciple also emerges as a symbolic figure who embodies the ideal relationship with Jesus that the Gospel hopes to make available to all its readers.

Thus the name of the author of this Gospel is unknown; however, the traditional designations of "John" for both the Gospel and its author will be used in this commentary, as well as the corresponding pronoun "he" to refer to the Evangelist. What *is* known about the author of this Gospel, is that he understood himself to be connected to the traditions about Jesus through the eyewitness testimony of the beloved disciple, that he held the beloved disciple's testimony to be true, and that he regarded the transmission of that testimony to be an act of faith ("He who saw this has testified so that you also may believe" [19:35]).

---

7. Bultmann is the important exception to this view. He maintained that the beloved disciple was only a symbolic figure. See Rudolph Bultmann, *The Gospel of John: A Commentary,* trans. G. R. Beasley-Murray, R. W. N. Hoarse, and J. K. Riches (Philadelphia: Westminster, 1971) 484.

JOHN'S USE OF SOURCES AND TRADITIONS

How is the reader to weigh the value and relative importance of source and composition theories for the interpretation of John? It is indisputable that the Fourth Evangelist drew on earlier traditions in the composition of his Gospel; he did not create the Gospel from whole cloth. It is critical, therefore, that the contemporary reader not be naive about the transmission of traditions in the first decades of the church, or about the composition process. Source and composition theories help the contemporary reader to recognize and remember that the development of NT literature did not move in one step from the time of Jesus to the written Gospels, but that there were many intermediate steps. It is the pivotal assumption of form criticism and all discussions of oral traditions that stories and teachings circulated in oral form to meet community needs—teaching, preaching, mission, worship, and probably also the entertainment value of telling good stories.

Such theories also stand as a caution to contemporary readers who may be tempted to perceive the faith traditions of the first decades of the church as monolithic or simplistic. Different communities had access to different streams of tradition. The Fourth Gospel, for example, draws explicit attention to the traditions that came to it through the distinctive witness of the beloved disciple. In addition, individual traditions were regarded as more helpful or essential to a community's life, depending on its social and religious setting and needs, much as in the preaching and teaching of the church today.

The most important source question is whether John knew and drew on the synoptic Gospels. A quotation from Clement of Alexandria offers the classic view of Johannine dependence on the Synoptics: "Last of all John, perceiving that the external facts had been made plain in the gospel, being urged by his friends and inspired by the Spirit, composed a spiritual gospel."[8] Clement recognized that the Gospel of John posed a decisive question about the interrelationship of history, theology, and interpretation. The solution that Clement proposed, and that remained the dominant view into the nineteenth century, was to assume Johannine use of the Synoptics. This solution confirmed the other canonical Gospels as the historical norm for the story of Jesus and rendered the differences between John and the Synoptics less problematic. John is simply exercising theological or "spiritual" freedom in his use of the other Gospels.

The most influential work to question the view that John depended on the other Gospels was that of Percival Gardner-Smith.[9] He carefully compared scenes held in common by John and the synoptic Gospels, and these comparisons led him to conclude that the interrelationship of the Gospels was best explained by the assumption that John used independent Jesus traditions that often resembled those in the Synoptics, not that John intentionally altered the synoptic Gospels.

---

8. Quoted in Eusebius *Ecclesiastical History* VI.xiv.7.
9. Percival Gardner-Smith, *Saint John and the Synoptic Gospels* (Cambridge: Cambridge University Press, 1938).

The work that was begun in Gardner-Smith's brief study was completed by C. H. Dodd in *Historical Tradition in the Fourth Gospel.* Dodd does a careful analysis of all of the Johannine passages that have any synoptic parallels and concludes that "behind the Fourth Gospel there lies an ancient tradition independent of the other gospels, and meriting serious consideration as a contribution to our knowledge of the historical facts concerning Jesus Christ."[10] Both Gardner-Smith and Dodd gave a prominent position to oral traditions about Jesus rather than explaining all overlaps among the Gospels in terms of dependence on written documents. The work of Gardner-Smith and Dodd thus made it possible to examine and interpret the Johannine traditions about Jesus on their own terms, not as being derivative of the Synoptics. They also pointed to John as an independent resource for information about Jesus.

Johannine independence from the synoptic Gospels has become the majority position in Johannine scholarship. Of the major twentieth-century commentaries on John written after Dodd (see Bibliography), only C. K. Barrett's work argues for Johannine dependence on Mark.[11] Johannine dependence on the Synoptics, especially Mark, has recently emerged as a fresh topic of debate,[12] but the exegetical evidence amassed by Dodd is difficult to overcome. It is the perspective of this commentary that John makes use of a stream of oral tradition that often overlaps with, but is nonetheless independent from, the traditions on which Mark and the other Gospels drew.

Another approach to source questions is to explain the distinctiveness of the Johannine traditions by appealing to other written sources. The classic lines of this approach to John were drawn by Rudolf Bultmann.[13] Bultmann understood the Fourth Evangelist to be a master literary craftsman who drew together three major sources in the composition of the Gospel: a passion-narrative source; a revelation-discourse source; and a signs source. The revelation-discourse source is Bultmann's most controversial proposal. It is the key to Bultmann's contention that a gnostic revealer-redeemer myth lies behind the Fourth Gospel's christology; the Prologue is the linchpin for this source. Bultmann maintained that John found this myth in the revelation-discourse source and rewrote it by making Jesus the redeemer. Bultmann's thesis of gnostic influence was very influential on German scholarship on John, although the suggestion of a revelation-discourse source has been largely rejected.

Bultmann's suggestion of a signs source as the source of the miracles recounted in John has received wider acceptance. The key elements in isolating this source are the occurrence of the noun "sign" (σημεῖον *sēmeion*) in the Gospel (e.g., 2:11; 4:54; 20:30), the enumeration of the two Cana miracles (2:11; 4:54), and the purported tension between

10. C. H. Dodd, *Historical Tradition in the Fourth Gospel* (Cambridge: Cambridge University Press, 1953) 423.

11. C. K. Barrett, *The Gospel According to St. John,* 2nd ed. (Philadelphia: Westminster, 1978).

12. See especially the work of Frans Neirynck, "John and the Synoptics," in *L'Evangile de Jean: Sources, redaction, theology,* ed. M. de Jonge, (Louvain: Louvain University Press, 1977) 73-106; and "John and the Synoptics: 1975–1990," in *John and the Synoptics,* ed. A. Deneaux (Louvain: Louvain University Press, 1992). For a judicious review of the question, see D. Moody Smith, *John Among the Gospels: The Relationship in Twentieth Century Research* (Minneapolis: Fortress, 1992).

13. Rudolf Bultmann, *The Gospel of John: A Commentary,* trans. G. R. Beasley-Murray, R. W. N. Hoare, and J. K. Riches (Philadelphia: Westminster, 1971).

the positive valuation of miracles in the source and the seemingly negative view of miracles in the Gospel (e.g., 4:48, but see Commentary on this verse). Robert Fortna, for example, following Bultmann's suggestions, has worked diligently for several decades to reconstruct "the Gospel of signs."[14]

The signs-source hypothesis, however, runs counter to the insights about the role and diversity of oral traditions proposed by Dodd and also overemphasizes the differences between the Johannine and Synoptic miracles. When one identifies the miracles in John—the wine miracle at the Cana wedding (2:1-11); the healing of the royal official's son (4:46-54); the healing of a lame man (5:1-18); the feeding of the five thousand (6:1-14); Jesus' walking on water (6:16-21); the healing of a blind man (9:1-41); the raising of Lazarus (11:1-44), and the miraculous catch of fish (21:1-14), one notices that with the single exception of the wine miracle at Cana, each of these miracles has some analogue in the synoptic tradition. Therefore, it seems more credible to postulate the common oral traditions about Jesus as the source of these stories than a fully formed signs source. That is, it seems more likely that John had access to an oral tradition that grouped together a series of miracle stories about Jesus than that he drew on a written signs collection. In addition, the signs-source hypothesis plays down the interrelationship of miracle and discourse throughout the Gospel (see, e.g., Commentary on chaps. 5; 6; and 9). Johannine scholars are divided on the hypothesis of a written signs source; some express skepticism about the viability of this hypothesis,[15] while others use the source as an exegetical tool in their commentary work.[16]

There was a final piece to Bultmann's source theory: an ecclesiastical redactor responsible for the final form of the Gospel. To this editor Bultmann attributed all sections of the Gospel that reflect later ecclesiastical issues, for example, the eucharistic section in 6:51-58. Although it is impossible to accept Bultmann's characterization of this editor and his concerns, because as the commentary below will argue, "ecclesiastical" concerns are not foreign to the theology of John, the thesis of a final editor or editors of the Gospel is shared by many Fourth Gospel scholars.

Raymond Brown, for example, proposes five distinct stages in the composition of John.[17] The stages are (stage 1) a body of traditional material; (stage 2) its development in the teaching and preaching of the Johannine community; (stage 3) its organization of this material into a Gospel narrative by the "evangelist" (perhaps the preacher of stage 2); (stage 4) a secondary edition by the evangelist; and (stage 5) a final editing by the redactor. Brown's theory has in its favor that it highlights the liveliness and fluidity of traditions

14. Robert T. Fortna, *The Gospel of Signs: A Reconstruction of the Narrative Source Underlying the Fourth Gospel* (Cambridge: Cambridge University Press, 1970); and *The Fourth Gospel and Its Predecessor: From Narrative Source to Present Gospel* (Philadelphia: Fortress, 1988).

15. E.g., Barrett, *The Gospel According to St. John*, 18, 77; Raymond E. Brown, *The Gospel According to John (I–IX)*, AB 29 (Garden City, N.Y.: Doubleday, 1966) xxxi; (but see also 1:195); George R. Beasley-Murray, *John*, WBC 36 (Waco, Tex.: Word, 1987) xl.

16. Schnackenburg, vol. 1, 67; Kysar, *John* 12-13. See also Kysar, *John the Maverick Gospel*, rev. ed. (Louisville: Westminster/John Knox, 1993).

17. Brown, *The Gospel According to John (I–XII)*, xxxiv-xxxix.

about Jesus in early Christian communities and emphasizes the intersection of the formation of the Gospel with the developing religious and pastoral needs of a particular community. Yet the precision with which he classifies the stages; the distinctions he makes among stages 3, 4, and 5; and his attempts in his commentary to distinguish which parts of the Gospel belong to which stage of composition cannot be supported adequately by the evidence of the Gospel text.

Source and composition theories place their emphasis on moving behind the text, that is, on the history of the text. These theories are thus valuable tools in reconstructing early Christian history, and they will be engaged in this commentary where appropriate; but tracking the composition history of John is not a priority of this commentary's interpretive work.

DATE OF COMPOSITION AND SOCIAL AND RELIGIOUS SETTING

$\mathfrak{P}^{52}$, an Egyptian papyrus fragment that dates from the early second century, contains the text of John 18:31-33, 37-38, suggesting that the Gospel was known in Egypt by 100 CE. In addition, John appears to have been in wide circulation by the middle of the second century CE. Heracleon wrote the first commentary on John around 150 CE (excerpts from this commentary are preserved in Origen's commentary on John).[18] Among the second-century church fathers, Irenaeus (180 CE) and Melito of Sardis (175 CE), both in Asia Minor, show indisputable knowledge of the Fourth Gospel, as do Bishop Polycrates (190) and the Muratorian Canon (180–200) from Rome. Tatian's *Diatesseron,* a Gospel harmony composed circa 175 CE, draws on texts from John and treats it with the same authority as he treats the synoptic Gospels. Moreover, Ignatius of Antioch may have had knowledge of John as early as the beginning of the second century. The manuscript evidence and the evidence of early church tradition thus suggest that the Gospel was completed no later than 100 CE.

In addition to this external evidence, the Gospel points to the crisis that may have precipitated its composition and hence provides additional assistance in arriving at a date. At three places in the Gospel, the expression "put out of the synagogue" occurs (9:22; 12:42; 16:2). In a highly influential study, J. Louis Martyn proposed that this phrase refers to a practice of excommunicating perceived heretics from the synagogue. This practice was formalized in the Benediction Against Heretics (Birkath ha-Minim), a benediction introduced into the synagogue liturgy sometime after the destruction of the Jerusalem Temple in 70 CE and probably between 85 and 95 CE.[19]

There is considerable scholarly debate about the precise contours and dating of this benediction (for the text of the benediction and a more detailed discussion of its implications for Fourth Gospel study, see Excursus "John 9:22 and the Benediction Against Heretics," 657-58). Nonetheless, this benediction offers an important example of the religious conflicts within first-century Judaism. The destruction of the Jerusalem

18. See Elaine Pagels, *The Johannine Gospel in Gnostic Exegesis: Heracleon's Commentary on John* (Atlanta: Scholars Press, 1972).

19. See J. Louis Martyn, *History and Theology in the Fourth Gospel,* 2nd ed. (Nashville: Abingdon, 1979).

Temple in 70 CE, the cultic center, meant a radical reorientation of Jewish religious life. Pharisees, priests, and Jewish Christians (or perhaps less anachronistically, Christian Jews), among others, struggled over religious identity and power. The benediction was the attempt of the pharisaical/rabbinic branch of Judaism to assert its control in the face of alternative forms of Judaism. This branch of post–70 CE Judaism ultimately did assert its control, emerging from these struggles as the dominant religious group within later Judaism.[20]

The religious turmoil within emergent Judaism after 70 CE is critical to the dating of the Fourth Gospel. In the Gospel's intense rhetoric about "the Jews" (see below and Reflections on John 8) and its predictions of expulsion, persecution, and martyrdom for believers, this intra-Jewish conflict is visible. The Fourth Evangelist and those for whom he wrote understood themselves to be a persecuted religious minority, expelled from the synagogue, their religious home, because of their faith in Jesus.[21] The pain of this intra-Jewish struggle is fresh and real for the Fourth Evangelist; many of Jesus' words in the Farewell Discourse can be read as intended to uphold this community in its struggles (see 15:18–16:3).

The publication of the benediction c. 90 CE marked the formalization of an intra-religious struggle that had been going on in many local communities prior to this date. The Gospel of John may stem from one such community, in which the practice of expulsion from the synagogue began almost immediately after the destruction of the Jerusalem Temple. The intensity of the conflict with the Jewish leadership, and the pivotal role it plays in shaping the religious and social identity of the community that read this Gospel, suggests 75–80 CE as the earliest possible date of composition; the external evidence, as noted above, makes a date much later than 100 CE unlikely. Thus the Gospel of John is roughly contemporaneous with Matthew, which was written in response to the same intra-Jewish struggles.

John thus belongs to and derives from the complex and multi-faceted cultural and intellectual milieu of first-century Judaism. The influence of this diversity of Jewish traditions on the Fourth Evangelist is evident throughout the Gospel. From beginning to end, the Gospel is shaped by the language and images of the OT. The opening words of the Gospel ("In the beginning . . .") are clearly intended to echo Gen 1:1. What is most striking about John's use of the OT is that the references to it are uniformly positive. For example, Jesus' description of his gifts are couched in the language of Scripture (cf., e.g., 6:32-33; Ps 78:24). Jesus' self-designation as "I AM" echoes the use of the divine name in the LXX of Second Isaiah (e.g., Isa 43:25; 51:12; 52:6). Indeed, the Scriptures are pointed to as bearing witness to Jesus (e.g., 5:39, 46). John's animosity to the Jewish religious authorities thus does not extend to Jewish religious traditions. He is thoroughly saturated in and shaped by the Jewish Scriptures.

Jewish wisdom traditions in particular pay a prominent role in John. These traditions, found in both canonical and extra-canonical Jewish documents (e.g., Proverbs, Sirach, Wisdom of Solomon), personify Wisdom as the presence of God's Word in the world (e.g., Prov 8:22,

20. See Shaye D. Cohen, *From the Maccabees to the Mishnah* (Philadelphia: Westminster, 1987).
21. See David Rensberger, *Johannine Faith and Liberating Community* (Philadelphia: Westminster, 1988).

34; Wis 7:22-26) and draw attention to God's Word as a source of nourishment and life (e.g., Prov 9:5; Sir 15:3; 24:21). One hears echoes of the idioms of the wisdom traditions in the Prologue (1:1-18) and throughout Jesus' discourses in John (e.g., 6:35; 7:37-38).

The discovery of the Qumran material has contributed to a broader understanding of the diversity of early and mid–first-century Judaism. The sharp dualistic language in John—light/darkness; good/evil—has counterparts in the documents of the Qumran sectarians. While it remains unclear how far one can postulate direct influence, at the very least the similarities between John and Qumran solidly locate the Gospel within the religious diversity of first-century Judaism.

In the first-century Mediterranean world, it was impossible to draw a rigid line between Judaism and Hellenism. The most important example of the rich conversation between Jewish and Greek thought is in the work of Philo of Alexandria, an early first-century Jew who wrote in Greek and was equally at home in Greek philosophy and Jewish Scripture. Philo has important similarities with John.[22] For example, "word" (λόγος *logos*) and "light" (φῶς *phōs*) figure prominently in the thought worlds of both Philo and John, and both were concerned with reinterpreting the Jewish scriptural traditions in the light of the circumstances in which they lived. Again, while direct influence of Philo on John cannot be demonstrated, Philo broadens our understanding of first-century Judaism and helps us to see John more clearly in its variegated Jewish context.

The question of gnostic influence on John needs to be examined in the light of the diversity of first-century Mediterranean Judaism. Just as one cannot draw a sharp line between Judaism and Hellenism in the first century, so also one cannot draw a sharp line between Judaism and Gnosticism. Much of what emerged as definitional for later Gnosticism—dualistic language, the pivotal role of light/dark imagery, the emphasis on knowledge—is found already in less developed forms in Jewish wisdom literature, Qumran, and Philo.[23] The proto-Gnostic tendencies in the Jewish traditions closest to the Fourth Gospel, as well as in the Fourth Gospel itself, may account in part for the important role John played in the theology of later Christian Gnostics (e.g., Valentinus and Heracleon).

The Gospel of John was thus written by a Jewish Christian for and in a Jewish Christian community that was in conflict with the synagogue authorities of its day (represented in the Gospel as "the Pharisees" or "the Jews"). The traditional identification of Ephesus as the place of the Gospel's composition fits this description, because Ephesus had a large and active Jewish community (see Acts 18–19), but nothing tells singularly in its favor either. Antioch and Alexandria, two Mediterranean cities with large Jewish populations, have also been proposed as the location of the Fourth Gospel. Nor is it possible to rule out

22. See, e.g., C. H. Dodd, *The Interpretation of the Fourth Gospel* (Cambridge: Cambridge University Press, 1953) 54-73; and Peder Borgen, "Philo," in *The Anchor Bible Dictionary* (New York: Doubleday, 1992) 5:333-42.

23. See Craig A. Evans, *Word and Glory: On the Exegetical and Theological Background of John's Prologue,* JSNTSup (Sheffield: JSOT, 1993).

a location in Palestine for the Fourth Evangelist and his community.[24] The place of the Gospel's origin, like its author, must remain unnamed; what is critical to the interpretation of John is the recognition of its origins in the religious life of first-century Judaism.

The preceding review articulates the historical-critical presuppositions of this commentary. Such historical-critical work is essential to the interpretation of John, as it is of any biblical book, because each book was written in a particular social and historical context. John reflects and arises out of the struggles and celebrations of an actual faith community. To ignore the first-century social, religious, and historical environment opens up the danger of interpreting John as if it were spoken directly to twentieth-century Christians, when it is not. It was written for first-century Jewish Christians whose world was in crisis because of their faith in Jesus as the decisive revelation of God. The good news of John for twentieth-century Christians is always mediated through this first community of readers. The contemporary reader, therefore, must be willing to engage in acts of theological and historical imagination when reading John; the reader must be willing to envision the experience of the first readers and the meaning of the Gospel for them.

A crucial illustration of this is John's language about "the Jews." As indicated already, and as will be discussed more fully in the Commentary on John 8, this language arises from conflicts between two different groups of first-century Jews: the community of the Fourth Gospel (Christian Jews) and the synagogue authorities. The intense enmity of this language is forged in the struggle for religious and community identity. And, most important, it is language spoken by one group of Jews to another, not by Gentile Christians about Jews. To recognize this social context is not to whitewash the problematic nature of much of this language. Rather, recognition of the socially determined nature and function of this language is essential for any responsible conversation about this language in a contemporary context. To appropriate this language into the modern situation of Jewish-Christian relations without attending to the inseparability of this language from the social world of Johannine Christians is unethical at best, tragic at worst. Awareness of the social, historical, and cultural contexts out of which John emerged, therefore, is essential not only for understanding what texts meant "then" but also for determining what texts mean "now."

THE STRUCTURE OF THE GOSPEL OF JOHN

It is conventional in Johannine scholarship to divide the Gospel of John into two parts: chaps. 1–12, commonly referred to as "the Book of Signs," and chaps. 13–20, commonly referred to as "the Book of Glory." John 21 is most often treated as an appendix or second ending to the Gospel. The reference to the arrival of Jesus' hour in John 13:1 thus serves as the dividing line between the two major sections, "Now before the festival of the Passover, Jesus knew that his hour had come to depart from this world and go to the

---

24. See J. Louis Martyn, "Glimpses into the History of the Johananine Community," in *L'Evangile de Jean, Sources, redaction, theologie,* ed. M. de Jonge (Louvain: Louvain University Press, 1977) 149-75.

Father." There is no question that John 13:1 marks a major turn in the Gospel narrative, because it initiates the enactment of the events of Jesus' hour, but this conventional division oversimplifies the contents of John 1–12 and the interrelationship of the events of Jesus' ministry and his "hour." Thus this commentary proposes an alternative structure for John. The exegetical rationale for this proposal is given in greater detail in the commentary itself; this introduction provides a general structural overview.

John 1:1-51, The Prelude to Jesus' Ministry. This section consists of two parts: a hymnic prologue (1:1-18) and a narrative prologue (1:19-51). Both of these sections function like the overture to an orchestral piece: They introduce a theme that will be developed throughout the remainder of the Gospel. Both sections have stylized structures that underscore their function as overture. John 1:1-18 begins the Gospel with a poetic celebration of Jesus' origin with God and his coming into the world. John 1:19-51, which narrates the witness of John the Baptist to Jesus (vv. 19-34) and the gathering of the first disciples (vv. 35-51), is composed as a series of four days that lay the groundwork for the unfolding of Jesus' ministry.

John 2:1–5:47, "The Greater Things": Jesus' Words and Works. Jesus' public ministry is narrated in two cycles: John 2:1–5:47 and John 6:1–10:42.[25] These chapters contain miracles and discourses by Jesus that point to the authority of Jesus' words and works—the wine miracle at Cana (2:1-11); the cleansing of the Temple (2:13-22); two healing miracles (4:46-54; 5:1-9); Jesus' conversations with Nicodemus (3:1-21) and the Samaritan woman (4:4-42)—and so fulfill his promise to his disciples that they would see "greater things" (1:50). Yet this cycle also contains the first story of Jesus' conflict with the Jewish authorities (5:9-47), a conflict that includes the decision to kill Jesus (5:18). This first cycle establishes the themes and tensions that characterize Jesus' public ministry in John—from the manifestation of Jesus' glory (2:1-11) to the rejection of that glory (5:9-47).

John 6:1–10:42, Jesus' Words and Works: Conflict and Opposition Grow. The second cycle of Jesus' public ministry follows the same pattern as the first—it begins with a miracle in Galilee, the feeding of the five thousand (6:1-15), and concludes with hostility to Jesus and renewed intention to kill him (10:31-39). The second cycle poses the same basic question as the first: Will people receive the revelation of God in Jesus? The difference between the two cycles is that the urgency of that question is highlighted as the hostility to Jesus increases.

John 11:1–12:50, The Prelude to Jesus' Hour. In most commentaries, John 11–12 is identified as the conclusion of Jesus' public ministry. This commentary proposes, however, that these two chapters form a unit in their own right in John. To read them simply as the conclusion of Jesus' ministry is to miss their narrative and theological significance in the overall development of the Gospel. Their primary function is to provide a bridge between the story of Jesus' ministry and that of his death (John 13–19). Just as

---

25. Most commentaries identify John 2:1–4:54 as a distinct unit in Jesus' ministry, because it begins and ends with a "sign" at Cana. This commentary proposes that the Cana miracles are not a unit in themselves, but only part of the first narrative cycle of Jesus' ministry. See also Kysar, *John*, 22-23, who identifies 2:1–5:47 as a unit.

John 1:1-51 stands as a prelude to Jesus' ministry, so also John 11–12 stands as the prelude to Jesus' hour. Many of the themes that will be developed fully in the narrative of Jesus' hour are anticipated here.

John 13:1–17:26, The Farewell Meal and Words of Jesus. John 13:1 signals a new orientation in the Gospel narrative; Jesus' hour, the time of his death, resurrection, and ascension, has arrived. From this point, the Gospel's focus will not waver from depicting and interpreting the events of Jesus' hour. John 13:1–17:26—which narrates the foot washing (13:1-20), Jesus' Farewell Discourse (14:1–16:33) and prayer (17:1-26)—provides the theological framework for interpreting the remainder of the Gospel.

John 18:1–19:42, "The Hour Has Come": Jesus' Arrest, Trial and Death. John 18–19 is the theological and narrative heart of the Gospel's depiction of Jesus' "hour." These chapters present the reader with the consummate portrait of Jesus as the one who willingly lays down his life for those he loves.

John 20:1-31, The First Resurrection Appearances. Jesus' hour consists of his death, resurrection, *and* ascension. John 20—Jesus' resurrection appearances, the gift of the Spirit, the ascension (alluded to, but not actually reported)—thus belongs to the narrative of Jesus' hour. It is not until Jesus' return to God (20:17) that his hour is completed.

John 21:1-25, Jesus' Resurrection Appearance at the Sea of Tiberius. This commentary proposes that John 21 be read as an integral part of the Gospel narrative (see Overview to John 21), rather than as an appendix or second ending. John 21:1-25 points toward the future life of the believing community and its continuing witness to Jesus.

JOHANNINE STUDY TODAY

The two most important figures in Fourth Gospel scholarship in the early and middle decades of the twentieth century were Rudolf Bultmann and C. H. Dodd. The contributions of Bultmann's work lay in the areas of source criticism and the literary history of the Fourth Gospel, history of religions (gnostic influence), and Johannine theology. As noted above, Dodd's major contribution was his investigation of the role of oral tradition in the shaping of the Gospel and his careful comparisons of John and the Synoptics. In addition to Dodd's demonstration of Johannine independence from the synoptic Gospels, Dodd was also a perceptive reader of Johannine literary and narrative technique, as the last third of *The Interpretation of the Fourth Gospel* demonstrates.[26]

In the decades since Bultmann and Dodd, the single most important work in Johannine studies is probably J. Louis Martyn's monograph *History and Theology in the Fourth Gospel.*[27] While others before Martyn had pursued the relationship of the Fourth Gospel to the synagogue, none had argued with such exegetical and methodological clarity. Nor had anyone so intentionally addressed the interaction between community and tradition in the formation of the Gospel. The task that Martyn sets for himself in the introduction to *History and Theology* makes this clear:

26. See C. H. Dodd, *The Interpretation of the Fourth Gospel* (Cambridge: Cambridge University Press, 1953).

27. J. Louis Martyn, *History and Theology in the Fourth Gospel* (Nashville: Abingdon, 1968; 2nd ed., 1979). See the comment by John Ashton, *Understanding the Fourth Gospel* (Oxford: Clarendon, 1993) 107.

Our first task . . . is to say something as specific as possible about the actual circumstances in which John wrote his gospel. How are we to picture daily life in John's church? Have elements of the peculiar daily experience left their stamp on the gospel penned by one of its members? May one sense even in the exalted cadences the voice of a Christian theologian who writes *in response to contemporary events and issues* which concern, or should concern, all members of the Christian community in which he lives?[28]

To meet his task, Martyn combines exegetical and historical analysis to conclude that many of the Gospel's dialogues and narratives are to be understood on two levels: (1) a witness to the time of Jesus and (2) a witness to the rearticulation of the tradition in response to events in the life of the Johannine community. As noted in the discussion above, the decisive event for this second level is the conflict of the Johannine community with the synagogue, perhaps in conjunction with the Benediction Against Heretics. In the preface to *History and Theology,* Martyn expressed his surprise that his research had led him away from previous convictions about links with Mandaean literature to the Jewish context he proposed.[29] When questions were asked about the everyday events with which the Gospel community was faced, the pivotal place of relations with Judaism reemerged.

Martyn's work decisively altered the landscape of Johannine studies in two ways. First, his analysis of the Jewish context out of which the Fourth Gospel developed remains the governing view of Johannine studies. Second, as a result of Martyn's work, and that of Raymond Brown in his commentary and subsequent monograph on the Johannine community,[30] the term "Johannine community" has become a commonplace in discussions of the Fourth Gospel. One need only survey dissertations of the 1970s and 1980s to see the prominence of studies that focus on the Johannine community.

In the decades since Martyn's and Brown's generative work about the Johannine community and its relationship to Judaism and early Christianity, two new areas of Johannine study have developed. One development was the move toward literary studies of the Gospel. In *The Anatomy of the Fourth Gospel,* the pioneer work in this field of Johannine scholarship, R. Alan Culpepper studies the literary characteristics of the Fourth Gospel and the narrative world created by them.[31] Literary-critical analysis asserts that the form and rhetorical devices of any given text must be taken with utmost seriousness and not regarded as incidental or extraneous. Studies of John's narrative structure, symbolism, irony, and imagery have enriched the encounter with the distinctive voice of the Fourth Gospel and have brought renewed vitality to exegetical work.[32]

A second important development in recent Johannine studies is the attention given

28. Ibid., 18.
29. Ibid., 11-12.
30. Raymond E. Brown, *The Community of the Beloved Disciple* (New York: Paulist, 1979).
31. R. Alan Culpepper, *The Anatomy of the Fourth Gospel* (Philadelphia: Fortress, 1983).
32. See, e.g., Paul D. Duke, *Irony in the Fourth Gospel* (Atlanta: John Knox, 1985); Gail R. O'Day, *Revelation in the Fourth Gospel* (Philadelphia: Fortress, 1986); Jeff Staley, *The Print's First Kiss: A Rhetorical Investigation of the Implied Reader in the Fourth Gospel,* SBLDS 82 (Atlanta: Scholars Press, 1988); Mark W. G. Stibbe, *John's Gospel* (New York: Routledge, 1994).

to the social world of the Gospel. This approach to John builds directly from the community history approach of Brown and Martyn, but does so with a concern for the dynamics of social and cultural factors that shaped the life of the community out of which the Gospel grew, rather than for the reconstruction of the community's history. David Rensberger's work *Johannine Faith and Liberating Community* is an important example of this approach.[33]

The student of the Gospel of John has at his or her disposal an embarrassment of riches. The Bibliography offers a sampling of the works on John to which readers of this commentary may turn for futher study.

33. See also Jerome Neyrey, *An Ideology of Revolt: John's Christology in Social-Science Perspective* (Philadelphia: Fortress, 1988); and Norman R. Petersen, *The Gospel of John and the Sociology of Light* (Valley Forge, Pa.: Trinity International, 1993).

BIBLIOGRAPHY

Commentaries

Barrett, C. K. *The Gospel According to St. John.* 2nd ed. Philadelphia: Westminster, 1978. A careful commentary on the Greek text of John that attends to textual, historical, and theological issues. Advocates Johannine dependence on Mark and Luke.

Beasley-Murray, George R. *John.* WBC 36. Waco, Tex.: Word, 1987. A critical commentary on the English text of John that combines attention to major scholarly work on John with the author's own historical and theological interests. Excellent bibliographies at the beginning of each chapter.

Brown, Raymond E. *The Gospel According to John.* AB 29 and 29A. New York: Doubleday, 1966, 1970. The definitive reference commentary on John that provides detailed coverage of introductory, textual, philological, historical, and theological issues. Also valuable for its reviews of the interpretation of John within the ancient and the modern church.

Bultmann, Rudolf. *The Gospel of John.* Philadelphia: Westminster, 1971. This monumental commentary remains the touchstone of Johannine interpretation. Despite its major problems— Bultmann's reconstruction of the "original" order of John and his hypothesis of Gnostic influence—this commentary is brilliant in both its exegesis and its articulation of the heart of Johannine theology.

Haenchen, Ernst. *John.* Hermeneia. 2 vols. Philadelphia: Fortress, 1984. This critical commentary on John was incomplete at the time of Haenchen's death and was edited into its final form by Ulrich Busse.

Hoskyns, E. C. *The Fourth Gospel.* Edited by F. N. Davey. London: Faber and Faber, 1947. This commentary was completed by F. N. Davey after Hoskyns's death in 1937. The introduction contains an invaluable essay on the interrelationship of history, theology, and interpretation in John. Hoskyns, like Bultmann after him, recognized the inseparability of exegesis and theology in the creation and interpretation of John.

Kysar, Robert. *John.* Augsburg Commentary on the New Testament. Minneapolis: Augsburg, 1986. A commentary especially directed to preachers and teachers.

Schnackenburg, Rudolf. *The Gospel According to St. John.* 3 vols. New York: Seabury, 1982. The most sweeping of all the commentaries on John, its particular areas of interest and strength are tradition-history, stylistic features, and theology. Like the work of Brown, this commentary is concerned with the history of composition and the place of John in the history of the church.

Studies on John

Bultmann, Rudolf. *The Theology of the New Testament*. New York: Scribner, 1955. This book's detailed treatment of Johannine theology establishes the contours of Johannine theology and remains the classic treatment of the subject.

Culpepper, R. Alan. *Anatomy of the Fourth Gospel: A Study in Literary Design*. Philadelphia: Fortress, 1983. This book studies the literary characteristics of John—plot, character, symbolism—in order to help the reader arrive at a clearer sense of how the Fourth Gospel tells its story.

Dodd, C. H. *Historical Tradition in the Fourth Gospel*. Cambridge: Cambridge University Press, 1963. This book is a comprehensive treatment of all of the passages in John that have any parallels in the synoptic tradition. Dodd's exegesis leads him to conclude that John does not depend on the Synoptics, but preserves an independent ancient tradition about Jesus.

————. *The Interpretation of the Fourth Gospel*. Cambridge: Cambridge University Press, 1953. The first third of this book reviews the religious and cultural background of John, and the second third reviews Johannine thought against that background. The book's final third offers a theologically and literarily insightful reading of John. Dodd is concerned with the structure and argument of John in its received form.

Käsemann, Ernst. *The Testament of Jesus: A Study of the Gospel of John in the Light of Chapter 17*. London: SCM, 1968. This important and much-debated study reads John through the lens of John 17. Käsemann sees the incarnation as a means of showing Jesus' glory and thus concludes that one finds in John evidence of "naive docetism."

Martyn, J. Louis. *History and Theology in the Fourth Gospel*. Nashville: Abingdon, 1968; 2nd ed., 1979. This is one of the most important books in Johannine studies. Its central thesis, that the Gospel of John is shaped by the Johannine community's struggles with the synagogue, is the governing view of the Gospel in contemporary scholarship. A very readable and exegetically insightful book.

Rensberger, David. *Johannine Faith and Liberating Community*. Philadelphia: Westminster, 1988. This book combines literary and sociological concerns in an attempt to interpret Johannine theology in the light of its struggles with the synagogue. Its emphasis is on the communal dimensions of Johannine faith.

Sloyan, Gerard S. *What Are They Saying About John?* New York: Paulist, 1991. This book offers the general reader a good introduction to Johannine scholarship. It begins with the commentaries of Hoskyns and Bultmann and surveys both commentaries and important monographs.

Smith, D. Moody. *The Theology of the Gospel of John*. Cambridge: Cambridge University Press, 1995. This book treats the theology of John in its historical and cultural context. An excellent introduction to Johannine theology.

OUTLINE OF JOHN

I. John 1:1-51, The Prelude to Jesus' Ministry

A. 1:1-18, The Prologue

B. 1:19-34, John's Testimony

C. 1:35-51, The First Disciples

II. John 2:1–5:47, The "Greater Things": Jesus' Words and Works

A. 2:1-12, The Wedding at Cana

B. 2:13–3:21, Jesus in Jerusalem
    2:13-22, The Cleansing of the Temple
    2:23-25, Interlude in Jerusalem
    3:1-21, Jesus and Nicodemus

C. 3:22–4:3, John's Final Testimony

D. 4:4-42, Jesus in Samaria

E. 4:43-54, The Healing of the Royal Official's Son

F. 5:1-47, A Sabbath Healing Miracle and Discourse
    5:1-18, The Miracle and Its Aftermath
    5:19-47, The Discourse

III. John 6:1–10:42, Jesus' Words and Works: Conflict and Opposition Grow

A. 6:1-71, The Bread of Life
    6:1-15, The Feeding of the Five Thousand
    6:16-24, Jesus Walks on Water
    6:25-71, Dialogue and Discourse on the Bread of Life
        6:25-34, Dialogue Between Jesus and the Crowd
        6:35-42, Jesus' First Discourse and the Crowd's Response
        6:43-52, Jesus' Second Discourse and the Crowd's Response
        6:53-59, Jesus' Third Discourse
        6:60-71, Conclusion: Jesus and His Disciples

B. 7:1–8:59, Conflict in Jerusalem
    7:1-13, Jesus Goes to Jerusalem
    7:14-36, Words of Conflict: Jesus' Teaching and Response
    7:37-52, Words of Conflict: Jesus' Teaching and Response
    [7:53–8:11, A Narrative of Conflict]
    8:12-30, Words of Conflict: Jesus' Teaching and Response
    8:31-59, Debate Between Jesus and His Jewish Opponents
        8:31-38, Freedom for the Descendants of Abraham
        8:39-47, Children of Abraham/Children of God
        8:48-59, Abraham and Jesus

C. 9:1–10:21, The Healing of the Blind Man (Miracle and Discourse)
    9:1-12, The Healing Miracle
    9:13-41, Dialogue and Interrogation
    10:1-21, The Shepherd Discourse

D. 10:22-42, Jesus at the Feast of Dedication

IV. John 11:1–12:50, The Prelude to Jesus' Hour

A. 11:1–12:11, Jesus' Hour Prefigured
    11:1-44, The Raising of Lazarus

JOHN 1:1-51

THE PRELUDE TO JESUS' MINISTRY

OVERVIEW

John 1:1-51 forms a three-part introduction to Jesus' ministry. John 1:1-18, traditionally known as the Prologue, begins the Fourth Gospel with a hymnic celebration of Jesus' origin and his coming into the world. John 1:19-34 narrates the initial witness of John the Baptist to Jesus, and John 1:35-51 narrates the gathering of Jesus' first disciples. The second and third parts of the introduction are structured as a series of four consecutive days, as the repeated expression "the next day" indicates (1:29, 35, 43). This division into four successive days is a literary device through which the Fourth Evangelist underscores the interrelatedness of these opening events. The three parts of John 1 together introduce themes that are decisive for interpreting John's story of Jesus' origin (1:1-5) and identity (1:14, 18, 29-34, 43-51); Jesus' relationship to God (1:1-2, 14, 18, 34, 35, 49, 51); Jesus' relationship to humankind (1:9-14, 16); the importance of witness to Jesus (1:7-8, 15, 19-28, 32-34); and the meaning of faith and discipleship (1:7, 12, 35-51).

JOHN 1:1-18, THE PROLOGUE

1 In the beginning was the Word, and the Word was with God, and the Word was God. [2]He was with God in the beginning.

[3]Through him all things were made; without him nothing was made that has been made. [4]In him was life, and that life was the light of men. [5]The light shines in the darkness, but the darkness has not understood[a] it.

[6]There came a man who was sent from God; his name was John. [7]He came as a witness to testify concerning that light, so that through him all men might believe. [8]He himself was not the light; he came only as a witness to the light. [9]The true light that gives light to every man was coming into the world.[b]

[10]He was in the world, and though the world was made through him, the world did not recognize him. [11]He came to that which was his own,

a5 Or darkness, and the darkness has not overcome   b9 Or This was the true light that gives light to every man who comes into the world

1 In the beginning was the Word, and the Word was with God, and the Word was God. [2]He was in the beginning with God. [3]All things came into being through him, and without him not one thing came into being. What has come into being [4]in him was life,[a] and the life was the light of all people. [5]The light shines in the darkness, and the darkness did not overcome it.

6There was a man sent from God, whose name was John. [7]He came as a witness to testify to the light, so that all might believe through him. [8]He himself was not the light, but he came to testify to the light. [9]The true light, which enlightens everyone, was coming into the world.[b]

10He was in the world, and the world came into being through him; yet the world did not know him. [11]He came to what was his own,[c] and

a Or [3]through him. And without him not one thing came into being that has come into being. [4]In him was life   b Or He was the true light that enlightens everyone coming into the world   c Or to his own home

515

NIV

but his own did not receive him. [12]Yet to all who received him, to those who believed in his name, he gave the right to become children of God— [13]children born not of natural descent,[a] nor of human decision or a husband's will, but born of God.

[14]The Word became flesh and made his dwelling among us. We have seen his glory, the glory of the One and Only,[b] who came from the Father, full of grace and truth.

[15]John testifies concerning him. He cries out, saying, "This was he of whom I said, 'He who comes after me has surpassed me because he was before me.'" [16]From the fullness of his grace we have all received one blessing after another. [17]For the law was given through Moses; grace and truth came through Jesus Christ. [18]No one has ever seen God, but God the One and Only,[b, c] who is at the Father's side, has made him known.

[a]13 Greek *of bloods*   [b]14 Or *the Only Begotten*   [c]18 Some manuscripts *but the only* (or *only begotten*) *Son*

NRSV

his own people did not accept him. [12]But to all who received him, who believed in his name, he gave power to become children of God, [13]who were born, not of blood or of the will of the flesh or of the will of man, but of God.

[14]And the Word became flesh and lived among us, and we have seen his glory, the glory as of a father's only son,[a] full of grace and truth. [15](John testified to him and cried out, "This was he of whom I said, 'He who comes after me ranks ahead of me because he was before me.'") [16]From his fullness we have all received, grace upon grace. [17]The law indeed was given through Moses; grace and truth came through Jesus Christ. [18]No one has ever seen God. It is God the only Son,[b] who is close to the Father's heart,[c] who has made him known.

[a]Or *the Father's only Son*   [b]Other ancient authorities read *It is an only Son, God,* or *It is the only Son*   [c]Gk *bosom*

COMMENTARY

The Gospel of John opens with one of the most challenging texts in the NT. The scope of John 1:1-18 is challenging, because the Fourth Evangelist begins the Gospel with the cosmic pre-existence of the Word and the Word's relationship to the world rather than with stories of Jesus' birth (Matt 1:1–2:23; Luke 1:1–2:52) or with the proclamation of John the Baptist (Mark 1:1-8; cf. John 1:6-8, 15). The form of John 1:1-18 also presents an interpretive challenge, because at many points the Prologue seems to have more in common with the cadences of early Christian hymns (e.g., Phil 2:5-11; Col 1:15-20) than with the prose of Gospel narratives. The reader of John 1:1-18 must grapple, therefore, with a wide range of issues, from the nature of its theological language, to its relationship to the rest of the Gospel of John, to its composition history, and relation to other Jewish and early Christian literature.

It is helpful for the reader of John 1:1-18 to have a picture of the overall movement of the Prologue as the first step in its interpretation. The Prologue consists of four parts: (1) 1:1-5, The

eternal Word is the Light and Life of Creation; (2) 1:6-8, John the Baptist witnesses to the Light; (3) 1:9-13, The Light, or Word, came into the World; and (4) 1:14-18, The Word became flesh and dwells among us.[34]

As these four divisions suggest, the Prologue is concerned with two different spheres of God's presence: (1) the eternal, the sphere of the cosmic Word of God, and (2) the temporal, the sphere of John the Baptist, the world, and the incarnate Word. The interaction between these two spheres is at the heart of the Prologue.

Three interrelated critical issues determine how one views the relationship among the parts of the Prologue: (1) the composition history of John 1:1-18; (2) the relationship of verses about John the Baptist (vv. 6, 8, 15) to the rest of the Prologue; and (3) the point at which the Prologue speaks of the incarnate Word.

The debate about the composition history of

34. This division is the same as that proposed by C. K. Barrett, *The Gospel According to St. John,* 2nd ed. (Philadelphia: Westminster, 1978) 149-50.

John 1:1-18 focuses on whether parts of the Prologue derive from an independent hymn that was modified to form the introduction to the Fourth Gospel, and on the provenance of the language and ideas of the Prologue. The poetic structure of some verses, especially vv. 1-5, and the distinctive theological vocabulary of 1:1-18 are cited as evidence of the incorporation of an earlier hymn. For example, "Word" (λόγος *logos*) is used as a christological term only in the Prologue (1:1, 14) and "grace" (χάρις *charis*) also occurs only in these opening verses of the Gospel (vv. 1, 14, 16-17).

Fourth Gospel scholarship is marked by a variety of reconstructions of the "original hymn." The criteria that govern these reconstructions range from a strict definition of poetic style to the commentator's assumptions about the theological intent of the Evangelist.[35] There is virtually total agreement that vv. 1-5 belong to the "original hymn," and that vv. 6-8, 15 are prose interpolations, but as far as the status of the remainder of the Prologue, what some scholars read as poetry, others read as the Evangelist's additions. The variety of reconstructions should caution the interpreter against basing a reading of the Prologue exclusively on any one reconstruction of the "original hymn." Moreover, as Barrett has wisely noted, scholars' lack of ability to arrive at a clear understanding of what is poetry or prose in the Prologue also suggests that it does not follow any strict definition of poetry. Indeed, rhythmic prose may be a better description of the style of the Prologue.[36] Interestingly, one finds a comparable variety of proposals about the structure of the Prologue from scholars who eschew source-critical questions and investigate the Prologue with literary methods.[37]

The provenance of the "original hymn" also divides scholars. There are three main scholarly hypotheses. First, in the early part of the twentieth century, Rudolf Bultmann argued that the Prologue is a revision of a *logos* hymn that originated in a Gnostic community that traced its origins back to John the Baptist (the Mandaeans).[38] This Gnostic hypothesis exerted tremendous influence on the study of the Prologue, even though the *Odes of Solomon* and the Mandaean literature that Bultmann cited postdated the Gospel of John. The publication of documents from Nag Hammadi stimulated renewed interest in the relationship between the Prologue and Gnosticism, although the Nag Hammadi documents, too, postdate the Fourth Gospel.[39]

Second, many scholars maintain that theories of a Gnostic provenance are unnecessary, because the Prologue can more helpfully be read against the backdrop of Judaism. C. H. Dodd, for example, while not actively engaging Bultmann's thesis, was one of the main proponents of an alternative provenance from which the Prologue grew: the Jewish wisdom tradition, including Philo's use of the term *logos*.[40] A Jewish provenance for the language and ideas of the Prologue has in its favor that the wisdom traditions predate the Fourth Gospel and that much of the Fourth Gospel is steeped in Jewish traditions (see the Introduction). Indeed, the Jewish wisdom tradition, both biblical and extra-biblical, has emerged as the governing view of the provenance of the language of the Prologue.[41]

35. See, for example, Rudolf Schnackenburg, *The Gospel According to St. John,* 3 vols. (New York: Seabury, 1982) 1:225-26. For his full treatment of the poetry of the Prologue, see his "Logos-Hymnus und johanneischer Prolog," *BZ* 1 (1957) 69-109. See also Rudolf Bultmann, *The Gospel of John: A Commentary,* trans. G. R. Beasley-Murray, R. W. N. Hoare, and J. K. Riches (Philadelphia: Westminster, 1971) 16-18. Brown provides a representative sampling of these efforts in *The Gospel According to John (I–XII),* AB 29 (Garden City, N.Y.: Doubleday, 1966) 22.

36. See Barrett, *The Gospel According to St. John,* 151; Ernst Haenchen, *John,* Hermenia, 2 vols. (Philadelphia: Fortress, 1984) 1:124; D. A. Carson, *The Gospel According to John* (Grand Rapids: Eerdmans, 1991) 112.

37. E.g., R. Alan Culpepper, "The Pivot of John's Prologue," *NTS* 27 (1980) 1-31; Jeffrey Staley, "The Structure of John's Prologue: Its Implications for the Gospel's Narrative Structure," *CBQ* 48 (1986) 241-64.

38. See Rudolf Bultmann, "The History of Religions Background of the Prologue to the Gospel of John," in John Ashton, ed., *The Interpretation of John* (Philadelphia: Fortress, 1986). This article was first published in 1923 in *Eucharisterion: Festschrift für Hermann Gunkel II.* Bultmann published a second, more detailed, article advocating this thesis, "Die Bedeutung der neuerschlossen mandaïschen und mandaïschen Quellen für das Verständnis des Johannesevangeliums," *ZNW* 24 (1925) 100-146.

39. For the contemporary discussion of Gnostic influence, see J. M. Robinson, "The Johannine Trajectory," in J. M. Robinson and H. Koester, ed., *Trajectories in Early Christianity* (Philadelphia: Fortress, 1971) 232-68; Kurt Rudolf, *Gnosis: The Nature and History of Gnosticism* (San Francisco: Harper & Row, 1983) 149, 382n. 48; G. Robinson, "The Trimorphic Protennoia and the Prologue of the Fourth Gospel," in J. E. Goehring et al., eds. *Gnosticism and the Early Christian World,* J. M. Robinson Festschrift (Sonoma, Calif.: Polebridge, 1990) 37-50.

40. C. H. Dodd, *The Interpretation of the Fourth Gospel* (Cambridge: Cambridge University Press, 1953) 272-85.

41. For a review of this development, see Robert Kysar, *The Fourth Evangelist and His Gospel: An Examination of Contemporary Scholarship* (Minneapolis: Augsburg, 1975). For more recent studies, see Peder Borgen, "The Prologue of John as Exposition of the OT," in Borgen, *Philo, John, and Paul: New Perspectives on Judaism and Early Christianity,* BJS 131 (Atlanta: Scholars Press, 1987) 75-102; Craig R. Koester, *The Dwelling of God: The Tabernacle in the Old Testament, Intertestamental Jewish Literature, and the New Testament,* CBQMS 22 (Washington, D.C.: Catholic Biblical Association, 1990); T. H. Tobin, "The Prologue of John and the Hellenistic Jewish Speculation," *CBQ* 52 (1990) 253-69; Craig A. Evans, *Word and Glory: On the Exegetical and Theological Background of John's Prologue,* JSNTSup 89 (Sheffield: Sheffield Academic Press, 1993).

Third, many scholars who accept a Jewish provenance for much of the language and ideas of the Prologue see the origin of the hymn itself within the Johannine community. For example, Haenchen, Brown, and Kysar argue that the writer of the Fourth Gospel has incorporated a hymn composed by a member of his community.[42]

It is also important to note that some scholars question the very notion of an "original hymn." Barrett and Carson argue that John 1:1-18 was specially written by the Evangelist himself to introduce the Fourth Gospel.[43]

Interpreters who read John 1:1-18 as an original hymn with prose interpolations give secondary status to the verses about John the Baptist (vv. 6-8, 15). It is suggested that these verses belonged originally with 1:19 and were displaced to accommodate the hymn. The presence of vv. 6-8, 15 is sometimes even cited as evidence of the Fourth Evangelist's misunderstanding of the "original hymn."[44] By contrast, scholars who question the notion of an "original hymn" view the John the Baptist verses as being essential to the understanding of the purpose of the Prologue.[45]

The way one interprets the place of the John the Baptist verses directly influences one's answer to the third critical question: At what point does the Prologue begin to speak about the historical Jesus (the incarnate Word)? The options are at v. 5, v. 10, or v. 14. It is clear that the most explicit statement of the incarnation occurs at v. 14, but is it the first? If one removes the John the Baptist verses, then it is possible to argue that vv. 1-5 focus on the cosmic Word; vv. 9-13 on the drama of God's Word with Israel; and that the historical Jesus becomes the subject of the Prologue only at v. 14.[46] If one includes the John the Baptist verses as being essential to the Prologue, however, then from v. 5 onward the Prologue must be read as pointing to the historical Jesus.

This commentary agrees with C. K. Barrett and others that John 1:1-18 was specially composed by the Evangelist as the beginning of the Fourth Gospel. It is highly likely that the Prologue does incorporate phrases from a pre-existent hymn, since all NT writers made use of earlier materials. Those phrases are no longer reclaimable in verse form, however. In John 1:1-18, the Fourth Evangelist has created something new out of two strands of early Christian tradition, both of which were probably familiar to his readers: a hymn that celebrated the cosmic origins and pre-existence of Jesus the Word, and the John the Baptist material, the traditional beginning point for the story of Jesus' ministry. The beginnings of Matthew and Luke employ a related technique, because also in those Gospels the evangelists affixed birth traditions to the John the Baptist material (Matt 1:1–3:17; Luke 1:1–3:20). The Fourth Evangelist has not simply affixed a tradition about Jesus' origin to the John the Baptist tradition, however, but has woven the two traditions together. It is incorrect to view the John the Baptist material as interpolations into an "original hymn," because the Evangelist fuses the two traditions together in order to orient his story to the theologically necessary beginning point of Jesus' ministry: Jesus' beginning *beyond* time and history in conjunction with his beginning *in* time and history. For the writer of John, the two belong together. The identification of possible phrases from an earlier hymn can be important if it helps to clarify the two strands of traditions the Evangelist brings together to create his distinctive Gospel beginning, but it works against a theologically coherent reading of the Prologue to insist on labeling part of the Prologue as hymnic and part as interpolation. The Fourth Evangelist's combination of the hymn tradition with the John the Baptist tradition is a deliberate strategy to establish the theological framework out of which the whole Gospel develops.

1:1-5. 1:1. The cosmic, transtemporal dimension of the Prologue receives its fullest expression in 1:1-5. John 1:1 contains three short phrases whose vocabulary and contents overlap. Each new phrase builds from the end of the preceding phrase in stairstep parallelism: "in the beginning was *the Word,* and *the Word* was with *God,* and *the Word* was *God.*" (The word order of the Greek text of v. 1*c* makes the

42. Ernst Haenchen, *John, Hermenia,* 2 vols. (Philadelphia: Fortress, 1984) 1:101, 125; Brown, *The Gospel According to John (I–XII),* 20-23; Robert Kysar, *John,* Augsburg Commentary on the New Testament (Minneapolis: Augsburg, 1986) 28.

43. See Barrett, *The Gospel According to St. John,* 151; Carson, *The Gospel According to John,* 111-12.

44. Haenchen, *John,* 1:128.

45. Morna Hooker, "John the Baptist and the Johannine Prologue," *NTS* 16 (1969–70) 354-58. See also Barrett, *The Gospel According to St. John,* 151; Carson, *The Gospel According to John,* 113.

46. See Kysar, *John,* 28-29; Haenchen, *John,* 1:113-15, 119. See also the important discussion of Ernst Käsemann, "The Structure and Purpose of the Prologue to John's Gospel," in *New Testament Questions of Today* (London: SCM, 1969) 138-52.

stairstep parallelism even more apparent: καὶ θεὸς ἦν ὁ λόγος [*kai theos ēn ho logos*].)

What is the origin of the term *logos,* "the Word"? In answering this question, it is important to remember that during the first century CE, the boundaries between different religions, philosophies, and cultures were fluid. One cannot draw a sharp line between Hellenism and Judaism, for example, because the two were in constant contact with each other in the eastern Mediterranean world. One should not be surprised, therefore, that *logos* appears in a variety of religions and philosophies with which the writer of John may have been familiar.

The most disputed claim is that the origins of the Fourth Evangelist's use of *logos* are to be found in Gnosticism.[47] As noted earlier, one can cite no Gnostic document in which *logos* appears that predates the Fourth Gospel, and so the argument for Gnostic influence is difficult to support. In fact, the line of influence from the Prologue to second-century Gnostic documents is much easier to substantiate.

Logos figures prominently in early Stoicism as the term for the rational principle of the universe, and that cosmological sense of *logos* is evident in John's Prologue. It is likely, however, that the Fourth Evangelist's reading of *logos* was more influenced by Jewish and early Christian interpretations of Stoicism than by Stoic philosophy directly.

The most fertile place to look for the background of *logos* is within Judaism. Philo is an excellent example of a Jewish contemporary of the Fourth Evangelist who melded Greek philosophy, particularly Stoicism and Platonism, with Jewish thought about God. In Philo, *logos* figures prominently as a way of speaking about the creative plan of God that governs the world.[48] Yet the Fourth Evangelist's use of *logos* to speak about Jesus does not seem to be directly derivative from Philo, but is a christocentric reading of the meaning of "the Word" in Judaism by someone steeped in the same Hellenistic culture.

The Prologue's picture of the role of the Word in creation and in human history thus draws on the Word of God in the OT. The creation accounts in Genesis are governed by God's spoken word; God spoke through the law at Sinai and through the prophets. The Word encompasses both word and deed, and that fits well with the image of *logos* in the Prologue. The Word also brings with it associations from the Jewish wisdom tradition. In Prov 8:22-31, for example, Wisdom has been God's companion "before the beginning of the earth," working alongside God to accomplish God's plan for humanity. In later Jewish wisdom traditions more directly influenced by Greek thought, "Wisdom" (σοφία *sophia*) becomes increasingly "a personal being standing by the side of God over against, but not unconcerned with, the created world."[49] The Fourth Evangelist makes an important shift in wisdom terminology, however. Wisdom (*sophia*) is a feminine noun in Greek, and indeed, is often clearly depicted as a female character in the wisdom literature (e.g., Prov 9:1-6; Sir 24:1-2, 28-29). By employing the term *logos,* a masculine noun, instead of *sophia,* the Fourth Evangelist reshapes the wisdom tradition to reflect the historical reality of the incarnation.[50]

In the use of *logos,* then, John has chosen a term familiar to both Jews and Greeks, but has used it in a new context with fresh meanings. John draws on the rich symbolism associated with *logos* and uses it as the lens through which he views the coming of Jesus into the world. The varieties of religious speculations that receive expression in *logos* in the Hellenistic world are subsumed by John into the revelation of God in Jesus.

John 1:1 stresses the eternal existence of the Word with God, an existence outside the bounds of time and history. The opening words of John 1:1, "in the beginning . . . ," recall the first words of Gen 1:1 (the Greek is identical with Gen 1:1 in the LXX), but they point to a time before the creation of the world. Creation is not spoken of until v. 3. As the Prologue unfolds, the eternal Word will not stay outside time and history, but will enter into the time-bound world. The contrast between the eternal and the temporal is seen in the

47. Rudolf Bultmann, *The Gospel of John: A Commentary,* trans. G. R. Beasley-Murray, R. W. N. Hoare, and J. K. Riches (Philadelphia: Westminster, 1971), 25-31.

48. E.g., Philo *Op. Mund.* 17-24.

49. Barrett, *The Gospel According to St. John,* 153. See also Wis 7:22, 27; Sirach 24.

50. For a discussion of gender questions and the role of *sophia* in the Fourth Gospel, see *Sophia and the Johannine Jesus,* JSNTSup 71 (Sheffield: Sheffield Academic Press, 1992).

Prologue in the contrast of the verb "to be" with the verb "to become" or "to come into being."[51]

There is a stairstep progression of thought as well as from among the three phrases of John 1:1. They move from the existence of the Word (v. 1*a*) to the relationship of the Word with God (v. 1*b*) to the identity of the Word as God (v. 1*c*). Verse 1*c* is the most difficult of the three phrases because of its affirmation "the Word was God." With these words, John affirms that the Word is fully God, just as Paul affirms in Phil 2:6 that Jesus "was in the form of God" and was equal to God. Through this phrase, John states that the Word is what God is and the Word does what God does. The Word thus "represents the self-expression of God," anticipating one of the central emphases of the Fourth Gospel.[52] When he says "the Word was God," John affirms the oneness of the Word and God (cf. John 10:30), not that the Word is a second God.

Verse 1 thus provides the ontological underpinnings of the Fourth Gospel's central claim that when one sees Jesus, one sees God; when one hears Jesus, one hears God (e.g., 5:37-38; 8:19; 14:9-11). The oneness of the Word and God means that the revelation spoken and enacted by the Word is indeed the revelation of God (cf. 1:18).

1:2. This verse recapitulates the three phrases of v. 1 and expresses them as one thought. This summary prepares the reader to move from the pre-existence and identity of the Word to the role of the Word in creation (v. 3) and the effect of the Word on what was created (vv. 4-5).

1:3-5. There is a punctuation problem at vv. 3-4. At issue is whether the phrase "what has come into being" (NRSV) belongs with the description of creation in v. 3 (NIV, NRSV alt.) or with the description of life in v. 4 (NRSV). The manuscript evidence and interpretations of the early church are divided on which punctuation is to be preferred, as is modern scholarship.[53] This commentary accepts the punctuation used in the NIV translation as the preferred reading. The repetition in the description of creation through the

Word in v. 3 ("without him nothing was made that has been made") is similar stylistically to the description of the Word in vv. 1-2. Moreover, the opening of v. 4, "In him [the Word] was life," introduces one of the Fourth Gospel's central claims about Jesus (e.g., 5:26; 6:35; 11:25; 14:6).

Verse 3 thus contains two statements about creation through the Word, one positive and one negative. The positive statement affirms that everything came into being through the Word (v. 3*a*). The second statement maintains that nothing was created without the Word (v. 3*b*). This positive/negative construction, an example of antithetical parallelism, underscores the role of the Word in all creation and hence the unity of all creation.

In vv. 4-5, the focus shifts from the created order in general to human beings. By affirming that "in him was life," the Prologue moves from the role of the Word in the one moment of creation to the ongoing, life-giving character of the Word. This ability to give and sustain life is symbolized by the light (cf. 8:12; 9:5; 11:9). The verb tenses that describe the interaction of light and darkness warrant attention. The light "shines," present tense, but the activity of darkness is narrated in the past tense. The verb tenses recall the initial moment when the light came into the world (past tense), yet also acknowledge the continuation of that light into the present (present tense).

The verb that describes the action of the darkness in v. 5 (καταλαμβάνω *katalambanō*) can be translated several ways. One translation renders the verb as "overcome" (NRSV) and thus denotes a struggle in which the light is victorious. A second translation renders the verb as "understood" (NIV) and denotes inability to recognize and understand what the light offers. Either translation is consonant with the rest of the Prologue.

1:6-8. Verse 6 introduces an actor from the human drama into the Prologue: John. John has a slightly different function in the Fourth Gospel than in the other Gospels. He is never identified as "the Baptist," nor is he ever called the forerunner of Jesus. Instead, John has one function in this Gospel: to witness to Jesus (v. 8).

The witness of John to the light is full of promise, because it contains the seeds of faith (v. 7). The description of John also contains a polemi-

---

51. For a fuller discussion of "being" and "becoming" in John 1:1-18, see Karl Barth, *Witness to the Word* (Grand Rapids: Eerdmans, 1986), and Frank Kermode, "St. John as Poet," *JSNT* 28 (1986) 3-16.

52. Kysar, *John,* 29.

53. Brown (*The Gospel According to John I–XII,* 6) agrees with the punctuation reflected in the NRSV, whereas Barrett (*The Gospel According to St. John,* 156-57), Haenchen (*John,* 1:113-14), and Schnackenburg (*The Gospel According to St. John,* 1:239-40) argue for the punctuation reflected in the NIV.

cal note, however. Verse 8 states quite clearly that John was not the light. The Fourth Evangelist thus removes any grounds for overvaluing the person of John by subordinating him to the "true light" (v. 9) (cf. 5:35). John was not a messianic figure, but a witness (see Commentary on 1:19-34).

As noted earlier, scholars debate whether v. 5 is a reference to the coming of Christ into the world. Some maintain that v. 5 is part of the "original" wisdom hymn and, therefore, refers only to the light of wisdom. The mention of John in vv. 6-8, however, indicates that whatever v. 5 may have meant in a hypothetical original hymn, the Fourth Evangelist wanted his readers to hear it as an allusion to the incarnation. The witness of John belongs to the story of Jesus. As the light enters the world, the focus shifts from the eternal Word to the historical. The transtemporal is wedded to concrete human experience through the person and witness of John.

1:9-13. 1:9. The NIV and the NRSV include v. 9 in the same paragraph with vv. 6-8. While the reference to the "true light" strengthens the refutation of John as the light (v. 8), v. 9 is best understood as introducing a new section of the Prologue. It carries forward from vv. 4-5 the notion that the light enlightens all people, but also explicitly states that the light was "coming into the world." Verse 9 thus contains a fresh allusion to the incarnation.

1:10. The text moves almost imperceptibly from the light as subject (neuter, v. 9) to the Word as subject (masculine, v. 10). This shift reflects the flexibility and fluidity of terminology used in the Prologue to speak of the Word. Life and light, the subjects of vv. 4-5, and 9, are two ways the Word expresses itself in the world. This is the first use of "world" (κόσμος *kosmos*) in the Gospel, a noun that will appear frequently throughout the Fourth Gospel. It is not a synonym for creation in general, but is used to refer specifically to humanity and its domain.

At first glance, v. 10*b* seems to be a reprise of v. 3, stressing both the temporality of creation ("came into being") and the role of the Word in creation. Verse 10*b* uses the language of v. 3, however, to make a fresh point. Its focus is on humanity, not creation in general, and it emphasizes that even the human domain was created through the agency of the Word. This emphasis

serves two purposes. First, it opposes the dualistic view of creation held by Gnosticism; even the human world belongs to the goodness and unity of creation. Second, it makes even more painful the rejection of the Word by the world in v. 10*c*. The world owes its very existence to the Word, but it did not know him. "To know" and its related term "to see" are key concepts in the Gospel of John. As the Gospel unfolds, whether people believe in Jesus will hinge on what they are able to know or to see.

1:11-13. These verses expand on v. 10*c*. Their focus moves from the Word to the fate of the Word in the world. Verse 11 narrates the drama of rejection. "His own" (ἴδιος *idios*) is used in two forms. It is used first in the neuter plural ("his own things"), which probably refers in general to the place of his own, the world he created; it is used, secondly, in the masculine plural to refer more specifically to "his own people"— either Israel and the Jewish people or more broadly the very humanity who came into being through the Word but nonetheless "did not receive him."

Verse 12 and its amplification in v. 13 express the salvific purpose of Jesus' ministry. When one believes in the name of Jesus, one is given power (NRSV; "right," NIV) to become a child of God. In graphic images, v. 13 contrasts the birth of a child of God with more conventional understandings of conception and birth. A child of God will not be born of blood or of sexual desire ("the will of the flesh," NRSV; "human decision," NIV). The expression "the will of man" refers to the role of sperm in conception, because the male was understood to be the carrier of new life. This section of the Prologue contains many themes that will feature prominently in the rest of the Gospel: light, life, knowledge, acceptance and rejection, the world, belief in Jesus, and new birth. It also heightens the interaction between the eternal and the temporal in two ways. First, the world's response to the Word is explicitly recounted as a drama of rejection and acceptance. Second, human beings, who belong to the temporal realm ("came into being," v. 10), are given a chance for life that depends on faith, not on temporal constraints. Despite the rejection in v. 11, vv. 9-13 end on a note of hope and promise.

1:14-18. 1:14. *Logos* appears in v. 14 for the first time since v. 1, as the Evangelist draws together all the threads of the hymn as it moves to its conclusion. Verse 14 states boldly what the reader of the Gospel has been assuming all along: the incarnation. Every word of v. 14 is important. It begins by announcing that the *logos,* the eternal Word, "became flesh." This is the first time the verb "to become" (γίνομαι *ginomai*) has been used of the Word; prior to v. 14, only the verb "to be" has been used. The verb changes in v. 14 in order to show that the Word has decisively moved from the eternal to the temporal. The historical Jesus is explicitly in the purview of the Prologue.

The meaning of "flesh" (σάρξ *sarx*) in v. 14*a* is an important point of discussion in Fourth Gospel scholarship. The range of interpretations is best represented in the contrasting views of Bultmann and Käsemann. Bultmann saw in v. 14*a* an affirmation of the full humanity of Jesus, understanding *sarx* as "the sphere of the human and the worldly as opposed to the divine."[54] It is in Jesus' "sheer humanity that he is the Revealer."[55] The core paradox of the incarnation, for Bultmann, is that the "glory" (δόξα *doxa*) can only be seen in the "flesh" (*sarx*).[56] Käsemann, by contrast, gave very little weight to the words of v. 14*a* because he felt that the Fourth Gospel did not portray Jesus as a believable human being; rather, he was "God striding across the earth."[57] The fact that the Word became flesh only means that the Word "entered the world of createdness" and took on flesh, not that he became fully human. Because Käsemann accented v. 14*c* ("and we have seen his glory"), he labeled the Fourth Gospel's christology "naive docetism."[58]

Bultmann's interpretation of v. 14*a* comes closer to the significance of the incarnation for the Fourth Gospel. At the heart of the incarnation for John is the reality that the glory is indeed revealed in Jesus' flesh (cf. 2:11). But v. 14*a* is weighted differently than Bultmann weighs it. The point of the incarnation is not that "the revealer is nothing but a man."[59] Rather, the use of *logos* in v. 14 draws the reader back to the first uses of *logos* in v. 1, and the juxtaposition of the two verses holds the key to the Fourth Evangelist's theology of incarnation.[60] "The Word was God" is now "The Word became flesh"; yet both statements remain valid. The Revealer, Jesus, is not a mere man, but is the Word of God made flesh, become human. The two statements of vv. 1 and 14 provide the theological basis for the whole Gospel (see Reflections).

Verse 14*b* also should be read alongside v. 1. "The Word was with God" is now "the Word . . . made his dwelling among us" (NIV). The Word who dwelt with God now dwells with "us," human beings like himself.[61] The introduction of the first-person plural pronoun in v. 14 is important. With its appearance, the perspective of the Prologue shifts from observation to confession: The Word lived among *us,* not simply in the world. The Prologue now claims the Word for the believing community. The note of confession continues in v. 14*c,* "we have seen his glory." The "we" does not refer to eyewitnesses but to the confessing community.

"To make one's dwelling" (σκηνόω *skēnoō,* v. 14*b*) is a verb rich with OT associations, because it recalls God's promise to dwell with God's people (Ezek 37:27 LXX). It comes from the same root as the noun for "tabernacle" or "tent" (σκῆνος *skēnos*), the place where God spoke to Moses (Exod 33:9) and where God's glory was seen (Exod 40:34).[62] This verb is the first in a series of images recalling Israel's Sinai experience (Exodus 19–40) that figure in the concluding verses of the Prologue ("glory," v. 14*c;* "law," v. 17; Moses, v. 17).

"Glory" (*doxa,* v. 14*c*) and "to glorify" (δοξάζω *doxazō*) figure prominently in the Fourth Gospel. John picks up the OT sense of "glory" as the manifest presence of God and confesses that this presence is now visible in Jesus. Yet, as noted

54. Rudolf Bultmann, *The Gospel of John: A Commentary,* trans. G. R. Beasley-Murray, R. W. N. Hoare, and J. K. Riches (Philadelphia: Westminster, 1971) 62.

55. Ibid., 63.

56. Ibid.

57. Ernst Käsemann, *The Testament of Jesus: A Study of the Gospel of John in the Light of Chapter 17* (London: SCM, 1968) 73.

58. Ernst Käsemman, "The Structure of John's Prologue," in *New Testament Questions of Today* (London: SCM, 1969) 148; *The Testament of Jesus,* 45, 66.

59. Bultmann, *The Gospel of John,* 62.

60. Marianne Meye Thompson, *The Humanity of Jesus in the Fourth Gospel* (Philadelphia: Fortress, 1988) 40.

61. Ibid.

62. Craig Koester, *The Dwelling of God: The Tabernacle in the Old Testament, Intertestamental Jewish Literature, and the New Testament* (Washington, D.C.: Catholic Biblical Association, 1989).

above, it is glory visible only in the humanity of the incarnate Word, the historical Jesus. As the Fourth Gospel's narrative unfolds, it will become clear that for the Fourth Evangelist, the fullest expression of Jesus' glory is found in his death, resurrection, and ascension (7:39; 12:16, 23, 28; 13:31). "The Father's only Son" is a characteristic Johannine way of speaking of the relationship between God and Jesus. It emphasizes Jesus' unique ("One and Only," NIV) relationship with God. "Full of grace and truth" echoes the Hebrew word pair "steadfast love" and "truth" (חסד *hesed* and אמת *'ĕmet*; e.g., Exod 34:6) that speaks of God's covenantal love and faithfulness. The concentration of OT language and imagery intensifies as the focus of the Prologue turns from the eternal Word to the incarnation.

1:15-17. These verses expand on the confessional note of v. 14*c*. John is the first witness to Jesus, and, therefore, it is appropriate that John's testimony be given as evidence of what "we have seen." The validity of John's witness is conveyed by the present tense verbs that introduce it ("John testifies . . . and cries out, saying . . . "). His witness is not locked in the past, but continues into the present. The two realms with which the Prologue is concerned, the eternal and the temporal, come together in v. 15. John, whose appearance in v. 6 introduced a concrete historical referent, bears witness in v. 15 to the pre-existence of Jesus ("he was before me"). John thus witnesses to the truth of v. 14, because he recognizes the pre-existent Word in the person of Jesus. Interestingly, John's witness in the synoptic Gospels only refers to Jesus as "the one who comes after me" (Matt 3:11; Mark 1:7; Luke 3:16); it contains no allusion to pre-existence.

Verses 16-17 return to the confession of the believing community. The community receives a share in the fullness of the Word. The grace and truth of the Word (vv. 14, 17) become the "grace upon grace" of the community's life. The double use of "grace" (χάρις *charis*) underscores the superabundance of gifts available to the believer through the incarnate Word. *Charis* occurs only four times in the Fourth Gospel, all in the Prologue. John establishes the theme of grace in the Prologue and then will illustrate it throughout the Gospel without naming it again.

Verse 17 places the gift of "grace upon grace"

in a specific historical context. The gift of the law through Moses (Exod 20:34) is placed next to a new gift: the grace and truth that came through Jesus Christ. Verse 17 does not disparage the previous gift, but points to the gift now available through Jesus Christ as something wondrously new.

Jesus Christ is named for the first time in the Gospel in v. 17. This ending of the Prologue recalls the hymn in Philippians where Jesus also is not named until the end of the hymn (Phil 2:10-11). The final note of celebration, and the most explicit statement of the community's embrace of the Word, includes the name of the one celebrated and praised.

1:18. This verse concludes the Prologue, but it also serves as an introduction to the Gospel narrative. It is central to understanding the Fourth Gospel, because it states explicitly John's understanding of Jesus' ministry and saving work: to make God known. The verb "to make known" (ἐξηγέομαι *exēgeomai*) shares the same Greek root as the noun for "exegesis," so this verse states that Jesus will bring out or interpret God.

This bold assertion is supported by three phrases that establish the uniqueness of the revelation of God in Jesus. First, John reminds the reader of an assumption well-known from the OT: No one has ever seen God. Second, John identifies Jesus as "God the only Son" ("the One and Only," NIV). This phrase has engendered controversy among even its earliest interpreters, because it is sometimes read as claiming that the Son is a second God. Interpreted in this way, this phrase threatens the monotheistic basis of Judaism and Christianity. Indeed, some manuscripts substitute "Son" for "God" to temper the claim of this phrase (these substitutions are reflected in the variants in the NRSV footnotes). Such tempering both misreads and weakens v. 18. This verse does not claim that the Son is a second God but that the only Son shares in the fullness of God, is fully God. This is the same claim made in v. 1*c*, "the Word was God." Third, v. 18 says that Jesus "is in the bosom of the Father." This phrase speaks of the intimate relationship between Father and Son. It, too, recalls an earlier verse of the Prologue, "the Word was with God" (v. 1*b*). In this last verse, then, the Prologue returns to its initial themes, but restates them in the concrete language of the Son and the Father instead of the Word and God. The reader of the Prologue has moved from the eternal Word to the grace and truth of the incarnate Word, Jesus Christ, and is now ready to enter the Gospel narrative.

The Gospel of John contains two overarching themes: Jesus' identity and the believer's identity in relationship to Jesus. Both of these themes are established in the Prologue. Vocabulary and im-ages introduced in the Prologue will recur throughout the Gospel—e.g., life (v. 4), light and darkness (v. 5), witness (v. 7), truth (v. 9, 17), world (v. 9), knowledge (v. 10), acceptance and rejection (vv. 11-12), children of God (v. 13), glory (v. 14), Father and Son (v. 18). John 1:1-18 introduces the reader to the life and ministry of Jesus, yet also encompasses the totality of that life.

REFLECTIONS

As noted in the Commentary, in John 1:1-18, the Fourth Evangelist has fused a variety of traditional materials—a hymnic tradition about the pre-existent Word, John the Baptist traditions, as well as many traditional images drawn from the OT—to orient his story of Jesus. Much of the content of the Prologue had familiar resonances for the Gospel's first readers, then, but none of it would have been familiar in this form. It is not enough for readers to recognize individual words or phrases of the Prologue; we must interpret them in the new context created by the Fourth Evangelist. And we can understand what that context is only when we have worked through the whole Prologue—and the whole Gospel! The interpreter thus discovers how to read and interpret the Prologue only by reading and interpreting it.

This reformulation of familiar material is seen most powerfully in the closing verses of the Prologue (1:14-18), in which the language about God and Word (1:1) is transformed to language about Father and Son (1:18). The Word became flesh (1:14) and the Word's name is Jesus Christ (1:17). The story of the Word is thus the story of Jesus; the story of Jesus is thus the story of the Word. This sweeping claim expresses the ontological reality out of which the Fourth Evangelist operates and against which every word of the Prologue is to be read. The Word becoming flesh is the decisive event in human history—indeed, in the history of creation—because the incarnation changes God's relationship to humanity and humanity's relationship to God. The incarnation means that human beings can see, hear, and know God in ways never before possible. The Father-Son relationship of God and Jesus is the key to this changed relationship. God's Son, because he is the incarnate Word, derives his identity from God (1:1, 18). The relationship between divine and human is transformed, because in the incarnation human beings are given intimate, palpable, corporeal access to the cosmic reality of God.

The newness wrought by God in Jesus is so dramatic that a conventional narrative of origins is insufficient. That is because the story *of* Jesus is not ultimately a story *about* Jesus; it is, in fact, the story of God. The Word's incarnation in Jesus redefines life, creation, and salvation, and in John 1:1-18 the Fourth Evangelist gives the Gospel reader the theological road map of God's self-revelation in Jesus. John 1:1-18 does not allow readers to distance themselves from that revelation, but instead draws the reader into the theological claims of the text.

Given the world-making significance of the incarnation for John, it is no wonder that he begins his Gospel with the words "in the beginning." As noted above, these words are intentionally evocative of the opening of Genesis 1. The priestly writers of the creation story in Genesis 1 took Israel back to the time before the created order, to the moment before God spoke creation into existence, and John does the same thing with his readers. "In the beginning" there was God and the Word, and the rest of the story unfolds from that relationship. John 1:3, like Genesis 1, views creation as belonging to God's Word. In the newly created order, life and light (v. 4) are the ways in which the Word, God's self-expression, is effective. John 1:1-4 evokes the wonder of creation, the gift of life, the power of the Word, and celebrates the mystery of revelation that transcends conventional limits of time and space. The resilience of the light that shines in the darkness (v. 5) is confirmation of the power of life available in the Word.

John reads the story of creation and God's Word through the lens of the incarnation, not simply OT traditions, however, so the story of creation gives way quickly to another story. The cosmological imagery of vv. 1-5 is wedded to concrete historical experience through the person and witness of John (vv. 6-8). The story of the Word, of God's self-expression, does not remain outside human experience but belongs to that experience. Moreover, the story of John the Baptist introduces faith and human response to the light into the story of the Word (v. 7).

In vv. 9-13, the joyous celebration of the Word and the light and life the Word offers gives way to the complex reality of human response. What does it mean not to accept the Word? In the context of the Prologue, it means not to see God in the Word, to deny that the Word is God's self-expression in the world. More specifically, in the context of vv. 6-8, it means not to accept that Jesus, to whom John the Baptist bears witness, is God's self-expression, that Jesus is the Word, the source of life and light for all people (vv. 4-5).

The rejection of the Word by Jesus' own people is restricted neither to the time of Jesus nor to that of the Fourth Gospel. The specific referent of "his own" is never explicitly identified in the Fourth Gospel (cf. 4:44). It stands as a figure for those on whom Jesus has some prior claim but who nonetheless reject him. In Jesus' time (and the time of the Fourth Evangelist) those on whom that prior claim had been made were the Jewish people, to whom the Word of God had been spoken before (cf. Heb 1:1), who had shared in God's story from "the beginning" (Gen 1:1). For contemporary Christians, however, the identification of Jesus' "own people," those on whom Jesus has prior claim, requires more interpretive work. The rejection of Jesus by those who have shared in the story of the incarnation from "the beginning" (John 1:1) is the true tragedy, and the church may sometimes find itself in the role of Jesus' rejecting "own."

Verses 12-13 highlight the tragedy of rejection by describing the fresh possibilities offered to those who believe. In these verses, the people who did receive Jesus are identified as those who "believed in his name." At this point in the Prologue, the name of the Word is Jesus, and those who receive Jesus thus believe that God is available in Jesus. This belief is the beginning of a new relationship with God, because those who believe are now children of God (1:12). Verses 12-13 thus express both the anthropological and the soteriological dimensions of the incarnation for the Fourth Evangelist; those who receive the incarnate Word become new people and enter into a new life with God (cf. 3:3-8).

The drama of rejection and acceptance of vv. 9-13 thus places a vivid choice before the reader: to either accept the Word and participate in a new relationship with God or reject the Word and receive nothing of the life and light the Word offers.

At v. 14, the Fourth Evangelist reveals where he stands in the drama of rejection and acceptance; he has received the Word. The Fourth Evangelist claims for himself and his community the wonder and mystery of the incarnation. The concluding section of the Prologue is neither neutral nor objective, but confesses, "We have seen his glory."

With the words "the Word became flesh and lived among us," the community recognized the bond that had been established between them and God as revealed in Jesus. God did not stay distant from them, remote and isolated; rather, in Jesus, God chose to live with humanity in the midst of human weakness, confusion, and pain. This bond holds for the contemporary Christian community as well. To become flesh is to know joy, pain, suffering, and loss. It is to love, to grieve, and someday to die. The incarnation binds Jesus to the "everydayness" of human experience. When the believing community confesses along with the Fourth Evangelist that the Word "lived among us," it affirms the link between the incarnation and its own humanness.

The reader is thus drawn into the confessions of v. 14c ("we have seen his glory") and v. 16 ("we have all received, grace upon grace"). This confessional language offers its vision of glory and its gifts of grace to each successive community that appropriates this text. In the Prologue, the first-century community rejoices in these gifts and opens up that joy to any others who wish to share their confessions. The joyous witness of the Prologue is spoken by those whose own experience has been decisively marked by the incarnation. John 1:14-18 is not theological speculation about the character of the incarnate Word, but the testimony of those whose lives have been changed by the incarnation.

John 1:1-18 appears in the church's lectionaries during the Christmas season. The lectionary thus asks the church to regard Jesus' coming into the world from the perspective of this text. This text contains none of the conventional elements of the Christmas story. Instead of manger, angels, and magi, John 1:1-18 presents the church with its explicit theological vision of the difference the incarnation makes in the life of the world.

JOHN 1:19-34, JOHN'S TESTIMONY

NIV

[19]Now this was John's testimony when the Jews of Jerusalem sent priests and Levites to ask him who he was. [20]He did not fail to confess, but confessed freely, "I am not the Christ.[a]"

[21]They asked him, "Then who are you? Are you Elijah?"

He said, "I am not."

"Are you the Prophet?"

He answered, "No."

[22]Finally they said, "Who are you? Give us an answer to take back to those who sent us. What do you say about yourself?"

[23]John replied in the words of Isaiah the prophet, "I am the voice of one calling in the desert, 'Make straight the way for the Lord.'"[b]

[24]Now some Pharisees who had been sent [25]questioned him, "Why then do you baptize if you are not the Christ, nor Elijah, nor the Prophet?"

[26]"I baptize with[c] water," John replied, "but among you stands one you do not know. [27]He is the one who comes after me, the thongs of whose sandals I am not worthy to untie."

a20 Or Messiah. "The Christ" (Greek) and "the Messiah" (Hebrew) both mean "the Anointed One"; also in verse 25.   b23 Isaiah 40:3
c26 Or in; also in verses 31 and 33

NRSV

19This is the testimony given by John when the Jews sent priests and Levites from Jerusalem to ask him, "Who are you?" 20He confessed and did not deny it, but confessed, "I am not the Messiah."[a] 21And they asked him, "What then? Are you Elijah?" He said, "I am not." "Are you the prophet?" He answered, "No." 22Then they said to him, "Who are you? Let us have an answer for those who sent us. What do you say about yourself?" 23He said,

"I am the voice of one crying out in the wilderness,

'Make straight the way of the Lord,'"

as the prophet Isaiah said.

24Now they had been sent from the Pharisees. 25They asked him, "Why then are you baptizing if you are neither the Messiah,[b] nor Elijah, nor the prophet?" 26John answered them, "I baptize with water. Among you stands one whom you do not know, 27the one who is coming after me; I am not worthy to untie the thong of his sandal." 28This took place in Bethany across the Jordan where John was baptizing.

29The next day he saw Jesus coming toward him and declared, "Here is the Lamb of God

a Or the Christ

NIV

[28]This all happened at Bethany on the other side of the Jordan, where John was baptizing.

[29]The next day John saw Jesus coming toward him and said, "Look, the Lamb of God, who takes away the sin of the world! [30]This is the one I meant when I said, 'A man who comes after me has surpassed me because he was before me.' [31]I myself did not know him, but the reason I came baptizing with water was that he might be revealed to Israel."

[32]Then John gave this testimony: "I saw the Spirit come down from heaven as a dove and remain on him. [33]I would not have known him, except that the one who sent me to baptize with water told me, 'The man on whom you see the Spirit come down and remain is he who will baptize with the Holy Spirit.' [34]I have seen and I testify that this is the Son of God."

NRSV

who takes away the sin of the world! [30]This is he of whom I said, 'After me comes a man who ranks ahead of me because he was before me.' [31]I myself did not know him; but I came baptizing with water for this reason, that he might be revealed to Israel." [32]And John testified, "I saw the Spirit descending from heaven like a dove, and it remained on him. [33]I myself did not know him, but the one who sent me to baptize with water said to me, 'He on whom you see the Spirit descend and remain is the one who baptizes with the Holy Spirit.' [34]And I myself have seen and have testified that this is the Son of God."[a]

[a] Other ancient authorities read *is God's chosen one*

COMMENTARY

1:19-28. John appeared as the first witness to Jesus in the Prologue (1:6-8, 15), and his witness begins the Gospel proper. On the first day (vv. 19-28), John testifies that he is not the light (1:8*a*); on the second day (vv. 29-34), John testifies to the light (1:8*b*).[63]

John 1:19 announces the theme of vv. 19-28: "This is the testimony given by John." "Testimony" or "witness" ($\mu\alpha\rho\tau\nu\rho\iota\alpha$ *martyria*) has religious and juridical dimensions, and both figure prominently in the Fourth Gospel. John's testimony to Jesus will lead others to faith, but it is also offered as evidence in a trial. John's interrogators in this passage are not curious passersby, but are a delegation sent by official Judaism (vv. 19, 22). The expression "the Jews" (οἱ Ἰουδαῖοι *hoi Ioudaioi*, v. 19) occurs repeatedly in the Fourth Gospel and has a wide range of meanings (see Introduction and Reflections on John 5:1-18 and John 8). Its most common usage, as in 1:19, is as a synonym for the Jewish religious establishment, which is the source of most of the opposition to Jesus' ministry in John.

The interrogation of 1:19-28 has a formal cast

and revolves around the question "Who are you?" (v. 19). The issue of John's identity must be resolved before the central question of the Gospel, Jesus' identity, can be addressed. The formal, emphatic beginning of v. 20 ("He confessed and did not deny it, but confessed") communicates the solemnity of John's response. John confesses, "I am not the Christ," even though he was not asked whether he was the Messiah. The Greek of John's denial (ἐγὼ οὐκ εἰμιν *egō ouk eimi*, "I am not") provides a pointed contrast with the language Jesus uses to speak about his identity in John (ἐγώ εἰμι *egō eimi*, "I am"). The rhetoric of John's denial thus reinforces its content; he is not the Christ.

Unlike the delegation's first question, the second and third supply predicates, "Are you Elijah?"; "Are you the prophet?" (v. 21). Elijah and the prophet were both figures upon whom some of the messianic expectations of Judaism came to rest. Elijah was transported into heaven without dying (2 Kgs 2:11), and many Jews expected his return as the harbinger of the messianic age (e.g., Mal 4:5). "The prophet" derives from the prophet-like-Moses of Deut 18:15. In the Qumran community, this prophet was seen as a messianic

63. C. H. Dodd, *Historical Tradition in the Fourth Gospel* (Cambridge: Cambridge University Press, 1963) 240.

figure, and similar expectations may lie behind the delegation's question.[64]

John's denials become increasingly terse. His denial that he is Elijah points to a major difference between the portrayal of John in the Fourth Gospel and the Synoptics. In Matthew (11:14; 17:10-13) and Mark (9:13), Jesus identifies John as Elijah; in Luke the angel announces to Zechariah that his son will be like Elijah (Luke 1:17). John is a witness to Jesus in the Fourth Gospel, however, and not a messianic figure. His response to the repeated question about his identity (v. 22) is to apply Isa 40:3 to himself (v. 23). In the synoptic Gospels, by contrast, Isa 40:3 is spoken about John (Matt 3:3; Mark 1:2-3; Luke 3:4). In the Fourth Gospel, John thus identifies himself as the voice who announces and gives witness.

Verse 24 begins a second stage of interrogation. In Jesus' time, the Pharisees were one among many groups of Jewish religious leaders, but by the time of the Fourth Evangelist, the Pharisees' successors, the rabbis, were the dominant group in Judaism. John draws attention to the Pharisaic presence in v. 24 in order to imply continuity between the authorities who opposed Jesus during his lifetime and the Jewish authorities who oppose the Johannine community (cf. the role of the Pharisees in John 9).

The question in v. 25 focuses on John's authority and his reasons for baptizing. John's answer shifts the focus away from baptism to Jesus (vv. 26-27). Verse 27 emphasizes the secondary position of the one who witnesses in relation to the one witnessed; not even slaves were required to undo their master's sandals. The Bethany of v. 28 should not be confused with the Bethany near Jerusalem (11:1).

1:29-34. In 1:19-28, John was unfraid to speak the truth about his identity and his ministry to officials from the religious establishment. In these verses, John boldy announces the truth to any who will hear. John 1:29-34 is structured to highlight John's testimony. First, the passage is dominated by verbs of witness: "see" (vv. 29, 32-34), "witness" (vv. 32, 34), "say" (vv. 29-30, 32, 34). Second, this passage consists almost entirely of direct discourse. The Fourth Evangelist does not talk about John's witness, but allows the

Gospel readers to hear John's witness for themselves. In 1:23, John identified himself as the voice of witness, and in 1:29-34 the reader hears that voice. Jesus first appears in the Fourth Gospel in v. 29, but in this scene he will stay on the sidelines and say nothing. The focus is on John's witness.

John identifies Jesus as "the Lamb of God who takes away the sin of the world" (v. 29). The singular of "sin" (ἁμαρτία hamartia) in v. 29 emphasizes the world's collective brokenness, not individual human sins. "Lamb of God" is rooted in OT imagery, but scholars are divided about its precise referents. In the mouth of John the Baptist, "lamb of God" might have referred to the conquering lamb found in post-biblical Jewish apocalyptic (for a Christian adaptation of the symbolism, see Rev 17:14).[65] The expression more likely recalls the servant songs of Second Isaiah (particularly Isa 53:7) or the Passover lamb, the cultic and liturgical symbol of Israel's deliverance (Exod 12:1-13).[66] In Judaism, the Passover lamb was not viewed as a sacrifice for sin, but the early church quickly reinterpreted Passover symbolism in the light of the eucharist (e.g., 1 Cor 5:7-8). Indeed, in the Fourth Gospel Jesus' crucifixion is linked to the slaughter of the paschal lamb. For example, the Fourth Evangelist links Jesus' unbroken legs at the crucifixion (19:33) with the Exod 12:46 teaching about the Passover lamb (19:36). Brown and Schnackenburg rightly suggest that the metaphor "lamb of God" cannot be explained by either the servant songs or the Passover lamb alone, but evokes them both.[67] John's title for Jesus in v. 29 (the first in a series of titles for Jesus in chap. 1) thus draws on a rich heritage of symbols to identify Jesus as the redeemer for the world's sin.

John testifies to Jesus' pre-existence, but his words sound more like a riddle than direct announcement. This verse echoes the testimony attributed to John in the Prologue (1:15) and express the christological claims of the early church, more than the testimony of a first-century Jewish prophet. John is thus confirmed as a valid

---

64. See, e.g., 1QS 9:11.

65. C. H. Dodd, *The Interpretation of the Fourth Gospel* (Cambridge: Cambridge University Press, 1953) 230-38.

66. C. K. Barrett, *The Gospel According to St. John,* 2nd ed. (Philadelphia: Westminster, 1978) 175-77.

67. Raymond E. Brown, *The Gospel According to John (I–XII),* AB 29 (Garden City, N.Y.: Doubleday, 1966) 60-63; Rudolf Schnackenburg, *The Gospel According to St. John,* 3 vols. (New York: Seabury, 1982) 1:298-301.

and reliable witness because he testifies to the truth of the claims of the church.

Verse 31 provides John's full answer to the question of v. 25: Why does he baptize? There is no notion of John's baptism of repentance (cf. Matt 3:1-12), because John's baptism belongs solely to his witness. This becomes even clearer in the account of Jesus' baptism in vv. 32-34. John is not depicted as an actor in Jesus' baptism; John's only role is to allude to it, for the text does not actually say that John baptized Jesus. God and the Spirit are the actors. Indeed, as vv. 31*a* and 33 make clear, John "knew" Jesus only because John had been told by God how to interpret the descent of the dove (v. 32).

John 1:29-34 ends with a formal statement of witness by John (v. 34). The verbs in v. 34, "see" (ὁράω *horaō*) and "witness" (μαρτυρέω *martyreō*), are in the perfect tense. The Greek perfect tense denotes a completed past action whose effect continues into the present. John's witness thus continues into the present. John recognizes Jesus as the "Son of God." To do so is to acknowledge Jesus' unique relationship with God and hence his ability to reveal God in ways never before available (cf. 1:14, 18).

The words of John the Baptist in 1:29-34 offer a rich witness to Jesus: He is the Lamb of God, the one who takes away the world's sin (v. 29), the pre-existent one (v. 30), the bearer of the Holy Spirit (v. 33), the Son of God (v. 34). The Fourth Evangelist's focus on John's role as witness contains an important theological affirmation, because witnessing is one beginning point of faith in this Gospel (e.g., 3:11, 32-36; 4:39). Yet this focus may also have a polemical edge. At the time of the Fourth Evangelist, there were persons who held to John the Baptist's teaching and baptism instead of Jesus' (Acts 18:25; 19:1-5). The Fourth Evangelist's insistence on John's role as witness and not messianic forerunner can be read in the light of this rivalry.

JOHN 1:35-51, THE FIRST DISCIPLES

NIV

[35] The next day John was there again with two of his disciples. [36] When he saw Jesus passing by, he said, "Look, the Lamb of God!"

[37] When the two disciples heard him say this, they followed Jesus. [38] Turning around, Jesus saw them following and asked, "What do you want?"

They said, "Rabbi" (which means Teacher), "where are you staying?"

[39] "Come," he replied, "and you will see."

So they went and saw where he was staying, and spent that day with him. It was about the tenth hour.

[40] Andrew, Simon Peter's brother, was one of the two who heard what John had said and who had followed Jesus. [41] The first thing Andrew did was to find his brother Simon and tell him, "We have found the Messiah" (that is, the Christ). [42] And he brought him to Jesus.

Jesus looked at him and said, "You are Simon son of John. You will be called Cephas" (which, when translated, is Peter[a]).

[a]42 Both *Cephas* (Aramaic) and *Peter* (Greek) mean *rock*.

NRSV

[35] The next day John again was standing with two of his disciples, [36] and as he watched Jesus walk by, he exclaimed, "Look, here is the Lamb of God!" [37] The two disciples heard him say this, and they followed Jesus. [38] When Jesus turned and saw them following, he said to them, "What are you looking for?" They said to him, "Rabbi" (which translated means Teacher), "where are you staying?" [39] He said to them, "Come and see." They came and saw where he was staying, and they remained with him that day. It was about four o'clock in the afternoon. [40] One of the two who heard John speak and followed him was Andrew, Simon Peter's brother. [41] He first found his brother Simon and said to him, "We have found the Messiah" (which is translated Anointed[a]). [42] He brought Simon[b] to Jesus, who looked at him and said, "You are Simon son of John. You are to be called Cephas" (which is translated Peter[c]).

[a] Or *Christ* [b] Gk *him* [c] From the word for *rock* in Aramaic (*kepha*) and Greek (*petra*), respectively

NIV

43The next day Jesus decided to leave for Galilee. Finding Philip, he said to him, "Follow me."

44Philip, like Andrew and Peter, was from the town of Bethsaida. 45Philip found Nathanael and told him, "We have found the one Moses wrote about in the Law, and about whom the prophets also wrote—Jesus of Nazareth, the son of Joseph."

46"Nazareth! Can anything good come from there?" Nathanael asked.

"Come and see," said Philip.

47When Jesus saw Nathanael approaching, he said of him, "Here is a true Israelite, in whom there is nothing false."

48"How do you know me?" Nathanael asked.

Jesus answered, "I saw you while you were still under the fig tree before Philip called you."

49Then Nathanael declared, "Rabbi, you are the Son of God; you are the King of Israel."

50Jesus said, "You believe*a* because I told you I saw you under the fig tree. You shall see greater things than that." 51He then added, "I tell you*b* the truth, you*b* shall see heaven open, and the angels of God ascending and descending on the Son of Man."

a50 Or Do you believe ...? *b51 The Greek is plural.*

NRSV

43The next day Jesus decided to go to Galilee. He found Philip and said to him, "Follow me." 44Now Philip was from Bethsaida, the city of Andrew and Peter. 45Philip found Nathanael and said to him, "We have found him about whom Moses in the law and also the prophets wrote, Jesus son of Joseph from Nazareth." 46Nathanael said to him, "Can anything good come out of Nazareth?" Philip said to him, "Come and see." 47When Jesus saw Nathanael coming toward him, he said of him, "Here is truly an Israelite in whom there is no deceit!" 48Nathanael asked him, "Where did you get to know me?" Jesus answered, "I saw you under the fig tree before Philip called you." 49Nathanael replied, "Rabbi, you are the Son of God! You are the King of Israel!" 50Jesus answered, "Do you believe because I told you that I saw you under the fig tree? You will see greater things than these." 51And he said to him, "Very truly, I tell you,*a* you will see heaven opened and the angels of God ascending and descending upon the Son of Man."

a Both instances of the Greek word for you in this verse are plural

COMMENTARY

1:35-42. John 1:35-51 (the third and fourth days), in which John's disciples follow Jesus, enact 1:7 ("He came as a witness to testify to the light, so that all might believe through him."). John's words to his disciples are not new (vv. 35-36); he previously identified Jesus as the lamb of God (v. 29). The significance of his witness is that the two disciples follow Jesus as a direct result of John's witness (v. 37). In the synoptic Gospels, the first disciples give up their work as fishermen to follow Jesus (Matt 4:18-22; Mark 1:16-20; Luke 5:1-11), but in the Fourth Gospel they give up a previous religious commitment as disciples of John.[68] Verses 35-37 probably reflect the historical reality that disciples of John were among the first to follow Jesus.

After his testimony, John simply disappears from

68. Barrett, *The Gospel According to St. John,* 179.

the scene. He is accorded no formal exit (cf. Nicodemus's disappearance from the text after 3:10). John has performed his function in the story, and, therefore, the story is finished with him. This will be true also at 3:24; John disappears from the Gospel narrative with no mention of his death. He has led others to Jesus, and his witness will now be replaced by his disciples' own experience of Jesus.

1:37-39. The verb "to follow" (ἀκολουθέω *akoloutheō,* v. 37) operates on two levels. It has a literal meaning in the story line, but it also serves as a metaphor for discipleship (see 8:12; 10:4, 27; 12:26; 13:36). Words with meanings that make sense on both a literal and a symbolic level occur frequently in the Fourth Gospel and are a distinctive trait of the Johannine literary style. Indeed, the entire dialogue between Jesus and his first two disciples in vv. 38-39 is suggestive of two levels of meaning.

Jesus initiates the conversation with the two disciples (v. 38*a*). His words make sense in the story line, but they also convey one of the central questions of this Gospel: What do people seek when they follow Jesus? Jesus' first words in the Gospel of John thus address the reader as well as the characters in the story. The disciples address Jesus as "Rabbi" (v. 38*b*). This transliteration of the Hebrew term occurs rarely in the NT (four times each in Matthew and Mark, eight times in John, never in Luke). Its use here evokes the actual speech patterns of the disciples. John translates the term because its Greek form (διδάσκαλος *didaskalos,* "teacher") would have been more familiar to readers who spoke Greek, and not Hebrew (or Aramaic).

The two disciples ask Jesus a question that works on the level of the story line (they want to know where Jesus stays), but the Greek word for "stay" (μένω *menō*) is also used in the Fourth Gospel to assert that the relationship of God, Jesus, and the Spirit with one another and with believers (e.g., 1:32, 33; 8:31, 35; 14:10, 17; 15) is permanent, not sporadic. This question, too, has theological overtones. Jesus does not answer the disciples' question directly, but issues an invitation that will allow them to find the answer for themselves (v. 39). The Johannine Jesus will often answer questions with indirection in order to allow those whom he encounters to discover the truth about Jesus for themselves (e.g., 4:9-10; 6:28-29; 18:35-38). The invitation to "come and see" is an offer to see Jesus with the eyes of faith (e.g., 1:46; 6:36; 9:35-41; 14:9). In v. 39*b*, the disciples respond precisely to Jesus' invitation; they come and see. Their vocation as disciples of Jesus begins. The reference to the "tenth hour" may be included as a point of demarcation to indicate a decisive beginning point for the disciples' new life.[69]

Significantly, the first two disciples are not given names in this call narrative. Their anonymity is reflective of the Johannine understanding of discipleship. The Fourth Gospel has a much less rigid and hierarchical understanding of discipleship than the synoptic Gospels do. Its circle of

disciples is broader. There is, for example, no formal catalogue of the twelve disciples in John.

1:40-42. The story of the two new disciples is incomplete until their witness brings others to Jesus (vv. 40-42). Andrew is named as one of the disciples in v. 40 in order to provide a link to the block of Petrine tradition preserved in vv. 41-42. Andrew's witness to Peter contains a new title, "Messiah." The Hebrew word "Messiah" (משיח *māšîaḥ*) occurs transliterated only here and 4:25 in the entire NT. As with "rabbi," the Greek form of the word ("Christ" [Χριστός *Christos*]) would be more familiar to John's readers.

The Fourth Evangelist places the tradition of Jesus' renaming Simon early in the Gospel narrative (v. 42; cf. Matt 16:17-19) in order to highlight Jesus' insight into Peter's future role in the church. In Matthew, the focus of the tradition is on Peter, but in John, Jesus' words are as much a revelation about Jesus' knowledge as they are about Peter's role. Jesus' omniscience will be highlighted at other points in the Fourth Gospel, most immediately in 1:47-49.

1:43-51. The fourth day ("the next day," v. 43) continues the call of Jesus' disciples. Jesus finds Philip and invites him to discipleship ("Follow me"). The identification of Philip by name and place (v. 44) provides a link to the passage about Andrew and Peter (vv. 40-42). The names of these three disciples are among the Twelve in all three synoptic lists (Mark 3:16-19 and par.).

1:45. Philip finds Nathanael and bears witness to Jesus, just as Andrew did with Peter in v. 40. Nathanael does not appear in any of the other Gospels and is absent from their lists of the Twelve. As noted earlier, John does not define discipleship in terms of the formal company of the Twelve. Philip's witness is in two parts. First, he identifies Jesus as the fulfillment of all Scripture (cf. Luke 24:27). Second, he identifies Jesus in the way one commonly distinguished one man from another: by naming his father, "Jesus, son of Joseph of Nazareth." This second identification articulates Jesus' putative human origins, but the truth of Jesus' origins was revealed in the Prologue: Jesus comes from God (1:1-2, 14, 18). The eyes of faith know that Joseph is not Jesus' father; God is (1:14, 18, 34). Philip's double identification of Jesus in v. 45 introduces a tension that will run throughout the Fourth Gospel: whether

---

69. Rudolf Schnackenburg, *The Gospel According to St. John,* 3 vols. (New York: Seabury, 1982) 1:309.

those who see Jesus will recognize the divine origins of this human being or think that knowledge of his human origins is the whole story (e.g., 6:42; 7:42).

1:46. For the first time in chap. 1, testimony to Jesus is met with resistance (v. 46a). Nathanael's resistance highlights the tension inherent in Philip's witness. Philip does not argue with Nathanael. Instead, he extends the same invitation to Nathanael ("come and see," v. 46b) that Jesus extended to his first disciples (v. 39b). Philip invites Nathanael to see for himself that the fulfillment of Scripture is indeed occurring in this human (son of Joseph) from Nazareth.

1:47-50. These verses comprise the longest conversation between Jesus and a disciple in chap. 1. Jesus reveals the most about himself to the one who expressed skepticism and doubt (cf. the Thomas story, 20:24-29). Jesus hails Nathanael as an "Israelite." The term *Israelite* occurs only in v. 47 in John and is used to convey Nathanael's model faithfulness. Jesus may praise Nathanael because he accepted Philip's invitation even though he had questions. "Israelite" has none of the ambiguities and shades of meaning that "Jew" carries with it in this Gospel. Jesus' words in v. 47 recall Ps 32:2 and its description of the righteous believer.

Jesus reveals more insight into Nathanael in v. 48. The precise meaning of his words is unclear. Scholars have speculated about the significance of the fig tree, but such speculation is tangential to John's emphasis here.[70] The focus of the story is on the fact of Jesus' superhuman knowledge and its effect on Nathanael. Nathanael correctly perceives Jesus' knowledge as an act of self-revelation and so comes to faith (vv. 49-50).

Nathanael's response to Jesus is more than witness ("this is . . . "); it is a confession ("You are . . . "). "Rabbi" links his response to the words of the first disciples (v. 38). "Son of God" (cf.1:34) is the central expression of Jesus' identity in the Fourth Gospel, because it recognizes Jesus' true origins. "King of Israel" is used as a term of mockery and derision in the passion narratives of Matthew (27:42) and Mark (15:32) but in John it is a positive term, expressing Jesus' significance for the people of God (see also 12:13).

Jesus' words to Nathanael in v. 50 are not a rebuke but a promise. These words, too, recall the story of Thomas (20:29). Jesus does not criticize the grounds of Nathanael's faith, but suggests that Nathanael is only at the beginning point of his faith in Jesus. The "greater things" Nathanael will see will be occasions for deepening faith.

1:51. "Very truly I say . . . " translates the Greek expression (ἀμὴν ἀμὴν λέγω *amēn, amēn, legō* . . .). A single *amēn* introduces some sayings of Jesus in the other Gospels (e.g., Matt 5:18; Mark 9:41; Luke 4:24), but the double *amēn* occurs only in John. Indeed, it is one of the distinctive marks of the speech patterns of the Johannine Jesus, occurring twenty-five times. Its solemn tones draw attention to the saying that follows. It is used to introduce a new thought (e.g., 5:24-25) or to mark the transition from dialogue to monologue (e.g., 3:11). The "you" to whom Jesus speaks in v. 51 is second-person plural, indicating that Jesus is speaking to a wider audience than Nathanael—i.e., also to the readers.

The plural pronoun may also suggest that the Son of Man saying originally circulated independently of this setting. In its present location, however, John 1:51 forms an appropriate conclusion to chap 1. John and his disciples have borne witness to Jesus, but v. 51 offers Jesus' own powerful promise of self-revelation. He identifies himself as the Son of Man. In the synoptic Gospels, this title is associated with Jesus' suffering and death (e.g., Matt 20:18; Mark 8:31; Luke 9:22), lowliness (e.g., Mark 10:45), and future coming (e.g., Matt 24:30; Mark 8:38; Luke 9:26), but v. 51 suggests that for John the Son of Man is the one who bridges the distance between heaven and earth (cf. 3:13; 6:62). This title thus continues the Fourth Evangelist's focus on the cruciality of the incarnation as the way in which God is made known to God's people.

Verse 51 is not a direct citation of any OT text, but is rich with allusions that the Fourth Evangelist reshapes. The verse combines images from the descent of the Son of Man in Dan 7:13 and Jacob's dream ladder in Gen 28:12. Much of the power of this use of the OT arises precisely because it defies a simple point-for-point correspondence with any one text. John's images thus stay constantly fresh and alive. The ladder of Gen 28:12 is replaced by the Son of Man, so that the

---

70. See Raymond E. Brown, *The Gospel According to John (I–XII)*, AB 29 (Garden City, N.Y.: Doubleday, 1966) 83.

Son of Man becomes the locus of God's activity on earth. The Son of Man becomes the place where the earthly and the heavenly, divine and human, temporal and eternal meet.

REFLECTIONS

John 1:19-51 focuses on two interrelated themes: the identity of Jesus and the meaning of discipleship. Both John the Baptist and Jesus' first disciples witness to Jesus' identity. The purpose of John's witness is to reveal Jesus, who is the source of redemption for the world (1:29-31). John first identifies Jesus with a traditional image, Lamb of God (1:29), but he complements that witness with the central claim of the Fourth Gospel: Jesus is the Son of God. The hope of redemption lies in recognizing Jesus as the Son of God. In many ways, then, John's witness makes the same move the Prologue does, claiming Jesus' relationship with God as the decisive category for understanding who Jesus is (cf. 1:18).

Yet "Son of God" is not the only christological title in John 1. The verses of John 1 overflow with such titles. If we move through chap. 1 in sequence, we find the following litany of titles:

> Lamb of God who takes away the sin of the world (v. 29)
> Son of God (v. 34)
> Lamb of God (v. 36)
> "Rabbi" (which translated means Teacher) (v. 38)
> "Messiah" (which is translated Anointed) (v. 41)
> Him about whom Moses in the law and also the prophets wrote (v. 45)
> Son of Joseph from Nazareth (v. 45)
> Rabbi (v. 49)
> Son of God (v. 49)
> King of Israel (v. 49)
> Son of Man (v. 51)

Why are there so many names for Jesus? Each disciple sees something different in Jesus and bears witness in his own way. Each disciple came to Jesus with differing expectations and needs—one needed a teacher, another the Messiah, another the fulfillment of Scripture—and each of these needs was met. Yet v. 51, Jesus' words about himself, suggests that none of these titles ultimately answers the question, Who is Jesus? The disciples' testimonies are only the beginning; they will see "greater things." The imagery of v. 51 suggests that the reality of God in Jesus outruns traditional categories and titles.

All the titles in John 1 must be read through the lens of the Prologue and, hence, through the lens of the incarnation. As the Gospel narrative progresses, the titles from chap. 1 will be replaced, expanded, transformed, or redefined by Jesus' words and works and ultimately by his death and resurrection. The rich variety of testimonies in chap. 1 is both cautionary and celebratory. It cautions the reader not to limit Jesus to preconceived categories and expectations but to keep one's eyes open for a surprising revelation of God. The church needs to attend to this caution, because it sometimes acts as if it has answered the last question about Jesus' identity and arrived at the definitive title for him. For example, when new images or metaphors for understanding Jesus and his relationship to the faith community arise in the church, they are often met with suspicion if not outright hostility for not being "orthodox" or being contrary to "tradition." Such absoluteness precludes fresh and vital calls to discipleship. The panoply of titles for Jesus in John 1 suggests that to insist on one name for Jesus is to miss the fullness of his identity.

Yet the sequence of succeeding witnesses in chap. 1 also celebrates the boundlessness of God's grace in Jesus. The litany of titles demonstrates the "fullness" from which the church is invited to receive "grace upon grace" (1:16). The christological richness of John 1:19-51 suggests that the list of titles for Jesus is open-ended. Just as each successive disciple in the narrative of John 1 had his needs and expectations met when he encountered Jesus, so also this text suggests that when the members of the contemporary faith community bring their new needs and expectations to Jesus, those needs will be met. As will be seen in the commentary below, the "I am" sayings (e.g., "I am the light of the world") point to a similar richness and boundlessness of God's grace in Jesus.

The christological focus of John 1:19-51 reveals much about the Fourth Evangelist's understanding of discipleship. The decision to be a disciple is inseparable from the decision one makes about Jesus' identity. John's entire ministry of baptism served the revelation of Jesus to Israel (1:31); what John does is determined by who Jesus is. As each new disciple comes to Jesus, the decision to follow Jesus is made in response to a statement about Jesus' identity (1:41, 45). Unlike the synoptic call narratives, where Jesus promises the disciples a change in their own lives (Matt 4:19; Mark 1:17; Luke 5:10), the focus of the call narratives in John is unwaveringly christological. The call narratives begin with the identity of Jesus, and any change for the disciples begins with recognizing and claiming Jesus. It is essential, therefore, that the Johannine call narratives be allowed to speak in their own voice and not be forced into the mold of the more familiar call narratives of the synoptic Gospels.

These stories remind the church that discipleship is an active engagement with Jesus. John 1:19-51 consists almost entirely of dialogue, so that the readers themselves become participants in the drama of discipleship. The reader becomes the audience for John's testimony. The reader is able to hear Jesus' initial question to the first disciples, "What are you looking for?" (v. 38), as a question addressed to the reader as well. One hears the variety of witnesses given by the disciples and can ponder Jesus' invitation to "Come and see." John does not report stories about discipleship but invites the reader to share in the call to discipleship. Moreover, these stories are dominated by verbs: *follow, see, seek, stay, find.* These verbs, too, emphasize that discipleship is active and involves interacting with Jesus.

In the last discipleship story of John 1, Nathanael moves from skepticism (v. 46) to bold christological confession (v. 49). What marks Nathanael as a disciple is that he knows who Jesus is, that he sees that the man from Nazareth is in fact the Son of God. Nathanael's declaration places him in the company of those who share in the confession "We have seen his glory" (1:14). One's identity as a disciple is grounded in the identity of Jesus.

THE "GREATER THINGS": JESUS' WORDS AND WORKS

OVERVIEW

John 2:1–5:47 is the first realization of the "greater things" promised by Jesus (1:51). The events of this unit—the two "signs" (2:1-11; 4:46-54), the cleansing of the Temple (2:13-22), Jesus' conversations with Nicodemus (3:1-21) and the Samaritan woman (4:4-42), the renewed witness of John (3:22-36), the healing of the man beside the pool (5:1-9)—all demonstrate the authority of Jesus' words and works. Jews and non-Jews, men and women all see and hear the "greater things" Jesus says and does. These chapters contain the full spectrum of responses to Jesus, from the faith of the disciples (2:11) to Jesus' rejection by the Jews (5:16-18). These chapters establish the central themes and tensions of the entire Gospel: the possibilities of new life and faith made available through the words and works of Jesus, and the decisions individuals are called to in the face of those possibilities. John 2:1–5:47 thus contains the drama of the Gospel of John in miniature and forms an appropriate beginning to the story of Jesus' ministry.

JOHN 2:1-12, THE WEDDING AT CANA

NIV

2 On the third day a wedding took place at Cana in Galilee. Jesus' mother was there, [2]and Jesus and his disciples had also been invited to the wedding. [3]When the wine was gone, Jesus' mother said to him, "They have no more wine."

[4]"Dear woman, why do you involve me?" Jesus replied. "My time has not yet come."

[5]His mother said to the servants, "Do whatever he tells you."

[6]Nearby stood six stone water jars, the kind used by the Jews for ceremonial washing, each holding from twenty to thirty gallons.[a]

[7]Jesus said to the servants, "Fill the jars with water"; so they filled them to the brim.

[8]Then he told them, "Now draw some out and take it to the master of the banquet."

They did so, [9]and the master of the banquet tasted the water that had been turned into wine.

[a]6 Greek *two to three metretes* (probably about 75 to 115 liters)

NRSV

2 On the third day there was a wedding in Cana of Galilee, and the mother of Jesus was there. [2]Jesus and his disciples had also been invited to the wedding. [3]When the wine gave out, the mother of Jesus said to him, "They have no wine." [4]And Jesus said to her, "Woman, what concern is that to you and to me? My hour has not yet come." [5]His mother said to the servants, "Do whatever he tells you." [6]Now standing there were six stone water jars for the Jewish rites of purification, each holding twenty or thirty gallons. [7]Jesus said to them, "Fill the jars with water." And they filled them up to the brim. [8]He said to them, "Now draw some out, and take it to the chief steward." So they took it. [9]When the steward tasted the water that had become wine, and did not know where it came from (though the servants who had drawn the water knew), the steward called the bridegroom [10]and said to him,

NIV	NRSV
He did not realize where it had come from, though the servants who had drawn the water knew. Then he called the bridegroom aside ¹⁰and said, "Everyone brings out the choice wine first and then the cheaper wine after the guests have had too much to drink; but you have saved the best till now." ¹¹This, the first of his miraculous signs, Jesus performed at Cana in Galilee. He thus revealed his glory, and his disciples put their faith in him. ¹²After this he went down to Capernaum with his mother and brothers and his disciples. There they stayed for a few days.	"Everyone serves the good wine first, and then the inferior wine after the guests have become drunk. But you have kept the good wine until now." ¹¹Jesus did this, the first of his signs, in Cana of Galilee, and revealed his glory; and his disciples believed in him. 12After this he went down to Capernaum with his mother, his brothers, and his disciples; and they remained there a few days.

COMMENTARY

The story of the wedding at Cana follows the standard form of a miracle story: vv. 1-2, Setting; vv. 3-5, Preparation for the Miracle; vv. 6-8, The Miracle; vv. 9-11, Conclusion. Verse 12 is a transition unit that links the Cana story to what follows.

Within this traditional form, the Fourth Evangelist has planted hints that the story is to be read as more than a typical miracle story. The reference to Jesus' hour in v. 4, for example, and to glory, signs, and faith in v. 11 point beyond the particulars of this story to themes of theological significance for the whole Gospel. Moreover, the Evangelist's placement of this miracle at the beginning of Jesus' ministry gives this story added significance. The miracle at Cana is the inaugural event of Jesus' ministry (cf. the Nazareth "inaugural sermon," Luke 4:16-30). Jesus inaugurates his ministry with a vivid enactment of the gift he has to offer.

2:1-2. The setting of the story is narrated leanly. The Fourth Evangelist provides the reader with only essential details: when (on the third day), where (Cana of Galilee), who (the mother of Jesus, Jesus, his disciples), why (a wedding feast). The reference to "the third day" locates the Cana story in the sequence of days begun in John 1 (vv. 29, 35, 43); the wedding should be understood as occurring three days after the day referred to at 1:43. The explicit linkage of the Cana miracle with the opening days of Jesus' ministry suggests that the Fourth Evangelist wants the reader to see that "the promise made by Jesus in 1:50 or 51 was fulfilled very soon."[71] Speculation on what lies behind the details of the setting (Why is Jesus' mother there? Who invited Jesus?) runs counter to the Evangelist's purpose in telling the story. Everything is subordinated to the heart of the story: the miraculous transformation of water into wine.

2:3-5. The preparation for the miracle establishes the problem that will evoke the miracle: The wine has run out. The lack of wine is communicated to Jesus by his mother (v. 3). (Mary is never referred to by name in John, but is always called "the mother of Jesus": 2:1, 3, 5, 12; 19:25). Jesus' mother asks nothing explicit of him in v. 3, but his response in v. 4 makes clear that her words carried an implied request. Jesus' mother assumed her son would somehow attend to the problem.

Jesus' words to his mother in v. 4a sound harsh to the modern ear, but they are neither rude nor hostile. Jesus frequently addresses women with the greeting "Woman" (e.g., Matt 15:28; Luke 22:57; John 4:21). The use of that form of address to speak to one's own mother is unusual, however. It creates a distance between Jesus and his mother by playing down their familial relation. It recalls Jesus' words in Mark 3:33, "Who are my mother and my brothers?" (NRSV). Attempts to see in the word "woman" (γυνή *gynē*) an allusion

71. Schnackenburg, *The Gospel According to St. John*, 1:325.

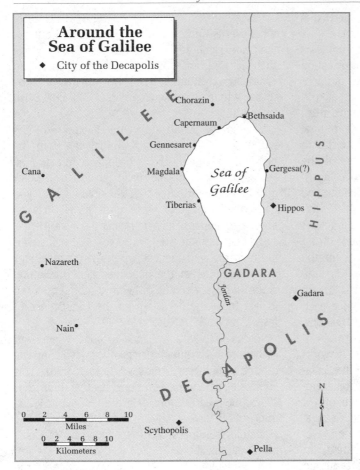

Around the Sea of Galilee

◆ City of the Decapolis

GALILEE

Cana

Nazareth

Nain

Chorazin

Capernaum

Gennesaret

Magdala

Tiberias

Bethsaida

Sea of Galilee

Gergesa(?)

HIPPUS

Hippos

GADARA

Jordan

Gadara

DECAPOLIS

0 2 4 6 8 10
Miles

0 2 4 6 8 10
Kilometers

Scythopolis

Pella

N

rification. Mary's concerns (v. 3) must be placed in the larger context of Jesus' death and resurrection. Verse 4 thus points the reader beyond this particular story to a broader theological context by asserting Jesus' freedom from all human control. Not even his mother has a privileged claim on him. Jesus' actions will be governed by the hour set by God, not by anyone else's time or will. Verse 4 also points beyond the immediate context by alluding to Jesus' passion. Any act of self-revelation by Jesus during his ministry is of a piece with Jesus' self-revelation at his "hour."

The preparation for the miracle concludes with the words of Jesus' mother to the servants, "Do whatever he tells you" (v. 5). Her words echo Pharaoh's words about Joseph in Gen 41:55, in which Pharaoh expresses unconditional confidence in Joseph's ability to resolve the situation of scarcity; they also give full authority to Joseph. The words of Jesus' mother do the same thing. She has not been dissuaded from her initial position that Jesus can do something about the lack of wine (v. 3), but in the light of Jesus' words in v. 4 she cedes the initiative for acting to Jesus. She continues to trust in Jesus' ability to act, but will not curtail his freedom.

2:6-8. The miracle itself begins with a description of the water jars. For the first time in this Gospel, the Fourth Evangelist provides copious detail—the number of jars, their composition, their purpose, and their size. Stone jars, in contrast to earthen jars, are free from the possibility of levitical impurity (Lev 11:33). The "rites of Jewish purification" probably refers to the ritual cleansing of hands at meals (cf. John 3:25). Even taking into account the possibility of a large gathering at the wedding, the quantity of stone jars and their capacity is unusual. Everything about v. 6 is overdrawn, from the description of the jars to the amount of narrative space the Evangelist devotes to the description. The narrative technique mirrors the size of the jars in order to

to Jesus' mother as the second Eve place more symbolic weight on this one word than the text can bear.[72] The expression translated "what concern is that to you and me?" like "Woman," is a formula of disengagement, not rudeness. It may have been a common expression in the Semitic world (cf. 2 Kgs 3:13; 2 Chr 35:21).

The reference to Jesus' hour in v. 4*b* explains why Jesus adopts a posture of disengagement toward his mother. While "hour" (ὥρα *hōra*) is used in the Fourth Gospel to indicate the passing of time (e.g., 1:39), it also is used metaphorically to refer to the time of eschatological fulfillment (e.g., 4:21, 23; 5:25, 28) and, most characteristically, to refer to the hour of Jesus' glorification—i.e., his death, resurrection, and ascension (see 7:30; 8:20; 12:23; 13:1; 17:1). Jesus' reference to his hour thus establishes a link between what Jesus does during his ministry and his glo-

72. E.g., Brown, *The Gospel According to John (I–XII)*, 108-9.

emphasize the extravagance of the miracle that is about to take place.

The Fourth Evangelist narrates the moments before (v. 7) and after (v. 8) the transformation of water into wine, but not the precise moment when the miracle occurs. New wine is created in the "old" vessels of the Jewish purification rites, symbolizing that the old forms are given new content (cf. Mark 2:21-22). It is inaccurate to describe this miracle as Jesus' rejection of the waters of purification and hence a symbol of Jesus' rejection of Judaism.[73] Rather, jars stood empty, waiting to be filled. Jewish vessels are filled with a wondrous new gift (cf. 1:17). This miracle is thus neither a rejection nor a replacement of the old, but the creation of something new in the midst of Judaism.

The jars from which the new wine is drawn (v. 8) were filled to the brim (v. 7). Since each jar had a large capacity (NIV, 20 to 30 gallons; NRSV, 20 or 30 gallons), Jesus turned an astonishing quantity of water into wine. It works against the story to try to explain away the magnitude of the transformation (by saying, for example, that only the water that was drawn out of the jars in v. 8 became wine), because its extravagance is at the heart of the miracle. The extravagant proportions here anticipate the extravagant proportions of the feeding of the five thousand (John 6:1-4). In both instances, the reader is shown the superabundance of gifts available through Jesus (cf. 1:16).

2:9-11. These verses form the conclusion to the miracle and offer public attestation to it. The steward of the feast indirectly verifies the miracle. The attestation to the miracle is in two parts. First, v. 9 attests to the source of the miracle. The expression "water that had become wine" is the first direct statement in the narrative of the miraculous transformation. Until this point, the transformation has been assumed but not stated. The reader of the story knows more than the steward, because the steward does not know the source of the wine. The servants do know the source of the wine, and in v. 9 they function as witnesses to the transformation (cf. the role of the neighbors in John 9:8-12). The question of where Jesus' gifts come from is pivotal in the Fourth Gospel (4:11; 6:5). Knowledge of the source

of Jesus' gifts is a step toward the knowledge of where Jesus himself comes from. Throughout the Fourth Gospel, John contrasts Jesus' knowledge that he is from God with the ignorance and erroneous certitudes about his origins held by those whom Jesus encounters (7:27-28; 8:14; 9:29-30).

Second, v. 10 attests to the goodness of the gift of wine. The steward's initial words to the bridegroom sound like a hospitality maxim, although no exact parallel has been found in other documents from the period. His final words, "you have kept the good wine until now," have a double meaning. They work on the level of the story line, but the steward's words also inadvertently witness to the deeper truth. He attributes the good wine to the beneficence of the bridegroom whose wedding is being celebrated, when in fact the wine derives from the beneficence of Jesus, the true bridegroom (3:29).

In the OT, an abundance of good wine is an eschatological symbol, a sign of the joyous arrival of God's new age (Amos 9:13; Joel 3:18). This eschatological symbolism suggests that John 2:1-11 can be read as more than the first act in Jesus' ministry. It also stands as the fulfillment of OT eschatological hopes, as the inaugural act of God's promised salvation.

A miraculous supply of wine as a sign of the presence of a god is a common motif in Greek folklore.[74] It seems unlikely, however, that the Fourth Evangelist has adopted a pagan legend and ascribed it to Jesus.[75] John 2:1-11 has too many distinctive Johannine traits and important theological overlaps with the miracle of the feeding of the five thousand in 6:1-15.

One must finally ask whether the gift of abundant good wine has eucharistic overtones. The story of John 2:1-11 is fully comprehensible without the eucharistic referent, but a eucharistic interpretation is consonant with the theme of the Cana miracle, the gift of grace that is available through Jesus. Moreover, it seems more than coincidental that two miracles whose central images are wine (John 2:1-11) and bread (6:1-15) are positioned so prominently in the structure of

73. C. K. Barrett, *The Gospel According to St. John,* 2nd ed. (Philadelphia: Westminster, 1978) 189.

74. See C. H. Dodd, *Historical Tradition in the Fourth Gospel* (Cambridge: Cambridge University Press, 1963) 224-25.

75. So Rudolf Bultmann, *The Gospel of John: A Commentary,* trans. G. R. Beasley-Murray, R. W. N. Hoare, and J. K. Riches (Philadelphia: Westminster, 1971) 118.

the Gospel (see Introduction). Eucharistic symbolism, therefore, seems possible as one level of meaning in John 2:1-11, but this symbolism must be read through the Johannine sacramental lens and not assessed according to the treatment of the eucharist in the synoptic Gospels or Paul's writings. (See Reflections at 6:25-71).

The steward's words in v. 10, while apt, still reside on the surface level of the miracle. The steward focuses on the wine, but the Evangelist wants the reader to see the transformation of water into wine for what it really is: a manifestation of Jesus' glory (v. 11). The Fourth Evangelist calls this miracle a "sign" (σημεῖον *sēmeion*) and further identifies it as Jesus' first sign. This designation, along with other occurrences of the word *sign* throughout the Fourth Gospel (e.g., 4:48, 54; 20:30), have led scholars to speculate about a possible sign-source upon which the Fourth Evangelist drew in the composition of his Gospel (see Introduction).

The first sign at Cana is a portent of things to come, because it points ahead to Jesus' "hour" (ὥρα *hōra*, v. 4), as well as to other signs (e.g., 4:54). The first sign at Cana is also a visible indicator of Jesus' authority because through it his glory is revealed. John uses the term *sign* to refer to Jesus' miracles, because for John the significance of the miracle does not rest solely in the act of the miracle itself, but in that to which the miracle points. That is, the deed reveals the doer and points to the significance of the deed as an act of eschatological salvation and God's abundance. The sign at Cana is identified as the "first" because it begins Jesus' self-revelation and models what is still to come. The Greek word for "first" in 2:11 (ἀρχή *archē*) means "beginning," rather than simply "the first in a sequence" (*prótē*).

Verse 11 makes specific that the miracle at the wedding in Cana points to Jesus' glory. In the OT, the manifestation of God's glory involves both a manifestation of God's power and a glimpse of the visible radiance of God (Exod 24:15-18; 34:29-35; 40:34-38). In the synoptic Gospels, the revelation of God's glory in Jesus is embodied in the story of the transfiguration (Mark 9:2-8 and par.). In the Fourth Gospel, however, there is no story of the transfiguration. God's glory is continually manifested in Jesus' life and ministry (1:14; 11:4, 40; 12:41; 17:22, 24). The ultimate moment of glorification occurs at Jesus' death, resurrection, and ascension (13:31; 17:5). Jesus' glory and his death are held in a dialectical relationship in the Fourth Gospel. This dialectic has already received expression in the tensions between the eternal and the historical, the human and the divine, that are at the heart of the Prologue.

REFLECTIONS

The central act in the story of the wedding at Cana is the miraculous transformation of water into wine. The contemporary reader, living in a rational, scientifically oriented age, may find this miracle puzzling at best, embarrassing and offensive at worst. Interpreters, therefore, often are tempted to talk around the miracle by focusing on other aspects of the text or to explain away the miracle by focusing on the differences between the biblical worldview and the modern worldview. In preaching this text, however, the preacher should not get caught up in an explanation or apology (just as the preacher should never succumb to the temptation to explain the resurrection). The essence of any miracle is that it shatters conventional explanations and expectations, and this miracle is no exception. It is incumbent upon the preacher not to diminish the extraordinariness of this story in any way. The christological revelation of this story must not be reduced to a discussion about the facticity of the miracle. Contemporary hearers of this story must be allowed to struggle with what this miracle says about Jesus.

The contrast between the responses of the steward and the disciples can help the contemporary Christian interpret and appropriate this text. Modern Christians distort and oversimplify when they assume that first-century people would have more immediately embraced the miraculous. The steward is perplexed by the sudden appearance of wine of such quality. He summons the bridegroom, the host of the party, because he assumes that the wine can be explained by conventional reasoning. He attributes the wine to the unprecedented hospitality of this man, but this miracle cannot be explained by an irregularity in etiquette. Rational explanations miss the mark. Jesus' disciples, by contrast, see in the miraculous abundance of good wine a sign of God's presence among them. They recognize the revelation of God in the prodigious flow of wine, and they recognize Jesus as the one who brought God to them. The miracle of the wine shatters the boundaries of their conventional world, and the disciples are willing to entertain the possibility that this boundary breaking marks the inbreaking of God. The steward tried to reshape the miracle to fit his former categories, while the disciples allowed their categories to be reshaped by this extraordinary transformation of water into wine, and so they "believed in him" (2:11) as the revealer of God.

John 2:1-11 poses hard questions for the interpreter, because the miracle challenges conventional assumptions about order and control, about what is possible, about where God is found and how God is known. Indeed, the impact of the miracle is lost if one does not entertain these and similar questions, because the force of the miracle derives precisely from its extraordinariness, from the dissonance it creates. If the contemporary reader does not experience a sense of dissonance when faced with this miracle, then the wonder of the miracle cannot be experienced either. To define one's response to this miracle in terms of whether one believes in miracles or in terms of the canons of modern science begs the question. Such interpretive moves are attempts to domesticate the miracle by making it adhere to conventional rules and definitions, whether those rules are the rules of science or of piety.

In the miracle in John 2:1-11, Jesus works an unprecedented act, the transformation of many gallons of water into good, rich wine. It is a miracle of abundance, of extravagance, of transformation and new possibilities. The grace the miracle offers and the glimpse of Jesus' glory it provides (2:11) run outside conventional expectations and place the reader at odds with how he or she thought the world was ordered. The interpretive task is not to put this miracle in a framework in which it "makes sense" (like the attempts of the steward in 2:9-10), but to free the faith community to receive the extraordinary gifts this miracle offers.

This story offers the interpreter a superabundance of theological themes and symbols. The challenge for the preacher is to navigate through these symbols without getting lost (or losing the text) in them. The symbolic richness creates the background and the foreground of this story, but is not its center. Its center is Jesus, his gift and his glory.

In the ancient lectionaries of the church, John 2:1-11 was read on Epiphany, a practice carried over into the Eastern church. In the Revised Common and Catholic lectionaries, this text is read at the beginning of the Epiphany season (Second Sunday After Epiphany, Year C). These liturgical placements of the text accurately reflect the christological focus of the story. The transformation of water into wine is significant because, in showing forth the unprecedented grace of Jesus, it reveals the glory of Jesus and anticipates his ultimate moment of glorification, his death, resurrection, and ascension.

The extravagance of Jesus' act, the superabundance of the wine, suggests the unlimited gifts that Jesus makes available. Jesus' ministry begins with an extraordinary act of grace, a first glimpse of the "greater things" to come (1:50). This story invites the reader to share in the wonder of this miracle, to enter into the joyous celebration made possible by Jesus' gift. The story invites the reader to see what the disciples see, that in the abundance and graciousness of Jesus' gift, one catches a glimpse of the identity and character of God. It is no wonder that the early Christian community confessed "from his fullness we have all received, grace upon grace" (1:16).

JOHN 2:13–3:21, JESUS IN JERUSALEM

OVERVIEW

At John 2:13, the scene shifts dramatically from the intimate setting of John 2:1-12, where Jesus is surrounded by family and friends, to the public arena: Jerusalem and the Temple. In John 2:13–3:21, Jesus comes "to his own" (1:11) in Jerusalem, the geographical and spiritual center of the Jewish faith. In 2:13-22, the Fourth Evangelist contrasts Jesus' authority with the authority of the temple cult. In 3:1-21, the Fourth Evangelist contrasts Jesus' teaching with the teaching of the Pharisees, personified in the teacher Nicodemus. This section thus places Jesus in direct contact with establishment Judaism, disclosing the perspectives and assumptions that will lead to ever deepening conflict.

John 2:13-22, The Cleansing of the Temple

NIV

13When it was almost time for the Jewish Passover, Jesus went up to Jerusalem. 14In the temple courts he found men selling cattle, sheep and doves, and others sitting at tables exchanging money. 15So he made a whip out of cords, and drove all from the temple area, both sheep and cattle; he scattered the coins of the money changers and overturned their tables. 16To those who sold doves he said, "Get these out of here! How dare you turn my Father's house into a market!"

17His disciples remembered that it is written: "Zeal for your house will consume me."*a*

18Then the Jews demanded of him, "What miraculous sign can you show us to prove your authority to do all this?"

19Jesus answered them, "Destroy this temple, and I will raise it again in three days."

20The Jews replied, "It has taken forty-six years to build this temple, and you are going to raise it in three days?" 21But the temple he had spoken of was his body. 22After he was raised from the dead, his disciples recalled what he had said. Then they believed the Scripture and the words that Jesus had spoken.

a17 Psalm 69:9

NRSV

13The Passover of the Jews was near, and Jesus went up to Jerusalem. 14In the temple he found people selling cattle, sheep, and doves, and the money changers seated at their tables. 15Making a whip of cords, he drove all of them out of the temple, both the sheep and the cattle. He also poured out the coins of the money changers and overturned their tables. 16He told those who were selling the doves, "Take these things out of here! Stop making my Father's house a marketplace!" 17His disciples remembered that it was written, "Zeal for your house will consume me." 18The Jews then said to him, "What sign can you show us for doing this?" 19Jesus answered them, "Destroy this temple, and in three days I will raise it up." 20The Jews then said, "This temple has been under construction for forty-six years, and will you raise it up in three days?" 21But he was speaking of the temple of his body. 22After he was raised from the dead, his disciples remembered that he had said this; and they believed the scripture and the word that Jesus had spoken.

Figure 9: Jewish Religious Festivals in John*

The festivals were times for "remembering"—that is, to liturgically recall and relive past events—as well as for feasting and celebrating. During all the pilgrimage festivals (Passover, Pentecost, and Tabernacles), huge crowds of pilgrims would congregate in Jerusalem (Josephus estimates as many as 2,700,000). Large numbers of animals were required, especially at Passover.

Sabbath
John 5:1-47; 7:14-24; 9:1-41

Celebrated from the earliest times of Israel's history, the sabbath is a visible sign of God's covenant with Israel and is listed among the religious festivals in Lev 23:1-3. The Old Testament associates the sabbath with both humanitarian and theological purposes.

"Keeping the sabbath holy" according to the Old Testament, meant no that work could be done: no food could be baked or broiled (Exod 16:23), no plowing or harvesting could be done (Exod 34:21), no firewood could be gathered (Num 15:32) or fires lit (Exod 25:3), no business dealings could be enacted (Amos 8:5; Neh 10:31; 13:15-18), and no burdens could be carried (Jer 17:21-22). The rabbis eventually distinguished thirty-nine classes of work forbidden on the sabbath. But at the same time, certain situations and types of work were exempt: cultic duties (e.g., circumcision, priestly duties), defensive warfare, and the saving of life among them. The rabbis also taught that God remained active on the sabbath for the physical and moral governance of the universe.

Passover-Unleavened Bread, 14-21 Nisan (March/April)
John 2:13-25; 6:1-71; 13:1–19:42

By New Testament times, the feasts of Passover and Unleavened Bread had been combined into a single, eight-day ceremony. On 14 Nisan, the Day of Preparation, the paschal lambs were slaughtered from 3:00 P.M. until 5:00 P.M. in the Temple. The Passover meal began at sundown (the beginning of the new day [15 Nisan]). The ritual consisted of eating the meal, recounting the story of the exodus and its meaning for the meal's participants, and singing songs of praise (drawn from the psalter). On the 16th of Nisan, the offering of first-fruits was made. During the festival, no leaven could be kept in a Jewish house, and only unleavened bread could be eaten.

The Passover feast commemorated Israel's liberation from Egypt, the fundamental event in its history. In addition, Passover was associated with the giving of manna and water in the wilderness, events symbolic of the giving of God's law (see Neh 9:13-15).

Feast of Tabernacles, 15-22 Tishri (September/October)
John 7:1–8:59

The Festival of Tabernacles (or Booths) originally celebrated the completion of the harvest, but eventually also came to commemorate God's protection of Israel during the time in the wilderness. In New Testament times, the festival had grown to an eight-day celebration centered at the Temple. The temple court and the streets of Jerusalem would be filled with temporary shelters. The first day of the festival was a day of solemn rest and worship. At the end of the day, four large lampstands, which lit the entire city of Jerusalem, were set up in the Court of Women; these lights symbolized the light of God. On days two through six (unless the day was a sabbath), there were daily sacrifices and at least three ritual processions. One involved the singing of the Hallel (Psalms 113–118), with the people carrying a citron in their left hands to symbolize the harvest, and a lulab (comprising three myrtle, two willow, and one palm branch tied in a bunch) in their right hands; these were waved during the singing of the first, the twenty-fifth, and the twenty-ninth verses of Psalm 118. During a second procession, called the *Simhat Bet ha-Sho'evah* ("The rejoicing of the place of water drawing"), the priests processed from the Temple to the pool of Siloam to draw water, returning through the Water Gate to pour the water on the altar as a libation; the marching was accompanied by singing, flute playing, dancing, and waving of branches. During the third procession, which was also accompanied by great revelry, the priests would light the giant lamps, after which the celebrating would continue far into the night. The seventh day, or "Great Day," included a procession during which people waved branches, marched around the altar seven times, and prayed for a good harvest in the coming year. Following the festival was a day of solemn worship on the eighth day.

The Feast of Dedication, 25 Kislev-1 Tevet (November/December)
John 10:22-49

The Feast of Dedication (or Hanukkah) commemorated God's deliverance of Israel from the oppression of Antiochus Epiphanes and the rededication of the altar and the cleansing of the Temple by the Maccabees. It is the only major festival without precedent in Jewish biblical tradition. It is thought that during New Testament times the celebration closely resembled that of the Feast of Tabernacles.

*See also Gale A. Yee, *Jewish Feasts and the Gospel of John* (Wilmington, Del.: Michael Glazier, 1989)

542

COMMENTARY

The cleansing of the temple narrative is found in all four Gospels (cf. Matt 21:12-13; Mark 11:15-19; Luke 19:45-48). The Gospel of John places the temple cleansing near the beginning of Jesus' ministry, whereas the synoptic Gospels associate it with his passion. It is unlikely that Jesus performed this bold act twice, so the two traditions probably narrate the same event. The synoptic chronology is the more historically reliable, because it is difficult to see how the Jewish religious authorities would have tolerated such a confrontational act at the beginning of Jesus' ministry. John moves the temple scene to the beginning of his Gospel because it serves a symbolic function for him. The temple cleansing in John completes the inaugural event begun with the Cana miracle. John 2:1-11 revealed the grace and glory of Jesus and the abundant new life Jesus offers. John 2:13-22 highlights the challenge and threat that new life poses to the existing order (cf. John 5:1-18).

The temple narrative in John consists of two parts: Jesus' actions in the Temple (vv. 14-17) and Jesus' saying about the destruction of the Temple (vv. 18-22). The temple narrative is set at Passover (v. 13); the expression "the Passover of the Jews" distances the Fourth Evangelist and his community from the religious observances of the Jewish community.

2:14-17. Jesus' actions in the Temple are narrated in one long complex sentence in the Greek text (vv. 14-16), which creates a mood of urgency and haste, thereby underscoring the intensity of Jesus' actions. Just as Jesus never hesitates as he moves through the Temple, so, too, vv. 14-16 never hesitate. John alone among the Gospels mentions sheep and cattle and the detail of Jesus' whip. John's picture of Jesus in the Temple is large and dramatic, as Jesus herds animals and people out of the temple court, pouring out money and overturning tables as he goes.

It is important to place the scene in the Temple in its proper religious and historical context. Cattle, sheep, and doves were required for burnt offerings in the Temple (see Leviticus 1 and 3). Since Passover was a pilgrimage feast, many of those coming to worship in the Temple would have journeyed a great distance and would not have brought animals with them. They needed to buy animals in Jerusalem in order to participate in temple worship. Similarly, the temple tax could not be paid in Greek or Roman coinage because of the human image (the emperor's head) on these coins (cf. Matt 22:15-22), and foreign coinage had to be changed into the legal Tyrian currency in Jerusalem. Therefore, the sale of animals and the changing of money were necessary if the worship of the cult was to proceed.

Christian interpretations that see this story principally as an illustration of the extortionist practices of the Jewish temple authorities disregard these realities of temple worship in Jesus' day. There were inevitable abuses of the temple system, but in vv. 14-16 Jesus confronts the system itself, not simply its abuses. This is apparent in the words he speaks to the dove sellers (v. 16). In the synoptic Gospels, Jesus quotes Isa 56:7 and Jer 7:11 (see Matt 21:13; Mark 11:17; Luke 10:46), verses that focus on the distortion of a place of worship into a "den of robbers." These OT verses are absent from John, however, and Jesus may allude instead to Zech 14:21 ("And there shall no longer be traders in the house of the LORD of hosts on that day" [NRSV]). In a play on the word for "house" (οἶκος *oikos*), Jesus complains that his Father's house has become a "house of trade." Since this trade was necessary to maintain the cultic system of sacrifice and tithes, Jesus' charge is a much more radical accusation in John than in the Synoptics. Jesus issues a powerful challenge to the very authority of the Temple and its worship (cf. 4:23-24).

In v. 17, the focus shifts to the disciples. They have no active role in this story, but function as interpretive witnesses (see v. 22). Psalsm 69:10 (English translation, Ps 69:9) serves as the lens through which the Fourth Evangelist wants the reader (like the disciples) to interpret Jesus' actions in the Temple. Verse 17 alters Ps 69:10 slightly, however, and that alteration is theologically significant. In the MT and most recensions of the LXX of Ps 69:10, the verb "consume" refers to past events, but in the disciples' recollection of the verse, the verb is translated as a future tense ("will consume me"). Psalm 69:10 thus functions as a prophecy of the time when Jesus will be consumed—that is, his crucifixion. Jesus' passion was read in the light of Psalm 69 by many NT writers (e.g., Matt 27:34, 48; Mark 15:23, 36; John 19:28; Rom 15:3). This use of Ps 69:10 gives the temple cleansing a christological emphasis. In the synoptic Gospels, the OT quotations draw attention to the Temple, but Ps 69:9 fixes the reader's attention on Jesus. John's temple story is ultimately about Jesus' fate, not the Temple's.

2:18-22. This christological focus is expanded in vv. 18-22. The Jews' demand for a sign (v. 18; cf. Mark 8:12; 1 Cor 1:22) is in reality a question about Jesus' authority. They use "sign" (σημεῖον *sēmeion*) in the sense of a warrant, not in the Johannine sense of a revelatory act. "The Jews" here represent those who question Jesus and do not know him. Jesus responds to their request with the saying about the destruction and rebuilding of the Temple (v. 19), which is not found on Jesus' lips in the synoptic Gospels, but is instead reported indirectly through the testimony of false witnesses at Jesus' trial (Matt 26:61; Mark 14:58) and in the taunting of Jesus on the cross (Matt 27:40; Mark 15:29; cf. Acts 6:14).

The Jews respond to Jesus' words about the Temple with disdain (v. 20). The rebuilding of the Temple was begun in approximately 19 BCE during the reign of Herod the Great. The reference to forty-six years of construction would suggest a date of 27 CE for this exchange between Jesus and the Jews. That date is historically plausible, since in John the temple incident occurs at the beginning of Jesus' ministry and Jesus' ministry lasts approximately three years.

Verses 18-20 are an example of the Johannine narrative technique of misunderstanding. The Jews respond to Jesus' words about the destruction and raising of the Temple with a very pragmatic protest (v. 20) that reveals that they understand only the surface meaning of Jesus' words (cf. Nicodemus, 3:3-5). The verb Jesus uses to speak of the raising of the Temple (ἐγείρω *egeirō*) points to a second, more symbolic level of meaning, however, because that verb is also used to speak of resurrection (John 2:22; 5:21; 12:1, 9, 17; 21:14).

Verse 21 makes the second level of meaning of Jesus' words is now made explicit. The Evangelist tells the reader that Jesus speaks of "the temple of his body." Since for Judaism the Temple is the locus of God's presence on earth, v. 21 suggests that Jesus' body is now the locus of God. Verse 21 recalls 1:51 where the Son of Man replaces Jacob's ladder as the locus of God's interaction with the world.

The Evangelist's commentary in v. 21 thus interprets the dialogue between Jesus and the Jews for the reader, so that the reader can discern the full meaning of Jesus' words and the nature of the misunderstanding between Jesus and the Jews. The Fourth Evangelist frequently interjects his own voice into the narrative of the Fourth Gospel to provide the reader with insight and information the characters in the stories do not have (e.g., 6:6; 11:13, 51-52; 12:6, 33). Verse 21 enables the reader to see the sign the "Jews" miss: Jesus has the authority to challenge the temple system because he is the locus of God's presence on earth.

Verse 22, like v. 17, focuses on the interpretive witness of the disciples; but unlike v. 17, it explicitly locates their witness after Jesus' resurrection. It recounts what the disciples "remembered." In John 14:26, Jesus promises that the Holy Spirit "will teach you all things and will remind you of everything I have said to you." In John, remembrance is active reflection on the past in the light of the resurrection with the aid of the Spirit. Such reflection leads to faith and deepened understanding (see 12:16). In 2:22, remembering the past with the aid of the Spirit reveals the truth of Scripture and Jesus' word in new ways. The combination of Scripture and Jesus' word in v. 22 shows that the early church began to grant Jesus' word the same authority it had already granted Scripture.

Verse 22 makes explicit the post-resurrection perspective from which the Gospel was written. Each of the Gospels is written from a post-resurrection perspective, but in John that perspective is intentionally integrated into the Gospel narrative. The distance between the disciples of Jesus in the Gospel stories and the disciples who read the Gospel stories is bridged by v. 22, because this verse points to a time beyond the end of the Fourth Gospel narrative, to a story that gets underway as the Fourth Gospel story draws to a close. Verse 22 points to the interpretive activity of believers as they remember and claim the stories and sayings of Jesus as their own.

REFLECTIONS

John 2:13-22 is popularly interpreted as an example of Jesus' anger and hence his humanity. Jesus' actions of taking the whip, herding out the animals, and overturning the tables are pointed to as evidence that Jesus could get angry. Such attempts to amass evidence to prove Jesus' humanity actually undercut the power of the incarnation, however. To focus on isolated attributes or emotions as proof of Jesus' humanity is in effect to seek after signs, to base one's faith on the surface evidence without perceiving the deeper reality. The underlying reality of the Fourth Gospel narrative is that "the Word became flesh" (1:14). Jesus' humanity thus pervades everything he says and does in his ministry. The scandal of John 2:13-22 is not Jesus' anger as proof of his humanity, but the authority this human being claims for himself through his words and actions.

Jesus, a complete outsider to the power structure of the Temple, issues a challenge to the authority of the Temple that quite literally shakes its foundations. Jesus throws the mechanics of temple worship into chaos, disrupting the temple system during one of the most significant feasts of the year so that neither sacrifices nor tithes could be offered that day. It is no wonder that the Jews who were gathered at the Temple asked for a sign to warrant his actions (2:18). Jesus was a human being just as they were; who was he to derail their worship?

Jesus explains his actions in the Temple by pointing to his death and resurrection (2:19-21). Jesus has the authority to challenge the authority of the Temple because his whole life bears testimony to the power of God in the world. John 2:13-22 is not about how Jesus' anger makes him like other people; instead, Jesus' bold, prophetic act in the Temple reinforces what 1:19-51 and 2:1-11 have already shown: There will be nothing hidden about Jesus' identity in John. Jesus is the locus of God's presence on earth, and God as known in Jesus, not the Temple, should be the focal point of cultic activity.

The far-reaching implications of Jesus' complaint and his actions in the Temple should caution the interpreter against advocating a one-dimensional theory of the superiority of Christianity over Judaism when expositing this text. Jesus is not against Judaism per se. John presents Jesus as an observant Jewish male who travels to Jerusalem at the pilgrimage feasts (2:13; 5:1; 7:10; 12:2). Jesus' challenge to the authority of the dominant religious institution in Judaism is not anti-Jewish, because it is in line with the institutional challenges of prophets like Amos and Jeremiah. Jesus challenges a religious system so embedded in its own rules and practices that it is no longer open to a fresh revelation from God, a temptation that exists for contemporary Christianity as well as for the Judaism of Jesus' day.

Jesus' dramatic actions in 2:13-16, through which he issued a radical challenge to the authority of the religious institutions of his day, issue a similar challenge to the institutionalism of the contemporary church. Christian faith communities must be willing to ask where and when the status quo of religious practices and institutions has been absolutized and, therefore, closed to the possibility of reformation, change, and renewal. The great danger is that the contemporary church, like the leaders of the religious establishment in the Gospel of John, will fall into the trap of equating the authority of its own institutions with the presence of God. All religious institutional embeddedness—whether in the form of temple worship, unjust social systems, or repressive religious practices—is challenged by the revelation of God in the life, death, and resurrection of Jesus.

John 2:23-25, Interlude in Jerusalem

NIV

NRSV

23Now while he was in Jerusalem at the Passover Feast, many people saw the miraculous signs he was doing and believed in his name.[a] 24But Jesus would not entrust himself to them, for he knew all men. 25He did not need man's testimony about man, for he knew what was in a man.

[a]23 Or and believed in him

23When he was in Jerusalem during the Passover festival, many believed in his name because they saw the signs that he was doing. 24But Jesus on his part would not entrust himself to them, because he knew all people 25and needed no one to testify about anyone; for he himself knew what was in everyone.

COMMENTARY

John 2:23-25 provides the transition from the temple narrative to the Nicodemus story. In these verses, the Fourth Evangelist contrasts the people's response to Jesus with Jesus' response to the people, thereby enabling the reader to see the people in Jerusalem through Jesus' eyes.

Many people in Jerusalem believed in Jesus on the basis of the signs he performed (v. 23). The Fourth Evangelist uses "signs" (σημεῖα *sēmeia*) here as a general designation for Jesus' works in Jerusalem. It is important to contrast 2:23 with 2:11. In 2:11, the miracle at Cana is called a sign, but the Evangelist also notes that Jesus manifested his glory in this sign. It is the manifestation of glory, not simply the sign itself, that leads to the disciples' faith. In 2:23 there is no indication that the people see the glory to which Jesus' signs point.

Verses 24-25 point out the inadequacy of faith based on signs as wondrous deeds alone; Jesus would not entrust himself to the people. The contrast between the people's faith (v. 23) and Jesus' response (vv. 24-25) is even sharper in the Greek text, because "believe" and "entrust" translate the same Greek verb (πιστεύω *pisteuō*). In other words, Jesus does not believe the people's belief.

Jesus' all-encompassing knowledge is the source of his distrust (vv. 24b, 25b). Jesus' knowledge of human nature was first highlighted in the call narratives of chap. 1 (Peter, 1:41-42; Nathanael, 1:47-50). The contrast between Jesus' knowledge and the knowledge of those around him is a central theme in the Fourth Gospel. Throughout the Fourth Gospel, people approach Jesus confident in their knowledge of themselves and of Jesus (see 3:2) and the encounter with Jesus challenges those certitudes (3:3-10). The only person whose knowledge is unchallenged in the Fourth Gospel narrative is Jesus. His knowledge of "what was in everyone," of his identity, and of God sets the standard by which all other knowledge is measured. Because of Jesus' knowledge, no one needs to testify to him (v. 25a), but other people, whose "knowledge" often blinds them to the truth (e.g., 9:24-34, 39-41), need witnesses to bring them to faith.

This interlude alerts the reader to some of the theological categories through which one is to read the Nicodemus story: the nature of faith and human response to Jesus, the relationship between faith and knowledge, and Jesus' ability to discern the adequacy of human response.

John 3:1-21, Jesus and Nicodemus

NIV

NRSV

3 Now there was a man of the Pharisees named Nicodemus, a member of the Jew-

3 Now there was a Pharisee named Nicodemus, a leader of the Jews. 2He came to-ish ruling council. [2]He came to Jesus at night and said, "Rabbi, we know you are a teacher who has come from God. For no one could perform the miraculous signs you are doing if God were not with him."

[3]In reply Jesus declared, "I tell you the truth, no one can see the kingdom of God unless he is born again.[a]"

[4]"How can a man be born when he is old?" Nicodemus asked. "Surely he cannot enter a second time into his mother's womb to be born!"

[5]Jesus answered, "I tell you the truth, no one can enter the kingdom of God unless he is born of water and the Spirit. [6]Flesh gives birth to flesh, but the Spirit[b] gives birth to spirit. [7]You should not be surprised at my saying, 'You[c] must be born again.' [8]The wind blows wherever it pleases. You hear its sound, but you cannot tell where it comes from or where it is going. So it is with everyone born of the Spirit."

[9]"How can this be?" Nicodemus asked.

[10]"You are Israel's teacher," said Jesus, "and do you not understand these things? [11]I tell you the truth, we speak of what we know, and we testify to what we have seen, but still you people do not accept our testimony. [12]I have spoken to you of earthly things and you do not believe; how then will you believe if I speak of heavenly things? [13]No one has ever gone into heaven except the one who came from heaven—the Son of Man.[d] [14]Just as Moses lifted up the snake in the desert, so the Son of Man must be lifted up, [15]that everyone who believes in him may have eternal life.[e]

[16]"For God so loved the world that he gave his one and only Son,[f] that whoever believes in him shall not perish but have eternal life. [17]For God did not send his Son into the world to condemn the world, but to save the world through him. [18]Whoever believes in him is not condemned, but whoever does not believe stands condemned already because he has not believed in the name of God's one and only Son.[g] [19]This is the verdict: Light has come into the world, but men loved darkness instead of light because their deeds were

[a]3 Or born from above; also in verse 7   [b]6 Or but spirit   [c]7 The Greek is plural.   [d]13 Some manuscripts Man, who is in heaven   [e]15 Or believes may have eternal life in him   [f]16 Or his only begotten Son   [g]18 Or God's only begotten Son

Jesus[a] by night and said to him, "Rabbi, we know that you are a teacher who has come from God; for no one can do these signs that you do apart from the presence of God." [3]Jesus answered him, "Very truly, I tell you, no one can see the kingdom of God without being born from above."[b] [4]Nicodemus said to him, "How can anyone be born after having grown old? Can one enter a second time into the mother's womb and be born?" [5]Jesus answered, "Very truly, I tell you, no one can enter the kingdom of God without being born of water and Spirit. [6]What is born of the flesh is flesh, and what is born of the Spirit is spirit.[c] [7]Do not be astonished that I said to you, 'You[d] must be born from above.'[e] [8]The wind[c] blows where it chooses, and you hear the sound of it, but you do not know where it comes from or where it goes. So it is with everyone who is born of the Spirit." [9]Nicodemus said to him, "How can these things be?" [10]Jesus answered him, "Are you a teacher of Israel, and yet you do not understand these things?

[11]"Very truly, I tell you, we speak of what we know and testify to what we have seen; yet you[f] do not receive our testimony. [12]If I have told you about earthly things and you do not believe, how can you believe if I tell you about heavenly things? [13]No one has ascended into heaven except the one who descended from heaven, the Son of Man.[g] [14]And just as Moses lifted up the serpent in the wilderness, so must the Son of Man be lifted up, [15]that whoever believes in him may have eternal life.[h]

[16]"For God so loved the world that he gave his only Son, so that everyone who believes in him may not perish but may have eternal life.

[17]"Indeed, God did not send the Son into the world to condemn the world, but in order that the world might be saved through him. [18]Those who believe in him are not condemned; but those who do not believe are condemned already, because they have not believed in the name of the only Son of God. [19]And this is the judgment, that the light has come into the world, and people

[a]Gk him   [b]Or born anew   [c]The same Greek word means both wind and spirit   [d]The Greek word for you here is plural   [e]Or anew   [f]The Greek word for you here and in verse 12 is plural   [g]Other ancient authorities add who is in heaven   [h]Some interpreters hold that the quotation concludes with verse 15

NIV	NRSV
evil. ²⁰Everyone who does evil hates the light, and will not come into the light for fear that his deeds will be exposed. ²¹But whoever lives by the truth comes into the light, so that it may be seen plainly that what he has done has been done through God."^a	loved darkness rather than light because their deeds were evil. ²⁰For all who do evil hate the light and do not come to the light, so that their deeds may not be exposed. ²¹But those who do what is true come to the light, so that it may be clearly seen that their deeds have been done in God."^a

[a]21 Some interpreters end the quotation after verse 15.

[a] Some interpreters hold that the quotation concludes with verse 15

COMMENTARY

In John 3:1-21, the focus shifts from the public arena to Jesus' interaction with an individual, Nicodemus. John 3:1-21 divides into two parts: vv. 1-10, the dialogue between Jesus and Nicodemus; and vv. 11-21, a discourse by Jesus. This text is the first instance of a common Johannine pattern of a central event, in this case a dialogue, followed by a discourse that draws general theological themes out of the particular event.

Scholars debate whether 3:16-21 should be read as words of the Johannine Jesus[76] or as a commentary by the Fourth Evangelist.[77] The ancient manuscripts contained no quotation marks. The NRSV and the NIV both punctuate the verses as the words of Jesus and indicate the alternative interpretation in a footnote. The reasons given for interpreting these verses as the Evangelist's commentary include the use of third-person pronouns to speak of Jesus and the presence of so many distinctly Johannine themes and expressions.[78] These arguments are not compelling for two reasons. First, Jesus cannot be eliminated as the speaker of these verses simply on the basis of pronoun use. There are many other instances in the Fourth Gospel in which Jesus speaks of himself in the third person, particularly in the context of Son of Man sayings (e.g., 1:51; 3:13-15; 8:28).

Second, and more theologically significant, the arguments against the Johannine Jesus as the speaker of these verses misread the theological intent and literary strategy of the Fourth Evangelist. At many points in the Gospel, the narrative

voices of the Johannine Jesus and the Fourth Evangelist overlap. Similar expressions and themes appear in the mouth of Jesus and in the Evangelist's commentary (e.g., 6:41 and 43; 9:22 and 16:2).[79] This similarity of voice derives from the Fourth Evangelist's understanding of himself as a faithful interpreter of Jesus' words and person. Everything in the Gospel bears the interpretive stamp of the Fourth Evangelist. As the narrator of Jesus' story, the Fourth Evangelist represents Jesus' words to a new generation of believers. As such, the Evangelist shares in one of the functions of the Paraclete, to keep Jesus' words alive for new and changing situations and communities of faith (cf. 16:12-13).

3:1-10. 3:1-2a. These verses present both positive and negative images of Nicodemus. On the positive side, Nicodemus, a Jewish leader (v. 1), seeks out Jesus. To seek Jesus, as noted earlier (1:38), is one of the first acts of discipleship in John. On the negative side, however, Nicodemus hides his seeking under the cloak of night (cf. the night visit of King Zedekiah and Jeremiah, Jer 37:16-21). This reference to the time of Nicodemus's visit is neither an incidental detail nor an attempt at historical verisimilitude. Rather, it provides a clue to the significance of this story for the Fourth Evangelist. "Night" (νύξ *nux*) is used metaphorically in the Fourth Gospel to represent separation from the presence of God (9:4; 11:10; 13:30). The symbolic significance of this night visit is confirmed by 3:19-21, which condemns those who prefer darkness to light.[80]

76. E.g., Raymond E. Brown, *The Gospel According to John (I–XII)*, AB 29 (Garden City, N.Y.: Doubleday, 1966) 149.
77. E.g., Rudolf Schnackenburg, *The Gospel According to St. John*, 3 vols. (New York: Seabury, 1982) 1:361.
78. Ibid., 1:381-82.

79. R. Alan Culpepper, *Anatomy of the Fourth Gospel: A Study in Literary Design* (Philadelphia: Fortress, 1983) 34-43.
80. Jouette M. Bassler, "Mixed Signals: Nicodemus in the Fourth Gospel," *JBL* 108 (1989) 638.

3:2b. The dialogue is initiated by Nicodemus's pronouncement about Jesus' identity in v. 2*b*, but Jesus' response in v. 3 shifts the initiative away from Nicodemus. As the dialogue unfolds, Nicodemus's speech is reduced to questions (vv. 4, 9), while Jesus' speeches become progressively longer, leading finally to the discourse that begins in v. 11.

Nicodemus's opening words to Jesus in v. 2*b* contain three positive acknowledgments of Jesus' identity. First, Nicodemus calls Jesus "Rabbi," an address that acknowledges Jesus as a teacher (cf. 1:38, 49). Second, Nicodemus acknowledges that Jesus is a "teacher come from God." Although "from God" is a traditional way of speaking of religious figures as God's emissaries (e.g., John the Baptist in 1:6), that Jesus' origin is from God is also a crucial christological affirmation in the Fourth Gospel (e.g., 1:1, 18; 3:31; 6:38; 7:28-29). Nicodemus's words here are like Caiaphas's words in 11:50: The full truth is unwittingly told. Third, Nicodemus speaks to Jesus in the first-person plural ("we know"). Nicodemus does not speak to Jesus simply as an individual, but as a leader of his community. The first-person plural implies that Nicodemus's community shares in his positive acknowledgment of Jesus.

Nicodemus's words are not unambiguously positive, however, because his insights into Jesus are based on Jesus' signs (v. 2*b*). From 2:23-25, the reader knows that Jesus will not entrust himself to those whose faith is based on signs. Nicodemus's confident assertion of who Jesus is ("we know . . . ") is thus immediately called into question by the warrants he offers for that knowledge: Jesus' signs. Moreover, Nicodemus assumes that he can explain what Jesus does through his preconceived categories of the possible ("no one is able . . . " v. 2). This certitude about what is and is not possible with God will be challenged as the dialogue with Jesus unfolds.

3:3. Jesus does not respond directly to Nicodemus's acknowledgment of him. Instead, he challenges Nicodemus with a teaching. Each of Jesus' teachings in John 3:1-11 begins with the introductory formula "Very truly, I tell you . . . " (ἀμὴν ἀμὴν λέγω *amēn, amēn legō*; see vv. 3, 5, 11). Jesus' teaching in v. 3 combines the traditional image of the kingdom of God with a new metaphor, "to be born ἄνωθεν" (*anōthen).*

The Greek word *anōthen* means both "from above" and "again," or "anew." This double meaning is possible only in Greek; there is no Hebrew or Aramaic word with a similar double meaning. The Johannine Jesus' words to Nicodemus in v. 3 are unavoidably and intentionally ambiguous because of the inherent double meaning of *anōthen.* This double meaning causes problems for translators of the Greek text, because there is no equivalent word with this double meaning in English. Thus the ambiguity of meaning is lost in English translations because they privilege one meaning of *anōthen* in the text ("from above," NRSV; "again," NIV) and relegate the second meaning to a footnote. This translation strategy communicates to the reader that the footnoted translation is a secondary definition, not an inherent meaning of the word. The translators thus decide for the reader that one reading is primary and the other secondary, when the Fourth Evangelist intends both to be heard simultaneously. Jesus' expression "to be born *anōthen,* to be born from above/again" challenges Nicodemus to move beyond surface meanings to a deeper meaning. When English translations resolve the tension in Jesus' words by reducing *anōthen* to one of its meanings, the challenge to Nicodemus (and to the reader) is lost. The intentional double meaning of *anōthen* must be kept in mind when reading this verse in order to discern Jesus' full meaning and the nature of Nicodemus's misunderstanding.

"To be born *anōthen"* speaks both of a time of birth ("again") and the place from which this new birth is generated ("from above"). "Kingdom of God" also has both temporal and spatial dimensions. The "kingdom of God" evokes both the time of God's reign and the place of God's realm. "Kingdom of God" is a frequent metaphor of eschatological newness in the synoptic Gospels (e.g., Mark 1:15; 4:26; Luke 4:43; 13:18), but in John it occurs only in the Nicodemus story (3:3, 5). The juxtaposition of "to be born *anōthen"* with the more traditional "kingdom of God" suggests that the new birth of which Jesus speaks is also an eschatological category. The new birth of which Jesus speaks gives new access to God (cf. 1 Cor 15:50).

3:4. Nicodemus is oblivious to the two levels of meaning in *anōthen.* He focuses on one meaning of "born *anōthen*" ("again") and protests that what Jesus calls for is physiologically impossible (v. 4). As in v. 2, Nicodemus's categories of what is possible intrude into the conversation. On the level that Nicodemus understands Jesus' words, Nicodemus's protest is correct. It is impossible for a grown man to reenter his mother's womb and be born a second time. Nicodemus's protest is ironic, however, because his words are correct and incontestable on one level, but that level stands in conflict and tension with what Jesus intends by the expression "to be born *anōthen*." Jesus' words speak of a radical new birth, generated from above, but Nicodemus's language and imagination do not stretch enough to include that offer.

3:5-8. Here Jesus provides a fresh set of images to move Nicodemus out of his misunderstanding. The expression "born of water and Spirit" (v. 5) interprets the phrase "to be born *anōthen*." For the reader of this Gospel in the Christian community, the reference to water and the Spirit carries with it images of baptism. The narrative also includes a listener, Nicodemus, who hears these words independent of any knowledge of Christian baptism, however.

Jesus' words about birth from water and Spirit are comprehensible without a baptismal referent if one attends carefully to the verb for "born" (the passive of γεννάω *gennaō*). In 3:4, Nicodemus drew Jesus' attention to the birthing process with his words about his mother's womb. The birth that Nicodemus envisions, the exit from the mother's womb, is quite literally a birth out of water. The breaking of the waters of birth announces the imminent delivery of a child. In v. 5 Jesus plays on Nicodemus's womb imagery to say that entrance into the kingdom of God will require a double birth: physical birth ("water") and spiritual rebirth ("Spirit").[81] New life will be born from water and Spirit, no longer only from water. Yet the spiritual rebirth also does not void the physical birth. Spirit and flesh are held together; this is not a docetic understanding of human existence before God (see Commentary on 6:63 also). Verse 6 supports this interpretation of v. 5, because its terms more directly underscore the two births of v. 5.

The early church understood baptism to be the sacramental enactment of Jesus' promise of new birth. A baptismal reading of 3:5-6 thus expands on the images of birth and new life already contained in the text. Indeed, the Fourth Evangelist was surely aware of the baptismal overtones for the church of the imagery in these verses.[82]

In v. 7, Jesus returns to his initial metaphor, "you must be born *anōthen*." The "you" is a second-person plural pronoun in the Greek, so that Jesus' requirement of fresh birth is now addressed to the "we" of Nicodemus's words in v. 2. Nicodemus resisted Jesus' words about new birth the first time Jesus spoke them (vv. 3-4) and, in v. 7*a* Jesus warns him against repeating that response.

In v. 8, Jesus uses the image of the wind to explain the birth of which he speaks. The Greek word for "wind" (πνεῦμα *pneuma*), like *anōthen*, has two inherent meanings; it means both "wind" and "spirit" (as does the Hebrew word [רוח *rûaḥ*]). Once again Jesus describes the new birth with a word that cannot be held to a single meaning. The word *pneuma* perfectly captures the essence of Jesus' message: the wind/spirit blows where it wills; human beings can detect its presence but cannot chart its precise movements. Jesus' offer of new birth is like the wind/spirit: a mystery beyond human knowledge and control.

3:9. Nicodemus responds to Jesus' words exactly as Jesus warned him not to, in amazement. Nicodemus's question in v. 9 is literally, "How is it possible for these things to happen?" Once again his preconceptions of what is possible intrude on the conversation (cf. 3:2, 4) and prevent him from embracing Jesus' words. One hears in Nicodemus's incredulous question an echo of Sarah's laugh in Gen 18:12. Nicodemus's words of resistance are the last words he speaks in this story, although he will appear twice more in John (7:50-52; 19:39-40).

3:10. Jesus responds to Nicodemus's resistance with a quick and penetrating irony that characterizes much of the dialogue in the Fourth Gospel (v. 10). In 3:2*b*, Nicodemus confidently asserted his knowledge of Jesus and God ("we know . . . "), and in 3:10 Jesus turns that confident assertion

---

81. Sandra M. Schneiders, "Born Anew [Jn 3:1-15]," *TToday* 44 (1987) 191-94.

82. See Schnackenburg, *The Gospel According to St. John,* 1:369; Ernst Haenchen, *John, Hermenia,* 2 vols. (Philadelphia: Fortress, 1984) 1:200; Bultmann, *The Gospel of John,* 138-39, took the words "water and" as evidence of an "ecclesiastical redaction," because for Bultmann, John has no interest in the sacraments.

back on Nicodemus. Neither Nicodemus's credentials (Pharisee, ruler of the Jews, teacher of Israel) nor his self-professed knowledge have brought him closer to understanding Jesus.

3:11-21. At v. 11, the text shifts from a dialogue to a monologue. As noted earlier, the phrase "very truly, I tell you" regularly introduces a new teaching by Jesus in John (e.g., 1:51; 3:3, 5; 5:24-25; 6:26) and often marks the shift from dialogue to monologue.[83] The dialogue between Jesus and Nicodemus alternated between Jesus' offer of new birth (vv. 3, 5-8) and Nicodemus's resistance (vv. 4, 9). The shift to the monologue allows Jesus' voice to silence the voice of resistance. Jesus' discourse runs through v. 21 and divides into two parts. Verses 11-15 interpret Jesus' offer of new birth through his death, resurrection, and ascension, and vv. 16-21 focus on the theme of judgment.

3:11-15. *3:11.* Jesus begins the discourse by speaking in the first-person plural. English translations of v. 11 mask the Greek word order. The translation "we speak of what we know" is smooth English, but the sentence literally reads, "what we know we say" (οἴδαμεν λαλοῦμεν *oidamen laloumen*). This word order is important because it means that the beginning of Jesus' discourse and Nicodemus's opening words to Jesus (v. 3) are the same: "we know. . . . " It is possible to read Jesus' words as a continuation of the irony of v. 10; Jesus parodies Nicodemus's assertion of his knowledge.

The first-person plural of v. 11 has another function. Jesus' words in v. 11 are all words of witness: we know; we see; we speak; we testify. In its immediate context, Jesus' "we" speaks for John the Baptist and the first disciples who have already borne witness to what they have seen. Jesus speaks for all those who have testified to this point in the Gospel narrative. In a broader context, however, Jesus' "we" speaks for the witness of the early church. This "we" stands in contrast to the "we" for whom Nicodemus speaks: the synagogue. The church's witness is contrasted with the non-responsiveness of the synagogue (note the second-person plural "you" in v. 11*b*). Nicodemus and his community are representative of all who do not receive the church's witness.

3:12. Jesus uses the expressions "earthly things" and "heavenly things" to summarize the witness that has already been given and the witness still to come (v. 12). "Earthly things" (τὰ ἐπίγεια *ta epigeia*) can be understood as referring to things about human beings, specifically the discussion of new birth in 3:3-8, whereas "heavenly things" (τὰ ἐπουράνια *ta epourania*) refers to things about God and Jesus to which Jesus has privileged access (1:18; 3:13) and that have not yet been revealed to Nicodemus and his community.

3:13. This verse establishes Jesus' authority as the source of "heavenly things": "No one has ascended into heaven except the one who descended from heaven, the Son of Man." This is the second time Jesus has spoken of himself as the "Son of Man" (see also 1:51) and both uses of the term are associated with language of heavenly ascent and descent. The Son of Man's privileged access to God is expressed in spatial terms: The Son of Man moves between heaven and earth and brings the two together.[84] The emphasis in this verse is on Jesus' descent. Jesus knows heavenly things because he has descended; this contrasts Jesus with other figures who were believed to have ascended and through their ascents received heavenly knowledge. For example, Moses went up the mountain and then descended with God's Word. The writings of Philo make clear that some Jews believed that Moses' ascent gave him special status before God.[85] Verse 13 underscores that Jesus first descended, then ascended.

Verse 13 refers to Jesus' ascension in the past tense. This verse thus presupposes an event that has not yet occurred in the Gospel narrative but is a reality for the post-resurrection church. This use of the past tense, like the disciples' remembering in 2:22, makes explicit the post-resurrection perspective from which the Gospel is written. By having Jesus bear witness to the ascension, the Fourth Evangelist places the witness of the early church in the mouth of Jesus and thus accords that witness greater authority and continuity.

3:14. The significance of the ascension of the

83. C. H. Dodd, *The Interpretation of the Fourth Gospel* (Cambridge: Cambridge University Press, 1953) 328.

84. Wayne A. Meeks, "The Man from Heaven in Johannine Sectarianism," *JBL* 91 (1972) 44-72; see also Godfrey C. Nicholson, *Death as Departure: The Johannine Descent-Ascent Schema* (Chico, Calif.: Scholars Press, 1983).

85. E.g., Philo *Life of Moses* 1.150; See Peder Borgen, "Philo of Alexandria," in *ABD* 5:340.

Son of Man is elaborated through an OT example (Num 21:8-9). The key to interpreting this analogy between Moses' lifting up of the serpent in the wilderness and the ascension of the Son of Man is the verb (ὑψόω *hypsoō*), meaning both "lift up" and "exalt." (The Hebrew verb נשא [*nāśā '*] has a similar double meaning; see the pun based on this verb in Gen 40:9-23.) Once again the Fourth Evangelist asks the reader to hold two meanings together simultaneously (see also 3:3, 7-8). As the serpent was lifted up in the wilderness, so the Son of Man must be lifted up on the cross. The double meaning of *hupsoō* implies, however, that the physical act of lifting up is also a moment of exaltation. That is, it is in the crucifixion that Jesus is exalted. John 3:14 is one of three statements about the "lifting up" of the Son of Man in John (see also 8:28; 12:32-34). These three sayings are the Johannine analogue to the three passion predictions in the synoptic Gospels (Mark 8:31; 9:31; 10:33-34; and par.).

The overlap of crucifixion and exaltation conveyed by v. 14 is crucial to Johannine soteriology, because the Fourth Evangelist understands Jesus' crucifixion, resurrection, and ascension as one continuous event. Verse 14 also contains a key to the theological grounding of the Evangelist's attraction to irony; the cross as humiliation is actually exaltation. This will become especially clear in the crucifixion narrative of John 18–19. The Fourth Gospel is often criticized for having an inadequate theology of the cross, but such criticism misconstrues the Johannine treatment of the crucifixion. As v. 14 makes clear, there is no exaltation apart from the crucifixion for John.

The overlap of crucifixion/exaltation also provides the context for interpreting the role of the ascent/descent language in v. 13 (and 1:51) and the Fourth Evangelist's use of the title "Son of Man." The Fourth Evangelist appropriates the traditional apocalyptic figure of the Son of Man (cf. Dan. 7:13) and invests it with his christological perspective. Ascent/descent language thus speaks of Jesus' relationship to God and to the world. The Son of Man's ascent to heaven is salvific, because he is the one who has descended from heaven, the very one whom the Prologue celebrates.

3:15. This verse makes explicit the salvific dimension of the crucifixion. (The lifting up of the serpent in Num 21:8-9 also has a salvific dimension.) Jesus'

offer of his life through being lifted up on the cross makes "eternal life" (ζωὴν αἰώνιον *zoēn aiōnion*) possible for those who believe. "Eternal life" is one of the dominant metaphors in the Fourth Gospel to describe the change in human existence wrought by faith in Jesus (e.g., 3:36; 4:14; 5:24; 6:27; 17:4). To have eternal life is to live life no longer defined by blood or by the will of the flesh or by human will, but by God (cf. 1:13). "Eternal" does not mean mere endless duration of human existence, but is a way of describing life as lived in the unending presence of God. To have eternal life is to be given life as a child of God. To speak of the newness available to the believer as "eternal life" shifts eschatological expectations to the present. Eternal life is not something held in abeyance until the believer's future, but begins in the believer's present. The focus on the crucifixion in 3:13-15 provides the key to interpreting Jesus' earlier metaphors of new birth and the kingdom of God. The offer of new life, "to be born *anōthen*," has only one source— Jesus' offer of his own life. The cross thus makes sense of the double meaning of *anōthen*. To be born *from above* is to be born *again* through the lifting up of Jesus on the cross.

3:16-21. Verse 16 provides the link between the two parts of the discourse. It sums up vv. 14-15 by reiterating the salvific dimensions of Jesus' death, but moves the argument forward with its reference to God's love. God gave Jesus to the world because God loves the world.

The verb translated "give" (δίδωμι *didōmi*) is regularly used in the Fourth Gospel to describe God as the source of what Jesus offers the world (3:35; 5:22, 26, 36). John 3:16 is the only place in the Fourth Gospel that says God "gave" his Son to the world; the more common expression is that God "sent" Jesus, as in 3:17. (Two Greek verbs meaning "to send" [πέμπω *pempō*] and [ἀποστέλλω *apostellō*] are used interchangeably; see 3:17; 4:34; 5:23-24, 30, 36-37; 6:38.) To "send" Jesus is more clearly associated with God's will for the world, whereas *didōmi* seems to be used in 3:16 to underscore that the incarnation derives from God's love for the world as well as from God's will.

"World" (κόσμος *kosmos*) in John refers most often to those human beings who are at odds with Jesus and God (1:10; 7:7; 15:18-19). The use of the term here suggests that God gives Jesus in love to all people, but only believers accept the gift. Verse 16 also reiterates the theme of eternal life from v. 15, but advances the argument by naming the alternative to eternal life: to perish. This verse makes clear that there is no middle ground in the Johannine vision. God's gift of Jesus, which culminates in Jesus' death, resurrection, and ascension, decisively alters the options available to the world. If one believes, one's present is altered by the gift of eternal life; if one does not believe, one perishes.

God's gift of Jesus to the world begins the judgment of the world. Verses 17-21 explain this judgment and exemplify what is known as John's "realized eschatology." To speak of realized eschatology means that God's judgment of the world is not a cosmic future event but is underway in the present, initiated by Jesus' coming into the world. God sends the Son into the world in love in order to save the world, not condemn it (v. 17). Yet the very presence of Jesus as incarnate Word in the world confronts the world with a decision, to believe or not to believe, and making that decision is the moment of judgment. If one believes, one is saved; if one does not believe, one condemns oneself unwittingly (v. 18).

Verses 19-21 portray this intricate balance between judgment and decision in the metaphorical language of light and darkness. This language recalls the language and imagery of the Prologue (1:5, 9-10). To love darkness more than light is the same as not believing, and it results in judgment (v. 19). The way a person acts in the presence of the light is the defining mark of a person's identity. Whether someone is good or evil is revealed solely by the decision he or she makes in the encounter with Jesus (vv. 20-21);[86] it is not predetermined in advance. "In the deci-

sion of faith or unbelief it becomes apparent what [a person] really is and . . . always was. But it is revealed in such a way that the decision is made only now."[87] Christology and anthropology are thus inseparably linked in the Fourth Gospel. Who people are is determined by their response to Jesus. These verses provide a telling conclusion to the Nicodemus narrative. Nicodemus did not believe (3:12); therefore, he remains in the darkness. He came to Jesus at night and will stay in the night.

The Fourth Gospel does include traditional understandings of eschatology and the final judgment (5:28-29), but judgment and eternal life as present tense are at the theological heart of this Gospel. It is crucial for the Fourth Evangelist that God's judgment of the world arises precisely out of God's love for the world. When God sent Jesus into the world, God presented the world with a critical moment of decision. God sent Jesus to save the world, but each person must decide whether to accept that offer of salvation. The world will thereby judge itself in its response to Jesus. Decision and self-judgment define Johannine eschatology. As Bultmann has written eloquently, the Fourth Gospel expresses "a radical understanding of Jesus' appearance as the eschatological event. This event puts an end to the old course of the world. As from now on there are only believers and unbelievers, so that there are also now only saved and lost, those who have life and those who are in death. This is because the event is grounded in the love of God, that love which gives life to faith, but which must become judgment in the face of unbelief."[88]

86. See Haenchen, *John*, 1:205.

87. Rudolf Bultmann, *The Gospel of John: A Commentary*, trans. G. R. Beasley-Murray, R. W. N. Hoare, and J. K. Riches (Philadelphia: Westminster, 1971) 159.

88. Ibid., 155.

REFLECTIONS

John 3:1-21 is a rich text, characterized by word play, misunderstanding, and irony in the dialogue of vv. 2-10 and by explicit theological reflection in the discourse of vv. 11-21. The very richness of the text complicates the task of the interpreter. There is a temptation to pare down John 3:1-21 to its "basic" elements—that is, either to summarize its story line (a Jewish religious authority comes to question Jesus) or its lesson (Jesus teaches about faith and judgment). Such summaries are easier to handle than the intricate dialogue and discourse of the text. This temptation is especially present for the preacher who is asked to present this rich text to a congregation in a limited amount of time. The interpreter needs to resist the temptation to distill this text to its essence or paraphrase its substance, however, because to do so does violence to the Johannine way of storytelling and risks losing the text's proclamation of the good news.

One of the distinctive characteristics of the Fourth Gospel narratives is that they forbid reduction. In these stories, in which action, dialogue, and discourse are closely intertwined, no one element stands in isolation. Rather, each element contributes to the narrative dynamic. This narrative dynamic involves the reader in an active process of reading and interpreting, as the reader is drawn into the conversations Jesus has with Gospel characters and tries to discover the meaning of Jesus' words. These narratives are constructed so that readers are led to their own encounters with Jesus through the words of the Gospel text (cf. 20:30-31). *How* John tells his story is thus an inseparable part of *what* he tells, because the narrative enables the reader to experience Jesus.[89]

In interpreting John 3:1-21, then, it is not enough to say on the basis of the discourse in vv. 11-21, for example, that this text is about faith, decision, and judgment, because that way of interpreting diminishes the full impact of the text. One needs the preceding dialogue, with Nicodemus's misunderstanding and Jesus' repeated offer of new images, to understand what the words of vv. 11-21 are really saying. The interpreter must attend to how John tells this story of Jesus and Nicodemus, how he moves the reader through the give and take between the two characters and thus affords the reader the chance to understand what Nicodemus can only misunderstand. Because the reader has participated in the dialogue between Jesus and Nicodemus, the words in vv. 11-21 are heard with more immediacy. Moreover, the reader has read the Prologue and attended to the witness of John, so that he or she has a wider theological context in which to place those words.

The interpreter, therefore, must allow the narrative dynamics of John 3:1-21 to shape an interpretation of the text. This mode of interpretation runs counter to some conventional appropriations of biblical texts and can be unsettling to the interpreter, because the interpreter must allow himself or herself to be reshaped by what the text says and does rather than reshaping the text to fit the interpreter's needs or preconceptions. This unsettling, however, mirrors what Jesus asks of Nicodemus in the story, because Jesus asks Nicodemus to let go of what he knows (3:2*a*) in order to be reborn through what Jesus has to offer (3:3, 5-8).

The use of the phrase "born again" in contemporary North American Christianity is instructive in this regard. This expression, which derives from Jesus' use of ἄνωθεν *anōthen* in 3:3 and 7, has become a slogan and rallying cry for an entire segment of contemporary Christian experience.[90] Indeed, the validity of a person's faith is frequently judged by whether one has been "born again." Born-again Christianity also exerts significant influence on discussions of politics and religion in North American culture. Yet this use of the expression occurs in isolation from its context in John 3 and with no attention to the complexities of the word *anōthen*. Rather, *anōthen* is flattened to have only one meaning, roughly equivalent to an individual's private moment of conversion.

Such contemporary Christians thus repeat the same mistake Nicodemus made: understanding the word *anōthen* on only one level. Nicodemus misunderstood the double dimensions of "born again" and "born from above" and so focused on physical rebirth. The priority given to "born again" in contemporary usage of John 3:3 and 7 also misunderstands the interrelationship of "born again" and "born from above" in Jesus' words. To interpret *anōthen* as describing spiritual rebirth through personal conversion can disregard the decisive christological dimension of *anōthen*: birth from

89. See Gail R. O'Day, *Revelation in the Fourth Gospel: Narrative Mode and Theological Claim* (Philadelphia: Fortress, 1986); *The Word Disclosed: John's Story and Narrative Preaching* (St. Louis: CBP, 1987) 16-28.

90. See Eric Gritsch, *Born Againism: Perspectives on a Movement* (Philadelphia: Fortress, 1982); Gail R. O'Day, "New Birth as a New People: Spirituality and Community in the Fourth Gospel," *Word and World* VIII (1988) 53-61.

above through the lifting up of Jesus on the cross (3:15). Contemporary usage of "born again" privileges anthropology over christology. That is, it emphasizes personal change more than the external source of that change: the cross. In Jesus' words in chap. 3, anthropology and christology are held in a delicate balance. That is, one cannot know the meaning of human life without grounding it in the reality of Jesus' life and the corporate dimension of that life. The irony of Nicodemus's response to Jesus' words is unwittingly operative whenever the church operates out of a single-level interpretation of *anōthen*.

By codifying the expression "born again" and turning it into a slogan, interpreters risk losing the powerful offer of new life contained in Jesus' words. Nicodemus and the reader are intended to struggle with the expression "born *anōthen*" in order to discern what kind of new birth is at the same time birth from above. In that struggle of interpretation, the reader is called to listen to all of Jesus' words in this text, not just a few of them. As the reader moves with Nicodemus and Jesus through this dialogue and into the discourse, a fresh and fuller understanding of "born *anōthen*" emerges. "Born *anōthen*" is complicated to interpret because its language and its promise transcend conventional categories. It envisions a new mode of life for which there are no precedents, life born of water *and* the Spirit, life regenerated through the cross of Jesus. If interpreters turn "born again" into a slogan, they domesticate the radical newness of Jesus' words and diminish the good news.

The challenge to interpreters of John 3:1-21, then, is to approach this text openly, not convinced that they already know what the text is about and what its words mean. If interpreters approach the Jesus of this text as Nicodemus approached him, confidently asserting what "we know . . . " (3:2), they may find, as Nicodemus did, that their certitudes and assumptions stand in the way of the full experience of Jesus this text offers. The Fourth Evangelist invites interpreters to allow the words of this text to play on them. This is a demanding invitation, because if accepted, it means that the interpreter must be willing to be changed by this text, to welcome new life on the terms offered by Jesus in this text. Belief in Jesus (3:16, 18) changes one's life so that one can, indeed, speak of being "born again," not because of an intrinsic change in human nature, but because of the new beginning that comes with a recognition of the full character of God that is revealed in Jesus. To believe in Jesus is to believe that Jesus is the Son of God and that God loved the world so much that God gave the Son as a gift. The God revealed in Jesus is a God whose love knows no bounds and who asks only that one receive the gift. If one receives the gift, one receives eternal life, because one's life is reshaped and redefined by the love of God in Jesus. The words about judgment with which the text concludes (3:17-21) underscore the seriousness of God's offer.

The seriousness of this text's invitation was grasped by African American slaves. Nicodemus's nighttime visit to Jesus offered an important biblical precedent for their own worship gatherings. Slaves were allowed to participate in formal Christian worship only at their masters' discretion; they were not allowed to have their own worship and rarely were allowed access to the Bible. Therefore, they held clandestine religious gatherings at night, a practice that continued after emancipation. The slaves saw in Nicodemus's night visit proof that it was possible to come to Jesus even when those in power forbade it.[91] Nicodemus was a model, someone who was willing to act on his own against the will of the authorities. The slaves' faith surpassed that of Nicodemus. Nicodemus's night visit was only exploratory, and in this story in John 3, he does not understand the invitation Jesus extends to him. The slaves, by contrast, understood and embraced what Jesus had to offer. They were willing to risk their safety and their very lives to come to Jesus. The slaves are a powerful example of those who "come to the light, so that it may be clearly seen that their deeds have been done in God" (3:21).

91. See the discussion of the importance of Nicodemus for African American religion in *Henry Ossawa Tanner,* introductory essay and catalogue chapters by Dewey F. Mosby; catalogue entries by Dewey F. Mosby and Darrell Sewell (Philadelphia: Philadelphia Art Museum, 1991) 168-71. Henry O. Tanner painted a work that depicts the night visit between Jesus and Nicodemus, *Nicodemus Visiting Jesus* (1899).

JOHN 3:22–4:3, JOHN'S FINAL TESTIMONY

NIV

²²After this, Jesus and his disciples went out into the Judean countryside, where he spent some time with them, and baptized. ²³Now John also was baptizing at Aenon near Salim, because there was plenty of water, and people were constantly coming to be baptized. ²⁴(This was before John was put in prison.) ²⁵An argument developed between some of John's disciples and a certain Jew*a* over the matter of ceremonial washing. ²⁶They came to John and said to him, "Rabbi, that man who was with you on the other side of the Jordan—the one you testified about—well, he is baptizing, and everyone is going to him."

²⁷To this John replied, "A man can receive only what is given him from heaven. ²⁸You yourselves can testify that I said, 'I am not the Christ*b* but am sent ahead of him.' ²⁹The bride belongs to the bridegroom. The friend who attends the bridegroom waits and listens for him, and is full of joy when he hears the bridegroom's voice. That joy is mine, and it is now complete. ³⁰He must become greater; I must become less.

³¹"The one who comes from above is above all; the one who is from the earth belongs to the earth, and speaks as one from the earth. The one who comes from heaven is above all. ³²He testifies to what he has seen and heard, but no one accepts his testimony. ³³The man who has accepted it has certified that God is truthful. ³⁴For the one whom God has sent speaks the words of God, for God*c* gives the Spirit without limit. ³⁵The Father loves the Son and has placed everything in his hands. ³⁶Whoever believes in the Son has eternal life, but whoever rejects the Son will not see life, for God's wrath remains on him."*d*

4 The Pharisees heard that Jesus was gaining and baptizing more disciples than John, ²although in fact it was not Jesus who baptized, but his disciples. ³When the Lord learned of this, he left Judea and went back once more to Galilee.

a25 Some manuscripts *and certain Jews* *b28* Or *Messiah* *c34* Greek *he* *d36* Some interpreters end the quotation after verse 30.

NRSV

22After this Jesus and his disciples went into the Judean countryside, and he spent some time there with them and baptized. ²³John also was baptizing at Aenon near Salim because water was abundant there; and people kept coming and were being baptized ²⁴—John, of course, had not yet been thrown into prison.

25Now a discussion about purification arose between John's disciples and a Jew.*a* ²⁶They came to John and said to him, "Rabbi, the one who was with you across the Jordan, to whom you testified, here he is baptizing, and all are going to him." ²⁷John answered, "No one can receive anything except what has been given from heaven. ²⁸You yourselves are my witnesses that I said, 'I am not the Messiah,*b* but I have been sent ahead of him.' ²⁹He who has the bride is the bridegroom. The friend of the bridegroom, who stands and hears him, rejoices greatly at the bridegroom's voice. For this reason my joy has been fulfilled. ³⁰He must increase, but I must decrease."*c*

31The one who comes from above is above all; the one who is of the earth belongs to the earth and speaks about earthly things. The one who comes from heaven is above all. ³²He testifies to what he has seen and heard, yet no one accepts his testimony. ³³Whoever has accepted his testimony has certified*d* this, that God is true. ³⁴He whom God has sent speaks the words of God, for he gives the Spirit without measure. ³⁵The Father loves the Son and has placed all things in his hands. ³⁶Whoever believes in the Son has eternal life; whoever disobeys the Son will not see life, but must endure God's wrath.

4 Now when Jesus*e* learned that the Pharisees had heard, "Jesus is making and baptizing more disciples than John" ²— although it was not Jesus himself but his disciples who baptized— ³he left Judea and started back to Galilee.

a Other ancient authorities read *the Jews* *b* Or *the Christ* *c* Some interpreters hold that the quotation continues through verse 36 *d* Gk *set a seal to* *e* Other ancient authorities read *the Lord*

COMMENTARY

In John 3:22–4:3, John the Baptist makes his final appearance in the Fourth Gospel. After John's initial testimony (1:19-34), Jesus' ministry among "his own" (1:11) began. He called his first disciples (1:35-51), performed his first miracle (2:1-11), and had his first confrontations with official Judaism (2:13–3:21). At 3:22, Jesus withdraws into the Judean countryside and will move next to the boundaries of Judaism (the Samaritan woman, 4:4-42). Before Jesus' ministry expands, however, John the Baptist will give his final witness. Jesus' first ministry among "his own" is thus framed by the witness of John (1:19-34; 3:22-36).

3:22-30. 3:22-24. In this passage, John claims that the ministries of Jesus and John overlapped. The narrator's aside in v. 24 about John's arrest makes certain that the reader sees that the ministries of John and Jesus take place concurrently. These parallel ministries provide the context for the complaint of John's disciples (v. 26) and John's renewed witness (vv. 27-30).

3:25. A disagreement between a "Jew" and John's disciples about purification precedes their complaint about Jesus. Verse 25 is awkward, because both its meaning and its relationship to the rest of the story are unclear. The substance of the disagreement about purification is never specified, nor is it even alluded to in the disciples' complaint to John (v. 26). Since "purification" can refer to Jewish ceremonial washing (cf. 2:6; note the NIV translation), the disagreement may have been triggered by the baptisms of Jesus and John, but the text does not make that clear. Nor does the text make clear the identity of the "Jew." Some manuscripts read "the Jews" here (see the NIV and NRSV footnotes), perhaps in an attempt to harmonize with John's use of "the Jews" elsewhere in the Gospel, but that emendation does not clarify the verse. The awkwardness of the expression "the Jew" has led to the suggestion that "Jew" is a textual corruption of "Jesus," and while that suggestion makes the best sense of the verse, there is no manuscript support for it.[92] The "Jew" may be a follower of Jesus, since John's disciples complain about Jesus and his followers,

but that interpretation, too, reads in more than the text supplies. The most that can be said confidently about this problematic verse is that it provides the pretext for the disciples' complaint in v. 26.

3:26. John's disciples' address, "Rabbi," indicates their respect for him as a teacher. Their words to John fall into two parts. First, they remind John of his earlier witness (v. 26*a*; see 1:19-34). Moreover, the disciples' recollection of John's testimony reminds the reader of 1:35-37, in which John witnesses to Jesus in the presence of his disciples. Second, the disciples' complaint to John about the success of Jesus' ministry (v. 26*b*) points to a rivalry between the followers of the two men, a rivalry that may have continued into the Evangelist's time (see Acts 19:1-7).

3:27-30. John employs three different strategies in answering his disciples' complaint. First, he uses an aphorism (v. 27) to correct their reading of the situation. This aphorism is another instance of words with a double meaning. As is typical of proverbial language, John's words offer a general truth rather than a truth specific to his disciples' complaint. That general truth is that a person can receive only what God gives to him or her. Yet this general truth also contains a truth specific to Jesus. A central theme throughout the Fourth Gospel is that those who come to Jesus are given him by God (6:39; 10:29; 17:9, 24), that what Jesus has is a gift from God (3:35; 17:2, 11).

Second, John turns the disciples' mention of his testimony back on them (v. 28); John himself testified that he was secondary to the Messiah. John's words in v. 28 are not a verbatim repetition, but a composite of many of his words in chap. 1 (1:20, 30, 36; cf. 1:6). John thus reminds his disciples that his own witness has anticipated the success of Jesus' ministry. Moreover, the reader too is put in the position of a witness; recalling the earlier words of John, one can testify that what John now says about himself and his earlier witness is true.

Third, John tells his disciples a parable (v. 29), thereby confirming his role as "rabbi." The parable of the bridegroom and his friend illustrates how

92. See the discussion in C. K. Barrett, *The Gospel According to St. John*, 2nd ed. (Philadelphia: Westminster, 1978) 221.

one person can rejoice at someone else's joy. The friend of the bridegroom occupies an important position at a Jewish wedding; he takes care of all the nuptial arrangements. Yet despite his prominence, the friend is always a secondary figure, because it is the bridegroom who is getting married, not the friend. It is not clear to what the parable refers when it speaks of the friend's hearing the bridegroom's voice; perhaps it means that the friend rejoices when he hears the bridegroom speak with the bride. The NIV attempts to clarify the meaning of the parable by supplying the verb "wait," for which there is no equivalent in the Greek text. In v. 29*b,* John draws an explicit lesson from the parable; like the friend, he is delighted with the greater response to Jesus.

While the primary purpose of the parable in v. 29 is to provide an illustration of shared joy, the parable also works on a second, symbolic level. In the OT, Israel is presented as the bride of God (Isa 61:10; Jer 2:2; Hosea 1–2); the use of bridal imagery here has potential christological implications as well. The parable can be read as raising the possibility of Jesus as the bridegroom of God's people.

In v. 30, John the Baptist builds on the three strategies of vv. 27-29 and offers his definitive response to the disciples' complaint: "He must increase, but I must decrease" (cf. Matt 11:11; Luke 7:28). What the disciples complain about is in reality part of God's plan ("must" [δεῖ *dei*]). From the very beginning John has testified that Jesus is greater than he is (1:27, 30), that John's ministry of baptism was for the purpose of revealing Jesus to Israel (1:31). The overlapping ministries of Jesus and John (3:22-24, 26) provide a concrete example of the truth to which John has testified from the beginning: John is not the light; Jesus is the light (1:8-9). Jesus' success is not an occasion for complaint but a reason for joy (v. 29*a*), because the ascendancy of Jesus' ministry marks the completion of John's work (v. 29*b*).

3:31-36. Verse 30 has another function: It also serves as the introduction to John's final witness to Jesus in vv. 31-36. Verses 31-36 resonate with Johannine subjects and characteristic expressions: Jesus' heavenly origins, the relationship between Jesus and God, faith and eternal life. As in vv. 16-21 (see Commentary above), the distinctive Johannine flavor and more general theological

orientation of these verses have led scholars to debate whose voice is speaking. Some interpret vv. 31-36 as the final witness of John the Baptist,[93] but other scholars maintain that these verses are either a displaced discourse of Jesus[94] or the Evangelist's commentary.[95] The NRSV presents this section as the Evangelist's commentary and thus does not place vv. 31-36 in quotation marks, whereas the NIV punctuates vv. 31-36 as the words of John the Baptist.

Verses 31-36 may have originated as an independent piece of theological reflection, but they are positioned in the narrative to serve as John's final witness. As was noted in the discussion of 3:16-21, the characters in the Fourth Gospel and the Evangelist's commentaries often share a common voice. In chap. 1, John the Baptist's witness sounds more like the early church's witness (e.g., 1:15, 30) than the words of a first-century Jewish itinerant prophet and reflects the Fourth Evangelist's understanding of the function of John the Baptist. John is the model witness, the unfailing herald of the truth about Jesus, and John's witness stretches from his own time to the church's time.

It is critical, therefore, to the portrait of John the Baptist in the Fourth Gospel that vv. 31-36 be read as his final witness. John's purpose is to bear witness to the light (1:7), and before he disappears from the narrative completely, he is given one final witness to speak. This witness draws out the theological implications of all that John has said in 1:19-34 and 3:27-30, but it also offers theological reflection on the early events of Jesus' ministry. It is appropriate that John should be the voice (1:23) of this theological witness, since he has been the principal interpreter of Jesus to this point in the Gospel narrative. John appeared on the scene, proclaiming Jesus as the redeemer of the world's sin (1:29), and he will exit proclaiming Jesus as the source of eternal life (3:36).

3:31-32. John's witness in vv. 31-36 contains two major subjects. First, vv. 31-32 continue the comparison of Jesus and John begun in 3:26-30.

93. Ernst Haenchen, *John, Hermenia,* 2 vols. (Philadelphia: Fortress, 1984) 210; and Barrett, *The Gospel According to St. John,* 219.

94. Raymond E. Brown, *The Gospel According to John (I–XII),* AB 29 (Garden City, N.Y.: Doubleday, 1966) 159-60; Rudolf Schnackenburg, *The Gospel According to St. John,* 3 vols. (New York: Seabury, 1982) 1:361, 380-92; Bultmann, *The Gospel of John,* 160.

95. See M. J. Lagrange, *Évangile selon Saint Jean* (Paris: Gabalda, 1948); theories also involve displacement.

Their relationship is presented in spatial categories: The one who comes "from above" is Jesus; the one who is "from the earth" is John (v. 31). In the Fourth Gospel, "earth" and "world" are not synonymous. "World" (κόσμος *kosmos*) usually depicts the sphere of human enmity to God (e.g., 15:18-19), and "earth" (γῆ *gē*) is used as a spatial contrast to heaven. John the Baptist cites Jesus' heavenly origin as proof of Jesus' superiority over him. Recognition of Jesus' heavenly origin is a central theme in the Fourth Gospel (3:13; 16:28). Unless one knows that Jesus is from God, one cannot fully grasp Jesus' identity (see 8:14; 9:29-31). The spatial categories in v. 31 recall the Nicodemus discourse (3:12), as does the use of "from above" (ἄνωθεν *anōthen*; see also 3:3, 7). The spatial categories make clear that *anōthen* is used in v. 31 to mean "from above." Jesus' superiority over John is also evident in their words. John can only speak of earthly things (v. 31), but Jesus, who is from heaven, testifies to everything he has seen and heard (v. 32*a*; cf. 3:11-13). Jesus' heavenly origin is the source and guarantee of all that he says.

In v. 32*b*, John's witness shifts to its second subject: the acceptance or rejection of Jesus' testimony. Verse 32*b* makes the sweeping statement, "no one accepts his testimony," directly contradicting v. 26 ("all are going to him"). Verses 26 and 32*b* must be understood as serving quite distinct purposes.[96] Verse 26 stresses Jesus' popularity in order to anticipate his increase and John's decrease. Verse 32*b* stresses Jesus' rejection in order to illustrate the Christian faith community's struggle with those who do not accept Jesus' witness (cf. 1:10-11). This struggle received narrative embodiment in the story of Nicodemus (3:1-21). Verse 32*b* overstates the rejection in order to emphasize the seriousness of the struggle.

3:33. This verse confirms that the absolute negative of v. 32*b* is hyperbole, because this verse assumes that someone accepts Jesus. The language of v. 33 communicates the importance of accepting Jesus' testimony. First, the verb "has certified" (lit., "to set one's seal to" [σφραγίζω *sphragizō*]) suggests the formal, binding dimension of accepting Jesus. Second, when one accepts Jesus' testimony, one certifies that "God is true." What is

at issue in faith in Jesus is the very character of God. In 1:18, the Fourth Evangelist identified Jesus as the one who makes God known, and v. 33 suggests that whoever accepts Jesus' testimony shares in that affirmation.

3:34-35. These verses provide three reasons why the character of God is revealed in Jesus' testimony. First (v. 34*a*), Jesus reveals the truth about God because he is sent by God (cf. 4:34; 5:24, 30; 12:45) and speaks God's words (cf. 14:10, 24; 17:8, 14). Second (v. 34*b*), Jesus has received the full gift of the Spirit of God. The subject of v. 34*b* is ambiguous in the Greek text, so that one could read either God or Jesus as the giver of the Spirit.[97] Ancient scribes attempted to resolve the ambiguity by supplying "God" as the subject in some manuscripts, and the context of v. 34*b* supports the scribes' interpretation. Verses 34-35 focus on what God has given Jesus, not on what Jesus gives. Moreover, God's gift of the Spirit to Jesus was confirmed in John the Baptist's account of the descent of the Spirit at Jesus' baptism (1:33). Third (v. 35), Jesus' relationship with God guarantees the validity of his witness about God (cf. 3:27; 13:3). Verse 35 is the first mention of the Father's love of the Son. This love will receive more attention as the Gospel proceeds (e.g., 5:20; 10:17; 15:9).

3:36. John concludes his witness with an explicit statement of the consequences of believing or not believing (see also vv. 15-16). The polarity of "believe"/"disobey" (πιστεύω *pisteuō*/ἀπειθέω *apeitheō*) is unusual (cf. 3:18, where the alternatives are "believe" or "not believe"). This is the only occurrence of "disobey" in John, the Synoptics, or the Johannine epistles. Its usage here suggests that unbelief is an act of will, of refusing Jesus' claims, a concept in keeping with the language of acceptance of vv. 32-33. The NIV translates *apeitheō* as "reject," and while that rendering may accurately capture the sense of the word here, it strains the Greek.

The alternative to "eternal life" in v. 36 is also unusual: "God's wrath" (ἡ ὀργὴ τοῦ θεοῦ *hē orgē tou theou*). This expression, like "disobey," occurs only here in John and is rare in the Synoptics.

96. Haenchen, *John*, 1:211.

97. For God as the giver of the Spirit, see Barrett, *The Gospel According to St. John*, 226; Bultmann, *The Gospel of John*, 164; for Jesus as the giver of the Spirit, see Brown, *The Gospel According to John (I–XII)*, 161-62.

It serves as an analogue to the language of "perish" and "condemnation" in John 3:16-18. Interestingly, in three out of its five Gospel occurrences, "God's wrath" is found in the mouth of John the Baptist (Matt 3:7; Luke 3:7; John 3:36). John the Baptist's final words in the Fourth Gospel reflect distinctive Johannine theological concerns, but they also convey a note of judgment that is consistent with the portrait of John the Baptist found elsewhere in the NT.

4:1-3. These verses provide a postscript to John's final witness. Verse 1 reiterates that Jesus' ministry is more successful than John's (cf. 3:26), but this success now implies conflict and tension with the Pharisees (cf. the Pharisees' careful interrogation of John the Baptist in 1:24-27). The specific danger posed by the Pharisees' knowledge of Jesus' success is not named, nor is it clear how a change in location removes Jesus from that danger (v. 3). Nonetheless, vv. 1 and 3 do anticipate the intensifying conflict and tension between Jesus and the Jewish religious establishment.

John 4:2 is perhaps the most awkward verse in the Gospel. It disrupts the grammar of vv. 1 and 3 (which are one sentence in the Greek) and directly contradicts the substance of 3:22, 26; 4:1. The NIV attempts to circumvent the awkwardness of v. 2 by rearranging the syntax of 4:1-3 (cf. the NRSV, which reflects the syntax of the Greek text), but such a rearrangement conceals the parenthetical nature of v. 2. Brown sees v. 2 as indisputable proof that several hands were responsible for the final form of the Fourth Gospel;[98] indeed, C. H. Dodd writes that v. 2 "ruins the sentence, and perhaps has better claim to be regarded as an 'editorial note' by a 'redactor' than anything else in the gospel except the colophon xxi.24-25."[99] The presence of v. 2 in the text can be explained only as the correction of a later editor who feared that the evidence that Jesus himself baptized disciples would support claims that Jesus was an imitator of John the Baptist (see 1:29-34).

98. Brown, *The Gospel According to John (I–XII)*, 164.
99. C. H. Dodd, *The Interpretation of the Fourth Gospel* (Cambridge: Cambridge University Press, 1953) 311.

REFLECTIONS

John the Baptist's joy at Jesus' success (3:29), even though that success marks the completion of John's work, reminds the reader that the success of the gospel takes precedence over the acclamation and acknowledgment of one's own ministry. The attitude of John's disciples (3:25-26) reflects the ministerial competition and turf battles that are commonplace in contemporary life, both in and out of the church. When others begin to contribute to effective ministries, it is often of overwhelming importance to those who first envisioned the particular ministry to remind "latecomers" of the program's roots and to continue to exercise control. Political leaders from the local to the global level jockey for position to receive credit for successful initiatives. John's disciples wanted him to reclaim his rightful spot, to disclaim Jesus as an interloper into his ministry of baptism, but John would have none of it. John did not need the credit; he did not want continuing acclamation; and he did not want to compete with Jesus. John's joy was complete because his ministry had revealed God's chosen one to Israel (1:31).

John's ministry thus ends on an odd note of triumph, a triumph marked by John's decrease and superfluity (3:30). John functioned as a midwife to Jesus' ministry, bearing witness to who Jesus was, opening people's eyes to Jesus' presence in their midst. Once Jesus' ministry had been born, John had no function. His witness was replaced by Jesus' own witness (3:32), and John rejoiced. It is often difficult for those who are engaged in the church's ministries to do what John did, to allow their witness to have a life of its own, to celebrate the success of their witness as a sign of the success of the gospel, not of their own success (cf. 1 Cor 9:15-18). John is a model disciple, because he was able to let go of his ministry for the sake of the gospel.

John is also a model disciple for the Fourth Evangelist because the content of his witness looks beyond itself to the witness of Jesus. John 3:31-36 marks a shift in emphasis in John's preaching from witness proclaimed to witness received. As John departs the scene, he confronts those who hear him with the responsibility of making their own decisions. John and Jesus have borne witness, but neither can guarantee that his witness will be accepted. Acceptance cannot be coerced, but each person who hears Jesus must decide whether to believe. In 3:36, John the Baptist delineated the consequences of this choice: eternal life or the enduring wrath of God. As in 3:15-21, there is no room for equivocation; the life of faith is all or nothing in the Fourth Gospel. When one accepts Jesus' testimony, one enters unqualifiedly into eternal life. When one disobeys, one endures God's wrath.

The absolute language of 3:36 conveys the seriousness of the faith decision—everything is at issue; everything is at stake. While these absolutes may at first glance seem oppressive, in reality they are ultimately liberating. Once one declares acceptance of Jesus' testimony and hence reveals who one is (cf. 3:20-21), then one is set free to live one's life reconstituted ("reborn," 3:3, 7) through the grace of God in Jesus. When one certifies that God is truth (3:33), the possibilities for life are limitless.

John's final witness bears the marks of his joyous celebration (3:29) as he proclaims the gifts of God available in Jesus (3:34-35) and the promise of new life Jesus offers to all (3:36). There is nothing subtle about John's final witness, but there was no subtlety to his earlier testimony either. John preaches with an urgency that recognizes the importance of accepting Jesus *now,* of making the decision that will lead to new life. The urgency of John's witness has not diminished over time; the moment of decision is as critical for modern Christians as it was for those who came to John in the wilderness. From first (1:9) to last (3:36), John is the voice of witness, calling those who hear to recognize Jesus and accept his testimony.

JOHN 4:4-42, JESUS IN SAMARIA

NIV

[4]Now he had to go through Samaria. [5]So he came to a town in Samaria called Sychar, near the plot of ground Jacob had given to his son Joseph. [6]Jacob's well was there, and Jesus, tired as he was from the journey, sat down by the well. It was about the sixth hour.

[7]When a Samaritan woman came to draw water, Jesus said to her, "Will you give me a drink?" [8](His disciples had gone into the town to buy food.)

[9]The Samaritan woman said to him, "You are a Jew and I am a Samaritan woman. How can you ask me for a drink?" (For Jews do not associate with Samaritans.[a])

[10]Jesus answered her, "If you knew the gift of God and who it is that asks you for a drink, you

NRSV

[4]But he had to go through Samaria. [5]So he came to a Samaritan city called Sychar, near the plot of ground that Jacob had given to his son Joseph. [6]Jacob's well was there, and Jesus, tired out by his journey, was sitting by the well. It was about noon.

[7]A Samaritan woman came to draw water, and Jesus said to her, "Give me a drink." [8](His disciples had gone to the city to buy food.) [9]The Samaritan woman said to him, "How is it that you, a Jew, ask a drink of me, a woman of Samaria?" (Jews do not share things in common with Samaritans.)[a] [10]Jesus answered her, "If you knew the gift of God, and who it is that is saying to you, 'Give me a drink,' you would have asked him, and he would have given you living water." [11]The woman said to him, "Sir, you have no bucket,

[a]9 Or *do not use dishes Samaritans have used*

[a] Other ancient authorities lack this sentence

would have asked him and he would have given you living water."

[11]"Sir," the woman said, "you have nothing to draw with and the well is deep. Where can you get this living water? [12]Are you greater than our father Jacob, who gave us the well and drank from it himself, as did also his sons and his flocks and herds?"

[13]Jesus answered, "Everyone who drinks this water will be thirsty again, [14]but whoever drinks the water I give him will never thirst. Indeed, the water I give him will become in him a spring of water welling up to eternal life."

[15]The woman said to him, "Sir, give me this water so that I won't get thirsty and have to keep coming here to draw water."

[16]He told her, "Go, call your husband and come back."

[17]"I have no husband," she replied.

Jesus said to her, "You are right when you say you have no husband. [18]The fact is, you have had five husbands, and the man you now have is not your husband. What you have just said is quite true."

[19]"Sir," the woman said, "I can see that you are a prophet. [20]Our fathers worshiped on this mountain, but you Jews claim that the place where we must worship is in Jerusalem."

[21]Jesus declared, "Believe me, woman, a time is coming when you will worship the Father neither on this mountain nor in Jerusalem. [22]You Samaritans worship what you do not know; we worship what we do know, for salvation is from the Jews. [23]Yet a time is coming and has now come when the true worshipers will worship the Father in spirit and truth, for they are the kind of worshipers the Father seeks. [24]God is spirit, and his worshipers must worship in spirit and in truth."

[25]The woman said, "I know that Messiah" (called Christ) "is coming. When he comes, he will explain everything to us."

[26]Then Jesus declared, "I who speak to you am he."

[27]Just then his disciples returned and were surprised to find him talking with a woman. But no one asked, "What do you want?" or "Why are you talking with her?"

and the well is deep. Where do you get that living water? [12]Are you greater than our ancestor Jacob, who gave us the well, and with his sons and his flocks drank from it?" [13]Jesus said to her, "Everyone who drinks of this water will be thirsty again, [14]but those who drink of the water that I will give them will never be thirsty. The water that I will give will become in them a spring of water gushing up to eternal life." [15]The woman said to him, "Sir, give me this water, so that I may never be thirsty or have to keep coming here to draw water."

16Jesus said to her, "Go, call your husband, and come back." [17]The woman answered him, "I have no husband." Jesus said to her, "You are right in saying, 'I have no husband'; [18]for you have had five husbands, and the one you have now is not your husband. What you have said is true!" [19]The woman said to him, "Sir, I see that you are a prophet. [20]Our ancestors worshiped on this mountain, but you[a] say that the place where people must worship is in Jerusalem." [21]Jesus said to her, "Woman, believe me, the hour is coming when you will worship the Father neither on this mountain nor in Jerusalem. [22]You worship what you do not know; we worship what we know, for salvation is from the Jews. [23]But the hour is coming, and is now here, when the true worshipers will worship the Father in spirit and truth, for the Father seeks such as these to worship him. [24]God is spirit, and those who worship him must worship in spirit and truth." [25]The woman said to him, "I know that Messiah is coming" (who is called Christ). "When he comes, he will proclaim all things to us." [26]Jesus said to her, "I am he,[b] the one who is speaking to you."

27Just then his disciples came. They were astonished that he was speaking with a woman, but no one said, "What do you want?" or, "Why are you speaking with her?" [28]Then the woman left her water jar and went back to the city. She said to the people, [29]"Come and see a man who told me everything I have ever done! He cannot be the Messiah,[c] can he?" [30]They left the city and were on their way to him.

31Meanwhile the disciples were urging him, "Rabbi, eat something." [32]But he said to them, "I

a The Greek word for *you* here and in verses 21 and 22 is plural
b Gk *I am*   c Or *the Christ*

NIV

²⁸Then, leaving her water jar, the woman went back to the town and said to the people, ²⁹"Come, see a man who told me everything I ever did. Could this be the Christ*?" ³⁰They came out of the town and made their way toward him.

³¹Meanwhile his disciples urged him, "Rabbi, eat something."

³²But he said to them, "I have food to eat that you know nothing about."

³³Then his disciples said to each other, "Could someone have brought him food?"

³⁴"My food," said Jesus, "is to do the will of him who sent me and to finish his work. ³⁵Do you not say, 'Four months more and then the harvest'? I tell you, open your eyes and look at the fields! They are ripe for harvest. ³⁶Even now the reaper draws his wages, even now he harvests the crop for eternal life, so that the sower and the reaper may be glad together. ³⁷Thus the saying 'One sows and another reaps' is true. ³⁸I sent you to reap what you have not worked for. Others have done the hard work, and you have reaped the benefits of their labor."

³⁹Many of the Samaritans from that town believed in him because of the woman's testimony, "He told me everything I ever did." ⁴⁰So when the Samaritans came to him, they urged him to stay with them, and he stayed two days. ⁴¹And because of his words many more became believers.

⁴²They said to the woman, "We no longer believe just because of what you said; now we have heard for ourselves, and we know that this man really is the Savior of the world."

*29 Or Messiah

NRSV

have food to eat that you do not know about." ³³So the disciples said to one another, "Surely no one has brought him something to eat?" ³⁴Jesus said to them, "My food is to do the will of him who sent me and to complete his work. ³⁵Do you not say, 'Four months more, then comes the harvest'? But I tell you, look around you, and see how the fields are ripe for harvesting. ³⁶The reaper is already receiving* wages and is gathering fruit for eternal life, so that sower and reaper may rejoice together. ³⁷For here the saying holds true, 'One sows and another reaps.' ³⁸I sent you to reap that for which you did not labor. Others have labored, and you have entered into their labor."

³⁹Many Samaritans from that city believed in him because of the woman's testimony, "He told me everything I have ever done." ⁴⁰So when the Samaritans came to him, they asked him to stay with them; and he stayed there two days. ⁴¹And many more believed because of his word. ⁴²They said to the woman, "It is no longer because of what you said that we believe, for we have heard for ourselves, and we know that this is truly the Savior of the world."

*Or 35. . . the fields are already ripe for harvesting. 36 The reaper is receiving

COMMENTARY

In John 4:4-42, Jesus' ministry enters a new stage. He leaves the confines of traditional Judaism and turns to those whom his Jewish contemporaries reckoned as outsiders and enemies: the Samaritans. The breach between Jews and Samaritans can be traced to the Assyrian occupation of northern Palestine (721 BCE; see 2 Kings 17), but the most intense rivalry began about 200 BCE. The source of the enmity be-

tween Jews and Samaritans was a dispute about the correct location of the cultic center (cf. John 4:20). The Samaritans built a shrine on Mt. Gerizim during the Persian period and claimed that this shrine, not the Jerusalem Temple, was the proper place of worship. The shrine at Mt. Gerizim was destroyed by Jewish troops in 128 BCE, but the schism between Jews and Samaritans continued (cf. John 4:9).

When Jesus meets the Samaritan woman at the well, he thus meets someone who stands in marked contrast to all that has preceded in the Gospel. For example, when Jesus spoke with Nicodemus in 3:1-21, he spoke with a named male of the Jewish religious establishment. When he speaks with the Samaritan woman, he speaks with an unnamed female of an enemy people.

John 4:4-42 is an important example of the complex interweaving of dialogue and narrative that characterizes much of the Fourth Gospel (see 6:1-71; 9:1-41; 11:1-44). This long passage consists of two main blocks of conversation (vv. 7-26, Jesus and the Samaritan woman, and vv. 31-38, Jesus and his disciples) surrounded by their narrative frames. The structure of the text can be outlined as follows:

4:4-6   Introduction: Jesus' arrival at the well

4:7-26   Conversation between Jesus and the Samaritan woman

4:27-30   Transition: Arrival of the disciples and departure of the woman

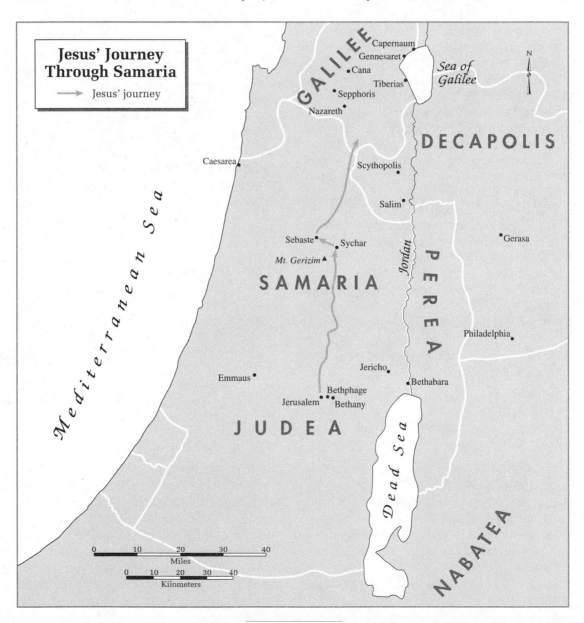

4:31-38 Conversation between Jesus and his disciples

4:39-42 Conclusion: Jesus and the Samaritan townspeople

Some of these sections may have originated as separate stories (e.g., the conversation with the disciples), but the Fourth Evangelist has carefully molded them together into one story. Each section either leads to what follows or builds on what precedes.

4:4-6. The introduction provides the setting for the narrative. Verse 4 links the Samaritan text to vv. 1-3; in order to get from Judea to Galilee (4:3), Jesus "had to go through Samaria." Scholars are fairly evenly divided on whether the necessity of this Samaritan journey is strictly geographical[100] or has theological overtones.[101] The geographical necessity of the trip is supported by Josephus who notes that the most expedient route from Judea to Galilee during the first century was through Samaria.[102] The word translated as "had to" (ἔδει *edei*), however, usually is associated in the Fourth Gospel with God's plan (e.g., 3:14, 30; 9:4). It seems best, therefore, to read the necessity of the journey through Samaria as both geographical and theological. Jesus' itinerary may have been governed by geographical expediency, but his stay in Samaria was governed by the theological necessity of offering himself to those whom social convention deemed unacceptable.

Verses 5-6 provide a detailed description of the location of Jesus' conversation with the woman. This description is important because of the OT imagery in which the geography is couched. The references to Jacob and his well introduce the patriarchal traditions that will figure prominently in the conversation between Jesus and the Samaritan woman (vv. 11-14). The description of Jesus' arrival at the well (v. 6*b*) also establishes the conditions of his request for water in v. 7. Jesus was tired from his journey, and he arrived at the well in the heat of the day ("about noon," NRSV; "about the sixth hour," NIV).

4:7-26. The dialogue between Jesus and the Samaritan woman consists of thirteen exchanges, one of the longest dialogues in the Gospel. It divides into two sections, each section introduced by a request/command by Jesus: (1) vv. 7-15 ("Give me a drink"); (2) vv. 16-26 ("Go, call your husband").

4:7. This verse begins with the arrival of the Samaritan woman at the well to draw water. Like vv. 5-6*a*, v. 7 is redolent with OT images that figure prominently in the rest of the narrative. First, Jesus' request for water recalls the story of Elijah and the widow of Sidon (1 Kgs 17:10-11). In both stories a man interrupts a woman engaged in household work to request a gesture of hospitality. The parallels between Elijah and Jesus suggest the image of Jesus as prophet, a theme that will occupy a pivotal place in Jesus' conversation with the woman (4:19).

Second, the scene of a man and a woman at a well recalls the betrothal stories of Isaac (Gen 24:10-61), Jacob (Gen 29:1-20), and Moses (Exod 2:15*b*-21). John 4:4-42 evokes these betrothal stories in order to rework their imagery, however. The story of the wedding feast (2:1-11) and John the Baptist's parable (3:29) have already introduced wedding imagery into the Fourth Gospel as images of eschatological joy and fulfillment. John 4:4-42 also raises the issues of eschatological fulfillment (vv. 21-26), but it transforms the messianic/bridal symbolism. In John 4:4-42, the Messiah comes not only to Israel, but also to those whom Israel marginalizes and despises. Unlike the OT well scenes, Jesus does not come to the well looking for a woman to be his bride, but for a witness who will recognize the Messiah and bring the despised people to him (vv. 34-38). What is most astonishing about John 4:4-42 is the fact that a Samaritan woman becomes that witness (vv. 28-30, 39-42).

4:9. The Samaritan woman responds to Jesus' request with amazement because it violates two societal conventions. First, a Jewish *man* did not initiate conversation with an unknown *woman.* Moreover, a Jewish teacher did not engage in public conversation with a woman ("Hence the sages have said: He that talks much with womankind brings evil upon himself and neglects the study of the law and at the last will inherit Gehenna.")[103] Second, Jews did not invite contact

---

100. C. K. Barrett, *The Gospel According to St. John,* 2nd ed. (Philadelphia: Westminster, 1978) 230.

101. Raymond E. Brown, *The Gospel According to John (I–XII)*, AB 29 (Garden City, N.Y.: Doubleday, 1966) 1:169.

102. Josephus *Antiquities of the Jews* 20.118; *The Jewish War* 2:232; *Life* 269.

103. See *p.ʾAbot* 1:5; cf. 4:27.

with Samaritans. The Fourth Evangelist's aside in v. 9c underscores the seriousness of the breach between Jews and Samaritans. A fear of ritual contamination (note the alternate translation of v. 9c in the NIV) developed into a prohibition of all social intercourse.

4:10. Instead of answering the woman's question directly, Jesus invites her to answer her question herself ("If you knew . . . "). If the woman could recognize the identity of the person with whom she speaks, a dramatic role reversal will take place. The woman would be the one who requests water. "Living water" (ὕδωρ ζῶν *hydōr zōn*) has two possible meanings. It can mean fresh, running water (spring water as opposed to water from a cistern), or it can mean life-giving water. Once again, the Fourth Evangelist intentionally uses a word with a double meaning (cf. 3:3, 7 and the expression "born again"/"from above" [ἄνωθεν *anōthen*]).

4:11-12. The Samaritan woman hears only the meaning "running water" in Jesus' words and so responds to his offer of living water with protests of logical and material impossibility (cf. Nicodemus, 3:4). It is not credible to her that a man who has just asked her for water because he was unable to acquire any for himself should now offer her fresh running water (v. 11a). Her protest leads to a question, "Where do you get that living water?" (v. 11b). This question, like other questions about the origins of Jesus' gifts (1:29; 2:9; 3:8; 6:5), is ironically charged. The question operates on two levels simultaneously—it makes sense to ask a man with no bucket where he will get water, but the question can also be asked of Jesus' gift of living water. The irony arises because the reader knows the appropriateness of the question on both levels, but the woman is aware only of the first, literal level of meaning.

The woman's question in v. 12 is a universally recognized instance of Johannine irony.[104] The immediate source of its irony is clear: For the Fourth Evangelist and most of his readers, Jesus is greater than Jacob, while the woman falsely assumes the opposite. (The question is introduced by the interrogative μὴ (*mē*) in the Greek text, a construction that anticipates a negative reply:

"You are not greater than Jacob, are you?" (cf. 8:53). Since Jesus has no visible means with which to draw water, the woman's question seems to imply that only a miracle similar to the one tradition attributed to Jacob at Haran could produce the water.[105] The woman responds to Jesus by challenging his ability to match the gift of one of the great forebears of the faith.

4:13-14. Jesus responds to the woman's challenge by focusing on the permanent effect of the two waters on thirst. Jacob's gift may have been miraculous and its abundance legendary (v. 12b), but it could not assuage thirst permanently (v. 13). Jesus' gift of living water will, however (v. 14). The contrast between the two waters recalls Isa 55:1-2 ("Ho, everyone who thirsts,/ come to the waters" [NRSV]). Jesus' description of his gift of water in v. 14 clarifies the meaning of the expression "living water": Jesus offers water that gives life. Those who drink from Jesus' water "will never thirst" (lit., "will not be thirsty forever"), because his water will become "in them a spring of water gushing up to eternal life" (v. 14). In John 7:37-39 Jesus' gift of living water is associated with the gift of the Spirit, and it is possible to see that connection in v. 14 as well.

4:15. The Samaritan woman responds enthusiastically to Jesus' words (v. 15a), but her enthusiasm misses the point. The motivation for her request—that she would no longer have to come back to the well (v. 15b)—shows that she has not yet grasped the radical nature of Jesus' gifts. She continues to see Jesus through her categories of physical thirst and miraculous springs, and so she does not understand the meaning of his "living water." Her request is ironic to the reader, because it is the right request for the wrong reasons (cf. 6:34).

On the one hand, then, v. 15 sounds a note of failure. Although by her request for water the Samaritan woman is ostensibly doing what Jesus had earlier said she should do (v. 10), she does not know for what she is asking or of whom she is asking it. She thinks that Jesus is a miracle worker who can provide her with extraordinary water. Her misperception is the source of the irony of her response for the reader, because the

---

104. E.g., Barrett, *The Gospel According to St. John*, 234; Brown, *The Gospel According to John (I–XII)*, 170.

105. José Ramón Díaz, "Palestinian Targum and New Testament," *NovT* 6 (1963) 76-77; Jerome Neyrey, "Jacob Traditions and the Interpretation of John 4:10-26," *CBQ* 41 (1979) 419-37.

conversation has led the reader to see that something more is at stake in these verses.

On the other hand, v. 15 sounds a note of hope, however nascent. The woman has gained considerable ground in this conversation. She has moved from seeing Jesus as a thirsty Jew who knowingly violates social convention to seeing him as someone whose gifts she needs. At the beginning of the conversation, Jesus' words about living water seemed preposterous to her, empty boasts by a man without a bucket (v. 11), but in v. 15, she believes that Jesus can give water that will assuage her thirst. The woman's openness to Jesus and her willingness to engage him in conversation stand in marked contrast to Nicodemus, who only greeted Jesus with amazement and resistance (3:4, 9). The Samaritan woman recognizes neither Jesus' true identity nor the fullness of his gifts, but in v. 15, she is willing to receive what she thinks he is offering and hence to acknowledge her need of him.

4:16-19. Jesus introduces a new topic in v. 16 in order to provide a fresh angle on his identity. In vv. 7-15, his invitation to the woman was couched in the metaphor of living water; in vv. 16-18, Jesus' invitation will be grounded in the woman's own life.

Verses 16-19 have been consistently misinterpreted, resulting in the popular portrait of this woman as a sinner. The text is not, as interpreters almost unanimously assume,[106] evidence of the woman's immorality. Jesus does not judge her; any moral judgments are imported into the text by interpreters. There are many possible reasons for her marital history other than her moral laxity. Perhaps the woman, like Tamar in Genesis 38, is trapped in the custom of levirate marriage (Deut 25:5-10; see also Luke 20:27-33), and the last male in the family line has refused to marry her. Significantly, the reasons for the woman's marital history intrigue commentators but do not concern Jesus.

One needs to read this story on its own terms. The conversation provides another example of Jesus' ability to see and know all things (cf. 1:48-50; 2:24). The woman's response to Jesus' request seems straightforward enough (v. 17*a*), but his reply (vv. 17*b*-18) causes the reader to reassess the woman's words. The reader accepts the woman's words at their face value, but Jesus penetrates beyond the surface level of her words to arrive at the truth about her life. It is not until Jesus indicates why the woman's words are true that the reader, too, knows the truth.

The conversation in vv. 16-19 is also a moment of revelation for the woman. Jesus' insight into her words and life leads her to declare him to be a prophet (v. 19). Her response recalls the response of Nathanael in 1:47-49. With both Nathanael and the Samaritan woman, a demonstration of perception and insight on Jesus' part leads to a christological confession.

4:20. In the light of her recognition of Jesus as a prophet, the woman puts before him the most pressing theological problem that stands between Jews and Samaritans: What is the right worship site, this mountain (Gerizim) or Jerusalem (v. 20)? The introduction of this topic is not, as commentators frequently argue, a psychological ploy, a classical evasion to turn the subject away from the embarrassing truth about her morals.[107] Nor is this theological topic and Jesus' response too difficult for the woman to understand.[108] By asking Jesus about the proper place of worship, the woman is not disengaging from Jesus. Rather, her inquiry about worship is an act of deepening engagement with Jesus, because she anticipates that the prophet Jesus will be able to speak an authoritative word on the subject.

4:21-24. The woman's words in v. 20 evoke a lengthy response from Jesus. The woman's comment reflects the present reality of Samaritan/Jewish relations, but in v. 21, Jesus directs her attention away from the present to the future. "The hour is coming" refers to the time of eschatological fulfillment (cf. 5:25, 28). In the eschatological age, the woman's categories will be obsolete, because neither the Samaritan ("this mountain") nor the Jewish site ("Jerusalem") will be the place of worship—both will be replaced in the eschatological age. Jesus' words in v. 21 also remind the woman of the object of worship: "the Father." The Samaritan/Jewish conflict so dominates the woman's perspective that her words to Jesus (v. 20) contain no reference to who is being worshiped.

---

106. E.g., Brown, *The Gospel According to John (I–XII)*, 171.

107. Ibid., 177; Robert Kysar, *John*, Augsburg Commentary of the New Testament (Minneapolis: Augsburg, 1986) 66.
108. Brown, *The Gospel According to John (I–XII)*, 176.

In v. 22, Jesus identifies himself with the Jews. The "you" of v. 22*a* is second-person plural, and the "you"/"we" contrast in that verse refers to Samaritans and Jews (cf. vv. 9, 20; the NIV translation, "you Samaritans," is an expansion; see also "you Jews" in 4:20). The Samaritans accepted only the Pentateuch as Scripture, and so from the Jewish perspective they had an incomplete picture of God ("You worship what you do not know").

In v. 22*b*, "salvation is from the Jews," Jesus affirms the positive role of the Jews in salvation history. The noun "Jew" is used positively here because it refers to the Jewish people as a whole (cf. 11:19, 45), not the Jewish religious authorities (1:19; 9:18, 22; see Reflections at 5:1-18 and chap. 8). Jesus reminds the woman of Israel's place as God's chosen people in order to caution her that by rejecting the Jews, she risks rejecting God's offer of salvation. This positive appraisal of the Jews has an ironic undertone when read in the context of the whole Gospel, because it points to one of the Gospel's central paradoxes. Salvation does originate from God's own people, the Jews, but some Jews do not receive that offer of salvation in Jesus. For example, the offer of salvation made by Jesus (a Jew) has been rejected by the Jew Nicodemus but will be accepted by the Samaritans (4:42).

The "but" with which v. 23 begins (NIV = "yet") marks a decisive turning point in Jesus' speech. In v. 21, the hour when conventional understandings of worship would change is coming; in v. 23, that hour is no longer merely anticipated but has arrived. The ordinary present has been transformed into the eschatological present. In the eschatological present, true worship is no longer defined by place, but as worship "in spirit and truth" (vv. 23-24). Worship of God in spirit and truth does not point to an internal, spiritualized worship but to a form of worship that reflects and is shaped by the character of God. That is, the historical problem of Jewish vs. Samaritan worship is transformed into the eschatological encounter with the presence of God. "God is spirit" (v. 24), not bound to any place or people, and those who worship God share in the spirit. Jesus' presence in the world initiates this transformation of worship, because Jesus' presence changes the moment of anticipation

("the hour is coming") into the moment of in-breaking ("and is now here").

4:25. The woman's response indicates that she has heard the eschatological promise of Jesus' words, but not the fulfillment. Jesus has spoken of the coming hour; the woman responds by speaking of the coming One. The Samaritans, like the Jews, expected a Messiah. The Samaritans called their Messiah *Ta'heb* ("the one who returns").[109] The Samaritans thought of the *Ta'heb* as a teacher, which may explain the statement "he will proclaim [explain] all things to us" (v. 25). The critical difference between Jesus' words and the woman's response, however, is that she does not grasp the eschatological immediacy of what Jesus says. To Jesus' vision of the inbreaking of the eschatological age, the Samaritan woman responds with traditional eschatological expectations of the future Messiah (cf. 11:23-26, where Martha voices similar expectations).

4:26. Jesus' response to the Samaritan woman's traditional eschatological affirmations is simple and bold: "I am, the one who is speaking to you" (v. 26; author's trans.). The NRSV and the NIV translations play down the boldness of Jesus' remarks by supplying a predicate ("he") for the "I am" saying that is not present in the Greek. When the predicate is supplied, the meaning of Jesus' words becomes, "I am the Messiah you expect." The "I am" of v. 26, however, is not simply Jesus' messianic self-identification. When Jesus speaks the "I am" in v. 26, these words make explicit connections with the divine name of Exod 3:14. Jesus thus speaks an absolute "I am" here, with no predicate (6:20; 8:24, 28, 58; 13:19; 18:6), in order to identify himself as the one in whom God is known (1:18). The absolute "I am" confirms the words of the Prologue, "the Word was with God, and the Word was God" (1:1). Jesus thus fulfills the Samaritan woman's messianic expectations at the same time as he transcends them.

4:27-30. This passage provides a bridge between Jesus' conversations with the woman and with his disciples (vv. 31-38). The disciples' reaction to Jesus is similar to the woman's initial response to him (v. 9): shock that Jesus would violate social conventions. Unlike the woman,

109. See Wayne A. Meeks, *The Prophet-King: Moses Traditions and the Johannine Christology* (Leiden: E. J. Brill, 1967) 216-57.

however, the disciples keep their questions to themselves.

4:28. The woman makes no response to Jesus' bold self-revelation, perhaps because of the disciples' return. She departs from the well, leaving her water jar behind. Like much narrative detail in the Fourth Gospel (e.g., 1:37-39), the detail about the jar works on two levels simultaneously. On the level of the plot line, the abandoned water jar provides a link between the two conversations at the well. The woman's jar will stand before Jesus and his disciples as they speak. Yet the detail also has meaning on a more theological level. The abandoned jar suggests that the woman's concern of v. 15, the desire for miraculous water, has been superseded by the revelation of Jesus' identity.

4:29. In response to her conversation with Jesus, the woman goes into town and bears witness to what she has heard. Her witness is three-fold. First, she invites her fellow townspeople to "come and see." This invitation is crucial in the Fourth Gospel (cf. 1:37-39, 46). It is an invitation to participate in the life of faith, to experience Jesus for oneself. Second, the woman offers her own experience as the basis of her witness, which here may build on the Samaritan expectation of a teaching Messiah (cf. v. 25). Third, she broaches the question of whether Jesus might be the Messiah. The NRSV accurately captures the tentativeness of the woman's words. (The question begins with the negative particle [μήτι *mēti*] in the Greek, a construction that anticipates a negative or contradicting response.) She cannot quite believe that Jesus is the Messiah, since he challenges her conventional messianic expectations (vv. 23-25), but her lack of certitude does not stand in the way of her witness. The woman's behavior stands in marked contrast to many characters in the Fourth Gospel who will insist on their own certitudes (e.g., Nicodemus, 3:9; the crowds, 6:25-34; the Pharisees, 9:24-34) and hence close themselves to what Jesus offers. The woman's witness brings the townspeople to Jesus (v. 30). Their movement toward him provides the backdrop for Jesus' conversation with his disciples.

4:31-38. Jesus' conversation with his disciples follows a similar pattern to his conversation with the woman, albeit abbreviated. It opens with a dialogue that revolves around a misunderstanding about the meaning of "food" (βρῶσις *brōsis*, vv.

31-33; cf. the misunderstanding about "living water" in vv. 10-15). This dialogue is followed by a longer speech by Jesus (vv. 34-38; cf. vv. 21-24) in which he offers a new way of thinking to his conversation partners. Both of these final speeches by Jesus have an eschatological orientation.

4:31-34. The disciples ask Jesus to eat the food that they have brought from town (v. 31; cf. v. 8), but Jesus does not accede to their request (v. 32). The disciples are confused by Jesus' words and assume that he must be referring to food that someone else had brought him (v. 33; cf. vv. 11-12). In v. 34, Jesus makes clear that the food that sustains him is his vocation: to do the will of the one who sent him and complete God's work. God is frequently described in the Fourth Gospel as the one who sent Jesus (e.g., 5:23-24, 30) and Jesus' mission is often characterized as doing the will and the work of God (5:30, 36; 6:38; 10:37-38). Jesus' description of his food is thus a crystallization of Johannine christology; food is the metaphor for Jesus' divine commission and the enactment of the relationship between Jesus and God. Verse 34 underscores that any discussion of Jesus' identity is meaningless apart from a discussion of his vocation. The necessity of Jesus' Samaritan sojourn (4:4) and his conversation with the woman (4:7-26) can be understood as examples of Jesus' "food," of doing the will and work of God, which sustains him.

4:35-38. The focus of Jesus' words now shifts slightly. Jesus has just spoken of his role in completing the work of the one who sent him; he then turns to a traditional biblical image of completion—the harvest (e.g., Isa 27:12; Joel 3:13). Harvest imagery is also found in the synoptic tradition (e.g., Matt 13:30, 39; Mark 4:29). Verses 35-38 are structured around two agricultural proverbs (vv. 35*a*, 37).

In v. 35*a*, Jesus draws his disciples' attention to a common agricultural saying ("Do you not say . . ."). This proverb has not been attested outside the Fourth Gospel, but it reflects agricultural life in ancient Palestine; there is a waiting period between seedtime and harvest. In v. 35*b*, Jesus informs his disciples that the waiting is over. Twice in v. 35*b*, Jesus exhorts his disciples to look around them: "Open your eyes and look at the fields." Jesus asks his disciples to attend carefully to the situation in which they find themselves, to read the data of their own experience instead of trusting in conventional wisdom (cf. 9:28-33, where the blind man's trust in his own experience is superior to conventional teachings). In their immediate context, Jesus' words draw the disciples' attention to the Samaritans who are coming to him (v. 30). The "crop" of Samaritan believers is proof that the harvest is ready.

Jesus' words in v. 35b are a metaphorical equivalent of what he said earlier to the Samaritan woman: "The hour is coming, and is now here" (v. 23). The conventional understanding is that one must wait for the Messiah/harvest (vv. 25, 35a). In reality, they are here now. Jesus' presence and his doing the will and work of the one who sent him makes the harvest of eschatological fulfillment a present reality (cf. the discussion of vv. 21-24).

Verse 36 continues the imagery of the immediacy of the harvest. The reaper is already at work, receiving wages, gathering fruit. Sower and reaper now share in the joy of the harvest (cf. Psalm 126; Isa 9:3). Interpreters are tempted to read v. 36 allegorically—that is, to establish the identity of the sower and the reaper. While such allegorical interpretations are often suggestive (e.g., God is the sower, Jesus the reaper),[110] all of them find the real meaning of v. 36 outside the context of the Samaria narrative. Instead of reading v. 36 as allegory, it is more helpful to read it parabolically.[111] That is, v. 36 does not point to specific sower and reaper figures outside the text, but offers a narrative illustration of the realized eschatology of which Jesus speaks in v. 35b. John the Baptist told the parable of the bridegroom and his friend to illustrate joy (3:29); Jesus now tells the parable of the sower and the reaper to illustrate the arrival of the eschatological present.

The second agricultural proverb occurs in v. 37. As with v. 36, interpreters get into difficulty when they try to establish the identities of the sower and the reaper. It is in the very nature of proverbial language to be suggestive of many applications. The primary function of v. 37, then, is also parabolic, not allegorical. The eschatological immediacy of the harvest does not mean an end to the distinct roles of sower and reaper. Verse

38 illustrates this reality from the disciples' own experience. The disciples share in a harvest of which they are not the primary workers. Verse 38 seems to point to the disciples' future, when they will be "sent" (ἀποστέλλω apostellō) by Jesus to continue his work (e.g., 17:18; 20:21). The immediate context of v. 38 suggests the Samaritan woman as one example of the "others" from whose work the disciples benefit.

In vv. 35-38, Jesus draws on traditional OT imagery of eschatological fulfillment, the harvest, and relates that harvest to the Samaritan mission. In 12:20-24, the beginning of the Gentile mission is also imbued with eschatological significance and illustrated with agricultural imagery. In John, unlike the Synoptics, the mission to outsiders does not wait until after Jesus' death. It is part of Jesus' own ministry. The Samaritan mission thus serves as a concrete example of Johannine realized eschatology. John 4 is the only NT evidence of a Samaritan mission during Jesus' ministry, although Acts corroborates the Samaritan mission of the early church (Acts 8:4-24).

4:39-42. John brings the Samaria narrative to a close by focusing on the success of the Samaritan mission. Verse 39 notes the faith in Jesus of many Samaritans and explicitly attributes the people's faith to the woman's "testimony" (μαρτυρία martyria). She, like John the Baptist, is a witness who brings people to faith in Jesus. Also like John the Baptist (3:30), the woman's witness diminishes in importance when the Samaritans have their own experience of Jesus (vv. 40-42). The Samaritans invite Jesus to stay with them, and he stays for two days (v. 40). The use of the verb for "stay" (μένω menō) recalls 1:38 and Jesus' meeting with his first disciples. To stay with Jesus is to enter into relationship with him (cf. 15:4, 7). Many more persons come to faith in Jesus as a result of this stay (v. 41), and in v. 42 those who believe acknowledge that their own encounter with Jesus supplants the woman's word. This is the model of witness and faith in the Fourth Gospel: The witness that leads to Jesus is replaced by one's own experience of Jesus.

The Samaritans' acclamation of Jesus as the savior of the world (v. 42) is the most sweeping christological confession yet encountered in the Gospel. Salvation may be from the Jews (v. 22b), but it is not limited to the Jews. Ethnic

---

110. So Rudolf Schnackenburg, *The Gospel According to St. John,* 3 vols. (New York: Seabury, 1982) 1:447.

111. Barrett, *The Gospel According to St. John,* 242.

and religious distinctions that figured prominently in this text (vv. 9, 20-22) are dissolved
in this recognition of the universality of salvation available in Jesus (cf. 3:17). The Samaritans' confession evidences the truth of Jesus'
words in vv. 21-24; the hour has indeed come
when neither this mountain nor Jerusalem will
define the worship of God.[112]

112. See Gail R. O'Day, *Revelation in the Fourth Gospel: Narrative
Made and Theological Claim* (Philadelphia: Fortress, 1986), for a more
detailed discussion of John 4:4-42.

REFLECTIONS

John 4:4-42 presents the interpreter with a text that from beginning to end transforms
conventional expectations and challenges the status quo. The setting of this narrative in Samaria
is a scandal that may have lost its force for modern readers, but would have been noted by
first-century readers. Jesus openly challenges and breaks open two boundaries in this text: the
boundary between "chosen people" and "rejected people," between male and female.

Verses 4-42 can be read helpfully alongside the parable of the good Samaritan (Luke 10:29-37).
In the Lukan text, the scandal is that the despised Samaritan is the neighbor, the agent of mercy
(Luke 10:37a). The Samaritan traveler touches the injured man's wounds as he nurses him (Luke
10:34), an obvious violation of the restriction against contact between Jews and Samaritans (John
4:9c). In Luke, Jesus holds up the Samaritan traveler as an example (10:37b), suggesting to his
listeners that acts of mercy should be governed by need and compassion (10:33), not by societal
conventions and fears. This passage conveys a similar challenge but in a more radical form, because
it is not a character in a parable who upsets social conventions but Jesus himself. Jesus initiates
contact with a Samaritan, asking her to attend to his need (v. 7). He then offers the Samaritan
woman the gift of God (v. 10) and reveals his identity to her (v. 26). He treats the Samaritan
woman—and later the Samaritan villagers—as a full human being, a worthy recipient of the grace
of God, not as the despised enemy from whom to fear contamination.

The preoccupation with protecting boundaries between the chosen and the despised peoples
is not limited to the Samaritan/Jewish conflict of the first century. Throughout human history,
people and nations have defined themselves over against other groups. The history of race
relations in the United States, the notion of racial purity that was at the ideological heart of
Hitler's Germany, the ethnic wars that wax and wane across the Middle East, Africa, Asia,
and Europe all have their roots in the same fears that divided Jews from Samaritans: the fear
of contamination (4:9c), the fear of sharing one's gift and privileged call (4:20) with others.

John 4:4-42 summons the church to stop shaping its life according to societal definitions of
who is acceptable and to show the same openness to those who are different that Jesus did
when he traveled in Samaria. The church is asked to cross boundaries as Jesus does instead
of constructing them. It does no good to cling to notions of a privileged people or a privileged
place, because Jesus has already ushered in a time when "you will worship the Father neither
on this mountain nor in Jerusalem" (4:21).

John 4:4-42 also challenges boundaries constructed on the basis of gender. The disciples'
astonishment in v. 27 does not derive from ethnic considerations but because Jesus speaks
with a *woman*. Jesus will not be governed by those fears and prejudices, either, and thus he
treats the woman as fully human.

The Commentary on John 4:4-42 highlights ways in which the woman's role in this text
has been misinterpreted because of imported assumptions about women's sexuality, intellect,
and interests. The interpreter must be very careful to return to the text and discover what
the Fourth Evangelist says about the woman, rather than pass on what one has always heard
about this text. The Samaritan woman is never judged as a sinner. On the contrary, she is
portrayed as a model of growing faith. As vv. 4-42 unfold, the reader sees the woman's faith

grow as she comes to entertain the possibility that Jesus might be the Messiah (4:29). Of even greater significance, however, the woman is portrayed as a witness (4:39). She invited her fellow townspeople to come and see Jesus.

The Samaritan woman's successful evangelization of her town belies the myth of the privileged position of men as witnesses and disciples. Because of her witness, the number of persons who believe in Jesus grows. Jesus treats her as a serious conversation partner, the first person in the Gospel to whom he makes a bold statement of self-revelation (v. 26). The Samaritan woman's story summons churches to reexamine the boundaries they set around women's witness and work.

Jesus' actions in John 4:4-42, as he embraces both Samaritans and women, are one example of the way this text challenges the status quo. Jesus' actions model alternatives for the faith community and show how human interrelationships are transformed in the eschatological present. Jesus' words in this passage also challenge the status quo. They do not attack it directly, but, like his actions, suggest what is possible in the new reality ushered in by his presence.

Jesus' words overflow with metaphor: living water, the hour, food, harvest. Each of these metaphors attempts to open reality in fresh ways for his conversation partners. Jesus wants to open the eyes of the Samaritan woman and his disciples so that they can see what is being offered to them in the present instead of continuing to view everything through the lens of old realities. Jesus wants the Samaritan woman to see who is speaking with her at *this* moment and the gifts that he offers (4:10). He wants her to see that the present moment is the time of eschatological fulfillment (4:23-24). Jesus wants his disciples to see that the harvest is ready *now,* contrary to popular understandings (4:35). In both conversations (4:7-26, 31-38), Jesus takes familiar images and fills them with new meaning in order to open up for his listeners the possibilities of a life defined by God's gifts. The metaphors of these verses keep the terms of the conversations always fresh, always suggestive, always open to new meanings in changing circumstances.

Everything is to be newly defined by the arrival of the hour, by the impingement of the eschatological future on the present. God's salvation is available now, to all who will receive it (cf. 2 Cor 6:2). Salvation will be offered on God's own terms, however, not necessarily in the form that those who wait on it have determined in advance. The Samaritans' acclamation of Jesus as savior of the world reminds the reader of that. The savior in whom they put their faith does not conform to their prior expectations. The reality of God's presence in Jesus redefines their previous categories.

The woman, the disciples, and the Samaritan villagers all received more from Jesus than their conventions and assumptions had led them to expect. One could say that once again Jesus transformed ordinary water into wine. An incredulous Samaritan woman becomes a witness to the gospel, Jesus' questioning disciples become co-workers in the harvest, the despised Samaritans spend two days with the "savior of the world." John 4:4-42 is a text of promise, of expectations overturned and surpassed. This text suggests that the life of faith and discipleship will be refreshed and reanimated by attending to Jesus' vision of transformed reality and, most important, to Jesus himself. Jesus' metaphors of living water and worship in spirit and truth invite the church to a new relationship to its God and to one another through his incarnate presence.

A final word needs to be said about the ways in which John 4:4-42 draws the reader into its story. The give and take of the dialogues, the play of irony and misunderstanding, and the rich metaphors invite the reader to take an active role in reading this text. The text does not position the reader as observer, nor does it simply present propositions to which the reader is to give assent. Rather, the narrative techniques of John 4:4-42 draw the reader into participation in the text. The invitation to discover Jesus' identity that Jesus extends to the woman (4:10) is extended to the reader also. The reader, like the Samaritan woman, experiences the shock of Jesus' insight into the woman's history (4:17-18). The reader hears the "I am" of v. 26 as spoken directly to him or her. In effect, by the end of the text, the reader has "stayed" with Jesus just as the Samaritan villagers do.

The active role John 4:4-42 gives the reader of this text should not be flattened in the appropriation of this text. That is, in interpreting this text, one needs to be careful not to rush too quickly to the resolution of the story—for example, by focusing too quickly on Jesus' self-revelation in v. 26 or the Samaritans' confession in v. 42. If the rich textures of the text are reduced to bare kernels, then the invitation it offers will be diminished.

The closing words of the Samaritan villagers hold the key to understanding the narrative techniques of this text. The Samaritans no longer need the secondary witness of the woman's word because "we have heard for ourselves" (v. 42). Effective witness does not replace the immediate experience of Jesus in the Fourth Gospel; it leads to that experience. John 4:4-42 is narrated so that the readers, too, can sense that they have heard Jesus for themselves. As a result of reading this text, one may come to recognize oneself as a "Samaritan"—one to whom the good news has come in unexpected places at unexpected times.

JOHN 4:43-54, THE HEALING OF THE ROYAL OFFICIAL'S SON

NIV

⁴³After the two days he left for Galilee. ⁴⁴(Now Jesus himself had pointed out that a prophet has no honor in his own country.) ⁴⁵When he arrived in Galilee, the Galileans welcomed him. They had seen all that he had done in Jerusalem at the Passover Feast, for they also had been there.

⁴⁶Once more he visited Cana in Galilee, where he had turned the water into wine. And there was a certain royal official whose son lay sick at Capernaum. ⁴⁷When this man heard that Jesus had arrived in Galilee from Judea, he went to him and begged him to come and heal his son, who was close to death.

⁴⁸"Unless you people see miraculous signs and wonders," Jesus told him, "you will never believe."

⁴⁹The royal official said, "Sir, come down before my child dies."

⁵⁰Jesus replied, "You may go. Your son will live."

The man took Jesus at his word and departed. ⁵¹While he was still on the way, his servants met him with the news that his boy was living. ⁵²When he inquired as to the time when his son got better, they said to him, "The fever left him yesterday at the seventh hour."

⁵³Then the father realized that this was the

NRSV

43When the two days were over, he went from that place to Galilee ⁴⁴(for Jesus himself had testified that a prophet has no honor in the prophet's own country). ⁴⁵When he came to Galilee, the Galileans welcomed him, since they had seen all that he had done in Jerusalem at the festival; for they too had gone to the festival.

46Then he came again to Cana in Galilee where he had changed the water into wine. Now there was a royal official whose son lay ill in Capernaum. ⁴⁷When he heard that Jesus had come from Judea to Galilee, he went and begged him to come down and heal his son, for he was at the point of death. ⁴⁸Then Jesus said to him, "Unless youᵃ see signs and wonders you will not believe." ⁴⁹The official said to him, "Sir, come down before my little boy dies." ⁵⁰Jesus said to him, "Go; your son will live." The man believed the word that Jesus spoke to him and started on his way. ⁵¹As he was going down, his slaves met him and told him that his child was alive. ⁵²So he asked them the hour when he began to recover, and they said to him, "Yesterday at one in the afternoon the fever left him." ⁵³The father realized that this was the hour when Jesus had said to him, "Your son will live." So he himself

ᵃ Both instances of the Greek word for *you* in this verse are plural

NIV	NRSV
exact time at which Jesus had said to him, "Your son will live." So he and all his household believed. ⁵⁴This was the second miraculous sign that Jesus performed, having come from Judea to Galilee.	believed, along with his whole household. ⁵⁴Now this was the second sign that Jesus did after coming from Judea to Galilee.

COMMENTARY

4:43-45. These verses provide an interlude between the Samaria narrative and the story of the royal official (vv. 46-54). Verse 43 serves two functions: It recalls Jesus' stay in Samaria ("after two days"; cf. v. 40), and it returns the focus to Galilee (cf. vv. 1-3). Verse 44 contains a proverb that seems to have been found in several strands of oral tradition. Mark 6:4 and Matt 13:57 preserve one form of the proverb, while Luke 4:24 and John 4:44 each preserves its own variants of the saying. (The proverb is also found in Oxyrhynchus Papyrus 1 and the *Gospel of Thomas* 31). The meaning of the proverb is the same in all of the versions: A prophet is without honor among his own.

But what is Jesus' "own country" (v. 44)? Ancient and modern interpreters debate whether it should be understood as Galilee or Judea.[113] The Fourth Gospel names Galilee as Jesus' native land (7:41, 52), but the conjunction "for" with which v. 44 begins suggests that Jesus' journey *to* Galilee demonstrates the truth of the proverb, and Jesus is welcomed in Galilee (vv. 45-54; see also 1:46-49; 2:1-11). Moreover, 4:1 implies that Jesus travels to Galilee to flee the Judean Pharisees. The context of v. 44 thus supports reading Judea as Jesus' "own country" here.

A careful reading of the proverb provides additional support. The Johannine version of the proverb is the only one of the four Gospel versions to modify "country" (πατρίς *patris*) with the adjective "one's own" (ἴδιος *idios*). The use of this

adjective recalls 1:11, "He came to what was his own [τὰ ἴδια *ta idia*], and his own people [οἱ ἴδιοι *hoi idioi*] did not accept him." John 1:11 and 4:44 say the same thing.[114] Jesus' "own country" does not refer to his *native* land, but to the place that is his own in God's plan of salvation: Judea and Jerusalem (cf. 4:22, "salvation is from the Jews"). Judea is Jesus' "own," but "his own people" reject him. He thus goes to others who do receive him (1:12): Samaritans (4:4-42) and Galileans (4:45-54). The importance of Jesus' movement away from Judea to Galilee is underscored by the repeated geographical references in the story of the royal official's son (4:46-47, 54). The Galileans' welcome in v. 45 is tied to Jesus' visit to Jerusalem (2:13-25) in order to underscore the contrast with the response of the Jerusalem Jews (2:23-25).

4:46-54. This passage follows the standard form of a miracle story. After an introductory verse (v. 46), the story falls into two parts: (1) vv. 47-50, the heart of the story, in which Jesus performs the miracle; and (2) vv. 51-53, the attestation of the miracle. John 4:46-54 is a story of healing at a distance. There are two stories of healing at a distance in the Synoptics as well: the centurion and his son (Matt 8:5-13; Luke 7:2-10) and the Syrophoenician (Canaanite) woman and her daughter (Matt 15:21-28; Mark 7:24-30). The Johannine story shares elements with both of these stories (cf. v. 47; Mark 7:26). The similarities suggest that the Johannine story is neither the creation of the Evangelist nor dependent on the Synoptic stories, but rather preserves a similar, but independent, piece of the Jesus tradition.[115]

---

113. Among ancient interpreters, Chrysostom maintained that Jesus' "own country" was Galilee, while Origen argued it was to be understood as Judea. For modern interpreters who argue for Galilee, see Raymond E. Brown, *The Gospel According to John (I–XII)*, AB 29 (Garden City, N.Y.: Doubleday, 1966) 187; Rudolf Bultmann, *The Gospel of John: A Commentary,* trans. G. R. Beasley-Murray, R. W. N. Hoare, and J. K. Riches (Philadelphia: Westminster, 1971) 204; for those who argue for Judea, see E. C. Hoskyns, *The Fourth Gospel* (London: Faber & Faber, 1947) 260-61; and C. K. Barrett, *The Gospel According to St. John,* 2nd ed. (Philadelphia: Westminster, 1978) 246.

114. Wayne A. Meeks, "Galilee and Judea in the Fourth Gospel," *JBL* 85 (1966) 164-65.

115. C. H. Dodd, *Historical Tradition in the Fourth Gospel* (Cambridge: Cambridge University Press, 1963) 188-95.

4:46. Verse 46a establishes the setting (Cana) and links the story to Jesus' earlier miracle in Cana. Verse 46b introduces a character unique to this story (a royal official) and describes the situation of need. The juxtaposition of the reference to the Cana miracle and the new situation of need leads the reader to anticipate another miracle. Scholars debate whether the royal official was a Gentile or a Jew.[116] His occupation and place of residence (Capernaum, a border town) allow for the possibility that he was a Gentile.

4:47. The miracle story proper begins in v. 47. The man's request for Jesus to "come down" (καταβαίνω katabainō) reflects the topography of the journey from Cana to Capernaum (see also vv. 49, 51). The Gospel narrative does not document any healing by Jesus prior to this story, but it has suggested that Jesus is the giver of life (e.g., vv. 13-14). The man's request thus provides the first occasion in the Fourth Gospel for Jesus to save life. In this way, vv. 46-54 anticipate the raising of Lazarus in chap. 11. In that story, Jesus will give life to someone not simply at the point of death but already dead.

4:48. Jesus' response in v. 48 is not directed exclusively to the royal official, because the "you" is a second-person plural. The combination "signs and wonders" (σημεῖα καὶ τέρατα sēmeia kai terata) is unique to John, although it is a traditional pairing found in the OT (e.g., Exod 7:3). It also occurs regularly in Acts (e.g., Acts 2:43; 5:12; 7:36). Scholars frequently assert that Jesus' words are a rebuke to those who base their faith on signs,[117] but Jesus' words have a more subtle purpose than that. If his words are simply a rebuke, then one would expect Jesus to refuse the man's request (cf. Matt 15:26; Mark 7:27), but he does not. Verse 48 may thus be helpfully read as astute observation on Jesus' part (cf. 1:47-49; 2:23-25; 4:16-19) and should be interpreted in the same vein as 2:3-4 in the first Cana miracle. Jesus will act, but his actions will not meet the expectations of "signs and wonders." His actions will be governed by his will (v. 34), not by human expectations and demand (see also 7:1-10).

4:49-50a. The royal official is not intimidated

by Jesus' response. Like Jesus' mother at Cana (2:5; cf. Mark 7:28), he holds firm (v. 49). He is motivated by compassion for his son and the urgency of this situation. Jesus' response to the man's renewed request is terse and to the point, "Go; your son will live" (v. 50a). The verb "live" (ζάω zaō) has a double meaning in this context; it is used to mean "recover from illness," and it also carries with it associations of Jesus' gift of life. Jesus does not accompany the royal official to see his son; the boy's recovery derives only from Jesus' word and promise.

4:50b-53. The man's belief in Jesus' word is demonstrated in the man's obedience. Jesus tells him to go (v. 50a), and he does. His departure for Capernaum begins the second part of the story, the attestation of the miracle. The servants provide evidence of the healing (vv. 51-52). Their words that "his child was alive" repeat Jesus' words of v. 50 and hence prove the power of Jesus' word to the father and the reader; what Jesus promised has, indeed, taken place. Jesus has given life. In v. 53a, the refrain "the son/child lives" is repeated for the third time in the story (see also vv. 50-51). The repetition of this phrase leaves no doubt that the focus of this story is on Jesus' promise and gift of life.

The man's realization that his son's healing did indeed result from Jesus' word (v. 53a) leads him and his whole household to faith (v. 53b). The phrase "he and his household" is unusual for John, but is reminiscent of the descriptions of Gentile conversions in Acts (Acts 10:2; 11:14; 18:8). The use of the expression here is probably influenced by the experience of the Christian community at the time of the Evangelist. The object of faith is not supplied in v. 53b, but when v. 53b is read in the light of v. 50, it becomes clear that now the man believes in Jesus, not only in Jesus' word.

4:54. The second Cana "sign" (v. 54), like the first one, results in the faith of those who witnessed it (v. 53; cf. 2:11; see the Introduction for a discussion of the "Signs Source"). Yet the story of the second miracle also contains a caution about faith based on "signs and wonders" (v. 48). How are these two perspectives to be reconciled? John 2:11 holds the interpretive key. Jesus' disciples saw him turn water into wine at Cana, but it was not the miracle in and of itself that led to their faith. Rather, they saw Jesus' glory in that

---

116. Gentile: Barrett, *The Gospel According to St. John*, 245; Jew: Brown, *The Gospel According to John (I–XII)*, 192.
117. E.g., Brown, *The Gospel According to John (I–XII)*, 195.

sign, and it was in Jesus, not the miracle, that they believed. In a similar way, the royal official moves beyond a preliminary faith in the miraculous power of Jesus' word (v. 50) to complete faith (v. 53). The two Cana signs are alike in that those who witness them are able to see the revelation of Jesus' identity in and through the miracle. The first Cana sign revealed Jesus' glory; the second reveals his ability to give life.

REFLECTIONS

The outcome of John 4:46-54 suggests that attention to the scandalous call of this text can have surprising results. The royal official approached Jesus with only one thing on his mind; his son was at the point of death, and Jesus might be the one to heal him. His reasons for seeking Jesus were desperation and basic need. Yet he ended up receiving much more than he could have hoped for and, indeed, much more than he knew he needed: the gift of his son's life *and* the gift of faith in Jesus. The royal official's faith was evoked by the care with which his needs were met, by the evidence of God's life-giving love in Jesus' act of physical healing.

This story raises the question of the relationship between signs and faith for the interpreter. This relationship rests at the theological heart of the Fourth Gospel. For the Fourth Evangelist, the fullness of a miraculous act is both in and beyond the miracle itself. That is, the person who interprets a miracle solely as a miraculous act will remain transfixed by and limited to the act itself—water turned into wine, a deathly ill boy revived, a miraculous feeding with bread (John 6). Jesus could be revered, perhaps even believed in on account of that act, but only as a miracle worker. What one would proclaim about Jesus from that perspective is, "Look what Jesus can *do.*" When a miraculous act is fully understood as a sign, however, what one would proclaim about Jesus is, "Look at *who Jesus is.*" He is the giver of abundant gifts (John 2:1-11); the giver of life (John 4:46-54). As the giver of abundance and life (cf. 10:10), Jesus points to (is a sign of) who God is, and this is the ground for faith.

It is thus the sight of God's presence in Jesus' acts that transforms them from miracles to signs. As such, the Johannine understanding of signs belongs to the Gospel's understanding of the incarnation. Signs hold together the physical and the spiritual, the immanent and the transcendent in the same way the incarnate Word does. In the flesh and blood of the incarnation, the fullness of God is available to humanity, but only if one is able to see the visible as pointing to the invisible (1:18). In the healing of a sick boy, the fullness of God is also available. The physical healing provides a glimpse of the character of God in Jesus.

Signs provide the opening to faith, then, when one recognizes that through them God is present and available in the tangible and corporeal realm of human life. It is not the miracle per se, but the glimpse of the presence of God at work with and in human experience that can lead to faith. To see God in Jesus' act of healing is to recognize the truth of the confession of 1:14, "The Word became flesh and lived *among us.*"

JOHN 5:1-47, A SABBATH HEALING MIRACLE AND DISCOURSE

OVERVIEW

John 5:1-47 consists of two basic parts: (1) vv. 1-18, a healing story (vv. 1-9a) and its aftermath (vv. 9b-18); and (2) vv. 19-47, a discourse by Jesus. This text thus follows a Johannine narrative pattern noted before (3:1-21), in which an event is followed by a discourse that draws out the theological implications of that event. By constructing the Gospel in this way, the Fourth Evangelist provides the reader with the theological categories through which to interpret the story of Jesus. In the case of John 5, those theological categories involve the introduction of the controversy between Jesus and the Jewish authorities.

John 5:1-18, The Miracle and Its Aftermath

NIV

5 Some time later, Jesus went up to Jerusalem for a feast of the Jews. ²Now there is in Jerusalem near the Sheep Gate a pool, which in Aramaic is called Bethesda*a* and which is surrounded by five covered colonnades. ³Here a great number of disabled people used to lie—the blind, the lame, the paralyzed.*b* ⁵One who was there had been an invalid for thirty-eight years. ⁶When Jesus saw him lying there and learned that he had been in this condition for a long time, he asked him, "Do you want to get well?"

⁷"Sir," the invalid replied, "I have no one to help me into the pool when the water is stirred. While I am trying to get in, someone else goes down ahead of me."

⁸Then Jesus said to him, "Get up! Pick up your mat and walk." ⁹At once the man was cured; he picked up his mat and walked.

The day on which this took place was a Sabbath, ¹⁰and so the Jews said to the man who had been healed, "It is the Sabbath; the law forbids you to carry your mat."

¹¹But he replied, "The man who made me well said to me, 'Pick up your mat and walk.'"

¹²So they asked him, "Who is this fellow who told you to pick it up and walk?"

¹³The man who was healed had no idea who it was, for Jesus had slipped away into the crowd that was there.

¹⁴Later Jesus found him at the temple and said to him, "See, you are well again. Stop sinning or something worse may happen to you." ¹⁵The man went away and told the Jews that it was Jesus who had made him well.

a2 Some manuscripts Bethzatha; other manuscripts Bethsaida
b3 Some less important manuscripts paralyzed—and they waited for the moving of the waters. 4From time to time an angel of the Lord would come down and stir up the waters. The first one into the pool after each such disturbance would be cured of whatever disease he had.

NRSV

5 After this there was a festival of the Jews, and Jesus went up to Jerusalem.

2Now in Jerusalem by the Sheep Gate there is a pool, called in Hebrew*a* Beth-zatha,*b* which has five porticoes. ³In these lay many invalids—blind, lame, and paralyzed.*c* ⁵One man was there who had been ill for thirty-eight years. ⁶When Jesus saw him lying there and knew that he had been there a long time, he said to him, "Do you want to be made well?" ⁷The sick man answered him, "Sir, I have no one to put me into the pool when the water is stirred up; and while I am making my way, someone else steps down ahead of me." ⁸Jesus said to him, "Stand up, take your mat and walk." ⁹At once the man was made well, and he took up his mat and began to walk.

Now that day was a sabbath. ¹⁰So the Jews said to the man who had been cured, "It is the sabbath; it is not lawful for you to carry your mat." ¹¹But he answered them, "The man who made me well said to me, 'Take up your mat and walk.'" ¹²They asked him, "Who is the man who said to you, 'Take it up and walk'?" ¹³Now the man who had been healed did not know who it was, for Jesus had disappeared in*d* the crowd that was there. ¹⁴Later Jesus found him in the temple and said to him, "See, you have been made well! Do not sin any more, so that nothing worse happens to you." ¹⁵The man went away and told the Jews that it was Jesus who had made him well. ¹⁶Therefore the Jews started persecuting Jesus, because he was doing such things on the sabbath. ¹⁷But Jesus answered them, "My Father is still working, and I also am working." ¹⁸For this

a That is, Aramaic   b Other ancient authorities read Bethesda, others Bethsaida   c Other ancient authorities add, wholly or in part, waiting for the stirring of the water; 4for an angel of the Lord went down at certain seasons into the pool, and stirred up the water; whoever stepped in first after the stirring of the water was made well from whatever disease that person had.   d Or had left because of

NIV	NRSV
¹⁶So, because Jesus was doing these things on the Sabbath, the Jews persecuted him. ¹⁷Jesus said to them, "My Father is always at his work to this very day, and I, too, am working." ¹⁸For this reason the Jews tried all the harder to kill him; not only was he breaking the Sabbath, but he was even calling God his own Father, making himself equal with God.	reason the Jews were seeking all the more to kill him, because he was not only breaking the sabbath, but was also calling God his own Father, thereby making himself equal to God.

COMMENTARY

The healing story of John 5:1-18 follows the conventions of the miracle story form—vv. 1-5 prepare for the miracle; vv. 6-9a narrate the miracle. External attestation of the miracle is provided indirectly by the controversy of vv. 9b-18, because it is the "Jews' " encounter with the healed man who is carrying his bed around on the sabbath that incites them against Jesus.

5:1-5. Verse 1 provides the temporal and geographical location for the story: in Jerusalem during one of the Jewish festivals. The text gives no clues as to which of the three pilgrimage festivals (Passover, Pentecost, or Tabernacles) it might be (see Fig. 9, "Jewish Religious Festivals in John," 542). Verses 2-3a provide a detailed description of the setting in Jerusalem (cf. 4:4-5). These two verses have suffered in transmission of the text and are rife with textual variants. The difference in the place names for the pool in the NRSV (Bethzatha) and NIV (Bethsaida) is a result of variants in the textual tradition. The most significant textual variant occurs between vv. 3a and 5. Some later manuscripts added the description of the angel stirring the waters (vv. 3b-4), but the oldest and most reliable witnesses do not contain these verses. As a result, vv. 3b-4 are printed only in the textual notes in both the NRSV and the NIV. Verses 3b-4 were probably added at a later date in order to explain v. 7 ("when the water is stirred") and reflected popular beliefs that spirits were responsible for the otherwise inexplicable bubbling of some pools of water. When the textual variants of vv. 2-3(4) are sorted through, what emerges is a picture of a pool in Jerusalem visited by a wide variety of invalids (v. 3a).[118]

Verse 5 introduces the central character of the healing story (other than Jesus): a man who had been sick for thirty-eight years. The verse does not specify the man's illness. The figure "thirty-eight years" is mentioned to indicate the seeming permanence of the man's affliction (cf. Mark 5:35; Luke 13:11).

5:6-9a. The healing miracle is initiated by Jesus (v. 6; cf. 9:6-7). His insight into the man's condition resembles his insight into Nathanael (1:47-48), the crowd in Jerusalem (2:23-25), and the Samaritan woman (4:16-18). (The NIV translation, "learned that," masks the text's emphasis on Jesus' insight by wrongly suggesting that he was informed of the man's condition.) Jesus asks the man if he wants to be "made well" (ὑγιὴς γενέσθαι; *hygiēs genesthai?*). This expression will function as a refrain throughout the rest of the story (vv. 9, 11, 14-15; cf. the use of "your son will live," 4:50-51, 53).

The man responds to Jesus' question the same way Nicodemus responded to Jesus' offer to be "born *anōthen*" ("from above"/"again"; 3:3-4)—with protests that Jesus' suggestion is impossible. The man interprets Jesus' question through his own presuppositions about how healing can be accomplished and, therefore, can only bemoan his predicament (v. 7). Jesus responds to the man's complaint with three imperatives: rise, take up your bed, walk (v. 8), the same three imperatives in Mark 2:9. Although there are similarities between

118. Archaeologists have excavated a pool in Jerusalem with five porticoes at St. Anne's Church that fits John's description (5:2). See Joachim Jeremias, *The Rediscovery of Bethesda* (Louisville: Southern Baptist Seminary, 1966).

this Johannine story and the story in Mark (cf. Mark 2:9-10; John 5:14), there are also significant differences. For example, the miracle in Mark 2 is enacted in response to the faith of the friends (2:5), whereas in John 5 there is no demonstration of faith. As with John 4:46-54, the Fourth Evangelist probably draws on a similar Jesus tradition, but his story is independent of Mark.

Verse 9a demonstrates the effectiveness of Jesus' healing words. The man was "made well" (cf. v. 6) and does exactly what Jesus commanded him. The miracle story proper thus ends on a note of triumph.

5:9b-18. Here John focuses on the aftermath of the miracle. Verse 9b introduces an element of which the reader had previously been unaware: The healing took place on the sabbath. This notation shifts the focus of the story from a straight miracle story to a conflict story. The concern with sabbath violation reflects an issue current in Jesus' time and in John's time. First-century Judaism defined community identity around three practices: circumcision, food laws, and sabbath observance. In Jesus' time, a challenge to the sabbath meant a challenge to the definition of covenant membership. This issue of community identity became even more sharply joined in the last quarter of the first century, because with the destruction of the Jerusalem Temple (70 CE) and the rise of early Christianity, Jews and Christians found themselves increasingly in conflict over religious systems and structures (see Reflections below).[119]

A shift in characters also occurs at this juncture. Verse 10 introduces "the Jews" into the story, and Jesus disappears until v. 14. The use of the phrase "the Jews" (οἱ Ἰουδαῖοι *hoi Ioudaioi*) in this passage is a banner example of the distinctive Johannine use of this term. It cannot refer to the Jewish people in general, since the man Jesus heals is certainly a Jew himself. Therefore, it refers to the Jewish authorities who oppose Jesus (see Reflections below).

The "Jews" accuse the man who has been healed of violating sabbath law; carrying a pallet constituted work.[120] It is commonly assumed that the man's response in v. 11 is intended to shift the blame for sabbath violation from himself to Jesus,[121] but nothing in the man's words necessitates that judgment. He simply gives a straightforward account of what happened to him and how he came to be carrying his bed (cf. 9:11, 15). Moreover, his words present the Jews (and the reader) with the two competing foci of this story: that he was "made well" and that healing is linked to a sabbath violation.

The Jews focus on only one of the two, the sabbath violation. They are concerned only to identify the person who instructed the man to pick up his bed and walk (v. 12). The Fourth Evangelist reminds the reader of both dimensions of the story, however, by repeating the epithet "the man who had been healed" (v. 13). The man can give no answer to the Jews' question, because he knows only that he was healed, not who was responsible. The question of Jesus' identity (v. 12), one of the key questions of the Gospel (e.g., 6:42; 7:28; 8:25), hangs unanswered.

Jesus, reentering the story in v. 14, takes the initiative and finds the man in the Temple (cf. 9:35). Jesus' words to the man are in two parts. First, Jesus confirms the reality of the healing, "you have been made well" (v. 14a). Second, Jesus speaks to the man about sin. In John, the verb "to sin" (ἁμαρτάνω *hamartano*) occurs elsewhere only in 9:2-3.[122] In Mark 2:5-10, Jesus links his healing of the paralytic man with the forgiveness of sins, yet in John 5:1-9a the healing does not seem to involve forgiveness of sins; so it seems wrong to read Jesus' words in v. 14 as embracing the traditional linkage of sin and illness (e.g., Job 5:17-18; Sir 38:15; 1 Cor 11:29-30; cf. John 9:2-3, where Jesus explicitly rejects that linkage). That is, v. 14 does not address the man's pre-healing condition. Jesus does not speak of what was required for healing but of the response to the healing already received; he urges that the man's healing should be more than physical. The man needs to be spiritually healthy also, as the expression "be made well" suggests. In chap. 9, physical blindness and sight will be played off against spiritual blindness and sight (9:39-41), and that dynamic is prefigured here.

119. See Jerome H. Neyrey, *An Ideology of Revolt: John's Christology in Social-Science Perspective* (Philadelphia: Fortress, 1988), 11; and Herold Weiss, "The Sabbath in the Fourth Gospel," *JBL* 110 (1991) 311-21.

120. See *m. Šabb.* 7.2: "The main classes of work are forty save one: . . . taking out aught from one domain into another."

121. E.g., Barrett, *The Gospel According to St. John,* 255; R. Alan Culpepper, *Anatomy of the Fourth Gospel: A Study in Literary Design* (Philadelphia: Fortress, 1983) 138.

122. The verb *hamartano* is also used at 8:11 in the non-Johannine story of 7:53–8:11.

Verse 15 is commonly read as an indication of the healed man's ingratitude; he responds to Jesus' healing by "turning him in" to the Jews.[123] Such a reading, however, judges the man's words by their consequences, not by the words themselves. A careful study of v. 15 suggests a different interpretation of the man's actions.[124] The verb used to describe the man's speech is "to announce" (ἀναγγέλλω *anangellō*). (The NIV and the NRSV both flatten this verb to the more general verb "to tell.") This verb occurs only four other times in the Fourth Gospel, and all four uses are positive. It is used once of the Messiah (4:25) and three times to describe the activity of the Paraclete (16:13-15). It is possible, then, to read the man's words as a positive announcement to the Jews. The Jews wanted to know who told the man to carry his bed around—that is, who encouraged him to violate sabbath law—but that is not what the man announces to them. Rather, he tells the "Jews" that "it was Jesus who had made him well." The man does not turn Jesus in for violating the sabbath law, but announces him as the man who has made him well.

The Jews remain uninterested in the healing, however. Although life-saving healing would be permissible on the sabbath, the healing of a disease that had lasted thirty-eight years could surely wait until sundown. Their sole concern remains the violation of sabbath law (v. 16). The man's announcement gives the Jews the evidence they need ("because of this") to persecute Jesus, but the man is not responsible for that outcome. At the very worst, the man is an unwitting pawn, unable to assess what the real issues are for the Jews (this is consistent with his attitude toward his healing in v. 7). Yet the man's actions in v. 15 may be an attempt to enact Jesus' words of v. 14—to live a whole life.

In vv. 10-16, then, two conversations have been taking place simultaneously. The Jews have been doggedly pursuing a conversation about sabbath violation (vv. 10, 12, 16), while the healed man and Jesus have been discussing healing and being made well (vv. 11, 14-15). Jesus' words in v. 17 address both conversations. He addresses the issue of work, the pivot of the Jews' concern about sabbath violation, but he does so to speak about his relationship with God, not to teach about the sabbath. If God continues to work on the sabbath, giving and sustaining life, so does Jesus. Jesus' response to the sabbath controversy is thus quite different in John than in the Synoptics. It provides an occasion for Jesus' self-revelation, not for teaching about the law (cf. Mark 2:27-28).

Jesus' words in v. 17 escalate the Jews' opposition from persecution to a decision to kill Jesus (v. 18). To Jesus' sabbath violation has been added the ultimate blasphemy: Jesus has made himself equal to God. The Jews have heard rightly the content of Jesus' words; he does speak of his unique relationship to God ("my father," v. 17; "his own [ἴδιον *idion*] father," v. 18) and does equate his work with God's work (cf. 4:34). They wrongly interpret those words, however, to be Jesus' assertion of his independence from God, of himself as another God, when Jesus means the exact opposite. His words in v. 17 stress his dependence on God.[125]

The claim Jesus makes for himself in 5:17 mirrors the christological confessions that led Johannine Christians into conflict with the synagogues. Also, Johannine Christians who confessed Jesus to be the incarnate Word, sharing fully in God's identity and work, were met with charges of blasphemy. Jesus' assertion of his identity with God in 5:17, even in the face of death threats, provided support to the Johannine community in their struggles.[126]

123. So Robert Kysar, *John,* Augsburg Commentary on the New Testament (Minneapolis: Augsburg, 1986) 78; C. K. Barrett, *The Gospel According to St. John,* 2nd ed. (Philadelphia: Westminster, 1978) 255.
124. See Jeffery L. Staley, "Stumbling in the Dark, Reaching for the Light: Reading Character in John 5 and 9," *Semeia* 53 (1991) 58-64.

125. Rudolf Bultmann, *The Gospel of John: A Commentary,* trans. G. R. Beasley-Murray, R. W. N. Hoare, and J. K. Riches (Philadelphia: Westminster, 1971) 245.
126. Neyrey, *An Ideology of Revolt,* 35.

REFLECTIONS

John 5:1-18 presents the reader with the first example of overt rejection of Jesus in the Fourth Gospel. The Gospel narrative has anticipated this rejection (1:11; 4:44), but its suddenness and intensity in this story are nonetheless surprising. Concern over violation of sabbath law escalates almost immediately into a resolve to kill Jesus. The Fourth Evangelist calls those who oppose Jesus in this story "the Jews," and interpreters must attend carefully to what John means by this expression lest they fall into a careless anti-Semitism. The interpreter must be careful to treat the "Jews" as characters in the story, not as an ethnic group. The "Jews" in this story are not Jesus' enemies because they are Jewish (cf. Jesus' assertion, "salvation is from the Jews," 4:22), but because they reject Jesus. That is, their Jewishness is not the issue; their response to Jesus is.

The "Jews" in John 5:1-18 make Jesus their enemy because he threatens their power, authority, indeed, their very perception of reality. The defense of the sabbath law is the defense of an entire system of ordering life and religious practice. It is the defense of a particular understanding of God and how God belongs in human experience, and of membership in a religious community. The "Jews" have too much to lose (and, therefore, much to defend) if Jesus is allowed to redefine God's presence in the world, so they choose to eliminate Jesus as a threat. The "Jews," the religious authorities with the power, close ranks rather than admit the possibility of a new way.

The rejection of Jesus in this story, then, is a rejection of the possibility of new and unprecedented ways of knowing God and ordering the life of faith. It is no accident that the Fourth Evangelist uses a healing story as the catalyst for this rejection (see also John 9), because a healing miracle simultaneously challenges conventional understandings of how the world is ordered and gives concrete embodiment to the new possibilities. The double foci of the dialogue of 5:9b-18 reinforces the double aspect of the miracle. The "Jews" focus on the challenge to the conventional order, whereas the healed man and Jesus focus on the new possibilities, the man's new life.

The contemporary analogue for the "Jews' " rejection is not found by looking for the rejection of Jesus by those outside the church, because in the Fourth Gospel, the "Jews" are Jesus' own people. The contemporary analogue is found instead by looking inside the church. The contemporary reader is thus invited by this text to examine when and by whom in contemporary church life the knowledge of God brought by Jesus is rejected because it is too challenging to existing religious systems and structures.

This is a delicate interpretive situation, because to engage in a battle of conflicting orthodoxies by pitting one "right" understanding of the good news against another is in reality a rejection of Jesus. Much damage and hurt have been done in the church by laity and clergy alike in the defense of the "right" position. Jesus' challenge, which the Jewish authorities rightly sensed and reacted against swiftly and intensely (5:18), is to the hegemony of any one group or position. Jesus brings God into human experience in ways that transcend and transform human definitions and categories.

John 5:1-18 illustrates this fact. Sabbath law, the specifics of which were defined and promulgated by human beings within the religious establishment, does not have the ultimate say about Jesus' activity in the world. If God is working, Jesus will keep working. In the contemporary church, issues of ordination, church governance, and baptismal and eucharistic practices often function as sabbath law functions for the "Jews" in this story: as the principal defining issues for membership in religious community and one's relationship to God. The reality of the incarnation of God's availability and presence in Jesus is the defining mark of the believing community for John, not the defense of particular practices.

There is no way to soften the rejection of Jesus in John 5:1-18. It is so powerful that even those not directly involved are drawn into its wake (e.g., the healed man in vv. 15-16). The question for the interpreter is whether to confront this rejection head-on and recognize where this dynamic plays itself out among Jesus' "own" today—that is, within the church itself.

John 5:19-47, The Discourse

NIV

¹⁹Jesus gave them this answer: "I tell you the truth, the Son can do nothing by himself; he can do only what he sees his Father doing, because whatever the Father does the Son also does. ²⁰For the Father loves the Son and shows him all he does. Yes, to your amazement he will show him even greater things than these. ²¹For just as the Father raises the dead and gives them life, even so the Son gives life to whom he is pleased to give it. ²²Moreover, the Father judges no one, but has entrusted all judgment to the Son, ²³that all may honor the Son just as they honor the Father. He who does not honor the Son does not honor the Father, who sent him.

²⁴"I tell you the truth, whoever hears my word and believes him who sent me has eternal life and will not be condemned; he has crossed over from death to life. ²⁵I tell you the truth, a time is coming and has now come when the dead will hear the voice of the Son of God and those who hear will live. ²⁶For as the Father has life in himself, so he has granted the Son to have life in himself. ²⁷And he has given him authority to judge because he is the Son of Man.

²⁸"Do not be amazed at this, for a time is coming when all who are in their graves will hear his voice ²⁹and come out—those who have done good will rise to live, and those who have done evil will rise to be condemned. ³⁰By myself I can do nothing; I judge only as I hear, and my judgment is just, for I seek not to please myself but him who sent me.

³¹"If I testify about myself, my testimony is not valid. ³²There is another who testifies in my favor, and I know that his testimony about me is valid.

³³"You have sent to John and he has testified to the truth. ³⁴Not that I accept human testimony; but I mention it that you may be saved. ³⁵John was a lamp that burned and gave light, and you chose for a time to enjoy his light.

³⁶"I have testimony weightier than that of John. For the very work that the Father has given me to finish, and which I am doing, testifies that the Father has sent me. ³⁷And the Father who sent me has himself testified concerning me. You have

NRSV

¹⁹Jesus said to them, "Very truly, I tell you, the Son can do nothing on his own, but only what he sees the Father doing; for whatever the Father[a] does, the Son does likewise. ²⁰The Father loves the Son and shows him all that he himself is doing; and he will show him greater works than these, so that you will be astonished. ²¹Indeed, just as the Father raises the dead and gives them life, so also the Son gives life to whomever he wishes. ²²The Father judges no one but has given all judgment to the Son, ²³so that all may honor the Son just as they honor the Father. Anyone who does not honor the Son does not honor the Father who sent him. ²⁴Very truly, I tell you, anyone who hears my word and believes him who sent me has eternal life, and does not come under judgment, but has passed from death to life.

²⁵"Very truly, I tell you, the hour is coming, and is now here, when the dead will hear the voice of the Son of God, and those who hear will live. ²⁶For just as the Father has life in himself, so he has granted the Son also to have life in himself; ²⁷and he has given him authority to execute judgment, because he is the Son of Man. ²⁸Do not be astonished at this; for the hour is coming when all who are in their graves will hear his voice ²⁹and will come out—those who have done good, to the resurrection of life, and those who have done evil, to the resurrection of condemnation.

³⁰"I can do nothing on my own. As I hear, I judge; and my judgment is just, because I seek to do not my own will but the will of him who sent me.

³¹"If I testify about myself, my testimony is not true. ³²There is another who testifies on my behalf, and I know that his testimony to me is true. ³³You sent messengers to John, and he testified to the truth. ³⁴Not that I accept such human testimony, but I say these things so that you may be saved. ³⁵He was a burning and shining lamp, and you were willing to rejoice for a while in his light. ³⁶But I have a testimony greater than John's. The works that the Father has given me

ᵃ Gk that one

NIV

never heard his voice nor seen his form, [38]nor does his word dwell in you, for you do not believe the one he sent. [39]You diligently study[a] the Scriptures because you think that by them you possess eternal life. These are the Scriptures that testify about me, [40]yet you refuse to come to me to have life.

[41]"I do not accept praise from men, [42]but I know you. I know that you do not have the love of God in your hearts. [43]I have come in my Father's name, and you do not accept me; but if someone else comes in his own name, you will accept him. [44]How can you believe if you accept praise from one another, yet make no effort to obtain the praise that comes from the only God[b]?

[45]"But do not think I will accuse you before the Father. Your accuser is Moses, on whom your hopes are set. [46]If you believed Moses, you would believe me, for he wrote about me. [47]But since you do not believe what he wrote, how are you going to believe what I say?"

[a]39 Or *Study diligently* (the imperative)   [b]44 Some early manuscripts *the Only One*

NRSV

to complete, the very works that I am doing, testify on my behalf that the Father has sent me. [37]And the Father who sent me has himself testified on my behalf. You have never heard his voice or seen his form, [38]and you do not have his word abiding in you, because you do not believe him whom he has sent.

[39]"You search the scriptures because you think that in them you have eternal life; and it is they that testify on my behalf. [40]Yet you refuse to come to me to have life. [41]I do not accept glory from human beings. [42]But I know that you do not have the love of God in[a] you. [43]I have come in my Father's name, and you do not accept me; if another comes in his own name, you will accept him. [44]How can you believe when you accept glory from one another and do not seek the glory that comes from the one who alone is God? [45]Do not think that I will accuse you before the Father; your accuser is Moses, on whom you have set your hope. [46]If you believed Moses, you would believe me, for he wrote about me. [47]But if you do not believe what he wrote, how will you believe what I say?"

[a] Or *among*

COMMENTARY

John 5:19-47 is the first fully developed discourse by Jesus in the Fourth Gospel. The discourse divides into two parts: (1) Verses 19-30 expand on v. 17 and elucidate the Father/Son relationship, and (2) vv. 31-47 focus on witnesses to Jesus. (This division of material differs from the NRSV, which divides at v. 29.)

5:19-30. This passage is an excellent example of the distinctive Johannine discourse style. It is built on a lean vocabulary base, the same few words occurring repeatedly—e.g., "father" (πατήρ *patēr,* vv. 19, 20, 21, 22, 23, 26), "son" (υἱός *huios,* vv. 19, 20, 21, 22, 23, 25, 26, 27), "judge" and "judgment" (κρίνω *krinō* and κρίσις *krisis,* vv. 22, 24, 27, 29, 30), and nouns and verbs from the root "life" (ζάω *zaō* and ζωή *zōē;* vv. 21, 24, 25, 26, 29). The repetitiveness of vocabulary and theme makes it difficult to outline vv. 19-30, because in many respects the discourse

moves forward and backward simultaneously. That is, the Fourth Evangelist advances the argument by placing what has been said before in a new context. It may be most helpful to think of John 5:19-30 as a web of closely interrelated themes. The Fourth Evangelist uses a similar technique of interwoven themes and motifs in the Prologue, the Farewell Discourse (chaps. 13–17), and most of the discourses in the Gospel (e.g., 6:35-59; 10:1-18).

5:19-20. The opening words of v. 19 ("Jesus gave them this answer") position the words that follow as an answer to the Jews' outrage in v. 18. Their concern is twofold: Jesus was breaking the sabbath and making himself equal to God (v. 18). Verses 19-20 address these concerns head-on by placing Jesus' work in the context of his complete dependence on God. Verses 19-20*a* depict the Son as incapable of doing anything apart from the model of the Father's own work. It is possible that vv. 19-20*a* are a parable that illustrates the apprentice relationship of father and son common to the Near Eastern culture of Jesus' time.[127] Jesus may be using this parable to introduce the general categories of father-son relationship, which the discourse will develop specifically about Jesus and God. Elsewhere in John, Jesus uses parabolic or proverbial language in this way to establish appropriate interpretive categories (e.g., 4:35-38). The parable of vv. 19-20*a* suggests that "the Jews" were partially correct, Jesus' relationship to God is that of a son to his "own father" (v. 18). They wrongly perceive Jesus' relationship with God as being of his own making, however. Like Phil 2:6 ("who, though he was in the form of God,/ did not regard equality with God/ as something to be exploited" [NRSV]), John 5:19-20 claims that Jesus' oneness with God is intrinsic to the identity he has shared with God from "the beginning" (1:1) and is of God's making, not Jesus'.

The promise that God will show the Son greater works (v. 20*b*) recalls Jesus' promise of 1:50 ("You will see greater things"). There "greater things" is linked to the Cana miracle; in 5:20 "greater works" is linked to the healing of 5:2-18. In both cases, the implication is that what Jesus does would be impossible apart from the workings of God.

5:21-22. These verses name the "greater works" that God will show Jesus. Verse 21 focuses on the work of giving life, v. 22 on the work of judgment. These two activities are works of God that Jewish tradition understood as continuing even on the sabbath.[128] God's ability to give life is at the center of OT faith (e.g., 1 Sam 2:6; 2 Kgs 5:7; Ezek 39:3-12). To give life to the dead has a double meaning, for "dead" can mean both physically and spiritually dead in John. Both meanings will figure in 5:19-30. Verse 21 makes clear that the Son now shares in the life-giving work of the Father ("for just as . . . so . . . "). Moreover, the Son has complete freedom in the enactment of that work ("for whom he wishes"). The truth of

v. 21 has already been demonstrated by the healing in 5:1-9. It was Jesus' wish to heal that led to the healing, not the man's request to be healed (5:6).

In v. 22, another activity traditionally associated with God is described as an activity of the Son: judgment (e.g., Pss 43:1; 109). Verse 22 declares that the Father has given the exercise of judgment to the Son. The truth of this claim was also demonstrated in the preceding healing story. When Jesus told the man to sin no more (5:14), Jesus was exercising his power of judgment. John 5:21-22 thus specifies how Jesus was working the works of God on the sabbath (cf. 5:17), while at the same time moving the conversation to a broader christological concern.

5:23. This verse articulates the purpose of the co-working of Father and Son. They share the same work so that they can be honored together. The radical claim here is that Jesus is to be honored as God is honored. Verse 23 thus provides further commentary on 5:1-18, because in the Jews' resolve to persecute and kill Jesus (5:16, 18), they actually dishonor the very God they claim to defend. In the ancient Mediterranean world, to dishonor the one sent is the same as dishonoring the sender (see also 8:49).[129]

5:24-25. These verses move from a description of the interrelationship of Father and Son to the soteriological significance of that relationship. Both verses begin with "Very truly, I say to you . . . " a rhetorical device that signals the introduction of an important new saying (see discussion of form in Commentary on 1:51). Verse 24 presents the possibility of eternal life in terms reminiscent of 3:18-21, 31-36. To hear Jesus' word and believe in God, like believing and doing what is true in 3:18-21 and accepting Jesus' testimony in 3:33, opens the gift of eternal life. The alternative is judgment (cf. 3:16, 19, 36). "Death" (θάνατος *thanatos*) and "life" (*zōē*) are used metaphorically in v. 24 to refer to spiritual life and death, so that v. 24 focuses on the present effects of belief in God. Verse 25 restates v. 24 in the idiom of realized eschatology. Like v. 24, its focus is on the present life of the believer. The language of the hour in v. 25 recalls

---

127. See C. H. Dodd, *Historical Tradition in the Fourth Gospel* (Cambridge: Cambridge University Press, 1963) 386n. 2; and "Une parabole caché dans le quatrième Évangile," *Revue d'Histoire et de Philosophie Religieuses* 2-3 (1962) 107-15.

128. For a discussion of Jewish debate about the meaning of God's sabbath rest (Gen 2:3), see Dodd, *The Interpretation of the Fourth Gospel*, 321-22, and Neyrey, *An Ideology of Revolt*, 25-29.

129. For a discussion of honor and shame in the ancient Mediterranean world, see Bruce Malina, *The New Testament World: Insights from Cultural Anthropology*, rev. ed. (Louisville: Westminster/John Knox, 1993) 28-40.

v. 23; traditional eschatological hopes are depicted as being fulfilled by the experience of Jesus in the present.

5:26-27. These verses provide further grounds for the soteriological claims of vv. 24-25. They return the focus to the relationship of the Father and the Son and away from the listener's faith experience. Verse 26 begins with the same grammatical construction as v. 21 ("for just as . . . so . . . ") and maintains that the Son has life because the Father saw to it that that be the case. Verse 26 focuses on the theme of life, v. 27 on the theme of judgment. These are the same themes found in vv. 21-22, but they are nuanced differently. Verses 26-27 focus more intensely on the *identity* of the Son, whereas vv. 21-22 focus on the *activity* of the Son. The Son's identity is given to him by the Father; he has life in himself because God gave it to him (v. 26); he is the Son of Man (cf. Dan 7:13) because God gave him authority to judge (v. 27).

5:28-29. It is difficult to determine whether the potential source of amazement in v. 28 ("Do not be astonished at this") is what has just preceded (that Jesus is the Son of Man, the eschatological figure, in the present) or what follows (the description of the final resurrection). This ambiguity may be intentional. Verses 28-29 draw on the language and imagery of future eschatology to describe the resurrection and the final judgment. The language appears to be deliberately contrasted with that of v. 25, in which the eschatological fulfillment is present, "the hour is coming, and is now here." In v. 28, the same language is used to point to future hopes, "the hour is coming" (cf. 4:21, 23). The spiritually dead of v. 25 become quite clearly the physically dead in v. 28 ("all who are in their graves"). The Son of God's voice in v. 25 becomes the Son of Man's voice in v. 28. Point for point, the pictures of realized eschatology in v. 25 and future eschatology in v. 28 mirror one another. Importantly, the decisive event in both eschatological scenarios is the same: hearing the voice of Jesus. The promise of both v. 25 and v. 28 anticipates the raising of Lazarus, when the power of Jesus' voice to transform death into life will be demonstrated (11:43-44).

The contrasting eschatological visions of vv. 25 and 28-29 have led commentators to propose that vv. 28-29 are a doublet of v. 25 from a separate stage of tradition[130] or the addition of a redactor

who wanted to correct John's eschatology with more traditional eschatological expectations.[131] Recourse to source theories to explain the relationship between the two eschatologies obscures the theological issues, however. As noted, the visions of v. 25 and vv. 28-29 have in common that both the eschatologically charged present and the anticipated future are presided over and determined by the presence of Jesus. As Neyrey helpfully suggests, in vv. 21-29, the Fourth Evangelist collected "a variety of old and new, Johannine and traditional eschatological statements" to show that Jesus has "God's full eschatological power." The combination of eschatological traditions is thus essential to the claims the Fourth Evangelist makes about Jesus.[132] One's life in the present is transformed from death to life when one hears the voice of Jesus (vv. 24-25). The future judgment is inaugurated by the voice of Jesus. Judgment is evoked by one's response to Jesus (cf. 3:18-21). Verse 29 is a reminder that one's decisions in the present also have future consequences.

The Fourth Evangelist never insists on the transformation of the present at the expense of the future.[133] The juxtaposition of vv. 24-25 and vv. 28-29 reminds the reader that past, present, and future all are given fresh meaning because of Jesus' presence in human experience. Traditional distinctions between present and future are insufficient to describe the new age inaugurated by Jesus. The Fourth Evangelist's eschatological vision pushes at the boundaries of conventional theological categories in the same way that it pushes at conventional language (e.g., his use of words with inherent double meanings). The wonder of Johannine eschatology is that it is able to hold present and future together in a shared vision. Jesus is the fulfillment of traditional eschatological expectations, but the Gospel writer fulfills them in such a way that they are redefined by the *present* reality of Jesus. Jesus is at the center of the believer's present and will be at the center of the believer's future also.

5:30. This verse provides a reprise of the central theme of 5:19-29: Jesus' dependence on God

130. Raymond E. Brown, *The Gospel According to John (I–XII)*, AB 29 (Garden City, N.Y.: Doubleday, 1966) 219-21.

131. Bultmann, *The Gospel of John*, 261.
132. Neyrey, *An Ideology of Revolt*, 31-33.
133. C. K. Barrett, *The Gospel According to St. John*, 2nd ed. (Philadelphia: Westminster, 1978) 68-70.

for his work. Verse 30 returns to v. 19: Jesus can do nothing without God. The expression "as I hear, I judge" addresses the Johannine theme of the relationship between the believer's decision and Jesus' judgment (see Commentary on 3:18-21). Jesus' judgment, whether in the present (vv. 24-25) or the future (vv. 28-29), is just because it derives from his enactment of God's will (cf. 4:34).

5:31-47. John 5:31 introduces the second part of the discourse (vv. 31-47) and shifts the focus to the grounds on which Jesus' claims of vv. 19-30 rest. John 5:31-47 divides into two parts: (1) vv. 31-40, which cite the witnesses who support Jesus' claims, and (2) vv. 41-47, which address the situation of unbelief into which those witnesses are offered.

5:31-40. *5:31-32.* As mentioned in the discussion of John 1:19-28, "witness" (μαρτυρία *martyria*) has both religious and juridical dimensions in the Fourth Gospel. John 5:31-47 highlights the juridical dimensions and is thus an explicit reminder of the trial motif that runs throughout the Fourth Gospel.[134] Jesus' acceptance or rejection by the world is frequently cast in juridical metaphors by the Fourth Evangelist. The trial motif will culminate in the sophisticated trial narrative of chaps. 18–19.

The charges of the "Jews" in 5:18 and their resolve to kill Jesus effectively place Jesus on trial. In vv. 19-30, Jesus spoke on his own behalf, but Jewish law holds that no man can bear witness on his own behalf.[135] In v. 31, therefore, Jesus explicitly states that he does not offer independent witness concerning himself, because that witness would not be true. The NIV's "valid" highlights the juridical intent of Jesus' words (his testimony to himself would not count as valid evidence). Additional witnesses are required. In vv. 33-40, Jesus will speak as his own defense attorney, presenting the witnesses who testify on his behalf.[136] The verb "witness" (*martyreō*) occurs seven times in 5:31-40 (vv. 31, 32 [twice], 33, 36, 37, 39); the noun form of the word (*martyria*) occurs four times (vv. 31, 32, 34, 36).

Jesus links his testimony with that of "another" in v. 32. The thrust of vv. 19-30 suggests that

Jesus is appealing to God's witness here. The commonality of work and purpose shared by the Father and the Son described in vv. 19-30 suggests a similar interrelationship of God's witness and Jesus' witness. The "Jews" objected to Jesus' description of his relationship with God (5:17-18), and Jesus must be prepared to counter similar objections to his claim to God's witness here. Jesus thus presents the witnesses who have testified to him during his ministry. He begins with John the Baptist (vv. 33-35), then reminds his listeners of his works (v. 36). He then reflects on God's witness in the light of the events of his ministry (vv. 37-38). He concludes by pointing to the witness of the Scriptures (vv. 39-40).

5:33-35. Jesus turns from God's witness (v. 32) to the witness of John the Baptist first because that is the witness the "Jews" themselves sought first. They sent messengers to John to test the truth of his witness (v. 33; 1:19-28). Jesus makes a claim for the truth of John's witness (cf. 5:31-32), but since in Johannine theology Jesus is the "truth" (14:6), his words may also mean that John witnesses to Jesus when he witnesses to the truth. Verse 34 is a disclaimer about the value of John's testimony for Jesus himself. Jesus does not need the testimony of John the Baptist, because Jesus knows the truth of God's witness (v. 32); but his listeners, who do not accept God's witness to Jesus, may be swayed by John's testimony (cf. related disclaimers at 11:42; 12:30). Verse 35 provides a summary of the ministry of John the Baptist. The description of John as a "lamp" (λύχνος *lychnos*) reinforces the claim of the Prologue that John was not the "light" (φῶς *phōs*, 1:8). As a lamp, John shone and gave off light, but his was a derivative brightness. Verse 35*b* may refer to the popularity of John's ministry, but that allusion also contains an implicit criticism of the "Jews."[137] They rejoiced for a while in John's presence, but they did not accept his testimony.

5:36. The second witness to which Jesus refers is his works (v. 36). Jesus' "works" (ἔργα *erga*) can be understood in a limited sense as referring to his miracles,[138] but the expression is used more generally in the Fourth Gospel to refer to all of

---

134. A. E. Harvey, *Jesus on Trial: A Study in the Fourth Gospel* (Atlanta: John Knox, 1977); Neyrey, *Ideology*, 10-24.

135. See *m. Ketub.* 2:9; cf. Deut 9:15.

136. Kysar, *John*, 85.

137. Josephus, *Antiquities of the Jews* 18.116-19.

138. See Brown, *The Gospel According to John (I–XII)*, 224.

Jesus' ministry (4:34).[139] Jesus' works bear witness to his relationship to the Father and to his vocation as the one whom God has sent, because God gave him the works to do. Verse 36 thus restates the themes of vv. 19-30. Jesus does what God has given him to do; Jesus completes God's own works (cf. 17:4, 23).

5:37-38. At v. 37, Jesus returns to God's witness (5:32), but he does so to criticize his listeners. The "Jews" have solicited the witness of John the Baptist (1:19-28) and have seen Jesus' works (2:23-25), yet they still "have never heard [God's] voice or seen [God's] form" (v. 37). No one has seen God except "God the only Son, who is close to the Father's heart, who has made him known" (1:18). The works of John the Baptist and Jesus have offered the "Jews" access to God through Jesus, but the "Jews" have rejected the very testimony that would lead them to Jesus and hence give them a glimpse of God. Verse 37 may contain an ironic allusion to the Sinai theophany (see Exod 19:9-11). Verse 38 makes Jesus' critique of his listeners' experience of God even more explicit and gives expression to the hallmarks of Johannine theology: faith in Jesus as the access to God (cf. 14:6-9) and the abiding presence of God and God's word (λόγος *logos*) with those who believe (cf. 15:1-11). It is possible that *logos* has a double meaning here: God's Word and Jesus as God's Word.

5:39-40. Jesus addresses the precipitating cause of the early church's crisis with the Jews: how to interpret Scripture. These verses also look forward to forthcoming conflicts between Jesus and "the Jews" (e.g., 7:21-24; 8:17-20). The expression "you search the scriptures" may be a technical term to describe rabbinic scriptural study. Verses 39-40 are an excellent example of the sophisticated use of irony in John. The irony revolves around the interpretation of "eternal life" and the role of Scripture. The "Jews" search the Scriptures because they think they are the source of "eternal life" (v. 39). The Scriptures bear witness to Jesus, but the "Jews" ignore their witness and choose not to come to Jesus "to have life" (v. 40). Since to the Johannine community Jesus is the source of eternal life, these verses depict the "Jews'" refusing the very thing for which they search.

In the first century, one dividing line between Jews and Christians was drawn over the proper interpretation of Scripture. Christians claimed that God's revelation in Jesus was continuous with and, indeed, the crowning point of God's revelation in Scripture, while the Jewish community denied that claim. Jesus' "defense" in 5:31-40 has the tone of the formal apologetic used in later disputes with the Jewish community and perhaps even in the formal defense of the Christian position (see, e.g., 15:26-27; 16:1-2, 8-11). The life situation of early Christians probably influenced the Fourth Evangelist's shaping of Jesus' words here.

5:41-47. At v. 41, the tone of Jesus' speech shifts. If Jesus is on trial in vv. 31-40, presenting witnesses as evidence in his defense, then the "Jews" are on trial in vv. 41-47. Jesus switches from defense attorney to prosecutor, citing the evidence of the "Jews'" unbelief against them. This shift is anticipated by the prevalence of second-person plural pronouns throughout vv. 31-40. Jesus' defense in 5:31-40 simultaneously presented his witnesses and looked toward his listeners' refusal to receive the testimonies offered. This is especially true of vv. 39-40, which have a dual function. In addition to completing the list of witnesses, these verses begin Jesus' frontal assault on his accusers. In vv. 41-47, the indictment of the listeners moves exclusively to the fore.

Verses 41-44 seem to develop from the claim of 5:34, which states that Jesus is not concerned with human acclaim, but cites the witnesses for the sake of the salvation of his listeners. The witnesses' reception remains an open question in 5:34, but in vv. 41-44, the Jews' rejection of the witnesses is assumed. Jesus once again renounces any interest in human praise (v. 41) and then turns to the Jews' behavior. The "Jews" do not love God (v. 42), a fact ("I know") demonstrated by their rejection of Jesus, who comes in God's name (v. 43*a*; cf. 1:11). The reference in v. 43*b* to the Jews' acceptance of "another" does not point to a specific messianic figure, but is cited as a general illustration of the Jews' blindness;[140] they are unable to discriminate truth from falsehood (cf. 3:21; 8:31-32, 42-47). Verse 44 returns to the theme of human praise, introduced in v. 41, and explicitly contrasts Jesus' attitude and that

139. See Bultmann, *The Gospel of John,* 265-66.

140. Kysar, *John,* 87.

of his listeners. His listeners' desire for human praise and approbation has taken precedence over seeking God's glory (cf. 12:43).

The discourse ends with a surprising twist. In vv. 41-44, Jesus has played the role of prosecutor, listing the charges against his listeners, but in v. 45, he declares that he will not be their accuser before God. Jesus cedes the role of accuser to Moses. Verses 45-47 are replete with irony. First, Moses, the author of the Torah (v. 47), the authority to which the Jewish leaders appeal in their adjudication of sabbath law, is in reality another witness to Jesus. Verses 46-47 reiterate the claim of vv. 39-40: The writings of Moses testify to Jesus, but the "Jews" do not accept this testimony. Second, and the source of an even more poignant irony, Moses has the role of the advocate for the people in the Jewish tradition; he is the one who stands in the breach between the people and God (see Exod 17:1-7; 32:30-34; Ps 106:23). According to the Johannine Jesus, however, the people's advocate, their hope (v. 45), will be their accuser instead, because al-though they claim to defend Moses' words, they actually reject them because they do not see that Scripture testifies to Jesus.

When the guarantor of the Jews' scriptural tradition is placed in the position of accuser, the intensity of the conflict between Jesus and the "Jews" is made clear. As chaps. 6–10 will show, there is no middle ground in this conflict, because entire belief systems and social constructs are at stake. By placing Moses on Jesus' side, the Fourth Evangelist denies the Jews their court of appeal. To be a disciple of Moses, the Fourth Gospel maintains, one must be a disciple of Jesus as well (cf. 9:28-29).

As the acrimony between Jesus and the "Jews" intensifies in the remainder of the Gospel, it is important to remember the historical setting out of which the Fourth Gospel emerged and the intense conflicts between the synagogue and the Johannine community (see Introduction). The acrimony is not directed to the Jewish people, but to those Jewish leaders who rejected Jesus and subsequently forced his followers out of the Jewish community.

REFLECTIONS

The Johannine discourses have their own distinctive place in the Fourth Gospel. They have few of the playful nuances of the Gospel narratives, none of the give and take found in conversations between Jesus and other characters. Instead, only one voice is heard in these discourses, the voice of Jesus, and his voice must guide the interpreter's handling of the discourse. The voice of Jesus explicitly declares the Gospel's theological and christological assumptions. The role given to Jesus in the discourses reveals a critical literary and theological strategy of the Fourth Evangelist: The character of Jesus within the Gospel narrative provides the warrants for the Evangelist's own theological perspective. The Johannine Jesus is cast as the interpreter of his own life and ministry. The job of the contemporary interpreter is to enable the voice of the Johannine Jesus to be heard in a fresh context.

In 5:19-47, the interpretive voice of the Johannine Jesus focuses on three overarching themes to which the interpreter should attend: the relationship of the Father and the Son; witnesses to Jesus; and resistance to the witnesses, which results in unbelief. In each of these three themes, the interpreter can note the interplay of two essential questions: Who is Jesus? and Who are human beings in the light of Jesus? The balance between these two questions is crucial for understanding the Fourth Gospel. From the perspective of the Fourth Gospel, Who is Jesus? must be addressed before the second question about human identity can even be asked. The discourse of 5:19-47 helpfully illustrates the interplay between these two questions.

In 5:19-30, the central concern is the relationship between God and Jesus. Eight of the twelve verses (5:19-23, 26-27, 30) focus on that relationship and hence on Jesus' identity. Who Jesus is can be answered by coming to a clearer understanding of Jesus' relationship to God. Jesus has received the gifts of life and judgment from God (5:21-22, 26-27); Jesus seeks to do the will of God (5:30). Sandwiched between these christological declarations are verses that focus on human response to Jesus (vv. 24-25, 28-29), on who people become in the light of Jesus. In vv. 24-25, for example, a person passes from spiritual death to life because of his or her response to Jesus. Those who hear Jesus receive new life (vv. 24-25, 28-29); those who deny Jesus, who do "evil" (5:29; cf. 3:20), are denied that life. If a person knows who Jesus is—recognizes him as sent by God (5:24)—that person receives a new identity. Jesus' identity and human identity are thus tightly intertwined, but the beginning point for the Fourth Gospel is always Jesus' identity.

A similar interplay of Jesus' identity and human identity is apparent in 5:31-47. In those verses, the presentation of the witnesses to Jesus (vv. 31-40) precedes discussion of the "Jews'" response to those witnesses (vv. 41-47). Each of the witnesses points to who Jesus is and provides a new occasion for response to Jesus and hence a transformed human identity. For example, Jesus recalls John the Baptist's witness in order that his listeners "may be saved" (v. 34). The Scriptures witness to Jesus and afford the "Jews" the chance for life (vv. 39-40). Verses 41-47 explore the ways in which the "Jews'" resistance to Jesus determines their identity. The witnesses should lead them to faith in Jesus, but they do not receive Jesus (v. 42). Their identities are shaped by the desire for human praise (vv. 41, 44) instead of by the love of God (v. 42).

The trial motif that dominates 5:19-47 highlights this interplay between Jesus' identity and human identity because it underscores the fact that a person is judged by the judgment he or she makes about Jesus. John 5:19-47 presents the evidence necessary to come to faith in Jesus and to be "reborn" into the life offered by God in Jesus. If one rejects the evidence, one loses the life. From the perspective of the Fourth Gospel, then, it is impossible to speak about human existence as a neutral, intellectual category. Human existence is completely defined and shaped by an individual's response to Jesus.

It is important that the interpreter of John 5:19-47 attend to the interplay of Jesus' identity and human identity in this text and honor the Fourth Gospel's presentation of this interrelationship. For this Gospel, one cannot understand human existence without first understanding who Jesus is. The discourse of 5:19-47 is an excellent example of the way in which christology pervades every aspect of the Fourth Gospel. Everything points to Jesus, who in turn points to God (1:18). The absolute centrality of Jesus in the Fourth Gospel often has the effect of distancing contemporary Christians who operate out of a lower christology than this Gospel. To questions like Who are we? or What are we to do? (cf. Luke 3:10), time and again the Fourth Gospel asks back, Who is Jesus? The Fourth Gospel does not catalogue specific actions to be renounced or embraced in the life of faith as, for example, Matthew and Luke do. The Fourth Gospel insists on one truth: "I have come in my Father's name" (5:43). The case for the life of faith rises or falls on that truth: "Very truly, I tell you, anyone who hears my word and believes in him who sent me has eternal life" (5:24).

John 5:19-47 speaks an important alternative to a church that sometimes thinks the words of the Bible are obsolete unless one can immediately identify their "relevance," unless those words can be turned into instructions for or illustrations of contemporary living. The testimony of this text resists such reduction because it is first and foremost a christological text. It holds up the extraordinary presence of Jesus to the community of faith and asks it to accept Jesus, to accept these witnesses that point to Jesus, and believe. The church needs texts like John 5:19-47 as part of its language of faith, texts that make the case for Jesus. The church needs texts—and moments of proclamation and teaching grounded in those texts—that announce who Jesus is, what Jesus does, what Jesus offers. John 5:19-47 reminds the church of the theological and christological grounds of its identity.

The Fourth Gospel's insistent witness to Jesus does not exist in isolation from the church. It is located in a canon that includes three other Gospel portraits of Jesus and epistolary reflections on the meaning of Jesus. In each of the books of the NT, the balance between the two questions Who is Jesus? and Who are human beings in response to Jesus? is different. The church must train its ears to listen to the distinctive voice and contribution of each of these NT witnesses. The Fourth Gospel, as exemplified in 5:19-47, puts the most weight on the first question, but the second question always follows. The Fourth Gospel is built around a high christology, but it is not a high christology devoid of human accountability. Rather, it is a high christology that demands human accountability.

John 5:19-47 is another example of the coalescing of literary form and theological function in the Fourth Gospel. This text about witness is itself a witness. It offers testimony to the intimate relationship of God and Jesus. It witnesses to the "great cloud of witnesses" that made Jesus known to the first generation of believers and prepared the way for witnesses to come. It witnesses to the cost of rejecting those witnesses, of the loss of spiritual rebirth. John 5:19-47 is not an easy text because of the absolute language of acceptance and rejection it employs and the directness of its christological reflections. The absolute language, however, reflects the earnestness of the Fourth Evangelist's witness. Because human identity is so dependent on Jesus' identity, everything is at stake in the recognition of Jesus as the sent one of God. By placing this witness in the mouth of Jesus, the Fourth Evangelist makes the acceptance or rejection of the witness more intense, because if one rejects the witness of these verses, one does indeed reject Jesus. The reader thus faces the same choices about Jesus that the characters in the story do. The interpreter's role is to enable the faith community who meets Jesus through this text to hear the witness and recognize the choices.

JOHN 6:1–10:42

JESUS' WORDS AND WORKS: CONFLICT AND OPPOSITION GROW

OVERVIEW

John 6 marks the beginning of a new section in the Fourth Gospel narrative. John 5 marked the completion of the first cycle of Jesus' ministry, from the manifestation of Jesus' glory to the rejection of that glory, and in John 6 the cycle begins anew. John 2:1–5:47 and 6:1–10:42 contain two often analogous portraits of Jesus' ministry. In many ways, no new theological themes are introduced in 6:1–10:42; instead, the theological themes from 2:1–5:47 are replayed in a new context: Jesus' authority and relationship to God, Jesus' ability to give life and judge, the consequences of faith or unbelief. The hostility and opposition to Jesus in response to these themes intensifies in chaps. 6–10, however, as the stakes climb.

This second major section in the Gospel, like the first, begins with a miracle in Galilee. To be more precise, chap. 6 begins with two Galilean miracles, the feeding of the five thousand (6:1-15) and Jesus walking on water (6:16-21). These two miracles inaugurate the second cycle just as the Cana miracle (2:1-11) inaugurated the first. In the Cana wine miracle and the feeding miracle, Jesus turns the ordinary into the extraordinary. In both miracles, Jesus provides a superabundance of gifts. The Cana miracle also revealed Jesus' glory to his disciples (2:11), and the theophany of 6:16-21 has that function in the second cycle. The two narrative cycles thus begin with miracles that show the grace and glory of Jesus. It is probably no accident that the two inaugural miracles involve wine and bread, the sacramental symbols of God's grace in Jesus (see Reflections at 6:35-71).

The two narrative cycles of Jesus' ministry also conclude analogously. A healing miracle (5:1-9a; 9:1-7) evokes conversation and controversy about Jesus' identity (5:6-18; 9:8-41), and the controversy concludes with a discourse by Jesus (5:19-

47; 10:1-42). Many details of the healing stories are similar: the healed man's inability to identify Jesus (5:13; 9:12), his questioning by the Jews (5:10-13; 9:13-17, 24), his focus on his own experience of being healed rather than on the Jews' theological concerns (5:15; 9:25), Jesus' finding the healed man at the end of the story (5:15; 9:35). In 5:18, the precise source of "the Jews'" rejection of Jesus is articulated: his relationship with the Father. In 10:30, that point is repeated, but the rejection of Jesus has intensified, "The Jews took up stones again to stone him" (10:31). The decision to kill Jesus (5:18) has evolved into action against him. The discourse of John 5 ends with a recital of witnesses to Jesus (John the Baptist, Jesus' works, God, Scripture), and those same witnesses are named in 10:31-42.

Many Johannine scholars propose that chaps. 5 and 6 should be reversed. Many commentaries even follow that transposed order in their analysis of John.[141] There are no manuscripts in which these chapters are transposed, however, so the transposition has to be posited for a stage before the final editing of the Gospel. The strongest arguments for transposition derive from geographical considerations: At the end of chap. 4, Jesus is in Galilee, in chap. 5 in Jerusalem; in chap. 6, he is back in Galilee with no mention of a journey from Jerusalem. If chaps. 5 and 6 are reversed, then Jesus' Galilean activities are concentrated in chaps. 4 and 6. Yet even those commentators who advocate transposition acknowledge that the move creates new difficulties while solving others. For example, the request of Jesus' brothers that

---

141. E.g., Rudolf Bultmann, *The Gospel of John: A Commentary,* trans. G. R. Beasley-Murray, R. W. N. Hoare, and J. K. Riches (Philadelphia: Westminster, 1971) 209-62; Rudolf Schnackenburg, *The Gospel According to St. John,* 3 vols. (New York: Seabury, 1982) 2:10-135; Gerard Sloyan, *John* (Atlanta: John Knox, 1988) 61-84.

he go to Jerusalem and show himself (7:3) loses much of its force if it follows the story of Jesus in Jerusalem in chap. 5.[142]

The structure of the Fourth Gospel proposed in this commentary assumes that the Gospel should be read in the sequence that is preserved in the manuscript traditions. The Fourth Evangelist was not recording an itinerary of Jesus' activity. Theological concerns, not geographical realism, determine the structure of the Fourth Gospel.

142. So Schnackenburg, *The Gospel According to St. John,* 2:7.

JOHN 6:1-71, THE BREAD OF LIFE

OVERVIEW

John 6 is a carefully crafted chapter, characterized by a tight interweaving of narrative and discourse. It follows the same basic pattern noted in chap. 5: miracle/dialogue/discourse. This pattern is more intricate in chap. 6, however, because the chapter narrates Jesus' self-revelation to two groups: the crowd and his disciples. Chapter 6, therefore, contains two miracles: one performed in front of the crowd and the disciples (6:1-15) and one performed in front of the disciples alone (6:16-21). This dual focus is reflected in the discourse material as well. In 6:35-59, Jesus speaks in the presence of the crowd and the disciples, but in 6:60-71 he speaks to his disciples alone.

John 6 can be outlined as follows:

6:1-15	Miracle (with crowd)
6:16-21	Miracle (with disciples alone)
6:22-24	Transition
6:25-34	Dialogue (crowd)
6:35-59	Discourse (crowd and disciples)
6:60-71	Conclusion (disciples alone)

John 6:1-15, The Feeding of the Five Thousand

NIV

6 Some time after this, Jesus crossed to the far shore of the Sea of Galilee (that is, the Sea of Tiberias), [2]and a great crowd of people followed him because they saw the miraculous signs he had performed on the sick. [3]Then Jesus went up on a mountainside and sat down with his disciples. [4]The Jewish Passover Feast was near.

[5]When Jesus looked up and saw a great crowd coming toward him, he said to Philip, "Where shall we buy bread for these people to eat?" [6]He asked this only to test him, for he already had in mind what he was going to do.

[7]Philip answered him, "Eight months' wages[a] would not buy enough bread for each one to have a bite!"

[a]7 Greek *two hundred denarii*

NRSV

6 After this Jesus went to the other side of the Sea of Galilee, also called the Sea of Tiberias.[a] [2]A large crowd kept following him, because they saw the signs that he was doing for the sick. [3]Jesus went up the mountain and sat down there with his disciples. [4]Now the Passover, the festival of the Jews, was near. [5]When he looked up and saw a large crowd coming toward him, Jesus said to Philip, "Where are we to buy bread for these people to eat?" [6]He said this to test him, for he himself knew what he was going to do. [7]Philip answered him, "Six months' wages[b] would not buy enough bread for each of them to get a little." [8]One of his disciples, Andrew, Simon Peter's brother, said to him, [9]"There is a boy here

[a] Gk *of Galilee of Tiberias*   [b] Gk *Two hundred denarii*; the denarius was the usual day's wage for a laborer

NIV

⁸Another of his disciples, Andrew, Simon Peter's brother, spoke up, ⁹"Here is a boy with five small barley loaves and two small fish, but how far will they go among so many?"

¹⁰Jesus said, "Have the people sit down." There was plenty of grass in that place, and the men sat down, about five thousand of them. ¹¹Jesus then took the loaves, gave thanks, and distributed to those who were seated as much as they wanted. He did the same with the fish.

¹²When they had all had enough to eat, he said to his disciples, "Gather the pieces that are left over. Let nothing be wasted." ¹³So they gathered them and filled twelve baskets with the pieces of the five barley loaves left over by those who had eaten.

¹⁴After the people saw the miraculous sign that Jesus did, they began to say, "Surely this is the Prophet who is to come into the world." ¹⁵Jesus, knowing that they intended to come and make him king by force, withdrew again to a mountain by himself.

NRSV

who has five barley loaves and two fish. But what are they among so many people?" ¹⁰Jesus said, "Make the people sit down." Now there was a great deal of grass in the place; so they*ᵃ* sat down, about five thousand in all. ¹¹Then Jesus took the loaves, and when he had given thanks, he distributed them to those who were seated; so also the fish, as much as they wanted. ¹²When they were satisfied, he told his disciples, "Gather up the fragments left over, so that nothing may be lost." ¹³So they gathered them up, and from the fragments of the five barley loaves, left by those who had eaten, they filled twelve baskets. ¹⁴When the people saw the sign that he had done, they began to say, "This is indeed the prophet who is to come into the world."

15When Jesus realized that they were about to come and take him by force to make him king, he withdrew again to the mountain by himself.

ᵃ Gk *the men*

COMMENTARY

The story of the miraculous feeding occupied a central place in the oral tradition about Jesus. It is the only miracle story that occurs in all four Gospels, and Matthew and Mark even tell the story twice (Matt 14:13-21; 15:32-39; Mark 6:30-44; 8:1-10; Luke 9:10-17). The pivotal place of this story in the traditions about Jesus means that it is not necessary to assume Johannine dependence on the synoptic Gospels, particularly Mark, here.[143] The Johannine version contains enough individual details that are essential to the story (e.g., the boy in v. 9) that it seems more likely that John drew on one of several versions of this story that circulated among the early Christians.[144]

The story of the miraculous feeding was popular in the early church because of the eucharistic interpretation to which it lent itself. The eucharistic interpretation receives a distinctive touch in John 6. The traditional eucharistic elements that feature in the synoptic tellings of the story (e.g., the traditional liturgical formula, Jesus took the loaves, blessed, broke, gave; Matt 14:19; 15:36; Mark 6:41; 8:6; Luke 9:16) are played down or are absent in John. The theological significance of Jesus' gift of himself in the bread is heightened, however (see Reflections at 6:60-71).

6:1-4. John 6:1-15 divides into two parts: (1) vv. 1-4, introduction, and vv. 5-15, the miracle story. Verses 1-4 serve as the introduction to the whole chapter and show evidence of having been constructed for the purpose of linking chap. 6 to the preceding narrative. The transition from v. 4 to v. 5 is rough, as is the relationship between vv. 3 and 15. Nonetheless, as strained as the composition of these verses seems, each verse of the introduction contributes something significant to the narrative that follows. Verse 1 establishes the location at the Sea of Galilee. Verse 2 introduces the theme of seeing signs, which will figure prominently in the rest of the chapter (see vv. 14,

143. As C. K. Barrett does, *The Gospel According to St. John,* 2nd ed. (Philadelphia: Westminster, 1978) 271.

144. For a full discussion of the history of the oral traditions of the miraculous feeding, see Raymond E. Brown, *The Gospel According to John (I–XII),* AB 29 (Garden City, N.Y.: Doubleday, 1966) 236-50.

26, 30). This verse also points back to the crowd's response in 2:23-25 and to the healing in 5:1-9. Jesus' retreat to the mountain with his disciples in v. 3 sets up the contrast between Jesus' self-revelation to his disciples and to the crowd, which, as noted, determines the structure of much of chap. 6. The reference to Passover in v. 4 introduces the exodus theme; exodus imagery figures prominently in vv. 5-59 (e.g., vv. 12, 31-32, 49, 58).

6:5-15. The miracle story proper contains elements standard in the miracle story form: an introduction (vv. 5-9), the miracle itself (vv. 10-11), the aftermath and results of the miracle (vv. 12-15). The miracle is initiated by Jesus (v. 5). Just as Jesus initiated contact with the Samaritan woman (4:9) and initiated the healing of the man by the pool (5:6), so also here he anticipates the hunger of the crowd. His question, "Where are we to buy food?" is asked to test Philip (v. 6). Jesus knows the answer to the question—he knows what he is going to do—and he wants to discover whether Philip does. As noted earlier, the whence of Jesus' gifts is an important christological question in the Fourth Gospel (e.g., 2:9; 4:11); if one knows the source of Jesus' gifts, one comes close to recognizing Jesus' identity (cf. 4:10). Neither Philip (v. 7) nor Andrew (vv. 8-9) is able to answer Jesus' question, however. Instead of seeing that Jesus' question is about himself, the two disciples interpret the question on the most conventional level and so give conventional answers: There is neither money nor food enough to feed so many people.

This exchange between Jesus and his disciples prepares for the miracle in several ways. Philip's and Andrew's responses communicate how daunting the size of the crowd is and hence the huge quantity of food that would be required to feed them. More important, the disciples' answers show how traditional categories cannot comprehend in advance what Jesus has to give. Conventional expectations offer no solutions to the crowd's needs; Jesus alone knows how to meet those needs.

The miracle is narrated succinctly in vv. 10-11. Verse 10 narrates an element standard to all of the accounts of the feeding: the order for the crowd to sit down (Matt 14:19; 15:35; Mark 6:39; 8:6; Luke 9:14). The size of the crowd was calculated by counting the number of men present. When one includes women and children in the count, the crowd is larger than five thousand persons (cf. Matt 14:21, which makes this explicit).

The miracle itself is narrated in v. 11. Jesus' actions do not reflect the more liturgically stylized actions of the synoptic accounts (e.g., Mark 6:41; Luke 9:16), but rather reflect the actions of a host at a Jewish meal. Jesus takes the food, gives thanks over it, and gives it to his "guests." Importantly, the Fourth Evangelist narrates Jesus' distributing the bread and fish himself, in contrast to the synoptic accounts, where the disciples distribute the food (e.g., Matt 14:19; Mark 6:41; Luke 9:16). Jesus' distribution of the food enhances the christological focus of this miracle: The gift of food comes from Jesus himself.

The gathering of twelve baskets full of fragments (v. 13) is standard in the tradition (Matt 14:20; Mark 6:43; Luke 9:17) and serves to emphasize the prodigiousness of the miracle; not only did the people eat their fill, but there were leftovers as well (cf. 2:6; 4:13-14). (Seven baskets of fragments are collected in Matt 15:37 and Mark 8:8). Jesus' words in v. 12 are unique to the Johannine version of the miracle and make an important connection between this story and the manna story of Exodus 16. In Exod 16:19, Moses asked that the people not leave any extra manna around, but the people disobeyed Moses and the leftover manna "bred worms and became foul" (Exod 16:20 NRSV). Jesus' words in 6:12 seem to caution against a repetition of Exodus 16. The connection between the feeding miracle and the manna story, so pivotal to 6:25-59, is thus introduced early on.

Verses 14 and 15 narrate the results of the miracle. The Fourth Gospel narrative has taught the reader to suspect any response to Jesus that is based on a surface reaction to signs (2:23-25; 4:48). The people's confession of Jesus as "the prophet who is to come into the world" (v. 14; cf. 4:25) is, therefore, ambiguous, because while it is an appropriate confession (cf. 4:19; 9:17), it rests on the evidence of signs. The people's confession continues the exodus imagery of the miracle, because it recalls the promise of a prophet like Moses of Deut 18:15.

In v. 15 Jesus displays his omniscience (cf. 1:48; 2:23-25; 4:16-18) by knowing in advance the crowd's intent. The people's desire to make Jesus king by force resolves the ambiguity of v.

14 and confirms that the people's response cannot be trusted. The kingship of Jesus is an important theme in the Fourth Gospel, first introduced in 1:49. Israel's desire for a king is part of its messianic expectations, the hope for a second David. Jesus will be "king" in the Fourth Gospel, but he will be king according to his definition of kingship (18:36-38), not forced to fit the world's definition. The kingship theme reaches its resolution in the crucifixion narrative of John 18–19. (See Reflections at 6:16-24.)

John 6:16-24, Jesus Walks on Water

NIV

¹⁶When evening came, his disciples went down to the lake, ¹⁷where they got into a boat and set off across the lake for Capernaum. By now it was dark, and Jesus had not yet joined them. ¹⁸A strong wind was blowing and the waters grew rough. ¹⁹When they had rowed three or three and a half miles,ª they saw Jesus approaching the boat, walking on the water; and they were terrified. ²⁰But he said to them, "It is I; don't be afraid." ²¹Then they were willing to take him into the boat, and immediately the boat reached the shore where they were heading.

²²The next day the crowd that had stayed on the opposite shore of the lake realized that only one boat had been there, and that Jesus had not entered it with his disciples, but that they had gone away alone. ²³Then some boats from Tiberias landed near the place where the people had eaten the bread after the Lord had given thanks. ²⁴Once the crowd realized that neither Jesus nor his disciples were there, they got into the boats and went to Capernaum in search of Jesus.

ª19 Greek *rowed twenty-five or thirty stadia* (about 5 or 6 kilometers)

NRSV

16When evening came, his disciples went down to the sea, ¹⁷got into a boat, and started across the sea to Capernaum. It was now dark, and Jesus had not yet come to them. ¹⁸The sea became rough because a strong wind was blowing. ¹⁹When they had rowed about three or four miles,ª they saw Jesus walking on the sea and coming near the boat, and they were terrified. ²⁰But he said to them, "It is I;ᵇ do not be afraid." ²¹Then they wanted to take him into the boat, and immediately the boat reached the land toward which they were going.

22The next day the crowd that had stayed on the other side of the sea saw that there had been only one boat there. They also saw that Jesus had not got into the boat with his disciples, but that his disciples had gone away alone. ²³Then some boats from Tiberias came near the place where they had eaten the bread after the Lord had given thanks.ᶜ ²⁴So when the crowd saw that neither Jesus nor his disciples were there, they themselves got into the boats and went to Capernaum looking for Jesus.

ª Gk *about twenty-five or thirty stadia*   ᵇ Gk *I am*
ᶜ Other ancient authorities lack *after the Lord had given thanks*

COMMENTARY

6:16-21. The story of Jesus walking on water appears in Matthew (14:22-32), Mark (6:45-51), and John, and in each case it follows the story of the feeding miracle. This suggests that the two stories were linked in oral tradition as a pair of Galilean miracles. John's account of the miracle is the shortest and the most simply constructed and cleanly narrated of the three versions. As is the case with 6:1-15, John does not seem dependent on Mark but rather preserves an independent variation of this core tradition.

Even in its lean narration, John 6:16-21 still contains the standard elements of a miracle story: vv. 16-18, introduction and preparation for the miracle; vv. 19-20, the miracle; v. 21, the aftermath of the miracle. Verses 16-18 establish the nighttime setting for the miracle (cf. Matt 14:23; Mark 6:47). In Matt 14:22 and Mark 6:45, Jesus orders the disciples to cross the lake, but in John the disciples go on their own initiative. In Matthew and Mark, Jesus watches the disciples' boat cross the rough sea (Matt 14:24; Mark 6:48), whereas in John the journey is narrated from the disciples' perspective. In John, therefore, the focus of the story is on the disciples' experience, and the story offers the reader a chance to share in that experience. Verse 17 anticipates the miracle that is about to occur ("and Jesus had not yet come to them"). Such proleptic statements are characteristic of the Johannine narrative style (e.g., 2:22; 11:2).

The miracle, like the introduction, is narrated from the disciples' perspective. There is no advance notice that Jesus is walking across the sea until the disciples see him (v. 19; cf. Matt 14:25; Mark 6:48). The Fourth Evangelist does not explain their fear (v. 19*b*) by saying that they thought they saw a ghost (so Matt 14:26; Mark 6:49). Rather, as v. 20 will confirm, the disciples are afraid because they "are awe-struck by the miracle of the manifestation of the divine."[145]

Jesus' words in v. 20 are the key to understanding the miracle of 6:16-21. The words "I am [ἐγώ εἰμι *egō eimi*]; do not be afraid" are found in all three accounts (Matt 14:27; Mark 6:50) and hence belong to the common fund of oral tradition, but they have a particular meaning in the christological context of the Fourth Gospel. A good case can be made that *egō eimi* should not be translated as a simple identification formula ("It is I," NIV and NRSV), but should be translated as an absolute *egō eimi* saying, "I am" (see Fig. 10, "The 'I AM' Sayings in John," 602). As Jesus walks across the water, he identifies himself to his disciples with the divine name, "I AM." The background for this use of the divine name can be found in the LXX of Second Isaiah (Isa 43:25; 51:12; 52:6). The Fourth Evangelist portrays Jesus as speaking the way Yahweh speaks in Second Isaiah.[146] This reading of *egō eimi* is supported by Jesus' second words to his disciples, "Do not be afraid." These words, too, are spoken by Yahweh in Second Isaiah. They are the words of the salvation oracle, words of comfort spoken to end the distress of God's people (e.g., Isa 43:1; 44:2, 8). "Do not be afraid" is also a standard element

145. Bultmann, *The Gospel of John,* 215.
146. Brown, *The Gospel According to John (I–XII),* 537.

of theophanies (e.g., Gen 15:1; Matt 28:5; Luke 2:10). Jesus' words in v. 20 confirm that his walking on water is a theophany and that this "manifestation of the divine" is the source of the disciples' fear.

The story comes to an end quickly in v. 21 with the sudden arrival of the boat at the shore. This sudden sea crossing is a second miracle: Jesus provided safe passage for his disciples. This miracle, too, is theophanic, because it recalls the safe passage God provides those in distress (e.g., Ps 107:30). The Fourth Gospel does not narrate the stilling of the storm (cf. Matt 14:32; Mark 6:51) because John 6:16-21 is not a nature miracle, a demonstration of Jesus' power over the forces of nature. It is a miracle of *theophany,* of the revelation of the divine in Jesus.

The theophanic focus of this narrative is confirmed by the density of OT allusions and images in this passage. In addition to the echoes of Second Isaiah in v. 20, the story builds on a variety of OT texts that describe God as the one who walks upon the water (Job 9:8 LXX) and who makes a path through the sea (Isa 43:2, 16; Pss 77:19; 107:23-32). God's dominion over the waters of chaos is a symbol in the OT of God's sovereignty and care, and in John 6:16-21 that symbolism is applied to Jesus. This story thus illustrates the truth of John 5:19-20: Jesus shares in God's work and identity. Many of the sea allusions in the OT texts that form the background of vv. 16-21 also contain allusions to Israel's safe crossing of the Reed Sea at the exodus (e.g., Isa 43:2), and those exodus allusions are appropriate for the setting of this miracle in John 6.

6:22-24. These verses form a transition narrative that serves several purposes. First, in terms of the mechanics of the story line, these verses narrate the movement of the crowd across the sea to Capernaum (v. 24) and set the stage for the dialogue and discourse that follow (vv. 25-59). Second, the detailed discussion of boats in vv. 22-24 and the crowd's confusion about Jesus' sea crossing provide indirect attestation to the miracle of vv. 16-21. Third, v. 23, with its reference to "the place where they had eaten the bread after the Lord had given thanks," links the two miracles in vv. 1-15 and 16-21 as part of one larger narrative. Finally, the crowd's ignorance about Jesus' whereabouts underscores that the theophany of vv. 16-21 was experienced only by the disciples.

REFLECTIONS

The two miracles of John 6:1-15 and 16-21 present the interpreter with two vivid enactments of the revelation of God's grace and glory in Jesus. On the one hand, this grace and glory are revealed outside conventional human experience and expectations—in the miraculous feeding of over five thousand people with five loaves and two fish; in Jesus' miraculous walking on water. On the other hand, the occasions where Jesus' grace is offered and his glory revealed are familiar occasions of human need—the need for food, the need for safety and rescue from danger. The fears and needs that Jesus' miracles meet belong to the common fund of human experience.

As in the healing of 4:46-54, Jesus' grace is not revealed in a "spiritual" gift, but in a tangible, physical gift. A hungry crowd sat on the grass and ate bread and fish. Their spiritual needs were not the presenting problem for Jesus; their physical needs were (6:5). The interpreter, therefore, needs to be careful lest he or she adopt a purely symbolic interpretation of John 6:1-15 and cast its corporeality aside. The miraculous feeding dramatically demonstrates that Jesus has gifts and resources to meet the full range of human needs. He supplies the daily bread that people need to sustain life (cf. Matt 6:11; Luke 11:3). The feeding of the crowd thus confirms that Jesus is the source of life (cf. 6:33, 35, 58).

Jesus' feeding miracle so impresses the crowd that they declare him to be a prophet (6:14) and intend to make him king (6:15). The crowd's reaction shows how difficult it is to receive Jesus' gifts on his terms without translating them immediately into one's own categories. Jesus' gift of food, the offer of his grace, provided the crowd with a glimpse of his identity, but they immediately tried to twist that identity to serve their own purposes. To make Jesus king is to take his grace and twist it to conform to pre-existent systems of power and authority. To make Jesus king is to judge him according to human glory (5:44) rather than to see in him God's glory. When Jesus withdrew from the crowd (6:15), he showed that he would offer his gift of grace without claiming worldly power. In that moment his glory was revealed, because true glory has nothing to do with worldly power. In John 6:1-15, Jesus' gift of grace thus becomes the vehicle for the revelation of his glory.

In John 6:16-21, by contrast, the revelation of Jesus' glory is the vehicle for his gift of grace. If the crowd's intention to make Jesus king distorts Jesus' glory, then Jesus' walking on water and his words to his disciples ("I am; do not fear") counterbalance that distortion with a true picture of his glory. In 6:16-21, Jesus reveals himself to his disciples as one with God, sharing in God's actions (e.g., Job 9:8; Isa 43:2), identifying himself with God's name (e.g., Isa 43:25), speaking God's words. Yet this manifestation of the divine in Jesus is not bravura, not a moment of glory for the sake of glory, but a moment of glory for the sake of grace. Jesus reveals himself to his disciples in order to allay their fears, to ensure their safe passage, to remind them that God has been, is, and will be their rescue. Jesus' glory is not revealed for power, but for grace-filled pastoral care.

These two miracle stories raise important questions about the balance between grace and glory. In 6:1-15, the heart of the story is Jesus' grace, Jesus' extraordinary, unprecedented gift. Yet the crowd is intrigued by the possibilities of glory, and they want to force Jesus to be king. John 6:16-21 narrates the most dramatic self-revelation of Jesus to this point in the Gospel; yet it occurs in the solitude of his disciples' fears. Jesus will not allow his grace to be controlled by the crowd's desire for glory, and so he hides himself. But he will not hold back his glory from those in need, because this is his mission: to make God known (1:18). How believers hold the grace and glory of Jesus in balance is critical to the life of faith. The grace is destroyed if one tries to harness it for false power and authority, and the glory is lost if one does not recognize its presence in the quiet places of Jesus' grace. Both the grace and the glory are essential to God's revelation in Jesus: "and we have seen his glory, the glory as of a father's only son, full of grace and truth" (1:14).

John 6:25-71, Dialogue and Discourse on the Bread of Life

OVERVIEW

As noted above, John 6:25-59 consists of a dialogue between Jesus and the crowd (vv. 25-34) and a three-part discourse by Jesus (vv. 35-59). John 6 concludes with a conversation between Jesus and his disciples. This lengthy section can be outlined as follows:

6:25-34 Dialogue between Jesus and crowd
6:35-42 Jesus' first discourse and "the Jews' " response
6:43-52 Jesus' second discourse and "the Jews' " response

6:53-59 Jesus' third discourse
6:60-71 Dialogue between Jesus and disciples

Since each of Jesus' three discourses is spoken in answer to "the Jews' " protests, vv. 35-59 acquire a dialogical cast. In that respect, these verses resemble the Farewell Discourse of John 14–16, which also incorporates the responses of Jesus' conversation partners into the discourse, more than they resemble the discourses of 3:11-21 or 5:19-47.

John 6:25-34, Dialogue Between Jesus and the Crowd

25When they found him on the other side of the lake, they asked him, "Rabbi, when did you get here?"

26Jesus answered, "I tell you the truth, you are looking for me, not because you saw miraculous signs but because you ate the loaves and had your fill. 27Do not work for food that spoils, but for food that endures to eternal life, which the Son of Man will give you. On him God the Father has placed his seal of approval."

28Then they asked him, "What must we do to do the works God requires?"

29Jesus answered, "The work of God is this: to believe in the one he has sent."

30So they asked him, "What miraculous sign then will you give that we may see it and believe you? What will you do? 31Our forefathers ate the manna in the desert; as it is written: 'He gave them bread from heaven to eat.'a"

32Jesus said to them, "I tell you the truth, it is not Moses who has given you the bread from heaven, but it is my Father who gives you the

a31 Exodus 16:4; Neh. 9:15; Psalm 78:24, 25

25When they found him on the other side of the sea, they said to him, "Rabbi, when did you come here?" 26Jesus answered them, "Very truly, I tell you, you are looking for me, not because you saw signs, but because you ate your fill of the loaves. 27Do not work for the food that perishes, but for the food that endures for eternal life, which the Son of Man will give you. For it is on him that God the Father has set his seal." 28Then they said to him, "What must we do to perform the works of God?" 29Jesus answered them, "This is the work of God, that you believe in him whom he has sent." 30So they said to him, "What sign are you going to give us then, so that we may see it and believe you? What work are you performing? 31Our ancestors ate the manna in the wilderness; as it is written, 'He gave them bread from heaven to eat.'" 32Then Jesus said to them, "Very truly, I tell you, it was not Moses who gave you the bread from heaven, but it is my Father who gives you the true bread from heaven. 33For the bread of God is that whicha

a Or he who

NIV	NRSV
true bread from heaven. ³³For the bread of God is he who comes down from heaven and gives life to the world." ³⁴"Sir," they said, "from now on give us this bread."	comes down from heaven and gives life to the world." ³⁴They said to him, "Sir, give us this bread always."

COMMENTARY

6:25-26. The crowd's question to Jesus at Capernaum (v. 25) reminds the reader that the crowd is ignorant of the miracle of vv. 16-21 (cf. vv. 22-24). The disciples (and the reader) know something about Jesus that the crowd does not. Jesus does not answer the crowd's question but instead redirects the conversation to the crowd's motive in seeking him (v. 26). Jesus' use of the noun "sign" (σημεῖον *sēmeion*) invites comparison with the two Cana signs (2:1-11; 4:46-54). The disciples saw the transformation of water into wine as a sign of Jesus' glory; the royal official saw the healing of his son as a sign of Jesus' ability to give life, and as a result they all believed in Jesus (2:11; 4:53). This crowd, Jesus says, can respond to the miracle only in terms of their full stomachs; they do not see it as a sign (cf. 6:30).

6:27. Jesus contrasts the crowd's work for food that perishes (they seek him because they ate their fill) with work for food that "endures for eternal life" (cf. Isa 55:2). The reference to food that perishes links this verse with Jesus' earlier admonition about the leftover bread fragments (6:12; "perish" and "be lost" translate the same Greek verb, ἀπόλλυμι [*apollymi*]) and the perishable manna of Exod 16:18-21. The food that endures to eternal life, much like the living water of 4:14, comes only from the Son of Man. The Son of Man is described as the one on whom "God the Father has set his seal." "To set one's seal" on something is to bestow a formal mark of identification, and v. 27 thus suggests that God marks the Son of Man as God's own. The father language of 6:27 recalls the same type of language in chap. 5 (e.g., 5:20-24, 26). The reference to the Son of Man as the giver of the imperishable food anticipates the themes of 6:35-59 because it places the gift of bread in an explicit christological context.

6:28-31. In v. 28, the crowd gives "work"

(ἐργάζομαι *ergazomai*) a new meaning. Jesus' admonition about laboring to *receive* a gift of imperishable food is transformed by the crowd into a question about their *performance* of works. The grace in Jesus' words disappears. In v. 29, Jesus attempts to return to his original use of "work" by defining it as faith in "him whom God has sent."

Throughout vv. 27-31, Jesus and the crowd use the same words but with very different meanings, another instance of the Johannine literary technique of misunderstanding. The crowd's questions in v. 30 repeat key words from vv. 26-29: "sign" (*sēmeion,* v. 26), "do" (ποιέω *poieō,* v. 28), "see" (εἴδετε *eidete,* v. 26, ἴδωμεν *idōmen,* v. 30), "believe" (πιστεύω *pisteuō,* v. 29), "work" (*ergazomai,* vv. 27-28). They shift the burden of who is to work from themselves (vv. 27-29) to Jesus (v. 30). The crowd's questions imply a contingency: They will do God's work only if Jesus does God's work first and performs a sign.

The crowd's request for a sign from Jesus is jarring. How can they make such a request immediately after the feeding miracle in which they shared (6:14, 26)? Jesus' words in v. 26 are confirmed: The crowd does not recognize the sign that has already been enacted before them. The crowd fleshes out its demands in v. 31 by appealing to their ancestors' experience in the wilderness. Their appeal is couched in the language of Scripture, although it is not an exact citation of any one text (cf. Ps 78:24; Exod 16:4, 15). The fact that the crowd, like their ancestors, have already been fed with miraculous bread underscores the irony of their demand.

6:32. At vv. 12 and 27, Jesus implicitly linked the feeding miracle with the manna story of Exodus 16; in v. 32, he does so explicitly. Jesus reworks four essential elements of v. 31: (1) the donor of the bread is God ("my Father"), not

Moses; (2) the gift of bread occurs in the present ("gives"), not the past; (3) the bread of which Jesus speaks is the *true* bread from heaven"; and (4) Jesus tells the crowd that they, not their ancestors, are the recipients of God's gift of the true bread from heaven ("gives you"). Jesus answers the crowd's demand for a sign (v. 30) by showing them that they have already received one. The contrasting gifts of v. 32, the exodus gift of manna and the present gift of the "true bread from heaven," recall the contrasting gifts of 1:17: "The law indeed was given through Moses; grace and truth came through Jesus Christ."

In a classic study of John 6, Peder Borgen demonstrated how Jesus' reinterpretation of the crowd's quotation of Scripture (6:31) can be most helpfully understood as midrash, a Jewish form of scriptural interpretation. According to Borgen, Jesus' words in v. 32 (and throughout the bread of life discourse, esp. also vv. 49-51, 58) are a deliberate exegesis of Ps 78:24. Borgen's work has become the definitive starting point for understanding the role of exodus imagery in the bread of life discourse.[147]

6:33. Jesus describes the "bread of God" with two predicates: "comes down from heaven" and "gives life to the world." These two predicates repeat what has already been said about Jesus in the Fourth Gospel. In 3:13, for example, the language of descent from heaven describes the activity of the Son of Man (cf. 3:31). In 5:21, Jesus is spoken of as the one who gives life (cf. 5:25-26). The description of the bread of God thus enables the Gospel reader (but not the crowd) to recognize that Jesus is the real subject of the conversation, not the feeding miracle alone. The conversation of 6:25-34, like that of 4:9-15, operates on two levels of meaning simultaneously and contains two understandings of the bread that comes down from heaven and gives life.

6:34. The crowd's request for bread in this verse reveals that they understand only one level of the conversation. The similarity between the crowd's request for bread and the Samaritan woman's request for water in 4:15 is unmistakable and universally recognized.[148] Like the Samaritan woman, the crowd of John 6 has understood one part of Jesus' words—that the bread of which he speaks is better than the bread given to their ancestors—but does not grasp why it is better. The bread of which Jesus speaks is not given "always," but is given once and for all in the very person of Jesus. (See Reflections at John 6:60-71.)

---

147. Peder Borgen, *Bread from Heaven: An Exegetical Study of the Concept of Manna in the Gospel of John and the Writings of Philo*, NovT 10 (Leiden: E.J. Brill, 1965). Borgen sees the role of midrash in John 6 as the key to the structure of the bread of life discourse.

148. E.g., Barrett, *The Gospel According to St. John*, 291; Brown, *The Gospel According to John (I–XII)*, 267; Schnackenburg, *The Gospel According to St. John*, 2:43.

John 6:35-42, Jesus' First Discourse and the Crowd's Response

NIV

35Then Jesus declared, "I am the bread of life. He who comes to me will never go hungry, and he who believes in me will never be thirsty. 36But as I told you, you have seen me and still you do not believe. 37All that the Father gives me will come to me, and whoever comes to me I will never drive away. 38For I have come down from heaven not to do my will but to do the will of him who sent me. 39And this is the will of him who sent me, that I shall lose none of all that he has given me, but raise them up at the last day. 40For my Father's will is that everyone who looks to the Son and believes in him shall have eternal life, and I will raise him up at the last day."

NRSV

35Jesus said to them, "I am the bread of life. Whoever comes to me will never be hungry, and whoever believes in me will never be thirsty. 36But I said to you that you have seen me and yet do not believe. 37Everything that the Father gives me will come to me, and anyone who comes to me I will never drive away; 38for I have come down from heaven, not to do my own will, but the will of him who sent me. 39And this is the will of him who sent me, that I should lose nothing of all that he has given me, but raise it up on the last day. 40This is indeed the will of my Father, that all who see the Son and believe in him may have eternal life; and I will raise them up on the last day."

NIV

[41]At this the Jews began to grumble about him because he said, "I am the bread that came down from heaven." [42]They said, "Is this not Jesus, the son of Joseph, whose father and mother we know? How can he now say, 'I came down from heaven'?"

NRSV

[41]Then the Jews began to complain about him because he said, "I am the bread that came down from heaven." [42]They were saying, "Is not this Jesus, the son of Joseph, whose father and mother we know? How can he now say, 'I have come down from heaven'?"

COMMENTARY

6:35. Jesus' first discourse opens with his bold self-revelation: "I am the bread of life." The bread the crowd requested is already before them and, Jesus proclaims, is the very person of whom they made their request. Verse 35 is the first occurrence of "I am" (ἐγώ εἰμι *ego eimi*) followed by a predicate nominative in the Fourth Gospel. The "I am" sayings form the distinctive core of Jesus' language of self-revelation in the Fourth Gospel (6:35, 48, 51; 8:12; 10:7, 9, 11, 14; 11:25; 14:6; 15:1, 5; see Fig. 10, "The 'I AM' Sayings in John," 602). In these "I am" sayings, Jesus identifies himself with symbols that come from the common fund of ancient Near Eastern religious and human experience----for example, bread (6:35, 48, 51), life (11:14), light (8:12), truth (14:16). Through these common symbols, Jesus declares that people's religious needs and human longings are met in him. These symbols also provide an alternative to the more traditional christological titles used to identify Jesus (e.g., the litany of titles in John 1), and suggest that no one title or tradition can contain the totality of Jesus' identity.[149]

Verse 35*b* expands on the claim of the "I am" saying. To come to Jesus and to believe in him are synonymous here (cf. 7:37), and v. 35*b* thus depicts in metaphorical language the results of faith in Jesus. Like the wine at Cana (2:1-11), the images of hunger and thirst in v. 35*b* have many symbolic overtones. They can be read in the context of the exodus imagery, already evoked in 6:31-32, because in the Israelites' wandering in the wilderness God provided for their hunger and thirst through the gifts of manna (Exodus 16) and water from the rock (Num 20:9-13).[150] The images also can be read through the lens of the Jewish wisdom traditions, where God's revelation is often represented as Israel's food and drink (Prov 9:5; Sir 24:21). Through that lens, the bread of life refers to Jesus' teaching and revelation.[151] Finally, the imagery of eating and drinking will become explicitly eucharistic in vv. 51-58, and it is possible to see eucharistic symbolism anticipated here.[152] The core meaning of the hunger/thirst imagery remains constant across the range of possible symbolisms: What people need for life is available in Jesus.

6:36-40. This passage expands on what it means to come to Jesus and believe. Xavier Leon-Dufour has shown that these five verses follow an ABCB'A' pattern (a chiasm):

A v. 36 seeing and not believing[153]
  B v. 37 Jesus will not drive away
    those who come to him
      C v. 38 I have come down
        from heaven
  B' v. 39 Jesus will lose nothing of all
    that God gives him
A' v. 40 seeing and believing

149. For a form-critical classification of the variety of "I am" sayings in John, see the lengthy footnote in Bultmann, *The Gospel of John,* 225-26n. 3. For ways in which the Fourth Gospel pushes at traditional christological titles, see George W. MacRae, "The Fourth Gospel and *Religionsgeschichte,*" *CBQ* 32 (1970) 13-14.

150. Schnackenburg, *The Gospel According to St. John,* 2:44.
151. Brown, *The Gospel According to John (I-XII),* 272-74.
152. Barrett, *The Gospel According to St. John,* 293.
153. Xavier Leon-Dufour, "Trois chiasmes johanninques," *NTS* 7 (1960-61) 251-53.

Figure 10: The "I AM" Sayings in John

Absolute "I AM" sayings without a predicate nominative:

4:26	Jesus said to her, "I AM, the one who is speaking to you."
6:20	But he said to them, "I AM; do not be afraid."
8:24	"I told you that you would die in your sins, for you will die in your sins unless you believe that I AM."
8:28	"When you have lifted up the Son of Man, then you will realize that I AM, and I do nothing on my own, but I speak these things as the Father instructed me."
8:58	"Very truly, I tell you, before Abraham was, I AM."
13:19	"I tell you this now, before it occurs, so that when it does occur, you may believe that I AM."
18:5, 7	Jesus replied, "I AM." When he said to them, "I am," they stepped back and fell to the ground.

"I AM" sayings with a predicate nominative:

6:35	"I am the bread of life. Whoever comes to me will never be hungry, and whoever believes in me will never be thirsty."
6:51	"I am the living bread that came down from heaven. Whoever eats of this bread will live forever; and the bread that I will give for the life of the world is my flesh."
8:12	"I am the light of the world. Whoever follows me will never walk in darkness but will have the light of life."
9:5	"I am the light of the world."
10:7, 9	"Very truly, I tell you, I am the gate for the sheep."
10:11, 14	"I am the good shepherd."
11:25-6	"I am the resurrection and the life."
14:6	"I am the way, and the truth, and the life."
15:1, 5	"I am the true vine, and my Father is the vinegrower."

The frame of the chiasm is the verbs "seeing" and "believing" (vv. 36, 40). The linkage of seeing and believing is at the heart of the Johannine understanding of faith (e.g., 4:48; 6:30; 20:25, 29). For the Fourth Evangelist, to see rightly is to believe. Verse 36 is a negative judgment on the crowd; their demand for a sign (v. 30) demonstrates that they see without truly seeing and, therefore, do not believe. (The expression "I said to you" in 6:36 does not point to any particular words of Jesus, but functions as a general allusion to themes of Jesus' teachings; see also 6:65.) Verse 40 concludes the passage with a counterbalancing positive statement of what one gains when one sees and believes: eternal life and resurrection on the last day. John 6:40 combines elements of realized eschatology ("eternal life") and more traditional eschatological expectations ("on the last day"). As in 5:24-25, 28-29, it is wrong to limit the Fourth Gospel to one view of eschatology, because at the heart of this Gospel's eschatology is the belief that faith in Jesus is determinative for the believer's present and future.

Verses 37 and 39 both announce that God's redemptive purpose and will is to bring people to Jesus and all that he offers. These two verses restate a theme encountered earlier in the Gospel (3:27)—those who come to Jesus are given to him by God—and further develop that theme by adding that Jesus will neither drive away (v. 37) nor lose (v. 39) anything that God gives him (cf. 10:28; 17:12). The word "all" (or "everything" [πᾶς pas]) in vv. 37 and 39 underscores that God's will for human salvation is inclusive in intent, not exclusive. God's salvific will also has eschatological dimensions, because Jesus' care of all whom God gives him extends to the resurrection "on the last day" (v. 39).

John 6:36-37, and 39-40 present the delicate balance between the human faith response (vv. 36, 40) and God's initiative in "giving" (δίδωμι *didōmi*) people to Jesus (vv. 37, 39). The key to maintaining the balance is expressed in v. 38: Jesus has come down from heaven (cf. 3:13) to make God's will visible and accessible to humankind. Faith in Jesus is impossible without God's initiating will for the world, but human beings retain responsibility for the decision they make in response to God's initiative (cf. 3:16-21). In vv. 36-40, that decision is expressed in terms of either seeing and not believing (v. 36) or seeing and believing (v. 40).

6:41-42. The crowd's response to Jesus' words is one of unbelief. For the first time in chap. 6, the crowd is identified as "the Jews." As Schnackenburg rightly notes, this shift in nomenclature indicates neither a textual seam nor a change of audience within the story.[154] Rather, the Fourth Evangelist intentionally uses the noun "Jews" to symbolize the crowd's resistance to Jesus. This crowd is of a piece with those who resisted Jesus in chap. 5. The verb "grumble" (γογγύζω *gongyzō*; "complain," NRSV) is carefully chosen by the Fourth Evangelist. It is used in the LXX to describe the Israelites' grumbling and complaints in the wilderness (e.g., Exod 15:24; 16:2, 7, 12; Num 11:1;

154. Rudolf Schnackenburg, *The Gospel According to St. John,* 3 vols. (New York: Seabury, 1982) 2:49.

14:2, 27; Ps 105:24-25; cf. 1 Cor 10:10). Verse 41 is another instance of exodus imagery at work in John 6; the crowd demonstrates the same recalcitrance as their forebears. The focus of the crowd's grumbling is Jesus' claim that he is the bread that has come down from heaven (v. 42).

John 6 has the heaviest concentration of language about Jesus' heavenly descent anywhere in the Fourth Gospel (6:33, 38, 41-42, 50-51, 58). Moreover, this descent language does not recur after this chapter. Descent language, introduced in 3:13, seems to be used in chap. 6 to solidify the connection between the manna miracle and Jesus' revelation of himself as the bread of life. The manna of Exodus 16 was bread that came down from heaven, but Jesus' claims of his own heavenly descent, coupled with the "I am" statement of v. 35, show him to be the *true* bread from heaven. Jesus, not the manna, is God's life-giving gift to the world (cf. 3:16; 6:32).

The "Jews" protest Jesus' claim and self-identification on the grounds that they know his parentage (v. 42). Although the Fourth Gospel contains no infancy narrative and makes no direct reference to the birth story traditions, it seems likely that 6:42 is an ironic allusion to those traditions (see also 7:41-42). Jesus is the son of God (1:17); his earthly family holds no key to his identity. The "Jews'" misplaced certitude about Jesus' origins blinds them to his true origins. (See Reflections at 6:60-71.)

John 6:43-52, Jesus' Second Discourse and the Crowd's Response

NIV

43"Stop grumbling among yourselves," Jesus answered. 44"No one can come to me unless the Father who sent me draws him, and I will raise him up at the last day. 45It is written in the Prophets: 'They will all be taught by God.'[a] Everyone who listens to the Father and learns from him comes to me. 46No one has seen the Father except the one who is from God; only he has seen the Father. 47I tell you the truth, he who believes has everlasting life. 48I am

a45 Isaiah 54:13

NRSV

43Jesus answered them, "Do not complain among yourselves. 44No one can come to me unless drawn by the Father who sent me; and I will raise that person up on the last day. 45It is written in the prophets, 'And they shall all be taught by God.' Everyone who has heard and learned from the Father comes to me. 46Not that anyone has seen the Father except the one who is from God; he has seen the Father. 47Very truly, I tell you, whoever believes has eternal life. 48I am the bread of life. 49Your ancestors ate the manna in the

NIV	NRSV
the bread of life. ⁴⁹Your forefathers ate the manna in the desert, yet they died. ⁵⁰But here is the bread that comes down from heaven, which a man may eat and not die. ⁵¹I am the living bread that came down from heaven. If anyone eats of this bread, he will live forever. This bread is my flesh, which I will give for the life of the world." ⁵²Then the Jews began to argue sharply among themselves, "How can this man give us his flesh to eat?"	wilderness, and they died. ⁵⁰This is the bread that comes down from heaven, so that one may eat of it and not die. ⁵¹I am the living bread that came down from heaven. Whoever eats of this bread will live forever; and the bread that I will give for the life of the world is my flesh." 52The Jews then disputed among themselves, saying, "How can this man give us his flesh to eat?"

COMMENTARY

6:43. Jesus now addresses the crowd for a second time. The Evangelist described the crowd's protests in v. 41 as "grumbling" (γογγύζω *gongyzō*), and Jesus refers to them with the same verb in v. 43. This repetition of the verb *gonguzō* establishes continuity between the perspective of the Evangelist and the Johannine Jesus by showing that they both see the crowd the same way.[155] This is another example of the overlap in the Fourth Gospel between the narrative voice of the Fourth Evangelist and Jesus (see Commentary on 3:16-21).

6:44-45. As is the habit of the Johannine Jesus (cf. 3:4-8), he does not directly address the subject of the crowd's grumbling. Instead, Jesus restates the central theological themes of the preceding discourse: God's initiative in drawing people to Jesus and the promise of resurrection on the last day (6:44; cf. 6:37, 39-40). In 6:45*a*, Jesus gives those themes scriptural support by appealing to "the prophets." The OT verse cited in v. 45*a* seems to be a paraphrase of the LXX of Isa 54:13, although its content also recalls Jer 31:33. The citation underscores God's initiative in making faith possible and the universality of God's actions ("they shall *all* be taught . . . "). The emphasis on God's role and the appeal to Scripture build on the list of witnesses developed in 5:31-40: Because Jesus' claims are grounded in God's work and identity, they cannot simply be dismissed as personal idiosyncrasy.[156]

In 6:45*b*, Jesus alludes to another theme of 6:36-40: the faith response. "Hearing" (ἀκούω *akouō*) and "learning" (μανθάνω *manthanō*) in v. 45*b* function analogously to "seeing" and "believing" in vv. 36 and 40; they are metaphors for human receptivity to what God offers. Verse 45*a* states that God's teaching is offered to all, but v. 45*b* suggests that only those who hear and learn what God teaches will come to Jesus. As in 6:36-40, God's initiative toward humanity is held in tension with human decision and response. The emphasis on teaching, hearing, and learning in vv. 44-45 suggests that the reason for the crowd's grumbling lies in their perception, not in Jesus' claims. God has taught them (v. 44), but they do not hear and learn (cf. 5:37).

6:46. Yet even those who learn from the Father do not see the Father. Verse 46 reasserts Jesus' unique relationship to God, recalling the conclusion of the Prologue (1:18). For the Fourth Evangelist, it is through Logos-Jesus alone that the believer has access to God the Father (5:23, 38, 42-43; 14:6-9).

6:47-48. The expression "very truly I tell you" (v. 47) signals the beginning of a new section in the discourse (cf. 5:19, 24-25; 6:32). Yet this section opens with a reprise of familiar Johannine themes: The believer receives eternal life (6:27, 40); Jesus is the bread of life (6:35). These themes provide the theological grounding for what follows. As in 5:19-30, here the Fourth Evangelist advances Jesus' argument by placing what Jesus has said previously in a new context. The interweaving and overlapping of theological themes evident here and throughout Jesus' discourses

155. R. Alan Culpepper, *Anatomy of the Fourth Gospel: A Study in Literary Design* (Philadelphia: Fortress, 1983) 41.
156. C. H. Dodd, *The Interpretation of the Fourth Gospel* (Cambridge: Cambridge University Press, 1953) 340.

help to create a cohesiveness of theological perspective throughout the Fourth Gospel.

6:49. Jesus returns to the crowd's challenge of 6:31 ("Your ancestors ate the manna in the wilderness"). Jesus repeats the crowd's words verbatim, with the important exception that "our ancestors" in v. 31, becomes "your ancestors" in v. 49. This change in pronouns distances Jesus from the crowd and their history. In v. 31, the crowd focused on the gift of the manna, but in v. 49 Jesus looks to the end of the exodus story. The very ancestors who ate the manna died as a result of their grumbling and unbelief (Num 14:21-23; Deut 1:35).

6:50-51. Jesus completes the comparison between the bread of heaven of which the crowd speaks and the bread of heaven of which he speaks. As noted already, Jesus' words in 6:32-33 can be seen as his reinterpretation of the OT scripture cited by the crowd in 6:31. In vv. 50-51, Jesus continues to interpret that citation, this time focusing on the verb "to eat" (ἐσθίω *esthiō*).[157] The manna eaten by the ancestors in the wilderness met the Israelites' immediate needs for sustenance, but did not satisfy ultimate human needs; the ancestors died (v. 49). The bread from heaven of which Jesus speaks, however, does satisfy ultimate human need. Those who eat the true bread from heaven (cf. 6:32) receive the gift of eternal life. The promise that no one will die (v. 50) is analogous to the promise that no one will hunger or thirst again (6:35).[158]

---

157. See Peder Borgen, *Bread from Heaven: An Exegetical Study of the Concept of Manna in the Gospel of John and the Writings of Philo,* NovT 10 (Leiden: E.J. Brill, 1965).

158. See C. K. Barrett, *The Gospel According to St. John,* 2nd ed. (Philadelphia: Westminster, 1978) 296.

In v. 51, Jesus takes his interpretation of the verb "to eat" one step further. He begins by repeating his self-identification as the bread from heaven (v. 51*a*). "Living bread" (a synonym for "bread of life"), like the "living water" of 4:10-14, is life-giving. To underscore this, Jesus then repeats that eating this bread will give eternal life (v. 51*b;* cf. v. 50). He concludes his words with a dramatic twist, however: "The bread that I will give for the life of the world is my flesh" (v. 51*c*).

What does it mean for Jesus to speak of the gift of his flesh for the life of the world? First, the language of v. 51*c* recalls both 1:14 ("and the Word became *flesh*") and 3:16 ("God so loved the *world* that he *gave* his only Son"). Verse 51*c* thus evokes the incarnation, the gift of Jesus' life out of God's love for the world. Second, it is possible to see an allusion to Jesus' death in the language of v. 51*c:* Jesus will give up his life, his flesh, as an expression of the same love manifest in the incarnation (10:17-19; 15:13). Finally, any Christian reader of v. 51, from the Fourth Gospel's first audience to the contemporary church, would hear eucharistic connotations in these words. The eucharistic imagery is not yet fully explicit (that will occur in vv. 52-58), but the direction of the imagery for the Christian reader is clear.

6:52. The "Jews" themselves make the first direct statement about eating Jesus' flesh, as they combine Jesus' words in vv. 51*b* and 51*c* into one statement. What shocks the crowd is that until Jesus' words in v. 51, Jesus' language has focused on the metaphor of the bread of life, but with v. 51 the metaphor shifts. The content of the crowd's protest in v. 52 makes clear that the sticking point is the language about flesh—namely, its use to refer to Jesus himself.

❖   ❖   ❖   ❖

EXCURSUS: JOHN 6:51*c*-58 IN CRITICAL SCHOLARSHIP

The language about "flesh" in v. 51*c* (and its development in vv. 53-58) is also a sticking point for Johannine scholarship and has made vv. 51-58 the most controversial and hotly debated verses in the Fourth Gospel. Bultmann, for example, maintains that the eucharistic references in these verses were imported into the text of the Fourth Gospel by a later editor in order to correct the anti-sacramental tendencies of the Fourth Evangelist.[159] This view of

---

159. Rudolf Bultmann, *The Gospel of John: A Commentary,* trans. G. R. Beasley-Murray, R. W. N. Hoare, and J. K. Riches (Philadelphia: Westminster, 1971) 138, 218-20. He makes the same claims for the references to water in John 3:5 (138).

the Fourth Gospel and sacramental theology is adhered to by other German Protestants. Haenchen, for example, maintains that any inclusion of the sacraments contradicts "the heart of [the Evangelist's] proclamation."[160] In contrast, D. A. Carson, a North American evangelical scholar, rejects the anti-sacramental reading, because he does not view vv. 51-58 as "profoundly sacramentarian at all." Lagrange, a French Catholic scholar, maintains that the allusion to the eucharist is evident in v. 51 and "could not be missed by anyone, except for Protestants who misconstrue the terms."[161] Raymond Brown adopts a middle-of-the-road position. He claims that vv. 51-58 are the sacramental double of the more teaching-revelation oriented bread of life discourse of vv. 35-50.[162] Both vv. 35-50 and vv. 51-58 preserve authentic Johannine traditions, but stem from different periods in the life of the Johannine community. Brown maintains that the two versions of the bread of life discourse complement each other along the lines of word and sacrament in the liturgy of the mass.[163]

The scholarly debate over John 6:51-58 is important to the reader of the Gospel of John because it reveals the presuppositions and assumptions out of which every interpreter works and how those assumptions affect interpretation. Sloyan, a Catholic scholar, has wisely observed about this discussion: "Some applaud the move to the sacramental plateau, others deplore it—but both seem to do so more on the basis of a Catholic or Reformation heritage than of hard data provided by the Fourth Gospel."[164] Schnackenburg, Barrett, and Beasley-Murray are noteworthy as scholars whose interpretation of these verses are guided by the "hard data" of the Fourth Gospel text.[165] A full discussion of Johannine eucharistic theology will follow in the Reflections at John 6:60-71, but a few comments are appropriate here with regard to the place of vv. 51-58 in the overall picture of chap. 6.

First, in order to have a clear vantage point from which to assess the divergent views of 6:51-58, it is important to look again at vv. 51-52 in their full narrative context. The crowd set the topic for Jesus' dialogue and discourse with its evocation of the manna miracle (6:31). In response, Jesus repeatedly stated that the manna was not the true bread from heaven; he is (6:35, 41, 48, 51a). The true bread from heaven gives life to the world, and as early as 6:35, Jesus suggested that eating the bread was the way to receive its gift of life (see also 6:49-50). In v. 51, then, Jesus takes the replacement of the manna with himself to its ultimate conclusion by equating his flesh with the bread of heaven. The "Jews'" protest in v. 52 indicates that they have followed the logic of the discourse, that they understand that Jesus himself now stands in place of the manna their ancestors ate.

It appears, then, that v. 51 does not mark a dramatic break from what preceded, but that the language and imagery of v. 51 are consistent with his preceding words and have been carefully prepared for. Readings that insist on a "faith-alone" or "sacrament-alone" outlook disregard the care with which themes and images overlap throughout the discourse of chap. 6.[166] This is particularly true for vv. 53-58. Key words and themes from 6:25-51 form the heart of this passage (see Commentary). On literary grounds, there is no compelling case for labeling these verses as secondary or even complementary to the "main" discourse of 6:35-51.[167] Rather, the language and style of vv. 53-58 suggest that those verses are an integral part of one continuous discourse.

Second, the scholarly debate about vv. 51-58 largely ignores the narrative structure of chap.

160. Ernst Haenchen, *John,* Hermenia, 2 vols. (Philadelphia: Fortress, 1984) 1:299.

161. D. A. Carson, *The Gospel According to John* (Grand Rapids: Eerdmans, 1991) 277; M.-J. Lagrange, *Évangile selon Saint Jean* (Paris: Gabalda, 1948) 183.

162. Raymond E. Brown, *The Gospel According to John (I–XII),* AB 29 (Garden City, N.Y.: Doubleday, 1966) 285-91.

163. Ibid., 290.

164. Gerard Sloyan, *John* (Atlanta: John Knox, 1988) 72.

165. Schnackenburg, *The Gospel According to St. John,* 2:58-60; Barrett, *The Gospel According to St. John,* 284; George R. Beasley-Murray, *John,* WBC 36 (Waco, Tex.: Word, 1987) 94-96.

166. Sloyan, *John,* 72.

167. See Bultmann, *The Gospel of John,* 234-37, labels them as secondary. Brown, *The Gospel According to John (I–XII),* 286-87, regards them as complementary.

6. Verse 51 does not mark the beginning of a new section; it is the conclusion of the second section of the bread of life discourse and is tightly linked to the "Jews' " protest in v. 52. As noted already, the "Jews' " protests serve as the pivot for each of the subsections of the discourse (6:35-42, 43-52, 53-59). Each section concludes with a statement by Jesus and the protest that it evokes from the Jews, so that the next section of the discourse builds on both the claim and the protest.[168] John 6:51-58 is no exception. Jesus' words in v. 51 evoke the "Jews' " protest (6:52), and beginning in v. 53 Jesus addresses the heart of their protest. John 6:51-52 thus prepare for the eucharistic language of 6:53-58. When vv. 51-58 are discussed as if they were an independent theological treatise on the eucharist, the narrative integrity of chap. 6 is destroyed, and an interpreter's sense of what constitutes theological coherence leads to explanations that appeal to independent traditions.

Third, there is a circular logic to questioning (or even rejecting) the eucharistic imagery of vv. 53-58 on the grounds that the Fourth Gospel contains no account of the institution of the eucharist comparable to that found in the Synoptics (Matt 26:26-29; Mark 14:22-25; Luke 22:14-23). It is possible that vv. 53-58 are the "institution text" in John, but presented in Johannine, not synoptic, categories. (See Commentary on 6:53-59 and Reflections at 6:60-71.)

168. Barrett, *The Gospel According to St. John*, 296.

❖   ❖   ❖   ❖

John 6:53-59, Jesus' Third Discourse

[53]Jesus said to them, "I tell you the truth, unless you eat the flesh of the Son of Man and drink his blood, you have no life in you. [54]Whoever eats my flesh and drinks my blood has eternal life, and I will raise him up at the last day. [55]For my flesh is real food and my blood is real drink. [56]Whoever eats my flesh and drinks my blood remains in me, and I in him. [57]Just as the living Father sent me and I live because of the Father, so the one who feeds on me will live because of me. [58]This is the bread that came down from heaven. Your forefathers ate manna and died, but he who feeds on this bread will live forever." [59]He said this while teaching in the synagogue in Capernaum.

[53]So Jesus said to them, "Very truly, I tell you, unless you eat the flesh of the Son of Man and drink his blood, you have no life in you. [54]Those who eat my flesh and drink my blood have eternal life, and I will raise them up on the last day; [55]for my flesh is true food and my blood is true drink. [56]Those who eat my flesh and drink my blood abide in me, and I in them. [57]Just as the living Father sent me, and I live because of the Father, so whoever eats me will live because of me. [58]This is the bread that came down from heaven, not like that which your ancestors ate, and they died. But the one who eats this bread will live forever." [59]He said these things while he was teaching in the synagogue at Capernaum.

COMMENTARY

6:53. The words "very truly I tell you" in v. 53 again mark the beginning of a new section. As in the earlier sections of the discourse (6:35-42, 43-51), this new section builds on what Jesus has said

before. "Eat of this bread" becomes the more explicit "eat the flesh of the Son of Man and drink his blood" in v. 53, and the emphasis of v. 53 is on what happens if one does not eat ("You have no life in you"). In Hebrew, the double formula "flesh and blood" emphasizes the corporeality of human existence,[169] and its use here is thus an affirmation of the incarnation of the Son of Man. For the Christian reader, however, the double formula has unmistakable eucharistic associations.

Verse 53 also builds on another of Jesus' earlier statements. It can be read as the fulfillment of the promise made in 6:27. The flesh and blood of the Son of Man are the food that endures for eternal life. The Son of Man is the one who has descended from heaven to give his life for the salvation of the world (3:13, 16). The gift of his flesh and blood belongs to that saving work; it is the food that gives eternal life.

The syntax of v. 53 ("unless . . .") makes clear that eating the flesh and drinking the blood of the Son of Man is a condition for receiving the gift of life. That Jesus' words focus on life should not surprise the reader; Jesus as the source of life has been a central theme of the first six chapters of the Gospel. What is new is the explicit linkage of participation in the eucharist to this gift of life. The strong emphasis on the eucharist reflects a shift in the primary audience to whom the Fourth Evangelist understands these words of Jesus to be addressed. The primary audience is no longer the audience in the story (the Jewish crowd), but the readers in John's own time. Such a shift is a regular part of the literary strategy of Fourth Evangelist (3:31-36; 6:60-71; 9:18-23). The Fourth Gospel narrative frequently plays itself out on a "two-level stage," so that the events in Jesus' life and the events in the life of the Evangelist's community are presented simultaneously.[170]

The insistence in v. 53 on both the fullness of the incarnation and the participation in the eucharist may be the Evangelist's attempt to counter developing docetic or gnostic tendencies within his community that wanted to deny the bodily aspects of Christ and of Christian experience. In that regard, it is noteworthy that nowhere in vv. 53-59 are the eucharistic elements of bread and wine mentioned. The Fourth Evangelist's focus remains on the flesh and blood of Jesus, not their sacramental representations, in order to under-

score Jesus' gift of his whole self, which is enacted in the eucharist (cf. 6:51).

6:54-55. Verse 54 is a positive statement of the condition expressed negatively in v. 53. The third-person Son of Man language gives way to first-person pronouns. Eating the flesh and blood of Jesus leads to the gift of eternal life and the promise of resurrection on the last day, complementary eschatological promises that run throughout the bread of life discourse (6:39-40, 44, 50-51). A comparison of vv. 40 and 54 shows that eating Jesus' flesh and drinking his blood parallels seeing the Son and believing in him. Participation in the eucharist and the faith decision are parallel in the Fourth Gospel, not either/or acts. Verse 55 states succinctly why Jesus' flesh and blood are the source of life. Jesus' flesh and blood thus fulfill the promise in 6:35 of food and drink that will end hunger and thirst.

6:56-57. These verses provide important clues to the distinctive Johannine eucharistic theology. Participation in the eucharist draws the believer into a relationship with Jesus. At the heart of v. 56 is the verb "to abide" (μένω *menō*). This verb expresses the interrelationship of Jesus and the believer that is the source of the believer's life (cf. 15.4). Yet the interrelationship of Jesus and the believer is actually an extension of the interrelationship of God and Jesus (6:57). Verse 57*a* builds on the claims of 5:21, 26-27: God shares God's life with Jesus. The one who eats Jesus (note the substitution in v. 57*b* of "me" for flesh and blood) receives life because that person shares in the life-giving relationship of God and Jesus (cf. 1:4). Johannine eucharistic theology is one of relationship and presence (see Reflections).

6:58. This verse serves as the conclusion to the whole bread of life discourse, tying together themes that have run throughout the discourse (e.g., 6:31, 37, 49-51*b*) with its final restatement of the life one receives from eating the bread from heaven. Verse 59 provides the Evangelist's formal note of conclusion. The reference to Capernaum corresponds to 6:24, although the synagogue was not referred to earlier. Jesus spoke the bread of life discourse, a christocentric reinterpretation of the manna story, in the traditional Jewish site of teaching and learning (cf. 6:45), the synagogue, the locus of "his own." (See Reflections at 6:60-71.)

169. Ibid., 299.
170. The clearest presentation of this Johannine characteristic is provided by J. Louis Martyn, *History and Theology in the Fourth Gospel* (Nashville: Abingdon, 1968; 2nd ed., 1979).

John 6:60-71, Conclusion: Jesus and His Disciples

NIV

⁶⁰On hearing it, many of his disciples said, "This is a hard teaching. Who can accept it?"

⁶¹Aware that his disciples were grumbling about this, Jesus said to them, "Does this offend you? ⁶²What if you see the Son of Man ascend to where he was before! ⁶³The Spirit gives life; the flesh counts for nothing. The words I have spoken to you are spirit*a* and they are life. ⁶⁴Yet there are some of you who do not believe." For Jesus had known from the beginning which of them did not believe and who would betray him. ⁶⁵He went on to say, "This is why I told you that no one can come to me unless the Father has enabled him."

⁶⁶From this time many of his disciples turned back and no longer followed him.

⁶⁷"You do not want to leave too, do you?" Jesus asked the Twelve.

⁶⁸Simon Peter answered him, "Lord, to whom shall we go? You have the words of eternal life. ⁶⁹We believe and know that you are the Holy One of God."

⁷⁰Then Jesus replied, "Have I not chosen you, the Twelve? Yet one of you is a devil!" ⁷¹(He meant Judas, the son of Simon Iscariot, who, though one of the Twelve, was later to betray him.)

a63 Or Spirit

NRSV

60When many of his disciples heard it, they said, "This teaching is difficult; who can accept it?" ⁶¹But Jesus, being aware that his disciples were complaining about it, said to them, "Does this offend you? ⁶²Then what if you were to see the Son of Man ascending to where he was before? ⁶³It is the spirit that gives life; the flesh is useless. The words that I have spoken to you are spirit and life. ⁶⁴But among you there are some who do not believe." For Jesus knew from the first who were the ones that did not believe, and who was the one that would betray him. ⁶⁵And he said, "For this reason I have told you that no one can come to me unless it is granted by the Father."

66Because of this many of his disciples turned back and no longer went about with him. ⁶⁷So Jesus asked the twelve, "Do you also wish to go away?" ⁶⁸Simon Peter answered him, "Lord, to whom can we go? You have the words of eternal life. ⁶⁹We have come to believe and know that you are the Holy One of God."*a* ⁷⁰Jesus answered them, "Did I not choose you, the twelve? Yet one of you is a devil." ⁷¹He was speaking of Judas son of Simon Iscariot,*b* for he, though one of the twelve, was going to betray him.

a Other ancient authorities read the Christ, the Son of the living God
b Other ancient authorities read Judas Iscariot son of Simon; others, Judas son of Simon from Karyot (Kerioth)

COMMENTARY

John 6:60-71 follows the same pattern as 6:25-59: The disciples protest (6:60; cf. 6:41-42, 52), and Jesus responds. Verses 60-71 can be subdivided into two units: (1) vv. 60-65, which focus on doubt and rejection among Jesus' disciples, and (2) vv. 66-71, which focus more narrowly on the faith response of the Twelve. The central theme of John 6:60-71 is the range of responses to Jesus among his followers: "grumbling" (v. 61), disbelief (v. 64), rejection (v. 66), confession of faith (vv. 68-69), and betrayal (vv. 64, 71). These verses form a poignant conclusion to chap. 6. In the face

of Jesus' most explicit and far-reaching offer of himself and the gift of life to those who believe, even many among his followers turn away.

6:60-62. The similarity between his disciples' protest and those of the crowd is established by the repetition of the verb "to grumble" (γογγύζω *gongyzō*; v. 61). Jesus' awareness of the disciples' grumbling is another example of his insight into human nature (cf. 1:47-48; 2:23-25). He issues a challenge to the disciples' doubt and resistance (vv. 61*b*-62). Jesus states the condition in v. 62 ("What if . . . ?") without giving its conclusion.

Will the ascension of the Son of Man increase the offense of Jesus' teachings or make sense of what offends the disciples now? Language about the ascent of the Son of Man is synonymous with language about Jesus' return to God (e.g., 3:13; 20:17) and thus points to the entire Easter event: death, resurrection, and ascension. Verse 62 also evokes the preexistence of the Son of Man (cf. 1:1-2, 18; 8:58) and Jesus' heavenly descent (3:13; 6:38, 51). Verse 62 thus suggests that the offense of Jesus' teaching must be contextualized in the sweep of his life, from incarnation to crucifixion and resurrection. The challenge of v. 62 is intentionally open-ended, because each person will make his or her own decision about the significance of this constellation of events.

John 1:51 offers a helpful analogue to 6:62. In both verses, the ascent of the Son of Man becomes the proving ground for the disciples' faith. In both verses, Jesus moves the disciples' immediate response, whether faith (1:50) or doubt (6:60), into a broader sphere. The ascent of the Son of Man—his death, resurrection, and ascension—transcends anything the disciples have yet experienced.

6:63. Jesus offers a new teaching. The contrast between spirit and flesh in this verse is taken by many scholars as the key to interpreting vv. 60-71 and the relationship of those verses to the rest of the chapter. Scholars who see the eucharistic language of vv. 51-58 as a secondary part of the discourse use the words of v. 63 ("the flesh is useless") to buttress their position.[171] (See Excursus "John 6:51c-58 in Critical Scholarship," 605-7.) How, they argue, could Jesus advocate giving and eating his flesh in vv. 51-58 and reject the value of flesh here? Verses 51-58 thus cannot belong to the core of Jesus' teaching in chap. 6, and the disciples in 6:60-71 can only be understood as protesting Jesus' words in 6:35-50, not those in 6:51-58.

Such a reading of the spirit/flesh contrast in v. 63, however, seems to misread both v. 63 and the eucharistic language of vv. 51-58. As Barrett correctly points out, Jesus' words about flesh in v. 63 make little sense if one rejects vv. 51c-58 as secondary, because the word "flesh" (σάρξ sarx) appears only in that section of the discourse

(6:51-56).[172] Why would Jesus correct a misperception about the significance of "flesh" if he had not taught about flesh previously? Therefore, it seems more probable that the teaching to which many of the disciples take offense (vv. 60-61a), and which Jesus addresses in v. 63, is indeed the teaching about eating Jesus' flesh.

The protesting disciples (like the "Jews" of v. 52) do not rightly perceive the flesh of which Jesus speaks. They see only Jesus' flesh; they do not see "the Word become flesh" (1:14). Jesus' words in v. 63 expose this misperception. The flesh as flesh *is* useless; only the Spirit gives life to the flesh, and the Spirit dwells in the Son of Man (cf. 1:33) and in the words that Jesus speaks.[173] Verse 63 recalls 1:13 and 3:4-8. A new life born of flesh and spirit is possible to those who believe, but if one limits one's understanding of life to one's preconceptions of what is possible in the flesh, one will receive nothing. Spirit and flesh must be held together; this is the heart of the incarnation.

John 6:63 thus continues the Johannine interpretation of the eucharist, begun in 6:51-58. Just as vv. 53-58 emphasize Jesus' flesh and blood in order to counteract developing docetic tendencies, so also v. 63 can be seen as counteracting another growing misperception in the Christian community: It counters the notion that the eucharist as a rite in and of itself has almost magical qualities, that the eucharistic elements themselves contain the key to eternal life. (Such an understanding of the eucharist may lie behind Ignatius's words: "breaking one loaf, which is the medicine of immortality, the antidote which results not in dying but in living forever in Jesus Christ.")[174] John 6:63 affirms that the flesh has salvific power only because it is inseparably bound to the life-giving, Spirit-filled words of Jesus. Jesus is not asking his disciples to eat flesh and drink blood; he is asking them to eat the Spirit-filled flesh and blood of the Son of Man (cf. 6:27).

6:64-65. Jesus knows that his words will not be believed by all of his disciples (v. 64). The foreknowledge of unbelief and betrayal leads Jesus to address again a theological theme that has run throughout chap. 6: the tension between divine

171. E.g., Bultmann, *The Gospel of John,* 287; Brown, *The Gospel According to John (I–XII),* 302-3.

172. Barrett, *The Gospel According to St. John,* 302.
173. Beasley-Murray, *John,* 96.
174. E.g., Ignatius *Ephesians* 20.2.

initiative and human choice (v. 65). Verse 65 reiterates the claim of 6:37, 39, 44: Access to Jesus is impossible without God's initiating act.

6:66-67. In v. 66, the rejection that Jesus foresaw takes place. That desertion is the direct catalyst for Jesus' question to the Twelve in v. 67 ("So Jesus asked. . . . " The NIV mutes this important connection). Verse 66 thus has a double function: to conclude the challenge to the disciples in vv. 60-65 and to introduce a new challenge for the Twelve. In v. 67, Jesus presents the Twelve with a choice. The relationship between divine initiative and human choice again comes to the fore (cf. v. 65). The Twelve must choose whether to accept or reject the offer God has made to them in Jesus.[175]

Verse 67 is the first time the expression "the twelve" (οἱ δώδεκα *hoi dōdeka*) occurs in the Fourth Gospel. That expression occurs infrequently in John—only in this passage (vv. 67, 70-71) and in one of the resurrection stories (20:24). The Fourth Evangelist has narrated no call of the Twelve (see 1:35-51), and he introduces the expression with no explanation. It seems likely that he assumes the expression's familiarity to his readers from other traditions about Jesus. Indeed, the reference to the Twelve and the prominent role of Peter in John 6:66-71 suggest that the Fourth Evangelist draws on traditions similar to those drawn on by the synoptic Gospels. John 6:67-71 is frequently referred to by scholars as the Johannine version of Peter's confession at Caesarea Philippi (Matt 16:13-20; Mark 8:27-33; cf. the related confession at Luke 9:18-20). The Fourth Evangelist's use of this tradition here can be compared to his use of Petrine traditions in 1:42-44.

175. Robert Kysar, *John,* Augsburg Commentary of the New Testament (Minneapolis: Augsburg, 1986) 112.

6:68-69. Simon Peter, given the role of spokesman for the Twelve, chooses to accept what is offered in Jesus (vv. 68-69). His words in v. 68 acknowledge that he has heard and learned (cf. 6:45) from the bread of life discourse, because he knows that Jesus has "words of eternal life" (cf. 6:63; see also 6:40, 47, 51, 54, 58). Verse 69 has the form of a confession of faith: "We have come to believe and know. . . . " "Believe" (πιστεύω *pisteuō*) and "know" (γινώσκω *ginōskō*) function as synonyms here, as they do in many places in the Fourth Gospel (e.g., 10:38; 14:7; 16:30). The use of both verbs intensifies Peter's confession. The christological title "the Holy One of God" occurs only here in the Fourth Gospel. John 10:36 speaks of Jesus as "the one whom the Father has sanctified" ("made holy" [ἡγίασεν *hēgiasen*]) and describes God's act of setting Jesus apart as God's emissary. Peter's confession of Jesus here shares that meaning (cf. 3:34; 4:34; 5:24, 30, 36, 38; 6:38).

6:70-71. Instead of embracing Peter's confession (cf. Mark 8:30, 33), Jesus raises again the question of election and choice. This time it is Jesus' act of election, not God's, on which Jesus focuses (v. 70). The verb "to elect" (ἐκλέγομαι *eklegomai*) refers exclusively to Jesus' selection of his followers in John (6:70; 13:18; 15:16, 19). Even election into the select group of the Twelve is no guarantee of a faith response, because one member of the Twelve is a devil. To speak of Judas (v. 71) as a devil (cf. 13:2, 27) means that Judas is drawn more to evil than to God (3:19-21). By alluding to the devil among the Twelve, Jesus warns Peter (and the reader) that a confession of faith will always be tested and, therefore, is always in jeopardy. Even among the Twelve, those who share in Peter's confession of v. 69 ("we believe"), the drama of belief and unbelief is acted out. Election is no substitute for the decision of faith.

REFLECTIONS

A basic theological tenet of the Fourth Gospel is that a sign alone is not an adequate ground for faith; the believer must come to understand the theological and christological truths revealed in that sign. (See Reflections on 4:46-54.) The structure of John 6 is governed by that theological conviction; the two miracles of 6:1-21 are followed by a dialogue and discourse (6:25-71) that give guidance in the proper interpretation of the "sign" (6:26, 30). The interpreter of John 6:25-71 thus does well to take his or her first interpretive clue from the Fourth Evangelist himself and read the dialogue and the bread of life discourse as a continuation of and commentary on the miracles of 6:1-21.

The length of John 6 makes handling this chapter as a totality a challenge. For example, vv. 1-69 spread over five Sundays in Year B in the Revised Common Lectionary (Propers 12-16). The preacher's task is to remember that each of the five lessons is only a piece of the whole, not an individual unit with a self-contained meaning.

The narrative strategy of the Fourth Evangelist works to remind the reader how tightly wedded the discourse of John 6 is to its narrative setting. For example, the crowd, so pivotal in vv. 25-34, does not disappear once the discourse begins, but twice interrupts Jesus' words (vv. 41-42, 52). These interruptions and Jesus' responses to them remind the reader that Jesus does not speak in a vacuum. His words belong to a particular occasion. He speaks to the same people who ate his miraculous gift of bread and fish, and his words offer them an interpretation of that miracle. "Bread" is thus not a disembodied concept in John 6, but is a concrete metaphor that springs from the miraculous feeding of 6:1-15 and the manna miracle of Exodus 16.

This interdependence of form and content in John 6 reflects the teachings that are at the heart of the discourse: Flesh and spirit belong together, and only when they are held together is life possible. On the one hand, without the Spirit, "the flesh is useless" (6:63), and the miraculous feeding of the five thousand will end the same way the manna miracle ended—with the death of those who ate the bread (6:49, 59a). The miraculous feeding is only that—a miraculous feeding—without the life-giving words of Jesus (6:63, 68). Those words enable people who eat the bread to see and believe (6:40) and hence live (6:51, 57-58). On the other hand, if the life-giving words of Jesus are separated from the fleshly reality of the miracle that preceded them, there is also no life. One must eat the bread, not simply respond to the teachings, in order to live (6:53, 58b). The miraculous gift of bread, both in the feeding of the five thousand and in Jesus' gift of his flesh for the life of the world, is as essential to John 6 as the teachings contained in it. The union between miracle and discourse, between sign and word is the narrative representation of the union of human and divine, flesh and spirit in the incarnation.

Nowhere is the maintenance of this union more critical (and, to many interpreters, more problematic) than in the interpretation of the eucharistic images and theology in John 6. As noted in the Commentary and Excursus sections above, many commentators find the presence of eucharistic images in John 6 at best tangential to the heart of the bread of life discourse, at worst antithetical to it. If, however, John 6:25-71 is read first of all as an essential part of the narrative that begins in 6:1-21 and not as an independent piece of theological reflection, then the eucharistic images concentrated in 6:51-58 can find their place in the full sweep of the bread of life discourse. The interpreter must begin with the miraculous feeding and Jesus' revelation of himself as the bread of heaven, not with the synoptic Gospels and an imported notion of normative eucharistic theology and practice in the early church. If interpreters of John 6 can free themselves from preconceptions about how a Gospel writer "should" present the eucharist, they will enjoy a fuller understanding of the bread of life discourse and of the eucharist.

To this end, it is essential that the interpreter honor the many levels of meaning in the bread metaphor in John 6. As noted throughout the Commentary on 6:25-71, the phrase "bread from heaven" is intentionally evocative of another bread from heaven: the manna with which the wandering Israelites were fed in the wilderness. The feeding miracle itself contains hints of this association (e.g., 6:12), and the dialogue and discourse make the association explicit (6:32-33, 48-50, 58). One level of meaning of the bread metaphor, then, links the bread of life discourse with the events of the exodus, both God's faithfulness in feeding Israel and the Israelites' recalcitrant grumbling. A second level of meaning builds on the language and images of Second Isaiah (e.g., Isa 50:10-11; 55:1-2). The bread from heaven represents the Word of God, which gives and sustains life (6:35, 63). In typical Johannine fashion, the very expression "from heaven" suggests these two levels of meaning, because it can mean both "come down from heaven" and "from God." The bread from heaven metaphor thus evokes two different gifts from God: the miraculous gift of actual food and the gift of God's Word.

When Jesus says, "I am the bread of life," these images of bread drawn from the scriptural tradition are transformed. The traditional metaphors are redefined by the *very person* of Jesus. Metaphors that pointed to God in the OT now point to God through Jesus. This focusing of the rich OT symbols on the person of Jesus is the context in which the eucharistic images are to be read and, indeed, out of which they grow.

For the Fourth Evangelist, the eucharistic images of 6:51-58 are the final stage in a progression of images that began with the manna in the wilderness. When Jesus says that his flesh is the "living bread that came down from heaven" (6:51), he is saying that he himself is the food that gives life, not the manna or the multiplied loaves. And it is through eating Jesus' flesh and drinking his blood, through the eucharist, that the believer partakes of this food.

To say that the bread metaphor in John 6 comes finally to represent Jesus' flesh and hence the eucharist does not mean that the exodus symbolism or the Word of God symbolism is voided. On the contrary, the whole range of symbolisms for bread remains in play throughout John 6. Jesus is the bread that people must eat to have life (6:53-56), and Jesus is also the bread to whom people must listen in order to have life (6:45, 63, 68). As has been noted repeatedly in this commentary, the Fourth Gospel is characterized by a linguistic richness and depth that defies reduction to a single meaning. The symbolic richness of the wine at Cana (2:1-11), Jesus' offer of new life to Nicodemus (3:1-15), and the living water (4:10-15) demonstrates that the Fourth Evangelist intends to expand, not restrict, the possibilities of life offered by Jesus. Jesus is the definitive point of access to God for the Fourth Evangelist (14:6), but there is no single approach to Jesus. Jesus can be met as the Holy One of God (6:69) and as the bread of life (6:35); as the presence of God who walks upon the water (6:20) and as the only one who has ever seen God (6:46).

The richness of the bread metaphor in John 6, then, is essential to the presentation of the eucharist. The manna in the wilderness, the Word of God that gives life, the multiplication of the loaves are all present when the believer eats Jesus' flesh and drinks his blood. One does not have to choose among the symbols and images, because all are at play in the eucharist for the Fourth Evangelist. The symbolic richness of the eucharist is one of the reasons why the eucharistic images are found in John 6 and not in the passion narrative (cf. Matt 26:26-29; Mark 14:22-25; Luke 22:14-23). The eucharist does not belong exclusively to Jesus' death for the Fourth Evangelist, but belongs to all of Jesus' life. Verse 51c does carry the association with Jesus' death, but the believer's participation in the eucharist marks more than Jesus' gift of his life in death. It marks the believer's full participation in all of Jesus' life and gifts. (See Commentary on John 13:1-20).

The sense of participation is conveyed in 6:56-57. When the believer eats Jesus' flesh and drinks his blood, the believer and Jesus abide together. Participation in the eucharist places the believer in relationship with Jesus, and the believer receives life through Jesus' abiding presence. The Fourth Evangelist does not draw a line of demarcation between participation in the eucharist and the faith response that many commentators, both Catholic and Protestant, seem to insist that he draw. Rather, what is definitional for faith in the Fourth Gospel is also definitional for the eucharist: the centrality of Jesus in the believer's life and the believer's relationship with Jesus.

Johannine eucharistic theology presents several challenges to the eucharistic theology and practices of many churches today. It challenges those Protestant churches that understand the eucharist primarily as a commemoration of Jesus' death or a meal of community fellowship. For the Fourth Evangelist, the eucharist is a meal of Jesus' presence, not primarily—if at all—a meal of remembrance. The eucharist is feeding on and being fed by *Jesus*. The "fellowship" derives first from the mutual indwelling of Jesus and the believer, and community is formed from those who share in Jesus' presence.

Johannine eucharistic theology also poses a challenge to those churches, Catholic and some

Protestant, that elevate the role of the person who presides at the eucharist. By placing his eucharistic theology in the context of the bread of life discourse rather than an institution narrative as found in the Synoptics, the Fourth Evangelist emphasizes the personal dimension of the sacrament rather than the institutionalization and institutional control of the sacrament. The eucharist is not Jesus' gift to an elite group of twelve who then mediate that gift to others; the eucharist is Jesus' direct gift to those who believe. The believer's participation in the eucharist thus revolves around Jesus' gift and the believer's relationship to Jesus, not on the mediation of the church.

The immediacy of Jesus' gift of the eucharist is anticipated in the feeding miracle (6:1-15). In 6:11, Jesus, not his disciples, distributes the bread and fish to the multitudes. In each of the Synoptic accounts, the disciples are responsible for the distribution of the food (Matt 14:19; Mark 6:41; Luke 9:16). The Johannine version thus places the emphasis on Jesus' own feeding of those who are hungry.

Everything in the Fourth Gospel, including the eucharist, is subsumed in the person of Jesus. This Gospel contains no traditional institution narrative, because such a narrative runs counter to the Fourth Evangelist's eucharistic theology. The Fourth Evangelist is not anti-sacramental. What he is against, it seems, is institutionalization of the sacraments, and commentators confuse that with an anti-sacramental attitude. The Fourth Evangelist places great theological value on the eucharist; it belongs to Jesus' gift of life (6:54-55). The eucharist, however, belongs to the believer, not to the church. It is for Jesus alone to give. All of Jesus' life is given to the believer when he or she eats Jesus' flesh and drinks his blood.

What does Johannine eucharistic theology offer the contemporary church? First, it provides a fresh perspective on ecumenical debates about who is welcome at the table. No church body can claim exclusive rights to Jesus' flesh and blood, because they are Jesus' alone to give. Second, the Johannine emphasis on the relationship between Jesus and the believer in the eucharist calls the church to ponder the role of the ordained clergy with respect to the eucharist. Johannine eucharistic theology seems to suggest that no one other than Jesus can control access to the eucharistic meal. Clergy may be given responsibility to ensure that believers are provided with opportunities to participate in the eucharist, but it is Jesus' presence, not clergy privilege, that governs the eucharist. Johannine eucharistic theology may provide a healthy vantage point from which to ask questions about power and access in the eucharistic life of many churches. Finally, the Fourth Evangelist's eucharistic theology may reinvigorate static divisions between word and sacrament in the life of the church. For the Fourth Evangelist, the eucharist belongs to and is inseparable from the revelation of God in Jesus. At the heart of both word and sacrament is the urgency for people to see God in Jesus and believe.

JOHN 7:1–8:59, CONFLICT IN JERUSALEM

OVERVIEW

John 7–8 take place in Jerusalem at the Feast of Tabernacles. These two chapters do not have the literary cohesiveness of some other Johannine texts (e.g., John 9:1-41) because they are composed of fragments of Jesus traditions that the Fourth Evangelist has brought together to create a picture of the increasing conflict between Jesus and his opponents. John 7–8 can be outlined loosely as follows:

[7:53–8:11 A Narrative of Conflict]
8:12-30   Words of Conflict: Jesus' Teaching and Response
8:31-59   Debate Between Jesus and His Jewish Opponents

In 7:1-52, the conflict between Jesus and his Jewish opponents is played out in a sequence of short scenes in which Jesus presses his case with the crowds at center stage (e.g., 7:25-31), while the Jewish leadership plots against him in the wings (7:32, 45-52).[176] In chap. 8, the mini-dramas eventually converge into one drama, as Jesus and his opponents engage in direct accusations and recriminations (8:31-59). The action in these chapters revolves around four central themes: (1) Jesus' identity as the one sent from God (7:16, 28-29, 33; 8:16, 18, 29, 42); (2) faithful interpretation of Jewish tradition (7:22-23, 47-52; 8:39-41, 52-58); (3) the faith decision Jesus' presence in the world demands and the division it causes (7:31, 40-44; 8:30-33,

176. C. H. Dodd, *The Interpretation of the Fourth Gospel* (Cambridge: Cambridge University Press, 1953) 347.

42-43, 47); and (4) the increasing threat to Jesus' life (7:1, 13, 19, 25, 30, 32, 44; 8:37, 40, 59).

The relationship of 7:53–8:11 to John 7 and 8 warrants special mention. This passage does not appear in the earliest Greek manuscripts of John, suggesting that the story did not belong originally to this Gospel. The origins of the Jesus tradition preserved in this passage are unclear, as is how it ended up in the Gospel of John. Given the uncertainty about the history of John 7:53–8:11, both the NIV and the NRSV print this text in brackets and inform the reader of its complicated textual history. To some extent, these verses disrupt the movement of John 7–8; the pattern of Jesus' teaching intermingled with the crowd's response recurs in 8:12 after the interruption of 7:53–8:11 (see the outline above). Yet one can also identify a logic to this particular placement of the tradition. John 7:53–8:11 contains a story that illustrates the confrontation and conflict between Jesus and the Jewish authorities that is at the heart of John 7–8, and this thematic connection may have led a later scribe to add the story after John 7:52 (see Commentary on this text below).

John 7:1-13, Jesus Goes to Jerusalem

NIV

7 After this, Jesus went around in Galilee, purposely staying away from Judea because the Jews there were waiting to take his life. ²But when the Jewish Feast of Tabernacles was near, ³Jesus' brothers said to him, "You ought to leave here and go to Judea, so that your disciples may see the miracles you do. ⁴No one who wants to become a public figure acts in secret. Since you are doing these things, show yourself to the world." ⁵For even his own brothers did not believe in him.

⁶Therefore Jesus told them, "The right time for me has not yet come; for you any time is right. ⁷The world cannot hate you, but it hates me because I testify that what it does is evil. ⁸You go to the Feast. I am not yet*a* going up to this Feast, because for me the right time has not yet come." ⁹Having said this, he stayed in Galilee.

a8 Some early manuscripts do not have yet.

NRSV

7 After this Jesus went about in Galilee. He did not wish*a* to go about in Judea because the Jews were looking for an opportunity to kill him. ²Now the Jewish festival of Booths*b* was near. ³So his brothers said to him, "Leave here and go to Judea so that your disciples also may see the works you are doing; ⁴for no one who wants*c* to be widely known acts in secret. If you do these things, show yourself to the world." ⁵(For not even his brothers believed in him.) ⁶Jesus said to them, "My time has not yet come, but your time is always here. ⁷The world cannot hate you, but it hates me because I testify against it that its works are evil. ⁸Go to the festival yourselves. I am not*d* going to this festival, for my time has not yet fully come." ⁹After saying this, he remained in Galilee.

a Other ancient authorities read was not at liberty   *b Or Tabernacles*   *c Other ancient authorities read* wants it   *d Other ancient authorities add* yet

NIV

¹⁰However, after his brothers had left for the Feast, he went also, not publicly, but in secret. ¹¹Now at the Feast the Jews were watching for him and asking, "Where is that man?"

¹²Among the crowds there was widespread whispering about him. Some said, "He is a good man."

Others replied, "No, he deceives the people." ¹³But no one would say anything publicly about him for fear of the Jews.

NRSV

10But after his brothers had gone to the festival, then he also went, not publicly but as it were*a* in secret. ¹¹The Jews were looking for him at the festival and saying, "Where is he?" ¹²And there was considerable complaining about him among the crowds. While some were saying, "He is a good man," others were saying, "No, he is deceiving the crowd." ¹³Yet no one would speak openly about him for fear of the Jews.

a Other ancient authorities lack *as it were*

COMMENTARY

John 7:1-13 can be subdivided into two sections: (1) vv. 1-10, Jesus and his brothers; and (2) vv. 11-13, initial response to Jesus in Jerusalem.

7:1-10. 7:1. John 7:1 links chap. 7 with chaps. 5–6. Verse 1*a* locates Jesus in Galilee, the site of John 6, and v. 1*b* points back to John 5 by reminding the reader why Judea is an inhospitable and dangerous place for Jesus. The verbal similarity between 7:1 and 5:18 is taken by some as evidence of the displacement of chaps. 5–6 (see the Overview to John 6), but displacement theories seem unnecessary here. One of the themes of this central section of the Fourth Gospel (chaps. 5–10) is the increasing hostility to Jesus. John 7:1 reminds the reader of the threat to Jesus' life that surfaced after Jesus' healing miracle in John 5. That threat provides the backdrop for the exchanges between Jesus and the "Jews" in chaps. 7–8.

7:2. The Feast of Tabernacles (Festival of Booths, NRSV) was originally a fall harvest festival that received theological significance in ancient Israel by its identification with the wilderness journey after the exodus (Lev 23:43, See Fig. 9, "Jewish Religious Festivals in John," 542). Tabernacles was a joyous festival; the people built booths in which they lived for seven days to celebrate the harvest and God's graciousness to them (see Deut 16:13-15; Lev 23:39-43). Leviticus 23:39 adds an eighth day of rest to the festival following the celebrations. The setting of John 7–8 at Tabernacles continues the exodus backdrop of John 6. Moreover, the Mishnah records that the liturgical rites of Tabernacles include water libation and torch-lit processions.[177] The images of water and light will figure in Jesus' teaching at Tabernacles (7:37-38; 8:12).

7:3-5. Tabernacles was one of three pilgrimage feasts observed during NT times (the other two were Passover and Pentecost), which partly explains the demand by Jesus' brothers that he go to Judea. Jesus' brothers (cf. 2:12) speak to him in imperatives ("leave here," "go," v. 3; "show yourself," v. 4) and propose that he regain his position with his disciples (cf. 6:66) through a public performance of works in Judea. The brothers' clamoring for works recalls the crowd's demand for a sign in 6:30. The brothers' insistence that Jesus act publicly also shows that they do not understand how Jesus makes himself known. The determining factor in Jesus' self-revelation is not whether it occurs in public or private, but whether those who see Jesus will understand and receive what he offers (e.g., 5:24, 40; 12:44-50). The Fourth Evangelist makes explicit the brothers' lack of faith in his comment in v. 5 (cf. Mark 3:21, 31-35).

7:6-9. Jesus' response to his brothers is framed by references to "his time" (vv. 6, 8). The noun "time" (καιρός *kairos*) occurs only in 7:6, 8 in the Fourth Gospel and is a synonym for the more common "hour" (e.g., 2:4; 7:30; 8:20; 12:23; 13:1). "My time" refers to the time of Jesus' glorification—his death, resurrection, and ascension. It is a time set for him by God, not by his brothers and their notions of time and expediency

177. See *m. Sukk.* 4:9–5:4.

(v. 6b). Jesus' self-revelation at any given moment belongs to the larger framework of the time of glorification, and that framework is not subject to his brothers' demands (cf. 2:4). The symbolic significance of Jesus' "time" is confirmed by the language of his refusal in v. 8. The verb "to go up" (ἀναβαίνω *anabainō*) is customarily used to describe the journey to Jerusalem (2:13; 5:1; 7:10; 11:55), but it also describes Jesus' ascension in John (3:13; 6:62; 20:17). The phrase "fully come" (πληρόω *pleroō*) is used to speak of the time of eschatological fulfillment (3:29; 15:11; 16:24). The root of Jesus' brothers' lack of understanding is that they do not understand his relationship to the world (vv. 4, 7). They think Jesus is someone who will impress the world with his works and thus cause the world to embrace him, but they are wrong. Jesus brings the world to the moment of judgment by testifying to the nature of the world's works (cf. 3:19-21).[178] As a result of Jesus' testimony, the world hates him. The difference in the world's response to Jesus' brothers (v. 7a) reinforces the brothers' distance from Jesus (cf. v. 5). This is the first explicit mention of the world's hatred of Jesus (cf. 15:18-25), but the "world" (κόσμος *kosmos*) has been portrayed as a sphere of enmity (1:10). The witness role Jesus claims for himself in v. 7 is the same role given to the Paraclete in 16:8-11. Jesus' work of bringing the world to judgment will continue in the activity of the Spirit within the post-resurrection community.

178. Rudolf Bultmann, *The Gospel of John: A Commentary,* trans. G. R. Beasley-Murray, R. W. N. Hoare, and J. K. Riches (Philadelphia: Westminster, 1971) 293.

7:10. Jesus' actions in v. 10 do not contradict his words in vv. 6-8. Rather, they confirm his independence from the dictates of his brothers. Jesus' brothers demanded that he go to Judea publicly and not in secret (vv. 3-4), but when he goes, he goes up "not publicly, but in secret."

7:11-13. This passage is framed by references to Jesus' Jewish opponents ("the Jews," vv. 11, 13), reminding the reader of the ever-present threat to Jesus. The "Jews" is not an ethnic designation in these verses, since the crowd of vv. 11-13 is itself Jewish, but is a symbol for Jesus' opponents. The crowd is divided in their response to Jesus (v. 12), and similar division will characterize the crowd's response throughout John 7 (e.g., 7:25, 31, 40-44). The Fourth Evangelist describes the crowd's comments as "complaining" (γογγύζω *gongyszō),* and this word choice repeats the description of the crowd and Jesus' disciples in chap. 6 (vv. 41, 43, 61). The use of this noun suggests that the complaining is a sign of doubt and recalcitrance, and even affirmations of Jesus (v. 12a) are untrustworthy.

The complaint brought against Jesus in v. 12b provides another glimpse of the two levels on which the Fourth Gospel unfolds. The charge of deceiving the people was a formal Jewish charge against Jesus in the late first and early second centuries CE.[179] In the use of "deceive" (πλανάω *planaō*) here, the Fourth Evangelist seems to be depicting events in Jesus' life in terms drawn from his and his community's experience (see also 9:22; 12:42; 16:2; Matt 27:63). (See Reflections at 7:37-52.)

179. See Justin *Dialogue with Trypho* 69; *m. Sanh.* 43a.

John 7:14-36, Words of Conflict: Jesus' Teaching and Response

NIV	NRSV
¹⁴Not until halfway through the Feast did Jesus go up to the temple courts and begin to teach. ¹⁵The Jews were amazed and asked, "How did this man get such learning without having studied?" ¹⁶Jesus answered, "My teaching is not my own. It comes from him who sent me. ¹⁷If anyone chooses to do God's will, he will find out whether	14About the middle of the festival Jesus went up into the temple and began to teach. ¹⁵The Jews were astonished at it, saying, "How does this man have such learning,^a when he has never been taught?" ¹⁶Then Jesus answered them, "My teaching is not mine but his who sent me. ¹⁷Anyone ^a Or *this man know his letters*

my teaching comes from God or whether I speak on my own. [18]He who speaks on his own does so to gain honor for himself, but he who works for the honor of the one who sent him is a man of truth; there is nothing false about him. [19]Has not Moses given you the law? Yet not one of you keeps the law. Why are you trying to kill me?"

[20]"You are demon-possessed," the crowd answered. "Who is trying to kill you?"

[21]Jesus said to them, "I did one miracle, and you are all astonished. [22]Yet, because Moses gave you circumcision (though actually it did not come from Moses, but from the patriarchs), you circumcise a child on the Sabbath. [23]Now if a child can be circumcised on the Sabbath so that the law of Moses may not be broken, why are you angry with me for healing the whole man on the Sabbath? [24]Stop judging by mere appearances, and make a right judgment."

[25]At that point some of the people of Jerusalem began to ask, "Isn't this the man they are trying to kill? [26]Here he is, speaking publicly, and they are not saying a word to him. Have the authorities really concluded that he is the Christ[a]? [27]But we know where this man is from; when the Christ comes, no one will know where he is from."

[28]Then Jesus, still teaching in the temple courts, cried out, "Yes, you know me, and you know where I am from. I am not here on my own, but he who sent me is true. You do not know him, [29]but I know him because I am from him and he sent me."

[30]At this they tried to seize him, but no one laid a hand on him, because his time had not yet come. [31]Still, many in the crowd put their faith in him. They said, "When the Christ comes, will he do more miraculous signs than this man?"

[32]The Pharisees heard the crowd whispering such things about him. Then the chief priests and the Pharisees sent temple guards to arrest him.

[33]Jesus said, "I am with you for only a short time, and then I go to the one who sent me. [34]You will look for me, but you will not find me; and where I am, you cannot come."

[35]The Jews said to one another, "Where does this man intend to go that we cannot find him? Will he go where our people live scattered among

who resolves to do the will of God will know whether the teaching is from God or whether I am speaking on my own. [18]Those who speak on their own seek their own glory; but the one who seeks the glory of him who sent him is true, and there is nothing false in him.

[19]"Did not Moses give you the law? Yet none of you keeps the law. Why are you looking for an opportunity to kill me?" [20]The crowd answered, "You have a demon! Who is trying to kill you?" [21]Jesus answered them, "I performed one work, and all of you are astonished. [22]Moses gave you circumcision (it is, of course, not from Moses, but from the patriarchs), and you circumcise a man on the sabbath. [23]If a man receives circumcision on the sabbath in order that the law of Moses may not be broken, are you angry with me because I healed a man's whole body on the sabbath? [24]Do not judge by appearances, but judge with right judgment."

[25]Now some of the people of Jerusalem were saying, "Is not this the man whom they are trying to kill? [26]And here he is, speaking openly, but they say nothing to him! Can it be that the authorities really know that this is the Messiah[a]? [27]Yet we know where this man is from; but when the Messiah[a] comes, no one will know where he is from." [28]Then Jesus cried out as he was teaching in the temple, "You know me, and you know where I am from. I have not come on my own. But the one who sent me is true, and you do not know him. [29]I know him, because I am from him, and he sent me." [30]Then they tried to arrest him, but no one laid hands on him, because his hour had not yet come. [31]Yet many in the crowd believed in him and were saying, "When the Messiah[a] comes, will he do more signs than this man has done?"[b]

[32]The Pharisees heard the crowd muttering such things about him, and the chief priests and Pharisees sent temple police to arrest him. [33]Jesus then said, "I will be with you a little while longer, and then I am going to him who sent me. [34]You will search for me, but you will not find me; and where I am, you cannot come." [35]The Jews said to one another, "Where does this man intend to go that we will not find him? Does he intend to go to the Dispersion among the Greeks and teach

---

[a]26 Or Messiah; also in verses 27, 31, 41 and 42

[a] Or the Christ   [b] Other ancient authorities read is doing

NIV	NRSV
the Greeks, and teach the Greeks? ³⁶What did he mean when he said, 'You will look for me, but you will not find me,' and 'Where I am, you cannot come'?"	the Greeks? ³⁶What does he mean by saying, 'You will search for me and you will not find me' and 'Where I am, you cannot come'?"

COMMENTARY

John 7:14-52 can be divided into two parts on the basis of the time references in vv. 14 and 37. Verses 14-36 take place "about the middle of the festival" (v. 14)—that is, on the third or fourth day. Verses 37-52 take place "on the last day of the festival" (v. 37).

7:14-15. Jesus thus begins to teach at Tabernacles in the middle of the festival, when the crowds are largest, and in the Temple, Judaism's most sacred place. The designation of the crowd as "the Jews" seems more to be a reminder of the distance between Jesus and the crowd (cf. 7:2, "the Jewish festival of Booths") than an indication of hostility at this point. The crowd questions how Jesus could "have such learning" when he has no formal training (cf. Mark 1:22).

7:16-20. Jesus' response shows that the crowd's question is really a christological question, because what Jesus says is inseparable from who Jesus is. Verses 16-18 echo the themes of the discourses in John 5: Jesus is the one sent from God (7:16, 18; cf. 5:24, 30, 36-38); God is the source of what Jesus says and does (7:16-17; cf. 5:19-22, 26-27); Jesus seeks God's glory, not his own (7:18; cf. 5:41-44).

Some scholars take the thematic overlap between John 5 and John 7:14-24 as evidence that Jesus' words in John 7 were originally part of the John 5 discourse.[180] This source-critical verdict seems both unnecessary and a misreading of the function of repetition in the Fourth Gospel. A core repertoire of themes is replayed throughout Jesus' teaching, and verbal similarity between different discourses does not automatically indicate source displacement or reduplication. Rather, each re-statement builds on what preceded.

John 7:17 and 19 highlight the decision with

which the Tabernacles crowd is faced: Will they recognize God's teaching in Jesus' words (7:17; cf. 5:37-39)? Will they act in accordance with their own law, Moses' gift to them (7:19; cf. 1:17, 5:45-47)? In v. 20, the crowd questions the truthfulness of Jesus' words and hence his authority to teach them about the law. In John, the noun "demon" (δαιμόνιον *daimonion*) occurs only in accusations against Jesus (7:20; 8:48-49, 52; 10:20-21). Jesus does not exorcise demons in John as he does in the synoptic Gospels (e.g., Matt 8:16, 28-34; Mark 1:34, 39; 7:24-30; Luke 4:41). For the Fourth Evangelist, the world's evil is revealed by its works and rejection of Jesus (e.g., 3:19-21; 7:7) rather than personified in demon possession (but note the description of Judas in 6:70; 13:2, 27).

7:21-24. Jesus' teaching in 7:21-24, like vv. 16-19, replays themes from John 5. The "one work" to which Jesus refers in v. 21 is the healing of 5:1-18. This healing is not the only work Jesus has performed to this point in his ministry (cf. 4:46-54), but it is the one work the Fourth Gospel records Jesus performing in Jerusalem, and it is a Jerusalem crowd to which Jesus now speaks (cf. 7:25).

In John 5, the healing precipitated a controversy about the sabbath law (5:10, 16, 18), and vv. 22-24 reflect on the same controversy. Jesus frames his argument around Jewish circumcision practice. Circumcision is mandated by Mosaic law (the aside about the patriarchs in v. 22 acknowledges that circumcision first appears in the patriarchal stories of Genesis [Gen 17:9-14], not the stories about Moses). To circumcise a Jewish male was to mark his membership in the covenant community, and he was considered incomplete without circumcision.[181] The male baby had to be circumcised on the eighth day of his life. If that day fell on the sabbath, then the need for circum-

180. Gerard Sloyan, *John* (Atlanta: John Knox, 1988) 86-87; Rudolf Schnackenburg, *The Gospel According to St. John,* 3 vols. (New York: Seabury, 1982) 2:130-31.

181. See *m. Ned.* 3:11.

cision overrode the prohibitions against work on the sabbath, and the baby was circumcised.[182]

In v. 23, Jesus employs a common rabbinic form of argumentation to argue from the lesser (circumcision) to the greater (healing); if one part of the body can be tended to on the sabbath in order to ensure a man's wholeness, why should the healing of the whole body not be possible? Verse 23 makes clear that Jesus' sabbath healing was not performed in order to overturn or break the sabbath law (cf. 5:18), but "to accomplish the redemptive purpose towards which the Law had pointed."[183]

Jesus concludes his argument with one of the central challenges of his ministry in the Fourth Gospel: to judge with "right judgment" (τὴν δικαίαν κρίσιν *tēn dikaian krisin*), not by appearances (v. 24). To the Jewish authorities, Jesus' healing appeared to be a violation of sabbath law, but in reality, when viewed with right judgment, it was a deepening fulfillment of the sabbath. Jesus challenges the crowd to judge with discrimination, to look carefully at what one sees and not judge according to what one expects to find or assumes one sees.

Verse 24 provides the interpretive key to the exchanges between Jesus and the crowd and authorities in chaps. 7–8, because most of the conflict and hostility from 7:25 arise from a misperception of Jesus' identity, from faulty judgment based on appearance (e.g., 7:25-27, 41-42; 8:15, 48, 53, 57). In addition, in the broader Gospel context, when one sees a sign simply as a miracle, one judges by appearance, and when one sees the sign as revealing the presence and identity of God, one judges with right judgment (cf. 2:11; 4:48; 6:26; 9:3; 11:4).

7:25-36. The focus of the narrative alternates between Jesus' teaching and the response of the crowd and the authorities to Jesus. His public teaching in the Temple ("openly" [παρρησία *parrēsia*]; cf. 7:4, 13) in the face of the authorities' death threat (cf. 7:2, 11, 19-20) leads the crowd to wonder whether Jesus might indeed be the Messiah (vv. 25-26; "the Christ," NIV). The wording of the Jerusalemites' question in v. 26 puts the onus of messianic identification on the authorities

themselves by raising the issue of what the authorities know. Verse 26 also seems to drive a wedge between "some of the people" and "the authorities" (cf. the authorities' attitude toward the crowd in 7:49). The theme of who knows what and who can claim certitude for their knowledge recurs throughout the discussion of Jesus' identity in chaps. 7–8 (e.g., 7:26-29; 8:52-55) and is an illustration of the theme of right judgment introduced in 7:24.

The debate about Jesus' messianic identity in vv. 26-27 (see also 7:31, 41-42) must be understood in the historical context of the first century. In the period immediately following the destruction of the Jerusalem Temple in 70 CE, both Jews and Christians engaged in intense debates over the meaning of messianic symbolism and how to recognize the Messiah.[184] The Johannine discussion of Jesus as Messiah is thus another example of the way in which the Fourth Gospel simultaneously addresses two historical periods. It presents the messianic debate as occurring among Jesus' contemporaries but shades the debate to reflect the messianic controversies in the Evangelist's own time period (see 7:12). The Fourth Evangelist's interpretation of Jesus as Messiah—that Jesus is the sent one of God, God's emissary, Son, and Word—interprets messianic symbolism in ways that differed from both Jewish and other Christian (e.g., the synoptic Gospels) interpretations of the Messiah.[185]

The messianic debate in v. 27 reflects a belief that the Messiah was in hiding somewhere and would reveal himself only in the last days.[186] Jesus could not really be the Messiah because the crowd knows his place of origin. In v. 28, however, Jesus boldly challenges ("Jesus cried out") the crowd's presumption of knowledge. The "whence" of Jesus is another example of the two levels of meaning operative in John. The crowd thinks it knows where Jesus is from because it knows his native land, but Jesus' native land has little to do with his real place of origin. Jesus' place of origin is from God (e.g., 1:1; 3:16-17, 31), and one will never understand who Jesus is (or what it means to speak of the Messiah) until one recognizes Jesus as

---

182. "And they may perform on the Sabbath all things that are needful for circumcision" (*m. Šabb.* 18:3). See also *m. Šabb.* 19:2.
183. C. K. Barrett, *The Gospel According to St. John,* 2nd ed. (Philadelphia: Westminster, 1978) 371.

184. See Wayne A. Meeks, *The Prophet-King: Moses Traditions and the Johannine Christology* (Leiden: E. J. Brill, 1967).
185. Gerard Sloyan, *John* (Atlanta: John Knox, 1988) 88.
186. See *Eth. Enoch* 69:29; 2 Esdr 7:28; 13:32.

having been sent by God (vv. 28-29). The key to deciphering Jesus' identity is clear: Know what Jesus knows, that he is sent by God (v. 29).

As earlier in chap. 7 (vv. 12-14), the response to Jesus' words is mixed, and once again the Fourth Evangelist uses the verb γογγύζω (gongyzō; translated in v. 32 as "mutter" or "whisper" rather than "complain") to describe the reaction (cf. 6:41, 43, 61; 7:12). "Many in the crowd" believed in Jesus (v. 31), but their faith is based on what Jesus does ("signs"), not on what he says or a clear recognition of his relationship to God. Verse 31 again focuses on how to recognize the Messiah (cf. 7:27, 40-42). Jewish literature does not state explicitly that the Messiah will be a miracle worker, but this verse may reflect the popular belief that the Messiah would perform miracles in the way Moses or Elijah did. The threat to Jesus' life (vv. 30, 32) is a constant element in the opening verses of chap. 7 (vv. 1, 11, 19, 25, 44-45), but this threat is balanced by the reminder that it is Jesus' hour, the time set for him by God, that governs his life, not human plans (v. 30).

John 7:33-36 contains another vignette of Jesus' teaching and the response it evokes. Jesus' words in vv. 33-34 anticipate one of the central motifs of the Farewell Discourse: Jesus will be present to the world only for a little while (13:33; 14:19; 16:16-19). This motif, whether spoken to the Jewish crowd or to Jesus' closest followers, underscores the ur-

gency of coming to faith in Jesus. As Bultmann has eloquently expressed it, "It is the *historical contingency of the revelation* which throws this terrible weight of responsibility on the hearer of the word. For the revelation is not generally available, but presents itself to [people] only at a certain limited time of its own choosing."[187] The urgency of making the faith decision is linked to the question of Jesus' identity, because Jesus is "going to him who sent me." Jesus will be inaccessible (v. 34) to those who do not recognize the relationship between Jesus and God and who cling to distorted notions of Jesus' origins.

The fact that the "Jews" are among those who cling to distorted notions is evidenced by their ironic questions in vv. 35-36. The "Jews" repeat Jesus' words to one another, explicitly admitting that they do not understand his meaning. The irony of their questions has two sources. First, they cling to a geographical definition of origin and place and, therefore, assume that Jesus is leaving them for another locale. The "Dispersion" (v. 35) refers to Jews who live outside of Palestine (note the NIV paraphrase). Second, and with a more profound irony for the reader of the Gospel, the interpretation that the "Jews" give to Jesus' words—that he is going to live among the Greeks and teach them—is an unconscious prophecy of the future of the Christian movement (cf. Caiaphas's unconscious prophecy, 11:49-52). (See Reflections at 7:37-52.)

187. Bultmann, *The Gospel of John*, 307.

John 7:37-52, Words of Conflict: Jesus' Teaching and Response

NIV

[37]On the last and greatest day of the Feast, Jesus stood and said in a loud voice, "If anyone is thirsty, let him come to me and drink. [38]Whoever believes in me, as[a] the Scripture has said, streams of living water will flow from within him." [39]By this he meant the Spirit, whom those who believed in him were later to receive. Up to that time the Spirit had not been given, since Jesus had not yet been glorified.

[a]37,38 Or / If anyone is thirsty, let him come to me. / And let him drink, [38]who believes in me. / As

NRSV

[37]On the last day of the festival, the great day, while Jesus was standing there, he cried out, "Let anyone who is thirsty come to me, [38]and let the one who believes in me drink. As[a] the scripture has said, 'Out of the believer's heart[b] shall flow rivers of living water.'" [39]Now he said this about the Spirit, which believers in him were to receive; for as yet there was no Spirit,[c] because Jesus was not yet glorified.

[a] Or *come to me and drink.* [38]The one who believes in me, as
[b] Gk *out of his belly*   [c] Other ancient authorities read *for as yet the Spirit* (others, *Holy Spirit*) *had not been given*

NIV

⁴⁰On hearing his words, some of the people said, "Surely this man is the Prophet."

⁴¹Others said, "He is the Christ."

Still others asked, "How can the Christ come from Galilee? ⁴²Does not the Scripture say that the Christ will come from David's family*a* and from Bethlehem, the town where David lived?" ⁴³Thus the people were divided because of Jesus. ⁴⁴Some wanted to seize him, but no one laid a hand on him.

⁴⁵Finally the temple guards went back to the chief priests and Pharisees, who asked them, "Why didn't you bring him in?"

⁴⁶"No one ever spoke the way this man does," the guards declared.

⁴⁷"You mean he has deceived you also?" the Pharisees retorted. ⁴⁸"Has any of the rulers or of the Pharisees believed in him? ⁴⁹No! But this mob that knows nothing of the law—there is a curse on them."

⁵⁰Nicodemus, who had gone to Jesus earlier and who was one of their own number, asked, ⁵¹"Does our law condemn anyone without first hearing him to find out what he is doing?"

⁵²They replied, "Are you from Galilee, too? Look into it, and you will find that a prophet*b* does not come out of Galilee."

a42 Greek *seed*   *b52* Two early manuscripts *the Prophet*

NRSV

40When they heard these words, some in the crowd said, "This is really the prophet." ⁴¹Others said, "This is the Messiah."*a* But some asked, "Surely the Messiah*a* does not come from Galilee, does he? ⁴²Has not the scripture said that the Messiah*a* is descended from David and comes from Bethlehem, the village where David lived?" ⁴³So there was a division in the crowd because of him. ⁴⁴Some of them wanted to arrest him, but no one laid hands on him.

45Then the temple police went back to the chief priests and Pharisees, who asked them, "Why did you not arrest him?" ⁴⁶The police answered, "Never has anyone spoken like this!" ⁴⁷Then the Pharisees replied, "Surely you have not been deceived too, have you? ⁴⁸Has any one of the authorities or of the Pharisees believed in him? ⁴⁹But this crowd, which does not know the law— they are accursed." ⁵⁰Nicodemus, who had gone to Jesus*b* before, and who was one of them, asked, ⁵¹"Our law does not judge people without first giving them a hearing to find out what they are doing, does it?" ⁵²They replied, "Surely you are not also from Galilee, are you? Search and you will see that no prophet is to arise from Galilee."

a Or *the Christ*   *b* Gk *him*

COMMENTARY

7:37-38. The reference to "the last day of the festival" marks the start of a new section. As noted, one of the central rites of the Tabernacles celebration was the water-libation, during which the priest circles the altar with freshly drawn water (see Fig. 9, "Jewish Religious Festivals in John," 542). The libations ended on the seventh day, but the Mishnah provides for an eighth day of rest and celebration as a final honoring of the Tabernacles feast.[188] The Mishnah gives no indication that the eighth day of the feast was any less important than the seventh. When Jesus speaks on "the last day," he may be speaking either on the seventh day as the water-libation is being performed, or

on the day after it has just been concluded. Jesus' words in vv. 37-38 have the same significance, regardless of the day on which they are set.[189] Like the water turned into wine in the Jewish purification jars of 2:8-11, the cultic setting of 7:37-38 suggests that old rites acquire new meaning because of the Word's incarnate presence in the world. Jesus' words in vv. 37-38, not the Jewish rites, are the culmination of the Tabernacles feast for the Fourth Evangelist.

The interpretation of Jesus' words in vv. 37-38 is complicated by two problems. First, it is unclear how Jesus' words are to be punctuated. The

188. See *m. Sukk.* 4:8-9; see also Lev 23:39.

189. C. K. Barrett, *The Gospel According to St. John,* 2nd ed. (Philadelphia: Westminster, 1978) 326.

central question is where to place a full stop: (a) after the word "drink" (πινέτω *pinetō,* as in the NIV translation); or (b) after the phrase "come to me" (ἐρχέσθω πρός με *erchesthō pros me,* as in the NIV variant provided in a footnote). The decision about punctuation affects the meaning of Jesus' words, because option (a) seems to position the believer as the source of living water in the quotation of v. 38, whereas punctuation (b) positions Jesus as the source of living water. (The NRSV opts to resolve the punctuation problem by adding words to the Greek text. The phrase "the one who believes" occurs once in the Greek but twice in the NRSV of v. 38 ["the one who believes in me," v. 38*a*; "out of the believer's heart," v. 38*b*]. The NRSV variant provided in a footnote is a more literal translation and is the same as the NIV. In both the main translation and the variant, the NRSV adheres to the meaning of option [a], and, indeed, in the main translation that decision about meaning determined the translation of vv. 37-38.)

A review of the history of interpretation of these verses shows that their punctuation has always vexed interpreters. The earliest manuscripts that include punctuation marks are divided in their readings (for example, 𝔓[66] follows punctuation [a], and Codex d and e follow punctuation [b]). The early church fathers, too, were divided. Origen, Chrysostom, Ambrose, Jerome, and Augustine punctuated the verses so that the believer was the source of living water; Justin and Hippolytus followed the second punctuation and identified Jesus as the source of living water. Modern interpreters continue to be divided on the punctuation of these verses.[190]

The punctuation decision is complicated further by the second interpretive problem of vv. 37-38: The words identified as Scripture in v. 38 appear nowhere in the OT. The quotation in v. 38 appears to be a composite of a variety of OT texts that refer to life-giving water, wisdom, or the Spirit (e.g., Prov 18:4; Isa 12:3; 43:19-20; 44:3; Jer 2:13; 17:13; Ezekiel 47; Zech 14:8) rather than one particular text. The words quoted in v. 38 are thus as ambiguous as the punctuation of the verses.

Because neither textual witnesses nor church fathers can resolve the ambiguity of vv. 37-38, the interpreter must rely on the context and content of Johannine theology to give clarity to these verses. Even that data is somewhat ambiguous. John 4:14 refers to living water becoming a spring within the believer, and thus could be read as supporting punctuation (a). Yet John 4:10 speaks of Jesus as the giver of the living water, and John 6:35 speaks of Jesus as the quencher of thirst, providing support for reading Jesus as the source of living water in 7:38. Moreover, a careful comparison of 4:14 and 7:37-38 shows that they make slightly different claims. John 4:14 does not speak of the believer as the source of living water for others. The weight of the Fourth Gospel evidence, then, seems to fall on the side of the second alternative, which sees Jesus as the source of living water. The Fourth Evangelist's commentary about the Spirit in v. 39 gives additional support to the christological reading of vv. 37-38, because in the Fourth Gospel the gift of the Spirit originates not with the believer, but with Jesus— or God (14:16, 26; 16:17; 20:20).

Schnackenburg has proposed a reading of vv. 37-38 that suggests that too much has been made of the punctuation problem with these verses. He demonstrates that the christological interpretation of vv. 37-38 is valid regardless of the way the verses are punctuated. Even if a full stop is placed after the word "drink," that does not mean that the believer is the source of living water in v. 38. Rather, that punctuation places the believer at the beginning of the next phrase for emphasis. As Schnackenburg translates, "If anyone believes in me, for him—as the Scripture says—rivers of living water will flow from [Jesus'] heart."[191] The advantage of Schnackenburg's proposal is that it returns the interpretive focus to the substance of Jesus' invitation and promise in vv. 37-38. In these verses, Jesus reiterates a promise that has resounded throughout the Gospel: Whoever believes in Jesus will receive new life (3:15-16; 5:24; 6:35, 40, 47).

7:39. Verse 39 gives an explicit statement of the Fourth Evangelist's understanding of the relationship between the gift of the Spirit and Jesus' "glorification." The gift of the Spirit becomes a reality in the believer's life only after Jesus' death, resurrection, and ascension (20:22). The bold wording of v. 39 ("for as yet there was no Spirit") gave rise to a textual variant that attempted to

---

190. For example, Barrett (ibid., 326-27) follows punctuation *a*; Bultmann (*The Gospel of John,* 303), punctuation *b*.

191. Rudolf Schnackenburg, *The Gospel According to St. John,* 3 vols. (New York: Seabury, 1982) 2:154.

soften its claim ("for the Spirit had not yet been given"). That variant misconstrues the Fourth Evangelist's pneumatology, however. The Fourth Evangelist is not denying the Spirit of God present in the OT. Indeed, the Spirit of God descended on Jesus at his baptism (1:34). The Fourth Evangelist is saying that the Spirit as it is known in the life of the church did not yet exist, because the Spirit of God is redefined in the light of Jesus' death, resurrection, and ascension.

7:40-44. Jesus' words engender another debate over his identity. Some in the crowd claim Jesus as the prophet—that is, the messianic prophet like Moses (v. 40; cf. 1:21, 25)—while others explicitly call him Messiah (v. 41a). Yet others in the crowd question whether Jesus could be the Messiah (vv. 41b-42). The crowd's doubt is based on the popular belief that the Messiah would come from Bethlehem (Mic 5:2; Matt 1:18–2:12). Interestingly, this belief contradicts the expectations alluded to in 7:27, that the Messiah's origins will be a mystery. Both beliefs were current in the first century, and the Fourth Evangelist may include both in the same story in order to highlight the inadequacy of all pre-existent definitions of the Messiah when applied to Jesus. Traditional messianic categories are inadequate because they rely on prior assumptions and expectations rather than judging Jesus on the basis of what he reveals about himself: that he is the one sent from God.

The debate about Galilee and Bethlehem in vv. 41b-42 takes on an additional significance when placed in the context of the traditions about Jesus' birth. Although the Fourth Evangelist narrates no birth stories, these two verses (see also 6:42) seem to allude to those traditions and serve ironically to undercut the crowd's claims. Not only does the crowd misconstrue the question of Jesus' origins (that his place of origin is from God, not from a city), but even when the question is framed in their terms, they get Jesus' place of origin wrong.

The division that has characterized the crowd's response throughout chap. 7 (vv. 12, 25, 31, 40-41) is explicitly named in v. 43. It receives a dramatic illustration in the renewed desire of some (but not all) to arrest Jesus (v. 44). Once again, however, the arrest attempt is ineffectual (cf. 7:30).

7:45-52. The narrative focus shifts from the crowd to the Jewish leaders. The return of the temple police empty-handed (v. 45) is further confirmation of the ineffectuality of their plans to arrest Jesus. The reason the police give for their failure (v. 46) echoes the crowd's response to Jesus' words in 7:15. The police thus witness to Jesus. The Pharisees' response to the police failure is to deride both the temple police and the crowd (7:47-49), deepening the split between themselves and the people (cf. 7:26). Their words repeat vocabulary and themes from the opening sections of John 7: "deceived" (v. 47; cf. 7:12), "know the law" (v. 49; cf. 7:19, 23).

The exchange with Nicodemus (7:50-52) provides ironic commentary on the Pharisees' words. Nicodemus, "who was one of them" (v. 50), raises a question about the law (v. 51), pointing out to his fellow Pharisees what their law actually teaches. His question suggests that it is the Pharisees' knowledge of the law that is a matter of doubt, not the crowd's (v. 49). Since Nicodemus "had gone to Jesus before" (v. 50), he alone among the Pharisees has given Jesus the hearing the law requires.

The Pharisees respond to Nicodemus the same way they responded to the temple police: by deriding him and asserting their superior knowledge of Scripture and the law (v. 52). Their appeal to Scripture ("search" [ἐραυνάω *eraunaō*]) ironically echoes Jesus' words to the Jewish leaders in 5:39. The claim that Scripture shows that no prophet will arise from Galilee is problematic, because 2 Kgs 14:25, for example, makes explicit mention of the Galilean origins of the prophet Jonah. The Pharisees' words are thus best understood as an allusion to the messianic expectations adduced in 7:41-42 and hence as evidence of their misperception of Jesus' origins. Far from being superior to the crowd, the Pharisees are subject to the same faulty judgment based on appearances (7:24).

REFLECTIONS

Independent fragments of tradition are brought together in John 7 (and 8) to form a coherent narrative of misunderstanding, resistance, and conflict. This conflict is key to the development of the Gospel story (note the repeated references to the threat to Jesus in John 7:1, 13, 19, 25, 30, 32, 44), but it also is key to the development of the Fourth Gospel's theology. All of the conversations in John 7 center on Jesus' identity and people's reaction to Jesus. Through the stories of conflict and opposition, through the various questions asked and divergent opinions expressed about Jesus (7:10-12, 15, 25, 35-36, 40-43, 45-52), the Fourth Evangelist emphasizes once more the cruciality of the decision one makes about Jesus.

The Fourth Evangelist's motives in combining the traditions he uses in John 7 (and that continue into John 8), then, are neither chronological (to chronicle Jesus' itinerary) nor psychological (to document the psychological motivation of Jesus' opponents) nor even purely literary (to tell a good story). His motive is primarily theological. That is, the narrative of John 7:1-52 (and 8:12-59) is shaped by the Fourth Evangelist's theological convictions. This is different from saying that the story of John 7–8 reflects the Fourth Evangelist's theological concerns, because in these chapters there is a complete absorption of story and theology.

Each conversation in John 7 underscores the contrast between the reality embodied in Jesus—that he is sent from God (7:16, 28, 33)—and the crowd's and the authorities' perception of that reality. Instead of allowing what they see in Jesus to redefine their understanding of God in the world, those who resist Jesus judge him according to pre-existent systems and structures that both cause and provide justification for their misperception. Jesus is measured against professed knowledge of who the Messiah will be (7:26-27, 41-42), of what Scripture says (7:48-52); the rigid certitude with which those expectations are held determines the judgment reached about Jesus. John 7:1-52 thus is configured to highlight the truth of 7:24, "Do not judge by appearances, but judge with right judgment."

Jesus' call for right judgment touches at the heart of the faith decision for the Fourth Evangelist. Jesus' coming into the world as the incarnate Word of God requires that one perceive reality differently. "The Word became flesh" (1:14); if one judges by appearances only, one risks stopping at the flesh and never recognizing God, who is present and available in that flesh. Judgment based on appearances risks reducing Jesus to fit who or what we think he should be rather than allowing his fullness, incarnate Word, to work its way on our systems and structures of perception.

It is not surprising, therefore, that the Fourth Gospel is characterized by the use of irony, symbol, and metaphor. The Fourth Evangelist uses literary devices that make it difficult for the reader to settle on surface meanings. Each use of irony, for example, creates incongruities and tensions between two levels of meaning. Irony asks the reader to make judgments and decisions about the relative value of stated and intended meaning in order to discover what is really being said. This invites reader participation in the Fourth Gospel's revelation of the truth about Jesus and God. Metaphor and symbol also involve two levels of meaning. The move from one level of meaning involves less tension than it does with irony, because a metaphor points in the direction of its meaning (see the discussion of the bread metaphor in the Commentary and Reflections on John 6). Nonetheless, the reader is asked to move from one level of meaning to a second level to which the metaphor or symbol points.[192] In all three uses of figurative language, the reader is an active participant in the text; in order to discover what is being revealed, he or she must "judge with right judgment." In this way, the experience of the Gospel reader parallels the experience of the characters in the Gospel story.

---

192. See R. Alan Culpepper, *Anatomy of the Fourth Gospel: A Study in Literary Design* (Philadelphia: Fortress, 1983); Gail R. O'Day, *Revelation in the Fourth Gospel* (Philadelphia: Fortress, 1986).

The centrality of "right judgment" also explains why there is so much repetition in Jesus' teaching in John. For the Fourth Evangelist, Jesus does not have fresh content to impart in each new revelation that the listener must learn and appropriate. Rather, the central christological and soteriological issue for the Fourth Evangelist is one's response to Jesus, his words and deeds. The core of Jesus' revelation is thus repeated over and over again throughout the Gospel: his identity as the sent one of God and the ways in which Jesus makes God visible and accessible to the world. The crux for faith is whether those who encounter Jesus and his words perceive and embrace this decisive truth about his identity.

Rudolf Bultmann overstated the case when he insisted that there is no content to Jesus' revelation in the Fourth Gospel and, therefore, the *fact* of Jesus' presence in the world alone is determinative of faith. Bultmann maintained that John "presents only the fact (*das Dass*) of the Revelation without describing its content (*ihr Was*)."[193] Jesus' statements about his identity and his relationship to God do provide content to his revelation, because they reveal something new about God and humanity's relationship to God. Bultmann was correct, however, to see the critical Johannine issue as a person's faith response, a person's decision for or against Jesus. The dividing line for the Fourth Evangelist is whether those who encounter Jesus recognize that God is decisively present in him.

John 7:1-52 is no exception to the repetitive character of Jesus' teaching in John. Much of what Jesus says in John 7 he has said before (cf. 7:16-18 and 5:19-22, 41-44) and will say again (cf. 7:33-34 and 13:33; 14:19). Again and again the reader meets the expression "the one who sent me" (7:16, 18, 28-29, 33), and again and again characters in the story do not perceive what this phrase means for Jesus' identity (7:27, 35-36). The result of misperception is not simply misunderstanding and miscommunication, however. Rather, misperception of Jesus' identity is a matter of life and death. It is a matter of life and death for Jesus, because the authorities' faulty perception leads to an intensification of the threat to Jesus' life (7:32). It is also a matter of life and death for those who encounter Jesus, characters in the Gospel and Gospel readers alike, because faulty perception of Jesus' identity removes one from Jesus' offer of salvation.

Embedded in the controversy dialogues and narratives of 7:1-52 is Jesus' offer of drink to everyone who believes, his promise of living water to everyone who thirsts (7:37-38). These verses focus on the link between salvation (living water) and coming to Jesus, on the relationship between the gift of the Spirit and belief in Jesus (7:38-39). The issue of right judgment thus points to the relationship between christology and soteriology in the Fourth Gospel. That is, when one judges with right judgment and recognizes who Jesus is, Jesus' gift of life becomes available (cf. 4:10; 6:35). Without right judgment, one will not receive new life.

The disagreements between Jesus and his opponents will become increasingly vitriolic as the Tabernacles scene continues into chap. 8. In John 7, the dividing line is drawn: Does one perceive that Jesus is sent from God or not? For the Fourth Evangelist there is no more crucial decision than the answer one gives to this question. The Fourth Evangelist's singular focus on this question may strike contemporary interpreters as odd or even offensive, because contemporary Christians are preoccupied with a broader array of questions about the life of faith. The Fourth Evangelist, however, wrote out of the conviction that if one could not decide about that question, there were no grounds for engaging other questions. For the Fourth Evangelist, everything hinged on right judgment, on seeing that God was decisively and newly available in the one whom God sent, Jesus.

---

193. Rudolf Bultmann, *Theology of the New Testament* (New York: Charles Scribner's Sons, 1955) 2:63-66, 83, 605.

[John 7:53–8:11, A Narrative of Conflict]

[The earliest manuscripts and many other ancient witnesses do not have John 7:53-8:11.]

⁵³Then each went to his own home.

8 But Jesus went to the Mount of Olives. ²At dawn he appeared again in the temple courts, where all the people gathered around him, and he sat down to teach them. ³The teachers of the law and the Pharisees brought in a woman caught in adultery. They made her stand before the group ⁴and said to Jesus, "Teacher, this woman was caught in the act of adultery. ⁵In the Law Moses commanded us to stone such women. Now what do you say?" ⁶They were using this question as a trap, in order to have a basis for accusing him.

But Jesus bent down and started to write on the ground with his finger. ⁷When they kept on questioning him, he straightened up and said to them, "If any one of you is without sin, let him be the first to throw a stone at her." ⁸Again he stooped down and wrote on the ground.

⁹At this, those who heard began to go away one at a time, the older ones first, until only Jesus was left, with the woman still standing there. ¹⁰Jesus straightened up and asked her, "Woman, where are they? Has no one condemned you?"

¹¹"No one, sir," she said.

"Then neither do I condemn you," Jesus declared. "Go now and leave your life of sin."

[[⁵³Then each of them went home,

8 ¹while Jesus went to the Mount of Olives. ²Early in the morning he came again to the temple. All the people came to him and he sat down and began to teach them. ³The scribes and the Pharisees brought a woman who had been caught in adultery; and making her stand before all of them, ⁴they said to him, "Teacher, this woman was caught in the very act of committing adultery. ⁵Now in the law Moses commanded us to stone such women. Now what do you say?" ⁶They said this to test him, so that they might have some charge to bring against him. Jesus bent down and wrote with his finger on the ground. ⁷When they kept on questioning him, he straightened up and said to them, "Let anyone among you who is without sin be the first to throw a stone at her." ⁸And once again he bent down and wrote on the ground.^a ⁹When they heard it, they went away, one by one, beginning with the elders; and Jesus was left alone with the woman standing before him. ¹⁰Jesus straightened up and said to her, "Woman, where are they? Has no one condemned you?" ¹¹She said, "No one, sir."^b And Jesus said, "Neither do I condemn you. Go your way, and from now on do not sin again."]]^c

^a Other ancient authorities add *the sins of each of them*
^b Or *Lord*   ^c The most ancient authorities lack 7.53—8.11; other authorities add the passage here or after 7.36 or after 21.25 or after Luke 21.38, with variations of text; some mark the passage as doubtful.

COMMENTARY

John 7:53–8:11 did not belong originally to the Gospel of John (see Overview to John 7:1–8:59), but found its way into some manuscripts of the Gospel at a later date.[194] The complicated textual history of this passage presents the reader with two preliminary interpretive decisions.

First, the Gospel reader should try to locate John 7:53–8:11 within the history of tradition. The literary evidence (style, syntax, vocabulary)

suggests that the story's origins are non-Johannine. For example, John 8:3 is the only occurrence of the noun "scribes" (γραμματεῖς *grammateis*) in the Fourth Gospel, although this noun is common in the other Gospels (Matt 5:20; 12:38; 23:2; Mark 2:16; 7:1, 5; Luke 5:21, 30; 11:53). The setting and form of the story, a controversy with Jewish leaders in the Temple, has more in common with the synoptic temple controversy stories (Matt 21:23-27; 22:15-22-33; Mark 11:27-33; 12:13-17-27; Luke 21:1-8, 20-40) than the long and involved debates between Jesus and the Jew-

---

194. For a review of the text-critical question, see Bruce Metzger, *A Textual Commentary on the Greek New Testament* (New York: United Bible Societies, 1975) 219-20.

ish authorities in John (e.g., 5:19-47; 8:12-58). Yet the literary evidence does not indicate conclusively that the synoptic tradition is the original home of this story either (although there is a long history of attributing this story to Luke).[195] The unknown origin of this story implies that even though some of its themes may be in keeping with Johannine theology (as will be discussed below), John 7:53–8:11 cannot be used judiciously to interpret Johannine thought.

Second, given the non-Johannine origins of 7:53–8:11, the interpreter must decide how seriously to attend to the canonical location of this story. Commentators on John decide that question in a variety of ways. Bultmann ignores the story altogether; Barrett treats it in an appendix; Brown and Schnackenburg treat it in its canonical location; Beasley-Murray treats it at the end of his discussion of John 7–8.[196] This commentary treats it in its canonical location, because its canonical Johannine context provides a useful interpretive framework for this otherwise contextless story.

7:53–8:1. These transition verses underscore the artificial placement of the story that follows. First, the identity of the group to which the phrase "each of them" refers is not clear. Second, 8:1 is the only reference to the Mount of Olives in the Fourth Gospel, whereas in the Synoptic tradition the Mount of Olives is a frequent resting spot for Jesus when he is near Jerusalem (Matt 21:1; 24:3; 26:30; Mark 11:1; 13:3; 14:26; see esp. Luke 21:37; 22:39).

8:2-6a. The story proper begins in v. 2 and consists of two parts: (1) vv. 2-6a, which establish the central conflict of the story, and (2) vv. 6b-11, which provide the resolution. The setting of this story in the Temple may have influenced its canonical location, because the Temple is the site of Jesus' teaching in John 7–8 (7:14, 28; 8:20, 59).

The scribes and Pharisees initiate the story's central conflict by bringing the "woman who had been caught in adultery" to Jesus (8:3). As noted earlier, this is the only occurrence of "scribes" in

the Fourth Gospel. John 8:4 is also the only time in which Jesus is addressed as "Teacher" (διδάσκαλε *didaskale*) in the Fourth Gospel (but note the translation of the Hebrew term "Rabbi" in 1:38; 20:16). "Teacher" is a common form of address for Jesus in the Synoptics (e.g., Matt 8:19; 12:38; 19:16; 22:16; Mark 9:17, 38; 10:17, 20, 35; 12:14, 19; Luke 3:12; 7:40; 10:25; 20:21, 28, 39). The address has an ironic tone here, because the Pharisees hope to undermine Jesus' teaching (8:2) with their question (cf. 8:6).

There are several irregularities in the scribes' and Pharisees' presentation of their legal case. First, they provide no witnesses to sustain the case that the woman was caught in the "very act" of adultery (cf. Deut. 17:6; 19:15). Jesus thus is not provided with the information necessary to adjudicate the law properly. Second, the scribes and Pharisees speak as if Mosaic law requires the death penalty for adulterous women only ("such women," v. 5) and completely ignore the fate of her male sexual partner. Mosaic law, however, makes explicit that both the man and the woman involved stand under the death penalty (Lev 20:10; Deut 22:22). In fact, the fundamental concern of Mosaic adultery laws is the protection and stability of men's property (i.e., their wives and their offspring), and the law is worded to focus primarily on men ("If a man commits adultery . . . " [Lev 20:10 NRSV]; "If a man is caught lying with the wife of another man . . . " [Deut 22:22 NRSV]). (Note also that the Mishnah explicitly mentions only the man's punishment by stoning for adultery).[197]

Verse 6a makes explicit what the legal irregularities of vv. 4-5 suggest: The scribes and Pharisees are not interested in Jesus' interpretation of Mosaic law but want only to entrap him. Both the law and the woman are merely foils for this primary goal of entrapment. The situation and language of testing and entrapment in v. 6a have more in common with the Synoptic traditions than with the rest of the Fourth Gospel (e.g., Matt 19:3; 22:18; Mark 10:2; 12:15).

8:6b-11. Jesus' response to the test is narrated in two remarkably balanced parts (vv. 6b-7, 8-11).

195. For a recent study of John 7:53–8:11 that advocates Lukan authorship, see Michel Gourges, " 'Moi non plus je ne condemne pas': Les mots et la theologie de Luc en Jean 8, 1-11," *SR* 19 (1990) 305-18.

196. See Barrett, *The Gospel According to St. John,* 589-92; Raymond E. Brown, *The Gospel According to John (I–XII),* AB 29 (Garden City, N.Y.: Doubleday, 1966) 1:335-38; Rudolf Schnackenburg, *The Gospel According to St. John,* 3 vols. (New York: Seabury, 1982) 2:162-71; George R. Beasley-Murray, *John,* WBC 36 (Waco, Tex.: Word, 1987) 143-47.

197. See *m. Sanh.* 7:4, 9. See also Judith Wegner, "Leviticus," in *The Women's Bible Commentary,* ed. Carol A. Newsom and Sharon H. Ringe (Louisville: Westminster/John Knox, 1992) 41; and *Chattel or Persons? The Status of Women in the Mishnah* (New York: Oxford University Press, 1988).

In both parts, Jesus makes a nonverbal response (bending down to write on the ground, vv. 6b, 8) and a verbal response (straightening up to speak, vv. 7, 10-11).

8:6b-7. Jesus' writing on the ground in v. 6b indicates his refusal to engage the question of vv. 4-5 as the scribes and Pharisees have posed it. The story gives no information about the content of what Jesus writes, because it is the act of writing itself that is important. Interpretations that attempt to supply the content of what Jesus writes miss the significance of Jesus' nonverbal response. In the Mediterranean world of Jesus' time, such an act of writing would have been recognized as an act of refusal and disengagement.[198]

The scribes' and Pharisees' continued pressing of their question (v. 7a) shows that they recognize Jesus' writing as an act of refusal, not as offering an answer. When Jesus finally straightens up and addresses them directly (v. 7b), he does not answer their legal question, but moves beyond the legal argument to the more encompassing issue of sin. The noun translated "the one without sin" (ἀναμάρτητος *anamartētos*) occurs only here in the NT, and the notion of sin that it conveys—that sin is linked to actions—is unusual for the Fourth Gospel. The more traditional Johannine understanding of sin is to link it with a person's refusal to recognize Jesus as the Logos (e.g., 8:24; 15:22-24). In 8:7, Jesus calls the scribes and Pharisees to accountability for their past actions and hence their own relationship to the law, which they had been willing to distort to press their case against Jesus.

8:8-11. Jesus' resumption of writing on the ground in v. 8 indicates that he is finished with the scribes and Pharisees. (The textual variant supplied in the NRSV footnotes is one example of early scribal efforts to supply content to Jesus' act of writing.) The actions of the scribes and Pharisees (and the rest of the crowd) in v. 9 answer the challenge Jesus posed to them; none of them is sinless. The elders' departure may be singled

198. See Gail R. O'Day, "John 7:53–8:11: A Study in Misreading," *JBL* 111 (1992) 632, 635-36.

out in this verse to highlight the fact that not even the most senior and revered members of the community are without sin.

Jesus straightens up to address the woman (v. 10) just as he did with the scribes and Pharisees in v. 7. His questions and the woman's response confirm what the reader knows from v. 9: There is no one left to condemn her. Jesus' words in v. 10 are the first time the woman has been directly addressed in the story. Prior to this verse, she has been only an object for the scribes and Pharisees to use in their entrapment of Jesus.

Jesus' words to the woman in v. 11 are a counterpoint to his words to the scribes and Pharisees in v. 7, where his words focused on how the scribes' and Pharisees' past (their sin) should inform their present actions. In v. 11, Jesus' words move beyond a focus on the relationship of past and present actions to the future (v. 11b). Jesus' words to the woman, "Do not sin again," also appear in 5:14 and seem to have the same meaning in both places. Jesus does not speak of what is required for acquittal (healing in 5:14) but urges that the acquittal that is freely given become the beginning point for a new life.

There are several possible reasons why John 7:53–8:11 received its canonical location. First, as noted in the Overview above, it provides a narrative illustration of the conflict that animates the dialogues of John 7–8. Second, one of the specific conflicts in John 7 is the proper interpretation of the law (7:19-24, 48-49), the conflict around which this particular story is built. Third, one can read this story as an illustration of 7:24: the difference between judging by appearance (the judgment of the scribes and Pharisees) or by right judgment (the judgment of Jesus). The theme of judgment continues into John 8 (e.g., 8:15-16). Its Johannine context thus suggests that John 7:53–8:11 is most effectively read as a story about Jesus' relationship to the law and the religious establishment rather than as a morality tale, as is frequently the case (see Reflections).

REFLECTIONS

John 7:53–8:11 is a vivid, powerful story whose hold on the imagination of its readers is not diminished by its complicated canonical history. Indeed, it is probably one of the most popular NT stories. Jesus' words in v. 7 about casting the first stone are repeated in an endless variety of contexts inside and outside the church, and they have achieved the status of a cultural adage rivaling any of Bartlett's quotations. They are used popularly as a check on moral self-righteousness. Popular interpretation also equates the substance of this story with its conventional title, "The Woman Caught in Adultery," and so reads the story in terms of Jesus' attitude toward sexuality.[199]

Yet do the popular appropriations of this story do it theological justice, or do they lead the interpreter into the trap of relying on what is said and remembered about a biblical story instead of attending to the story itself? When John 7:53–8:11 is read either as a cautionary tale against self-righteous judgment or as a story about Jesus' leniency toward adulterous women, the radical claim of this story and its christological focus are diminished or completely lost.

What is striking about John 7:53–8:11 is the way in which Jesus negotiates the scribes' and Pharisees' test. As the Commentary has noted, Jesus' writing on the ground signaled his unwillingness to engage their categories and hence his unwillingness to allow them to exercise any control in the situation. When Jesus does speak, he speaks to the situation of the scribes and Pharisees as well as to the woman. The scribes and Pharisees brought the woman to Jesus as an object to be manipulated for their own ends, but Jesus treats the woman and the scribes and Pharisees as theological equals, each as human beings to whom words about sin can be addressed (vv. 7, 10-11). Jesus offers all his conversation partners in this story the opportunity to break with old ways, where the power of condemnation and death are determinative, and to enter a world marked by freedom and acquittal. The woman is invited to embrace a new future that will allow her to live as a free woman, not a condemned woman. The scribes and Pharisees are invited to give up the categories according to which they had defined and attempted to control life, because their presumed control leads only to the distortions of vv. 4-6.

John 7:53–8:11 is thus a radical story in which Jesus puts his authority up against the claims of the Jewish religious establishment. It is a story of Jesus' grace and mercy, as the dominant thread of Christian interpretation has held since Augustine,[200] but Jesus offers this grace in a very particular social and religious context. His words to both the scribes and Pharisees and the woman have a political and theological, rather than a predominantly moral, dimension. By his very presence, Jesus challenges the law and the power of those who claim the authority to interpret the law. Jesus' identity calls the scribes' and Pharisees' social position and theological authority into question. Jesus brings the promise of freedom to all—scribes, Pharisees, the woman—but that freedom demands a renunciation of old ways and former claims.

In interpreting John 7:53–8:11, then, it is important for the reader to move beyond popular appropriations of this story to its christological core. This story is about neither the scribes' and Pharisees' "sin" of self-righteousness nor the woman's sexual sin; rather, it is about the challenge to embedded religious authority that Jesus brings and the possibilities of new life that arise from that challenge. Jesus places his authority to forgive and to offer freedom over against the religious establishment's determination of the categories of life and death.

---

199. A recent comment by John Updike illustrates this popular interpretive bent: "The Bible is actually rather soft on lust. Jesus' plea for the adulterous woman and his fondness for female company, low and high, give a genial tinge to his ministry" ("Even the Bible Is Soft on Sex," *New York Times Book Review* XCVIII, no. 25 [June 20, 1993]).
200. Augustine, Homily XXXIII, in *Homilies on the Gospel According to St. John* (London: F. & J. Rivington, 1848) 1.477.

John 8:12-30, Words of Conflict: Jesus' Teaching and Response

NIV	NRSV
[12]When Jesus spoke again to the people, he said, "I am the light of the world. Whoever	12Again Jesus spoke to them, saying, "I am the light of the world. Whoever follows me will never

follows me will never walk in darkness, but will have the light of life."

¹³The Pharisees challenged him, "Here you are, appearing as your own witness; your testimony is not valid."

¹⁴Jesus answered, "Even if I testify on my own behalf, my testimony is valid, for I know where I came from and where I am going. But you have no idea where I come from or where I am going. ¹⁵You judge by human standards; I pass judgment on no one. ¹⁶But if I do judge, my decisions are right, because I am not alone. I stand with the Father, who sent me. ¹⁷In your own Law it is written that the testimony of two men is valid. ¹⁸I am one who testifies for myself; my other witness is the Father, who sent me."

¹⁹Then they asked him, "Where is your father?"

"You do not know me or my Father," Jesus replied. "If you knew me, you would know my Father also." ²⁰He spoke these words while teaching in the temple area near the place where the offerings were put. Yet no one seized him, because his time had not yet come.

²¹Once more Jesus said to them, "I am going away, and you will look for me, and you will die in your sin. Where I go, you cannot come."

²²This made the Jews ask, "Will he kill himself? Is that why he says, 'Where I go, you cannot come'?"

²³But he continued, "You are from below; I am from above. You are of this world; I am not of this world. ²⁴I told you that you would die in your sins; if you do not believe that I am *the one I claim to be,ᵃ* you will indeed die in your sins."

²⁵"Who are you?" they asked.

"Just what I have been claiming all along," Jesus replied. ²⁶"I have much to say in judgment of you. But he who sent me is reliable, and what I have heard from him I tell the world."

²⁷They did not understand that he was telling them about his Father. ²⁸So Jesus said, "When you have lifted up the Son of Man, then you will know that I am *the one I claim to be* and that I do nothing on my own but speak just what the Father has taught me. ²⁹The one who sent me is with me; he has not left me alone, for I always do what pleases him." ³⁰Even as he spoke, many put their faith in him.

walk in darkness but will have the light of life." ¹³Then the Pharisees said to him, "You are testifying on your own behalf; your testimony is not valid." ¹⁴Jesus answered, "Even if I testify on my own behalf, my testimony is valid because I know where I have come from and where I am going, but you do not know where I come from or where I am going. ¹⁵You judge by human standards;ᵃ I judge no one. ¹⁶Yet even if I do judge, my judgment is valid; for it is not I alone who judge, but I and the Fatherᵇ who sent me. ¹⁷In your law it is written that the testimony of two witnesses is valid. ¹⁸I testify on my own behalf, and the Father who sent me testifies on my behalf." ¹⁹Then they said to him, "Where is your Father?" Jesus answered, "You know neither me nor my Father. If you knew me, you would know my Father also." ²⁰He spoke these words while he was teaching in the treasury of the temple, but no one arrested him, because his hour had not yet come.

21Again he said to them, "I am going away, and you will search for me, but you will die in your sin. Where I am going, you cannot come." ²²Then the Jews said, "Is he going to kill himself? Is that what he means by saying, 'Where I am going, you cannot come'?" ²³He said to them, "You are from below, I am from above; you are of this world, I am not of this world. ²⁴I told you that you would die in your sins, for you will die in your sins unless you believe that I am he."ᶜ ²⁵They said to him, "Who are you?" Jesus said to them, "Why do I speak to you at all?ᵈ ²⁶I have much to say about you and much to condemn; but the one who sent me is true, and I declare to the world what I have heard from him." ²⁷They did not understand that he was speaking to them about the Father. ²⁸So Jesus said, "When you have lifted up the Son of Man, then you will realize that I am he,ᶜ and that I do nothing on my own, but I speak these things as the Father instructed me. ²⁹And the one who sent me is with me; he has not left me alone, for I always do what is pleasing to him." ³⁰As he was saying these things, many believed in him.

ᵃ Gk *according to the flesh*   ᵇ Other ancient authorities read *he*   ᶜ Gk *I am*   ᵈ Or *What I have told you from the beginning*

COMMENTARY

The pattern evident in John 7:1-52 continues in 8:12-30: short scenes in which Jesus' teaching places him in conflict with his Jewish conversation partners. Like the mini-dramas in chap. 7 (see Overview), in 8:12-30 the Fourth Evangelist once again combines a variety of Jesus traditions to create a narrative that is shaped by theological intentions. John 8:12-30 can be subdivided into two smaller units: vv. 12-20 and vv. 21-30. Each of the subdivisions begins in a similar way ("again," vv. 12, 21), and each ends with the Evangelist's report on the response to Jesus' teaching (the inability to arrest Jesus, v. 20; the faith of "many," v. 30).

8:12-20. 8:12. The "I am" saying with which Jesus begins his teaching in v. 12 is one in a series of "I am" sayings in the Fourth Gospel (see Fig. 10, "The 'I AM' Sayings in John," 602). As noted above (see 7:2), light was an important element in the celebration of the Feast of Tabernacles. The Mishnah describes the lighting of four large lampstands in the Temple Court of the Women at the close of the first festival day.[201] These lampstands produced so much light that "there was not a courtyard in Jerusalem that did not reflect the light of the Beth ha-She'ubah."[202] Celebrants at Tabernacles danced before those candlesticks with "burning torches,"[203] adding even more light to their joyous celebration. As with the words about water in 7:37-38, here Jesus is declaring himself to be the true fulfillment of Tabernacles joy when he declares himself to be the light of the world.[204] Old rites are once again transformed by Jesus' incarnate presence (cf. 2:6-11). The Tabernacles light illuminated all of Jerusalem, but Jesus is the light of the world.[205]

Light is a frequent image in the OT. Light was God's first creation (Gen 1:3-4). In the exodus tradition (which forms part of the background of the Tabernacles festival; see Commentary on 7:2), God went before Israel in the wilderness as a pillar of fire at night "to give them light" (Exod 13:21

NRSV; see also Ps 105:39; Wis 18:3). The associations of light with the exodus (see also God's self-revelation to Moses in the burning bush) provide continuity between 8:12 and the exodus traditions evoked in John 6. Light is also a frequent OT symbol of theophany (e.g., Gen 15:17; Exod 19:18; Ps 104:2; Ezek 1:4). In the wisdom tradition, light is a symbol for the law or the Word of God (Ps 119:105; Prov 6:23; Wis 18:4) and for Wisdom itself (Prov 8:22).

Light also figured as a symbol of God or God's Word in Hellenistic Judaism, especially Philo, Qumran, and Gnosticism.[206] "Light" as a religious symbol thus had broad currency in the Mediterranean world,[207] but the Fourth Evangelist gives that symbol new meaning by identifying it with the revelation of God in Jesus (cf. discussion of *logos* in Commentary on 1:1-18).

The use of light symbolism in the Fourth Gospel provides the final context within which to place Jesus' words in 8:12*a*. In 1:4-10, light is the central image for the presence of the Word in the world. "Light" (φῶς *phōs*) and "life" (ζωή *zōē*; see 8:12*b*) are identified in 1:4 as two ways in which the Word expresses itself in the world. Light and life are signs of the Word's relationship to the world; they are the ways in which humanity experiences the incarnate Word. "World" (κόσμος *kosmos*) is used neutrally in 8:12*a* (cf. 1:19); it is not the sphere of enmity and conflict (1:10; 7:7), but the place where God's offer of life in Jesus is available (3:16-17). Jesus' own words in 8:12*a* thus confirm the christological and soteriological claims of the prologue.

John 8:12*b* makes explicit the soteriological dimensions of Jesus as the light. The presence of Jesus as the light of the world presents the world with two choices: to follow Jesus and have "the light of life" or to walk in darkness (cf. 3:19-21; 11:9; 12:35-36). "Follow" (ἀκολουθέω *akoloutheō*) is the language of discipleship (1:37-38, 40, 43), which in John involves recognition of and response to Jesus' offer of life (10:27-28; see also 10:4-5).

---

201. See *m. Sukk.* 5.2.
202. Ibid., 5.3.
203. Ibid., 5.4
204. Charles H. Talbert, *Reading John: A Literary and Theological Commentary on the Fourth Gospel and the Johannine Epistles* (New York: Crossroad, 1992) 143-53.
205. Rudolf Schnackenburg, *The Gospel According to St. John*, 3 vols. (New York: Seabury, 1982) 2:189.

206. Bultmann claimed Gnosticism was the decisive influence on John, but as with his claims about *logos*, could cite no Gnostic documents in which "light of the world" appeared. See Rudolf Bultmann, *The Gospel of John: A Commentary*, trans. G. R. Beasley-Murray, R. W. N. Hoare, and J. K. Riches (Philadelphia: Westminster, 1971) 342n. 5.
207. See C. K. Barrett, *The Gospel According to St. John*, 2nd ed. (Philadelphia: Westminster, 1978) 335-37.

8:13-18. The Pharisees respond to Jesus' invitation by questioning the validity of Jesus' self-witness (cf. 7:32, 45-52). Their words recall Jesus' own words about self-witness in 5:31. As noted at 5:31, Jewish law held that a man's witness on his own behalf is not legally admissible evidence; he must have the witness of two other men.[208] In 5:31-40, therefore, Jesus presented other witnesses on his behalf. This time Jesus responds to the Pharisees' complaint with a strategy that at first glance contradicts his earlier words. It is a misreading of the contradiction to explain it by different layers of tradition, however.[209] In 5:31-40, Jesus conducted his self-defense according to the juridical categories of his opponents; he ceded them their interpretation of the law and their definition of witness. In the present text, Jesus distances himself from his opponents' categories ("your law," v. 17) and counters with his juridical categories. The "even if . . . " with which vv. 14 and 16 begin draws attention to the conflicting juridical perspectives.[210] The heavy concentration of the adjective "valid" in this section (ἀληθής *alēthēs*, 8:13-14, 17; and ἀληθινός *alēthinos*, 8:16, are used interchangeably here) points to the heart of the juridical debate: Only one perspective can be "valid" or true. This juridical debate reflects the church/synagogue debates at the time of the Fourth Evangelist about the validity of Jesus' claims (cf. 5:31-40; 7:12*b*; 15:26-27; 16:1-2, 8-11).

Jesus' knowledge of his origin and his destination (v. 14) validates his self-witness, because it derives from his relationship to God and his whole career as the Word. The Greek verb translated "going" (ὑπάγω *hypagō*) regularly speaks of Jesus' departure from this world through his death, resurrection, and ascension (7:33; 8:21; 13:3, 33, 36; 14:28; 16:5, 10). Jesus' words, therefore, are not self-interested witness. Rather, Jesus is the only one who can bear witness "on his behalf," because he is the only one who has seen God and can make God known (1:18).[211] Because his opponents do not share Jesus' knowledge (v. 14*b*), they cannot recognize the validity of his witness.

The distance between Jesus and his opponents is further underscored by the difference in their approach to judgment (vv. 15-16). To judge "by human standards" is literally to judge "according to the flesh" (κατὰ τὴν σάρκα *kata tēn sarka*).[212] It is because Jesus' opponents judge solely by what is visible that they do not recognize his divine origins (cf. 7:24). Jesus' statement that he judges no one (v. 15*b*) seems to contradict his earlier statements (5:30). His words in v. 16 further heighten the contradiction: Does he judge or not? The answer, as happens frequently in the Fourth Gospel, is both/and, not either/or. Jesus was sent by God for salvation, not judgment (3:16), but Jesus' witness has an intrinsic eschatological dimension, because it evokes decision and judgment (3:17-21).[213] When a moment of judgment occurs, Jesus' judgment, like the witness out of which it arises, is valid, because he judges at one with the God who sent him (5:22, 27), the same God who sent him for salvation. Once again, the validity (truth) of what Jesus does derives from his relationship with God (cf. 7:17-18).

Verses 17-18 end Jesus' argument with an ironic twist. He meets the Pharisees' demand for two witnesses by offering himself and God. He returns to the categories of 5:32ff., but now includes his self-witness. The irony arises because Jesus gives the Pharisees what they ask for, but in terms they can neither recognize nor receive because they judge "according to the flesh" (cf. 5:40-44).

8:19. For the Gospel reader, the Pharisees' question in v. 19 is also an instance of irony. They ask about the location of Jesus' father, so that he can present himself as a witness, but their question reveals a more profound ignorance about the identity of God and the relationship of God and Jesus. Jesus' response confirms the Pharisees' real ignorance. Verse 19*b* contains the key to Johannine christology and theology: To know Jesus is to know God (cf. 14:6-7).

8:20. The unit concludes with an echo of 7:30. It is the time set for Jesus by God that governs Jesus' life, not human intentions. The reference to the temple treasury as the place where Jesus teaches provides an additional connection to the

---

208. See *m. Ketub.* 2.9; Deut. 17:6; 19:15; cf. John 8:17.
209. So Jerome H. Neyrey, *An Ideology of Revolt: John's Christology in Social-Science Perspective* (Philadelphia: Fortress, 1988) 52, 58.
210. Bultmann, *The Gospel of John,* 278.
211. Cf. ibid., 279.

212. John 8:15 is the only non-Pauline usage of the expression "according to the flesh" in the NT. Paul regularly uses this expression, but without the definite article before *sarx* (e.g., Rom 1:3; 4:1; 1 Cor 1:26, 2 Cor 1:17; Gal 4:23).
213. See George R. Beasley-Murray, *John,* WBC 36 (Waco, Tex.: Word, 1987) 129.

Feast of Tabernacles, because the Temple treasury was located next to the Court of the Women, the site of the Feast's light celebration.

8:21-30. When Jesus resumes speaking ("again" [πάλιν *palin*], v. 21), his words replay the theme of his departure from 8:14. In 8:12-20 the validity of Jesus' witness was the lens through which to view his identity; in vv. 21-30, Jesus' departure—that is, his death, resurrection, and ascension—now becomes the lens (8:21-22, 28).

8:21. Jesus' words echo 7:33-34. His emphasis on the consequence of his departure for the "Jews" ("you will die in your sin") conveys the limits of Jesus' availability and offer of salvation (cf. 16:33-34). "To die in your sin" is synonymous with the darkness of v. 12*b*. The use of "sin" in the singular suggests that sin is not measured by individual actions, but is instead the central and decisive sin of not recognizing God in Jesus (cf. 1:29; 8:24; 9:41; 15:22-24; 16:9).[214] Brown helpfully relates this understanding of sin to the unforgivable sin of not receiving the Holy Spirit in the Synoptics (Mark 3:29).

8:22. As in 7:35-36, the "Jews" misunderstand Jesus' words about his departure. Their questions have a harder edge than in chap. 7, however, because suicide was a serious offense in Judaism. The person who had committed suicide was forbidden regular burial rites and "the souls . . . go to darkest Hades, and God, their father, will visit the sins of the evil-doers on their descendants."[215] The "Jews'" questions (as in 7:35-36) also are ironic, because they are an unwitting prophecy of the theological truth of Jesus' death in John. Jesus will indeed lay down his life of his own accord (10:17-18; 15:13).

8:23. Jesus explains the source of the "Jews'" lack of comprehension: They are defined by their place of origin just as Jesus is defined by his, and the two stand in opposition to one another (cf. 8:14). The expression "from below" (ἐκ τῶν κάτω *ek tōn katō*) may be a play on the Jews' allusion to suicide in v. 22. Jesus will not be relegated to below (Hades) because he is from above. The spatial dualism of v. 23*a* recalls 3:31 (see also 19:11, 23), as well as Jesus' invitation to Nicode-

mus in 3:3, 7. To enter the kingdom of God (3:3) or not to die in sin (8:22), one must be from above, not below,not of this world (cf. 1:12-13). The "Jews" are thus distinguished from Jesus' disciples who do not belong to the world (15:19; 17:6, 14, 16).

8:24. Jesus reiterates his words of 8:21 ("I told you"). The plural "sins" (ἁμαρτίαι *hamartiai*) is not a significant change from v. 21; it reminds the "Jews" that the one central sin underscored earlier can nonetheless be manifested in individual actions (cf. 3:19-21). The only alternative to dying in sin is to believe that "I am" (v. 24*b*). The NRSV supplies a pronoun as a predicate ("I am he") and the NIV offers a paraphrase ("I am the one I claim to be"), but these translations ignore or alter the use of an absolute ἐγώ εἰμι (*egō eimi*) saying in the Greek (cf. 4:26; 6:20; see also Fig. 10, "The 'I AM' Sayings in John," 602). Jesus makes a bold claim for himself here, and he sets very high stakes for faith. He identifies himself with the divine name (see Exod 13:14; Isa 43:25; 51:12; 52:6 LXX) to testify that he and God are one (1:1; 10:30). To move from death to life, the Jews must recognize Jesus as the incarnate Logos of God (cf. 8:19).

8:25a. The Jews' question here may be the most ironically charged of all the questions in John 7–8 (cf. 7:35, 42; 8:19). It shows a complete misunderstanding of the *egō eimi* saying. They think Jesus has merely omitted the predicate in an identification saying and grasp none of the theological overtones. The irony is profound, because in their ignorance they ask the critical christological question of the Gospel: Who is Jesus?

8:25b. There is no consensus for the translation of this verse (note the disparity between the NIV and the NRSV). Two translation difficulties render the meaning of this sentence obscure. First, it is not clear whether the Greek word ὅτι (*hoti*) is used as an interrogative and thus introduces a question (NRSV), or whether it should be read as a relative pronoun (ὅ τι *ho ti*) and hence simply translated as "that" or "what." Second, it is not clear how the adverbial expression τὴν ἀρχήν (*tēn archēn*) is to be translated (e.g., "at all," NRSV; "all along," NIV; or "from the beginning," NRSV alt.). This translation ambiguity means that Jesus' words can be read as an affirmation (NIV) or a rebuke (NRSV). Against the NRSV translation is the fact that v. 25*b* introduces a new section of Jesus'

214. See Raymond E. Brown, *The Gospel According to John (I–XII)*, AB 29 (Garden City, N.Y.: Doubleday, 1966) 350.

215. Josephus *The Jewish War* 3.375; Schnackenburg, *The Gospel According to St. John*, 2:198.

speech, and the NRSV rendering seems more appropriate to the end of a conversation. A translation with a meaning similar to that of the NIV is favored by most recent commentators.[216] The solution may lie with the reading found in one of the oldest manuscripts, $\mathfrak{P}^{66}$, which contains words missing in other manuscript traditions, "What I told you from the beginning I am also telling you."[217] This translation provides a smooth transition to v. 26 and contains a suggestive echo of the Prologue (1:1).

8:26-27. Verse 26 restates themes from earlier discourses, particularly Jesus as the one sent by God (5:37-38; 6:29, 39, 57) and God as the source of Jesus' words (3:34; 7:16). These themes underscore Jesus' relationship with God as the decisive factor in who Jesus is and what he does, but Jesus' audience does not grasp this central theological reality (v. 27).

8:28. Jesus' departure is depicted in v. 28 in the distinctly Johannine idiom for Jesus' death, resurrection, and ascension: "lifted up" (ὑψόω *hypsoō*). As noted at 3:14, *hypsoō* means both "lift up" and "exalt." This is the second of three statements about the lifting up of the Son of Man in John (see 3:14; 12:32-34), analogous to the three passion predictions in the Synoptic tradition (Mark 8:31; 9:31; 10:33-34; and par.).

The title "Son of Man" draws attention to Jesus as an eschatological figure (cf. 5:28), and v. 28 highlights this element of judgment in two ways. First, Jesus places responsibility for his lifting up on his audience ("When you have lifted up . . . "). In contrast, in 3:14 and 12:32-34 "lifted up" is in the passive voice, suggesting God's agency.[218] There is an ironic dimension to this responsibility, because in lifting up Jesus to kill him, his opponents participate in his exaltation. Second, the lifting up of the Son of Man is a moment of judgment because it confronts the Jews with the truth of Jesus' identity. Verse 28 gives the crucifixion/resurrection/ascension an explicit revelatory significance, "You will realize that I am" (author's trans.; once again the NIV and the NRSV mute the Greek use of an absolute *egō eimi*). The lifting up will also confirm

what Jesus has been saying all along: He does nothing on his own (5:19, 30) and speaks what God has taught him (7:16).

Scholars debate whether v. 28 should be read as a prophecy of judgment (i.e., it will be too late for the Jews)[219] or a promise (i.e., the Jews will realize the truth).[220] Yet an either/or reading of v. 28 seems to overlook the nature of decision in the Fourth Gospel, which always holds together the two dimensions of salvation and judgment.[221] The significance of Jesus' words in v. 28 is that they point to a time after his lifting up, when the truth will be revealed to the Jews (note the future tense, "you will know" [γνώσεσθε *gnōsethe*]). The knowledge gained through the lifting up thus "falls in the age of the Spirit-Paraclete."[222] Verse 28 looks beyond the Gospel narrative to the future experience of Christians and Jews. The lifting up, therefore, is not simply the culmination of Jesus' self-revelation, but is the beginning of the witness of the community with the aid of the Paraclete. Many of the verbs used to describe Jesus' activity in 8:12-20 will also be used to describe the work of the Paraclete (15:26; 16:11, 13).

8:29. The lifting up also will show the constancy of God's presence with Jesus (v. 29). This constancy distinguishes God's relationship to Jesus from humanity's relationship to Jesus during his lifetime. Jesus' disciples will leave him "alone" (μόνος *monos*) at the cross, but God will not (cf. 16:32). Jesus' "pleasing actions" (τὰ ἀρεστά *ta aresta*) are not a prerequisite for God's presence; rather, they are an inevitable outcome of their relationship of God and Jesus. Because God and Jesus are united by love (3:35; 15:9), Jesus is intrinsically pleasing to God. The love commandment of the Farewell Discourse (13:34; 15:12) opens this aspect of God and Jesus' relationship to include the disciples. When the disciples act in and out of this love, they, too, share in "pleasing actions" (cf. 1 John 3:22).

8:30. The conclusion to the unit ("many believed" [πολλοὶ ἐπίστευσαν *polloi episteusan*]) stands in marked contrast to the reference to

216. Beasley-Murray, *John*, 125-26; Brown, *The Gospel According to John (I–XII)*, 347-48; but see Barrett, *The Gospel According to St. John*, 343, who plays down the translation difficulty and favors a third option: "I am from the beginning what I tell you."

217. Brown, *The Gospel According to John (I–XII)*, 348.

218. Schnackenburg, *The Gospel According to St. John*, 2:202.

219. Bultmann, *The Gospel of John*, 349-50; Brown, *The Gospel According to John (I–XII)*, 351; Barrett, *The Gospel According to St. John*, 344.

220. E. C. Hoskyns, *The Fourth Gospel* (London: Faber & Faber, 1947) 336-37.

221. Schnackenburg, *The Gospel According to St. John*, 2:202-3.

222. Beasley-Murray, *John*, 132.

Jesus' arrest that concluded vv. 12-20. The juxtaposition of the two conclusions highlights the divided response among those who hear Jesus (cf. 7:43).

John 8:31-59, Debate Between Jesus and His Jewish Opponents

OVERVIEW

John 8:31-59 has been called the *locus classicus* of Johannine theology.[223] In these verses, the Fourth Evangelist lays bare what he perceives to be the fundamental lines of debate and disagreement between Judaism and Christianity. The disagreement between Jesus and the Jews is no longer depicted in terms of response to a particular event—for example, a healing (John 5) or the feeding miracle (John 6)—but the basic theological differences themselves become the presenting issue.

The dialogue of 8:31-59 is virtually seamless, each verse building on what precedes to convey the intensification of the theological debate. Neyrey identifies the forensic quality of this unified debate, noting that 8:31-59 reads as a trial of Jewish objections to Jesus.[224] At issue is the truth of Jesus' testimony (8:32, 40, 45-46, 55) and the falsehood of those who oppose him (8:44-45). The repeated references to Abraham (8:33, 37, 39-40, 52-53, 56, 58) are the only such references in the Fourth Gospel and provide a key to the development of the debate.[225] The references to Abraham cluster around two distinct but interrelated themes: Abraham's relationship to Jesus' interlocutors (vv. 31-38) and to Jesus (vv. 48-59). The debate will show that one's relationship to Abraham is ultimately determined by one's relationship to God (vv. 39-47). Like the midrash on Moses and manna in John 6:25-51 (see Commentary above), vv. 31-59 can be read as a midrash on the Abraham tradition and the meaning of being an heir to Abraham.

The references to Abraham suggest the following subunits within the debate:

8:31-38   Freedom for the Descendants of Abraham
8:39-47   Children of Abraham/Children of God
8:48-59   Abraham and Jesus

---

223. C. H. Dodd, *Historical Tradition in the Fourth Gospel* (Cambridge: Cambridge University Press, 1963) 330.
224. See Neyrey, *An Ideology of Revolt,* 43-48.

225. See Dodd, *Historical Tradition in the Fourth Gospel,* 330; Horacio E. Lona, *Abraham in Johannes 8: Ein Beitrag zur Methodenfrage* (Bern: Lang, 1976); Jeffrey S. Siker, *Disinheriting the Jews: The Use of Abraham in Early Christian Controversy with Judaism from Paul Through Justin Martyr* (Ann Arbor, Mich.: University Microfilms, 1989).

John 8:31-38, Freedom for the Descendants of Abraham

NIV	NRSV
[31]To the Jews who had believed him, Jesus said, "If you hold to my teaching, you are really my disciples. [32]Then you will know the truth, and the truth will set you free."	[31]Then Jesus said to the Jews who had believed in him, "If you continue in my word, you are truly my disciples; [32]and you will know the truth, and the truth will make you free." [33]They
[33]They answered him, "We are Abraham's descendants[a] and have never been slaves of anyone. How can you say that we shall be set free?"	answered him, "We are descendants of Abraham and have never been slaves to anyone. What do you mean by saying, 'You will be made free'?"
[34]Jesus replied, "I tell you the truth, everyone who sins is a slave to sin. [35]Now a slave has no permanent place in the family, but a son belongs to it forever. [36]So if the Son sets you free, you	[34]Jesus answered them, "Very truly, I tell you, everyone who commits sin is a slave to sin. [35]The slave does not have a permanent place in the household; the son has a place there forever. [36]So if the Son makes you free, you will be free indeed.
*a33 Greek *seed*; also in verse 37*	

636

will be free indeed. ³⁷I know you are Abraham's descendants. Yet you are ready to kill me, because you have no room for my word. ³⁸I am telling you what I have seen in the Father's presence, and you do what you have heard from your father.ᵃ"

ᵃ38 Or presence. Therefore do what you have heard from the Father.

³⁷I know that you are descendants of Abraham; yet you look for an opportunity to kill me, because there is no place in you for my word. ³⁸I declare what I have seen in the Father's presence; as for you, you should do what you have heard from the Father."ᵃ

ᵃ Other ancient authorities read you do what you have heard from your father

COMMENTARY

8:31-32. These verses identify Jesus' audience as "the Jews who believed in him." The harsh nature of the debate that follows raises questions about this identification. Many commentators propose that the expression is a gloss by a later editor to link 8:31ff. with the conclusion of v. 30 ("many believed").[226] A more helpful suggestion is to see the expression as another glimpse of the two levels on which the Gospel unfolds (see also 5:31-40; 9:1-41), pointing beyond the narrative setting to the Evangelist's own time. Yet even when this assumption is made, the identification remains problematic. Some scholars take the reference to believing Jews as a polemic against Jews within the Evangelist's time who believed in Jesus but remained advocates of Jewish religious practices.[227] Other scholars maintain that the faith to which vv. 30-31 refer is inadequate and that the purpose of the ensuing debate is to test it and show its inadequacy.[228]

Such readings, however, tend to overlook the relationship of 8:31-59 to the rest of chaps. 7–8. These verses are the theological climax of all that has preceded. The identification of Jesus' audience here as "the Jews who believed in him" does not point to a specific historical audience either in the Gospel or in the Evangelist's time, but serves to highlight the intensity of the theological debate between Jews and Jewish Christians. Jews who professed faith in Jesus in the Fourth Evangelist's time encountered theological arguments like those voiced by Jesus' opponents in these verses. The debate is given full rein here, with Jesus prevail-

ing, to show how the Christian claims could stand up to Jewish counterarguments.[229]

Verses 31-32 contain an "if" clause (v. 31a) followed by three apodoses (vv. 31b, 32a, 32b) that introduce the promises that motivate the debate. The condition ("if") is expressed with two distinctive Johannine terms, μένω (menō "continue in," NRSV) and λόγος (logos "word"). The centrality of Jesus' word is highlighted in several ways in vv. 31-59: The frequent use of logos (vv. 31, 37, 43, 51-52, 55); three occurrences of "very truly, I say to you" (vv. 34, 51, 58); and Jesus' repeated references to his speaking (vv. 38, 43, 45-46, 55). Menō denotes a permanent relationship between Jesus' listeners and his word (cf. the use of menō in 15:4, 7, 10). All that Jesus promises in v. 32 depends on the listener's continuing relationship to Jesus' word.

The three promises are each built around the root "truth" (ἀλήθεια alētheia) and are inextricably intertwined. The liberating power of the truth is unknowable apart from being Jesus' disciple, which in turn depends on one's relationship to Jesus' word. The truth and freedom that Jesus promises are not abstract principles, but like light and life (e.g., 1:4-5, 9; 8:12), are bound to the Word. The truth is the presence of God in Jesus (e.g., 8:14-19, 27-28). Freedom can be interpreted in a variety of contexts in Jewish tradition, as v. 33 will show, but its root context is the exodus to freedom out of slavery in Egypt. The introduction of "freedom" (ἐλευθερόω eleutheroō) in v. 32 thus suggests a reinterpretation of the exodus tradition through

226. E.g., Brown, The Gospel According to John (I–XII), 354-55.
227. C. H. Dodd, Historical Tradition in the Fourth Gospel (Cambridge: Cambridge University Press, 1963) 379.
228. Hoskyns, The Fourth Gospel, 336-37; Bultmann, The Gospel of John, 433.

229. Rudolf Schnackenburg, The Gospel According to St. John, 3 vols. (New York: Sebury, 1982) 2:204-5; Beasley-Murray, John, 103.

the lens of the truth of God in Jesus (see also the reinterpretation of exodus imagery in John 6).

8:33. Jesus' reinterpretation of freedom evokes resistance in his listeners. They rebut his words by appealing to their heritage as descendants (σπέρμα *sperma*) of Abraham (cf. Matt 3:9; Luke 3:8). This appeal will develop into the central paradox of the debate: Is it possible to claim Abraham while rejecting Jesus (e.g., vv. 37, 39-40, 47, 53, 57)? The Jews' rebuttal of Jesus' words is another instance of Johannine use of misunderstanding. Jesus spoke of freedom as the result of knowing the truth, but when the Jews repeat Jesus' words in v. 33*b*, they misquote him, leaving out the reference to truth. Instead, they interpret Jesus' words as if they themselves were a misreading of Jewish heritage. The Jews' words can be read on two levels. First, they can be read as a statement that the Jews' descent from Abraham already guarantees their spiritual freedom, so that they have no need of what Jesus offers.[230] Second, their words can be read as a reflection on Jewish history.[231] In this reading, the hyperbole of the Jews' denial heightens the poignant irony of their words: Israel's history is characterized by periods of slavery and captivity, and the situation in which the Jews currently find themselves, as subjects of the Roman Empire, is yet one more situation of slavery. In their desire to distance themselves from Jesus, they have already begun the process of distancing themselves from their own history (cf. 19:15).

8:34-38. Jesus addresses the two prongs of the Jews' protest (and misunderstanding): freedom and their descent from Abraham. Jesus first corrects his listeners' misunderstanding of freedom and slavery. The solemn formula with which v. 34 begins ("Very truly, I tell you") marks the introduction of a new teaching (cf. 5:24-25). Freedom is a gift; one cannot lay claim to freedom by virtue of one's heritage; one's identity as slave or free is determined by what one does, not by who one claims to be (cf. 3:19-21). "Slave to sin" is thus synonymous with "die in your sin(s)" (8:21, 24).

The short parable of v. 35 illustrates the relationship among status, inheritance, and freedom (for other short parables in John, see 3:29; 5:19;

11:9-10). The images in this short parable belong to the common stock of Jesus' parables: slave, household, son (cf. Matt 21:33-46; 22:1-14),[232] but they seem also to have more specific associations in their use here. The images of son and slave in this verse recall the story of Ishmael and Isaac (Gen 16:15; 21:9-21) and the struggle over inheritance (cf. Gal 4:21-31). The use of "forever" (εἰς τὸν αἰῶνα *eis ton aiōna*) points to the eschatological dimension of freedom and links the promise of freedom with the other eschatological gifts Jesus promises (e.g., 6:35).

The christological focus of Jesus' words about freedom and slavery moves to the foreground in v. 36. Jesus repeats the promise of freedom from v. 32, substituting "Son" for "truth," and thus makes explicit the link between truth and Jesus' identity. If one recognizes the truth of Jesus' identity, that he is the Son (cf. 1:18; 3:16, 35-36; 5:23; 6:40; 8:28), then freedom is possible. The shift in imagery from Abraham's son in the parable of v. 35 to God's Son in v. 36 anticipates the argument of vv. 39-47.

In vv. 37-38, Jesus directly engages the Jews' protest of v. 33 ("descendants [*sperma*] of Abraham"). He grants them their claim (v. 37*a*), but contrasts the claim with their behavior (v. 37*b*). The desire to kill Jesus has been a constant part of the fabric of chaps. 7-8 (7:1, 25, 30, 44-45; 8:20), and Jesus now identifies that desire with the absence of any relationship to his word (cf. v. 31*a*). The claim to relationship with Abraham must be measured against the relationship with Jesus.

Verse 38 compares the respective relationships of Jesus and his listeners to the "Father." This verse presents two translation problems. First, the verse has several important textual variants. In v. 38*a* Jesus repeats a claim made many times in the Gospel, that he speaks what he has seen with the Father (1:18; 3:32; 8:26). In order to heighten the contrast between Jesus and his listeners, some ancient manuscripts add a personal pronoun here ("my Father"), but the oldest manuscripts ($\mathfrak{P}^{66.75}$) omit the pronoun. The most significant textual variant occurs in v. 38*b*. As in v. 38*a*, some manuscripts add a personal pronoun before "Father" ("your father," NIV), in order to heighten the contrast. Again the oldest manuscripts ($\mathfrak{P}^{66.75}$) do not contain the personal pronoun, and the

---

230. C. K. Barrett, *The Gospel According to St. John,* 2nd ed. (Philadelphia: Westminster, 1978) 345.

231. Brown, *The Gospel According to John (I–XII)*, 355; Beasley-Murray, *John*, 133.

232. See Dodd, *Historical Tradition in the Fourth Gospel,* 380; Brown, *The Gospel According to John (I–XII)*, 355.

reading without the pronoun should thus be accepted as the preferred reading (NRSV). Second, one has to decide whether to translate the verb "do" (ποιεῖτε *poieite*) in v. 38*b* as an indicative ("you do," NIV) or an imperative ("you should do," NRSV). When the verb is translated as an indicative, it becomes an indictment of the Jews' behavior, whereas when it is translated as an imperative, it continues the challenge Jesus posed to his listeners in v. 31.

The best reading of v. 38 is without personal pronouns and with *poieite* translated as an imperative ("do").[233] At this point in the debate, the issue is whether the Jews will embrace their inheritance as descendants of Abraham and recognize the Father whom they share with Jesus. The addition of personal pronouns forecloses this possibility, because the pronouns explicitly identify distinct fathers for Jesus and the Jews. As the debate progresses in vv. 39-47, the difference in fathers will be unambiguously announced, but in vv. 31-38 the possibility of obedience remains open. (See Reflections at 8:48-59.)

233. So Brown, *The Gospel According to John (I–XII)*, 356.

John 8:39-47, Children of Abraham/Children of God

[39]"Abraham is our father," they answered.

"If you were Abraham's children," said Jesus, "then you would[a] do the things Abraham did. [40]As it is, you are determined to kill me, a man who has told you the truth that I heard from God. Abraham did not do such things. [41]You are doing the things your own father does."

"We are not illegitimate children," they protested. "The only Father we have is God himself."

[42]Jesus said to them, "If God were your Father, you would love me, for I came from God and now am here. I have not come on my own; but he sent me. [43]Why is my language not clear to you? Because you are unable to hear what I say. [44]You belong to your father, the devil, and you want to carry out your father's desire. He was a murderer from the beginning, not holding to the truth, for there is no truth in him. When he lies, he speaks his native language, for he is a liar and the father of lies. [45]Yet because I tell the truth, you do not believe me! [46]Can any of you prove me guilty of sin? If I am telling the truth, why don't you believe me? [47]He who belongs to God hears what God says. The reason you do not hear is that you do not belong to God."

a39 Some early manuscripts *"If you are Abraham's children," said Jesus, "then*

[39]They answered him, "Abraham is our father." Jesus said to them, "If you were Abraham's children, you would be doing[a] what Abraham did, [40]but now you are trying to kill me, a man who has told you the truth that I heard from God. This is not what Abraham did. [41]You are indeed doing what your father does." They said to him, "We are not illegitimate children; we have one father, God himself." [42]Jesus said to them, "If God were your Father, you would love me, for I came from God and now I am here. I did not come on my own, but he sent me. [43]Why do you not understand what I say? It is because you cannot accept my word. [44]You are from your father the devil, and you choose to do your father's desires. He was a murderer from the beginning and does not stand in the truth, because there is no truth in him. When he lies, he speaks according to his own nature, for he is a liar and the father of lies. [45]But because I tell the truth, you do not believe me. [46]Which of you convicts me of sin? If I tell the truth, why do you not believe me? [47]Whoever is from God hears the words of God. The reason you do not hear them is that you are not from God."

a Other ancient authorities read *If you are Abraham's children, then do*

COMMENTARY

8:39a. This verse functions as a transition from the first to the second unit of the debate. The Jews' appeal to Abraham shifts the focus from the Jews as descendants of Abraham (vv. 33, 37) to Abraham as father. The noun "father" (πατήρ *patēr*) occurs frequently in vv. 39-47 (vv. 39, 41, 42, 44 [3x]), and significantly is always used in relationship to the question of the Jews' father, never Jesus'.[234] This is highly unusual for the Fourth Gospel, where the subject of Jesus' identity as God's Son is a crucial theological theme. Verses 39-47 will go on to show that the Jews' appeal to Father Abraham without appealing to Jesus' Father calls the Jews' inheritance into question.

8:39b-41a. Jesus rebuts the Jews' appeal to Abraham by focusing on their actions. His words in v. 39*b* are reminiscent of the teaching of John the Baptist in Matt 3:9 (see Luke 3:8 also). In both instances, a claim to Abrahamic paternity is held up to the standards of one's works, with the clear implication that the inheritance is conditional (cf. Rom 9:6-8). The Mishnah provides additional evidence of the importance of Abraham as a measure of discipleship: "A good eye and a humble spirit and a lowly soul—[they in who are these] are the disciples of Abraham our father."[235]

The condition in v. 39*b* is difficult to translate because it is a mixed condition in the Greek; the verb in the protasis ("if" clause) is in the present tense ("are"; see the NIV variant), while the verb in the second clause is in the past tense. The NIV and the NRSV resolve the translation difficulty by accepting the readings of variant manuscripts and placing both verbs in the past tense. This translation decision mutes the intensity of the condition, however. Some manuscripts try to resolve the grammar of this verse by turning the second verb into an imperative (NRSV alt.). This, too, changes the meaning of the text, because it makes it roughly synonymous with v. 38, rather than an advance in the debate. The Greek would be more accurately translated, "If you *really* are children of Abraham, then you would be doing. . . . "[236]

Jesus no longer tells the Jews what to do (v. 38); he now observes what they neglect to do.

The shift from "descendants" of Abraham (σπέρμα *sperma*) to "children" of Abraham (τέκνα *tekna*) in v. 39, introduces a new theological metaphor into the debate. "Children" is used only twice in the Fourth Gospel apart from this verse, and in both instances it refers to "children of God" (1:12; 11:52). Its use here suggests that the ultimate focus of the conversation is on relationship to God, not to Abraham.

In v. 40, the Jews' attempt to kill Jesus is measured against two standards. First, it is measured against God's truth, which Jesus speaks. Verse 40 thus returns to the theme with which the debate began in v. 31, remaining in Jesus' word and knowing the truth, and it shows once again that the Jews do not meet the conditions Jesus set for them (cf. v. 37). Second, it is measured against the model of Abraham himself. The reference to Abraham's actions recalls the faithfulness of Abraham to the truth of God (Gen 12:1-9; 15:1-6; cf. Rom 4:16-25), but it may also intend a more specific contrast between the murderous actions of the Jews and the hospitality for which Abraham was renowned (Gen 18:1-15; cf. Heb 13:2).[237]

Verse 41*a* marks an important shift in Jesus' words to the Jews from invitation to act (v. 38) to observation of actions (vv. 39-40) to indictment (v. 41*a*). This shift mirrors the shift to greater antagonism between the conversation partners. The ambiguity in the use of "father" also moves one step closer to resolution here, because v. 41*a* makes clear that Jesus is distinguishing the Jews' father from Father Abraham and, it seems, from his Father.

8:41b. The Jews recognize Jesus' indictment and intensify their defense of their heritage by turning their appeal from Father Abraham (vv. 33, 39) to Father God (v. 41). In the OT, "fornication" (Greek, πορνεία *porneia*) was a symbol for idolatry (e.g., Hos 1:2; 2:4-5; 4:13-14) and so the Jews' claim to legitimacy is a claim about their relationship to the one God.[238] Some scholars read the words "we are not illegitimate children" as an

234. Gilbert L. Bartholomew, *An Early Christian Sermon-Drama: John 8:31-59* (Ann Arbor, Mich.: University Microfilms, 1974) 19-20.

235. *m. 'Abot.* 5:19.

236. Bruce M. Metzger, *A Textual Commentary on the Greek New Testament* (New York: United Bible Societies, 1975) 225.

237. So Brown, *The Gospel According to John (I–XII)*, 357.

238. See Beasley-Murray, *John*, 135; Rudolf Schnackenburg, *The Gospel According to St. John*, 2:212.

attack on Jesus for the rumors about his birth,[239] but this seems unlikely given that the Jews remain on the defensive (cf. v. 48, where the Jews go on the offensive). They respond to Jesus' indictment by defending their relationship to God. Therefore, it seems that for the first time in the debate, the Jews come close to understanding Jesus' words.

8:42-47. Three times the Jews have appealed to their paternity, and three times Jesus has rebutted them:

A. Appeal (v. 33)	we are descendants of Abraham
Rebuttal (v. 37)	I know that you are descendants of Abraham, *but . . .*
B. Appeal (v. 39*a*)	Abraham is our father
Rebuttal (v. 39*b*)	*If* you were children of Abraham . . .
C. Appeal (v. 41*b*)	We have one father, God himself
Rebuttal (v. 42)	*If* God were your father . . .

Just as the Jews' inheritance from Abraham is conditional on their actions (vv. 39*b*-40), so also Jesus' final rebuttal (vv. 42-47) asserts that their inheritance from God is, too.

8:42. The parallelism between vv. 39*b*-40 and v. 42 shows that to do the works of Abraham is to love Jesus (cf. vv. 56-58), and one's status as a child of God depends on that love (cf. 1:13). One's relationship to Jesus is the measure of one's relationship to God because of Jesus' relationship to God. Verse 42*b* returns to theological motifs that have resounded throughout the earlier dialogues of chaps. 5, 7, and 8: Jesus comes from God (e.g., 5:43; 7:28); Jesus is sent by God (e.g., 5:24, 30; 7:16, 29, 33; 8:16, 18, 29). The phrase "now I am here" translates the Greek verb ἥκω (*hēkō*). This verb was used to speak of the arrival of a divine figure into the world and may have those connotations here (cf. 1 John 5:20).[240]

8:43. This verse returns to the opening challenge of the debate (v. 31)—the only way to be

a disciple of Jesus is to stay in his word—and asserts "the Jews'" failure to meet that challenge. The Jews' failure to understand Jesus' "language" (λαλιά *lalia*) has been demonstrated by the many instances of their misunderstanding in this debate (vv. 33, 39, 41) and is here attributed by Jesus to their inability to hear his word (λόγος *logos*) (cf. 5:38).[241]

8:44. The discussion of paternity reaches its painful conclusion in vv. 44-47; the Jews are neither Abraham's nor God's children, but are children of the devil. The sharp contrast between children of God and children of the devil in this verse is shocking to the contemporary Gospel reader, but it was not without precedent in intra-Jewish debates at the time of both Jesus and the Fourth Evangelist.

The following passage from *m. ʾAbot* 5:19, quoted in part at v. 39, needs to be cited in full here in order to show the intensity of debate within Judaism around the meaning of faithful discipleship:

> He in whom are these three things is of the disciples of Abraham our father; but [he in whom are] three other things is of the disciples of Balaam the wicked. A good eye and a humble spirit and a lowly soul—[they in whom are these] are of the disciples of Abraham our father. An evil eye, a haughty spirit, and a proud soul—[they in whom are these] are of the disciples of Balaam the wicked. How do the disciples of Abraham our father differ from the disciples of Balaam the wicked? The disciples of Abraham our father enjoy the world and inherit the world to come, as it is written, *That I may cause those that love me to inherit substance and that I may fill their treasuries.* The disciples of Balaam the wicked inherit Gehenna and go down to the pit of destruction, as it is written, *But thou, O God shalt bring them down into the pit of destruction; bloodthirsty and deceitful men shall not live out half their days.*

While this Mishnah passage does not explicitly contrast disciples of Abraham with children of the devil, it does use very harsh language to describe those who do not do the works of Abraham, language that includes the promise of eternal damnation and identifies those who do not do Abraham's works with wickedness.

Qumran texts provide the most useful ana-

239. See C. K. Barrett, *The Gospel According to St. John,* 2nd ed. (Philadelphia: Westminster, 1978) 348; Raymond E. Brown, *The Gospel According to John (I–XII),* AB 29 (Garden City, N.Y.: Doubleday, 1966) 357.

240. E.g., Origen *Contra Celsum VII* 9.

241. Cf. Jerome H. Neyrey, *An Ideology of Revolt: John's Christology in Social-Science Perspective* (Philadelphia: Fortress, 1988) 44.

logues to the intensity of rhetoric in 8:44.[242] First, they provide a glimpse of the religious diversity of late Second Temple Judaism (150 BCE—70 CE) and hence flesh out the picture of the Judaism of Jesus' day. Second, and most germane for John 8, these documents show the harsh language used by a Jewish sectarian group to express its relationship to others within Judaism who opposed its beliefs and practices. For example, the Habakkuk Commentary sets the Teacher of Righteousness and his followers in opposition to those who have deserted the community to follow the Wicked Priest.[243] This enemy of the community is said to have defiled God's temple and is repeatedly called "the Liar" and "the Spouter of Lies." A passage in one of the Thanksgiving Hymns illustrates the intensity of the rhetoric well:

> And they, teachers of lies and seers of falsehood,
> have schemed against me a devilish scheme,
> to exchange the Law engraved on my heart by
> Thee
> for the smooth things (which they speak) to Thy
> people . . .
> But Thou, O God,
> dost despise all Satan's designs;
> it is Thy purpose that shall be done
> and the design of Thy heart that shall be established for ever.
>
> As for them, they dissemble,
> they plan devilish schemes.
> They seek Thee with a double heart
> and are not confirmed in the truth.
> A root bearing poisoned and bitter fruit
> is in their designs.[244]

These examples from Jewish literature set the polemic of v. 44 in its cultural context. The Fourth Evangelist, like the Qumran community, understood his community to be engaged in a struggle over the proper interpretation of Jewish tradition. This cultural context does not diminish the harshness of the attack but enables the contemporary reader to hear it in a context closer to that in which the earliest Gospel readers heard it. This language, like other debates between Jesus and the "Jews" in the Fourth Gospel, provides a glimpse into the theological debates of the Fourth

Evangelist's own time. The intensity of the rhetoric reflects the intensity of the theological and social struggle. (See Introduction and Reflections at 8:48-59.)

The harsh language of Jesus' charge in v. 44 builds on the distinction he already made in 8:23: Jesus and the Jews have different origins. The reference to the devil as the enemy here is the first mention of the devil as the ultimate enemy,[245] a perspective that will be emphasized more in the Farewell Discourse (13:2, 27; 14:30; 16:11; see also 12:31, 17:15).

The beginning of v. 44 is notoriously difficult to translate. A literal translation would read, "You are from the father of the devil," because the definite article appears before both "father" and "devil" in the Greek. This literal translation does not fit the Fourth Evangelist's argument, however. As the rest of the verse makes clear, Jesus is not concerned with speculation about the devil's origins, but with the devil himself as the Jews' father.[246] The Fourth Evangelist seems to include the extra definite article in order to highlight the word *father* and thus make clear that the play on that word has reached its conclusion. The only father to whom the Jews can make an appeal is the devil.

Earlier statements about the Jews' actions (e.g., 8:34, 38, 40-41) culminate in the statement that "you choose to do [ποιέω *poieō*] your father's desires." This accusation must be placed in the context of earlier discussions about the work of God in John. In 6:29, Jesus states that the work of God is to "believe in him whom he has sent." The Jews' unbelief means that they do not do God's work. By framing the argument in terms of the work of God and the work of the devil, the Fourth Evangelist reminds the reader that the decision to believe in Jesus is an eschatological decision that reveals one's ultimate relationship to God and God's judgment (cf. 3:17-21).

The description of the devil in v. 44 draws heavily on Jewish scriptural traditions. The language about the devil as a murderer from the beginning probably alludes to the temptation story (Genesis 3), when as a result of the serpent's

---

242. See Gerard Sloyan, *John* (Atlanta: John Knox, 1988) 102.
243. See 1QpHab.
244. 1QH IV, 7. Sloyan cites part of this hymn text in his own translation. This translation is from G. Vermes, *The Dead Sea Scrolls in English,* 3rd ed. (London: Penguin, 1987) 175.

245. See Brown, *The Gospel According to John (I–XII),* 364.
246. Rudolf Bultmann, *The Gospel of John: A Commentary,* trans. G. R. Beasley-Murray, R. W. N. Hoare, and J. K. Riches (Philadelphia: Westminster, 1971) 318-20. See BDF, 268.

activity, death was introduced and humans lost the gift of immortality. Wisdom 2:23-24 (NRSV) shares this view of the creation story:

for God created us for incorruption,
and made us in the image of his own eternity,
but through the devil's envy death entered the
  world,
and those who belong to his company experience it.

There may also be an allusion here to the Cain story (Gen 4:8-16), the Bible's first murder,[247] but such an allusion seems secondary to a primary reference to the introduction of death into human experience. The "Jews'" desire to kill Jesus (v. 37) thus mirrors the desires of the first murderer, their father the devil. The phrase "from the beginning" recalls John 1:1 ("in the beginning") and heightens the contrast between Jesus and the devil. Jesus is the Logos from the beginning; the devil, a murderer.[248]

The language used to describe the devil's relationship to the truth continues this contrast. The verb phrase "does not stand" (οὐκ ἕστηκεν *ouk estēken*) functions as the opposite of "remain" (μένω *menō*; cf. v. 31)—that is, unlike Jesus and his disciples, the devil has no relationship to the truth. To say that the truth is not in the devil further emphasizes the devil's distance from God and Jesus, because Jesus is God's truth (8:31; 14:6). The reference to the devil's lies may be another allusion to Genesis 3 and the serpent's lying words. The

phrase "for he is a liar and the father of lies" implicitly contrasts God as the Father of truth and the devil as the father of lies.

8:45-47. This passage links truth and falsehood to belief and unbelief. Like the devil, "the Jews" do not recognize the truth; indeed, it is Jesus' very truthfulness that precludes the Jews' access to him (vv. 45-46). The Jews' inability to hear the words of God in Jesus reveals their distance from the truth and hence from God (v. 47). This is not a new theme in the Gospel of John (cf. 3:17-21; 5:38, 42; 6:45; 7:17-18, 28; 8:19), but it is stated here in its most absolute form. The proving ground of one's identity and relationship to God is one's acceptance of Jesus as God's Word (1:12-13), as God's Son (3:16, 18, 36; 5:23-24; 6:40, 46; 8:19), as the one whom God has sent (5:24, 36-37; 6:29; 7:28-29). The "Jews" reject the truth of God that Jesus offers them, and in the theological world of the Fourth Evangelist, this means that they reveal that they are not God's children.

This middle section of the debate (vv. 39-47) thus ends with Jesus' assertion that the "Jews" have failed the challenge of v. 31 and hence are outside of its promises. This debate can be read as an extended illustration of 3:19-21: "And this is the judgment, that the light has come into the world, and people loved darkness rather than light because their deeds were evil."[249] (See Reflections at 8:48-59.)

---

247. Brown, *The Gospel According to John (I–XII)*, 358.
248. See Barrett, *The Gospel According to St. John*, 349.

249. See Beasley-Murray, *John*, 142.

John 8:48-59, Abraham and Jesus

NIV	NRSV
48The Jews answered him, "Aren't we right in saying that you are a Samaritan and demon-possessed?"	48The Jews answered him, "Are we not right in saying that you are a Samaritan and have a demon?" 49Jesus answered, "I do not have a demon; but I honor my Father, and you dishonor me. 50Yet I do not seek my own glory; there is one who seeks it and he is the judge. 51Very truly, I tell you, whoever keeps my word will never see death." 52The Jews said to him, "Now we know that you have a demon. Abraham died, and so did the prophets; yet you say, 'Whoever keeps my word will never taste death.' 53Are you greater
49"I am not possessed by a demon," said Jesus, "but I honor my Father and you dishonor me. 50I am not seeking glory for myself; but there is one who seeks it, and he is the judge. 51I tell you the truth, if anyone keeps my word, he will never see death."	
52At this the Jews exclaimed, "Now we know that you are demon-possessed! Abraham died and	

NIV

so did the prophets, yet you say that if anyone keeps your word, he will never taste death. [53]Are you greater than our father Abraham? He died, and so did the prophets. Who do you think you are?"

[54]Jesus replied, "If I glorify myself, my glory means nothing. My Father, whom you claim as your God, is the one who glorifies me. [55]Though you do not know him, I know him. If I said I did not, I would be a liar like you, but I do know him and keep his word. [56]Your father Abraham rejoiced at the thought of seeing my day; he saw it and was glad."

[57]"You are not yet fifty years old," the Jews said to him, "and you have seen Abraham!"

[58]"I tell you the truth," Jesus answered, "before Abraham was born, I am!" [59]At this, they picked up stones to stone him, but Jesus hid himself, slipping away from the temple grounds.

NRSV

than our father Abraham, who died? The prophets also died. Who do you claim to be?" [54]Jesus answered, "If I glorify myself, my glory is nothing. It is my Father who glorifies me, he of whom you say, 'He is our God,' [55]though you do not know him. But I know him; if I would say that I do not know him, I would be a liar like you. But I do know him and I keep his word. [56]Your ancestor Abraham rejoiced that he would see my day; he saw it and was glad." [57]Then the Jews said to him, "You are not yet fifty years old, and have you seen Abraham?"[a] [58]Jesus said to them, "Very truly, I tell you, before Abraham was, I am." [59]So they picked up stones to throw at him, but Jesus hid himself and went out of the temple.

[a] Other ancient authorities read *has Abraham seen you?*

COMMENTARY

Verses 48-59 have more of a dialogic cast than do the earlier parts of the debate—there are six changes of speaker in this unit (vv. 48, 49, 52, 54, 57, 58) in contrast to three in vv. 31-38 (vv. 31, 33, 34) and four in vv. 39-47 (vv. 39*a,* 39*b,* 41*b,* 42). Jesus' listeners are identified as "the Jews" in v. 48 for the first time since their identification as "the Jews who had believed in him" in v. 31. The repeated references to the "Jews" in the remainder of the debate (vv. 52, 57) reinforce that the debate is now between unmasked antagonists. Verse 48 thus signals a new turn in the debate. In vv. 31-47, Jesus' listeners responded to Jesus' words by defending themselves and their heritage (vv. 33, 39, 41); in v. 48 they go on the offensive and turn their words against Jesus. The focus will stay on Jesus until the end of the debate.

8:48. The "Jews" attack Jesus with the same charges that he earlier used against them. Just as Jesus denied their claims to be children of Abraham (v. 39) and called them children of the devil (v. 44), so also the Jews now deny Jesus' place as a child of Abraham by calling him a Samaritan and identifying him with the "demonic" (δαίμων *daimōn*; cf. 7:20). In addition to this turn to "mutual name calling" in the "Jews'" accusations,[250] the specific content of the rejection of Jesus' Jewish heritage is important. By labeling Jesus a Samaritan, the "Jews" link him with a social group perceived by establishment Judaism as covenant outsiders.[251] Yet the Samaritans understood themselves as true inheritors of the promises of Abraham, whose claims to that inheritance were rejected and denied by Jerusalem Judaism. The accusation that Jesus has a demon occurs elsewhere in the Gospel traditions (Matt 9:34; 12:24; Mark 3:22; Luke 11:15; John 10:20), but this is the only place where Jesus is accused of being a Samaritan.

8:49a. Although Jesus rebuts the charge of having a demon, he ignores the charge of being a Samaritan.[252] The Samaritans have a much more visible and positive role in the Fourth Gospel than in the other Gospels (e.g., John 4). While this is often taken as evidence of interest by Johannine Christians in a Samaritan mission,[253] it may reflect

250. Neyrey, *An Ideology of Revolt,* 46.
251. Ibid., 47.
252. See Sloyan, *John,* 104.
253. E.g., ibid.

the identification of Johannine Jewish Christians with the Samaritans' relationship to Jerusalem Judaism. The Johannine Christians, like the Samaritans, understood themselves to be the inheritors of the promises of Abraham and Moses (5:46-47; 6:32, 49-50, 58; 7:22-24; 8:39, 56; 9:28), but were denied those claims by establishment Judaism (in Fourth Gospel parlance, the "Jews"). The labeling of Jesus as a Samaritan here may be another glimpse into the two levels of the Gospel. Jesus himself is labeled a covenant outsider by those within the covenant community in order to portray him as sharing the social experience of the Fourth Evangelist and his community.

8:49b-51. Jesus repudiates the charge of demon possession by appealing to his relationship with God. The language of "honoring" (τιμάω timaō) in v. 49b needs to be read alongside 5:23. This argument rests on the notion of "honor" in the ancient Mediterranean world, and the assumption that the one sent is the same as the sender. The treatment one gives the emissary is thus equal to one's treatment of the Sender.[254] By dishonoring Jesus, the "Jews" dishonor God and prove the truth of Jesus' accusations in v. 47; they are not from God. The language about seeking his own glory (v. 50a) recalls arguments against seeking one's own glory in chaps. 5 and 7 (5:41, 44; 7:18). Because Jesus' glory comes from God (v. 50b) and thus is not of his own making (cf. 1:14; 17:5, 22, 24), an attack on Jesus is also an attack on God.

The reference to God as judge (v. 50b) highlights the eschatological dimension of the Jews' lack of true relationship with God. Life and death reside with the One who seeks Jesus' glory, and in the Jews' dishonoring of Jesus, they risk God's condemnation (cf. 3:17-18; 5:22; 8:16; 12:47-48). The "very truly" saying (ἀμὴν ἀμήν amēn, amēn) of v. 51 makes this eschatological dimension even more explicit. The condition, "whoever keeps my word," recalls the opening condition of v. 31 ("if you continue in my word") and suggests that truth, freedom, and the end of death belong together as Jesus' eschatological gifts. Just as once the devil introduced death (v. 44), so also now

Jesus' word removes death from human experience (cf. 5:24-25; 6:40, 47, 58; 11:25-26).

8:52-53. The "Jews" continue on the offensive in vv. 52-53. In vv. 33 and 39, the Jews appealed to Abraham to defend their own identity, and here they appeal to Abraham to attack Jesus' identity. The Jews interpret Jesus' words about death as foolish words about immortality, which can easily be disproved by appeal to the deaths of Abraham and the prophets. Such an appeal to refute Jesus is ironic in the light of v. 44, since the very deaths to which the Jews make appeal can be traced to the devil's introduction of death. They thus align themselves with the devil's work in order to prove that Jesus has a demon. The Jews' question in v. 53a is also ironic. It is introduced by an interrogative particle that assumes a negative response (μὴ mē; cf. the Samaritan woman's question about Jacob in 4:12): "You are not greater than our father Abraham, who died, are you?" But for the Fourth Evangelist and most of his readers, the question can only be answered positively. In attempting to refute Jesus, the Jews inadvertently underscore the truth about him.

The Jews' final question to Jesus in v. 53b reveals another misunderstanding. The Jews respond to Jesus' words as if they were an instance of self-aggrandizement. A literal translation of their question would read, "What do you make yourself?" The NIV and NRSV translations of this question render the brusqueness of the Greek into smooth English, but they mask its connection with larger Johannine themes about Jesus' identity by eliminating the reflexive pronoun. The occasion for the discourse in John 5 was the Jews' misperception that Jesus was "making himself equal to God" (5:18); the opening dialogue in chap. 8 addressed the question of Jesus' bearing witness to himself. In both cases, Jesus' response was to show that he does nothing on his own, that God, not Jesus, "makes" something of Jesus (5:19, 30-31; 8:17-18; cf. 7:28-29).

8:54-57. Jesus once again disputes the Jews' interpretation of his words by dismissing language of self-glorification (v. 54; cf. 5:41, 44; 12:43) and repeating the claim of v. 50, that God is the one who glorifies him. Jesus' ironic identification of the God who glorifies him as the God to whom the Jews earlier made appeal (v. 41) sets the stage for his renewed critique of the Jews in v. 55.

254. For a discussion of honor and shame in the ancient Mediterranean world, see Bruce Malina, *The New Testament World: Insights from Cultural Anthropology,* rev. ed. (Louisville: Westminster/John Knox, 1993) 28-40.

The fullest indictment of the Jews in v. 55 is Jesus' identification of them as liars. In v. 44, the devil was identified as a liar and his words as lies; the use of "liar" in v. 55*b* makes clear that the Jews share fully in the devil's nature (vv. 44 and 55 are the only occurrences of the noun ψεύστης [*pseustēs*, "liar"] in the Fourth Gospel). The link between the devil and the "Jews" is complete. Jesus' truthfulness comes from his knowledge of God (v. 55*a*), "the Jews'" lies from their knowledge of the devil and distance from God.

Jesus' appeal to Abraham in v. 56 is an important turn in the debate, because it is the first time in 8:31-59 that Jesus himself appeals to Father ("ancestor," NRSV) Abraham. Prior to this verse, the Jews have appealed to Abraham to prove the truth of their claims (8:33, 39, 53), but now Jesus uses Abraham as a witness against the Jews to prove the truth of his claims.[255] Note that Abraham is identified as *your* father Abraham, the second-person plural pronoun further emphasizing the distance between Jesus and the Jews (cf. 8:53).

Verse 56 seems to build on two Jewish traditions. First, the references to Abraham's happiness ("rejoiced," "was glad") recall the play on the name of Isaac (which means "he laughs"; see Gen 17:17-19; 18:9-15; 21:6) and later Jewish traditions that interpreted Abraham's laughter about Isaac's birth as a sign of his joy.[256] Second, the reference to Abraham's foreknowledge of Jesus builds on midrashic traditions that the future was revealed to Abraham by God.[257] Paul may build on a similar tradition when he writes of Abraham, "And the scripture . . . declared the gospel beforehand to Abraham" (Gal 3:8 NRSV).

The past tense "he saw" (εἶδεν *eiden*, v. 56*b*) is ambiguous. Does it refer to Abraham's lifetime or to a revelation by God to Abraham after his lifetime? The "Jews" clearly understand Jesus' words as referring to Abraham's lifetime and treat them with disdain. Their rebuke of Jesus in v. 57 recalls 2:19-21, where the "Jews" also misinterpret a christological saying of Jesus by hearing it only through a chronological filter. The reference to "fifty years" is not a statement of Jesus' exact age, but is meant to show the ludicrousness of Jesus' words. The manuscript evidence is divided on whether the end of the verse should be read "and have you seen Abraham" or "has Abraham seen you" (see the NRSV footnote). The preferred reading accentuates the Jews' misunderstanding, because it focuses on the impossibility of a life span overlap between Abraham and Jesus.

8:58. Jesus' response to the Jews makes clear that the deciding issue is not one of overlapping life spans. Rather, Jesus is making a significant claim about his relationship with God. The "very truly" (*amēn, amēn*) with which Jesus' words begin mark them as introducing a new teaching. In this case, it is the culminating teaching of the whole debate. The core of Jesus' pronouncement resides in the absolute "I am" (ἐγώ εἰμι *egō eimi*) saying (i.e., with no predicate nominative supplied), which is used in two ways in this verse.

First, the contrast between "was" and "am" recalls the opening verses of the Prologue and their claims for the pre-existence of the Word (1:1-3). As in the Prologue, the pivot of the verb use is the contrast between the time-bound and the eternal. The verb translated "was" in v. 58 is the Greek verb γενέσθαι (*genesthai*), and could be translated literally as "became" or "came into being." As in the Prologue (cf. 1:3, 6, 14), the verb relates to the created order, to that which is limited by time. Abraham's time was finite and time-bound. When Jesus says, "Before Abraham *was*, I *am*," therefore, he is pointing to his pre-existence with God beyond the bounds of time.

Second, the use of the absolute *egō eimi* echoes 4:20; 6:20; and 8:24, 28 (see Fig. 10, "The 'I AM' Sayings in John," 602). As in those verses, the absolute *egō eimi* here is to be understood as Jesus' identifying himself with the divine name, "I AM" (see Commentary on 8:24). These words express Jesus' unity with God and restate another claim of the Prologue (1:1). Jesus' words thus prove the ironic truth of the Jews' words in 8:53: Jesus *is* greater than Abraham because Jesus is one with God.

8:59. As in 5:18, where Jesus' claims about his relationship with God intensified the Jews' intention to kill him, here, too, Jesus' claim to oneness with God leads to an attempt on his life (v. 59). Execution by stoning was the punishment

255. Horacio E. Lona, *Abraham in Johannes 8: Ein Beitrag zur Metodenfrage* (Bern: Lang, 1976) 418.
256. Cf. *Jub.* 14:21; 15:17; 16:19-20; Philo *Mut. Nom.* 154-69.
257. E.g., *Gen. Rab.* 44:25; Barrett, *The Gospel According to St. John*, 351-52; Rudolf Schnackenburg, *The Gospel According to St. John*, 3 vols. (New York: Seabury, 1982) 2:221-22.

prescribed for blasphemy in the OT (Lev 24:13-16; cf. John 10:31). The description of Jesus' escape in v. 59*b* strains credulity; how could he hide safely among his adversaries in the Temple? This comment by the Fourth Evangelist needs to

be taken as a stylized observation intended to reinforce his comments in 7:30 and 8:20 that Jesus can neither be arrested nor killed because "his hour had not yet come."

REFLECTIONS

John 8 presents the reader of the Gospel of John with some of the Gospel's most difficult interpretive issues. The Jesus who emerges from these verses speaks with staggeringly sharp invective to his opponents and holds nothing back in his attack on his theological adversaries. It is very difficult to harmonize this picture of Jesus with the images of him that shape our theological imaginations: Jesus as the one who eats with outcasts and sinners, who cares for the lost sheep, who is the model of how we are to love. Complicating this picture of Jesus is the fact that he speaks this scathing language to a group John identifies as the "Jews," so that Jesus' words in this chapter have become a pivotal text in discussions of Christian anti-Semitism.

Because this text has played such a controversial role in shaping Jewish-Christian relationships, it is the interpreter's moral responsibility to look the language of this chapter and the image of Jesus squarely in the face.[258] It does no good simply to whitewash the intensity of the invective, nor does it do any good to continue to treat the anti-"Jews" language in this text as if it were license for anti-Semitism. The interpreter is called to ask hard questions of this text in order to discover what it is saying and what it is not saying. The interpreter must work diligently and carefully to understand the text in its original social and historical context in order to avoid making simplistic and destructive extrapolations to contemporary church settings. The commentary has attempted to provide the interpreter with some of the historical, social, and cultural contexts necessary to begin this work. This Reflections section will begin by reviewing the historical and social data as they pertain directly to the appropriation of this text and then, on the basis of this review, to examine the critical issues with which this text confronts the interpreter.

Two historical/social issues bear directly on the appropriation of John 8: the relationship of the Johannine community to establishment Judaism and the role of invective in first-century intra-Jewish debates. As has been noted many times in this commentary, the relationship between Johannine Jewish Christians and Judaism is one of the decisive issues for the shape and perspective of the Fourth Gospel. Throughout the Gospel, Jesus' antagonists are regularly identified as the "Jews." The work of J. Louis Martyn and others has helped us to see that a rupture(s) with the synagogue occurred sometime in the last quarter of the first century that decisively changed the fabric of Johannine Christians' religious lives.[259]

Prior to the decisive break, Johannine Christians were able to hold together their participation in the liturgical and cultural world of Judaism and their faith in Jesus. (It is important to note that this joint identity was not unique to Johannine Christians. For example, in Acts 2, Luke depicts the developing Christian community as participating in temple worship as well as conducting their own worship services.) The exact course of events that led to the break cannot be charted, but the destruction of the Jerusalem Temple in 70 CE was one of the pivotal factors.[260]

---

258. For a discussion of the ethics of biblical interpretation, see Elisabeth Schüssler Fiorenza, "The Ethics of Biblical Interpretation: Decentering Biblical Scholarship," *JBL* 107 (1988) 3-17.

259. J. Louis Martyn, *History and Theology in the Fourth Gospel* (Nashville: Abingdon, 1968); David Rensberger, *Johannine Faith and Liberating Community* (Philadelphia: Westminster, 1988); see a review of Martyn's influence in John Ashton, *The Interpretation of the Fourth Gospel* (Oxford: Oxford University Press, 1993).

260. Jewish-Christian status under Roman rule also had an effect on Jewish-Christian relations in the late first century (see, e.g., Acts 18 and the reference to the expulsion of Jews from Rome), but for the Fourth Gospel, intra-Jewish concerns are pivotal.

Without the Temple, Judaism was forced to reconstitute itself around a different center, and the Jewish Scriptures became that center. The synagogues, therefore, took on more importance, because they were the sites where Scripture was taught and preached. Moreover, those Jews who professed faith in Jesus also took the Scriptures to be of the utmost importance, because they understood Jesus to be the fulfillment of God's promises as made known to God's people through Scripture. The conflict was joined, therefore, around the question of who could lay claim to God's promises and to the status of God's people. This conflict is apparent in the adversarial language of Matthew 23, for example, but the group of Christians who seemed to have experienced this conflict and struggle most intensely in their day-to-day lives was the community of Christians for whom the Fourth Gospel was written. The Fourth Gospel makes repeated reference to Christians' being cast out of the synagogue (9:22; 12:42; 16:2) and the fear and danger this produced in the community's life.

The Johannine Christians thus understood themselves to be outcasts, people whom the Jewish establishment no longer considered to be Jews, a community forcibly removed from its roots and the symbols that formed its identity. Their self-identity was as a marginalized community that stood powerless in the face of the power of the dominant religious group, the Jews. The Gospel of John contains many attempts by the Fourth Evangelist to reclaim his community's relationship to its Jewish roots. The Fourth Evangelist makes repeated references to Jewish feasts and demonstrates the ways in which Jesus is the true fulfillment of those feasts (e.g., 7:37-38; 8:12). Most of the Fourth Evangelist's primary metaphors and images are drawn from the language of the Jewish Scriptures, and John 4, 6, and 8 revolve around comparisons between Jesus and Jacob, Moses, and Abraham, respectively. The wealth and depth of Jewish scriptural allusions in the Fourth Gospel show that the Fourth Evangelist is not antagonistic to Jewish traditions. Rather, he is antagonistic to the Jewish power structures and political forces that have attempted to cut his community off from these traditions.

The virulent language of chap. 8 must be read against this backdrop of being cast out of the synagogue, of being excluded from the religious centers that had once helped to define one's religious and communal identity. The language of this chapter is the language of the minority group spoken in protest to the majority culture. The Johannine Jewish Christians had no way to back up this language—that is, they had no power to take any actions comparable to their own exclusion from the synagogue. They were outnumbered by the Jewish community and had no political resources at their disposal. Their only "power" rested in the force of their rhetoric, in their ability to denounce those who had excluded them.

In the Commentary on 8:44-47, Qumran texts were cited in order to place the invective of these verses in their full cultural context. The Qumran community, too, used very strong language to speak against other Jews whom they sensed were depriving them of their religious heritage and polluting God's promises to God's people. One important difference between the Qumran sectarians and the Johannine community is that the Qumran sectarians initially chose to exclude themselves from the Jerusalem community, whereas the Johannine community was forcibly excluded. The persecution that the Qumran community endured after their separation, however, was not of its choosing and positioned them as a community oppressed by establishment Judaism, like the community for which the Fourth Evangelist wrote. The Qumran analogue is important, because it helps the interpreter to see how the language about the Jews in chap. 8 functions as intra-Jewish invective in its own cultural and historical setting.[261]

What is the significance of this historical context for the contemporary interpreter of John 8? First, it reminds the interpreter that one must attend to the specific situation of a biblical text in order to make the move to potential contemporary appropriations. The issues in John 8 have a very specific cultural context, and the only way that this text can have a place in

---

261. Cf. Luke T. Johnson, "The New Testament's Anti-Jewish Slander and the Conventions of Ancient Polemic," *JBL* 108 (1989) 419-41.

the life of the church is if the specificity of that original context is honored. One must understand the originating context and then look for modern analogues to that context. That is especially critical with a text, like this one, that has had such a disturbing place in the history of interpretation.

Second, attention to the historical and social contexts of John 8 compels the interpreter to work more carefully at assessing the *function* of the negative language for the original readers and thus assists the interpreter in distinguishing among the many painful issues with which this text confronts the modern reader. It helps the interpreter to see that simple condemnations of Johannine anti-Semitism, for example, do not begin to touch the complexity of this text. In order to honor the complexity of this text, the interpreter must begin to think separately about two distinct issues that are often treated as one issue in contemporary conversations about this text: (1) the relation of John 8 to Christian anti-Semitism; and (2) the social function of religious invective. It is to the contemporary dimensions of these two issues for the life of Christian faith that we now turn.

1. As the historical review made clear, the Fourth Evangelist understood his community to be persecuted by the power and theological politics of the Jewish establishment. Moreover, this community was itself without power in the face of what it understood to be its oppressors. The harshly negative language about the Jews in this chapter, then, needs to be taken first and foremost as the language of a group without the means—economic, political, military (note the references to the police sent by the Pharisees in 7:32, 45; cf. also 18:3)—to act out its virulence. It is the language of a Jewish-rooted minority that is no longer allowed to claim its Judaism, speaking against those who have denied them their heritage.

When the words of John 8 become the weapons contemporary Christians use in a crusade against Judaism, this critical social fabric is overlooked and, indeed, distorted. First, contemporary Christians have come a long way from the intimate ties with Judaism that shaped the Johannine community. The majority of Christians today are Gentile by heritage, not Jewish, and so the language of John 8 belongs to a context foreign to contemporary Christian experience. When Jesus speaks about the Jews the way he does in John 8, giving voice to the Johannine community's needs and anger, it is intra-family language. Contemporary Gentile Christians who use this language against Jews are not members of the family and hence their language carries a different weight. Contemporary Christians have not been hurt by the Jewish religious establishment the way the Johannine Christians perceived themselves to be, rejected by those they took to be their brothers and sisters in faith, so that the pathos that drove this language in its own context is missing in ours.

Second, and more crucially, Christians, particularly in North America and Europe, are no longer the minority group, rejected by the Jewish religious establishment because of their beliefs, but are the majority group whose religious practices and values dominate contemporary culture. The balance of power between Christians and Jews is the exact opposite of the situation in which the Fourth Evangelist lived and wrote, and for contemporary Christians to point to John 8 as justification for their attitude toward Judaism is a false and dangerous appropriation of the biblical text.

The danger of the misappropriation of the Fourth Gospel's type of invective in a situation where the power relationships between Christians and Jews are reversed was tragically evident in the actions of the Third Reich toward Europe's Jewish population. In that situation, the Germans had the military, economic, and political power to act out the language of hate. It was no longer a question of a minority group's using strong language to defend its right to exist and worship as it chose, but the majority culture's exercising its might to exterminate a less powerful group it found offensive and falsely perceived as a threat.

For the Fourth Evangelist, the situation was one of a spiritual and theological battle, in which the Jewish religious authorities were dictating the shape of the Johannine Christians' faith lives. No such situation holds today; Christianity is not at risk because of Judaism, and for contemporary Christians to overlook this critical social distinction is to do misservice to the gifts and promises of God that Jews and Christians share. The Fourth Evangelist experienced his community as being on the verge of losing access to those gifts, and so the Johannine Jesus speaks with intensity about the Christians' claim to those gifts and promises as distinct from Jewish claims. Jewish-Christian relations are completely different today, however, and the Fourth Gospel's invective against the Jews has no meaning in a world where Christian claims and practices rest secure.

2. When the questions of anti-Semitism and religious invective are distinguished from one another, it becomes possible to look at the social and theological function of the language of John 8 as an issue in its own right. One then can ask how this language serves the needs of this religious community. What does this language accomplish? What are its implications for contemporary Christian communities?

As noted earlier, the primary theological function of the invective in John 8 is to defend the Christian community's claims against the perceived assault of the Jewish religious establishment. Its closely related social function is to establish the identity of this faith community over against those who deny the community's right to exist. The absolute character of this language and the sharp lines it draws between those who share the community's beliefs and those who do not are frequently pointed to by scholars as evidence of the *sectarian* quality of Johannine faith.[262] That is, the Johannine community understood itself as a minority religious group at odds with the dominant religious culture. If Johannine sectarianism is perceived as a primarily intra-Christian phenomenon, then the description is not altogether apt, because Johannine christology and theology are not wholly distinct from other early Christian traditions. If, however, Johannine sectarianism is perceived as Jewish sectarianism, as the above discussion would suggest, then the designation is both apt and helpful in clarifying the social function of the invective in John 8. The way in which the minority, religiously oppressed community of the Fourth Gospel grounded its identity was to reject those who had rejected them first and so establish the boundaries of their community.

The social intent that drives the invective of John 8 is not an isolated phenomenon. On the contrary, the rigidity of community identification it reflects and the language of hate that often accompanies it is evident across the globe in racial, ethnic, and religious conflicts. The divisions between Catholics and Protestants in Ireland is an excellent example of the odd mix of religion, power politics, and community identity that fuels the invective of John 8.

The invective of John 8 confronts the interpreter with very disturbing questions—questions whose answers may be even more difficult to determine than the questions about John 8 and the "Jews." The primary question is this: Is it necessary to exclude others so absolutely and hatefully in order to establish community identity? This may have been the only avenue that presented itself to the Fourth Evangelist and his community, but is it the only avenue available to us? The NT contains a variety of models of community formation. Paul, for example, who also struggled earnestly with the relation of the developing Christian community and Judaism, developed a model of community formation that attempted to break down barriers rather than to strengthen them (e.g., Gal 3:28). Contemporary Christians, therefore, have a rich set of options as they think about their identity as a faith community, options that move beyond the strident language of John 8.

For an oppressed community like that for whom the Fourth Evangelist wrote, the language of John 8 may have restored a sense of their own power and dignity in the face of persecution. It may be that for communities in similar situations, this language still presents a viable model

---

262. For a general discussion of Johannine sectarianism, see Wayne A. Meeks, "The Man from Heaven in Johannine Sectarianism," *JBL* 91 (1972) 44-72. For a discussion of Johannine sectarianism with particular attention to its relationship to Judaism, see David Rensberger, *Johannine Faith and Liberating Community* (Philadelphia: Westminster, 1988) 27-29, 135-44.

of community. Yet even when the language is contextualized that way, one still feels a sense of pain and regret at the damage that language like that found in John 8 can cause. The invective found in John 8, and the misuse that later generations of Christians made of it, may bear its most powerful witness as a cautionary tale for present and future Christian communities.

JOHN 9:1–10:21, THE HEALING OF THE BLIND MAN (MIRACLE AND DISCOURSE)

OVERVIEW

John 9:1–10:21 contains two well-known blocks of the Fourth Gospel that are frequently handled as two discrete units: the healing of the man born blind (9:1-41) and the "good shepherd" discourse (10:1-21). The division of this material into two discrete units owes more to adherence to the external (and secondary) markers of chapter division than it does to the text of the Fourth Gospel itself, because the Fourth Gospel text makes no break whatsoever between 9:41 and 10:1; both belong to the same speech of Jesus. This absence of a clear break suggests that Jesus' words in 10:1-18 should be read as a discourse to the Pharisees of 9:40.[263]

When John 9 and 10 are read together, they can be seen as following the common Johannine pattern of event, dialogue, and discourse (cf. the use of this pattern in John 3 and 6) and more particularly, as paralleling the pattern of healing, dialogue, and discourse used in John 5:[264]

	JOHN 5	JOHN 9–10
Healing miracle	5:1-9	9:1-12
Dialogue	5:10-18	9:13-41
Discourse by Jesus	5:19-47	10:1-18

John 10:19-21 supports linking 10:1-18 with John 9, because these verses narrate the response of the "Jews" to Jesus' words in 10:1-18 (v. 19) and to the healing miracle (v. 21). John 9:39-41 functions as a bridge section; these verses can be read as concluding the dialogue section, but they also serve as the introduction to the discourse of 10:1-18 (cf. the relationship of 5:17-18 to 5:19-30).

John 9:1–10:21 has several distinguishing literary features. First, after the blind man receives his sight in 9:6, Jesus is absent from the story until 9:35. This is Jesus' longest absence in the Fourth Gospel narrative. Through Jesus' absence, the Fourth Evangelist moves the healed man and his witness into narrative prominence and turns the focus of the story to people's response to Jesus. Second, 9:1-40 seems to be shaped by the law of twos from classical Greek drama: No more than two characters (or character groups) speak on stage at the same time.[265] The use of this technique heightens the sense of drama as the events of the chapter unfold.

263. C. H. Dodd, *The Interpretation of the Fourth Gospel* (Cambridge: Cambridge University Press, 1953) 356; E. C. Hoskyns, *The Fourth Gospel* (London: Faber & Faber, 1947) 366; George R. Beasley-Murray, *John*, WBC 36 (Waco, Tex.: Word, 1987) 148.

264. This grouping of vv. 8-12 with the miracle story differs from those treatments of John 9:1-41 that divide the text into seven scenes (vv. 1-7, 8-12, 13-17, 18-23, 24-34, 35-38, 39-41. See, e.g., Martyn, *History and*

Theology, 26-27. I propose this division because it seems to honor the function of these verses as attestation to the miracle. Moreover, the seven scenes can only be maintained if one overlooks the links between the end of chap. 9 and the beginning of chap. 10.

265. J. Louis Martyn, *History and Theology in the Fourth Gospel* (Nashville: Abingdon, 1968; 2nd ed., 1979) 26; George MacRae, *Invitation to John* (Garden City, N.Y.: Doubleday, 1978) 125.

John 9:1-12, The Healing Miracle

NIV

9 As he went along, he saw a man blind from birth. ²His disciples asked him, "Rabbi, who sinned, this man or his parents, that he was born blind?"

³"Neither this man nor his parents sinned," said Jesus, "but this happened so that the work of God might be displayed in his life. ⁴As long as it is day, we must do the work of him who sent me. Night is coming, when no one can work. ⁵While I am in the world, I am the light of the world."

⁶Having said this, he spit on the ground, made some mud with the saliva, and put it on the man's eyes. ⁷"Go," he told him, "wash in the Pool of Siloam" (this word means Sent). So the man went and washed, and came home seeing.

⁸His neighbors and those who had formerly seen him begging asked, "Isn't this the same man who used to sit and beg?" ⁹Some claimed that he was.

Others said, "No, he only looks like him."

But he himself insisted, "I am the man."

¹⁰"How then were your eyes opened?" they demanded.

¹¹He replied, "The man they call Jesus made some mud and put it on my eyes. He told me to go to Siloam and wash. So I went and washed, and then I could see."

¹²"Where is this man?" they asked him.

"I don't know," he said.

NRSV

9 As he walked along, he saw a man blind from birth. ²His disciples asked him, "Rabbi, who sinned, this man or his parents, that he was born blind?" ³Jesus answered, "Neither this man nor his parents sinned; he was born blind so that God's works might be revealed in him. ⁴We[a] must work the works of him who sent me[b] while it is day; night is coming when no one can work. ⁵As long as I am in the world, I am the light of the world." ⁶When he had said this, he spat on the ground and made mud with the saliva and spread the mud on the man's eyes, ⁷saying to him, "Go, wash in the pool of Siloam" (which means Sent). Then he went and washed and came back able to see. ⁸The neighbors and those who had seen him before as a beggar began to ask, "Is this not the man who used to sit and beg?" ⁹Some were saying, "It is he." Others were saying, "No, but it is someone like him." He kept saying, "I am the man." ¹⁰But they kept asking him, "Then how were your eyes opened?" ¹¹He answered, "The man called Jesus made mud, spread it on my eyes, and said to me, 'Go to Siloam and wash.' Then I went and washed and received my sight." ¹²They said to him, "Where is he?" He said, "I do not know."

a Other ancient authorities read *I*   *b* Other ancient authorities read *us*

COMMENTARY

Stories of Jesus' giving sight to a blind man are found in all of the Gospels (cf. Matt. 9:27-31; 20:29-34; Mark 8:22-26; 10:46-52; Luke 18:35-42), and the story in John 9 shares elements with many of these other stories. These common elements include the man's being a beggar (cf. Mark 10:46-52), the use of spittle (cf. Mark 8:22-26), and Jesus' touching the man's eyes (cf. Matt 12:22-37). As with the healing stories of John 4:46-54 and 5:1-9*a*, however, John does not seem to be directly dependent on any of the synoptic traditions but uses an independent story from a fund of Jesus traditions. In the telling of this miracle story, the Fourth Evangelist includes the formal ele-

ments of a miracle story: the situation of need (vv. 1-5), the miracle (vv. 6-7), and the attestation to the miracle (vv. 8-12). The first and third elements are greatly expanded from the conventional miracle story form in order to serve the Fourth Evangelist's dramatic and theological purposes in this story.

9:1-5. The opening phrase of 9:1, "as he walked along," is vague, providing no concrete time or location for the story that is about to unfold, suggesting that the Fourth Evangelist intends the story of the blind man to be read in continuity with the preceding chapters. Jesus' claim to be the light of the world (8:12) is repeated in 9:5, and the healing miracle in chap. 9 stands as a demonstration of this claim. In addition, the Mishnah identifies Siloam, the water in which the blind man bathes (v. 7), as the source of the water for the water libations of the Tabernacles feast.[266] Finally, chaps. 9–10 build on Jesus' denunciation of the "Jews" in chap. 8. The intense conflict between the healed man and the Pharisees (esp. 9:24-34) dramatizes the theological arguments of the earlier debate.

Verses 1-5 narrate the situation of need that evokes the miracle, but they provide an interesting twist on the traditional miracle story form. The man's blindness is stated as a fact in v. 1, but he is not an active character in the story until v. 7. He makes no request of Jesus to be healed (cf. 4:46-54), nor does Jesus engage in any conversation with him about his healing (cf. 5:1-9a). Rather, the blind man's initial narrative function is as the catalyst for the conversation between Jesus and his disciples in vv. 2-5. (This is the first appearance of Jesus' disciples in the Gospel since 6:60-71 and their first mention since 7:3. The disciples would have been a superfluous presence in chaps. 7–8, where the focus was on establishing the lines of conflict between Jesus and the Jewish religious authorities.)

The disciples' question in v. 2 reflects traditional Jewish speculation on the relationship of illness and sin (cf. 5:14). The notion that a parent's sins are visited on the children was common in Jewish reflections on the causes of suffering. Because he was blind from birth, however, any sin the man himself might have committed would need to have been committed before he was born. This line of reasoning was also not unknown in first-century Judaism, because the enmity of Jacob and Esau in the womb had given rise to midrashic speculation on the possibility of sin before birth.[267]

Jesus' words in vv. 3-5 turn the conversation away from the disciples' conventional theodicy concerns. In the Fourth Gospel, "sin" is not a moral category about behavior, but is a theological category about one's response to the revelation of God in Jesus (8:21, 24; cf. 9:39-41; 16:9; see Reflections). The man's blindness, therefore, is not an occasion for reflection on sin and causality, but

is an occasion with revelatory significance. The "need" that evokes the miracle, then, is not the man's blindness, but the need for God's works to be made manifest. It is interesting to compare Jesus' words in v. 3 with the framing of the Cana miracle story in 2:1-11. In that story, the revelatory dimension of the miracle is brought out explicitly at the end (2:11), but here the reader is told what to look for before the miracle occurs.

"Works" (ἔργα *erga*) has two ranges of meaning in the Fourth Gospel, both of which occur in vv. 3-4. First, as in v. 3, "works" describes what Jesus does as the one through whom God's works are accomplished (cf. 4:34; 10:25, 37; 14:10; 17:4). Second, the Fourth Evangelist also defines God's work as belief in Jesus (6:28-29; 14:12; cf. 8:39-42), and this is the usage in v. 4. The manuscript evidence is divided on whether v. 4a should read "We must work" or "I must work," and this may reflect a confusion over which meaning of "works" is intended here. The oldest manuscripts support "we" instead of "I" and thus confirm the turn toward the disciples' work in v. 4. Some manuscripts correct "the one who sent me" to read "the one who sent us" in order to make the two pronouns in v. 4a agree, but "me" is the preferred reading. "The one who sent me" is Jesus' most frequent way of speaking about God in the Fourth Gospel (cf. 5:24, 30, 37; 7:16; 8:16), and its use here affirms the disciples' share in God's work.

The metaphorical use of "day" and "night" in v. 4b signals the contingency of Jesus' presence as the Logos.[268] Day will come to an end with the arrival of Jesus' hour (see the use of "night" in 13:30). Day and night are paired in 11:9-10 with a similar metaphorical meaning. Verse 5 makes the metaphor and its contingency ("as long as") explicit: Jesus' presence in the "world" (κόσμος *kosmos*) is the light that makes God's work possible (cf. 8:12).

9:6-7. The opening phrase of v. 6 links Jesus' words with the actions that follow, making clear that Jesus' words in vv. 2-5 are intended as the prologue to the miracle. The miracle itself is narrated leanly. The healing power of clay made with spittle (v. 6) was a popular element in healing stories in the Greco-Roman world.[269] Only

---

266. See *m. Sukk.* 4:10.

267. See Hermann L. Strack and Paul Billerbeck, *Kommentar zum Neuen Testament aus Talmud und Midrash* (München: Beck, 1924) 2:527-29.

268. Cf. Rudolf Bultmann, *The Gospel of John: A Commentary,* trans. G. R. Beasley-Murray, R. W. N. Hoare, and J. K. Riches (Philadelphia: Westminster, 1971) 332.

269. E.g, Tacitus *History,* 4.18.

Mark has Jesus use spit and clay in healings (7:33; 8:23); Matthew and Luke avoid that detail in their healing stories, probably because of its popular associations with magic. Jesus' making of clay takes on an additional significance in this story, because kneading was one of the thirty-nine categories of work explicitly forbidden on the sabbath (v. 14; cf. *m. Šabb.* 7.2).

The Fourth Evangelist's translation of the Hebrew word "Siloam" links the healing waters of Siloam with Jesus himself. Throughout the Fourth Gospel, Jesus is referred to as the one who is sent by God (e.g., 7:28-29; 10:36; 12:45). Since Siloam was the source of the water used during the Tabernacles feast, the translation of the pool's name here seems to underscore the point made in 7:37-39: Jesus is the source of Tabernacles fulfillment, not the traditional Jewish rites (see Commentary on 7:37-39). The healing does not occur in Jesus' presence; like the healing of 4:46-54, it is a healing at a distance. There is no further contact between Jesus and the blind man until 9:35.

9:8-12. These verses complete the third element of the miracle story form, the attestation to the miracle. As with vv. 1-5, the Fourth Evangelist takes great liberties within this formal element to serve his narrative purposes. These verses employ the traditional motif of witnesses to a miracle,[270] but while the neighbors of the blind man attest to the man's healing and hence conclude the miracle story, their questions about the healing also anticipate and, indeed, set the stage for the next section of the narrative:[271] the interrogation of the blind man by the Pharisees.

The neighbors' disagreement about the blind man's identity and his healing (vv. 8-9) positions the healed man to serve as his own witness and to provide his own attestation to the miracle. In v. 9b, the man is depicted as repeatedly identifying himself ("kept saying" [ἔλεγεν *elegen*]; the verb is in the imperfect tense) as the former blind man; in v. 11, he gives a full accounting of the miracle. Even though he was silent in vv. 1-7, the man's words in vv. 9b-11 show that he was fully attentive to what was happening to him. Moreover, unlike the man in chap. 5, the blind man knows the identity of the man who healed him (v. 11; cf. 5:13). His ignorance of Jesus' whereabouts (v. 12) draws the reader's attention to Jesus' absence from the narrative. (See Reflections at 9:13-41.)

270. Rudolf Bultmann, *History of the Synoptic Tradition,* 2nd ed. (Oxford: Blackwell, 1968) 225.
271. Cf. Bultmann, *The Gospel of John,* 333.

John 9:13-41, Dialogue and Interrogation

[13]They brought to the Pharisees the man who had been blind. [14]Now the day on which Jesus had made the mud and opened the man's eyes was a Sabbath. [15]Therefore the Pharisees also asked him how he had received his sight. "He put mud on my eyes," the man replied, "and I washed, and now I see."

[16]Some of the Pharisees said, "This man is not from God, for he does not keep the Sabbath."

But others asked, "How can a sinner do such miraculous signs?" So they were divided.

[17]Finally they turned again to the blind man, "What have you to say about him? It was your eyes he opened."

The man replied, "He is a prophet."

[18]The Jews still did not believe that he had been blind and had received his sight until they

[13]They brought to the Pharisees the man who had formerly been blind. [14]Now it was a sabbath day when Jesus made the mud and opened his eyes. [15]Then the Pharisees also began to ask him how he had received his sight. He said to them, "He put mud on my eyes. Then I washed, and now I see." [16]Some of the Pharisees said, "This man is not from God, for he does not observe the sabbath." But others said, "How can a man who is a sinner perform such signs?" And they were divided. [17]So they said again to the blind man, "What do you say about him? It was your eyes he opened." He said, "He is a prophet."

[18]The Jews did not believe that he had been blind and had received his sight until they called the parents of the man who had received his sight [19]and asked them, "Is this your son, who you say

NIV

sent for the man's parents. ¹⁹"Is this your son?" they asked. "Is this the one you say was born blind? How is it that now he can see?"

²⁰"We know he is our son," the parents answered, "and we know he was born blind. ²¹But how he can see now, or who opened his eyes, we don't know. Ask him. He is of age; he will speak for himself." ²²His parents said this because they were afraid of the Jews, for already the Jews had decided that anyone who acknowledged that Jesus was the Christ*a* would be put out of the synagogue. ²³That was why his parents said, "He is of age; ask him."

²⁴A second time they summoned the man who had been blind. "Give glory to God,*b*" they said. "We know this man is a sinner."

²⁵He replied, "Whether he is a sinner or not, I don't know. One thing I do know. I was blind but now I see!"

²⁶Then they asked him, "What did he do to you? How did he open your eyes?"

²⁷He answered, "I have told you already and you did not listen. Why do you want to hear it again? Do you want to become his disciples, too?"

²⁸Then they hurled insults at him and said, "You are this fellow's disciple! We are disciples of Moses! ²⁹We know that God spoke to Moses, but as for this fellow, we don't even know where he comes from."

³⁰The man answered, "Now that is remarkable! You don't know where he comes from, yet he opened my eyes. ³¹We know that God does not listen to sinners. He listens to the godly man who does his will. ³²Nobody has ever heard of opening the eyes of a man born blind. ³³If this man were not from God, he could do nothing."

³⁴To this they replied, "You were steeped in sin at birth; how dare you lecture us!" And they threw him out.

³⁵Jesus heard that they had thrown him out, and when he found him, he said, "Do you believe in the Son of Man?"

³⁶"Who is he, sir?" the man asked. "Tell me so that I may believe in him."

a22 Or *Messiah*   *b24* A solemn charge to tell the truth (see Joshua 7:19)

NRSV

was born blind? How then does he now see?" ²⁰His parents answered, "We know that this is our son, and that he was born blind; ²¹but we do not know how it is that now he sees, nor do we know who opened his eyes. Ask him; he is of age. He will speak for himself." ²²His parents said this because they were afraid of the Jews; for the Jews had already agreed that anyone who confessed Jesus*a* to be the Messiah*b* would be put out of the synagogue. ²³Therefore his parents said, "He is of age; ask him."

24So for the second time they called the man who had been blind, and they said to him, "Give glory to God! We know that this man is a sinner." ²⁵He answered, "I do not know whether he is a sinner. One thing I do know, that though I was blind, now I see." ²⁶They said to him, "What did he do to you? How did he open your eyes?" ²⁷He answered them, "I have told you already, and you would not listen. Why do you want to hear it again? Do you also want to become his disciples?" ²⁸Then they reviled him, saying, "You are his disciple, but we are disciples of Moses. ²⁹We know that God has spoken to Moses, but as for this man, we do not know where he comes from." ³⁰The man answered, "Here is an astonishing thing! You do not know where he comes from, and yet he opened my eyes. ³¹We know that God does not listen to sinners, but he does listen to one who worships him and obeys his will. ³²Never since the world began has it been heard that anyone opened the eyes of a person born blind. ³³If this man were not from God, he could do nothing." ³⁴They answered him, "You were born entirely in sins, and are you trying to teach us?" And they drove him out.

35Jesus heard that they had driven him out, and when he found him, he said, "Do you believe in the Son of Man?"*c* ³⁶He answered, "And who is he, sir?*d* Tell me, so that I may believe in him." ³⁷Jesus said to him, "You have seen him, and the one speaking with you is he." ³⁸He said, "Lord,*e* I believe." And he worshiped him. ³⁹Jesus said, "I came into this world for judgment so that those who do not see may see, and those who do see may become blind." ⁴⁰Some of the Pharisees near

a Gk *him*   *b* Or *the Christ*   *c* Other ancient authorities read *the Son of God*   *d* *Sir* and *Lord* translate the same Greek word   *e* *Sir* and *Lord* translate the same Greek word

NIV

37Jesus said, "You have now seen him; in fact, he is the one speaking with you."

38Then the man said, "Lord, I believe," and he worshiped him.

39Jesus said, "For judgment I have come into this world, so that the blind will see and those who see will become blind."

40Some Pharisees who were with him heard him say this and asked, "What? Are we blind too?"

41Jesus said, "If you were blind, you would not be guilty of sin; but now that you claim you can see, your guilt remains."

NRSV

him heard this and said to him, "Surely we are not blind, are we?" 41Jesus said to them, "If you were blind, you would not have sin. But now that you say, 'We see,' your sin remains."

COMMENTARY

John 9:13-41 divides into five scenes: (1) vv. 13-17, the "blind" man and the Pharisees; (2) vv. 18-23, the "Jews" and the man's parents; (3) vv. 24-34, the man and the Pharisees/"Jews"; (4) vv. 35-38, Jesus and the man; (5) vv. 39-41, Jesus and the Pharisees. This five-scene structure shows that this central dialogue section consists of two types of dialogue scenes: scenes in which the Pharisees/Jews have the lead role in the dialogue (vv. 13-34) and scenes in which Jesus has that role (vv. 35-41).

9:13-17. The three scenes in which the Jewish authorities have the lead role are scenes of interrogation. The first of these, vv. 13-17, is the Pharisees' initial interrogation of the blind man. This interrogation scene introduces the conflict over sabbath violation (vv. 14, 16). Kneading was an activity explicitly forbidden on the sabbath (see Commentary on v. 6).[272] As in 5:1-18, the concern with sabbath violation reflects an issue current in Jesus' time. To violate the sabbath law was to challenge the laws that bound the Jewish covenant community together and the Pharisees' authority as interpreters of those laws (see Commentary on 5:9b-18). Jesus' violation of a sabbath prohibition is thus seen by some of the Pharisees as evidence of Jesus' distance from God (v. 16a). This conclusion resounds with irony (as the blind man will point out in v. 33), because the correct interpretation of the healing is as the revelation of God's works (v. 3). Some of the Pharisees, however, link this healing with other miraculous acts Jesus has performed (note the use of the plural

"signs" [σημεῖα *sēmeia*], v. 16b; cf. the words of Nicodemus the Pharisee in 3:2). This schism among the Pharisees (v. 16c) echoes the divided response of the blind man's neighbors (vv. 8-9; cf. 7:12, 25-27, 31, 40-43).

Like the preceding scene with the neighbors (vv. 8-12), the Pharisees' interrogation of the man provides an opportunity for the blind man to bear witness to his healing (v. 15). There is a progression in the man's witness; in v. 11, he identified his healer simply as "the man called Jesus," but in this scene he identifies Jesus as a prophet (v. 17; cf. 4:19). The man's growing awareness of the truth of Jesus' identity (see vv. 30-33, 36, 38) underscores one of the story's central theological themes: Blindness is not determined simply by seeing or not seeing, but by recognizing the revelation of the works of God in Jesus (cf. v. 3, 41).

9:18-23. In the second interrogation scene, the authorities turn their attention to the man's parents. The authorities are identified as the "Jews" in this scene (v. 18), not Pharisees (cf. vv. 13, 15-16). This change in nomenclature ties John 9 into the debates of John 8 (cf. 8:48, 57) and highlights the formal nature of the inquiry. The authorities question both the man's identity and his healing (vv. 18-19), because if they can show that he was never blind, then the whole question of the miracle can be dismissed.[273] The parents confirm that their son was indeed born blind (v. 20) and that they know nothing about the

272. See *m. Šabb.* 7:2.

273. Bultmann, *The Gospel of John,* 335.

manner in which he received his sight (v. 21*a*). In v. 21*b,* the parents disclaim any knowledge of *who* opened their son's eyes, even though the authorities had not explicitly mentioned any healer in their questions. The parents' third answer thus points to the motivation behind the authorities' questions; their fundamental concern is with Jesus, not with the identity of the blind man.

The parents terminate the interrogation by suggesting that the authorities ask the man himself about the healing (vv. 21*c-d*). In 9:22-23, the Fourth Evangelist inserts two verses of commentary that interpret the parents' response to the reader. The parents' words are attributed to their fear of "the Jews." "Jews" is clearly used here in its specialized sense as "Jewish authorities," since the parents must be Jews themselves or they would not be members of the synagogue. In three other places in John (7:13; 19:38; 20:19), "fear of the Jews" is mentioned as the cause of people's silence and secrecy about Jesus. The Evangelist's commentary in 9:22 offers more than a generalized allusion to the parents' fear of the Jewish authorities, however. The Evangelist specifies the source of this fear: "for the Jews had already agreed that anyone who confessed Jesus to be the Messiah would be put out of the synagogue." This explanation introduces data that seems to point explicitly beyond the confines of the story line to the life of the Johannine community.

Verse 22 contains many elements that have drawn the attention of scholars interested in reconstructing the social context in which the Fourth Gospel was written: the formal tone to the word "agreed" (συντίθεμαι *syntithemai*); the formal language of confession (ὁμολογέω *homologeō*) that focuses on the confessing of Jesus as the Christ; and the expression "put out of synagogue,"

which translates the Greek word ἀποσυνάγωγος (*aposynagōgos*).

The most important work done on this passage is that of J. Louis Martyn, whose investigations into John 9 changed the shape and scope of Johannine scholarship.[274] Through a careful and detailed exegetical analysis of 9:22, Martyn proposed that the agreement to put out of the synagogue those who confessed Jesus as the Messiah refers to the Benediction Against Heretics that was introduced into the synagogue liturgy sometime after 70 CE and probably between 85 and 95 CE (see Introduction). On the basis of this benediction, Martyn concluded that the Fourth Gospel was written at the end of the first century CE in and to a community that was being expelled from the synagogue, and that this conflict with the synagogue decisively shaped the Johannine story of Jesus. To support this view of the role of the synagogue, Martyn points to the two other uses of "put out of the synagogue" in John (12:42; 16:2). This is the only occurrence of this word anywhere in the NT or in Jewish and Christian writers of the period.

Martyn's exegesis of 9:22 also led to his critical insight that the conflict with the authorities in John 9 provides the banner example of the two levels on which the Fourth Evangelist was writing the Gospel. The Evangelist frames vv. 18-23 so that the community for whom the Gospel was written can see its own experience reflected in the experience of the characters in the story. On one level, the story portrays a conflict with the religious authorities in Jesus' own day, but it is told in idioms (e.g., "afraid of the Jews," "be put out of the synagogue") that also communicate directly on the level of the community's own experience of conflict and persecution.

274. See Martyn, *History and Theology in the Fourth Gospel.*

❖　　❖　　❖　　❖

EXCURSUS: JOHN 9:22 AND THE BENEDICTION AGAINST HERETICS

The Benediction Against Heretics can be found as the twelfth in a list of nineteen benedictions in the contemporary Jewish prayer book, but because the prayer book was heavily censored in the Middle Ages, this version is not a reliable version of the one introduced by the first-century rabbis. A more reliable text, although its exact age is difficult to determine, is a version of the Benediction found in the Cairo Genizah in 1896: "For the apostates let there be no hope and let the arrogant government be speedily uprooted in our days. Let the Nazarenes [Christians] and the Minim [heretics] be destroyed in a moment and let them be blotted out of the Book of Life and not be inscribed together with the righteous. Blessed art thou, O Lord, who humblest the proud!"[275]

Martyn's precise linkage of 9:22 with the benediction against heretics has been questioned on a number of points. The questions cluster largely around issues of the dating of the twelfth benediction and the reliability of the reference to Christians in the Cairo version of the benediction. Scholars have pointed out that the words of the benediction were not fixed by the late first century and that the prayer must be read in the context of the changes within late first-century Judaism itself. Prior to the destruction of the Jerusalem Temple by the Romans in 70 CE, Judaism had many avenues of expression, which included Pharisaic/rabbinic, Sadducean, apocalyptic, nationalistic (Zealot), and Christian.[276] After the destruction of the Temple, however, the Pharisaic/rabbinic branch moved into ascendancy and began to establish standards of Jewish orthodoxy along its lines. The original form of the prayer was probably directed against heretics in general—that is, all Jews who do not adhere to the Pharisaic/rabbinic line, rather than exclusively against Christians, with the explicit reference to Christians added after the first century.[277]

This does not mean, of course, that the community for which the Fourth Evangelist wrote could not have experienced the general malediction against heretics as directed specifically against them. What it does mean, however, is that one must be careful about how closely one links the social setting of the Fourth Gospel to one particular interpretation of the benediction. While the shape of the conflict between the Johannine community and the synagogue might not be explained point for point for correspondence between John 9:22 and the wording of the Benediction Against Heretics, Martyn's basic understanding of the social circumstances that gave rise to the Fourth Gospel holds true: This community experienced expulsion from the synagogue as a fact of its religious life, and it laid the responsibility for that expulsion on the Jewish authorities—i.e., the Pharisees (see Reflections on John 8).[278]

275. The first published translation of this text was in S. Schecter, "Genizah Specimens," *JQR* old series 10 (1898) 197-206, 654-59. This translation is the one quoted by Martyn, *History and Theology*, 58.
276. Daniel J. Harrington, "The Problem of 'the Jews' in John's Gospel," *Explorations* 8, 1 (1994) 3-4.
277. Steven T. Katz, "Issues in the Separation of Judaism and Christianity After 70 CE: A Reconsideration," *JBL* 103 (1984) 69-74.
278. David Rensberger, *Johannine Faith and Liberating Community* (Philadelphia: Westminster, 1988) 22-29.

❖   ❖   ❖   ❖

9:24-34. In the third and final interrogation scene, the authorities are identified only with the pronoun "they." They are clearly the same group identified as the Pharisees who interrogated the man in vv. 13-17, but the motivation for the second interrogation is also clearly linked to the parents' words to the "Jews" in v. 21 ("so" [οὖν *oun*], v. 24). The authorities thus have the dual identity of Pharisees/"Jews" in this scene, underscoring the fluidity of levels in the telling of this story.

Twice in this interrogation scene the authorities hold their knowledge up to the man and expect him to accept their positions (vv. 24, 29). Each time, however, the man counters with his own knowledge (vv. 25, 30-33). The fact that the man holds his ground in the face of the

Jewish authorities gives this interrogation scene a markedly different cast from the preceding two (vv. 13-17, 18-23). The authorities try to intimidate the man with their status and knowledge, but he will not be intimidated.

9:24-25. "Give glory to God" (v. 24) is a traditional oath formula, through which a person is enjoined to tell the truth (e.g., Josh 7:19) or confess one's sin (e.g., 1 Sam 6:5; Jer 13:16) as evidence of one's worship of God. The Jewish authorities' appeal to these words in this context resounds with irony, however, since, from the Johannine perspective, this is exactly what the man will do in the course of this conversation with the authorities. He will acknowledge God's glory in the healing work of Jesus (vv. 30-33; cf.

1:14; 2:11; 11:4), while the authorities will turn their backs on this manifestation of God's glory.

The "we know" with which the Jewish authorities express their certitude that Jesus is a sinner recalls Nicodemus's assertion of his knowledge about Jesus in 3:2. In both places, the expression carries the weight of official Pharisaic authority. The grounds for calling Jesus a sinner is his violation of the sabbath law (cf. v. 16).

The man does not engage the Jewish authorities in the category of their expertise (what constitutes sin according to the law; v. 25a), but instead contrasts their claim with the reality of his experience and hence his knowledge (v. 25b). His refusal to bend to their knowledge is in itself a challenge to their authority, as is the content of his words. The man's insistence on what he knows confronts the Jewish authorities with a contradiction inherent in their definition of sin; their focus on the violation of the law precludes a focus on the healing (cf. 5:10-15; 7:21-24).

9:26-27. The Jewish authorities' renewed interrogation about what occurred in the healing (v. 26; cf. vv. 15, 19) could be seen as a fulfillment of their responsibility to gather as much evidence as possible in order to decide a case (cf. Nicodemus's request that Jesus be granted a full hearing in accordance with the law, 7:51), but their opening words in v. 24 make clear that their minds are made up. In reality, the renewed questioning serves only to uncover potential inconsistencies in the man's testimony and gather additional evidence against Jesus.[279]

Verse 27 reveals that the man has not been fooled into believing that the authorities' repeated questions have anything to do with a judicious search for information. The mock earnestness of the man's response in v. 27 is a consummate example of Johannine ironic understatement, as he cleverly turns the authorities' inquiries against them. For the first time in this series of interrogations, the Jewish authorities become the interrogatees, rather than the interrogators (v. 27b-c). The staged guilelessness of the man's final question in v. 27c is calculated to taunt the authorities. One can imagine the pleasure with which the audacity of the man's question would be read by a community who saw its own story being played out in these verses.

9:28-29. The use of the verb "revile" (λοι-δορέω *loidoreō*) in v. 28 to describe the authorities' response marks the end of any pretense of objective inquiry on their part. This is the only occurrence of this verb in any of the Gospels; its three other NT occurrences convey the sense of serious insult (Acts 23:4) and suggest situations of persecution and abuse (1 Cor 4:12; 1 Pet 2:23).

In Jewish literature, "disciple of Moses" occasionally appears as a designation for the rabbis.[280] By using this designation of themselves here, the Jewish authorities stress their faithfulness to the Mosaic law. The disdain with which the authorities contrast the man's status as a disciple of Jesus (v. 28, lit., "you are a disciple of that one") with their own status makes clear that to them, one can be either a disciple of Moses or a disciple of Jesus, but not both. From the perspective of the Fourth Gospel, however, in order to be fully faithful to Moses and the promises of God to Moses, one must be a disciple of Jesus. Discipleship of Jesus as the true enactment of Mosaic discipleship was suggested in 5:45-47, where Moses was shown to be a witness to the revelation of God in Jesus. For the Fourth Gospel, faithfulness to the grace and truth available in Jesus, not faithfulness to the law, is the decisive mark of true discipleship (1:17; see also 7:21-24).

The authorities continue their rebuke of the man by pointing to the superiority of Moses' relationship to God (v. 29). That God spoke to Moses is a mainstay of the Pentateuchal narrative (e.g., Exod 33:11; Num 12:2, 8). This assertion by the authorities becomes an ironic claim for the reader of the Gospel, however, because while God may indeed have spoken to Moses, Jesus is the Word of God made flesh (1:14). The authorities' self-professed ignorance of Jesus' origins continues a theme that was prominent in John 7–8 (e.g., 7:28, 41-42; 8:23). They assume Jesus' origin is simply a matter of geography and do not perceive the theological dimension of Jesus' origins, that he comes from God (cf. 8:14). Through their assertion of their knowledge in v. 29 (cf. v. 24), the authorities in reality reveal more about their ignorance than they intend. Interestingly, one of the most vivid depictions of Jesus' origins occurs in the reworking of the Mosaic

---

279. See Bultmann, *The Gospel of John,* 336; Rudolf Schnackenburg, *The Gospel According to St. John,* 3 vols. (New York: Seabury, 1982) 2:251.

280. See texts cited in Hermann L. Strack and Paul Billerbeck, *Kommentar zum Neuen Testament aus Talmud und Midrash* (München: Beck, 1924) 2:535.

traditions in John 6, in which Jesus is identified as the true bread from heaven (6:32-35, 49-51, 58).

9:30-33. The man's opening words in v. 30 show that he is not governed by the fear that shaped his parents' response to the authorities (vv. 21-23). Instead, he goes on the offensive in vv. 30-33, once again confronting the authorities with the contradictions in their own positions (cf. v. 25). First, he turns the authorities' assertion of their lack of knowledge of Jesus' origins ("you do not know," v. 30; "we know," v. 31) back on them by reminding them of one of the conventional theological beliefs of Judaism: that God does not listen to sinners but to the righteous (v. 31; cf. Job 35:13; Ps 66:18; Prov 15:29; Isa 1:15). The description in v. 31 of those to whom God listens is noteworthy, because it combines a traditional Hellenistic description of piety ("one who worships God" [θεοσεβής *theosebēs*]) with a traditional Jewish description ("obeys his will").[281] Second, the man confronts the authorities with the scale of the miracle. His completely unprecedented healing (v. 32) makes sense only if God is the source of the healing (v. 33; cf. 3:2). The traditional teachings of Judaism should thus lead one to recognize the works of God revealed in this healing (9:3).

9:34. The Jewish authorities correctly characterize the man's words to them as teaching; he has indeed taken over their role as teacher of the faith. The authorities reject his teaching on the same grounds that they attempted to dismiss Jesus' healing: The man is a sinner. In the case of the man, however, the case for his sin is not built around sabbath violation, but around the traditional linkage of sin and illness (cf. 9:2). Jesus had dismissed this linkage as the appropriate category through which to interpret the man's blindness (9:3-5), and the authorities' continued adherence to this category is further proof of their distance from the revelation of God in Jesus. The expediency that drives the authorities is also exposed in this charge, because while earlier they rejected his blindness as a way of dismissing the miracle (vv. 18-19), now they accept his blindness as a way of dismissing the man as a sinner.[282]

The notice that the authorities "drove out" (ἐκβάλλω *ekballō*) the man can be read in the more limited sense that they expelled him from their presence as a way of bringing the conversation to a close. In the light of v. 22, however, the authorities' action should be seen as the enactment of the agreement referred to there. The interrogation scenes close with an action that dramatizes the breach in relationship between the Jewish authorities and Jews who align themselves with Jesus.

9:35-38. In the fourth dialogue scene, the focus shifts to Jesus. Verse 35 sets up an explicit contrast between Jesus' initiative in finding the man (cf. 5:14) and the authorities' action in driving him out. Jesus' action underscores his words of 6:37: "anyone who comes to me I will never drive away [*ekballō*]" (see also 10:4). This contrast between the authorities and Jesus introduces a theme that will be developed further in the discourse of 10:1-21.

Jesus' question in v. 35 contains an emphatic use of the pronoun "you" in Greek (σύ *su*), thus intentionally contrasting the beliefs of the man with the beliefs of the authorities. In Jewish usage, the Son of Man refers to a future figure whose coming will mark the beginning of God's final judgment (e.g., Enoch 49:4; 61:9; 69:27). The Fourth Gospel has transformed that traditional eschatological usage, however, so that Jesus is the Son of Man whose eschatological judgment is already underway in the present (e.g., 3:14-15; 5:27). Just as the Samaritan woman was confronted by Jesus with the possibility of the anticipated Messiah's being already present (4:25-26), so also the healed man is confronted by Jesus with the possibility that the future judge is already present. To this point in John 9, the theme of the judgment evoked by the light of the world (9:5; cf. 3:17-21; 12:31-36) has largely been implicit. Jesus' question makes this theme explicit as he asks the man whether he recognizes in his healer "the *eschatological* bringer of salvation."[283] The man's response in v. 36 suggests that once the Son of Man is pointed out to him, he is ready to accept the transformation of eschatological categories that Jesus proposes.

Jesus' words of self-identification in v. 37 (cf. 4:26) lead to the man's confession of faith (v. 38). This confession is the culmination of the man's progression in faith that has run throughout chap. 9. He first acknowledged Jesus simply as the man

---

281. See Bultmann, *The Gospel of John,* 337; C. K. Barrett, *The Gospel According to St. John,* 2nd ed. (Philadelphia: Westminster, 1978) 364.
282. Bultmann, *The Gospel of John,* 337.

283. Ibid., 338.

who had healed him (v. 11), then identified him as a prophet (v. 17), then as a miracle worker from God (vv. 30-33). This progression marks a deepening of the man's gift of sight, from the gift of physical sight to spiritual and theological sight. He now knows who and what he sees in Jesus. "Worship" (προσκυνέω *proskyneō*) is used in John to speak of the worship of God (4:20-24; 12:20). When the man worships Jesus, then, he is acknowledging the presence of God in Jesus and thus ironically fulfills the authorities' demand that he give glory to God (v. 24). With this act of worship, the man's role in the story is completed and he disappears from the narrative (cf. the "exits" of Nicodemus and John the Baptist at 3:9, 36).

Like the rest of chap. 9, vv. 35-38 work on two levels simultaneously. When Jesus finds the expelled man and leads him to a christological confession, the story points through the actions of the characters to the lives of the readers and suggests that if believers are cast out of the synagogue because of their allegiance to Jesus, they will not be left to fend for themselves. Their confession of Jesus will secure them in community with him at the same time as it excludes them from their former religious home.

9:39-41. In the final dialogue scene (vv. 39-41), the focus shifts from the healing miracle itself to the purpose of Jesus' ministry as revealed in that miracle. As noted in the Overview, this scene has a double function. The direct conversation between Jesus and the Jewish authorities concludes the controversy over the healing that dominated 9:13-38, but the new focus also introduces the discourse that follows in 10:1-18. In v. 39, Jesus defines the eschatological purpose of his incarnation ("I came into this world for judgment so that . . . "). As in 3:18-21, Jesus' coming into the world as the light (9:5; cf. 1:9; 12:46) is the moment of judgment, the moment of division.

This reference to judgment here confirms Jesus' identification as the Son of Man in vv. 35-38. It is as the light that Jesus initiates the judgment that characterizes the Son of Man. Sight and blindness are not defined by one's physical sight, but by one's openness to the revelation of God in Jesus. The metaphorical use of sight and blindness to refer to spiritual openness was well known in OT literature, particularly in Isaiah (see esp. Isa 6:10; 42:18-25; cf. also Wis 2:21; Mark 4:12).

The NRSV translation of v. 40 perfectly captures the tone of the Pharisees' question in response to Jesus' pronouncement. In the Greek, the question is introduced by the interrogative particle μή (*mē*) to indicate that the Pharisees are anticipating a negative response to their question. That is, they expect Jesus to affirm that they are exempt from the judgment he describes in v. 39.

Jesus' answer in v. 41 completely undercuts the Pharisees' position. He inverts their definition of sin by explicitly discounting any link between physical blindness and sin (v. 41*a*), and then labeling them with the category that they have attempted to place on him and the blind man throughout John 9, sinner. Sin is defined by neither the presence of an illness (9:2, 34) nor the violation of the law (9:16, 24) but by one's resistance to Jesus. Throughout the preceding dialogue, the Jewish authorities, who have their physical sight, repeatedly insisted on their knowledge about who Jesus could and could not be (vv. 16, 24, 29) and by so doing showed themselves to be closed to Jesus as the light of the world and hence blind. By contrast, the man who had been born blind received his physical sight, but his true sight came as he moved through his ignorance (vv. 12, 25) to recognize Jesus as the Son of Man, as the light of the world. In their immovable insistence on their own rectitude, shown once again in their question of v. 40, the Pharisees demonstrate their own blindness and hence judge themselves (cf. 3:19-20).

REFLECTIONS

As noted in the Introduction, one of the distinctive traits of the Fourth Gospel is the indissoluble union of story and theological interpretation in its telling of the story of Jesus. For the Fourth Evangelist, to tell the story of Jesus is also always to tell what that story means for the reader. As noted in the Commentary and Reflections on John 5 and 6, the Johannine technique of accompanying stories of Jesus with an interpretive discourse is one way in which the union of story and theological interpretation is evident in the Gospel narrative.

John 9:1–10:21 contains such an interpretive discourse (10:1-18), which will be discussed below. On other occasions, however, the Fourth Evangelist embeds the interpretation directly into the telling of the story itself. The Commentary and Reflections on John 4 noted the ways in which the form of that story was inseparable from and in direct service of the content of the story. There was no accompanying discourse because narrative and theology were interwoven in the dramatically constructed scenes between Jesus and the Samaritan woman and Jesus and his disciples.

In John 9:1-41, narrative and theology are more seamlessly interwoven than in any of the other Johannine texts. John 9:1-41 is the most accomplished example of the Fourth Evangelist's use of drama to meld story and interpretation. The Fourth Evangelist structured the story around a succession of short scenes that give John 9 the feel of a drama, facilitating the development of the story and highlighting the tension between characters. The entire story unfolds within the bounds of this drama. The readers are positioned as the audience at a play; none of the characters ever speaks words that address the readers' situation directly. Instead, readers are invited to see their experience within the drama that is being enacted before their eyes. Even the Evangelist's interpretive commentary in 9:22-23 does not speak directly to the links between the parent's situation and the reader's situation but is intended to ensure that the reader will make the connection.

As noted in the Commentary, Martyn has seen in the dramatic structure and style of John 9:1-41 the clues to the two historical levels on which the Gospel is written. The Fourth Evangelist tells a story that is about a situation and characters at the time of Jesus, but the story is told in such a way that it is also about a situation and characters at the time of the Evangelist. For example, the role of Jesus in 9:35-38 can be read as a model for the role of the Christian preacher in the time of the Fourth Evangelist.[284]

One can move Martyn's seminal observation in a slightly different direction by looking at the dramatic style of the two levels of John 9 from the perspective of preaching. By inviting the readers to see their experience in the drama being enacted before their eyes, the Fourth Evangelist employs an indirect method of proclaiming the good news of Jesus and his significance for his readers that is common in narrative preaching. Indeed, several scholars, most especially Raymond Brown and Barnabas Lindars, have proposed that homilies preached in the Johannine community may lie behind many of the texts in the Gospel, and John 9 lends considerable support to that view. When one thinks of John 9 as a sermon, one notes that John 9 adheres to one of the central tenets of narrative preaching: It *shows* what it wants to *tell*.[285]

By letting the drama of John 9 show how the story of Jesus narrated there speaks to the reader's own experience, instead of breaking out of the story and explaining its significance to and for the reader more directly, the Fourth Evangelist is creating a situation in which the Gospel can be "overheard" by the reader.[286] Fred Craddock has identified the two key elements in overhearing as "distance (I am an anonymous listener, reader, viewer, unrelated to the event) and participation (I am drawn in by identification with persons and conditions within the event)."[287] Both of these elements are at work in John 9, and it is possible to interpret the two levels that Martyn has identified so clearly as the Fourth Evangelist's strategy for overhearing. The element of distance is seen in the completeness of the story that unfolds in the drama of John 9; the story makes sense as a story of Jesus that has no relation to those who read or listen to the story. The element of participation is present in the clues that the Fourth Evangelist embeds in the story to guide the listeners to recognize that they are also overhearing their own story. For example, when the authorities are called "the Jews" instead of "Pharisees" (v. 18), the Evangelist points beyond Jesus' story to the readers' story, as do his comments in vv. 22-23. But, as is critical for overhearing, those clues leave the reader the freedom to translate the story of John 9 into their own experience.

284. J. Louis Martyn, *History and Theology in the Fourth Gospel* (Nashville: Abingdon, 1968; 2nd ed., 1979).
285. See, for example, Barbara Brown Taylor, "Preaching the Body," in *Listening to the Word: Essays in Honor of Fred B. Craddock,* ed. Gail R. O'Day and Thomas G. Long (Nashville: Abingdon, 1993).
286. "Overhearing" as an approach to preaching is developed by Fred B. Craddock, *Overhearing the Gospel* (Nashville: Abingdon, 1978).
287. Ibid., 115.

It is interesting to reflect on the Fourth Evangelist's selection of this strategy to address a situation so vital and painful to the life of his community. One function of the drama of John 9 is clearly to offer comfort, encouragement, and hope to the community in its struggles with the synagogue, but this comfort must be found within the story itself (e.g., the audacity of the man in vv. 24-34 and the "happy ending" of vv. 35-38). The Gospel offers no direct words of encouragement; even Jesus' pronouncement in v. 41 is completely clothed in metaphor with no specific referents. Later in the Gospel, Jesus will say words about exclusion from the synagogue that are more directly addressed to the reader's situation (16:2-3), but here, the good news is available to the reader only through overhearing.

This example of overhearing has much to offer contemporary interpreters of this text. The drama, the dialogues, the tension in the Fourth Evangelist's depiction of the conflict with the Jewish authorities cannot be flattened in the interpreter's appropriation of this text, because to flatten the narrative dynamics of John 9 is to destroy the overhearing that is at the heart of the story. This text thus challenges the interpreter to find strategies of indirect communication similar to the Fourth Evangelist's own, so that contemporary readers or listeners, like those in the Johannine community, are invited to find their own experiences in the story of John 9.

1. What good news can be overheard in the drama of John 9? In crucial ways, vv. 1-41 are a dramatization of John 3:16-21. In those verses, the Fourth Evangelist lays out the heart of his eschatology, describing how the incarnation has decisively altered eschatological expectations. God's judgment is no longer reserved for a future age, because the presence of Jesus in the world brings the world to the critical moment of decision. The offer of God's love, available to the world in the presence of Jesus, God's Son, is the eschatological moment. Good and evil are defined solely by people's response to Jesus; the good are those who come to the light, the evil those who scorn the light.

The healing miracle of John 9:1-41, then, is not simply a story that shows the revelation of the works of God in Jesus' gift of sight (v. 3). Rather, the Fourth Evangelist uses this healing story to portray the eschatological truth of Jesus' incarnation palpably and poignantly. Light and darkness are no longer merely concepts, but are embodied in the characters of John 9. In the blind man's journey from physical blindness to spiritual sight, the reader is able to watch as someone comes to the light and is given new life. In the Jewish authorities' journey from physical sight to spiritual blindness, the reader is able to watch as they close themselves to the light and place themselves under judgment. Through the drama of John 9, the reader is able to share in the eschatological reality of Jesus' presence.

2. The dramatic structure of John 9 intensifies what may be the most profound theological irony of this text: The authorities, who positioned themselves as judges of others, finally bring themselves under judgment as sinners. Throughout John 9, the Jewish authorities insist on their right to judge both the healed man and Jesus as sinners (9:16, 24, 34). When the healed man confesses his faith in Jesus as the Son of Man, he acknowledges Jesus as the eschatological judge, whose judgment renders the authorities' judgment impotent. Because of the obvious focus of John 9 on sight and blindness, knowledge and ignorance, its focus on sin is often overlooked. This is a serious omission, because the presentation of sin in John 9 is pivotal to any interpretation of sin in John.

The theme of sin is introduced in the opening verses of John 9, when the disciples attempt to link the man's blindness to sin (see also v. 34). The theme of sin reappears in the Pharisees' opening conversation about Jesus' miracle. To many of them, Jesus' violation of the sabbath marks him as a sinner (9:16; see also vv. 24, 31). To both the disciples and the Pharisees, sin is a moral category, primarily defined in relation to actions.

John 9:1-41 redefines sin by showing that it is exclusively a theological, not moral, category. The key to this redefinition is found in Jesus' words in v. 41. The Pharisees' assertion of their own sight is the basis for Jesus' judgment of them as sinners. The Pharisees do have physical sight; the sight they lack is the ability to see God revealed in Jesus (cf. 9:3), and their refusal to acknowledge this "blindness" on their part proves that they are sinners. Why? Because in the Fourth Gospel, sin is defined not by what one does, but almost exclusively by one's relationship to Jesus, and more specifically, by whether one believes that God is present in Jesus.

Jesus "takes away the sin of the world" (1:29) by the fact of his coming into the world. By giving the world access to the light and love of God, Jesus takes away the world's sin because he makes it possible for the world to redefine its relationship with God. For this reason, "sin" occurs almost exclusively in the singular in John (see Commentary on John 8:21). The world's sin is its refusal to believe in Jesus (16:9). There is a circular logic to the Johannine notions of sin and salvation that John 15:22 and 24 articulate explicitly: "If I had not come and spoken to them, they would not have sin; but now they have no excuse for their sin. . . . If I had not done among them the works that no one else did, they would not have sin."

The Johannine notion of sin is thus intimately tied to its understanding of judgment and eschatology as expressed in 3:18-21. Sin only occurs in response to Jesus. If the Pharisees of John 9 had not been given the opportunity to see, then they would not be blind. But because they had seen Jesus' works and still refused to receive God's revelation in Jesus, they remain in sin. They have turned down Jesus' offer of salvation and so bring themselves under judgment.

Johannine soteriology cannot be understood unless interpreters of John allow "sin" to be heard in Johannine terms without automatically subsuming it into other NT definitions of sin. The Johannine understanding of sin and salvation contributes an important voice to Christian theology, because it provides an alternative to what is often posited as normative in discussions of salvation. In those discussions, sin is used primarily as a moral category to refer to people's actions that are opposed to the will of God, and Jesus redeems people from their sins through the expiation of his death. The Johannine understanding of sin opens up to a very different understanding of the salvific function of Jesus' death. Salvation from sin is primarily a result of Jesus' *life,* not his death, because it is the very life of Jesus as God's Son and incarnate Word that makes it possible for people to move from sin to eternal life.

This Johannine view of sin and salvation can be a difficult one for contemporary Christians to grasp, because the expiatory view of sin and the exclusive linkage of salvation with Jesus' death so dominate conversations within the church. Yet the church loses a powerful witness if it ignores or silences this Johannine voice. First, the Gospel of John invites Christians to reevaluate the criteria by which one defines sin and by which people are judged. The Fourth Gospel, as dramatized in John 9, reduces sin to its christological, and hence *theological,* essence. Sin is fundamentally about one's relationship with God, and for the Fourth Evangelist, the decisive measure of one's relationship with God is one's faith in Jesus. This flies in the face of views that want to define sin in relation to right actions and thereby establish the norms for judgment. To the Fourth Evangelist, these norms for judgment are very lean: Believe in the revelation of God in Jesus. Judgment is therefore based not on what people do, as the disciples and the Pharisees in John 9 assumed, but on people's embrace of God in Jesus. The only way to be excluded from Jesus' offer of salvation is to turn one's back on that offer. This is a radical and liberating notion of sin and salvation, one that not surprisingly makes many people uncomfortable, because it removes the establishment of norms of behavior from the category of sin. From the Johannine perspective, it is not the Christian community's responsibility, just as it was not the Pharisees', to judge anyone's sins, because the determination of sin rests with God and Jesus, and the individual and is determined by faith, not actions. The Johannine Gospel is thus the most radical example of salvation by grace anywhere in the NT.

Second, the Johannine understanding of sin and judgment invites the Christian community to reexamine its understanding of salvation and redemption. The Fourth Gospel quite explicitly relocates the offer of salvation to Jesus' life and moves away from a narrow focus on Jesus' death. The Gospel is unequivocally clear: Jesus' incarnation, not the expiation of his death, brings salvation from sin. This, too, can be discomfiting to people who think that an expiatory understanding of salvation is the "only" Christian view. Yet again, to overlook the Johannine view is to miss a powerful witness and resource for the life of faith. The Gospel of John invites Christians to recognize the transformative power of the love of God made manifest in the incarnation and to shape their lives accordingly. This is why Johannine eschatology puts its primary emphasis on Jesus' coming into the world. To reject Jesus is to reject the love of God in Jesus and so to pass from the possibility of salvation to judgment (cf. 3:16-17). Therefore, the Pharisees' announcement of their sight, when in fact they have not seen God in Jesus, marks their sin and the "blind" man's embrace of Jesus as the Son of Man marks his salvation. Judgment and salvation are not lodged with Jesus' death; they belong to Jesus' life. (For more on the significance of the death of Jesus in John, see Reflections on 12:20-36.)

The story of the blind man has been used as a symbol of faith and new life throughout the history of the church. The healing of the blind man appears as a baptismal symbol in second-century frescoes in the catacombs in Rome (as do the stories of the Samaritan woman and the healing of the man in John 5). These same stories were used in Lenten baptismal liturgies dating at least as far back as the fourth and fifth centuries. The blind man's movement from darkness to light and his confession of his faith in Jesus provided a vehicle through which the church could celebrate the power of new life that begins in baptism. The blind man's words in John 9:25 also offer eloquent testimony to the transforming power of God's grace in the hymn "Amazing Grace": "I once was blind, but now I see."

John 10:1-21, The Shepherd Discourse

NIV

10 "I tell you the truth, the man who does not enter the sheep pen by the gate, but climbs in by some other way, is a thief and a robber. [2]The man who enters by the gate is the shepherd of his sheep. [3]The watchman opens the gate for him, and the sheep listen to his voice. He calls his own sheep by name and leads them out. [4]When he has brought out all his own, he goes on ahead of them, and his sheep follow him because they know his voice. [5]But they will never follow a stranger; in fact, they will run away from him because they do not recognize a stranger's voice." [6]Jesus used this figure of speech, but they did not understand what he was telling them.

[7]Therefore Jesus said again, "I tell you the truth, I am the gate for the sheep. [8]All who ever came before me were thieves and robbers, but the sheep did not listen to them. [9]I am the gate; whoever enters through me will be saved.[a] He will come in and go out, and find pasture. [10]The thief comes only to steal and kill and destroy; I have come that they may have life, and have it to the full.

[a]9 Or kept safe

NRSV

10 "Very truly, I tell you, anyone who does not enter the sheepfold by the gate but climbs in by another way is a thief and a bandit. [2]The one who enters by the gate is the shepherd of the sheep. [3]The gatekeeper opens the gate for him, and the sheep hear his voice. He calls his own sheep by name and leads them out. [4]When he has brought out all his own, he goes ahead of them, and the sheep follow him because they know his voice. [5]They will not follow a stranger, but they will run from him because they do not know the voice of strangers." [6]Jesus used this figure of speech with them, but they did not understand what he was saying to them.

[7]So again Jesus said to them, "Very truly, I tell you, I am the gate for the sheep. [8]All who came before me are thieves and bandits; but the sheep did not listen to them. [9]I am the gate. Whoever enters by me will be saved, and will come in and go out and find pasture. [10]The thief comes only to steal and kill and destroy. I came that they may have life, and have it abundantly.

[11]"I am the good shepherd. The good shepherd lays down his life for the sheep. [12]The hired hand,

NIV

[11]"I am the good shepherd. The good shepherd lays down his life for the sheep. [12]The hired hand is not the shepherd who owns the sheep. So when he sees the wolf coming, he abandons the sheep and runs away. Then the wolf attacks the flock and scatters it. [13]The man runs away because he is a hired hand and cares nothing for the sheep.

[14]"I am the good shepherd; I know my sheep and my sheep know me— [15]just as the Father knows me and I know the Father—and I lay down my life for the sheep. [16]I have other sheep that are not of this sheep pen. I must bring them also. They too will listen to my voice, and there shall be one flock and one shepherd. [17]The reason my Father loves me is that I lay down my life— only to take it up again. [18]No one takes it from me, but I lay it down of my own accord. I have authority to lay it down and authority to take it up again. This command I received from my Father."

[19]At these words the Jews were again divided. [20]Many of them said, "He is demon-possessed and raving mad. Why listen to him?"

[21]But others said, "These are not the sayings of a man possessed by a demon. Can a demon open the eyes of the blind?"

NRSV

who is not the shepherd and does not own the sheep, sees the wolf coming and leaves the sheep and runs away—and the wolf snatches them and scatters them. [13]The hired hand runs away be- cause a hired hand does not care for the sheep. [14]I am the good shepherd. I know my own and my own know me, [15]just as the Father knows me and I know the Father. And I lay down my life for the sheep. [16]I have other sheep that do not belong to this fold. I must bring them also, and they will listen to my voice. So there will be one flock, one shepherd. [17]For this reason the Father loves me, because I lay down my life in order to take it up again. [18]No one takes[a] it from me, but I lay it down of my own accord. I have power to lay it down, and I have power to take it up again. I have received this command from my Father."

[19]Again the Jews were divided because of these words. [20]Many of them were saying, "He has a demon and is out of his mind. Why listen to him?" [21]Others were saying, "These are not the words of one who has a demon. Can a demon open the eyes of the blind?"

[a] Other ancient authorities read *has taken*

COMMENTARY

The discourse of John 10:1-18 continues the words of Jesus begun at 9:41 and is positioned in the narrative as Jesus' reflection on what has just taken place with the blind man and the Phari- sees/"Jews." As noted in the Overview to 9:1– 10:21, this combination of miracle, dialogue, and discourse is common in the Fourth Gospel. John 10:1-18 has a transitional function in the overall movement of the Gospel.[288] It is the last full discourse of Jesus' public ministry; Jesus' next major discourse is the Farewell Discourse of John 14:1–16:33, which is directed to his disciples.

The Fourth Evangelist uses the expression "very truly, I say to you" to mark the two parts of the discourse (vv. 1-6, 7-18). Verses 1-6 consist

of the "figure of speech" (vv. 1-5), followed by the Evangelist's interpretive comment (v. 6). Verses 7-18 consist of a series of four "I am" statements (vv. 7-16), followed by a conclusion (vv. 17-18).

10:1-6. Scholars are divided on whether vv. 1-5 contain one unified figure of speech[289] or whether it is the fusing of two distinct figures.[290] Those who argue for two figures see these verses as preserving two parables, one about entering the sheepfold (vv. 1-3a), a second about the shepherd (vv. 3b-5). A sharp division between the two parts

288. Rudolf Bultmann, *The Gospel of John: A Commentary,* trans. G. R. Beasley-Murray, R. W. N. Hoare, and J. K. Riches (Philadelphia: Westminster, 1971) 363.

289. E.g., George R. Beasley-Murray, *John,* WBC 36 (Waco, Tex.: Word, 1987) 166-67.
290. E.g., C. H. Dodd, *Historical Tradition in the Fourth Gospel* (Cambridge: Cambridge University Press, 1963) 382-85; Raymond E. Brown, *The Gospel According to John (I–XII),* AB 29 (Garden City, N.Y.: Doubleday, 1966) 391-92; Robert Kysar, *John,* Augsburg Commentary of the New Testament (Minneapolis: Augsburg, 1986) 159-60.

of vv. 1-5 does not seem warranted by the text, however, because all of vv. 1-5 focuses on the shepherd and his relation to the flock. In vv. 1-3*a,* the shepherd comes to the sheep, and in vv. 3*b*-5 the sheep recognize the shepherd. A positive image of the shepherd (vv. 2-4) is contrasted with the negative image of thief, bandit, and stranger (vv. 1, 5).[291]

The expression "very truly, I tell you" (v. 1) serves two rhetorical functions. First, it marks the shift from dialogue to monologue (cf. 3:11; 5:19), and second, it indicates a new movement in the argument (cf. 5:24-25; 6:26, 34; 8:34). Instead of continuing to address the Pharisees' situation directly (9:41), Jesus addresses it more obliquely through his use of figurative language (cf. Jesus' use of the parable of the lost sheep in Luke 15:3-7).

10:1-3a. Verses 1-2 are one sentence in the Greek text, marked by a carefully balanced antithetical parallelism that establishes the identity of the shepherd (v. 2) by first establishing who he is not (v. 1). The pivot of the antithesis is the way one enters the sheepfold. The one who has "authorized access"[292] (i.e., enters by the gate) is the shepherd; the one without authorized access is a thief and a bandit. The fact that the shepherd has authorized access is confirmed by the gatekeeper's opening the gate for him (v. 3*a*).

10:3b-5. In vv. 3*b*-5, the figure expands from the identification of the shepherd to the sheep's recognition and response to the shepherd. Verses 3*b*-4 use a chiastic parallelism built around images of hearing and movement to develop the positive image of the shepherd and the sheep:

v. 3*b*	A	"hear his voice," "calls his own sheep by name"
	B	"and leads them out"
v. 4	B′	"brought out all his own," "goes ahead of them," "the sheep follow him"
	A′	"they know his voice"

The intimacy of the relationship between the shepherd and the sheep is demonstrated by the sheep's ability to recognize the shepherd's voice

(vv. 3*b*-4) and the shepherd's ability to call "his own" by name (v. 3*b*). To call the sheep by name may refer to the practice of giving pet names to individual sheep[293] or it may simply mean to call each sheep individually. As a result of this intimacy, the sheep will follow the shepherd.

The dominant imagery of v. 5 is also hearing and motion, but it is used to the opposite effect in this verse. Just as the intimacy of the shepherd/sheep relationship was defined by voice and movement, so also the absence of such intimacy with the stranger is defined by voice ("they do not know the voice of strangers") and movement ("will not follow a stranger"; "will run from him"). In and of itself, then, the figure is not hard to understand. It presents a fairly simple picture of the work of the shepherd and his flock that corresponds to the pastoral practices of the Mediterranean world. For example, sheepfolds were usually constructed adjoining the house and had a separate entrance gate. The only access to the sheepfold was through this gate. If the flock was large enough to require more than one shepherd, an undershepherd might be assigned the task of watching the sheepfold door at night. The roles of each of the characters in the figure are well defined and limited: The shepherd has the largest role, coming to the sheep, calling them by name, and leading them; the sheep respond to the shepherd (or refuse to respond to the stranger); and the thief, the bandit, and the stranger reflect potential threats to the sheep and hence the economic livelihood of the shepherd.

10:6. The Evangelist's commentary in v. 6 makes clear, however, that Jesus' words are to be understood as more than a depiction of Palestinian pastoral practices. First, the Evangelist explicitly labels Jesus' words a "figure of speech" (παροιμία *paroimia*). *Paroimia* is a difficult word to translate precisely. In the LXX, *paroimia* is used to translate the Hebrew word that means "proverb" (משל *māšāl*; e.g., Prov 1:1). The only NT usage of the Greek word *paroimia* outside of John (2 Pet 2:22) clearly means "proverb," because it is used to introduce a quotation from the book of Proverbs. Yet the Hebrew word *māšāl is* also translated by the Greek word for "parable" (παραβολή *parabolē*) in the LXX, and in some texts it is clear

---

291. Jurgen Becker, *Das Evangelium des Johannes* (Gutersloh: G. Mohn, 1979) 325.

292. Beasley-Murray, *John,* 168.

293. So Brown, *The Gospel According to John (I–XII),* 385.

that *parabolē* and *paroimia* are synonyms (e.g., Sir 47:17). One of the other meanings of the Hebrew word *māšāl* is "riddle." The translation "figure of speech" is an attempt to capture the open-endedness of *paroimia* that the word "proverb" rarely conveys in English.

It is in the very nature of the general language and images of proverbs to be suggestive of many meanings. Sirach 39:3 is instructive in this regard: "He seeks out the hidden meanings of proverbs" (NRSV). In v. 6, then, the Evangelist is drawing the reader's attention to Jesus' use of language whose meaning intentionally resides below the surface level, as in 4:35-38 and 12:24. In the other two uses of *paroimia* in John (16:25, 29), speaking in "figures of speech" is contrasted with speaking "plainly" (παρρησία *parrēsia*). *Paroimia* thus points to a way of speaking that encompasses, but is not limited to, a particular literary form such as parable or proverb.[294]

Second, the Evangelist informs the reader in v. 6 that the Pharisees do not understand what Jesus says. One has to ask whether within the narrative framework of John 9:1–10:21, the Pharisees could have interpreted this "figure of speech," or if Jesus used it intentionally to preclude interpretation (cf. Mark 4:11-12). The images of sheep and shepherd were frequently used with metaphorical significance within the OT. Traditionally, God is understood as the shepherd and God's people as sheep (e.g., Pss 23:1; 74:1; 79:13; 80:1; 95:7; 100:3). Of particular importance for the background of Jesus' use of pastoral imagery here is Ezekiel 34, in which the kings of Israel are the bad shepherds who endanger and exploit the flock (Ezek 34:1-10); God is the good shepherd who will rescue the sheep and who will place them in the care of "my servant, David" (v. 23)—that is, a restored monarchy (Ezek 34:11-31).

When Jesus' figure of speech is read in the context of 9:1-41, it seems clear that Jesus is positioning the Pharisees in the role of thief, bandit, and stranger. Their conduct toward the blind man (cf. 9:34) has demonstrated that they do not have the flock's best interest at heart, whereas Jesus' conduct toward the man has shown him to be the shepherd who comes to the sheep (cf. 9:35) and to whom the sheep respond

(cf. 9:36-38). It is this use of the pastoral imagery that the Pharisees did not understand, because as the teachers and leaders of Israel (cf. 3:2, 10), they would think of themselves in the role of shepherd, not thief or stranger.

To the reader of the Gospel, the figure of speech of vv. 1-5 has an even wider range of associations. The language of vv. 1-5 not only draws the reader into OT pastoral imagery, but also carries echoes of Johannine themes—for example, "his own" (vv. 3-4; cf. 1:11), hear his voice (v. 3; cf. 5:37; 12:47).[295] These echoes open up to the more explicitly christological use of the same pastoral imagery in vv. 7-16.

10:7-18. A commonly held view of the relationship between vv. 1-5 and vv. 7-18 is that vv. 1-5 should be seen as a parable, and vv. 7-18 as the parable's allegorical (and perhaps secondary) explanation (analogous to the relationship of the parable of the sower in Mark 4:1-9 to its interpretation in 4:13-20).[296] There are several problems with this interpretive move. First, there is no one-to-one correspondence between the figure of vv. 1-5 and Jesus' words in vv. 7-16. Many of the elements of vv. 1-5 are ignored in vv. 7-16 (e.g., the gatekeeper, the stranger) and new ones are introduced (the hired hand, the wolf). Jesus continues to use pastoral imagery in vv. 7-16, but uses it to move in a new direction. Second, this interpretive move tends to read the "I am" statements in isolation from the use of figurative language in other discourses and "I am" statements in John (e.g., 6:35; 8:12; 15:1).[297]

A comparison with John 6 is especially helpful in guiding the interpretation of John 10:7-16.[298] Jesus' words in John 6 also consist of a series of "I am" statements (6:35, 41, 48, 51) followed by theological expansion (6:36-40, 43-47, 49-50). In John 6, Jesus' self-revelation is couched in the language of bread and built around images from the exodus tradition to show that he was the true fulfillment of Mosaic hopes (see Commentary

294. See Kim E. Dewey, *"Paroimai* in the Gospel of John," *Semeia* 17 (1980) 81-99.

295. See E. C. Hoskyns, *The Fourth Gospel* (London: Faber & Faber, 1947) 371-72.

296. E.g., Brown, *The Gospel According to John (I–XII)*, 391.

297. Robert Kysar, "Johannine Metaphor—Meaning and Function: A Literary Case Study of John 10:1-18," *Semeia* 53 (1991) 81-111, attempts to read John 10:1-18 in the light of Johannine metaphor, but even he isolates this discourse and does not relate it to other Johannine discourses. Interestingly, the shepherd imagery also receives barely a notice in Culpepper's discussion of Johannine symbolism in *Anatomy of the Fourth Gospel*, another example of the idiosyncratic treatment this text receives.

298. Hoskyns, *The Fourth Gospel*, 367.

on John 6). A similar use of language and imagery is at work in John 10:7-16. In his reworking of the images of OT pastoral imagery, Jesus shows how he is the one who meets the needs of the sheep.

The second part of the discourse begins like the first, with the use of "very truly, I say to you" to indicate a new development in the discourse. Verses 7-16 divide into two parts, each part containing a pair of "I am" statements by Jesus that are accompanied by brief explanations. Verses 7-10 are built around Jesus' self-identification as the gate for the sheep (vv. 7, 9), and vv. 11-16 around his self-identification as the good shepherd (vv. 11, 14).

10:7-10. Verses 7, 9, and 10*b* present the positive image of Jesus as the gate; vv. 8 and 10*a* present the contrasting negative image of the thief. In vv. 1-2, the gate was the means of authorized access to the sheepfold and was introduced in order to distinguish the one who had authorized access, the shepherd, from those who did not, thieves and bandits. In vv. 7-10, by contrast, the primary point of reference for the gate imagery is the effect of the gate on the sheep themselves. When Jesus identifies himself as the gate for the sheep (v. 7), he points to the ways in which one's place in the sheepfold, and hence one's identity as a member of the flock, is determined exclusively by one's relationship to Jesus as the gate. One enters the fold through Jesus.

Those who enter the fold by ways other than the gate are thieves and bandits (v. 8; cf. v. 1). Some of the earliest manuscripts omit the phrase "before me" (πρὸ ἐμοῦ *pro emou*) in the description of the thieves and bandits in v. 8 in an attempt to soften the seeming rejection of all OT figures. "All who came before me" cannot imply a sweeping rejection of OT figures, however, because Jesus has earlier referred to both Moses and Abraham as positive witnesses to him (5:45-46; 8:56).[299] Rather, it refers to those like the Jewish leaders in John 5 (vv. 39-40, 47) and 9 (vv. 28-29) who discount these witnesses to Jesus and thus attempt another means of access to the sheepfold. The sheep do not listen to them, since they have not entered through the gate and thus do not belong in the fold (v. 8*b*).

That Jesus' self-identification as the gate is primarily oriented to the life of the sheep is made even clearer in vv. 9-10. Jesus explicitly identifies himself as the means to salvation (v. 9; cf. 14:6). Verse 9 incorporates OT imagery in its description of Jesus as the gate. The promise of entering through the gate to find salvation echoes Ps 118:19-20 and identifies Jesus as the point of access to God for the flock. The promise of finding pasture recalls the pastoral imagery of Ps 23:2 and Ezek 34:14. Jesus' promise of pasture in v. 9 also recalls his earlier promises of gifts of water (4:14; 7:37) and bread (6:35) that will end thirst and hunger. The three verbs identified with the thief in v. 10*a* all have to do with the destruction and death of the flock, whereas v. 10*b* restates one of the central affirmations of the Gospel: Jesus comes to bring life (e.g., 3:16; 5:24; 6:40, 51; 11:25; 20:31).

The imagery of the gate, then, has both christological and ecclesiological significance (see Reflections below). By addressing the grounding of the community's life in Jesus, vv. 7-10 introduce themes that will dominate the Farewell Discourse (14:1–16:33). These community concerns fit well after the drama of John 9, in which the Pharisees attempted to destroy community by driving out the healed man (9:34; cf. 10:4), and Jesus moved to restore it (9:35-38).

10:11-16. At v. 11, the focus shifts to Jesus' self-revelation as the good shepherd. The identification of Jesus as the shepherd was implicit in the figure of speech in vv. 1-5, but it is made explicit for the first time here. As in vv. 7-10, the positive image of the good shepherd (vv. 11, 14-16) is contrasted with a negative image, that of the hired hand (vv. 12-13).

The "I am" saying of v. 11*a* is explained exclusively in metaphorical language in vv. 11*b*-13. That is, after the initial use of a first-person singular pronoun, Jesus never refers to himself directly again. Instead, he draws on images derived from the OT to explain what he means by "good shepherd." The adjective "good" (καλός *kalos*) also has the meaning "model" or "true," and the reference point for what constitutes a model shepherd is set by the image of God as the good shepherd in Ezekiel 34. According to Ezek 34:11-16, God the good shepherd cares for the sheep, rescuing them from the places to which they have been scattered, feeding them, and tending to the weak, the injured, and the lost. By identifying

299. Bultmann, *The Gospel of John,* 376.

himself as the good shepherd of Ezekiel 34, Jesus thus identifies himself as fulfilling God's promises and doing God's work (cf. 4:34; 17:4).

Verse 11*b* pushes beyond the imagery of Ezekiel 34 in its reference to the shepherd's willingness to lay down his life for the sheep. A possible OT antecedent may lie in the messianic oracle of Zech 13:7-9, in which the death of the shepherd is required so that the flock can be purified.[300] Verse 11*b* may also have points of contact with Palestinian shepherding practices; a good shepherd may indeed have to give up his life to prevent the decimation of his flock by wild animals. Yet the reference to the shepherd's laying down his life is cast in a distinctive Johannine idiom (10:15, 17-18; 13:37-38; 15:13; 1 John 3:16), so that the reader of the Gospel cannot help hearing in Jesus' words an allusion to his own death. Verses 15 and 17-18 will make those associations with the death of Jesus explicit, but at this point Jesus stays within the metaphor of shepherding. He works to build the interpretive frame of reference before he turns more directly to his own life and death.

The image of the hired hand in vv. 12-13 has many echoes of the image of the bad shepherd in Ezek 34:5-6, 8-10. It also recalls descriptions of the bad shepherd in Jer 23:1-3 and Zech 11:15, 17. The common denominator in these OT portraits of the bad shepherd and the picture of the hired hand is the shepherd's primary concern for his own well-being at the expense of the flock's well-being. In each of these portraits, the flock is scattered and devoured by animals as a result of the shepherd's neglect. This picture of the hired shepherd's lack of concern for the sheep (v. 13) stands in marked contrast to the picture of the good shepherd, who cares for the sheep to the point of laying down his life for them.

Jesus' self-revelation in vv. 14-16 weaves back and forth seamlessly between figurative and nonfigurative speech. Jesus begins by once again identifying himself with the image of the good shepherd (v. 14), but explains that image primarily by making reference to his ministry and relationship to God, rather than by staying within the images of sheep and shepherd as he did in vv. 11-13. This move between figurative and non-

figurative speech results in some ambiguity in interpreting Jesus' words. This ambiguity is immediately evident in v. 14*b*. When Jesus speaks of his relationship with his own, he may be speaking within the shepherding figure (cf. vv. 3-4), but the expressions "my own" (τὰ ἐμά *ta ema*) and "his own" (οἱ ἴδιοι *hoi idioi*) also describe Jesus' relationship to his followers in John (e.g., 1:11; 13:1; 17:9-10). Verse 14*b* suggests that the line between metaphorical and direct speech is very thin in this section of the discourse.

This is especially evident in the use of the verb for "know" (γινώσκω *ginōskō*) in vv. 14*b*-15*a*. Jesus' words in v. 14*b* may be read as an elaboration of the shepherd imagery of vv. 4-5, but v. 15*a* explicitly moves outside of the shepherd imagery by pointing to Jesus' relationship to the Father. Verse 15*a* provides a working definition of knowledge in John: Knowledge is not a cognitive category, but is a category of relationship. The true measure and model of knowledge is God's and Jesus' mutual knowledge. Jesus is thus the good shepherd not simply because of his relationship to the sheep, but also because of his relationship to God.

Verse 15*b* makes the connection of Jesus' death and the shepherd's death (cf. v. 11) explicit. The juxtaposition of vv. 15*a* and 15*b* suggests again that Jesus lays down his life not simply because of his relationship to the sheep (as in the image of the shepherd in v. 11) but because of his relationship with God. The reference in v. 16 to other sheep has particular relevance in the setting of Jesus' conversation with the Pharisees. Jesus is suggesting here that his flock is not limited to the sheep of Israel[301] and that the community created by his death will include people from outside of Israel (cf. 12:32). The mark of this expanded flock will be that "they will listen to my voice," a trait that distinguishes the flock from the Jewish leaders who neither listen to nor know Jesus' voice (cf. 8:43; 10:6). To hear Jesus' voice is the mark of faithfulness to Jesus and his word (cf. 5:24; 10:27; 12:47).

The final image of v. 16 returns fully to the sheep metaphor. The vison of a united flock recalls the final promise of Ezek 34:31: "You are my sheep, the sheep of my pasture and I am your God" (NRSV). Jesus once again positions himself

300. Rudolf Schnackenburg, *The Gospel According to St. John,* 3 vols. (New York: Seabury, 1982) 2:295.

301. See Beasley-Murray, *John,* 171; C. K. Barrett, *The Gospel According to St. John,* 2nd ed. (Philadelphia: Westminster, 1978) 376.

as the fulfillment of promises traditionally associated with God. Jesus the good shepherd will bring about unity in the flock through his relationship with God and his death (v. 15).

10:17-18. This unit forms the conclusion to the discourse. In these verses, the shepherd metaphor is abandoned completely and Jesus speaks directly about his death and relationship with God. These verses focus on three theological themes that are essential to understanding the death of Jesus in John. First, vv. 17 and 18c place Jesus' death fully in the context of his relationship with God. Verse 17 contains the first linkage of "love" (ἀγαπάω agapaō) with Jesus' death in the Fourth Gospel. God's love for the world (3:16) and for Jesus (3:35; see also 17:24) are already known to the reader, and v. 17 adds a new dimension to that love. God loves Jesus because Jesus lives out God's commandment fully (v. 18). In the Fourth Gospel, the core commandment that Jesus gives his disciples is that they love one another *just as he has loved them* (13:34). The sign of Jesus' love for them is that he is willing to lay down his life for them (cf. 13:1; 15:13). Jesus thus obeys the same commandment from God that he passes on to his disciples, to live fully in love. It is wrong to read the phrase "for this reason" (διὰ τοῦτό dia touto, v. 17) as saying that Jesus wins the Father's love through his death; rather, his death is the ultimate expression of the love relationship that already exists and defines who he is and how he enacts God's will for the world.

Second, vv. 17-18 make clear that Jesus' laying down his life is an act he freely chooses as an expression of his obedience to God (vv. 17b, 18a). Jesus is not a victim in death nor a martyr against his will, but is in control of his own death (v. 18b; see 19:11, 17). The Gospel story has already demonstrated this in the authorities' inability to arrest Jesus (7:30, 44) and his control of the hour (2:4; 7:30; 8:20).[302]

Third, vv. 17-18 point to the inseparability of Jesus' death and resurrection in John. Jesus' enactment of God's work is incomplete until he returns to the Father through his resurrection and ascension (13:1; 17:1, 4-5). Jesus reveals God's will for the world not only in his death, but also in his victory over death through his return to God. When Jesus lays down his life, therefore, it is to the end of taking it up again. In vv. 17-18, Jesus speaks of himself as the agent of both his death and his resurrection (cf. 2:19-21). That is, whereas elsewhere in the NT God raises Jesus (e.g., Acts 2:24; 10:40; 1 Cor 15:15; Gal 1:1), here Jesus speaks of taking up his own life again. The "power" (ἐξουσία exousia) that Jesus has to lay down his life and to take it up again is given to him by God (see 17:2 and Jesus' statement about Pilate's "power" at 19:11). These verses point to the complete union of God and Jesus in their work (cf. 4:34), a union that receives explicit expression at 10:30.

10:19-21. The schism among the "Jews" in response to Jesus' words (v. 19) recalls the schism among them in response to his healing of the blind man (9:16). In 9:16a, some attempted to discredit Jesus by calling him a sinner; here the charge is demon possession (v. 20; cf. 7:20; 8:48). Others are willing to trust the evidence of the miracle itself (9:16b; v. 21). Verses 19-21 make clear that the Fourth Evangelist intends the healing and the discourse to be assessed in the light of each other. A decision about Jesus' identity must hold together both his words and his works.

302. See Jerome H. Neyrey, *An Ideology of Revolt: John's Christology in Social-Science Perspective* (Philadelphia: Fortress, 1988) 71.

REFLECTIONS

The image of Jesus as the good shepherd has a perennial hold on Christian imagination and piety. Some of the most popular pictures of Jesus are those that depict him as a shepherd, leading a flock of sheep.[303] This picture of Jesus has influenced the church's images of its leaders, so that in many traditions the ordained minister is referred to as the "pastor," and ministerial care of the congregation is referred to as "pastoral care." Behind both of these understandings of ministerial vocation is the sense that the minister is called to lead in the image

303. See James P. Martin, "John 10:1-10," *Int.* 32 (1978) 171.

of Jesus' leadership, to be the shepherd as Jesus is shepherd. Because these images play such an important role in the life of the church, it is critical for the interpreter of John 10 to distinguish among the various uses of shepherd imagery in the NT. The move to pastoral images of ministry, for example, belongs more to other NT texts (e.g., John 21:15-19; Acts 20:28-29; 1 Pet 5:2-3) than to the interpretation of John 10. The pastoral images of John 10 are primarily christological and ecclesiological, focusing on Jesus' identity and his relationship to the sheep.

Because the picture of Jesus as good shepherd has such a rich tradition in the life of the church (for other NT examples of this image, see Heb 13:20; 1 Pet 2:25; 3:4), there is a tendency to read John 10 as if Jesus' self-revelation as the good shepherd is the only christological image in the discourse. As a result, the christological imagery of the gate (vv. 7-10) is subsumed into the imagery of the good shepherd (vv. 11-16). This move runs contrary to the text itself, however. The two "I am" statements of John 10 present the reader with two christological images whose theological integrity must be preserved. When the shepherd image is emphasized in isolation from the gate image, the picture of Jesus in John 10 becomes too easy to appropriate and loses its christological edge. When the gate imagery is dropped, the christological focus of the shepherd imagery can become anthropocentric. That is, Jesus as the good shepherd becomes a model for other shepherds who would lead the "sheep." The text becomes as much about "us" as leaders as it is about Jesus as the shepherd. When the gate imagery is retained, however, this slide from the christological to the anthropocentric is more difficult.

The heavy concentration of OT pastoral images in this discourse, particularly images associated with God in the OT texts, points the reader to the discourse's christological heart: Jesus is the fulfillment of God's promises to God's people. Yet Jesus is more than the good shepherd for whom Israel waits (Ezekiel 34), because he is also the gate for the sheep. Jesus is the way to life (the gate), and he leads the way to life (the good shepherd). While these are closely related, they are not the same thing. Jesus is the way to life because he is himself life (v. 10; cf. 14:6). Jesus leads the way to the life because he lays down his own life (vv. 11, 14-15). These are non-transferrable attributes; they derive from the heart of Jesus' identity as the one sent by God.

The "I am" statements of John 10, then, deepen the array of images of Jesus available to the church. The images of Jesus as the gate and the good shepherd are intensely relational; they have no meaning without the presence of the sheep. These "I am" statements do not simply reveal who Jesus is, but more specifically reveal who Jesus is in relationship to those who follow him. The identity of Jesus and the identity of the community that gathers around him are inextricably linked.

The relational dimension of the christological images provides the bridge to the ecclesiological dimension of this imagery. The identity of the community is determined by the shepherd's (Jesus') relationship to it and its relationship to the shepherd (Jesus). There is, then, an anthropological dimension to the shepherd discourse, but it is an anthropology completely dependent on the discourse's christology and expressed exclusively in communal terms. For the community of faith, human identity is determined by Jesus' identity. Who Jesus is with and for the community determines who the community is.

What image of community life does this discourse present? Nowhere in this discourse are any who follow Jesus depicted as shepherds or even assistant shepherds. Rather, all who gather around Jesus receive their identity as members of the flock. The community that gathers around Jesus are the ones who share in the mutual knowledge of God and Jesus, whose relationship to Jesus is modeled on Jesus' relationship to God (v. 15). Listening to Jesus' voice is the source of its unity (v. 16). By taking Jesus as its point of access to God, the community receives abundant life (v. 10).

Most important, however, the community that gathers around Jesus receives its identity through Jesus' gift of his life for them. In the end, to be a member of Jesus' flock is to know oneself as being among those for whom Jesus is willing to die. The christological and ecclesiological images of the shepherd discourse become one around the death of Jesus. The death of Jesus also holds together the metaphors of gate and shepherd and shows how Jesus can be both things. In the freely chosen act of his death, Jesus shows the way to life (gate) and offers abundant life by the example of his love (shepherd). It is important that Jesus says he lays down his life for *the* sheep, not for *his* sheep (v. 15), just as in 6:51 he speaks of giving his flesh for the life of the world. It is an inclusive, rather than an exclusive, gift, just like God's love for the world (3:16). Jesus makes the love of God fully available by expressing that love in his death (vv. 17-18).

The shepherd discourse thus provides the contemporary church with the occasion to reflect on several critical theological themes. First, it asks the church to attend to the christological heart of its identity. Who the church is cannot be separated from who Jesus is. Reflection on church identity, then, always needs to be part of a serious christological conversation, a conversation that takes Jesus' gift of his life as its starting point. Second, this discourse provides an occasion to reassess the assumptions that accompany the use of shepherd and pastoral imagery within the church, particularly about the church's leaders. When that imagery sets the church's "shepherds" apart from the rest of the sheep, the power of the pastoral imagery of community in John 10 is diminished, if not lost. Jesus uses pastoral imagery in this discourse to depict the lives of all believers, not just some, in relationship to him.

Finally, the discourse provides the church with a fresh vantage point from which to reflect on community practices. What does it mean for the church to live as Jesus' sheep? What does a church that understands itself as Jesus' sheep look like? How will its identity be manifested in the world? Jesus the good shepherd chose to make his identity manifest to the world through his death. The shepherd discourse calls the church to live out its life according to the model of community envisioned here by Jesus, a model grounded in the mutuality of love embodied in the relationship of Jesus and God. This model of community will be developed further in the Farewell Discourse, but the first glimpse of the community for which Jesus gave his life is available in this text.

JOHN 10:22-42, JESUS AT THE FEAST OF DEDICATION

NIV

22Then came the Feast of Dedication[a] at Jerusalem. It was winter, 23and Jesus was in the temple area walking in Solomon's Colonnade. 24The Jews gathered around him, saying, "How long will you keep us in suspense? If you are the Christ,[b] tell us plainly."

25Jesus answered, "I did tell you, but you do not believe. The miracles I do in my Father's name speak for me, 26but you do not believe because you are not my sheep. 27My sheep listen to my voice; I know them, and they follow me. 28I give them eternal life, and they shall never

NRSV

22At that time the festival of the Dedication took place in Jerusalem. It was winter, 23and Jesus was walking in the temple, in the portico of Solomon. 24So the Jews gathered around him and said to him, "How long will you keep us in suspense? If you are the Messiah,[a] tell us plainly." 25Jesus answered, "I have told you, and you do not believe. The works that I do in my Father's name testify to me; 26but you do not believe, because you do not belong to my sheep. 27My sheep hear my voice. I know them, and they follow me. 28I give them eternal life, and they will

a22 That is, Hanukkah   b24 Or *Messiah*

a Or *the Christ*

NIV

perish; no one can snatch them out of my hand. [29]My Father, who has given them to me, is greater than all[a]; no one can snatch them out of my Father's hand. [30]I and the Father are one."

[31]Again the Jews picked up stones to stone him, [32]but Jesus said to them, "I have shown you many great miracles from the Father. For which of these do you stone me?"

[33]"We are not stoning you for any of these," replied the Jews, "but for blasphemy, because you, a mere man, claim to be God."

[34]Jesus answered them, "Is it not written in your Law, 'I have said you are gods'[b]? [35]If he called them 'gods,' to whom the word of God came—and the Scripture cannot be broken— [36]what about the one whom the Father set apart as his very own and sent into the world? Why then do you accuse me of blasphemy because I said, 'I am God's Son'? [37]Do not believe me unless I do what my Father does. [38]But if I do it, even though you do not believe me, believe the miracles, that you may know and understand that the Father is in me, and I in the Father." [39]Again they tried to seize him, but he escaped their grasp.

[40]Then Jesus went back across the Jordan to the place where John had been baptizing in the early days. Here he stayed [41]and many people came to him. They said, "Though John never performed a miraculous sign, all that John said about this man was true." [42]And in that place many believed in Jesus.

[a]29 Many early manuscripts *What my Father has given me is greater than all* [b] *34* Psalm 82:6

NRSV

never perish. No one will snatch them out of my hand. [29]What my Father has given me is greater than all else, and no one can snatch it out of the Father's hand.[a] [30]The Father and I are one."

[31]The Jews took up stones again to stone him. [32]Jesus replied, "I have shown you many good works from the Father. For which of these are you going to stone me?" [33]The Jews answered, "It is not for a good work that we are going to stone you, but for blasphemy, because you, though only a human being, are making yourself God." [34]Jesus answered, "Is it not written in your law,[b] 'I said, you are gods'? [35]If those to whom the word of God came were called 'gods'—and the scripture cannot be annulled— [36]can you say that the one whom the Father has sanctified and sent into the world is blaspheming because I said, 'I am God's Son'? [37]If I am not doing the works of my Father, then do not believe me. [38]But if I do them, even though you do not believe me, believe the works, so that you may know and understand[c] that the Father is in me and I am in the Father." [39]Then they tried to arrest him again, but he escaped from their hands.

[40]He went away again across the Jordan to the place where John had been baptizing earlier, and he remained there. [41]Many came to him, and they were saying, "John performed no sign, but everything that John said about this man was true." [42]And many believed in him there.

[a] Other ancient authorities read *My Father who has given them to me is greater than all, and no one can snatch them out of the Father's hand* [b] Other ancient authorities read *in the law* [c] Other ancient authorities lack *and understand*; others read *and believe*

COMMENTARY

John 10:22-42 brings the second cycle of Jesus' public ministry (6:1–10:42) to a close. John 7:1–10:21 is located at or around the Feast of Tabernacles (7:2, 14, 37). Verse 22 indicates that Jesus is still in Jerusalem, but the time of year has changed. Tabernacles was celebrated in late September/early October, the Feast of Dedication in December (see Commentary on 10:22-23; see Fig. 9, "Jewish Religious Festivals in John," 542). Yet 10:26-28 uses language and images drawn from the discourse of 10:1-18, and Jesus seems to

assume that his listeners will recognize its meaning. How is the chronological gap between the two halves of John 10 to be understood?

It is important to remember that the Fourth Evangelist has located 10:22-39 in the narrative with an eye primarily to the Gospel reader's sense of theological coherence, not the demands of chronology. First, from a narrative perspective, the audiences of vv. 1-18 and vv. 22-39 are linked despite the time difference. In both instances, Jesus is speaking to members of the Jewish religious establishment in Jerusalem, called the "Jews" in both texts (10:19, 24, 31, 33). The issue of Jesus' identity vis-à-vis the Jewish religious establishment has been a constant theme since 7:1, and the similarities between vv. 1-18 and vv. 22-39 underscore that theme here for the reader (cf. the relationship between 5:1-18 and 7:19-24).

Second, in addition to the thematic overlap with 10:1-18, Jesus' words in 10:22-39 also revisit themes from the discourses of John 5 and 6 (cf., e.g., 10:28 and 6:37, 39; 10:30 and 5:17). Each of the four witnesses to which Jesus appealed in 5:31-49 is appealed to again in this section: his works (10:25, 32, 37-38; cf. 5:36), God (10:29, 30, 36; cf. 5:37), Scripture (10:34-36; cf. 5:37), John the Baptist (10:40-42; cf. 5:35). It is not necessary, therefore, to explain the similarities between 10:22-42 and the preceding unit by theories of text displacement[304] or by locating all of John 10 at the Feast of Dedication.[305] Rather, 10:22-42 serves as a climax of many earlier themes,[306] and indeed is the theological conclusion to Jesus' public ministry.

10:22-39. These verses have the cast of a formal interrogation of Jesus by the "Jews." Verses 24-31 focus on the identity of Jesus as the Messiah and vv. 32-39 on Jesus as the Son of God. These two parts follow the same narrative pattern: The "Jews" confront Jesus about his identity (vv. 24, 33); Jesus answers (vv. 25-30, 34-38), each time speaking about his relationship with God; and in response to Jesus' words, the "Jews" react violently (vv. 31, 39). (The paragraph break at v. 30 in both the NIV and the NRSV undercuts the structure of these units.)

Much of the text in these verses recalls material found in the narratives of the trial before the Sanhedrin in the synoptic Gospels. For example, the demand that Jesus clarify whether he is the Messiah in v. 24 is similar to Luke 22:67, and the charge of blasphemy in v. 33 is similar to charges of blasphemy in Mark 14:64 (cf. Matt 26:65). In Mark 14:61, the high priest inquires whether Jesus is "the Messiah, the Son of the Blessed One" (NRSV; cf. 10:24, 36). That the

Johannine material has points of similarity with both Markan and distinctly Lukan traditions suggests that the Fourth Evangelist had access to traditional Jesus material similar to that used by the other evangelists, and not that he depends directly on one or the other or even both.[307] Moreover, it is consistent with the treatment of passion traditions in other Johannine texts to find this interrogation material outside of the passion narrative proper. The location of the narrative of the cleansing of the Temple in John 2 and the eucharistic traditions in John 6, both outside of their synoptic location within the passion narrative, suggests that the Fourth Evangelist was quite intentional about crossing the strict division that the synoptic Gospels maintain between Jesus' passion and the rest of his ministry (see Commentaries on 11:53 and 12:27).[308]

10:22-23. The scene is set for the conversations that follow. The Feast of Dedication (v. 22) is the Jewish festival of Hanukkah. It celebrates the liberation of Jerusalem from the reign of the Syrian (Seleucid) king Antiochus Epiphanes. Antiochus had defiled the Jerusalem Temple in 167 BCE by building an altar to his own gods within the Temple sanctuary (1 Macc 1:54-61), and in 165 BCE Judas Maccabeus and his brothers regained control of the Temple and rededicated it to the God of Israel (1 Macc 4:36-58). The eight-day feast takes place in the month of Chislev (December), as did the original rededication (1 Macc 4:56; 2 Macc 10:1-8) and is marked by the lighting of lamps and rejoicing (1 Macc 4:59; 2 Macc 1:8-9, 18).

The Feast of Dedication could be celebrated away from Jerusalem because it was not one of the pilgrimage feasts. Its mention in v. 22, then, does not give a reason for Jesus' presence in Jerusalem (cf. 7:1-10). Instead, its mention here, along with the realistic notation about winter, draws attention to the passing of time since the Feast of Tabernacles and Jesus' continuing presence in Jerusalem. The reference to Solomon's portico (v. 23) adds a realistic detail to the picture,

304. Rudolf Bultmann, *The Gospel of John: A Commentary,* trans. G. R. Beasley-Murray, R. W. N. Hoare, and J. K. Riches (Philadelphia: Westminster, 1971) 312-13.

305. Schnackenburg, *The Gospel According to St. John,* 2:275-76.

306. C. H. Dodd, *The Interpretation of the Fourth Gospel* (Cambridge: Cambridge University Press, 1953) 362; Barrett, *The Gospel According to St. John,* 387.

307. C. H. Dodd, *Historical Tradition in the Fourth Gospel* (Cambridge: Cambridge University Press, 1963) 92; *The Interpretation of the Fourth Gospel,* 361-62.

308. David Rensberger, *Johannine Faith and Liberating Community* (Philadelphia: Westminster, 1988) 75-77; Wilhelm Wilckens, *Die Entstehungsgeschichte des vierten Evangeliums* (Zollikon: Evangelisher Verlag, 1958). See also A. E. Harvey, *Jesus on Trial: A Study in the Fourth Gospel* (Atlanta: John Knox, 1977).

because the area of the Temple so known was located on the eastern side of the Temple and so would have been the most protected area of the Temple precincts in winter.[309]

10:24. A literal translation of the "Jews'" question in v. 24a would be, "How long are you taking away our life?" Even though both the NIV and the NRSV translate the phrase as "keep us in suspense," there is little evidence of the idiom's use with that meaning in other literature. In modern Greek, the idiom means, "How long will you continue to annoy us?" and there are ancient examples of that meaning of the idiom as well.[310] Because the idiom is difficult to translate precisely, scholars are divided on whether the question expresses suspense and a genuine desire to have the issue resolved[311] or irritation and hostility.[312] Since the idiom follows on the heels of John 8–9, irritation seems more likely.

The similarities between v. 24b and Luke 22:67 have already been noted (see Commentary above). The request that Jesus speak "plainly" (παρρησία *parrēsia*; cf. 7:4) about his Messiahship has a particular relevance in this context, because his last public discourse was a "figure of speech" (παροιμία *paroimia*, 10:6; see also 16:25-33). As noted in the Commentary on 10:1-18, the shepherd figure, which dominates that discourse, is a metaphor for the restored rule of God in the OT, and so it has messianic implications.

John 10:24 is the only place in the Gospel where Jesus is asked directly whether he is the Messiah. This inquiry into Jesus' messianic identity at the close of his public ministry provides an intriguing balance to the "Jews'" interrogation of John the Baptist (1:19-28), which serves as the prelude to Jesus' ministry. In both the opening and closing moments of Jesus' public ministry, the "Jews" are concerned with whether the Messiah is among them (see also 7:26-27, 31, 41-42; 12:34). The significant difference between 1:19-28 and 10:24 is that now Jesus is being interrogated directly. The Samaritan woman recognizes that Jesus may be the Messiah (4:25, 29), and Martha confesses that he is the Messiah (11:27); but in neither of

those instances does Jesus endorse their identification of him. Instead, he claims more for himself than the title "Messiah" (4:26; 11:25-26, 40). That is also the case in Jesus' response to the "Jews" here.

10:25-30. Jesus' response in vv. 25-29 demonstrates the truth of his opening words ("I have told you") because in these verses he repeats claims he has already made in other speeches to the "Jews" (e.g., 5:31-47; 8:28-29, 38). In v. 25, he returns to the theme of his works as witness (5:36). It is unfortunate that the NIV has chosen to translate ἔργα (*erga*) as "miracles" instead of "works" because that translation limits what Jesus means when he speaks of his works in the Gospel of John. While "works" certainly includes Jesus' miracles (cf. 7:21), it is not limited to them. The purpose of Jesus' ministry is to do the works God has given him to do (4:34; 5:20; 9:3; 17:4). John 14:10 makes clear that Jesus does not draw a strict line between words and works, and Bultmann has rightly seen that "works" refers to "Jesus' revealing activity as a whole."[313]

Jesus' words in vv. 26-29 confront the "Jews" with the Johannine paradox of faith and election, expressed here in the metaphors of the shepherd discourse (cf. 10:3-4, 10, 12, 14, 16). To believe is to belong to those who hear Jesus' voice and receive eternal life (cf. 5:24), but one cannot hear Jesus' voice unless one is given to him by God (cf. 6:37, 39). The Greek text of v. 29a is confused and impossible to reconstruct with certainty; the NIV and the NRSV present the two main alternatives. The basic difference in the syntax of the variants is whether the subject of v. 29a is taken to be God (NIV; NRSV footnote) or what God has given Jesus (NRSV; NIV footnote).[314] Both meanings are possible in the context, although an affirmation about the greatness of God (NIV), rather than the community, seems more appropriate in the light of vv. 29b and 30.

The parallelism between what Jesus says of himself in v. 28b and of God in v. 29b (the sheep are secure in the hands of each) underscores the fact that Jesus and God do the same work; what is true of the work of one is true of the work of

---

309. Josephus *Antiquities* 15.398-402; cf. Acts 3:11; 5:12.
310. Barrett, *The Gospel According to St. John,* 380.
311. E.g., Kysar, *John,* 166.
312. Schnackenburg, *The Gospel According to St. John,* 2:305.

313. Bultmann, *The Gospel of John,* 390.
314. For a full discussion of all the manuscript options, see C. K. Barrett, *The Gospel According to St. John,* 2nd ed. (Philadelphia: Westminster, 1978) 381-82.

the other. Jesus gives explicit expression to this inseparable unity of work in 10:30: "The Father and I are one." It is critical that the contemporary interpreter read v. 30 in the context of Johannine theology and not through the lens of the christological controversies of the second through fourth centuries or of the trinitarian doctrine that developed out of those controversies (see Reflections). The Greek word "one" (ἕν *hen*) is neuter, not masculine, so that Jesus is not saying that he and God are one person, nor even of one nature or essence. Rather, he is saying that he and God are *united* in the work that they do. It is impossible to distinguish Jesus' work from God's work, because Jesus shares fully in God's work. John 10:30 presents in summary form what Jesus said at length about his relationship with God in 5:17, 19-30. God gives life; Jesus gives life (5:21; 10:28). God judges; Jesus judges (5:22; 9:39). Jesus' words in v. 30 do not add anything to that earlier discourse, but respond to the "Jews'" request that he speak "plainly."

John 10:30 affirms what Jesus' "works" have already shown: that Jesus shares in God's work and power. His unity with God thus provides the answer to the Messiah question (v. 24); Jesus is both more than and other than traditional expectations for the Messiah. His power is not that of a political liberator who will restore Israel; it is the very power of God. God shares with Jesus God's eschatological power over life, death, and judgment.[315]

10:31. The "Jews" respond to Jesus' words in the same way they did to his comparable words at 5:17, with the intent to kill him (cf. 5:18). They recognize, as they did at 5:18 and 8:58-59, that Jesus is claiming equality with God. Stoning was a more appropriate response at 8:59, however, because there Jesus did pronounce the name of God (8:58), the only explicit grounds for blasphemy as a capital offense stated in the Mishnah.[316] He does not do that here.

10:32. Jesus' question to the "Jews" in v. 32 moves immediately to the grounds for their attempted stoning. He once again presents them with the witness of his works (cf. v. 25). The adjective "good" (καλός *kalos*) is concentrated in John 10 (vv. 11, 14, 32-33),[317] so that it seems likely that the description of Jesus' works as "good" is intended to recall his earlier description of himself as the good shepherd.

10:33. The only occurrence of the formal charge of blasphemy in the Fourth Gospel is this verse (cf. Matt 26:65; Mark 14:64). The definition of blasphemy does not fit the description of blasphemy in either Leviticus or the Mishnah, but focuses instead on the same issue that provoked the "Jews" at 5:18, that Jesus is making himself God. As at 5:18, the "Jews" are both right and wrong in what they hear Jesus saying. They correctly hear his claims to equality of relationship with God, but they wrongly hear it as an equality of his own making (cf. Phil 2:6-11).

10:34-36. Jesus employs an intricate argument from Scripture to show that his equality with God is of God's making, not Jesus'. He introduces his argument in v. 34*a* with the phrase "your law" for rhetorical effect. Jesus wants his adversaries to recognize that their charge of blasphemy will be undone by their own Scripture. Jesus' parenthetical reminder of the immutability of Scripture in v. 35*b* serves the same purpose. His appeal to Scripture here exemplifies his claim of 5:39 that Scripture bears witness to him. "Law" (νόμος *nomos*) is used to refer to Scripture in general, not simply to the books of the law (cf. 15:25; 1 Cor 14:21).

Jesus' argument in vv. 34-36 employs several exegetical techniques common to first- and second-century Jewish exegesis.[318] Jesus' exegesis may seem strained to contemporary exegetes, but it falls solidly within the range of exegetical approaches of first-century Judaism. Therefore, it is wrong to read Jesus' exegesis in vv. 34-36 as a parody of Jewish exegesis.[319]

First, Jesus cites only the first half of Ps 82:6, even though he clearly presupposes the rest of the verse ("children of the Most High, all of you") in his argument (see v. 36). Second, in rabbinic argumentation, a comparison could be made between two biblical texts simply on the presence of the same word in both texts, even if the words

---

315. Jerome H. Neyrey, *An Ideology of Revolt: John's Christology in Social-Science Perspective* (Philadelphia: Fortress, 1988) 69-71.
316. See *m. Sanh.* 7:5; cf. Lev 24:11, 15-16.

317. The only occurrence of *kalos* outside of John 10 is in the description of the wine at 2:10.
318. See Raymond E. Brown, *The Gospel According to John (I–XII)*, AB 29 (Garden City, N.Y.: Doubleday, 1966) 409-10.
319. Bultmann, *The Gospel of John*, 389.

occur in distinct contexts and with quite different meanings. Jesus employs this technique when he compares "gods" to God (vv. 35-36). Third, his main line of argumentation follows the common rabbinic pattern of arguing from the lesser to the greater. That is, if Scripture speaks of human beings who receive the Word of God as gods, how can it be blasphemy for Jesus to speak of himself as God's Son? For the Gospel reader, there may be an additional level of meaning in this argument from the lesser to the greater, because Jesus not only receives the Word of God like those of whom Ps 82:6 speaks, but he *is* the Word of God (1:1, 14).[320]

Jesus' self-description in v. 36 answers the Jews' blasphemy charge, because it points to God as the author of Jesus' identity and vocation, not Jesus himself. By speaking of himself as the one whom God "has sanctified" (ἁγιάζω *hagiazō*), Jesus identifies himself as the Holy One of God, the one set apart by God (cf. 6:69; 17:19). His identity as the one whom God "has sent" (ἀποστέλλω *apostellō*) into the "world" (κόσμος *kosmos*) is well documented throughout the Gospel (e.g., 3:17; 17:18, 21, 23). As in 10:30, Jesus' use of the title "Son of God" here is a distillation of his description of his relationship with God in 5:19-30. As God's Son, Jesus does what the Father gives him to do.

10:37-38. Jesus once again appeals to the witness of his works (cf. 5:36; 10:25, 32). Barrett has pointed out an interesting similarity between Jesus' line of argumentation in v. 37 and 8:39-41. In 8:39-41, the "Jews'" claim to descent from Abraham was disproved by their works; in 10:37, Jesus applies the same standards to himself. His "sonship and apostleship could be disproved by deeds not congruent with them."[321] On the surface, Jesus' appeal in vv. 37-38 contradicts his

opening words to the "Jews" in v. 26. In that verse, the "Jews'" belief was precluded because they did not belong to his sheep, but in v. 38, they are presented with faith as a decision they can make. The juxtaposition of these verses returns to the theme that received its fullest expression in 6:36-40, the delicate balance of human decision and divine initiative in one's response to Jesus. The pivot, as in 6:36-40, is God's relationship with Jesus. Faith in Jesus is impossible without God's initiating act in sending his sanctified Son into the world (10:36; cf. 1:32-34), but humans are responsible for recognizing the work and presence of God in Jesus (10:38).

John 10:38*b* expresses the unity of Father and Son in the language of intimacy and indwelling (cf. 1:1; 14:10; 17:21, 23). As in 10:30, the emphasis is on the indissoluble union of the two. As before, this claim to oneness with the Father provokes Jesus' antagonists to action (v. 39). The notation that he "escaped from their hands" recalls 7:20 and 8:20; even though Jesus' control of "the hour" is not mentioned, it is clearly implied. The expression also echoes Jesus' claim for the security of the sheep in 10:28-29. Jesus, like the sheep, will not be snatched from the Father's hand.

10:40-42. These verses return Jesus to the place where John the Baptist first bore witness to him (1:28). His retreat serves two purposes. First, Jesus removes himself from Jerusalem and Judea in order to return there to meet his death at a time of his own choosing (11:7-9),[322] thus underscoring his words about his death in 10:17-18. Second, it moves the witness of John the Baptist into view for the last time. John is depicted as the model witness to Jesus, whose testimony is true (cf. 5:33) and leads people to Jesus (vv. 41-42; cf. 1:37). The public ministry of Jesus ends where it began: with the testimony of John.

---

320. For more detailed discussions of John 10:34-36 as midrash on Ps 82:6, see Neyrey, *An Ideology of Revolt,* Appendix 2, 221-24; Richard Jungkuntz, "An Approach to the Exegesis of John 10:34-36," *CTM* 35 (1964) 556-65.

321. Barrett, *The Gospel According to St. John,* 386.

322. Ibid., 379.

REFLECTIONS

John 10:22-42 brings the interpreter face to face with the decisive theological issue of this Gospel: the relationship of God and Jesus. As the commentary has shown, this passage says nothing about this relationship that has not been said before, but it says it in direct and concise formulations: "The Father and I are one"; "the Father is in me and I in the Father."

There is a temptation to interpret these words according to the norms of later trinitarian doctrine, to read them according to what they became in the life of the church, rather than what they say in their own context. To do so, however, is to distort and diminish the theological and christological witness of this important text. The Gospel of John was an important resource for the theologians of the second and third centuries as they struggled to think through the interrelationship of the three persons of God, but their questions were not the Fourth Evangelist's questions, nor were their intrachurch controversies his.[323] As the Commentary on 10:30 shows, John was talking about the functional unity of God and Jesus in their work and power, not a metaphysical unity of nature and person. Later christology expressed this unity metaphysically by speaking of the one nature or substance, categories absent from John. The Fourth Evangelist's primary concern was to articulate the relationship of God and Jesus in the context of Jewish-Christian relations, not Christian-Christian relations in the debates over christology.

The most important difference between the discussions of the early church fathers and the Fourth Evangelist about the relationship of God and Jesus is that the church fathers were developing doctrine and the Fourth Evangelist was telling a story.[324] This does not mean that the Fourth Evangelist's reflections are inherently any less theological, but because they are cast in a story, they have a very different theological intent. John 10:30 and 38 thus belong to John's story of Jesus and cannot be abstracted from that context without altering their meaning. When Jesus says, "I and the Father are one," it does not come as any surprise to the Gospel reader, because that reality has been acted out throughout the Gospel narrative. Jesus has done the works of God, spoken the words of God, identified himself with the I AM of God. The relationship of God and Jesus is not a metaphysical puzzle for the Fourth Evangelist, but evidence of God's love for the world (3:16-17). The wonder of the incarnation is that God is palpably available to the world in the person of Jesus, that those who believe in Jesus, who see the works of God in Jesus, have access to God in ways never before possible (14:7-11).

The question of the identity of the persons of God and Jesus would make no sense to the Fourth Evangelist, because he is clear throughout that Jesus' incarnation and presence in the world are wholly the result of God's initiative: God gave; God sent. The two distinct characters, God and Jesus, are essential to John's proclamation of the gospel. In fact, much of the trinitarian conversation about natures and persons would probably sound to the Fourth Evangelist like the "Jews'" erroneous charge of blasphemy in 10:33, a conversation that misses the point about the unity of God and Jesus.

One non-negotiable point that John and the early framers of doctrine have in common, however, is that Jesus' relationship to God is the crux and stumbling block of Christian faith. For the Fourth Evangelist, that relationship is the dividing line between Jews and Christians, and hence is the focal point of most of the controversy between Jesus and the religious authorities. For the second-, third-, and fourth-century theologians, it was the dividing line between orthodoxy and heresy. For contemporary Christians, it is the source of Christians' distinctive religious identity in their conversations with one another and with people of different religious faiths.

In the Fourth Gospel, Jesus does not claim to be a second God or somehow to replace God or to "make himself" God. Rather, Jesus claims to know God as no human has ever known God, to be one with God in will and work for the salvation of the world. This truth, and the believer's experience of it, is the ultimate shaping factor in the Fourth Gospel narrative.

---

323. See T. E. Pollard, "The Exegesis of John x.30 in the Early Trinitarian Controversies," *NTS* 3 (1956–57) 334-49.

324. See the discussion of primary and secondary languages of faith in George Lindbeck, *The Nature of Doctrine: Religion and Theology in a Post-Liberal Age* (Philadelphia: Westminster, 1984).

Everything, from the hymnic beginning (1:1-18) to Thomas's confession at 20:28, works to show forth the incarnate presence of God in Jesus.

It thus requires a significant amount of interpretive imagination and effort to allow John 10:22-42 to speak to the church about the relationship of God and Jesus in its own voice, and not in the voice of church doctrine. In order to understand Jesus' claims in 10:30 and 38 about his relationship with God, it is critical that the interpreter keep them grounded in the whole story of the Fourth Gospel. Jesus' acts of healing and giving life, his words of teaching all demonstrate and embody the presence of God in the world. Taken out of that larger context, the theological and christological claims of John 10:30 and 38 become doctrinal propositions. Within that narrative context, however, they have a life and vitality that they cannot have as doctrinal propositions. They serve to guide the reader back into the story of Jesus, to remind the reader of the shape and character of the "grace upon grace" (1:16) that is available when Jesus makes God known.

JOHN 11:1–12:50

THE PRELUDE TO JESUS' HOUR

OVERVIEW

I t is conventional to locate the major division in the structure of the Gospel of John at 13:1. That verse is correctly seen as signaling the beginning of the narrative of Jesus' "hour"—his death, resurrection, and ascension. According to this division, John 11 narrates the concluding "sign" of Jesus' public ministry, John 12 the concluding words of the public ministry. This commentary proposes, however, that the significance of chaps. 11–12 in the Fourth Gospel narrative is lost when it is taken as the conclusion to the public ministry. As the Commentary on John 10:22-42 discussed, those verses represent the theological conclusion to Jesus' public ministry.[325]

John 11–12, therefore, stand as a bridge between Jesus' ministry and his hour.[326] They belong neither to the public ministry nor to the story of Jesus' hour, but constitute their own section within the Gospel narrative. John 11–12 move the public ministry into the context of Jesus' death.

John 11–12 have an analogous function to that of John 1:1-51. Just as 1:1-51 stands as the prelude to Jesus' ministry, chaps. 11–12 stand as the prelude to Jesus' hour. As has been seen, many of the themes that are enacted in chaps. 2–10 were anticipated and telegraphed first in 1:1-51. It is the same with John 11–12. Just as 1:1-51 prepared the reader to enter the story of Jesus' ministry, so also chaps. 11–12 prepare the reader to enter the story of his death and resurrection.

---

325. In the Commentary above, Jesus' retreat beyond the Jordan and the appeal to the witness of John the Baptist in 10:40-42 were seen as establishing a symmetry between the beginning and end of Jesus' public ministry. It is not necessary to claim, as Brown does (Raymond E. Brown, *The Gospel According to John [I–XII]*, AB 29 [Garden City, N.Y.: Doubleday, 1966] 414), however, that these verses were the end of the public ministry in the original Gospel outline and that John 11–12 are an addition at a later stage of composition. This view misconstrues the role of John 11–12 in the Gospel narrative.

326. Cf. Rudolf Bultmann, *The Gospel of John: A Commentary,* trans. G. R. Beasley-Murray, R. W. N. Hoare, and J. K. Riches (Philadelphia: Westminster, 1971) 392.

JOHN 11:1–12:11, JESUS' HOUR PREFIGURED

OVERVIEW

John 11:1–12:11 consists of three interrelated sections: (1) 11:1-44, the raising of Lazarus; (2) 11:45-54, the decision to kill Jesus; (3) 11:55–12:11, Jesus' anointing at Bethany. The decision to kill Jesus is made in direct response to the raising of Lazarus (11:46-48, 53), and Jesus'

anointing at Bethany occurs in the shadow of that decision (12:7-11). It is important that John 11:1-44 be read in this broader context, and not as an isolated text, because the story of the raising of Lazarus is incomplete without its aftermath.

John 11:1-44, The Raising of Lazarus

NIV

11 Now a man named Lazarus was sick. He was from Bethany, the village of Mary and her sister Martha. ²This Mary, whose brother Lazarus now lay sick, was the same one who poured perfume on the Lord and wiped his feet with her hair. ³So the sisters sent word to Jesus, "Lord, the one you love is sick."

⁴When he heard this, Jesus said, "This sickness will not end in death. No, it is for God's glory so that God's Son may be glorified through it." ⁵Jesus loved Martha and her sister and Lazarus. ⁶Yet when he heard that Lazarus was sick, he stayed where he was two more days.

⁷Then he said to his disciples, "Let us go back to Judea."

⁸"But Rabbi," they said, "a short while ago the Jews tried to stone you, and yet you are going back there?"

⁹Jesus answered, "Are there not twelve hours of daylight? A man who walks by day will not stumble, for he sees by this world's light. ¹⁰It is when he walks by night that he stumbles, for he has no light."

¹¹After he had said this, he went on to tell them, "Our friend Lazarus has fallen asleep; but I am going there to wake him up."

¹²His disciples replied, "Lord, if he sleeps, he will get better." ¹³Jesus had been speaking of his death, but his disciples thought he meant natural sleep.

¹⁴So then he told them plainly, "Lazarus is dead, ¹⁵and for your sake I am glad I was not there, so that you may believe. But let us go to him."

¹⁶Then Thomas (called Didymus) said to the rest of the disciples, "Let us also go, that we may die with him."

¹⁷On his arrival, Jesus found that Lazarus had already been in the tomb for four days. ¹⁸Bethany was less than two miles*a* from Jerusalem, ¹⁹and many Jews had come to Martha and Mary to comfort them in the loss of their brother. ²⁰When Martha heard that Jesus was coming, she went out to meet him, but Mary stayed at home.

a18 Greek fifteen stadia (about 3 kilometers)

NRSV

11 Now a certain man was ill, Lazarus of Bethany, the village of Mary and her sister Martha. ²Mary was the one who anointed the Lord with perfume and wiped his feet with her hair; her brother Lazarus was ill. ³So the sisters sent a message to Jesus,*a* "Lord, he whom you love is ill." ⁴But when Jesus heard it, he said, "This illness does not lead to death; rather it is for God's glory, so that the Son of God may be glorified through it." ⁵Accordingly, though Jesus loved Martha and her sister and Lazarus, ⁶after having heard that Lazarus*b* was ill, he stayed two days longer in the place where he was.

⁷Then after this he said to the disciples, "Let us go to Judea again." ⁸The disciples said to him, "Rabbi, the Jews were just now trying to stone you, and are you going there again?" ⁹Jesus answered, "Are there not twelve hours of daylight? Those who walk during the day do not stumble, because they see the light of this world. ¹⁰But those who walk at night stumble, because the light is not in them." ¹¹After saying this, he told them, "Our friend Lazarus has fallen asleep, but I am going there to awaken him." ¹²The disciples said to him, "Lord, if he has fallen asleep, he will be all right." ¹³Jesus, however, had been speaking about his death, but they thought that he was referring merely to sleep. ¹⁴Then Jesus told them plainly, "Lazarus is dead. ¹⁵For your sake I am glad I was not there, so that you may believe. But let us go to him." ¹⁶Thomas, who was called the Twin,*c* said to his fellow disciples, "Let us also go, that we may die with him."

¹⁷When Jesus arrived, he found that Lazarus*b* had already been in the tomb four days. ¹⁸Now Bethany was near Jerusalem, some two miles*d* away, ¹⁹and many of the Jews had come to Martha and Mary to console them about their brother. ²⁰When Martha heard that Jesus was coming, she went and met him, while Mary stayed at home. ²¹Martha said to Jesus, "Lord, if you had been here, my brother would not have died. ²²But even now I know that God will give you whatever you ask of him." ²³Jesus said to her,

a Gk him   *b Gk he*   *c Gk Didymus*   *d Gk fifteen stadia*

NIV

[21]"Lord," Martha said to Jesus, "if you had been here, my brother would not have died. [22]But I know that even now God will give you whatever you ask."

[23]Jesus said to her, "Your brother will rise again."

[24]Martha answered, "I know he will rise again in the resurrection at the last day."

[25]Jesus said to her, "I am the resurrection and the life. He who believes in me will live, even though he dies; [26]and whoever lives and believes in me will never die. Do you believe this?"

[27]"Yes, Lord," she told him, "I believe that you are the Christ,[a] the Son of God, who was to come into the world."

[28]And after she had said this, she went back and called her sister Mary aside. "The Teacher is here," she said, "and is asking for you." [29]When Mary heard this, she got up quickly and went to him. [30]Now Jesus had not yet entered the village, but was still at the place where Martha had met him. [31]When the Jews who had been with Mary in the house, comforting her, noticed how quickly she got up and went out, they followed her, supposing she was going to the tomb to mourn there.

[32]When Mary reached the place where Jesus was and saw him, she fell at his feet and said, "Lord, if you had been here, my brother would not have died."

[33]When Jesus saw her weeping, and the Jews who had come along with her also weeping, he was deeply moved in spirit and troubled. [34]"Where have you laid him?" he asked.

"Come and see, Lord," they replied.

[35]Jesus wept.

[36]Then the Jews said, "See how he loved him!"

[37]But some of them said, "Could not he who opened the eyes of the blind man have kept this man from dying?"

[38]Jesus, once more deeply moved, came to the tomb. It was a cave with a stone laid across the entrance. [39]"Take away the stone," he said.

"But, Lord," said Martha, the sister of the dead man, "by this time there is a bad odor, for he has been there four days."

a27 Or Messiah

NRSV

"Your brother will rise again." [24]Martha said to him, "I know that he will rise again in the resurrection on the last day." [25]Jesus said to her, "I am the resurrection and the life.[a] Those who believe in me, even though they die, will live, [26]and everyone who lives and believes in me will never die. Do you believe this?" [27]She said to him, "Yes, Lord, I believe that you are the Messiah,[b] the Son of God, the one coming into the world."

[28]When she had said this, she went back and called her sister Mary, and told her privately, "The Teacher is here and is calling for you." [29]And when she heard it, she got up quickly and went to him. [30]Now Jesus had not yet come to the village, but was still at the place where Martha had met him. [31]The Jews who were with her in the house, consoling her, saw Mary get up quickly and go out. They followed her because they thought that she was going to the tomb to weep there. [32]When Mary came where Jesus was and saw him, she knelt at his feet and said to him, "Lord, if you had been here, my brother would not have died." [33]When Jesus saw her weeping, and the Jews who came with her also weeping, he was greatly disturbed in spirit and deeply moved. [34]He said, "Where have you laid him?" They said to him, "Lord, come and see." [35]Jesus began to weep. [36]So the Jews said, "See how he loved him!" [37]But some of them said, "Could not he who opened the eyes of the blind man have kept this man from dying?"

[38]Then Jesus, again greatly disturbed, came to the tomb. It was a cave, and a stone was lying against it. [39]Jesus said, "Take away the stone." Martha, the sister of the dead man, said to him, "Lord, already there is a stench because he has been dead four days." [40]Jesus said to her, "Did I not tell you that if you believed, you would see the glory of God?" [41]So they took away the stone. And Jesus looked upward and said, "Father, I thank you for having heard me. [42]I knew that you always hear me, but I have said this for the sake of the crowd standing here, so that they may believe that you sent me." [43]When he had said this, he cried with a loud voice, "Lazarus, come out!" [44]The dead man came out, his hands and

aOther ancient authorities lack and the life   bOr the Christ

NIV

⁴⁰Then Jesus said, "Did I not tell you that if you believed, you would see the glory of God?"

⁴¹So they took away the stone. Then Jesus looked up and said, "Father, I thank you that you have heard me. ⁴²I knew that you always hear me, but I said this for the benefit of the people standing here, that they may believe that you sent me."

⁴³When he had said this, Jesus called in a loud voice, "Lazarus, come out!" ⁴⁴The dead man came out, his hands and feet wrapped with strips of linen, and a cloth around his face.

Jesus said to them, "Take off the grave clothes and let him go."

NRSV

feet bound with strips of cloth, and his face wrapped in a cloth. Jesus said to them, "Unbind him, and let him go."

COMMENTARY

John 11:1-44 has a much more complex structure than any of the previous miracle stories in John. It does not follow the common Johannine pattern of miracle/dialogue/discourse (cf. John 5; 9–10). The miracle concludes, rather than begins, the story: vv. 1-16, introduction: Lazarus' illness and death; vv. 17-37, preparation for the raising of Lazarus; vv. 38-44, the raising of Lazarus.

Even though the presenting issue of the story is Lazarus's illness and death (cf. 11: 1-5), only a fraction of the story is given over to the raising of Lazarus. The bulk of the story focuses on Jesus' conversations with characters in preparation for the raising of Lazarus: with the disciples (vv. 7-16), with Martha (vv. 20-27), and with Mary and the "Jews" (vv. 28-37). There is no concluding discourse. Instead, narrative and discourse are tightly interwoven. In this regard, the style and structure of John 11:1-44 resemble that of John 4:4-42 in which narrative and discourse also are woven together.

The raising of Lazarus is recounted only in the Gospel of John. It serves as the catalyst for Jesus' death, a role played by the cleansing of the Temple in the synoptic Gospels (see Commentary on 2:13-21). Its absence from the synoptic Gospels should not be taken as proof that the Fourth Evangelist made up this story. Each of the other Gospels recounts the story of the raising of Jairus's daughter (Matt 9:18-26; Mark 5:21-43 Luke 8:40-

56), a story not found in John, so that it is clear that a story about Jesus' raising someone from the dead is common to all of the Gospel traditions (see also Luke 7:11-17, 22; Matt 11:5). There is no question that the Fourth Evangelist has shaped the story of the raising of Lazarus to fit his theological purposes, but this does not mean that the core of the story, the raising of Lazarus, did not come to him from oral traditions about Jesus.

Lazarus is the name of the poor man in the parable in Luke 16:19-31. The presence of the name "Lazarus" in a parable that focuses on a potential return from the dead (Luke 16:27-31) has led some scholars to suggest that John 11:1-44 is simply a historicizing of the parable and, therefore, of no independent value as a Jesus tradition.[327] The literary characteristics of Jesus' parables argue against this view, however. The presence of the name "Lazarus" in the Lukan parable is highly unusual; indeed, Luke 16:19-31 is the only one of Jesus' parables in any of the Gospels in which a character has a name. It seems literarily more credible, therefore, to suggest that the name "Lazarus" enters the parable under the influence of the Jesus tradition that lies behind John 11:1-44.[328]

327. See C. K. Barrett, *The Gospel According to St. John,* 2nd ed. (Philadelphia: Westminster, 1978) 389.

328. See C. H. Dodd, *Historical Tradition in the Fourth Gospel* (Cambridge: Cambridge University Press, 1963) 228; Brown, *The Gospel According to John (I–XII),* 428-29; George R. Beasley-Murray, *John,* WBC 36 (Waco, Tex.: Word, 1987) 199-200.

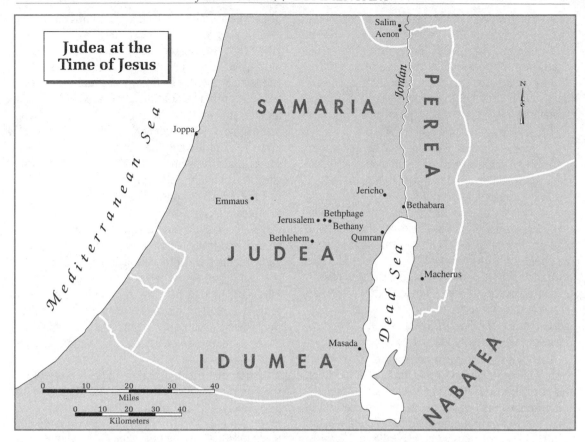

Judea at the Time of Jesus

11:1-16. The introduction consists of two units: (1) vv. 1-5, which set the scene, and (2) vv. 6-16, in which Jesus interprets Lazarus' death in the context of his own life and death.

11:1. The Bethany mentioned here is not the Peraean Bethany to which Jesus retreated in 10:40 (cf. 1:28); it is a Judean town in close proximity to Jerusalem (v. 18). The synoptic Gospels also identify this Judean Bethany as the place where Jesus stayed immediately prior to and during his passion week visit to Jerusalem (cf. Matt 21:17; Mark 11:1, 11-12; Luke 19:29). John is alone among the Gospels in identifying this village with Mary and Martha. This reference may preserve an accurate tradition-historical reminiscence; that is, early Christian tradition identified Bethany primarily as the place of Mary's anointing of Jesus (11:2; 12:1-8). The two sisters also appear in Luke, although without any indication of their geographical origins (Luke 10:38-42). The presence of the two sisters in both Luke and John does not necessarily indicate Johannine depend-

ence on Luke.[329] It is more likely that the two sisters appeared in traditions to which Luke and John both had access. Lazarus is identified in relationship to his sisters (v. 1*b*), and the description of his sister Mary occupies the center of vv. 1-2.

11:2. Verse 2*a* gives a proleptic identification of Mary; the anointing to which it refers will not be recounted until 12:3. It is conventional to read this verse as an editorial gloss inserted to clarify which of the many Marys known in Christian tradition is meant here,[330] but it is not necessary to attribute this verse to a later editor. First, this proleptic identification is similar to the proleptic identification of Andrew as Simon Peter's brother in 1:40. The Fourth Evangelist assumes that his readers are familiar with these characters from their place in Christian tradition. Second, and more important, this proleptic identification serves a narrative and theological function. Mary's anointing of Jesus in 12:1-8 is explicitly linked

329. So Barrett, *The Gospel According to St. John,* 46, 390.
330. E.g., Brown, *The Gospel According to John (I–XII),* 423.

with the preparation of Jesus' body for burial (12:3, 8). By pointing forward to Mary's role in this anointing, the Fourth Evangelist moves Jesus' death into the forefront of the Lazarus story. The connections between the Lazarus story and Jesus' death will become even more explicit in the remainder of the introductory verses.

11:3. The sisters' message recalls the words of Jesus' mother in 2:3; although they merely inform Jesus of the situation and make no direct request of him, some action on Jesus' part seems to be expected. The identification of Lazarus as "he whom you love" (ὅν φιλεῖς *hon phileis*) has led some to link Lazarus with the "beloved disciple" who appears in chaps. 13–21,[331] but that linkage does not hold up to the scrutiny of the text itself. Jesus loves this whole family (v. 5), not simply Lazarus. A comparison of the verbs in v. 3, "love" (φιλέω *phileō*), and v. 5, "love" (ἀγαπάω *agapaō*) suggests that for the Fourth Evangelist the two verbs function as synonyms (cf. 21:15-17).

11:4. Jesus' response turns the focus away from the illness per se to the illness as an occasion for revelation (cf. 9:3). Jesus' words are theologically dense. First, v. 4*a* points toward the end of the story. Lazarus's illness is not ultimately about death, because Jesus will give life to Lazarus. Second, this gift of life will reveal the glory of God (cf. 1:14; 2:11). That is, in it the character and identity of God will be visible. Third, by linking this glory with the Son of God, Jesus continues to use the theological categories that shaped his controversy with the "Jews" in 10:22-39. This gift of life will be revelatory of Jesus' relationship with God. Finally, the "glorification" of Jesus in John refers to his death, resurrection, and ascension (e.g., 12:16, 23, 28; 13:31; 17:1, 4). Jesus thus makes an explicit connection between Lazarus's illness and his own death (cf. 11:2). There is, then, an irony to Jesus' words in v. 4, because while the illness will not end in Lazarus's death, it will end in his.

11:5-6. Verse 5 functions as a concluding affirmation of Jesus' love for the family when it is read with the preceding verses. Read with what follows, however, this affirmation is jarring and disjunctive. The conjunctions with which v. 6

begins ("so when he heard . . ." author's trans.) explicitly counterpoise Jesus' love and his delay. (The NRSV moves the conjunctions to the beginning of v. 5; the NIV paraphrases them as "yet" and softens the disjunction.) Jesus' delay needs to be interpreted alongside his response to his mother and brothers in 2:4 and 7:6-10; as Bultmann says, "The work of Jesus has its own hour."[332] The juxtaposition of vv. 5 and 6 underscores that not even his love for this family will alter the unfolding of the events of his hour.

11:7-15. By choosing the time for his return to Judea (v. 7), Jesus also chooses the time for his death (v. 8).[333] The disciples' question in v. 8 emphasizes Jesus' decision in the face of unambiguous danger and probable death (cf. 10:31, 39; see also 8:59). Jesus' decision recalls his words in 10:17-18, in that he "lays down" his life freely. Jesus will explain his decision to return to Judea to his disciples in two ways, in relation to his own life and death (vv. 9-10) and in relation to Lazarus's death (vv. 11-15).

Jesus' rhetorical question in v. 9*a* refers to the common Jewish practice of dividing the day into twelve hours of daylight and twelve of night. He uses this image in vv. 9*b*-10 to explain his decision. Just as the hours of daylight are limited, so, too, are the hours for Jesus' work (cf. 9:4). He must be about his work while it is still day and will not be hindered by whatever dangers Judea holds. Jesus' answer recalls the Johannine use of "hour" (ὥρα *hōra*) as a metaphor for the time of Jesus' death (e.g., 2:4; 7:30; 8:20; 12:23; 13:1; 17:1). Yet because Jesus has already identified himself as the light of the world (8:12; 9:5), these verses can also be read as referring to the disciples' relationship to Jesus (cf. 3:19-21; 12:35, 46). Just as the time for Jesus to work is limited, so also the time for them to move from darkness to the light of Jesus is limited. The prospect of Jesus' death, or their own deaths (cf. v. 16), is not the stumbling block; walking apart from the light is (cf. Isa 8:14-15).

Verses 11-12 are an extended word play about Lazarus's death. The narrative has not yet reported his death, and Jesus' knowledge of it

331. Floyd Filson, "Who Was the Beloved Disciple?" *JBL* 68 (1949) 83-88; J. N. Sanders, "Those Whom Jesus Loved: St. John xi.5," *NTS* 1 (1954–55).

332. Bultmann, *The Gospel of John*, 398.

333. Ibid., 398; Barrett, *The Gospel According to St. John*, 379, 391; C. H. Dodd, *The Interpretation of the Fourth Gospel* (Cambridge: Cambridge University Press, 1953) 367.

is another instance of his ability to know all things (cf. 1:48; 4:16-18; 6:6). "Fallen asleep" (κοιμάομαι *koimaomai,* v. 11) has a literal meaning of "sleep," but is also used frequently in the NT as a euphemism for death (e.g., Matt 27:52; 1 Cor 7:39; 11:30; 15:6, 18, 20, 51; 1 Thess 4:13-15). "To awaken him" (ἐξυπνίζω *exypnizō*) plays on that double meaning. The disciples' misunderstanding of Jesus' words (v. 12) contains its own word play. The disciples do not understand why Jesus would risk his life by returning to Judea if Lazarus is only "asleep" (cf. the "Jew' " misunderstanding of Jesus' death at 8:21-22). The word translated as "get better" (NIV) or "be all right" (NRSV) is the future passive of the Greek verb σώζω (*sōzō*). In relation to illness, the passive of *sōzō* does have the meaning of "recover," but other meanings of the verb are often implied as well.[334] In Markan healing stories, for example, the verb also conveys its theological meaning of "save" or "deliver" (e.g., Mark 5:28, 34; 10:52), and that double meaning seems to be at play in v. 12.

Word play and misunderstanding are common literary techniques in the Fourth Gospel (e.g., 3:3-4, 8, 14; 4:10-11, 31-34). What is unusual about the misunderstanding of vv. 11-12 is that the Fourth Evangelist so quickly resolves it (vv. 13-14). First, he inserts an explanatory comment to the reader (v. 13), lest the reader miss the tension in the conversation between Jesus and his disciples. Second, v. 14 resolves the misunderstanding within the story line itself. "Plainly" (παρρησία *parrēsia*) is clearly used here to contrast Jesus' direct description of Lazarus's death with his figurative description of it in v. 11 (cf. 10:24; 16:25, 29).

In v. 15, Jesus gives his delay and Lazarus's death a theological interpretation. Not only is Lazarus's death an occasion for revelation (v. 4), but it also is an occasion for the disciples to come to faith (cf. the same combination of revelation and faith in 2:11). Like v. 4, v. 15 anticipates the miracle with which the story ends.

11:16. Thomas's response in v. 16 is ambiguous. Does he mean that the disciples should die with Jesus or with Lazarus? This ambiguity mirrors the two explanations Jesus has given for his Judean trip, his life and death and Lazarus's. "Twin" (NRSV; the NIV retains the Greek word

for "twin" [Δίδυμος *Didymos*]) is the meaning of the Semitic name "Thomas," translated for the Gospel's Greek readers (cf. 1: 38, 41-42). This meaning of the name "Thomas" gave rise in Gnostic circles to the belief that Thomas was Jesus' twin.[335] Thomas is mentioned in all of the synoptic lists of disciples (Matt 10:3; Mark 3:18; Luke 6:15; see also Acts 1:13), but has his most prominent role in John (see also 14:5; 20:24-29; 21:2). In this verse, Thomas epitomizes the obedient disciple, but his obedience has an ironic edge to it, because he cannot yet fully understand what the Judean trip will entail for Jesus and his disciples.

11:17-37. The middle section of the Lazarus story (vv. 17-37) is its theological heart. It consists of an introduction (vv. 17-19), followed by two scenes: Jesus and Martha (vv. 20-27); and Jesus and Mary and her fellow mourners, the "Jews" (vv. 28-37).

11:17. Verse 17 provides confirmation of Jesus' knowledge of Lazarus's death (vv. 11, 14). The four-day period to which it refers underscores the finality of the death (cf. v. 39). According to popular Jewish belief at the time of Jesus, the soul hovered around the body in the grave for three days after death, hoping to reenter the body. But after the third day, when the soul "sees that the color of its face has changed," the soul leaves the body for good.[336]

11:18-19. The geographical information in v. 18 serves two purposes. First, it reminds the reader how close Jesus now is to Jerusalem, the place where his life is at risk (10:31, 39; 11:8). Second, it suggests that the "Jews" referred to in v. 19 come from Jerusalem. The presence of fellow mourners was an expected courtesy within Jewish religious and social practice.[337] The fellow mourners have a more important narrative function than that of consoling the sisters, however, as they will serve as witnesses to the miracle (vv. 31, 36-37, 45-46). At v. 19, "the Jews" seems to be a neutral designation for Jewish mourners (see also vv. 31, 33), but at vv. 36-37 and 45-46, the division among these "Jews" about Jesus echoes the division among the "Jews" elsewhere in the Gospel (e.g., 10:19-21), when "the Jews" refers to a resistant and hostile crowd.

---

334. BAGD, 798.

335. E.g., *The Acts of Thomas* 1, 31.
336. See *Gen. Rab.* 100 [64a]. See also Hermann L. Strack and Paul Billerbeck, *Kommentar zum Neuen Testament aus Talmud und Midrash* (München: Beck, 1924) 2:544-45. See also Andre Neher, *The Exile of the Word* (Philadelphia, Jewish Publication Society of America, 1981) 24.
337. Strack-Billerbeck, *Kommentar zum Neuen Testament,* 4:592-607.

11:20. Verse 20 returns the narrative focus to the two sisters of vv. 1-5. Scholars have tended to evaluate the characterization of Martha and Mary in this verse according to the portrait of the sisters in Luke 10:38-39, identifying Martha with activity and Mary with passivity,[338] but the characterization does not seem as close as these scholars maintain.[339] It is a misreading to label Mary's behavior in v. 20 as passivity. Instead, she stays in the house to continue the mourning rituals with her fellow mourners.

11:21-22. Martha's greeting to Jesus makes the implied request of v. 3 explicit; she had expected Jesus to do something. Commentators are reticent to identify Martha's words here as a complaint, seeing in them only an expression of regret and faith in Jesus as a healer.[340] To overlook their edge of complaint, however, is to overlook the thoroughgoing Jewishness of Martha's remarks. Complaint belonged to the language of faith in Judaism (e.g., Psalms 4; 6; 13; 22) and does not cast doubts on Martha's piety. On the contrary, the edge of complaint in v. 21 gives greater impact to Martha's statement of confidence in Jesus in v. 22. "Even now," in the face of Lazarus's death, Martha's confidence is undiminished. Martha's words are framed as a confession, "I know . . ."[341] (see also Martha's words in vv. 24, 27; cf. 9:31) and can be read as her assessment of Jesus as a righteous man to whom God will listen in prayer.[342] The truth of Martha's assertion runs deeper than that, however, because God has given all things into Jesus' hands (3:35; 10:29).

11:23-24. Jesus' response to Martha (v. 23) is intentionally open-ended and thus susceptible to misunderstanding. Since it supplies no time frame for the resurrection of which it speaks, it can be read as a general affirmation of the future resurrection of the dead. This is how Martha interprets it (v. 24). The belief in the general resurrection of the dead can be traced back in the Bible to

Dan 12:2. Pharisaic Judaism held to this belief, although the Sadducees denied it (Acts 23:6-8; Mark 12:18-27 and par.) Martha thus affirms her belief in one of the tenets of her faith. Her understanding of the resurrection is grounded in traditional eschatological expectations. The expression "on the last day" (ἐν τῇ ἐσχάτῃ ἡμέρᾳ *en tē eschatē hēmera*) is distinctively Johannine (e.g., 6:39-40, 44, 54), occurring nowhere else in the NT.

11:25-26. In the "I am" statement of v. 25*a,* Jesus identifies himself as the fulfillment of eschatological expectations. The promise of resurrection and life is not lodged in some distant event, but is available already in the person of Jesus. The discourse of John 5:19-30 focused on how God's gift of the works of judgment and life to Jesus marked Jesus' presence in the world as the decisive eschatological event, and this "I am" statement serves as the culmination of the themes begun there. By announcing that he is both the resurrection and the life, Jesus affirms his sovereignty over the present and future lives of believers.[343]

This double dimension is brought out in vv. 25*b-*26*a.* These verses consist of two tightly constructed parallel phrases, built around the verbs "believe" (πιστεύω *pisteuō*), "live" (ζάω *zaō*), and "die" (ἀποθνῄσκω *apothnēskō*). The hinge of both phrases is the expression "the one who believes in me":

the one who believes in me and dies→yet lives

the one who lives and believes in me→never dies

The focus of v. 25*b* is the effect that believing in Jesus has on the believer's death; the focus of v. 26*a,* the effect it has on the believer's life.[344]

The two phrases spell out what it means for Jesus to be the resurrection (v. 25*b*) and the life[345] (v. 26*a*) and are not synonymous.[346] For Jesus to be the resurrection means that physical death has no power over believers; their future is deter-

---

338. Barrett, *The Gospel According to St. John,* 394; Brown, *The Gospel According to John (I–XII),* 433.

339. Rudolf Bultmann, *The Gospel of John: A Commentary,* trans. G. R. Beasley-Murray, R. W. N. Hoare, and J. K. Riches (Philadelphia: Westminster, 1971) 401n. 4.

340. E.g., Rudolf Schnackenburg, *The Gospel According to St. John,* 3 vols. (New York: Seabury, 1982) 2:329: "No criticism of Jesus for not coming sooner is implied."

341. Bultmann, *The Gospel of John,* 401.

342. E. C. Hoskyns, *The Fourth Gospel* (London: Faber & Faber, 1947) 402.

343. Some of the oldest manuscripts (e.g., 𝔓[45]) omit the words "and the life." Text critics tend to accept the longer reading and to explain the omission as an attempt to harmonize with v. 24, which only mentions the resurrection. See Bruce M. Metzger, *A Textual Commentary on the Greek New Testament* (New York: United Bible Societies, 1975).

344. See Gail R. O'Day, *The Word Disclosed: John's Story and Narrative Preaching* (St. Louis: CBP, 1987) 88-89.

345. See C. H. Dodd, *The Interpretation of the Fourth Gospel* (Cambridge: Cambridge University Press, 1953) 364-65.

346. Despite Bultmann, *The Gospel of John,* 403; Schnackenburg, *The Gospel According to St. John,* 2:831; Barrett, *The Gospel According to St. John,* 396.

mined by their faith in Jesus, not by their death (cf. 5:28-29; 6:39-40, 44, 54). For Jesus to be the life means that the believer's present is also determined by Jesus' power for life, experienced as his gift of eternal life (cf. 3:16, 36; 5:24; 6:47; 10:28; 17:2).

Jesus' words in vv. 25-26 are the critical theological lens for interpreting the raising of Lazarus and, indeed, for understanding the Fourth Gospel's eschatological categories (see Reflections). In v. 25*a*, he makes a christological claim that redefines traditional Jewish eschatological expectations; in vv. 25*b*-26*a*, he unfolds the soteriological implications of that claim. His question to Martha, then, in v. 26*b*, is also the critical question for the reader, because unless one believes in Jesus and his word, the transformed life he offers is rendered void.

11:27. Martha's response to Jesus is couched in the formal language of confession. "I believe" is the perfect tense of the verb πιστεύω (*pisteuō*), used in the Fourth Gospel to communicate formal confession of faith (e.g., 6:69; 20:29). The sequence of christological titles recalls the sequence of titles in John 1 (vv. 41, 49). The title "Messiah" is an appropriate response to what Jesus has said, because the expected Messiah was the main carrier of Jewish eschatological hopes (cf. 4:25; 7:26-27, 41-42; 10:24). So, too, is the designation of Jesus as the Son of God. Jesus' words in vv. 25-26 about his power over life and death are revelatory of his unique relationship with God (5:21-29; 10:17-18). Martha's confession is thus of the status of the confessions of Peter (6:68-69) and Thomas (20:28) and anticipates the narrator's own witness to Jesus in 20:31.

Scholars are divided over whether "the one who is coming into the world" should be taken as a third title[347] or simply as modifying the first two.[348] Two considerations argue for reading it as a third title. First, it returns to the theme of eschatological expectation that has dominated Jesus' conversation with Martha. Second, it echoes the distinctly Johannine designation of Jesus as the one who comes into the world (e.g, 1:9-11; 3:31; 6:51; 7:29; 8:23).

11:28-37. The conversation between Martha and Jesus ends on the high note of Martha's confession; any additional conversation would be anticlimactic to the theological intent of the dialogue. For this reason, Jesus' request to see Mary is reported secondhand by Martha (v. 28) and serves as the introduction to the next scene (vv. 28-37), rather than as the conclusion to the former. The scene between Mary and Jesus is conventionally seen by commentators as a pale imitation of the preceding scene with Martha.[349] Indeed, Schnackenburg writes, "Mary . . . gives the impression of being nothing more than a complaining woman."[350] Such views of the relationship between the two scenes arise from the erroneous assumption that the exchange between Mary and Jesus is the focal point of vv. 28-37, when the scene itself signals quite strongly that this is not the case. Any exchange between Jesus and Mary is intentionally aborted by the Fourth Evangelist's mention of the presence of "the Jews" in v. 33. The narrative attention given to the whereabouts of the "Jews" (vv. 31, 33, 36-37) suggests that the scene was never intended to narrate a private encounter between Jesus and Mary, but to identify the public tensions that arise from the encounter of Jesus and the "Jews."

11:28-31. Martha's words to Mary (v. 28) and Mary's response to them (v. 29) provide one of the first illustrations of the truth of Jesus' words in 10:3 and 16: Mary shows herself to be one of Jesus' sheep in that she goes to him when he calls (cf. 11:43-44; 20:16-18). Martha's efforts at a private conversation (v. 28) and Mary's hasty departure to Jesus (v. 29) will not yield a private meeting between Jesus and one of "his own," however. In vv. 30-31, the Fourth Evangelist interrupts the movement of the story and moves the focus from Mary to the "Jews." Jesus' location outside the village is restated (v. 30) in order to underscore the fact that Jesus has not yet come into the "Jews' " presence. The lengthy description of the scene from the "Jews' " own perspective (v. 31) makes clear that whatever happens next in the narrative will be public. (Verse 31 seems even lengthier and more of an interruption in the Greek text, because it is one complex sentence that slows down the pace of the story.)

11:32. It is not a sign of the use of different strata of tradition that Mary greets Jesus with the same words her sister used (v. 32).[351] The initial

347. E.g., Barrett, *The Gospel According to St. John*, 397.
348. E.g., Schnackenburg, *The Gospel According to St. John*, 2:332.

349. See Brown, *The Gospel According to John (I–XII)*, 433.
350. Schnackenburg, *The Gospel According to St. John*, 2:333.
351. Brown, *The Gospel According to John (I–XII)*, 433.

message to Jesus had come from both sisters (v. 3); both shared the expectation that Jesus would intervene on their brother's behalf. Mary's greeting displays the same combination of complaint and confidence in Jesus as a healer that her sister's did (see Commentary on 11:21). That Mary falls at Jesus' feet (NIV; the NRSV erroneously translates πίπτω [piptō, "to fall"] as "kneel") is further evidence of her devotion to Jesus and seems intended to draw the anointing of 12:1-8 into this story once again (see also v. 2).

11:33-35. These verses are among the most difficult to understand in the Gospel. From the earliest patristic interpreters of this text, commentators have struggled to interpret the words about Jesus' emotions in these verses. This difficulty has even influenced the way v. 33 is translated. The differences between the NIV and the NRSV translations are instructive in this regard. The NIV translates the verb ἐνεβριμήσατο (*enebrimēsato*) as "deeply moved," the NRSV as "greatly disturbed." The NIV translates the verb ἐτάραξεν (*etaraxen*) as "troubled," the NRSV as "deeply moved." The two translations suggest that the verbs are synonymous and that they have to do with the depths of Jesus' compassion (esp. "deeply moved"). However, they are more interpretation than translation, because the Greek verbs do not have these meanings. The first verb (ἐμβριμάομαι *embrimaomai*) connotes anger and indignation, not compassion. In its LXX and other NT usages, it has this meaning consistently (e.g., Dan 11:30 LXX; Matt 9:30; Mark 1:43; 14:5). The primary meaning of the second verb is "agitated" or "troubled" (ταράσσω *tarassō*; the NIV is more accurate here) and is used here to underscore the intensity of Jesus' emotion.

The NIV and the NRSV thus tend to sentimentalize Jesus' emotions in v. 33, turning them from anger to compassion. This tendency to soften Jesus' emotions is evident in the very earliest manuscripts as well. 𝔓[45], for example, avoids the direct statement that Jesus was indignant ("He was disturbed in spirit like being angry"). Interestingly, German translations of this text, following Luther's initial translation, tend to render the verbs as verbs of anger.[352]

The evidence of the Greek text, then, seems incontestable that Jesus is described as angry in v. 33. But why do the tears of Mary and the "Jews" arouse Jesus' anger and indignation? The main explanations offered for Jesus' anger conclude that Jesus was angry at the unbelief of Mary and the Jews[353] or that Jesus was angry at the evidence of the power of sin and death in the world.[354] There are two significant variations on the latter suggestion. Chrysostom suggested that Jesus was angry at the prospect of his own death and his upcoming battle with Satan, much as he was in the Garden of Gethsemane in Mark (14:33). Barrett adds to Chrysostom's suggestion, seeing in Jesus' anger evidence of the theme of the messianic secret. In addition to being troubled by the approaching end of his ministry, Jesus is angry because he feels pressed to reveal himself through the raising of Lazarus.[355]

None of the above suggestions resolves all of the issues in v. 33. To say that Jesus is angry at death, either his own or the power of death in general, is to overlook the powerful evidence of vv. 4, 15, 25-26, and 40 that Jesus understands Lazarus's death as a joyous occasion for the revelation of the glory of God and Jesus' power as the resurrection and the life. The suggestion that Jesus is angry at the lack of faith fits the context better. Jesus may be angry that the "Jews," those who are not his own, have intruded onto the scene. The introductory verses repeatedly stress the intimacy of Jesus' relationship with Lazarus and his sisters (vv. 3, 5, 11). Jesus rejoiced that Lazarus's death would be an occasion for his disciples to come to faith (v. 15). Perhaps this miracle was to be for his intimates, much like the foot washing in 13:1-20, and his last words in 14:1–17:26 are only for "his own." Now Jesus is angry that it must be shared with those who do not believe that he is the Son of God.

The "you" in v. 34 is second-person plural, not singular; Jesus is speaking to the crowd, not to Mary alone. This exchange confirms that Lazarus's death is no longer a family matter; it is a public matter. "Laid" (τίθημι *tithēmi*) functions as a technical expression for burial (cf. 19:41-42; 20:2, 13, 15).

352. See Beasley-Murray's excellent review of the translation history of v. 33. George R. Beasley-Murray, *John,* WBC 36 (Waco, Tex.: Word, 1987) 192-93.

353. Bultmann, *The Gospel of John,* 406; E. C. Hoskyns, *The Fourth Gospel* (London: Faber & Faber, 1947) 404-5; Beasley-Murray, *John,* 193.
354. See Brown, *The Gospel According to John (I–XII),* 435.
355. Barrett, *The Gospel According to St. John,* 399.

Jesus' anger in v. 33 informs the interpretation of his tears in v. 35. It is again important that the tears not be sentimentalized. Nor should one point to these tears as evidence of Jesus' "humanity." As noted in the Reflections on the cleansing of the Temple (2:13-22), it goes against the Fourth Evangelist's understanding of the witness of the incarnation (cf. 1:14) to point to an isolated emotion as "proof" of Jesus' humanity. Jesus' tears come in direct response to the invitation to "Come and see" where Lazarus is buried (v. 34b); these tears are thus positioned in the story as Jesus' public acknowledgment of the pain that death causes in human life. As Schnackenburg notes, "The scale of Jesus' act can only be recognized if the bitterness of physical death is not minimized."[356]

11:36-37. The interpretation offered by the "Jews" in v. 36 should not be taken as an accurate interpretation of Jesus' tears. Throughout the Fourth Gospel, the response of the crowd, particularly when they are called "the Jews," is not to be trusted. They are neither faithful witnesses to nor interpreters of Jesus (cf. 7:35-36; 12:29). This verse serves as a further signal not to sentimentalize Jesus' emotions in this scene, as does the division of opinion noted in v. 37. Verse 37 establishes continuity between Jesus as the light (9:5) and Jesus as the resurrection and the life (11:25; cf. 1:4), but it also links the "Jews" who bore witness to Jesus' healing of the blind man with the "Jews" here. Although some commentators read the "Jews' " words in v. 37 as a statement of faith in Jesus,[357] a comparison with other instances of divided response to Jesus in the Gospel suggests that v. 37 is spoken hostilely (e.g., 7:12; 9:16; 10:19-21).

11:38-44. 11:38. The final scene begins with Jesus' arrival at Lazarus's tomb. Jesus' emotions are described with the same verb used in v. 33, "disturbed" (*embrimaomai*), so that again Jesus' anger and indignation are being described, not his compassion. This anger supports reading the "Jews' " words in v. 37 as expressing doubt and hostility. The description of the tomb suggests that it was built into rocks.[358]

---

356. Rudolf Schnackenburg, *The Gospel According to St. John,* 3 vols. (New York: Seabury, 1982) 2:337.

357. E.g., Raymond E. Brown, *The Gospel According to John (I–XII),* AB 29 (Garden City, N.Y.: Doubleday, 1966) 426; C. K. Barrett, *The Gospel According to St. John,* 2nd ed. (Philadelphia: Westminster, 1978) 400-401.

358. As opposed to a vertical shaft dug into the ground; see the descriptions of such tombs in *m. Mo'ed Qat.* 1:6; *m. B. Bat.* 6:8; and Matt 27:60.

11:39. Martha's protest in v. 39b interrupts Jesus as he initiates the miracle (v. 39a), thus heightening the suspense. Her words (and her description as "the sister of the dead man") draw attention to the reality of death that confronts Jesus at the tomb. Jewish burial did not involve embalming, as it did in Egypt (see Gen 50:2-3, 26). The body was anointed with perfume and wrapped (cf. 12:7; 19:40), but after four days the effect of the perfume would be rendered null by the odor of the body's decomposition. The reference to "four days" also underscores the reality of the death (see on v. 17).

Martha's assumptions about the reality and power of death govern her response to Jesus (cf. the ways in which Nicodemus's assumptions about the birth process informed his response to Jesus in 3:3-9). Even her exemplary confession of faith at 11:27 could not prepare her for the fullness of Jesus' identity and gifts.

11:40. Jesus' response to Martha in v. 40 is an amalgam of his words in vv. 4, 15, and 25-26. They thus pull together everything that Jesus has said in this story about the revelatory significance of the miracle he is about to perform. The synthetic nature of this question makes clear that the Fourth Evangelist intends this question to be heard by the readers as directed to them as well as to Martha (cf. the question in v. 26b). It reminds the reader and those gathered at the tomb of the theological categories through which the upcoming miracle must be viewed.

11:41-42. Jesus' own actions in vv. 41-42 add to the suspense surrounding the miracle. After the stone is removed (v. 41a), Jesus stops to pray. Verse 41b contains two elements that are characteristic of Jesus' prayer in John: Jesus lifts up his eyes (cf. 17:1) and addresses God as "Father" (cf. 12:28; 17:1). The vocative of "father" (πάτερ *pater*) is also used by Jesus in his prayers in the synoptic Gospels (Matt 26:39, 42; Mark 14:36; Luke 10:21; 22:42; 23:43, 46). This is the first time in John that Jesus has directly addressed God as "Father." Jesus' prayer is one of thanksgiving (εὐχαριστέω *eucharisteō*) for his relationship with God. Some commentators have been bothered by this prayer, taking it to be a "show" prayer, intended solely to influence the listeners (cf. v. 42) and not as an expression of any piety on

Jesus' part.[359] Such views proceed from the assumption that this prayer is intended as intercession or petition, when, in fact, it is a prayer of thanksgiving. Wilcox has helpfully observed how Jesus' words in v. 41*b* echo Ps 118:21 ("I thank you that you have answered me . . . ").[360] As a prayer of thanksgiving, this prayer is a powerful acknowledgment from Jesus to God of the relationship to which Jesus has repeatedly appealed throughout his ministry. He does not need to make individual prayer requests of God, because he lives in constant communion with God and in the certainty of his relationship with God. In this prayer, as in the prayer of John 17, Jesus models the confidence in God to which he will summon his disciples in the Farewell Discourse (14:13-14; 15:7, 16; 16:23-24, 26).[361] As Bultmann writes, "In him that which is promised to his followers as eschatological possibility is realised."[362]

Jesus' prayer in vv. 41-42 is also an act of doxology. Jesus wants to direct the eyes of those who gather at the tomb, like his own eyes, toward God, not toward Jesus himself, so that God's glory will be seen in the miracle (vv. 4, 40). Jesus prays so that those gathered at Lazarus's tomb may recognize what Jesus knows: that he does nothing on his own, that everything he does is God's action in and through him. Whether the bystanders hear the words of Jesus' prayer is thus a moot point. What is critical is that they (and the reader) recognize that he puts himself in a prayerful relationship with God.

This prayer needs to be read alongside Jesus' discourses in 5:19-30 and 10:32-39.[363] Jesus spoke those discourses in response to the Jews' charges that he was making himself God. Jesus' prayer is another demonstration of the complete falsity of those charges. He has said that he does nothing without God, and now he demonstrates it.[364] Everything that Jesus says and does has been given to him by God (5:19-20). God is the one who has given him power over life and death (5:21), the power to raise the dead (5:25-29; see also 6:39-40), and this prayer serves to locate the upcoming miracle with God.

11:43-44. As is typical in the Fourth Gospel, the miracle itself is narrated leanly (cf. 2:7-8; 5:8-9; 9:6-7). Yet even this lean narration has layers of theological meaning. Jesus' summons to Lazarus in v. 43 recalls Jesus' words in 5:28 and 10:3; it is Jesus' voice to which Lazarus responds. Jesus' words also echo the words of the Servant in Isa 48:9 to those who are bound and in darkness.[365]

The Fourth Evangelist creates a startling visual image of Lazarus's exit from the tomb (v. 44*a*). First, he is referred to as "the dead man," not as Lazarus, again to emphasize the sweep of the miracle Jesus has performed (cf. v. 39). Second, he is still bound in his grave clothes.[366] These details, too, underscore the magnitude of the miracle of the raising of Lazarus by concretizing the hold that death had on him. They do not point away from it to a secondary miracle—that is, Lazarus walks even though his feet are bound.[367] It is also possible that the description of the burial clothes anticipates the story of Jesus' resurrection. In that story, the burial clothes also will be described in vivid detail (20:6-7). The difference is that Lazarus arose still dressed in the clothes of death, dependent on the voice of Jesus to achieve his freedom from death (vv. 43-44*b*), but Jesus arises completely free of death.

359. A. Loisy, *Le Quatrième Évangile* (Paris: Alphonse Picard, 1903) 651.
360. M. Wilcox, "The 'Prayer' of Jesus in John xi.41b-42" *NTS* 24 (1977–78) 128-32.
361. E. C. Hoskyns, *The Fourth Gospel* (London: Faber & Faber, 1947) 406.
362. Rudolf Bultmann, *The Gospel of John: A Commentary*, trans. G. R. Beasley-Murray, R. W. N. Hoare, and J. K. Riches (Philadelphia: Westminster, 1971) 409.
363. See also Barrett, *The Gospel According to St. John*, 403, and Jerome H. Neyrey, *An Ideology of Revolt: John's Christology in Social-Science Perspective* (Philadelphia: Fortress, 1988), 90-92 for a discussion of the relationship between 11:1-44 and 5:15-30.

364. Bultmann, *The Gospel of John*, 408.
365. Sandra Schneiders, "Death in the Community of Eternal Life: History, Theology, and Spirituality in John 11," *Int.* 41 (1987) 55.
366. See *m. Šabb.* 23:4 for a reference to burial wrappings.
367. E.g., Hoskyns, *The Fourth Gospel*, following Basil; perhaps C. K. Barrett, *The Gospel According to St. John*, 2nd ed. (Philadelphia: Westminster, 1978) 403.

REFLECTIONS

As a first step in reflecting on this text, it is important to acknowledge the question that many hearers of the story of the raising of Lazarus will ask: Did this really happen? As the

Overview discussed, there is no more reason to reject this story on tradition-historical grounds than there is to reject any of the other Gospel stories of Jesus raising someone from the dead or, indeed, of any of the accounts of Jesus' miracles. Yet the question of whether it happened is usually not merely a question about the historicity of the event; beneath it lies a question about the very metaphysical possibility of the event. That is, the question that lingers in many hearers' minds is "Can we really believe that something like this happened?"

For some people, even those who are eyewitnesses of events that others around them attribute to the miraculous, it is simply impossible to accept that the supernatural can overlap with the natural, that anything can occur for which there is no rational explanation. It is always a matter of reason over faith, of the known over the "might be." Yet for many people, the experiences of their lives have led them to accept that there is genuine mystery in the world, that the world is full of evidence that the supernatural does overlap with the natural, that the line between the two is permeable. For religious people, this mystery, the overlap between the natural and the supernatural, is seen as evidence of God's transcendence of the categories by which God's creatures understand the world to be ordered and of God's intervention in the workings of creation. It is thus a question of faith whether one can acknowledge the possibility and, indeed, reality of God's miraculous intervention in creation.

It is against this background that the question, "Could it happen?" of the Lazarus story can be engaged. There is no way to prove the "facts" of this miracle. Rather, the Fourth Evangelist (and all the Gospel writers) confronts his readers with the ultimate clash between views of historical and metaphysical reality in order to lead them to make a decision about how they understand the world to be ordered. The only answer to the question of whether this miracle could have occurred is another question: Can we believe that God, acting through Jesus, has power over the course of life and death?

The Fourth Evangelist engages this question head on in John 11:1-44. As noted in the Commentary, the theological heart of this story is in vv. 25-26, because these verses explain the meaning and import of the miracle of vv. 43-44. The miracle of the raising of Lazarus from the dead concretely illustrates the truths that Jesus declares in vv. 25-26, but it is these truths, not the miracle, that have the lasting significance for the life of faith.[368]

What truths do these verses offer the reader? First, they offer the truth of the identity of Jesus. When Jesus identifies himself with the images of the resurrection and the life (v. 25a), he uses those metaphors to give concrete expression to his unity with the Father, to show what it means that Jesus and God are one. Even though this "I am" saying has a predicate nominative supplied, it is closer in meaning to the absolute "I am" sayings (those without a predicate nominative; see also Fig. 10, "The 'I AM' Sayings in John," 602), because Jesus' self-revelation as the resurrection and the life points to his sharing fully in the power of God.[369] The magnitude of this claim cannot be overstated, because it announces that God's power over life and death, a central belief of OT faith (e.g., 2 Kgs 5:7; Ezek 39:3-12) is now shared with Jesus (see Commentary on 5:21-29). When one sees and hears Jesus, one does not see and hear God in some static sense (as frequently seems to be communicated in doctrinal formulations), but one sees God's will for the salvation of the world at work in the world.

Jesus' self-revelation as the resurrection and the life is the decisive eschatological announcement of this Gospel. His full share in God's power over life and death marks the beginning of God's new age, the age in which God's hope for the world becomes a reality. What God wills and hopes for the life of the world is now available in Jesus—that is, the defeat of death's power to remove people from life with God. Who Jesus is, not only what Jesus does (i.e., the works of God as in John 9), marks this decisive shift in God's relationship

368. See E. C. Hoskyns, *The Fourth Gospel* (London: Faber & Faber, 1947) 402.
369. See Neyrey, *An Ideology of Revolt*, 88, for a discussion of the difference between this "I am" statement and the other predicate nominative "I am" statements.

with the world. As the resurrection and the life, Jesus defeats death in the future and in the present. The power of death to separate people from God is reduced to nothing by the presence of the power of God in Jesus. This defeat is no longer merely eschatological promise; it is eschatological reality.

Jesus defeats the power of death because in him the world meets the power of the love of God incarnate (cf. Rom 8:35-39). God's full sharing of power over life and death with Jesus is an expression of God's love for Jesus and for the world. Because God loves Jesus, God has given all things to him (3:35), culminating in the power over life and death. Because God loves Jesus, God has given him the glory that is revealed in the raising of Lazarus, in the defeat of death (11:4; 17:24). Because God loves the world, God gives Jesus to the world for its salvation (3:16-17), so that the world might come to know fully God's love for it and live grounded in that love (17:23). Jesus' own death is a measure of this love (10:17; 15:12), because in it Jesus' power as the resurrection and the life comes to fullest expression.

Yet this decisive christological announcement is only half of the truth that vv. 25-26 offers the Gospel reader. These verses also offer readers the opportunity to claim that truth for their own lives. Significantly, then, who Jesus is in relationship to God is linked with who Jesus is for believers. As noted in the commentary, the hinge of the parallel phrases in vv. 25b and 26a is the expression "the one who believes in me." Jesus' words point to the "So what?" of his identity for the life of the believer.

Verses 25b and 26a are the most far-reaching promise anywhere in the Gospel of what relationship with Jesus offers those who embrace it. They are of a piece with the promises of living water (4:10, 14; 7:37-38), living bread (6:33, 35, 51), and even eternal life (3:15; 6:47; 10:28), but they supersede all those earlier promises by confronting head on the question of death.[370] They are not idle words of hope, because they name the greatest threat to full relationship with God: death. They offer a vision of life to the believer in which his or her days do not need to be reckoned by the inevitable power of death, but instead by the irrevocable promise of life with God. The two parts of vv. 25b and 26a invite the believer to a vision of life in which one remains in the full presence of God during life and after death. The physical reality of death is denied power over one's life with God, as is the metaphysical reality of death.

This promise is also an invitation, made explicit in Jesus' question in v. 26b. The way to experience the power of God's love for the world that defeats death, to receive the promises of God as the reality of God, is to believe in Jesus. When Jesus asks Martha, "Do you believe this?" he asks her to believe both that he is the resurrection and the life and that as the resurrection and the life he defeats the power of death. That is, he asks her whether she believes in the fullness of his relationship with God and the effects of that relationship on the life of the world.

Faith, therefore, is not assent to a series of faith statements, but assent to the truth of Jesus' relationship with God and the decisive change that relationship means for the lives of those who believe. Schnackenburg has eloquently expressed what it means to answer yes to Jesus' question of v. 26b: "The content [of faith] is what Jesus means for believers, and therefore faith is fundamentally an attachment to this messenger of God. . . . The relevance of faith lies not in the power of faith as such, but in the fact that faith creates communion with Jesus and that through Jesus believers receive the gift of life."[371]

Jesus' claim in vv. 25-26, the claim to which he invites Martha's (and the church's) assent, is that the eschatological reality of God that is present in Jesus has decisively altered human experience of life and death. Martha confesses her faith in Jesus as the Son of God (v. 27), yet v. 39 shows that she is not really convinced about the "So what?" of her christological confession. Martha's attempt to stop Jesus from opening Lazarus's tomb (v. 39) shows that the full impact of that eschatological claim is beyond her comprehension (see Commentary).

---

370. See Schneiders, "Death in the Community of Eternal Life."
371. Schnackenburg, *The Gospel According to St. John*, 2:332.

694

Martha serves as a mirror for the contemporary Christian, because the church responds to Jesus' claims of vv. 25-26 in ways that often are as hesitant as Martha's words in v. 39.

For example, Jesus' "I am" statement of v. 25a, one of the christological high points of the Gospel, loses much of its eschatological and soteriological significance if the only time the church engages it is at Easter or funerals. The church preaches about death and resurrection at the time of death, but shies away from such topics in the midst of life. Yet it is in the everyday rhythms of life that the church most needs to talk about Jesus' power as the resurrection and the life, so that death can indeed lose its sting. To proclaim the power of resurrection only at the time of death is both to impoverish the proclamation and to weaken the power of its witness in the face of death. There is thus a critical need to include conversations about death and the theological significance of Jesus as the resurrection and the life in the ongoing theological reflection of the church, not just in its reflection about death.

In the moment of crisis, at the funeral of a loved one, the immediate need is for pastoral care and reassurance about the power of the resurrection. Indeed, funerals do provide gospel witness to the power of God in Jesus. But a funeral is not the moment for believers to reassess their lives in the light of the new eschatological reality in which the incarnation enables the church to live, because the power of grief and loss is so palpable. Why, then, does the church so often save its most powerful proclamation about death and resurrection for funerals?

Jesus' powerful announcement to Martha suggests that the church needs to embrace Jesus as the resurrection and the life not only at times of death, but also in the daily moments of human lives, because these moments, too, whether one names them so or not, are also lived in the face of death. John 11 asks the church to reflect that Jesus is the resurrection and the life not just for the crisis moment of death, but for all moments in life. Jesus as the resurrection and the life is the decisive eschatological announcement, because he announces that the world is now definitively under God's care and power. John 11:25-26 invites the church to claim that death is indeed an inescapable part of the believer's life, but that it also belongs to the ongoing, life-giving power of God in Jesus ("even though they die, will live," v. 25b). And Jesus' words here invite the church to claim that God's life-giving power in Jesus is the power that determines the believer's existence, not the power of death ("everyone who lives and believes in me will never die"). John 11 thus offers a promise about how those who believe in Jesus will live their lives, not just about how they will end them.

It is the church's responsibility to reintegrate death into the mainstream of its theological and pastoral reflection and experience. The goal of such a reintegration is not to eliminate the pain at the death of those we love—that would be a gnostic exercise in denial—but to help the church experience the life of faith grounded in the affirmation that Jesus is the resurrection and the life. The promises of God in Jesus offered in the face of death can equip the church to understand the promises of God in Jesus offered in the midst of life.

John 11:45-54, The Decision to Kill Jesus

NIV

[45]Therefore many of the Jews who had come to visit Mary, and had seen what Jesus did, put their faith in him. [46]But some of them went to the Pharisees and told them what Jesus had done. [47]Then the chief priests and the Pharisees called a meeting of the Sanhedrin.

"What are we accomplishing?" they asked.

NRSV

[45]Many of the Jews therefore, who had come with Mary and had seen what Jesus did, believed in him. [46]But some of them went to the Pharisees and told them what he had done. [47]So the chief priests and the Pharisees called a meeting of the council, and said, "What are we to do? This man is performing many signs. [48]If we let him go on

NIV

"Here is this man performing many miraculous signs. ⁴⁸If we let him go on like this, everyone will believe in him, and then the Romans will come and take away both our place*ᵃ* and our nation."

⁴⁹Then one of them, named Caiaphas, who was high priest that year, spoke up, "You know nothing at all! ⁵⁰You do not realize that it is better for you that one man die for the people than that the whole nation perish."

⁵¹He did not say this on his own, but as high priest that year he prophesied that Jesus would die for the Jewish nation, ⁵²and not only for that nation but also for the scattered children of God, to bring them together and make them one. ⁵³So from that day on they plotted to take his life.

⁵⁴Therefore Jesus no longer moved about publicly among the Jews. Instead he withdrew to a region near the desert, to a village called Ephraim, where he stayed with his disciples.

ᵃ48 Or temple

NRSV

like this, everyone will believe in him, and the Romans will come and destroy both our holy place*ᵃ* and our nation." ⁴⁹But one of them, Caiaphas, who was high priest that year, said to them, "You know nothing at all! ⁵⁰You do not understand that it is better for you to have one man die for the people than to have the whole nation destroyed." ⁵¹He did not say this on his own, but being high priest that year he prophesied that Jesus was about to die for the nation, ⁵²and not for the nation only, but to gather into one the dispersed children of God. ⁵³So from that day on they planned to put him to death.

⁵⁴Jesus therefore no longer walked about openly among the Jews, but went from there to a town called Ephraim in the region near the wilderness; and he remained there with the disciples.

ᵃ Or our temple; Greek our place

COMMENTARY

11:45-46. These transitional verses provide corroboration of the miracle (cf. 2:9-10; 5:10-18; 9:8-12), and hence can be read as the conclusion to the preceding miracle story. Jesus' actions cause division among the "Jews," continuing a pattern found elsewhere in the Gospel (cf. 7:40-41, 43; 9:16; 10:19). The contrast between "many" (πολλοὶ *polloi*) in v. 45 and "some" (τινές *tines*) in v. 46, suggests that more "Jews" believe in Jesus as a result of the raising of Lazarus than those who denounce him. Yet, more important, vv. 45-46 also move the story forward from the raising of Lazarus to the formal decision to kill Jesus. The report given to the Pharisees in v. 46 is explicitly identified as the reason for the council meeting in v. 47 ("so . . . " [οὖν *oun*], NRSV; the NIV masks the causal link between the two verses).

11:47a. At the time of Jesus, the members of the Sanhedrin were chief priests, elders, and scribes; the Pharisees were not official members and, therefore, had no authority to call the council together (cf. v. 47). Yet it is also true that the

Pharisees had a *de facto* voice in Sanhedrin deliberations, because during this period most of the scribes were Pharisees.[372] The Pharisees' unofficial power may explain why the combination "chief priests and Pharisees" (rather than "scribes"; cf. Mark 14:1, 43, 53; Luke 19:47; 20:1, 19; 22:2, 66; 23:10) is the Fourth Gospel's standard designation for the Jewish leadership when it acts as a formal, deliberative body (7:32, 45; 18:3).[373] Moreover, as noted earlier (see Commentary on 1:24), it was the descendants of the Pharisees with whom the Fourth Evangelist was in conflict; and so his word choice focuses on the branch of Judaism that was most recognizable to his readers (cf. the alternation of the terms "Pharisees" and "Jews" in chap. 9).

11:47b-48. The chief priests and Pharisees' question in v. 47*b* can be translated as either a rhetorical question (NIV) or a deliberative ques-

372. See, e.g., Josephus *Antiquities of the Jews* 15.3.
373. Ernst Bammel, *"Ex Illa itaque die consilium fecerunt . . .* (John 11:53)," in Ernst Bammel, ed., *The Trial of Jesus: Cambridge Studies in Honor of C. F. D. Moule* (London: SCM, 1970) 21.

tion (NRSV). The continuation of their speech in v. 48 suggests that the question is not merely rhetorical; they are looking for a solution to their dilemma. The dilemma is expressed in terms of the political consequences of Jesus' popularity. The Sanhedrin's political concerns here are for their own self-interest. The emphatic placement of the first-person plural pronoun in the Greek makes this clear. A more literal translation that accurately conveys the leadership's concerns is "The Romans will come and take away from us the holy place and the nation" (cf. NIV). The leaders are not concerned about the destruction of Jerusalem by the Romans (NRSV),[374] but their own loss of power within the religious and political system. This loss of power was indeed a concern of the ruling Jewish establishment pre–70 CE.[375] Were Jesus to attract more of a following, like the crowd that attempted to make him king (6:15) or the crowd that will hail him as king when he enters Jerusalem (12:12-19), the Romans would hold the Jewish leadership responsible for this disturbance and take away their power.[376] To read the leadership's words this way adds a level of irony to this scene, because the post–70 CE Gospel reader knows that the truth of the Sanhedrin's concerns ran deeper than they anticipated.

11:49-50. Caiaphas is identified as "high priest that year" (v. 49). Many scholars see this apparent reference to Caiaphas's yearly appointment as an example of the Fourth Evangelist's ignorance of Jewish customs, because the office of high priest came with lifetime tenure.[377] Yet some scholars think that the reference to an annual appointment is not a mistake by the Fourth Evangelist, but a nod to the realities of Jewish life in the Roman Empire. That is, even though the high priesthood was a lifetime appointment,

during Roman rule the high priest held office only at the discretion of the Roman governor; thus the priest could not count on a lifetime appointment.[378] The temporal reference may thus introduce another note of irony into the passage by reminding readers of the tenuous hold the high priest had on his office, despite his claims to power, an irony that is developed further in vv. 51-52 (cf. 19:10-12). Indeed, Caiaphas's term did not last his lifetime, because he was deposed at the end of Pilate's term as governor (18–36 CE).[379]

Since Origen, however, another interpretation of the words "in that year" has been suggested: to translate them emphatically, "for that year." This translation draws attention to this particular year of Caiaphas's high priesthood, the year of Jesus' death, and does not speak about the duration of his term.[380] The Fourth Evangelist wants the reader to identify Caiaphas's priesthood with *that* year, regardless of when else he may have been high priest. This reading has much in its favor. In particular, the repeated use of the phrase "that year" in relation to Caiaphas (see also v. 51; 18:13) suggests that the Evangelist intends more than a reference to the length of the high priestly term.

The abrasiveness of Caiaphas's opening words in v. 49 matches Josephus's portrait of the tenor of conversations at Sanhedrin meetings.[381] His words in v. 50 are a model of political realism and expediency,[382] and they speak to the leadership's self-interest. They are offered in the form of an aphorism, and similar aphorisms are well documented in the ancient Mediterranean world. Beasley-Murray, for example, cites the following saying from *Gen. Rab.* 94, 60a: "It is better that this man be killed than that the totality be punished on his account."[383]

11:51-52. The irony that has underlaid much of this passage comes to its fullest expression in the commentary in vv. 51-52. The narrator informs the reader that Caiaphas's words are not

374. So Brown, *The Gospel According to John (I–XII)*, 442; Barrett, *The Gospel According to St. John*, 406.

375. See Ernst Bammel, "Ex Illa itaque die consilium fecerunt . . . (John 11:53)."

376. Hoskyns, *The Fourth Gospel*, 410; Ernst Haenchen, *John*, Hermenia, 2 vols. (Philadelphia: Fortress, 1984) 2:75; George R. Beasley-Murray, *John*, WBC 36 (Waco, Tex.: Word, 1987) 196. For further discussion of Jewish/Roman political interactions around the death of Jesus, see the Commentary on John 18:28–19:16.

377. See Bultmann, *The Gospel of John*, 410n. 10; Haenchen, *John*, 2:75. Priestly appointments in cities in Asia Minor were one-year term appointments, so the suggestion is made that the Fourth Evangelist confused the Jewish and pagan customs. See also C. H. Dodd, "The Prophecy of Caiaphas: John xi 47–53," in *Neotestamentica et Patristica: Eine Freudengabe, Herrn Professor Dr. Oscar Cullman zu seinem 60. Geburtstag*, NovTSup 6 (Leiden: E. J. Brill, 1962) 141.

378. See "Ex Illa itaque die consilium fecerunt . . . (John 11:53)," 39; Beasley-Murray, *John*, 197.

379. Josephus *Antiquities of the Jews* 28. 35, 95.

380. So, e.g., Brown, *The Gospel According to John (I–XII)*, 440; Barrett, *The Gospel According to St. John*, 446; Schnackenburg, *Der Evangelist Johannes*, 2:348.

381. Josephus *The Jewish War* 2.166.

382. Bultmann, *The Gospel of John*, 411.

383. Beasley-Murray, *John*, 196-97. See also Hermann L. Strack and Paul Billerbeck, *Kommentar zum Neuen Testament aus Talmud und Midrash* (München: Beck, 1924) II:540; Bammel, *The Trial of Jesus*, 26-27.

simply the political realism that he intends, but are inspired, albeit unintentional, prophecy about the true meaning of Jesus' death. The oracular power of the high priesthood can be traced back to the beginning of the institution, because included in the priestly regalia were the lots of Urim and Thummin, which guided the priest in oracular decisions (e.g., Exod 28:30; Lev 8:8; Deut 33:8; 1 Sam 14:41-42). Josephus wrote about the oracular powers of John Hyrcanus when he was high priest;[384] so the notion of the priest's prophetic powers was not unknown at the time of the Fourth Evangelist. What is striking about the Fourth Evangelist's appeal to this tradition in v. 51, however, is that he uses it to show how the power of the priesthood can witness to the truth of Jesus even as it works actively to suppress it. The Fourth Evangelist's attitude toward Caiaphas here is like that of Second Isaiah to Cyrus; even those who do not know God can be God's instruments for salvation (Isa 45:4-5).

In addition to revealing the ironic dimension of Caiaphas's desire for political expediency, the Fourth Evangelist's commentary in vv. 51-52 provides the reader with theological categories through which to assess Jesus' upcoming death. At 1:12, "children of God" are defined as those who receive Jesus and believe in his name. At 8:28 Jesus told the "Jews" that at his death they would "realize that I am." Both of these ideas are brought together in v. 52, when the Fourth Evangelist identifies the purpose of Jesus' death as the gathering of God's dispersed children into one (see also 12:32). The Fourth Evangelist's commentary recalls Jesus' image in 10:15-18 of himself as the shepherd who lays down his life for the one flock. Jesus' death will be the dividing line between those who believe in his name, recognize God in him, and hence show themselves as children of God and those who do not. These categories will be expanded upon in the Farewell Discourse.

This vision of the purpose of Jesus' death has its own irony because the Fourth Evangelist's language in v. 52 plays on Jewish hopes for the restoration of the true Israel. One of Israel's eschatological hopes is the gathering together of all the tribes of Israel who have been dispersed throughout the Mediterranean world (e.g, Isa 43:5-6; 60:6; Jer 31:10; Ezek 34:12), and the Fourth Evangelist names Jesus as the agent of that gathering. Verse 52 makes clear that the Fourth Evangelist's eschatological vision is not for a merely national restoration, however, but for a truly inclusive gathering of all of God's children. The arrival of the Greeks in 12:20 (see below) confirms that this gathering includes Jews and Gentiles.

11:53. The Sanhedrin leadership were persuaded by Caiaphas's argument of expediency, unaware of the implications of his prophecy. The word translated as "planned" (βουλεύομαι *bouleuomai*) has the meaning of a formal decision. This verse echoes 5:18 (see also 7:1, 25; 8:37, 40), with the important difference that the death threat has moved from intention to official decision and resolve. These verses thus serve as the formal prelude to the narrative of Jesus' death in John 18–19.

11:54. Jesus' retreat to Ephraim (v. 54) is explicitly linked to the Sanhedrin's decision ("therefore"). As at 10:40, Jesus' retreat signals the reader that Jesus' arrest and death will occur according to his time and plan, not the Sanhedrin's. He retreats until his hour arrives with the Passover (12:23; 13:1). Ephraim was located in the Judean outlands, further signaling that Jesus does not retreat to escape his death (cf. 11:8-10), but to control its time.

---

384. See Josephus *Antiquities of the Jews* 13.282-83, 299; *The Jewish War* 1.68.

REFLECTIONS

The Commentary on 11:45-54 noted the repeated instances of irony in the Fourth Evangelist's presentation of the Sanhedrin's decision to kill Jesus. This use of irony raises two important issues for the Gospel interpreter. First, it confronts the interpreter with the paradox of Jesus' raising of Lazarus as the catalyst for his death sentence. In the synoptic Gospels, Jesus' cleansing of the Temple is the catalyst for his death sentence (see Commentary on 2:13-21), but by explicitly naming the Lazarus miracle as the precipitating cause of the Sanhedrin meeting, the Evangelist expands the arena of Jesus' threat to the Jewish authorities' power. That is, Jesus' challenge is not interpreted simply as his challenge to the political power of the religious establishment; it is presented as a challenge to the very way in which the presence of God is known and approached in the world. Jesus' raising of Lazarus demonstrated that all of Jesus' claims about his unity with God are true: He does share God's power for life; he does embody the fulfillment of God's promises (see Commentary on 11:1-44).

The governing irony of the juxtaposition of the Lazarus miracle and the Sanhedrin decision is that even as the authorities resolve to kill Jesus, they are powerless in the presence of the one who is the resurrection and the life. Before performing the miracle, Jesus explicitly stated that Lazarus's illness was not for death, but for the glory of God (11:4). Faced with that glory, the religious leadership nonetheless resorts to planning his death. Jesus' gift of life is the most radical and dangerous threat to the authorities' power, yet all of their political machinations will only enhance Jesus' power for life, not impede it. The truth of who Jesus is and what Jesus gives exceeds all hopes and anticipations, and because Jesus' gift of life redefines the power of death, all agents of death are rendered impotent in his presence. The Fourth Evangelist's ironic commentary tells the reader that this decision for death contains the seeds of life for those who believe. It is a brilliant way of reinforcing the bold message of 11:1-44: Because Jesus is the resurrection and the life, death has lost its sting.

Yet this thoroughly ironic treatment of Jesus' death sentence confronts the interpreter with a second issue: How is the relationship between "history" and "interpretation" to be negotiated in this text? The Evangelist's interpretive work is undisguised in this passage; he provides explicit narrative commentary on the theological meaning of the event he is recounting (vv. 51-52); he arranges details of the story to highlight his ironic reading. Yet as the Commentary on these verses has shown, they also offer glimpses of the workings of the Sanhedrin that stand up well next to other sources about life in first-century Palestine under Roman rule.

It is critical that the interpreter of the Fourth Gospel not fall into the anachronistic trap, shaped by Enlightenment understandings of science and history, of drawing a line between history and interpretation. The Fourth Evangelist did not separate recounting the story from interpreting the story, and that unity of purpose shapes all aspects of the Gospel. Details that give the reader a glimpse into the religious life of early and mid–first-century Palestine, stories that come from common traditions about Jesus, find their way into this Gospel, but they do so through the Fourth Evangelist's literary and theological lens. The irony with which the account of Caiaphas's pronouncement is laced is evidence not that the Fourth Evangelist had no regard for history, or even that he made the story up, but rather that he understood God's purposes to be at work *even in* history and constructed his narrative so that his readers could see that, too.

John 11:55–12:11, Jesus' Anointing at Bethany

NIV

⁵⁵When it was almost time for the Jewish Passover, many went up from the country to Jerusalem for their ceremonial cleansing before the Passover. ⁵⁶They kept looking for Jesus, and as they stood in the temple area they asked one another, "What do you think? Isn't he coming to the Feast at all?" ⁵⁷But the chief priests and

NRSV

55Now the Passover of the Jews was near, and many went up from the country to Jerusalem before the Passover to purify themselves. ⁵⁶They were looking for Jesus and were asking one another as they stood in the temple, "What do you think? Surely he will not come to the festival, will he?" ⁵⁷Now the chief priests and the Pharisees

NIV

Pharisees had given orders that if anyone found out where Jesus was, he should report it so that they might arrest him.

12 Six days before the Passover, Jesus arrived at Bethany, where Lazarus lived, whom Jesus had raised from the dead. [2]Here a dinner was given in Jesus' honor. Martha served, while Lazarus was among those reclining at the table with him. [3]Then Mary took about a pint[a] of pure nard, an expensive perfume; she poured it on Jesus' feet and wiped his feet with her hair. And the house was filled with the fragrance of the perfume.

[4]But one of his disciples, Judas Iscariot, who was later to betray him, objected, [5]"Why wasn't this perfume sold and the money given to the poor? It was worth a year's wages.[b]" [6]He did not say this because he cared about the poor but because he was a thief; as keeper of the money bag, he used to help himself to what was put into it.

[7]"Leave her alone," Jesus replied. "₁It was intended₁ that she should save this perfume for the day of my burial. [8]You will always have the poor among you, but you will not always have me."

[9]Meanwhile a large crowd of Jews found out that Jesus was there and came, not only because of him but also to see Lazarus, whom he had raised from the dead. [10]So the chief priests made plans to kill Lazarus as well, [11]for on account of him many of the Jews were going over to Jesus and putting their faith in him.

[a]3 Greek a litra (probably about 0.5 liter)   [b]5 Greek three hundred denarii

NRSV

had given orders that anyone who knew where Jesus[a] was should let them know, so that they might arrest him.

12 Six days before the Passover Jesus came to Bethany, the home of Lazarus, whom he had raised from the dead. [2]There they gave a dinner for him. Martha served, and Lazarus was one of those at the table with him. [3]Mary took a pound of costly perfume made of pure nard, anointed Jesus' feet, and wiped them[b] with her hair. The house was filled with the fragrance of the perfume. [4]But Judas Iscariot, one of his disciples (the one who was about to betray him), said, [5]"Why was this perfume not sold for three hundred denarii[c] and the money given to the poor?" [6](He said this not because he cared about the poor, but because he was a thief; he kept the common purse and used to steal what was put into it.) [7]Jesus said, "Leave her alone. She bought it[d] so that she might keep it for the day of my burial. [8]You always have the poor with you, but you do not always have me."

9When the great crowd of the Jews learned that he was there, they came not only because of Jesus but also to see Lazarus, whom he had raised from the dead. [10]So the chief priests planned to put Lazarus to death as well, [11]since it was on account of him that many of the Jews were deserting and were believing in Jesus.

[a]Gk he   [b]Gk his feet   [c]Three hundred denarii would be nearly a year's wages for a laborer   [d]Gk lacks She bought it

COMMENTARY

11:55-57. These verses link the decision to kill Jesus (11:53) with the upcoming Passover, the context for the final events in Jesus' ministry (12:1, 12, 20; 13:1). This is the third Passover mentioned in John (see 2:13, 23; 6:4). The need for purification prior to celebrating Passover (v. 55) accurately represents Jewish cultic practices (cf. Num 9:10; 2 Chr 30:17-18; Josephus *The Jewish War* 1.229; see also Acts 21:24, 26; 24:18). The tension attendant on this last Passover is underscored by vv. 56-57. The crowd's questions (v. 56)

are intentionally ambiguous; it is unclear whether those who look for Jesus have positive or malicious intent (cf. 7:11). The language of v. 57 is an explicit reminder of the formal death threat under which Jesus stands: "chief priests and Pharisees" recalls the official body that passed the death sentence (cf. v. 47, 53); and the verbs "give orders", "report", and "arrest" are legal terms.[385]

385. Ernst Bammel, ed., "Ex Illa itaque die consilium fecerunt . . . (John 11:53)," in *The Trial of Jesus: Cambridge Studies in Honor of C. F. D. Moule* (London: SCM, 1970) 33.

12:1-8. 12:1. The story of Jesus' anointing is narrated here. The time referent locates the anointing in the same week as Passover and thus serves as a reminder of the proximity of Jesus' hour. The identification of Bethany as the site of Jesus' raising of Lazarus (v. 1) also directs the reader's attention toward Jesus' hour, because this miracle precipitated the death sentence under which Jesus now stands (cf. 11:47, 53, 57). Jesus' return to Bethany, the place from which he had retreated in response to this death sentence (11:54), also suggests movement toward his hour.

12:2. The Evangelist does not specify who gave the dinner for Jesus; the naming of Lazarus, Martha, and Mary supports the assumption that the dinner is at the home of this family whom Jesus loves (cf. 11:5). Outside of this verse, the word "dinner" (δεῖπνον deipnon) is used exclusively in John to refer to Jesus' last dinner with his disciples (13:2, 4; 21:20). As the discussion of vv. 3-8 will show, this dinner has many echoes of that meal.

12:3-8. Two anointing traditions are preserved in the canonical Gospels. The first, found in Mark 14:3-9 (and followed by Matt 26:1-13), is associated with the events of Jesus' passion and narrates the anointing of Jesus' head by a woman as preparation for his burial (Matt 26:12; Mark 14:8). The second, found in Luke 7:36-49, narrates the anointing of Jesus' feet and has no associations with Jesus' burial. It exemplifies the woman's love and respect for Jesus (Luke 7:44-47) and evokes Jesus' forgiveness of her sins (Luke 7:48-49). The story in John 12:3-8 includes elements from both traditions. For example, Mary anoints Jesus' feet, as in the tradition preserved in Luke, yet her anointing is explicitly linked with Jesus' burial, as in the tradition preserved in Mark.

The Fourth Evangelist seems to have combined the two traditions into one story in composing his story of the anointing.[386] It is not necessary to postulate Johannine dependence on the synoptic Gospels for this story,[387] but rather acquaintance with the two traditions that lie behind all of the Gospel anointings (see Commentary on 4:46-54 and 6:1-21). The Fourth Evangelist carefully com-

bined details from the two anointing traditions because both stories had details that served his theological purposes.

The anointing itself is narrated in v. 3. Both John and Mark point to the quality of the perfume (cf. Mark 14:3), but only John mentions the quantity. To many commentators, Mary's actions seem merely an awkward echo of the woman in Luke 7; they note that the woman's action of wiping her tears from Jesus' feet with her hair fits the Lukan story, but such a gesture seems out of place in the Johannine account.[388] Careful attention to the Fourth Evangelist's word choice in narrating Mary's actions, however, suggests that the action of wiping Jesus' feet is essential to the Johannine account. The verb "to wipe" (ἐκμάσσω ekmassō; see also 11:2) is the same verb used to describe Jesus' wiping of his disciples' feet at the foot washing in John 13:5. Mary's anointing and wiping of Jesus' feet thus point toward Jesus' foot washing at the farewell meal.[389] Like the stories of the raising of Lazarus (11:1-44) and the Sanhedrin's decision to kill Jesus (11:45-54), this story prefigures critical events in Jesus' hour.

The reference to the pervasiveness of the fragrance of the perfume (v. 3b) signals the extravagance of Mary's act; a pound of expensive perfume would, indeed, overwhelm the house! Yet this reference to the perfume's fragrance may have additional significance. At 11:39, Martha attempted to stop Jesus at Lazarus's tomb because of the stench that would come out of the tomb. Through Mary's act, the stench of death that once lingered over this household has been replaced by the fragrance of love and devotion.

In the Markan anointing, an unnamed group protests the woman's waste of the perfume (Mark 14:5), but in John the protest is voiced by Judas alone (v. 4). The major role played by Judas in the anointing story (vv. 4-6) further suggests that the Fourth Evangelist intends the reader to link Mary's anointing with the events of the farewell meal (cf. 13:2, 26, 29). The lengthy description of Judas in v. 4 serves two purposes. First, it makes the connection with Jesus' death explicit (see also 6:71; 18:2, 5), and second, it delegitimates Judas's protest before he even speaks. What

386. So, e.g., Raymond E. Brown, *The Gospel According to John (I–XII)*, AB 29 (Garden City, N.Y.: Doubleday, 1966) 450-52; Robert Kysar, *John*, Augsburg Commentary of the New Testament (Minneapolis: Augsburg, 1986) 325-26n. 17.

387. So C. K. Barrett, *The Gospel According to St. John*, 2nd ed. (Philadelphia: Westminster, 1978) 410-11.

388. So Rudolf Schnackenburg, *The Gospel According to St. John*, 3 vols. (New York: Seabury, 1982.

389. See Kysar, *John*, 187.

might be a reasoned complaint about the expenditure of money (cf. Matt 26:8) is shown to be untrustworthy by the Evangelist's commentary. Judas's words in v. 5 nonetheless underscore the extravagance of Mary's act; she has spent a year's wages (NIV) on this act of devotion.

The delegitimation of Judas continues in v. 6. This verse provides a detail about Judas that will be repeated at 13:29; he was the keeper of the common purse. Greed was one of the early church's explanation for Judas's treachery (e.g., Matt 26:15), and v. 6 can thus be read as continuing the vilification of Judas in early Christian tradition. Yet the details of this description seem to serve another purpose as well. Judas is labeled a "thief" (κλέπτης *kleptēs*), the same word used to describe the one who threatens the flock in 10:1, 8, 10. The expression "not because he cared about the poor" echoes the description of the hired hand's lack of care for the sheep (10:13). The use of these words suggests that the description of Judas is intended to point the reader toward the proper context in which to place Judas's actions. When he betrays Jesus, he also betrays the sheep.

Verses 3-6 thus narrate two distinct responses to the arrival of Jesus' hour. Mary is the model of faithful discipleship, Judas unfaithful.[390] Jesus' words in vv. 7-8 validate Mary's response. The grammar of the Greek text of v. 7 is difficult. Verse 7*b* begins with an elliptical purpose clause (lit., "in order that [ἵνα *hina*] she might keep it"). The NRSV resolves the difficulty by supplying the verb phrase "she bought it," but these words are not in the Greek text and their addition limits the scope of Jesus' response. The NIV comes closer to the meaning of the Greek text because it emphasizes the centrality of the purpose clause. Two other instances of a *hina* purpose clause

without a clear protasis clarify the meaning of Jesus' words here. At both 9:3 and 11:4, an elliptical *hina* purpose clause is used to announce the purpose of Jesus' revelatory acts. Here, the same construction is used to announce the revelatory significance of *Mary's* act. The anointing in Mark 14 is the only anointing Jesus' body receives for its burial, but in John, there will be another anointing at the time of Jesus' burial (19:38-42). The significance of Mary's act is that it anticipates that final anointing. Jesus' words in v. 7 thus interpret Mary's act as confirming the impending arrival of his hour.

Jesus' words in v. 8 are identical to Matt 26:11 (cf. Mark 14:7). This verse is absent from some manuscripts and may have been added to others by a scribe to harmonize with the Matthean account.[391] It alludes to the commandment to care for the poor in Deut 15:11, and in Matthew and Mark it clearly rebuffs the protest about money and waste. Yet this verse takes on a distinct meaning in the Johannine context and as such may point again to the Evangelist's creative use of tradition. It reminds the disciples of the limited time of Jesus' presence among them and the urgency to respond to Jesus while he is still here (cf. 11:9-10). Mary has recognized this limitedness and responded to it.

12:9-11. These verses form an appropriate conclusion to all three stories of 11:1–12:11 by reiterating the link between Jesus' raising of Lazarus and the threat to Jesus' life. The authorities' fears (11:48) come true; "many of the Jews" desert and believe in Jesus (v. 11). The danger that the authorities perceive in Jesus' miracle is underscored by their decision to put Lazarus to death also; there can be no public reminders of what Jesus has done.

---

390. Elisabeth Schüssler Fiorenza, *In Memory of Her: A Feminist Reconstruction of Christian Origins* (New York: Crossroad, 1983) 330.

391. So Brown, *The Gospel According to John (I–XII)*, 449; Barrett, *The Gospel According to St. John*, 415.

REFLECTIONS

The Commentary on 12:1-8 identified Jesus' anointing by Mary as anticipatory of two events in Jesus' hour: Jesus' washing of his disciples' feet at the last supper and Jesus' burial. Perhaps because the linkage with Jesus' burial is an interpretation shared by Mark and Matthew, commentators have focused almost exclusively on this aspect of the story. Yet it is in the link between the anointing and the foot washing that the Fourth Evangelist's distinctive theology can be seen most clearly, and the full meaning of this story is lost when that linkage is overlooked.

In the foot washing (see Commentary and Reflections on 13:1-20), Jesus will wash his disciples' feet as an expression of his love for them (13:1), as a way of drawing them into his life with God (13:8). He will also ask them to repeat this act of service for one another (13:14-15). What Jesus will do for his disciples and will ask them to do for one another, Mary has already done for him in 12:3. In Mary, then, the reader is given a picture of the fullness of the life of discipleship. Her act shows forth the love that will be the hallmark of discipleship in John and the recognition of Jesus' identity that is the decisive mark of Christian life.

Mary's act of discipleship is brought out even more strongly in the contrast with Judas in this scene. Judas does not respond to the impingement of Jesus' hour with an act of love for Jesus, but with self-centered disdain. Judas's response leads to the destruction of the flock, whereas Mary's actions model the life of love that should characterize Jesus' sheep.

The power of the witness of Mary's discipleship in this story is that she knows how to respond to Jesus without being told. She fulfills Jesus' love commandment before he even teaches it (e.g., 13:34-35); she embraces Jesus' departure at his hour before he has taught his followers about its true meaning (e.g., 14:2-4; 16:19-24). In the story of the raising of Lazarus, she responded to Jesus' calling for her (11:28-29), thus showing that she was one of Jesus' own. In the anointing, she shows what it means to be one of Jesus' own. She gives boldly of herself in love to Jesus at his hour, just as Jesus will give boldly of himself in love at his hour.

The Commentary and Reflections on John 11:1-44 discussed Jesus' raising of Lazarus as the eschatological announcement of the fullness of God available in Jesus and the fullness of life Jesus makes available to those who believe. Mary's anointing of Jesus is the companion eschatological act, because it is the eschatological announcement of the promise of discipleship. That is, if in the raising of Lazarus, Jesus is fully revealed, then in Mary's anointing of Jesus, faithful discipleship is fully revealed. Mary's act of anointing illustrates the Evangelist's eschatological vision of the new life to be lived by those who embrace Jesus' life and death and become children of God (1:12; 11:53).

Jesus' words about discipleship in the Farewell Discourse will make explicit what this story shows: Discipleship is defined by acts of love and one's response to Jesus. It is important, therefore, in the appropriation of John 12:1-8 in the life of the church to acknowledge that the Fourth Evangelist names a woman as the first to embody the love that is commanded of all disciples. The Fourth Evangelist's eschatological vision of a community shaped by love and grounded in relationship to Jesus is first enacted by a female disciple who by conventional standards has no claim to that position (cf. the disciples' response to Jesus' conversation with a woman in 4:27). Discipleship in the Fourth Gospel does not conform to some of the church's stereotypical assumptions about the composition of Jesus' circle of disciples. For example, the Twelve as a fixed group of male disciples are nearly invisible in this Gospel (see 6:67-71). Jesus' disciples are persons, like Mary, whom he loves and who love him and live out that love (e.g, 13:35; 15:9-10, 12-17; 17:26).

Figure 11: Chronology of the Holy Week and Resurrection Appearances in the Gospels

	Matthew		**Mark**	
Saturday				
Sunday			Mark 11:1-11	Triumphal entry Looks around Goes to Bethany
Monday	Matt 21:1-17	Triumphal entry "Cleanses" Temple Cures the blind and the lame Goes to Bethany	Mark 11:12-19	Curses fig tree "Cleanses" Temple Conspiracy against Jesus Leaves city

Tuesday	Matt 21:18–25:46	Curses the fig tree, which withers
		Jesus in the Temple:
		  Question about authority
		  Three parables
		  On paying taxes
		  Question about the resurrection
		  The Great Commandment
		  Question about David's Son
		  Denunciation of scribes and Pharisees
		  Lament over Jerusalem
		Leaves the Temple
		Destruction of the Temple foretold
		On the Mount of Olives
		  Discourse on the end of the age
		  Signs of the end
		  Persecutions foretold
		  Desolating Sacrilege
		  Coming of the Son of Man
		  Lesson of the fig tree
		  Necessity for watchfulness
		  Faithful and unfaithful slave
		  Two parables
		  Judgment of the Gentiles
			Mark 11:20–13:37	Discovers withered fig tree
				Jesus in the Temple:
				  Question about authority
				  Three parables
				  On paying taxes
				  Question about the resurrection
				  The Great Commandment
				  Question about David's Son
				  Denunciation of scribes
				  Widow's offering
				Leaves the Temple
				Destruction of the Temple foretold
				On the Mount of Olives
				  Discourse on the end of the age
				  Signs of the end
				  Persecutions foretold
				  Desolating Sacrilege
				  Coming of the Son of Man
				  Lesson of the fig tree
				  Necessity for watchfulness

Wednesday	Matt 26:1-16	Plot to kill Jesus Anointing in Bethany Betrayal by Judas	Mark 14:1-11	Plot to kill Jesus Anointing in Bethany Betrayal by Judas
Thursday	Matt 26:17-75	**Day of Preparation*** Last supper Prayer at Gethsemane Betrayal and arrest Trial before the Sanhedrin Peter's denial	Mark 14:12-72	**Day of Preparation*** Last supper Prayer at Gethsemane Betrayal and arrest Trial before the Sanhedrin Peter's denial
Friday	Matt 27:1-61	**Day of Passover** Suicide of Judas Trial before Pilate Barabbas released Jesus mocked Crucifixion, death, and burial	Mark 15:1-47	**Day of Passover** Trial before Pilate Barabbas released Jesus mocked Crucifixion, death, and burial
Saturday	Matt 27:62-66	Guard placed at tomb		
Sunday	Matt 28:1-15	Resurrection Angel appears to the women Jesus appears to the women Report of the guard	Mark 16:1-8	Resurrection Discovery of empty tomb Angel appears to the women The women say "nothing to anyone"
			Mark 16:9-21	Jesus appears to Mary Magdalene Jesus appears to "two of them" Jesus appears to the Eleven Jesus' ascension
Later Events	Matt 28:16-20	Great Commission to the eleven in Galilee		

*The Day of Preparation could refer to preparing for the sabbath (as in Matthew, Mark, and Luke) or preparing for a festival (cf. Matt 26:17; Mark 14:12; Luke 22:8). Only in John does it refer to both, since, according to John's chronology, the Passover fell on the sabbath the year of Jesus' death. The Day of Preparation, like the festival itself, began at sundown of the previous evening.

Luke-Acts		John		

Luke-Acts

(No time reference is given for these events.)

Luke 19:28–22:12	Triumphal Entry Lament over Jerusalem

"Cleanses" Temple

Question about authority
Parables
On paying taxes
Question about the resurrection
The Great Commandment
Question about David's Son
Jesus denounces the scribes
The widow's mite

Destruction of the Temple foretold
Destruction of Jerusalem foretold

Coming of the Son of Man
Lesson of the fig tree
Need to be alert

"Every day he was teaching in
   the temple" (Luke 21:37)

Plot to kill Jesus

Betrayal by Judas

John

John 12:1-11	Mary anoints Jesus in Bethany Plot to kill Jesus	**Saturday**
John 12:12-50	Triumphal entry Greeks come to see Jesus Jesus speaks about his death Response to Jesus "Then Jesus cried out . . ."	**Sunday**

Luke 22:7-65	**Day of Preparation*** Last supper Dispute about greatness Prayer on Mt. of Olives Betrayal and arrest Jesus brought to High Priest's house Peter's denial Jesus mocked

John 13:1–18:27	Jesus washes disciples' feet Jesus' final discourse Jesus and disciples go to a garden Betrayal and arrest Trial before High Priest Peter's denial	**Thursday**

Luke 22:66–23:56*a*	**Day of Passover** Trial before Sanhedrin Trials before Herod and Pilate Barabbas released Crucifixion, death, and burial

John 18:28–19:42	**Day of Preparation*** Trial before Pilate Crucifixion, death, and burial	**Friday**

Luke 23:56*b*	"They rested on the sabbath"

	Day of Passover	**Saturday**

Luke 24:1-49	Resurrection Discovery of empty tomb Two men "in dazzling clothes" appear to the women Peter visits the tomb Jesus appears in Emmaus Jesus appears to the disciples

John 20:1-23	Resurrection
	Jesus appears to Mary Magdalene
	Peter and the Beloved Disciple visit
	  the tomb
	Jesus appears to the disciples
	  (without Thomas)
		Sunday

Acts 1:3-11	"Forty Days Later" Jesus' ascension at Bethany

John 20:26-29	"One week later" Jesus appears to the Eleven	**Later Events**
John 21:1-25	"After these things" Jesus appears in Galilee	

JOHN 12:12-19, JESUS' ENTRY INTO JERUSALEM

NIV

¹²The next day the great crowd that had come for the Feast heard that Jesus was on his way to Jerusalem. ¹³They took palm branches and went out to meet him, shouting,

"Hosanna!ᵃ"

"Blessed is he who comes in the name of the Lord!"ᵇ

"Blessed is the King of Israel!"

¹⁴Jesus found a young donkey and sat upon it, as it is written,

¹⁵"Do not be afraid, O Daughter of Zion;
  see, your king is coming,
    seated on a donkey's colt."ᶜ

¹⁶At first his disciples did not understand all this. Only after Jesus was glorified did they realize that these things had been written about him and that they had done these things to him.

¹⁷Now the crowd that was with him when he called Lazarus from the tomb and raised him from the dead continued to spread the word. ¹⁸Many people, because they had heard that he had given this miraculous sign, went out to meet him. ¹⁹So the Pharisees said to one another, "See, this is getting us nowhere. Look how the whole world has gone after him!"

ᵃ13 A Hebrew expression meaning "Save!" which became an exclamation of praise   ᵇ13 Psalm 118:25, 26   ᶜ15 Zech. 9:9

NRSV

12The next day the great crowd that had come to the festival heard that Jesus was coming to Jerusalem. ¹³So they took branches of palm trees and went out to meet him, shouting,

"Hosanna!
  Blessed is the one who comes in the name
    of the Lord—
  the King of Israel!"

¹⁴Jesus found a young donkey and sat on it; as it is written:

¹⁵ "Do not be afraid, daughter of Zion.
  Look, your king is coming,
    sitting on a donkey's colt!"

¹⁶His disciples did not understand these things at first; but when Jesus was glorified, then they remembered that these things had been written of him and had been done to him. ¹⁷So the crowd that had been with him when he called Lazarus out of the tomb and raised him from the dead continued to testify.ᵃ ¹⁸It was also because they heard that he had performed this sign that the crowd went to meet him. ¹⁹The Pharisees then said to one another, "You see, you can do nothing. Look, the world has gone after him!"

ᵃ Other ancient authorities read with him began to testify that he had called . . . from the dead

COMMENTARY

Jesus' triumphal entry into Jerusalem is narrated in all four Gospels (see also Matt 21:1-11; Mark 11:1-10; Luke 20:29-40). All four versions share a common core: Jesus is greeted by a crowd waving branches and shouting the words of Ps 118:25; Jesus rides a donkey during the entry. Beyond this common core, however, the differences between the Johannine account and those in the other Gospels are especially pronounced. For example, the Johannine version is considerably briefer than those of the other three Gospels, narrating only the entry itself and containing no account of the preparation for the entry and the procuring of the donkey (cf. Matt 21:1-7; Mark 11:1-7; Luke 19:29-35). Given the

number of significant differences in John's version of the entry, a theory of Johannine dependence on Mark for this story[392] seems neither tenable nor necessary. Rather, the recounting of Jesus' entry in all four Gospels is best interpreted as evidence of the prominent place the entry occupied in early Christian traditions about Jesus.

12:12-15. The entry is narrated in vv. 12-15. Verses 12-13 focus on the crowd; vv. 14-15 on Jesus.

12:12. This verse explicitly connects the entry story with the preceding narratives. First, the

392. So Barrett, *The Gospel According to St. John,* 416.

entry is located on the day after the anointing ("the next day"). Since the anointing took place six days before Passover (v. 1), a Saturday, the entry takes place on Sunday. John alone among the Gospels specifies the day of the week of Jesus' entry, and the church has followed this chronology in its liturgical celebration of Palm Sunday. Second, the identification of the "great crowd" points back to the crowds of 11:55-56 and 12:9 and is a reminder of the numbers that Jesus is attracting (cf. 11:48).

12:13. John is also alone among the Gospels in identifying the branches waved by the crowd as palm branches (cf. Matt 21:8; Mark 11:8; there is no mention of branches in Luke). Since the Maccabean period, palm branches were symbols of national triumph and victory (e.g., 2 Macc 10:7; 1 Macc 13:51). The palm branches thus suggest that the crowd greets Jesus as their national hero. The crowd's opening words in v. 13*b* combine words from two verses of Psalm 118: "Hosanna" (v. 24 [v. 25 English]) and "Blessed be the one who comes in the name of the Lord" (v. 25 [v. 26 English]). These words occur in all four Gospel accounts and match the wording of the LXX of Psalm 118 exactly. One can also detect in the entry narrative echoes of the liturgical instructions of Ps 118:26*b* (v. 27 NRSV and other English trans.): "Bind the festal procession with branches." Psalm 118 is a royal psalm sung in thanksgiving for victory in battle; vv. 19-29 of the psalm provide the instructions for the liturgical celebration of the return of the triumphant king to the Temple. The use of Psalm 118 suggests that John 12:13 is to be read as the reenactment of this psalm's liturgical celebration of a royal triumph.

The Fourth Evangelist further reinforces the royal dimension of the crowd's greeting by adding the words "the King of Israel" to the traditional greeting from Psalm 118 (cf. the additions that each of the Gospels makes to Psalm 118: Matt 21:9; Mark 11:9-10; Luke 19:38). These words come from Zeph 3:15. Zephaniah 3:14-15 is similar to the enthronement psalms (e.g., Psalms 95–99), which celebrate God's heavenly enthronement as King. The use of Zeph 3:15 here highlights the people's hope in Jesus as the one who will restore God's kingdom in their nation. The fact that the Jerusalem crowd reacts to Jesus as their national savior corroborates the

authorities' fears about Rome's response to Jesus' popularity (11:48).

This is not the first time Jesus has been hailed as king in the Fourth Gospel. In the panoply of christological titles of John 1, Nathanael proclaims Jesus to be the King of Israel (1:49). Jesus responds to Nathanael's announcement by promising that he will see "greater things than these" (1:50), suggesting that Nathanael's understanding of Jesus' kingship will be changed by the reality of Jesus' ministry. Perhaps closest to the crowd's response here are the actions of the Galilean crowd at 6:14-15. In response to Jesus' miraculous feeding, the people wanted to make Jesus king "by force," but Jesus escapes from them. They, like the crowd here, misunderstand the nature and purpose of Jesus' power. The theme of Jesus' kingship will reach its conclusion in the passion narrative (see 18:33–19:22).

12:14-15. The focus now turns to Jesus. In the synoptic Gospels, Jesus' riding on a donkey precedes the acclamation by the crowd (cf. Matt 21:1-7; Mark 11:1-7; Luke 19:29-34), but in John it follows the acclamation and is positioned as a corrective to the crowd's misunderstanding of the nature of Jesus' kingship. The story of the procurement of the donkey is streamlined into the words "Jesus found a young donkey" (v. 14). Jesus' action is interpreted in the citation from Zech 9:9 (v. 15; cf. Matt 21:5), affirming that Jesus is king, but not the warrior king whom the crowd greets with palm branches. He is instead the king who embodies the eschatological vision of Zech 9:9: "Triumphant and victorious is he,/ humble and riding on a donkey, on a colt, the foal of a donkey" (NRSV).

The Fourth Evangelist has altered the opening words of Zech 9:9 from "Rejoice," to "Do not be afraid." The words "Do not be afraid" occur in many places in the OT canon, most frequently in the poetry of Isaiah, where they announce the beginning of the reign of God and the fulfillment of God's eschatological promises (e.g., Isa 35:4; 40:9; 41:14). They are also associated with theophanies (e.g., Gen 15:1). Of particular importance for v. 15 is the occurrence of those words at Zeph 3:16. The allusion to Zephaniah 3 here provides a further corrective to the crowd's perception of Jesus. They incorrectly used the words of Zephaniah 3 to greet Jesus as their political savior;

the Fourth Evangelist makes a renewed appeal to Zephaniah 3 to show that Jesus comes as the presence of God among them, but not as the conquering hero.

12:16. The disciples saw what the reader sees—the crowd greets Jesus with palm branches, Jesus responds by sitting on a donkey—but the meaning of these events was unclear to them until after Jesus' glorification. That is, it is only from the perspective of Jesus' death, resurrection, and ascension that the real meaning of Jesus' kingship can be comprehended. For the disciples to remember means that they reflect on the past in the light of the resurrection with the aid of the Spirit (cf. 14:26). As at 2:22, remembering the past with the aid of the Spirit reveals the truth about Scripture and Jesus' actions (see Reflections). John has assisted the reader in that "remembering" by supplying his commentary in v. 15.

12:17-19. These verses integrate the entry narrative into the larger unit of John 11–12 by returning to a theme from 11:47-53: the authorities' fear of Jesus' popularity. Verses 17-18 point to two groups that now follow Jesus: those who were present at the Lazarus miracle (v. 17) and those who have heard reports of the miracle (v. 18; cf. 4:39-42). The Pharisees themselves testify to the fulfillment of their fears in v. 19 (cf. the Pharisees' complaint in Luke 19:39). Their confession of helplessness ("you can do nothing") answers their own question of 11:47 ("What are we to do?"). Their hyperbolic announcement that the "world" (κόσμος *kosmos*) has gone after Jesus provides ironic testimony to the truth of Caiaphas's prophecy (11:50-52). The Pharisees, the Jewish authorities, unwittingly confirm one of the central tenets of the Gospel: Jesus came to save the world (3:16-17); he is the Savior of the world (4:42). Their words thus provide a fitting conclusion to the entry narrative, in which the crowd has wrongly greeted Jesus as their national hero (cf. 11:48).

REFLECTIONS

As noted in the Commentary, the church follows the Fourth Gospel's lead in naming its liturgical celebration of Jesus' entry into Jerusalem Palm Sunday. The waving of palm branches and the occurrence of the entry on a Sunday are only mentioned in John. The church follows the Fourth Gospel's lead in another aspect of its Palm Sunday celebration as well. When the church celebrates Palm Sunday correctly, it is doing the very thing that is reported about the disciples in v. 16: It is remembering the past through the lens of Jesus' death, resurrection, and ascension. That is, Palm Sunday is not merely a commemoration of a past event; it is, rather, the liturgical *remembrance* through which Jesus' entry becomes real for the present-day worshiping community.

In v. 16, the Fourth Evangelist rightly reminds the reader that the individual pieces of Jesus' life and ministry will assume their final shape only when they are reflected on after Jesus' glorification—after the fullness of Jesus' identity is revealed, after the full extent of Jesus' love for his own is made manifest. By including this explicit reminder in the middle of telling the story of Jesus, the Fourth Evangelist identifies the church's work of interpretation and reflection as an essential part of the gospel message. That is, he acknowledges that the work of interpretation and reflection is an act of faith, done through the gift of the Spirit and informed by the recognition of God's defeat of the power of death through the death, resurrection, and ascension of Jesus. Moreover, the Fourth Evangelist affirms that only when one consciously and intentionally engages in such reflection can the full truth of Jesus be grasped.

How, then, can the church's celebration of Palm Sunday be such an act of reflection and remembrance? When the church celebrates Palm Sunday, when it shouts, "Hosanna! Blessed is the one who comes in the name of the Lord," it is not participating in a victory march. Palm Sunday is not one more excuse for a parade; it is, rather, a moment for communal reflection on Jesus' identity. The life of the church derives from the life and love of Jesus, and the Palm Sunday liturgy invites the church to remember the shape and character of that life and love. The liturgy of the church uses Palm Sunday as the occasion to focus its life on the events of Jesus' death, resurrection, and ascension, because Palm Sunday is also Passion Sunday. Like Jesus' disciples in 12:16, the church can understand the meaning of Jesus' entry—and its identity as liturgical reenactor of that entry—only by remembering it in the light of the rest of the story.

It is noteworthy that after the two events that traditionally mark the beginning of Jesus' journey to his death (the cleansing of the Temple and the entry), the Fourth Evangelist appends the same commentary about remembering (2:22; 12:16). Although some scholars explain this with an appeal to sources,[393] a more theologically suggestive explanation is that the Fourth Evangelist wanted to underscore for the reader the incompleteness of traditions about Jesus, even those that are most well-known, when they are interpreted apart from the full story of Jesus' glorification. These two notices about remembering, taken in conjunction with Jesus' teaching about the role of the Paraclete in bringing the community to remembrance (14:26), reveal a great deal about the Fourth Evangelist's understanding of his own interpretive work. His Gospel narrative is itself an act of remembering, of reflecting on the whole story of Jesus from a post-glorification perspective, and of allowing that perspective to govern his interpretation.

393. So Schnackenburg, *The Gospel According to St. John,* 2:377; possibly Brown, *The Gospel According to John (I–XII),* 463.

JOHN 12:20-36, JESUS INTERPRETS HIS DEATH

NIV

20Now there were some Greeks among those who went up to worship at the Feast. 21They came to Philip, who was from Bethsaida in Galilee, with a request. "Sir," they said, "we would like to see Jesus." 22Philip went to tell Andrew; Andrew and Philip in turn told Jesus.

23Jesus replied, "The hour has come for the Son of Man to be glorified. 24I tell you the truth, unless a kernel of wheat falls to the ground and dies, it remains only a single seed. But if it dies, it produces many seeds. 25The man who loves his life will lose it, while the man who hates his life in this world will keep it for eternal life. 26Whoever serves me must follow me; and where I am, my servant also will be. My Father will honor the one who serves me.

27"Now my heart is troubled, and what shall I say? 'Father, save me from this hour'? No, it was for this very reason I came to this hour. 28Father, glorify your name!"

Then a voice came from heaven, "I have glorified it, and will glorify it again." 29The crowd that was there and heard it said it had thundered; others said an angel had spoken to him.

30Jesus said, "This voice was for your benefit,

NRSV

20Now among those who went up to worship at the festival were some Greeks. 21They came to Philip, who was from Bethsaida in Galilee, and said to him, "Sir, we wish to see Jesus." 22Philip went and told Andrew; then Andrew and Philip went and told Jesus. 23Jesus answered them, "The hour has come for the Son of Man to be glorified. 24Very truly, I tell you, unless a grain of wheat falls into the earth and dies, it remains just a single grain; but if it dies, it bears much fruit. 25Those who love their life lose it, and those who hate their life in this world will keep it for eternal life. 26Whoever serves me must follow me, and where I am, there will my servant be also. Whoever serves me, the Father will honor.

27"Now my soul is troubled. And what should I say—'Father, save me from this hour'? No, it is for this reason that I have come to this hour. 28Father, glorify your name." Then a voice came from heaven, "I have glorified it, and I will glorify it again." 29The crowd standing there heard it and said that it was thunder. Others said, "An angel has spoken to him." 30Jesus answered, "This voice has come for your sake, not for mine. 31Now is the judgment of this world; now the ruler of this

NIV

not mine. ³¹Now is the time for judgment on this world; now the prince of this world will be driven out. ³²But I, when I am lifted up from the earth, will draw all men to myself." ³³He said this to show the kind of death he was going to die.

³⁴The crowd spoke up, "We have heard from the Law that the Christ*a* will remain forever, so how can you say, 'The Son of Man must be lifted up'? Who is this 'Son of Man'?"

³⁵Then Jesus told them, "You are going to have the light just a little while longer. Walk while you have the light, before darkness overtakes you. The man who walks in the dark does not know where he is going. ³⁶Put your trust in the light while you have it, so that you may become sons of light." When he had finished speaking, Jesus left and hid himself from them.

a34 Or *Messiah*

NRSV

world will be driven out. ³²And I, when I am lifted up from the earth, will draw all people*a* to myself." ³³He said this to indicate the kind of death he was to die. ³⁴The crowd answered him, "We have heard from the law that the Messiah*b* remains forever. How can you say that the Son of Man must be lifted up? Who is this Son of Man?" ³⁵Jesus said to them, "The light is with you for a little longer. Walk while you have the light, so that the darkness may not overtake you. If you walk in the darkness, you do not know where you are going. ³⁶While you have the light, believe in the light, so that you may become children of light."

After Jesus had said this, he departed and hid from them.

a Other ancient authorities read *all things*   *b* Or *the Christ*

COMMENTARY

12:20. The arrival of the Greeks marks the beginning of a new section. These "Greeks" (Ἕλληνες *Hellēnes*) are to be distinguished from Greek-speaking Jews (Ἑλληνίσται *Hellēnistai*; cf. Acts 6:1; 9:29; 11:20). Because they have made the pilgrimage to Jerusalem for the Passover feast, they may be Gentile proselytes, but what the Fourth Evangelist intends to underscore is that they are non-Jews, representatives of the Gentile world. Their request to see Jesus confirms the Pharisees' unconscious prophecy of 12:19; the world is indeed going after Jesus.

12:21-22. The prominent role of Philip and Andrew in vv. 21-22 can helpfully be compared with the call narratives of 1:35-46, in which they also play prominent roles.[394] Jesus greeted the first disciples (one of whom was Andrew, 1:40) with the invitation "Come and see" (1:39); Philip called Nathanael with the same invitation (1:46). The Greeks' request to "see" Jesus, a conventional way to request a meeting (cf. Luke 8:20; 9:9; Acts

28:20), can thus also be read as their desire to become disciples. Because Andrew and Philip were the first to receive the invitation to discipleship directly from Jesus (1:39, 43), their presence in vv. 21-22 establishes a connection between the call of the first Jewish disciples and the arrival of the first Gentile disciples.

12:23. Just as the raising of Lazarus and Jesus' anointing by Mary both prefigured Jesus' glorification, so, too, does this arrival of the Greeks. It prefigures the church's future mission to the Gentiles and the inclusion of Gentiles in God's promises. As such, it points to the fulfillment of the eschatological promises of universal salvation (cf. 4:42). This proleptic glimpse of that future marks the arrival of Jesus' hour (v. 23) because it is through Jesus' glorification—his death and resurrection, his return to God—that God's promises for God's people are fulfilled. Jesus' hour is the decisive eschatological dividing line. The future to which the arrival of the Greeks points requires Jesus' death (cf. 10:15-16).

12:24-36. Jesus' announcement of the arrival of his hour (v. 23) is followed by a series of teachings about the meaning of his death (vv. 24-26, 32) and the urgency of the hour (vv. 27, 30, 32, 35-36). These teachings are punctuated

---

394. The two most frequent explanations for the prominence of Philip and Andrew are: (1) They are the only two disciples who were known solely by Greek names, and (2) these verses may allude to an actual role that the two played in the Gentile mission. (So, e.g., Schnackenburg, *The Gospel According to St. John*, 2:382; Barrett, *The Gospel According to St. John*, 422).

by responses from the crowd (vv. 29, 34). The Fourth Evangelist uses the same compositional technique employed in John 7 to construct this narrative about Jesus' death.

12:24-26. Jesus introduces the first set of teachings about his death (vv. 24-26) with a brief agricultural parable (v. 24; cf. 4:35-36). The seed imagery recalls the parables of sowing found in the Synoptics (Matt 13:3-32; Mark 4:3-20, 26-32; Luke 8:5-15), but this Johannine agricultural figure seems to be independent of any in the synoptic tradition.[395] The agricultural figure that most closely resembles v. 24 is 1 Cor 15:37-38, but the purpose of the two figures is quite distinct. Paul uses the seed imagery to illustrate the resurrection of the body, whereas Jesus uses the imagery to interpret his own death.

The significance of this parable for understanding Jesus' death lies in the contrast between remaining solitary (μόνος μένει *monos menei*; "just a single grain" [NRSV]) and "bearing much fruit" (πολὺν καρπὸν φέρει *polyn karpon pherei*). In John, "fruit" is Jesus' metaphor for the life of the community of faith (see 15:1-8; the NIV ["many seeds"] masks this important point). Jesus thus uses the seed parable to show that the salvific power of his death resides in the community that is gathered as a result of it (cf. 10:15-16; 11:51-52). Verse 24 states metaphorically what v. 32 will state directly and as such is an appropriate response to the Greeks' request; one comes to Jesus through his death.[396]

Verse 25 records one of the best-attested sayings of Jesus; in addition to this verse, some form of the saying occurs five times in the synoptic Gospels (Matt 10:39; 16:25; Mark 10:39; Luke 9:24; 17:33). While all of the occurrences share the basic pattern of an antithetical parallelism that highlights contrasting attitudes toward one's life, there are also significant differences among the sayings. The significant number of variations within the synoptic tradition and between the Synoptics and John argues against any theory of literary dependence and for multiple attestations of this saying in the oral tradition.[397] The differ-ences also point to the ways each evangelist adapted this Jesus saying to serve his Gospel.

Verse 25 must be read against the backdrop of Jesus' death (vv. 23-24). The word for "life" (ψυχή *psyche*) is common to the tradition (e.g., Mark 8:35; Luke 9:24; 17:33), but it takes on particular significance here, because it is the same word used by Jesus to describe his gift of his life (10:11, 15, 17; see also 15:13). To love one's life is the opposite of Jesus' own action; it places one outside of the community shaped by Jesus' gift of his life (*psyche*) and leads to the loss of that life (v. 25*a*). This is reinforced in the antithesis of v. 25*b*. To hate one's life in "this world" is to declare one's allegiance to Jesus (cf. 15:18-19) and so to receive his gift of eternal life (cf. 3:16; 6:40; 10:28; 17:2). Peter's profession of his purported willingness to give up his life for Jesus (13:37-38) and his subsequent denial of Jesus (18:15-18, 25-27) illustrate v. 25*a*; his reclaiming of his love and service for Jesus in 21:15-19 illustrate v. 25*b*.

Verse 26 also has analogues in the synoptic tradition (Matt 10:38; Mark 8:34; Luke 14:27). While the synoptic versions establish a condition for following Jesus ("taking up one's cross"), the Johannine version contains both condition (v. 26*a*) and promise (v. 26*b* and *c*). Since Jesus' ultimate service is the gift of his life in love, v. 26*a* calls the disciples to love as he loves and hence to serve as he serves.[398] What it means to be Jesus' servant will be enacted in the foot washing of 13:1-20 (see the Commentary there). Verse 26*a* builds on the antithesis of v. 25 and again points to the link between Jesus' death and membership in the community of disciples. Verse 26*b* affirms that the disciple is not only called to follow Jesus to his death, but also is offered the promise of following Jesus through his death to share in his glorification. This promise anticipates the promises of the Farewell Discourse: Jesus and the believer will always remain together (e.g., 14:2-4, 18-20; 17:23-24). Verse 26*c*, too, is an "unambiguous statement of promise."[399] It is the only time in the Gospel that God is spoken of as honoring someone, and it anticipates the mutuality of relationship among God, Jesus, and believer promised in the Farewell Discourse.

395. C. H. Dodd, *Historical Tradition in the Fourth Gospel* (Cambridge: Cambridge University Press, 1963) 366-69.

396. Rudolf Bultmann, *The Gospel of John: A Commentary,* trans. G. R. Beasley-Murray, R. W. N. Hoare, and J. K. Riches (Philadelphia: Westminster, 1971) 424.

397. See the detailed analyses in Dodd, *Tradition,* 338-43, and Raymond E. Brown, *The Gospel According to John (I–XII),* AB 29 (Garden City, N.Y.: Doubleday, 1966) 473-74.

398. Interestingly, the only other use of the verb for "serve" (διακονέω *diakoneō*) in John is at 12:2, where Martha does the very thing Jesus calls for here: She serves him.

399. Bultmann, *The Gospel of John,* 425.

12:27-28a. The focus returns to Jesus' hour. There are echoes of the Gethsemane agony scene in these verses, but it is not necessary to postulate Johannine dependence on Mark 14:32-42 to explain the use of these echoes.[400] Rather, these verses are an ironic play on the tradition of Jesus' agony at his death, which is handled quite differently in Mark. Unlike the Markan text, the focus of vv. 27-28a is on the immediacy and urgency of Jesus' hour ("now"), not on his struggle in the face of that hour.

The only words of "agony" that Jesus speaks in v. 27a are an allusion to Ps 42:5, 11 (Psalm 41 LXX; cf. Mark 14:34). The Fourth Evangelist's use of this psalm as the vehicle for Jesus' words of agony is one indicator of his ironic handling of the tradition, because Psalm 42 affirms the psalmist's trust in God. By evoking this psalm, the Fourth Evangelist communicates that Jesus trusts in God at his hour. A second indication of the Evangelist's ironic handling of the agony tradition is in the parallel prayers of vv. 27b and 28a. The first prayer, framed as a question ("And what should I say?"), is never prayed by Jesus and stands as a parody of the prayer associated with Jesus' agony in the garden (Mark 14:36).[401] The second prayer, "Father, glorify your name," is the true prayer for the hour. Jesus lays down his life of his own free will (10:18); he embraces his hour as an expression of his love for God and the moment of God's glorification.

Verses 27-28 are an excellent example of the way the Fourth Evangelist takes traditional material and reshapes it to fit the theological vision that drives the Gospel. An "agony" scene cast in the idiom of the tradition as recorded in Mark would make no sense in this Gospel, because God's will and Jesus' will have always been the same. There is no internal struggle in the face of his death, because Jesus recognizes the hour as the ultimate purpose of his ministry. It is the final revelation of his relationship with God.

12:28b. The appropriateness of Jesus' prayer is confirmed by the voice from heaven. The past, present, and future of God's self-revelation in Jesus are brought together in this verse. The publicly audible answer to Jesus' prayer testifies to God's involvement in the events of the hour (cf. vv. 29-30). "I have glorified [my name]" points to what God has already done in Jesus and should be understood as referring to the events leading up to and including the inception of the hour. It may also contain a specific reference to the Lazarus story (cf. 11:4). "I will glorify it again" points to the hour and its aftermath. Verses 27-28 anticipate Jesus' prayer in John 17 in which the past, present, and future of God's glorification of Jesus are also combined.

12:29-33. Verse 29 is commonly interpreted as a classic example of Johannine misunderstanding, in which the crowd completely misses the point.[402] The crowd's response may be more ambiguous than simple misunderstanding, however.[403] Thunder was a common religious symbol for the voice of God (e.g., Exod 4:23; Ps 29:3-9), and angels were traditionally understood as God's messengers (e.g., Gen 16:7; 18:2-8; 19:1; Luke 1:11, 26; 2:9). The crowd's hearing the voice of God as either thunder or an angel's voice suggests that the crowd recognized that they were witnesses to an epiphany, some revelation of the divine, but that they did not grasp that they witnessed the unmediated presence of God in God's relationship to Jesus. Jesus' words in v. 30 underscore that this is indeed what the crowd has missed. They suggest that the voice should be heard as the partner to Jesus' prayer in 11:41-42, external attestation of the relationship between God and Jesus.

Verses 31-32 focus on Jesus' death as the decisive eschatological event, through which both negative (v. 31) and positive (v. 32) judgment are enacted.[404] Verse 31 underscores the eschatological immediacy and urgency of Jesus' hour (note the repetition of "now") and the inevitability of judgment. "This world" will be judged in its response to Jesus at his hour (see 3:18-19). The judgment of this world is expressed in more traditional eschatological imagery in v. 31b. The expression "the ruler of this world" occurs only in John (see also 14:30; 16:11), but similar imagery

---

400. C. K. Barrett, *The Gospel According to St. John,* 2nd ed. (Philadelphia: Westminster, 1978) 424-25.

401. But see ibid., 425; and George R. Beasley-Murray, *John,* WBC 36 (Waco, Tex.: Word, 1987) 212, who contend that Jesus actually prays this prayer here.

402. E.g., Bultmann, *The Gospel of John,* 430; Brown, *The Gospel According to John (I–XII),* 468.

403. George W. MacRae, *Invitation to John* (Garden City, N.Y.: Doubleday, 1978) 154.

404. See Rudolf Schnackenburg, *The Gospel According to St. John,* 3 vols. (New York: Seabury, 1982) 2:390-93; Beasley-Murray, *John,* 213.

is used elsewhere in the NT (cf. Matt 4:8-9; 2 Cor 4:4; Eph 2:2; 6:12) and Qumran literature[405] to refer to the devil, the embodiment of opposition to God. Verse 31*b* thus names the cosmic implications of Jesus' hour; it marks the defeat of the power of evil in the world (cf. 13:2, 27; 16:33).

Verse 32 is the third prediction of the "lifting up" of Jesus (see also 3:14; 8:28). The double meaning of "lifted up" (ὑψόω *hypsoō*) is again at play here. To be lifted up "from the earth" can be read as a description of the physical act of crucifixion (as the Evangelist underscores with his comment at 12:33; cf. 18:32), but it can also be read as a description of Jesus' exaltation (uplifting, literally) in his return to God. The positive effect of Jesus' hour is described in sweeping terms ("draw all people") and highlights the universal offer of salvation available in Jesus. It is people's response to this offer that sets limits, not Jesus himself (cf. 12:46-48).

12:34. The crowd's misunderstanding of Jesus' words recalls crowd misunderstanding in 7:26-27, 41-42: conventional teachings and expectations about the Messiah stand in the way of receiving Jesus. "Law" refers to Scripture in general, not strictly to the Torah (cf. 10:34), and the text alluded to here may be Ps 89:37 (36, English), which states that the line of David will continue forever.[406] What is most interesting about the crowd's response is that they have not completely misunderstood Jesus (cf. v. 29). They are the ones who introduce both "Messiah" and "Son of Man" into the conversation; Jesus has used neither of those terms in his passion prediction. The

Fourth Evangelist thus suggests that the crowd grasps some of the eschatological implications of Jesus' words, but not enough. The distance between Jesus and the crowd is captured in their final question. Jesus has been speaking about himself as the Son of Man since v. 23, but the crowd has not realized this.

12:35-36. Jesus turns from direct speech about his death to a metaphorical description of his ministry. He never speaks about himself directly in these verses, but instead cloaks everything in the metaphor of light and darkness. These verses build on Jesus' earlier uses of this metaphor (3:19-21; 8:12; 9:5; 11:9-10; cf. 1:4-9). The choice for those who listen to Jesus is clear: Receive the new life he offers ("become children of light") or remain lost in the darkness.

Verses 35-36 do not address the crowd's question about the Son of Man directly, but instead offer a compelling, indirect response to the crowd's continuing misunderstanding and distance from Jesus. First, Jesus once again underscores the temporal urgency of the situation. "For a little longer" points to the contingency of Jesus' ministry (cf. 7:33; 13:33; 14:19; 16:16-18). Second, the light/darkness metaphor continues the theme of judgment and response to Jesus. These verses, therefore, function as a concluding appeal for faith in Jesus as a response to the urgency of the hour.

Jesus' departure in v. 36*b* enacts the contingency of his ministry and creates a dramatic pause in the Gospel narrative. Although the voice of Jesus will be heard in vv. 44-50 (see Commentary below), this departure marks the end of his teaching prior to his hour. Jesus hides from the crowd because the moment of decision has arrived.

---

405. See 1QM 1:1, 5, 13; 14:9; 1QS 1:18; 2:5, 19.

406. This idea was first suggested by van Unnik and has achieved consensus recognition. See W. C. van Unnik, "The Quotation from the OT in John 12:34," *NovT* 3 (1959) 174-79.

REFLECTIONS

John 12:20-36 is the most concentrated collection of sayings on the death of Jesus in the Gospel of John and, therefore, provides the interpreter with an appropriate place to reflect on the meaning of the death of Jesus in this Gospel. Theological inquiry about Jesus' death and its soteriological efficacy is most frequently identified as "atonement theology." Before looking at the Johannine understanding of the death of Jesus, it will be helpful to review the theologies of atonement that have shaped and continue to shape the life of the church.[407]

It is conventional to speak of three atonement theologies that have had the most influence

---

407. This review of the three theologies of atonement follows the pattern suggested by Douglas John Hall in his thorough review of theologies of the atonement in *Professing the Faith: Christian Theology in a North American Context* (Minneapolis: Fortress, 1993) 413-34, 463-80.

on the church's understanding of the death of Jesus. These three models are commonly identified as (1) the ransom or "classical" theory, in which Jesus' death is understood as the act of ransom (payment) that bought the world its freedom from sin and death;[408] (2) the substitutionary or sacrificial victim model, in which Christ's death is understood as the sacrifice necessary to atone for human guilt and sin;[409] and (3) the "moral influence" theory, in which Jesus' death is understood as a model of moral behavior because it reveals to humanity how much God loves them.[410]

None of the traditional atonement theologies presents a soteriology that accords with that offered in the Fourth Gospel. Theologies of ransom or substitution are wholly absent from this Gospel's understanding of the cross. For example, as the discussion of John 10:1-21 pointed out (see Reflections there), Jesus is not a victim at his death, but is in complete control (see 12:27-28 also). Abelard's theology of Jesus' death on the cross as the demonstration of God's love captures part of the Fourth Gospel's soteriology, but as the discussion below will suggest, it overlooks the demand for human response and decision that is an essential part of Jesus' "glorification" in John.

In reflecting on the Johannine understanding of the death of Jesus, it is important to begin by remembering that theologies of atonement are in actuality theologies of reconciliation—that is, they attempt to explain how God and humanity were reconciled to one another in Jesus' death. There is a disheartening tendency in theological conversations in the contemporary North American church to subsume all models of reconciliation under the umbrella of "sacrifice."[411] Sacrifice is one way of understanding reconciliation, but not the only way. Jesus' sayings in John 12:23-36 suggest an alternative model of reconciliation, one that is built around the restoration of relationship.

The Commentary on 12:24 noted that Jesus' death is described as both necessary and life-giving because as a result of it community is formed ("much fruit"). The discipleship teachings in vv. 25-26, which in the synoptic traditions define discipleship exclusively as taking up one's cross, instead define discipleship as serving Jesus and make clear that the goal of such service is restored relationship with God and Jesus. The passion prediction in 12:32 also focuses on relationship, that through Jesus' death all people will be drawn to him. Finally, in the concluding teaching of vv. 35-36, community is described as "becoming children of light."

Throughout the Gospel, this new relationship to God and one's fellow human beings is described in the metaphors of new birth and new or eternal life (e.g., 3:3-8; 4:14; 5:24; 6:40, 47, 54; 10:28; 17:3). Jesus' glorification is the final step in the offer of this new life, because through Jesus' death, resurrection, and ascension God's relationship to the world itself is irrevocably changed. The world that lives in opposition to Jesus ("this world") is judged by Jesus' death, and its power overcome (vv. 25, 31). Jesus' death has this effect, not because it is a sacrifice that atones for human sin, but because it reveals the power and promise of God and God's love decisively to the world.

What is striking about John 12:23-36 is that the connection between Jesus' death and the life of the believing community is repeatedly stressed. The faith community consists of those who redefine the meaning of life on the basis of Jesus' death (vv. 24-26). The faith community is the fruit of Jesus' death; it is what shows forth Jesus' love to the world (see also 13:34-35). It is the transformative potential of Jesus' death for those who believe that leads to the repeated

---

408. The most influential statement of this view of the atonement for the contemporary church is Gustaf Aulen, *Christus Victor: An Historical Study of the Three Main Types of the Idea of the Atonement,* trans. A. G. Herbert (London: SPCK, 1953).

409. The most influential expressions of this theology of atonement are the works of Anselm and Calvin.

410. The original proponent of this understanding of the atonement was Abelard, but this theory achieved its popularity in liberal North American churches through the works of the Social Gospel theologians and others who looked to Jesus as a source of moral inspiration.

411. The resistance that feminist critiques of the substitutionary model of atonement receive in the church is a disturbing example of the hold that this model has on popular Christian imagination. Feminist suggestions of alternative models are labeled a distortion of the tradition, heretical, or worse. For one such suggestion, see Delores Williams, *Sisters in the Wilderness: The Challenge of Womanist God Talk* (Maryknoll, N.Y.: Orbis, 1993).

expressions of temporal urgency in 12:23-36. It is critical to believe in Jesus so that one can share in the gift of his life—the gift that leads to eternal life, to the confident assurance of God's and Jesus' abiding presence.

A strong note of tension and judgment is implicit in this urgency, because for Jesus' death to effect reconciliation with God one must make the decision to believe in Jesus. That is, Jesus' death offers reconciliation to all people, but one must decide to accept this offer. This element of tension is lacking in all of the dominant theologies of atonement, and, as a result, the balance between the human and the divine is skewed. That is, there is a tendency for discussions of atonement to favor either the side of divine initiative (ransom, sacrifice) or of human embrace of God's love (moral influence), but in the Fourth Gospel, the focus remains steadfastly on the inseparable interrelationship of the divine and human, an interrelationship that is most fully expressed in the incarnation.

At the heart of the Johannine understanding of the death of Jesus is the recognition that it is of a piece with the life of Jesus. Jesus' death is an expression of his relationship with God, which began "at the beginning." For the Fourth Gospel, then, a theology of reconciliation does not focus exclusively on the death of Jesus, but on the incarnation itself—the life, death, and resurrection of Jesus—and on the interrelationship of God and Jesus in love that the incarnation reveals.

The Fourth Gospel, then, makes two important contributions to the ongoing conversation about reconciliation. First, it suggests a way of understanding reconciliation that takes *relationship* as a serious theological category. Jesus' death is the ultimate expression of his relationship to God and to his own people (10:16-18). The decision to believe is the decision to become a partner in that relationship, to become a member of a community that is bound to God and Jesus as they are bound to each other, and whose relationship to one another is an extension of the God/Jesus relationship. Second, the Fourth Gospel insists on placing the incarnation as the starting point for any conversation about atonement and reconciliation and not isolating Jesus' death on the cross as the sole moment of reconciliation. Jesus' glorification, the events of his "hour," complete what began in the incarnation (cf. 12:28), but the incarnation itself is the locus of reconciliation.

JOHN 12:37-50, THE EPILOGUE TO JESUS' MINISTRY

NIV	NRSV
[37]Even after Jesus had done all these miraculous signs in their presence, they still would not believe in him. [38]This was to fulfill the word of Isaiah the prophet:	[37]Although he had performed so many signs in their presence, they did not believe in him. [38]This was to fulfill the word spoken by the prophet Isaiah:

"Lord, who has believed our message
  and to whom has the arm of the Lord been
    revealed?"[a]
	"Lord, who has believed our message,
	  and to whom has the arm of the Lord been
	    revealed?"

[39]For this reason they could not believe, because, as Isaiah says elsewhere:	[39]And so they could not believe, because Isaiah also said,

[40]"He has blinded their eyes
  and deadened their hearts,
so they can neither see with their eyes,
  nor understand with their hearts,
  nor turn—and I would heal them."[b]
	[40] "He has blinded their eyes
	  and hardened their heart,
	so that they might not look with their eyes,
	  and understand with their heart and
	    turn—
	  and I would heal them."

[a]38 Isaiah 53:1   [b]40 Isaiah 6:10

NIV

[41] Isaiah said this because he saw Jesus' glory and spoke about him.

[42] Yet at the same time many even among the leaders believed in him. But because of the Pharisees they would not confess their faith for fear they would be put out of the synagogue; [43] for they loved praise from men more than praise from God.

[44] Then Jesus cried out, "When a man believes in me, he does not believe in me only, but in the one who sent me. [45] When he looks at me, he sees the one who sent me. [46] I have come into the world as a light, so that no one who believes in me should stay in darkness.

[47] "As for the person who hears my words but does not keep them, I do not judge him. For I did not come to judge the world, but to save it. [48] There is a judge for the one who rejects me and does not accept my words; that very word which I spoke will condemn him at the last day. [49] For I did not speak of my own accord, but the Father who sent me commanded me what to say and how to say it. [50] I know that his command leads to eternal life. So whatever I say is just what the Father has told me to say."

NRSV

[41] Isaiah said this because[a] he saw his glory and spoke about him. [42] Nevertheless many, even of the authorities, believed in him. But because of the Pharisees they did not confess it, for fear that they would be put out of the synagogue; [43] for they loved human glory more than the glory that comes from God.

[44] Then Jesus cried aloud: "Whoever believes in me believes not in me but in him who sent me. [45] And whoever sees me sees him who sent me. [46] I have come as light into the world, so that everyone who believes in me should not remain in the darkness. [47] I do not judge anyone who hears my words and does not keep them, for I came not to judge the world, but to save the world. [48] The one who rejects me and does not receive my word has a judge; on the last day the word that I have spoken will serve as judge, [49] for I have not spoken on my own, but the Father who sent me has himself given me a commandment about what to say and what to speak. [50] And I know that his commandment is eternal life. What I speak, therefore, I speak just as the Father has told me."

[a] Other ancient witnesses read when

COMMENTARY

John 12:37-50 serves as the epilogue to Jesus' public ministry. It divides into two parts: (1) vv. 37-43, the Evangelist's commentary on Jesus' ministry, and (2) vv. 44-50, a summary discourse by Jesus.

12:37-43. The Evangelist struggles with the same dilemma that drives Paul in Romans 9–11: How does one account for the rejection of Jesus by his "own" (cf. 1:11)? This was a serious theological dilemma for Jews who understood Jesus to be the fulfillment of God's eschatological promises to Israel. The problem is stated quite succinctly in v. 37, and the Evangelist's explanation for the lack of faith is in two parts, vv. 38-41 and 42-43.

In vv. 38-41, the Fourth Evangelist mounts an argument from Scripture built around two quotations from Isaiah. Verse 38 is an exact quotation of the LXX of Isa 53:1 (cf. the use of the same

verse in Rom 10:16). In this context, it provides a useful summary of Jesus' ministry—"message" evokes Jesus' words, "the arm of the Lord," his works. The second Scripture quotation is Isa 6:10 (v. 40). This passage played an important role in early Christian attempts to explain lack of faith in Jesus, appearing in some version in all four Gospels and Acts (see Matt 13:14-15; Mark 4:12; Luke 8:10; Acts 28:26-27).

The introduction to Isa 6:10 in v. 39 makes clear that the crowd's inability to believe is not the result of the prophet's work, as is the case in Isa 6:9-13, but is part of God's plan for salvation history (cf. the use in Acts). The Evangelist eliminates any reference to hearing and ears from the quotation in v. 40, thereby placing the emphasis on seeing and knowing, two pivotal Johannine themes. The people's obduracy is thus in line with the Johannine definition of sin as spiritual blindness (9:39-41). That the Isa 6:10 quotation is to be understood as a prophecy of God's work in Jesus is made explicit by the concluding comment in v. 41. This verse alludes to the broader context of Isaiah 6, in which the prophet experiences a theophany (vv. 1-5). The link to the vision of Isaiah 6 is stated even more directly in textual variants of v. 41 that read "when" (ὅτε *hote*) instead of "because" (ὅτι *hoti*; see the NRSV footnote). The Fourth Evangelist interprets this theophany as a vision of God's glory, and hence as a vision of the glory of the Logos (cf. 1:14; 17:5; see also the reference to Abraham in 8:56-58).

It is significant that while the synoptic Gospels place the Isa 6:10 quote in Jesus' mouth, the Fourth Evangelist positions this explanation as the later reflection of the believing community.[412] In vv. 38-41, the Fourth Evangelist thus demonstrates the "remembering" he describes at 2:22 and 12:16.

The argument from Scripture in vv. 38-41 places its theological emphasis on the side of divine initiative and determination as an explanation for unbelief. That is, the rejection of Jesus and unbelief among God's people is part of God's plan for salvation history, not a sign of the failure or unreliability of God's promises. That the Fourth Evangelist is not arguing for simple predestination, however, is made clear by the explanation for unbelief offered in vv. 42-43. In those verses, the emphasis is on human choice. As at 6:37-40 (see Commentary), the Fourth Evangelist maintains the tension between divine initiative and human freedom.

Verses 42-43 offer an explanation for unbelief that acknowledges the sociopolitical realities of the conflict between Judaism and emerging Christianity. Nicodemus is one example of an "authority" who believes in Jesus but does not confess his faith (7:50; cf. 19:39-41), but the real intent of v. 42 is to point to the conflict with the Jewish religious establishment in the Evangelist's own day. As at 9:22 (see also 16:2), the two levels on which the Fourth Evangelist is writing are revealed; he describes the unbelief in Jesus' time in categories drawn from the experience of his readers.[413] Verse 43 explicitly identifies the fear of confessing one's

faith in Jesus as a human choice (cf. 5:44). The reference to the "glory that comes from God" links vv. 42-43 to the argument from Isaiah in vv. 38-41 and brings the contrast between faith and unbelief into even sharper relief.[414] Because of a fear of political power and loss of prestige ("human glory") and security ("be put out of the synagogue"), some choose against the experience of God revealed in Jesus. To love human glory is equivalent to loving one's life and so removes one from the promises that come as a result of Jesus' glorification (see 12:23-26).[415]

12:44-50. Like the discourse at 3:16-21, these verses are an independent discourse by Jesus that the Fourth Evangelist has intentionally positioned as the epilogue to Jesus' ministry and the prelude to his hour. These verses are not displaced from another discourse,[416] but instead stand on their own as an overview of the dominant themes of Jesus' ministry. These verses add no new teachings to the Gospel; rather, they read as a compendium of all that has preceded. They serve to present the reader with the theological issues necessary to make his or her own decision about Jesus (see Reflections).

The brief introduction to the discourse ("Jesus cried out," v. 44*a*) places weight on these words as a proclamation (cf. 1:15; 7:28, 37). Verses 44-45 and 49-50 provide a frame for the discourse and proclaim the central theological claim of Jesus' ministry: that Jesus makes God known (1:18; cf. 8:19), that faith in Jesus is ultimately faith in God. Jesus says or does nothing on his own, but speaks the words that God has given him to say (cf. 5:30; 6:38; 7:16-17; 8:28). In significant ways, these framing verses restate the claims of the Prologue: Jesus is one with God (1:1-2; cf. 5:19-24; 10:30, 38), the incarnate Logos of God (1:14; cf. 5:37-38; 10:36). They also point forward to Jesus' words in the Farewell Discourse (e.g., 14:7, 9-11, 20; 15:15). The center verses, vv. 46-48, restate the central soteriological claim of Jesus' ministry: Jesus has come as light into the world (cf. 1:4-5; 8:12; 9:5; 12:35-36) to save the world (cf. 3:16-17). They also restate the paradoxical nature of judgment in the Fourth Gospel:

412. Brown, *The Gospel According to John (I–XII)*, 485.
413. See J. Louis Martyn, *History and Theology in the Fourth Gospel* (Nashville: Abingdon, 1968; 2nd ed., 1979) 40-41.

414. Barrett, *The Gospel According to St. John*, 433.
415. See C. H. Dodd, *The Interpretation of the Fourth Gospel* (Cambridge: Cambridge University Press, 1953) 380.
416. So Bultmann, *The Gospel of John*, 313.

Jesus comes not to judge, but his presence will evoke judgment because of the response people make to his word (cf. 3:18; 5:24; 8:15, 26; 9:39). This soteriological claim, too, points forward to the Farewell Discourse (e.g., 14:23-24; 15:22-24). This concluding discourse thus succinctly states the heart of the Johannine gospel.

REFLECTIONS

In order to understand the narrative and theological function of this epilogue, it is helpful to envision this section along the analogy of the theater. With Jesus' exit at 12:36, the curtain has come down on his public ministry. In vv. 37-43, the Evangelist, "the playwright," reveals himself directly to the audience and comments on the dilemma with which the first "act" ends: Why do Jesus' own reject him? After he completes his speech, he, too, disappears behind the curtain, and the stage is completely empty and dark. The voice of Jesus is then heard (vv. 44-50), crying out to the darkened theater from the wings, his own voice providing the final commentary on the drama that has played itself out before the audience. When Jesus finishes speaking, the audience is once again alone in the darkness, with Jesus' offer of salvation ringing in their ears.

John 12:37-50 thus provides a poignant conclusion to the story of Jesus' public ministry, as this passage makes the drama of faith or unbelief the reader's own. By placing the final summation of the gospel of Jesus' public ministry in Jesus' mouth, the Fourth Evangelist positions Jesus as the final authority on the significance of his own ministry. By placing this summation in an independent discourse, free from any specific temporal or geographical location, the Fourth Evangelist creates a situation that speaks directly to the reader's own situation. That is, the Gospel reader does not hear Jesus' words as being directed first to Peter or to Martha, for example, but as spoken to the reader directly.

This epilogue also positions the reader to enter the story of Jesus' hour. The ultimacy of Jesus' ministry is laid bare both in the Evangelist's words of judgment and in Jesus' concluding proclamation. The reader is faced with a simple alternative: to believe in Jesus as the incarnate Word of God, or not to believe. The Fourth Evangelist allows no possibility of hedging this decision; to believe is life, to reject Jesus is to incur judgment. As the reader moves into the story of Jesus' glorification, of his death, resurrection, and ascension, the reader is inescapably aware of what is at stake in that story.

JOHN 13:1–17:26

THE FAREWELL MEAL AND DISCOURSE

OVERVIEW

John 13:1 marks a significant shift in the orientation of the Fourth Gospel's narrative. Prior to this verse, Jesus' hour has been anticipated (2:4; 7:30; 8:20) or acknowledged as imminent (12:23, 27), but 13:1 signals its arrival. The rest of the Gospel will narrate the unfolding of the events of Jesus' hour. The events narrated in John 13:1–17:26 are all situated at Jesus' final meal with his disciples before his arrest (18:1-12). These chapters consist of three large units: (1) 13:1-38, the foot washing and subsequent dialogues between Jesus and his disciples; (2) 14:1–16:33, Jesus' farewell discourse; and (3) 17:1-26, Jesus' prayer.

The chronology of the events of the last days of Jesus' life in John differs from that of the synoptic Gospels (see Fig. 11, "Chronology of the Holy Week and Resurrection Appearances in the Gospels," 704-5). Both John and Mark (followed by Matthew and Luke) agree that the trial and crucifixion took place on Thursday evening/Friday, but they disagree on the relationship of those events to the Passover celebration. In the Synoptics, the meal in the upper room is explicitly positioned as the meal on the first evening of Passover (Mark 14:12, 14, 16), whereas in John the final meal occurs "before the festival of Passover" (13:1). This means that in the synoptic Gospels, the crucifixion of Jesus takes place on the first full day of the Passover festival, whereas in John it occurs on the day before Passover, or the Day of Preparation (19:31, 42).

Both chronologies imbue the death of Jesus with symbolic significance vis-à-vis the Passover. In the synoptic chronology, the symbolism comes from presenting the institution of the eucharist as the Passover meal. In John, the symbolism comes from linking the crucifixion of Jesus with the slaughter of the Passover lambs (19:14, 36). The differences between these two chronologies are impossible to resolve cleanly, and it is not possible to recover the "correct" chronology, because the handling of tradition in both cases seems to show theological coloration. Scholars who favor the synoptic chronology tend to do so because they accept as normative the Synoptic portrait of the institution of the eucharist.[417] The Johannine chronology is equally plausible, however, and may resolve some of the tensions attendant upon the trial's taking place on a holy day.[418] As a point of comparison, the Pauline tradition does not specify whether the last supper was a Passover meal (1 Cor 11:23-26), but it does refer to the death of Jesus as the sacrifice of the paschal lamb (1 Cor 5:7).

417. E.g., Barrett, *The Gospel According to St. John,* 48-51.
418. Raymond E. Brown, *The Gospel According to John (XIII–XXI),* AB 29A (Garden City, N.Y.: Doubleday, 1966) 555-56.

JOHN 13:1-38, THE FAREWELL MEAL

OVERVIEW

The displacement of eucharist traditions to John 6 and John's eucharistic theology is discussed at length in the Commentary and Reflections on John 6:25-59 and need not be repeated here. The Fourth Evangelist has chosen to narrate the farewell meal in a way that highlights his understanding of the events of Jesus' hour as the full expression of Jesus' love.

On a surface reading, the constituent elements of John 13:1-38 are easy to identify: vv. 1-11, the foot washing; vv. 12-20, discourse by Jesus on service; vv. 21-30, Jesus prophecies his betrayal; vv. 31-38, the love commandment and prophecy of Peter's denial. The links between these units are explicitly signaled in the narrative (v. 12: "After he had washed their feet . . . he said to them"; v. 21: "After saying this Jesus was troubled in spirit and declared . . . "; v. 31: "When he had gone out, Jesus said . . . "). The Fourth Evangelist thus presents the four sections of 13:1-38 as interlocking pieces that depict the events at the farewell meal.

Such complex interrelationships among units in a lengthy text are not unusual in the Fourth Gospel (see, for example, the Commentary on John 6; 9–10; 11). The examples of John 6 and 9:1–10:21 provide the closest analogues in understanding the structure of John 13. Chapter 6 consists of a series of dialogues and brief discourses by Jesus that interpret an "event," the feeding of the five thousand. A similar series of dialogues is found in John 13. As noted in the Commentary on John 9:1–10:21, John 9:39-41 serves as both the conclusion to the dialogue with the Pharisees and the introduction to the discourse (10:1-18). John 13:31-38 has a similar double function; it concludes the dialogue scenes between Jesus and his disciples and introduces the discourse.

As the Commentary to follow will show, when John 13:1-38 is read as an interconnected series of passages, the interpreter is able to note the recurrence of certain themes throughout all four units. In particular, the theme of discipleship dominates these verses (e.g., vv. 8, 10, 14-17, 34-35), as does the tension between Jesus' gift of himself in love and the betrayal and rejection of that gift by those whom Jesus loves (e.g., vv. 11, 18-19, 21-30, 36-38).

John 13:1-11, The Foot Washing

NIV

13 It was just before the Passover Feast. Jesus knew that the time had come for him to leave this world and go to the Father. Having loved his own who were in the world, he now showed them the full extent of his love.[a]

[2]The evening meal was being served, and the devil had already prompted Judas Iscariot, son of Simon, to betray Jesus. [3]Jesus knew that the Father had put all things under his power, and that he had come from God and was returning to God; [4]so he got up from the meal, took off his outer clothing, and wrapped a towel around his waist. [5]After that, he poured water into a basin and began to wash his disciples' feet, drying them with the towel that was wrapped around him.

[6]He came to Simon Peter, who said to him, "Lord, are you going to wash my feet?"

[7]Jesus replied, "You do not realize now what I am doing, but later you will understand."

[8]"No," said Peter, "you shall never wash my feet."

Jesus answered, "Unless I wash you, you have no part with me."

a1 Or he loved them to the last

NRSV

13 Now before the festival of the Passover, Jesus knew that his hour had come to depart from this world and go to the Father. Having loved his own who were in the world, he loved them to the end. [2]The devil had already put it into the heart of Judas son of Simon Iscariot to betray him. And during supper [3]Jesus, knowing that the Father had given all things into his hands, and that he had come from God and was going to God, [4]got up from the table,[a] took off his outer robe, and tied a towel around himself. [5]Then he poured water into a basin and began to wash the disciples' feet and to wipe them with the towel that was tied around him. [6]He came to Simon Peter, who said to him, "Lord, are you going to wash my feet?" [7]Jesus answered, "You do not know now what I am doing, but later you will understand." [8]Peter said to him, "You will never wash my feet." Jesus answered, "Unless I wash you, you have no share with me." [9]Simon Peter said to him, "Lord, not my feet only but also my hands and my head!" [10]Jesus said to him, "One who has bathed does not need to wash, except

a Gk from supper

⁹"Then, Lord," Simon Peter replied, "not just my feet but my hands and my head as well!"

¹⁰Jesus answered, "A person who has had a bath needs only to wash his feet; his whole body is clean. And you are clean, though not every one of you." ¹¹For he knew who was going to betray him, and that was why he said not every one was clean.

for the feet,ᵃ but is entirely clean. And youᵇ are clean, though not all of you." ¹¹For he knew who was to betray him; for this reason he said, "Not all of you are clean."

ᵃ Other ancient authorities lack *except for the feet*   ᵇ The Greek word for *you* here is plural

COMMENTARY

13:1. This verse introduces Jesus' hour and hence the larger narrative of the events of Jesus' death, resurrection, and ascension (see Overview to 13:1–17:26), but it also introduces the specific events of the farewell meal. It establishes two frameworks for the events that are about to be narrated. The first is an external framework; the events of the farewell meal are located in the context of the Passover festival (see Fig. 9, "Jewish Religious Festivals in John," 542). This is the third Passover festival mentioned in John (see also 2:13, 23; 6:4), and the Fourth Gospel narrative has been signaling the approach of this final Passover since 12:1 (see also 12:9, 12, 20). The second framework could be called an "internal" framework, because the Fourth Evangelist enables the reader to view the events of the farewell meal from the perspective of Jesus' knowledge and love.

John 13:1 is one long sentence in Greek (although both the NIV and the NRSV punctuate it as two sentences), in which Jesus' knowledge of his hour and his love for his own are expressed in three participial clauses that introduce the one finite verb clause of the sentence, "He loved them to the end." Each of these three verb clauses deserves serious attention. The first clause (v. 1*b*: "Jesus, knowing that this hour had come . . . ") must be interpreted alongside the verses in the Prologue that describe Jesus' coming into the world and his relationship to God (e.g., 1:1-5, 10-14, 18). Jesus' hour marks the end of his ministry in "this world" and his return to the Father. The full significance of Jesus' return to God will be brought out in the discourse in 14:1–16:33. Jesus' knowledge of his relationship to God has been a theme throughout his ministry (e.g., 5:17, 19; 7, 28-29; 8:54-55; 10:38)

and 13:1*b* makes clear that the end of his life will be governed by the same knowledge (cf. 18:4; 19:28).

The second clause (v. 1*c*: "Having loved his own who were in the world . . . ") offers a description of Jesus' ministry to this point. Like v. 1*b*, it both recalls the Prologue (cf. 1:10-13) and anticipates the Farewell Discourse and prayer (cf. 15:9-17; 17:6-19). Jesus' own are those whom he knows and loves (cf. 10:14; 15:13); they are those "in the world" who have embraced God's gift of Jesus (cf. 3:16-17).

Jesus' knowledge of his hour and his continuing love for his own provide the backdrop for 13:1*d*. The Greek expression used to describe Jesus' love (εἰς τέλος *eis telos*) can be translated two different ways, as a comparison between the NRSV and the NIV shows. It can be translated as a temporal expression ("to the end," NRSV), or as referring to the quality of Jesus' love ("the full extent," NIV). The Fourth Evangelist probably intended both meanings to be heard here, because it was in loving his own "to the end" that the "full extent" of Jesus' love is revealed. The English translation "fully" or even the more literal "to completion" would thus more adequately capture the multivalence of the Greek. Jesus' love for his own will be demonstrated in the foot washing, but it will receive its full and final expression in his gift of his life (15:13).

13:2-5. Verses 2-3 introduce the foot washing, and vv. 4-5 narrate the foot washing proper. Again, although these verses are punctuated as three separate sentences in the NIV and the NRSV, they are one long, complex sentence in the Greek text (so the RSV). Verses 2-3 contain no finite verbs, and instead consist of a series of participial clauses that introduce the finite verbs of vv. 4-5 ("he got up . . . began to wash"). While the breaks in the English translations make for smoother syntax, unfortunately they also serve to play down the interrelationship and interdependence of the introduction to the foot washing and the act itself.

13:2. The evening meal that is already in progress and the devil's decision about Judas's betrayal of Jesus both provide the context for the statement about Jesus' knowledge in v. 3 and the foot washing in vv. 4-5. This combination is important, for it signals a tension between fellowship and betrayal that will recur throughout 13:1-38. The reference to the devil and Judas in v. 2 is more ambiguous than the English translations suggest. It is not clear from the Greek whether the devil has put it into his own heart that Judas will betray Jesus or into Judas's heart. Although the reference to Satan and Judas in v. 27 would support the first reading, the significance of the comment is the same regardless of the reading: The events of the last supper are enacted against the backdrop of a cosmic struggle between the powers of good and evil that will be manifested in Judas's betrayal of Jesus (cf. 12:31; 14:30).

13:3. The narrator once again takes the reader inside the mind of Jesus (cf. v. 1). This interior perspective provides an interesting juxtaposition with v. 2, which took the reader inside the "mind" of the devil. Jesus' knowledge in v. 3 expresses the essence of his ministry: that everything he has is given to him *by God* and that his home from whence he comes and to which he returns is *with God*. These two theological realities have formed the center of Jesus' words and works throughout the Gospel (see, e.g., 3:13; 6:37-38; 8:23; 10:29) and will form the center of Jesus' words and works at the farewell meal and in his death and resurrection (see, e.g., 14:2, 28; 16:28; 17:2, 4-5, 24).

13:4-5. The description of the foot washing is given in almost exaggerated detail; each action is narrated in something approaching "real" time. That is, the space given to narrating Jesus' preparation for and initiation of the foot washing is

equivalent to the time that would elapse in the enactment of the events themselves. The details are intended to draw the reader's attention to the absurdity of the event, an absurdity that will be reinforced by Peter's comments in vv. 6-8.[419] Yet the details also provide important clues to the theological significance of the foot washing for the Fourth Evangelist. First, the verb used to describe Jesus' "removal" (τίθημι *tithēmi*) of his clothes in v. 4 is the same verb used by Jesus to describe laying down his life (10:15, 17-18; cf. 10:11; 13:37-38; 15:13). The Fourth Evangelist's verb choice thus signals the connection between the foot washing and Jesus' gift of his life.[420] Second, the description of Jesus' "wiping" (ἐκμάσσειν *ekmassein*) the disciples' feet with the towel (v. 5) links the foot washing with the anointing (see Commentary on 12:1-8).

Foot washing was practiced in both Jewish and Greco-Roman contexts in the ancient Mediterranean world. It had three main functions: (1) personal hygiene; (2) an act of hospitality; or (3) a cultic act.[421] Since the foot washing in John 13 occurs in the context of a meal, the practice of foot washing as hospitality provides the most helpful analogue in interpreting the Johannine text. Foot washing was a way of welcoming one's guests; a person's feet would become dusty during the journey, and the host offered water so that guests could wash their feet (e.g., Gen 18:4; 19:2; 43:24; Luke 7:44; *Joseph and Asenath* 7.1; *Odyssey* 19.308-319).[422] The foot washing was normally performed by the guests themselves, or by servants at the behest of the host, so that foot washing as service is closely linked with foot washing as hospitality. The combination of service and hospitality is particularly strong in Abigail's words to David in 1 Sam 25:41.

When Jesus washes his disciples' feet, then, he combines the roles of servant and host. When Jesus wraps himself with the towel, he assumes

419. Rudolf Bultmann, *The Gospel of John: A Commentary,* trans. G. R. Beasley-Murray, R. W. N. Hoare, and J. K. Riches (Philadelphia: Westminster, 1971) 466.

420. Barrett, *The Gospel According to St. John,* 439.

421. See Arland J. Hultgren, "The Johannine Footwashing (13:1-11) as Symbol of Eschatological Hospitality," *NTS* 28 (1982) 541-42; and John Christopher Thomas, *Footwashing in John 13 and the Johannine Community,* JSNTSup 61 (Sheffield: Sheffield Academic Press, 1991) 26-58.

422. For more examples, see Hultgren, "The Johannine Footwashing," and Thomas, *Footwashing in John 13 and the Johannine Community.*

the garb and position of the servant,[423] but the act of hospitality that he offers is the prerogative of the host. This odd combination of roles prompts Peter's protest in v. 6. Moreover, foot washing normally occurred before food was served (e.g., Gen 24:32-33; Judg 19:21), not in the middle of the meal.

13:6-10. The dialogue between Jesus and Peter clarifies the nature of Jesus' striking gesture of hospitality.

13:6-8a. One can infer from v. 6 neither that Jesus washed Peter's feet first (so Augustine) nor that he came to Peter last (so Origen). Rather, as is common across the Gospels, Peter speaks as the representative disciple.[424] Jesus' response to Peter in v. 7 points to a time when Jesus' gesture will be comprehensible to him. The future to which Jesus alludes is the time after his return to the Father (cf. vv. 1 and 3). Jesus' words here anticipate his use of a similar expression in the Farewell Discourse (cf. 14:29; 16:4, 25-28) to remind his disciples that what he teaches them will become comprehensible to them only after his "hour." As at 2:22 and 12:16, the Holy Spirit will lead the disciples to understanding in the future (14:25-26). The NIV captures the emphatic denial in Peter's words in v. 8a; Jesus' words in v. 7 notwithstanding, Peter will not allow Jesus to assume the role of a servant (cf. Peter's response to Jesus at Mark 8:31-33).

13:8b. Jesus' response holds the key to understanding the foot washing. Jesus' washing of Peter's feet is stipulated as a necessary condition for Peter's "share" (μέρος *meros*) with Jesus. To have a share with Jesus is to have fellowship with him,[425] to participate fully in his life. The foot washing is "a symbolic act of eschatological hospitality,"[426] through which Jesus shares his home—that is, the Father's home (cf. 1:1; 14:2)—with his disciples. The foot washing is an *eschatological* act because through it Jesus manifests the unity and intimacy of God, Jesus, and the believer that marks full relationship with God (e.g., 15:1-10). It draws the disciple into the love that marks God's and Jesus' relationship to each other and to the world (3:16, 35; 14:23, 31;

17:23-24, 26). Through the foot washing, Jesus unites the believer with him as he enters the events of his hour (cf. 13:1, 3).[427] If one removes oneself from this act, then one removes oneself from Jesus and the promises of God. To have Jesus wash one's feet is to receive from Jesus an act of hospitality that decisively alters one's relationship to Jesus and, through Jesus, to God.

One's share with Jesus, then, is the gift of full relationship with him, which he offers in the foot washing, a relationship that opens the believer to Jesus' eschatological gift of eternal life (see Reflections below). The salvific dimension of the foot washing, therefore, is lodged in the relationship with Jesus that it offers, not in the foot washing as an act of ritual purification (see Commentary on 13:10) nor as representative of the disciples' "cleansing in the sacrificial blood of Christ."[428]

13:9. Peter's insistence that Jesus wash more than his feet is uttered as emphatically as his earlier refusal to allow Jesus to wash him at all (v. 8a). The hyperbole of the rhetoric in both instances draws attention to Peter's continuing misunderstanding of the foot washing. The request that his head and hands be washed suggests that Peter locates the value of the foot washing in the cleansing power of the water and not in Jesus' offer of relationship.

13:10. That Jesus rejects Peter's interpretation of the foot washing is clear (v. 10); what is not clear is the precise meaning of his words. The interpretation of Jesus' words is complicated by the uncertainty of the wording of v. 10a. Two versions of this verse are found in the manuscript tradition: a longer version (printed in the NIV and NRSV texts) and a shorter version that lacks the phrase "except for the feet" (NRSV variant).[429] The longer version seems to say that the washing of one's feet is a secondary or extra activity, done only to supplement one's bath. This reading of the foot washing is clearly at odds with Jesus' words in v. 8 and probably entered the textual tradition under the influence of those interpreters in the early church who misinterpreted the foot washing in John as symbolic of Christian

423. George R. Beasley-Murray, *John*, WBC 36 (Waco, Tex.: Word, 1987) 233.
424. Bultmann, *The Gospel of John*, 466.
425. Ibid., 468.
426. Hultgren, "The Johannine Footwashing," 542.

427. Bultmann, *The Gospel of John*, 468.
428. C. K. Barrett, *The Gospel According to St. John*, 2nd ed. (Philadelphia: Westminster, 1978) 436.
429. For example, the shorter version is accepted by Origen, Tertullian, and Tatian.

baptism.[430] In this view, the overall bath to which Jesus refers in v. 10a is baptism, and the foot washing refers to additional acts of penance for sins after baptism. Even though modern translations employ the longer version of the verse, modern scholars are close to unanimity in their view that the shorter reading should be accepted as authentic.[431]

Even when the shorter reading of v. 10a is followed, Jesus' words in this verse remain difficult to interpret. First, what is the relationship between the verbs "to bathe" (λούω louō) and "to wash" (νίπτω niptō)? Jesus seems to be underscoring a contrast for Peter that challenges his misunderstanding of the foot washing. Since the verb louō is frequently associated with ritual bathing,[432] Jesus may be challenging Peter's assumption about the purifying effects of the water itself. The foot washing is not about water per se; it is about entering into relationship with Jesus by receiving his gesture of hospitality. Peter does not need a ritual bath; he needs to have his feet washed by Jesus. Inattention to the distinction between bathing and washing in this verse may also have contributed to the addition of the words "except for the feet."

Second, what does Jesus mean by "clean" (καθαροί katharoi, v. 10b)? The announcement of cleanliness is made in the second-person plural, so that it includes all who are present at the foot washing, not just Peter. This announcement anticipates Jesus' words in the Farewell Discourse, "You are already cleansed [katharoi] by the word that I have spoken to you" (15:3). When 13:10 and 15:3 are read together, it becomes clear that the cleanliness of which Jesus speaks is accomplished by one's reception of Jesus' word, not by the ritual cleansing Peter envisions and requests. In 13:10, Jesus' "own" are clean through their reception of his enacted word, in 15:3, through their reception of his spoken word.[433] Verse 10 thus supplements Jesus' words in v. 8, focusing attention on the participatory and relational dimensions of the foot washing.

13:11. The Evangelist inserts his commentary in v. 11 to ensure that the Gospel readers recognize Jesus' disclaimer at the end of v. 10b as an allusion to the betrayal. The fact that the one who is not clean is the one who will betray Jesus confirms that cleanliness has to do with one's relationship to Jesus and acceptance of the foot washing, not with the cleansing power of the water itself. To be unclean is not to be unwashed, for Judas belongs to the circle of those whose feet Jesus washed. Rather, to be unclean is to turn away from union and intimacy with Jesus. As at the earlier prediction of the betrayal (6:70-71), the mention of Judas's betrayal reminds the reader that even election as one of Jesus' "own" (13:3), one whom he loves completely, is no guarantee of a faith response.[434] In order to have one's share with Jesus (v. 8), one must choose to accept the gesture of love that Jesus makes in the foot washing. The introduction (v. 2) and conclusion (v. 11) to the narrative of the foot washing together place Jesus' act of hospitality, service, and love in the inescapable context of his betrayal. (See Reflections at 13:12-20.)

---

430. To read the foot washing as a type of baptism is to misread the foot washing by overemphasizing the role of water in this text. See, e.g., Oscar Cullmann, *Early Christian Worship* (London: SCM, 1953). The salvific dimension of the foot washing comes not from the water, but from Jesus' assuming the role of one who washes feet. Even when the rite of foot washing was included in early church baptisms, there was disagreement among the church fathers as to the relative status of foot washing. See E. C. Hoskyns, *The Fourth Gospel* (London: Faber & Faber, 1947) 443-46. For a review of scholarship on baptism and foot washing, see Raymond E. Brown, *The Gospel According to John (XIII–XXI)*, AB 29A (Garden City, N.Y.: Doubleday, 1966) 556-68; and Beasley-Murray, *John*, 234-35.

431. Hoskyns, *The Fourth Gospel*, 438-39; Bultmann, *The Gospel of John*, 469-71; Barrett, *The Gospel According to St. John*, 441-42; Rudolf Schnackenburg, *The Gospel According to St. John*, 3 vols. (New York: Seabury, 1982) 3:20-22; Brown, *The Gospel According to John (XIII–XXI)*, 566-68; Beasley-Murray, *John*, 229.

432. See BAGD, 480, 2b for examples.

433. Bultmann, *The Gospel of John*, 470-71; Beasley-Murray, *John*, 234.

434. Bultmann, *The Gospel of John*, 473.

John 13:12-20, Discourse by Jesus on Communal Service

NIV

12When he had finished washing their feet, he put on his clothes and returned to his place. "Do you understand what I have done for you?" he asked them. 13"You call me 'Teacher' and 'Lord,' and rightly so, for that is what I am. 14Now that I, your Lord and Teacher, have washed your feet, you also should wash one another's feet. 15I have set you an example that you should do as I have done for you. 16I tell you the truth, no servant is greater than his master, nor is a messenger greater than the one who sent him. 17Now that you know these things, you will be blessed if you do them.

18"I am not referring to all of you; I know those I have chosen. But this is to fulfill the scripture: 'He who shares my bread has lifted up his heel against me.'ᵃ

19"I am telling you now before it happens, so that when it does happen you will believe that I am He. 20I tell you the truth, whoever accepts anyone I send accepts me; and whoever accepts me accepts the one who sent me."

ᵃ18 Psalm 41:9

NRSV

12After he had washed their feet, had put on his robe, and had returned to the table, he said to them, "Do you know what I have done to you? 13You call me Teacher and Lord—and you are right, for that is what I am. 14So if I, your Lord and Teacher, have washed your feet, you also ought to wash one another's feet. 15For I have set you an example, that you also should do as I have done to you. 16Very truly, I tell you, servantsᵃ are not greater than their master, nor are messengers greater than the one who sent them. 17If you know these things, you are blessed if you do them. 18I am not speaking of all of you; I know whom I have chosen. But it is to fulfill the scripture, 'The one who ate my breadᵇ has lifted his heel against me.' 19I tell you this now, before it occurs, so that when it does occur, you may believe that I am he.ᶜ 20Very truly, I tell you, whoever receives one whom I send receives me; and whoever receives me receives him who sent me."

ᵃ Gk slaves ᵇOther ancient authorities read ate bread with me
ᶜ Gk I am

COMMENTARY

John 13:12-20 is a discourse spoken by Jesus after the foot washing (v. 12a). It is conventional to identify these verses as the "interpretation" of the foot washing,[435] but scholars are divided over the relationship of this "interpretation" to the foot washing narrative. The division arises because the discourse seems to move in a different direction from vv. 1-11. In vv. 12-20 Jesus speaks of the foot washing as an act the disciples are to imitate (cf. vv. 14-15), whereas in vv. 1-11 he speaks of the foot washing as an act that they are to receive (v. 8). Some scholars conclude that the interpretation in vv. 12-20 is a secondary, "moralizing" addition to the primary foot washing narrative of vv. 1-11.[436]

If one approaches the relationship of vv. 1-11 and vv. 12-20 from the perspective of the broader relationship of the four scenes of John 13 (see Overview), however, one gets a different picture. The Fourth Evangelist follows the foot washing (vv. 1-11) with three scenes between Jesus and his disciples (vv. 12-20, 21-30, 31-38), not one scene. These three scenes together focus on the community that is created when Jesus washes his disciples' feet.[437] The entire supper sequence places positive and negative images of relationship with Jesus before the reader and so sets the stage for the discourse of 14:1–16:33.

13:12-15. Jesus teaches about the foot washing and its implications for the life of the believing community. His introductory question in v. 12 is a rhetorical device, intended to draw the disciples'

435. E.g., Brown, *The Gospel According to John (XIII–XXI),* 569; Barrett, *The Gospel According to St. John,* 443.

436. E.g., Brown, *The Gospel According to John (XIII–XXI),* 562.

437. Cf. Bultmann, *The Gospel of John,* 478-79.

attention to the central paradox of the foot washing: that he, their master (lord) and teacher, assumed the role of the servant (vv. 13-14a; cf. Luke 22:27). The one in the position of teacher and lord could expect service from his followers, and the foot washing reverses this pattern. In vv. 14-15, Jesus issues two imperatives for the disciples. The imperative in v. 14 refers explicitly to the foot washing and is developed as a logical argument from the greater to the lesser; what is true for the teacher and lord must also be true for the disciples. The inclusion of foot washing among the list of a widow's "good works" in 1 Tim 5:10 suggests that this imperative was followed by some early Christian communities. Verse 15 reframes the imperative in the more general language of "example," a reframing that anticipates the love commandment of 13:34-35.

13:16-20. The focus shifts to more general teachings on discipleship and relationship to Jesus. These verses are framed by two "very truly" (ἀμὴν ἀμήν amēn, amēn) sayings (vv. 16, 20). At the center of these verses is Jesus' prediction of his betrayal by a member of his intimate circle (vv. 18-19).

The saying in v. 16 reinforces the imperatives of vv. 14-15 by reminding the disciples of the relative roles of servant and master. A similar teaching is also found in the synoptic tradition (Matt 10:24-25; Luke 6:40). The teaching is located in quite distinct contexts in each of its three Gospel occurrences, and that, coupled with the variations among the three versions of the saying, suggests that this saying circulated orally in variant forms.[438] The precise meaning of Jesus' words in v. 17 is unclear. "These things" may refer to his double imperative in vv. 14-15. If that is the case, the disciples will be blessed if they follow the example of Jesus in love and service.

Jesus' teaching on the foot washing includes another prediction of the betrayal (v. 18; cf. vv. 10b-11). In both instances, Jesus' knowledge of his betrayer is stressed (vv. 11, 18a). This emphasis serves two purposes. First, Jesus' knowledge

confronts the reader with the painful truth about the betrayal. Jesus is not betrayed by a stranger, but by someone whom he has chosen (cf. 6:70), to whom he has offered himself fully in love. Verses 12 and 14 pointed to those listening to Jesus as the recipients of his paradoxical service ("what I have done to you"; "I, your Lord and Teacher, have washed your feet"), yet one of them will reject that service. The quotation of Ps 41:9 in v. 18b underscores the intimacy of the betrayal; Jesus' betrayer is one who has broken bread with him.[439]

Second, Jesus' knowledge of his betrayer reveals that Jesus is in control of the events leading up to his death, that no one is taking his life from him (cf. 10:17-18). Jesus prepares his disciples in advance for what is coming (v. 19; cf. 14:29; 16:1, 4-5) so that when the events of his hour unfold, "you may believe that I am." Jesus' use of an absolute ἐγώ εἰμι (egō eimi, v. 19; the NRSV and NIV wrongly supply a predicate nominative, "he") announces his claim of oneness with God (cf. 6:20; 8:24). Jesus wants his disciples to recognize that in his betrayal, death, and resurrection the fullness of his identity will be revealed (see also 8:28).

Verse 20 focuses on the mutuality of relationships among Jesus, God, and those whom Jesus sends. This verse, like 13:16, resembles a teaching of Jesus found in Matthew (10:40). The meaning of the two verses is similar, although the vocabulary is quite distinct (e.g., Matthew and John use different verbs for "to receive"). The relationship of the two texts thus seems best explained by access to variant forms of the saying in the oral tradition rather than by any literary dependence. What God has done for Jesus (sent him into the world, 3:17, 23; 6:38), Jesus now does for the disciples (cf. 17:18). The disciples share fully in Jesus' work, which means that they share fully in God's work (cf. 4:34; 5:17). For the disciples to do what Jesus has done, then, is a way to make visible the unity and intimacy with God and Jesus that their participation in the foot washing symbolized.

---

438. See C. H. Dodd, *Historical Tradition in the Fourth Gospel* (Cambridge: Cambridge University Press, 1963) 335-38; Brown, *The Gospel According to John (XIII–XXI)*, 569-70.

439. Bultmann, *The Gospel of John*, 478.

REFLECTIONS

The foot washing, like all of Jesus' works in John, needs to be understood as an act of self-revelation. The extended introduction (vv. 1-3) opens the revelatory dimension of the foot washing to the reader. Like the introductions that precede the healing of the blind man in John 9 and the raising of Lazarus in John 11, these opening verses show the reader what to look for in the story that follows. In John 13:1-3, the reader is cued to look for a revelation of Jesus' relationship with God (vv. 1a and 3) and his love for his "own" (v. 1b). Indeed, when Jesus washes his disciples' feet, thereby welcoming them into his "home" with God, Jesus' union with God and his "own" is revealed.

Just as the miracle at the Cana wedding (2:1-11) initiated Jesus' ministry with a parabolic act that revealed Jesus' glory, so also the foot washing initiates Jesus' hour with a parabolic act that reveals Jesus' love. Both are christological signs pointing beyond the particular event to the truth of Jesus' identity. The Cana miracle revealed the abundance of life and gifts that Jesus has to offer (see Commentary and Reflections on John 2:1-11); the foot washing reveals the promise of full relationship with God and Jesus that is offered to those whom Jesus loves. By washing his disciples' feet, Jesus enters into an intimate relationship with the disciples that mirrors the intimacy of his relationship with God. It is an intimacy that discomfits Peter, because it overturns all his conventional assumptions of roles and propriety (vv. 6, 8). Yet it is only by accepting Jesus in the surprising role of loving host *and* intimate servant that one has a "share" with him, that one receives the love of God incarnate.

As noted in the commentary, the salvific offer of the foot washing is found in the intimacy of union with Jesus that it makes available. The essence of the foot washing is Jesus' offer of himself in love; the transformative power of the foot washing is in the gracious and hospitable service of Jesus. God's love for the world in sending Jesus (3:16) is here enacted in Jesus' love for his own. The interrelationship of God, Jesus, and the believer will be the subject of the discourse of 14:1–16:33, but it is enacted in the foot washing narrative first. The foot washing reveals Jesus' unfettered love for the disciples, and it is this love that holds the promise of new life for the disciples. The call for the disciples is to allow themselves to be ministered to in this way, to accept Jesus' gesture of love fully.

In 13:1-11, Jesus asks nothing of the disciples other than that they place themselves completely in his hands (cf. 13:3), that they discard their images of who he is and how one comes to God and give themselves to his ministrations. He asks that they enter into relationship with him on his terms, that they allow their relationship with him to be defined by God's love and God's love alone. They are to allow Jesus to lead them in love, much like the image of the good shepherd in John 10. The foot washing removes the possibility of distance between Jesus and his followers, and brings them face to face with the love of God for them. Peter's initial responses (vv. 6, 8) and the mention of Judas's betrayal (vv. 2, 11) make clear that accepting this gesture of love and hospitality is indeed a challenge for those who follow Jesus.

There is a tendency in contemporary church appropriation of the foot washing narrative to begin and end one's interpretation of this text with vv. 12-15. That is, in most conversations about this text within the church, the foot washing is held up as an example of humble service that those who follow Jesus are called to imitate. While there is no question that John 13:12-15 does present the foot washing as a model for communal service, those verses are one piece of a much larger picture.

The call to service in this text cannot be separated from the call to participation with Jesus in vv. 1-11. One can follow Jesus' example (v. 15) only if one has already experienced Jesus' loving service for oneself. The call of vv. 12-15 is to embody the love and service of Jesus for one another. In the community's embodiment and enactment of Jesus' love, the community reveals Jesus' identity to the world. It is critical that this christological dimension be understood as definitional for the foot washing. Jesus does not simply issue a general call for service; he issues a call to give as he gives, to love as he loves.

Bultmann has articulated more clearly and powerfully than any other commentator the relationship between Jesus' act of love and the call to communal service. In commenting on the relationship between vv. 1-11 and vv. 12-20 he writes:

> The explicit theme of the first section is the fellowship with Jesus; this is shown to be grounded in an event that contradicts the natural reason, namely in the service rendered by Jesus, the binding power of which will prove itself . . . if [the disciple] is prepared to base his life on this event and on it alone. The second section adds that this fellowship of the disciples with Jesus at the same time opens up a fellowship amongst themselves, and that for the former to exist, the latter must be made a reality through the disciples' action.[440]

When the faith community embodies Jesus' love, it not only reveals his identity, but it also assumes a new identity for itself, shaped by Jesus' identity. The references to the betrayal that are woven into the foot washing narrative sound a cautionary note about this new identity. Jesus' act toward us in love presents the community with a choice: One can embrace Jesus' gift to us and embody one's embrace of that gift through one's own acts of love, or one can turn one's back on Jesus' gift of love. We can enter into community with Jesus and with one another, or we can reject that community.

440. Ibid., 478-79.

John 13:21-30, Jesus Prophesies His Betrayal

21After he had said this, Jesus was troubled in spirit and testified, "I tell you the truth, one of you is going to betray me."

22His disciples stared at one another, at a loss to know which of them he meant. 23One of them, the disciple whom Jesus loved, was reclining next to him. 24Simon Peter motioned to this disciple and said, "Ask him which one he means."

25Leaning back against Jesus, he asked him, "Lord, who is it?"

26Jesus answered, "It is the one to whom I will give this piece of bread when I have dipped it in the dish." Then, dipping the piece of bread, he gave it to Judas Iscariot, son of Simon. 27As soon as Judas took the bread, Satan entered into him.

"What you are about to do, do quickly," Jesus told him, 28but no one at the meal understood why Jesus said this to him. 29Since Judas had charge of the money, some thought Jesus was telling him to buy what was needed for the Feast, or to give something to the poor. 30As soon as Judas had taken the bread, he went out. And it was night.

21After saying this Jesus was troubled in spirit, and declared, "Very truly, I tell you, one of you will betray me." 22The disciples looked at one another, uncertain of whom he was speaking. 23One of his disciples—the one whom Jesus loved—was reclining next to him; 24Simon Peter therefore motioned to him to ask Jesus of whom he was speaking. 25So while reclining next to Jesus, he asked him, "Lord, who is it?" 26Jesus answered, "It is the one to whom I give this piece of bread when I have dipped it in the dish."[a] So when he had dipped the piece of bread, he gave it to Judas son of Simon Iscariot.[b] 27After he received the piece of bread,[c] Satan entered into him. Jesus said to him, "Do quickly what you are going to do." 28Now no one at the table knew why he said this to him. 29Some thought that, because Judas had the common purse, Jesus was telling him, "Buy what we need for the festival"; or, that he should give something to the poor. 30So, after receiving the piece of bread, he immediately went out. And it was night.

[a] Gk dipped it   [b] Other ancient authorities read Judas Iscariot son of Simon; others, Judas son of Simon from Karyot (Kerioth)   [c] Gk After the piece of bread

COMMENTARY

John 13:21-30 is explicitly tied to the preceding scene with the words, "After saying this . . . " (v. 21). The reader is thus intended to read this narrative of betrayal in the context of the foot washing and Jesus' teaching about community. The intimacy of the setting at the supper continues in this scene and, indeed, is reinforced by many of the details of these verses (e.g., vv. 23-26).

13:21. Verse 21 is the first explicit announcement of the betrayal in the supper scene (cf. the narrator's statement in v. 2, and Jesus' allusions in vv. 10, 18-19). The notation that "Jesus was troubled in spirit" (v. 21a) once again takes the reader "inside" Jesus (cf. 13:1, 3). The verb for "troubled" (ταράσσω *tarassō*) normally refers to anger or indignation (cf. 11:33), and that seems to be the emotional state described here. The narrator may preface the betrayal prediction with a mention of Jesus' anger in order to underscore the disparity between Jesus' offer of himself in love in the foot washing and the rejection of that offer by one of his own. The gravity of Jesus' announcement is signaled in two ways to the reader: the use of the verb "to testify" (μαρτυρέω *martyreō*) to introduce Jesus' remarks and the "very truly, I tell you" with which Jesus' words in v. 21 begin. Both mark these words as a solemn and prophetic announcement of the betrayal.

13:22. The reference to the disciples' uncertainty (v. 22) renders the scene from the perspective of those who are gathered around Jesus. This verse functions as an important reminder that even though the significance of the prediction of the betrayal is apparent to Jesus and to the Gospel readers (cf. 6:64, 71; 12:4; 13:2, 11), it is not yet comprehensible to the disciples (cf. vv. 28-29). Jesus' announcement, coupled with the disciples' response, is recounted at the last supper scene in all four Gospels (see Matt 26:21-25; Mark 14:18-21; Luke 22:21-23). All four seem to preserve a similar core tradition, but, with the exception of Matthew and Mark, do not seem to depend on one another.[441] The Fourth Evangelist nowhere

says how many of Jesus' disciples were present at this supper gathering. Scholars who assume that those present at this meal were the Twelve impose the Synoptic understanding of discipleship on the Johannine narrative.[442]

13:23-25. The questioning of Jesus by his disciples (vv. 23-25) is narrated with much more detail in John than in the other Gospels. These verses introduce a new character into the Fourth Gospel narrative, "the disciple whom Jesus loved." This disciple was not mentioned in the narrative of Jesus' ministry, but he will play a prominent role in the narrative of Jesus' hour (19:26-27; 20:2-10; see also 21:7, 20-23). This disciple is never named, but is always identified solely in terms of Jesus' love for him. The disciple may have been recognizable to the first readers, and John 19:35 and 21:24 suggest that it is this disciple to whom the community points as the guarantor of its witness to Jesus (see Introduction). Nonetheless, the anonymity of this disciple suggests that the Fourth Evangelist understands the significance of this disciple to rest in his relationship to Jesus, not in his own identity.

The opening description of the beloved disciple in v. 23 draws particular attention to his relationship with Jesus. He is described as "reclining in the bosom of Jesus" (v. 23, author's trans.) This description of the beloved disciple's relationship to Jesus mirrors exactly the description of Jesus' relationship to God in 1:18. "As Jesus is in the bosom of the Father, so the Beloved Disciple lies in the bosom of the Son; thus the concrete position of the disciple marks the verity that the true disciples are in Jesus as Jesus is in the Father."[443] The position of the beloved disciple at the supper thus anticipates Jesus' teachings about discipleship in the Farewell Discourse (e.g., 14:20; 15:4-5).

The beloved disciple is paired with Simon Peter in this scene, as he is frequently in the narrative of Jesus' hour.[444] This pairing probably points to the prominence of both disciples for the Johannine community (see Commentary on John 20:2-10). The description of the disciples reclining at the

---

441. Brown, *The Gospel According to John (XIII–XXI)*, 577; Bultmann, *The Gospel of John*, 478; Dodd, *Historical Tradition in the Fourth Gospel*, 52-54.

442. So Barrett, *The Gospel According to St. John*, 445.
443. E. C. Hoskyns, *The Fourth Gospel* (London: Faber & Faber, 1947) 443.
444. The only exception is 19:26-27.

meal suggests that the diners sat on cushions or couches on the floor, not at the table. One would recline on one's left side, leaving the right hand free for eating. In v. 25, the beloved disciple is described as leaning back into Jesus to ask his question, which would suggest that he was sitting at Jesus' right side. Although scholars have tried to recreate the seating arrangement of the rest of the disciples from these verses,[445] the text provides no data to support those constructions. One can tell nothing from v. 24 about where Peter or Judas was seated. The NIV incorrectly translates v. 24 as if Peter asks the beloved disciple a question; the Greek text says only that Peter "nodded" to him (νεύω *neuō*) and through that motion indicated that the beloved disciple should inquire of Jesus.

13:26. In Matt 26:22 and Mark 14:19, each of the disciples in turn asks Jesus whether he is the betrayer (in Luke 22:23, the disciples ask one another, but not Jesus). In John, the beloved disciple is given the prominent role of the lone questioner. Jesus' answer in v. 26, like his words at 13:18, underscores the contrast between the intimacy of the meal and the presence of the betrayer. Jesus' words and actions in v. 26 reinforce that the betrayer is one of Jesus' intimates; he is one to whom Jesus offers food as a gesture of friendship and hospitality, even though Jesus knows that Judas is the one who will betray him.[446]

13:27. Like v. 2, v. 27 reminds the reader of the cosmic dimensions of the betrayal. The description of Satan's entering Judas suggests that Judas's defection from the community of love and friendship that surrounds Jesus is a result of demonic possession. That is, the critical players in the betrayal are Jesus and the devil, not Jesus and Judas.[447] The Gospel of John, unlike the Synoptics, has narrated no stories of exorcisms in Jesus' ministry. The battle with demonic forces and evil is saved until the consummate battle of Jesus' own hour. Importantly, even in this consummate bat-

tle, Satan's work is framed by Jesus' initiative: Jesus offers the food to Judas and instructs him to proceed quickly.

13:28-29. These verses remind the reader that the other disciples remain outsiders to the full scope of the cosmic dimensions of the betrayal. The disciples' ignorance of what transpires between Jesus and Judas is not a narrative "weakness," included as a way of "exonerating the Eleven for complicity in Judas' sin."[448] Rather, by highlighting the disciples' ignorance (note the use of the verb "know" [γινώσκω *ginōskō*] in v. 28), Jesus' singular knowledge of the events of his hour is again underscored (cf. 13:1, 3). Indeed, the suppositions that the disciples reach about Jesus' words to Judas are plausible at the surface level (cf. 12:6) and continue the Johannine theme of misunderstanding into Jesus' hour. Just as the disciples misunderstood Jesus' words about his food at 4:31-33 and his words about Lazarus's death at 11:11-12, so also they misunderstand and misperceive Jesus' words at this crucial moment. Their misunderstanding will continue into the discourse of John 14–16 (e.g, 14:5, 8; 16:29-33).

13:30. Ironically, even in betrayal, Judas is obedient to Jesus; he leaves "immediately," fulfilling Jesus' urging for haste in v. 27. Jesus remains in control of the events of his hour (cf. 10:17-18). The notation "And it was night" has many layers of meaning. First, this notation underscores the truth of Judas's identity. By removing himself from Jesus, he has demonstrated that he loves the darkness more than the light and so cuts himself off from Jesus' offer of life (cf. 3:17-21). Second, one of the core elements of Jesus' teaching is that he is the light of the world (8:12; 9:5) and that day and light are the times for his work in the world (9:4; 11:10). Judas's actions usher in the time that brings Jesus' presence as the light of the world to a close. Yet, finally, this verse also brings home the truth of the Prologue (1:5): "The light shines in the darkness, and the darkness did not overcome it."[449] (See Reflections at 13:31-38.)

445. See, e.g., Raymond E. Brown, *The Gospel According to John (XIII–XXI)*, AB 29A (Garden City, N.Y.: Doubleday, 1970) 574.
446. George R. Beasley-Murray, *John*, WBC 36 (Waco, Tex.: Word, 1987) 238.
447. Rudolf Bultmann, *The Gospel of John: A Commentary*, trans. G. R. Beasley-Murray, R. W. N. Hoare, and J. K. Riches (Philadelphia: Westminster, 1971) 482.

448. C. K. Barrett, *The Gospel According to St. John*, 2nd ed. (Philadelphia: Westminster, 1978) 447.
449. See also Bultmann, *The Gospel of John*, 483.

John 13:31-38, The Love Commandment and Prophecy of Peter's Denial

³¹When he was gone, Jesus said, "Now is the Son of Man glorified and God is glorified in him. ³²If God is glorified in him,ᵃ God will glorify the Son in himself, and will glorify him at once.

³³"My children, I will be with you only a little longer. You will look for me, and just as I told the Jews, so I tell you now: Where I am going, you cannot come.

³⁴"A new command I give you: Love one another. As I have loved you, so you must love one another. ³⁵By this all men will know that you are my disciples, if you love one another."

³⁶Simon Peter asked him, "Lord, where are you going?"

Jesus replied, "Where I am going, you cannot follow now, but you will follow later."

³⁷Peter asked, "Lord, why can't I follow you now? I will lay down my life for you."

³⁸Then Jesus answered, "Will you really lay down your life for me? I tell you the truth, before the rooster crows, you will disown me three times!"

ᵃ32 Many early manuscripts do not have *If God is glorified in him.*

³¹When he had gone out, Jesus said, "Now the Son of Man has been glorified, and God has been glorified in him. ³²If God has been glorified in him,ᵃ God will also glorify him in himself and will glorify him at once. ³³Little children, I am with you only a little longer. You will look for me; and as I said to the Jews so now I say to you, 'Where I am going, you cannot come.' ³⁴I give you a new commandment, that you love one another. Just as I have loved you, you also should love one another. ³⁵By this everyone will know that you are my disciples, if you have love for one another."

³⁶Simon Peter said to him, "Lord, where are you going?" Jesus answered, "Where I am going, you cannot follow me now; but you will follow afterward." ³⁷Peter said to him, "Lord, why can I not follow you now? I will lay down my life for you." ³⁸Jesus answered, "Will you lay down your life for me? Very truly, I tell you, before the cock crows, you will have denied me three times."

ᵃ Other ancient authorities lack *If God has been glorified in him*

COMMENTARY

As noted in the Overview to John 13, vv. 31-38 can be read as either the conclusion to the series of last supper scenes between Jesus and his disciples that begins with the foot washing[450] or as the introductory section of the Farewell Discourse.[451] Scholars who argue for reading 13:31-38 as the introduction to the discourse note that the themes introduced by these verses are the central themes of the rest of the discourse and that these verses fit the pattern that continues in 14:1-24: words of Jesus punctuated by questions by the disciples (cf. 14:5, 8, 22). Yet the beginning of v. 31 ("When he had gone out, Jesus said . . . "; v. 31a) suggests that this scene is to be read first in conjunction with what has preceded. The scenes between Jesus and his disciples in 13:1-38 focus on what it means to be Jesus' own; the supper began with a symbolic gesture by Jesus that embodied what it means to be in relationship with Jesus (vv. 1-5), followed by a sequence of dialogues and teachings of Jesus that draw out the meaning of this relationship. John 13:31-38 brings those dialogues to a close by providing a final definition of Jesus' "own" and thereby setting the stage for the discourse whose ultimate concern is the interrelationship of Jesus and his own.[452]

450. Robert Kysar, *John,* Augsburg Commentary on the New Testament (Minneapolis: Augsburg, 1986) 449; R. Alan Culpepper, "The Johannine *Hypodeigma:* A Reading of John 13:1-38," *Semeia* 53 (1991) 134.

451. Brown, *The Gospel According to John (XIII–XXI),* 608-9; Beasley-Murray, *John,* 244; Hoskyns, *The Fourth Gospel,* 447.

452. Barrett, *The Gospel According to St. John,* 449, suggests that 13:31-38 be read as a unit complete unto itself that functions as a farewell discourse in miniature, anticipating in both form and content the discourse that follows in John 14–16. Rudolf Schnackenburg, *The Gospel According to St. John,* 3 vols. (New York: Seabury, 1982) 3:48-58, also treats 13:31-38 as a distinct unit.

John 13:31-38 divides into two parts: (1) vv. 31-35, a teaching by Jesus, and (2) vv. 36-38, a dialogue between Jesus and Peter. Jesus' teaching clusters around two topics: (1) Jesus' glorification and departure (vv. 31-33) and (2) the commandment that the disciples love one another (vv. 34-35).

13:31-32. The "now" with which Jesus' words in v. 31 begin marks a decisive turn in the narrative. The supper scene opened with the narrator's commentary that Jesus knew that his hour had come (13:1; see 13:3 also), and with Jesus' words at v. 31 this knowledge is made public (cf. his remarks at the arrival of the Greeks, 12:23). The disciples are thus given access to the knowledge that motivated Jesus' actions toward them in the foot washing.

Verses 31-32 are complex to interpret. Their complexity arises because the verb "to glorify" (δοξάζω *doxazō*) is repeated five times, but the temporal framework in which the verb is used shifts from past to future. This seeming temporal confusion is intentional, because in these verses Jesus' and God's mutual glorification is depicted as a reality that is underway *even as* Jesus speaks. The arrival of the hour is now the governing narrative and theological reality of the Gospel. Past, present, and future are redefined in the light of the arrival of the hour. Jesus' announcement in 13:31 thus heralds the arrival of the eschatological hour (cf., "the hour is coming and now is," 4:23; 5:24).[453]

The eschatological import of Jesus' announcement is underscored by his use of the title "Son of Man" here. "Son of Man" is the christological title with the strongest eschatological associations in the Fourth Gospel (5:27; 8:28; 12:23) and is most explicitly linked with Jesus' descent and ascent—that is, his coming from and returning to God (1:51; 3:13-14; 6:62; 12:32-34).

The mutual glorification of God and Jesus was initiated in the incarnation (1:14)—that is, in the incarnation, the presence of God in Jesus becomes visible to the world (cf. 17:24). Jesus' words and works continued the mutual glorification (2:11; 7:18; 8:54; 11:4), but the decisive moment of glorification is the unfolding of the events of Jesus' hour. In that hour, in Jesus' death on a cross and

return to God, the full glory of God and Jesus will be revealed (see also 17:1). Who God is, who Jesus is, and who they are to each other and to the believer is fully revealed in Jesus' death, resurrection, and ascension.

13:33. As Jesus himself notes, his words to his disciples about his imminent departure do not differ from his earlier words to the "Jews" (7:33-34; 8:21). What is different is the significance of that departure for the hearers. When Jesus spoke to the "Jews," those in power who opposed him, he pointed to his return to God as a moment of judgment and condemnation. Here, his departure is presented to his disciples as the seal of their new relationship with God, with Jesus, and with one another. At 1:12, the Prologue announced that "to all who received him, who believed in his name, he gave power to become children of God." When Jesus addresses his followers as "little children," he acknowledges the truth of the Prologue's claims. Verse 33 is the only place in the Fourth Gospel where Jesus' followers are explicitly addressed as "little children" (τεκνία *teknia*), a common form of address for members of the believing community in 1 John (2:1, 12, 28; 3:7, 18; 4:4; 5:21).

13:34-35. The intimacy of "little children" sets the framework for Jesus' teaching in these verses. The commandment of v. 34 builds on Jesus' words to his disciples after the foot washing (13:15); his love for them has provided them with the model of how they are to relate to one another. In order to understand why this is a new commandment, it is important to look at how "commandment" (ἐντολή *entolē*) is used elsewhere in the Gospel. At 10:18, Jesus' decision to lay down his life is described as his enactment of God's commandment; at 14:31 and 15:12, Jesus' obedience to God's commandment is the mark of Jesus' love for God. For Jesus to keep God's commandment is for Jesus to enact his love of God in words and works (cf. 12:49-50).

What is new, therefore, is not the commandment to love, because that commandment lies at the heart of the Torah (Lev 19:18; Deut 6:4; cf. Mark 12:28 and par.). Rather, what is new is that the commandment to love derives from the incarnation (see 3:16). The "new" turn in the commandment of 13:34 is that Jesus' "own" are asked to enter into the love that marks the relationship

453. Gail R. O'Day, " 'I have overcome the world' (John 16:33): Narrative Time in John 13–17," *Semeia* 53 (1991) 153-66.

of God and Jesus. Their participation in this relationship will be evidenced the same way that Jesus' is: by acts of love that join the believer to God (cf. 14:15, 21, 23; 15:12). Keeping this commandment is the identifying mark of discipleship (v. 35), because it is the tangible sign of the disciples' abiding in Jesus (15:10).

13:36. Simon Peter, like the "Jews" before him (7:35-36; 8:22), does not understand Jesus' words about his departure (v. 36a). Jesus' response in v. 36b anticipates the prophecy of Peter's future in 21:18-19, but they also correct Peter's misperception of the nature of Jesus' departure. Jesus leaves his disciples in order to complete God's work and make a new life with God possible for them (cf. 14:2-3), and they cannot follow him into that life until the events of the hour are completed (that is, after the full sequence of death, resurrection, and ascension).[454] Verse 36a thus evokes a time after the hour, a theme that will recur throughout the discourse (e.g., 16:7, 16-24).

13:37-38. The centrality of the prediction of Peter's denial of Jesus (vv. 37-38) to early Christian traditions about Jesus' death is evident in the inclusion of some version of this prediction in all four Gospels (see Matt 26:30-35; Mark 14:26-31; Luke 22:31-34). The common elements in all four versions are Peter's announcement of his willingness to die for Jesus, the prediction of Peter's triple denial, and the reference to the cock's crowing. Matthew and Mark contain almost identical versions of the

denial, but the distinctiveness of both the Johannine and the Lukan treatments of the prediction argue against any theories of literary dependence on one another or on the Markan tradition.[455]

The distinctiveness of the Johannine treatment of the denial is the language it uses to speak of Peter's death and its placement in the story. The expression "lay down my life for you" echoes directly Jesus' description of the good shepherd at 10:11 and of himself at 10:17-18. Peter thus presents himself as willing to keep Jesus' commandment, to do what he has done (13:15), to love as he loves (13:34-35). Yet, as Jesus' prediction of the denial makes clear, Peter's enthusiasm is possible only because he does not understand the full demand of Jesus' hour (cf. Peter's words at 13:9). Faced with that demand, he will deny Jesus. What Jesus predicts of Peter here he will predict of all his disciples at 16:32: They will all desert him at his death (cf. Matt 26:31; Mark 14:27).

The pathos of the prediction of Peter's denial is increased in John by its location at the foot washing and immediately following the love commandment. This dialogue between Jesus and Peter serves notice to the disciples (and the reader) that in significant ways Judas is not an isolated case. While the betrayal may be the most dramatic case of refusing to remain with Jesus, Peter's denial underscores that the decision to be one of Jesus' "own" is always at risk.

---

454. Cf. Bultmann, *The Gospel of John,* 596-97.

455. C. H. Dodd, *Historical Tradition in the Fourth Gospel* (Cambridge: Cambridge University Press, 1963) 55-56.

REFLECTIONS

When John 13 is read as a unit, it provides the reader with a dramatic and tensive presentation of the meaning of discipleship. The chapter begins with a demonstration of love by Jesus that is misunderstood by Peter (13:1-11), and it closes with a commandment to love in the light of Jesus' hour, which is also misunderstood by Peter (13:31-38). In between these two scenes are two conversations that focus on the opposite poles of discipleship: 12:12-20, which raises up the possibility of community grounded in love and service, and 12:21-30, which raises up the reality of betrayal *even within* this community.

The tension of John 13 invites the reader to look at the commandment to love one another with fresh eyes. As 13:35 makes clear, this commandment is the hallmark of discipleship, yet it seems that the radical call of this commandment is often missed. The ethical demand of this commandment, which focuses so specifically on love *within* and *among* members of the faith community, is often dismissed as "easier" or "softer" than the ethical demand to love one's neighbor as oneself (Matt 19:19; 22:39; Mark 12:31) or to love one's enemies (Matt 5:44; Luke 6:27-35). Moreover, this is the only commandment that Jesus explicitly identifies for his disciples and insists that they keep, so that again, the Johannine ethic can be seen as somewhat diminished when read next to the broad range of ethical imperatives in the Sermon on the Mount.

Yet the very narrative in which this commandment is lodged suggests that there is nothing easy about keeping the commandment to love one another. Jesus' teachings on love and discipleship are unrelentingly placed in the context of his betrayal and death in John 13. The example to which the love commandment points is the love of Jesus for his disciples, a love that will receive its fullest and final expression in his death. Jesus' followers, therefore, are exhorted to love one another as fully as he loves them, a love that may indeed find its expression in the laying down of one's life. To model one's love on a love whose ultimate expression is the gift of one's life is to model one's love on a love that has no limits, that knows no boundaries and restrictions. To interpret Jesus' death as the ultimate act of love enables the believer to see that the love to which Jesus summons the community is not the giving *up* of one's life, but the giving *away* of one's life. The distinction between these prepositions is important, because the love that Jesus embodies is grace, not sacrifice. Jesus gave his life to his disciples as an expression of the fullness of his relationship with God and of God's love for the world. Jesus' death in love, therefore, was not an act of self-denial, but an act of fullness, of living out his life and identity fully, even when that living would ultimately lead to death.

One of the most powerful contemporary North American examples of a life that followed fully Jesus' model of limitless love is that of Martin Luther King, Jr. His death came not because he chose to give up his live for others, but because he chose to live the love of Jesus fully. In sermons from near the end of his life, it is apparent that King knew full well the jeopardy into which his ministry put his life, but to live out the love of Jesus carried with it the threat of death from which King did not shy away. Like Jesus, he put no limits on his love. Bishop Oscar Romero, too, did not choose to give up his life, but he chose to love his "sheep" fully, which ultimately meant laying down his life for them.

To love one another as Jesus loves us does not automatically translate into one believer's death for another, nor does it mean to deny oneself for others. Jesus did not deny himself; he lived his identity and vocation fully. Rather, to love one another as Jesus loves us is to live a life thoroughly shaped by a love that knows no limits, by a love whose expression brings the believer closer into relationship with God, with Jesus, and with one another. It is to live a love that carries with it a whole new concept of the possibilities of community.

That the love commandment is directed internally—to members of the community—does not make it easier to keep. Indeed, the wisdom of this commandment as the sole explicit commandment of Jesus in this Gospel is made abundantly clear by a review of the history of the church in any era. The church's witness in the world is always hurt and diminished by the hatred and lack of love that marks Christians' dealings with one another. It is no easy task for Christians to love one another. In many ways, it is easier to love one's enemies, because one might not have to deal with them every day. Jesus promised that the community's love for one another would be a signal to people ("everyone," v. 35) that they were Jesus' disciples, yet that signal is crippled daily by the divisions and discord within the Christian community.

The betrayal that haunts John 13 (vv. 2, 11, 18, 21-30) points to the destructiveness of living against Jesus' love, as does the prediction of Peter's denial. The very story of John 13 thus points to the cost and challenge of living a life that keeps one commandment: to love one another as Jesus loved us. The commandment opens up the possibility of community with God and Jesus and community with one another, but it is not an easy word to keep.

JOHN 14:1–16:33, THE FAREWELL DISCOURSE

OVERVIEW

As noted in the Overview to John 13:1–17:26, John 14:1–16:33 is the centerpiece of the three units that compose the Johannine account of the farewell meal (13:1-38; 14:1–16:33; 17:1-26). As the centerpiece, the Farewell Discourse needs to be read in the light of what both precedes and follows it. The common Johannine narrative pattern, noted repeatedly throughout this commentary, is that of event/dialogue/discourse (e.g., John 5; 6; and 9). Read from one perspective, the Farewell Discourse coheres with this pattern, because Jesus' teachings in John 14–16 do indeed draw out themes that are introduced by the foot washing and the dialogues that follow it.

Yet the primary orientation of the Farewell Discourse is not to an event that preceded it, but to an event whose arrival is imminent—that is, Jesus' death, resurrection, and ascension. In John 14–16, Jesus explains the significance of his departure to his disciples and points them toward the life that they will lead after his hour. The Farewell Discourse thus interprets an event *before* it happens and as such marks a decisive variant on the familiar Johannine narrative style. It is as the interpretation of Jesus' death that John 14–16 derives the name the "Farewell Discourse," because in preparing his disciples for his departure, Jesus' words here do indeed function as his farewell to his own.

Critical Issues in Reading the Farewell Discourse. The delineation of the boundaries and structure of the Farewell Discourse presents the interpreter with several critical issues. The first, as noted in the Commentary on 13:31-38, is where to mark the beginning of the discourse. There is no sharp break between 13:31-38 and 14:1; indeed, John 14:1 is presented as the continuation of the words of Jesus that begin at 13:38.[456] Yet there is nonetheless a significant shift between 13:38 and 14:1, because Jesus' words in 13:38 are addressed specifically to

Peter, whereas at 14:1 they are addressed to all of the disciples, as the use of the second-person plural pronoun indicates (cf. the shift in personal pronouns in the move from dialogue to discourse in 3:11). The discourse will be peppered with questions by the disciples (e.g, 14:5, 8), but after 13:38 Jesus' responses will always address the circumstances of all his disciples, not simply those of the individual petitioner.[457] (Note the use of the second-person plural in Jesus' response to Thomas at 14:7 and to Philip at 14:9). This commentary, therefore, proposes that John 14:1 marks the beginning of the discourse.

A second critical determination is where to end the discourse. Although Jesus' words in 17:1-25 share the same narrative setting with the discourse, there is a significant shift in Jesus' intended audience between 16:33 and 17:1. The formal markers at 17:1 (see Commentary on John 17) make clear that Jesus ceases speaking to his disciples and addresses his words to God in prayer. Therefore, although John 17:1-25 shares many themes with the discourse and has a formal relationship to the preceding discourse unit (see "The Genre of the Farewell Discourse" below), this shift in audience argues for interpreting Jesus' prayer as a discrete textual unit within the larger farewell meal narrative.

The third and most complex critical issue is how to assess the interrelationship of the various units of the discourse. Even in the most cursory reading of the Farewell Discourse, the interpreter is struck by both the density of the material, particularly evident in the repetition of key sayings by Jesus (e.g., 14:13-14; 15:7, 16; 16:23-24) and by some apparent contradictions. The most glaring surface contradiction is Jesus' summons to depart at 14:31, followed not by departure, but by an extension of the discourse. Another set of apparent contradictions is the variety of verb tenses Jesus uses to speak of his departure. He speaks of the events of his hour in the past tense (cf. 16:33),

456. Many commentators, therefore, identify 13:31ff. as the beginning of the discourse. See the list in the Commentary on 13:31-38.

457. Cf. Brown, *The Gospel According to John (XIII–XXI),* 608.

as imminent (e.g., 14:3), and as underway even as he speaks (e.g., 16:15, 28). Commentators have struggled with the significance of these repetitions and seeming contradictions for centuries and have proposed a variety of solutions to the interpretive puzzle they pose.[458]

Three approaches have dominated the critical conversation. The first, a more traditional approach, assumes that Jesus and his disciples did indeed depart the supper at 14:31 and that the speeches in John 15–17 were spoken as he and his disciples walked to the Garden of Gethsemane.[459] The introduction to 18:1 ("After Jesus had spoken these words, he went out . . . ") calls this proposal seriously into doubt. The second, advanced most thoroughly by Bultmann but also by others,[460] suggests that the repetitions and contradictions are the result of the displacement of the discourse at some stage in its composition and/or transmission. The contents of the discourse must therefore be rearranged in order to return it to its original order. For example, Bultmann proposes that the original order of the discourse was 13:1-30; 17; 13:31-35; 15–16; 13:36–14:31. Yet, as with all displacement theories (see the discussion of the order of John 5 and 6 above), these rearrangements create their own set of interpretive problems. Bultmann's rearrangement overlooks many of the introductory features of John 14 as well as the concluding features of John 17.

The third approach proposes that John 14–16 (or 13:31–16) contains two alternative versions of the Farewell Discourse. The repetitions and structure of the discourse are thus explained in terms of its redactional history. That is, John 14:1-31 preserves one version of Jesus' farewell words to his disciples, John 15:1–16:33 a second. The call to depart in John 14:31 is viewed as the conclusion to the first discourse, which has been revised

and added to in 15:1ff. This redactional approach is the consensus among recent Fourth Gospel scholars,[461] although they disagree over the particulars of who wrote the second version (i.e., whether the Evangelist or a later editor) and who added it (again, whether the Evangelist or a later editor).

The redactional solution is arguably the cleanest solution to the composition history of the discourse, yet it, too, is not without problems. First, one is led to ask whether the contents of the discourse really necessitate such a thoroughgoing redactional proposal. The purported intent of the redactional proposal is to account for the repetitions and logical inconsistencies and contradictions within the Farewell Discourse. Yet a careful reading of the "first" and "second" discourses identified by these scholars reveals that even within these supposed discrete units, one still encounters repetitiveness and awkward transitions between and within units (note, for example, the shift from future to present tense in the description of the disciples' pain in 16:20-22). The theory of two full versions of the Farewell Discourse seems an attempt to impose an externally determined logic on the discourse rather than accepting its repetitiveness and circularity of logic and development as essential to both its form and narrative and theological purpose. Circularity of logic and repetition is a distinctive trait of the discourses in John (cf. the Commentary on 5:19-47) and their use in the crowning discourse of the Gospel should be expected.[462]

One also has to ask whether this redactional approach gives inordinate weight to one verse, 14:31. There are two significant inconsistencies in the way this verse is handled in the two-discourse theory. First, the redactional solution assumes a slavish handling of the Jesus traditions that the rest of the Gospel neither demonstrates nor supports. The Fourth Gospel shows a remarkable freedom in the way it handles traditions (cf., for example, the displacement of the cleansing of the temple narrative to the opening of Jesus' ministry). There is little support from the rest of

458. For a recent review of the history of research on the structure and composition of the Farewell Discourse, see Fernando Segovia, *The Farewell of the Word: The Johannine Call to Abide* (Minneapolis: Fortress, 1991) 21-47.

459. Examples of this approach among contemporary commentators include Ernst Haenchen, *John 2: A Commentary on the Gospel of John Chapters 7–21*, (Philadelphia: Fortress, 1984) 128; and D. A. Carson, *The Gospel According to John* (Grand Rapids: Eerdmans, 1991) 477-79.

460. Bultmann, *John*, 459-61. For a review of scholars prior to Bultmann who proposed a variety of displacement theories (e.g., Wellhausen, Bacon, Bernard, Wendt), see W. F. Howard, *The Fourth Gospel in Recent Criticism and Interpretation* (London: Epworth, 1931)

461. Rudolf Schnackenburg, *The Gospel According to St. John*, 3:90-91; Brown, *The Gospel According to John (XIII–XXI)*, 581-94; Barrett, *The Gospel According to St. John*, 454-55; Beasley-Murray, *John*, 223-24; Kysar, *John*, 219-20; Segovia, *The Farewell of the Word*, 319-28.

462. See George A. Kennedy, *New Testament Interpretation Through Rhetorical Criticism* (Chapel Hill: University of North Carolina Press, 1984) 73-85.

the Gospel for the view that because the first version of the discourse ended with the words in 14:31, the Evangelist (or a later editor) had to include it here. Second, the two-discourse theory assumes that neither the Evangelist nor a later editor (depending on whom commentators credit with the redaction) noticed the disjunction between 14:31 and 15:1 that is so glaringly obvious to modern interpreters. Again, the only way to explain this authorial/editorial lapse is to appeal to a slavish adherence to tradition.

The problem of 14:31 is not easy to resolve. Yet were not such emphasis given to 14:31, one wonders whether the break between John 14 and 15–16 would seem so glaring. There are interpretations of the Farewell Discourse that attempt to take 14:31 as one verse in the discourse and not as *the* decisive verse for the discourse. Hoskyns, for example, explains the verse in terms of tradition history, and Dodd offers a symbolic reading of the verse.[463] In this respect, they are following the interpretive traditions of the early church theologians (e.g., Cyril of Alexandria; see Commentary below). In more contemporary criticism, attempts are made to read the discourse as a whole, and thus to arrive at its meaning without dependence on the theory of two discourses.[464]

There is no doubt that the Fourth Evangelist has brought together in John 14:1–16:33 traditions that originally existed independently of this one long unit. In that regard, the combination of traditions in the Farewell Discourse is no different from the combination of traditions in the discourses of John 5; 7–8. Therefore, it does not seem necessary to postulate two distinct versions of the Farewell Discourse to explain the composition history and structural complexities of the Farewell Discourse. Instead, one finds in these chapters a combination of many once distinct units of tradition whose prior history is not recoverable. Just as the Fourth Evangelist brought together distinct units of tradition in John 5 to form a discourse that focused on the relationship of God and Jesus and in John 7–8 to focus on the conflict between Jesus and the Jewish authorities, so also here he has brought together traditions to

focus on Jesus' death and the disciples' future. Jesus' death confronted the early church with two immediate crises: the meaning of Jesus' death on a cross and his absence from his followers. It is the pastoral and theological genius of the Fourth Evangelist that he positioned the Farewell Discourse to be Jesus' response to those crises.

The Genre of the Farewell Discourse. In reading the Farewell Discourse, one needs to consider its relationship to a genre of literature well documented in the ancient Mediterranean world—that of the farewell or last testament of a famous man. In the OT, one finds this form in Jacob's farewell and blessing of his twelve sons (Genesis 49), in Joshua's farewell address (Joshua 22–24), and in David's farewell and instructions to Solomon and the royal court (1 Chronicles 28–29). The most extended example of the farewell address is in Deuteronomy, in which the entire book is cast as Moses' farewell speeches to his people. This literary form also occurs in extra-canonical Jewish literature, particularly those books like *The Testaments of the Twelve Patriarchs* and *Jubilees,* which retell and expand the stories of the Pentateuch; in Greek and Roman literature (e.g., the death of Socrates in Plato's *Phaedo*); and elsewhere in the NT (e.g., Paul's farewell at Miletus, Acts 20:17-38).

Some of the defining characteristics of this form include the gathering of family and/or followers by the dying or departing man, the announcement of approaching death or departure, prophecies and/or promises and blessings, a review of the man's life, the naming of a successor, final instructions, and a prayer.[465] Each of these characteristics appears in the Farewell Discourse, and there can be little doubt that the Fourth Evangelist has composed the narrative of the events at the supper with the farewell speech form in view.[466] Fernando Segovia has suggested that the entire sup-

---

463. E. C. Hoskyns, *The Fourth Gospel* (London: Faber & Faber, 1947) 464-65; C. H. Dodd, *The Interpretation of the Fourth Gospel* (Cambridge: Cambridge University Press, 1953) 408-9.

464. See Yves Simoens, *La Gloire d'Aimer* (Rome: Biblical Institute Press, 1980).

465. The most important studies of the farewell form include Johannes Munck, "Discours d'adieu dans le Nouveau Testament et dans la litterature biblique," in *Aux sources de la tradition chrétienne: Melanges offerts a M. Maurice Goguel* (Neuchatel and Paris: Delachaux & Niestle, 1950) 155-70; H.-J. Michel, *Die Abschiedsrede des Paulus an die Kirche Apg 20, 17-38* (Munich: Kosel, 1973); and William S. Kurz, "Luke 22:14-38 and Greco-Roman and Biblical Farewell Addresses," *JBL* 104 (1985) 251-68; and *Farewell Addresses in the New Testament* (Collegeville, Minn.: Liturgical Press, 1990).

466. So, e.g., Brown, *The Gospel According to John (XIII–XXI),* 597-601; Beasley-Murray, *John,* 222-23; Schnackenburg, *The Gospel According to St. John,* 3:57.

per scene should be read as a farewell type of scene, a suggestion that helpfully draws together both the genre of the farewell testament and the narrative setting.[467]

In addition to identifying the formal characteristics of the farewell speech in general, the most instructive comparison may be between the Johannine Farewell Discourse and the farewell speeches of Moses in Deuteronomy.[468] Through the literary device of the farewell speech in Deuteronomy, the traditions of Sinai and Moab are given a fresh hearing, a "re-presentation," in a new setting, because they are presented as being spoken in *this* moment for *this* people (cf. Deut 5:1-3; 8:1; 30:1-20).[469] Deuteronomy was not written for a people about to enter the promised land, however, but was written centuries after Moses for a people who had long lived in the land. The farewell speeches in Deuteronomy invite the readers of eighth- and seventh-century BCE Israel to see themselves as if they were the people on the plains of Moab. Moreover, by using this narrative strategy, the author(s) of Deuteronomy give Mosaic sanction to their interpretive work.

The Fourth Evangelist has a similar aim with the Farewell Discourse. Jesus speaks with confidence and knowledge about the events of the future, about his relationship with God and his disciples, about the advent of the Paraclete, and about the disciples' future. The voice of Jesus in the Farewell Discourse is the voice of one who says, "But take courage; I have conquered the world!" (16:33). Jesus' victory over the world in his death, resurrection, and ascension is the governing theological reality of this discourse, and, indeed, this theological perspective accounts for many of the seeming contradictions in the discourse (see Commentary on 14–16). The voice of Jesus that speaks in the Farewell Discourse is, therefore, that of the risen and victorious Jesus.[470] Just as the words of Moses in Deuteronomy are addressed beyond their narrative setting to the later readers of the book, so also the words of

Jesus in the Farewell Discourse, even though set at the farewell meal and hence prior to Jesus' hour, move beyond this narrative setting to address his followers in the time after his hour.

What is the narrative and theological significance of having a farewell discourse that is spoken from the perspective of the risen Jesus, grounded in his victory over the world (16:33)? First, just as the Deuteronomic authors used the voice of Moses to sanction their own interpretive work, so also the Fourth Evangelist uses the voice of Jesus to give sanction to his. The community's future is envisioned in Jesus' voice, not the Evangelist's own. The Fourth Evangelist has chosen to disclose the future of the community of faith by grounding it in the present voice of Jesus in the discourse. Second, the voice of the risen Jesus that resounds in the Farewell Discourse communicates the central eschatological truth of this Gospel: The hour is coming and now is. That is, by addressing the disciples' present (i.e., the time before the hour) with words that are grounded in the victory of the hour, the Fourth Evangelist makes the transformative eschatological presence of Jesus a reality for both the disciples and the Gospel reader. In constructing this discourse, which glides without notice from past to present to future, the Fourth Evangelist shows how God's new age is already shaping the disciples' lives through the farewell promises and assurances of Jesus. The future for which they wait is already underway, because Jesus' "future" victory is in fact the present reality.

Units and Themes of the Farewell Discourse. The Farewell Discourse can be divided into four broad units: (1) 14:1-31, "I will not leave you orphaned"; (2) 15:1-17, "Abide in my love"; (3) 15:18–16:4*a*, "I have chosen you out of the world"; (4) 16:4*b*-33, "It is to your advantage that I go away."

The first and last units (14:1-33; 16:4*b*-33) contain teachings of Jesus punctuated by questions from his disciples, whereas the middle two units (15:1-17; 15:18–16:4*a*) consist exclusively of Jesus' teaching. The governing theme of each unit is signaled in the paragraph above by a key saying of Jesus from that unit. John 14:1-31 focuses primarily on themes of consolation and assurance for the disciples in the light of Jesus' departure and return to the Father. This unit emphasizes Jesus' relationship to God and the implications of

467. Segovia, *Farewell of the Word,* 1-20.

468. See A. Lacomara, "Deuteronomy and the Farewell Discourse," *CBQ* 36 (1974) 65-84.

469. See Gerhard von Rad, "Ancient Word and Living Word: The Preaching of Deuteronomy and Our Preaching" *Int.* 15 (1961) 3-13; and Martin Noth, "The Interpretation of the Old Testament: I. The Representation of the Old Testament in Proclamation," *Int.* 15 (1961) 50-60.

470. See Gail R. O'Day, " 'I have overcome the world' (John 16:33): Narrative Time in John 13–17," *Semeia* 53 (1991) 153-66.

that relationship for the disciples, as well as the promise of the Paraclete (14:16-17, 26). John 15:1-17 contains the extended metaphor of the vine and its branches (15:1-11), as well as a restatement of the love commandment (15:12-17). Together these two sections articulate the theme of abiding love. John 15:18–16:4a focuses on the believers' relationship to the world and contains another promise of the Paraclete (15:26-27). John 16:4b-33 returns to the themes of consolation and assurance in the face of Jesus' departure, but with a particular focus on the role of the Paraclete in offering that consolation (16:7-15).

John 14:1-31, "I Will Not Leave You Orphaned"

OVERVIEW

John 14:1-31 consists of a sequence of Jesus' teachings that address the themes of Jesus' departure and its significance for his followers. As is the case with the entire Farewell Discourse (see the Overview above), this unit does not develop according to a strict linear logic. Rather, its logic is more circular, developing its perspective through repetition of key themes and words—e.g., verbs for "coming" and "going" (14:2-6, 12, 18, 28, 30); for "believe" (πιστεύω *pisteuō,* 14:1, 10-12, 29); for "know" (14:4-5, 7, 9, 17, 20); for "see" (14:7, 17, 19); for "remain" (μένω *menō,* 14:10, 17, 25); for "love" (ἀγαπάω *agapaō,* 14:15, 21, 23-24, 28); Jesus' relationship to the Father (14:6-13, 16, 20-21, 23, 26, 28, 31). This repetitiveness creates a web of interwoven themes and motifs (see Commentary on 5:19-30) that resists clean outlining. The Commentary below is divided into three sections: (1) vv. 1-11; (2) vv. 12-24; and (3) vv. 25-31, in order to faciliate the analysis and interpretation of the text.

John 14:1-11, "I Am the Way, and the Truth, and the Life"

NIV

14 "Do not let your hearts be troubled. Trust in God[a]; trust also in me. ²In my Father's house are many rooms; if it were not so, I would have told you. I am going there to prepare a place for you. ³And if I go and prepare a place for you, I will come back and take you to be with me that you also may be where I am. ⁴You know the way to the place where I am going."

⁵Thomas said to him, "Lord, we don't know where you are going, so how can we know the way?"

⁶Jesus answered, "I am the way and the truth and the life. No one comes to the Father except through me. ⁷If you really knew me, you would know[b] my Father as well. From now on, you do know him and have seen him."

⁸Philip said, "Lord, show us the Father and that will be enough for us."

a1 Or You trust in God   b7 Some early manuscripts If you really have known me, you will know

NRSV

14 "Do not let your hearts be troubled. Believe[a] in God, believe also in me. ²In my Father's house there are many dwelling places. If it were not so, would I have told you that I go to prepare a place for you?[b] ³And if I go and prepare a place for you, I will come again and will take you to myself, so that where I am, there you may be also. ⁴And you know the way to the place where I am going."[c]

⁵Thomas said to him, "Lord, we do not know where you are going. How can we know the way?" ⁶Jesus said to him, "I am the way, and the truth, and the life. No one comes to the Father except through me. ⁷If you know me, you will know[d] my Father also. From now on you do know him and have seen him." ⁸Philip said to him, "Lord, show us the Father, and we will be satisfied."

a Or You believe   b Or If it were not so, I would have told you; for I go to prepare a place for you   c Other ancient authorities read Where I am going you know, and the way you know   d Other ancient authorities read If you had known me, you would have known

NIV

⁹Jesus answered: "Don't you know me, Philip, even after I have been among you such a long time? Anyone who has seen me has seen the Father. How can you say, 'Show us the Father'? ¹⁰Don't you believe that I am in the Father, and that the Father is in me? The words I say to you are not just my own. Rather, it is the Father, living in me, who is doing his work. ¹¹Believe me when I say that I am in the Father and the Father is in me; or at least believe on the evidence of the miracles themselves."

NRSV

⁹Jesus said to him, "Have I been with you all this time, Philip, and you still do not know me? Whoever has seen me has seen the Father. How can you say, 'Show us the Father'? ¹⁰Do you not believe that I am in the Father and the Father is in me? The words that I say to you I do not speak on my own; but the Father who dwells in me does his works. ¹¹Believe me that I am in the Father and the Father is in me; but if you do not, then believe me because of the works themselves."

COMMENTARY

14:1. Jesus' opening words to his disciples (vv. 1-4) begin with three imperative clauses (v. 1). The verb for "troubled" (ταράσσω *tarassō,* v. 1*a*) translates a verb used three times previously in the Gospel to describe Jesus' condition of distress (11:33; 12:27; 13:21). In each of these three uses, the verb refers primarily to Jesus' agitation and disturbance in the face of the power of death and evil, not simply to his sadness. The same meaning of "troubled" applies here, and it is important that the opening imperative of v. 1 not be excessively sentimentalized. Jesus does not speak to the disciples' personal sadness at his death, but instead exhorts them to stand firm in the face of his departure, when the events may look to them as if evil and death are having their way. It is a rallying cry for strength. Peter's denial, predicted in 13:38, can be seen as an illustration of how the disciples will act if they surrender to their troubled hearts.

The two final verbs ("believe . . . believe" [πιστεύετε *pisteuete*]) could be translated either as indicatives (i.e., "you believe . . . ") or imperatives. The introductory imperative of v. 1*a* suggests that all three verbs in the verse should be read as imperatives, as in both the NIV and the NRSV. These final two imperatives build on the christological core of Jesus' ministry, the unity of Jesus and God (10:30; cf. 12:44), and provide the theological grounding for the opening exhortation. The disciples' faith in the relationship of God and Jesus will empower them to rejoice in the events of Jesus' hour (14:28), because through the eyes of faith they will recognize Jesus' hour as the culmination of his enactment of God's work, as the defeat of the ruler of the world (12:31; 14:30).

14:2-3. In vv. 2-3, Jesus turns from exhortation to promise. Jewish traditions that identify the "Father's house" with a heavenly dwelling place clearly lie behind the imagery of v. 2*a* (e.g., Pss 2:4; 66:1; 113:5-6; 123:1; Isa 66:1),⁴⁷¹ but it is critical to the interpretation of Jesus' words here that the reference to "my Father's house" not be taken as a synonym for heaven.⁴⁷² Instead, this reference to the Father's house needs to be read first in the context of the mutual indwelling of God and Jesus, a form of "residence" that has been repeatedly stressed from the opening verses of the Gospel (e.g., 1:1, 18). Throughout the Gospel, location has consistently been a symbol for relationship. For example, in 1:18, a description of Jesus' physical location (in the bosom of the Father) communicates the intimacy of Jesus' relationship with God. Jesus' description as one who comes from heaven (3:31; 6:41, 51; cf. 3:12-13) confirms his origins with God. To know where Jesus is from is to know his relationship with God. The parable about the relative place of the son and the slave in the house in John 8:35-36 confirms that God's house is about relationship and not exclusively about location (see also 2:16). It is in this relationship, as much as in any heavenly dwelling per se, that there are "many rooms."

The noun translated "dwelling place" (μονή

---

471. See also especially Philo *Som.* 1, 256.
472. C. K. Barrett, *The Gospel According to St. John,* 2nd ed. (Philadelphia: Westminster, 1978) 457.

monē, "room" in the NIV) also points to the relational dimension of Jesus' imagery. While it, too, appears in Jewish literature as a reference to heavenly dwellings for the faithful,[473] it takes on additional meaning in the Johannine context. This noun is derived from the verb "remain" or "to dwell" (μένω *menō*), a verb used in the Fourth Gospel to describe the mutuality and reciprocity of the relationship of God and Jesus (14:10; 15:10). The use of this noun here (see also 14:23) points to the inclusion of others in this relationship, this "house." Jesus uses the domestic imagery to say, "My return to God will make it possible for you to join in the relationship that the Father and I share" (cf. 20:18). The promise of v. 2*a* is thus verbal confirmation of what Jesus enacted in the foot washing; the disciples are welcome in the Father's house (see Commentary on 13:1-8).

Verse 2*b* is difficult to translate with certainty (note the differences between the NIV and the NRSV). The main question is how to translate the Greek conjunction ὅτι (*hoti,* "that" or "for"), which follows the words "told you" in most manuscripts. The array of options chosen by translations and commentators evidences the lack of consensus about this verse. The NIV follows the text tradition that omits the conjunction altogether and places a complete stop after "you."[474] The NRSV footnote translates *hoti* as "for" and positions Jesus' words about his preparation of a place for the disciples as proof of the truth of v. 2*a.*[475] The NRSV translates *hoti* as "that" and so punctuates v. 2*b* as a question. The interrogative reading of the NRSV seems doubtful, however, since 14:2-3 is the first and only time in John that Jesus speaks of preparing a place for his disciples. Jesus' words about preparing a place are the core promise of these verses and are not offered as a test of the disciples. The NIV and the NRSV footnotes, therefore, seem the better reading because they position Jesus' preparation of a place for the disciples as the grounding of Jesus' assurance about "the Father's house."

The expression "I will come again" (v. 3) evokes the traditional early Christian expectation of the second coming of Jesus and signals the eschatological orientation of these verses. To turn Jesus' promise here into language about Jesus' coming to the individual believer at the believer's death is to misconstrue the eschatological significance of this promise.[476] His return will be the enactment of the eschatological announcement of the Lazarus story, "I am the resurrection and the life" (11:25; see Commentary and Reflections on John 11:1-44). It is the ultimate witness to the power of God over life and death,[477] and it is this power that is the mark of the new age. Jesus' return announces that nothing, not even death, can separate Jesus and his "own" from God (cf. Rom 8:38-39). Jesus' promised return to his disciples thus functions as the seal of the new eschatological reality ushered in by the events of his hour. Jesus' promise to take his own to himself is the promise of the arrival of the hoped-for age, which is marked by reunion and reconciliation with God, by inhabiting one's "place" in God's home.

Verses 2-3 thus draw on the traditional imagery of heaven as God's home to describe the new reality that Jesus' death, resurrection, and ascension make available to the believer. He reinterprets this traditional imagery, however, to reflect his eschatological perspective (cf. this text, e.g., with the use of heaven imagery in 1 Thess 4:13-18). The language about place promises the disciples a share in Jesus' relationship with God (cf. 13:8), a share that is made explicit in the concluding promise of v. 3: "so that where I am, there you may be also." This promise of the advent of the eschatological age marked by full communion with God is the Johannine vision of the "kingdom of God" (cf. 3:3, 5; see Reflections on Johannine eschatology at 16:25-33).

14:4-5. Verse 4 is transitional; on one level its language about Jesus' departure seems to continue the theme of vv. 1-3, but as vv. 6-7 will make clear, Jesus is actually introducing a new topic in this verse. Jesus' words here shift their focus away from the destination of Jesus' journey to a new term, "the way" (ἡ ὁδός *hē hodos*). The word order of the Greek text reinforces this shift, "And where I am going, you know the way" (author's

473. See, esp. Enoch 39:4.
474. So Raymond E. Brown, *The Gospel According to John (XIII–XXI),* AB 29A (Garden City, N.Y.: Doubleday, 1970) 619-20.
475. So George R. Beasley-Murray, *John,* WBC 36 (Waco, Tex.: Word, 1987) 241, 243; Barrett, *The Gospel According to St. John,* 457.

476. See Rudolf Bultmann, *The Gospel of John: A Commentary,* trans. G. R. Beasley-Murray, R. W. N. Hoare, and J. K. Riches (Philadelphia: Westminster, 1971) 600-603; Barrett, *The Gospel According to St. John,* 457.
477. Cf. Beasley-Murray, *John,* 251.

trans.). Thomas, however, does not perceive the shift in Jesus' words. He, like Peter in 13:36, remains confused about where Jesus is going (v. 5; cf. Thomas's misunderstanding at 11:16), and interprets "the way" and "where I am going" as synonyms, both pointing to Jesus' destination. The "I am" (ἐγώ εἰμι *egō eimi*) saying in v. 6*a* reveals the extent of Thomas's misunderstanding. "The way" is not a geographical term, as Thomas has perceived it, but is instead a description of the revelatory work of Jesus. To "know the way" is thus synonymous with knowing Jesus himself.

14:6a. As with the other "I am" sayings for which a predicate is supplied (e.g., 6:35; 8:12; 9:5; 11:25; 15:1; see Fig. 10, "The 'I AM' Sayings in John," 602), Jesus identifies himself in v. 6*a* with a symbol, "the way," that is at home in the variety of religions and cultures that intersected with one another in the eastern Mediterranean world (cf. the discussion of the term *logos* in the Commentary on John 1:1). For example, Bultmann, noting the prominence of language about the way in Mandean literature, proposed that the decisive religious influence on the Fourth Evangelist's use of "way" was Gnosticism.[478] As with Bultmann's suggestion about the origins of *logos*, however, the absence of any gnostic documents that predate the Gospel weakens his suggestion. Indeed, there is a stronger likelihood that some of the second-century gnostic literature contains echoes of the Gospel of John.[479] C. H. Dodd suggested that the source of the term "way" was to be found in the philosophy of the hermetic literature, a body of literature produced in Egypt that worked through the philosophical dimensions of religious life and faith.[480] Yet, as with the Mandean literature, the Hermetic literature postdates the Gospel of John. In both gnostic and hermetic literatures, one sees evidence of the richness of religious discourse in the Mediterranean world in the first and second centuries, but these parallels do not readily translate into clearly defined streams of influence.

As with *logos*, the background for the Fourth Evangelist's use of "the way" is to be found within Judaism.[481] Within the Jewish wisdom tradition, "way" (דרך *derek*) denotes the life-styles of the

"wise" (those who live in accordance with the teaching of the sages [Prov 2:8, 20]) and the "wicked" (those who flaunt wisdom [Prov 2:12, 14]). In the Psalms, "way" is used as a metaphor to describe a life lived either in accordance with the law or the will and desire of God (e.g., Ps 119:1, 3, 5, 27, 33). In this context (see also, e.g., Ps 86:11; Tob 1:3), "way" is not used strictly as the route to somewhere else (as in the Mandean and Hermetic literature), but as an expression of the faithful person's unity with God. The following quotation from a Palestinian targum provides an interesting example of the metaphorical use of "way" within first-century synagogal Judaism: "Better is Torah for the one who attends to it than the fruits of the tree of life: Torah which the Word of the Lord has prepared in order that it may be kept, so that man may live and walk by the paths of the way of the life of the world to come."[482] The combination of "way" and "life" in this passage is noteworthy, as is its eschatological orientation. These examples from biblical and post-biblical Judaism show that "way" as a metaphor for life with God was present within Judaism and thus available for adaptation by the Fourth Evangelist.

The distinctiveness of the Johannine appropriation of "way" (*hodos*) rests in its combination with the predicates that follow ("truth" [ἀλήθεια *alētheia*] and "life" [ζωή *zōē*]) and in its singular identification with the person of Jesus. As with the two "I am" sayings in John 10 ("gate," 10:7, 9; "good shepherd," 10:11, 14), in v. 6*a* Jesus reveals himself to be simultaneously the *access to* and the *embodiment of* life with God. "Truth" and "life" thus function as appositives in relation to the leading noun, "way"—that is, they clarify how and why Jesus is "the way."[483] These two nouns are not general abstract nouns, but are nouns whose specific christological content has been demonstrated throughout Jesus' life and ministry. To recognize Jesus as the truth is to affirm that as the Word made flesh, Jesus makes the truth of God available to the world (1:14, 17-18; cf. 5:33). It is to acknowledge that one's relationship with Jesus is relationship with the liberating truth of God (8:31-32), that Jesus' life and min-

478. Bultmann, *The Gospel of John*, 602-6.
479. E.g., *The Gospel of Thomas*.
480. C. H. Dodd, *The Interpretation of the Fourth Gospel*, 48-51.
481. Brown, *The Gospel According to John (XIII–XXI)*, 628-29.

482. See Targum Ps-J., Gen. 3.24, cited by Craig A. Evans, *Word and Glory: On the Exegetical and Theological Background of John's Prologue*, JSNTSup 89 (Sheffield: JSOT, 1993) 116.
483. Brown, *The Gospel According to John (XIII–XXI)*, 621; Rudolf Schnackenburg, *The Gospel According to St. John*, 3 vols. (New York: Seabury, 1982) 3:64-65.

istry are the ultimate witness to God's truth (18:37). Jesus is the "way," the promise of the possibility of unity with God, because in him one meets the truth of God.

When Jesus identifies himself as "the life," he is repeating the self-revelation that formed the heart of the Lazarus narrative (see Commentary on 11:25). As at 11:25, this saying claims God's life-giving powers for Jesus, and so serves as the key eschatological announcement of the Gospel. Jesus is life (cf. 1:4), because Jesus brings God's gift of life to the world (e.g., 3:15-16; 5:21, 26; 10:28-29; 11:25-26; 12:50). Jesus is "the way," because he is the access point to God's promise of life.

14:6b-7. The three predicate nominatives of the "I am" saying of v. 6*a* thus all point to the unity of Jesus and God in the work of salvation. This unity is stated directly in the absolute language of v. 6*b*. This verse, and its positive restatement in v. 7, voices the irreducible heart of Johannine theology (see Reflections below). The christological claim of vv. 6*b*-7 was first introduced in the concluding affirmation of the Prologue (1:18) and sounded throughout Jesus' discourses (e.g., 5:19-29; 7:28-29; 8:24-29, 54-58;

10:30, 34-38; 12:44-45). This is the heart of the good news for the Fourth Evangelist, that in Jesus, the incarnate Word, the Son of God, one can see and know God in a manner never before possible.

14:8-11. Jesus' claims in v. 7 have been the stumbling block for his conversation partners throughout the Gospel (5:37-38; 8:25-27, 42; 10:25-30), and Philip's request in v. 8 shows that they are no less of a stumbling block for his "own." Philip does not understand the nature of Jesus' self-revelation, that the incarnation is the ultimate revelation of God. Even Jesus' explicit announcement in v. 7 is not enough for Philip. Yet Jesus can offer nothing more than he has already made available to Philip and the others (v. 9). His words and works offer corroborating witness to God's presence in him (vv. 10-11; cf. 5:36-37; 7:16-17; 10:37-38; 12:48-50), but in the end the decisive question is whether Philip and the disciples believe in Jesus as the tangible, enfleshed presence of God. "Believe" (πιστεύω *pisteuō*) occurs three times in vv. 10-11, and the repetition of this verb shifts the focus from Jesus' revelation of God to the disciples' acceptance of it. This unit ends by returning to the exhortation with which it began, "Believe in God, believe also in me" (14:1; cf. vv. 10, 11).

REFLECTIONS

Rudolf Schnackenburg has rightly identified John 14:6-7 as "the high point of Johannine theology."[484] These verses announce in clear language the theological conviction that drives the Fourth Evangelist's work, "No one comes to the Father except through me." These words express the Fourth Evangelist's unshakable belief that the coming of Jesus, the Word made flesh, decisively altered the relationship between God and humanity. These words affirm that Jesus is the tangible presence of God in the world and that God the Father can be known only through that incarnate presence. Humanity's encounter with Jesus the Son makes possible a new experience of God as the Father.

Yet the very clarity and decisiveness of the Fourth Evangelist's conviction here have turned these words into a weapon with which to bludgeon one's opponents into theological submission. These words are used as a litmus test for Christian faith in myriad conversations and debates within the contemporary church. They are taken by some as the rallying cry of Christian triumphalism, proof positive that Christians have the corner on God and that people of any and all other faiths are condemned. They are seen by others as embarrassingly exclusionary and narrow-minded, and they are pointed to as evidence of the problems inherent in asserting Christian faith claims in a pluralistic world.

How is the contemporary Christian to interpret this central claim of the Fourth Gospel? It is of the utmost importance that before the interpreter decides to accept or reject the Fourth Gospel's affirmation, embrace or distance oneself from its theological view, the Fourth Evangelist

484. Schackenburg, *Der Evangelist Johannes,* 3:65.

be allowed to have his say. That is, it is incumbent upon the contemporary interpreter to engage in an act of theological imagination when interpreting this passage, to try to envision the theological claim the Fourth Evangelist might have been making in *his* context instead of assessing these words as if they were spoken directly to the contemporary context.

Jesus' claim that "no one comes to the Father except through me" is the joyous affirmation of a religious community that does, indeed, believe that God is available to them decisively in the incarnation. This claim has been announced from the opening lines of the Gospel, "No one has ever seen God. It is God the only Son, who is close to the Father's heart, who has made him known" (1:18). In many ways, John 14:6 is both truism and tautology, because, following John 1:18, it is indeed only through the incarnation that the identity of God as Father is revealed. John 14:6 is not a general metaphysical statement about "God"; Jesus does not say "No one comes to God except through me," but "No one comes to the *Father* except through me," and the specificity of that theological nomenclature needs to be taken seriously. John 14:6 is the very concrete and specific affirmation of a faith community about the God who is known to them because of the incarnation. As noted in the Reflections on the Prologue, the incarnation changes everything for the Fourth Evangelist, because through it humanity's relationship to God and God's relationship to humanity are decisively altered. The incarnation has redefined God for the Fourth Evangelist and those for whom he writes, because it brings the tangible presence of God's love to the world. "God" is not a generic deity here; God is the One whom the disciples come to recognize in the life and death of Jesus. When Jesus says "no one," he means "none of you."[485] In John 14:6, then, Jesus defines God for his disciples; the Fourth Evangelist defines God for the members of his faith community.

It is important to try to hear this joyous, world-changing theological affirmation in the first-century context of the Fourth Gospel. This is not, as is the case in the twentieth century, the sweeping claim of a major world religion, but it is the conviction of a religious minority in the ancient Mediterranean world.[486] It is the conviction of a religious group who had discovered that its understanding of the truth of God carries with it a great price (see Reflections on John 8:31-59). This conviction has led them into conflict with the Judaism that previously had been their sole religious home, and so they have had to carve out a new religious home for themselves, a home grounded in the incarnation. It is possible to hear an element of defiance in the proclamation of 14:1-11, a determination to hold to this experience and knowledge of God against all opposition and all pressure to believe otherwise. In the unambiguous words of John 14:6-7, the Fourth Gospel declares where it stands in the first-century intra-Jewish debate about the character of God and the identity of God's people.

What is often labeled in 14:1-11 as excessively exclusionary would be described more accurately as *particularism.* That is, the claims made in John 14:6 express the particularities of the Fourth Evangelist's knowledge and experience of God, and membership in the faith community for which he writes and which he envisions does indeed hinge on this claim. This claim has distanced them from their prior religious home, and thus it will shape their new one (cf. 14:2-4). The particularism of John 14:6-7 does *de facto* establish boundaries; it says, "This is who we are. We are the people who believe in the God who has been revealed to us decisively in Jesus Christ." To be included in the circle of Jesus' "own," one must recognize Jesus for who he is, which means recognizing the revelation of God in him.

The claim of John 14:6-7 becomes problematic when it is used to speak to questions that were never in the Fourth Gospel's purview. To use these verses in a battle over the relative merits of the world's religions is to distort their theological heart. It is a dangerous and destructive anachronism to cite John 14:6-7 as the final arbiter in discussions of the relative

---

485. See Paul Minear, *John: The Martyr's Gospel* (New York: Pilgrim, 1984) 108-10.
486. See David Rensberger, "Sectarianism and Theological Interpretation in John" (paper presented at the annual meeting of the SBL, Chicago, Ill., November 1994).

merits of different religions' experiences and understanding of God. The Fourth Gospel is not concerned with the fate, for example, of Muslims, Hindus, or Buddhists, nor with the superiority or inferiority of Judaism and Christianity as they are configured in the modern world. These verses are the confessional celebration of a particular faith community, convinced of the truth and life it has received in the incarnation. The Fourth Evangelist's primary concern was the clarification and celebration of what it means to believe in Jesus (cf. 14:1, 10-11). The theological vision articulated here expresses the distinctiveness of Christian identity, and it is as people shaped by this distinctiveness that Christians can take their place in conversations about world religion. Indeed, the Prologue's claims about the Logos (1:1-3) provide an opening for conversations about how one encounters the divine.

When one brackets out the questions that contemporary Christians falsely import into these verses, there is nothing outrageous or offensive about the claims made here. Rather, at the heart of Christianity is this affirmation of the decisive revelation of God in the incarnation. John 14:6 can thus be read as the core claim of Christian identity; what distinguishes Christians from peoples of other faiths is the conviction given expression in John 14:6. It is, indeed, through Jesus that Christians have access to their God.

John 14:12-24, "If You Love Me, You Will Keep My Commandments"

NIV

12I tell you the truth, anyone who has faith in me will do what I have been doing. He will do even greater things than these, because I am going to the Father. 13And I will do whatever you ask in my name, so that the Son may bring glory to the Father. 14You may ask me for anything in my name, and I will do it.

15"If you love me, you will obey what I command. 16And I will ask the Father, and he will give you another Counselor to be with you forever— 17the Spirit of truth. The world cannot accept him, because it neither sees him nor knows him. But you know him, for he lives with you and will be[a] in you. 18I will not leave you as orphans; I will come to you. 19Before long, the world will not see me anymore, but you will see me. Because I live, you also will live. 20On that day you will realize that I am in my Father, and you are in me, and I am in you. 21Whoever has my commands and obeys them, he is the one who loves me. He who loves me will be loved by my Father, and I too will love him and show myself to him."

22Then Judas (not Judas Iscariot) said, "But, Lord, why do you intend to show yourself to us and not to the world?"

a17 Some early manuscripts and is

NRSV

12Very truly, I tell you, the one who believes in me will also do the works that I do and, in fact, will do greater works than these, because I am going to the Father. 13I will do whatever you ask in my name, so that the Father may be glorified in the Son. 14If in my name you ask me[a] for anything, I will do it.

15"If you love me, you will keep[b] my commandments. 16And I will ask the Father, and he will give you another Advocate,[c] to be with you forever. 17This is the Spirit of truth, whom the world cannot receive, because it neither sees him nor knows him. You know him, because he abides with you, and he will be in[d] you.

18"I will not leave you orphaned; I am coming to you. 19In a little while the world will no longer see me, but you will see me; because I live, you also will live. 20On that day you will know that I am in my Father, and you in me, and I in you. 21They who have my commandments and keep them are those who love me; and those who love me will be loved by my Father, and I will love them and reveal myself to them." 22Judas (not Iscariot) said to him, "Lord, how is it that you will reveal yourself to us, and not to the world?"

a Other ancient authorities lack me   b Other ancient authorities read me, keep   c Or Helper   d Or among

NIV

²³Jesus replied, "If anyone loves me, he will obey my teaching. My Father will love him, and we will come to him and make our home with him. ²⁴He who does not love me will not obey my teaching. These words you hear are not my own; they belong to the Father who sent me."

NRSV

²³Jesus answered him, "Those who love me will keep my word, and my Father will love them, and we will come to them and make our home with them. ²⁴Whoever does not love me does not keep my words; and the word that you hear is not mine, but is from the Father who sent me."

COMMENTARY

14:12-14. The expression "very, truly, I tell you" with which v. 12 begins signals the introduction of a new teaching (vv. 12-14) into the discourse (cf. 5:24-25). This new teaching builds on the theme of faith in Jesus that was prominent in 14:1-11, but moves it in a new direction by focusing on the ways in which belief in Jesus empowers the believing community. Jesus has declared throughout his ministry that the works that he does are God's works, not his own (5:20, 36; 10:37-38; 14:10), that his work is to complete God's work (4:34; 17:4). Verse 12a includes those who believe in Jesus in that mutuality of work; the disciples' works will be Jesus' works in the same way that Jesus' works are God's (cf. 17:18; 20:21). In relation to Jesus, "works" refers to all the acts of his ministry, the purpose of which is always to make known "the power and character of God."[487] For the disciples to share in Jesus' works, then, is for them to share in the revealing of God to the world.

Verses 12b-14 underscore the links between the believers' works and Jesus' own work. First, the success of the disciples' works is directly dependent on Jesus' departure to the Father (v. 12b). When Jesus returns to the Father, his work in the world is completed (cf. 19:30). The events of Jesus' hour—his death, resurrection, and ascension—show forth the fullness of his love for God and the fullness of God's love for the world (cf. 3:16-17; 10:17-18; 14:31). The disciples' works, which will be done *after* the events of the hour, are therefore greater because they will reveal the completed story of the Word made flesh and hence the fullness of God's love. Their works thus are not greater than Jesus' works because of

anything intrinsic to the disciples themselves, but because they belong to the new eschatological age ushered in by Jesus' hour. As such, they continue the glorification of God through Jesus that was the purpose of Jesus' own works (v. 13b; cf. 5:44; 11:4; 17:4).

Second, Jesus' repeated promise in vv. 13-14 that he will answer the believers' prayers makes explicit that it is Jesus who acts in and through the disciples and their works (note the repetition of the expression "I will do"). Their works in reality are Jesus' works.[488] Jesus does not specify the nature of the disciples' works in vv. 12-14, but vv. 15-24 suggest that they are to be works that spring from one's love of God and Jesus, and as such continue the love that is at the heart of Jesus' own works.

14:15-24. These verses describe two dimensions of the believer's love relationship with Jesus: (1) the inseparability of one's love of Jesus and the keeping of his commandments (vv. 15, 21, 23-24) and (2) the abiding and indwelling of the presence of God, even after Jesus' death and departure with those who love him (vv. 16-20, 22-23).

14:15. A comparison of vv. 15 and 21 with vv. 23-24 shows that "commandments" (ἐντολαί *entolai,* vv. 15, 21), "word" (λόγος *logos,* v. 23), and "words" (λόγοι *logoi,* v. 24) are all synonyms. They point to the totality of what Jesus says and reveals about God. In order to interpret Jesus' words about keeping his commandments/word in these verses, they need to be placed alongside Jesus' earlier teachings about faithfulness to his word. Jesus regularly cites faithfulness to his words as the mark of belonging to him (e.g., 5:38; 8:31, 37, 51; 12:47-48; cf. 6:67-69). John 13:34-

487. C. K. Barrett, *The Gospel According to St. John,* 2nd ed. (Philadelphia: Westminster, 1978) 460.

488. Bultmann, *The Gospel of John,* 611.

35 makes clear that the sign of faithfulness to Jesus' commandments is to live a life of love grounded in Jesus' own love. Here Jesus conjoins those two aspects of keeping his commandments. When vv. 15 and 21a are read together, it becomes clear that the protasis of v. 15a does not introduce a conditional sentence, but introduces two parallel clauses that together define what it means to love Jesus. To love Jesus is to keep his commandments; to keep Jesus' commandments is to love him.

Jesus' words also point to the ways in which the disciples' love and obedience to Jesus determine their relationship with God. As with Jesus' words about the disciples' works in v. 12, his words in vv. 21 and 23 open up the distinctiveness of his love relationship with God to include the disciples. The disciples will share in the Father's love as a result of their love of Jesus (vv. 21, 23; cf. the negative statement in v. 24). This mutual love of God, Jesus, and the disciples provides the context in which the three promises of the indwelling of the divine presence in the community are to be heard: the promise of the Paraclete (vv. 16-17); of Jesus' return (vv. 18-20); and of the advent of God and Jesus (v. 22-23).

14:16-17. This is the first occurrence of the noun παράκλητος (*paraklētos*) in the Fourth Gospel. This noun derives from the verb παρακαλέω (*parakaleō*), which has a wide range of meanings that include "to exhort and encourage," "to comfort and console," "to call upon for help," and "to appeal." The noun form can mean "the one who exhorts," "the one who comforts," "the one who helps," and "the one who makes appeals on one's behalf." The Fourth Evangelist seems to draw on the whole range of meanings in the variety of functions attributed to the Paraclete in the five Paraclete passages in the Farewell Discourse (see also 14:26; 15:26; 16:8-11, 12-15).[489] The difficulty of choosing among these meanings is reflected in the various English translations of the noun *paraklētos*—e.g, "Comforter" (KJV), "Advocate" (NRSV), "Counselor" (NIV). It seems better, therefore, to translate *paraklētos* as "Paraclete" (as NJB) rather than settle on one English noun, because the Greek reader would have heard the

resonances of all the meanings that are lost to the contemporary reader when one English noun is privileged.

Jesus identifies his request to God as the origin of God's gift of the Paraclete (v. 16a). Yet in the other Paraclete passages, the relationship between God and Jesus will be nuanced slightly differently; John 14:26 most closely resembles 14:16, but at 15:26 and 16:7, Jesus speaks of himself as the one who sends the Paraclete. This interchange of the roles of God and Jesus in the description of the Paraclete's origins is not a theological inconsistency in the discourse, but rather is a further demonstration of the theological truth that undergirds this Gospel: God and Jesus are united and share fully in the work that they do (cf. 5:17, 19; 10:30, 37-38).

The use of the adjective "another" (ἄλλος *allos*) to modify "Paraclete" in v. 16a suggests that Jesus was also a Paraclete (cf. 1 John 2:1, where Jesus is explicitly identified as Paraclete). "Paraclete" thus is not simply another name for the Spirit, but is a particular way of describing the functions of the Spirit, functions held in common with Jesus. What the Paraclete does is not new, but is a continuation of the work of Jesus. This can be seen clearly in the description of the Paraclete as the Spirit of truth in v. 17. To call the Paraclete the "Spirit of truth" is to identify the Paraclete as more than a true—i.e., truthful—Spirit. As the Spirit of truth, the Paraclete shares in the work of Jesus, because Jesus is the truth (14:6). The work of the Paraclete is thus to keep the truth of Jesus present to the world after Jesus' departure (cf. 16:7-11). As with the unity of God and Jesus in their work, the relationship between Jesus and the Paraclete is also defined by the unity of their work.

The response of the world to the Paraclete's presence echoes the response of the world to the incarnation itself, a division between those who receive and those who do not (cf. 1:10-13). Yet the focus of vv. 16-17 is not ultimately on this division, but on the assurance that the presence of the Paraclete gives to Jesus' "own." Knowledge of the Paraclete is defined as the Paraclete's abiding with the believing community (v. 17b). The Paraclete is repeatedly described in ways that emphasize its presence in and relationship with the faith community: "will be with you forever";

---

489. George Johnston, *The Spirit-Paraclete in the Gospel of John* (Cambridge: Cambridge University Press, 1970).

"abides with you"; and "will be in you." The Paraclete ensures that the revelation of God in the incarnation does not end with Jesus' death and return to God. (Excursus on the Paraclete follows 16:12-15.)

14:18-20. The second promise of continuing presence is Jesus' promise of his own return (vv. 18-20). "Orphan" (ὀρφανός *orphanos*) was a common metaphor to describe disciples left without their masters,[490] but the use of the metaphor here has a special poignancy in the light of the familial and domestic imagery that runs throughout Jesus' words to his own (e.g., 13:33; 14:2-3, 10-14; 15:9-11; 16:21-24, 27). Jesus' promise that he will not leave the disciples orphaned recalls his use of the address "little children" in 13:33 and is an assurance that the intimacy of that familial relationship is not undercut by Jesus' departure. His promise to return (v. 18*b*) thus immediately counters any possible perception of Jesus' death as his abandonment of his own.

The primary referent of this promise to return is Jesus' Easter appearances; indeed, vv. 18-20 are the first in a series of promises made by Jesus in the Farewell Discourse that find fulfillment in the stories of John 20–21 (see also 14:27; 16:16, 20, 22). Verse 19 provides an anticipatory description of the post-resurrection appearances (e.g., "you will see me"; "because I live"). As in the promise of the Paraclete at v. 17, Jesus' promise of his Easter return also makes a distinction between the world and the believing community (see also 15:18-25; 16:8-11; 17:6-25). Jesus' resurrection life gives life to the believers (v. 19*b*), because it is the ultimate demonstration that Jesus is indeed "the resurrection and the life" (see 11:25-26).

The language in vv. 18-20 also highlights the eschatological dimension of the promise; "I am coming" recalls the traditional language of the parousia (cf. 14:3); "in a little while" evokes the interim period before the time of eschatological fulfillment (cf. 16:16-22; Isa 26:20); "on that day" evokes the time of eschatological fulfillment (cf.

16:23, 26; Isa 4:2; Mark 13:32).[491] The notion of the parousia is transformed here, however. The events of Jesus' hour, his departure and return, usher in a new age with God, an age in which the full mutuality and intimacy of God, Jesus, and believers will be experienced (v. 20).

The promise of Jesus' Easter return needs to be read in concert with the preceding promise of the Paraclete (vv. 16-17). The advent of the Paraclete does not render Jesus himself superfluous, nor does it supersede him. Rather, the Paraclete's presence will make the events of the resurrection available beyond their limited moment in time. It is through the Paraclete that the eschatological fulfillment of Jesus' hour becomes an experience for all believers, not just those of the first generation (see Reflections below).

14:21-24. The interrelatedness in the life of the believing community of the love of Jesus, the keeping of Jesus' commandments, and the indwelling of the divine presence is evident in the third promise of presence (vv. 22-23). In v. 21*c,* Jesus links his love for those who love him with his self-revelation, but Judas's question in v. 22 shows that he misunderstands this linkage. Judas, like Jesus' brothers at 7:3-4, is looking for a messianic sign that will impress the world,[492] and he does not recognize Jesus' love as the theophany for which he seeks (cf. Philip's misunderstanding at 14:8). The name of this second Judas does not occur in any synoptic lists of the twelve disciples. John 14–16 does not explicitly restrict the disciples present at the discourse to the Twelve, however; therefore, it is a misguided exercise to try to harmonize this name with those lists.

As is typical of Jesus' teaching (cf. 3:4-8; 4:12-14; 14:5-7), he does not address Judas's misunderstanding directly, but instead restates his words about love and revelation (v. 23). When the disciples live in love, and thereby keep Jesus' word, they experience the love of God, and it is through that love that they will also experience the indwelling of God and Jesus. The noun translated as "home" in v. 23 is the same Greek word translated as "dwelling place" in v. 2 (μονή *monē*). In 14:2-3, faith in Jesus leads to the disciples' full communion with God and Jesus in the Father's "dwelling place," and at v. 23, love

490. E.g., the disciples of Socrates at his death, *Phaedo,* 116*a*. For rabbinic examples, see Hermann L. Strack and Paul Billerbeck, *Kommentar zum Neuen Testament aus Talmud und Midrash* (München: Beck, 1924) 2:562.

491. Brown, *The Gospel According to John (XIII–XXI),* 640; Beasley-Murray, *John,* 258.

492. Brown, *The Gospel According to John (XIII–XXI),* 647.

of Jesus leads to the same end. To love Jesus is to live with God and Jesus—that is, to enter into relationship with them (cf. 15:9-10, 12), to come home. The revelation of God in Jesus is explicitly linked to the community's love of Jesus and God's love of them (cf. 3:16). The abiding presence of God and Jesus within the community is thus both the foundation and the result of the community's love. This section of the discourse concludes with a warning about how this presence can be forfeited by not living out one's love of Jesus (v. 24; cf. v. 15).

REFLECTIONS

All of Jesus' words in vv. 12-24 address the shape of the community's life after the events of Jesus' hour and as such are intimately connected to the farewell situation. The following statement from Bultmann helps to place this section of the discourse in its appropriate theological context: "The question therefore which activates the section vv. 15-24 is this: what is this love, which is directed to Jesus? And this question, too, has to be understood in the context of the 'farewell situation.' Can the disciples still love him, when he has gone? Can the next generation love him, without having had a personal relationship with him?"[493]

"Can the disciples still love him, when he has gone?" John 14:12-24 answers yes to this question, but it may be a yes that surprised even Jesus' first disciples. The disciples can still love Jesus, but neither by clinging to a cherished memory of him nor by retreating into their private experience of him. Rather, they can continue to love Jesus *by doing his works* (vv. 12-14) and *by keeping his commandments* (vv. 15-24). That is, when they move outside of their own private experience of Jesus, when they live what Jesus has taught them and demonstrated in his own life, *then* they will find themselves once again in his love.

Jesus' teachings to the disciples here about love chart the continuation of his own life into the life of his followers. Jesus lived out God's love of him by keeping God's commandments, by making God known to the world, by offering God's promise of salvation to the world, by loving fully, even to the extent of laying down his life. Jesus' union with God was not a private, mystical union, in which their love for one another was only self-beneficial—that is, for the glory of God and Jesus alone with no eye to the life of God's creation. On the contrary, the love of God and Jesus was a public love, first revealed to the world in the incarnation and repeatedly revealed in Jesus' words and works throughout his ministry. The glorification of God and Jesus in Jesus' works was for the sake of those to whom Jesus came, so that they might believe and come to share in the love of God and Jesus.

The believer's union with God and Jesus is possible after Jesus' death, resurrection, and ascension, but like the union of God and Jesus, it is not a private, mystical union of the believer with his or her God. Jesus' words in vv. 12-24 consistently point to the communal nature of union and relationship with him after the end of his earthly ministry. The promises of divine presence are promises made to the community, not to the individual. All of the personal pronouns in these verses are second-person plural, not singular. Jesus does not promise the Paraclete, or his own return, or the home-making of God and Jesus to individuals (14:23), but to a community who lives in love. God, Jesus, and the Paraclete are inseparably interconnected with one another, as the promise of God's sending the Paraclete in response to Jesus' request shows (v. 16), and they come together to those who love, to those who mirror the divine communion in their human communion with one another.

When Jesus' disciples follow his own model of love, then, it is possible for relationship with Jesus to extend beyond the first generation of believers. Relationship with Jesus does not depend on physical presence, but on the presence of the love of God in the life of the community. And the love for God is present whenever those who love Jesus keep his

493. Bultmann, *The Gospel of John,* 613.

commandments (v. 21, 23), when they continue to live out the love that Jesus showed them in his own life and death. Since in the Farewell Discourse Jesus speaks to the time after his hour, the reader of the Gospel is placed in the same situation as the narrative audience. That is, the contemporary reader must also discover what it means to have relationship with Jesus in his absence. The insistence of these verses on love as the sign of fidelity to Jesus and the way to communion with God, Jesus, and the Paraclete suggests that the believing community in any generation will enter into relationship with Jesus only when it takes on and lives out the love of the incarnation.

John 14:25-31, "Rise, Let Us Be on Our Way"

NIV

25"All this I have spoken while still with you. 26But the Counselor, the Holy Spirit, whom the Father will send in my name, will teach you all things and will remind you of everything I have said to you. 27Peace I leave with you; my peace I give you. I do not give to you as the world gives. Do not let your hearts be troubled and do not be afraid.

28"You heard me say, 'I am going away and I am coming back to you.' If you loved me, you would be glad that I am going to the Father, for the Father is greater than I. 29I have told you now before it happens, so that when it does happen you will believe. 30I will not speak with you much longer, for the prince of this world is coming. He has no hold on me, 31but the world must learn that I love the Father and that I do exactly what my Father has commanded me.

"Come now; let us leave."

NRSV

25"I have said these things to you while I am still with you. 26But the Advocate,a the Holy Spirit, whom the Father will send in my name, will teach you everything, and remind you of all that I have said to you. 27Peace I leave with you; my peace I give to you. I do not give to you as the world gives. Do not let your hearts be troubled, and do not let them be afraid. 28You heard me say to you, 'I am going away, and I am coming to you.' If you loved me, you would rejoice that I am going to the Father, because the Father is greater than I. 29And now I have told you this before it occurs, so that when it does occur, you may believe. 30I will no longer talk much with you, for the ruler of this world is coming. He has no power over me; 31but I do as the Father has commanded me, so that the world may know that I love the Father. Rise, let us be on our way."

a Or Helper

COMMENTARY

John 14:25-31 concludes this first unit of the discourse by recapitulating most of the themes of vv. 1-24. Its summary quality is pointed to by many scholars as support for their view that 14:1-31 is the original version of the discourse (see Overview to 14:1–16:33). Yet it is not at all uncommon in the discourses of this Gospel for the Evangelist to advance the discourse by returning to and summarizing earlier themes (e.g., 5:19-31; 6:35-59), and the use of that technique here should be evaluated in relation to the overall stylistic tendencies of the Gospel,

and not primarily in the service of a redactional theory.

14:25. The expression "I have said these things to you" occurs repeatedly in the Farewell Discourse as a transitional sentence both to draw together earlier teachings and to introduce a new teaching (16:1, 4, 6, 25, 33; cf. 17:1, 3). The use of the verb "remain" (μένω menō) here does not speak of the mutual indwelling of God, Jesus, and the Paraclete (14:10, 17), but of Jesus' physical presence. This verse serves as a reminder that regardless of the abiding presence of God and

Jesus with the disciples (14:23), the concrete reality of Jesus' physical departure from them remains unchanged.

14:26. The second promise of the Paraclete emphasizes the continuity between what Jesus says while he is present and what the Paraclete will teach in Jesus' absence. Verse 26 is quite specific about the precise nature of the Paraclete's teaching: The Paraclete will "remind" the disciples of Jesus' teachings. "To remind" (ὑπομιμνῄσκω *hypomimnēskō*) occurs only here in the Fourth Gospel, but a related passive form, "to remember" (μιμνῄσκομαι *mimnēskomai*), occurs at 2:22 and 12:16. These two verses are important for understanding what the Paraclete's work of reminding—that is, causing to remember—looks like in the life of the believing community. At 2:22 and 12:16, the Fourth Evangelist notes that after Jesus' resurrection, the disciples "remembered" what Jesus had said and done, and they were brought to deeper understanding and faith. The Paraclete does not teach new things, but keeps Jesus' own teachings alive in the post-resurrection community.

The primary description of Jesus in this Gospel is as the one whom the Father sent, and God's sending of Jesus is associated with his mission to complete God's work (e.g., 3:17; 4:34; 6:38; 7:29; 8:29; 10:36; 12:44; 14:24). The notation that God will send the Paraclete in Jesus' name indicates that the Paraclete, too, shares in God's work (cf. 5:43). Verse 26 is the only place in John where the Paraclete is referred to as the "Holy Spirit." It is important that this reference be read in its Johannine context and not with the full weight of later trinitarian theology. The Fourth Gospel's description of the interrelationship of Father, Son, and Paraclete is the seed bed from which trinitarian doctrine grew, but the doctrinal formality of those later articulations should not be read back into the description of the Spirit/Paraclete in the Fourth Gospel. "The Holy Spirit" is one of the ways the Fourth Evangelist describes the presence of the Paraclete in the believing community, but not the only or even the primary way. (See Excursus "The Paraclete," 774-78.)

14:27. Jesus' words of assurance to his disciples contain a new promise. Verse 27*a* is the first occurrence of the word "peace" (εἰρήνη *eirēnē*) in the Fourth Gospel. In the OT, "peace" (שׁלוֹם *šālôm*) was a conventional leave-taking address (e.g., 1 Sam 1:17), but Jesus is not simply saying farewell to his disciples with this promise of peace. In the context of Jesus' death, the verb "to leave" (ἀφίημι *aphiēmi*) takes on the meaning of a bequest, and its use here provides an interesting counterpoint with its use in v. 18. In that verse, Jesus promised not to leave (*aphiēmi*) the disciples "orphans," and his promise of his peace supports that earlier promise. The disciples will not be orphans—that is, they will not be alone—because they will live in the peace of Jesus (cf. 16:33). The peace that Jesus offers is not the world's peace—neither the false promise of security (e.g., Jer 6:14) nor the end of conflict. The peace that Jesus gives is *his* peace, a peace that derives from the heart of Jesus' life. The peace of Jesus is "the all-embracing sphere of his life (see v. 19), his love (vv. 21, 23), his joy (15:11; 16:22; 17:13)."[494] The gift of peace rests at the center of Israel's eschatological hopes (e.g., Isa 52:7; 54:10; Ezek 37:26-28; Zech 9:10) and is now available in Jesus.

The promise of Jesus' peace is not an occasion for complacency, however, as is seen by Jesus' repetition of the exhortation with which the discourse opened (v. 27*c*; cf. 14:1). The addition of the second imperative in v. 27*d* (lit., "Let them not be cowardly [δειλιάτω *deiliatō*]") reinforces the fact that these are not sentimental imperatives, simply telling the disciples not to worry, but call the disciples to find strength to face the new circumstances in which Jesus' departure places them.

14:28. Verse 28*a* points back to v. 3 and once again brings the disciples face to face with the reality of Jesus' departure. Jesus' words to the disciples about their love in v. 28*b* are expressed as an unreal condition ("if you loved me, you would rejoice . . . "). Some manuscripts soften the sentence by changing the Greek verb into a real condition (that is, a statement of the disciples' actual love for Jesus), but the unreal condition is essential to its meaning. Jesus' words ask the disciples to look at their understanding of the nature and meaning of love in their relationship with Jesus: Do they love only for their own benefit, or can they love for Jesus' benefit as well? If they are able to be generous in their love, then

494. Rudolf Schnackenburg, *The Gospel According to St. John,* 3:84.

they will rejoice.[495] Jesus' words here recall the parable of the bridegroom told by John the Baptist at 3:29-30. Like the friend of the bridegroom, the disciples should love Jesus enough to rejoice that he completes his work by returning to the Father.

Jesus' statement "the Father is greater than I" became a pivotal text in the christological controversies of the third and fourth centuries CE. In order to understand what Jesus is saying to his disciples about his departure, however, his words need to be read independently of the use made of them by Arius and the answers to Arius offered by either Athanasius and Origen or Cyril of Alexandria and Augustine.[496] John 14:28 is not about the creation of the Son, nor is it in any way about the metaphysical nature of the relationship of God and Jesus. Rather, as with 10:30 and 38, these words speak to the relationship of God and Jesus to each other in the work that they share.

First, God is the one who sent Jesus, the incarnate Word, into the world to do God's work. God has given Jesus his words to say and works to do (cf. 5:19-20). As the one sent by God, Jesus cannot be greater than the one who sent him (13:16). God, as the originator of Jesus' saving work, is greater than he is. Second, all of Jesus' life and ministry have been to make God known (1:18). Jesus' reminder of the Father's greatness is a reminder that Jesus' life is all about God, not about himself. It is a cause for rejoicing when Jesus returns to the Father, because his revelation of the character of God is completed.

14:29-31. This section of the Farewell Discourse is brought to a close by an announcement of the cosmic significance of Jesus' departure. Verse 29 repeats almost verbatim Jesus' words at 13:19; in both instances, Jesus wants his disciples to recognize that the events of the hour belong to his revelation of God and so are an occasion for faith. Verses 30-31 focus on the struggle with the world that is at the heart of Jesus' death and departure. The "ruler of this world" (v. 30) is an apocalyptic expression, depicting the devil, the embodiment of evil and opposition to God. The cosmic conflict with God's opponent will be waged at Jesus' death, but it is a conflict whose outcome is known and assured ("has no power over me"). As at 12:31, the inevitability

of the judgment of the world in Jesus' death is stressed (see also 16:11).

The powerlessness of the ruler of this world is contrasted in v. 31 with Jesus' obedience to God's commandment. God's commandment is for Jesus to give eternal life to the world and is grounded in God's love for the world (3:16-17). The contrast between the two antagonists in the cosmic battle could not be more clearly drawn: the ruler of this world, who embodies everything that is opposed to God, and Jesus, the Son of God, whose actions demonstrate his love for God.

As noted in the Overview to 14:1–16:33, the last phrase of 14:31 ("Rise, let us be on our way") is one of the most controversial in Fourth Gospel scholarship. The difficulty with the verse is that while it seems to be instructions from Jesus to his disciples to depart, no change of location is noted until 18:1. Also as noted in the Overview, the consensus solution to this problem is to postulate that 14:31 was the original conclusion to the discourse and is, indeed, a direction to depart and that chaps. 15–17 are later additions to this original discourse. Yet this consensus solution is not without difficulties, the most glaring of which is that it seems to assume that what is now such an obvious disjunction to critical commentators would have been unnoticed or ignored by the person (or persons) who appended chaps. 15–17 to 14:31. In addition, this solution asks three brief words in the Greek text to support a major critical hypothesis.

Scholars who have attempted to wrestle with the text as it is, without recourse to either a displacement or an editorial theory, are rare. Among major commentators of John, only Hoskyns and Dodd can be included in that group. Hoskyns interprets 14:31*d* as the Johannine echo of Mark 14:42 ("Get up, let us be going. See, my betrayer is at hand").[497] The Fourth Gospel has no scene of Jesus' "agony" in the Garden of Gethsemane (Matt 26:30-35; Mark 14:32-42; Luke 22:39-46), and much of the material from the Gethsemane traditions has echoes in other places in John (see, e.g., the Commentary on John 12:27-28). Dodd, too, appeals to Mark 14:42 in interpreting John 14:31*d*.[498] As

495. Raymond E. Brown, *The Gospel According to John (XIII–XXI)*, AB 29A (Garden City, N.Y.: Doubleday, 1970) 654.

496. For a discussion of the exegesis of this text in the christological controversies, see T. E. Pollard, "The Exegesis of John x.30 in the Early Trinitarian Controversies," *NTS* 3 (1956–57) 334-49.

497. E. C. Hoskyns, *The Fourth Gospel* (London: Faber & Faber, 1947) 462, 464-65.

498. C. H. Dodd, *The Interpretation of the Fourth Gospel* (Cambridge: Cambridge University Press, 1953) 406-9; *Historical Tradition in the Fourth Gospel* (Cambridge: Cambridge University Press, 1963) 68, 72.

v. 30 makes clear, in John, Jesus' real enemy is the devil, not Judas, and the battle with that enemy has already been joined. In that context, then, with this concluding exhortation Jesus summons his disciples to enter into the conflict with him.

Given the reworking and displacement of traditional passion material throughout the Fourth Gospel (e.g., 2:13-22; 6:51-60; 11:53), the suggestions of Hoskyns and Dodd have more merit than they are usually accorded.[499] The advantage of these suggestions is that they require the interpreter to read John 14:31*d* in its present position in the discourse and not dismiss it simply as a faulty editorial seam. They also require the interpreter to look at the exhortation not simply as a misplaced instruction to depart, but as an exhortation that might have theological content. From

Jesus' opening words in 14:2, spatial language has doubled for relational language throughout this chapter (see, e.g., 14:6-7). It is consonant, therefore, with the language about place in John 14 to interpret the words "on our way" (ἐντεῦθεν *enteuthen*) as being about relationship with Jesus at his hour, as much as they are about physical location. The first-person plural pronouns of 14:31*d* include the disciples in the eschatological moment of Jesus' departure and mark the ushering in of the promise of 14:3—Jesus will take his disciples to himself, and thus to their place and home with God. John 14:31*d* thus ends this first unit of the discourse on a note of eschatological triumph quite in keeping with the rest of vv. 30-31. The impotence of the ruler of this world is a reality; the disciples' home and full relationship with God beckons. Indeed, this note of eschatological triumph provides the theological foundation for the continuation of the discourse in John 15–16.

---

499. Note the dismissal of these positions by Brown, *The Gospel According to John (XIII–XXI)*, 657; Barrett, *The Gospel According to St. John*, 454; Beasley-Murray, *John*, 263, all of whom advocate the two-discourse theory.

REFLECTIONS

The governing theological and pastoral concern of John 14:1-31 is to prepare the community of Jesus' followers for life in his absence. This theme is captured most poignantly in the promise of Jesus to his disciples in John 14:18: "I will not leave you orphaned; I am coming to you." This promise speaks directly to the disciples' fear and despair—that they will be left alone, that the new life and hope for a future that Jesus has given them will end when his physical presence among them ends, that they will be left like children without parents, with no one to care for them, with no one to love and no one to love them—as they face the inevitability of Jesus' departure.

It is the wonder of the Farewell Discourse that on the eve of Jesus' own death, he pauses to speak to the disciples about their fears, anxieties, and despair. The words he offers in John 14 are not simplistic offers of comfort and assurance, however, but derive from his knowledge of the love of God for him and his "own," and his confidence in the triumph of that love over "the ruler of this world." In John 14, Jesus moves the disciples beyond the present moment in which they are living into the future that is grounded in the certitude of the resurrection and the gift of the Spirit. He offers them a vision of a future shaped by the promises of God, in which God is always present to them—through their love for one another and through the communal indwelling of God, Jesus, and the Paraclete. Over and over again in John 14, Jesus sounds the note that the disciples will not face the future alone, that the gift God has given to them in Jesus will not terminate with the end of Jesus' life, but will take on new shape when, under the guidance of the Paraclete, they live out God's commandment to love.

The Farewell Discourse will spell out in specific detail the adversity and strife that the followers of Jesus will experience on account of their love for him (e.g., 15:20; 16:1-2), but the focus of this opening section of the discourse is on the theological resources available to them so that they will believe that they will triumph as Jesus has triumphed. Jesus calls them to recognize the indomitable power of the love of God that Jesus has made known to them.

One way to think about Jesus' words in John 14 (and the rest of the Farewell Discourse) is as Jesus' preaching to his gathered followers. Jesus offers his disciples the good news of the love of God and of the abiding presence of God with them, even when the circumstances of their lives would indicate otherwise. In the face of the evidence that says that the battle is lost, that death will claim Jesus, and that the hope Jesus offered them is thereby nullified, Jesus speaks words of renewed hope and assurance, "Do not let your hearts be troubled, and do not let them be afraid" (14:27). The speaking of the assurance of God's presence against the fears of the world can be traced back into the temple liturgy of Israel and the exilic preaching of Second Isaiah. In the temple liturgy, the priest's spoken word, "Do not be afraid," marked the turn from despair to hope in Israel's laments (e.g., Psalm 13; Lam 3:55-57). In the preaching of Second Isaiah, it was the insistent refrain of that same salvation oracle, "Do not be afraid," that led the exiles to believe that a new future with God was possible (e.g., Isa 41:8-13; 43:1-7; 44:1-5). In the preaching of Jesus in the Farewell Discourse, that refrain thus occurs again, summoning disciples to believe in a life shaped not by Jesus' absence, but by the unending presence of God.[500]

Both the form and substance of John 14 provide powerful resources for the life and faith of the contemporary church. Its form, the offer of a confident word of hope to meet one's fears, is often neglected in the theological and pastoral debates that sometimes threaten to consume the life of the church. Its substance, that God's presence will not be defeated by any distress, can give the church renewed strength and hope to live as the people of God. Jesus' words in the Farewell Discourse offer his first followers and contemporary believers the possibility of a world in which hope overcomes despair, God's presence overcomes anxiety about God's absence, and in which the present holds in it the seeds of a fresh future shaped by love, not fear.

500. See Gail R. O'Day, "Towards a Biblical Theology of Preaching," in *Listening to the Word,* ed. Gail R. O'Day and Thomas G. Long (Nashville: Abingdon, 1993) 17-32.

John 15:1-17, "Abide in My Love"

15 "I am the true vine, and my Father is the gardener. [2]He cuts off every branch in me that bears no fruit, while every branch that does bear fruit he prunes[a] so that it will be even more fruitful. [3]You are already clean because of the word I have spoken to you. [4]Remain in me, and I will remain in you. No branch can bear fruit by itself; it must remain in the vine. Neither can you bear fruit unless you remain in me.

[5]"I am the vine; you are the branches. If a man remains in me and I in him, he will bear much fruit; apart from me you can do nothing. [6]If anyone does not remain in me, he is like a branch that is thrown away and withers; such branches are picked up, thrown into the fire and burned. [7]If you remain in me and my words remain in you, ask whatever you wish, and it will be given

[a]2 The Greek for *prunes* also means *cleans.*

15 "I am the true vine, and my Father is the vinegrower. [2]He removes every branch in me that bears no fruit. Every branch that bears fruit he prunes[a] to make it bear more fruit. [3]You have already been cleansed[a] by the word that I have spoken to you. [4]Abide in me as I abide in you. Just as the branch cannot bear fruit by itself unless it abides in the vine, neither can you unless you abide in me. [5]I am the vine, you are the branches. Those who abide in me and I in them bear much fruit, because apart from me you can do nothing. [6]Whoever does not abide in me is thrown away like a branch and withers; such branches are gathered, thrown into the fire, and burned. [7]If you abide in me, and my words abide in you, ask for whatever you wish, and it will be done for you. [8]My Father is glorified by this, that

[a] The same Greek root refers to pruning and cleansing

NIV

you. [8]This is to my Father's glory, that you bear much fruit, showing yourselves to be my disciples.

[9]"As the Father has loved me, so have I loved you. Now remain in my love. [10]If you obey my commands, you will remain in my love, just as I have obeyed my Father's commands and remain in his love. [11]I have told you this so that my joy may be in you and that your joy may be complete. [12]My command is this: Love each other as I have loved you. [13]Greater love has no one than this, that he lay down his life for his friends. [14]You are my friends if you do what I command. [15]I no longer call you servants, because a servant does not know his master's business. Instead, I have called you friends, for everything that I learned from my Father I have made known to you. [16]You did not choose me, but I chose you and appointed you to go and bear fruit—fruit that will last. Then the Father will give you whatever you ask in my name. [17]This is my command: Love each other."

NRSV

you bear much fruit and become[a] my disciples. [9]As the Father has loved me, so I have loved you; abide in my love. [10]If you keep my commandments, you will abide in my love, just as I have kept my Father's commandments and abide in his love. [11]I have said these things to you so that my joy may be in you, and that your joy may be complete.

[12]"This is my commandment, that you love one another as I have loved you. [13]No one has greater love than this, to lay down one's life for one's friends. [14]You are my friends if you do what I command you. [15]I do not call you servants[b] any longer, because the servant[c] does not know what the master is doing; but I have called you friends, because I have made known to you everything that I have heard from my Father. [16]You did not choose me but I chose you. And I appointed you to go and bear fruit, fruit that will last, so that the Father will give you whatever you ask him in my name. [17]I am giving you these commands so that you may love one another."

[a] Or be   [b] Gk slaves   [c] Gk slave

COMMENTARY

John 15:1-17 contains the final "I am" sayings in the Gospel (vv. 1, 5) and introduces the governing metaphor of this unit: the vine and its branches. This metaphor is developed most fully in vv. 1-6, so that many scholars see these opening verses as an independent figure, similar to the figure of the sheepfold in John 10:1-5. For example, Brown proposes that 15:1-6 belongs to the genre of puzzle or riddle (מָשָׁל *māšāl*, see the discussion of this term at 10:6), a genre well-documented in Hebrew literature.[501] He further proposes that this vineyard *māšāl* originated in another context and was located secondarily in the Farewell Discourse. Based on this understanding of the figurative language in vv. 1-6, Brown divides 15:1-17 into two parts: (1) vv. 1-6, the figure, and (2) vv. 7-17, its exposition and application. Brown thus notes an exact analogy between the structure of John 10:1-18 (vv. 1-5, the figure; vv. 7-18, exposition and application) and John 15:1-17.[502]

This understanding of the literary character of John 15:1-17 has several major limitations, however. First, as is the case with the pastoral imagery of John 10, the vineyard imagery is not as self-contained in vv. 1-6 as Brown's analysis would suggest. The imagery recurs in v. 8 ("bear much fruit") and v. 16 ("bear fruit"), suggesting that the line between figure and exposition of the figure cannot be drawn cleanly. The problematic nature of the line between figure and exposition in this text can be seen in the variety of scholarly proposals on how to subdivide vv. 1-17 into its component parts.[503] Second, even within vv. 1-6, the line between figure and exposition is not completely clean. In vv. 3-5, Jesus repeatedly uses second-person plural pronouns to open up the vineyard figure to appeal directly to his listeners' experience. The interweaving of third- and second-

---

501. Brown, *The Gospel According to John (XIII–XXI)*, 668; followed by Schnackenburg, *The Gospel According to St. John*, 3:108; Beasley-Murray, *John*, 269.
502. Brown, *The Gospel According to John (XIII–XXI)*, 665-67.

503. For example, Bultmann, *John*, 529; Kysar, *John*, 238; and Segovia, *The Farewell of the Word*, 127-31 identify vv. 1-8 and 9-17 as the two parts, while Schnackenburg, *The Gospel According to St. John*, 3:75-96 divides the unit in two at v. 11.

person pronouns throughout vv. 1-6 under-cuts Brown's view that the "third person dominates the imagery" of these verses and thus raises questions about his isolation of this figure from the rest of the discourse.[504] Third, Brown's analysis overlooks the distinctive role of the "I am" sayings in 15:1-6. His analogy with 10:1-18 breaks down at this point,[505] because in 10:1-18 the "I am" sayings are found in vv. 7-18, the section that develops the figure, whereas in John 15, they are found in the figure itself. The "I am" statements of 15:1, 5 are thus treated almost as independent sayings and not integrated fully into their literary and theological context. In both 10:7-18 and 15:1-17, the "I am" sayings are more generative of the content and shape of the discourses in which they are embedded than Brown's analysis allows.

Barrett and Dodd come closer to understanding the literary character of the discourse of 15:1-17. Because Barrett eschews any generic identification of this passage and speaks instead of "John's reflection upon the traditional image [the vine],"[506] Dodd's comments are more helpful. Dodd does not attempt to subdivide this unit into figure and interpretation, but instead notes the complete integration of figurative language and language that speaks directly of Jesus and his disciples throughout this unit. "The language indeed changes to and fro between the literal and the metaphorical in a way which would be bewilder-ing, if the reader were not conscious all through that all the statements made really refer to Christ and his disciples, under the symbol of a vine and its branches, rather than to any earthly vine."[507]

Dodd's observation suggests that any attempt to differentiate sharply between figurative and "literal" (language that speaks directly of Jesus and his situation) in this discourse is a distortion of the very nature of this discourse. That is, the categories of figure and exposition are an external imposition on the way the Fourth Evangelist uses language and develops his theology. The Fourth Evangelist uses metaphor as one of the primary language tools in constructing his discourses, so that the word pictures he creates are inseparable

from the theology he is communicating (cf. the Commentary on 10:1-21). The correct analogy to draw between chaps. 10 and 15, then, is between the discourse of 10:7-18 (with its four "I am" sayings) and 15:1-17 (with its two "I am" sayings), because each of those texts is a discourse that is shaped and governed by its metaphorical content. In each text, there is continual movement be-tween the metaphorical and the "literal."

15:1. Jesus' words at 15:1 are the beginning of a lengthy monologue (see Overview to John 14:1–16:33). The transition from 14:31 to the "I am" statement of 15:1 is abrupt, but no more abrupt than many other transitions in earlier dis-courses in the Gospel (see, e.g., the transitions from 9:41 to 10:1; 13:38 to 14:1).

In the "I am" (ἐγώ εἰμι *egō eimi*) saying of 15:1*a* (see Fig. 10, "The 'I AM' Sayings in John," 602), Jesus once again identifies himself with a symbol common to the religions of the Mediter-ranean world, and scholarly debate again focuses on whether the symbol of the vine derives pri-marily from Gnosticism or Judaism. The case for Gnostic influence is particularly weak with regard to the vine metaphor, however. When one studies the parallels adduced from Mandaean texts,[508] it becomes clear that the ideas of these later texts have been read back into John 15 by scholars. For example, Bultmann identifies the vine of 15:1 with the Mandaean "tree of life,"[509] but as Schnackenburg has rightly pointed out, the word *life* appears nowhere in John 15:1-17.[510] In addi-tion, to maintain the claim of Gnostic influence, the interpreter must focus exclusively on the vine as a symbol for Jesus and disregard the develop-ment of the vine imagery as a symbol for the community in 15:1-17.

When one turns to Judaism, one finds vineyard symbolism that is consonant with the use of the symbol in John 15. In Sir 24:16-17, for example, Wisdom compares herself to a vine: "Like the vine I bud forth delights,/ and my blossoms become glorious and abundant fruit" (NRSV). The song of

504. Brown, *The Gospel According to John (XIII–XXI)*, 667.
505. As he himself notes in passing, ibid., 666.
506. Barrett, *The Gospel According to St. John*, 2nd ed. (Philadelphia: Westminster, 1978) 471.
507. Dodd, *Interpretation*, 136.

508. E.g., "We are a vine, the vine of life, a tree on which there is no lie, the tree of praise, from the odor of which each man receives life" (*Ginza* 59.39–60.2). See the list of texts in Eduard Schweizer, *Ego Eimi . . . Die Religionsgeschichtliche Herkunft und theologische Bedeuting der Johan-nesischen Bildreden, zugleich ein Beitrag zur Quellenfrage des vierten Evangeliums* (Göttingen: Vandenhoeck & Ruprecht, 1939) 39-41; fol-lowed by Bultmann, *The Gospel of John*, 530-31.
509. Bultmann, *The Gospel of John*, 529.
510. Schnackenburg, *Der Evangelist Johannes*, 3:98.

the vineyard (Isa 5:1-7) offers the parade example of "vine" as a symbol for the people of God. In this text, "the house of Israel and the people of Judah" are explicitly identified as "the vineyard of the Lord" (v. 7). The failure of Judah to live in justice and righteousness is expressed through the metaphor of yielding fruit: God, the planter, expected grapes, but Judah produced only wild grapes (vv. 2, 4). These verses also make use of the language of clearing away (v. 5) and pruning (v. 6) to describe God's actions toward the vineyard. Similar imagery reappears in Jer 2:21; Ezek 19:10-14; and Hos 10:1 (cf.Ps 80:8-19; Isa 27:2-6; Ezek 15:1-8; 17:7-8). Vine imagery remained a symbol for Israel in rabbinic Scripture interpretation,[511] as well as in the synoptic Gospels (Matt 21:33-46; Mark 12:1-12; Luke 20:9-16). The vine imagery in John 15:1-17 should thus be read in the context of the rich use of this symbol in Jewish Scriptures and tradition.[512]

As with the symbols of the other "I am" statements, the traditional symbol of the vine is wholly redefined by its christological content. Jesus does not simply adapt the vine imagery in order to suggest that he is now the true Israel, however. In order to understand what Jesus means when he identifies himself as the vine in vv. 1 and 5, one must read the two "I am" sayings in conjunction with the additional predicates that follow them. In v. 1, Jesus' self-identification is lodged in the context of his relationship with God, in v. 5 in the context of his relationship with the community of his followers. When Jesus speaks of himself as the vine, then, his words are not only self-revelatory, but are revelatory of the interrelationship of God, Jesus, and the community in the life of faith as well. All three elements— gardener, vine, and branches—are essential to the production of fruit. The repetition of the "I am" saying in vv. 1 and 5 positions Jesus as the middle ground between God and the community.

When Jesus speaks of "my Father" as the gardener in v. 1, he expresses in agricultural imagery the truth that he stated directly to his disciples in 14:28, "the Father is greater than I." It is the same truth that lies behind the father/son

parable of 5:19-20: God is the source and guiding hand that governs Jesus and his work (cf. 4:36-37; 10:28-30). Like the true light (1:9) and the true bread from heaven (6:32), Jesus is the "true" (ἀληθινός *alēthinos*) vine because he comes from the Father (cf. 17:3, "the only true [*alēthinos*] God").

15:2. Like the song of the vineyard in Isaiah 5, v. 2 depicts the role of God the gardener in the judgment of the vineyard (cf. esp. Isa 5:5-6). The description of God's actions toward both unproductive and productive branches involves a word play that is difficult to reproduce in an English translation. The verb for "prune" (καθαίρω *kathairō*) in v. 2*b* is a compound form of the root verb "to remove" (αἴρω *airō*), which is used in v. 2*a*. Beasley-Murray's translation of the two verbs ("cuts off"/ "cuts clean") may come closest to giving the English-language reader a sense of how the Greek reader would have heard this verse.[513] "To bear fruit" is a common image in the OT to speak of the community's faithfulness (e.g., Ps 1:3), but it is important to ask what that metaphor means in the specific context of the Farewell Discourse. When John 15:2 is read in the light of 14:1-31, "bearing fruit" emerges as another way to speak about the works of love that are required of Jesus' followers (14:12, 15, 21, 23). The unproductive branches of which v. 2 speaks are those people *within* the Christian faith community who do not bear fruit in love. This verse is not a polemic against Jewish apostasy,[514] nor does it point back to Judas's betrayal.[515] Its concern is with those people who are already in relationship with Jesus ("every branch in me").[516]

15:3-4. The verb *kathairō* has the double meaning of "to prune" and "to cleanse" (note the NIV and NRSV footnotes), so that with this verb the Fourth Evangelist can simultaneously evoke agricultural realism and theological truth.[517] Jesus' words in vv. 3-4*a* build on this double meaning and equate "cleansing" with staying in relationship to Jesus and his word ("abide in me as I abide in you"). Jesus' abiding in the disciples

---

511. E.g., *Lev. Rab.* 36:2, a midrash on Psalm 80.
512. For a thorough listing of the Jewish parallels to John 15, see Craig A. Evans, *Word and Glory: On the Exegetical and Theological Background of John's Prologue,* JSNTSup 89 (Sheffield: JSOT, 1993) 37-45.

513. George R. Beasley-Murray, *John,* WBC 36 (Waco, Tex.: Word, 1987) 266.
514. Brown, *The Gospel According to John (XIII–XXI),* 666.
515. E. C. Hoskyns, *The Fourth Gospel* (London: Faber & Faber, 1947) 471.
516. Barrett, *The Gospel According to St. John,* 473.
517. Dodd, *Interpretation,* 136.

provides the grounds for their faithfulness to him. These verses recall the foot washing in John 13, where cleansing was also identified as being in relationship with Jesus (to have a "share" with Jesus, 13:8-10). The return to the agricultural metaphor in v. 4*b* reinforces that relationship with Jesus is the key to bearing fruit. Note that the branch's relationship to the vine is described with the same verb that describes the disciples' relationship to Jesus, "to abide" (μένω *menō*). Agricultural imagery and more direct theological language are completely intertwined in these opening verses of John 15.

15:5-6. The "I am" saying with which v. 5 begins explicitly links the community's self-identity with Jesus' identity. This linkage is reinforced in v. 5*c-d*, which restates the claim of v. 4. The vivid description in v. 6 of the removal and disposal of branches is set in antithetical parallelism to Jesus' positive words about abiding and bearing fruit in v. 5. The language of this verse is an accurate representation of the pruning and clearing of a vineyard (cf. Ps 80:16; Ezek 15:1-8; Matt. 13:30). It builds on the agricultural imagery of v. 2, but in that verse the focus is on God's actions as gardener (as amplification of v. 1*b*), whereas in v. 6 the focus is on the branches themselves (as amplification of v. 5*b*).

15:7-10. These verses are an excellent example of the interweaving of themes that characterize the Farewell Discourse. In these verses, the themes of John 14 are revisited in the context of the vineyard imagery of 15:1-6. For example, v. 7 echoes the promises of 14:13-14, but explicitly links the promise of answered prayer with the community's abiding with Jesus (cf. 14:16 also). Verse 8 reaffirms the claim of 14:12-14 that the community's works continue the glorification of God that characterizes Jesus' own works. The community's works are depicted in the agricultural imagery of vv. 1-6, "bear fruit." The two verb clauses in v. 8*b*, "bear much fruit" and "become my disciples," are complementary aorist subjunctives, but they are not synonyms. To bear fruit—that is, do works of love—is the tangible sign of discipleship (cf. 13:34-35). The NIV translation correctly communicates the relationship of the two verbs in v. 8*b*, but it does so by paraphrasing the Greek text. Verses 9-10 make the connections between John 14 and 15 explicit; the

ground of the community's abiding with Jesus is the love that God and Jesus share with each other and that the community is called to enact (cf. 14:20-24, 31).

15:11. The refrain with which v. 11 begins ("I have said these things to you") marks a transition in the discourse (cf. 14:25; 16:1, 25). Jesus' words about joy complement his words to the disciples about their joy in 14:28. The unity and mutuality that love makes possible, symbolized by the unity of vine and branches, leads to full joy (cf. 3:29-30; 16:24; 17:13).

15:12-17. This passage builds on what precedes, but focus even more directly than vv. 1-11 on what it means for the disciples to live out Jesus' love. Verse 12 is a direct restatement of the love commandment of 13:34 and sets the theme for all that follows. Verse 13 is the most explicit statement in the Gospel of what it means to love as Jesus loves. Jesus' words in v. 13 echo the ideal of friendship as expressed in classical Greek philosophy (e.g., both Plato and Aristotle point to death for others as the noble ideal), but the classical ideal is given new content through the life and death of Jesus. That Jesus' death is the ultimate demonstration of his love has been implied in 10:17-18, in the foot washing narrative of John 13, and in the love commandment itself, but is only now stated directly.

The word translated "friend" (φίλος *philos*) in vv. 13-15 is from the verb "to love" (φιλέω *phileō*). The Fourth Gospel uses the two Greek verbs for "love" (ἀγαπάω *agapaō* and *phileō*) interchangeably (cf., e.g., 13:2 and 20:2; 5:20 and 10:17), so when Jesus speaks of friends here, he is really saying "those who are loved" (cf. the description of Lazarus at 11:3, 11). The English noun "friend" does not fully convey the presence of love that undergirds the Johannine notion of friendship. Verse 14 makes it even clearer that Jesus is not simply appealing to the noble ideal of friendship in v. 13, but to an understanding of friendship wholly grounded in Jesus' particular love. A comparison of 14:15 and 21 with 15:14 suggests that to be Jesus' friend and to love Jesus are synonymous, because both are defined as keeping Jesus' commandments.

At the foot washing, Jesus spoke of his relationship to his disciples with the servant/master metaphor (13:13-16), but as his hour draws even closer that relationship changes (v. 15). Jesus' disciples are now his friends, because he has kept nothing about God from them (cf. 16:25). Jesus has involved the disciples in the intimacy of his relationship with God (e.g., 14:2, 23, 31; 15:9). Again, in the context of the Farewell Discourse and the restatement of the love commandment in 15:12, "everything that I have heard from my Father" has to be interpreted as referring to the love of God and Jesus that receives its full expression in Jesus' death. It is the events of Jesus' hour that determine the change in status from servants to "those who are loved" (cf. 19:26-27).

The language of friendship is immediately contextualized by language of election in v. 16a. This language of election does not speak of the election of the Twelve,[518] because there is no indication anywhere in the Farewell Discourse of the number and composition of the circle that is present with Jesus on this last evening. Rather, Jesus reminds the disciples (including the readers) that their place with him is the result of his initiative, not theirs; relationship with Jesus is ultimately a result of God's grace (cf. 6:37-39, 44).

Jesus follows this reminder of election with a reminder of commission and vocation (v. 16b). "Appointed" translates the Greek verb τίθημι (tithēmi), the verb used in v. 13 to speak of laying down one's life (see also 10:11, 17-18). This verb thus depicts the disciples' commission as grounded in Jesus' gift of his life. The description of the disciples' commission returns to the agricultural imagery with which John 15 began ("bear fruit"). The language of appointment and commission in this verse suggests a possible mission dimension to bearing fruit: The disciples are commissioned by Jesus to go and do works of love (cf. 17:18; 20:21). Jesus describes the disciples' works as "fruit that will last" (μένω menō), suggesting that their works, too, will attest to the abiding presence of and union with God and Jesus. This verse may also contain an allusion to the lasting character of the church as evidence of Jesus' continuing presence (cf. the description of the Paraclete at 14:16-17). As a final guarantee of the community's union with God and Jesus, Jesus repeats his promise of answered prayer (v.

16c; cf. 15:7). Jesus prays to God with full confidence that he is heard and will be answered (see Jesus' prayers at 11:41-42; 12:28-30; 17:1-26), and he promises the disciples that they can pray with that same confidence. They thus share fully in Jesus' relationship with God, further evidence that they are Jesus' "friends."

The repetition of the love commandment in v. 17 provides a frame with Jesus' words in v. 12. This verse explicitly restates the theme of the preceding unit, but it also serves as a transition to the next section of the Farewell Discourse, 15:18–16:4a. In that section, the focus shifts from the love within the community to the hate and strife the community will experience in its dealings with "the world." Two themes that occupy a prominent place in the farewell setting, the love commandment and the theme of the abiding presence and relationship (menō) of God and Jesus with the community are thus brought to their joint conclusion in John 15:1-17. These themes will be picked up again in Jesus' culminating prayer in John 17 (vv. 21, 23, 26), but Jesus will not speak to his disciples again about either loving or abiding.

Many scholars debate whether eucharistic significance should be accorded the vine symbolism of John 15:1-17,[519] but that debate seems to misread the function of this image in the Farewell Discourse. The farewell meal is governed in the Fourth Gospel by the foot washing, not by the institution of the eucharist (see Commentary on John 6). As noted in the Commentary on John 13, the foot washing is an act through which the disciples share in Jesus' presence and that provides a model for their own acts of love. The vine image thus provides the crowning symbol for the life of a community who lives out the love that Jesus shared with it in the foot washing and in his death. The intermingling of the branches in the vine and the gardener's attentive care to the fruitfulness of the branches create the quintessential visual image of the life of the Christian community that is shaped by love and grounded in God's presence.

---

518. So Brown, *The Gospel According to John (XIII–XXI)*, 683.

519. E.g., E. C. Hoskyns, *The Fourth Gospel* (London: Faber & Faber, 1947) 474-75; Beasley-Murray, *John*, 269, argue for a connection between this imagery and the eucharist.

REFLECTIONS

John 15:1-17 poses challenging questions to the contemporary Christian community about its self-identity. What does it mean for the church to live as the branches of Christ the vine? What would "church" look like if it embraced this model for its corporate life?

1. First, the image of community that emerges from John 15:1-17 is one of interrelationship, mutuality, and indwelling. To get the full sense of this interrelationship, it is helpful to visualize what the branches of a vine actually look like. In a vine, branches are almost completely indistinguishable from one another; it is impossible to determine where one branch stops and another branch starts. All run together as they grow out of the central vine. What this vine image suggests about community, then, is that there are no free-standing individuals in community, but branches who encircle one another completely. The fruitfulness of each individual branch depends on its relationship to the vine, nothing else. What matters for John is that each individual is rooted in Jesus and hence gives up individual status to become one of many encircling branches.

The communal life envisioned in the vine metaphor raises a strong challenge to contemporary Western models of individual autonomy and privatism. At the heart of the Johannine model is social interrelationship and corporate accountability. The vine and branches metaphor exhorts the community to steadfastness in its relationship to Jesus, a steadfastness that is measured by the community's fruits (vv. 4-5). To bear fruit—that is, to act in love—is a decidedly corporate act. It is "rooted" in Jesus' love for the community (v. 9) and issues in the community's embrace of that love as the central commandment of its own life (vv. 10, 12, 17). To live as the branches of the vine is to belong to an organic unity shaped by the love of Jesus. The individual branch is subsumed into the communal work of bearing fruit, of living in love and so revealing itself to be one of Jesus' disciples (vv. 8, 16). To live according to this model, then, the church would be a community in which members are known for the acts of love that they do in common with all other members. It would not be a community built around individual accomplishments, choices, or rights, but around the corporate accountability to the abiding presence of Jesus and corporate enactment of the love of God and Jesus.

2. Second, the metaphor of the vine suggests a radically non-hierarchical model for the church. As the description of a vine and its branches suggests, no branch has pride of place; no one branch can claim precedence or privilege over any other. The descriptions of the cutting and pruning of the branches in 15:2 and 6 underscore this point. Fruitfulness is the only differentiation among branches, and the discernment of fruitfulness falls to the gardener (God) alone, not to any of the branches. It is the gardener's role to prune and shape the vine to enhance fruitfulness. All branches are thus the same before God, distinguishable only by their fruit. There is neither status nor rank among the branches. Hierarchy among the branches of the vine is precluded, because all members grow out of the one central vine and are tended equally by the one gardener.[520]

This dimension of John's metaphor also poses some serious challenges to the ways in which institutional church life is understood and maintained. For the Fourth Gospel, there is only one measure of one's place in the faith community—to love as Jesus has loved—and all, great and small, ordained and lay, young and old, male and female are equally accountable to that one standard. Were the church to shape itself according to the Johannine metaphor, it would be a community in which decisions about power and governance would be made in the light of the radical egalitarian love of the vine image.

520. See Gail R. O'Day, "John," in *The Women's Bible Commentary,* Carol A. Newsom and Sharon H. Ringe ed. (Louisville: Westminster/John Knox, 1992) 303.

3. Third, this metaphor is stark in its anonymity. That is, the visual image of the branches lacks any and all distinctions in appearance, character, or gifts. The anonymity of this image is brought into sharp relief when compared with another NT ecclesial metaphor, the Pauline metaphor of the church as the body of Christ. First Corinthians 12 is irresistible in the anatomical fantasy it puts before the Corinthians: talking feet and ears, entire bodies composed exclusively of ears or eyes or noses. Unlike the Johannine metaphor, the Pauline image does not remove the differences among the various members of the body, but actually points to those differences as definitional of what it means to be a body. Each member is able to see the place that his or her individual gifts occupies in the corporate body (1 Cor 12:12-13, 27-30). Paul holds together the oneness of Christ and the diversity of gifts and members in the body metaphor.

The Johannine metaphor undercuts any celebration of individual gifts, and this, too, challenges contemporary Western understandings of personality, individualism, and self-expression. Were the church to live as the branches of Christ, individual distinctiveness would give way to the common embodiment of love. The distinctiveness of the community would derive solely from its relationship to God and Jesus, not the characteristics or even gifts of its members. The mark of the faithful community is how it loves, not who are its members. There is only one gift, to bear fruit, and any branch can do that if it remains with Jesus.

John 15:18–16:4a, "I Have Chosen You Out of the World"

NIV

[18]"If the world hates you, keep in mind that it hated me first. [19]If you belonged to the world, it would love you as its own. As it is, you do not belong to the world, but I have chosen you out of the world. That is why the world hates you. [20]Remember the words I spoke to you: 'No servant is greater than his master.'[a] If they persecuted me, they will persecute you also. If they obeyed my teaching, they will obey yours also. [21]They will treat you this way because of my name, for they do not know the One who sent me. [22]If I had not come and spoken to them, they would not be guilty of sin. Now, however, they have no excuse for their sin. [23]He who hates me hates my Father as well. [24]If I had not done among them what no one else did, they would not be guilty of sin. But now they have seen these miracles, and yet they have hated both me and my Father. [25]But this is to fulfill what is written in their Law: 'They hated me without reason.'[b]

[26]"When the Counselor comes, whom I will send to you from the Father, the Spirit of truth who goes out from the Father, he will testify about me. [27]And you also must testify, for you have been with me from the beginning.

a20 John 13:16   b25 Psalms 35:19; 69:4

NRSV

[18]"If the world hates you, be aware that it hated me before it hated you. [19]If you belonged to the world,[a] the world would love you as its own. Because you do not belong to the world, but I have chosen you out of the world—therefore the world hates you. [20]Remember the word that I said to you, 'Servants[b] are not greater than their master.' If they persecuted me, they will persecute you; if they kept my word, they will keep yours also. [21]But they will do all these things to you on account of my name, because they do not know him who sent me. [22]If I had not come and spoken to them, they would not have sin; but now they have no excuse for their sin. [23]Whoever hates me hates my Father also. [24]If I had not done among them the works that no one else did, they would not have sin. But now they have seen and hated both me and my Father. [25]It was to fulfill the word that is written in their law, 'They hated me without a cause.'

[26]"When the Advocate[c] comes, whom I will send to you from the Father, the Spirit of truth who comes from the Father, he will testify on my behalf. [27]You also are to testify because you have been with me from the beginning.

a Gk were of the world   b Gk Slaves   c Or Helper

NIV

16 "All this I have told you so that you will not go astray. ²They will put you out of the synagogue; in fact, a time is coming when anyone who kills you will think he is offering a service to God. ³They will do such things because they have not known the Father or me. ⁴I have told you this, so that when the time comes you will remember that I warned you. I did not tell you this at first because I was with you."

NRSV

16 "I have said these things to you to keep you from stumbling. ²They will put you out of the synagogues. Indeed, an hour is coming when those who kill you will think that by doing so they are offering worship to God. ³And they will do this because they have not known the Father or me. ⁴But I have said these things to you so that when their hour comes you may remember that I told you about them.

"I did not say these things to you from the beginning, because I was with you."

COMMENTARY

John 15:18–16:4a moves the Farewell Discourse in a new direction. For the first time in the discourse, Jesus addresses the believing community's relationship to those outside the community. This picture of the community's relationship to the world stands in stunning contrast to the picture of its internal relationships. Where its internal relationships are governed by love (14:15, 21, 23; 15:12, 17), its relationship with the world will be governed by hate (15:18-19, 23-25), persecution (15:20; 16:2*a*), and death (16:2*b*). David Rensberger has convincingly argued that the Fourth Evangelist intentionally placed the traditions in 15:18–16:4a in this location in the Farewell Discourse to complement the love traditions of John 15:1-17. The call to love as Jesus loves receives its most crucial test when the community meets the world's hatred (see Commentary on 16:3).[521]

The synoptic Gospels, too, contain teachings on the world's hatred and persecution of the Christian community. These traditions appear in two clusters. In all three Synoptics they form part of the eschatological discourse, in which Jesus teaches his disciples about the signs of the end of the age (Matt 24:1-36, esp. vv. 9-14; Mark 13:1-37, esp. vv. 9-13; Luke 21:5-36, esp. vv. 12-19). Matthew and Luke also preserve another set of traditions about persecution of the faithful; in Matthew they are found in the discourse of 10:1-42, in which Jesus commissions and instructs the Twelve (see Matt 10:17-23; cf. also Matt 5:10-

11) and appear in an abbreviated form in Jesus' instructions to his disciples in Luke 12:1-12 (see Luke 12:11-12; cf. also Luke 6:22-23). The Johannine persecution traditions seem to be independent of both of these synoptic clusters. The presence of persecution traditions in all four Gospels, however, points to the role that the experience of persecution played in the formation of early Christian self-identity.

There is some scholarly debate over the boundaries of this third unit of the Farewell Discourse. Barrett, for example, breaks the unit at 15:27, while Bultmann argues that the theme of the community's relationship to a hostile world continues through 16:4*b*-11.[522] Two factors argue for dividing the discourse at 16:4*a*. First, 16:4*b*-6 introduces the theme of the concluding section of the discourse, Jesus' departure from the community. The promise of the Paraclete in 16:7-11 speaks of the *Paraclete's* relationship to the world, not the community's, and is offered as evidence of why the community should not sorrow at Jesus' departure. Second, John 16:4*a* marks the end of Jesus' monologue that began at 15:1. At 16:5-6, Jesus again engages in dialogue with his disciples.[523] The majority of scholars, therefore, end this unit at John 16:4*a*.[524]

521. David Rensberger, *Johannine Faith and Liberating Community* (Philadelphia: Westminster, 1988) 79.

522. C. K. Barrett, *The Gospel According to St. John,* 2nd ed. (Philadelphia: Westminster, 1978) 479-80; Rudolf Bultmann, *The Gospel of John: A Commentary,* trans. G. R. Beasley-Murray, R. W. N. Hoare, and J. K. Riches (Philadelphia: Westminster, 1971) 547-48.

523. Fernando Segovia, *The Farewell of the Word: The Johannine Call to Abide* (Minneapolis: Fortress, 1991) 173.

524. So Raymond E. Brown, *The Gospel According to John (XIII–XXI),* AB 29A (Garden City, N.Y.: Doubleday, 1970) 693; George R. Beasley-Murray, *John,* WBC (Waco, Tex.: Word, 1987) 270; Rudolf Schnackenburg, *The Gospel According to St. John,* 3 vols. (New York: Seabury, 1982) 3:92-93.

John 15:18–16:4a can be divided as follows: (1) 15:18-25, the world's hatred of the community; (2) 15:26-27, the promise of the Paraclete; and (3) 16:1-4a, the enactment of the world's hatred.

15:18-25. 15:18-20. Jesus' opening words in v. 18 present the disciples with an inescapable reality of their life as the community of his followers: They will experience the world's hatred (cf. 1 John 3:13). The inescapability of this hatred is underscored by the grammar of v. 18; the sentence is a real condition (i.e., "if the world hates"), not an unreal condition (i.e., "if the world were to hate you"). Jesus does not follow this announcement with easy words of comfort, but instead exhorts the disciples to a full understanding of the sources of this hatred ("be aware" [γινώσκετε ginōskete]). The disciples must recognize what is at issue in their conflict with the world, because that knowledge will enable them to stand firm in the face of persecution (see 16:1, 4a).

Verses 18b-20 identify one source of the world's hatred of the community: It is an extension of the world's hatred of Jesus. The verb "to hate" (μισέω miseō) is in the perfect tense in v. 18b; the hatred of Jesus began in the past, but its effect continues into the present. The world's hatred of Jesus extends to the disciples because of their relationship with him (v. 19). The noun "world" (κόσμος kosmos) occurs five times in v. 19, and this heavy concentration highlights the contrast between the community and the world. Although "world" is sometimes used neutrally in John to name God's created order (e.g., 3:16), here it clearly is used to represent what is opposed to God's work and presence in Jesus (cf. 7:7). The antithetical parallelism of Jesus' words in v. 19a-b further underscores the contrast between Jesus' followers and the world. The language of love in v. 19a is an ironic play on the love language of the Farewell Discourse, because in order to receive the world's love instead of its hatred, the community would have to renounce its share in Jesus' love (cf. the possible ironic play in the contrast between the world's "own" and Jesus' "own"; cf. also 1:11). Verse 19b builds on the election language of 15:16. When Jesus chose the disciples to be his own, he also chose them out of the world (see also 17:6, 9). The picture of the community's relationship to the world in v. 19 is sharply dualistic. Jesus does not belong to this world (8:23), and neither do his disciples. As a result, both incur the world's hatred (17:14).

Verse 20 gives concrete expression to the truths stated in abstractions in vv. 18-19. Verse 20a is a direct quote of Jesus' words in 13:16 (see also Matt 10:24; Luke 6:40). By recalling this teaching, Jesus recalls the entire foot washing for his disciples and thereby places that act of service and love in a new context. Jesus' words here may at first seem to contradict 15:15 ("I do not call you servants any longer . . . but I have called you friends"), but they actually complement them. Jesus reminds the disciples that friendship does not preclude the demands of service. If the disciples share in Jesus' love and gifts, then they must also share in the consequences of that love and those gifts (cf. v. 20b). The double conditions in v. 20b (if they persecuted me/ will persecute you; if they kept my word/ will keep yours) suggest that the "mission of the church will result in the same twofold response as the work of Jesus himself."[525]

15:21. This is a transitional verse. Verse 21a summarizes the essence of vv. 18-20; the world's hatred of the disciples is "on account of my name"—that is, not because of the disciples themselves, but because of Jesus and their identification with him (cf. Matt 5:11; 24:9; Mark 13:13; Luke 21:17). Verse 21b provides the interpretive key to the remainder of the discourse by identifying another source of the world's hatred of the disciples: its fundamental ignorance of the identity of God as the one "who sent me [Jesus]." Not to know the one who sent Jesus is not to recognize the work and will of God in Jesus' works, not to recognize that to see and know Jesus is to see and know God (e.g., 1:18; 4:34; 7;16-17, 28-29; 8:18-19; 9:4; 10:36; 12:45; 14:7). The world hates Jesus (and by extension, his disciples), because the world does not know that the one who sent Jesus is "the only true God" (17:3; cf. 16:3). As always in the Fourth Gospel, the core issue is ultimately theological (cf. 1:18; 5:18; 10:30, 38; 14:6).

15:22-24. These verses explain how the world's lack of recognition of the true identity of God is equivalent to their hatred of both Jesus and God. These three verses consist of a pair of

525. Barrett, *The Gospel According to St. John,* 480.

parallel sayings (vv. 22-23; v. 24) that show the interrelatedness of "hate" and "sin" (ἁμαρτία *hamartia*) in the Gospel of John. Without the advent of Jesus and his words (v. 22) and works (v. 24*a*) into the world, then the world would be without sin (v. 22, 24*a*). But because Jesus has made God available to the world through his words and works (e.g., 10:32, 38; 14:10) and the world does not recognize God in Jesus, therefore the world is without excuse for its lack of faith and hence its sin (v. 22*b*). To see and reject Jesus is to hate both Jesus and the God whom he reveals to be the Father (vv. 23, 24*b*). Verses 22-24 state directly what was enacted indirectly through the drama of the healing of the blind man in John 9 (see Commentary and Reflections there).

There is an unavoidable and probably intentional circularity to this presentation of sin and hate. Jesus "takes away the sin of the world" (1:29) by providing the world with access to the life-giving presence of God. To reject this offer of life is by definition to die in one's sin (8:21, 24). The advent of Jesus thus simultaneously exposes the world's sin and provides the only means of removing that sin (cf. 3:16-21). For the Fourth Gospel, "sin" is defined by whether one believes that God is present in Jesus, that Jesus is the incarnate Word of God (see 16:9). "Hate," therefore, is not simply enmity or intense dislike. In the Fourth Gospel, "hate" describes a life shaped by the rejection of the revelation of God in Jesus (cf. 3:20), in the same way that "love" describes a life shaped by the embrace of the revelation of God in Jesus. "To have sin [*hamartia*]" and "to hate" (*miseō*) thus are presented as synonyms in vv. 22-24. To relate to God through hate, not love, is the ultimate definition of sin.

15:25. Jesus brings his discussion of the world's hatred to a close with a quotation from Scripture (v. 25). The words Jesus quotes appear at Pss 35:19 and 69:4, so it is difficult to determine with certainty which psalm Jesus is invoking here. The introductory phrase with which Jesus sets up the quote points to its significance as the conclusion of his argument. First, the introduction provides the first explicit identification of the adversaries to whom Jesus refers when he speaks of "the world." The quotation from Jewish Scripture and Jesus' designation of it as "their law" (cf. the expression "your law" at 8:17, 10:34) make

clear that "the world" is to be understood as the Jewish leaders who oppose Jesus. This will be brought out even more fully in 16:1-4*a*. Second, Jesus positions the Jewish leaders' own Scripture to bear witness against them. He used Scripture in a similar way at 5:39, 46-47, and 10:34.

15:26-27. Jesus' third promise of the advent of the Paraclete (see also 14:16-17, 26) provides an interlude between the two depictions of the hate the faith community will experience (vv. 18-25; 16:1-4*a*). As in the earlier promises, the interrelationship of Jesus and God in the sending of the Paraclete is evident in 15:26. Indeed, v. 26 contains two parallel clauses that speak of both Jesus and God as the originating agents of the Paraclete ("I will send to you from the Father"; "who comes from the Father").[526] Both share in the Paraclete's mission, just as both shared in Jesus' mission (e.g., 4:34). The verb "to come from" (NRSV) or "to go out from" (NIV; ἐκπορεύομαι *ekporeuomai*) is analogous to the verb "to send" (πέμπω *pempō*) here. It does not refer to the eternal "procession" of the Spirit as is found in the classic trinitarian creeds of the church (e.g., the expression "who proceeds from the Father and the Son" in the Nicene Creed). John 15:26 is not a description of the metaphysical unity of God and the Spirit, but of God as the source of the Paraclete's presence with and mission to the believing community.[527]

This third promise introduces a new function of the Paraclete, "to testify" (μαρτυρέω *martyreō*) about Jesus.[528] In assigning this function to the Paraclete, Jesus places the Paraclete in a long line of witnesses to him that include John the Baptist (1:7, 19, 32, 34; 5:33), the Samaritan woman (4:40), Jesus' works and words (5:36; 8:14, 18; 10:25), the Scriptures (5:39), and even God (5:37). In the context of witnessing, the identification of the Paraclete as the "Spirit of Truth" (cf. 14:17) takes on added significance. As noted at 14:17, this epithet indicates the continuity between the Paraclete and Jesus (who is the truth, 14:6), but it also marks the continuity of the Paraclete's witness with these other witnesses.

---

526. Schnackenburg, *The Gospel According to St. John,* 3:118.
527. See Beasley-Murray, *John,* 276; Brown, *The Gospel According to John (XIII–XXI),* 689.
528. The decision of the translators of the NRSV to translate "about me" (περὶ ἐμοῦ *peri emou*) as "on my account" is difficult to explain, since it changes the meaning of Jesus' words and is inconsistent with the use of the preposition *peri* after the verb "to witness" (*martyreō*) elsewhere in the Gospel. See, for example, 1:7, 15; 5:31, 32, 36-37; 8:14, 18.

John the Baptist testified to the truth (5:33), and during Jesus' trial before Pilate, Jesus will describe his mission as testifying to the truth (18:37).

John 15:27 provides the link between this promise of the Paraclete and the framing verses about the world's hatred. The presence of the Paraclete as a witness with the community provides the grounds for Jesus' exhortation to the community that they, too, must be witnesses. As 16:1-4*a* will make explicit, the community will endure persecution as a result of its faith. The promise of the Paraclete, who will be a co-witness to Jesus alongside the community, is offered as encouragement and a reminder that they will not be alone in their trials and that they can stand firm in what they believe (see 16:1).

The witness of the Paraclete and that of the community are not two distinct acts; rather, the community's witness is the visible sign of the Paraclete's work as witness. The witness of each provides continuity between the ministry of Jesus and the ministry of the church. The warrant for the community's witness is that they have been with Jesus "from the beginning" (cf. Acts 1:21-22; 10:39) and provide historical continuity between the earthly ministry of Jesus and the church's own ministry after Jesus' death (cf. 1 John 1:1-2; see also 4:14). Interestingly, Hoskyns suggests that the phrase "from the beginning" refers to conversion (so 1 John 2:24; 2 John 6) and should not be restricted to a historical connection with Jesus.[529] Since in the Fourth Gospel "in the beginning" is used to introduce the story of Jesus' relationship with God (1:1) and not his earthly ministry, there may be some grounds for Hoskyns's claim. That is, the expression refers to the beginning of one's relationship with Jesus.

One further dimension of the Paraclete teaching in vv. 26-27 needs to be mentioned. The function accorded the Paraclete in 15:26-27 is quite close to Jesus' words about the role of the Spirit in the synoptic teachings on persecution: to speak with and for the community when it is brought before its adversaries (Matt 10:20; Mark 13:11; Luke 12:12). The synoptic teachings bring out the forensic context of the Spirit's witness more explicitly than John 15:26-27, although the forensic context is clearly assumed in the description of the community's persecution in 16:2 and

provides the background for the fourth promise of the Paraclete in 16:8-11.

16:1-4a. John returns to the theme of the world's hatred and depicts the community's persecution in much more vivid and concrete language than that found in 15:18-25. This passage is framed by the refrain "I have said these things to you" (16:1, 4*a*; cf. 14:25; 15:11; 16:33). In both instances "these things" refers to Jesus' teachings about the world's hatred and persecution of the community. The refrain focuses the hearers' attention on Jesus' words, but more important, it alerts the hearers to Jesus' intention in speaking them: to bolster the disciples and their faith in the face of persecution. "To stumble" (σκανδαλίζω *skandalizō*) is used in 16:1 to mean to fall away from their faith in Jesus (note the NIV's "go astray"), and Jesus offers his teachings as encouragement against such defection (cf. 6:60-61). If the disciples "remember" (μνημονεύω *mnēmoneuō*) Jesus' teaching at the time of their persecution (v. 4*a*), they will be able to recognize (with the aid of the Paraclete, 14:26) that their persecution is in continuity with Jesus' own ministry and teachings and not an annulment of all that they heard from him.

Within this rhetorical frame, Jesus presents the disciples with a harsh picture of the life that awaits them because of their faith in him. At 9:22 and 12:42, the expression "put out of the synagogue" (ἀποσυνάγωγος *aposynagōgos*) was found in the Evangelist's comments; at 16:2 it occurs for the first and only time in the mouth of Jesus. The use of this term in 16:2*a* points once again to the two-level nature of the teachings of Jesus in John. Predictions about the persecution of the faith community are common to all of the Gospels (e.g., Mark 13:9-13), but in John those predictions are cast in language that mirrors the persecution experienced by the Fourth Evangelist's community. (See Excursus "John 9:22 and the Benediction Against Heretics," 657-58, for a discussion of the community's expulsion from the synagogue.)

Yet excommunication is not the full extent of the persecution that Jesus predicts for the faith community. The expression "the hour is coming when . . ." sets the context for the prediction of martyrdom that follows. Even though both the NRSV and the NIV translate the Greek particle ἵνα (*hina*) as "when," it is not used simply to

---

529. Hoskyns, *The Fourth Gospel,* 482.

mark time in 16:2*b,* but conveys a sense of purpose. Its use here parallels that at John 12:23, "the hour has come for [*hina*] the Son of Man to be glorified."[530] "The hour" and its arrival are the distinctly Johannine metaphor for Jesus' death, resurrection, and ascension, for his completion of God's work (12:23; 13:1; 17:1-5). "The hour is coming" also is used in the Gospel to refer to the time of eschatological fulfillment (e.g., 4:21, 23; 5:25, 28). With respect to Jesus' life, those two meanings of "hour" are indistinguishable, because the hour of Jesus' death, resurrection, and ascension is the decisive eschatological moment, the time when God's plan for the world's salvation is fulfilled. When Jesus speaks of the disciples' deaths with the metaphor of "the hour," he implies that the disciples share his hour with him, with all its eschatological implications (see also 16:4*a*).[531]

The expression "service (worship) to God" (λα-τρεία *latreia*) is used in the NT to refer to Jewish worship (Rom 9:4; Heb 9:1, 6). Like the reference to the community's excommunication from the synagogue in 16:2*a,* it points to the Johannine community's conflict with the Jewish religious leadership as the cause of its persecution (cf. Acts 6:8–8:1*a*; 23:12-15; Gal 1:13). The identification of the motivation for this persecution as worship also focuses on the theological roots of the conflict and persecution: division over what constitutes faithfulness to God and who can lay claim to knowing the true identity of God. This is brought out even more sharply by v. 3 (cf. 15:21). To know neither the Father nor Jesus is to be ignorant of the meaning of the incarnation, because it is in the incarnation that one comes to know the Father (14:7). From the perspective of the Fourth Evangelist, what is at stake in the persecution and martyrdom of the Christian faith community is the very identity of God.

Jesus' prediction of persecution and martyrdom in 16:2 must be read in the context of his earlier teachings in the Farewell Discourse. The contrast between the world's murderous hatred of the faith community and the love to which Jesus enjoins the community is striking. The persecution for which Jesus prepares the disciples will be the ultimate test of whether they will love one another as Jesus loves them (13:34-35; 15:12, 17), because the threat of martyrdom will present the disciples with the same situation that Jesus faced: the giving up of one's life for one's friends (15:13; cf. 10:11, 15, 17). As Rensberger has seen, The disciples' "love for one another indicates the reality of their faith in Jesus, just as the world's hatred of them reflects its rejection of him."[532] Neither "love" nor "hate" is an abstract proposition in the Fourth Gospel, but is the concrete embodiment of one's relationship to Jesus and God.

---

530. Paul S. Minear, *John: The Martyr's Gospel* (New York: Pilgrim Press, 1984) 26.

531. E. C. Hoskyns, *The Fourth Gospel* (London: Faber & Faber, 1947) 483; Minear, *John,* 26.

532. David Rensberger, *Johannine Faith and Liberating Community* (Philadelphia: Westminster, 1988) 79.

REFLECTIONS

John 15:18–16:4*a* brings the contemporary reader face to face with some of the most complex issues raised by the sectarianism of the Fourth Gospel, because in these verses the lines between the faith community and the "world" are more sharply drawn than anywhere else in the Gospel. The Reflections on John 8 discussed one aspect of Johannine sectarianism, the Johannine community's self-identity as an oppressed Jewish sect and how that self-identity led to the antagonism to the Jewish authorities that is evident throughout the Gospel. The Johannine community's relationship to establishment Judaism is clearly a factor in the depiction of persecution in 15:18–16:4*a* (15:21, 25; 16:2-3), but the community's adversaries are named more generally here as "the world." This choice of nomenclature highlights the radical heart of Johannine sectarianism.

At the center of Johannine ecclesiology is a communal self-understanding that intentionally and unflinchingly positions itself over against the ways of "the world."[533] The Johannine

---

533. For a full treatment of the implications of Johannine sectarianism for contemporary theology, see ibid., 135-52. My comments are shaped by Rensberger's insights.

community will not accept the terms by which the world would have it live, because the world denies the one thing that it knows to be the truth: "No one has ever seen God. It is God the only Son, who is close to the Father's heart, who has made him known" (1:18). This community derives its identity from this truth and from the new relationship with God and one another that is now possible because of the revelation of God in Jesus. The Johannine Jesus calls his followers to recognize that they belong to him and makes clear that to belong to Jesus precludes any membership in the world. The Johannine community, therefore, understands itself to be living in opposition to the ways of the world.

What are the ethical implications of reading this sectarian vision in the contemporary context? Does this Johannine sectarian vision of Christians' relationship to the world have anything of value to contribute to contemporary discussions of Christian identity? Or is it so bound by the particular social context in which the Johannine community found itself that it can make no contribution to contemporary ecclesiology?

In order to answer these questions, the interpreter must begin by acknowledging the negative and potentially destructive aspects of this sectarian vision. First, the Johannine claims about its knowledge of God and the world's ignorance of God can lend itself to a rigid dogmatism and misplaced triumphalism in the contemporary context (see Reflections on John 14:1-11). Second, world-denying language can all too easily be confused with life-denying language. That is, the Johannine language about the world can be misinterpreted as a call to extreme asceticism or as a renunciation of life. In this regard, it is crucial to note that at 17:15 Jesus says, "I am not asking you to take them out of the world." Not belonging to the world does not mean absenting or hiding oneself from the world, nor, as 17:15 makes clear, is it a metaphor for speaking about death. To translate the Johannine language about the world into language about death or ascetic renunciation is to spiritualize this language and to rob it of its radical countercultural edge. Third, as the Fourth Gospel rhetoric itself shows, when a group's self-identity is so sharply framed in opposition to others, there is a tendency to dehumanize or even demonize one's adversary (e.g., John 8:31-47). When this dehumanizing is taken to extremes, it makes a sham of the love commandment that lies at the heart of Johannine theology.

Contemporary interpreters cannot dismiss these negatives lightly, nor can they dismiss the ways in which sectarian language like that found in John 15:18–16:4*a* has been used irresponsibly and destructively in the history of the church. Yet neither can contemporary interpreters allow these negatives to provide them with an easy excuse for not engaging the challenges raised by this text. John 15:18–16:4*a* challenges the contemporary church to reject the way the world does business and to present the world with an alternative, an alternative grounded in the love of God revealed in Jesus.

Jesus calls his followers to reject "business as usual," to reject the ways of the world that stand in opposition to his ways—to his revelation of the love of God in his life and death. The effect of this call is the very opposite of ascetic renunciation or withdrawal from the world. Rather, John 15:18–16:4*a* challenges the Christian community to be fully present in the world while at the same time not following the dictates of the world. Because the faith community does not belong to the world, it is not governed by the world's categories and expectations. When the church chooses to play the world's games, by the world's rules, the church risks losing everything, because when the church is judged "successful" according to the world's standards, it acts as if it belongs to the world instead of like it was chosen out of the world (15:19). In many ways, this Johannine vision can be understood through H. Richard Niebuhr's category of "Christ against culture."[534]

The community will call the world and its culture into question by its radical obedience

534. H. Richard Niebuhr, *Christ and Culture* (New York: Harper and Bros., 1951).

to the one commandment Jesus set before it: "Just as I have loved you, you also should love one another. By this everyone will know that you are my disciples, if you have love for one another" (13:34-35). This love cannot be separated from its source in God and Jesus. The community's love and presence in the world are defined by the incarnation, including the hour. Just as Jesus' hour overcomes the power of the world (12:31; 16:33), so also the community's continuing embrace of the model of Jesus' life and death in its own life has the promise of overcoming the world.

The world's hatred of this community can be seen as a direct response to the threat this community's love and witness pose to its ways of doing business. It is important to note that "hate" is never used in John to describe the community's response to the world; it is used exclusively to describe the world's response to Jesus and his followers. If hate begins to shape the Christian community's response to the world, then it is acting in opposition to the incarnate love of God.

These verses thus challenge the contemporary church to shape its life according to the standards of the incarnation and not according to the standards of the world. They challenge the church to call into question all of the world's practices that do not show forth the love of God as known in the life and death of Jesus. Yet they also challenge the church to do this without redefining itself in terms of hate.

John 16:4*b*-33, "It Is to Your Advantage That I Go Away"

NIV

[4] I have told you this, so that when the time comes you will remember that I warned you. I did not tell you this at first because I was with you.

[5] "Now I am going to him who sent me, yet none of you asks me, 'Where are you going?' [6] Because I have said these things, you are filled with grief. [7] But I tell you the truth: It is for your good that I am going away. Unless I go away, the Counselor will not come to you; but if I go, I will send him to you. [8] When he comes, he will convict the world of guilt[a] in regard to sin and righteousness and judgment: [9] in regard to sin, because men do not believe in me; [10] in regard to righteousness, because I am going to the Father, where you can see me no longer; [11] and in regard to judgment, because the prince of this world now stands condemned.

[12] "I have much more to say to you, more than you can now bear. [13] But when he, the Spirit of truth, comes, he will guide you into all truth. He will not speak on his own; he will speak only what he hears, and he will tell you what is yet to come. [14] He will bring glory to me by taking

[a]8 Or *will expose the guilt of the world*

NRSV

[4] But I have said these things to you so that when their hour comes you may remember that I told you about them.

"I did not say these things to you from the beginning, because I was with you. [5] But now I am going to him who sent me; yet none of you asks me, 'Where are you going?' [6] But because I have said these things to you, sorrow has filled your hearts. [7] Nevertheless I tell you the truth: it is to your advantage that I go away, for if I do not go away, the Advocate[a] will not come to you; but if I go, I will send him to you. [8] And when he comes, he will prove the world wrong about[b] sin and righteousness and judgment: [9] about sin, because they do not believe in me; [10] about righteousness, because I am going to the Father and you will see me no longer; [11] about judgment, because the ruler of this world has been condemned.

[12] "I still have many things to say to you, but you cannot bear them now. [13] When the Spirit of truth comes, he will guide you into all the truth; for he will not speak on his own, but will speak

[a] Or *Helper*   [b] Or *convict the world of*

NIV

from what is mine and making it known to you. [15]All that belongs to the Father is mine. That is why I said the Spirit will take from what is mine and make it known to you.

[16]"In a little while you will see me no more, and then after a little while you will see me."

[17]Some of his disciples said to one another, "What does he mean by saying, 'In a little while you will see me no more, and then after a little while you will see me,' and 'Because I am going to the Father'?" [18]They kept asking, "What does he mean by 'a little while'? We don't understand what he is saying."

[19]Jesus saw that they wanted to ask him about this, so he said to them, "Are you asking one another what I meant when I said, 'In a little while you will see me no more, and then after a little while you will see me'? [20]I tell you the truth, you will weep and mourn while the world rejoices. You will grieve, but your grief will turn to joy. [21]A woman giving birth to a child has pain because her time has come; but when her baby is born she forgets the anguish because of her joy that a child is born into the world. [22]So with you: Now is your time of grief, but I will see you again and you will rejoice, and no one will take away your joy. [23]In that day you will no longer ask me anything. I tell you the truth, my Father will give you whatever you ask in my name. [24]Until now you have not asked for anything in my name. Ask and you will receive, and your joy will be complete.

[25]"Though I have been speaking figuratively, a time is coming when I will no longer use this kind of language but will tell you plainly about my Father. [26]In that day you will ask in my name. I am not saying that I will ask the Father on your behalf. [27]No, the Father himself loves you because you have loved me and have believed that I came from God. [28]I came from the Father and entered the world; now I am leaving the world and going back to the Father."

[29]Then Jesus' disciples said, "Now you are speaking clearly and without figures of speech. [30]Now we can see that you know all things and that you do not even need to have anyone ask you questions. This makes us believe that you came from God."

NRSV

whatever he hears, and he will declare to you the things that are to come. [14]He will glorify me, because he will take what is mine and declare it to you. [15]All that the Father has is mine. For this reason I said that he will take what is mine and declare it to you.

[16]"A little while, and you will no longer see me, and again a little while, and you will see me." [17]Then some of his disciples said to one another, "What does he mean by saying to us, 'A little while, and you will no longer see me, and again a little while, and you will see me'; and 'Because I am going to the Father'?" [18]They said, "What does he mean by this 'a little while'? We do not know what he is talking about." [19]Jesus knew that they wanted to ask him, so he said to them, "Are you discussing among yourselves what I meant when I said, 'A little while, and you will no longer see me, and again a little while, and you will see me'? [20]Very truly, I tell you, you will weep and mourn, but the world will rejoice; you will have pain, but your pain will turn into joy. [21]When a woman is in labor, she has pain, because her hour has come. But when her child is born, she no longer remembers the anguish because of the joy of having brought a human being into the world. [22]So you have pain now; but I will see you again, and your hearts will rejoice, and no one will take your joy from you. [23]On that day you will ask nothing of me.[a] Very truly, I tell you, if you ask anything of the Father in my name, he will give it to you.[b] [24]Until now you have not asked for anything in my name. Ask and you will receive, so that your joy may be complete.

[25]"I have said these things to you in figures of speech. The hour is coming when I will no longer speak to you in figures, but will tell you plainly of the Father. [26]On that day you will ask in my name. I do not say to you that I will ask the Father on your behalf; [27]for the Father himself loves you, because you have loved me and have believed that I came from God.[c] [28]I came from the Father and have come into the world; again, I am leaving the world and am going to the Father."

[29]His disciples said, "Yes, now you are speak-

[a] Or will ask me no question   [b] Other ancient authorities read Father, he will give it to you in my name   [c] Other ancient authorities read the Father

NIV	NRSV
³¹"You believe at last!"*a* Jesus answered. ³²"But a time is coming, and has come, when you will be scattered, each to his own home. You will leave me all alone. Yet I am not alone, for my Father is with me. ³³"I have told you these things, so that in me you may have peace. In this world you will have trouble. But take heart! I have overcome the world." *a 31 Or "Do you now believe?"*	ing plainly, not in any figure of speech! ³⁰Now we know that you know all things, and do not need to have anyone question you; by this we believe that you came from God." ³¹Jesus answered them, "Do you now believe? ³²The hour is coming, indeed it has come, when you will be scattered, each one to his home, and you will leave me alone. Yet I am not alone because the Father is with me. ³³I have said this to you, so that in me you may have peace. In the world you face persecution. But take courage; I have conquered the world!"

COMMENTARY

The final section of the Farewell Discourse begins at 16:4*b* (see Commentary on 15:18–16:4*a* for discussion of the reasons for this division). This section returns to the themes with which the Farewell Discourse opened in John 14: Jesus' departure and its effect on the disciples' future. The farewell situation governs both 14:1-31 and 16:4*b*-33. The thematic overlap between chaps. 14 and 16 leads some scholars to suggest that 14:1-31 and 16:4*b*-33 are duplicate discourses—that is, two versions of the same tradition.[535] Yet, as discussed in the Overview to John 14:1–16:33, this solution to the composition of the Farewell Discourse tends to discount the role of repetition as a literary technique throughout the Fourth Gospel. There are undeniable echoes of John 14 in Jesus' teachings in 16:4*b*-33 (e.g., John 14:13-14; 16:23-24), but one does not need to resort to a complex redactional theory to explain them. Rather, as in other discourses in the Fourth Gospel, the Farewell Discourse employs a web-like construction. The argument of the discourse often moves forward by moving backward, by returning to what has been said before and restating it in a new context.

There are subtle yet important distinctions in the way the farewell theme is handled in John 14 and 16. John 14:1-31 introduces the theme of absence and departure and focuses on words of assurance and consolation. It is as if Jesus is

assuring his disciples that the future is possible *even though* he is leaving them (14:1-4, 18, 27). John 16:4*b*-33, by contrast, brings Jesus' farewell instructions to a conclusion and focuses less on assurance and more on the shape of the future itself. In these verses, Jesus is showing his disciples that his departure is necessary *so that* they can fully embrace the future. He repeatedly points them to the benefits of his departure (16:7, 22-27, 33).

John 16:4*b*-33 can be divided into three parts. The first part, vv. 4*b*-7*a,* reintroduces the theme of Jesus' departure and the disciples' response to it. This introduction is followed by two sections that show why Jesus' departure is to the disciples' advantage: vv. 7*b*-15, which contain two new teachings about the advent of the Paraclete; and vv. 16-33, which focus on Jesus' victory over the world in which the disciples will share.

16:4b-7a. Jesus' reflection on his own words once again marks a transition in the discourse (v. 4*b;* cf. 14:25; 15:11; 16:2, 4*a,* 12). "These things" ("all this," NIV) refers to Jesus' prediction of the community's persecution in 15:18–16:4*a,* but it also applies more generally to all of Jesus' teachings in the Farewell Discourse, particularly his teaching about his departure. Verses 4*b* and 5*a* highlight the contrast between the time of Jesus' ministry ("from the beginning"; "I was with you," v. 4*b*) and the present moment of the hour ("now" [νῦν *nun*], v. 5*a;* cf. 12:31; 13:31; 17:13). The arrival of the hour, of Jesus' death, resurrec-

535. Most notably Raymond E. Brown, *The Gospel According to John (XIII–XXI),* AB 29A (Garden City, N.Y.: Doubleday, 1970) 588-97.

tion, and ascension, determines what Jesus teaches his disciples (cf. 12:23; 13:1; 17:1).

Verses 5*b*-7*a* introduce the theme of 16:4*b*-33: the disciples' "sorrow" (λύπη *lypē*) at Jesus' departure. Although many scholars point to v. 5*b* as evidence of the compositional problems in the Farewell Discourse,[536] Jesus' complaint here ("none of you asks me . . . ") does not contradict 13:36 and 14:5, but is primarily a rhetorical device. Jesus is not really concerned with the disciples' questions about his departure, but refers to their present speechlessness as a way of introducing their "situation of sorrow."[537] As Dodd suggests about v. 5*b*, Jesus reproaches the disciples, "not because they are not enquiring about his destination, but because in spite of knowing that he is going to the Father they are dismayed about the future."[538]

The disciples' "sorrow" (*lypē*) at Jesus' teaching about his departure (note the repetition of "these things" in 16:6) provides the occasion for his words in this final unit of the Farewell Discourse. In 14:1-31 Jesus offers the assurance of his peace to the disciples' troubled hearts (14:1, 27); in 16:4*b*-33 he now offers their sorrowful hearts reasons for rejoicing (see 16:20-22).[539] Verse 7*a* confirms this intent. The expression with which this verse begins, "I tell you the truth," can be read simply as a solemn asseveration, synonymous with the more common expression "very truly I tell you." Yet the noun "truth" (ἀλήθεια *alētheia*) may also suggest that Jesus' promise that his death is to the disciples' advantage is grounded in the truth of Jesus' revelation of God (cf. 1:17; 3:33; 8:45-46; 14:6). At 14:28, Jesus urged his disciples to love him enough to see his death as a reason for rejoicing, because through it Jesus completes God's work. Here he urges the disciples to see the good in it for them as well.

16:7b-15. 16:7b-11. These verses contain the fourth promise of the Paraclete in the Farewell Discourse (cf. 14:16-17, 26; 15:26-27; 16:12-15). The two conditional clauses of v. 7*b-c* identify Jesus' departure as the prerequisite for the advent of the Paraclete. At 7:39, the Evangelist explained to the reader that the gift of the Spirit could not occur until after Jesus' glorification, and v. 7*b* places that same claim in the words of Jesus himself. The Paraclete's ministry is to make Jesus and his work present and available for the community in his absence. Since Jesus' death, resurrection, and ascension complete his revelation of God (17:1-5), his departure must precede the advent of the Paraclete. Verse 7*b* thus defines the relationship between Jesus and the Paraclete; the Paraclete's work cannot be undertaken until Jesus' work is completed. Verse 7*c* identifies Jesus as the sole sender of the Paraclete. This identification does not contradict earlier references to the mutual involvement of God and Jesus in the sending of the Paraclete (cf. 14:16, 26; 15:26), but rather is worded this way to highlight the inseparable bond between Jesus' departure and the advent of the Paraclete.

Verses 8-11 paint a vivid picture of the Paraclete's activity in the world. The picture is clearly one of a trial, in which the Paraclete has the role of prosecuting attorney and the world is the defendant, standing before the believing community. The trial motif has been prevalent throughout the Gospel of John, although prior to this passage, the focus has been on Jesus himself as prosecutor and judge (e.g., 3:19; 8:26; 9:39; cf. 12:47-48). Jesus' active role as judge of the world will reach its dramatic climax in his trial before Pilate (see Commentary on 18:28–19:16), and 16:8-11 shows how that role will be ceded to the Paraclete after Jesus' departure. The Paraclete's share in the judgment of the world is another example of how the Paraclete continues the work of Jesus.

It is important to note the distinction between the juridical roles of the Paraclete in 15:26-27 and 16:8-11.[540] In 15:26-27, the Paraclete's role is that of the defense counsel, bearing witness with and for the community in the world's case against it. This shift in roles confirms the importance of not limiting the translation of *Paraclete* to one English noun (e.g., "Advocate"; see above at 14:16) and of noting the variety of functions that define the Paraclete's presence and ministry in the faith community (see Excursus "The Paraclete," 774-78.

---

536. So Rudolf Bultmann, *The Gospel of John: A Commentary,* trans. G. R. Beasley-Murray, R. W. N. Hoare, and J. K. Riches (Philadelphia: Westminster, 1971) 459, 558n. 2; and Brown, *The Gospel According to John (XIII–XXI),* 583, 710, who make this verse one of the key pieces in their compositional theories.

537. Rudolf Schnackenburg, *The Gospel According to St. John,* 3 vols. (New York: Seabury, 1982) 3:126; note the use of the present tense "asks" (ἐρωτᾷ *erōta*), so C. K. Barrett, *The Gospel According to St. John,* 2nd ed. (Philadelphia: Westminster, 1978) 485.

538. C. H. Dodd, *The Interpretation of the Fourth Gospel* (Cambridge: Cambridge University Press, 1953) 413.

539. Λύπη (*lypē*) is translated as "pain" by both the NIV and the NRSV in 16:20-22.

540. See Dodd, *The Interpretation of the Fourth Gospel,* 414.

The precise contour of the Paraclete's role is more difficult to identify than its broad forensic function. The key difficulty is how to translate the central verb phrase in v. 8 (ἐλέγξει . . . περί *elegxei . . .peri*). The verb ἐλέγχω (*elegchō*) can be translated either as "expose" (as at 3:20) or "convict" (as at 8:46). The NRSV ("prove the world wrong about") and the NIV ("convict the world of guilt in regard to") both adopt the basic meaning of "convict," although they must paraphrase this verse in order to communicate that meaning (neither the word "wrong" nor "guilt" appears in the Greek). "Expose" seems a better translation, however, because it has the same double meaning as the Greek verb: both "bring to light" and "hold up to reprobation."[541] To say that the Paraclete will expose the world regarding sin, righteousness, and judgment means that the Paraclete will bring out into the open the true meaning of sin, righteousness, and judgment and hold the world accountable to those standards. As in 15:18-25, "world" is not a neutral term, but means "that which is opposed to God in Jesus."

The Paraclete's exposure of the world is narrated in a strict symmetrical pattern in vv. 9-11; each verse opens with the key noun, followed by a *hoti* clause ("that" or "because") that simultaneously "exposes" the meaning of the noun and the world's relation to it. In each instance, the exposure has a christological core. Sin, righteousness, and judgment thus are not abstract concepts, but derive their meaning from the life and death of Jesus.

Verse 9 provides the Gospel's most straightforward statement of the Johannine understanding of "sin" (ἁμαρτία *hamartia*). As has been noted already (see Reflections on John 9), for the Fourth Gospel, sin is a theological, not a moral, category. The world's sin is not to believe in Jesus—that is, not to believe that Jesus is the incarnate Logos of God (cf. 8:24; 15:22-24). The present tense verb in the expression "they do not believe" (οὐ πιστεύουσιν *ou pisteuousin*) shows that the Fourth Evangelist's primary concern is with the world's ongoing rejection of the revelation of God in Jesus, not simply with one particular rejection of Jesus by the Jewish power structure.

The noun "righteousness" (δικαιοσύνη *dikaiosynē*) occurs only in this passage in the Fourth

Gospel (16:8, 10). The juridical context of vv. 8-11 suggests that it is used in the legal sense of what is right and just, as in the use of the adjective "righteous" (δίκαιος *dikaios*) to modify "judgment" at 5:30 and 7:24. In the context of the world's trial by the Paraclete, then, righteousness should be read as synonymous with "vindication," and not as referring to the believer's justification by faith, an interpretation overly influenced by the Pauline use of the term (e.g., Rom 4:25).[542]

Righteousness is exposed in two ways (v. 10). First, Jesus' death is not defeat, as the world assumes. Rather, his death shows forth the righteousness ("rightness") of God, because in death Jesus goes to God and completes his work. This will be confirmed in Jesus' address of God as "righteous [*dikaios*] Father" at 17:25. Second, the disciples no longer see Jesus. This expression here does not refer to the contingency of the revelation (as, for example, 7:33-34; 8:21; 13:31). Nor is it related to Jesus' abiding presence with his disciples, and therefore is not followed by a promise that the disciples will see him again (14:19; 16:16-19). Rather, Jesus' absence is offered as corroboration of his departure and hence the seal of his vindication.

The trial motif governs the interpretation of v. 11 as well. This verse brings to prominence the cosmic and eschatological dimensions of the world's trial; the ultimate judgment is the judgment of "the ruler of the world" (see also 12:31; 14:30). The verb "judge" (κέκριται *kekritai*; "condemn," NRSV, NIV) is in the perfect tense. The NIV captures the meaning of the Greek perfect tense well: The ruler of the world was judged in the past (at Jesus' hour), and that judgment continues into the present. In Jesus' death, resurrection, and ascension, the ruler of the world, the devil, the embodiment of all that is opposed to God, is defeated and God is victorious. The life and death of Jesus are ultimately about the governance of the world. It is important to read v. 11 in the light of v. 8, which says that the Paraclete *"will expose* the world concerning . . . judgment." The future tense, like the perfect tense of "to judge," shows that the Paraclete continues God's eschatological judgment beyond the time of

541. E. C. Hoskyns, *The Fourth Gospel* (London: Faber & Faber, 1947) 484.

542. John Calvin, *The Gospel According to St. John 11–21 and First John,* 1:18; *Calvin's Commentaries* (Grand Rapids: Eerdman's, 1959).

Jesus' life and death into the life of the faith community. The world is continually judged by God's work in Jesus.

16:12-15. The focus shifts from the role of the Paraclete in the world to the functions of the Paraclete within the faith community (cf. 14:16-17, 26). Verse 12 sets the context for the fifth and final Paraclete teaching in the Farewell Discourse (vv. 13-15). Jesus confronts the disciples with the constraints that time imposes on his teaching to them and points them toward their own futures. The verb "to bear" (βαστάζω *bastazō*) is normally used to refer to the physical act of supporting or bearing a heavy load (e.g., Matt 3:11; 20:12; Mark 14:13; Luke 7:14; Acts 3:2; Rom 11:18). Here it is used metaphorically to point to the burden of the disciples' future. The future will test them in ways that they cannot now anticipate; Jesus, therefore, can teach the disciples nothing more about the future in the present moment. Bultmann moves to the heart of Jesus' words here when he writes, "The believer can only measure the significance and claims of what he has to undergo when he actually meets it. He anticipates the future in faith, not foreknowledge."[543]

This does not mean, however, that Jesus' teachings have come to an end for the disciples nor that they will have to face the future without the supporting words of Jesus. Jesus' words about the Paraclete in vv. 13-15 show the disciples how, even in his absence, their futures fall within his providence. The functions of the Paraclete spelled out in these verses will ensure that the disciples do not face the future alone (cf. 14:18), unequipped with the necessary words of Jesus. The Paraclete will carry Jesus' teachings into the future.

As at 14:17 and 15:26, the title "Spirit of Truth" (v. 13) underscores the reliability of the Paraclete and points to his link with Jesus, who is the truth (14:6). Verse 13 describes two interrelated functions of the Spirit of Truth in the future life of the community. First, "he will guide you into all the truth" (v. 13*a*). The verb "to guide" (ὁδηγέω *hodēgeō*) occurs only here in John and is a compound verb from the roots "way" (ὁδός *hodos*) and "lead" (ἄγω *agō*), thus literally "lead in the way." This verb is used in the Psalms (LXX) to point to the instructional role

of God (cf. Pss 25:5, 9; 85:10) in leading the community into right and faithful behavior. In Wis 9:11 and 10:10, it is used to describe the teaching function of Wisdom. This verb thus points to the teaching role the Paraclete will have in the future life of the faith community. Its combination with "truth" is a direct echo of 14:6, "I am the way, and the truth, and the life," and thus specifies the content of the Paraclete's teaching. To say that the Paraclete will guide the disciples into all the truth is to say that in the future the Paraclete will lead the community into the life-giving revelation of God in Jesus.

Verse 13*b* offers the warrants for the Paraclete's guidance ("for"): The Paraclete will not be an independent witness to the truth, but speaks what he will hear. The textual witnesses are divided over whether "hear" (ἀκούω *akouō*) is in the present or future tense. The future tense fits the context best, because Jesus is describing the future activity of the Paraclete. The future tense is the reading preferred by the Nestle-Aland[27] edition of the Greek text, although the NIV and the NRSV both opt for the present tense variant. This description of the Paraclete echoes earlier descriptions of Jesus (7:16-17; 8:26, 40; 12:49-50), in which Jesus is described as speaking what he hears from God, and is thus another example of the continuity between Jesus and the Paraclete.

Second, the Paraclete "will declare to you the things that are to come" (v. 13*c*). The verb "to declare" (ἀναγγέλλω *anangellō*) means to proclaim what has been heard (cf. 4:25; 16:25)[544] and as such builds on the claim of v. 13*b*. It is not a verb of prophecy or prediction, and thus does not describe the Paraclete as one who foretells the future. Rather, it highlights the proclamatory function of the Paraclete within the community. "The things that are to come" may refer specifically to the events of Jesus' hour (which the Paraclete will help to interpret to the community; cf. 2:22; 12:16), but it also refers to the community's future, to the events for which Jesus cannot prepare them now (v. 12). The Paraclete thus will proclaim the teachings of Jesus to them in the new and changing circumstances of their lives. That is, Jesus' words are not locked

---

543. Bultmann, *The Gospel of John*, 573.

544. P. Jouon, "Le verbe Anagellô dans St. Jean," *RSR* (1938) 234-35; Brown, *The Gospel According to John (XIII–XXI)*, 708; Schnackenburg, *The Gospel According to St. John*, 3:135.

in the disciples' past, restricted to a particular historic moment. Nor does Jesus' death rob future believers of the chance to receive the word of Jesus in the changing circumstances of their lives. The promise of v. 13c is that the presence of the Paraclete in the life of the community will ensure that all believers' futures are open to fresh proclamations of Jesus' words.

The repetition of the expression "he will take what is mine" in vv. 14-15 supports the definition of *anangellō* as "to declare what has been heard." These verses offer supplementary definitions of what it means to speak of the Paraclete as the one who will declare what he has heard. First, in v. 14, Jesus describes the Paraclete's declaration

to the community of "what is mine" as an act of glorification. Jesus' words and actions glorified God, made visible the identity of God (1:14, 18; 17:4-6), and the Paraclete's proclamation will do the same for Jesus. This description again underscores continuity between Jesus' ministry and the Paraclete's ministry. Second, in v. 15 Jesus returns to one of the central affirmations of his ministry ("All that the Father has is mine"; cf. 5:19-20) in order to underscore the grounding of the Paraclete's ministry. For the Paraclete to take what is Jesus' is for the Paraclete to participate in the fullness of Jesus' revelation of God and then to declare that fullness to succeeding generations of disciples.

❖   ❖   ❖   ❖

EXCURSUS: THE PARACLETE

The Farewell Discourse places a rich portrait of the Paraclete before the Gospel reader. As the Commentary on the five Paraclete passages has shown (14:16-17, 26; 15:26-27; 16:7-11, 12-15), the Paraclete is intimately tied to Jesus' preparation of his disciples for their life after his return to God. In none of the other Gospels does the Spirit play such a central role in the teaching of Jesus. Furthermore, by speaking of the Spirit as the Paraclete, the Fourth Evangelist seems to be attempting to free his portrait from early Christian preconceptions of the nature of the Spirit in order to get a fresh hearing for the role the Spirit plays in the life of the believing community. For example, John does not identify the presence of the Spirit in the Christian community with specific spiritual gifts (cf. 1 Cor 12:1-11, 27-28; 14:1-33; Acts 2:4). The Gospel does not portray the Spirit as actively directing the activities of the believing community (cf. Acts 8:29, 39; 10:19; 11:12; 13:2, 4), nor does it point to the role of the Spirit in baptism (cf. Acts 2:38; 8:16-17; 10:44-48). The portrait of the Paraclete in the Farewell Discourse is thus one of the most substantive and distinctive theological contributions of this Gospel, and it warrants the interpreter's careful reflection.

The Commentary has discussed the details of the Johannine portrait of the Paraclete. Two aspects of that portrait can be singled out as the basis for theological reflection on the Paraclete: the Paraclete as the continuing presence of Jesus in the post-resurrection community and the Paraclete as teacher and witness.

THE PARACLETE AS THE PRESENCE OF JESUS

It is impossible to overstate the crisis that the believing community faced as a result of Jesus' death. The shape and scope of this crisis can be illustrated by looking at the conversation between Jesus and Peter at 6:67-68. At 6:67, Jesus asked the Twelve whether they, too, wanted to leave him because of the difficulty of his teachings. In response, Peter replied, "Lord, to whom can we go? You have the words of eternal life" (6:68). Peter, speaking for the disciples, recognized the life-giving power of Jesus' revelation. At Jesus' death, the disciples face the inversion of the situation proposed at 6:67: Jesus is leaving them, and Peter's question becomes even more poignant, "Lord, to whom can we go?" Is Jesus' death the end of his "words of eternal life"?

Figure 12: Paraclete Passages in the Gospel of John*

14:16-17   "And I will ask the Father, and he will give you another Counselor to be with you forever—the Spirit of truth. The world cannot accept him, because it neither sees him nor knows him. But you know him, for he lives with you and will be in you."

14:26   "But the Counselor, the Holy Spirit, whom the Father will send in my name, will teach you all things and will remind you of everything I have said to you."

15:26   "When the Counselor comes, whom I will send to you from the Father, the Spirit of truth who goes out from the Father, he will testify about me.

16:7-11   "But I tell you the truth: It is for your good that I am going away. Unless I go away, the Counselor will not come to you; but if I go, I will send him to you. When he comes, he will convict the world of guilt in regard to sin and righteousness and judgment; in regard to sin, because men do not believe in me; in regard to righteousness, because I am going to the Father, where you can see me no longer; and in regard to judgment, because the prince of this world now stands condemned."

16:12-15   "I have much more to say to you, more than you can now bear. But when he, the Spirit of truth, comes, he will guide you into all truth. He will not speak on his own; he will speak only what he hears, and he will tell you what is yet to come. He will bring glory to me by taking from what is mine and making it known to you. All that belongs to the Father is mine. That is why I said the Spirit will take from what is mine and make it known to you."

*Scripture quotations are from the NIV.

It is important to be clear about the theological dimension of this crisis. In John, Jesus' revelation of God hinges on the recognition that Jesus is the incarnate Logos, the Son of God. Jesus' revelation of God is not a general, abstract revelation of the character of God. The essence of God cannot be abstracted from the incarnation and represented as some general notion of the "divine." Rather, the reality of the incarnation is the essence of Jesus' revelation of God. It is in the Word become flesh, in God's gift of his Son, that believers come to know who God is. That is, the incarnation has brought believers into new relationship with God and has opened up the possibility of their becoming children of God (1:12-13). Jesus' death and departure thus presented the disciples, and the church, with a crisis far greater than simply the loss of their teacher and friend. Jesus' death and return to God marked the end of the incarnation. If the revelation of God is lodged in the incarnation, what happens when Jesus is gone? Was Jesus' revelation of God possible for only the first generation of believers, available only to those who had physical contact with Jesus and his ministry? Was Jesus' revelation of God thus limited to one particular moment in history, or does it have a future?

It is the theological genius of the Fourth Evangelist to present the Paraclete as the solution to this crisis. Throughout Jesus' words about the Paraclete, the emphasis repeatedly falls on the Paraclete as the one who will continue Jesus' work after his absence, as the one who will make it possible for the experience of God made known and available in the incarnation to be known after Jesus' death. The Commentary on the Paraclete passages repeatedly noted the ways in which the description of the Paraclete echoed the Gospel's description of Jesus. For example, the verbs "to witness" and "to abide," both identified in the Gospel with the life and ministry of Jesus, are associated with the Paraclete in the Farewell Discourse ("witness" [μαρτυρέω *martyreō*], e.g., 3:32; 8:13-18; 15:26-27; "abide" [μένω *menō*], e.g., 14:17, 25; 15:4). The Paraclete is explicitly described as speaking the words of Jesus and reminding the disciples of Jesus' teaching (14:26; 15:13-15). The Paraclete's origins are explicitly linked to the agency of God and Jesus, and the Paraclete is described as being sent by God and given by God (14:16, 26), verbs that are also used to describe Jesus' advent into the world (e.g., 3:16; 4:34; 6:38; 12:44-45). The very language of these promises thus establishes the connections between the ministry of Jesus and the ministry of the Paraclete. The Paraclete is positioned as the link between the historical ministry of Jesus and the future life of the church after Jesus' death.

Through the promise of the Paraclete, the Fourth Evangelist is able to portray Jesus' death, resurrection, and ascension not as the end, but as the beginning of a new era in the life of the believing community. Indeed, in 16:7-8, Jesus goes so far as to speak of his departure as being for the disciples' good, so that they will be able to share in the advent of the Paraclete. Future generations of believers are not left alone, bereft of the experience of God made known in the incarnation, because the Paraclete takes that experience of God and extends it beyond the limits of Jesus' life and death. The Paraclete makes it possible for all believers to share in the good news of the incarnation, because the Paraclete makes Jesus present to believers, even though Jesus is now physically absent.

The promise of the abiding presence of the Paraclete highlights the interconnection of all aspects of the Johannine theological vision. In addition to clarifying the Johannine understanding of the Spirit (its pneumatology), the Paraclete passages also contribute to the Fourth Evangelist's portrait of Jesus and point to the writer's understanding of the nature of Christian community. As the Farewell Discourse is at pains to make clear, Jesus' death will not leave the disciples orphaned, because Jesus and God will send the Paraclete to the believing community. Jesus will leave the world, but the disciples will not (17:11, 15), and the promise of the Paraclete shows Jesus as one who will continue to support his followers for perpetuity. The promise of the Paraclete thus stands as a testament to the reliability of Jesus and his love, because Jesus has not ignored the future of those who will live on after he leaves them. It is a stunning portrait of Jesus that has at its heart a conviction about the abiding presence of Jesus with those whom he loves and who love him. Jesus is, indeed, the good shepherd who loves and cares for his own both in his death (10:17-18; 13:1, 35; 15:12-13) and beyond.

The promise of the Paraclete thus provides the ultimate definition of what Jesus means when he says, "Abide in me as I abide in you" (15:4). The presence of the Paraclete means that there are no temporal or spatial limits on Jesus' love and on believers' access to that love. The love of God made known in the incarnation continues into the life of the community through the gift of the Paraclete. What is critical about the promise of the Paraclete is that Jesus and God send the Paraclete to the *community,* not to individuals. Readings of the Fourth Gospel that emphasize the individual believer's mystical relationship to Jesus through the Spirit distort the Johannine picture of the Paraclete. The Paraclete is not a private possession, nor is its presence discernible as an internal experience of the individual believer. The Paraclete is given to and known in the community. Because the Paraclete is the presence of Jesus after Jesus' departure, it is not simply a subjective experience of "God," but is always linked to the revelation of God made known in the incarnation. The Paraclete keeps the community grounded in Jesus' revelation of God, not in an individual's private experience of God. The Paraclete is thus the unifying mark of Christian community, because it gives all believers access to Jesus.

THE PARACLETE AS TEACHER AND WITNESS

Jesus' teachings in the Farewell Discourse consistently depict the Paraclete as teacher and witness, and this depiction illuminates the role of the Paraclete in forming and shaping Christian community. Two passages are especially important in this regard. First, at 14:26, Jesus says that the Paraclete will "remind you of all that I have said to you." As noted in the Commentary, this verse points both to the connection between what Jesus said and what the Paraclete will say (see also 16:14) and to the nature of the Paraclete's teaching role. For the Paraclete, to teach is to remind the community of what Jesus himself said. Second, at John 16:12-13, Jesus says, "I still have many things to say to you, but you cannot bear them now. When the Spirit of Truth comes, he will guide you into all the truth." In these verses, as the Commentary suggested, Jesus points to the importance of fresh encounters with the words of Jesus, given at the time of need, not in advance of that time, and identifies the Paraclete as the medium of those encounters.

These descriptions of the Paraclete are pivotal for contemporary Christian communities of faith, because they point to the ways in which the Paraclete enables past, present, and future to converge in the life of the church. The Paraclete enables the words of Jesus to resound afresh in ever-changing circumstances. On the one hand, the Paraclete's role is essentially *conserving.* That is, the Paraclete enables the Christian community, at any time in its life, to reach back to the teachings of Jesus and "remember," to bring Jesus' teachings to life afresh with new understanding (see Reflections on 12:12-18). On the other hand, the Paraclete's role as teacher is also *creative.* The Paraclete enables the word of Jesus to move forward from its moment in history to the present life of the church. The Paraclete gives new meanings to the teachings of Jesus as the changing circumstances of faith communities and the world demand.

The words of Jesus that community members are able to receive before a crisis are quite distinct from the words that the community is able to receive during or after a crisis. For example, if someone tried to tell an adolescent what he or she would need to hear from Jesus to endure what life will bring at thirty, fifty, or seventy years of age, the adolescent would not be able to "bear" them. The words of Jesus that a community will need to endure the destruction of a church building by fire would also be insupportable in advance of the event. The words of Jesus that the community needs to hear to make sense of the church's place in changing social and economic circumstances are likewise unbearable in advance, because there is no context for such words in advance of the situation of need. The Fourth Evangelist portrays the Paraclete as the guarantee that the words of Jesus will always be available as fresh words for any and all futures.

The Paraclete thus ensures that there is an ongoing communication between Jesus and contemporary communities of faith. As with the Gospel's emphasis on the abiding presence of the Paraclete, this interpretation of the Paraclete's role as teacher and witness is also a stroke of theological genius. This understanding of the Paraclete as teacher both honors the integrity of the historical ministry of Jesus and at the same time recognizes that Jesus' ministry must always be interpreted in order to keep its offer of God alive.

The Paraclete's teaching, witness, and interpretation can take many forms in the life of the faith community. The first place where the reader of the Fourth Gospel experiences the work of the Paraclete is in the Gospel narrative itself. In telling his story of Jesus, the Fourth Evangelist shares in the work of the Paraclete. He does indeed "remind" his readers of what Jesus said and did, thus carrying the teachings of Jesus forward from the past into the present. But in his reminding, he also places the story of Jesus into conversation with the circumstances in which his readers live, so that they are able to hear Jesus' words as if he were speaking to their own lives and needs. The two levels of many of the Gospel's narratives, in which Jesus' relationship to the Jewish authorities of his day melds with the Jewish controversies of the Evangelist's time (e.g., John 5:31-46; 7:11-13; 9:22-41), can be interpreted as the work of the Paraclete, to show that Jesus' story is both a past event and a contemporary story.[545] The Fourth Evangelist understands, perhaps better than any other evangelist, that story and interpretation, history and theology, are inseparably linked in the life of Jesus and the church and that is incumbent upon the faith community to engage in disciplined conversation between the story of Jesus and their own stories.

The contemporary Christian also experiences the Paraclete in the preaching of the church. Each time a preacher attempts to proclaim the Word of God in a new circumstance, he or she shares in the work of the Paraclete. At its heart, preaching belongs to the ongoing conversation among past, present, and future in the life of the church. Like the work of the Paraclete, preaching is both conserving and creative. It is at the same time both old and new, past tense and contemporary. The preacher is bound both to the traditions of the church, so that his or her work is an act of reminding, and to the present moment, so that his or her work is also an act of discovering how the Word of God speaks in a new day. The gift and presence of the Paraclete allows both the preacher and the congregation to share in a fresh experience of the Word of God.

545. J. Louis Martyn, *History and Theology in the Fourth Gospel* (Nashville: Abingdon, 1968; 2nd ed., 1979) 143-51.

❖   ❖   ❖   ❖

16:16-33. As noted in the Commentary above, John 16:7b-33 provides two responses to the disciples' sorrow at Jesus' impending departure (vv. 7b-15 and vv. 16-33). Jesus' words in v. 16 provide the transition between these two responses, because they turn the focus from the Paraclete back to Jesus' departure per se, the theme with which he began in vv. 5-7a.

16:16. Jesus has used the expression "a little while" (μικρόν *mikron*) to speak of the imminence of his departure and hence the limited time of his presence (7:33; 13:33; cf. 12:35). Against this background, it is clear that the adverb *mikron* in v. 16a refers to the time leading up to Jesus' death. With the second *mikron* in v. 16b, however, Jesus points beyond his death to the disciples' future experience of Jesus ("you will see me again"). In the context of the Farewell Discourse, this second "a little while" seems to refer to the time between Jesus' death and his resurrection appearances.

In the OT, the expression "a little while" is often used to refer to the interval of intense

eschatological expectation and to evoke the imminence of God's new age (e.g, Isa 10:25; 26:20; 29:17). The prominence of OT imagery, particularly from Isaiah, in 16:21 (see below) supports reading Jesus' words in v. 16b against that background. Some interpreters (e.g., Augustine), therefore, find a reference to the resurrection too limiting and instead see *mikron* as referring to the time before the parousia, Jesus' Second Coming.[546] These interpreters rightly emphasize the eschatological dimension of Jesus' promise here, but misread the Johannine understanding of the resurrection. For John, the hour—Jesus' death, resurrection, and ascension—is the eschatological event, marking the beginning of God's new age, and as such the significance of the resurrection appearances extends beyond the experiences of his first disciples on Easter day (see below on 16:22 and 20:1-29).[547]

16:17-18. The disciples' confused questioning

546. Brown, *The Gospel According to John (XII–XXI)*, 729-30, in a quite different vein, takes this verse as a reference to the Paraclete.
547. Rudolf Schnackenburg, *The Gospel According to St. John,* 3 vols. (New York: Seabury, 1982) 3:156.

underscores the ambiguity of Jesus' words in v. 16. These verses are the first time the disciples have spoken since 14:22, although at this juncture they speak only among themselves (v. 17) and do not address their words directly to Jesus (cf. v. 19). Their questions to one another link the two parts of the discourse in John 16, because not only do they repeat the immediately preceding words of Jesus from v. 16, but they also repeat his words of v. 10 ("because I am going to the Father"; cf. the similar function of the disciples' questions to one another at 4:27). Their questions show that they have recognized that Jesus is speaking to them about his departure, but that the meaning of that departure still remains beyond their grasp. Their continual repetition of Jesus' words sounds almost like stammering (note the NIV's correct translation of the Greek imperfect at v. 18, "they kept asking"). The language of vv. 17-18 conveys the disciples' inarticulateness in the face of Jesus' departure and thereby confirms Jesus' words of vv. 5b-6: the disciples' sorrow at Jesus' departure seems to have rendered them speechless.

16:19. Jesus' knowledge of the disciples' questions points again to his ability to know "what was in everyone" (2:25; cf. 1:47-48; 6:15, 61; 13:11). As is typical of the teaching of Jesus throughout this Gospel, Jesus does not answer their questions directly, but instead moves their questions in a new direction (cf. 3:2-9; 4:12-14). The expression "very truly, I tell you" with which v. 20 begins is used once again to introduce a new teaching (cf., e.g., 3:3, 5; 5:24-25; 8:34). The teaching that follows in vv. 20-24 addresses the disciples' sorrow (λύπη *lypē*; "pain," NRSV; "grief," NIV) and its resolution.

16:20. Verse 20a depicts the contrasting effect of Jesus' death on his disciples and the world (cf. 15:18–16:4a). The verbs "to weep" (κλαίω *klaiō*) and "to mourn" (θρηνέω *thrēneō*) describe the lamentation and grieving at a death (John 11:31, 33; 20:11; Luke 7:13; 7:32; 8:52; 23:27; see also Jer 22:10). The contrast between mourning and rejoicing in v. 20 recalls the contrast in the blessing and woe of Luke 6:21 and 25 between the disciples of Jesus and their adversaries. Jesus immediately promises the transformation of the disciples' sorrow into joy in v. 20b, but will not address its counterpart, the transformation of the

world's joy into its opposite, until the final words of the discourse (16:33).[548]

16:21. Jesus employs a short parable to illustrate the relationship between present sorrow and future joy in the disciples' experience. In John's Gospel, Jesus often draws on proverbs or short parables to illustrate his claims (e.g., 4:37-38; 5:19-20; 8:35; 10:1-5; 12:24).[549] Dodd offers an excellent analysis of the form of this parable, noting the formal balance of its composition: two parts that each have the same pattern, "when A occurs, B occurs, because C has occurred."[550] In v. 21a, the interrelated elements are labor, pain, and the time of delivery; in v. 21b, the mother's delivery of the child shifts the balance between pain and joy. This parable, which draws on a common life experience, thus serves as an apt illustration of Jesus' teaching about sorrow and joy.

Yet this parable is much more than a general illustration. Its imagery, while reflective of ordinary experience, draws on a wealth of OT imagery in which the metaphor of childbirth is used to describe the advent of God's salvation. Of particular relevance are two texts from Isaiah. Isaiah 26:17 employs the childbirth metaphor to describe the experience of God's people as they await God's deliverance. (As noted above, an echo of Isa 26:20 can be heard in Jesus' words in v. 16.) In Isa 66:7-17, the metaphor of childbirth is used to envision the restoration of Jerusalem. Both of these texts use the childbirth metaphor as a communal metaphor; it evokes the experience of the people of God as they move from suffering to renewed joy.

The language of v. 21 has other theological resonances. First, the Greek word translated "pain" (*lypē*) is an unusual word to describe a woman's pain at childbirth, since it is normally a word for emotional, not physical, pain. Its use here is probably to call the disciples' (and the reader's) immediate attention to the connections Jesus is establishing between the conventional parable and the particularities of the disciples' situation at Jesus' departure. Second, Jesus speaks of the woman's time of delivery as "her hour." This use of "hour" evokes both Jesus' own hour

---

548. E. C. Hoskyns, *The Fourth Gospel* (London: Faber & Faber, 1947) 488.

549. See C. H. Dodd, *Historical Tradition in the Fourth Gospel* (Cambridge: Cambridge University Press, 1963) 366-87, for a full discussion of Jesus' use of these literary forms in John.

550. Ibid., 370.

(2:4; 8:20; 12:23; 13:1) and the anticipated eschatological hour (4:21, 23; 5:25, 28). Third, the noun θλῖψις (*thlipsis*, "anguish") is used to describe the woman's ordeal in labor. This noun, normally translated "tribulation," is usually used in apocalyptic contexts to describe the suffering and persecution the community will endure in advance of the inbreaking of God's kingdom (e.g., Matt 24:9, 21, 29; Mark 13:19, 24; Acts 14:22; Rom 8:35).

In this parable, then, Jesus draws on OT childbirth imagery to communicate the eschatological transformation that will occur within the faith community as a result of his death. The disciples will become a new people, a people of joy. Images of birth are important metaphors in the Fourth Gospel to describe the new life that Jesus makes available to those who believe (1:12-13; 3:3-10; cf. "little children" at 13:33). The imagery of childbirth is especially significant in the context of the Farewell Discourse, because it is, indeed, new birth for the disciples that will be effected through Jesus' death and resurrection (see Commentary on 20:17). It is a distortion of the parable to interpret its symbolism as depicting the birth of the Messiah, along the analogy of Rev 12:2-5, because such a view misreads the essential communal referent of the metaphor.[551] As in the Isaiah texts, the woman stands as a symbol for the community, suffering through tribulation in order to receive God's awaited salvation and new life.

16:22. Jesus makes the direct comparison between the parable and the disciples' sorrow ("so you have sorrow now"). He identifies his reappearance to them as the act that will transform their sorrow to joy. Jesus' words seem to be a promise of his resurrection appearances, and, indeed, in John 20 Jesus' appearance will cause Mary to cease weeping (20:16) and cause the other disciples to rejoice (20:20). The Easter stories thus show the reliability of Jesus' farewell promise and the truth of his words. Jesus' promise in v. 22 is the perfect complement to v. 6 (cf. the relationship between 14:1 and 27), and at the same time seems to contain a deliberate allusion to Isa 66:14 ("You shall see, and your heart shall rejoice" [NRSV]). The wording of the promise in v. 22 ("I will see you again") highlights Jesus'

initiative toward the disciples in the resurrection (cf. the wording of 16:16). Verse 22 ends with a statement of the permanence of the disciples' joy. Like the birth of the child in the parable, Jesus' resurrection will irreversibly change the course of the disciples' lives.

16:23-24. As at 14:20, "on that day" (v. 23*a*) underscores the connection between Jesus' resurrection and the time of eschatological fulfillment. Because of Jesus' resurrection, the disciples have entered into eschatological joy. The sign of this eschatological joy will be their lack of questions (v. 23*a*).

The precise meaning of Jesus' promise here depends on how one interprets the Greek verb ἐρωτάω (*erōtaō*). The NRSV gives it the meaning of "petition" ("ask nothing of me"). According to this reading, vv. 23-24 form one teaching about the believers' petitions. This reading seems unlikely, however, since the expression "very truly, I tell you" with which v. 23*b* begins always introduces a new teaching in John and so marks a shift in Jesus' teaching. The more common meaning of *erōtaō* is "to ask questions," and this is the meaning accepted by the NIV and most scholars (see also the NRSV footnote).[552] "On that day" the confused, anxious, and stammering questions that have marked the disciples' relationship to Jesus during his ministry (e.g, 6:9; 11:8; 13:6, 25, 36) and especially during the Farewell Discourse (14:5, 22; 16:17-18) will cease. As Bultmann has eloquently stated, this is *"the eschatological situation:* to have no more questions! . . . This is to say that the believers live in *joy;* because it is the nature of joy that all questioning grows silent, and nothing needs explaining."[553]

In vv. 23*b*-24, Jesus describes a second characteristic of eschatological joy: answered prayer (cf. 14:13-14; 15:7, 16). Answered prayer is a sign of eschatological joy because it is a sign that the disciples share fully in Jesus' relationship with God. The manuscript evidence is divided over whether the phrase "in Jesus' name" should be linked with the disciples' asking (the reading fol-

---

551. So Raymond E. Brown, *The Gospel According to John (XIII–XXI)*, AB 29A (Garden City, N.Y.: Doubleday, 1970) 731-32.

552. For example, Hoskyns, *John*, 489; Bultmann, *John*, 583; Brown, *The Gospel According to John (XIII–XXI)*, 722-23; Barrett, *The Gospel According to St. John*, 494.

553. Rudolf Bultmann, *The Gospel of John: A Commentary*, trans. G. R. Beasley-Murray, R. W. N. Hoare, and J. K. Riches (Philadelphia: Westminster, 1971) 583.

lowed by the NIV and the NRSV) or God's response (NRSV footnote). Both readings emphasize the interrelationship of God, Jesus, and the community in prayer. As a sign of God's new age, the disciples can pray, like Jesus, in the full confidence that God hears their prayers. This confidence in prayer will be enacted for the disciples in Jesus' prayer of 17:1-16.

16:25-33. *16:25.* The final section of the Farewell Discourse is introduced by the transitional expression "I have said these things to you" (v. 25*a;* see also 14:25; 15:11; 16:4). The Greek noun translated "figures of speech" by the NRSV (παροιμίαι *paroimiai*) can refer to a range of literary forms, including parable, proverb, and riddle (see Commentary on 10:6). Its use in the plural in v. 25*a* (as opposed to the singular at 10:6; 16:29) suggests that it is being used adverbially (note the NIV's "figuratively")—that is, it describes a general mode of speaking rather than a specific literary form.[554] "These things," therefore, should not be read as referring simply to the parable of 16:21, but to all of Jesus' teaching in the Farewell Discourse.[555]

On the surface level, the contrast to which Jesus points in v. 25*b* is clear. In the Fourth Gospel, "plainly" (παρρησία *parrēsia*) is used to characterize the public cast of Jesus' ministry (e.g., 7:26; 18:20), but it is also used to describe direct speech (10:24-25; 11:14). Jesus thus accentuates the difference between the present, when he speaks in "figures of speech" (*paroimiais*), and the future, when he will speak "plainly" (*parresia*). But the real emphasis of this verse is not on Jesus' mode of speaking per se, but on the changes that will be accomplished by "the hour." The expression "the hour is coming" (cf. 4:21; 5:28) makes clear that the eschatological vision that shapes Jesus' words in vv. 19-24 continues in vv. 25-28. In vv. 23-24, Jesus gave two promises of the disciples' participation in eschatological joy: the end of their need to ask questions (v. 23*a*) and their answered prayer (vv. 23*b*-24). In vv. 25-28, Jesus moves those eschatological promises

to their conclusion. Verse 25 complements v. 23*a*, vv. 26-27 complement vv. 23*b*-24, and v. 28 states the grounds of all of Jesus' eschatological promises.

Jesus' promise in v. 25 is not a general promise about direct speech, but is a very particular promise about his revelation of the Father. Jesus' hour—his death, resurrection, and ascension—completes his revelation of God and as such marks a decisive change in the believer's access to God. "The hour is coming" when Jesus' revelation of God will be "plain" because "the hour is coming" when Jesus will return to God (13:1). What has been anticipated during Jesus' life will be fully available as a result of his hour. Jesus' promise in v. 25*b* thus confirms his promise in v. 23*b*: the disciples will not need to ask questions because Jesus' revelation will be "plain." Jesus' promise in v. 25*b* must also be read alongside his promises of the Paraclete in 14:25 and 16:12-15. The verb "I will tell" (ἀπαγγέλλω *apangellō*) in 16:25 echoes the verb used to describe the future work of the Paraclete in 16:13-15: "he will declare" (ἀναγγέλλω *anangellō*).[556] The Paraclete will give the disciples access to Jesus' full revelation of God after Jesus' return to God (cf. 16:7).

16:26-27. The eschatological dimension of Jesus' promises is reinforced by the opening words of v. 26, "on that day" (cf. 14:20; 16:23). Verses 26-27 place the eschatological promise of answered prayer (cf. vv. 23*b*-24) in the context of God's love for those who love Jesus. The disciples' prayer is grounded in their relationship with Jesus ("you will ask in my name," v. 26*a*), and Jesus' disclaimer of his own role in their petitioning confirms the strength of this relationship. Jesus is not renouncing his role as petitioning mediator with God in v. 26*b,* as his prayer in John 17 shows (cf. 14:16). Rather, his words here accentuate the authenticity of the disciples' own relationship with God and the claim that relationship has on God.

Verse 27 specifies the character of this relationship: love. The vision of a community shaped by love, intimacy, and mutuality that formed the core of Jesus' teaching in 15:1-17 receives its fullest expression here by explicitly naming God as a member of that community. Just as Jesus and the disciples are friends, "loved ones" (φίλοι *philoi,* 15:13-15), so also God and the disciples are friends,

---

554. Luis Rubio Moran, "Revelacion en enigmas y revalacion en claridad," *Salmanticensis* 19 (1972) 118.

555. C. H. Dodd, *The Interpretation of the Fourth Gospel* (Cambridge: Cambridge University Press, 1953), restricts this phrase to 16:19-21, but the consensus view among Johannine scholars is that it refers to the entire discourse (e.g., Brown, *The Gospel According to John (XIII–XXI),* 735; Schnackenburg, *The Gospel According to St. John,* 3:162.

556. George R. Beasley-Murray, *John,* WBC 36 (Waco, Tex.: Word, 1987) 287.

united by love.[557] The disciples' love of Jesus is not a prerequisite for God's love of them, however. Rather, v. 27 points to the organic connection between the believers' love of Jesus and God's love of them, a connection that mirrors the organic connection between Jesus and his followers (14:20-24; 15:10). Both verbs in v. 27 ("have loved" [πεφιλήκατε *pephilēkate*] and "have believed" [πεπιστεύκατε *pepisteukate*]) are in the perfect tense, pointing to the duration through time of the disciples' love and faith. Verse 27 is the ultimate eschatological vision of union with God.

16:28. This verse is a summary of the Johannine Gospel. It returns to the theme first hinted at in 1:51 ("angels of God ascending and descending upon the Son of Man") and first stated fully at 3:13 ("No one has ascended into heaven except the one who descended from heaven, the Son of Man"). Both halves of v. 28 are essential to the Fourth Evangelist's theology. Verse 28*a,* which emphasizes Jesus' origins with and from God, is the key to the Fourth Evangelist's understanding of the incarnation and Jesus' revelation of God. Verse 28*b,* which emphasizes Jesus' return to God, is the key to the Fourth Evangelist's ecclesial and eschatological vision, because Jesus' return completes his revelation of God, makes possible the gift of the Paraclete, and so opens up the community to the possibility of a new relationship with God and with one another. In the context of the Farewell Discourse, this summary serves to remind the disciples and the readers that it is not enough to focus on Jesus' origins with God. Jesus' descent must be complemented by his ascent; his story is incomplete without his death and departure. Verse 28 thus brings the discourse of John 16 back to its beginnings in vv. 5-7; Jesus' departure is indeed to the disciples' advantage.[558]

16:29-30. In contrast to the questions that have previously characterized their contributions to the farewell conversation (e.g., 14:5, 22), the disciples respond to Jesus with boldness and certainty in these verses. Their confidence is readily apparent in the NRSV translation of the opening exclamation of v. 29: "Yes, now you are speaking plainly." The disciples repeat Jesus' words from v. 25

almost verbatim, thus offering a seemingly appropriate response, but the few differences between their words and Jesus' original words are telling and offer another example of Johannine irony.[559] First, as noted already, *paroimia* is used in the plural in v. 25 ("figures of speech"). The disciples, however, respond to Jesus' words as if only one figure of speech is in view. The disciples' confident response to Jesus' words, then, misinterprets the words' central premise. By using "figure" in the singular, the disciples seem to assume that the contrast of which Jesus speaks is between the parable of v. 20 and the "plain" words of vv. 25-28. Second, and much more significant, the disciples completely overlook the eschatological dimension of Jesus' words. Jesus pointed to a time in the future when he would speak plainly, a time after his departure, but the disciples respond as if the present moment is already the time of Jesus' plain speaking. They misconstrue the meaning of "figures," because of their exclusive focus on their present conversation with Jesus.

The irony of the disciples' response becomes even clearer in v. 30, which opens with a hyperbolic statement of confidence ("Now we know that you know all things") and ends with a confession of faith ("by this we believe"). The irony of v. 30 arises because the disciples think they are making an appropriate confession, but they are not. First, v. 30*a* seems to refer to Jesus' ability to discern their questions at v. 19. Their "knowledge" about Jesus is not based on anything he said about mutuality of relationship among God, Jesus, and the believer as a result of Jesus' departure (vv. 26-28), but is instead based on his omniscience. Jesus spoke of the disciples' love for him (v. 27), but they respond solely in terms of knowledge. Second, in v. 30*b* the disciples' confession of faith only acknowledges Jesus' words about his origins with God (cf. Nicodemus's opening words at 3:2); it says nothing about his departure. This omission underscores the incompleteness of their bold confession, because they do not acknowledge the necessity of Jesus' death and departure to complete his revelation of God.

16:31-32. Jesus' words in v. 31, "Now you believe," ironically echo the disciples' words in

557. See Barrett's powerful observation, *The Gospel According to St. John,* 2nd ed. (Philadelphia: Westminster, 1978) 496, that v. 27 shows how the Father stands within "the unique circle of love."

558. Rudolf Schnackenburg, *The Gospel According to St. John,* 3:163.

559. For a fuller discussion of the ironic dimensions of this conversation, see Gail R. O'Day, *Revelation in the Fourth Gospel: Narrative Mode and Theological Claim* (Philadelphia: Fortress, 1986) 104-9.

vv. 29-30 and shatter any illusions about the adequacy of their confession. Verse 31 is not introduced by an interrogative particle or adverb, so it is unclear whether Jesus' words should be read as a statement or a question. The Nestle-Aland[27] text punctuates the sentence as a question, and that is the reading followed by the NRSV and the majority of scholars. The NIV, however, punctuates it as a statement. If v. 31 is punctuated as a statement, it is important to remember that Jesus is mocking the disciples' earlier confession, not congratulating them. The emphatic use of "now" (ἄρτι *arti*) parodies the disciples' emphatic use of "now" (νῦν *nun*), and the repetition of "believe" (πιστεύω *pisteuō*) challenges their confession.

The disciples' words assumed that the time of eschatological fulfillment of which Jesus spoke had already arrived, and in vv. 31-32 Jesus reorients them to the true meaning of "the hour." "Now" is not the time of glib confessions; "now" is the hour of death and betrayal. The shift in Jesus' words from "The hour is coming" (v. 25) to "The hour is coming, indeed it has come" (v. 32) points to the link between the time of eschatological fulfillment and Jesus' death. The hour that is upon Jesus and his disciples is the hour of Jesus' death, and the disciples' confession in v. 30, with its omission of any mention of Jesus' return to God, shows that they still do not recognize the significance of the hour. This lack of recognition and comprehension is poignantly underscored by Jesus' prediction of the disciples' abandonment of him at his death. This prediction is cast in language that echoes Zech 13:7: "Strike the shepherd, that the sheep may be scattered" (NRSV). Matthew and Mark also use this tradition from Zechariah to predict the disciples' abandonment of Jesus (Matt 26:31; Mark 14:27), but the prophecy has special poignancy in the Fourth Gospel because of its echoes of the scattering of the herd in the good shepherd discourse (John 10:12).

Jesus' prediction of the disciples' abandonment is rendered even more poignant by the contrast in v. 32 between the disciples' relationship with Jesus and God's relationship with Jesus. Scholars are divided on whether the Fourth Evangelist intends Jesus' affirmation of God's presence in v. 32 as a correction of the "cry of dereliction" found in the synoptic tradition (Matt 27:46; Mark 15:34). Hoskyns and Barrett, for example, maintain that v. 32 is a deliberate correction, but Jesus' words do not need to be read with that polemical note here. The Farewell Discourse has repeatedly emphasized that Jesus' hour brings the disciples into the union that he shares with God (e.g., 14:20; 15:9-10, 16) and has promised the disciples lasting relationship with God and Jesus (e.g., 14:18, 23), but the disciples do not hold to that relationship at the moment of Jesus' death. Jesus does, however; even at his death, he knows that God is with him (cf. 8:29).

16:33. Jesus once again reflects on his own words ("I have said these things to you") as a way of bringing the discourse to its conclusion. Verse 33 makes clear why and how Jesus' gift of his peace is not like the world's peace (cf. 14:27). The disciples' relationship with Jesus ("in me you may have peace"), the significance of which has been spelled out for them over and over again in the Farewell Discourse, enables them to experience peace even in the face of the world's "persecution" (θλῖψις [*thlipsis*]; cf. 16:21). The disciples' place in the world and the world's power over them is transformed because of Jesus. This is stated in absolute terms in the ringing announcement with which the Farewell Discourse closes, "But take courage; I have conquered the world!" Jesus' peace is the definitive eschatological gift, because it marks the ultimate defeat of the powers of the world (κόσμος *kosmos*) that stand in opposition to God (cf. 12:31; 14:30-31). Jesus' words of hope and reassurance in the Farewell Discourse thus are not idle words of hope, but are grounded in the reality of the guaranteed victory of God's love in Jesus. The language of victory in John 16:33 is very similar to Paul's language in 1 Cor 15:57, but the eschatological perspective is different. For Paul, the victory is future, but for John, it is already present.

REFLECTIONS

In John 16:33, the eschatological perspective that has governed the Farewell Discourse is stated explicitly. Jesus' "future" victory—his glorification in the events of his hour—is indeed the present reality. The Jesus who speaks in the Farewell Discourse is the Jesus who has already conquered the world; the voice of Jesus that reassures the disciples and points them to their future is the voice of the risen Jesus. John 14–16 is an ingenious eschatological discourse, because it brings God's future into the present of the Gospel narrative by announcing that *this* is the moment of victory. John 16:33 announces that God's new age, initiated by Jesus' victory over the world, has entered the present. Jesus' victory over the world thus transforms conventional understandings of present and future.[560]

Much has been said in this commentary about the richness of Johannine eschatology (see, e.g., Commentary on 5:24-28; 11:25-26). It simplifies the eschatological options in the NT to characterize them as "realized" versus "future" eschatology, because by definition eschatology has to do with the future, with "the last things." Johannine eschatology is no exception, because it, too, is concerned with the future. What varies among the different eschatological perspectives in the NT is the relationship between present and future in the eschatological vision. In some eschatologies, the emphasis is on the present's giving way to the future (e.g., 1 Cor 15:23-28), whereas in others the emphasis is on the future's breaking into and transforming the present. Johannine eschatology belongs to the second category, but that does not mean that the Fourth Gospel portrays all of the possibilities of God's future as "realized" in the present moment. On the contrary, as John 16:16-33 shows quite clearly, Johannine eschatology points to the confidence with which Christians can face into the future, knowing that God's sovereign presence in and governance of the present *and* the future is assured.

When contemporary Christians think about eschatology, then, they come face to face with some of the core questions of Christian faith: How does the believer move from the present to the future? What is God's place in that future? What is the nature of Christian hope? John 16:16-33 provides the interpreter with one perspective from which to engage those questions, because it is above all an eschatological text. In this concluding section of the Farewell Discourse, Jesus offers the disciples (and the readers) ways to imagine the possibilities of life beyond the present moment and points them toward their future life with God.

Key to the Johannine eschatological vision is the cosmic significance of Jesus' hour—his death, resurrection, and ascension. Just as the "beginning" (1:1) of the Jesus story, the incarnation, has cosmic significance (see Reflections on 1:1-18), so, too, has the conclusion of the Jesus story. Jesus loved his own "to the end" (13:1), and because of that love the believers' futures are forever altered. The last things, like the first things, are redefined by the incarnation. In the return of the Logos, the Son, to the Father, the world is decisively changed. Indeed, the world is conquered by Jesus, the ruler of the world rendered powerless (14:30) by the fullness of Jesus' love made manifest in the gift of his life. The full possibilities of life with God are revealed in Jesus' death, resurrection, and ascension, because death did not defeat Jesus. Rather, Jesus defeated death, laying down his life to take it up again (10:17-18), laying down his life in love so that he could return his life to God in love and so open to all believers the possibility of communion and union with God (16:27-28; 17:23). Jesus repeatedly stresses the necessity and advantage of his departure in John 14–16 (e.g., 14:28; 16:7, 28), because without his death and departure the cosmic changes begun at the incarnation are incomplete. Without Jesus' death and departure, the old order remains in place. With Jesus' death and departure, the old order is judged and peace and joy take its place (14:30-31; 16:8-11, 23-24, 33), even in the face of persecution (16:1-3).

That Jesus' offer of eschatological peace and joy is not an instance of "cheap grace" is evidenced by the repeated references to suffering and persecution in the Farewell Discourse (15:18–16:4*a*, 20-22, 33). This persistent reminder of the persecution the community will endure and the courage that will be required of them belies any easy labeling of Johannine eschatology as "realized eschatology." The Farewell Discourse does not paint a picture of the

560. See Gail R. O'Day, " 'I have overcome the world' (John 16:33): Narrative Time in John 13–17," *Semeia* 53 (1991).

Christian life devoid of present hardship and trial, in which all of God's promises are fully actualized in the present moment. The prediction of the disciples' abandonment of Jesus at his hour underscores this (v. 32). Just as Jesus' victory over the world could not be effected without his death, so also the believers' share in Jesus' victory will be accompanied by suffering, sorrow, and pain.

What the Farewell Discourse does promise is that the movement from present sorrow to future joy is possible and, indeed, guaranteed as a result of Jesus' victory in his hour. It is this guarantee, the sure, unshakable confidence in Jesus' victory over the world and the peace that the victory makes possible, that provides the grounds for Christian hope. Hope is not idle speculation about the future, about what might be or what might happen, although contemporary parlance often reduces "hope" to that range of expectations. Rather, Christian hope is the conviction, grounded in the victory of Jesus' death and resurrection, that one's present and future belong to God and that, as a result, all things are possible (16:23-24). The measure of what is possible in the present is the victory of Christ (16:33). The measure of what is to be hoped for is the promises of Christ (16:23, 26-28). Both the present and the future are redefined by Jesus' death and resurrection and are held together in a delicate balance. When one lives in hope, the present moves toward the promises and possibilities of the future, and the future transforms the sorrows and seeming impossibilities of the present.

The Fourth Gospel's distinctive contribution to the church's conversation about hope and the future is the value that it places on the present moment as the arena in which God's future is already underway. For the Fourth Evangelist, the decisive Easter proclamation is "In the world you face persecution. But take courage; I have conquered the world!" Jesus' victory over the world is neither partial nor only anticipated, no matter what present struggles, suffering, and sorrow suggest. Because of that decisive and absolute victory, both the present and the future are now the locus for the enactment of the promises of God. John 16:16-33 invites the faith community to enter the eschatological domain of its life, to embrace God's future that has been opened up for them even in the present moment because of Jesus' death and departure.

JOHN 17:1-26, JESUS' FAREWELL PRAYER

NIV	NRSV
17 After Jesus said this, he looked toward heaven and prayed:	**17** After Jesus had spoken these words, he looked up to heaven and said, "Father, the hour has come; glorify your Son so that the Son may glorify you, [2]since you have given him authority over all people,*[a]* to give eternal life to all whom you have given him. [3]And this is eternal life, that they may know you, the only true God, and Jesus Christ whom you have sent. [4]I glorified you on earth by finishing the work that you gave me to do. [5]So now, Father, glorify me in your own presence with the glory that I had in your presence before the world existed.
"Father, the time has come. Glorify your Son, that your Son may glorify you. [2]For you granted him authority over all people that he might give eternal life to all those you have given him. [3]Now this is eternal life: that they may know you, the only true God, and Jesus Christ, whom you have sent. [4]I have brought you glory on earth by completing the work you gave me to do. [5]And now, Father, glorify me in your presence with the glory I had with you before the world began.	
[6]"I have revealed you*[a]* to those whom you gave me out of the world. They were	[6]"I have made your name known to those whom you gave me from the world. They were yours, and you gave them to me, and they have

[a]6 Greek your name; also in verse 26

[a] Gk flesh

NIV

yours; you gave them to me and they have obeyed your word. [7]Now they know that everything you have given me comes from you. [8]For I gave them the words you gave me and they accepted them. They knew with certainty that I came from you, and they believed that you sent me. [9]I pray for them. I am not praying for the world, but for those you have given me, for they are yours. [10]All I have is yours, and all you have is mine. And glory has come to me through them. [11]I will remain in the world no longer, but they are still in the world, and I am coming to you. Holy Father, protect them by the power of your name—the name you gave me—so that they may be one as we are one. [12]While I was with them, I protected them and kept them safe by that name you gave me. None has been lost except the one doomed to destruction so that Scripture would be fulfilled.

[13]"I am coming to you now, but I say these things while I am still in the world, so that they may have the full measure of my joy within them. [14]I have given them your word and the world has hated them, for they are not of the world any more than I am of the world. [15]My prayer is not that you take them out of the world but that you protect them from the evil one. [16]They are not of the world, even as I am not of it. [17]Sanctify[a] them by the truth; your word is truth. [18]As you sent me into the world, I have sent them into the world. [19]For them I sanctify myself, that they too may be truly sanctified.

[20]"My prayer is not for them alone. I pray also for those who will believe in me through their message, [21]that all of them may be one, Father, just as you are in me and I am in you. May they also be in us so that the world may believe that you have sent me. [22]I have given them the glory that you gave me, that they may be one as we are one: [23]I in them and you in me. May they be brought to complete unity to let the

NRSV

kept your word. [7]Now they know that everything you have given me is from you; [8]for the words that you gave to me I have given to them, and they have received them and know in truth that I came from you; and they have believed that you sent me. [9]I am asking on their behalf; I am not asking on behalf of the world, but on behalf of those whom you gave me, because they are yours. [10]All mine are yours, and yours are mine; and I have been glorified in them. [11]And now I am no longer in the world, but they are in the world, and I am coming to you. Holy Father, protect them in your name that you have given me, so that they may be one, as we are one. [12]While I was with them, I protected them in your name that[a] you have given me. I guarded them, and not one of them was lost except the one destined to be lost,[b] so that the scripture might be fulfilled. [13]But now I am coming to you, and I speak these things in the world so that they may have my joy made complete in themselves.[c] [14]I have given them your word, and the world has hated them because they do not belong to the world, just as I do not belong to the world. [15]I am not asking you to take them out of the world, but I ask you to protect them from the evil one.[d] [16]They do not belong to the world, just as I do not belong to the world. [17]Sanctify them in the truth; your word is truth. [18]As you have sent me into the world, so I have sent them into the world. [19]And for their sakes I sanctify myself, so that they also may be sanctified in truth.

20"I ask not only on behalf of these, but also on behalf of those who will believe in me through their word, [21]that they may all be one. As you, Father, are in me and I am in you, may they also be in us,[e] so that the world may believe that you have sent me. [22]The glory that you have given me I have given them, so that they may be one, as we are one, [23]I in them and you in me, that they may become completely one, so that the world may know that you have sent me and have loved them even as you have loved me. [24]Father, I desire that those also, whom you have given me, may be with me where I am, to see my glory, which you have given me because you loved me before the foundation of the world.

NIV

world know that you sent me and have loved them even as you have loved me.

²⁴"Father, I want those you have given me to be with me where I am, and to see my glory, the glory you have given me because you loved me before the creation of the world.

²⁵"Righteous Father, though the world does not know you, I know you, and they know that you have sent me. ²⁶I have made you known to them, and will continue to make you known in order that the love you have for me may be in them and that I myself may be in them."

NRSV

²⁵"Righteous Father, the world does not know you, but I know you; and these know that you have sent me. ²⁶I made your name known to them, and I will make it known, so that the love with which you have loved me may be in them, and I in them."

COMMENTARY

Jesus' prayer in John 17:1-26 is the final scene of his farewell meal with his disciples. Since the sixteenth century, the traditional title of this prayer has been "Jesus' high priestly prayer." This title highlights the role of Jesus as intercessor in this prayer, but it minimizes the intrinsic connections between this prayer and the preceding discourse.[561]

By concluding his narration of the farewell with this prayer, the Fourth Evangelist is adhering to the conventions of the farewell genre (see Overview to John 14:1–16:33). In biblical literature, for example, Moses' farewell speeches in Deuteronomy conclude with a hymn of praise to God (the Song of Moses, Deut 31:30–32:47) and Moses' blessing of the Israelites (Deuteronomy 33). Many of the farewell speeches of the patriarchs in *Jubilees* end with prayer,[562] as do farewell speeches found in Jewish apocalyptic literature.[563] The farewell prayer is thus well documented in the religious literature of the ancient Mediterranean world and would have been a familiar genre to the first readers of the Gospel.

The prayer in John 17, however, is not the conventional prayer of a dying man. Indeed, Jesus' farewell, as John 14–16 has underscored, is about the full constellation of the events of Jesus' hour—death, resurrection, and ascension—not simply his death. The prayer of John 17 is thus not a death-bed prayer, but the prayer of the One on the verge of willingly laying down his life and thus completing God's work (17:1-5).

The Fourth Evangelist has crafted and positioned Jesus' farewell prayer to stand as the theological climax of the Fourth Gospel. First, within the prayer of John 17, the reader hears echoes of themes from all of Jesus' preceding discourses (cf., e.g., 17:2 and 5:21; 17:12 and 6:39; 17:16 and 15:19; 17:20-21 and 10:16; 17:23 and 14:21-23),[564] as well as echoes of the Prologue (cf. 17:2 and 1:12; 17:5 and 1:1-2, 14; 17:3 and 1:17; 17:24 and 1:1-3, 14; 17:25 and 1:10; for details, see the Commentary below). The Jesus who speaks in this prayer is familiar to the Gospel reader as the incarnate Logos, the Son of God the Father.

Second, Jesus' prayer stands between his words to his disciples in the Farewell Discourse and the beginning of the passion story (chaps. 18–19). The prayer thus stands at the pivotal turn into the events of the hour and needs to be read in the context of Jesus' last announcement in 16:33, "I have overcome the world." This prayer is not a universal and timeless prayer of Jesus,[565] but one decisively

561. This title was given to the prayer by David Chytraeus. As early as the fourth century, however, Cyril of Alexandria already labeled Jesus the "High Priest" in this prayer. Although this title correctly conveys Jesus' role as intercessor, it also inappropriately reads the notion of Jesus' cultic sacrifice into this prayer. See Commentary v. 19.

562. E.g., Moses, *Jub.* 1:19-21; Noah, *Jub.* 10:3-6.

563. E.g., the prayer of Baruch in *2 Baruch* and the prayer of Ezra in *4 Esdras*. C. H. Dodd has noted that many of the dialogues in the *Hermetica* often end with a prayer or a hymn. See Dodd, *The Interpretation of the Fourth Gospel*, 420-23. Bultmann, of course, also notes parallels in Mandaean documents. See Bultmann, *The Gospel of John*, 489n. 8.

564. Dodd, *The Interpretation of the Fourth Gospel*, 417.

565. So Brown, *The Gospel According to John (XIII–XXI)*, 747.

grounded in and shaped by Jesus' hour. Jesus prays in the confidence of the eschatological victory of his hour, and the temporal perspective of his prayer is governed by that eschatological reality. In this prayer, Jesus speaks of his departure as already accomplished (17:11-12), imminent (17:1, 5), and even underway as he speaks (17:11, 13). The shifting temporal perspective of the prayer, which brings past, present, and future together into one narrative moment, shows that conventional understandings of time are redefined by this "hour." Form and content work together in John 17 to communicate the eschatological impact of Jesus' hour.[566] Dodd's comment that the prayer "in some sort *is* the ascent of the Son to the Father" overstates the case, but it nonetheless captures the theological and narrative significance of this prayer for the Johannine story of Jesus.[567]

In the Farewell Discourse, Jesus repeatedly spoke of the disciples' complete confidence in God's response to their prayer as a sign of eschatological newness and possibility (14:13-14; 15:16; 16:23-24, 26-27). When Jesus prays in John 17 he models this confidence of asking and receiving and so enacts the eschatological reality of union with God. The prayer of John 17 thus represents the relationship between God and Jesus. As Dodd writes so eloquently, "We still need something which will represent the archetypal union of the Son with the Father; and this is supplied in the only way in which such union can be truthfully represented in human terms."[568] In this prayer, then, the reader is given a glimpse of the intimacy that marks the union of God and Jesus, for Jesus stops addressing his disciples directly and addresses himself to God. The Johannine story of Jesus will move to its conclusion as it began, with Jesus "close to the Father's heart" (1:18).

Most scholars suggest that the prayer should be divided according to the person or groups for whom Jesus prays, but even with that beginning point, scholars are unable to reach any agreement as to the division of the prayer into its constituent parts. Westcott, for example, argued that the prayer has three parts: Jesus prays for himself (vv. 1-5), for his disciples (vv. 6-19), and for the church (vv. 20-26).[569] Brown follows Westcott's basic structure, but

suggests that the three parts of the prayer are vv. 1-8, 9-19, 20-26, thus producing sections of equal length.[570] Other scholars argue for a four-part division, with some seeing vv. 6-8 as a distinct unit,[571] and others seeing vv. 24-26 as a distinct unit.[572] Many suggest even more intricate divisions based on stylistic rather than content considerations.[573]

This commentary suggests the following threefold division of the prayer: (1) vv. 1-8, Jesus prays for his glorification; (2) vv. 9-23, Jesus prays for the faith community; (3) vv. 24-26, Jesus prays for the eschatological union of Father, Son, and believers. In many ways, however, it is best to read the prayer as an indivisible unit. As is characteristic of the Johannine literary style, the prayer has a lean vocabulary base, and its thought is developed through repetition, expansion, and elaboration of key themes. The same themes run from the beginning to the end of the prayer (cf. 17:5, 25). In this way, the form of the prayer mirrors its central theme, the unity of Father, Son, and believers. The interrelationship of the different sections of this prayer may thus be the consummate example of the coherence of form and content in the Fourth Gospel and should be honored in the interpretation of the prayer.

17:1-8. 17:1a. In the opening section of Jesus' prayer, he prays for himself and his work. Verse 1*a*, the narrator's introduction of the prayer, contains two important signals to the reader about the words of Jesus that follow. First, throughout the Farewell Discourse Jesus repeatedly used the expression "I have said these things" to indicate a transition in his words (14:25; 15:11; 16:1, 4, 6, 25, 33). In v. 1, this same expression is used by the narrator in his commentary ("After Jesus had spoken these words") to refer to the Farewell Discourse and mark the transition to the prayer. Words that the reader has come to recognize as a refrain within the story are now used to com-

---

566. See Gail R. O'Day, " 'I have overcome the world' (John 16:33): Narrative Time in John 13–17," *Semeia* 53 (1991) 163-64.

567. Dodd, *The Interpretation of the Fourth Gospel,* 419.

568. Ibid., 419.

569. B. F. Westcott, *The Gospel According to St. John* (London: Clarke, 1880) 237-38.

570. Raymond E. Brown, *The Gospel According to John (XIII–XXI),* AB 29A (Garden City, N.Y.: Doubleday, 1970) 749-50.

571. So C. H. Dodd, *The Interpretation of the Fourth Gospel* (Cambridge: Cambridge University Press, 1953) 417.

572. So Rudolf Schnackenburg, *Der Evangelist Johannes: Wie er spricht, denkt und glaubt: Ein Kommentar* (Stuttgart: Calwer, 1948) 3:168-69. Barrett suggests a fourfold division with vv. 25-26 as the concluding unit. See C. K. Barrett, *The Gospel According to St. John,* 2nd ed. (Philadelphia: Westminster, 1978) 499.

573. E.g., A. Laurentin, *"We'attah—kai nun.* Formule characteristique des textes juridiques et liturgiques (a propos de Jean 17:5)," *Biblica* 45 (1964) 168-94, 413-32; Jürgen Becker, "Aufbau, Schichtung, und theologiegeschichtliche Stellung des Gebetes in Johannes 17," *ZNW* 60 (1969) 56-83; Mark Appold, *The Oneness Motif in the Fourth Gospel* (Tübingen: J.C.B. Mohr [Paul Siebeck], 1976).

ment on the story from outside. Second, to look up to heaven is a formal posture of prayer (cf. 11:41-42; Ps 123:1; Mark 6:41; Luke 18:13). The narrator's description of Jesus thus underscores the shift that has taken place in the story; Jesus no longer includes those around him in his range of vision. His words, like his eyes, will be directed to God. The reader, like the disciples in the story, is placed on the outside, looking in as Jesus prays.

17:1b-5. The first words of Jesus' prayer in v. 1*b* indicate both the One to whom the prayer is addressed and the occasion for the prayer. Jesus will use the direct address "Father" (πάτερ *pater,* the vocative) six times in this prayer (see also v. 5, 11, 21, 24, 25; 11:41; 12:27-28). Jesus' reference to the arrival of the hour complements the narrator's announcement of the arrival of the hour at 13:1. The entire farewell meal has been enacted under the imminence of the hour, but this is the first time during the meal that Jesus himself has spoken explicitly of its arrival (cf. 12:23, 27).

Verses 1*b*-5 are framed by Jesus' repeated petition, "Glorify your Son" (v.1) /"me" (v. 5), which recalls Jesus' words at 13:31-32 (cf. 12:23, 28). The contrast between the prayer of Jesus at Gethsemane on the eve of his death (Mark 14:34-36 and par.) and this petition is stark (see also Commentary on 12:27-28); the Johannine Jesus experiences no "agony" at his hour, because he recognizes the hour as the ultimate purpose of his work and the completion of his revelation of God. This petition also acknowledges that Jesus' glory, like the rest of his ministry (cf. vv. 2, 24), derives from God.

Jesus' opening petition is followed by three dependent clauses, the syntax of vv. 1*c*-2 thus confirming the necessity of God's glorification of Jesus for the completion of Jesus' work. The first dependent clause ("so that the Son may glorify you") emphasizes the theological dimension of God's glorification of Jesus at his hour. In Jesus' death, resurrection, and ascension, the glory of God—God's identity—will be made visible (cf. 8:28). The second and third dependent clauses (v. 2) emphasize the soteriological dimension of Jesus' glorification.[574] The expression "authority over all flesh" (πάσης σαρκός *pasēs sarkos,* v. 2*a*) recalls God's gift of the eschatological power of giving life and judgment to Jesus (5:21-27). "All flesh,"

a Hebraic expression for "all people" (cf. NIV and NRSV) also has echoes of 1:14. Jesus' authority over "all flesh" is exercised in his own enfleshment—that is, in the incarnation. Jesus' eschatological powers are evidenced in his gift of eternal life "to all whom you have given me" (v. 2*b;* cf. 1:12). Verse 2 thus points to God as the source of everything for Jesus and the faith community (cf. vv. 6, 9-10, 22, 24; 6:37).

"Eternal life" (ζωῆς αἰώνιος *zōēs aiōnios*) is the primary description of the gift that Jesus brings to those who believe in him in chaps. 1–12 (e.g., 3:15; 4:14; 6:27, 68; 10:10; see also 1:4), but vv. 2*b* and 3 are the only occurrences of "eternal life" in John 13–21. In the last half of the Gospel, when Jesus is speaking only to his "own," language of love replaces the language of eternal life as the primary imagery to speak about the life of the believing community. Jesus' death, resurrection, and ascension reveal the extent and nature of the love that shapes his relationship with God and his "own," and thus reveal the character and identity of God (cf. 13:1, 34-35; 15:12). Jesus' glorification completes the revelation of God as Father and hence "the only true God" (see Commentary and Reflections on 14:6-8). To know this God is to have eternal life (v. 3; cf. 3:16; 5:24; 6:40; 10:28). This verse does not emphasize knowledge per se, but emphasizes the revelation of God in the incarnation. The knowledge of which v. 3 speaks is thus neither gnostic nor metaphysical; it must be interpreted through the love manifested in Jesus' life and death (see vv. 23, 26).

Most scholars label v. 3 an editorial gloss inserted to clarify the meaning of "eternal life," and thus not part of the prayer.[575] The strongest evidence for reading the verse as a gloss is the use of the name "Jesus Christ," which appears elsewhere in the Gospel only at 1:17. Barrett regards v. 3 as a parenthetical comment by the Evangelist rather than a gloss.[576] Barrett's interpretation correctly identifies the Evangelist's motive, but plays down the narrative and theological significance that v. 3 is deliberately cast as part of Jesus' prayer (note the second-person singular pronoun, "that they may know *you"*). Verse 3 should be interpreted like 3:16-21 (see Commentary there), as another example of the way in which the Fourth

---

574. The NIV masks the interdependence of these clauses by punctuating v. 2 as a separate complete sentence.

575. See Brown, *The Gospel According to John (XIII–XXI),* 741; Schnackenburg, *The Gospel According to St. John,* 3:172. Brown thinks the verse reflects a "confessional or liturgical formula of the Johannine church."

576. Barrett, *The Gospel According to St. John,* 503.

Evangelist meshes his theological voice with Jesus' voice.

In v. 4, Jesus reviews his ministry. He emphasizes his work as the completion of God's work (4:34; 5:36; cf. 5:17; 10:37-38; 14:31) and as the revelation of God's glory (7:18; 11:4, 40; cf. 2:11). The work of God that Jesus has completed will be described in vv. 6-8. The "And now" with which v. 5 begins returns the prayer to the moment of Jesus' hour. Jesus' repeated reference in the petition of v. 5 to being in God's presence makes clear that the ultimate goal of Jesus' hour is his return to God (see 13:1; 14:28; 16:7). Verse 5 returns the reader to the theological world of the Prologue (1:1-18), in which the Logos was with God before creation (1:1-3).

❖   ❖   ❖   ❖

EXCURSUS: JESUS' RETURN TO GLORY

How is one to interpret this reference to Jesus' return to his pre-existent glory? In his famous study of John 17, Käsemann claimed that this chapter shows that the Fourth Gospel is concerned with protology ("first things"), not eschatology, and that the incarnation "does not mean complete, total entry into the earth, into human existence, but rather the encounter between the earthly and the heavenly." For Käsemann, "the accepted Word of God produces an extension of the heavenly reality on earth. . . . This unity between Father and Son is the quality and mark of the heavenly world."[577] Yet Bultmann interpreted John 17:5 to show the exact opposite:

The evangelist has depicted the work of Jesus in such a way that it can only, and should only, be understood in the light of the end: as eschatological event. . . .

. . . The δοξασθείς [*doxastheis,* "the one who is glorified"] is at the same time and always the σάρξ γενόμενος [*sarx genomenos,* "the one who became flesh"]. His is both the exaltation and the humiliation, and the humiliation is not obliterated through the return into the heavenly δόξα [*doxa,* "glory"] (v. 5). . . .

. . . Jesus' δοξασθῆναι [*doxasthēnai,* "glorification"] consists in two things: first in his earthly life becoming the eschatological event . . . and secondly, it consists in the world's recovering the character of creation by means of the same eschatological event.[578]

Bultmann's perspective more accurately reflects the Johannine understanding of Jesus' pre-existent glory. To speak of Jesus' return to God and the glory that he had before creation does not negate the incarnation, but rather reinforces its scandal. As in Phil 2:6-11, here the pre-existent Logos shared in God's identity. In distinction from the Philippians hymn, however, where Paul puts the emphasis on Jesus' emptying himself of his pre-existent status in the incarnation, John makes an even more radical claim that the incarnation is an act of fullness (1:16), so that "we have seen his glory" in the Word become flesh. That is, "Whoever has seen me has seen the Father" (14:9). For Jesus to return to his preexistent glory, the incarnation must come to an end; Jesus must die. Through his death, which demonstrates his love for his own, this glory is extended to the lives of the believing community (cf. 17:24). Jesus' love "to the end" (13:1) makes his return to God possible, and this love decisively changes the lives of those who believe "that I am in the Father and the Father is in me" (14:11). What Käsemann overlooks in his study of John 17 is the essential link between this prayer and Jesus' death, and the emphasis in the Farewell Discourse on the community's share *while in the world* in the intimacy, mutuality, and love of the Father/Son relationship.

577. Ernst Käsemann, *The Testament of Jesus: A Study of the Gospel of John in the Light of Chapter 17* (London: SCM, 1968) 65, 69.
578. Rudolf Bultmann, *The Gospel of John: A Commentary,* trans. G. R. Beasley-Murray, R. W. N. Hoare, and J. K. Riches (Philadelphia: Westminster, 1971) 493, 496.

❖   ❖   ❖   ❖

17:6-8. As noted in the Commentary above, there is much scholarly ambivalence about the function of vv. 6-8 in Jesus' prayer. Scholars who link these verses with vv. 9ff. interpret them as the introduction to Jesus' intercessions for his disciples, whereas scholars who link them with vv. 1-5 interpret them as Jesus' review of his work and the conclusion of his petitions for his glorification.[579] This commentary follows the latter option, because the rhetoric of v. 9 ("I am asking . . . ") seems to mark a shift in the focus of Jesus' request of God. Either grouping allows for a credible reading of the prayer, however. Like so many passages in the Fourth Gospel (e.g., 5:17-18; 9:39-41), vv. 6-8 are best interpreted as having a double function. Jesus' words about his disciples and their relationship to God belong at the same time to his words about his own relationship with God.

In vv. 6-8, Jesus continues what he began in v. 4, to describe the work through which he has glorified God on earth. Jesus summarizes his entire ministry in his statement "I revealed/made known your name" (v. 6*a*; see also v. 26). Jesus does not use "name" (ὄνομα *onoma*) in a narrow sense to refer to a particular name of God (e.g., "Father" or "I AM");[580] rather, he uses it more broadly to stand for the character and identity of God (cf. Ps 22:23 [22]; Isa 52:6; the NIV follows this understanding of *onoma* when it translates "your name" simply as "you"). Jesus' words are thus a confirmation of the claim of the Prologue, "It is God the only Son, who is close to the Father's heart, who has made God known."[581]

Verses 6*b*-8 describe those to whom Jesus revealed God's name. Verse 6*b* returns to a theme introduced in v. 2, that Jesus' disciples were given to him by God. This verse points to both divine initiative ("you gave me from the world"; "they were yours and you gave them to me") and human response ("they have kept your word") as

constitutive of the faith community (see also 6:37-39, 44; 15:16-17). Verses 7-8 stress the community's knowledge of the relationship between God and Jesus, knowledge that they have received from Jesus' revelation (v. 8*a*). The tautology of v. 7 underscores its central truth, that God is the source of everything Jesus has. This truth is reinforced in v. 8*a* ("the words that you gave me"; cf. 5:19; 12:49) and in the two parallel statements about Jesus' origins with God in vv. 8*b-c* (cf. 11:42; 16:27-28). Indeed, vv. 6-8 repeatedly emphasize God as the One who gives and from whom Jesus comes. In the context of the prayer, Jesus' review of his ministry in vv. 6-8 reminds God (and the disciples and readers who overhear the prayer) of the connection between the community's life and God's gift, a connection to which Jesus will make appeal in the intercessions that begin in v. 9.

17:9-23. Verse 9 begins the central section of Jesus' prayer, in which he turns from his own glorification to intercessions for the future life of his followers. Most commentators subdivide these intercessions, distinguishing between Jesus' prayer for his first disciples (vv. 9-19) and for later generations of believers (vv. 20-23).[582] This distinction misreads the nature of Jesus' prayer, however. The line between "historical" disciples and "future" disciples is blurred throughout the prayer. The prayer does distinguish between the community's life with the physical presence of Jesus (v. 12) and without that presence (v. 11), but like the Farewell Discourse, this distinction applies to *all* community life after the hour, not just the life of the first disciples. The intercessions of vv. 9-23 are tightly interrelated and depict the full life of the faith community after Jesus' hour; in vv. 11*b*-16, Jesus prays for God's safeguarding of the community in the world; in vv. 17-19, Jesus prays for God's authorization of the community's work in the world; and in vv. 20-23, Jesus prays for the success of the community's work in the world. In John 17:9-23, present and future are not to be sorted out along a linear time line, but are to be read through the lens of Jesus' hour. Just as the imminence of Jesus' hour determines the

---

579. Commentators who link vv. 6-8 with vv. 9ff. include C. K. Barrett, *The Gospel According to St. John,* 2nd ed. (Philadelphia: Westminster, 1978) 499, 505; Rudolf Schnackenburg, *The Gospel According to St. John,* 3 vols. (New York: Seabury, 1982) 3:169; and George R. Beasley-Murray, *John,* WBC 36 (Waco, Tex.: Word, 1987). Those who link vv. 6-8 with vv. 1-5 include E. C. Hoskyns, *The Fourth Gospel* (London: Faber & Faber, 1947) 498-99; and Raymond E. Brown, *The Gospel According to John (XIII–XXI),* AB 29A (Garden City, N.Y.: Doubleday, 1970) 750.

580. For "Father," Beasley-Murray, *John,* 298; for "I am," see Brown, Brown, *The Gospel According to John (XIII–XXI),* 755; Dodd, *The Interpretation of the Fourth Gospel,* 417n. 2.

581. Barrett, *The Gospel According to St. John,* 505.

582. So Brown, *The Gospel According to John (XIII–XXI),* 749, 773-74; Schnackenburg, *The Gospel According to St. John,* 3:169, 188-89; Barrett, *The Gospel According to St. John,* 499; Hoskyns, *The Fourth Gospel,* 505. Robert Kysar, *John,* Augsburg Commentary of the New Testament (Minneapolis: Augsburg, 1986) 255, is one of the few commentators who reads vv. 9-23 as unified intercessions.

---

language about Jesus' departure (see Overview), so it also determines the language about the faith community. The fact that this prayer simultaneously holds Jesus' present and future disciples in view is another example of how this prayer is *eschatological* prayer.

17:9-11a. John 17:9-11*a* provides a general introduction to the intercessions. Verse 9 is unambiguous about the subjects for whom Jesus prays. He prays for those whom he described in vv. 6-8, those whom God gave him, and not for the world. Jesus' words have a harsh ring to the modern reader, who may hear v. 9 in the context of contemporary thought about the place of the church in a secular society or the church's responsibility to the world. In order to interpret this verse properly, however, the reader must not read it in the light of these modern conversations, but according to the theological perspective of the Fourth Gospel. "World" (κόσμος *kosmos*) is not a synonym for "earth" (cf. v. 2) or "creation" here (cf. vv. 5, 24), but stands for the sphere of enmity to God (e.g., 1:10-11; 7:7; 12:31; 15:18-19; 16:8-11). Since the world does not know God (15:21, 24; 16:3), Jesus' prayer to God for the world *as world* is precluded by definition. As Barrett has articulated aptly, "To pray for the *kosmos* would be almost an absurdity, since the only hope for the *kosmos* is precisely that it should cease to be the *kosmos*."[583] Verses 20-23 show that Jesus does have a sense of mission to the world and hope that the world will come to know the love of God (cf. 3:16), but his prayers can only be for the work of the community in the world, not for the world itself.

Although both the NIV and the NRSV punctuate v. 10 as a separate sentence, in the Greek, vv. 9-10 are one sentence that identifies those for whom Jesus does pray. Verses 9*b*-10*a* reinforce that the community belongs mutually to God and to Jesus and that the impetus for this mutuality of possession rests with God. The beginning of the faith community's life is once again located with the gift of God (cf. 3:35; 6:37, 39; 10:29; 13:3). Verse 10*b* is the first time in the Gospel that the community is identified as a locus of Jesus' glorification (cf. 2:11; 8:54; 11:4; 13:31-32). For Jesus to be glorified in the community means that the identity of Jesus is made visible

in them. As 13:34-35 makes clear, the identity of Jesus is made visible in the community when they love one another as he has loved them. Verse 10*b* helps clarify the importance of Jesus' review of his ministry in vv. 4, 6-8. The formation of a community based in the mutuality and intimacy of the relationship of God and Jesus belongs to Jesus' completion of God's work.

Verse 11*a* identifies the occasion for Jesus' intercessions. As a result of the hour (v. 1*b*), Jesus leaves the world to go to God, while his disciples remain in the world. The three present tense verbs of v. 11*a* communicate the ongoing effect of Jesus' departure to God (instead of "I am no longer [οὐκέτι εἰμί *ouketi eimi*]," the NIV incorrectly translates "I will remain no longer"; see also v. 13*a*). Jesus' absence from the world and return to God are the defining realities of the future lives of his disciples (see also 14:3, 28; 16:7, 10, 28).

17:11b-16. The intercessions begin with Jesus' renewed address to God (v. 11*b*; cf. vv. 1, 5). The adjective "holy" (ἅγιος *hagios*) occurs rarely in John. Aside from three pairings with "Spirit" (1:33; 14:26; 20:22), it occurs only here and at 6:69. Its usage here may reflect the influence of the liturgical language of the Fourth Evangelist's time, as the same address to God occurs in the eucharistic prayer of the *Didache*, a document roughly contemporaneous with the Fourth Gospel.[584] To be holy is to be set apart. This address to God is particularly appropriate at this point in Jesus' prayer because the intercessions that follow include Jesus' request that God "sanctify," "make holy" (ἁγιάζω *hagiazō*), the disciples (vv. 17-19).

Verses 11*b*-16 consist of a focal request, that God protect the disciples "in your name" (v. 11*b*), and its elaboration and expansion (vv. 12-16). Jesus' revelation of God's name—that is, God's identity and character—shaped the identity of the faith community during his ministry (vv. 6-8), and he now asks that God keep secure the community's grounding in that name.[585] The purpose of this request ("so that" [ἵνα *hina*]) is to ensure the unity of the faith community, which mirrors ("just as" [καθώς *kathos*]) the unity of God and Jesus

583. Barrett, *The Gospel According to St. John,* 506.

584. "We give thanks to you, Holy Father, for your holy name" (*Did.* 10.2; cf. Matt 6:9; Luke 11:2).

585. The NIV is an awkward paraphrase of the Greek. It seems to treat the name almost as a talisman in this verse. This translation is at odds with its translation of "name" (ὄνομα *onoma*) in v. 6.

(cf. 10:30). The community's life after the hour is thus entrusted by Jesus to God.

Verses 12-16 provide two rationales for Jesus' intercession. First, Jesus was responsible for the safeguarding of the community during his ministry, so his departure necessitates that this work now be entrusted to God (vv. 12-13). Jesus' description of his own safeguarding of the community in v. 12a repeats almost verbatim his request of God in v. 11b; the rhetoric of these verses thus points to the protection of the community in God's name as another example of the work that God and Jesus share (cf. 5:17, 19). Jesus' self-description in v. 12b contains important echoes of the shepherd discourse in John 10. Jesus presents himself as the good shepherd, under whose care none of the flock is "lost" or "destroyed" (ἀπώλετο apōleto, 10:28; cf. 10:10). That Judas's betrayal does not void Jesus' promise of protection and care is underscored by Judas's description in v. 12b as "the one destined to be lost." The only other NT occurrence of this expression, which is more accurately translated as "the son of destruction" (ὁ υἱὸς τῆς ἀπωλείας ho huios tēs apōleias) is in an apocalyptic prediction in 2 Thess 2:3: "For that day will not come unless the rebellion comes first and the lawless one is revealed, the son of destruction" (author's trans.). Its use here highlights the eschatological dimension of the betrayal and anticipates the reference to "the evil one" in v. 15. (cf. 13:2, 27). The reference to the betrayal as a fulfillment of Scripture (see also 13:19) further underscores that the betrayal does not void the security of Jesus' care (see also 6:70-71), but belongs to God's plan.

The "but now" with which v. 13 begins confirms that Jesus' departure to God is indeed the motivation for this intercession, as does Jesus' use of the refrain "I speak these things in the world" (cf. 14:25; 16:4b). Jesus' intercession for God's protection, spoken at his hour, shares in the eschatological vision articulated by the Farewell Discourse; the unity with God and Jesus that this intercession anticipates is a mark of the fullness of the disciples' eschatological joy (v. 13b; 15:11; 16:20-24).

The second rationale for Jesus' intercession is the community's relationship to the world (vv. 14-16). As in 15:18–16:4a, the community's relationship to the world is sharply dualistic; neither Jesus nor the disciples belong to this world, and as such they incur the world's hatred (vv. 14, 16; 15:19; cf. 7:7). Verse 15 renews the intercession for protection from v. 11b. "The evil one" (see also Matt 6:13) is synonymous with "the ruler of this world" and is the personification of the cosmic forces in the world that are opposed to God (cf. 12:31; 14:30; 16:11). Judas's betrayal of Jesus, to which v. 12 has already alluded, is one example of the destructive power of "the evil one" within the circle of Jesus' chosen ones (cf. 6:70-71; 13:1, 27). The prediction of persecution and martyrdom in 16:1-4a also points to the threat the world and its hatred of the faith community poses to the community's unity. It is for the preservation of this unity in the face of the cosmic power of evil that Jesus seeks God's help. The community needs this protection because it is to live out its identity and vocation in the world (v. 15a).

17:17-19. Jesus' second intercession (vv. 17-19) builds directly from vv. 15-16 and gives more specific shape to the community's vocation in the world. As in the intercession of vv. 11b-16, vv. 17-19 consist of the central request (v. 17a) and its elaboration (vv. 17b-19). "Sanctify" (hagiazō), like the related adjective "holy" (hagios, v. 11), means "to set apart for sacred work or duty." In the LXX, it designates the consecration of someone for priestly (e.g., Exod 28:41) or prophetic (e.g., Jer 1:5) service. In its only other Fourth Gospel usage (10:36), hagiadzō clearly means to be set apart for God's work. In that verse, Jesus describes himself as "the one whom the Father has sanctified and sent into the world." In the intercession of v. 17, then, Jesus is asking God to do for the disciples what he has already done for him: set them apart for God's work in the world. "In the truth" refers to the truth of God revealed in the life and ministry of Jesus (1:14; 8:32; 14:6; 16:13; cf. the similar meaning of "in your name," vv. 6, 11-12). Verse 17b ("your word is truth") echoes two central claims of this Gospel—Jesus is God's Word (1:1-2, 14) and the truth (14:6)—and thus confirms that "truth" is to be interpreted christologically here. It is through the disciples' share in Jesus' distinctive revelation of God that they are set apart for their work in the world.

Verse 18 parallels the missions of Jesus and the disciples in the world and reinforces the link between sanctification and sending (cf. 10:36). Throughout the Gospel, Jesus refers to himself as the one whom God has sent into the world, and v. 18 explicitly gives the faith community a share in that mission. Those who receive Jesus' revelation of God also share in the work God has given Jesus to do (see also 14:12; 20:21). Through their sanctification and their sending, the disciples continue Jesus' work in the world. The faith community will continue Jesus' revelation of God to the world (see vv. 20-23).

As the repetition of v. 17*a* in v. 19*b* makes clear, Jesus' words in v. 19 elaborate the initial intercession. "Sanctify," therefore, must be read in the context of its meaning in 10:36 and v. 17. For Jesus to sanctify himself means that he sets himself apart for God's work. The reflexive pronoun is unusual, since God is normally identified as the one who sets apart, but it is thoroughly in keeping with Johannine usage. Verse 19 offers one more example of Jesus' full share in God's work (4:34; 5:17, 19-30; 10:30, 38) and also fits with the Johannine picture of Jesus as the one who is fully in control of his life and death (e.g., 10:17-18). Yet most commentators ignore the clear continuity between the use of "sanctify" in vv. 17 and 19, and instead interpret "sanctify" in terms of the cultic consecration and sacrifice of animals in the OT (e.g., Exod 13:2; 28:41; 29:1-46; Deut 15:19, 21). With this interpretation of "sanctify," v. 19 becomes primarily a reference to Jesus' self-sacrifice in his death. For example, Brown goes so far as to say that "John xvii 19 has Jesus consecrating himself, seemingly as a victim." Hoskyns reads v. 19 as referring to the saving efficacy of Jesus' blood.[586]

Do Jesus' words about his self-sanctification for the sake of his disciples refer to his death? Yes, but it must be remembered that in the Fourth Gospel, Jesus' death is not an isolated event, nor is it portrayed as the sacrifice of a victim (see Reflections on John 12:20-36). First, throughout the Farewell Discourse and prayer, Jesus speaks of the full constellation of the events of his hour, culminating in his return to God (e.g., 14:2-3, 28; 16:16, 28). When Jesus speaks of his self-sanctification, he does not speak simply of setting himself apart for his death, but of joyously embracing the completion of his revelation of God *in the events of the hour* (cf. 14:28, 31). Second, when Jesus speaks of his self-sanctification, he is speaking of setting himself apart for the full mission for which God has sent him into the world, not simply his death. His words in v. 19 are both retrospective and prospective. That is, Jesus looks back to what he has already done and forward to what he is about to do. Jesus' entire mission, his completion of the work of God in his life, death, resurrection, and ascension, enables the sanctification of the faith community (v. 19*b*), because it is in Jesus' entire mission that the full truth of God is revealed to them.

17:20-23. Jesus expands the circle for whom he prays. In vv. 7-19, Jesus prayed for those who took on his work in the world; in vv. 20-23, Jesus prays for those who come to believe through that work. The contrast in v. 20 between "these" and "those who believe in me on account of their word" is not between the first generation of believers and all future generations of believers, but between those in any generation who already believe and those who do not believe but may come to believe on account of the witness of the faith community. In vv. 20-23, Jesus turns his attention to the world and expresses his desire that the world will come to share in the knowledge of God that marks the life of the faith community (vv. 21, 23).[587] In these verses, the "world" (κόσμος *kosmos*) is not portrayed as actively hating the community (cf. 15:18-19; 17:14), but as receiving the community's witness.

As in the intercessions of vv. 9-16 and vv. 17-19, vv. 20-23 consist of a central intercession (vv. 20-21) and its elaboration (vv. 22-23). The syntax of v. 21 is complex; it contains four dependent clauses (vv. 20-21 are one sentence in the Greek text). The first dependent clause ("that they may all be one") is Jesus' core prayer for the unity of the faith community. With this request, Jesus prays that those who come to believe in him will share in the same communal identity as those who brought them to faith (cf. v. 11). The definition of this unity is supplied by the second dependent clause ("just as . . . " [καθώς *kathōs*]). The unity for which Jesus prays is not intrinsic to the community itself, but derives from the primal

---

586. Brown, *The Gospel According to John (XIII–XXI),* 767; Hoskyns, *The Fourth Gospel,* 502-4. See also Schnackenburg, *The Gospel According to St. John,* 3:187-88. Even Barrett, who notes that "sanctify" must mean the same thing in both vv. 17 and 19, ignores his own counsel and reads the preparation of sacrificial victims into v. 19.

587. Paul S. Minear, "Evangelism, Ecumenism, and John 17," *TToday* 35 (1978) 5-13; *John: The Martyr's Gospel* (New York: Pilgrim, 1984).

unity of Father and Son. For the community to be "one" means that they mirror the mutuality and reciprocity of the Father/Son relationship (cf. 10:38; 14:10, 20).

The third dependent clause in v. 21 ("that they may also be in us") shows that this unity will be more than simple mirroring, however. The community will experience oneness because they share in the mutuality and reciprocity of the Father/Son relationship (cf. 14:23; 15:8-10). Jesus' words about the community's oneness in this prayer never stand apart from his affirmation of the unity of the Father and Son (17:11, 21-23). The oneness sayings thus present a vision for the theological grounding of the identity of the community that is theirs by virtue of the relationship of God and Jesus (see Reflections). There is no "one" for the community without the "we" of the Father and Son.

The final dependent clause in v. 21 points to the purpose of the community's oneness. This oneness—the share in and enactment of the unity that defines the relationship of God and Jesus—will offer a witness to the world about the revelation of God in Jesus. In this final clause, Jesus prays that through the community's unity, the world will come to believe what the community already believes, that Jesus is the one whom God has sent (3:17; 5:24, 36; 7:28-29; 8:18-19; 12:45, 49).

Like vv. 20-21, vv. 22-23 are one sentence in the Greek (so NRSV) and have the same syntax: an initial independent clause ("The glory . . . I have given them," v. 22a) and four dependent clauses. "Glory" (δόξα $doxa$) links this intercession with Jesus' opening petition for himself (vv. 1-5) and refers to the full revelation of God made known in Jesus. God's glory marks the beginning and end of the incarnation (1:14; 13:31-32; 17:1, 25), and v. 22 makes clear that it will also mark the life of the faith community. In Jesus' glorification, in the events of the hour, the character and identity of God are made known through Jesus' love for God (14:30) and his own (13:1, 34-35; 15:12).

The first dependent clause ("that they may be one") repeats the prayer for oneness from v. 21. The community's oneness depends on Jesus' gift to them of God's glory. That is, the community's oneness derives from the character and identity of God revealed to them in Jesus' life and death. The second dependent clause ("just as we are one; I in them and you in me") also echoes v. 21 and

points once again to mutuality, intimacy, and reciprocity as definitional of the community's oneness. The ultimate measure of reciprocity is the love of God and Jesus for each other and for the community as enacted in Jesus' hour (cf. 13:34-35).[588]

The third dependent clause ("that they may be completely one") points to the theme of eschatological fulfillment with which the prayer will conclude (vv. 24-26). The verb "to complete" (τελειόω $teleioō$) is normally associated in the Fourth Gospel with Jesus' completion of God's work (4:36; 5:34; 17:4; see also 13:1; 19:30), so that the oneness that v. 23b envisions is the perfection of the revelation of God in the world. The community's oneness will complete God's work in the same way that Jesus' life and death did. The community will be able to undertake this work because of the glory Jesus has given them (v. 22a).

The final dependent clause states the ultimate purpose of the community's oneness. As at v. 21, it is to serve as a witness to the world. Verse 23d states explicitly what was implied in the rest of vv. 22-23: that the community's oneness bears witness to the love of God. The community's oneness, like the incarnation itself, makes visible and tangible the love of God. Verse 23d also states directly what was conveyed by the repeated formulas of mutuality and reciprocity in vv. 20-23: God's love for the community is the same as God's love for Jesus. Jesus' prayer is that God, Jesus, and the faith community will truly be one in love.

17:24-26. Jesus' prayer intensifies in its conclusion. First, he addresses God directly as "Father" twice (vv. 24-25), giving these verses a sense of increased urgency and intimacy.[589] Second, Jesus' language of intercession changes in v. 24. Instead of the more conventional prayer language of "asking" (ἐρωτάω $erōtaō$; vv. 9, 15, 20), Jesus employs the language of volition, "I want . . . " (θέλω $thelō$). This shift in language is significant, because Jesus does not seek to do his own "will" (θέλημα $thelēma$), but God's will (4:34; 5:30; 6:38-39). In addition, at 5:21, the only other place in the Fourth Gospel where $thelō$ is used to describe Jesus' own actions, the Son's gift of life "to whomever he wishes [θέλει $thelei$]" is an example of his enactment of the eschatological powers God has given him. The language of

---

588. Schnackenburg, *The Gospel According to St. John*, 3:191.
589. Ibid., 3:439n. 84.

volition at the conclusion of this prayer, then, underscores the confidence with which Jesus speaks to God and anticipates God's response. Third, Jesus' description of those for whom he prays, "those also, whom you have given me," removes all distinctions between those who already have faith and those who are brought to faith. All believers ultimately depend on the gift and grace of God (6:37; 17:2, 9).

The intercession of v. 24 ("that [they] may be where I am") is a prayer for the eschatological union of God, Jesus, and the faithful. This is not a prayer for the union of the individual believer with Jesus after the believer's death, although many commentators insist on importing this notion into this verse.[590] Rather, "the conclusion of the prayer is pure eschatology."[591] The vision of v. 24, like that of 14:2-3 and 23, is of the radical indwelling of God, Jesus, and believers that will be the sign of God's new age. It points to a hoped-for future that transcends and transforms human and divine community, but it is a communal future eschatological vision, not a private individualistic vision.

The expansion of this core intercession in the remainder of v. 24 is the crowning eschatological statement of the prayer, "to see my glory, which you have given me because you loved me before the foundation of the world." Jesus' words express a desire for the faith community to share in the glory that God and the Logos shared "in the beginning" (1:1-3; cf. 17:5). This hope transcends the limits of time and history and returns the reader to the world of the Prologue. Indeed, v. 24 translates the claims of the Prologue into the language of the Farewell Discourse: The glory of the pre-existent Logos derives from the love of God. The hope of the eschatological age is that the faith community will come face to face with that love (cf. 1 Cor 13:11-13). Its first full taste of that love comes in Jesus' hour.

The address with which v. 25 begins, "Righteous Father" (πατέρ δίκαιε *pater dikaie*), con-firms the eschatological character of the prayer's conclusion. The adjective "righteous" occurs rarely in the Fourth Gospel and always in the context of judgment (5:30; 7:24; see also "righteousness," 16:8, 10). This usage suggests that by addressing God as "Righteous Father," Jesus is pointing to God as the eschatological judge and handing the work of judgment and salvation back to God. In vv. 25-26, Jesus reviews his ministry one last time and places the future of both the world and the faith community in God's hands.

The eschatological dividing line remains whether or not one knows the Father and that the Father sent Jesus (v. 25; cf. 3:19-21; 8:21-24; 16:8-11). As the rhetoric of v. 25 shows, Jesus is positioned between God and the world, because he knows the Father and has been sent by him into the world. Verse 26 summarizes the work of Jesus' ministry ("made your name known to them"; cf. v. 6), but it also points to the future work of Jesus ("will make it known"). This verse thus confirms one of the central themes of the Farewell Discourse: Jesus' death and departure does not end his presence and work with the faith community. Jesus' work continues in the work of the Paraclete (14:26; 15:26; 16:13-15) and Jesus is present in the indwelling of God, Jesus, and the community when the community lives out the love of the incarnation (13:34-35; 14:21-23; 15:9-10, 12-17).

As in v. 24, Jesus' last words in the prayer leave no doubt about the defining role of love in the relationship of God, Jesus, and the community. Love is not simply an affective category, but moves to the heart of the character and identity of God. The love of God for Jesus, the love of the Father for the Son, will continue in the life of the faith community, and through this love Jesus also will be present to the community (v. 26b). The community will become the locus of God's love in the world, just as the incarnate Logos was that locus. Jesus' ultimate enactment of that love is in his gift of his life (13:1, 34-35; 14:30; 15:12-13; 17:1-2). The words with which the prayer of John 17 end, then, are the perfect transition to the story of Jesus' hour.

590. Raymond E. Brown, *The Gospel According to John (XIII–XXI)*, AB 29A (Garden City, N.Y.: Doubleday, 1970) 779-80; Rudolf Schnackenburg, *The Gospel According to St. John*, 3:195.

591. E. C. Hoskyns, *The Fourth Gospel* (London: Faber & Faber, 1947) 506. Also, C. K. Barrett, *The Gospel According to St. John*, 2nd ed. (Philadelphia: Westminster, 1978) 514.

REFLECTIONS

The crucial beginning point in the interpretation and theological appropriation of John 17 may seem like an obvious one: chap. 17 is Jesus' prayer to God on the eve of his death. Yet, despite its seeming obviousness, this narrative reality often is ignored in the interpretation of this chapter. For example, the verses about unity (vv. 20-23) are often treated in the ecumenical movement as Jesus' directives about Christian unity, with little or no attention paid to the context of those words in the Fourth Gospel—that is, that they are Jesus' words to God, not to the community. In order to interpret faithfully John 17, the interpreter must pay attention both to what this text says and to the form and context in which it says it. The awareness that John 17 is cast consistently as prayer from beginning to end is essential to its role in the Johannine story of Jesus. The beginning point in any interpretation of John 17 must be the acknowledgment that the words in this chapter are portrayed not as Jesus' instructions to the community, but as Jesus' words offered to God in prayer.

As noted in the commentary, 17:1 leaves no doubt that Jesus is no longer speaking to his disciples, but is speaking instead to God. This is a radical shift from the rest of the farewell meal. Beginning with the foot washing, Jesus has been engaged in give and take with his disciples, instructing them and explicitly preparing them for his departure and their lives in his absence. The disciples have been full participants in John 13–16, but at 17:1, all that changes. Throughout chap. 17, Jesus speaks exclusively to God; the community is spoken of only in the third person. Jesus never turns from God to address the disciples directly. Their only narrative function is as those for whom Jesus prays. The disciples in the story thus have the same role as the Gospel readers—all participate in this prayer only by the privilege of overhearing.[592] To ignore the difference in the way the disciples are addressed in John 17 and the rest of the Farewell Discourse is to do a disservice to the prayer form and the narrative world the Fourth Evangelist has created. Jesus and God must be allowed this narrative moment of intimate communication; the disciples and the reader must stand on the outside, overhearing.

1. When the narrative presentation of John 17 as prayer governs the text's interpretation, three theological themes come to the fore. First, on the eve of his death, *Jesus speaks to God on behalf of the faith community.* Jesus entrusts the hope for the future of his followers to God in prayer. Throughout the Farewell Discourse, Jesus has made promises to the disciples—and the reader—about the future, and in this prayer, Jesus entrusts that future to God. It is a striking theological move. Instead of entrusting the community's future to the community itself, Jesus entrusts that future to God. Jesus' final words before the hour are not last-minute instructions to the community about what it should do in Jesus' absence; instead, his words turn the future of the community over to God.

Jesus' prayer for the community, then, models how the community is to understand and receive its identity in the world. It is to understand that its life rests in and depends on God's care. In this prayer, Jesus does not supply pragmatic directives on how to arrive at church unity or how to recognize the face of the "evil one" in the world. Rather, Jesus places the church's future in the hands of God and invites the church to listen in on that conversation. The church's future is thus shown to be God's, not ours. That is, the future of the church ultimately does not depend on or derive from the church's own work, but rests with God. When contemporary readers overhear this prayer, they are brought face to face with the sovereign grace of God.

By positioning Jesus' last words as a prayer, the Fourth Evangelist makes it possible for all generations of believers to hear and experience the love that Jesus and God have for them. To successive generations of believers, this prayer communicates the theological vision that lies at the heart of the life of faith. Jesus hands those whom he loves back to God and holds God to God's promises for this community. The Fourth Evangelist tells the story of Jesus' hour so that

---

592. For a discussion of overhearing, see Fred B. Craddock, *Overhearing the Gospel* (Nashville: Abingdon, 1978).

this articulation of Jesus' love and hope for his "own" provides the lens for interpreting Jesus' life and death. Indeed, Jesus does not leave his followers orphaned, because he has called on God on their behalf, asking God to give them what God has already given Jesus. In this prayer, Jesus puts into words what he will enact in his death, the totality of his love for his "own."

In reflecting on this prayer, then, and its appropriation in the life of the church, it is critical that the church remind itself that it is the recipient of Jesus' prayer. Jesus, "the only Son, who is close to the Father's heart," prays that God will be present in the life and mission of the faith community. Jesus has entrusted the church to God's protective care and loving kindness. It is interesting to ponder how the Christian community's self-definition would be changed if it took as its beginning point, "We are a community for whom Jesus prays."

2. Second, in this prayer, the reader overhears *the intimacy of Jesus' relationship with God.* The language in the prayer creates a tone of intimacy, for the whole prayer is built around an I/you axis of communication. God's presence is actively invoked and drawn upon by Jesus in John 17; Jesus either speaks to God using second-person pronouns or addresses God as "Father." Jesus is close enough to God (cf. 1:18) that he can lay his petitions and intercessions before the Father in the confidence that he will be heard. At Jesus' hour, he turns to the One who sent him and loves him.

It is, perhaps, at first glance contradictory that this intimate portrait of the relationship of God and Jesus is found in a prayer to which the reader has only indirect access. Yet it is the very indirectness of the reader's access to this prayer that gives it its narrative and theological power. Jesus' prayer, offered in the confidence that God is present and hears, is the appropriate vehicle to bring to conclusion the interaction of Father and Son that has so dominated the Fourth Gospel. Throughout the Gospel, Jesus has insisted that he and God are engaged in ongoing conversation (3:34-35; 11:42; 12:49; 14:24), and this prayer embodies that truth.

As is the nature of prayer, Jesus is bold enough to hold God to God's promises:[593] You have given, you have sent, you have loved; now keep, sanctify, let them be one. In this prayer, Jesus opens up his relationship with the Father to include the community by calling on the character and identity of God, which is known to him and in which he desires the community to share. In this prayer, then, the community is able to hear what it means that Jesus is the Son of God, the incarnate Logos, that Jesus shares in God's glory. Jesus' prayers and desires for those whom he loves are at one with God's desires. This prayer enables the faith community to hear how Jesus and God love each other and work together for the future of the community in the world.

John 17 shows the church its share in the intimacy of the incarnation. Yet the church's share in this intimacy is not cause for facile triumphalism, because John 17 is unshakably lodged in the story of Jesus' hour. The relationship between the Father and Son that this prayer reveals is ultimately grounded in Jesus' death. It is not merely because of the exigency of tradition or genre conventions that at the end of the farewell meal, prior to the unfolding of the events of the hour, Jesus addresses himself directly to God in prayer. As he moves toward his death, Jesus entrusts his own future to God.

3. Third, when contemporary readers overhear this prayer, they are given a glimpse of life with God that transcends conventional limits and expectations. This prayer invites the reader to contemplate *the eschatological possibility of life with God.* This prayer points the faith community toward a future in which God's governance and care of them is complete, in which the experience of God's love for them is realized. It is this eschatological vision that makes day to day life possible, because, as this prayer is a reminder, God is responsible for the nurture of the future. This eschatological vision, too, is not cause for facile triumphalism, because it is grounded in the inescapable reality of Jesus' hour. Yet this prayer invites the faith community to believe, as Jesus believed at his hour, that "the love with which you have loved me may be in them, and I in them."

593. See Karl Barth, *Prayer,* trans. Sara F. Terrien (Philadelphia: Westminster, 1952).

"THE HOUR HAS COME":
JESUS' ARREST, TRIAL, AND DEATH

OVERVIEW

I t is clear from Paul's letters that the story of the death of Jesus formed the heart of early Christian proclamation (1 Cor 11:23; 15:3-5; cf. also the centrality of the story of Jesus' death in the sermons of Acts; e.g., 3:12-26; 10:34-43). It is not surprising, therefore, that one finds a basic similarity in the passion narratives of all four Gospels (see Fig. 11, "Chronology of the Holy Week and Resurrection Appearances in the Gospels," 704-5). Each Gospel narrates Jesus' betrayal, arrest, trial, crucifixion, and burial. Yet the four Gospels share more than just the basic outline. For example, all Gospels narrate Jesus' retreat with his disciples to a garden and the subsequent arrival of Judas; the crowd's demand for the release of Barabbas; the casting of lots for Jesus' clothes; and the burial request of Joseph of Arimathea.

The breadth and depth of passion material shared by the Gospels suggest that more than the preaching of the early church lies behind the Gospel passion narratives, but what occupied the middle ground between the early church's preaching on the death of Jesus and the fully developed Gospel passion narratives is a point of much debate and discussion in NT scholarship. The primary source and historical questions concern the interplay of oral and written pre-Gospel passion traditions, the existence of a pre-Markan passion source, and the influence of Mark's passion narrative on the other three Gospels.[594] As noted in the Introduction, this commentary assumes the independence of John from the synoptic Gospels. The similarities in the passion narratives of John and the Synoptics are best

explained as deriving from an overlap in the traditions to which each of the evangelists had access, not as a result of the Fourth Evangelist's use of any of the other Gospel passion narratives as his source.

Yet there are also significant differences among the Gospel passion narratives. Some of these differences can be attributed to the varieties of passion traditions circulating in earliest Christianity to which individual evangelists had access, and some can be attributed to the theological emphases of each Gospel. Each Gospel thus presents its own distinctive treatment of the death of Jesus. In the passion narrative, the reader encounters the complex interrelationship of tradition and interpretation perhaps more acutely than anywhere else in the Gospels (see Reflections on John 11:45-53).

The Johannine story of Jesus' death is the story of Jesus' hour, toward which the whole Gospel has been moving (2:4; 7:30; 8:20; 13:1). When read in this light, it becomes clear that the traditional nomenclature of "passion narrative" is actually a misnomer for the story of Jesus' death in the Fourth Gospel. "Passion" refers to Jesus' suffering, and in the Fourth Gospel, Jesus is not presented as the one who suffers. Rather, as the Fourth Evangelist has repeatedly underscored in the Gospel, Jesus' death is the hour of his exaltation (3:13-14; 8:28; 12:32) and glorification (12:23; 13:31-32; 17:1). Jesus goes to his death willingly (10:17-18; cf. 15:13), not as the suffering victim, but as the one in control. Jesus' control over the events of his hour is one of the central themes of each episode in John 18–19 (see Commentary below). Moreover, for the Fourth Evangelist, Jesus' hour includes his death, resurrection, and ascension. Even though John 18–19 can be read as a discrete narrative unit, it is not a

---

594. For an exhaustive treatment of the historical and source questions about the Gospel passion narratives, see Raymond E. Brown, *The Death of the Messiah: From Gethsemane to the Grave. A Commentary on the Passion Narratives in the Four Gospels,* 2 vols. (New York: Doubleday, 1994).

discrete theological unit. The post-resurrection appearances, the gift of the Spirit, and the ascension narrated in John 20 conclude the story of Jesus' hour. That story begins with Jesus' death, but it will not be completed until he returns to the Father (16:28; 20:18).

The Fourth Evangelist's understanding of the hour shapes the framing of John 18–19. In John 13–17, the Fourth Evangelist dramatically slowed down the pace of the story, so that Jesus could interpret his death to his disciples before it took place. It is as if the Fourth Evangelist put the enactment of the hour on hold, so that the disciples—and the readers—could grasp its significance (see Overview to John 14:1–16:33). At 18:1 the narrative focus turns from Jesus' interpretation of the hour to the events of the hour, and the pace of the story accelerates. Indeed, chaps. 18–19 unfold rapidly, moving quickly toward Jesus' death and burial. Once the hour is underway, there is no narrative pause for explanation.

John 18:1–19:42 consists of five discrete units: (1) 18:1-12, the arrest; (2) 18:13-27, the interrogation by Annas; (3) 18:28–19:16a, the trial before Pilate; (4) 19:16b-37, the crucifixion and death; (5) 19:38-42, the burial. The dramatic pace of these chapters is controlled by the narrator's references to the shifts in Jesus' physical location after he is arrested and bound at 18:12. Indeed, these references to Jesus' movement mark the unit divisions (18:13: "they took him to Annas"; 18:28: "they took Jesus . . . to Pilate's headquarters"; 19:16b-17: "so they took Jesus, and carrying his cross by himself . . . "; 19:40, "they too, the body of Jesus" [cf. 19:38]).

It is clear from this outline that the centerpiece of John 18–19 is the trial before Pilate. Not only does it occupy the literal center of these chapters, but also it is their longest sustained scene. As the Commentary below will show, it is the Fourth Evangelist's literary and theological masterpiece. This carefully structured trial provides the conclusion to the theme of judgment that has been central to the Fourth Gospel. Employing some of the Gospel's most painful irony, John 18:28–19:16a shows that it is the world, not Jesus, who is on trial.

JOHN 18:1-12, THE ARREST

NIV

18 When he had finished praying, Jesus left with his disciples and crossed the Kidron Valley. On the other side there was an olive grove, and he and his disciples went into it.

²Now Judas, who betrayed him, knew the place, because Jesus had often met there with his disciples. ³So Judas came to the grove, guiding a detachment of soldiers and some officials from the chief priests and Pharisees. They were carrying torches, lanterns and weapons.

⁴Jesus, knowing all that was going to happen to him, went out and asked them, "Who is it you want?"

⁵"Jesus of Nazareth," they replied.

"I am he," Jesus said. (And Judas the traitor was standing there with them.) ⁶When Jesus said, "I am he," they drew back and fell to the ground.

⁷Again he asked them, "Who is it you want?"

And they said, "Jesus of Nazareth."

⁸"I told you that I am he," Jesus answered. "If you are looking for me, then let these men go."

NRSV

18 After Jesus had spoken these words, he went out with his disciples across the Kidron valley to a place where there was a garden, which he and his disciples entered. ²Now Judas, who betrayed him, also knew the place, because Jesus often met there with his disciples. ³So Judas brought a detachment of soldiers together with police from the chief priests and the Pharisees, and they came there with lanterns and torches and weapons. ⁴Then Jesus, knowing all that was to happen to him, came forward and asked them, "Whom are you looking for?" ⁵They answered, "Jesus of Nazareth."[a] Jesus replied, "I am he."[b] Judas, who betrayed him, was standing with them. ⁶When Jesus[c] said to them, "I am he,"[b] they stepped back and fell to the ground. ⁷Again he asked them, "Whom are you looking for?" And they said, "Jesus of Nazareth."[a] ⁸Jesus answered, "I told you that I am he.[b] So if you are looking for me, let these men go." ⁹This was to fulfill the

[a] Gk the Nazorean   [b] Gk I am   [c] Gk he

NIV

⁹This happened so that the words he had spoken would be fulfilled: "I have not lost one of those you gave me."ᵃ

¹⁰Then Simon Peter, who had a sword, drew it and struck the high priest's servant, cutting off his right ear. (The servant's name was Malchus.)

¹¹Jesus commanded Peter, "Put your sword away! Shall I not drink the cup the Father has given me?"

¹²Then the detachment of soldiers with its commander and the Jewish officials arrested Jesus. They bound him

ᵃ9 John 6:39

NRSV

word that he had spoken, "I did not lose a single one of those whom you gave me." ¹⁰Then Simon Peter, who had a sword, drew it, struck the high priest's slave, and cut off his right ear. The slave's name was Malchus. ¹¹Jesus said to Peter, "Put your sword back into its sheath. Am I not to drink the cup that the Father has given me?"

12So the soldiers, their officer, and the Jewish police arrested Jesus and bound him.

COMMENTARY

18:1-3. These verses set the scene for the arrest. The introductory phrase, "After Jesus had spoken these words" (v. 1a), echoes Jesus' familiar refrain from the Farewell Discourse (14:25; 15:11; 16:1, 4, 25; the NIV paraphrase "praying" obscures this connection). As at 17:1, the narrator moves this refrain into his own commentary to signal a transition in the story. John 18:1a signals the completion of the farewell meal and discourse and the first change of physical location since 13:1 (see Commentary on 14:31).

The Fourth Evangelist names neither the specific garden to which Jesus and his disciples depart (cf. "Gethsemane," Matt 26:36; Mark 14:32), nor the general location as the Mount of Olives (Matt 26:30; Mark 14:26; Luke 22:39), but speaks more broadly of the Kidron Valley. The Kidron Valley (lit., "the winter-flowing Kidron"; the brook had water only in winter) was on the east side of Jerusalem, the same direction as the Mount of Olives. The location of the arrest site in John is thus consonant with that found in the Synoptics, but its description probably reflects the independent tradition on which the Evangelist draws.⁵⁹⁵ (The NIV translation of "garden" (κῆπος *kēpos*) as "olive grove" is thus an unnecessary attempt to harmonize the Johannine narrative with the other Gospel accounts). The verbs of motion in v. 1 ("entered" [εἰσέρχομαι *eiser-*

chomai]) and v. 4 ("went out" [ἐξέρχομαι *exer-chomai*] NIV) suggest a formal demarcation of the boundaries of the garden, probably a wall (see Commentary on v. 4).

The reference to Judas's knowledge of the garden (v. 2) underscores a theme from John 13: The betrayer was one of Jesus' inner circle (cf. 13:18, 21-30; see also 6:70-71). It is this knowledge that positions him as the guide for the arresting forces. The Gospel of John alone among the Gospels portrays both Roman and Jewish soldiers at the arrest. The Greek word translated "detachment of soldiers" (σπεῖρα *speira*) always refers in the NT to Roman soldiers, either a "cohort" (600 soldiers) or a "maniple" (200 soldiers; see Matt 27:27; Mark 15:16; Acts 10:1; 21:31; 27:1). The other group of arresting officers, "police from the chief priests and Pharisees," were involved in an earlier unsuccessful attempt to arrest Jesus (7:32, 45). The presence of the Roman soldiers is taken by many commentators to be historically impossible, on the grounds that the Roman governor would never turn over his troops to the Jewish authorities.⁵⁹⁶ Yet the historical plausibility of their presence can also be argued.⁵⁹⁷ The Roman government maintained troops in the

596. So Schnackenburg, *The Gospel According to St. John*, 3:222; Barrett, *The Gospel According to St. John*, 518.

597. So Brown, *The Gospel According to John XIII–XXI*, 808; *The Death of the Messiah*, 1:248-51; Beasley-Murray, *John*, 332; Dodd, *Historical Tradition in the Fourth Gospel*, 73-74.

595. Dodd, *Historical Tradition in the Fourth Gospel*, 67-68; Brown, *The Gospel According to John (XIII–XXI)*, 806-7.

Antonia fortress, which overlooked the Temple, for the express purpose of maintaining order.[598] It does not necessarily strain historical credibility to think that the Roman governor might have made troops available to the Jewish authorities to help prevent a possible riot occasioned by Jesus' arrest (cf. 11:48), especially with the increased crowds at Passover (11:55; 12:9). However one decides this historical question, it is clear that the Fourth Evangelist portrays the conjoined Roman and Jewish interest in Jesus' arrest from the very beginning of the story.[599]

The mention of the lanterns and torches (v. 3b), necessary equipment for a nighttime arrest in a garden, underscores that Judas's arrival with the arresting officers is the night to which the narrator referred at 13:30. At the same time, the lanterns and torches are an ironic reminder of the true impotence of Jesus' opponents, because the soldiers, equipped with artificial lights, come to arrest the "light of the world" (8:12; 9:5).[600] Yet the reader knows that "the light shines in the darkness, and the darkness did not overcome it" (1:5). The reference to weapons also sounds an ironic note, because it signals a misperception of the necessity of force in Jesus' arrest, a misperception shared by Jesus' own disciples (see vv. 10-11, 36).

18:4-6. Verse 4 sets the theme that will govern the arrest narrative. As at 13:1, the narrator reminds the reader of Jesus' knowledge of the events of his hour. Jesus' supernatural knowledge of persons and events has been repeatedly emphasized throughout the Gospel (1:47-49; 2:24; 4:17; 6:6, 64). Verse 4 leaves no doubt as to who is in control of Jesus' arrest; hundreds of soldiers have approached the walled garden that Jesus and his disciples have entered, and Jesus exits the enclosure to meet the soldiers. His question to the soldiers is the same as the question he asked the first disciples who followed him (see Commentary on 1:38). Instead of seeking relationship with Jesus, however, the soldiers are seeking to kill him (cf. the expression "seek to kill" at 5:18; 7:1, 20; 8:37; 10:39; 11:8, 56), but as with those first disciples, the initiative still rests with Jesus. Jesus' actions in v. 4 fulfill his words of 10:18, "No one

takes [my life] from me, but I lay it down of my own accord."

Verse 5 further highlights Jesus' initiative in his arrest. The soldiers respond to Jesus' question, identifying him by his geographical place of origin (cf. 1:45-46), and Jesus acknowledges that he is the one for whom they look (v. 5a). The aside about Judas in v. 5b also reinforces Jesus' initiative. Unlike the synoptic Gospels, where Judas initiates the arrest by kissing Jesus (Matt 26:47-50; Mark 14:43-46; cf. Luke 22:47-48), in John's Gospel Judas stands inactively with the arresting forces. This aside may also underscore that Judas, once a member of Jesus' circle of disciples, now stands with those who oppose Jesus.

The centerpiece of vv. 5-6 is the "I am" (ἐγώ εἰμι *egō eimi*) with which Jesus responds to the soldiers in v. 5a. The NIV and the NRSV both supply a predicate nominative ("he") that is not present in the Greek text and translate Jesus' words as a simple formula of self-identification (cf. 9:9). Yet the repetition of the *egō eimi* in v. 6a and the description of its effect on the soldiers in v. 6b show that these words are much more than a formula of self-identification. They should be interpreted, like the *egō eimi* at 4:26; 6:20; and 8:28, as another instance of Jesus' use of the absolute *egō eimi* formula (see Fig. 10, "The 'I AM' Sayings in John," 602). That is, with these words Jesus identifies himself, not simply as the one for whom the soldiers seek, but with the divine name "I AM" (Isa 43:25; 51:12; 52:6 LXX). Even at Jesus' arrest, he reveals himself to be the incarnate Logos of God. That Jesus' words are to be interpreted as a theophany is confirmed by the soldiers' response. To fall prostrate on the ground is a conventional response to a theophany (e.g., Ezek 1:28; Dan 10:9; Acts 9:3-4; Rev 1:17). The soldiers' response may also be a reminder of their powerlessness before the power of God (cf. Pss 27:2; 56:9).[601]

18:7-9. After the theophany of v. 6, the movement toward Jesus' arrest resumes. Verses 7-8a repeat v. 5, emphasizing once again Jesus' control and initiative. In Jesus' request that the soldiers let his disciples go (v. 8b), Jesus shows that he is the good shepherd who will lay down his life for his sheep (10:11, 15). The words of Jesus quoted

---

598. See Josephus *Antiquities of the Jews* 19.9.2.

599. David Rensberger, *Johannine Faith and Liberating Community,* 90, 102n. 18.

600. Paul Duke, *Irony in the Fourth Gospel* (Atlanta: John Knox, 1985) 109.

601. Rudolf Schnackenburg, *The Gospel According to St. John,* 3 vols. (New York: Seabury, 1982) 3:224.

in v. 9 do not match precisely any one of his previous teachings (see also 6:35, 65; 10:25, 36), but clearly echo both 10:28-29 and 6:39 ("I should lose nothing of all that he has given me, but raise it up on the last day"; cf. also 6:37; 17:12). Many commentators see this verse's seeming emphasis on the physical well-being of the disciples as a misreading of the Jesus teaching it cites and so attribute it to a later redactor.[602] This attribution seems unnecessary, however, because the focus of vv. 8b-9 is not on the disciples themselves, but on Jesus' demonstrated concern for them that is available in all situations.[603] The reference to the fulfillment of Jesus' words (see also 18:32) points to the trustworthiness of Jesus' promises (cf. also the fulfillment of 14:27 in 20:19; 16:22 in 20:20).

18:10. This verse preserves a tradition also found in the synoptic Gospels, in which one of Jesus' disciples cuts off the ear of the high priest's slave (Matt 26:51; Mark 14:47; Luke 22:50). Each of the four Gospels works its own variation on this tradition, however. In Luke, for example, Jesus heals the servant's ear (22:51), whereas in Matthew and Mark the disciple's action provides the occasion for Jesus' teaching on the nature of his arrest and is linked with the flight of the disciples (Matt 26:51-56; Mark 14:48-50). John alone provides the names of the disciple (Simon Peter) and the servant (Malchus) involved. The addition of Peter's name probably reflects a later development in the tradition. For the Fourth Evangelist, Peter is frequently positioned as the spokesman for the disciples (e.g., 6:68-69), and this scene should be read in that light. His overreaction to the troops recalls his overeager response to Jesus at the foot washing (13:9; cf. also Peter's jumping into the lake at 21:7), and his misunderstanding of the nature of Jesus' arrest is consonant with Peter's earlier misunderstanding of the meaning of Jesus' death (13:36-38). The addition of the name "Malchus" may also be a later elaboration of the tradition, but it nonetheless has the ring of reminiscence (cf. v. 26).

18:11. Jesus' response to Peter clarifies the nature of Peter's misunderstanding (cf. Jesus' correction of Peter at 13:7, 10, 38). As Jesus will state explicitly in the trial before Pilate, it is not necessary to fight Jesus' arrest with force (cf. 18:36), because Jesus comes to the hour of his own accord. The cup is a metaphor for Jesus' suffering and death in the Synoptics (see Matt 20:22; Mark 10:38-39; Luke 22:50) and is central to the tradition of Jesus' agony in the garden (Matt 26:39; Mark 14:36; Luke 22:42). Jesus' words in v. 11, like 12:27-28, are an ironic reworking of that tradition. In v. 11, Jesus does not pray that the cup will pass from him, but describes the cup as the gift of the Father.[604] Jesus freely accepts this gift because it is essential to his completion of the work God has given him to do (cf. 3:27, 35; 5:22, 26-27; 6:37; 12:49).

18:12. The arrest itself is narrated leanly and swiftly. The exaggerated use of force by Jesus' opponents—all of the soldiers and their leader are depicted as being involved in the arrest—reinforces the theme of the enemies' misperception of the nature of Jesus' arrest. He is bound and thus nominally under their control, but as the rest of chaps. 18–19 will show, he nonetheless remains in control of events. The NIV and the NRSV translation "Jewish police" is an unfortunate and inexact translation choice. The text literally reads "the police of the Jews," and a comparison with the description of the officers in v. 3 makes clear that "the Jews" is used in its technical Johannine sense here as a synonym for the Jewish leadership. Verse 12 is a transitional verse; it concludes the arrest, but it also serves as the introduction to the interrogation before Annas (vv. 13-27; vv. 12-13 are one sentence in the Greek text).

---

602. So Rudolf Bultmann, *The Gospel of John: A Commentary,* trans. G. R. Beasley-Murray, R. W. N. Hoare, and J. K. Riches (Philadelphia: Westminster, 1971) 640. Raymond E. Brown, *The Gospel According to John (XIII–XXI),* AB 29A (Garden City, N.Y.: Doubleday, 1970) 811, also attributes the verse to a final editor, without clearly specifying his reasons.

603. So also C. H. Dodd, *Historical Tradition in the Fourth Gospel* (Cambridge: Cambridge University Press, 1963) 432; Schnackenburg, *The Gospel According to St. John,* 3:226.

604. C. K. Barrett, *The Gospel According to St. John,* 2nd ed. (Philadelphia: Westminster, 1978) 522.

REFLECTIONS

John 18:1-12 is the last appearance of Judas in the Fourth Gospel. The central paradox of Judas's character was introduced in the very first mention of him in the Gospel, "for he, though one of the twelve, was going to betray him" (6:71). Judas has a featured role in three scenes in the Gospel: the anointing at Bethany (12:1-18), the farewell meal (13:1-30), and the arrest (18:1-12). In each of these scenes, the Fourth Evangelist repeatedly places this paradox before the reader: Judas was one of those closest to Jesus, and yet he betrayed him. The Fourth Evangelist wants to make sure that the reader understands the extent of the betrayal; Judas sat at table with Jesus, had his feet washed by Jesus, and nonetheless turned against him. The Gospel of John does not narrate Judas's negotiations with the Jewish authorities over his payment for betraying Jesus (cf. Matt 26:14-16; Mark 14:10-11; Luke 22:3-6), nor is the Gospel interested in what happens to Judas after the arrest. Once Judas's act of betrayal is accomplished, he simply disappears from the scene (cf. Matt 27:3-10; Acts 1:16-20).

As crass as Judas's betrayal of Jesus for thirty pieces of silver seems, at least that story allows one to identify in Judas's greed a clear motive for his betrayal. The Gospel of John does not give the reader that option. The only details about Judas that have any relevance for the Fourth Evangelist are those that pertain to his relationship with Jesus. Everything else is theologically beside the point. The pain and pathos of the betrayal in John are presented unfiltered; the reader must grapple with the reality that one of Jesus' intimates betrayed him (see also 6:64, 70-71). Judas was offered relationship with Jesus, the incarnate presence of the love of God. Judas was offered membership in Jesus' flock, but Judas chose instead to align himself with Satan, the ruler of the world, the enemy of God (13:2, 27).

The story of Judas confronts the contemporary reader with very difficult theological issues, because it asks the reader to acknowledge and accept the reality of evil in the world. There are no ulterior motives for Judas's betrayal; he simply came under the sway of evil: "And this is the judgment, that the light has come into the world, and people loved darkness rather than light because their deeds were evil" (3:19). It would be much more palatable for many contemporary readers if one could impute psychological motivations to Judas's betrayal, but the Fourth Gospel does not allow that route. Instead, the Fourth Evangelist insists on putting Judas's betrayal on the cosmic stage and asks the reader to see in Judas's betrayal the human surrender to the power of evil.

Judas's betrayal, then, is the story of failure—of human failure to resist the pull of evil, of human failure to embrace God's gift of love and life. Judas's failure is far from the end of the story. In Jesus' death, resurrection, and ascension, "the ruler of this world" is defeated (14:30; 16:33), but the pathos of the betrayal lingers, because even within the framework of that victory, people of faith still have to choose. Will they side with the defeated ruler of the world or will they side with the victory of God? The choice should be simple, but the story of Judas remains as an object lesson to show that it is not. Judas was one of Jesus' intimates, included in Jesus' promises of life, and he nonetheless chose the way of death.

JOHN 18:13-27, THE INTERROGATION BY ANNAS

13and brought him first to Annas, who was the father-in-law of Caiaphas, the high priest that year. 14Caiaphas was the one who had advised the Jews that it would be good if one man died for the people.

15Simon Peter and another disciple were following Jesus. Because this disciple was known to the high priest, he went with Jesus into the high

13First they took him to Annas, who was the father-in-law of Caiaphas, the high priest that year. 14Caiaphas was the one who had advised the Jews that it was better to have one person die for the people.

15Simon Peter and another disciple followed Jesus. Since that disciple was known to the high priest, he went with Jesus into the courtyard of

NIV

priest's courtyard, [16]but Peter had to wait outside at the door. The other disciple, who was known to the high priest, came back, spoke to the girl on duty there and brought Peter in.

[17]"You are not one of his disciples, are you?" the girl at the door asked Peter.

He replied, "I am not."

[18]It was cold, and the servants and officials stood around a fire they had made to keep warm. Peter also was standing with them, warming himself.

[19]Meanwhile, the high priest questioned Jesus about his disciples and his teaching.

[20]"I have spoken openly to the world," Jesus replied. "I always taught in synagogues or at the temple, where all the Jews come together. I said nothing in secret. [21]Why question me? Ask those who heard me. Surely they know what I said."

[22]When Jesus said this, one of the officials nearby struck him in the face. "Is this the way you answer the high priest?" he demanded.

[23]"If I said something wrong," Jesus replied, "testify as to what is wrong. But if I spoke the truth, why did you strike me?" [24]Then Annas sent him, still bound, to Caiaphas the high priest.[a]

[25]As Simon Peter stood warming himself, he was asked, "You are not one of his disciples, are you?"

He denied it, saying, "I am not."

[26]One of the high priest's servants, a relative of the man whose ear Peter had cut off, challenged him, "Didn't I see you with him in the olive grove?" [27]Again Peter denied it, and at that moment a rooster began to crow.

[a]24 Or *(Now Annas had sent him, still bound, to Caiaphas the high priest.)*

NRSV

the high priest, [16]but Peter was standing outside at the gate. So the other disciple, who was known to the high priest, went out, spoke to the woman who guarded the gate, and brought Peter in. [17]The woman said to Peter, "You are not also one of this man's disciples, are you?" He said, "I am not." [18]Now the slaves and the police had made a charcoal fire because it was cold, and they were standing around it and warming themselves. Peter also was standing with them and warming himself.

[19]Then the high priest questioned Jesus about his disciples and about his teaching. [20]Jesus answered, "I have spoken openly to the world; I have always taught in synagogues and in the temple, where all the Jews come together. I have said nothing in secret. [21]Why do you ask me? Ask those who heard what I said to them; they know what I said." [22]When he had said this, one of the police standing nearby struck Jesus on the face, saying, "Is that how you answer the high priest?" [23]Jesus answered, "If I have spoken wrongly, testify to the wrong. But if I have spoken rightly, why do you strike me?" [24]Then Annas sent him bound to Caiaphas the high priest.

[25]Now Simon Peter was standing and warming himself. They asked him, "You are not also one of his disciples, are you?" He denied it and said, "I am not." [26]One of the slaves of the high priest, a relative of the man whose ear Peter had cut off, asked, "Did I not see you in the garden with him?" [27]Again Peter denied it, and at that moment the cock crowed.

COMMENTARY

John 18:13-27 contains two blocks of material: (1) Jesus' interrogation before Annas (vv. 19-24); and (2) Peter's denials (vv. 17-18, 25-27). Jesus' trial before the Jewish authorities is recounted in three different ways in the Gospels. Mark (followed closely by Matthew) narrates an evening meeting of the Sanhedrin at which Jesus is tried (Mark 14:55-65; see also Matt 26:57-68), and a morning meeting in which the Sanhedrin decides to hand Jesus over to Pilate (Mark 15:1, 3; see also Matt 27:1-2). Luke mentions no evening meeting and narrates a morning Sanhedrin session in which Jesus is tried and handed over to Pilate (Luke 22:66–23:2). The Fourth Gospel narrates no formal trial of Jesus by the Sanhedrin. Instead, it recounts Jesus' interrogation by Annas, the father-in-law of the high priest (vv. 13-14, 19-23), and makes only fleeting reference to Jesus' appearance before the high priest Caiaphas (v. 24). To compound the difficulty, John refers to both Annas (vv. 15-16, 19, 22) and Caiaphas (vv. 13, 24) as the "high priest." The attempt to harmonize the Synoptic and Johannine accounts can be seen in some parts of the manuscript tradition of John 18:13-27, in which scribes rearranged the verses in order to present Caiaphas as the one who interrogates Jesus.[605]

Does the Fourth Evangelist preserve a distinctive tradition about Jesus' trial in John 18:13-27? In order to answer that question, it is important to place both Annas and Caiaphas in their historical context (see Fig. 13, "High Priests During New Testament Times," 807).[606] Annas was high priest from 6 to 15 CE, but his influence did not end when his term ended. In addition to being the father-in-law of Caiaphas (who was high priest from 18 to 36 CE), five of Annas's sons, as well as a grandson, succeeded him as high priest. It is clear from reading Josephus that Annas was the most influential member of the high priestly family for the early and mid first century CE.[607] Indeed, in Josephus one finds Annas referred to with the title "high priest" after his term had ended,[608] a practice that may be reflected in John's use of that title for Annas in 18:15-16, 19, 22. Luke also testifies to Annas's continuing influence, for he twice speaks jointly of the high priesthoods of Annas and Caiaphas (Luke 3:2; Acts 4:6).

Given Annas's influence, it is not implausible that he would have had a role in the interrogation of Jesus and that his role was remembered in a tradition to which the Fourth Evangelist had access. Raymond Brown suggests that the meeting before Annas was like a police interrogation that immediately follows the arrest of a suspect, with Annas in the role of interrogator, and there is a certain historical plausibility to Brown's presenta-

tion.[609] As high priest, Caiaphas would have had the official role of presiding over the Sanhedrin session. The reference to Jesus' transfer from Annas to Caiaphas in v. 24 suggests that the tradition on which the Fourth Evangelist drew for his story of the death of Jesus included meetings with both Annas and Caiaphas. Other than this allusion, however, the Fourth Evangelist accords this meeting with Caiaphas no place in the story.

Against this tradition-historical background, the interpreter may then ask: (1) Why does the Fourth Evangelist omit any account of a Sanhedrin trial? and (2) Why does he showcase the informal meeting before Annas? The Fourth Evangelist's acknowledgment of a meeting before the high priest may have been necessitated by the tradition, but to narrate it more fully would have served no dramatic or theological purpose in the Fourth Gospel narrative. Jesus' formal legal relationship with the Jewish authorities had been concluded at 11:47-53. The Sanhedrin had already met and passed a death sentence against Jesus at 11:53 (see Commentary); to repeat that decision now would be anticlimactic (cf. the Fourth Evangelist's moving of the cleansing of the Temple narrative to the beginning of Jesus' ministry). Moreover, not only had the death sentence already been passed, but also Jesus' formal questioning by the Jewish leadership had been incorporated into the narration of Jesus' ministry (see esp. 5:16-18; 10:22-39).[610] The dramatic focus of John 18–19, therefore, shifts to the trial before Pilate. Yet the Fourth Evangelist nonetheless allows Jesus to speak one more word to the Jewish religious establishment. As the Commentary to follow will show, the Fourth Evangelist may have found an interview with Annas in the tradition, but the content of the interview bears throughout the distinctive theological stamp of the Fourth Evangelist.

In all four Gospels, Jesus' appearance before the Jewish authorities is linked with Peter's denials, but the narrative presentation of the interrelation-

605. The most dramatic rearrangement of the text occurs in Sinaitic Syriac (fourth/fifth century CE), in which the text is written as vv. 13, 24, 14-15, 19-23, 16-18, 25-27. This rearrangement positions Caiaphas as the interrogating high priest, but creates more problems than it solves by altering the relationship of Peter's denials to Jesus' interrogation and by making Annas completely superfluous to the story.
606. Josephus *Antiquities of the Jews* 18.26-35.
607. Ibid., 20.198.
608. Ibid., 18.95.

609. Raymond E. Brown, *The Death of the Messiah,* 2 vols. (New York: Doubleday, 1994) 2:408, 424-26. See also C. H. Dodd, *Historical Tradition in the Fourth Gospel* (Cambridge: Cambridge University Press, 1963) 93-95. Barrett takes an opposite approach, seeing in the Johannine account a variation on the two Sanhedrin sessions in Mark. See Barrett, *The Gospel According to St. John*, 523-34.
610. Hans Windisch, *Johannes und die Synoptiker. Wollte der vierte Evangelist die älteren Evangelien ergänzen oder ersetzen?* (Leipzig: J. C. Hinrichs, 1926) 82; Bultmann, *The Gospel of John,* 644.

Figure 13: High Priests During New Testament Times

High Priests / Dates of Tenure	Rulers who controlled appointments to the High Priesthood	Historical events
Joezer ben Boethus[1] (23–5 BCE) Eleazer ben Boethus[1] (?–?) Jesus ben Sei (?–?) Joezer ben Boethus (?–6 CE) (reinstated)	**Herod the Great**[10] (Matthew 2; Luke 1:5) **Herod Archelaus** (4 BCE–6 CE) (Matt 2:22)	
Annas ben Seth[2] (6–15) (Luke 3:2; John 18:13, 24; Acts 4:6)	**Quirinius, governor of Syria** (Luke 2:2)	
Ishmael ben Phiabi[3] (15–16 ?) Eleazar ben Anan[2] (16–17?) Simeon ben Kimhit[4] (17–18) **Joseph Caiaphas**[5] (18–36) (Matt 26:3, 57; Luke 3:2; John 11:48; 18:13, 24; Acts 4:6)	Valerius Gratus, procurator of Judea	
	Pontius Pilate,[11] procurator of Judea (26–36) (Matthew 27; Mark 15; Luke 13:1, 23; John 18–19; Acts 3:13; 4:27; 13:28; 1 Tim 6:13)	Era of **Jesus'** Ministry (c. 28–33) Apostles arrested and flogged (Acts 5:17-42) Stoning of **Steven** (Acts 6:1–8:2) **Paul**'s Conversion (c. 34)
Jonathan ben Anan[2] (36–37) (Acts 4:6) Theophilus ben Anan[2] (37–41)	Vitellius, governor of Syria	
Simeon ben Boethus[1] (41–?) Matthias ben Anan[2] (?–?) Elionaeus ben Cantheras[6] (43–44) Joseph ben Kimhit[4] (44–47)	**Agrippa I** (Acts 12:1-4, 20-23)	Execution of **James, son of Zebedee** (c. 44) (Acts 12:1-2)
Ananias ben Nedebeus (47–59) (Acts 22:30–23:10; 24:1)	Herod of Chalcis	Council in Jerusalem (c. 51) (Acts 15) **Paul**'s arrest and imprisonment in Jerusalem and Caesarea (c. 59/60) (Acts 21:27– 26:32)
Jonathan ben Anan[2] (reinstated?) Ishmael ben Phiabi[3] (59–61) Joseph ben Simeon[4] (61–62) Annas ben Anan[7] (62) Joshua ben Damnai (62–63?) Joshua ben Gamaliel[8] (63–65?) Mattathias ben Tehophilus[2] (65–67) Phannias ben Samuel[9] (67–70)	**Agrippa II** (Acts 25:13–26,32)	Martyrdom of **Paul** (c. 62) Martyrdom of **James** (62) Martyrdom of **Peter** (c. 64) Jewish Revolt (66) Siege of Jerusalem; Temple destroyed (70)

1. The Boethus family
2. The bet Hanan family.
3. The Phiabi family.
4. The Kimhit family.
5. Member of the bet Hanan family by marriage.
6. According to Josephus a member of the Boethus family; according to the Talmud, a separate family.
7. The bet Hanan family; served as High Priest for only three months; responsible for the execution of James, the brother of Jesus.
8. Member of the Boethus family by marriage.
9. Appointed by the Zealots, by lot, during the Jewish Revolt.
10. Herod appointed seven High Priests during his thirty-three-year reign.
11. Pontius Pilate never exercised his rights to appoint or depose a high priest.

Bold Type: Persons mentioned in the New Testament

ship of these two events varies. In Luke 22:54-62, Peter's denials are narrated in full before Jesus' interrogation even begins, whereas in Mark (followed by Matthew), the scene for the denials is set before Jesus' trial (Matt 26:58; Mark 14:54), but the denials themselves are not narrated until after the trial (Matt 26:66-75; Mark 14:66-72). The juxtaposition of the two events is much more dramatic in the Gospel of John. In keeping with the Fourth Evangelist's penchant for structuring a story along the lines of a drama (e.g., John 9:1-39; 18:28–19:16), the Fourth Evangelist presents Jesus' appearance before Annas and Peter's denial as a three-act drama. The three acts are jointly introduced by vv. 13-16, which establish the characters and setting, and then proceed as follows: vv. 17-18, Peter's first denial; vv. 19-24, Jesus' interrogation by Annas; vv. 25-27, Peter's second and third denials. As the Commentary will show, by structuring the scene this way, the Fourth Evangelist heightens the irony and pathos of Peter's denials and the boldness of Jesus' response.

18:13-16. As noted above, vv. 13-16 introduce the scenes that follow; vv. 13-14 set the stage for Annas's interrogation of Jesus, and vv. 15-16 for Peter's denials. The relation of Annas and Caiaphas to the office of high priest was discussed above. (For a discussion of the phrase "high priest that year," see Commentary on 11:49-50). In v. 14, the narrator reminds the reader of Caiaphas's role at the earlier Sanhedrin meeting (11:46-53). This reminder confirms that the death sentence from that meeting (11:53) provides the decisive context for the interpretation that follows. By reminding the reader of Caiaphas's unconscious prophecy about the expediency of Jesus' death (11:50-52), v. 14 also sets the following proceedings within the ironic framework of that earlier scene, in which even the high priest was shown to be a witness to the truth of Jesus. The Fourth Evangelist thereby undercuts the juridical force of the interrogation before it even begins.

Verses 15-16 explain Peter's presence at the interrogation. In the synoptic Gospels, Peter alone follows Jesus and gains access to the courtyard on his own (Matt 26:58; Mark 14:54; Luke 22:54), but in John, Peter is accompanied and assisted by "another disciple." Many scholars argue that the unnamed disciple in vv. 15-16 is the beloved disciple, who is also paired with Peter at 13:23-

25; 20:1-10; and 21:15-23.[611] To support this view, one can point to 20:2, where the beloved disciple is referred to as "the other disciple, the one whom Jesus loved." Yet 18:15 refers to "another disciple," not *the* other disciple," and it is hard to explain why the Fourth Evangelist would not have more clearly identified the disciple in vv. 15-16 as "the disciple whom Jesus loved" if that were the disciple he meant.[612]

The identity of this disciple is at best a secondary concern, however, for his importance lies solely in his narrative function: to gain Peter admittance to the high priest's courtyard. To underscore this function, the disciple's acquaintance with the high priest is mentioned twice in these verses. Scholars frequently ask how a Galilean fisherman could be an acquaintance of the high priest,[613] but this very question reveals several interpretive prejudices. First, it assumes that "disciple" (μαθητής *mathētēs*) is equivalent to "one of the twelve," an assumption that is not in keeping with the use of "disciple" in the Gospel of John; John's notion of discipleship is much broader than that (see 1:35-51). Second, it plays down the evidence of social diversity among Jesus' followers. The references to Joseph of Arimathea and Nicodemus at Jesus' burial (19:38-40) suggest that Jesus attracted disciples from a broad spectrum of class and political groupings in Judea.

18:17-18. These verses narrate Peter's first denial. As in the other three Gospels, Peter's first questioner is a female servant (Matt 26:69; Mark 14:67; Luke 22:56). The woman's question in v. 17*a* is introduced in the Greek text with the interrogative particle (μή *mē*), which normally indicates that a negative response is expected (cf. the use of *mē* at 4:12; 8:53; 9:41); this usage is accurately reflected in the NIV and the NRSV. The very wording of the woman's question thus provides Peter with the opportunity to deny that he is one of Jesus' disciples, which he does immediately (v. 17*b*). The words of Peter's denial, "I am not" (οὐκ εἰμί *ouk eimi*; see also 18:25) are the antithesis of Jesus' words of self-identification and revelation from 18:1-12, "I am" (ἐγώ εἰμι *egō eimi*; vv. 5-6, 8). Jesus freely and boldly

611. E.g., George R. Beasley-Murray, *John,* WBC 36 (Waco, Tex.: Word, 1987) 324.

612. So Schnackenburg, *The Gospel According to St. John,* 3:235.

613. So Barrett, *The Gospel According to St. John,* 526.

declares who he is, but Peter, the representative disciple, cannot even claim discipleship. This contrast will be heightened in the two scenes that follow (vv. 19-24, 25-27).

Verse 18 adds narrative richness to the scene in the courtyard with its description of the charcoal fire and the cold (cf. Mark 14:54; Luke 22:55), but this verse also adds dramatic tension. The group warming itself at the fire includes the temple police, the very group involved in the arrest of Jesus (vv. 3, 12). The description of Peter standing with the police seems a deliberate echo of the description of Judas, who stood with the police at 18:5. As at 13:36-38, the Fourth Evangelist reminds the reader that the line between outright betrayal of Jesus and denial of one's relationship with him is a thin one (see Reflections below).

18:19-24. Annas is referred to with the honorific title "high priest" (see Commentary above) in the interrogation scene. His questioning is reported to the reader only in the narrator's commentary; there is no direct speech of Annas in this scene. The focus is on the speech of Jesus. As noted above, John 18:19-24 appears to have been deliberately shaped by the Evangelist to highlight his narrative and theological intents.

Jesus' words hold the key to understanding the Evangelist's intent in this scene. Jesus confronts Annas with the relationship of his teaching ministry to Judaism, "I have spoken openly to the world [κόσμος *kosmos*]; I have always taught in synagogues and in the temple, where all the Jews [οἱ Ἰουδαῖοι *hoi Ioudaioi*] come together. I have said nothing in secret" (v. 20). Most scholars misread these words, seeming to read them simply as the Johannine version of Jesus' words in Mark 14:49 ("Day after day I was with you in the temple teaching, and you did not arrest me" [NRSV]) and hence as a general statement about the public nature of Jesus' ministry. Raymond Brown, for example, interprets Jesus' words in v. 20 along the analogy of "Wisdom speaking publicly to men," going so far as to translate Jesus' words in verse format.[614] Jesus' words in v. 20 are not a general defense of the public nature of his ministry, however, but are his final challenge to the Jewish authorities.

First, in the context of Jesus' hour, "world" cannot simply be read as a synonym for "everywhere." Rather, Jesus is claiming to have spoken publicly even among those who did not receive him and, indeed, who hated him (cf. 15:18-20). Second, Jesus summarizes his teaching ministry by pointing to those occasions when he has taught in the official sites of Judaism. Verse 20 is an accurate description of Jesus' teaching ministry in John. John 5 and 7–10 are all located in the Jerusalem Temple precincts, as is John 2:13-22 (cf. also Jesus' conversation with Nicodemus, "a leader of the Jews," 3:1-21). John 6:25-59 is located in the synagogue at Capernaum. Jesus is indeed on record as having kept nothing secret in his public pronouncements to establishment Judaism. Third, and perhaps most telling, is Jesus' use of the expression "the Jews." "The Jews" does not refer simply to the Jewish people here, but instead is used in the distinctive Johannine sense of the Jewish authorities (see discussion of "the Jews" at 1:19; 5:1-18; 9:22). The presence of this Johannine idiom in the words of Jesus points to John 18:19-23 as a two-level drama in which Johannine Jewish Christians are invited to see their experience of official Judaism in the experience of Jesus.

When the two levels of John 18:19-23 are held in view, the subjects of Annas's interrogation—Jesus' disciples and his teaching—take on added significance. Questions about Jesus' disciples and his teachings fit the context of Jesus' own time, but they also fit well the Evangelist's time. In John 9:28, one of the charges made against the man born blind was "You are his disciple, but we are disciples of Moses." Annas's question may thus echo the questions asked of Jesus' later disciples about their relationship to Jesus.[615] Similarly, the early Christian narratives about martyrs record that the martyrs were asked about their teachings.[616] The Fourth Evangelist has framed Jesus' interrogation scene to stand as a model for the Johannine community's experience of trial and interrogation.

As the blind man does with the authorities in John 9, Jesus turns Annas's questions back on him (cf. 9:27). Jesus has already spoken fully in the presence of official Judaism (v. 21); Annas should,

614. Brown, *The Gospel According to John (XIII–XXI)*, 825. See also Brown, *The Death of the Messiah*, 1:415.

615. Schnackenburg, *The Gospel According to St. John*, 3:238.
616. Barrett, *The Gospel According to St. John*, 527.

therefore, inquire of them, not of Jesus. The impotence of the Temple authorities in the face of Jesus' witness is symbolized by the action of the police officer (v. 22). As earlier in the garden, the police still wrongly assume that force will bring Jesus into line. Jesus' response in v. 23 recalls his earlier words to "the Jews" at 8:46 and positions his words as the arbiter of right or wrong, guilt or innocence. Annas's only response to Jesus' challenge is to send him on to Caiaphas (v. 24). Jesus' words dominate the interrogation, and neither the high priest's questions nor the police officer's blow can rob them of their power.

18:25-27. The dramatic focus returns to Peter with the narration of his second and third denials (cf. vv. 15-18). Verse 25a picks up exactly where v. 18 left off in order to show the continuity between the first denial and this new scene. The reader is to envision Jesus' interrogation and Peter's denials as occurring simultaneously. The second question and denial (v. 25b-c), as at v. 17, focus on Peter's discipleship. The question is again introduced by mē, and Peter's negative response

is intensified by the use of the verb phrase "he denied it and said." In the third question and denial (vv. 26-27), the Fourth Evangelist's dramatic sense is evident. Peter's questioner is not an anonymous bystander as in the other Gospel accounts (Matt 26:73; Mark 14:70; Luke 22:59), but is someone who had a reason to remember Peter, as the slave was related to the man "whose ear Peter had cut off." Unlike the first two questions, the question this slave asks Peter is not introduced by the interrogative particle mē. That is, this third question does not expect a negative response, because the questioner knows that the true answer from Peter is yes. Peter's third denial is thus given an added poignancy, because he denies his very presence in the garden to someone who had witnessed him there.

Unlike the synoptic Gospels (Matt 26:75; Mark 14:72; Luke 22:61-62), John has no narrative commentary on Peter's denial. The framing of Jesus' boldness before Annas with Peter's denials is commentary enough, and the reader is left to make the connections between this scene and Jesus' prediction of Peter's denial at 13:36-38.

REFLECTIONS

John 18:13-27, like 18:1-12, presents the reader with two contrasting images. One is the image of Jesus, who willingly offers himself to those who come to arrest him and boldly answers those who interrogate him. The other is the image of Jesus' disciples who betray and deny the one who so freely gives his life for them. The other characters in these scenes, the Roman soldiers, the temple police, even Annas and Caiaphas, merely provide the background against which this drama between Jesus and his own is acted out.

Judas's betrayal of Jesus is the more dramatic action, but Peter's denial may be the most haunting. Judas's betrayal bears testimony to the power of evil and so is a reminder of the cosmic drama that is acted out in Jesus' life and death (see Reflections on 18:1-12). Peter's denials are not placed on such a grand stage, however. Instead, Peter's denials occupy that gray area, marked not by outright betrayal, but by compromise and acquiescence to personal expediency, self-protection, and fear.

Peter's denials are even more painful and haunting when they are placed in their wider context in the Gospel narrative. At the farewell meal, Jesus acted out his love for his disciples in the foot washing, addressing Peter individually about his share in Jesus' life (13:6-10). In the Farewell Discourse, Jesus reassured his disciples about his abiding presence with them and declared his love for them (e.g., 14:18, 21-23; 15:12-15). In the farewell prayer, Jesus prayed to God on his disciples' behalf, placing their caretaking and their future in God's hands, expressing his hopes for the fullness of their lives with God and one another (17:20-26). Jesus showed the truth and trustworthiness of his words with his actions in the garden, when he asked the soldiers to let his disciples go. In front of Annas he showed that he would, indeed, lay down his life of his own accord when he challenged

Annas with the truth of his ministry. Yet with the farewell words of Jesus still echoing in his ears, Peter cannot even publicly claim his place as Jesus' disciple.

The Fourth Evangelist thus places before the reader two models of how the faithful can meet adversity and trial: the model of Jesus, who holds nothing back for the sake of those he loves, and the model of Peter, who holds everything back for his own sake. In the theological idiom of this Gospel, these two models provide fresh access to Jesus' commandment to love one another as he has loved us (13:34-35). The fullest embodiment of that commandment is to lay down one's life for another (15:12), a promise Peter foolishly and lightly made at 13:36-38. But in John 18:13-24, the reader is given a painful glimpse of the limits of Peter's love and yet one more demonstration of the limitlessness of Jesus' love.

In the context in which the Fourth Evangelist wrote, of community oppression and persecution because of one's faith (see 16:1-4), Peter's denials clearly show how easy it is to lose heart (cf. 14:1), how easy it is to remove oneself from the embrace of Jesus' love. In the contemporary North American setting, in a social context far removed from that of Johannine Jewish Christians, the temptation to deny one's place with Jesus remains real and perhaps even more insidious. Under what social and personal pressure will one turn one's back on Jesus' love, will one equivocate about discipleship?

In Holy Week liturgies, the passion narrative from one of the Gospels is frequently presented as a dramatic reading, with the congregation taking the part of the crowd who clamors for Jesus' crucifixion. It is a vivid moment in the liturgy, in which each congregant is indirectly asked to consider the part he or she plays in the crucifixion of Jesus. It is tempting to envision a Holy Week liturgy in which John 18:13-27 would be presented as a dramatic reading, with the congregation taking Peter's part: "Are you one of his disciples? . . . *I am not.*" For most Christians, the moment of betrayal of Jesus' love does not come in the dramatic announcement, "Crucify him!" but in the more subtle denial of allegiance to the one who gives his life for us, of infidelity to the ever faithful love of Jesus.

JOHN 18:28–19:16*a*, THE TRIAL BEFORE PILATE

NIV

28Then the Jews led Jesus from Caiaphas to the palace of the Roman governor. By now it was early morning, and to avoid ceremonial uncleanness the Jews did not enter the palace; they wanted to be able to eat the Passover. 29So Pilate came out to them and asked, "What charges are you bringing against this man?"

30"If he were not a criminal," they replied, "we would not have handed him over to you."

31Pilate said, "Take him yourselves and judge him by your own law."

"But we have no right to execute anyone," the Jews objected. 32This happened so that the words Jesus had spoken indicating the kind of death he was going to die would be fulfilled.

33Pilate then went back inside the palace, sum-

NRSV

28Then they took Jesus from Caiaphas to Pilate's headquarters.*a* It was early in the morning. They themselves did not enter the headquarters,*a* so as to avoid ritual defilement and to be able to eat the Passover. 29So Pilate went out to them and said, "What accusation do you bring against this man?" 30They answered, "If this man were not a criminal, we would not have handed him over to you." 31Pilate said to them, "Take him yourselves and judge him according to your law." The Jews replied, "We are not permitted to put anyone to death." 32(This was to fulfill what Jesus had said when he indicated the kind of death he was to die.)

33Then Pilate entered the headquarters*a* again, summoned Jesus, and asked him, "Are you the

a Gk *the praetorium*

NIV

moned Jesus and asked him, "Are you the king of the Jews?"

[34]"Is that your own idea," Jesus asked, "or did others talk to you about me?"

[35]"Am I a Jew?" Pilate replied. "It was your people and your chief priests who handed you over to me. What is it you have done?"

[36]Jesus said, "My kingdom is not of this world. If it were, my servants would fight to prevent my arrest by the Jews. But now my kingdom is from another place."

[37]"You are a king, then!" said Pilate.

Jesus answered, "You are right in saying I am a king. In fact, for this reason I was born, and for this I came into the world, to testify to the truth. Everyone on the side of truth listens to me."

[38]"What is truth?" Pilate asked. With this he went out again to the Jews and said, "I find no basis for a charge against him. [39]But it is your custom for me to release to you one prisoner at the time of the Passover. Do you want me to release 'the king of the Jews'?"

[40]They shouted back, "No, not him! Give us Barabbas!" Now Barabbas had taken part in a rebellion.

19 Then Pilate took Jesus and had him flogged. [2]The soldiers twisted together a crown of thorns and put it on his head. They clothed him in a purple robe [3]and went up to him again and again, saying, "Hail, king of the Jews!" And they struck him in the face.

[4]Once more Pilate came out and said to the Jews, "Look, I am bringing him out to you to let you know that I find no basis for a charge against him." [5]When Jesus came out wearing the crown of thorns and the purple robe, Pilate said to them, "Here is the man!"

[6]As soon as the chief priests and their officials saw him, they shouted, "Crucify! Crucify!"

But Pilate answered, "You take him and crucify him. As for me, I find no basis for a charge against him."

[7]The Jews insisted, "We have a law, and according to that law he must die, because he claimed to be the Son of God."

[8]When Pilate heard this, he was even more afraid, [9]and he went back inside the palace. "Where do you come from?" he asked Jesus, but Jesus gave him no answer. [10]"Do you refuse to

NRSV

King of the Jews?" [34]Jesus answered, "Do you ask this on your own, or did others tell you about me?" [35]Pilate replied, "I am not a Jew, am I? Your own nation and the chief priests have handed you over to me. What have you done?" [36]Jesus answered, "My kingdom is not from this world. If my kingdom were from this world, my followers would be fighting to keep me from being handed over to the Jews. But as it is, my kingdom is not from here." [37]Pilate asked him, "So you are a king?" Jesus answered, "You say that I am a king. For this I was born, and for this I came into the world, to testify to the truth. Everyone who belongs to the truth listens to my voice." [38]Pilate asked him, "What is truth?"

After he had said this, he went out to the Jews again and told them, "I find no case against him. [39]But you have a custom that I release someone for you at the Passover. Do you want me to release for you the King of the Jews?" [40]They shouted in reply, "Not this man, but Barabbas!" Now Barabbas was a bandit.

19 Then Pilate took Jesus and had him flogged. [2]And the soldiers wove a crown of thorns and put it on his head, and they dressed him in a purple robe. [3]They kept coming up to him, saying, "Hail, King of the Jews!" and striking him on the face. [4]Pilate went out again and said to them, "Look, I am bringing him out to you to let you know that I find no case against him." [5]So Jesus came out, wearing the crown of thorns and the purple robe. Pilate said to them, "Here is the man!" [6]When the chief priests and the police saw him, they shouted, "Crucify him! Crucify him!" Pilate said to them, "Take him yourselves and crucify him; I find no case against him." [7]The Jews answered him, "We have a law, and according to that law he ought to die because he has claimed to be the Son of God."

[8]Now when Pilate heard this, he was more afraid than ever. [9]He entered his headquarters*a* again and asked Jesus, "Where are you from?" But Jesus gave him no answer. [10]Pilate therefore said to him, "Do you refuse to speak to me? Do you not know that I have power to release you, and power to crucify you?" [11]Jesus answered him, "You would have no power over me unless it had

a Gk *the praetorium*

NIV

speak to me?" Pilate said. "Don't you realize I have power either to free you or to crucify you?"

[11]Jesus answered, "You would have no power over me if it were not given to you from above. Therefore the one who handed me over to you is guilty of a greater sin."

[12]From then on, Pilate tried to set Jesus free, but the Jews kept shouting, "If you let this man go, you are no friend of Caesar. Anyone who claims to be a king opposes Caesar."

[13]When Pilate heard this, he brought Jesus out and sat down on the judge's seat at a place known as the Stone Pavement (which in Aramaic is Gabbatha). [14]It was the day of Preparation of Passover Week, about the sixth hour.

"Here is your king," Pilate said to the Jews.

[15]But they shouted, "Take him away! Take him away! Crucify him!"

"Shall I crucify your king?" Pilate asked.

"We have no king but Caesar," the chief priests answered.

[16]Finally Pilate handed him over to them to be crucified.

So the soldiers took charge of Jesus.

NRSV

been given you from above; therefore the one who handed me over to you is guilty of a greater sin." [12]From then on Pilate tried to release him, but the Jews cried out, "If you release this man, you are no friend of the emperor. Everyone who claims to be a king sets himself against the emperor."

13When Pilate heard these words, he brought Jesus outside and sat*a* on the judge's bench at a place called The Stone Pavement, or in Hebrew*b* Gabbatha. [14]Now it was the day of Preparation for the Passover; and it was about noon. He said to the Jews, "Here is your King!" [15]They cried out, "Away with him! Away with him! Crucify him!" Pilate asked them, "Shall I crucify your King?" The chief priests answered, "We have no king but the emperor." [16]Then he handed him over to them to be crucified.

So they took Jesus;

a Or *seated him*   *b* That is, *Aramaic*

COMMENTARY

John 18:28–19:16*a* is the supreme example in the Fourth Gospel of the Fourth Evangelist's use of dramatic structure, irony, and symbolism in the service of theological interpretation. Jesus' trial before Pilate is the theological and dramatic climax of the story of Jesus' hour.

Like the Pharisees' interrogation of the blind man in John 9, Jesus' trial before Pilate is struc-

tured as a drama. The trial narrative opens with an introductory verse (18:28) that establishes the time and location for the drama. This introduction is followed by seven scenes:[617]

617. The division into seven scenes is almost universally recognized and accepted by Johannine scholars. The only major exception is Bultmann, who grouped 19:1-7 as one scene and thus only had six scenes in the trial.

	Location	Characters
Scene 1 (18:29-32)	Outside	Pilate and "the Jews"
Scene 2 (18:33-38*a*)	Inside	Pilate and Jesus
Scene 3 (18:38*b*-40)	Outside	Pilate and "the Jews"
Scene 4 (19:1-3)	(Inside)	Jesus and the soldiers
Scene 5 (19:4-7)	Outside	Pilate, Jesus, and "the Jews"
Scene 6 (19:8-12)	Inside	Pilate and Jesus (and "the Jews")
Scene 7 (19:13-16*a*)	Outside	Pilate, Jesus, and "the Jews"

As the outline makes clear, the drama is enacted on two stages, one outside Pilate's headquarters, one inside. These two stages serve several literary and theological purposes. First, throughout the trial, Pilate is depicted as scurrying back and forth between "the Jews" who remain outside, and Jesus, who remains inside the headquarters (note the verbs of motion that introduce each scene—e.g., 18:29: "Pilate went out to them"; 18:33: "Then Pilate entered the headquarters again . . . ").[618] This split stage thus robs Pilate of any narrative stability and thereby calls into question his authority as judge. Second, even when the dramatic focus is on Pilate and Jesus inside the headquarters, the offstage presence of "the Jews" reminds the reader of what is at stake in the trial (as with the split stages of John 7).[619] Third, the staging supports the theological movement of the trial. As the trial moves to its conclusion, the boundaries between the two stages become more permeable and "both the personages and the places move nearer to each other."[620] That is, in scene 5, all of the major characters are positioned on the outside stage; in scene 6, the voice of "the Jews" penetrates into the inside stage (19:12), and in scene 7, all of the major characters are together outside again.

As with his sophisticated use of literary techniques in John 18:28–19:16a, the Fourth Evangelist also employs history and tradition to serve his theological intentions. This does not mean that the Fourth Evangelist creates this trial narrative out of whole cloth, however. For example, the question with which Pilate begins his interrogation of Jesus, "Are you the King of the Jews?" (18:33), is also Pilate's initial question to Jesus in all of the other Gospels (Matt 27:11; Mark 15:2; Luke 23:3). This exchange (cf. also Jesus' response, "You say that I am a king," 18:37) thus seems to belong to the common traditions about Jesus' trial (cf. Matt 27:11-14; Mark 15:1-5; Luke 23:1-6), but John develops it to fit his theological interpretation.

This trial narrative also showcases the intersection of religion and politics in mid–first-century Judea. The portrait of the complicity of the Jewish leadership and the Roman procurator in John 18:28–19:16a may provide the most vibrant picture of any of the Gospels of the complex relationship of Jews and Romans in the decades leading up to the revolt of 70 CE.[621] This element of the Johannine trial is often ignored, with most Johannine commentators viewing John's picture of Pilate through the lens of later Christian apologetic toward Rome and not through the lens of first-century Jewish/Roman relations. This is seen most clearly in commentators' descriptions of Pilate as a sympathetic character in John.[622] As the Commentary below will suggest, this insistence on reading Pilate sympathetically distorts the dynamics of the Johannine trial and diminishes the full scope of its portrait of Jesus as judge and king.

The trial before Pilate ultimately has a christological focus, as both Pilate and "the Jews" are brought to judgment by Jesus the eschatological judge and king. Themes from John 5:19-31 and John 10 provide its theological backdrop. The complete integration of literary technique, tradition, and interpretation that is at the heart of John 18:28–19:16a is another example of the inseparable unity of form and content in the Gospel. Through its ironic juxtapositions and intricate staging (see Commentary below), the reader is drawn into the narrative and shares in its cosmic reversal of judgment.

18:28. As noted in the Overview to John 13–17, in John, Jesus' trial before Pilate occurs on the Day of Preparation for the Passover, the 14th of Nisan, before the first Passover meal is eaten, whereas in the synoptic Gospels it occurs on the 15th of Nisan, the day after the first Passover seder has been celebrated. Verse 28 makes clear that the Passover meal still lies in the future and that the trial begins early in the morning of the Day of Preparation (see also 19:14). Those who bring Jesus to the Roman headquarters but refuse to enter are identified only with

618. John 19:1-3 contains no explicit reference to Pilate's return inside, but that he does is made clear by the verb at 19:4: "Pilate went out again. . . . "
619. C. H. Dodd, *Historical Tradition in the Fourth Gospel* (Cambridge: Cambridge University Press, 1963) 96-97.
620. Rudolf Schnackenburg, *The Gospel According to St. John,* 3 vols. (New York: Seabury, 1982) 3:242.

621. Dodd, *Historical Tradition in the Fourth Gospel,* 120; Wayne A. Meeks, *The Prophet-King: Moses Traditions and the Johannine Christology* (Leiden: E. J. Brill, 1967) 63-81; David Rensberger, "The Politics of John: The Trial of Jesus in the Fourth Gospel," *JBL* 103 (1984) 395-411; David Rensberger, *Johannine Faith and Liberating Community* (Philadelphia: Westminster, 1988) 87-106.
622. So, e.g., Raymond E. Brown, *The Gospel According to John (XIII–XXI),* AB 29A (Garden City, N.Y.: Doubleday, 1970) 860, 864, 877, 890; *The Death of the Messiah,* 1:750, 830, 844-45; Schnackenburg, *The Gospel According to St. John,* 3:248-49, 256-57, 263; Barrett, *The Gospel According to St. John,* 530-31, 533, 538.

the vague pronoun "they" (αὐτοί *autoi*) in vv. 28-30; at v. 31, however, they will be explicitly identified as "the Jews." As will become clear as the trial narrative progresses, "the Jews" refers specifically to the Jewish religious leadership in John 18:28–19:16 and not to the Jewish people in general (see esp. 19:6-7, 12, 15).

The key detail in v. 28 is the narrator's note about ritual defilement. There is a historically plausible explanation for this note. The Mishnah stipulates that dwelling places of Gentiles are unclean, perhaps resulting from Gentile burial practices,[623] and Num 9:9-11 has a provision for

eating the Passover meal a month late if one has been rendered ritually unclean by contact with a corpse. The narrator's comment is not intended to give a note of historical accuracy to the scene, however, but to establish its theological irony. The trial narrative opens with "the Jews' " insistence on ritual purity and their meticulous attention to the demands of their faith, and it will end with their complete denial of the claims of that faith (19:15).[624] The attentiveness to ritual purity also provides the rationale for the Fourth Evangelist's use of the literary device of the two stages.

623. See m. Oholoth 18.7

624. George W. MacRae, *Invitation to John* (Garden City, N.Y.: Doubleday, 1978) 209.

❖   ❖   ❖   ❖

EXCURSUS: JOHN'S PORTRAYAL OF PILATE

Pilate, who first appears at v. 29, was the Roman procurator of Judea from 26 to 36 CE. The image of Pilate that emerges from the Jewish and Roman accounts of his procuratorship is that of a mean-spirited and hard ruler, who scorned his Jewish subjects.[625] The portrait of Pilate in the synoptic Gospels is more benign, probably under the influence of pro-Roman Christian apologetic. In Matthew, for example, Pilate is portrayed as being completely guiltless in the death of Jesus (Matt 27:24-26); in Luke he is portrayed as being convinced of Jesus' innocence (Luke 23:4, 13-16, 22-25). As will be shown below, the Johannine portrait in the trial narrative is more consistent with the character of Pilate in the non-Christian accounts; therefore, it is a mistake to see the Pilate of John 18–19 through the lens of the synoptic Gospels. The Pilate who emerges from these chapters is antagonistic and scornful of "the Jews," but that does not mean he is Jesus' ally, searching to convince the Jewish authorities of Jesus' innocence.[626] Rather, Pilate, like the Jewish leaders in 11:46-53, is driven primarily by political expedience. He is portrayed as being singularly unconcerned with questions of guilt or innocence (e.g., 18:31, 38; 19:10), and he involves himself in Jesus' trial as a means "to humiliate 'the Jews' and to ridicule their national hopes by means of Jesus."[627] There is no pro-Roman, anti-Jewish apologetic in the portrayal of Pilate's role in Jesus' death. Pilate's response to Jesus and his culpability are foregrounded in this trial in order to show the extent of Jesus' judgment over the world.

625. Josephus *Antiquities of the Jews* 18.35, 55-62, 88-89; Philo *Legatio ad Gaium* 38; Tacitus *Annals* 15, 44).
626. A representative example of this approach to Pilate would be Schnackenburg, who writes: "Pilate seeks to save [Jesus] right up to the last minute" (*The Gospel According to St. John,* 3:263). So also Barrett and Brown.
627. Rensberger, *Johannine Faith and Liberating Community,* 92.

❖   ❖   ❖   ❖

18:29-32, Scene One: "What Accusation Do You Bring?" The conversation between Pilate and "the Jews" in 18:29-32 pivots on the question of who will be accountable for the death penalty in Jesus' case. In the first exchange (vv.

29-30), "the Jews' " answer to Pilate's inquiry into the charges against Jesus is really a non-answer and as such shifts responsibility for adjudicating Jesus' case back to Pilate. Yet at a theological level, their response points to what is at issue for the Evangelist in the trial. The Greek of 18:30 would be translated literally as "Were this one not doing wrong [κακὸν ποιῶν *kakon poiōn*]?" and recalls 3:19-21, in which the contrast between doing evil and doing what is true is determined by one's relationship to the light. By "handing over" Jesus, the Jewish authorities attempt to remove the light that brings them into judgment (cf. the use of "hand over" [παραδίδωμι *paradidōmi*] at 18:35-36; 19:11, 16, 30).

Pilate tries to extricate himself from the apparent parochialism of this case ("judge him according to your law," v. 31a), but "the Jews" respond that Jesus' capital offense removes him from their jurisdiction (v. 31b). "The Jews' " response in v. 31b is consistent with the description of the Sanhedrin's meeting in 11:46-53, at which Caiaphas argued that Jesus should be killed in order to protect the leaders' political standing and power vis-à-vis the Roman government. The question of whether the Sanhedrin had jurisdiction over death-penalty cases under Roman rule is therefore largely immaterial to the interpretation of v. 31,[628] because the Jewish leaders are making a political gesture to Rome here. An internal Jewish resolution of the situation is inadequate if the chief priests want to secure their standing with Rome; Jesus must receive a death sentence from the Roman government.

Verse 32 confirms that Jesus will not die by stoning (cf. 8:59; 10:31; 11:8), but by crucifixion, the Roman method of execution. Verse 32 is the only time in the trial narrative in which the Fourth Evangelist interrupts the story to provide explicit theological commentary; Jesus' crucifixion at the hands of the Roman government is to be interpreted in the light of Jesus' earlier predictions of his death at 3:14; 8:28; and 12:32 (cf. esp. 12:33). The maneuvering of Pilate and "the Jews" in reality is in the service of Jesus' exaltation and return to God.

18:33-38a, Scene Two: "Are You the King of the Jews?" 18:33. The question about Jesus' kingship with which Pilate begins his interrogation of Jesus in v. 33 is found in all of the Gospel accounts of the trial (Matt 27:11; Mark 15:2; Luke 23:3). The Fourth Evangelist takes this traditional passion component, however, and develops it into the governing motif of the trial. "King" (βασιλεύς *basileus*) occurs nine times in

the trial before Pilate (18:33, 37 [twice], 39; 19:3, 12, 14, 15 [twice]; see also its usage at 19:19 and 21), its heaviest concentration anywhere in the Fourth Gospel.[629] The prominence of the kingship motif underscores the intersection of religion and poli- tics in the trial narrative. Political sedition fell under the jurisdiction of the Roman courts, and Pilate's questioning about Jesus' political claims points to the Roman awareness of the potential threat Jewish messianic hopes posed to their governance. Yet, for the Fourth Evangelist, the kingship motif also has theological significance, and throughout the trial he plays the political and theological meanings of kingship off one another.

18:34. As is typical of Jesus throughout the Fourth Gospel, he responds to Pilate's question with a question of his own (v. 34; cf. 3:9-10; 11:8-9; 14:8-9). Jesus' words move to the heart of Pilate's depiction in this trial, for they question whether Pilate can act on his own, or only in response to others. In addition, Jesus' question signals the direction the rest of the trial will take, because he turns the tables on Pilate and positions himself as the interrogator.[630]

18:35. Pilate's response to Jesus is also pivotal in interpreting both Pilate's character in this trial and its political undertones. His initial question is introduced with the Greek interrogative particle μήτι (*mēti*, a compound form of μή *mē*), which anticipates a negative response, and its sense is accurately reflected in the NRSV, "I am not a Jew, am I?" In this question, Pilate expresses his disdain for the Jews. This disdain, consistent with the description of Pilate in Josephus (see Excursus "John's Portrayal of Pilate," 815), will govern his dealings with the Jewish authorities in the remainder of the trial (see 18:39; 19:5, 14-15). Pilate's reference to "your own nation [ἔθνος *ethnos*] and high priests" in v. 35b recalls the Sanhedrin's meeting in 11:48-52, the only other place where *ethnos* occurs in John, and reinforces the role of political expediency and self-interest in the "handing over" of Jesus.

Pilate's question in v. 35a is also an example of the Fourth Evangelist's use of theological irony in this trial. For the Fourth Evangelist, "the Jews" represent the world's resistance to the revelation

---

628. For a thorough discussion of this question, see Brown, *The Death of the Messiah*, 1:348-72.

629. Its only other occurrences are at 1:49; 6:15; 12:13, 15.
630. Paul Duke, *Irony in the Fourth Gospel* (Atlanta: John Knox, 1985) 129.

of God in Jesus. Pilate anticipates a negative answer to his question, but the trial will show that in fact Pilate is "a Jew," that he belongs with those who reject Jesus.[631] Pilate's question is thus similar to the Pharisees' question at 9:40 ("Surely [*mē*] we are not blind, are we?"), in which the false certitude expressed in the question will be ironically exposed by one's response to Jesus.

18:36-38a. Here Jesus will address the two questions Pilate has asked him: "Are you a king?" (v. 33) and "What have you done?" (v. 35). Jesus' responses are negative and positive counterparts; in v. 36, he defines his kingship by stating what it is not; in v. 37, he gives a positive description of what he has done. Although both the NIV and the NRSV translate βασιλεία (*basileia*) as "kingdom," a more accurate translation would be "kingship" or perhaps "reign." Jesus is describing the nature and function of his kingship, not a place. When Jesus says, "My kingship is not of this world," or "not from here," he is referring to its origin, not its location. The Fourth Gospel has repeatedly emphasized that Jesus originates from God (3:31; 8:23, 42; 16:28), and his kingship has the same origins (cf. 15:19). The difference between Pilate's and Jesus' understanding of kingship is underscored in v. 36*b,* which provides an illustration of the contrast between belonging to God and belonging to "this world." The word translated "followers" (ὑπηρέται *hypēretai,* lit. "servants") is the same word used elsewhere to describe the temple police (e.g., 18:3, 12, 18, 22; 19:6), so that Jesus is ironically contrasting his "officers" and the temple officers. His kingship, unlike that of the king Pilate serves (cf. 19:12, 14-16), is not secured by force (cf. 18:11).

In v. 37*a,* Pilate returns to his original question (see v. 33), and the emphatic wording of the renewed question suggests that he understands that his earlier political assumptions have been confirmed; Jesus does claim to be "king." Jesus' response, "You say that I am a king" (v. 37*b*), is similar to his response to Pilate in the Synoptics (Matt 27:11; Mark 15:2; Luke 23:3). Jesus neither directly affirms nor denies Pilate's words (contrary

to the NIV), but once again returns responsibility for decision to Pilate.

Verse 37*c-d* is a distillation of theological themes that have run throughout the Gospel. First, it stresses the connection between Jesus' origin with God and his witness to the truth (e.g., 3:31-36; 8:14-18, 42, 46; 14:6; 17:17). "For this I was born" and "for this I came into the world" are synonyms that place Jesus' kingship in the familiar Johannine idiom of Jesus' mission in the world (see also 3:17, 19; 6:38; 9;39; 12:46-47; 16:28) and affirm that the origins of Jesus' kingship are not "of this world." Second, the expression "Everyone who belongs to the truth listens to my voice" recalls the claims of the shepherd discourse of John 10 (vv. 3-4, 16, 27); to "belong to the truth" is thus to be one of Jesus' sheep. In addition, at 8:31, knowing the truth and being Jesus' disciple were presented as synonyms. To "belong to the truth" is to recognize in Jesus the truth of God, to see the fullness of God revealed in Jesus, to hear the words of God in Jesus' voice (cf. 5:42; 8:47; 12:49-50).

It is important to remember that pastoral imagery had political overtones in Israel; shepherd was a common metaphor for king (e.g., Ezek 34:1-31; see Commentary on 10:1-6). By introducing motifs from the shepherd discourse into the trial, then, the Fourth Evangelist points the reader to the proper theological context in which to interpret the discussion of Jesus' kingship. Jesus is the good shepherd, the one who who lays down his life for the sheep (10:11, 17-18).[632] Verse 37 also interprets Jesus' kingship in the light of his role as the eschatological judge. Jesus' presence in the world and the word of truth that he speaks are the moment of judgment and decision for the world (5:22, 27; 12:46-48). Although Jesus is nominally on trial here, he is the one who testifies to the truth, and the world is judged by its response to his witness (3:19; 9:39).

It is in the context of Jesus as eschatological judge, as the one who testifies to the truth that Pilate's much-debated question in v. 38*a* ("What is truth?") must be heard and evaluated. In the immediate context of the legal proceedings against Jesus, Pilate's question seems to provide one more example of his contempt for the case that has

631. Meeks, *The Prophet-King,* " 'Am I a Jew?'—Johannine Christianity and Judaism," in *Christianity, Judaism and Other Greco-Roman Cults: Studies for Morton Smith at Sixty,* ed. Jacob Neusner, 4 vols. (Leiden: E. J. Brill, 1975) 1:163-86.

632. Meeks, *The Prophet-King,* 68.

been brought before him. Nothing in the portrait of Pilate in John 18–19 supports reading this question as evidence of Pilate's desire to acquit Jesus.[633] The real significance of Pilate's question, however, lies in what it signals to the reader, and here again, one finds a consummate example of Johannine theological irony, because Pilate's very question contains its own answer. In asking this question of the one who is the truth (14:6), Pilate unknowingly reveals that he does not belong to the truth, that he does not listen to Jesus' voice. Pilate shows that he is not one of Jesus' sheep and thus begins to answer his question of v. 35, "I am not a Jew, am I?"[634]

18:38b-40, Scene Three: "Not This Man, but Barabbas." Pilate does not wait for a reply to his question about truth, but immediately exits the headquarters and returns outside to "the Jews" (v. 38*b*), further suggesting that his question is not serious. The tradition about the release of Barabbas is found in all four Gospels (see Matt 27:15-26; Mark 15:6-15; Luke 23:18-25), although there is no other attestation to this practice of Passover release. The Barabbas scene is narrated quite differently in John than in the other Gospels, however. First, this scene occurs at a different place in the trial narrative. In all of the other Gospels, it occurs at the climax of Pilate's deliberation, whereas here it (and the scourging in 19:1-3, see Scene 4 below) has been placed near the middle of the proceedings. Second, it is a much more abbreviated scene than in the other three Gospels; there is almost no description of Barabbas's crime (cf. Mark 15:6; Luke 23:19), no mention of his actual release (cf. Matt 27:26; Mark 15:15; Luke 23:25), and a truncated dialogue between Pilate and "the Jews" (cf. Mark 15:9-14; Luke 23:14-23). The Johannine account also gives very little attention to Pilate's motivation for the release or his conviction of Jesus' innocence (cf. Matt 27:18, 19, 23-24; Mark 15:10, 14-15; Luke 23:20, 22, 24).

The scene thus is streamlined to have one focus: the choice between "the King of the Jews" and Barabbas. Pilate's disdain for "the Jews" is once again signaled in his taunting use of the title

"King of the Jews" for Jesus (v. 39). The identification of Barabbas is terse, simply the one word "bandit" (λῃστής *lēstēs*). On the basis of Barabbas's description in the synoptic Gospels as a political criminal and the use of the noun "bandit" to describe political revolutionaries in Josephus,[635] many scholars assume that the Fourth Evangelist is focusing on Barabbas as a political criminal here as well (note the NIV paraphrase, "Barabbas had taken part in a rebellion"). Bultmann, for example, sees this scene as further illustrating the hypocrisy of the Jewish authorities, who, having denounced Jesus to Rome as an alleged political criminal, now seek the release of a real political criminal.[636] Yet the ultimate significance of the noun "bandit" seems to lie elsewhere for the Fourth Evangelist. The same noun is used in the shepherd discourse to describe those who threaten the sheep and come before Jesus (10:1, 8). The choice between Jesus and Barabbas is thus the choice between the good shepherd and the bandit, and in choosing Barabbas, the "Jews" once again demonstrate that they do not belong to Jesus' sheep. This scene thus continues the theme of the shepherd/king from the previous scene.[637]

19:1-3, Scene Four: "Hail, King of the Jews." As already noted, the Fourth Evangelist locates the account of Jesus' flogging and mocking in the middle of the trial. In Mark 15:15*b*-20 and Matt 27:26*b*-31, the flogging and mocking of Jesus by the Roman soldiers immediately precedes his execution.[638] As such, it is narrated in its appropriate legal and procedural location, for flogging was normally a preliminary to crucifixion.[639] In locating this scene in the middle of the trial, the Fourth Evangelist radically alters its function. The Roman soldiers' actions are not an act of torture and humiliation meted out to a criminal after his sentence, because Jesus' trial is still in progress and no verdict has yet been reached. Many scholars, guided by their assumptions that throughout this trial Pilate is seeking to persuade "the Jews" of Jesus' innocence, see in the flogging an attempt by Pilate to dissuade the Jews from

633. Barrett seems to read Pilate's question this way. See C. K. Barrett, *The Gospel According to St. John,* 2nd ed. (Philadelphia: Westminster, 1978) 538.
634. Meeks, *The Prophet-King,* 67, sees v. 35 as being fully answered in this verse.
635. E.g., Josephus *The Jewish War* 2.253-54, 585.
636. Rudolf Bultmann, *The Gospel of John: A Commentary,* trans. G. R. Beasley-Murray, R. W. N. Hoare, and J. K. Riches (Philadelphia: Westminster, 1971) 657-58.
637. Meeks, *The Prophet-King,* 68.
638. Lukes narrates no flogging, although Pilate alludes to it twice (Luke 23:16, 22).
639. See, e.g, Josephus *The Jewish War* 5.449.

their determination to seek the death penalty for Jesus. That is, Pilate hopes that the Jews will accept Jesus' beating as sufficient punishment.[640] Yet "the Jews" are not witnesses to this scene; they are outside the headquarters, and the flogging and abuse occur inside (cf. 19:4). The actions of John 19:1-3 are thus narrated for the Gospel readers alone, so the clue to the placement of this scene must be sought within the Fourth Evangelist's dramatic and theological purposes.

As with the Barabbas tradition, the Fourth Evangelist has streamlined the narrative of Jesus' flogging and mistreatment by the Roman soldiers to showcase his theological interpretation. First, the Johannine account is briefer than those in Mark and Matthew, and it has one focal point: the dressing of Jesus in royal attire and the soldiers' acclamation of him as "King of the Jews" (vv. 2-3). Second, the Fourth Evangelist nowhere labels the soldiers' actions and words as "mocking" (cf. Matt 27:29, 31; Mark 15:20). Instead, the soldiers' actions stand on their own, their interpretation left to the reader. Third, and most important, the Fourth Evangelist does not record that the soldiers strip Jesus of the royal garb and return him to his own clothes (cf. Matt 27:31; Mark 15:20). Rather, John 19:5 makes clear that Jesus stays dressed in the royal garb for the remainder of the trial.

The Fourth Evangelist thus has transformed the tradition of Jesus' mockery by the Roman soldiers into a narrative of Jesus' investiture as king.[641] As the middle scene in the drama, John 19:1-3 is the turning point in the trial narrative. From this point on, Jesus' kingship becomes a visible and tangible part of the proceedings; when Pilate presents Jesus to the "Jews" in 19:4-7, 13-16, he presents to them a man dressed in the garb of a king. John 19:1-3 thus sets the stage for the ultimate enactment of Jesus' kingship, his exaltation on the cross (see vv. 19-21), his gift as the good shepherd of his life for his own.

19:4-7, Scene Five: "Here Is the Man."

This is the first of two scenes in which Pilate brings Jesus outside the headquarters in order to present him to "the Jews" (see also vv. 13-16). Both are scenes of high drama, in which all of the protagonists of the trial are together on one stage: Jesus, dressed as a king, is silent, while Pilate and "the Jews" debate his fate.

19:4-5. The presentation of Jesus is narrated in three parts in vv. 4-5: (1) Pilate's words of introduction (v. 4); (2) Jesus' appearance (v. 5a); and (3) Pilate's declaration, "Here is the man" (v. 5b). The juxtaposition of vv. 4 and 5 makes it difficult to see how Pilate's words in v. 4 could be taken as a serious statement of Jesus' innocence; that Pilate presents Jesus to "the Jews" dressed in royal garb is disdainful both of "the Jews" and of Jesus. Pilate's words in vv. 4-5 contain no pity for Jesus, nor is his purpose "to make the person of Jesus appear to the Jews as ridiculous and harmless."[642] Rather, Pilate flaunts his authority as the Roman procurator and parodies the political claims and aspirations of the Jewish leadership. The purpose of his words and actions seems to be to taunt the Jews and their messianic pretensions.[643] These verses are the real mockery in the Johannine trial, and the object of the mockery is the Jewish leadership. Pilate's actions in vv. 4-5 border on the farcical, as the Roman procurator toys with "the Jews" and their "king."

Pilate's declaration in v. 5 is one of the most famous (and most discussed) lines from the Fourth Gospel. On the level of the story line, as indicated earlier, Pilate's words seem to communicate his disdain for the whole notion of a Jewish kingship. Yet Pilate's words may also work on a second level, providing the reader with yet another indication of the nature of Jesus' kingship. It is possible, for example, that the words "Here is the man [ὁ ἄνθρωπος ho anthrōpos]" are intended to echo the description of Jesus as "the Son of Man" (ὁ υἱός τοῦ ἀνθρώπου ho huios tou anthrōpou).[644] In the Fourth Gospel, "Son of Man" is associated with Jesus' death (e.g., 3:14; 8:28; 12:23, 32-34), but it is also used to describe Jesus as the eschato-

640. So Barrett, *The Gospel According to St. John*, 530; Bultmann, *The Gospel of John*, 659; Brown, *The Gospel According to John (XIII–XXI)*, 886; Duke, *Irony in the Fourth Gospel*, 132.

641. Josef Blank, "Die Verhandlung vor Pilatus Jo 18:28–19:16 im Lichte johanneischer Theologie," *Biblische Zeitschrift* 3 (1959), 60-81; Ignace de la Potterie, "Jesus, King and Judge According to John 19:13," *Scripture* 13 (1961) 97-111 (originally published in *Biblica* 41 [1960] 117-47); Meeks, *The Prophet-King*, 68-69; Duke, *Irony in the Fourth Gospel*, 132.

642. So Bultmann, *The Gospel of John*, 659. See also Schnackenburg, *The Gospel According to St. John*, 3:255-56.

643. David Rensberger, *Johannine Faith and Liberating Community* (Philadelphia: Westminster, 1988) 94.

644. C. H. Dodd, *Historical Tradition in the Fourth Gospel* (Cambridge: Cambridge University Press, 1963) 97.

logical judge (e.g., 5:27-28). To the Gospel reader, then, Pilate inadvertently presents Jesus to "the Jews" as the eschatological judge, thereby undercutting his own authority as judge and ironically revealing the true nature of this trial. Pilate's presentation of Jesus thus may resemble Caiaphas's unconscious prophecy about the meaning of Jesus' death at 11:50; even those who seek to destroy Jesus unintentionally witness to the truth about him.

19:6a. The reaction of the Jewish leadership to the sight of Jesus dressed as a king is swift and intense. Unlike the synoptic Gospels where the crowd clamors for Jesus' crucifixion (Matt 27:22-23; Mark 15:13-14; Luke 23:18, 21, 23), in John it is only the formal leadership and their henchmen. "The Jews" and "chief priests" are used interchangeably in John 18–19 (e.g., 19:6-7, 14-15). The elimination of any role for the crowd and the exclusive focus on the participation of the leadership again point to the political slant John gives this trial and clarify who he identifies as Jesus' antagonists. The double cry, "Crucify! Crucify!" (NIV; the NRSV supplies the pronoun that is absent in the Greek text) confirms the chief priests' intention that Jesus die at the hands of a Roman court.

19:6b. Pilate's response in v. 6b mocks this intention. The Jewish leadership had no authority to carry out a crucifixion; that method of execution belonged to the jurisdiction of the Roman legal system. Pilate thus taunts the Jewish leadership with their dependence on his granting the merits of their case against Jesus and threatens to disregard their demands.

19:7. "The Jews" then allude to the law against blasphemy, which prescribes death by stoning for blasphemers (Lev 24:13-16; see also *m. Sanh.* 7.5). "The Jews" have already tried to stone Jesus for blasphemy twice (8:59; 10:31), and their charge of blasphemy here, "He has made himself the Son of God" (author's trans.), is almost identical to their charges of blasphemy against Jesus at 5:18 and 10:33. "The Jews'" appeal to the blasphemy law is ironic in the light of 18:31, where they disowned their legal right to enact a death penalty, and marks a new turn in their dealings with Pilate. As the Roman procurator of Judea, Pilate was required to honor local customs, and the Jewish leadership seems to remind him of that responsibility here.[645]

That is, "the Jews" remind Pilate of his stake in this trial and its potential political implications for him. In v. 7, the Jewish leadership thus is portrayed as willing to exploit the claims of their faith in the service of political expediency. They respond to Pilate's taunting of their dependence on his judicial role by reminding him of the limits on his juridical freedom (see also 19:12).

19:8-12, Scene Six: "You Would Have No Power Over Me." 19:8-9. Verse 8 provides the first explicit reference to Pilate's reaction to the proceedings. Although the Greek expression (μᾶλλον ἐφοβήθη *mallon ephobēthē*) can be translated as a comparative ("even more afraid," NIV; or "more afraid than ever," NRSV), this translation is problematic, because v. 8 is the first time Pilate's fears have been mentioned. Many scholars get around this difficulty by reading fear back into many of Pilate's earlier words and actions in the trial, but this interpretive move borders on excessive psychologizing about the character and motives of the Johannine Pilate.[646] It thus seems preferable to translate the expression as an intensive— Pilate became "very much afraid."[647]

Verses 8-9 are one sentence in the Greek text (so NIV), so that Pilate's fear is clearly positioned as the motivation for his reentering the headquarters and interrogating Jesus. What is not as clear is the reason for this fear. Pilate's fear may derive from the "Jews'" introduction of religious categories in v. 7. That is, the possibility that he might be in the presence of a divine man, "the Son of God," evokes Pilate's fears.[648] This interpretation, however, assumes that Pilate would honor and respect "the Jews'" language about God, an assumption that the text does not otherwise support. A more likely explanation for Pilate's fears is political. If, as suggested, the Jewish leadership's motivation in introducing the blasphemy charge in v. 7 is political, not primarily religious, then it may be that very political threat that evokes Pilate's fears. Pilate is afraid because he recognizes that the situation in which he finds himself may place his political future in jeopardy (see also 19:12). In this regard, as Brown has observed, Pilate is

---

645. See Philo *Legatio ad Gaium* 38. So Raymond E. Brown, *The Gospel According to John (XIII–XXI)*, AB 29A (Garden City, N.Y.: Doubleday, 1970) 890-91.

646. E.g., Rudolf Schnackenburg, *The Gospel According to St. John*, (Stuttgart: Calwer, 1948) 3:260; Bultmann, *The Gospel of John*, 661n. 2.
647. So Barrett, *The Gospel According to St. John*, 542.
648. Dodd, *Historical Tradition in the Fourth Gospel*, 114; Schnackenburg, *The Gospel According to St. John*, 3:260; most dramatically, Duke, *Irony in the Fourth Gospel*, 133.

similar to Caiaphas at 11:48-53.[649] Both leaders, secular and religious, are anxious and fearful about what Jesus means to their power and authority.

Pilate's question about Jesus' origins in v. 9 initiates a new probe into Jesus' identity in response to the Jewish charge of blasphemy (cf. Pilate's inquiry into Jesus' origins in Luke 23:5-7), but for the Fourth Gospel reader, this question has additional meaning. The question of Jesus' origins is one of the most important christological and theological issues in the Gospel, and the reader knows that the correct answer to the question "Where are you from?" is "From God" (e.g., 1:1-3, 18; 3:34; 6:33; 7:29; 16:27-28). Pilate's ignorance of this answer thus further identifies him with "the Jews" (see 18:35), whose ignorance of Jesus' origins is a theme throughout the Gospel (7:27-28; 8:14; 9:29; cf. also 6:42; 7:41-42). Jesus' silence (cf. Matt 27:14; Mark 15:5) allows the implications of Pilate's question to linger for the reader; Jesus has already answered the question of his origins for Pilate (18:36-37), and Pilate rejected that answer with his question, "What is truth?" No further answer is possible.

19:10-11. The conversation between Pilate and Jesus in these verses supports reading the potential loss of power as the cause of Pilate's fears, since these verses focus on the meaning and source of power. These verses parallel the exchange about kingship in 18:35-38, for both exchanges contrast power that is based in human institutions with true power, which resides with God. The wording of Pilate's challenge to Jesus in v. 10 is very important, because it is a direct echo of Jesus' own language about his death in 10:17-18. There, Jesus says, "No one takes it [my life] from me, but I lay it down of my own accord. I have power [ἐξουσία *exousia*] to lay it down, and I have power [*exousia*] to take it up again." The reader, therefore, knows that Pilate's claims to power in 19:10 are false; the judicial power to which Pilate appeals is a sham, because authority over Jesus' life and death rests with Jesus.

Jesus makes this explicit in his response in v. 11. The English wording of v. 11*a* is ambiguous, but the Greek makes clear that Jesus is not saying that *power* is given to Pilate from above, but that

the *exercise* of power over Jesus is given to him from above (cf. 3:27). God has given power and authority to judge to Jesus (5:27), not to Pilate. Indeed, God has given Jesus "power [*exousia*] over all flesh" (17:2). Pilate's exercise of power, therefore, is only as an instrument in the service of God and Jesus in the fulfillment of Jesus' hour.

The reference to "sin" (ἁμαρτία *hamartia*) in v. 11*b* is about neither legal nor moral culpability in the death of Jesus, but is a theological statement about relationship to God. Jesus' words in v. 11*b*, therefore, do not reflect pro-Roman Christian apologetic that wants to minimize the culpability of Pilate in the death of Jesus,[650] but must be interpreted in the light of the Johannine understanding of sin. In the Fourth Gospel, "sin" is defined by whether one believes that God is fully present in Jesus, whether one believes that to see Jesus is to see God (14:9; see Reflections on John 9). To have the greater sin, then, is to have the greater blindness to the revelation of God in Jesus.

Jesus ascribes the "greater sin" to "the one who handed me over to you." Prior to the trial narrative, the verb "to hand over" or "to betray" (παραδίδωμι *paradidōmi*) was used exclusively to refer to Judas's betrayal (e.g., 6:64; 12:4; 13:2, 11, 21; 18:2, 5). In the trial narrative, however, this verb no longer refers to Judas, whose part in the events of the hour has been played and therefore has disappeared from the story, but refers to the Jewish leadership (18:30, 35-36), as it does here. At this point in the trial narrative, "the Jews" do have the greater sin, because in handing Jesus over to Pilate they have definitively rejected the revelation of God in Jesus. That is, they have the greater blindness to the presence of God in Jesus, especially because they claim to know God (5:39; 8:41; 9:29; 10:33; cf. 9:39-41). By the end of the trial, however, when Pilate himself hands Jesus over to be crucified (19:16*a*), Pilate will share their sin, because he, too, will have rejected the revelation of God in Jesus. He will be fully a "Jew."

19:12. This verse marks the decisive dramatic turn in the trial narrative. In v. 12*a*, the narrator informs the reader of Pilate's intention to release Jesus. Where earlier Pilate had only been toying with "the Jews" about Jesus' release, now he

---

649. Brown, *The Gospel According to John (XIII–XXI)*, 891.

650. So Schnackenburg, *The Gospel According to St. John*, 3:261-62; Brown, *The Gospel According to John (XIII–XXI)*, 893.

intends it in earnest. Pilate himself never expresses this intention, yet in v. 12*b*, "the Jews" know of Pilate's plan. The appearance of the narrator's comments in the words of characters in the story heightens the drama of the moment, for it is as if the Jews know Pilate's plans as soon as he does and are one step ahead of him. As in 19:7, "the Jews" remind Pilate of the political constraints on his juridical options. "Friend of the emperor" may already have been used as an official title in this period, granted in recognition of loyalty and service to the emperor.[651] Even if it is not used as a title here, the meaning of "the Jews' " warning is clear: If Pilate releases this man who has been handed to him on charges of political sedition, he may find himself accused of sedition.

Pilate's interrogation of Jesus occurs inside the headquarters, out of sight of the Jewish authorities, yet their words to Pilate in v. 12*b* penetrate into this stage. The divide between the two stages is decisively breached, preparing for the final reunion of all the protagonists in vv. 13-16. The staging heightens the effect of "the Jews' " words, because their seeming omniscience gives almost ominous power to their warning. The immediate juxtaposition of the narrator's comments in v. 12*a* and the Jews' response in v. 12*b* thus places Pilate and his decision with respect to Jesus in the spotlight. The moment for Pilate's decision has arrived.

19:13-16a, Scene Seven: "Here Is Your King." This scene is the solemn and tragic conclusion to the trial narrative. The solemnity with which the Evangelist perceives this moment is indicated by both the formal identification of the site (note that both its Greek and Aramaic names are provided in v. 13) and the detailed accounting of the day and time (v. 14*a*; see below). As at 19:8, "the Jews' " words are explicitly positioned as the motivation for Pilate's actions ("When Pilate heard these words . . . ").

19:13. What Pilate does when he brings Jesus out of the headquarters is a controversial point in Fourth Gospel scholarship. The controversy stems from whether the verb (ἐκάθισεν *ekathisen*) should be translated as an intransitive verb, describing an action without a direct object

("Pilate sat on the judge's seat" [NIV, NRSV]), or as a transitive verb, requiring a direct object to complete its meaning ("Pilate seated [Jesus] on the judge's seat" [NRSV alt.]). Both translations are grammatically possible, so the question must be resolved on other grounds. Those scholars who argue for the intransitive translation make their case largely on the grounds of historical probability. That is, they deem it historically improbable that Pilate would have mocked the judicial process at this point by placing Jesus, the accused, on the seat from which the judge was to voice his verdict.[652] This reading once again assumes that Pilate is still intent on releasing Jesus, when in fact this scene continues and intensifies Pilate's mockery of the Jewish authorities from 19:4-7 (see Commentary on vv. 14*b* and 15*b*). It is fully in keeping with the character of the Johannine Pilate for him to taunt the Jews at this critical point by seating Jesus, still dressed in the purple robe and crown of thorns, on the judge's seat.[653]

This commentary agrees with those scholars who support the transitive reading of *kathidzō*.[654] For Pilate to seat Jesus on the judge's seat lends a profound irony to the scene that accords with the theological and dramatic intent of the trial narrative. Pilate, who intends to mock Jesus and the Jews by placing Jesus on the judge's seat, unknowingly places him in his rightful place as judge. Read in this light, the staging of the final, climactic scene telegraphs its theological content: Jesus is the true judge and king. It also confirms Jesus' words of v. 11, that Pilate exercises his authority only in the service of God and Jesus.

19:14. The charade of parading Jesus out one more time dressed as a king is Pilate's answer to the Jews' warning about Pilate's loyalty to the

---

651. Ernst Bammel, "*philos tou kaisaros* (John 19:12)," *Theologie Literaturzeitung* 77 (1952) 205-20.

652. E.g., Bultmann, *The Gospel of John,* 664; Schnackenburg, *The Gospel According to St. John,* 3:263-64; Brown, *The Gospel According to John (XIII–XXI),* 880-81, who writes, "the seriousness of Roman law militates against such buffoonery." See also Raymond E. Brown, *The Death of the Messiah,* 2 vols. (New York: Doubleday, 1994) 1:844, appendix III D.

653. It is also interesting to note that the soldiers "seat" (καθίζω *kathizō*) Jesus on the judgment seat and mock him as judge and king as part of Jesus' mockery in the *Gospel of Peter.* "And they dressed him in purple and seated him upon the judgment seat, saying, 'Judge justly, King of Israel' " (5.7) and Justin's *Apology:* "They seated him upon the judge's seat, and said, 'Judge us' " (I.35).

654. The most important and thorough presentation of this position is Ignace de la Potterie, "Jesus, roi et juge d'après Jn 19, 13: *ekathisen epi bematos,*" *Biblica* 41 (1960) 217-47. See also Meeks, *The Prophet-King,* 73-76; Duke, *Irony in the Fourth Gospel,* 134-35; and George W. MacRae, *Invitation to John* (Garden City, N.Y.: Doubleday, 1978) 210. Barrett, *The Gospel According to St. John,* 544, argues that the Fourth Evangelist was conscious of both meanings.

emperor in v. 12. By presenting Jesus as "your King" in v. 14*b*, Pilate once again mocks the Jews' messianic pretensions and any threat they might pose to Roman rule (cf. 19:4-5). As with the seating of Jesus on the judge's seat, Pilate's words also have a profound theological irony. In his mocking and derision, Pilate, like Caiaphas at 11:49, unconsciously speaks the truth about Jesus: He is the king (cf. 1:49).

The reference to the day and hour in v. 14*a* deserves special mention. As noted earlier (see Overview to John 13–17), the Johannine chronology for the trial and crucifixion differs from that of the Synoptics. In John, as 19:14 makes explicit, the trial and crucifixion occur on the Day of Preparation, the 14th of Nisan. According to John, the legal proceedings begin early in the morning (18:28) and last until noon ("the sixth hour," NIV). Most scholars assume that John is trying to establish a connection between the death of Jesus and the slaughter of the Passover lamb with this notation,[655] and while that association may be implied at 19:36, it is not the association intended here. Rather, as de la Potterie and Meeks have carefully observed, John is not noting the time of Jesus' crucifixion in v. 14 (as in Mark 15:25, "nine o'clock in the morning"), but the time of Pilate's announcement of Jesus as king.[656] By linking Jesus' presentation as judge and king with noon on the Day of Preparation, the Fourth Evangelist positions this scene to coincide with the time when regulations for the Passover feast go into effect.[657] As Jerusalem prepares to celebrate the Passover, "the Jews" are presented with their king.

19:15. This Passover context provides the necessary theological and dramatic background for "the Jews'" rejection of Jesus in v. 15. Note again that as in v. 6, it is the religious leadership, not a crowd, who rejects Jesus and calls for his crucifixion (v. 15*a*). Pilate's taunt in v. 15*b* sets up the dramatic conclusion of the trial narrative in v. 15*c*. When the chief priests answer Pilate, "We have no king but the emperor," the trial reaches its tragic and pathos-filled end. With this reply, the chief priests renounce everything that gives them their distinctive identity as God's people.

First, in professing allegiance to the Roman emperor, the chief priests ironically renounce all their messianic hopes and aspirations. At 8:33, "the Jews" said to Jesus, "We are descendants of Abraham and have never been slaves to anyone" (see Commentary on 8:33), but here they renounce that defining freedom and enslave themselves to Rome. Second, at the heart of Israel's faith is the claim that God is the only king (e.g., Judg 8:23; 1 Sam 8:7; Isa 26:13). In shouting, "We have no king but the emperor," the chief priests thus deny their God. One of the theological themes of Passover is the celebration of God as judge and king, a theme captured in the following hymn from a Passover liturgy:

> From everlasting to everlasting thou art God
> Beside thee we have no king, redeemer, or
>   savior,
> No liberator, deliverer, provider
> None who takes pity in every time of distress
>   and trouble
> We have no king but thee.[658]

In their zeal to reject Jesus, the chief priests have rejected the very God whom they purport to serve.

19:16a. With the chief priests' words, the drama has been played out. The narrator adds no interpretive comment, for such comment would be superfluous; the pathos of the moment speaks for itself. The trial narrative ends with the very understated report that Pilate handed Jesus over to the chief priests to be crucified (v. 16). As noted, in handing Jesus over, Pilate joins "the Jews" in their rejection of God in Jesus. Pilate and "the Jews" have both gotten what they wanted—"the Jews" have rid themselves of Jesus and secured their place with Rome (cf. 11:48-53), and Pilate has maneuvered the Jewish authorities into renouncing their messianic aspirations and so secured his place with Rome—but at a great cost (see Reflections).

---

655. Rudolf Bultmann, *The Gospel of John: A Commentary,* trans. G. R. Beasley-Murray, R. W. N. Hoare, and J. K. Riches (Philadelphia: Westminster, 1971) 664n. 5, 677; E. C. Hoskyns, *The Fourth Gospel* (London: Faber & Faber, 1947) 525; C. K. Barrett, *The Gospel According to St. John,* 2nd ed. (Philadelphia: Westminster, 1978) 545; Raymond E. Brown, *The Gospel According to John (XIII–XXI),* AB 29A (Garden City, N.Y.: Doubleday, 1970) 895.

656. de la Potterie, "Jesus, roi et juge," 244ff.; Meeks, *The Prophet-King,* 76n. 3.

657. See *m. Pesahim* 1.4-5.

658. Wayne A. Meeks, *The Prophet-King: Moses Traditions and the Johannine Christology* (Leiden: E. J. Brill, 1967) 71. The dating of this hymn is uncertain, but even if this very hymn was not part of the seder in first-century Palestine, it captures the theological intent of the celebration.

REFLECTIONS

At John 12:46-49, in the epilogue to his public ministry, Jesus states the role of judgment in his ministry: "I have come as light into the world, so that everyone who believes in me should not remain in the darkness. I do not judge anyone who hears my words and does not keep them, for I came not to judge the world, but to save the world. The one who rejects me and does not receive my word has a judge; on the last day the word that I have spoken will serve as judge, for I have not spoken on my own, but the Father who sent me has himself given me a commandment about what to say and what to speak."

These words of Jesus provide the critical theological categories through which to interpret the trial of John 18:28–19:16a, because they help the interpreter to understand that the real trial is not whether or not Jesus will be judged guilty of a capital offense, but whether or not Pilate and the Jewish religious leadership will be judged by Jesus' word. In order to understand the ways in which the trial before Pilate brings the theme of judgment to its conclusion, it will be useful to examine how the conduct and fate of the central characters in the trial narrative (the Jewish leaders, Pilate, Jesus) through the lens of Jesus' words in 12:46-49.

1. *The Jewish Leaders.* For the Jewish leaders, the trial narrative is the capstone on the theological conflict that has characterized the relationship between Jesus and "the "Jews" throughout the Gospel narrative. The theological conflicts of John 5 and 7–10 form the background of this trial scene, but their content is not repeated here. As Jesus made clear in his words to Annas in 18:20-21, he has already spoken openly to "the Jews" about God, and they have rejected his revelation; there is no need to rehearse the differences further. As if to underscore this point, Jesus and the Jews do not speak to one another in the trial. They each speak only to Pilate.

The critical moment of judgment for the chief priests comes in vv. 14-16, which is also the final opportunity for decision. Jesus stands before them, their king, and Pilate puts the crucial question to them, "Shall I crucify your King?" The chief priests' answer is the most painful moment in the Gospel, for as the Commentary noted, in their zeal to destroy Jesus, they have denied the very God in whom their lives are grounded.

For the Fourth Evangelist, the decisive theological issue that divides the Jewish leadership and Johannine Jewish Christians is how one defines relationship with God. The Jewish leadership is emblematic of active rejection of Jesus, of the insistence that there is another way to God, and for the Fourth Evangelist, such a perspective is a lie (see Commentary and Reflections on 8:31-59). For the Fourth Evangelist, as the Gospel repeatedly makes clear, Jesus redefines relationship with God: "No one comes to the Father except through me" (see Reflections on John 14). The Fourth Evangelist's understanding of judgment is derived directly from this understanding of God. Those who come to God through Jesus are not judged, but come to eternal life. Those who reject the offer of God in Jesus are by definition judged, because they have closed themselves off from God. In 19:15, the Fourth Evangelist gives narrative shape to this understanding of judgment; he allows the reader to witness a moment of judgment. It is the decisive eschatological moment: In rejecting Jesus as king, the Jewish leadership at the same time reject God as king and are, therefore, judged.

The Fourth Evangelist does not append any explicit word of judgment at the end of this scene, because none is needed. Through their own words and their rejection of Jesus, the Jewish leaders have judged themselves, and that judgment lingers in the narrative without comment. They were offered salvation and invited into the presence of God, but chose condemnation instead (cf. 3:18). They heard Jesus' words but did not keep them (12:47). From the perspective of the Fourth Evangelist, "the Jews' " rejection of Jesus is a tragedy of monumental proportions, because they have lost everything.

It is important to note that there is neither joy nor exultation in the Fourth Evangelist's depiction of this moment. It is instead a moment of sheer loss, whose impact echoes in the narrative silence. The Fourth Evangelist does not gloat, but instead "the Jews' " announcement feels almost funereal. They have disclaimed their God; who could rejoice? It is critical that the contemporary interpreter read this presentation of the Jewish leadership's rejection of Jesus and denial of their God as the final expression of the Fourth Evangelist's theological conflict with Judaism and not as a statement about Jewish responsibility for the death of Jesus. The death of Jesus is not the tragedy for the Fourth Evangelist; "the Jews' " loss of their relationship with God is. John 19:15 is a crystallization of what has been apparent throughout the Gospel: For the Fourth Evangelist, everything is at stake in the decision one makes about the revelation of God in Jesus.

2. *Pilate.* The character of Pilate introduces a new element into the Fourth Gospel's theme of judgment. Prior to John 18:28–19:16a, Jesus' only antagonists have been "the Jews," and their part in the trial narrative builds on their other encounters with Jesus throughout the Gospel. "The Jews" provide the background in this trial, but Pilate and his response to Jesus occupy the foreground in the trial narrative. By giving Pilate such prominence in the trial narrative, the Fourth Evangelist asks the reader to look at Jesus and the decision about Jesus in a new light. In this trial, the Fourth Evangelist opens up the arena of Jesus' testimony to include the broader world. Just as he moved outside the traditional boundaries of Judaism and testified to a Samaritan woman in John 4, so also here Jesus testifies to a representative of the Roman government who is clearly shown to be wanting, who does not respond to the word of truth that Jesus brings and indeed is in his very person.

The role of Pilate shows that the "world" (κόσμος *kosmos*), the sphere of enmity toward Jesus, is not limited to "the Jews," and that "Jew" is not an ethnic designation. The eschatological scope of Jesus' hour and the judgment that comes with it (cf. 8:21-28) is highlighted in Pilate's rejection of Jesus. Pilate, a "ruler of the world," is judged by Jesus' hour just as the Jewish religious leadership is judged.

Pilate's exchanges with Jesus in the trial (18:33-38a; 19:8-11) are a perfect illustration of Jesus' words at 12:48: "The one who rejects me and does not receive my word has a judge; on the last day the word that I have spoken will serve as judge." Jesus' words to Pilate move to the heart of his ministry and revelation of God: "My kingdom is not from this world"; "For this I came into the world, to testify to the truth"; "You would have no power over me unless it had been given you from above." Pilate's question, "What is truth?" signals his rejection of Jesus and his words. When Pilate hands Jesus over to be crucified, he puts into action the rejection that has characterized his response to Jesus throughout the trial. He has never heard Jesus; he has never listened to Jesus' voice.

The word that Jesus has spoken does indeed stand as judge, because it is Jesus' word that has shown the limits of Pilate's purported judgment, power, and authority. Pilate attempts to exercise his power and authority over Jesus, but instead, Pilate's power and authority diminish as the trial unfolds. His questions and responses to Jesus draw attention to his distance from any true command of power, authority, and truth. The trial narrative presents the reader with a ruler who has all the accoutrements of power and office (note the soldiers at his disposal), with the legal authority to take away life, but who nonetheless stands powerless in the face of true power, authority, and life. Jesus testifies to the truth; Pilate builds a case around mockery and political expedience. The power of this ruler of the world is exposed as empty.

Pilate, then, is not a victim in this trial, nor is he some hapless innocent, trapped by the machinations of the Jewish leadership.[659] Rather, Pilate is a man, like so many others in this

---

659. So Bultmann, *The Gospel of John,* 657-59, 662n. 6, 665 ("Pilate falls victim to the Jews"); Schnackenburg, *Der Evangelist Johannes,* 3:249, 263, 265; Brown, *The Gospel According to John (XIII–XXI),* 893-94.

Gospel, to whom Jesus speaks the truth about himself and God. Pilate is given the opportunity to make his decision about Jesus—not his *legal* decision, but his *theological* decision. That is, by speaking the truth to Pilate, Jesus puts Pilate on trial. Pilate is asked to decide whether he will receive Jesus' word, whether he will identify himself with those who "have the love of God" in them (5:42), or whether he will turn his back on God.

When John 18:28–19:16a is read as part of the Good Friday lessons (Year C), it may be Pilate who should occupy the church's attention as it meditates on the significance of the trial. The "Jews'" rejection of Jesus is a tragedy that brings a theological conflict to its painful conclusion, and its pathos is palpable. The presentation of Pilate in this trial gives the interpreter a different angle on response to Jesus, however. Pilate makes it impossible to isolate "the Jews" as the enemies and rejecters of Jesus, because by the end of the trial Pilate is fully complicit with them. Pilate's encounter with and rejection of Jesus are completely played out on this one stage; Pilate both receives Jesus' witness and rejects it and him in the course of this one story. The reader thus is able to experience the drama of decision making and to reflect on its consequences. In his rejection, Pilate reveals who he is, that he loves the darkness more than the light, that he belongs to those who reject the revelation of God in Jesus. This image of the world's rejection of Jesus puts hard and searching questions before the church, because it is another reminder that the real issue on Good Friday is not who is responsible for the death of Jesus, but the many ways in which the revelation of God in Jesus can be rejected.

3. *Jesus.* Juridical imagery and metaphors have dominated the presentation of the life and ministry of Jesus in the Fourth Gospel. John the Baptist's proclamation about Jesus is repeatedly identified as "witness" or "testimony" (e.g., 1:7, 15, 19, 34; 3:26; 5:33). Jesus speaks of his words and works as testimony that the Father has sent him (e.g., 3:32; 5:36), and God, too, is said to bear witness on Jesus' behalf (5:37; 8:18). Jesus' life and ministry have been presented through the metaphor of a trial, in which the world is presented with the truth of God in Jesus and is asked to respond (3:33; 5:33; 8:31, 45; 14:6; 15:26; 17:17). Jesus both bears witness and is the one to whom witness is born in this "trial," because Jesus both speaks God's words and is God's Word. His mission (what Jesus says and does) and his identity (who Jesus is) are inseparable in the Gospel. Both belong to his revelation of the character and identity of God. When Jesus tells Pilate that his mission is to testify to the truth (18:37), he is also speaking about his identity as the truth.

In addition to juridical language about witness, language about judgment also dominates the Johannine portrait of Jesus' ministry. Jesus is identified as the Son of Man, who in the Fourth Gospel is the agent of God's eschatological judgment (5:27; 9:35). The lifting up of the Son of Man is the moment of the world's judgment (3:13-15; 8:28; 12:34). Jesus is also the light of the world, whose very advent into the world is the moment of judgment and division (8:12; 9:5; 12:46; cf. 9:39).

In the trial before Pilate, then, the juridical metaphors and imagery about Jesus are brought to their dramatic conclusion. Story line and theology completely coalesce, because the "trial" becomes both metaphorical and actual. On one level, Jesus is on trial for his life, but on another, and for the Fourth Evangelist, the most important level, the world is on trial for its life. The world thinks it is judging Jesus, but in reality, Jesus is judging it, and he judges the world both by what he says and does and by who he is. In the trial narrative, then, the inseparability of Jesus' mission and identity is most acute.

Jesus bears witness to the truth in what he says, enacting his words of 12:49, "for I have not spoken on my own, but the Father who sent me has himself given me a commandment about what to say and what to speak." As was noted in the discussion of the Jewish religious leaders and Pilate, this witness is also an act of judgment, because it evokes decision from those who hear. The world has to declare itself for or against Jesus, and in declaring itself against Jesus, the world falls under his judgment and the judgment of God (3:36; 5:22, 27-28,

45; 8:21-29, 42-47; 12:31, 48-50; 16:8-11). But Jesus also bears witness to the truth in who he is. As he stands before Pilate and the Jewish authorities, dressed in the raiment of a king, his presence bears witness to the truth of his identity. He is the king, not the kind of claimant to power that Pilate fears, but the good shepherd-king, who is about to lay down his life for those he loves.

From the perspective of the participants in the trial narrative, Jesus plays two roles: the accused, on whom a verdict is to be rendered, and the mocked and humiliated "king," an object of derision and scorn. From the perspective of the Fourth Evangelist, Jesus also plays two roles in the trial narrative: the eschatological judge and the good shepherd-king. In the ironic tension between these two sets of roles lies the theological heart of the trial narrative. At the end of the trial, when Jesus is handed over to be crucified, Pilate and the Jewish religious leaders think that the moment of judgment on Jesus has finally arrived, that his "kingship" has come to an end. Yet it is not the moment of Jesus' judgment, but theirs. Nor is it the end of Jesus' kingship, but the prelude to his exaltation and final "enthronement" on the cross (19:17-22).

The pathos of this trial is lodged in its portrait of Pilate and the Jewish leaders, not of Jesus. The end of this trial is a tragedy for Jesus' antagonists, because they have turned their backs decisively and absolutely on Jesus' gift of eternal life, of his gift of the love of God, but it is not a tragedy for Jesus. As Jesus says at 12:27, "No, it is for this reason that I have come to this hour." The trial before Pilate is a magnificent portrait of the love of God incarnate in Jesus, flinching neither from testifying to the truth nor from laying down his life. The trial, like the crucifixion that immediately follows (19:17-37), does not represent defeat for Jesus, because it belongs to his moment of glorification. The Fourth Evangelist is masterful in crafting the trial narrative so that the theological significance of Jesus and his death is always before the reader. Such an approach does not minimize the "reality" of Jesus' death, but it insists that the fact of Jesus' trial and crucifixion is only part of the story. To understand the death of Jesus, one must recognize that the man who died on that cross was the loving shepherd, the witnessing judge, the incarnate Word who did not hesitate in laying down his life for those he loved.

JOHN 19:16*b*-37, THE CRUCIFIXION

NIV

[16]Finally Pilate handed him over to them to be crucified.

So the soldiers took charge of Jesus. [17]Carrying his own cross, he went out to the place of the Skull (which in Aramaic is called Golgotha). [18]Here they crucified him, and with him two others—one on each side and Jesus in the middle.

[19]Pilate had a notice prepared and fastened to the cross. It read: JESUS OF NAZARETH, THE KING OF THE JEWS. [20]Many of the Jews read this sign, for the place where Jesus was crucified was near the city, and the sign was written in Aramaic, Latin and Greek. [21]The chief priests of the Jews protested to Pilate, "Do not write 'The King of the Jews,'

NRSV

[16]Then he handed him over to them to be crucified.

So they took Jesus; [17]and carrying the cross by himself, he went out to what is called The Place of the Skull, which in Hebrew[a] is called Golgotha. [18]There they crucified him, and with him two others, one on either side, with Jesus between them. [19]Pilate also had an inscription written and put on the cross. It read, "Jesus of Nazareth,[b] the King of the Jews." [20]Many of the Jews read this inscription, because the place where Jesus was crucified was near the city; and it was written in Hebrew,[a] in Latin, and in Greek. [21]Then the chief

[a] That is, *Aramaic*   [b] Gk *the Nazorean*

NIV

but that this man claimed to be king of the Jews."

²²Pilate answered, "What I have written, I have written."

²³When the soldiers crucified Jesus, they took his clothes, dividing them into four shares, one for each of them, with the undergarment remaining. This garment was seamless, woven in one piece from top to bottom.

²⁴"Let's not tear it," they said to one another. "Let's decide by lot who will get it."

This happened that the scripture might be fulfilled which said,

"They divided my garments among them
 and cast lots for my clothing."[a]

So this is what the soldiers did.

²⁵Near the cross of Jesus stood his mother, his mother's sister, Mary the wife of Clopas, and Mary Magdalene. ²⁶When Jesus saw his mother there, and the disciple whom he loved standing nearby, he said to his mother, "Dear woman, here is your son," ²⁷and to the disciple, "Here is your mother." From that time on, this disciple took her into his home.

²⁸Later, knowing that all was now completed, and so that the Scripture would be fulfilled, Jesus said, "I am thirsty." ²⁹A jar of wine vinegar was there, so they soaked a sponge in it, put the sponge on a stalk of the hyssop plant, and lifted it to Jesus' lips. ³⁰When he had received the drink, Jesus said, "It is finished." With that, he bowed his head and gave up his spirit.

³¹Now it was the day of Preparation, and the next day was to be a special Sabbath. Because the Jews did not want the bodies left on the crosses during the Sabbath, they asked Pilate to have the legs broken and the bodies taken down. ³²The soldiers therefore came and broke the legs of the first man who had been crucified with Jesus, and then those of the other. ³³But when they came to Jesus and found that he was already dead, they did not break his legs. ³⁴Instead, one of the soldiers pierced Jesus' side with a spear, bringing a sudden flow of blood and water. ³⁵The man who saw it has given testimony, and his testimony is true. He knows that he tells the truth, and he testifies so that you also may believe. ³⁶These

a24 Psalm 22:18

NRSV

priests of the Jews said to Pilate, "Do not write, 'The King of the Jews,' but, 'This man said, I am King of the Jews.'" ²²Pilate answered, "What I have written I have written." ²³When the soldiers had crucified Jesus, they took his clothes and divided them into four parts, one for each soldier. They also took his tunic; now the tunic was seamless, woven in one piece from the top. ²⁴So they said to one another, "Let us not tear it, but cast lots for it to see who will get it." This was to fulfill what the scripture says,

"They divided my clothes among themselves,
 and for my clothing they cast lots."
²⁵And that is what the soldiers did.

Meanwhile, standing near the cross of Jesus were his mother, and his mother's sister, Mary the wife of Clopas, and Mary Magdalene. ²⁶When Jesus saw his mother and the disciple whom he loved standing beside her, he said to his mother, "Woman, here is your son." ²⁷Then he said to the disciple, "Here is your mother." And from that hour the disciple took her into his own home.

28After this, when Jesus knew that all was now finished, he said (in order to fulfill the scripture), "I am thirsty." ²⁹A jar full of sour wine was standing there. So they put a sponge full of the wine on a branch of hyssop and held it to his mouth. ³⁰When Jesus had received the wine, he said, "It is finished." Then he bowed his head and gave up his spirit.

31Since it was the day of Preparation, the Jews did not want the bodies left on the cross during the sabbath, especially because that sabbath was a day of great solemnity. So they asked Pilate to have the legs of the crucified men broken and the bodies removed. ³²Then the soldiers came and broke the legs of the first and of the other who had been crucified with him. ³³But when they came to Jesus and saw that he was already dead, they did not break his legs. ³⁴Instead, one of the soldiers pierced his side with a spear, and at once blood and water came out. ³⁵(He who saw this has testified so that you also may believe. His testimony is true, and he knows[a] that he tells the truth.) ³⁶These things occurred so that the scripture might be fulfilled, "None of his bones shall be broken." ³⁷And again another passage of scrip-

a Or there is one who knows

NIV	NRSV
things happened so that the scripture would be fulfilled: "Not one of his bones will be broken,"*a* *37*and, as another scripture says, "They will look on the one they have pierced."*b*	ture says, "They will look on the one whom they have pierced."
a36 Exodus 12:46; Num. 9:12; Psalm 34:20 *b37* Zech. 12:10	

COMMENTARY

John 19:16b-37 has much material in common with the other Gospel accounts of Jesus' crucifixion and death, the most important of which include the inscription of the charge against Jesus (Matt 27:27; Mark 15:26; Luke 23:38; John 19:19) and casting lots for Jesus' clothes (Matt 27:35; Mark 15:24; Luke 23:34; John 19:23-25a). Yet the Fourth Evangelist handles these traditions quite differently from the synoptic authors. The events between Jesus' crucifixion and his death are narrated in a different order in John (cf. the narrative location for the casting of lots in each of the Gospels). Details that receive only a passing mention in the other Gospels receive a fuller treatment in John (e.g., the inscription; the lots; and the women at the cross, which John develops into the scene with Jesus' mother and the beloved disciple, vv. 25-27); some aspects of the synoptic accounts—for example, any mocking of Jesus on the cross—are absent. There are also details found in John alone (e.g., the piercing of Jesus' side, vv. 34-35). The similarities and differences support the view that the Fourth Evangelist is drawing on a tradition that at times overlaps with, but is independent from, those on which the synoptic authors draw.

The Johannine account of Jesus' crucifixion and death is arranged to highlight the dignity and self-control of Jesus at his death. None of the more dramatic elements of the crucifixion story in the Synoptics are found in John: the sun does not darken (Matt 27:45; Mark 15:33; Luke 23:44); the curtain of the Temple is not torn in two (Matt 27:51; Mark 15:38; Luke 23:45); there are no earthquakes (Matt 27:51) or opened tombs (Matt 27:52-53). These details contribute to a mood of chaos and confusion, a mood out of keeping with Jesus' dignity at his death. Old Testament citations are given a prominent role (vv. 24, 28, 36, 37)

as one way of underscoring the solemnity of the event. The Fourth Evangelist takes traditional material about Jesus' death and shapes it to fit his understanding of Jesus' death as the hour at which he completes God's work (v. 30).

John 19:16b-37 is narrated as a series of five episodes:[660] (1) vv. 16b-22, the crucifixion of "the King of the Jews"; (2) vv. 23-24, casting lots for Jesus' clothes;[661] (3) vv. 25-27, the beloved disciple and Jesus' mother; (4) vv. 28-30, Jesus' death; (5) vv. 31-37, the piercing of Jesus' side.

19:16b-22. 19:16b-18. The first episode in the crucifixion narrative divides into two parts: (1) the report of the crucifixion of Jesus (vv. 16b-18) and (2) the debate over the inscription on the cross (vv. 19-22). Verse 16b marks the official beginning of the execution, as the Roman soldiers take charge of Jesus (the NIV removes the ambiguity of the pronoun "they" in v. 16b by supplying the noun "soldiers"; cf. 19:18, 23, 25). The place of execution, Golgotha, was located outside the city (note the verb "went out," v. 17a). It may have been called "The Place of the Skull" because of its dome-like shape. Unlike the synoptic Gospels, in which Simon of Cyrene is compelled by the soldiers to carry Jesus' cross (Matt 27:32; Mark 15:21; Luke 23:26), Jesus carries his cross "by himself" (ἑαυτῷ *heautō*). That the criminal carried his own cross to his execution is well-documented in Roman literature and, indeed, was the common practice.[662] If the Fourth Evangelist is drawing on an independent tradition that

660. Brown argues for a chiastic structure to John 19:16b-42, but the correspondences that he notes between scenes seem forced and not at all self-evident in the narrative. See Brown, *The Gospel According to John (XIII–XXI),* 911-12.

661. The verse division of the NIV, in which the episode with the soldiers concludes in v. 24, follows that of the Nestle-Aland[27] text and is to be preferred over that chosen by the NRSV.

662. See the list of references in Bultmann, *The Gospel of John,* 668n. 3.

makes no mention of Simon, he is not altering the synoptic tradition.[663] On one level, then, the reference to Jesus' carrying his own cross simply reflects Roman criminal procedures, but to the reader of the Gospel, this reference carries a deeper significance. Jesus again demonstrates that he is in total command of the events of the hour (10:17-18; 18:5, 8, 20-21; see also 19:28).

As in all of the Gospels, the narration of the actual moment of crucifixion—that is, the moment when Jesus is nailed to the cross—is narrated with extreme brevity and restraint (v. 18; Mark 15:24). None of the gruesome details of this cruel form of death is recounted; the notice that Jesus was crucified is enough. The Fourth Evangelist's account is the leanest of all, giving no description of the two men crucified with Jesus other than to note their presence, a notice required by the tradition. His description of the location of the crosses is vivid in its simplicity; it reads literally, "one there and one there, and Jesus in the middle."

19:19-22. In vv. 19-22, the Fourth Evangelist takes a detail common to all of the Gospel accounts of Jesus' crucifixion, the inscription of the charges against Jesus, and develops it to underscore his interpretation of Jesus' crucifixion as the defining moment in his kingship. The importance of the inscription for the Fourth Evangelist is evidenced in the amount of narrative space given over simply to its description (vv. 19-20). On the legal level, the inscription "Jesus of Nazareth, the King of the Jews" (v. 19), stands as the formal charge against Jesus of political sedition (see also Matt 27:27; Mark 15:26; Luke 23:38). The legal formality is underscored by the Fourth Evangelist's use of the term τίτλος (*titlos*), which is a transliteration into Greek of the official Latin term *titulus* ("inscription," NRSV, or "notice," NIV). Criminals were often required to wear the *titulus* with their charges inscribed on it around their neck on the way to their place of execution.[664]

On the theological level, however, this inscription positions the kingship motifs from the trial before Pilate (18:28–19:16*a*) as the interpretive lens through which to view Jesus' crucifixion. The double meaning of ὑψόω (*hypsoō*), introduced into the Gospel story at 3:14 (see Commentary there), finally comes fully into play; in the "lifting" up of Jesus on the cross, he is "exalted" as king. Verse 20 highlights the public character of Jesus' exaltation as king. First, Jesus is publicly displayed as "king" before "many of the Jews." "Jews" seems to be used in vv. 19-22 in its general sense of "Jewish people," not in its distinctive Johannine sense of "Jewish leaders" (cf. v. 21, "the chief priests of the Jews"). The leadership's attempt to end the public's exposure to Jesus (11:48) has failed. Second, the inscription is written in all three languages current in Judea during Roman rule: Aramaic (the Semitic vernacular), Latin (the official language of the Roman Empire), and Greek (the language of commerce). The inscription that Jesus is the "King of the Jews" is thus a universally comprehensible announcement. In the lifting up of Jesus on the cross, the truth of Jesus' prediction about his death is confirmed: "When I am lifted up from the earth, I will draw all people to myself" (12:32; see also 11:52). On the cross, Jesus is revealed as "the Savior of the world" (4:42).

In vv. 21-22, Pilate exacts his final humiliation of the Jewish leaders. It is a moment of profound irony, because the leaders, who had tried to appease Rome by denouncing Jesus as a political criminal and by renouncing loyalty to any governance but Rome, have won nothing. Jesus will be crucified as their king. Pilate's insistence on the immutability of his inscription is not evidence of his recognition of the legitimacy of Jesus' claims; it is Pilate's assertion of control over his Jewish subjects. Pilate's assertion of control is also ironic, because the trial has shown that his power is false. The pretensions to power of both the Jewish leaders and Pilate are overshadowed by Jesus' enthronement on the cross: "For as the Crucified, Jesus is really the king; the kingly rule, awaited in hope, is not as such destroyed, but established in a new sense; the cross is the exaltation and glorification of Jesus."[665]

19:23-24. It was common practice at a Roman execution for the clothes of the executed criminal to fall to the executioners as spoil. Each of the four Gospels interprets the soldiers' division of

---

663. So, e.g., C. H. Dodd, *Historical Tradition in the Fourth Gospel* (Cambridge: Cambridge University Press, 1963) 124-25. Barrett maintains that John corrects the Markan version. See C. K. Barrett, *The Gospel According to St. John,* 2nd ed. (Philadelphia: Westminster, 1978) 548.
664. See, e.g., Suetonius *Caligula* 32; *Domitian* 10; Cassius *Dio* 54.8.

665. Bultmann, *The Gospel of John,* 669.

Jesus' clothing as a fulfillment of Ps 22:18 (Matt 27:34; Mark 15:24; Luke 23:34; John 19:23-24). The synoptic Gospels use language from Ps 22:18 when they refer to the division of the clothes (e.g., the vocabulary used in Mark 15:24 for "divide" and "cast lots" is the same as that in the LXX of Psalm 22), but John is the only Gospel to provide a narrative illustration of Ps 22:18 and to cite the verse from the LXX in full. The narrative of the soldiers' actions, in which Jesus' clothing is disposed of in two stages, seems to represent a misunderstanding of the function of synonymous parallelism in the psalm. The two halves of Ps 22:18 describe the same action twice, but the Fourth Evangelist's narrative interprets the verse as referring to two distinct acts. This misunderstanding may derive in part from the LXX use of two different nouns for "clothing" in each clause of Ps 22:18 (ἱμάτιον *himation*; ἱματισμός *himatismos*). One finds a similar misunderstanding of Semitic synonymous parallelism at Matt 21:2-9, where Matthew understands Zech 9:9 as referring to two animals, not one.

This episode seems to have no distinctive theological significance for the Fourth Evangelist other than what it had for all of the evangelists: its fulfillment of Scripture (v. 24). Even in something as mundane as the disposition of Jesus' clothes, God's plan for salvation is at work. The fulfillment of Scripture is given prominence in the Johannine crucifixion account (see also vv. 28, 36-37), perhaps to underscore that Jesus' death is not a defeat, but God's victory over the world (cf. 16:33). Many interpreters have attempted to find a distinctive Johannine emphasis in this pericope, but their efforts seem forced. For example, both ancient and modern interpreters have drawn on Josephus's description of the seamless tunic of the high priest to interpret v. 23 as a reference to Jesus the high priest.[666] Yet the noun "tunic" (χιτών *chitōn*) is used exclusively in the NT to refer to a person's inner garment (worn next to the skin; e.g., Mark 6:9; 14:63; Luke 3:11; 6:29; 9:3), and v. 23 suggests nothing more than that common usage. The seamlessness of the garment is mentioned simply to explain why lots had to be cast for it (v. 24a), and thus

fulfill the Evangelist's understanding of Ps 22:18b. Another reading suggests that the seamless garment represents the unity of Christ and believers, but this, too, seems to overstate the case.[667]

19:25-27. The third episode opens with the notice of the women standing near the cross (v. 25). All of the Gospels mention the presence of women at the crucifixion, but in the synoptic Gospels, the women are mentioned after the death of Jesus and are said to stand at a distance (Matt 27:55-56; Mark 15:40-41; Luke 23:49). The syntax of v. 25 is ambiguous, as the differences between the NIV and the NRSV show. The NRSV interprets the verse as referring to three women (Jesus' mother; his mother's sister, Mary the wife of Clopas; and Mary Magdalene), whereas the NIV interprets the verse as referring to four women: an unnamed pair and a named pair. The NIV is to be preferred, because one of the functions of v. 25 seems to be to contrast the four women with the four soldiers of vv. 23-24 (v. 24c and v. 25 are explicitly connected in the Greek text by the use of a μὲν . . . δὲ [*me . . . de*] construction, translated as "meanwhile").[668]

The list of women in John 19:25 differs from the lists in Mark 15:40 and Matt 27:56 (Luke does not name the women); the only name they share in common is Mary Magdalene (for the role of Mary Magdalene at Jesus' hour, see Commentary on 20:1-18). Although attempts have been made to reconcile the Johannine list with the Synoptics, Barrett's comment sounds an important cautionary note, "Identifications are easy to conjure but impossible to ascertain."[669] The diversity of the lists suggests the richness of the tradition about the faithful women who attended Jesus at his death.

"The disciple whom he loved" is introduced abruptly in v. 26. On a surface level, it is possible

666. Josephus *Antiquities of the Jews* 3.161. Among modern interpreters, see especially Brown, *The Gospel According to John (XIII–XXI)*, 912, 920-21.

667. Among modern interpreters, see E. C. Hoskyns, *The Fourth Gospel* (London: Faber & Faber, 1947) 529; Barrett, *The Gospel According to St. John*, 550. The most influential ancient statement of this view is Cyprian *On the Unity of the Church* 7.

668. See especially Rudolf Schnackenburg, *The Gospel According to St. John*, 3 vols. (New York: Seabury, 1982) 3:273, 276.

669. Barrett, *The Gospel According to St. John*, 551. See, e.g., the attempts in Brown, *The Gospel According to John (XIII–XXI)*, 904-6; and *The Death of the Messiah*, vol. 2. Such attempts must always remain inconclusive, a bit arbitrary, and, indeed, unnecessary, because the Synoptic lists do not present themselves as either exhaustive or definitive (note that Mark and Matthew preface the list of names with the words "among them").

to read vv. 26-27 as a scene of filial devotion; at the moment of death, Jesus attends to the care of his mother. Yet the very formality of the scene and the symmetry of Jesus' words to his mother and the beloved disciple suggest that the scene has a deeper meaning for the Evangelist. The symbolic and theological significance of vv. 26-27 is a topic of much debate among Johannine interpreters, and much of the debate seems to divide along Catholic and Protestant lines. Catholic interpreters tend to emphasize the role of Jesus' mother in this scene, seeing her as symbolic of the Mother of the Church, the New Eve, or the New Israel.[670] Protestant interpreters tend to put the emphasis on the role of the beloved disciple as a symbol of the church and faithful discipleship.[671]

It is important to interpret vv. 26-27 in the light of the roles of Jesus' mother and the beloved disciple within the Fourth Gospel narrative and not through the lens of later mariological and ecclesial teachings. The only other appearance of Jesus' mother in the Fourth Gospel is at the wedding in Cana (2:1-11), the beginning of Jesus' ministry. Jesus' address of his mother as "Woman" in both scenes suggests that the reader is to connect 2:1-11 and 19:26-27. The "disciple whom Jesus loves" was last mentioned at 13:25, inquiring about the identity of the betrayer; he will appear again as a witness to the empty tomb (20:1-10; see also 19:35; 21:20-23). It, therefore, is possible to interpret Jesus' mother as representing the sweep of Jesus' incarnate ministry from beginning to end, and the beloved disciple as representing those for whom Jesus gives his life in love at his hour and who are commanded to love in the same way. When Jesus entrusts his mother and the beloved disciple to each other, then, the Fourth Evangelist points to Jesus' death as the link between the past of Jesus' ministry (represented by Jesus' mother) and the movement of that ministry into the future (represented by the beloved disciple).

John 19:26-27 also symbolizes the beginning of the creation of the new family of God. At 1:12-13, believers were promised a future as "children of God," and in response to Jesus' words, the beloved disciple takes Jesus' mother "to his own home" ($\epsilon i \varsigma$ $\tau \grave{\alpha}$ $i \delta \iota \alpha$ *eis ta idia*; cf. 1:11; 16:32). The beloved disciple's action is located explicitly at "that hour," suggesting that the events of Jesus' hour—his death, resurrection, and ascension— make this new family a reality (see also 20:17).

19:28-30. These verses narrate Jesus' death. His knowledge "that all is now finished" (v. 28) links Jesus' death with the beginning of his hour, when Jesus' knowledge of the arrival of his hour (13:1) and its significance (13:3) was also explicitly noted. The verb "to finish" ($\tau \epsilon \lambda \acute{\epsilon} \omega$ *teleō*) occurs only at 19:28 and 30, but it is synonymous with the verb "to complete" ($\tau \epsilon \lambda \epsilon \iota \acute{o} \omega$ *teleioō*), which is used to describe Jesus' mission: to complete God's work (4:34; 5:36; 17:4). As it has throughout the Gospel, the term "all" ($\pi \acute{\alpha} \nu \tau \alpha$ *panta*) refers to everything that God has given Jesus (cf. 3:35; 5:20; 13:3; 15:15; 17:7). Jesus is thus depicted as facing the moment of death with the knowledge that he has completed the work God has given him.

The scripture to which v. 28*b* refers seems to be Ps 69:22, which in the LXX contains the same words for "sour wine" ($\breve{o} \xi o \varsigma$ *oxos*) and "thirst" ($\delta \iota \psi \acute{\alpha} \omega$ *dipsaō*) as are used here. All of the Gospels interpret the offer of sour wine to Jesus on the cross through the lens of this psalm (see also Matt 27:48; Mark 15:36; Luke 23:36), but the Johannine treatment is distinctive. First, as in the treatment of Ps 22:18 in John 19:23-24, John provides a fuller narrative illustration of the psalm and is alone in referring explicitly to its fulfillment. Second, in the synoptic Gospels, someone in the crowd takes the initiative to offer Jesus a drink, but in John, Jesus takes the initiative with his words, "I am thirsty." Third, in the Synoptics, the offer of vinegar is a mocking gesture, but there is no mockery in John. Jesus remains a figure of dignity.

On the most mundane level, Jesus' thirst acknowledges the pain that accompanies his death by crucifixion. On a deeper level, his words recall his question to Peter at the arrest, "Am I not to drink the cup that the Father has given me?" (18:11).[672] Jesus' thirst thus symbolizes his willingness to embrace his death, and the offer of sour wine takes on an ironic note as one more example of the world's misunderstanding of him.

670. E.g., Raymond E. Brown, *The Gospel According to John (XIII–XXI)*, AB 29A (Garden City, N.Y.: Doubleday, 1970) 913, 924-26.

671. E.g., Beasley-Murray, *John*, 349-50; Barrett, *The Gospel According to St. John*, 552.

672. Schnackenburg, *The Gospel According to St. John*, 3:283; Brown, *The Gospel According to John (XIII–XXI)*, 930.

Jesus thirsts for God's cup and is offered sour wine. There also may be a related ironic contrast between the "good wine" at Cana through which Jesus revealed his glory (2:9, 11) and the "sour wine" that he receives at his glorification. The world falsely attempts to assuage the thirst of the One who is himself the source of "living water" (4:10, 13-14; 7:37-38). Interpretations that associate offering vinegar on a branch of hyssop to Jesus with the sprinkling of the blood of the Passover lamb on lintels and doorposts with a bunch of hyssop (Exod. 12:22) stretch the textual evidence, however.[673]

With the final fulfillment of Scripture accomplished in the offer of sour wine, Jesus himself announces what the narrator signaled in v. 28: "It is finished" (v. 30*a*). Jesus' death is not a moment of defeat or despair (cf. the last words of Jesus on the cross at Matt 27:46; Mark 15:34), but a moment of confidence in his completion of God's work in the world (17:4). Jesus' death on the cross is the final expression of his love for his own (cf. 13:1; 15:13) and his love for God (14:30-31). Jesus' death itself is narrated with dignity and restraint. The poignancy of the moment is conveyed by the simple notation that "he bowed his head."

Verse 30*c* literally reads, "he handed over [παρέδωκεν *paredōken*] his spirit." As in Matt 27:50, "spirit" (πνεῦμα *pneuma*) is used here as a synonym for "life." On the basis of 7:39, some commentators read v. 30*c* as a description of Jesus' gift of the Spirit to the believers who stand near the cross.[674] But according to 7:39, the gift of the Spirit comes after Jesus' glorification, which includes his resurrection and ascension. Moreover, Jesus' gift of the Holy Spirit is fully and explicitly narrated at 20:22. The theological significance of v. 30*c* does not lie in the noun "spirit," but in the verb "hand over." In the trial narrative, both the Jewish leaders and Pilate "handed over" Jesus to be crucified (18:30, 35-36; 19:11, 16, 30; cf. also the references to Judas at 13:2, 11, 21), thinking themselves the agents of Jesus' death, but in the end, Jesus hands himself over. The truth of Jesus' words in 10:18,

"No one takes it from me, but I lay it down of my own accord," is confirmed.

19:31-37. The Fourth Evangelist now provides his final interpretation of Jesus' death on a cross. The events narrated in these verses have no parallels in the synoptic Gospels. This passage is quite straightforward in its narration of the disposition of the bodies on the crosses in vv. 31-33. The "Jews'" desire to remove the bodies from the crosses before the sabbath (v. 31*a*) reflects the legislation in Deut 21:22-23, that the bodies of hanged criminals should be removed from the scaffolding by nightfall (cf. Josh 8:29). The "day of preparation" does not have particular reference to Passover preparation here, but refers in general to the sabbath vigil (sundown Thursday to sundown Friday). The reference to the "special Sabbath" (NIV)—i.e., that this sabbath is also the Passover (cf. NRSV)—underscores the importance and urgency of the request for "the Jews."

The reference to Pilate in this scene and the burial scene that follows (vv. 38-42) is a reminder that the crucifixion lay within the jurisdiction of the Roman courts. There is an ironic symmetry between v. 31 and 18:28, the introduction to the trial narrative. Jesus' death is framed by the Jewish leaders' preoccupation with religious ritual and propriety and their dependence on Roman rule to practice their own customs.

The request that the legs of the crucified men be broken and the soldiers' subsequent actions (vv. 32-33) depict a common practice at crucifixions. Death by crucifixion could last for days, and the criminals' legs often were broken as a way of hastening death. That Jesus' legs were not broken, reported in v. 33 in straight narration, will be given theological significance in v. 36. The motivation for the soldier's piercing of Jesus' side (v. 34) is not important to the Evangelist; the significance of the piercing lies in the result, "and at once blood and water came out." The commentary that follows in v. 35 about the reliability of the eyewitness to this event underscores its importance, as does the Scripture quotation in v. 37.

19:34-35. The emphasis on the eyewitness and his truthfulness in v. 35 confirm that the reader is to understand the flow of blood and water from Jesus' side as something that actually happened. Although the eyewitness is not explicitly identified in v. 35, it is almost unanimously

---

673. Scholars who advocate the Passover symbolism here include Barrett, *The Gospel According to St. John,* 553; and Brown, *The Gospel According to John (XIII–XXI),* 930. Scholars who reject this symbolism include Dodd, *Historical Tradition in the Fourth Gospel,* 123n. 2; Schnackenburg, *The Gospel According to St. John,* 3:284; Bultmann, *John,* 674.

674. So Barrett, *The Gospel According to St. John,* 554; Hoskyns, *John,* 532. See also Brown, *The Gospel According to John (XIII–XXI),* 931.

assumed by Fourth Gospel scholars that he is the "disciple whom Jesus loved." This disciple was explicitly positioned at the foot of the cross (vv. 26-27), and the reliability of his testimony will be evoked again in similar language at 21:25. Verse 35 refers to the eyewitness in third-person language and thus seems to distinguish between the beloved disciple as the source of information about this incident and the author of the Gospel account (see Introduction). Several scholars see v. 35 as a later addition to the Fourth Gospel, added to enhance the authority of the beloved disciple, but nothing in the text supports or necessitates positing an author other than the Evangelist.[675]

It is physiologically possible that blood and a clear liquid that might be described as water could flow from a chest wound immediately after death. Yet it is clear from the stated purpose of the eyewitness's testimony ("that you also may believe," v. 35) that more than a report of medical data is at stake here. By drawing attention to this flow of blood and water, the Fourth Evangelist seems first and foremost to be confirming the reality of Jesus' death. First John 5:6-8 draws on this language of blood and water in the service of its anti-docetic polemic in a way consistent with 19:34, but the theological intent of 19:34 extends beyond an anti-docetic apologetic. The Word became flesh (1:14), and at this moment, with blood and water flowing from Jesus' dead body, the fleshliness of the Word receives its most vivid and poignant demonstration.

The attention that the Fourth Evangelist gives to the flow of blood and water suggests that he also attached symbolic significance to it. Jesus is the source of "living water" in the Gospel (4:10, 12-14; 7:37-38). In the eucharistic imagery of 6:53-58, his blood, too, is identified with his gift of life (6:53-55). It is thus possible to read a second level of meaning into v. 34: that life flows out of Jesus' death.[676] Patristic and medieval exegetes read 19:34 as symbolizing the foundation of the sacraments of eucharist ("blood") and baptism ("water"). Although, as already noted, echoes of John 6 can be heard here, the Evan-

gelist's emphasis seems less on the sacraments per se and more on Jesus' death as a source of life.

19:36-37. In these verses, the Fourth Evangelist appends scriptural commentary on the preceding scene. The quotation in v. 36 does not occur in that precise form anywhere in the OT. The Fourth Evangelist may be referring to Exod 12:10 (LXX) or 12:46, verses that proscribe the breaking of the bones of the Passover lamb.[677] If this is the text the Fourth Evangelist has in mind, then he is setting up a correspondence between the death of Jesus and the slaughter of the Passover lamb. There is, however, another OT text that is closer in wording to v. 36 than the Passover texts: Ps 34:20 (33:21 LXX), "[The Lord] keeps all their bones;/ not one of them will be broken" (NRSV). The Fourth Evangelist has already employed two psalms in his presentation of Jesus' death (Pss 22:18; 69:10), and a strong case can be made that he employs a third one here.[678] Psalm 34 is a hymn of thanksgiving and praise for deliverance, and v. 20 praises God's protection of the righteous ones. In interpreting Jesus' death as a fulfillment of this Scripture, the Fourth Evangelist focuses attention on God's victory in Jesus and thus highlights God's sovereignty even in Jesus' death.

The OT citation in v. 37 confirms this reading. The text cited there is Zech 12:10, although in a version that differs slightly from both the LXX and the MT. Like the psalter, Zechariah 9–14 was an important theological resource in the early church's interpretation of Jesus' death (e.g., the use of Zech 9:9 at Matt 21:5; Mark 11:12; John 12:15; the use of Zech 13:7 at Matt 26:31; Mark 14:27; John 16:32). Zechariah 12:10-14 portrays Jerusalem's lament over the death of the king it has martyred. Zechariah 12:10 is a text both of mourning and of hope, for in the midst of death, God pours out "a spirit of compassion and supplication on the house of David and the inhabitants of Jerusalem, so that, when they look on the one whom they have pierced, they shall mourn for him, as one mourns for an only child, and weep bitterly over him, as one weeps for a firstborn" (NRSV). The Fourth Evangelist's citation of this

675. E.g., Schnackenburg, *The Gospel According to St. John,* 3:287, 291. Bultmann, *John,* attributed both vv. 34*b* and 35 to the ecclesiastical redactor, because he understood v. 34*b* as depicting the symbolic foundation of the sacraments of eucharist and baptism.

676. Barrett, *The Gospel According to St. John,* 558; Brown, *The Gospel According to John (XIII–XXI),* 949-50.

677. So Brown, *The Gospel According to John (XIII–XXI),* 952-53; Barrett, *The Gospel According to St. John,* 553, 558; Hoskyns, *John,* 533. These commentators also link this verse with John the Baptist's announcement at 1:29 ("Here is the lamb of God that takes away the sin of the world"), even though the Passover lamb did not have expiatory significance in Judaism. See Commentary on 1:29 and Reflections below.

678. See especially Dodd, *Historical Tradition in the Fourth Gospel,* 42-44, 131-37.

passage may be intended as a final judgment on "the Jews," who, in looking at Jesus on the cross, the executed king, still do not see the revelation of God (cf. 8:28). The full context of Zech 12:10 suggests, however, that it is cited as a word of hope for the reader, as confirmation that even in death, when one looks on the One who is pierced, one sees God's only child, the firstborn (cf. 1:18). (See Reflections at 19:38-42.)

JOHN 19:38-42, THE BURIAL

NIV

38Later, Joseph of Arimathea asked Pilate for the body of Jesus. Now Joseph was a disciple of Jesus, but secretly because he feared the Jews. With Pilate's permission, he came and took the body away. 39He was accompanied by Nicodemus, the man who earlier had visited Jesus at night. Nicodemus brought a mixture of myrrh and aloes, about seventy-five pounds.[a] 40Taking Jesus' body, the two of them wrapped it, with the spices, in strips of linen. This was in accordance with Jewish burial customs. 41At the place where Jesus was crucified, there was a garden, and in the garden a new tomb, in which no one had ever been laid. 42Because it was the Jewish day of Preparation and since the tomb was nearby, they laid Jesus there.

[a]39 Greek *a hundred litrai* (about 34 kilograms)

NRSV

38After these things, Joseph of Arimathea, who was a disciple of Jesus, though a secret one because of his fear of the Jews, asked Pilate to let him take away the body of Jesus. Pilate gave him permission; so he came and removed his body. 39Nicodemus, who had at first come to Jesus by night, also came, bringing a mixture of myrrh and aloes, weighing about a hundred pounds. 40They took the body of Jesus and wrapped it with the spices in linen cloths, according to the burial custom of the Jews. 41Now there was a garden in the place where he was crucified, and in the garden there was a new tomb in which no one had ever been laid. 42And so, because it was the Jewish day of Preparation, and the tomb was nearby, they laid Jesus there.

COMMENTARY

The Johannine account of Jesus' burial has two emphases: (1) the men who prepare Jesus' body for burial (vv. 38-39*a*) and (2) the elegance and dignity of the preparation and burial (vv. 39*b*-42). Each of the Gospels names Joseph of Arimathea as the person who buries Jesus (see Matt 27:57; Mark 15:43; Luke 23:50-52). Luke and Mark identify Joseph as a member of the Sanhedrin, Matthew as a disciple of Jesus. In identifying Joseph as a secret disciple of Jesus, the Fourth Evangelist links him with the Jewish authorities of 12:24-43 who, because of a fear of losing their political power and position within the synagogue, will not confess their faith in Jesus. At Jesus' death, however, Joseph is willing to make his faith public, even going to the Roman authorities to request Jesus' body for burial (cf. Mark 15:43-45 and par.). The language used to describe Joseph echoes the conflicts between the Jewish religious authorities and the audience for whom the Evangelist writes (cf. 9:22; 16:2) and suggests that the Fourth Evangelist intends his readers to see Joseph's boldness and reverence for Jesus as a model for their own discipleship.

The introduction of Nicodemus in v. 39 confirms that the Fourth Evangelist sees the willingness to bury Jesus as evidence of one's willingness to give public expression to one's faith. The cross-reference to Nicodemus's initial night visit (3:1-21) leaves no doubt that the reader is intended to carry the whole story of Nicodemus forward into this burial scene. In his two previous appearances (see 3:1-21; 7:50-52), Nicodemus is an ambiguous figure, showing interest in Jesus, but never confessing his faith. At Jesus' death, Nicodemus, like Joseph, abandons neutrality and secrecy and acts out his love and reverence for Jesus (cf. 12:1-8). The actions of these two men demonstrate the truth of Jesus' three predictions about the salvific effect of his crucifixion (3:14-15; 8:28; 12:32): his "lifting up" is a decisive moment of judgment through which Joseph and Nicodemus come to "realize that I AM."

The prodigious amount of burial spices (v. 39*b*, "one hundred" [λίτρας *litras*] are the equivalent of seventy-five pounds, so the NIV) recalls the excessive quantity of perfume at 12:3. Here, as in Mary's anointing, the excess symbolizes the love the two men have for Jesus. In coming forward to bury Jesus, Joseph and Nicodemus, like Mary, show themselves to be Jesus' disciples, those who love Jesus and live out that love (13:35). This love is further enacted in the care and dignity with which Jesus' body is prepared for burial (v. 40). Not only are the requirements of a proper Jewish burial adhered to, but also the combination of spices and linen burial clothes is normally accorded only to people of wealth or prominence (cf. the elegance of the Johannine description with Mark 15:46). The pristine condition of the garden tomb also underscores the dignity of this burial (v. 41).

The explanation for the use of this pristine tomb echoes the motivation for "the Jews' " request in v. 31. The contrast between the two verses is quite pointed, however. In 19:31, the impending sabbath provides the motivation to mutilate the bodies and further hasten the deaths of the executed men, whereas in 19:42 it is the motivation for an act of reverence and love. Details about the closing of the tomb (e.g., Matt 27:60-61; Mark 15:46-47) are not important to the Fourth Evangelist, because as it has been throughout the Gospel, the focus is on Jesus. The note that "they laid Jesus there" (v. 42) thus gives finality to the burial.

REFLECTIONS

The Commentary on John 19:16*b*-42 noted the ways in which the Fourth Evangelist narrates Jesus' death with dignity, respect, and solemnity. There is none of the turmoil of the Synoptic accounts—no jeering crowds, no loud cry when Jesus dies (see Commentary above). The Fourth Evangelist provides no narrative details that will distract from the essential focus of the crucifixion story: Jesus' serene and controlled gift of his life in love.[679] The dignity and serenity of Jesus' death in John does not minimize the "reality" of that death, however. To the contrary, on many occasions, this dignity adds to the poignancy of Jesus' death—the simple statement "I am thirsty" (v. 28), the restrained note that Jesus bowed his head (v. 30), the care with which Joseph and Nicodemus attend to Jesus' dead body (vv. 39-42). The Fourth Evangelist never lets the reader forget that the crucifixion narrative is at its core the story of the end of a human life.

In the same way, the Fourth Evangelist never lets the reader forget that the crucifixion narrative also marks the completion of Jesus' work of making God known to the world. The explicit references to the fulfillment of Scripture, the highest concentration of fulfillment formulas anywhere in the Fourth Gospel, repeatedly reinforce that the drama being acted out in Jesus' death belongs to God's plan and work of salvation. Jesus' death does not abrogate God's offer of life and love; rather, it brings that offer to fruition.

The key to the dignity and serenity that surround Jesus' death in John are the words "It is finished" (v. 30). Jesus dies with a public proclamation of the completion of his mission on his lips. The words he speaks on the cross in Mark 15:34 (and Matt 27:46), "My God, my God, why have you forsaken me?" are a theological impossibility for the Johannine Jesus. God and Jesus are united in work and in love, and that unity is strengthened, not broken, at Jesus' death. Jesus' death fills him neither with despair nor a sense of abandonment by God, because he knows that he has lived fully the life and mission God gave him to live. He revealed the truth of God to an often hostile world, knowing from the very beginning of his ministry that such words and works could cost him his life (2:19-21; 5:18; 7:30; 8:37, 59; 10:31; 11:8), but also knowing that his life and work on earth were for the glorification of God (17:4).

In Jesus' death, then, the reader is confronted one last time with both the wonder and

679. See George W. MacRae, *Invitation to John* (Garden City, N.Y.: Doubleday, 1978) 213-14.

the poignancy of the incarnation. Jesus is the Son of God, the one sent by God into the world to save the world by revealing God's love. And Jesus is also the man who will die on a cross, bleeding from his pierced side, wrapped in linen cloths and laid to rest in a garden tomb. Because Jesus is human, because he can and will die, he can reveal the fullness of God's love in ways never before possible, because he reveals God's love in categories that derive from human experience. In his death, Jesus gave up what human beings hold most dear—life—and he gave it up because he chose to do so in love. Jesus lays down his life in love for those whom he loves, and the meaning of both "life" and "love" are redefined. Life becomes an expression of love, the ultimate gift. Love, love unto death, becomes the only true source of life. Jesus' gift of his life on the cross is the ultimate gesture of generosity and grace. It is, indeed, pure gift—not required of him, but offered by him, so that we may understand the full extent of God's love for the world.

When scholars interpret John's portrayal of Jesus' death through the lens of the slaughter of the Passover lamb (see Commentary on 19:36), and thus point to the sacrificial nature of his death and the cleansing power of his blood, they overlook the pivotal role of love in Jesus' death and misread the Passover lamb. The Passover lamb is not an expiatory sacrifice, but is a symbolic reenactment of "the passover of the LORD" (Exod 12:11 NRSV). The blood on the doorposts marked the inhabitants who lived within as God's protected ones. The lamb's blood thus serves as a sign that one belongs to God, not an act of expiation or atonement. If there is any link between Jesus' death and the slaughter of the Passover lamb, it is not in terms of Jesus' death as an expiatory sacrifice, but as the new sign of what it means to be marked as God's people. To share in Jesus' death, to love as Jesus loves, is the new sign of "the passover of the Lord," of a new exodus to freedom and life (cf. 8:31).

It is to this powerful and poignant gift of his life in love that Jesus asks his followers to conform their lives (cf. 13:34-35; 15:12-17). The crucifixion and the love commandment go hand in hand, because it is impossible to understand what Jesus' love is if it is separated from his death on the cross. The resurrection stories will affirm the transformative power of this love to reshape the world, but it is to the crucifixion that one must look to understand Jesus' love, and hence to understand who Jesus and God are. In the poignancy of Jesus' death on the cross, he lives out the life for which he was born and into which he was sent by bearing his ultimate witness to the truth (cf. 12:27; 18:37). And the truth is this: Jesus will give what is most precious, to us and to God.

The crucifixion stands as a reminder that the love of God is neither "soft" nor simply affective. Love is not simply an emotion, but it defines the very essence of character and identity. To say that God is love (e.g., 17:26; 1 John 4:7-8, 16), to say that Jesus is love (e.g., 13:34; 14:21; 15:9) is to say that they love without limits, that they love "to the end" (13:1). They also love freely. If Jesus' followers are to love one another as "I have loved you," then they must love one another with a love that derives from and is shaped by Jesus' gift of his life on the cross. This is no easy task or goal. If the fullness of God is revealed in the incarnation (cf. 14:6) and the crucifixion brings the work of the incarnation to fulfillment, then for Jesus' followers to love as he loves means to embrace the cross as the ultimate measure of fidelity to God—to give without counting, to love without restraint. When the author of 1 John writes, "There is no fear in love, but perfect love casts out fear" (4:18 NRSV), it is to the love of Jesus on the cross that he refers. If we love enough to know that we will give our life, our all, to those we love, what is there to fear? To live in, and out of, such love is to live fully in the presence of God.

How is the ordinary believer to live in the face of such a commandment, in the face of such a model of what it means to love? There is no simple or easy answer, but there is the story of Jesus' own life and death to which the believer and the believing community can and must always return. In this story of Jesus' love, one can catch glimmers of what it means to be a community of love, to see and know God fully in the midst of life and death. In the cross, we come to understand what the Evangelist celebrates when he says, "From his fullness we have all received, grace upon grace" (1:16).

THE FIRST RESURRECTION APPEARANCES

OVERVIEW

First Cor 15:4-5 provides a synopsis of the Easter preaching of the early church: "he was raised . . . and "he appeared." These two kernels of tradition are given narrative form in the empty tomb and resurrection appearance stories of the Gospels. Each of the Gospels begins at a similar place with its resurrection accounts—the early Sunday morning visit to Jesus' tomb, the presence of Mary Magdalene, the stone removed from the tomb opening, the appearance of an angel (or angels)—but after this visit, each Gospel goes its own way in recounting resurrection traditions.[680] Mark narrates only the empty tomb tradition (16:1-8 resurrection appearances were appended in the additions of Mark 16:9-20); Matthew, Luke, and John recount their own appearance stories. Moreover, the sequence of resurrection appearances noted in 1 Cor 15:5-8 does not correspond to any of the Gospel accounts of Jesus' resurrection appearances. Attempts to isolate and reconstruct "authentic" sources of the resurrection stories, therefore, may distort the

early church's own approach to this material. The remarkable variation among the Gospels suggests that the early church had a rich tradition of resurrection stories and that the evangelists employed narrative and theological freedom in incorporating these traditions into their Gospels.

The resurrection stories in John occur in two narrative clusters: chaps. 20 and 21. (For a discussion of the critical questions surrounding John 21 and its relationship to the rest of the Fourth Gospel narrative, see the Overview to that chap.) John 20 contains three stories that are narrated in a precise chronological sequence:

vv. 1-18 Sunday morning: The empty tomb and Jesus' appearance to Mary Magdalene

vv. 19-23 Sunday evening: Jesus' appearance to the gathered disciples (without Thomas)

vv. 24-31 One week later: Jesus' appearance to Thomas and the gathered disciples

680. C. H. Dodd, *Historical Tradition in the Fourth Gospel* (Cambridge: Cambridge University Press, 1963) 140-42.

JOHN 20:1-18, THE EMPTY TOMB AND THE APPEARANCE TO MARY MAGDALENE

NIV

20 Early on the first day of the week, while it was still dark, Mary Magdalene went to the tomb and saw that the stone had been removed from the entrance. ²So she came running to Simon Peter and the other disciple, the one

NRSV

20 Early on the first day of the week, while it was still dark, Mary Magdalene came to the tomb and saw that the stone had been removed from the tomb. ²So she ran and went to Simon Peter and the other disciple, the one whom

NIV

Jesus loved, and said, "They have taken the Lord out of the tomb, and we don't know where they have put him!"

³So Peter and the other disciple started for the tomb. ⁴Both were running, but the other disciple outran Peter and reached the tomb first. ⁵He bent over and looked in at the strips of linen lying there but did not go in. ⁶Then Simon Peter, who was behind him, arrived and went into the tomb. He saw the strips of linen lying there, ⁷as well as the burial cloth that had been around Jesus' head. The cloth was folded up by itself, separate from the linen. ⁸Finally the other disciple, who had reached the tomb first, also went inside. He saw and believed. ⁹(They still did not understand from Scripture that Jesus had to rise from the dead.)

¹⁰Then the disciples went back to their homes, ¹¹but Mary stood outside the tomb crying. As she wept, she bent over to look into the tomb ¹²and saw two angels in white, seated where Jesus' body had been, one at the head and the other at the foot.

¹³They asked her, "Woman, why are you crying?"

"They have taken my Lord away," she said, "and I don't know where they have put him." ¹⁴At this, she turned around and saw Jesus standing there, but she did not realize that it was Jesus.

¹⁵"Woman," he said, "why are you crying? Who is it you are looking for?"

Thinking he was the gardener, she said, "Sir, if you have carried him away, tell me where you have put him, and I will get him."

¹⁶Jesus said to her, "Mary."

She turned toward him and cried out in Aramaic, "Rabboni!" (which means Teacher).

¹⁷Jesus said, "Do not hold on to me, for I have not yet returned to the Father. Go instead to my brothers and tell them, 'I am returning to my Father and your Father, to my God and your God.'"

¹⁸Mary Magdalene went to the disciples with the news: "I have seen the Lord!" And she told them that he had said these things to her.

NRSV

Jesus loved, and said to them, "They have taken the Lord out of the tomb, and we do not know where they have laid him." ³Then Peter and the other disciple set out and went toward the tomb. ⁴The two were running together, but the other disciple outran Peter and reached the tomb first. ⁵He bent down to look in and saw the linen wrappings lying there, but he did not go in. ⁶Then Simon Peter came, following him, and went into the tomb. He saw the linen wrappings lying there, ⁷and the cloth that had been on Jesus' head, not lying with the linen wrappings but rolled up in a place by itself. ⁸Then the other disciple, who reached the tomb first, also went in, and he saw and believed; ⁹for as yet they did not understand the scripture, that he must rise from the dead. ¹⁰Then the disciples returned to their homes.

11But Mary stood weeping outside the tomb. As she wept, she bent over to look*a* into the tomb; ¹²and she saw two angels in white, sitting where the body of Jesus had been lying, one at the head and the other at the feet. ¹³They said to her, "Woman, why are you weeping?" She said to them, "They have taken away my Lord, and I do not know where they have laid him." ¹⁴When she had said this, she turned around and saw Jesus standing there, but she did not know that it was Jesus. ¹⁵Jesus said to her, "Woman, why are you weeping? Whom are you looking for?" Supposing him to be the gardener, she said to him, "Sir, if you have carried him away, tell me where you have laid him, and I will take him away." ¹⁶Jesus said to her, "Mary!" She turned and said to him in Hebrew,*b* "Rabbouni!" (which means Teacher). ¹⁷Jesus said to her, "Do not hold on to me, because I have not yet ascended to the Father. But go to my brothers and say to them, 'I am ascending to my Father and your Father, to my God and your God.'" ¹⁸Mary Magdalene went and announced to the disciples, "I have seen the Lord"; and she told them that he had said these things to her.

a Gk lacks *to look*   *b* That is, *Aramaic*

COMMENTARY

John 20:1-18 consists of three parts: (1) vv. 1-2, introduction; (2) vv. 3-10, the empty tomb; (3) vv. 11-18, Jesus' appearance to Mary Magdalene.

20:1-2. As in the other Gospels, the first visit to Jesus' tomb occurs "early on the first day of the week, while it was still dark"—that is, on Sunday morning (Mark 16:2 and par.; the first day of the week was sundown Saturday to sundown Sunday). Mary Magdalene is accompanied by other women in the synoptic Gospels (Matt 28:1; Mark 16:1; Luke 24:10), but in John she comes to the tomb alone (v. 1). In addition to her role in the passion and Easter narratives (see Matt 27:56, 61; Mark 15:40, 47; John 19:25; cf. Luke 23:49), Mary Magdalene appears in Luke 8:2, where she is identified as a Galilean woman from whom Jesus had exorcised seven demons. It is important to distinguish the Gospel portrait of Mary Magdalene from the traditions that developed about her in the patristic and medieval periods.[681] There is no biblical foundation for the popular portrait of her as a "sinful" woman or prostitute. Instead, as v. 18 will show, Mary Magdalene is the first disciple to proclaim the good news of Easter.

Mary interprets the removal of the stone from the tomb as evidence that someone has stolen Jesus' body (v. 2; cf. Matt 27:63-66; 28:11-14). Her haste in running to Peter and the beloved disciple communicates her sense of urgency and anticipates their similar haste and urgency in running back to the tomb (v. 4). The first-person plural pronoun ("we") in her report suggests that Mary understands herself to be expressing the puzzle of the empty tomb for all of Jesus' followers, not for herself alone (cf. v. 13).[682] In confessing her ignorance of Jesus' whereabouts ("we do not know where they have laid him"), Mary ironically echoes one of the decisive misunderstandings of Jesus' ministry: whence Jesus comes and where he is going (e.g., 7:33-36; 8:21-23).[683]

20:3-10. Mary's report of the empty tomb provides the catalyst for the second scene; her own story will resume in vv. 11-18. John 20:3-10 is the second pairing of Peter and the beloved disciple in the Gospel (cf. 13:21-30; see also John 21). Peter has functioned as the representative of Jesus' disciples throughout the Gospel; the full range of discipleship has been embodied by Peter: confession of faith (6:67-69), misunderstanding and misplaced enthusiasm (13:6-10, 36-38; 18:10-11), denial (18:15-18, 25-27). The disciple "whom Jesus loved" is singularly identified with the events of Jesus' hour (see also 13:21-30; 19:26-27, 35). He is always identified by his relationship to Jesus and never by his name. Peter has many roles in the Fourth Gospel, but the beloved disciple has only one role: to embody the love and intimacy with Jesus that is the goal of discipleship in John.

The details about these two disciples' running to the tomb give a vividness to the narrative (v. 4). There is something almost droll about the interactions of the two disciples outside the tomb. The beloved disciple hesitates to enter the tomb (v. 5), but Peter, whose actions in the Fourth Gospel are consistently characterized by an excess of enthusiasm (13:9; 18:10; 21:7), does not hesitate (v. 6a). The history of interpretation of these verses is intrigued by these details. For example, some commentators interpret the notation that the beloved disciple outran Peter to the tomb as evidence that the beloved disciple was younger than Peter.[684] Bultmann suggested that Peter represented Jewish Christianity and the beloved disciple Gentile Christianity, so that in these verses, one sees that "the first community of believers arises out of Jewish Christianity, and the Gentile Christians attain to faith only after them."[685] Still other scholars construct elaborate theories about vv. 4-6 as a narrative depiction of the ecclesial rivalry between Petrine and Johannine Christianity.[686] Most of these theories lead away from the Fourth Evangelist's focus on the significance of the empty tomb.

681. See Susan Haskins, *Mary Magdalen: Myth and Metaphor* (New York: Harcourt Brace, 1994) for a thorough treatment of this question.

682. It is not necessary to postulate that the first-person plural pronoun arises from the Fourth Evangelist's slavish adherence to an earlier tradition in which Mary had companions at the tomb. So, e.g., Raymond E. Brown, *The Gospel According to John (XIII–XXI)*, AB 29A (Garden City, N.Y.: Doubleday, 1970) 984, 1000.

683. Paul Minear, " 'We Do Not Know Where . . . ' John 20:2," *Int.* 30 (1976) 125-39.

684. See, e.g., most recently, the notes on 20:4 in the New Oxford Annotated NRSV.

685. Rudolf Bultmann, *The Gospel of John: A Commentary*, trans. G. R. Beasley-Murray, R. W. N. Hoare, and J. K. Riches (Philadelphia: Westminster, 1971) 685.

686. See the discussion in Brown, *The Gospel According to John (XIII–XXI)*, 1004-1007.

There is a dramatic progression to the discovery of the evidence of the empty tomb: Mary sees the stone that has been removed from the tomb's opening (v. 1); the beloved disciple notices the linen cloths (v. 5; cf. 19:40); Peter sees the linen cloths and the head wrapping (vv. 6b-7).[687] With Peter's evidence, the narrative begins to move toward the resolution of Mary's confusion and misunderstanding expressed in v. 2. The Evangelist describes in great detail what Peter sees when he enters the tomb. There may be an apologetic intent here, a defense against charges that the tomb was empty because Jesus' body was stolen. The evidence of the burial cloths suggests that the body has not been stolen; grave robbers would not have unwound the body from its wrappings. But the description of the burial cloths has a more important theological function. At Lazarus's exit from the tomb (11:44), his burial cloths were also described in great detail; the same word for "head cloth" (σουδάριον soudarion) occurs in 11:44 and 20:7. Lazarus emerged from the tomb still wrapped in his grave cloths, and he depended on Jesus' command to free himself from the wrappings; but in 20:6-7, Jesus' grave cloths remain behind in the empty tomb. The details of the grave cloths thus point to the theological resolution of Mary's misunderstanding: No one has taken Jesus away; he has left death behind (cf. 10:18).

The dramatic progression of evidence continues with the beloved disciple's entrance into the tomb in v. 8 and reaches its theological conclusion: "he saw [εἶδεν eiden] and believed [ἐπίστευσεν episteusen]." Yet this statement about the beloved disciple's belief is not without interpretive difficulties. First, the text supplies no object of the disciple's faith. Some commentators (e.g., Augustine) suggest that this verse means simply that the beloved disciple believed Mary's report that the tomb was empty. It is unlikely that the Fourth Evangelist would use the verb "to believe" to mean simply "acknowledge" or "give assent to," as it has more theological weight that that throughout the Gospel (e.g., 1:12; 3:15, 18; 5:38; 11:25-26; 12:46; 14:1, 10-11). Second, the interpretive commentary in v. 9 suggests that the disciples' understanding of the resurrection re-

mains incomplete ("for as yet they did not know").

It is important to remember that vv. 3-10 relate an empty-tomb story, not a story of a resurrection appearance. What the beloved disciple believes, then, is the evidence of the empty tomb: not merely that the tomb is empty, but that its emptiness bears witness that Jesus has conquered death and judged the ruler of this world (12:31; 14:30; 16:33). The beloved disciple's faith is as complete as faith in the evidence of the empty tomb can be. To say that the beloved disciple believes in the resurrection is to rush the story,[688] however, as v. 9 reminds the reader. Jesus' glorification is not yet over; the disciples have not yet experienced Jesus' resurrection, nor has Jesus ascended to the Father (cf. 20:17). Only after Jesus is glorified, when the Paraclete is given to the community, will the disciples understand and remember the Scripture (2:22; 12:12; cf. 14:26). It may be for this reason that the story notes that the disciples simply return home from the empty tomb (v. 10). Jesus has not yet appeared to give his post-resurrection commissions and instructions (vv. 17, 21-22).

20:11-18. 20:11-13. The reintroduction of Mary Magdalene is abrupt; her return to the tomb is presupposed by v. 11 but is never narrated (cf. the abrupt shift of narrative focus to Peter in the courtyard at 18:25). Verses 11-13 resume the traditional account of Mary Magdalene's discovery of the empty tomb, but they contain several distinctive Johannine emphases. First, John is the only Gospel in which Mary "weeps" (κλαίω klaiō) at the tomb. The repeated references to her weeping (vv. 11, 13, 15) recall Jesus' words at 16:20a ("Very truly, I tell you, you will weep [κλαύσετε klausete] and mourn, but the world will rejoice") and thus set the stage for the fulfillment of Jesus' promise of 16:22 ("So you have pain now; but I will see you again, and your hearts will rejoice, and no one will take your joy from you"; see also 16:20b). As noted in the Commentary on the Farewell Discourse, many of Jesus' promises in those chapters find their narrative fulfillment in the resurrection stories of John 20 (see also Commentary on vv. 19-23). Second, the angels make no Easter announcement, but only draw renewed

687. Rudolf Schnackenburg, *The Gospel According to St. John,* 3 vols. (New York: Seabury, 1982) 2:311.

688. So, e.g., ibid., 3:312; Barrett, *The Gospel According to St. John,* 561, 563-64.

attention to Mary's grief. The announcement of the significance of the resurrection belongs to Jesus (vv. 17-18), not to an intermediary messenger. Mary's response to the angels is a reiteration of her words at v. 2, but she now speaks exclusively of the cause of her own grief, not the community's confusion.

Finally, John alone among the Gospels locates the angels as "sitting where the body of Jesus had been lying, one at the head and the other at the feet" (v. 12; cf. Matt 28:2; Mark 16:5; Luke 24:4). This explicit link between the angels' location and Jesus' body may contain an echo of Jesus' opening eschatological promise of angels ascending and descending on the Son of Man (1:51). These angels are not messengers, but are evidence of the inbreaking of the promised new age in Jesus' death and resurrection.

20:14. The dramatic and theological heart of this story is vv. 14-18. Verse 14 establishes the story's dramatic tension; the reader knows what Mary does not: that the person she sees is Jesus. This setting increases the reader's participation in the story that is about to unfold, because the reader is positioned to anticipate the moment of recognition. Luke 24:15-16 creates a similar dynamic of anticipation and recognition in the Emmaus road story.

20:15. Jesus' questions (v. 15*a*) reinforce the drama of mistaken identity. They are questions that one might reasonably expect a gardener to ask in these circumstances, and so there is a certain logic to Mary's response (v. 15*b*). But for the reader, who knows that the questioner is the risen Jesus and not the gardener, the exchange between Jesus and Mary is another example of Johannine misunderstanding. Indeed, as Barrett has written, "This is the supreme example of the device, for it is not a metaphor but Jesus himself who is mistaken."[689] For example, Jesus' question, "Who are you looking for?" works on two levels. On the level of the plot line, it can be interpreted, as Mary does, as pertaining to Mary's search for Jesus' body. But this question repeats the first words spoken by Jesus in the Gospel (1:38). Jesus' words to the first people who seek him at the beginning of his ministry and to the first person who seeks him after the resurrection thus contain the same invi-

tation to discipleship. Mary's response to "the gardener" is also a supreme example of Johannine misunderstanding and irony. Mary, like the Samaritan woman at the well, is ignorant of who is speaking to her, and so she does not understand the implications of her own question (cf. 4:10). From a theological perspective, it is, indeed, Jesus who has "carried him away," for it is Jesus who has the power to take up his own life again (10:18), but Mary thinks only of the disposition of a corpse.

20:16. The lean narration of the moment of recognition contributes to its poignancy. Mary turned toward Jesus once before (v. 14), but his speaking her name enables her to recognize him this time. The Aramaic word ῥαββουνί (*rabbouni*) is a personal address or form of endearment of the word for "rabbi," teacher or master. This interchange between Jesus and Mary reveals him as the good shepherd; he knows his sheep by name, and they respond to his voice (10:3-4, 14, 16, 27; cf. Isa 43:1). The promised transformation from weeping and pain to joy has been accomplished through the word and presence of Jesus (16:20-22).

20:17. This verse contains the first commands of the risen Jesus. Jesus' first command (v. 17*a*) is a prohibition. The present imperative, "Do not hold on to me," may prohibit either an action already in progress or an intention to act. That is, Jesus' words do not necessarily assume that Mary is already holding on to him (cf. Matt 28:9), but only that he has perceived her intention to do so. Jesus' prohibition here is not a general prohibition against touching his resurrected body (cf. his invitation to Thomas in v. 27), but a very specific prohibition against "holding on to" (ἄπτω *haptō*) Jesus at this moment and hence interfering with the unfolding of the events of the hour.

For the Fourth Evangelist, Jesus' glorification consists of his death, resurrection, and ascension. The Johannine metaphor for Jesus' glorification, "lifted up" (ὑψόω *hypsoō*), holds together all three parts of Jesus' "exaltation." Jesus' glorification begins when he is lifted up on the cross, but it will not be complete until he returns to God. The awkwardness of Jesus' words, "I have not yet ascended to the Father," arises from the awkwardness of having to give linear, narrative shape to something that transcends and transforms tempo-

---

689. C. K. Barrett, *The Gospel According to St. John,* 2nd ed. (Philadelphia: Westminster, 1978) 564.

ral categories for the Evangelist.[690] That is, John must try to communicate his understanding of Jesus' glorification as a transtemporal event within the narrative constraints of the traditional stories of Jesus' death, resurrection, and ascension as three distinct chronological events. The conversation between Jesus and Mary in the garden is the Fourth Evangelist's attempt to give narrative shape to a theological reality.

The pivotal importance of Jesus' return to the Father is stated positively in v. 17b. Jesus commands Mary to go and proclaim the good news of his ascension, not the promise of future post-resurrection appearances (cf. Matt 28:7; Mark 16:7).[691] In announcing his ascent to God, Jesus announces the completion of his glorification; his distinctive identity as the eschatological Son of Man is confirmed by his ascent (3:13; 6:62). His return to the Father is a moment of great rejoicing (14:28; 17:13). Because Jesus has promised to "prepare a place for you" (14:2), his ascension ensures the ultimate fulfillment of his promises to those he loves. In returning to the Father, Jesus makes it possible for his disciples to share fully in his relationship with God. That is underscored in the expression "my Father and your Father, my God and your God." This double-identification formula confirms that what was true of Jesus'

relationship with God is now true of the disciples' relationship with God (cf. 14:23; 15:8-11, 16; 16:23-27; 17:20-26).

The Prologue announced that to all who believed in Jesus, he gave "power to become children of God" (1:13), and Jesus' words at 20:17 identify the completion of his glorification as the source of that new identity. To underscore the creation of the new family of God, Mary is instructed to announce the news of the ascension to "my brothers." Through this metaphorical use of the noun "brother" (ἀδελφός adelphos), Jesus' disciples are now recognized as members of his family. The noun adelphos is not gender limiting here, but is used inclusively to identify all of Jesus' disciples as his family (cf. the NRSV's translation of ἀδελθοί [adelphoi] as "the community" at 21:23).

20:18. That discipleship is not restricted to men in John is amply demonstrated by the role accorded to Mary in v. 18. She is the first witness to the resurrection, announcing both the fact of the resurrection ("I have seen the Lord") and the content of Jesus' message ("he had said these things to her"). The two names with which Mary speaks of Jesus in vv. 11-18 ("Rabbouni" and "Lord") recall Jesus' words at the farewell meal, "You call me Teacher and Lord—and you are right, for that is what I am" (13:13), and further confirm her portrayal as one of Jesus' disciples.

690. Brown, *The Gospel According to John (XIII–XXI)*, 1014; Schnackenburg, *The Gospel According to St. John*, 3:318-19.
691. Bultmann, *The Gospel of John*, 688.

REFLECTIONS

Each of the resurrection stories in John provides the Gospel reader with a different angle on what it means to meet the risen Jesus. In this first story (20:1-18), the reader is given two scenes through which to ponder the resurrection: the empty tomb and Mary's encounter with the risen Jesus.

1. The empty tomb narrative runs counter to sentimental notions of the resurrection and reunion with Jesus. Peter and the beloved disciple are given nothing but the evidence of an empty tomb. The effect of that evidence on Peter is not stated in the text, but its impact on the beloved disciple is clear, "he saw and believed." No angelic announcement accompanies the glimpse into the empty tomb, no reassuring words that Jesus has risen, that he has gone before them. In Mark 16:1-8, the women have the verbal witness of the angels, and they nonetheless flee the tomb in terror and amazement. In John there is only the stark emptiness of the tomb and the telltale presence of Jesus' abandoned burial clothes; yet the beloved disciple believes.

How can the evidence of an empty tomb lead to faith? In what may sound like a theological tautology, the beloved disciple believed because he already believed. That is, because the beloved disciple believed in Jesus and the trustworthiness of his promises about himself and

God (e.g., 14:1-3, 18-20, 23; 16:33), when he saw the empty tomb, he knew what it signaled: that Jesus had conquered death. The beloved disciple did not know what form Jesus' conquest of death had taken; he did not know how Jesus' conquest of death would be manifested among the living; he did not even know how to speak about what he saw in the tomb. All he knew was what the burial cloths told him: that Jesus had defeated death.

Stories of empty tombs confront the Christian community with the crux of resurrection faith: whether to believe in Jesus' defeat of death without corroborating evidence, without stories of visits with the risen Jesus. The short ending of the Gospel of Mark leaves the reader to ponder the empty tomb and to come to his or her own decision about the power of God in Jesus to overcome death. In John 20:3-10, the Fourth Evangelist presents the reader with a character who embodies that faith, who does not "judge by appearances," but "with right judgment" (7:25). It is important that the contemporary Christian community heed this story and linger with the witness of the empty tomb before moving ahead to stories of the risen Jesus.

2. The second scene—Mary Magdalene in the garden with Jesus (vv. 11-18)—contains one of the NT's most poignant images of the grace and delight of the resurrection: the moment of recognition when Mary hears Jesus call her by name. In that moment, Mary abandons her grief and turns to her teacher with expectancy. It is, as the Commentary noted, the demonstration of the truth of Jesus' promise that he would see his followers again, that their grief at his absence would turn to joy, that he would not leave his followers orphaned (16:20-22; 14:18-20). This scene captures in one narrative moment all of the joy the church experiences when it exults on Easter Sunday, "Christ is risen, he is risen indeed!"

Yet this moment of pure joy is the beginning, not the end, of Mary Magdalene's encounter with the risen Jesus. Although the church loves to celebrate Easter through the lens of stories of resurrection appearances, John 20:17 suggests another way of marking Jesus' victory on the cross. The good news that Jesus commands Mary to proclaim is not that he is risen, but that he is *"ascending to my Father and your Father, to my God and your God."* This is not meant to minimize the resurrection, but to note that for the Fourth Gospel the appearances of the risen Jesus are neither the counterpart to the cross nor the climax of the story. The cross brings the incarnation to a close, but the story of the Logos finds its conclusion only in Jesus' return to God, which is the counterpart to the descent from heaven (3:13, 31; 6:38; 8:23). This return makes new life possible for the believing community (14:28; 16:28), because Jesus' ascent to God renders permanent that which was revealed about God during the incarnation. The love of God embodied in Jesus was not of temporary duration, lasting only as long as the incarnation. Rather, the truth of Jesus' revelation of God receives its final seal in his return to God. Cross/resurrection/ascension is the decisive eschatological event for the Fourth Evangelist, because it forever changes the way God is known in the world and makes God's new age a reality.

Language of ascension and return to God, so pivotal in the Fourth Gospel's proclamation of the good news, can sound foreign and excessively transcendent to contemporary believers. In a church culture that often insists on privileging the anthropocentric dimensions of faith—that is, that insists on translating everything in terms of what it means "for us"—it is often difficult to know what to do with the Fourth Gospel's unwavering christological and theological foci. For the Fourth Evangelist, as the Prologue makes clear, everything begins with God and with Jesus' relationship to God (1:1-5), and there can be no conversation about "us" until there is a conversation about "them"—God and Jesus. The source of new life lies with God as revealed in Jesus, and for the Fourth Evangelist, there is no short cut around serious theological reflection about the identity of God and Jesus.

Yet that serious theological reflection is always linked for the Fourth Evangelist with the gifts of life and love that God and Jesus bring to those who believe, and his understanding of the ascension is no exception. Indeed, the new life that Jesus brings may receive its most explicit expression anywhere in the Gospel in Jesus' announcement of his ascension: "I am ascending to my Father and your Father, to my God and your God." It is an astonishing announcement, as Jesus himself translates what his ascension means "for us": Through Jesus' ascension, the believing community receives a new identity. His ascension is the confirmation that the believing community now knows God as Jesus knows God, that Jesus has opened up the possibility of new and full relationship with God. The intimacy of Jesus' relationship with God the Father, as in 1:18, now marks the believing community's relationship with God.

Jesus' announcement in v. 17 is every bit as poignant and transforming as his speaking Mary's name in v. 16, indeed more so. Verse 16 demonstrates the power and intimacy of relationship with Jesus for one of his sheep, but in v. 17 that power and intimacy is opened up for all members of the community. Jesus' promises in the Farewell Discourse all pointed in the direction of this ascension announcement, that the love that God and Jesus have for each other would be opened up by Jesus' death, resurrection, and ascension to include the believing community. This announcement is the ultimate "So what?" of Easter. Jesus' death on the cross, his revelation of his and God's love, his resurrection and ascension are indeed ultimately about us, because they open up for those who believe fresh possibilities of life as children of God. But even as they are ultimately about us, they must also ultimately be about God, because it is only as one sees God in Jesus that one can know what it means to live as God's child.

JOHN 20:19-23, JESUS' FIRST APPEARANCE TO THE GATHERED DISCIPLES

NIV

¹⁹On the evening of that first day of the week, when the disciples were together, with the doors locked for fear of the Jews, Jesus came and stood among them and said, "Peace be with you!" ²⁰After he said this, he showed them his hands and side. The disciples were overjoyed when they saw the Lord.

²¹Again Jesus said, "Peace be with you! As the Father has sent me, I am sending you." ²²And with that he breathed on them and said, "Receive the Holy Spirit. ²³If you forgive anyone his sins, they are forgiven; if you do not forgive them, they are not forgiven."

NRSV

19When it was evening on that day, the first day of the week, and the doors of the house where the disciples had met were locked for fear of the Jews, Jesus came and stood among them and said, "Peace be with you." ²⁰After he said this, he showed them his hands and his side. Then the disciples rejoiced when they saw the Lord. ²¹Jesus said to them again, "Peace be with you. As the Father has sent me, so I send you." ²²When he had said this, he breathed on them and said to them, "Receive the Holy Spirit. ²³If you forgive the sins of any, they are forgiven them; if you retain the sins of any, they are retained."

COMMENTARY

The story of Jesus' appearance to the disciples in John 20:19-23 can be subdivided into two parts: (1) vv. 19-20, the appearance of the risen Jesus, and (2) vv. 21-23, the disciples' commissioning by the risen Jesus. This section has elements in common with Luke 24:36-43: Both occur on Sunday evening; Jesus greets the disciples with the same words; and in both Jesus displays the wounds of his crucifixion to the gathered disciples. The common elements do not point to a common source behind the two stories, however, as the stories themselves are quite distinct, but they do suggest strongly that in John 20:19-23 the Fourth Evangelist is using a story that came to him in the tradition.

845

20:19-20. It is important to note that these verses identify those gathered together with the general term "disciples" (μαθηταί *mathētai*). They are never identified as the Eleven (the Twelve minus Judas), and it is a mistake to read this gathering of disciples in the light of the more closed notion of the Twelve that operates in the synoptic Gospels (e.g., Matt 28:16-20). The Fourth Evangelist rarely speaks of the Twelve (6:67, 70-71; 20:24). The gathering of disciples in vv. 19-23, like that at the farewell meal, probably included the core group, but there is no indication that it was limited to them. This gathering of disciples, like that in chaps. 13–16, represents the faith community in general, not the apostolic leadership.

John 20:19-23 is linked with the preceding story in the garden by the use of the emphatic expression "that day" (v. 19), although the disciples' fearful conduct indicates that they have not credited Mary's report (cf. Luke 24:11). The locked doors may be mentioned to heighten the drama and supernatural effect of Jesus' entrance into the room (v. 19*b*; cf. v. 26; Luke 24:37), but their primary importance for the Fourth Evangelist is found in the phrase "for fear of the Jews." This expression derives from the Johannine community's conflicts with the Jewish authorities of their day (see Commentary on 9:22); the Fourth Evangelist thus intends his readers to see their own experience reflected in this story of the first disciples. Jesus' greeting, "Peace be with you" (cf. Luke 24:36) is a conventional greeting (e.g., Rom 1:7; 1 Cor 1:3; 2 Cor 1:3; Gal 1:3), but it has an additional function in v. 19. With these words, Jesus fulfills another of his promises from the Farewell Discourse: the gift of his peace (14:27). This peace is given to a community who will experience the world's hatred and persecution (15:18-25). The gift of this peace to the disciples who have locked themselves away "for fear of the Jews" is an explicit reminder to the reading community that they need not face the Jewish authorities anxiously, but can do so with the peace of Jesus.

Jesus' presentation of his hands and side (cf. 19:34) in v. 20 is similar to his self-presentation in Luke 24:38-40, although in abbreviated form. A fuller self-presentation is saved until the Thomas story for greater dramatic effect (vv. 25, 27). Like Jesus' calling Mary by name in v. 16, his displaying his body to them underscores the continuity between the earthly and the risen Jesus. In Luke, the motivation for this presentation is explicitly stated: The disciples were afraid that Jesus was a ghost (24:37). There is no explicit motivation for Jesus' actions in John; a motivation like the Lukan motivation seems to be assumed, however, since it is not until after Jesus shows the disciples his hands and side that they rejoice (cf. Luke 24:41). The disciples' joy, like the end of Mary's weeping in v. 16, is the fulfillment of Jesus' promise in 16:20-22 that the disciples' pain will turn to joy when they see him again. The narrator's confessional perspective is revealed in his designation of Jesus as "the Lord" in his commentary in v. 20.

20:21-23. Jesus' repeated greeting (v. 21*a*) is not simply reduplicative. The disciples can receive Jesus' words as his gift of peace and not simply as a greeting only after they recognize that the person who speaks to them is "the Lord" (v. 20). Jesus' words in v. 21*b* are a direct echo of his prayer at 17:18. The syntax of both verses clearly positions the Father's sending of Jesus (e.g., 3:17; 4:34; 5:36; 10:36; 14:24; 17:3, 8) as an analogue for Jesus' sending of the community. Jesus thus commissions the faith community to continue the work God sent him to do.

Jesus' breathing on the disciples (v. 22) is explicitly linked with his words in v. 21 ("When he had said this . . . "), so that the gift of the Spirit is presented as that which empowers the community to continue Jesus' work. The Spirit was promised for the time after Jesus' glorification (7:37-39), and at v. 22 that moment has arrived. The verb "to breathe" (ἐμφυσάω *emphysaō*) occurs only here in the NT, and its usage clearly evokes the description of God's breathing the breath of life into the first human in Gen 2:7. It also recalls the description of the breath of life in Ezek 37:9 (see also the description of God in Wis 15:11: "and breathed a living spirit into them" [NRSV]). Jesus' breathing the Holy Spirit on his disciples thus is described as a new, second creation. The image of new life provides an important link with Jesus' announcement in 20:17. Those who believe in Jesus receive new life as children of God (cf. 3:3-10), and the Holy Spirit is the breath that sustains that new life. (For a discussion of this text as the Johannine "Pentecost," see Reflections.)

The commissioning scene closes with Jesus' words in v. 23 about forgiving and retaining sins. This is a very complex verse to interpret. Its vocabulary is unusual for the Fourth Gospel; this is the only occurrence of the verbs "to forgive" (ἀφίημι *aphiēmi*) and "to retain" (κρατέω *krateō*) in the Gospel. C. H. Dodd proposed that this verse was an independent form of the teaching about binding and loosing in Matt 18:18 (cf. Matt 16:19),[692] but as shall be seen below, while this may explain its traditional roots, the adaptation of this teaching into the Johannine setting gives it a quite different meaning from the Matthean version. Also, this verse has had a controversial role in the history of the church, as church leaders have debated its significance for the practices of baptism and penance. For example, it was a crucial text in the Council of Trent's defense of the sacrament of penance and the role of ordained clergy in granting absolution from sins, and it is often used in discussions of the relationship between rituals of repentance and the rite of baptism.[693]

It is critical in the interpretation of v. 23, therefore, that this verse be heard in its Johannine context and not be read anachronistically through the lens of the Reformation. First, Jesus' words in v. 23 are addressed to the entire faith community, not to its apostolic leaders. Any discussion of this verse, therefore, must be grounded in an under-standing of forgiveness of sins as the work of the entire community. Second, the community's enactment of Jesus' words in v. 23 depends on both Jesus' words of sending in v. 21 and the gift of the Holy Spirit in v. 22. The forgiveness of sins must be understood as the Spirit-empowered mission of continuing Jesus' work in the world. Third, although vocabulary of forgiveness and retaining is foreign to John, "sin" (ἁμαρτία *hamartia*) is not. Because the community's work is an extension of Jesus' work, v. 23 must be interpreted in terms of Jesus' teaching and actions about sin. The crucial texts in this regard are 3:19-21; 8:21-24; 9:39-41; and 15:22-24. In John, sin is a theological failing, not a moral or behavioral transgression (in contrast to Matt 18:18). To have sin is to be blind to the revelation of God in Jesus (see Reflections on John 9). Jesus brings people to judgment by his revealing work and presence in the world.

In v. 23, then, Jesus commissions the community to continue the work of making God in Jesus known in the world and thereby to bring the world to the moment of decision and judgment with regard to sin (cf. 15:22-24). The description of the Paraclete's activity in 16:8-9 supports this reading of 20:23, because the Paraclete is to "prove the world wrong about sin . . . because they do not believe in me." When the believing community receives the Spirit in v. 22, they are empowered to carry out this work of the Paraclete.[694] Jesus' words in v. 23 are a more specific form of his words in v. 21: The community is to continue what God sent Jesus to do.

692. C. H. Dodd, *Historical Tradition in the Fourth Gospel* (Cambridge: Cambridge University Press, 1963) 347-49.

693. For an excellent treatment of the place of John 20:23 in the history of the church, see Brown, *The Gospel According to John (XIII–XXI)*, 1041-45.

694. See ibid., 1042-43, and Bultmann, *The Gospel of John*, 692-93.

REFLECTIONS

John 20:19-23 occurs as a text for both Easter and Pentecost text in the church's lectionary. The preaching cycles of the church year thus recognize that in this text one meets the risen Jesus, and so they use this text as a vehicle for the Easter message. But the account of the gift of the Spirit also makes this story an appropriate Pentecost text, because in it one finds the Johannine version of the beginning of the church's post-Easter life.

It is important to recognize that the Easter/Pentecost division in the liturgical life of the church reflects the story line of Luke-Acts and does not reflect the Johannine understanding of the relationship of the resurrection and the gift of the Holy Spirit. For the Fourth Gospel, as John 20:19-23 makes clear, the gift of the Spirit and the articulation of the community's mission are intimately and inseparably tied to the resurrection and ascension of Jesus. When the church celebrates Easter, it also celebrates the beginnings of its mission. When the church celebrates the beginning of its mission and its empowerment with the Spirit, it also celebrates Easter. For John, the church's ongoing life as a community of faith, as the people who continue Jesus' work in the world, derives from Jesus' Easter promises and gifts.

This is reinforced in John 20:19-23 by the number of promises from the Farewell Discourse that find their fulfillment in this story. In the Farewell Discourse, Jesus promised his followers a life shaped by joy, a life grounded in the gift of his peace, a life guided by the work of the Paraclete/Spirit, and when each of these promises is fulfilled in 20:19-23, the distance between Easter and Pentecost is collapsed. The church's identity as a people is shaped by the gifts it receives from the risen Jesus, gifts he promised as a way of ensuring his continuing presence among them.

Perhaps the most difficult part of this Easter/Pentecost story concerns precisely what Jesus commissions the faith community to do. Just as Jesus was sent by the Father, so also he sends the community (v. 21), but the content of the church's work is only alluded to. The combination of vv. 22-23 suggests that the faith community is to be a people shaped by Jesus' gift of the Spirit and that the mark of that gift will be the power to forgive or retain sins. As the Commentary discussed, however, forgiving sins does not involve forgiving moral transgressions (nor does retaining sins involve retaining moral transgressions), but it involves bearing witness to the identity of God as revealed in Jesus. If the interpreter combines vv. 22-23 with Jesus' commandment to love one another in 13:34-35, a possible picture of the church's mission emerges. By loving one another as Jesus loves, the faith community reveals God to the world; by revealing God to the world, the church makes it possible for the world to choose to enter into relationship with this God of limitless love. It is in choosing or rejecting this relationship with God that sins are forgiven or retained. The faith community's mission, therefore, is not to be the arbiter of right or wrong, but to bear unceasing witness to the love of God in Jesus.

The resurrection story of John 20:19-23 thus provides a fresh vantage point from which the church can preach and teach the story of its own beginnings. The beginning of the community's life is not separated from the story of Easter; indeed, in John, the gift of the Spirit and the commissioning of the church occur on Easter Sunday evening. The Johannine Easter narratives are a reminder that the church's life is intimately bound to Jesus' life, death, and resurrection. To celebrate the resurrection, the Fourth Gospel suggests, is also to celebrate the beginnings of the church's mission in the world. Jesus lives, not because he can walk through locked doors and show his wounds to frightened disciples, but because he breathes new life into those disciples through the gift of the Spirit and commissions them to continue his work.

JOHN 20:24-31, JESUS' APPEARANCE TO THOMAS

NIV

24Now Thomas (called Didymus), one of the Twelve, was not with the disciples when Jesus came. 25So the other disciples told him, "We have seen the Lord!"

But he said to them, "Unless I see the nail marks in his hands and put my finger where the nails were, and put my hand into his side, I will not believe it."

26A week later his disciples were in the house again, and Thomas was with them. Though the

NRSV

24But Thomas (who was called the Twin[a]), one of the twelve, was not with them when Jesus came. 25So the other disciples told him, "We have seen the Lord." But he said to them, "Unless I see the mark of the nails in his hands, and put my finger in the mark of the nails and my hand in his side, I will not believe."

26A week later his disciples were again in the house, and Thomas was with them. Although the

[a] Gk Didymus

NIV

doors were locked, Jesus came and stood among them and said, "Peace be with you!" [27]Then he said to Thomas, "Put your finger here; see my hands. Reach out your hand and put it into my side. Stop doubting and believe."

[28]Thomas said to him, "My Lord and my God!"

[29]Then Jesus told him, "Because you have seen me, you have believed; blessed are those who have not seen and yet have believed."

[30]Jesus did many other miraculous signs in the presence of his disciples, which are not recorded in this book. [31]But these are written that you may[a] believe that Jesus is the Christ, the Son of God, and that by believing you may have life in his name.

a31 Some manuscripts *may continue to*

NRSV

doors were shut, Jesus came and stood among them and said, "Peace be with you." [27]Then he said to Thomas, "Put your finger here and see my hands. Reach out your hand and put it in my side. Do not doubt but believe." [28]Thomas answered him, "My Lord and my God!" [29]Jesus said to him, "Have you believed because you have seen me? Blessed are those who have not seen and yet have come to believe."

30Now Jesus did many other signs in the presence of his disciples, which are not written in this book. [31]But these are written so that you may come to believe[a] that Jesus is the Messiah,[b] the Son of God, and that through believing you may have life in his name.

aOther ancient authorities read *may continue to believe*   bOr *the Christ*

COMMENTARY

20:24-25. These verses form a bridge between the appearance story in vv. 19-23 and the appearance to Thomas in vv. 26-29. The story in vv. 19-23 gave no hint that Thomas was missing from the scene; by informing the reader of this detail after the fact (v. 24), the Evangelist gives an additional significance to that earlier story (cf. the way the late notice that Jesus' healings in John 5 and 9 took place on the sabbath shifted the emphasis in those stories). A story of the commissioning of the faith community now functions to showcase the question of faith in the resurrection. Thomas has appeared twice previously in the Fourth Gospel (11:16, where he is also identified as the Twin, and 14:5; see also 21:2). That he was one of the Twelve accords with his identification in the synoptic Gospels (Matt 10:3; Mark 3:18; Luke 6:15).

The disciples' announcement to Thomas in v. 25a is the same announcement that Mary Magdalene made to them in v. 18. Thomas will not believe their announcement (v. 25b), but it is important to note that the disciples did not seem to believe Mary's earlier announcement either. Only when Jesus appeared to the disciples (v. 19) and showed them his hands and his side (v. 20) did they recognize "the Lord" and rejoice. In

rejecting the verbal witness to the resurrection, then, Thomas is acting no differently from the other disciples. Thomas's demands in v. 25b are worded graphically, and the demand for concrete evidence is heightened by his insistence on touching Jesus' hands and side, but in essence what he demands as the conditions of his belief, tangible proof of the resurrection, is what Jesus himself gave the disciples in v. 20.

20:26-29. Thomas's demands set the stage for Jesus' appearance in these verses. The description of the gathering and of Jesus' entrance in v. 26 mirror v. 19, with two exceptions. First, the elimination of the expression "the fear of the Jews" may suggest that through the gift of the Holy Spirit (v. 22), fear is now removed (cf. 14:27). Second, Thomas's presence is explicitly noted, reinforcing that Thomas will now receive what he missed in the earlier appearance. Indeed, after Jesus' communal greeting in v. 26, the focus of the story rests exclusively on Jesus and Thomas.

In v. 27, Jesus offers to give Thomas exactly what he demanded; his words parallel Thomas's demands in v. 25. Although the word "doubt" is indelibly linked with Thomas in the popular interpretation of this story, the word occurs nowhere in vv. 24-29 (contrary to the NIV and the

NRSV). A literal translation of v. 27b reads, "Do not be unbelieving [ἄπιστος *apistos*] but believing [πιστός *pistos*]." This is the only occurrence of this pair of adjectives in the Fourth Gospel, and their contrast is important. Jesus exhorts Thomas to move from a position of unbelief to belief. This story does not focus on doubt and skepticism, but on the grounds of faith. Jesus will meet the conditions that Thomas set for his belief; indeed, he explicitly identifies his offer of himself as the motivation for Thomas's move from unbelief to belief.

Jesus' offer of himself to Thomas evokes the most powerful and complete confession of Jesus in the Fourth Gospel: "My Lord and my God!" (v. 28). In confessing Jesus as his Lord and God, Thomas acknowledges the truth of the words that Jesus spoke to him in 14:7 ("If you know me, you will know my Father also. From now on you do know him and have seen him"; cf. 14:9: "Whoever has seen me has seen the Father."). As Bultmann has correctly noted, this confession acknowledges that Jesus' return to the Father is now complete, that Jesus shares in God's glory "that I had in your presence before the world existed" (17:5).[695] The language of this confession affirms the central truth with which the Gospel began: "The Word was with God, and the Word was God" (1:1). Thomas sees God fully revealed in Jesus.

It is not touching Jesus that leads Thomas to this confession of faith, but Jesus' gracious offer of himself. Although many commentators read Jesus' words and gestures in v. 27 as slightly sarcastic and an attempt to shame Thomas, no exegetical evidence supports such an interpretation.[696] Jesus is not attempting to shame Thomas, but is giving Thomas what he needs for faith, as he has done so many times in the Gospel (e.g., 4:10-26; 5:6-9; 9:35-38; 11:1-42). Were Jesus attempting to shame Thomas here, Thomas's confession in v. 28, the high point of the Gospel's christological confessions, would be narratively and theologically weakened. Why would a character whom Jesus has shamed be given the most powerful confession in the Gospel? Would

shame really be the theological impetus for such a confession? To the contrary, v. 27 is another demonstration of the truth of 1:16: "From his fullness we have all received, grace upon grace" (see Reflections).

The manuscript evidence is unclear whether v. 29a should be punctuated as a question (NRSV) or a statement (NIV), but the punctuation does not decisively alter the meaning of the verse. Jesus' words in v. 29a contain a direct and seemingly intentional echo of the words with which he concluded his first conversation with his disciples at 1:50. In response to Nathanael's "seeing and believing," Jesus promised that even greater things would be revealed to the disciples, including the eschatological vision of the Son of Man (1:51). Jesus' words at 20:29 contain a related promise that belief will not be limited to those who see what Thomas has seen. Jesus does not disparage the faith of the first disciples, which was grounded in sight.[697] The Fourth Gospel has repeatedly pointed to the importance of that witness (see esp. 19:35) and to the word of the first disciples as a source of faith for others (17:20-21). Actually, v. 29 is intended to reassure future generations of believers that having seen Jesus—that is, being a first-generation witness—is not a prerequisite for faith. The joy of the first disciples at the sight of the risen Lord is explicitly stated in v. 20; the blessing in v. 29 includes future generations in that joy.[698]

20:30-31. These verses mark a shift in style of the Gospel narrative. The narrator now speaks directly to his readers (v. 31; cf. 19:35). Because of this direct address and the reference to "many other signs" in v. 30, nearly all modern scholars maintain that John 20:30-31 is the original conclusion to the Gospel, and that John 21 is a postscript or addendum.[699] Raymond Brown's assessment of these verses summarizes this critical position: "The air of finality in these two verses justifies their being called a conclusion despite the fact that in the present form of the Gospel a whole chapter follows."[700] It is important to note that it

695. Bultmann, *The Gospel of John*, 695.
696. E.g., Brown, *The Gospel According to John (XIII–XXI)*, 1046; Bultmann, *The Gospel of John*, 694; Schnackenburg, *The Gospel According to St. John*, 3:331.
697. So Bultmann, *The Gospel of John*, 696.
698. Brown, *The Gospel According to John (XIII–XXI)*, 1049.
699. Robert Fortna, *The Gospel of Signs: A Reconstruction of the Narrative Source Underlying the Fourth Gospel*, SNTSMS 11 (Cambridge: Cambridge University Press, 1979), proposed that these verses formed the conclusion of the signs source.
700. Brown, *The Gospel According to John (XIII–XXI)*, 1049.

is only modern interpreters who note the decisive "air of finality" about these verses. In the first eighteen centuries of the church's interpretation of this Gospel, commentators assumed that vv. 30-31 concluded the stories in John 20 and that 21:1-25 was the conclusion of the Gospel (for a fuller discussion of the relationship of John 21 to the rest of the Gospel, see the Overview to John 21). Of major twentieth-century commentators on John, Hoskyns stands alone in maintaining that 20:30-31 concludes the resurrection stories of John 20 and not the entire Gospel.[701] The evidence in support of reading vv. 30-31 as the conclusion to John 20 (and not the original conclusion of the Gospel), however, is stronger than the critical consensus allows.

First, the intrusion of the narrator's voice directly into the storytelling (vv. 30-31) is not unusual in the Fourth Gospel; indeed, it is one of the distinctive traits of the Fourth Evangelist's narrative style. For example, at 11:51-52 the narrator interprets the story of Caiaphas and the Sanhedrin in order to ensure that the reader understands the full meaning of Caiaphas's prophecy; at 2:22 and 12:16, the narrator makes explicit connections to the disciples' situation after Jesus' glorification; at 12:33, the narrator interprets Jesus' words about his death for the reader (see also 18:32); and at 19:35, the narrator comments on the source and veracity of the testimony in 19:34. The narrator's words in 20:30-31 belong to this same category of interpretive comment; the Fourth Evangelist interrupts the flow of the narrative to ensure that the reader grasps the significance of what has just been recounted. On this basis, John 21 is not an addendum.

The Fourth Evangelist uses the narrator's comments in vv. 30-31 to underscore for his readers that Jesus' blessing in v. 29b is addressed to them; "you," the readers, are among "those who have not seen." The manuscript evidence is divided on whether the verb "to believe" (πιστεύω *pisteuō*) in v. 31 should be read as an aorist subjunctive

("that you may come to believe," NRSV) or a present subjunctive ("that you may believe," NIV; i.e., "continue to believe"). The aorist subjunctive can be read as suggesting that the Gospel is a missionary document, intended to bring people to faith, the present subjunctive that the Gospel is intended to support and sustain the faith of those who already believe. Such distinctions, especially dependent as they are on the variation of one letter in the manuscripts, impose too strict a set of alternatives for the purpose of the Fourth Gospel. For identifying the intended audience of the Gospel, the rest of the Gospel does not support such a strict choice between coming to faith for the first time or continuing in faith.

Second, according to the majority opinion, "many other signs [σημεῖα *sēmeia*]" in v. 30 is a summary statement of all of Jesus' activity in the Gospel. By reading the reference to signs in v. 30 so broadly, however, one misses the importance of this verse in clarifying the Evangelist's understanding of both the resurrection appearances and signs. Rather than referring to Jesus' entire ministry, the narrator is identifying the events of John 20 as signs.[702] Note that also in 2:11 and 4:54 the reader is not informed that the miracles Jesus performed were "signs" until the end of the story (so also 12:18). In addition, in 2:18-20 Jesus himself pointed to his resurrection as a sign.[703] The narrator's comments about signs in v. 30 thus echo the narrative commentary of 2:21-22, in which the disciples' faith is linked to the completion of the events narrated in John 20.

To identify Jesus' resurrection appearances as signs means that, like Jesus' other signs, the theological truth of the resurrection appearance lies not in the appearance itself, but in that to which it points. That is, the resurrection appearance stories are about something other than Jesus' miraculous return from death. In vv. 1-10, the theological truth that is revealed by the empty tomb is Jesus' victory over death and the ruler of this world; in vv. 11-18, the revealed truth is Jesus' continuing presence as the good shepherd; in vv. 19-23, Jesus' appearance to the disciples points to the gift of the Spirit/Paraclete and the truth of his promises in the Farewell Discourse.

701. E. C. Hoskyns, *The Fourth Gospel* (London: Faber & Faber, 1947) 549-50. The hold of the modern critical consensus is apparent in the way Brown refers to Hoskyns's position: "Hoskyns . . . is one of the few modern critical writers who refuses to interpret xx 30-31 as a conclusion" (Brown, *The Gospel According to John (XIII–XXI)*, 1057). The following articles also challenge the critical consensus: H. Thyen, "Aus der Literatur zum Johannesevangelium," TR 42 (1977) 213-61; Stephen S. Smalley, "The Sign in John 21," *NTS* 20 (1974) 275-88; Paul S. Minear, "The Original Functions of John 21," *JBL* (1983) 85-98.

702. Hoskyns, *The Fourth Gospel*, 550; Minear, "The Original Functions of John 21," 88-90.

703. Minear, "The Original Functions of John 21," 90.

In each of these stories, were Jesus' appearance taken only as a miracle and not as a "sign," its revelatory power would be lost. This is most dramatically clear in vv. 24-29. Thomas sees through the physical miracle that he demands (v. 25) to that to which it points: the full revelation of God in Jesus (v. 28). Jesus' resurrection appearance to Thomas is thus a sign in the fullest Johannine sense, because it points to God in Jesus and so leads to faith (cf. 2:11).

Third, the truth to which the "signs" of Jesus' resurrection appearances point is not his return from death, but *the completion of his hour.* This is confirmed in the statement of purpose in v. 31: "that you may come to believe that Jesus is the Messiah, the Son of God." It is not Jesus' resurrection appearances per se that reveal this truth, but his resurrection appearances as a sign of his return to God in glory. That is what Thomas's confession affirms (see Commentary on v. 28). The reader, like Thomas and the other disciples, is not summoned merely to believe in the resurrection, but to believe in the revelation of Jesus'

identity and relationship with God, of which the resurrection is a sign. Read in this way, the narrator's words in vv. 30-31 about the resurrection appearances as signs clarify the significance of the other signs in the Gospel as well.

In vv. 30-31, the narrator speaks directly to the reader so that the reader can recognize that he or she, too, can interpret the signs of Jesus' resurrection and come to faith. It is not physical sight and signs that are decisive for faith, but the truth they reveal. The contrast between signs "which are not written" in v. 30 and "these are written" in v. 31 underscores for readers who live after the first generation that the words of the Gospel text will lead to faith in Jesus and through that faith to new life (v. 31). Verse 31 thus identifies two interdependent purposes of the resurrection stories: (1) christological, to bring the reader to faith in the identity of Jesus as the Son of God, and (2) soteriological, to offer the reader the experience of new life that is available because the work of Jesus' hour has been completed.

REFLECTIONS

1. John 20:24-29 is acknowledged almost universally as the story of "Doubting Thomas." This epithet for this disciple and his story, which falsely isolates Thomas from the rest of the disciples, has the unfortunate effect of foreclosing any fresh hearing of this text. To focus so narrowly and negatively on Thomas's doubt in the interpretation of this text is to miss the point of this story. The center of this story is Jesus, not Thomas.

At the heart of this story is Jesus' generous offer of himself to Thomas. Thomas had established the conditions for his faith: He must be allowed to touch Jesus' wounds. The Johannine Jesus does not censure Thomas for these conditions, but instead makes available to him exactly what he needs for faith. Thomas *should* have been able to believe in the disciples' resurrection proclamation, just as the disciples should have been able to believe in Mary's proclamation. But Thomas's faith is more important than the grounds of his faith, so Jesus presents his post-resurrection body to Thomas and exhorts him, "Do not be unbelieving but believing." He gives Thomas a sign and asks him to see and believe. This palpable offer of Jesus' grace leads Thomas to a confession of faith. Jesus' offer of his wounds to Thomas is of a piece with his calling Mary by name in 20:16; it is another demonstration of his care for his sheep.

Jesus' love for his own did not end with his death, but determines all future interactions between Jesus and the community of his followers. Jesus' love and care for his own are evident in the blessing with which the Thomas story concludes (20:29). In this blessing, the Fourth Evangelist reminds all readers—his first readers, who were a generation removed from these resurrection appearances, and all later readers, no matter how many centuries removed—that knowledge of and relationship with Jesus is not limited to his first disciples.

John 20:24-29 is a story of hope and promise, not judgment and reprimand. It stands as a pledge and promise to later generations that they, too, will experience the grace of God in

Jesus. As bold as Jesus' gesture to Thomas is in 20:26-28, Jesus' care for the faith of those who come after Thomas, who will not see, is equally without limit and measure.

2. As noted in the Commentary, 20:30-31 spells out the implications of Jesus' blessing in v. 29 for later generations of believers, for those who have not seen and yet believe. These verses provide an important glimpse into the Evangelist's understanding of himself as a theologian and the Gospel text as a vehicle for faith. By drawing explicit attention to the role of the resurrection stories in bringing people to faith, the Evangelist suggests that the Gospel narrative itself gives its readers the words that make faith in Jesus possible for those who live after the first generation of disciples. These verses present the Gospel narrative itself as the locus of revelation for later generations.[704]

By ascribing this revelatory role to the Gospel, the Fourth Evangelist completely eliminates all grounds for thinking that second-, third-, or sixtieth-generation believers are at any disadvantage to the first generation of disciples. From the perspective of the Fourth Evangelist, the answer to the old hymn question "Were you there when they crucified my Lord?" would be yes, so long as it is understood that yes is not a yes to a kind of historicism or historical reenactment, but a yes to the full experience of God in Jesus that is available in the Gospel stories. The revelation of God in Jesus is grounded in history, but it transcends history through precisely this narrative.

The revelation of God in Jesus is ever present, ever new, and ever available because of the work of the Spirit/Paraclete. In claiming the revelatory role of his own account of Jesus, the Fourth Evangelist confirms the presence of the Paraclete at work with him (see Excursus "The Paraclete," 774-78). As storyteller, theologian, pastor, teacher, interpreter, the Fourth Evangelist opens up the words and works of Jesus so that all experience of God in Jesus is immediate, so that each new generation of believers has equal access to Jesus and his revelation of God.

John 20:30-31 raises several important issues for contemporary debates about the authority of Scripture. First, this passage suggests that the authority and "truth" of Scripture is not to be secured by debates about verbal inerrancy and critically verified "facts." Rather, the truth of Scripture lies in its power to make the presence of God in Jesus available to the faith community in each successive generation. Any and all attempts to equate and identify the reconstruction (or deconstruction) of the events of Jesus' life with the authority of Scripture miss the point. Such attempts would, for the Fourth Evangelist, fall into the category of demanding signs—falsely equating the fact with its meaning and theological truth. Second, by identifying the locus of revelation in the Gospel narrative, by ascribing a soteriological purpose to the things that "are written," these verses call the Christian community to reexamine its identity as a people shaped by the biblical text. These verses suggest that an engagement with the biblical text, with its offer and interpretation of God, is vital to the life of faith. In preaching and teaching these texts, in meditating on them in prayer, it is, indeed, possible to believe without having seen.

704. See Gail R. O'Day, *Revelation in the Fourth Gospel: Narrative Mode and Theological Claim* (Philadelphia: Fortress, 1986) 93-94.

JOHN 21:1-25

JESUS' RESURRECTION APPEARANCE AT THE SEA OF TIBERIUS

OVERVIEW

The consensus of scholarly opinion is that John 21:1-25 is a secondary addition to the Fourth Gospel and that it should be interpreted as a postscript or epilogue to the Gospel. Scholars are divided on whether the material in John 21 was added later by the Evangelist himself or by a redactor, although the latter theory is more widely held.[705] It is important to note, however, that all of the extant manuscripts of the Gospel of John, including the ancient $\mathfrak{P}^{66}$, contain chap. 21. Unlike John 7:53–8:11, where the manuscript evidence supports identifying this passage as a later addition (see Commentary there), no manuscript evidence exists that the Gospel of John ever circulated without chap. 21. In addition, the case for the secondary status of this chapter cannot be made conclusively on the grounds of differences in vocabulary and syntax from the rest of the Gospel. Bultmann's assessment of the linguistic evidence is representative of the position of most scholars who advocate the redactional status of John 21: *"Language and style* admittedly afford no sure proof. . . . As to the *vocabulary,* the fact that a series of terms are met only in ch. 21 is accidental and conditioned by the material."[706]

The secondary status of John 21, therefore, is argued on two basic grounds: (1) John 20:30-31 brings the Gospel to a close, and (2) Jesus' post-resurrection appearances in John 21 introduce an ecclesial focus that is secondary and anticlimactic to the concerns of John 1–20.[707] The Commentary

on 20:30-31 has already questioned the consensus view of the function of those verses and proposed that they be read as the conclusion to the resurrection stories in John 20 and not as the original conclusion to the entire Gospel. As with the critical consensus about 20:30-31, there is a circularity in the argument that 21:1-25 is secondary; the decision about the status of chap. 21 is largely based on how it fits scholars' theological preconceptions about how the Gospel of John should end. Beasley-Murray, for example, writes that John 21 "has an emphasis on the situation of the Church and its leaders beyond anything in the body of the Gospel."[708] The very wording of this assessment, however, presupposes that chap. 21 does not constitute part of the "body" of the Gospel.

Again, Hoskyns stands virtually alone among twentieth century commentators of John in advocating that 21:1-25 belongs to the original plan of the Gospel (cf. Commentary on 20:30-31). He perceives the ecclesial focus of the chapter as essential to, rather than detracting from, the ending of the Fourth Gospel.[709] Paul Minear also has questioned the consensus view, arguing that the stories about the disciples in John 21 provide the necessary conclusion to themes introduced earlier in the Gospel.[710]

There is a distinction between the focus of John 20 and that of John 21, but it is a distinction that is integral to the scope and movement of the Gospel narrative. In 20:1-31, the narrative and theological focus rests on the completion of Jesus'

---

705. Barrett, Brown, Bultmann, Dodd, and Schnackenburg all argue that a redactor wrote John 21.

706. Rudolf Bultmann, *The Gospel of John: A Commentary,* trans. G. R. Beasley-Murray, R. W. N. Hoare, and J. K. Riches (Philadelphia: Westminster, 1971) 700.

707. See, e.g., the arguments in Raymond E. Brown, *The Gospel According to John (XIII–XXI),* AB 29A (Garden City, N.Y.: Doubleday, 1970) 1077-1082.

708. George R. Beasley-Murray, *John,* WBC 36 (Waco, Tex.: Word, 1987) 396.

709. E. C. Hoskyns, *The Fourth Gospel* (London: Faber & Faber, 1947) 550.

710. Paul S. Minear, "The Original Functions of John 21," *JBL* (1983) 91-98. See also those scholars cited at note 701.

glorification. Thomas's proclamation, "My Lord and my God" (20:28), signals the fulfillment of Jesus' prayer of 17:1-5; Jesus is glorified in God's presence. But Jesus' prayer at his hour looks beyond his own glorification to the future life of the believing community (17:6-26), and the stories of John 21 point explicitly to that future. It is inaccurate, therefore, to state that John 21:1-25 introduces ecclesial concerns that are not integral to the Gospel. In John 16:2-3, for example, Jesus predicted the future persecution and martyrdom of members of the community, predictions that are revisited in the stories

of Peter and the beloved disciple in 21:15-24. Throughout chaps. 13–17, Jesus spoke of his hopes and promises for the life of the faith community (e.g., 14:12; 15:12-27; 17:17-18, 20; cf. 19:26-27), and John 21:1-25 offers a narrative conclusion to those hopes.

John 21:1-25 is narrated as one continuous scene at the Sea of Tiberius. It consists of two parts: (1) vv. 1-14, Jesus appears to the gathered disciples, (2) vv. 15-24, Jesus speaks to Peter about his future and that of the beloved disciple. Verse 25 is the formal conclusion of the Gospel.

JOHN 21:1-14, JESUS APPEARS TO THE GATHERED DISCIPLES

NIV

21 Afterward Jesus appeared again to his disciples, by the Sea of Tiberias.[a] It happened this way: [2]Simon Peter, Thomas (called Didymus), Nathanael from Cana in Galilee, the sons of Zebedee, and two other disciples were together. [3]"I'm going out to fish," Simon Peter told them, and they said, "We'll go with you." So they went out and got into the boat, but that night they caught nothing.

[4]Early in the morning, Jesus stood on the shore, but the disciples did not realize that it was Jesus.

[5]He called out to them, "Friends, haven't you any fish?"

"No," they answered.

[6]He said, "Throw your net on the right side of the boat and you will find some." When they did, they were unable to haul the net in because of the large number of fish.

[7]Then the disciple whom Jesus loved said to Peter, "It is the Lord!" As soon as Simon Peter heard him say, "It is the Lord," he wrapped his outer garment around him (for he had taken it off) and jumped into the water. [8]The other disciples followed in the boat, towing the net full of fish, for they were not far from shore, about a hundred yards.[b] [9]When they landed, they saw a

a[1] That is, Sea of Galilee   b[8] Greek *about two hundred cubits* (about 90 meters)

NRSV

21 After these things Jesus showed himself again to the disciples by the Sea of Tiberias; and he showed himself in this way. [2]Gathered there together were Simon Peter, Thomas called the Twin,[a] Nathanael of Cana in Galilee, the sons of Zebedee, and two others of his disciples. [3]Simon Peter said to them, "I am going fishing." They said to him, "We will go with you." They went out and got into the boat, but that night they caught nothing.

[4]Just after daybreak, Jesus stood on the beach; but the disciples did not know that it was Jesus. [5]Jesus said to them, "Children, you have no fish, have you?" They answered him, "No." [6]He said to them, "Cast the net to the right side of the boat, and you will find some." So they cast it, and now they were not able to haul it in because there were so many fish. [7]That disciple whom Jesus loved said to Peter, "It is the Lord!" When Simon Peter heard that it was the Lord, he put on some clothes, for he was naked, and jumped into the sea. [8]But the other disciples came in the boat, dragging the net full of fish, for they were not far from the land, only about a hundred yards[b] off.

[9]When they had gone ashore, they saw a

a Gk *Didymus*   b Gk *two hundred cubits*

NIV

fire of burning coals there with fish on it, and some bread.

¹⁰Jesus said to them, "Bring some of the fish you have just caught."

¹¹Simon Peter climbed aboard and dragged the net ashore. It was full of large fish, 153, but even with so many the net was not torn. ¹²Jesus said to them, "Come and have breakfast." None of the disciples dared ask him, "Who are you?" They knew it was the Lord. ¹³Jesus came, took the bread and gave it to them, and did the same with the fish. ¹⁴This was now the third time Jesus appeared to his disciples after he was raised from the dead.

NRSV

charcoal fire there, with fish on it, and bread. ¹⁰Jesus said to them, "Bring some of the fish that you have just caught." ¹¹So Simon Peter went aboard and hauled the net ashore, full of large fish, a hundred fifty-three of them; and though there were so many, the net was not torn. ¹²Jesus said to them, "Come and have breakfast." Now none of the disciples dared to ask him, "Who are you?" because they knew it was the Lord. ¹³Jesus came and took the bread and gave it to them, and did the same with the fish. ¹⁴This was now the third time that Jesus appeared to the disciples after he was raised from the dead.

COMMENTARY

The Evangelist has combined elements from two types of traditions in this story of Jesus' appearance to his disciples on the beach: a story of a miraculous catch of fish (cf. Luke 5:1-11) and a recognition story (cf. Luke 24:30-35). The result is a post-resurrection appearance story that follows the standard conventions of a miracle story: vv. 1-3, setting and preparation for the miracle; vv. 4-6, the miracle; vv. 7-14, the attestation of the miracle/recognition of Jesus. The miraculous catch of fish thus functions analogously to the miracle at the wedding in Cana (2:1-11); in both stories the miracle is the vehicle for an epiphany. Jesus' first and last revelatory acts in the Gospel narrative are thus both miracles of abundance in Galilee.

21:1-3. Like the introduction to the Cana miracle story (2:1-2), vv. 1-2 establish the time, location, and characters of the miracle story. The tight chronological sequence of 20:1-29 (Sunday morning, v. 1; Sunday evening, v. 19; one week later, v. 26) gives way to the more general phrase "after these things" (cf. the temporal relationship between the carefully enumerated days of John 1:19-51 and the opening of the Cana story). All the resurrection appearances in John 20 are located in Jerusalem (as is also the case in Luke 24), but the appearance in John 21 takes place in Galilee at the Sea of Tiberius. Matthew also re-

cords a Jerusalem resurrection appearance (28:9-10), followed by a Galilean appearance (Matt 28:16-19; cf. Mark 16:7). The Sea of Tiberius (the Sea of Galilee) was near the site of the miraculous feeding of John 6:1-14; there are important echoes of this earlier story in 21:9-13. The temporal openness and shift in location from chap. 20 to chap. 21 may indicate that Jesus' presence is not limited to his appearances in that first week in Jerusalem, but is available to the disciples wherever and whenever they gather.

The verb "to show [oneself]" or "to reveal" ($\phi\alpha\nu\epsilon\rho\acute{o}\omega$ *phaneroō,* v. 1) is an important verb in the Fourth Gospel. It is associated with the revelatory dimension of Jesus' miracles at 2:11 and 9:3, and it is used to summarize the purpose of Jesus' ministry at 1:31 and 17:6. The repetition of the expression "Jesus showed himself" at the beginning and end of v. 1 thus underscores for the reader that the miracle story that follows is an epiphany and should be interpreted in the light of the revelatory acts of Jesus' ministry (the NIV incorrectly paraphrases v. 1*b* and eliminates the second use of *phaneroō*).[711]

Verse 2 lists seven disciples. Simon Peter and Thomas figured prominently in the resurrection stories of John 20 (vv. 3-10, 24-29). John 21 is

711. See Stephen S. Smalley, "The Sign in John 21" *NTS* 20 (1974) 275-88.

the first time Nathanael has appeared since the call narrative of 1:45-50. At 1:50, Jesus promised Nathanael that he would see "greater things," and his reappearance in the closing epiphany of the Gospel signals the fulfillment of that promise. The beloved disciple, who will play a prominent role at v. 7, is not explicitly mentioned in v. 2. He could be one of the sons of Zebedee (who are mentioned here for the only time in the Fourth Gospel) or one of the two unnamed disciples with whom the list ends. The fact that the beloved disciple is consistently unnamed in the Gospel argues in favor of the latter (see Introduction).

In interpreting v. 3, most commentators focus on the disciples' motivation for the fishing trip and what it says about their relationship to Jesus. Hoskyns, for example, sees v. 3 as a sign of the disciples' complete apostasy and a fulfillment of Jesus' prediction of 16:32; the disciples have scattered to their own homes and abandoned Jesus. Brown sees this verse as an indication of the disciples' aimlessness. In stark contrast, Barrett interprets the scene through the lens of the synoptic call narratives (Matt 4:18-22; Mark 1:16-20; Luke 5:10) and sees the fishing trip as a symbolic enactment of the commission of John 20:21. Schnackenburg, however, eschews entering "into the difficult problems as to how the disciples behaved after Jesus' death, whether they stayed in Jerusalem or returned to Galilee, etc.," and wisely recommends that one interpret v. 3 by "staying with the text."[712] Verse 3 plays a critical role in the miracle story per se, because it establishes the situation of need that Jesus' miracle will correct: the disciples' inability to catch any fish (v. 3*b*; cf. 2:3; 6:5).

21:4-6. These verses narrate the miracle, and the first characteristics of the recognition story also appear here. For example, the introduction of Jesus in v. 4 recalls the recognition story of John 20:11-18; the reader knows that the man on the beach is Jesus, but the disciples do not (cf. also Luke 24:15-16). The juxtaposition of the night of unsuccessful fishing (v. 3) and Jesus' morning appearance (v. 4) may be intended to evoke the theological symbolism of the contrast between day

and night, light and darkness (1:5; 9:4; 11:9-10; 12:35-36; 13:30).

Jesus' opening words in v. 5 express the familial intimacy ("children" [παιδία *paidia*]) that is now a reality because of Jesus' hour (20:17; cf. his use of "little children" [τεκνί α *teknia*] at 13:33). Given John's propensity for synonyms, not much can be made of the vocabulary difference between 13:33 and 21:5. The two nouns are used interchangeably throughout 1 John (e.g., 1 John 2:1, 12, 14, 18, 28).

Jesus' question to the disciples in v. 5 is introduced with the interrogative particle (μή τι *mē ti*) and thus anticipates a negative response (note the NRSV; cf. 4:12; 8:53; 9:40; 18:17). There is an underlying irony to this question, because Jesus initiates his contact with the disciples by asking them for food, but in the end will give food to them (vv. 9, 12-13). This pattern recalls Jesus' exchange with the Samaritan woman in John 4:7-16. Jesus initially requested a drink from the woman (4:7), but in the end he offered her living water (4:13-14).

The miracle proper is narrated in v. 6. The miracle, a prodigious catch of fish, occurs in response to Jesus' word and command (cf. 4:50, 53; 5:8; 11:43). The great quantity of fish (v. 6*b*) will be reemphasized in vv. 8 and 11.

21:7-14. This miraculous catch of fish is the direct catalyst for the beloved disciple's recognition of Jesus (v. 7*a*). His announcement of Jesus' identity is couched in the language of the Easter proclamation: "It is the Lord" (cf. 20:18, 20, 25, 28). The two earlier Galilean miracles provide a clue in identifying what it is about the catch of fish that evokes the beloved disciple's recognition. In the Cana miracle (2:1-11), the disciples saw Jesus' glory in the abundance of good wine; the feeding miracle of 6:1-14 also points to the abundance of Jesus' gifts. In this miracle, too, the beloved disciple recognizes the abundance of fish as deriving from the fullness of Jesus' gifts (cf. 1:14, 16).

The focus on the beloved disciple and Peter in v. 7 anticipates vv. 15-24. The portrayal of their responses to the miracle is consistent with their responses to the empty tomb (20:3-10). The beloved disciple is again the first to recognize what he sees (cf. 20:8), while Peter responds with his characteristic eagerness (v. 7*b*; 20:6; cf. 13:9;

---

712. Hoskyns, *The Fourth Gospel,* 552; Brown, *The Gospel According to John (XIII–XXI),* 1096; C. K. Barrett, *The Gospel According to St. John,* 2nd ed. (Philadelphia: Westminster, 1978) 579; Rudolf Schnackenburg, *The Gospel According to St. John,* 3 vols. (New York: Seabury, 1982) 3:353.

18:10). The NIV correctly captures the meaning of the Greek of v. 7*b*. The image of Peter dressing himself in order to jump into the water paints a comical picture of his impetuosity; he is caught between his desire to greet Jesus with proper respect (that is, fully clothed) and his eagerness to greet him immediately. The reference to their proximity to shore and the other disciples' more restrained conduct in v. 8 highlights Peter's buffoonish enthusiasm.

21:9. Verses 9-13 focus on Jesus' identity as the source of life for the disciples. This identity is highlighted in two interrelated scenes: Jesus' offer of a meal to his disciples (vv. 9, 12-13) and the attestation of the abundance of the miracle (vv. 10-11). The meal of v. 9 is the same food as that of 6:1-14, "fish" (ὀψάριον *opsarion*) and "bread" (ἄρτος *artos*). Jesus' preparation of this meal for his disciples confirms that he is the giver of gifts, the source of life-sustaining nourishment (4:13-14; 6:35, 51; 7:37; 10:9).

21:10-11. Jesus' command to the disciples in v. 10 is a narrative device to introduce a final description of the catch of fish. The threefold description of the size of the catch in v. 11 ("full of large fish"; "a hundred fifty-three of them"; "though there were so many, the net was not torn") leaves no doubt that it is the magnitude of the catch to which the Evangelist wants to direct the reader's attention. The magnitude of the catch confirms that Jesus has performed a great miracle and, as noted above, points to the abundance of Jesus' gifts. Yet the amount of narrative space devoted to the size of the catch has suggested to many interpreters that additional symbolism is intended. In particular, the significance of the number "a hundred fifty-three" has intrigued interpreters since the earliest days of the church. Augustine, for example, proposed two ways of reading this number that still govern more recent interpretations. First, he proposed a mathematical explanation. The number 153 is obtained when all of the integers from 1 to 17 are added together; this mathematical fact thus suggests the completeness of the number 153 itself.[713] Second, he suggested, as had earlier patristic writers (e.g., Cyril of Alexandria), that the number should be

read allegorically. Augustine proposed that the number was a symbol of the Trinity, and while this specific allegorical reading is rejected by scholars, other allegorical interpretations are proposed. The most common suggestion is that the number stands for the totality of the church.[714] In addition to these symbolic readings, some scholars propose that the number 153 preserves the memory of an eyewitness who counted the fish.[715]

The symbolic relationship between the miraculous catch of fish and the disciples' mission does not seem to lie in the description of the quantity of fish, however, but in Peter's action in hauling in the net. The verb "to haul" (ἕλκω *helkō*; see also v. 6) is the same verb used in 6:44 to describe those who come to Jesus from God ("No one can come to me unless *drawn* by the Father who sent me") and in 12:32 to describe the salvific effect of Jesus' death ("And I, when I am lifted up from the earth, will *draw* all people to myself"). The use of this verb with reference to the disciples and the catch of fish suggests that they now join God and Jesus in drawing people to Jesus. The catch of fish, then, marks the extension of God and Jesus' work into the disciples' work. This story thus stands as the narrative fulfillment of Jesus' promises to his disciples in the Farewell Discourse that they will share in his works (14:12; 15:5, 7-8, 16; cf. 17:18, 20-21).

21:12-14. The disciples recognize Jesus as the Lord and, therefore, do not question him about his identity (v. 12) points to the fulfillment of another of Jesus' farewell promises about the community's life after his glorification (16:23). The fellowship of the meal in v. 13 confirms the intimacy of the relationship between the risen Lord and his disciples (cf. Luke 24:30-35, where the meal is the moment of recognition).[716] The description of Jesus' actions as host of the meal (v. 13) echoes the description of his actions at the feeding of the five thousand (6:11). Some manuscripts complete the allusion to 6:11 by adding the clause "when he had given thanks." As in the Cana miracle of 2:1-11 and the meal at 6:1-14, the early church saw eucharistic symbolism in this meal. Since in the Gospel of John the eucharist

713. Augustine *In Jo. tr.* CXXII.8. Hoskyns, *The Fourth Gospel,* 553-54, and Barrett, *The Gospel According to St. John,* 581, propose a similar reading. For a review of the history of interpretation of this verse, see Beasley-Murray, *John,* 401-4.

714. Augustine *In Jo.* XII. For modern allegorical readings, see, e.g., Hoskyns, *The Fourth Gospel,* 554.

715. Brown, *The Gospel According to John (XIII–XXI),* 1076.

716. Schnackenburg, *The Gospel According to St. John,* 3:359.

is understood as Jesus' gift to the believer and an expression of relationship with Jesus (see Commentary and Reflections on John 6), a eucharistic reading is consonant with the themes of this story.

The enumeration of Jesus' appearances in v. 14 includes the appearances to the gathered disciples in 20:19-29, but excludes the appearance to Mary Magdalene in 20:11-18 (cf. Paul's list of appearances in 1 Cor 15:3-7, which also does not mention the women). The repetition of the verb *phaneroō* at the conclusion of the story (here translated as "appeared"; cf. v. 1) affirms that the fishing miracle is an epiphany.

JOHN 21:15-25, JESUS, PETER, AND THE BELOVED DISCIPLE

NIV

[15]When they had finished eating, Jesus said to Simon Peter, "Simon son of John, do you truly love me more than these?"

"Yes, Lord," he said, "you know that I love you."

Jesus said, "Feed my lambs."

[16]Again Jesus said, "Simon son of John, do you truly love me?"

He answered, "Yes, Lord, you know that I love you."

Jesus said, "Take care of my sheep."

[17]The third time he said to him, "Simon son of John, do you love me?"

Peter was hurt because Jesus asked him the third time, "Do you love me?" He said, "Lord, you know all things; you know that I love you."

Jesus said, "Feed my sheep. [18]I tell you the truth, when you were younger you dressed yourself and went where you wanted; but when you are old you will stretch out your hands, and someone else will dress you and lead you where you do not want to go." [19]Jesus said this to indicate the kind of death by which Peter would glorify God. Then he said to him, "Follow me!"

[20]Peter turned and saw that the disciple whom Jesus loved was following them. (This was the one who had leaned back against Jesus at the supper and had said, "Lord, who is going to betray you?") [21]When Peter saw him, he asked, "Lord, what about him?"

[22]Jesus answered, "If I want him to remain alive until I return, what is that to you? You must follow me." [23]Because of this, the rumor spread among the brothers that this disciple would not

NRSV

15When they had finished breakfast, Jesus said to Simon Peter, "Simon son of John, do you love me more than these?" He said to him, "Yes, Lord; you know that I love you." Jesus said to him, "Feed my lambs." [16]A second time he said to him, "Simon son of John, do you love me?" He said to him, "Yes, Lord; you know that I love you." Jesus said to him, "Tend my sheep." [17]He said to him the third time, "Simon son of John, do you love me?" Peter felt hurt because he said to him the third time, "Do you love me?" And he said to him, "Lord, you know everything; you know that I love you." Jesus said to him, "Feed my sheep. [18]Very truly, I tell you, when you were younger, you used to fasten your own belt and to go wherever you wished. But when you grow old, you will stretch out your hands, and someone else will fasten a belt around you and take you where you do not wish to go." [19](He said this to indicate the kind of death by which he would glorify God.) After this he said to him, "Follow me."

20Peter turned and saw the disciple whom Jesus loved following them; he was the one who had reclined next to Jesus at the supper and had said, "Lord, who is it that is going to betray you?" [21]When Peter saw him, he said to Jesus, "Lord, what about him?" [22]Jesus said to him, "If it is my will that he remain until I come, what is that to you? Follow me!" [23]So the rumor spread in the community[a] that this disciple would not die. Yet Jesus did not say to him that he would not die, but, "If it is my will that he remain until I come, what is that to you?"[b]

a Gk *among the brothers*   *b* Other ancient authorities lack *what is that to you*

NIV

die. But Jesus did not say that he would not die; he only said, "If I want him to remain alive until I return, what is that to you?"

²⁴This is the disciple who testifies to these things and who wrote them down. We know that his testimony is true.

²⁵Jesus did many other things as well. If every one of them were written down, I suppose that even the whole world would not have room for the books that would be written.

NRSV

²⁴This is the disciple who is testifying to these things and has written them, and we know that his testimony is true. ²⁵But there are also many other things that Jesus did; if every one of them were written down, I suppose that the world itself could not contain the books that would be written.

COMMENTARY

The opening words of v. 15 ("When they had finished breakfast") explicitly link John 21:15-25 to the preceding scene and position it as a continuation of the same appearance by Jesus. These verses narrate a conversation between the risen Jesus and Peter; vv. 15-19 focus on Peter himself, and vv. 20-24 focus on the beloved disciple. Peter has been a prominent figure since the opening call narrative of John 1 (see 1:40-42; 6:66-71; 13:6-10, 24, 36-38; 18:10-11, 15-27; 20:3-10), the beloved disciple since the farewell meal (13:21-27; 19:26-27; 20:3-10; see also 19:35). This final scene of the Fourth Gospel concludes the stories of these two disciples by depicting the shape of their lives after Jesus' glorification. They stand as two specific examples of the continuation of Jesus' work in the work of the community.

21:15-17. The threefold pattern of the conversation between Jesus and Peter in these verses seems intended to counterbalance Peter's three denials of Jesus, predicted by Jesus at 13:38 and narrated in 18:15-27. In these verses, Peter is enabled to move beyond his previous relationship with Jesus and claim the unity, intimacy, and mutuality with God and Jesus, promised to believers in the Farewell Discourse. These verses point to a future for Peter that is based on his relationship with Jesus after, rather than before, Jesus' hour.

Verse 15 establishes the basic pattern that is repeated with minimal variation in vv. 16-17: Jesus' question of Peter's love for him; Peter's affirmation of his love; Jesus' charge to feed/care for his sheep. The name "Simon son of John,"

used in all three verses, provides an important link with Peter's first appearance in the Fourth Gospel. The risen Jesus' use of this name repeats the words he spoke when he first met Peter ("You are Simon son of John," 1:42) and once more portrays Jesus as the good shepherd who knows the name of his sheep (cf. 20:16). Two different verbs for "to love" are used in vv. 15-17: ἀγαπάω (agapaō, vv. 15a, 16a) and φιλέω (phileō, vv. 15b, 16b, 17). These verbs are used as synonyms throughout the Gospel, with no difference in meaning. For example, both verbs are used to speak of "the disciple whom Jesus loved" (ἠγάπα ēgapa, 13:23; ἐφίλει ephilei, 20:2); God's love of Jesus (ἀγαπᾷ agapa, 10:17; φιλεῖ philei, 5:20); God's love for the disciples (ἀγαπήσει agapēsei, 14:23; philei, 16:27); and the disciples' love of Jesus (agapa, 14:23; πεφιλήκατε pephilēkate, 16:27). There is no reason, therefore, to ascribe gradations of meaning to their usage here (as the NIV does). The Evangelist's propensity for synonyms is also evident in the variation "lambs"/"sheep" and "feed"/"tend."

Several exegetical details warrant individual attention. First, Jesus' initial question contains a comparison between Peter's love for Jesus and that of the other disciples ("more than these," v. 15a). On a literary level, by mentioning other disciples, this phrase provides a bridge between vv. 1-14 and vv. 15-24.[717] This comparison also may place Jesus' question in the context of Peter's earlier conduct at the farewell meal. Peter earlier

---

717. Bultmann, *The Gospel of John*, 711; Brown, *The Gospel According to John (XIII–XXI)*, 10.

falsely boasted "more than these" about his willingness to lay down his life for Jesus (13:37).[718] Peter ignores the comparison in his response (v. 15b). Second, the language of Peter's affirmation of his love for Jesus highlights a distinctly Johannine theme: Jesus' knowledge of everything (v. 17b), which has characterized his portrayal in John (e.g., 1:48; 2:24; 6:6, 64; 13:1; 18:4, 28; cf. 16:30).

Jesus' charge to Peter in vv. 15-17 is regularly interpreted as Peter's pastoral and apostolic commission. That is, in these verses Jesus appoints Peter to be the shepherd of his flock.[719] In Matt 16:16-19, Jesus positions Peter as the foundation of the church, but it is not as clear as most commentators assume that John 21:15-17 has an analogous function. The charge to "feed my sheep" should be interpreted in the light of Jesus' commandments to his disciples in the Farewell Discourse, not Matt 16:18-19. These verses do not point to Peter as Jesus' distinctive successor, but as embodying what is true of all of Jesus' disciples. These verses position Peter as a model of what it means to live out one's love of Jesus.

The heart of vv. 15-17 lies in the relationship between Peter's love for Jesus and the charge to feed Jesus' sheep. When Jesus translates Peter's love for him into the charge "feed my sheep," he is reminding Peter of his words in 13:34-35; "Just as I have loved you, you also should love one another. By this everyone will know that you are my disciples, if you have love for one another." In his charge to Peter, Jesus is reminding him to keep that commandment, to put his love for Jesus into practice by feeding/tending Jesus' sheep. Jesus does not hand his sheep over to Peter's singular care,[720] but instead reminds Peter of what it means to love Jesus. Jesus is calling Peter to love Jesus' sheep as he has loved them (cf. 10:11-18). In that call, as Minear has rightly seen, one finds the fulfillment of yet another of Jesus' farewell promises: "They who have my commandments and keep them are those who love me; and those who love me will be loved by my Father, and I will love them and reveal myself to them" (14:21).[721]

21:18-19. The expression "very truly I say" (ἀμὴν ἀμὴν λέγω *amēn amēn legō*) in v. 18 marks the introduction of a new teaching. This teaching, as v. 19a makes explicit, is a prediction of Peter's martyrdom and takes the form of a short parable, a teaching form common in the Fourth Gospel (e.g., 3:29; 4:36; 8:35). *First Clement* 5.4 also refers to Peter's martyrdom. Verse 18a-b is constructed in strict antithetical parallelism; the three terms of v. 18a ("younger"/"fasten your own belt"/"go wherever you wished") are matched by their exact opposite in v. 18b ("grow old"/"stretch out your hands, someone else will fasten belt"/"take you where you do not want to go"). Since many of the early church theologians interpreted OT references to stretching out one's arms (e.g., Exod 17:12; Isa 65:2) as foreshadowing the crucifixion,[722] most scholars see in the expression "stretch out your arms" a specific reference to Peter's death by crucifixion.[723] The verb ζωννύω (*zōnnyō*; "fasten your belt," NRSV; "dress," NIV) literally means "to gird," so the NRSV seems closer to the Greek. The verb's precise meaning in this context is not clear; it may contain an allusion to the binding of criminals to the cross or the fettering of criminals on their way to execution. Its general meaning, however, is to contrast the freedom of Peter's youth with the captivity that will mark his old age and death.

The wording of the narrator's interpretive commentary at v. 19a is identical to the commentary on the manner of Jesus' death at 12:33 and 18:32. The link between Peter's death and Jesus' death is made even more explicit by the phrase "by which he would glorify God." Jesus glorified God through his death (7:39; 12:16; 13:31-32; 14:13; 17:1-5), and now Peter will share in that work.

Jesus' command to Peter, "Follow me" (v. 19b), is a general invitation to discipleship; to follow Jesus is to be one of his sheep (10:4, 27). This command is also a more specific invitation to martyrdom and death (see also 12:26). At the farewell meal, Jesus predicted that Peter could not follow him now, but would follow afterward (13:36); the invitation in v. 19b marks the arrival of that moment. At 13:37, Peter expressed his

---

718. So Barrett, *The Gospel According to St. John*, 584; Schnackenburg, *The Gospel According to St. John*, 3:362.

719. E.g., ibid., 3:363-65; Barrett, *The Gospel According to St. John*, 584. See the helpful discussion of this passage in relation to Matt 16:16-19 in Beasley-Murray, *John*, 406-7.

720. Schnackenburg, *The Gospel According to St. John*, 3:363.

721. Paul S. Minear, "The Original Functions of John 21," *JBL* (1983) 92.

722. E.g., *The Epistle of Barnabas* 12.2, 4.

723. The one major exception to this is Rudolf Bultmann, *The Gospel of John: A Commentary*, trans. G. R. Beasley-Murray, R. W. N. Hoare, and J. K. Riches (Philadelphia: Westminster, 1971) 713.

willingness to lay down his life for Jesus, a boast that Jesus rejected (13:38). Verses 18-19 show that now Peter is able to do what he could not do before: lay down his life in love.

Jesus' words to Peter in vv. 18-19 thus complement and complete the conversation in vv. 15-17. As the good shepherd, Jesus was willing to lay down his life for the sheep (10:11, 15). At 15:12-14, Jesus commanded his disciples to enact that same love for one another. In 21:15-19, the Fourth Evangelist brings the Gospel's portrait of Peter to a close by pointing to his fidelity to Jesus' commandment. Peter, like the beloved disciple, is to be known by his share in Jesus' love. Peter's authority for the readers of the Fourth Gospel thus does not derive from his "office," but from the fullness of his love for Jesus and Jesus' own.

21:20-21. These verses are a narrative bridge constructed to shift the focus from Peter to the beloved disciple and to introduce Jesus' saying in v. 22. The identification of the beloved disciple in v. 20 makes an explicit reference to his first appearance in the Gospel at the farewell meal (cf. the identification of Nicodemus at 19:39). This identification reminds the reader of the beloved disciple's role as witness to Jesus' hour.

21:22-24. Verse 22 records a saying of Jesus about the future of the beloved disciple; vv. 23-24 are the narrator's comments on the meaning of this saying and the ongoing significance of the beloved disciple. Together they underscore the importance of the beloved disciple for the community for whom this Gospel was written. The most obvious meaning of the saying in v. 22—that the beloved disciple would be alive at Jesus' second coming—is labeled a rumor and misinterpretation in v. 23. This saying may record a tradition similar to that found in Mark 9:1; it is recorded not for its eschatology, however, but to address concerns about the beloved disciple.

First, v. 23 indicates that the saying of v. 22 was misinterpreted as a prediction that the beloved disciple would not die. Although v. 23 does not say so explicitly, the narrator's comments seem to be occasioned by the death of the beloved disciple, which necessitated the narrator's direct address of the false rumors that had spread about the disciple. The tradition recorded in v. 22 does not use language of life or death, but, in distinctly Johannine vocabulary, says that the beloved disci-

ple will "remain" (μένω menō). In v. 24, the narrator will address how the beloved disciple does indeed remain in the community even after he has died. Second, Jesus' saying about the beloved disciple is spoken to Peter, not to the beloved disciple. In its present narrative context, then, v. 22 highlights the separate fates of two prominent disciples: one for whom discipleship is characterized by laying down his life (Peter), and one for whom it is not. Jesus' rebuke of Peter's question (cf. 2:4) and his reiteration of the command to follow suggest that the two disciples are not to be compared and measured against each other. Rather, the future of each disciple—Peter, to follow to death; the beloved disciple, to remain—is shown to be Jesus' will.[724]

Barrett is alone among major Johannine commentators in correctly noting the intrinsic connection between v. 24 and the preceding verses about the beloved disciple.[725] The narrator's words in v. 24 are analogous to his commentary in v. 19a; in both he interprets for the reader Jesus' teaching about the key disciples. In v. 19a he makes sure that the reader recognizes that Peter is going to die a martyr's death and so live out his love for Jesus. In v. 24, the narrator makes sure that the reader recognizes that even though the beloved disciple does not die a martyr's death, he nonetheless bears witness to Jesus. His witness is the foundation of the very Gospel through which the readers experience Jesus. The beloved disciple's death does not diminish his standing in the community, because his witness remains. Peter's ministry is marked by his death; the beloved disciple's is marked by this Gospel.

Verse 24 warrants careful examination because of the role it plays in decisions about the authorship of the Gospel (see Introduction). First, one must examine the relationship between the expressions "who is testifying to these things" and "has written them." If John 21 is held to be an integral part of the Gospel, then v. 24 cannot be read as the words of a redactor pointing back to the written work of another "author." As the verse is constructed, the reference to writing is given as corroboration of the beloved disciple's witness. That is, the beloved disciple is pivotal to

724. Ibid., 716.
725. C. K. Barrett, *The Gospel According to St. John,* 2nd ed. (Philadelphia: Westminster, 1978) 583.

the community, not merely because he provides the oral testimony of an eyewitness, but because his testimony has found its way into the written form of this Gospel. By corroborating the beloved disciple's witness, v. 24a stresses the connection between this Gospel and the beloved disciple's witness, while at the same time seeming to attribute the actual authorship of this Gospel to someone other than the beloved disciple himself. John 21:24 thus has the same function as 19:35: to point to the beloved disciple as the source of the traditions about Jesus that are interpreted in the Gospel.

Second, who is the "we" of v. 24b? Again, if John 21 is taken as an integral part of the Gospel, this "we" cannot be read as a reference to the redactor. Instead, this "we" should be read in the light of the "we" of 1:14-18.[726] This "we" is the voice of the confessing community that claims that the testimony of the beloved disciple is truthful. As a truthful witness whose words remain, the beloved disciple stands as another example of the work and presence of the Paraclete in the community (cf. 14:16-17; 15:26; 16:13).

21:25. The direct voice of the narrator is interjected into the commentary in the Gospel's concluding verse ("I suppose . . . "; cf. the direct address to the readers in 20:30-31). The hyperbole of this last verse reflects a rhetorical convention common among Greek and Jewish writers in the ancient Mediterranean world.[727] The following saying, attributed to Rabbi Johanan ben Zakkai, a contemporary of the Fourth Evangelist, employs the same convention and helps to illumine the Evangelist's intent in the concluding verse: "If all heaven were a parchment, and all the trees produced pens, and all the waters were ink, they would not suffice to inscribe the wisdom I have received from my teachers; and yet from the wisdom of the wise I have enjoyed only so much as the water a fly which plunges into the sea can remove."[728] Verse 25 is thus a statement of authorial humility, in which the Fourth Evangelist distinguishes his work in writing the Gospel and interpreting traditions about Jesus from the witness of the beloved disciple. He, the Evangelist, is only one among an innumerable many who will write about and interpret the traditions about Jesus.

726. Minear, "Original Functions," 95.

727. See, e.g., Philo de posteritate Caini 144.

728. Hermann L. Strack and Paul Billerbeck, *Kommentar zum Neuen Testament aus Talmud und Midrash* (München: Beck, 1924) 2:587. This is Hoskyns's translation, *The Fourth Gospel* (London: Faber & Faber, 1947) 561.

REFLECTIONS

As has been noted repeatedly throughout this commentary, theology and christology are inseparably interwoven in the Fourth Gospel. The clearest statement of that is found in John 14:8: "Whoever has seen me has seen the Father." It is equally true that theology, christology, and ecclesiology are interwoven. The clearest statement of this interrelationship may be the prayer of John 17, in which Jesus prays to God for the future of the believing community.

Concerns about the faith community's future, therefore, are not secondary to the Fourth Evangelist, but are an integral part of his understanding of who Jesus is. In the opening verses of the Gospel (1:14-18), the "we" of the faith community bear witness to the gifts it has received from Jesus (see Commentary). Almost one-fifth of the Fourth Gospel narrative (chaps. 13–17) is devoted exclusively to Jesus' words about the future of the faith community after his glorification. How will the community live in his absence? What shape will their lives take? How will they endure persecution and the world's hatred? How will they experience Jesus' presence? What will be their identity as a people of faith? Jesus addresses these and other questions with words of hope and promises of his presence. As noted in the Commentary and Reflections on the Farewell Discourse, the Fourth Evangelist gives these concerns pride of place in the Gospel by locating them in the teachings Jesus spoke *before* his hour, "so that when it does occur, you may believe" (14:29; see also 15:11; 16:1).

The stories in John 21 belong to this constellation of theological concerns. They show the reading community what the promises of the Farewell Discourse mean for them by illustrating the disciples' lives *after* Jesus' hour. The stories in John 21 are not resurrection stories per se, because their focus is not on Jesus' resurrection and ascension—that was the theological heart of John 20. Rather, the focus of John 21 moves beyond Jesus' resurrection to the future of which he spoke in the Farewell Discourse. This chapter invites the reader to envision how the community of disciples can continue to experience Jesus' post-glorification presence and carry his work forward.

As noted in the Commentary, the opening story of John 21:1-14 has important points of continuity with the miracles of Jesus' ministry, especially the turning of water into wine at Cana and the feeding of the five thousand. The abundant catch of fish and the breakfast on the beach both suggest that Jesus' gifts continue even after the events of "his hour." This story is a narrative testimony to the truth of the community's testimony in 1:16: "From his fullness we have all received, grace upon grace." The vast quantity of fish in the disciples' net and the gracious meal of bread and fish show that God's gift is available in the risen Jesus just as it was in the incarnate Jesus. Just as Jesus' ministry was inaugurated with a miracle of unprecedented abundance (2:1-11), so, too, is the church's ministry. John 21:1-14 is thus a story of celebration for the post-resurrection community, because it demonstrates for the community that its life is grounded in an experience of God's fullness and unprecedented, unexpected gift.

This joyous story provides the backdrop for the call to discipleship that Peter receives in 21:15-19. Jesus' gifts in his miracles are only signs of his ultimate gift—the gift of his life in love—and Jesus calls Peter to share in that gift. It is noteworthy that Jesus' commissions to Peter in this story, both to feed his sheep and to follow him, are grounded in and derive from Peter's love of Jesus. It is in the post-resurrection community's love for Jesus that he continues to be fully known. To love Jesus is to know Jesus, because, as Jesus' words to Peter make clear, to love Jesus is to shape one's life according to Jesus' life. The threefold question, answer, and commission in vv. 15-17 underscore that words of love must be matched by a life of love. Peter's love of Jesus will be evidenced when he cares for Jesus' sheep, not apart from that care.

The life to which Jesus summons Peter, and that, indeed, Peter lived, requires of him an act of love that matches Jesus' act: the gift of his life. Peter models for the faith community the ultimate fidelity to Jesus' words, because he fulfills Jesus' core commandment, that his disciples love one another as he has loved them. When Peter three times answers, "Yes, I love you," he is not simply giving lip service to his love for Jesus, but is in essence pledging his life. Peter is who Jesus calls his followers to be, a disciple who puts no limits on his love, who will, like Jesus, love "to the end" (13:1).

What does such a model of love and discipleship mean for the post-resurrection community? If Peter is the model, if a life that is willing to embrace martyrdom fulfills Jesus' commandments to his followers, then what about those believers who do not lay down their lives in love, who are not martyrs for the faith? Are they excluded from the circle of Jesus' gifts? It may be some of these very questions that the exchange between Jesus and Peter in John 21:21-22 addresses. When Peter, the martyr, asks Jesus in v. 21 about the beloved disciple, a man who did not die a martyr's death, the dilemma of how one loves Jesus is placed before the reader. Is the beloved disciple's witness and discipleship invalidated because his life ended without his laying down his life in love?[729] As noted, Jesus' combination rebuke/recommission to Peter in v. 22 suggests that such questions and comparisons are beside the point. Peter is to be about the business of his discipleship, and the beloved disciple is to be about his. Indeed, v. 24 avers quite strongly that the beloved disciple's witness is invaluable to the life of the faith community.

John 21:15-25 thus surfaces a genuine ecclesial dilemma. That Jesus repeatedly calls his disciples to a life of love shaped by his own gift of his life is incontestable; yet not all

---

729. Paul S. Minear, *John: The Martyr's Gospel* (New York: Pilgrim, 1984) 160-61.

discipleship will be marked by the disciple's laying down his or her life. The extent of the dilemma is readily seen in John 21 because the beloved disciple, the figure through whom the readers of this Gospel have a distinctive connection with Jesus, was not martyred. How is the church to live with this dilemma?

It is critical that both sides of the dilemma be acknowledged. On the one hand, it is very easy in the contemporary North American church to soften Jesus' call to lay down one's life in love, to see it as a figure of speech or an ideal far removed from the day-to-day realities and struggles of the life of faith. But the history of the church is full of people who knew that Jesus' words were real, who answered the call to love Jesus and one another fully with their lives. Nor is such love a relic of the church's past. Love that knows no limits, including the limit of one's own life, also shapes the discipleship of the contemporary church. Martin Luther King, Jr., and Bishop Oscar Romero are the most obvious and well-known examples of love that knew no limits, but when one pays careful attention, one regularly notices stories of Christian disciples who give their lives in love: nuns and priests who have stayed at their ministries in Central America and war-torn Eastern Europe, knowing that it will cost their lives; doctors and nurses in hospitals and health-care facilities in impoverished and embattled countries around the world who will not leave those for whom they care; martyrs of religious persecution across the globe. It is crucial that contemporary Christians remember this form of discipleship.

On the other hand, it is easy to minimize all forms of discipleship that do not involve laying down one's life. What, one is tempted to think, is the significance of my struggle to live the love of Jesus in my small ways when compared to those who lay their lives on the line daily? What is the worth of my witness when weighed against the witness of someone's death? The words about the beloved disciple in vv. 20-24 insist that his love for Jesus was not to be devalued because his witness took the form of reporting traditions about Jesus and not martyrdom.

Perhaps the story of John 21:1-14 provides the key to working through this ecclesial dilemma. The stories of John 21 begin, not with Peter's call to martyrdom or the praise of the beloved disciple's witness, but with a story of Jesus' gracious gifts. Jesus gave gifts to all of the disciples in the boat: Peter, the martyr; the beloved disciple, the witness; Thomas and Nathanael, who wanted to see to believe (1:47-50; 20:24-29); to the sons of Zebedee and the unnamed disciples, about whom the Gospel records nothing except that they are disciples. For all of these people, whose discipleship would take varied forms, Jesus provided a miraculous catch of fish and hosted breakfast on the beach. Those who will give up their lives in love, those who struggle daily in what may seem the smallest places to bear witness to Jesus' love—all receive Jesus' gifts. The discipleship of the believing community, John 21 suggests, begins with the affirmation and celebration of the gifts of God in Jesus; the embodiment of that graciousness in the life of faith provides the measure of faithful discipleship.

Transliteration Schema

HEBREW AND ARAMAIC TRANSLITERATION

Consonants:

א	=	ʾ	ט	=	ṭ	פ or ף	=	p
ב	=	b	י	=	y	צ or ץ	=	ṣ
ג	=	g	כ or ך	=	k	ק	=	q
ד	=	d	ל	=	l	ר	=	r
ה	=	h	מ or ם	=	m	שׂ	=	ś
ו	=	w	נ or ן	=	n	שׁ	=	š
ז	=	z	ס	=	s	ת	=	t
ח	=	ḥ	ע	=	ʿ			

Masoretic Pointing:

Pure-long			Tone-long			Short			Composite		
הָ	=	â	ָ	=	ā	ַ	=	a	ֲ	=	ă
ֵי	=	ê	ֶ	=	ē	ֶ	=	e	ֱ or ֳ	=	ĕ
or ִי	=	î				ִ	=	i			
or וֹ	=	ô	ֹ	=	ō	ָ	=	o	ֳ	=	ŏ
or וּ	=	û				ֻ	=	u			

GREEK TRANSLITERATION

α	=	a	ι	=	i	ρ	=	r
β	=	b	κ	=	k	σ or ς	=	s
γ	=	g	λ	=	l	τ	=	t
δ	=	d	μ	=	m	υ	=	y
ε	=	e	ν	=	n	φ	=	ph
ζ	=	z	ξ	=	x	χ	=	ch
η	=	ē	ο	=	o	ψ	=	ps
θ	=	th	π	=	p	ω	=	ō

INDEX OF MAPS, CHARTS, AND ILLUSTRATIONS

INDEX OF EXCURSUSES

ABBREVIATIONS

General

BCE	Before the Common Era
CE	Common Era
c.	circa
cent.	century
cf.	compare
chap(s).	chapter(s)
LXX	Septuagint
MS(S)	manuscript(s)
MT	Masoretic Text
OL	Old Latin
NT	New Testament
OT	Old Testament
v(v).	verse(s)

Names of Biblical Books (with the Apocrypha)

Gen	Nah	1–4 Kgdms	John
Exod	Hab	Add Esth	Acts
Lev	Zeph	Bar	Rom
Num	Hag	Bel	1–2 Cor
Deut	Zech	1–2 Esdr	Gal
Josh	Mal	4 Ezra	Eph
Judg	Ps (Pss)	Jdt	Phil
1–2 Sam	Job	Ep Jer	Col
1–2 Kgs	Prov	1–4 Macc	1–2 Thess
Isa	Ruth	Pr Azar	1–2 Tim
Jer	Cant	Pr Man	Titus
Ezek	Eccl	Sir	Phlm
Hos	Lam	Sus	Heb
Joel	Esth	Tob	Jas
Amos	Dan	Wis	1–2 Pet
Obad	Ezra	Matt	1–3 John
Jonah	Neh	Mark	Jude
Mic	1–2 Chr	Luke	Rev

Names of Pseudepigraphical and Early Patristic Books

As. Mos.	*Assumption of Moses*
Did.	Didache
1-2-3 Enoch	Ethiopic, Slavonic, Hebrew *Enoch*
Jub.	*Jubilees*
Pss. Sol.	*Psalms of Solomon*
T. Dan	*Testament of Dan*
T. Issachar	*Testament of Issachar*

Names of Dead Sea Scrolls and Related Texts

Q	Qumran
1Q, 2Q, etc.	Numbered caves of Qumran, yielding written material; followed by abbreviation of biblical or apocryphal book
1QH	*Hôdāyôt* (*Thanksgiving Hymns*) from Qumran Cave 1
1QS	*Serek hayyahad* (*Rule of the Community, Manual of Discipline*)
1QSa	Appendix A (*Rule of the Congregation*) to 1QS

To distinguish the same-named tractates in the Mishna, Tosepta, Babylonian Talmud, and Jerusalem Talmud, *m., t., b.,* or *y.* precedes the title of the tractate.

ʾAbot	ʾAbot
B. Bat.	Baba Batra
B. Qam.	Baba Qamma
Git.	Gittin
Hor.	Horayot
Ketub.	Ketubot
Mo'ed Qat.	Mo'ed Qatan
Nazir	Nazir
Ned.	Nedarim
Pesah.	Pesahim
Qidd.	Quddusin
Šabb.	Šabbat
Sanh.	Sanhedrin
Sukk.	Sukka
Tamid	Tamid
Yoma	Yoma (= Kippurim)

Other Rabbinic Works

Rab.   *Rabbah* (following abbreviation of biblical book)

Greek Manuscripts and Ancient Versions

Papyrus Manuscripts
$\mathfrak{P}^{45}$ Third-century Greek Papyrus manuscript of the Gospels
$\mathfrak{P}^{52}$ Second-century Greek manuscript fragment of John 18:31-33, 37-38
$\mathfrak{P}^{66}$ Second or third-century Greek Papyrus manuscript of John (incomplete)
$\mathfrak{P}^{69}$ Late second-century Greek Papyrus manuscript of the Gospel of John
$\mathfrak{P}^{75}$ Third-century Greek Papyrus manuscript of the Gospels

Lettered Uncials
א   Codex Sinaiticus, fourth-century manuscript of LXX, NT, *Epistle of Barnabas,* and *Shepherd of Hermas*
A   Codex Alexandrinus, fifth-century manuscript of LXX, NT, 1 & 2 Clement, and Psalms of Solomon
B   Codex Vaticanus, fourth-century manuscript of LXX and parts of the NT
C   Codex Ephraemi, fifth-century manuscript of parts of LXX and NT
D   Codex Bezae, fifth-century bilingual (Greek and Latin) manuscript of the Gospels and Acts
K   Ninth-century manuscript of the Gospels
L   Eighth-century manuscript of the Gospels
W   Washington Codex, fifth-century manuscript of the Gospels (also called the Freer Gospels)
X   Codex Monacensis, ninth or tenth-century miniscule manuscript of the Gospels
Θ   Koridethi Codex, ninth-century manuscript of the Gospels
Ψ   Athous Laurae Codex, eighth- or ninth-century manuscript of the Gospels (incomplete), Acts, The Catholic and Pauline Epistles, and Hebrews

Numbered Uncials
0181   Fourth or fifth-century partial manuscript of Luke 9:59-10:14

Numbered Minuscules
75   Eleventh century manuscript

Ancient Versions
d   The Latin text of Codex Bezae
e   Codex Palatinus, fifth century Latin manuscript of the Gospels

Other Abbreviations
f^1 Family 1: miniscule manuscripts belonging to the Lake Group (1, 118, 131, 209, 1582)
f^{13} Family 13: miniscule manuscripts belonging to the Ferrar Group (13, 69, 124, 174, 230, 346, 543, 788, 826, 828, 983, 1689, 1709)
א*   The original reading of Codex Sinaiticus
א¹   The first corrector of Codex Sinaiticus
א²   The second corrector of Codex Sinaiticus
D*   The original reading of Codex Bezae
D²   The second corrector (c. fifth century) of Codex Bezae

ABBREVIATIONS

Commonly Used Periodicals, Reference Works, and Serials

AB	Anchor Bible
ANF	The Ante-Nicene Fathers
BAGD	W. Bauer, W. F. Arndt, F. W. Gingrich, and F. W. Danker, *Greek-English Lexicon of the NT*
BDF	F. Blass, A. Debrunner, and R. W. Funk, *A Greek Grammar of the NT*
BJS	Brown Judaic Studies
BZ	*Biblische Zeitschrift*
CBQ	*Catholic Biblical Quarterly*
CBQMS	Catholic Biblical Quarterly--Monograph Series
CTM	*Concordia Theological Monthly*
FFNT	Foundations and Facets: New Testament
HTR	*Harvard Theological Review*
IDB	*Interpreter's Dictionary of the Bible*
IDBSup	Supplementary volume to *IDB*
Int	*Interpretation*
JBL	*Journal of Biblical Literature*
JNES	*Journal of Near Eastern Studies*
JPS	Jewish Publication Society
JQR	*Jewish Quarterly Review*
JSNTSup	Journal for the Study of the New Testament--Supplement Series
JSOT	*Journal for the Study of the Old Testament*
JTS	*Journal of Theological Studies*
LCL	Loeb Classical Library
NIGTC	The New International Greek Testament Commentary
NJB	New Jerusalem Bible
NovT	*Novum Testamentum*
NTS	*New Testament Studies*
RSR	Recherches de science religieuse
RevExp	Review and Expositor
SNTSMS	Society for New Testament Studies Monograph Series
SR	*Studies in Religion/Sciences religieuses*
TDNT	G. Kittel and G. Friedrich (eds.), *Theological Dictionary of the New Testament*
TToday	*Theology Today*
WBC	Word Biblical Commentary
ZNW	*Zeitschrift für die neutestamentamentliche Wissenschaft*